History of the Arabic Written Tradition

Volume 2

Handbook of Oriental Studies

Handbuch der Orientalistik

SECTION ONE

The Near and Middle East

Edited by

Maribel Fierro (*Madrid*)
M. Şükrü Hanioğlu (*Princeton*)
Renata Holod (*University of Pennsylvania*)
Florian Schwarz (*Vienna*)

VOLUME 117/2

The titles published in this series are listed at *brill.com/ho1*

History of the Arabic Written Tradition

VOLUME 2

By

Carl Brockelmann

Translated by

Joep Lameer

TUTA SUB AEGIDE PALLAS · 1683 ·

BRILL

LEIDEN | BOSTON

Originally published as *Geschichte der Arabischen Litteratur* in 1898 and 1902.
Subsequent editions by Brill between 1937 and 1943, and in 1996.

Library of Congress Cataloging-in-Publication Data

Names: Brockelmann, Carl, 1868–1956, author. | Lameer, Joep, translator. | Witkam, J. J., writer of preface.
Title: History of the Arabic written tradition / by Carl Brockelmann ; translated by Joep Lameer ; with a preface by Jan Just Witkam.
Other titles: Geschichte der arabischen Litteratur. English | Handbook of Oriental studies. Section one, Near and Middle East (2014) ; vol. 117.
Description: Leiden ; Boston : Brill, 2016. | Series: Handbook of Oriental studies. Section one, The Near and Middle East ; volume 117 | Originally published as Geschichte der Arabischen Litteratur in 1898 and 1902 — Title page verso of volume 1. | Includes bibliographical references.
Identifiers: LCCN 2016032425 (print) | LCCN 2016041105 (ebook) | ISBN 9789004323308 (hardback : alk. paper) | ISBN 9789004326262 (E-book) | ISBN 9789004323308 (hardback) | ISBN 9789004326316 (hardback) | ISBN 9789004334618 (hardback) | ISBN 9789004335806 (hardback) | ISBN 9789004335813 (hardback)
Subjects: LCSH: Arabic literature—History and criticism.
Classification: LCC PJ7510 .B713 2016 (print) | LCC PJ7510 (ebook) | DDC 892.7/09—dc23
LC record available at https://lccn.loc.gov/2016032425

Typeface for the Latin, Greek, and Cyrillic scripts: “Brill”. See and download: brill.com/brill-typeface.

ISSN 0169-9423
ISBN 978-90-04-32631-6 (hardback)
ISBN 978-90-04-32632-3 (e-book)

This book is printed on acid-free paper and produced in a sustainable manner.

Printed by Printforce, the Netherlands

Contents

THIRD BOOK
The Decline of Islamic Literature

First Section From Mongol Rule Until the Conquest of Egypt by Sultan Selīm I in the Year 1517 3

Introduction 3

Chapter 1. Egypt and Syria 6
- 1 *Poetry and Rhymed Prose* 7
- 2 *Philology* 21
- 3 *Historiography* 30
  - A Individual Biographies 30
  - B Collective Biographical Works 33
  - C Local and National History 38
  - D Universal History 46
- 4 *Popular Literature in Prose, Anthologies, and Folk Tales* 56
- 5 *Ḥadīth* 63
  - A *ʿIlm al-ḥadīth wa-ʿilm al-rijāl* 63
  - B Biographies of the Prophet 71
  - C Collections of *Ḥadīth* and Edifying Works 74
- 6 *Fiqh* 79
  - A The Ḥanafīs 79
  - B The Mālikīs 86
  - C The Shāfiʿīs 88
  - D The Ḥanbalīs 106
  - E The Shīʿa 111
- 7 *Sciences of the Qurʾān* 112
- 8 *Dogmatics and uṣūl al-dīn* 119
- 9 *Mysticism* 121
- 10 *Mathematics* 131
- 11 *Astronomy* 133
- 12 *Geography and Cosmography* 138
- 13 *Politics and Public Administration* 142
- 14 *Militaria, Hunting, and Agriculture* 144
- 15 *Medicine and Veterinary Science* 146
- 16 *Zoology* 148
- 17 *Music* 149

18 *Occult Sciences* 149
19 *Encyclopaedias and Polyhistors* 150
I *Fann al-tafsīr wa-taʿalluqātuhu wal-qirāʾāt* 155
II *Fann al-ḥadīth wa-taʿalluqātuhu* 157
III *Fann al-fiqh wa-taʿalluqātuhu* 165
IV *al-Ajzāʾ al-mufrada fī masāʾil makhṣūṣa ʿalā tartīb al-abwāb* 166
V *Fann al-ʿarabiyya wa-taʿalluqātuhu* 169
VI *Fann al-uṣūl wal-bayān wal-taṣawwuf* 170
VII *Fann al-taʾrīkh wal-adab* 171

Chapter 2. Iraq and al-Jazīra 174
1 *Poetry and Rhymed Prose* 174
2 *Philology* 176
3 *Historiography* 176
4 *Ḥadīth* 177
5 *Fiqh* 178
A The Ḥanafīs 178
B The Mālikīs 178
C The Shāfiʿīs 178
D The Ḥanbalīs 179
E The Shīʿa 180
6 *Sciences of the Qurʾān* 182
7 *Dogmatics* 183
8 *Mysticism* 183
9 *Mathematics* 184
10 *Astronomy* 186
11 *Music* 187
12 *Medicine* 187

Chapter 3. North Arabia 188
1 *Poetry and Rhymed Prose* 188
2 *Historiography* 188
3 *Ḥadīth* 192
4 *Fiqh* 193
A The Ḥanafīs 193
B The Mālikīs 193
5 *Sciences of the Qurʾān* 193
6 *Mysticism* 194
7 *Mathematics* 196
8 *Geography* 196

Chapter 4. South Arabia 198
1 *Poetry* 198
2 *Philology* 199
3 *Historiography* 201
4 *Fiqh* 203
A The Ḥanafīs 203
B The Shāfiʿīs 203
C Sayyid Muḥammad b. Ibrāhīm b. ʿAlī b. al-Murtaḍā b. al-Mufaḍḍal b. al-Hādī b. al-Wazīr 203
D The Zaydīs 204
5 *Sciences of the Qurʾān* 207
6 *Mysticism* 208
7 *Medicine* 208
8 *Horse Breeding* 209
9 *Occult Sciences* 209
10 *Encyclopaedias* 209

Chapter 5. Iran and Tūrān 211
1 *Poetry and Rhymed Prose* 211
2 *Philology* 212
3 *Historiography* 215
4 *Ḥadīth* 215
5 *Fiqh* 216
A The Ḥanafīs 216
B The Shāfiʿīs 220
C The Shīʿa 220
6 *Sciences of the Qurʾān* 221
7 *Dogmatics* 226
8 *Mysticism* 226
9 *Philosophy* 231
10 *Politics* 235
11 *Mathematics* 236
12 *Astronomy* 237
13 *Medicine* 239
14 *Encyclopaedias and Polyhistors* 239

Chapter 6. India 247
1 *Philology* 247
2 *Historiography* 247
3 *Fiqh, Ḥanafī* 247

4 *Qur'ānic Exegesis* 248
5 *Mysticism* 248

Chapter 7. The Turks of Rūm and the Ottoman Empire 250
1 *Philology* 250
2 *Historiography* 251
3 *Fiqh, Ḥanafī* 252
4 *Sciences of the Qur'ān* 255
5 *Dogmatics* 257
6 *Mysticism* 259
7 *Medicine* 262
7a *Mathematics and Astronomy* 262
8 *Occult Sciences* 263
9 *Encyclopaedias and Polyhistors* 263

Chapter 8. North Africa 266
1 *Poetry* 266
2 *Philology* 267
3 *Historiography* 269
A Local History 269
B History of the Ibāḍīs 270
C Histories of Dynasties 270
D Universal History 272
4 *Ḥadīth* 274
5 *Fiqh, Mālikī* 275
6 *Sciences of the Qur'ān* 277
7 *Dogmatics* 279
8 *Mysticism* 283
9 *Politics* 286
10 *Mathematics* 287
11 *Astronomy* 288
12 *Travelogues* 288
13 *Medicine* 289
14 *Music* 289
15 *Alchemy and Occult Sciences* 290
16 *Eroticism* 290

Chapter 9. Spain 291
1 *Poetry and Belles Lettres* 291
2 *Philology* 292
3 *Historiography* 292
4 *Fiqh, Mālikī* 295
5 *Sciences of the Qurʾān* 296
6 *Mysticism* 297
7 *Politics* 297
8 *Mathematics and Astronomy* 297
9 *Travelogues and Geographies* 298
10 *Medicine* 299
11 *Sports* 299

Second Section From the Conquest of Egypt by Sultan Selīm I in 1517 to the Napoleonic Expedition to Egypt in 1798 301

Introduction 301

Chapter 1. Egypt and Syria 303
1 *Poetry and Rhymed Prose* 304
2 *Philology* 320
3 *Historiography* 325
A Individual Biographies 325
B Collective Biographical Works 326
C Local and National History 331
D Chronicles 335
E Universal History 337
4 *Popular Works and Anthologies* 339
5 *Ḥadīth* 341
6 *Fiqh* 349
A The Ḥanafīs 349
B The Mālikīs 359
C The Shāfiʿīs 363
D The Ḥanbalīs 371
E The Shīʿa 372
7 *Sciences of the Qurʾān* 374
8 *Dogmatics* 379
9 *Mysticism* 383
10 *Homilies and Paraenesis* 409
11 *Philosophy* 410
12 *Politics* 410

13 *Mathematics* 411
14 *Astronomy* 411
15 *Travelogues and Geographies* 415
16 *Hunting and Militaria* 419
17 *Music* 419
18 *Medicine* 419
19 *Occult Sciences* 422
20 *Encyclopaedias and Polyhistors* 423

Chapter 2. Al-Jazīra, Iraq, and Bahrain 430
1 *Poetry* 430
2 *Philology* 431
3 *Historiography* 431
4 *Fiqh* 433
A The Ḥanafīs 433
B The Shāfiʿīs 433
C The Shīʿa 433
5 *Sciences of the Qurʾān* 434
6 *Dogmatics* 435
7 *Mysticism* 435
7a *Philosophy* 436
8 *Travelogues* 436

Chapter 3. North Arabia 437
1 *Poetry* 437
2 *Philology* 439
3 *Historiography* 440
4 *Ḥadīth* 443
5 *Fiqh* 447
A The Ḥanafīs 447
B The Mālikīs 447
C The Shāfiʿīs 448
D Ḥanbalīs and Wahhābīs 451
6 *Sciences of the Qurʾān* 451
7 *Dogmatics* 451
8 *Mysticism* 452
9 *Philosophy* 454
10 *Mathematics* 454
11 *Astronomy* 454
12 *Travelogues and Geographies* 455
13 *Encyclopaedias and Polyhistors* 455

Chapter 4. South Arabia 461
1 *Poetry and Belles Lettres* 461
2 *Philology* 464
3 *Historiography* 464
4 *Ḥadīth* 467
5 *Fiqh* 468
A The Shāfiʿīs 468
B The Zaydīs 470
6 *Sciences of the Qurʾān* 472
7 *Dogmatics* 473
8 *Mysticism* 473
9 *Astronomy* 474
10 *Occult sciences* 474

Chapter 5. Oman, East Africa, and Abyssinia 475
A *Oman* 475
B *East Africa* 476
C *Abyssinia* 476

Chapter 6. Iran and Tūrān 477
1 *Poetry and Belles Lettres* 477
1b *Philology* 477
2 *Ḥadīth* 477
3 *Shīʿī fiqh and kalām* 479
4 *Sciences of the Qurʾān* 479
5 *Mysticism* 480
6 *Philosophy* 480
8 *Mathematics and Astronomy* 481
10 *Medicine* 481
11 *Encyclopaedias and Polyhistors* 482

Chapter 7. India 484
1 *Philology* 484
2 *Historiography* 484
3 *Belles Lettres* 484
4 *Ḥadīth* 485
5 *Fiqh, Ḥanafī* 485
6 *Sciences of the Qurʾān* 486
7 *Dogmatics* 486
8 *Mysticism* 487

9 *Philosophy* 489
10 *Travelogues* 490
11 *Encyclopaedias* 491

Chapter 8. The Malay Archipelago 492

Chapter 9. Rumelia and Anatolia 493
1a *Philology* 493
2 *Historiography* 495
3 *Popular Prose* 501
4 *Ḥadīth* 502
5 *Fiqh, Ḥanafī* 503
6 *Sciences of the Qurʾān* 512
7 *Dogmatics* 517
8 *Mysticism* 522
9 *Politics* 525
10 *Astronomy* 526
11 *Medicine* 527
12 *Music* 528
13 *Agriculture* 528
14 *Occult Sciences* 528
15 *Encyclopaedias and Polyhistors* 529

Chapter 10. The Maghreb 536
1 *Adab* 536
2 *Philology* 537
3 *Historiography* 537
4 *Popular Prose* 540
5 *Ḥadīth* 541
6b *Fiqh, Mālikī* 542
7 *Sciences of the Qurʾān* 543
8 *Dogmatics* 543
9 *Mysticism* 544
9a *Philosophy* 545
10 *Mathematics and Astronomy* 546
11 *Travelogues and Geographies* 547
12 *Medicine* 548
13 *Warfare* 548

Chapter 11. The Sudan 549

Third Section From the Napoleonic Expedition to Egypt in 1798 until the Present Day 551

Chapter 1. Egypt 551
1 *Poetry and Rhymed Prose* 553
2 *Philology* 557
3 *Historiography* 559
4 *Popular Prose* 562
5 *Ḥadīth* 563
6 *Fiqh* 564
A The Mālikīs 564
B The Ḥanafīs 565
C The Shāfiʿīs 565
7 *Dogmatics* 566
8 *Mysticism* 567
9 *Paraenesis* 568
10 *Mathematics* 569
11 *Travelogues and Geographies* 569
12 *Encyclopaedias* 570

Chapter 2. Syria 571
1 *Poetry* 571
2 *Philology* 573
3 *Historiography* 574
4 *Islamic Theology and Mysticism* 574

Chapter 3. Mesopotamia and Iraq 576

Chapter 4. Mecca (North Arabia) 577

Chapter 5. South Arabia 580

Chapter 6. Oman 582

Chapter 7. Persia 583

Chapter 8. Afghanistan 584

Chapter 9. India 585

Chapter 11. Istanbul 586

|THIRD BOOK 1

The Decline of Islamic Literature

From Mongol Rule Until the Conquest of Egypt by Sultan Selīm I in the Year 1517

Introduction

Alongside the ʿAbbāsid caliphate, which had long since crumbled to dust, the Mongol onslaught also wiped out the majority of the petty states that had been feeding on the former's remains. But together with the rotting remains of a moribund world, the Mongol steeds also trampled any of the seeds that could have permitted a successful future cultural development; even up to the present day, the Near East has not recovered from these calamities. From that time on, Iraq and Iran, once the centres of the intellectual and material culture of the Islamic world, lay almost entirely barren. Egypt and Syria have taken their place, and still offer Arabic literature a tolerable home, and towards the end of this period, India witnessed a flourishing of culture that was on a par with that of Syria or Egypt. However, due to Turkish and Mongol domination, the influence of Persian lore was all-embracing, so there was little room for contributions to Arabic literature. In Asia Minor, the Ottoman empire rose to power.
| However, intense battles for its sheer existence would absorb all the energy 4
of this nascent state, so it had little time to promote intellectual pursuits. In
North Africa, | Arabic literature clung to a miserable existence under Berber 4
rule, while in Spain one region after another was lost to the Christians, the result of an unwholesome proliferation of petty states and endless intra-Muslim bickering. At the end of this period, even Granada, the last Arab city, fell into Christian hands. Nevertheless, this isolated outpost provided fertile ground for Arabic literature until the very end.

Brilliant intellectual feats are, however, nowhere recorded. None of the versifiers—still abundant in number—was able to break through the barriers of form and matter of the ancient versifying techniques in an effort to explore new ways of reaching higher goals. The traditional forms of the *muwashshaḥ* and the *zajal*, though much employed in this period, were frowned upon as mere distractions by the literati. The only things produced in philology were textbooks and lexicons, of which a mere fraction are genuinely useful. The sole field to have shown advancing activity was historiography as, under the auspices of royal patronage, (near-)contemporary history boomed, while the more remote past was not entirely neglected either. However,

 | DOI 10.1163/9789004326323_002

opinions and approaches showed hardly any progress. Ibn Khaldūn’s philosophy of history is a lone exception, although his *magnum opus* is nothing more
than a compilation, unworthy of its brilliant *Muqaddima*. At the hands of able
5 *udabā’*, popular literature followed well-trodden paths. | Traditional themes
received their final form in collections of tales and romances, of which later
generations altered but minor details, or so it seems. In theology there was
absolutely no possibility of coming up with anything new. The interpretation
5 of the Qur’ān | and the now almost completely barren field of dogmatics merely
fed on the legacy of the past, while, in a sad contrast to what its spiritual founders had once envisioned, mysticism petrified into a raving hodgepodge of formulae sanctioned by the dervish orders. With the exception of delirious verses in imitation of the famous masters, these produced only polemical tracts on the details of their rituals, as well as saints’ lives brimming with miracle stories. The only thing legal experts were able to do was to constantly rehash the material that had been assembled by their ancestors; it was impossible for them to further develop the field. Mathematics and natural sciences edged near to extinction; the former produced only elementary textbooks that were focussed on the needs of specialists in inheritance law, while, among the *muwaqqit*s of the large mosques, astronomy became a parish discipline of limited practical purpose. It was the privilege of a Mongol ruler of Persia, Ulugh Beg, to briefly resuscitate the great scientific traditions of the past, although the natural sciences ended up as alchemical amusements and fantasies, while geography ended up in fabulous cosmologies and pilgrim’s books. There was only one branch of literature that, while not originating in this period, was pursued with greater vigour than ever before: books on warfare. These found a favourable reception at the court of the Mamlūks, who were very much focused on everything military. The decline of literature was finally—and regretably—confirmed by the bustling activity of the polymaths, the most notorious representative of whom was the writing “monster” al-Suyūṭī, who wrote books on the entire spectrum of human interest of his time, from the secrets of the word of God and the merits of the flea, all the way to the joys of copulation.

6 6 | Despite the fragmentation of the caliphate, | it was still possible to
present the Arabic literature of the previous period in a single large tableau. In this period, however, this is no longer feasible, as each of the different regions went its own way. It is correct that the Mamlūk empire still attracted a number of foreign literati, just as Iraq had done in the past, and the madrasas of Damascus and Cairo hosted many students from the Maghreb

and Iran,[1] but apart from this the differences in intellectual outlook between the various countries were hardly less pronounced than those that existed between the various medieval European states. As such, our account must, from now on, be region by region.

1 On the popularity of the people from the Maghreb in Damascus and the various ways in which they made a living in spiritual or in worldly service, see Ibn Baṭṭūṭa, I, 239.

Chapter 1. Egypt and Syria

While the eastern part of the Muslim world suffered the initial brunt of the Mongol invasions, and groaned under their barbaric rule, Egypt and Syria enjoyed a tolerable measure of prosperity under the Ayyūbids and their sucessors, the Turkish and Circassian Mamlūks. But even the best of these rulers hardly had any interests apart from maintaining their armies and building sumptuous edifices. There was never such a thing as a regular administration, and that which did exist only collected taxes. But even such poor management, stretching across the centuries, did not entirely exhaust the still-abundant internal resources of these countries, especially as the blessings of Levantine
7 trade continued to supplement internal revenue.[1] And despite their terrible |
7 plunder of Damascus, even Tīmūr's | hordes were unable to bring that city to
its knees in the same way as Hūlāgū's Mongols had done to its eternal rival Baghdad some 150 years earlier. It was only towards the end of this period, under the Burjī Mamlūks, that culture embarked upon a rapid decline and literary interest started to wane. At court and amongst those who were close to the government, the never-ending uncertainty of the political situation, in which no ruler had enough time to fully govern as almost all of them died from unnatural causes, resulted in an uncertainty over life and property that was only comparable to that which hung over the heads of the old aristocracy during the darkest days of the Roman Empire. Even the most capable and hard-working men only rarely survived more than three years in office, and many a *qāḍī* could be appointed and deposed over ten times during his career. Scholars working as teachers in madrasas were no better off; even in the East there can hardly have been a time when the intrigues surrounding the nominations to these posts were more intense than at this time. There are reports of rival scholars being forced to swap a professorial chair every two years—some even more often—merely as a consequence of the favour or whim of the ruler. If people did not despair under such circumstances this was due to Muslim fatalism, combined with the easy-going nature of the people of the Orient. Anybody taking an active part in public life could hardly ever enjoy the leisure time needed for the mental focus required for serious literary production. Furthermore, there were the moral constraints imposed by the orthodox *fuqahā'*, who ruthlessly persecuted even such a pious and God-fearing man as the Ḥanbalī Ibn Taymiyya, simply because he did not accept their doctrine on each and every point. So, while much paper was covered with ink in Syria and

1 The great importance of trade in those days may also be inferred from the fact that, as well as statesmen and scholars, biographical dictionaries often include major players in trade.

Egypt during this period, | precious little was written that was anything more 8
than a subsitute for something older that had been lost. | While in the literary 8
arena the leading role was still played by the Arabs, the Turks, who had a firm hold over politics, started to provide some serious competition.

DK: *Kitāb al-durar al-kāmina fī aʿyān al-miʾa al-thāmina* by Ibn Ḥajar al-ʿAsqalānī, d. 852/1448 (p. 67), 4 vols., Hyderabad 1348/9.

MT: *Muntakhab min Taʾrīkh Quṭb al-Dīn al-Nahrawānī al-Ḥanafī*, d. 990/1582 (p. 381), Leid. 1045.

RA: *Kitāb al-rawḍ al-ʿāṭir fī-mā tayassara min akhbār ahl al-qarn al-sābiʿ ilā khitām al-qarn al-ʿāshir* by Sharaf al-Dīn b. Ayyūb al-Nuʿmānī, d. 999/1590 (p. 289), Berl. 9886.

ḤS: Khwandamīr, d. 942/1525, *Ḥabīb al-siyar* (in Persian) (Tehran 1271), vol. III, lith. Bombay 1857.

ShN: *al-Shaqāʾiq al-Nuʿmāniyya fī ʿulamāʾ al-dawla al-ʿUthmāniyya* by Ṭāshköprīzāde, d. 968/1560 (p. 425), printed in the margin of Ibn Khallikān, Cairo 1299.

1 *Poetry*[1] *and Rhymed Prose*[2]

1. Shihāb al-Dīn Aḥmad b. ʿAbd al-Malik al-ʿAzāzī, who was born in Qalʿat ʿAzāz in 633/1235, was a merchant who lived near the market of the Circassians in Cairo. He died in 710/1310. He was a productive poet, especially of *muwashshaḥāt*.

Fawāt I, 48, Hartmann, *Muw.* 84/5. *Dīwān* Fātiḥ 3838, Cairo ^{1}IV, 247, ^{2}III, 134.

2. Abū ʿAbdallāh Muḥammad b. Dānīyāl b. Yūsuf Shams al-Dīn al-Mawṣilī al-Khuzāʿī was a linguist and ophtalmologist from Cairo. As a poet, he emulated Ibn al-Ḥajjāj (I, 81). At the beginning of his career he had attempted to give literary form to the popular shadow play. He died on 12 Jumādā II 710/7 November 1310.

| *Fawāt* II, 190 (with many samples of his poetry and the impossible statement 9
that he died in 608), *Orient.* II, 316, Wüst. *Gesch.* 383. 1. *Urjūza fī quḍāt Miṣr*, 99 *rajaz* verses, with an appendix by al-Suyūṭī up to the the year 886/1481, Berl.
9814,$_7$.—2.–4. see Suppl. (4. Garr. 1105). | 9

1 For Sufi poets, see § 9.

2 Since the two genres were, without exception, practised by the same people, it is not possible to separate them.

2a. Muḥammad b. ʿUmar Makkī ʿAbd al-Ṣamad b. Aḥmad al-Umawī al-Miṣrī Ṣadr al-Dīn b. al-Wakīl (b. al-Muraḥḥal, b. al-Khaṭīb) was born in Damietta (or, according to others, in Ushmūn) in Shawwāl 665/June–July 1267. After completing his studies he was, from the age of twenty, active as a *muftī*, taught at various madrasas in Cairo and Hama, and was also involved in the controversy surrounding Ibn Taymiyya. However, his main interest was poetry, and in his works he often borrowed from the ancient masters; as such, he once congratulated al-Malik al-Nāṣir on the construction of a new castle with a *qaṣīda* that he had taken from al-Taʿāwīdhī. He died in Cairo on 24 Dhu ʾl-Ḥijja 716/20 March 1317.

DK IV, 115/23. *Dīwān* see *Br. Mus. Quart.* VI, 97. He called his *muwashshaḥāt* collection *Ṭirāz al-dār*, following the example of Ibn Sanāʾ al-Mulk (I, 304). He left a *Kitāb al-ashbāh wal-naẓāʾir* that was unfinished, and a commentary on the *Kitāb al-aḥkām* of ʿAbd al-Ḥaqq (I, 458, 10, 2).

3. Shams al-Dīn Aḥmad b. Abi ʾl-Maḥāsin Yaʿqūb b. Ibrāhīm b. Abī Naṣr al-Ṭayyibī al-Asadī, who was born in Bukhārā in 649/1251 and died in Tripoli in Syria in 717/1317.

Poems, Gotha 2196,$_{4}$.

4. Taqī al-Dīn ʿAbdallāh b. Aḥmad b. Tammām b. Ḥassān al-Tallī al-Ḥanbalī al-Ṣāliḥī was born in 635/1237 and died on 3 Rabīʿ II 718/5 June 1318.

Poems, Gotha 1296,$_{12}$.

5. Shams al-Dīn Muḥammad b. al-Ḥasan al-Ṣāʾigh al-Ḥanafi, born in 645/1247, was a philologist who lived in the goldsmiths' quarter of Damascus. He died on 3 Shaʿbān 725/16 July 1325 (or, according to others, in 721/1321).

10 | *Fawāt* II, 188. Poems, Gotha 2296.

6. Despite being a Shīʿī and philologist by profession, ʿAlī b. al-Muẓaffar b. Ibrāhīm b. ʿUmar b. Zayd al-Kindī al-Wadāʿī, Kātib al-Wadāʿa, was, nevertheless, a *shāhid* (assessor) in the *dīwān* of the Umayyad mosque in Damascus. He died in 726/1326.

Fawāt II, 87, Ibn al-Qāḍī, *Durrat al-ḥijāl* II, 428,$_{1220}$. Poems, Gotha 2196,$_{13}$, Ambros. 68,$_{x}$ (RSO III, 582). His huge compilatory work on linguistics entitled *al-Tadhkira al-Kindiyya*, of which he bequeathed a copy written in his own hand to the Sumaysāṭiyya madrasa in Damascus, is unlikely to have ever circulated as a book.

7. ʿAbd al-Laṭīf b. ʿAbdallāh al-Suʿūdī Sayf al-Dīn, who died in 736/1335.

Some *qaṣīda*s, Berl. $7846_{,4}$.

8. ʿAlāʾ al-Dīn ʿAlī b. Muḥammad b. Salmān b. Ghānim al-Maqdisī was an influential independent scholar and poet in Damascus, who died in 737/1336 in Tabūk.

Fawāt II, 77. A *qaṣīda* on Ibn Taymiyya (p. 100), Berl. $7847_{,1}$.

9. Muḥammad b. Abī Bakr b. Ibrāhīm b. al-Nabīh was born around 662/1264, became a *qāḍī* in Homs in 718/1318, then in Tripoli and Aleppo, | and finally was 10
a professor at the Shaʾmiyya madrasa in Damascus. He died there in 745/1344.

Subkī, *Ṭab.* II, 44, DK III, 398, no. 1062. 1. A *qaṣīda*, Berl. 7848.—2. *ʿUmdat al-sālik wa-ʿuddat al-nāsik*, Alex. Fun. $126_{,2}$ (only Ibn al-Nabīh).

10. Abu ʾl-Ẓarāʾif Ibrāhīm b. ʿAlī b. Ibrāhīm al-Miʿmār al-Ḥāʾik al-Miṣrī Ghulām al-Nuwayrī, who died in 749/1348 (see Suppl.).

Fawāt I, 31, RA 10v. Selected poems, Esc. ^{2463}, Pet. 139.[3]

| 11. Fakhr al-Dīn Abū Bakr b. Muḥammad al-Ḥakkāk al-Ṣūfī, who was active in 11
Syria around 752/1351.

Dīwān al-qaṣāʾid al-ḥumayniyyāt wal-mukassarāt, Gotha 2303, Esc. $^2374_{,1}$, Patna I, $197_{,1771}$ (see Suppl.).

12. Muḥammad b. Yūsuf b. ʿAbdallāh Shams al-Dīn al-Khayyāṭ al-Ḥanafī al-Shādhilī al-Ḍafḍaʿ was born in Damascus in Rajab 693/June 1294 and became a court poet for al-Malik al-Nāṣir (r. 709–41/1309–40) in Cairo. Returning from one of his pilgrimages, he died on 14 Muḥarram 756/30 January 1355.

DK IV, 300/2, RA 233r, Ibn Ḥabīb, *Orient.* II, 402. *Dīwān*, containing mostly religious poems, Esc. ^{2346}; another, alphabetical collection, ibid. 347; another

3 Zayn al-Dīn b. al-Wardī, d. 749/1349, see p. 140.

collection, ibid. 460; a poem in 61 verses on the great fire of Damascus of 740/1339, Leid. 362.

13. Muḥammad b. Wafāʾ al-Shādhilī, d. 765/1363, see Suppl.

14. Jamāl (Shihāb) al-Dīn Muḥammad b. Muḥammad b. al-Ḥasan b. Nubāta al-Fāriqī al-Ḥudhāqī al-Miṣrī died in hospital in Cairo in Ṣafar 768/January–
11 February 1366. | Sultan al-Nāṣir Ḥasan (r. 755–62/1354–61) had given him an administrative position in the city, but soon relieved him of it because of his old age.

DK IV, 216/23, RA 224r, al-Suyūṭī, *Ḥusn al-muḥ.* I, 329. *Orient.* II, 419, Wüst. *Gesch.* 430, Hartmann *Muw.* 42 (on his father al-Ṣafadī, *al-Wāfī* I, 270). According to Ibn Baṭṭūṭa I, 160, his ability in *muqaṭṭaʿāt* was greater than in *qaṣīdas*.—1. *Dīwān* in various recensions, Berl. 7681/3, Gotha 2304, Vienna 483, Upps. 144, Leid. 734, de Sacy 153, Br. Mus. Suppl. 1086 (compiled by Muḥammad b. Ibrāhīm al-Bashtakī, d. 830/1427, like AS 3874), Bodl. I, 1213, Köpr. 1249, Cairo ^{1}IV, 236, 306, ^{2}III, 113, Patna I, $196_{,1762}$, print. Alexandria n.d.—2. *al-Qaṭr al-Nubātī*, selections from his *Dīwān*, Paris $2234_{,4}$, Alex. Adab 131.—3. *Taʿlīq al-dīwān*, a collection of ordinances, letters, epistolary opening formulas, and congratulations from the year 743/1342, Berl. 8640.—4. *Sūq al-raqīq*, erotic poems,
12 Esc. ^{2}449, Paris $3362_{,3}$(?).—5. | Individual poems, Gotha 26i, $2196_{,16}$.—6. *Sajʿ al-muṭawwaq*, poetic sketches of eminent scholars and aesthetes of his time, with samples of letters written to them by the author at various times, which often include their answers, Berl. 8645, f. 47r/79r, 9870, AS 3843, f. 121r/6v, 4045 (autograph dated 719), Alex. Adab $128_{,11}$, Cairo ^{1}IV, 262.—7. *Farāʾid al-sulūk fī maṣāyid al-mulūk*, a poem in *rajaz*, Berl. $8158_{,4}$.—8. *Muntakhab al-hadiyya min al-madāʾiḥ al-nabawiyya*, Köpr. 1397.—9. *Maṭlaʿ al-fawāʾid wa-majmaʿ al-farāʾid*, stylistic samples in prose and verse, Paris 3344.—10. *Sulūk duwal al-mulūk*: a. on the merits of kings; b. their duties towards themselves; c. towards their family and relatives; d. towards the people; e. towards the army, Krafft 474
12 (wrongly attributed to another author). |—11. Alphabetically ordered excerpts from his correspondence, *Tarsīl*, Esc. ^{2}548, $567_{,3}$.—12. *Mufākhara bayna ʾl-sayf wal-qalam* Copenhagen $231_{,10}$, Cambr. 415/7.—13. *Khuṭba fī taʿẓīm shahr Rajab* Gotha $44_{,34}$.—14. *Sharḥ al-ʿuyūn fī Sharḥ Risālat b. Zaydūn*, see vol. I, 325.—15. *al-Mukhtār min shiʿr b. al-Rūmī*, Suppl. I, 125.—16. *Talṭīf al-mizāj min shiʿr b. al-Ḥajjāj*, see vol. I, 81.

15. Abu ʾl-Walīd Ismāʿīl b. Muḥammad b. Muḥammad b. ʿAlī b. ʿAbdallāh b. Hāniʾ b. ʿĀmir Sarī al-Dīn al-Lakhmī al-Andalusī al-Ghanāṭī al-Mālikī was born

in 708/1308 in Granada, went to Syria via Egypt, and settled in Hama, where he became chief Mālikī *qāḍī*, and to where he returned after holding the same office in Damascus for two years and two months. Towards the end of his life he moved to Cairo, where he died in Rabīʿ II 771/November 1369.

RA 61r. *Kitāb al-badīʿ fī waṣf al-rabīʿ*, a selection from the works of Spanish poets only, Esc. ^{2}353.

15a. Ḥusayn b. Muḥammad b. ʿAlī al-Musawwadī wrote, in 767/1365:

Al-Mawāhib al-qadriyya fī madḥ khayr al-bariyya, Alex. Fun. 133,$_{6}$; another *qaṣīda*, ibid. 7.

16. Aḥmad b. ʿAlī b. ʿAbd al-Kāfī b. ʿAlī b. Tammām b. Yūsuf b. Tammām Bahāʾ al-Dīn Abū Ḥāmid al-Subkī | al-Miṣrī al-Shāfiʿī was born on 20 Jumādā II 13
719/9 August 1319 and studied in Cairo and Damascus. When his father Taqī al-Dīn (p. 86) became a *qāḍī* in Damascus, he, at the age of just 20, was given professorships at the Manṣūriyya, Sayfiyya, and Ḥakkāriyya madrasas in the city, thanks to a recommendation by the famous scholar ʿIzz al-Dīn b. Jamāʿa (p. 72). Having then taught at the Turbat al-Shāfiʿī and the Khashshābiyya and Shaykhūniyya madrasas in Cairo, he became a *muftī* at the Dār al-ʿadl and, in Shaʿbān 763/June 1362, *qāḍī* of Syria. Having worked again as a madrasa professor for a time, he was then made the military judge in Cairo. He died in Rajab 773/4 February 1372 in Mecca, to where he was a regular visitor.

RA 25v, al-Suyūṭī, *Ḥusn al-muḥ.* I, 246. 1. Riddle poem on the Nile, with an answer by Ṣalāḥ al-Dīn al-Ṣafadī (31. 3), Berl. 6111, 7866.—2.–4. see Suppl.—5. *Hadiyyat al-musāfir ila ʾl-nūr al-sāfir*, a *qaṣīda* in *thāʾ* in praise of the Prophet, composed on 30 Rabīʿ II 773/9 November 1371 in *al-Rawḍa al-sharīfa*, Cairo ^{2}III, 430, also attributed to his father (see. p. 88,$_{9,17}$). For his brother Tāj al-Dīn, see p. 89.

17. Shihāb al-Dīn Abu ʾl-ʿAbbās Aḥmad b. Yaḥyā b. Abī Ḥajala al-Tilimsāni al-Ḥanbalī, the grandson of the famous Sufi, was born in Tlemcen in 725/1325. After making the pilgrimage and visiting | Damascus he became provost of 13
the Sufi monastery that had been founded by Manjak at the gates of Cairo. As a poet he emulated ʿUmar b. al-Fāriḍ (I, 305). He died of the plague on 30 Dhu ʾl-Qaʿda 776/2 May 1375.

A short autobiography from his *Kitāb magnāṭīs al-durr al-nafīs* is on the title
page of the edition of no. 1, C. 1305; *DK* I, 331, no. 828, *RA* 27r, al-Suyūṭī, *Ḥusn
al-muḥ.* I, 329, Ibn Ḥabīb, *Orient.* II, 440, Wüst. in *Lüddes Ztschr.* I, 57, *Gesch.*
437. 1. *Dīwān al-ṣabāba*, tales of famous lovers with a selection of erotic poems,
Berl. 8373/4, Gotha 2305/8 (where other MSS are listed), Paris 3348/59, 5915,
14 6296, Algiers 1824, Br. Mus. Suppl. | 1113, AS 3595/6, Cairo [1]IV, 248, [2]III, 135, print.
C. 1279, 1291, 1305, in the margin of *Tazyīn al-aswāq* by Dā'ūd al-Anṭākī, 1308.
See E. Garcia Gomez, *El Ṭawq* de Ibn Ḥazm y *al-Dīwān al-ṣ.*, *al-Andalus* VI,
1941, 65/72.—Abstracts: a. Ismā'īl b. al-Ṣā'igh al-Ḥalabī, ca. 830/1427, Berl. 8375,
Vienna 394.—b. Anon., Berl. 8376.—2. *Sukkardān al-sulṭān al-Malik al-Nāṣir*, an
anthology on the meaning of the number seven for the country, the history, the
ruler, and the inhabitants of Egypt, composed in 757/1356, Berl. 8377/8, Gotha
1658/66 (where other MSS are listed), Garr. 207, AS 4038/42, Dāmād Ibr. 951,
Cairo [1]V, 68, *Bull. de Corr. Afr.* 1884, p. 12, no. 20, print. Būlāq 1288.—3. *al-Ṭāri' 'ala
'l-Sukkardān*, Paris 3360; from this and from nos. 1 and 2 the author compiled a
number of *qaṣīdas* in praise of al-Malik al-Nāṣir entitled *Naql al-kirām fī madḥ
al-maqām*, with five tales at the end of each *bāb* entitled *'Iqd al-bāb wa-dhikr
mā fīhi min faṣl al-khiṭāb*, Gotha 2138/9.—4. *Qaṣā'iḍ* on the fall of Alexandria
in the year 771/1369 (sic?), on the Nile, and on Rawḍa, Berl. 7866,$_{2-4}$, see ḤKh
III, 5161.—5. *Manṭiq al-ṭayr*, an anthology, abstracts Berl. 8379, from which are
maqāmas in ibid. 8554,$_{1}$.—6. *Sulwat al-ḥazīn fī mawt al-banīn*, Berl. 2260.—7.
Jiwār al-akhyār fī dār al-qarār, Yeni 701 (title corrupted), Alex. Mawā'iẓ 13, Cairo
[1]II, 153, V, 41, [2]I, 284.—8. *al-Ṭibb al-masnūn fī daf' al-ṭā'ūn*, Cairo [1]VII, 588.—9.
Inshā' wāḥid al-a'dād, Köpr. 705.—10.–14. see Supp.—15. *al-Tadhkīr bil-mawt
wa-sukna 'l-qubūr wal-khurūj minhā wal-nushūr*, Bursa, Ulu Cami Taş. 161.

18. Shams al-Dīn Abū 'Abdallāh Muḥammad b. Aḥmad b. 'Alī b. Jābir al-Ḥawwārī al-Andalusī al-A'mā (Ḍarīr, Kafīf), who was born in Spain in 698/1299, went to Egypt, with his compatriot Aḥmad b. Yūsuf al-Ghanāṭī (p. 111) made the Ḥajj, then travelled to Damascus and Aleppo, and finally went to al-Bīra on the Euphrates. He died there in Jumādā II 780/October 1378.

DK III, 339, no. 900, Maqq. I, 916. 1. *Badī'iyyat al-'imyān* or *al-Ḥulla al-siyarā
fī madḥ khayr al-warā*, Berl. 7353, Alex. Fun. 94,$_{7}$, on which was written the
14 commentary *Ṭirāz al-Ḥulla wa-shifā' al-'illa* by his friend | Aḥmad b. Yūsuf (see
above), Br. Mus. 1693, Esc. [2]327, Cairo [1]IV, 302, [2]II, 203.—2. *Kitāb al-ghayn fī
15 madḥ sayyid al-kawnayn*, an alphabetical collection of laudatory poems | on the
Prophet, Berl. 7867.—3. *Wasīlat al-ābiq*, a list of the *aṣḥāb* and *tābi'ūn* in *rajaz*
verse in the manner of Abū Nu'aym (I, 445), Algiers 1658.—4. Three *qaṣīdas*

on prosody and rhyme, Paris $4452_{,1-3}$.—5. Grammar in verse, ibid. 5.—6. A *maqṣūra* in praise of the Prophet, ibid. 7 = (?) *Qaṣīda fī madḥ al-nabī*, Cairo ^{2}III, 288 = (?) *al-Rawḍ al-mamṭūr fī naẓm al-maqṣūr*, Br. Mus. Or. 7471, 1 (DL 60).—7. A *qaṣīda* on the difference between *maqṣūr* and *mamdūd*, Paris $4452_{,8}$.—8. A *qaṣīda* on the difference between *ẓāʾ* and *ḍād*, ibid. 9, on which a commentary by al-Ruʿaynī, ibid. 11.—9. A *qaṣīda* on *muthallath*, ibid. 12 = *Ghāyat al-marām fī tathlīth al-kalām* in 272 verses, Sbath $1203_{,2}$.—10. *Naẓm Faṣīḥ Thaʿlab*, see I, 121.—11. *al-Minḥa fi ʾkhtiṣār al-Mulḥa*, ibid. $329_{,5}$.—12.–16. see Suppl.

19. Burhān al-Dīn Abū Isḥāq Ibrāhīm b. ʿAbdallāh al-Qīrāṭī was born in Ṣafar 726/January 1326, and moved to Cairo in 766/1364, where he had literary relations with Ibn Nubāta. He then went to live in Mecca, where he died in Rabīʿ II 781/July 1379.

DK I, 31, no. 77, *RA* 4v, al-Suyūṭī, *Ḥusn al-muḥ.* I, 329. 1. *Dīwān* entitled *Maṭlaʿ al-nayyirayn*, Berl. 7868, Paris 3209, Br. Mus. Suppl. 1087, Garr. 91, Cairo ^{1}IV, 325, ^{2}II, 359.—2. Individual poems, Gotha 26, f. 131v, Pet. Ros. $95_{,3}$.—3. Anthology (*taḥrīr*), Berl. 7869/70, cf. ʼ71, Leid. 736.—4. *al-Wishāḥ al-mufaṣṣal wal-funūn al-muwaṣṣal fī khulq al-shabāb al-mukhaṣṣal*, a collection of works on love and lovers, in poetry and in prose, Gotha 2168.—5. see Suppl.

20. ʿAlī b. ʿĪsā b. Muḥammad b. Abī Mahdī al-Fihrī al-Bastī moved to Aleppo in 760/1359 (?), where he was to be a teacher of *ḥadīth* and Arabic, where he taught Sibṭ b. al-ʿAjamī, and where he was active as a preacher in the months of Rajab, Shaʿbān and Ramaḍān. Later he went to Alexandria and then to Bursa, where he attained great wealth. He died there in 786/1384.

DK III, 92, 205 (with the impossible statement that he died in 719). *Zahrat al-ādāb wa-tuḥfat uli ʾl-albāb*, completed in 764/1363, Alex. Adab 76 (which has al-Busuṭī, the basis of Suppl. III, 1247).

21. ʿIzz al-Dīn ʿAlī b. al-Ḥusayn b. Abī Bakr al-Mawṣilī | al-Dimashqī lived in 16
Damascus and, for a short period, in Aleppo. He died in 789/1387.

DK III, 43, no. 99. *Badīʿiyya*, a poem to illustrate various rhetorical figures, which is an imitation of a poem with the same title by Ṣafī al-Dīn al-Ḥillī (d. 750/1349, p. 159), Berl. 7354, self-commentary Cairo ^{1}IV, 302, ^{2}II, 184.

22. Aḥmad b. Muḥammad b. al-ʿAṭṭār al-Dunaysarī moved from writing *fiqh* to
15 *adab*, composed panegyrics on the great figures of his time, | and wrote various popular works. He died in Rabīʿ II 794/March 1392.

DK I, 287, no. 732. 1. *Qaṣīdas*, Berl. 7877.—2.The *hamziyya* in *Qūt al-nadīm*, Gotha 2318, was probably taken from his *al-Muwashshaḥāt*; cf. Hartmann, *Muw.* 30.

23. Fakhr (Majd) al-Dīn Abu ʾl-Faraj ʿAbd al-Raḥmān b. ʿAbd al-Razzāq b. Makānis al-Qibṭī al-Ḥanafī, who was born in 745/1344, succeeded his brother Karam al-Dīn ʿAbd al-Karīm in the office of *nāẓir al-dawla*, but it was not long before he had to step aside for ʿAlam al-Dīn Yaḥyā. As the vizier of Syria he accompanied Sultan al-Ẓāhir Barqūq to Aleppo. When he was on his way from Damascus to Egypt to assume the vizierate there, he was poisened and died in Bilbīs, on 12 Dhu ʾl-Ḥijja 794/31 October 1392.[4]

DK II, 330, no. 2304, Ibn Ḥabīb, *Orient.* II, 445, 479 ff, al-Suyūṭī, *Ḥusn al-muḥ.* I, 330, Hartmann, *Muw.* 40. 1. *Dīwān*, compiled by his son Faḍlallāh Majd al-Dīn, d. 822/1419, Berl. 7874, Munich 534, Paris 3210/1, Br. Mus. Suppl. 1088, Cairo ^{1}IV, 313, ^{2}III, 112, Esc. ^{2}342/3, Calcutta p. 23, no. 1023.—2. *Bahjat al-nufūs al-awānis bi-mukhtaṣar dīwān al-Majd b. Makānis* by ʿAbdallāh b. ʿAbdallāh b. Salama al-Idkāwī (p. 283), completed in 1182/1768, Gotha 2309.—3. Two *rajaz* poems, instructions on how to conduct one's life: a. *ʿUmdat al-ḥurafāʾ wa-qudwat*
17 *al-ẓurafāʾ*, b. *al-Laṭāʾim* | *wal-ashnāf*, mixed with tales, Leid. 737 (where other MSS are listed, see Suppl.).—4. Individual poems, Berl. 7876, Vienna 486.—5. A poem on ethics, Brit. Mus. $640,_3$ = (?) *Waṣiyya*, Cairo ^{1}VII, 145, ^{2}III, 435.—6. See Suppl.

23a. Shams al-Dīn Abū ʿAbdallāh Muḥammad b. ʿAbdallāh b. Muḥammad al-Khaffāf, who died after 797/1395.

Badhl al-istiṭāʿa fī madḥ ṣāḥib al-shafāʿa, which does not only contain poems on the Prophet, but also on many other subjects, including the famine of the year 797 and the death of Nāṣir al-Dīn b. Bint Maylaq (Suppl. II, 148), Copenhagen 276, AS 3917 (*WZKM* XXVI, 85, Ritter).

24. Zayn (Sharaf) al-Dīn Jārallāh Abū Saʿīd Shaʿbān b. Muḥammad al-Qurashī al-Shāfiʿī al-Āthārī, d. 828/1425, see Suppl.

4 Corrupted to 864 in Casiri I, 160, Nicoll-Pusey II, 549, Cairo ^{1}IV, 314, ^{2}III, 256.

1. *Miftāḥ bāb al-faraj*, his *dīwān*, mostly poems in praise of the Prophet, applying various metres and rhetorical figures, divided into a *muqaddima*, 10 *aqsām* and a *khātima*, each of which has its own preface, and most of which are imitations of the *Burda* (I, 308) and the poems of al-Ḥillī (p. 159), Leid. 739.—2. *Badīʿ al-badīʿ fī madīḥ al-shafīʿ*, Berl. 7356, Paris 3248,$_{9}$.—3. *al-ʿIqd al-badīʿ fī madḥ al-shafīʿ*, composed in 808/1405, Berl. 7357, Esc. ^{2}470,$_{7}$.—4. A *badīʿiyya* without title, Berl. 7358.—5. *Badīʿ al-badīʿ fī madḥ al-shafīʿ*, ibid. 7359/60.—6. *al-Ḥalāwa al-sukkariyya*, a didactic poem on grammar in 100 *rajaz* verses, composed in 806/1403 in India, with a commentary entitled *al-Qilāda al-jawhariyya*, composed in 821/1418 in al-Ṣāliḥiyya near Damascus, Berl. 6760, Paris 4165, Cairo ^{1}IV, 87, ^{2}II, 149.—7. *Kifāyat al-ghulām fī iʿrāb al-kalām*, on syntax, in 1000 *rajaz* verses, Berl. 6761, Cairo ^{2}II, 154.—8. *al-Wāfī fī ʿilm al-ʿarūḍ wal-qawāfī* in verse, Cairo ^{1}IV, 200.—9. *Urjūza fī ṣināʿat al-kitāba*, Garr. 96.

24a. Jalāl al-Dīn Abū ʿAbdallāh Muḥammad b. Aḥmad b. Sulaymān b. Yaʿqūb b. Khaṭīb Dārayyā al-Anṣārī al-Khazrajī al-Dimashqī was born on 15 Rabīʿ I 745/28 July 1344 and died in Rabīʿ I 810/August 1407.

RA 225r. 1. A *qaṣīda*, Berl. 788,$_{2}$.—2. *Unmūdhaj murāsalāt*, composed in 760/1359 in Damascus, Garr. 2196.

| 25. Abu ʾl-Maḥāsin Taqī al-Dīn Abū Bakr ʿAlī b. ʿAbdallāh b. Ḥijja al-Ḥamawī 18
al-Qādirī al-Ḥanafī, born in 767/1366 in Hama, was also called al-Azrārī because
he had worked as a button maker | in his youth. Later he made a study tour to 16
Mosul, Damascus, and Cairo. On his way back he witnessed the great fire of Damascus, which took place during the siege of the city by al-Ẓāhir Barqūq[5] in 791/1390, and on which he wrote a letter to Ibn Makānis. During the reign of al-Muʾayyad Shaykh (815–24/1412–21) he was appointed as a *munshiʾ* in the *dīwān* by the privy secretary Nāṣir al-Dīn al-Bārizī. In 822/1419 he accompanied Crown Prince Ibrāhīm on his campaign in Asia Minor.[6] After the death of his patron he returned to Hama in 830/1427, dying there on 25 Shaʿbān 837/7 April 1434.

RA 80v, *MT* 85v. 1. *Badīʿiyyat b. Ḥijja*, an imitation of the *Burda* (I, 308), in praise of the Prophet, employing all rhetorical devices, with the self-commentary *Taqdīm Abī Bakr* or *Khizānat al-adab wa-ghāyat al-arab*, completed in 826/1423, Berl. 7361/4, Ms. or. quart. 2049, Gotha 2595/6 (where other MSS

5 See Weil, *Gesch. der Chalifen* IV, 565.
6 Ibid. V, 144.

are listed), Paris 3206$_{,4}$, 3207$_{,2}$, 3213/7, Br. Mus. Suppl. 985$_{,i}$, Esc. ^{2}294, AS 4053,
Patna I, 195$_{,1750}$, print. Calcutta 1230 (at the end of the *Dīwān al-Mutanabbī*),
Būlāq 1273, C. 1291, 1304; cf. Mehren *Rhet.* 12.—Commentaries: a. Ibn Kannān, d.
1153/1740 (p. 299), Berl. 7366.—b. ʿUthmān b. Ṭāhir, ibid. 7367.—c. Muḥammad
b. Aḥmad al-Samannūdī, Paris 3218.—d. *al-ʿIqd al-badīʿ fī fann al-badīʿ* by Būlus
ʿAwwād, Beirut 1881 (Sarkis 1395).—2. *Thubūt al-ḥujja ʿala ʾl-Mawṣilī wal-Ḥillī
li-Ibn Ḥijja*, a critical exposition of the *Badīʿiyya* of Ṣafī al-Dīn al-Ḥillī and of
ʿIzz al-Dīn al-Mawṣilī (no. 21), and a demonstration that the one written by the
author himself is of greater merit, Berl. 7369.—3. *Taʾhīl al-gharīb*, an anthology of ancient and modern poets, Gotha 2156, Br. Mus. 768, Esc. ^{2}395 (fragm.),
NO 3701, Cairo ^{1}IV, 213, ^{2}III, 41.—4. *al-Thamarāt al-shahiyya min fawākih
al-Ḥamawiyya* (*wal-zawāʾid al-Miṣriyya*), his collection of his own poems,
19 | Berl. 7891, Munich 531, Esc. ^{2}293, 436, 428$_{,4}$, Garr. 918, Alex. Fun. 198$_{,1}$.—
5. *Majra ʾl-sawābiq*, panegyrical poems on race horses, partly by him, and partly
by Ibn Nubāta (p. 11), the Spaniard Ibn al-Khaṭīb, d. 776/1374 (p. 260), and
others, Gotha 1335.—6. Individual *qaṣīdas*, Berl. 7892/3.—7. *Qahwat al-inshāʾ*,
letters and certificates composed on the order of Egyptian sultans, Berl. 8644,
Tüb. 69$_{,i}$, Leid. 353, Cambr. 53, Paris 4438, Naples, Cat. 240, Algiers 1898, NO
4308, Cairo ^{1}IV, 292, ^{2}III, 294.—8. Two letters to al-Damāmīnī, d. 827/1424
(p. 32), Leid. 366.—9. The letter to Ibn Makānis, mentioned above, Berl.
9784.—10. *Thamarāt* (*Thimār*) *al-awrāq*, with a *Dhayl* by the author, an anthology, Berl. 8382/3, Ms. or. Oct. 3979, Gotha 2152/5 (where other MSS are listed),
Paris 3529/43, Algiers 1872$_{,2}$, NO 3757, AS 4848, Alex. Adab 29, Cairo ^{1}IV, 223,
303, ^{2}III, 73, printed in the margin of the *Muḥāḍarāt al-udabāʾ* of Rāghib,
17 Būlāq 1287, 1300 (*OB* I, 910); | on which a *Dhayl* by Muḥammad b. Muḥammad
al-Sābiq al-Ḥamawī, ca. 850/1446, Berl. 8384, Br. Mus. 766$_{,2}$, Cairo ^{1}IV, 303,
^{2}III, 155.—11. *Taghrīd al-Ṣādiḥ*, selected sayings, aphorisms, and admonitions from *al-Ṣādiḥ wal-bāghim* by Ibn al-Habbāriyya, d. 504/1110 (see I, 293),
Berl. 7894/8.—12. *Azhār al-anwār*, a collection of short poems and anecdotes,
mostly belletristic, and mainly from Ibn Khallikān, Berl. 8385.—13. *Risāla fi
ʾl-sikkīn*, Copenhagen 231$_{,8}$.—14. *Multaqaṭāt*, traditions (author?), Berl. 1393.—
15. *Bulūgh al-marām min Sīrat b. Hishām wal-Rawḍ al-unuf wal-iʿlām*, a revision of Ibn Hishām's biography of the Prophet and of the commentary on it
by al-Suhaylī (I, 526), Berl. 9568.—16. *Bulūgh al-murād min al-ḥayawān wal-
nabāt wal-jamād*, an augmented imitation of al-Damīrī's (d. 808/1405, see p. 138)
Ḥayāt al-ḥayawān, Vienna 1444.—17. *Kashf al-lithām ʿan wajh al-tawriya wal-
istikhdām*, on the rhetorical style figures mentioned in the title (Mehren 105/7),
written as a supplement to the *Faḍḍ al-khitām ʿani ʾl-tawriya wal-istikhdām*
by Ṣalāḥ al-Dīn al-Ṣafadī, d. 764/1362 (p. 31), Berl. 7344, Gotha 2824, Leid.
237, Pet. AM (Gottwaldt p. 4).—18. *Burūq al-ghayth*, an abstract of al-Ṣafadī's

commentary on the *Lāmiyyat al-ʿAjam* (I, 284), Leid. 659/60.—19. *Laṭāʾif al-talṭīf* see vol. I, $81_{,11}$.—19a.–22. see Suppl.—23. *Rashf al-manhal*, a *takhmīs* on a *qaṣīda* by al-Ḥasan b. ʿAlī b. Muḥammad b. Maḥmūd b. ʿAbd al-Qādir al-Jīlānī, a counterpart to an earlier *takhmīs* by Badr al-Dīn al-Ṣāḥib, Garr. 97.

| 26. Al-Qāḍī ʿAbd al-Karīm b. Dirghām al-Ṭarāʾifī, who flourished around 20
853/1449.

1. *Mukhammasāt fī madḥ al-nabī*, 29 *takhmīs* of 20 strophes each, Berl. 7904/5.—2. *Abkār al-afkār fī madḥ al-nabī al-mukhtār*, Cairo ^{1}IV, 201, ^{2}III, 3.

27. ʿIzz al-Dīn ʿAbd al-Raḥīm b. Muḥammad b. Abi ʾl-Furāt al-Qāhirī, Qāḍī al-Jawra, was born in Cairo in 759/1358, lived from 834/1430 until 838/1434 in his hometown, and died in Dhu ʾl-Ḥijja 851/February 1448.

Kattānī, *Fihris* II, 274. 1. *Dīwān*, Berl. 7900.—2. *Mukhtaṣar sharḥ Qayd al-sharāʾid wa-naẓm al-farāʾid*, see p. 79, 6.

28. Muḥammad b. Abī Bakr b. Abi ʾl-Wafāʾ al-Ḥusaynī al-Maqdisī Tāj al-Dīn Abu ʾl-Wafāʾ b. Taqī al-Dīn, ca. 857/1453.

Dīwān, alphabetically arranged, Berl. 7906, AS 3922/3, ʿUm. $5766_{,2}$, Cairo ^{2}III, 156.[7]

29. Nūr al-Dīn Abu ʾl-Ḥasan ʿAlī b. Sūdūn (Sawdūn) al-Bashbughāwī[8] was born in Cairo in 810/1407, studied there, and then moved to Syria. He died in Damascus in 868/1464 (see Suppl.).

| MT 77r, Hartmann, *Muw.* 56. 1. *Nuzhat al-nufūs wa-muḍḥik al-ʿabūs*, a col- 18
lection of poems, mostly of a humorous nature, Berl. 7909/10, Leipz. 567/8, Copenhagen 222, Bodl. I, 424 (cf. II, 581, 619), Paris 3220, Esc. ^{2}450, Madr. 207 (Gg 251), Garr. 105, Patna I, $207_{,1847}$, lith. C. 1280. The wide circulation of these poems is illustrated by the many quotations in the *Hazz al-quḥūf* of Abū Shādūf (p. 278), see Hartmann, loc. cit.—2. *Qurrat al-nāẓir wa-(fī) nuzhat al-khāṭir*, a revision of the same collection, in which sobriety and pleasantry are separated, Gotha 2159/60, Esc. ^{2}368, Cairo ^{1}IV, $291_{,2}$, ^{2}III, 277.—3. See Suppl.—4. Two *maqāmas*, Berl. $8554_{,3}$.—5. *al-Fawāʾid al-laṭīfa* (see Suppl.), also Alex. Adab 137.

7 Al-Nawājī, d. 859/1455, see p. 56.

8 Like this, according to the autograph in Pusey 619, cf. Hartmann, *Muw.* 56.

30. ʿĪsā b. Muḥammad b. ʿĪsā al-Maqdisī wrote, in 873/1468:

21 | *Kitāb al-jawhar al-maknūn fi ʾl-sabʿa funūn*, a collection of his poems in the seven more recent metres (cf. H. Gies, Diss. Leipzig 1879), Esc. ^{2}459.

31. Abu ʾl-Ṭayyib (Abu ʾl-ʿAbbās) Shihāb al-Dīn Aḥmad b. Muḥammad b. ʿAlī b. al-Ḥasan al-Ḥijāzī al-Qāhirī al-Khazrajī al-ʿUbādī was born after 800/1397 (or, according to others, in Shaʿbān 790/August 1388), studied under Ibn Ḥajar al-ʿAsqalānī (d. 852/1448, p. 67), but then turned exclusively to belles lettres, supposedly because he had undermined his health by taking too much anacardia. He died on 8 Ramaḍān 875/12 March 1471 (or, according to others, in 874).

MT 79v, al-Suyūṭī, *Ḥusn al-muḥ.* I, 330. 1. *al-Lumʿa al-Shihābiyya min al-burūq al-Ḥijāziyya*, selections of his poems, Esc. ^{2}475.—2. *Rawḍ al-ādāb*, an anthology of poems completed on 17 Muḥarram 826/1 January 1423; a. *Fi ʾl-muṭawwalāt*, b. *Fi ʾl-muwashshaḥāt wal-azjāl*, c. *Fi ʾl-maqāṭīʿ*, d. *Fi ʾl-nathriyyāt*, e. *Fi ʾl-ḥikāyāt*, Vienna 400, Leid. 510, Br. Mus. 1104/5, Suppl. 1119, AS 4017/8, Garr. 213, Patna I, $199_{,1781}$, print. Bombay 1898 (Sarkis 1151).—3. *Kunnās al-ḥawārī fi ʾl-ḥisān min al-jawārī*, Copenhagen $220_{,4}$, print. as no. 2 of a *Majmūʿa*, C. 1326 (Alex. Adab 130/1).—4. *Jannat al-wildān fi ʾl-ḥisān min al-ghilmān*, ibid. 3, in *Majmūʿa* no. 1.—5. *al-Zanjabīl al-qāṭiʿ fī ṭayy (waṭʾ) dhāt al-barāqiʿ*, a poem, Berl. $7912_{,2}$, Bol. $459_{,9}$.—6. *Nayl al-rāʾid fi ʾl-Nīl al-zāʾid*, which lists the various levels of the Nile from the Hijra until 876 (sic), with, at the beginning, a list of the nilometers of different ages and of the years in which the Nile did not reach the necessary level to fertilise the land, Paris 2271 (autograph), Br. Mus. 1328, Patna I, $286_{,2334}$.—7. *Qalāʾid al-nuhūr min jawāhir al-buḥūr*, mnemonic verses in different metres, Berl. 7159/60, Gotha $39_{,11}$, Garr. 511, in *Majmūʿa* no. 3.—8.–10. see Suppl.—11. *Nadīm al-kaʾīb wa-ḥabīb al-ḥabīb*, a *dīwān* and anthology, Daḥdāḥ 243 = Berl. Brill M. 168.

32. ʿAbd al-Qādir b. Abī Bakr b. Khiḍr al-Dumāṭī (Dumāṣī) al-Shāfiʿī, who was born in 842/1438, wrote, in 886/1481:

19 | 1. *al-Muntakhab al-yasīr min al-dīwān al-kabīr*, Esc. ^{2}473.—2. *al-Durr al-muntaqā*, a collection of poems, Copenhagen 378.—MT 71r.

22 | 33. Shihāb al-Dīn Abu ʾl-ʿAbbās Aḥmad b. Muḥammad b. al-Hāʾim al-Manṣūrī was born in al-Manṣūra in 799/1396 and died in 887/1482.[9]

9 ḤKh confuses him with the jurisconsult and mathematician of the same name, d. 815/1412, p. 125, see Rieu, Add. 773r (ad 260v), 780 (ad 480r).

Al-Suyūṭī, *Ḥusn al-muḥ.* I, 331. 1. *Dīwān*, arranged alphabetically by himself and published in 825/1422, Vienna 487, Paris 3312, Esc. ^{2}372, 419,$_2$ (cf. 442), Madr. 222.—2. A *qaṣīda* on the Prophet, Esc. ^{2}442,$_1$.

34. ʿAlam al-Dīn Shākir b. ʿAbd al-Ghanī b. al-Jīʿān, who was born in 790/1388, was of Coptic descent, worked as a *mustawfī* in the *Dīwān al-jaysh* and died on 14 Rabīʿ II 882/27 July 1477.

1. A book in prose and verse that he wrote to console himself following the death of his brother al-Muʿizz al-Saʿdī Ibrāhīm in 864/1459, Br. Mus. 638,$_1$.—2. *Masāʾil al-dumūʿ ʿalā mā tafarraqa min al-jumūʿ*, an elegy, ibid. 2.

35. Tāj al-Dīn ʿAbd al-Wahhāb b. Aḥmad b. Muḥammad b. ʿAbdallāh b. Ibrāhīm b. Abī Naṣr Muḥammad b. ʿArabshāh b. Abī Bakr al-Qurashī al-ʿUthmānī al-Anṣārī al-Saʿdī al-Khazrajī al-Ḥanafī was born on 22 Shawwāl 813/18 February 1411 in Ḥajjī Tarkhān (Astrakhan)[10] in Qipchāq territory. He was the son of the biographer of Tīmūr, d. 854/1450, went with his father to Damascus, and thence to Cairo, dying in 901/1495.

1. *Shifāʾ al-kalīm bi-madḥ al-nabī al-karīm*, a *badīʿiyya* with an introduction and conclusion in prose, Gotha, 3,$_7$.—2. A *waṣiyya* of Sufic character, Berl. 4011.—3. *Laṭāʾif al-ḥikam*, aphoristic verses from older poets, ibid. 8187.—4. A dervish song in praise of God and other *qaṣīdas*, ibid. 7923,$_4$.—5. *al-Jawhara al-waḍīʾa takhmīs al-qaṣīda al-Sharīfiyya al-ʿAlawiyya*, on *Munājāt ʿAlī*, composed in Dhu ʾl-Qaʿda 900/August 1495, Gotha 4,$_2$.—6. *Shurb riyāḍ al-taʿbīd zulāl muzn al-tawḥīd*, a didactic poem on *uṣūl al-dīn*, ibid. 4,$_1$.—7. A didactic poem on the differences between the Meccan and Medinan suras, ibid. 3.—8. *Kashf al-kurūb dhikr awliyāʾ Allāh aʿlām | al-ghurūb*, in prose and verse, ibid. 4.—9. Poem about 23
the prophets from Adam to Muḥammad. composed in Cairo in Muḥarram 887/February—March 1482, ibid. 5.—10. *Ashraf al-ansāb nasab afḍal al-anbiyāʾ wa-aʿẓam al-aḥbāb*, a genealogical *rajaz* poem in 50 verses | on the prophets, the 20
time between each of them, and on Muḥammad being the noblest, composed in 888/1483, Berl. 2531.—11. *Ashraf al-rasāʾil wa-aẓraf al-masāʾil*, a *rajaz* work on the wives, children, and family (*aṣhār*) of Muḥammad, composed in 892/1487, ibid. 8160,$_1$, with some smaller poems and a *takhmīs*.—12. *Risālat al-anjāb fī dhikr al-khilāfa li-afḍal al-aṣḥāb*, a *rajaz* work on the first four successors of the Prophet, ibid. 9697.—13. *Murshid al-nāsik li-adāʾ al-manāsik*, ca. 1200 *bayts*, rhyming on *Allāh*, on the pilgrimage to Mecca, Gotha 4,$_6$.—14.–16. see Suppl.

10 On the pronunciation, see Ibn Baṭṭūṭa ii, 410.

36. Aḥmad b. Muḥammad b. Muḥammad b. Abī Bakr al-Qudsī Shihāb al-Dīn b. ʿUbayya, d. 905/1499.

Part of a collection of poems, Berl. 7924.

37. Al-Ḥusayn b. Aḥmad b. al-Ḥusayn al-ʿAzāzī al-Ḥalabī Shihāb al-Dīn, d. 912/1506.

Dīwān, beginning Berl. 7927, see Hartmann, *Muw.* 85.

38. ʿAlī b. Muḥammad b. ʿAbdallāh b. Mulayk al-Ḥamawī al-Dimashqī al-Fuqqāʿī al-Ḥanafī ʿAlāʾ al-Dīn Abu ʾl-Ḥasan, who was born in 840/1436 in Hama, initially made a living in Damascus as a trader in beer (*fuqqāʿ*). He later turned to the study of *fiqh* and poetry, dying in Shawwāl 917/January 1512.

RA 198v. 1. *Dīwān*, edited by Abū b. Muḥammad Ḥāmid al-Ṣafadī, Br. Mus. $630_{,1}$.—2. Individual *qaṣīdas*, Berl. 7930.—3. A poetic anthology, Gotha 2162.

39. Muḥammad al-Ḥalabī Rashīd, a student of al-Suyūṭī, ca. 920/1514.

An alphabetically ordered collection of *qaṣīdas* by later poets, Berl. 8204.

40. Ibrāhīm b. Muḥammad b. Abī Bakr al-Murrī al-Maqdisī Burhān al-Dīn Abū Isḥāq b. Abī Sharīf, d. 923/1517, see Suppl.

24 | 1. A *qaṣīda* on his longing for Cairo, Berl. $7933_{,4}$.—2. *Tafsīr al-āyatayn* ($2_{,257}$, $39_{,53}$) *wal-ḥadīth*, AS 393 (Ritter).

41. Qānsūh al-Ghūrī (Ghawrī), the penultimate Circassian Mamlūk sultan, ascended to the throne in 906/1500 and died in 922/1516 near Marj Dābiq, in the battle against the Ottoman sultan, Selīm I.

21 | Weil, *Gesch. der Chal.* v 385/416, Hartmann, *Muw.* 73. 1. *Dīwān*, Copenhagen 280.—2. *al-Munaqqaḥ al-ẓarīf ʿala ʾl-muwashshaḥ al-sharīf*, two *muwashshaḥs*, with *ḥadīths* regarding the power and glory of princes, published by al-Suyūṭī on the occasion of the celebrations surrounding the sultan's accession to power, Gotha $56_{,4}$.—3. See Suppl. and M. Awad, *Actes du XXe congr. intern. des Or.*, Brussels 1938 (1940), p. 320. Mention is made there of a work called *Nafāʾis al-majālis al-sulṭāniyya* by Ḥusayn b. Muḥammad al-Ḥusaynī, who lived at his court for 18 months, and of the discussions carried on by him, as well as of a Turkish translation of the *Shāhnāme* he commissioned from Ḥusayn b. Hasan

Muḥammad al-Ḥusaynī al-Āmidī, and of the Arabic and Turkish poems by the sultan, following the *Nafāʾis* and Ṭabbākh's *Taʾrīkh Ḥalab*.

2 *Philology*

1. It seems that Aḥmad b. ʿAlī b. Masʿūd flourished at the beginning of the eighth century.

Marāḥ al-arwāḥ, a popular textbook on grammar, is, in the MSS (see Berl. Ms. or. oct. 3874/5, Gotha 194,$_2$, BDMG 66a, Garr. 422/5, Qawala II, 47), usually accompanied by *al-Taṣrīf al-ʿIzzī* (I, 336), and it was printed in this way in Istanbul 1233, Būlāq 1240 and other printings (*BO* I, 130ff, II, 131f, Euting 1562), and separately in lith. Kanpur 1885, Delhi 1887, 1893, Lahore 1887.—Commentaries: 1. Aḥmad b. Dunqūz, from the time of Meḥmed II (r. 855–86/1451–81), Munich 759, Copenhagen 193, Pet. 155, Paris 4185/6, Br. Mus. 498, Garr. 429/30, Alex. Adab 28, Qawala II, 41/3, print. Istanbul 1306, C. 1309, glosses by Dāʾūd al-Ashkashī (?), Alex. Adab 4.—2. *Rāḥ al-arwāḥ* by Yūsuf b. ʿAbd al-Malik b. Bakhshāyish, composed in 839/1435, Algiers 27.—3. *al-Falāḥ* by Ibn Kamālpāsha, d. 940/1533 (p. 449), Qawala II, 45, print. Istanbul 1289, in the margin of *OB* VI, 4857.—4. *al-Miftāḥ* by Ḥasan Pāshā, ca. 800/1397, Munich 758, Vienna 204, Pet. 153 Garr. 426/8, Alex. Adab 8.—| 5. ʿAbd 25
al-Raḥmān b. Khalīl al-Rūmī, Krafft 54.—6. ʿAbd al-Mahdī al-Ḥanafī, Delhi 1883, 1886.—7. Anon., Leipz. p. 335, no. 7, Krafft 55, Pet. 154.—8. (also Berl. Ms. or. Oct. 3798, Garr. 431)—9.–11. See Suppl. (10. *Fatḥ al-fattāḥ*, Alex. Adab 10).

2. Around the same time Shams al-Dīn ʿAbd al-Muʾmin b. Muḥammad al-Barkamūnī flourished.

Lubb al-lubāb fī ʿilm al-iʿrāb, Ind. Off. 899. Commentaries: 1. *Khulāṣat al-iʿrāb* by Yūsuf b. Jamāl ʿAlawī, ibid. 900.—2.–5. See Suppl.

2a. Abu ʾl-Ḥasan ʿAlī b. Khalaf b. ʿAlī b. ʿAbd al-Wahhāb, who probably wrote around 700/1300.

Mawārid al-bayān, on rhetoric and *inshāʾ*, ḤKh VI, 130,$_{23334}$, undated, Fātiḥ 4128.

3. Jamāl al-Dīn Abu ʾl-Faḍl Muḥammad b. Mukarram b. ʿAlī b. Manẓūr al-Anṣārī al-Khazrajī al-Ifrīqī, who was born in 630/1232, was a *qāḍī* in Tripoli for a time, before dying in Cairo in Shaʿbān 711/1311. He supposedly left no fewer than 500 volumes of abstracts of historical and philological works.

DK IV, 262, no. 725, al-Suyūṭī, *Ḥusn al-muḥ.* I, 307, Wüst. *Gesch.* 384. 1. *Lisān al-ʿArab*, a dictionary summarising the contents of the *Tahdhīb*, *Jamhara* (I, 114), *Ṣaḥāḥ* (I, 133), *Muḥkam* (I, 376), and *Nihāya* (I, 439), in 20 vols., Būlāq 1300/8, C. 1348ff,[1] from where ʿAbd al-Qayyūm Muḥammad, *Fahāris Lisān al-ʿArab* I, *Asmāʾ al-shuʿarāʾ*, Lahore 1938.—2. *Nithār al-azhār fi ʾl-layl wal-nahār wa-aṭāyib awqāt al-aṣāʾil wal-asḥār wa-sāʾir mā yashtamil ʿalayhi min kawākibihi*
22 *al-falak al-dawwār*, Cairo [1]IV, 335, [2]III, 403. |—3. *Mukhtaṣar Taʾrīkh madīnat Dimashq li-Ibn ʿAsākir*, see I, 403.—4. *Mukhtaṣar Taʾrīkh Baghdād lil-Samʿānī*, see I, 402.—5. *Mukhtaṣar Jāmiʿ al-mufradāt* (?), see I, 648.—6., 7. see Suppl.—8. *Ikhtiṣār Kitāb al-ḥayawān lil-Jāḥiẓ*, Esc. [2]901.

26 | 3a. Muḥammad b. Muṣṭafā b. Zakariyyāʾ al-Dawrakī al-Ṣulghurī Fakhr al-Dīn al-Ḥanafī was born in 631/1234 in Dawrak, lectured at the Ḥusāmiyya in Cairo, and was for a time *muḥtasib* in Gaza. He died in 713/1313.

DK IV, 259, no. 715, Suyūṭī, *Bughya*, 106. For his works, see Suppl. II, 924, no. 94. Al-Suyūṭī cites a *Qaṣīda fī qawāʿid lisān al-Turk*.

3b. Ṣafī al-Dīn al-Urmawī, d. 723/1323 (see Suppl.).

2. *al-Irshād ilā waqf al-aʿdād*, Patna II, 559,$_{2924,2}$.

3c. Nāṣir al-Dīn Shafīʿ Abu ʾl-Faḍl b. Nur al-Dīn Abu ʾl-Ḥasan ʿAlī b. ʿImād al-Dīn Abu ʾl-Faḍl ʿAbbās al-Kinānī was born in 649/1252 and died in 730/1330.

Al-Raʾy al-ṣāʾib fī ithbāt mā lā budda minhu lil-kātib, Garr. 2195.

4. Abū Ḥafṣ ʿUmar b. ʿAlī b. Sālim b. Ṣadaqa al-Lakhmī al-Iskandarī Tāj al-Dīn b. al-Fākihānī, a Mālikī *faqīh* and philologist, made the pilgrimage from Damascus in 730/1330 and then, having gone to Alexandria, died in 731/1331 (or, according to others, in 734/1334).

DK III, 178, no. 418, Ibn Farḥūn, *Dībāj*, C. 1329, 186/7. 1. *al-Ishāra fi ʾl-naḥw*, ḤKh [1]I, 308, 768, [2]I, 98 with a commentary Pet. AMK 922, on which is *Taʿlīqa mukhtaṣara*, Gotha 314.—2.–5. See Suppl. (2. also Patna I, 148,$_{1425}$).

5. Jalāl al-Dīn Abu ʾl-Maʿālī Muḥammad b. ʿAbd al-Raḥmān b. ʿUmar Khaṭīb Dimashq al-Qazwīnī was born in 666/1267 in Asia Minor, studied *fiqh*, and

---

1 According to d'Ohsson, *Allgemeine Schilderung des Osman. Reiches* I, 573 (G. Jacob, *Beduinenleben* [2]XXXV) it was printed in Istanbul as early as the eighteenth century (?).

became a *qāḍī* there before he was even twenty years old. When his brother became a *qāḍī* in Damascus he accompanied him there and became a preacher at the main mosque. In 724/1324 he became a *qāḍī* there himself, and in 727/1327 he was promoted to chief *qāḍī* of Egypt. In this position he was able to exert considerable influence on the government of Sultan al-Malik al-Nāṣir.
However, the outrageous extravagance of his son | ʿAbdallāh, on account 27
of whom al-Nāṣir had already paid off debts amounting to 30,000 dinars in 724/1324, caused him to be transferred back to Damascus, where he died soon after as a result of a stroke, on 15 Jumādā I 739/1338.

DK IV, 3, no. 3, *ḤS* III, 2, 9, Ibn Baṭṭūṭa I, 210. 1. *Talkhīṣ al-miftāḥ*, see vol. I, 335.—2. *al-Īḍāḥ fi 'l-maʿānī wal-bayān*, on rhetoric, Gotha 2786 (where other MSS are listed), Esc. $^{2}261_{,1}$, Garr. 552.—Commentaries: a. Jamāl al-Dīn Muḥammad b. Muḥammad al-Āqsarāʾī, ca. 775/1375, Esc. $^{2}258$.—b. Anon., on the *shawāhid*, ibid. 249.—c. Shams al-Dīn al-Niksārī, Bol. 393, Alex. Nahw. 2.

5a. Muḥammad b. ʿAlī al-Anṣārī (see Suppl.).

Al-Manzaʿ al-badīʿ, Berl. Ms. or. oct. qu. 2055.

6. Badr al-Dīn al-Ḥasan b. Qāsim b. ʿAbdallāh b. ʿAlī al-Murādī b. Umm Qāsim, who died in 749/1348.

1. *Kitāb al-janā* (*jany*) *al-dānī fī ḥurūf al-maʿānī* Berl. Ms. or. oct. 3873, Gotha 317 (fragm.), Esc. $^{2}78$, Ibr. Pāshā 1053, Alex. Naḥw 8.—2. *Jumal al-iʿrāb*, on phrases that substitute a noun and are therefore subject to inflection, Leid. 215, Bank. XX, 2116.—3. 8 *kāmil* verses on different types of phrases, with a commentary by Ibrāhīm b. al-Ḥasan, Berl. 6877.—4. *Sharḥ Alfiyyat b. Mālik*, see vol. I, 360.—5.–11. see Suppl. (10. autograph, Fātiḥ Waqf Ibr. 71, Ritter).

| 7. ʿAbdallāh b. Yūsuf b. ʿAbdallāh b. Yūsuf b. Aḥmad b. ʿAbdallāh b. Hishām 23
Jamāl al-Dīn Abū Muḥammad, born in Dhu 'l-Qaʿda 708/April 1308, was initially a Ḥanafī, but then became a Shāfiʿī, and in this capacity he was made a professor of *tafsīr* at al-Qubba al-Manṣūriyya in Cairo. However, because he could not find a job at a madrasa, he changed again to be a Ḥanbalī, and was then given a job at one of their madrasas. He died on Friday 5 Dhu 'l-Qaʿda 761/18 September 1360.

DK II, 308, no. 2248, *RA* 148v, al-Suyūṭī, *Ḥusn al-muḥ.* I, 309. 1. *Qaṭr al-nadā wa-ball al-ṣadā*, on grammar, with a commentary, Gotha 238/9 (where other MSS
are listed), BDMG | 67b, Alex. Fun. $110_{,1}$, Sbath 200, Mosul $39_{,241}$, $44_{,50/1}$, $148_{,132}$, 28
$163_{,343}$, $224_{,207}$, $244_{,323/4}$, Patna I, $169_{,1566}$, Garr. $450/_{2}$, Philadelphia 31, print.

Tunis 1281, C. 1274, among others. *Ibn Hijam, La pluie de rosée et l'étanchement du soif, traité de flexion et de syntaxe, trad. par* A. Goguyer, Leiden 1887.—Commentaries: a. *Mūjib al-nidāʾ* by ʿAbdallāh b. Aḥmad al-Fākihī, d. 972/1564 (p. 380), composed in 924/1518, Gotha 331 (where other MSS are listed), Leid. 216, Ind. Off. 968, Alex. Naḥw $35_{,4}$, 39, Cairo ^{1}IV, 108, ^{2}II, 156, Makr. 54.—Glosses: *α* Yāsīn b. Zayn al-Dīn al-ʿAlīmī al-Ḥimṣī al-Shāfiʿī, d. 1061/1651, Paris 4154, Garr. 453/4, Alex. Naḥw 12, print. C. 1299, 1307.—*β–ζ* see Suppl. (*β* read: ʿAlī b. ʿAbd al-Qādir al-Nabtītī, d. after 1060/1650, *Muḥ.* III, 161, Suppl. II, 950, Cairo ^{1}IV, 21. *ε* print. Jerusalem 1320, Alex. Naḥw 12).—b. Aḥmad b. Muḥammad al-Sijāʿī al-Shāfiʿī, d. 1190/1776 (p. 323), Berl. 6741, print. Būlāq 1289, C. 1306 and 1323, on which glosses by Muḥammad al-Anbābī, C. 1310, 1305/6, *taqrīr* by Sayyid al-Sharshīmī al-Sharqāwī, completed in 1272/1856, Alex. Naḥw 7.—c. Anon. *Murqiṣ al-akhyār, Iʿrāb Q. al-n.*, Makr. 55.—d. Glosses on the commentary of the author by Aḥmad b. Aḥmad al-Daljamūnī, twelfth cent., Cairo ^{1}IV, 48, ^{2}II, 103.—e. Ismāʿīl b. al-Shaykh Tamīm al-Jawharī, Gotha 330.—f. Moulvi Irtiza Alikhan, Madras 1889.—g. On selected passages by Ṣādiq b. ʿAlī b. Ḥasan al-Ḥusaynī, d. 855/1451, Berl. 6742/3, on the *shawāhid*, Cairo ^{2}II, 129.—h. On the *shawāhid*: *β* Muḥammad b. Aḥmad al-Shirbīnī, d. 977/1569 (p. 320), Berl. 6745.—*α–ε* see Suppl.—*ζ Maʿālim al-ihtidāʾ* by ʿUthmān b. Makkī al-Zabīdī, C. 1324.—*η* Anon., Mosul $79_{,12}$, $186_{,293}$.—i. Anonymous commentaries and glosses, Berl. 6737/40, de Jong $11_{,9}$.—k.–t. see Suppl.—u. Glosses by Yūsuf al-Mālikī al-Fayshī, d. 1061/1651 (Muḥ. IV, 510), Vat. V. $830_{,7}$, Alex. Naḥw 12.—v. *Hadiyyat al-arīb li-aṣdaq al-ḥabīb* by Abū ʿAbdallāh Muḥammad ʿĀshūr al-Ṭāhir, Naqīb al-ashrāf bi-Tūnis, d. 1284/1867, C. 1296.—Versification by Sulaymān b. ʿAbdallāh b. Shāwī Bek al-ʿUbaydī al-Ḥimyarī, ca. 1178/1764, Berl. 6746.—11 commentaries, 5 glosses, and 3 versifications are listed in Ahlw. 6747.

2. *Mughni 'l-labīb ʿan kutub al-aʿārīb*, composed in 749/1348–756/1355 in Mecca, Berl. 6725/6, Ms. or. qu. 2060, BDMG 80, Munich 736/8, Paris 4155/7, 6418, Br. Mus. 516, Suppl. 976/8, Ind. Off. 966, de Jong, 20, Pet. Ros. 141, Esc. ^{2}48, 97/8, 131, 202, Algiers 120/5, Garr. 445/6, Köpr. 1502, NO 4630/45, AS 4587/8, Cairo ^{1}IV,
29 110, ^{2}II, 160, Makr. 87, Qawala II, 121, Mosul $70_{,260}$, $148_{,135}$, $164_{,261}$, $224_{,215}$, Patna | I, $174_{,1609/10}$, print. Tehran 1274, C. 1302, 1305, 1307, among others—Commentaries: a. *Tuḥfat al-gharīb* by Muḥammad b. Abī Bakr al-Damāmīnī, d. 827/1424 (p. 32), Berl. 6727/8, Leid. 217, Ind. Off. 967, Esc. ^{2}203, Garr. 447, A. Taymūr *RAAD* III, 341, Patnā I, $162_{,1527}$, another, unfinished, Munich 739, Cairo ^{1}IV, 75, Garr. 448.—b. *al-Munṣif min al-kalām* by Aḥmad b. Muḥammad al-Shumunnī, d. 872/1467 (p. 82), Esc. ^{2}49, 50, 204, Cairo ^{1}IV, 114, ^{2}II, 165, Mosul $40_{,254}$, Patna I, $175_{,1614}$, print. Istanbul 1305.—c. *al-Fatḥ al-qarīb*, on the *shawāhid* by al-Suyūṭī, d. 911/1505, Berl. 6729/30, cod. Weil, Esc. ^{2}51, Paris 4158, Cairo ^{1}IV, 71, ^{2}II, 129, Qawala II, 91, Patna I, $169_{,1353}$, print. C. 1322, 1324, among others.—d. Anon,. on the *shawāhid*,

composed in 1056/1646, Algiers 126/7.—e. Muḥammad b. Muḥammad al-Amīr, d. 1232/1817 (p. 485), Makram 15, Qawala II, 71, print. C. 1299, 1310.—f. Glosses by Muḥammad b. ʿArafa al-Dasūqī, d. 1230/1815 (Suppl. II, 737), Būlāq 1286, C. 1306.—g. Notes by Aḥmad b. Muḥammad Dardīr, Gotha 333.—h.–n. see Suppl.—o. *Muntahā amal al-arīb* by Aḥmad b. Muḥammad b. ʿAlī b. al-Mollā, d. 990/1582, Qawala II, 124. |—Abstracts: a. Muḥammad b. ʿAbd al-Majīd al-Shāfiʿī 24
al-Suʿūdī, tenth cent., Esc. ^{2}170.—b. Abū ʿAbdallāh Muḥammad b. Muḥammad b. Haydūn(?), ibid. $244_{,2}$.—c. Muḥammad b. Muṣṭafā Āqkirmānī, d. 1174/1760 (see Suppl.), Alex. Naḥw. 39.—d. Anon., Patna I, $173_{,1604}$.—14 commentaries, 2 versifications, 4 abstracts, and 1 adaptation, Ahlw. 6731.

3. *al-Iʿrāb ʿan qawāʿid al-iʿrāb*, Berl. 6705/6, Gotha 318/9 (where other MSS are listed), Hamb. Or. Sem. 120, Garr. 455, Alex. Fun. $171_{,10}$, Qawala II, 59, Sbath 916, Mosul $241_{,245a}$, Teh. I, 15, II, 310, cf. de Sacy, *Anth. gramm.* 73/92, 155.—Commentaries: a. Muḥammad b. Sulaymān al-Kāfiyajī, d. 879/1474 (p. 114), Berl. 6707/8, Garr. 457.—b. *Muwaṣṣil al-ṭullāb* by Khālid b. ʿAbdallāh al-Azharī, d. 905/1499 (p. 33), Berl. 6709/10, Gotha 324/5 (where other MSS are listed), Hamb. Or. Sem. $75_{,1}$, Garr. 458, Cairo ^{1}IV, 116, ^{2}II, 108, Qawala II, 125, Makr. 60, Alex. Naḥw 20, 43, Mosul $241_{,243b}$, cf. de Sacy, *Anth. gr.* 185, print. C. 1292, 1308.—Glosses by Abū Bakr al-Shanawānī, d. 1019/1610 (p. 285), Cairo ^{1}IV, 119, ^{2}II, 173, by Muḥammad b. ʿAbd al-Raḥmān al-Ḥamawī, completed in 1031/1622, Alex. Naḥw 11, Cairo ^{2}II, 95 (see Suppl.).—c. Muḥammad b. Yaḥyā al-Maqdisī, d. 923/1517, Berl. 6712, Gotha 321.—d. Aḥmad b. Muḥammad al-Zīlī al-Shamsī, completed in 967/1559, Berl. 6713/4, Pet. 191, AMK 922, Paris $4006_{,4}$, Br. Mus. Suppl. 974, Alex. Naḥw 13, Cairo ^{1}IV, 48.—e. *Tawḍīḥ al-iʿrāb*, by Maḥmūd b. Ismāʿīl al-Kharparī | (Khirtibirtī), before 1055/1645, Berl. 6715, Leipz. $27_{,2}$, de 30
Jong $19_{,2}$, Paris $4006_{,5}$, 4148/9, 6551.—f. Glosses on b. by Aḥmad b. Muḥammad al-Zurqānī d. before 1061/1651), Berl. 6716, Paris 4147, Alex. Fun. $96_{,3}$.—h. *Laṭāʾif al-iʿrāb*, an analysis of the Qurʾān passages cited, written by Ḥājjī Bābā b. ʿAbd al-Karīm al-Ṭūsiyawī during the reign of Meḥmed II (855–86/1451–81, p. 223), Paris 4150.—i. Anon., Berl. 6719/22, Gotha 323, Sbath 747.—k. On the *shawāhid*, by al-Bijāʾī, d. 866/1461, Berl. 6717.—m.–u. see Suppl. (n. Alex. Naḥw 13, q. Qawala II, 119).—Abstracts: a. by the author himself, *al-Nukat*, Gotha 320.—b. *al-Qawāʿid al-ṣughrā*, by the author, with the commentary *Aqrab al-maqāṣid* by ʿIzz al-Dīn b. Jamāʿa, d. 819/1416 (p. 94), Alex. Naḥw 3.—Versifications by: a. Aḥmad b. Muḥammad b. al-Hāʾim, d. 815/1412 (p. 91), composed in 795/1393, Berl. 6718.—b. *al-Ṣila wal-ʿāʾid bi-naẓm al-Q.* by Muḥammad b. Sālim b. Wiṣāl, Ambr. A. 43_{iv} (*RSO* III, 275).—c.–i. see Suppl. (i. Anon., also Gotha 327).—k. *Muwaṣṣil al-ṭullāb* by ʿUllaysh, d. 1299/1881 (p. 486), Makr. 60.—4 commentaries and 3 versifications in Ahlw. 6724.

4. *Shudhūr al-dhahab fī maʿrifat kalām al-ʿArab*, a book on grammar with a commentary, Berl. 6732/3, Munich 744, Paris 2677,$_{11}$, 4161, 4192, Br. Mus. Suppl. 971/3, Esc. ^{2}47,$_2$, Algiers 131, BDMG 79, AS 4543, Alex. Naḥw 45, Fun. 142,$_6$, Cairo ^{1}IV, 68, 100, ^{2}II, 127, Makr. 39, Garr. 459, Mosul 148,$_{138}$, 189,$_{101b}$, print. Būlāq 1253, C. 1289, 1299, 1310, among others. Commentaries: a. *Sharḥ al-ṣudūr li-sharḥ zawāʾid al-Shudhūr*, according to ḤKh IV, 19, 1, by al-Ḥasan b. Abī Bakr al-Ḥalabī, d. 836/1432, Esc. ^{2}489,$_2$, by Muḥammad b. ʿAbd al-Dāʾim al-Birmawī, d. 831/1427 (p. 95), following Alex. Naḥw 36, Qawala II, 92.—b. Zakariyyāʾ al-Anṣārī, d. 926/1520 (p. 99), Berl. 6734/5, Hamb. Or. Sem. 49,$_2$.—c. Ibn al-Mollā, composed in 995/1587, Pet. 189.—d. ʿAbd al-Malik b. Ḥusayn al-Isfarāʾinī, d. 1037/1627 (p. 380), Cairo ^{1}IV, 78, ^{2}II, 138, Patna I, 171,$_{1585}$.—e. Glosses by Muḥammad b. Muḥammad al-Amīr, d. 1232/1817 (p. 468), Cairo ^{2}II, 94, print. C. 1272.—f. On the *shawāhid* by Muḥammad ʿAlī al-Fayyūmī, C. 1304.—g.–o. see Suppl.—p. *al-Durr al-manthūr ʿalā Sharḥ al-Sh.* by Muḥammad Manṣūr al-Yāfiʿī al-Ḥanafī, completed in 1237/1821, Alex. Naḥw 16.—q. Anon., Sbath 183, 195, Mosul 224,$_{206}$.—10 commentaries and 2 versifications are listed in Ahlw. 6736.

5. *Mūqid al-adhhān wa-mūqiẓ al-wasnān*, on difficult aspects of grammar, Berl. 6748/9, Paris 4115,$_2$, 4162, Alex. Fun. 188,$_3$, Cairo ^{1}VII, 69, 104, 172, 598.—
31 6. *Alghāz*, grammatical riddles, dedicated to Sultan al-Malik | al-Kāmil, d. 757/1356, Berl. 6750/1, Alex. Fun. 133,$_{10}$, on which glosses by Aḥmad Sayf al-Ghazzī al-Ḥanafī, Cairo ^{2}II, 94, print. C. 1304.—7. *al-Rawḍa al-adabiyya fī shawāhid ʿulūm al-ʿarabiyya*, following Ibn Jinnī's *K. al-lumaʿ* (I, 131), Berl. 6752.—8. *al-Jāmiʿ al-ṣaghīr fi ʾl-naḥw*, Paris 4159, a commentary by Ismāʿīl b. Ibrāhīm al-Yamanī, completed in 932/1525, Paris 4160.—9. *Risāla fi ʾntiṣāb* (*Iʿrāb*) *lughatan wa-faḍlan wa-iʿrāb* (*waṣṭilāḥan*) *khilāfan wa-ayḍan wal-kalām ʿalā hālummā jarran*, Berl. 6886, Cairo ^{1}IV, 53, 59, VII, 564, ^{2}II, 111, 254, Qawala II, 86.—10. On the noteworthy use of the accusative in 9 passages in the Qurʾān, Berl. 6884.—11. A grammatical treatise on difficult passages in the Qurʾān, composed in 747/1346, Esc. ^{2}86,$_6$.—12. *Fawḥ al-shadhā fī masʾalat kadhā*, a reworking of *al-Shadhā fī aḥkām kadhā* by his teacher Abū Ḥayyān, Leid. 219, 220,
25 Köpr. 1593.—13. *Masāʾil fi ʾl-naḥw wa-ajwibatuhā*, Leid. 221. | 14. *Sharḥ al-qaṣīda al-laghziyya fi ʾl-masāʾil al-naḥwiyya*, Leid. 226.—15. *Sharḥ Bānat Suʿād*, see vol. I, 39.—16. *Awḍaḥ al-masālik fī sharḥ Alfiyyat b. Mālik*, see vol. I, 360.—17. *Shawārid al-mulaḥ wa-mawārid al-minaḥ*, on how to attain sainthood, Berl. 2097,$_7$.—18. *Mukhtaṣar al-Intiṣāf*, see vol. I, 346.—19. *Risāla fī tawjīh al-naṣb*, Alex. Fun. 188,$_5$, (= 11?).—20.–24. see Suppl.

8. Aḥmad b. Muḥammad b. ʿAlī al-Muqriʾ al-Fayyūmī, who died after 770/1368.

Kitāb al-miṣbāḥ al-munīr fī gharīb al-Sharḥ al-kabīr, originally glosses on al-Rāfiʿī's commentary on the *Wajīz* by al-Ghazzālī (I, 543), later augmented into a general lexicon of legal literature, Berl. 6976, Gotha 406/7 (where other MSS are listed), Br. Mus. Suppl. 867/9, Cairo ^{1}IV, 187, Patna I, 189,$_{177}$, print. Būlāq 1281, C. 1278, 1305, Kanpur 1288, among others; cf. Mehren, *ZDMG* 27, 204 ff.

9. Muḥammad b. Muḥammad b. ʿAbd al-Karīm al-Shāfʿī al-Mawṣilī al-Baladī al-Baʿlī, who was born in 699/1299 in Baalbek, was a preacher at the Umayyad mosque in Damascus. He died in 774/1372 in Tripoli, having become wealthy through his activity in the booktrade.

DK IV, 188, no. 504, *JA* s. IX, v. 3, p. 305. *Lawāmiʿ al-anwār fī naẓm gharīb al-Muwaṭṭaʾ wa-Muslim*, 300 *rajaz* verses on difficult expressions in the *ḥadīth* works of | Mālik (I, 185) and Muslim (I, 167), Berl. 10166/7, Gotha 588, Esc. ^{1}476 32
(now lost), Patna I, 58,$_{591}$.

10. Shams al-Dīn Muḥammad b. ʿAbd al-Raḥmān b. ʿAlī b. al-Ṣāʾigh al-Ḥanafī al-Zumurrudhī, who was born before 710/1310, was a student of Abū Ḥayyān. He wrote countless philogical works while he was a military judge, a *muftī* at the Dār al-ʿadl, and a professor at the Ṭūlūnid mosque. He died on 10 Shaʿbān 776/15 January 1375.

DK III, 499, no. 1347, Ibn Quṭlūbughā, no. 191. 1. *Kitāb al-mirqāh fī iʿrāb lā ilāha illa 'llāh*, Cairo ^{1}VII, 631, ^{2}I, 158.—2. Hunting poems, Berl. 7866,$_{7}$.

11. Shams al-Dīn Muḥammad b. Abī Bakr al-Khabīṣī, d. 801/1398.

Al-Muwashshaḥ, Sharḥ al-Kāfiya, see Suppl. I, 532,$_{7}$.

12. Shihāb al-Dīn Abu 'l-ʿAbbās Aḥmad b. Muḥammad b. Muḥammad b. ʿAlī al-Aṣbaḥī al-ʿUnnābī al-Andalusī began his studies in Spain, then moved to Cairo to continue them with Ibn Ḥayyān (p. 109), before finally settling in Damascus, where he died in Muḥarram 776/June 1374.

| *DK* I, 298. *Nuzhat al-abṣār*, detailed metrics, completed in 749/1348, Berl. 26
7129.—2. *al-Wāfī fī maʿrifat al-qawāfī*, on the theory of rhyme, ibid. 7130.

13. ʿAbdallāh b. Aḥmad al-Bishbīshī, who was born in 762/1361 and died in Alexandria in 820/1417.

ʿAlī Mubārak, *Khiṭaṭ* IX, 65ff. *Kitāb al-tadhyīl wal-takmīl li-ma ʾstuʿmila min al-lafẓ al-dakhīl*, on foreign words, Cod. Landberg, see Vollers, *ZDMG* 50, 609.

14. Muḥammad b. Abī Bakr b. ʿUmar b. Abī Bakr b. Muḥammad b. Sulaymān b. Jaʿfar al-Makhzūmī al-Iskandarī al-Mālikī al-Damāmīnī Badr al-Dīn was born in Alexandria in 763/1362. He studied there and in Cairo, before moving to Damascus in 800/1398, from where he made the pilgrimage. After his return he
33 became a preacher at the principal mosque | in Alexandria. He later founded a weaving mill, which he mortgaged heavily. When it burned down he ran away from his creditors to the Ṣaʿīd, but was arrested and brought to Cairo. There, Ibn Ḥijja al-Ḥamawī (p. 18) and the privy secretary Nāsir al-Dīn al-Bārizī helped him to pay off his debts, while the latter got him the job of *qāḍī* for the Mālikīs.[2] After a second pilgrimage in 819/1416 he went to Yemen in 820 where he gave lectures in the mosque of Zabīd. From there he travelled to India, acquired great wealth, and died in Shaʿbān 827/July 1424 in Gulbarga.

RA 213v, al-Suyūṭī, *Ḥusn al-muḥ*. I, 311. 1. *Kitāb al-qawāfī*, on metrics, with a commentary by Muḥammad b. ʿUthmān b. ʿUmar al-Balkhī (p. 193), Leid. 225, Ind. Off. 972/3.—2. *Jawāhir al-buḥūr fī ʾl-ʿarūḍ*, on which a commentary by Muḥammad b. Ibrāhīm b. Luʾluʾ al-Zarkashī (p. 456), composed in 882/1477, is preserved in MS Algiers 239.—3. *Sharḥ al-Qaṣīda al-rāmiza lil-Khazrajī*, completed in 817/1414, see I, 380.—4. *Iẓhār al-taʿlīl al-mughlaq li-wujūb ḥadhf ʿāmil al-mafʿūl al-muṭlaq*, Leid. 231,$_1$.—5. *Sharḥ Mughni ʾl-labīb*, p. 29.—6. *Nuzūl al-ghayth*, a confutation of al-Ṣafadī's mistakes in his commentary on the *Lāmiyyat al-ʿajam* (I, 285), composed in 794/1392 in Cairo, Leid. 657/8, Upps. 103, Esc. ^{2}325, 560, Cairo ^{1}IV, 338, ^{2}III, 410, Mosul 278,$_{59,3}$ (autograph dated 795), favourable opinions on it in Berl. 39, for a rebuttal see vol. I, 285.—7. *al-Fatḥ al-rabbānī fī ʾl-radd ʿala ʾl-Binbānī*, a refutation of the
27 attacks of | Minhāj al-Binbānī, whom he had become acquainted with as an emissary to Abu ʾl-Fatḥ Aḥmad Shāh b. Muḥammad Shāh b. Muẓaffar Shāh,[3] a. against the pronunciation of this name, b. against his attacks on particular passages from his work *Maṣābīḥ al-Jāmiʿ* about Bukhārī (I, 164) and from the beginning of his commentary on the *Tashīl*, Leid. 1752.—8. A sermon, in which the names of the suras are used in an artful manner, Berl. 3953,$_4$.—9. *Shams al-maghrib fī ʾl-murqiṣ wal-muṭrib*, a handbook for writing letters, Berl. 8643.—10. *al-Manhal al-ṣāfī*, see p. 193.—11.–13. see Suppl.

2 According to al-Suyūṭī he was a professor of *iqrāʾ* and *naḥw* at the Azhar.

3 This is according to MS RA; however, Muḥammad b. Aḥmad b. Muẓaffar of Gujarāt 816–55/1413–51 must be meant, see Lane-Poole, *Dynasties* 313.

| 15. Aḥmad b. ʿAbbād b. Shuʿayb al-Qināʾī al-Qāhirī Shihāb al-Dīn Abu ʾl-ʿAbbās 34
al-Khawwāṣ, who died in 858/1454[4] as imam of the Quṭbiyya in Cairo.

Al-Kāfī fī ʿilmay al-ʿarūḍ wal-qawāfī, Berl. 7131/2, Paris 2357,$_{5}$, Garr. 506/7, Alex. ʿArūḍ 3, 4, Fun. 128, Patna I, 191,$_{1729}$, lith. C. 1273, 1276, 1297, Cairo ^{1}VII, 336, 339, 454, 605, ^{2}I, 605.—Commentaries: 1. ʿAbd al-Raḥmān b. ʿĪsā al-Murshid al-Wajāhī, b. 975/1567, d. 1037/1628, composed in 1004/1595, Berl. 7133.—2. Khalīl b. Wālī b. Jaʿfar al-Ḥanafī, ibid. 7134/5, Gotha 368, Br. Mus. 637, Alex. ʿArūḍ 6.—3. ʿUmar b. Ḥusayn al-Āmidī, composed in 1162/1749, Berl. 7136.—4. Muḥammad al-Damanhūrī, d. 1288/1871 (p. 478), *Irshād al-shāfī*, C. 1301, *Mukhtaṣar*, composed in 1230/1825, Berl. 7137, Makram 55, Patna I, 191, 1730, print. C. 1281, Būlāq 1285.—5. Anon., Br. Mus. Suppl. 993, Garr. 509.—6.–10. see Suppl. (6. Alex. ʿArūḍ 3; 7. Garr. 508).—11. *Mawāhib al-kāfī ʿala ʾl-Tibr al-ṣāfī fī naẓm al-kitāb al-musammā al-Kāfī etc.* by Ibrāhīm b. Muḥammad al-Ṣūfī al-Wādī al-Muṣābiʿ al-Shabāṭī al-Sharīf, Tunis 1323.

15a. See Suppl. Autograph of both works, AS 4330.

16. Zayn al-Dīn Khālid b. ʿAbdallāh b. Abī Bakr al-Azharī al-Jarjāwī, who died on 14 Muḥarram 905/26 August 1499 in Cairo.

RA II, 123r. 1. *al-Muqaddima al-Azhariyya fī ʿilm al-ʿArabiyya*, with a self-commentary, Gotha 335/6 (where other MSS are listed), BDMG 84/5, Garr. 461/2, Patna I, 170,$_{1583}$, print. Būlāq 1252.—Glosses: a. al-Ḥasan b. al-ʿAṭṭār, d. 1250/1834, Krafft 43, print. Būlāq 1284, C. 1307.—b. ʿAlī b. Ibrāhīm al-Ḥalabī, d. 1044/1634, p. 307, Algiers 177,$_{1}$, Alex. Naḥw 27.—c. Abū Bakr b. Ismāʿīl al-Shanawānī, d. 1019/1610 (p. 285), Tüb. 60, Paris 4194, Alex. Naḥw 10.—d. Abu ʾl-Najāʾ, C. 1312.—e.–k. see Suppl. (f. Alex. Naḥw 9, Makram 32. i. Muḥammad Qūsh b. Yūsuf b. Ibrāhīm al-Gharqī, d. 1232/1817, Alex. Naḥw 34).—l. Muḥammad b. Saʿd b. ʿAyyād, completed in 1253/1837, Alex. Naḥw 34.—2. *al-Alghāz al-naḥwiyya*, Rabat 518,$_{3}$, Cairo ^{1}VII, 59, 199, ^{2}II, 79.—3. *Muwaṣṣil* | *al-ṭullāb ilā qawāʿid* 35
al-iʿrāb, p. 29.—4. *Sharḥ al-Ājurrūmiyya*, p. 238.—5. *Tamrīn al-ṭullāb fī ṣināʿat al-iʿrāb*, I, 362.—6. *Sharḥ al-Muqaddima al-Jazariyya*, p. 202.—7.–14. see Suppl.

17–20. See Suppl. (18.2 *Rafʿ etc.* Berl. 7170/1, *Dafʿ etc.* Garr. 510).

---

4 This is according to Ahlw., who follows al-Sakhāwī; Freytag, *Verskunst* § 36, n. 10, followed by Pertsch and Rieu, gives 729 as the year of death, due to confusion with the Shāfiʿī al-Qūnawī, p. 86.

28 | 3 *Historiography*

A Individual Biographies[1]

1. Shāfiʿ b. ʿAlī b. ʿAbbās b. Ismāʿīl b. ʿAsākir al-Kinānī al-ʿAsqalānī, who was born in Dhu ʾl-Ḥijja 649/February 1252, studied *ḥadīth* and became a secretary in the *dīwān*. Although blinded after being hit by an arrow at the battle of Homs in 680/1281,[2] he was very productive as an historian and an *adīb*. He died on 24 Shaʿbān 730/13 June 1330.

DK II, 184, no. 1922, *Orient.* II, 351. Wüst. *Gesch.* 396. *Al-Manāqib al-sariyya al-muntazaʿa min al-Sīra al-Ẓāhiriyya*, a prose abstract of Ibn ʿAbd al-Ẓāhir's (d. 692/1293) biography of Baybars (see I, 388).

2. In Egypt, Shams al-Dīn al-Shujāʿī wrote, around 745/1344:

Taʾrīkh al-sulṭān al-Malik al-Nāṣir Muḥammad b. Qalāwūn wa-banīhi, a part of this originally very extensive work, on the years 737–45/1336–44, is preserved in MS Berl. 9833, Wüst. *Gesch.* 415.

3. Muḥammad b. ʿAqīl wrote, in 785/1383:

Al-Durr al-naḍīd fī manāqib al-Malik al-Ẓāhir Abī Saʿīd (Barqūq, d. 801/1399), with an introduction on the just ruler and Barqūq's predecessors from Sultan al-Muʿizz ʿIzz al-Dīn Aybak, d. 665/1447, Berl. 9817.

36 | 4. Muḥammad b. Muḥammad b. Aḥmad b. Ṣaṣarrāʾ, who came from a Damascene family of scholars and flourished around 801/1399.

Wüst. *Gesch.* 449. *Al-Durra al-muḍīʾa fi ʾl-dawla al-Ẓāhiriyya*, a history of Sultan Barqūq, 784–801/1382–98, Bodl. I, 849.

5. Abu ʾl-ʿAbbās Aḥmad b. Muḥammad b. ʿAbdallāh b. ʿArabshāh Shihāb al-Dīn al-Dimashqī al-Ḥanafī was born in Damascus on 15 Dhu ʾl-Ḥijja 791/6 November 1392. When the city was conquered by Tīmūr, he, his mother, and
29 his siblings were taken prisoner and hauled off to Samarqand, | where he studied theology and philology with al-Jurjānī (p. 216) and Ibn al-Jazārī (p. 201). Once he had acquired a thorough knowledge of Turkish and Persian, he went

1 For histories of Muḥammad and other prophets, see § 5.

2 Weil, *Gesch. der Chal.* V, 126.

to al-Khīṭa in 811/1408 to complete his education. From there he went with his family to Khwārizm and Dasht, where he studied *fiqh* for several years in Ḥājjī Ţarkhān (Astrakhan), and where his son Tāj al-Dīn (p. 22) was born. Passing through the Crimea, he then went to Adrianople where he became the privy secretary to the Ottoman sultan Meḥmed I. After the latter's death in 824/1421 he returned to Damascus in Rabīʿ II 825/April 1422, living solely off his writings. In 832/1429 he made the pilgrimage to Mecca, and in 840/1429 moved to Cairo. When Jaqmaq rose to power there in 842/1438 he had him incarcerated on accusations of slander; apparently Jaqmaq had been angered by the fact that he had not obeyed his order to come to Damascus from Adrianople, where he had then been the emir. Although released because of an illness after just five days, he died twelve days later, on 15 Rajab 854/25 August 1450.

Biography, Gotha $94_{,7}$, Freytag, *Ebn Arabschah* XXV, Wüst. *Gesch.* 488, *MT* 16r. 1. *ʿAjāʾib al-maqdūr fī nawāʾib Tīmūr*, in spite of its panegyric form, is an often spiteful account, Berl. 9731/2, Ms. or. quart. 2133, Gotha 1840/2 | (where other 37
MSS are listed), Un. Eg. 11049, Patna I, $289_{,2339/40}$, print. C. 1285, 1305. *Ahmedis Arabsiadis vitae et rerum gestarum Timuri historia, ed. lat. vert.* J. Golius, Leiden 1636, second and third editions by Jacob Meyer, Oxford 1703/4, ed. S.H. Manger, Leeuwarden 1767/72, *Histoire du grand Tamerlan, trad. par* Pierre Vattier, Paris 1658. —2. *al-Taʾlīf al-ṭāhir fī shiyam al-Malik al-Ẓāhir al-Qāʾim bi-nuṣrat al-ḥaqq Abī Saʿīd Jaqmaq*, composed in 843/1439, in two parts: a. a mirror for princes; b. a detailed history of the years 841–3/1437–9, Br. Mus. Suppl. 559/60, see *JRAS* 1907, 395ff.—3. *Fākihat al-khulafāʾ*, a mirror for princes in the form of animal fables in rhymed prose, adapted from the Persian *Marzbānnāme* (see no. 4) (see Chauvin, *Bibl.* II, 11, Houtsma, *ZDMG* 52, 359), Berl. 8390/1, Gotha 2696/8 (where other MSS are listed), Köpr. 1345, Yeni 877, NO 4137/8, AS 3320/1, 4154, | Serāi A. II, 3104, Cairo ^{1}IV, 288, print. Mosul 1869, Būlāq 1276, C. 1300, 30
1303, *Fructus imperatorum et jocatio ingeniorum*, ed. G.G. Freytag, 2 vols., Bonn 1832.—4. *Marzubānnāme*, the same content as 3, originally by Marzubān b. Rustam b. Sharwīn, the prince of Ṭabaristān towards the end of the fourth cent., composed in the dialect of his country, translated into New Persian by Saʿd al-Dīn-i Warāwīnī between 607–22/1210–25, and translated into Arabic by him, Gotha 2692 (where other MSS are listed), Paris 3524, lith. C. 1277.— 5. *Jalwat al-amdāḥ al-jamāliyya fī ḥullatay al-ʿarūḍ al-ʿarabiyya*, on the syntax of particles in 183 verses, Berl. 6764.—6. *Tarjumān al-mutarjam etc.* see Suppl. vol. II. Serāi A II, 88, (see *Türk. Mečm.* III, 182).

5a. An anonymous *Sīrat al-ṣulṭān al-shahīd al-Malik al-Ẓāhir Jaqmaq* (r. 842–57/1438–53), Serāi 2992 (from the library of Sayf al-Dīn Inal, 857–65/1453–61).

6. Badr al-Dīn Abu 'l-Faḍl (Abū ʿAbdallāh) Muḥammad b. Abī Bakr b. Aḥmad b. Qāḍī Shuhba al-Asadī al-Dimashqī al-Shāfiʿī, who died in Ramaḍān 874/March 1470.

Wüst. *Gesch.* 491. 1. *al-Durr al-thamīn fī manāqib Nur al-Dīn* (Maḥmūd b. Zengī), Br. Mus. Suppl. $487_{,\mathrm{viii}}$, Pet. AM 175, Alex. Ta'r. 65.—2. *al-Tuḥfat al-bahiyya fī sharḥ al-Ushnuhiyya fi 'l-farā'iḍ*, composed in 832/1428, see I, 489.—3. *Mukhtaṣar Kitāb al-ḥayawān* of al-Damīrī (p. 138), Bodl. I, 503.

38 | 7. In the year 877/1472 an unidentified author wrote:

Ta'rīkh al-Malik al-Ashraf Qā'ītbāy, with a history of his predecessors from Ṣalāḥ al-Dīn onwards, Paris 5916, Bodl. I, 800 (wrongly attributed to al-Suyūṭī), Br. Mus. Suppl. 561/2, Cairo ^{1}V, 23, excerpts from Baybars' expedition against Rhodes and Cyprus are in A. Wahrmund, *Jahresber. der k. k. öff. Lehranstalt für or. Spr.* Vienna 1883.

8. Al-Ḥasan b. Aḥmad b. ʿArabshāh, the son of Shihāb al-Dīn (no. 5) wrote, around 900/1494:

Īḍāḥ al-ẓulm wa-bayān al-ʿudwān fī ta'rīkh al-Nābulusī al-khārij al-khawwān, a biography in rhymed prose of Ibrāhīm al-Nābulusī, who lived around 850/1446 and who is depicted as a cruel and unjust tyrant who ruled Damascus, Berl. 9779.

9. Abu 'l-Baqā' b. Yaḥyā b. al-Jīʿān, who died in 902/1496.

1. *al-Qawl al-mustaẓraf fī safar mawlāna 'l-Malik al-Ashraf*, on Qā'ītbāy's trip to Syria in 882/1477, Esc. $^{2}1708_{,4}$, Cairo V ^{1}114, ^{2}299 (see Suppl.).—2. *Ṭawāliʿ al-budūr fī taḥwīl al-sinīn wal-shuhūr*, AS 2665, Cairo ^{1}V 264.

10. In order to regain the favour of Qānṣūh Ghūrī, an unidentified author wrote, in 923/1517:

Al-ʿUqūd al-jawhariyya fi 'l-nawādir al-Ghūriyya, a collection of historical anecdotes with events from Ghūrī's life, AS 3312/3 (Ritter).

| B Collective Biographical Works[1] 31

1. Abū Isḥāq Ibrāhīm b. Aḥmad b. Muḥammad b. Maʿālī al-Rāqiʿī al-Dimashqī Burhān al-Dīn, a Ḥanbalī preacher who died in 703/1303.

1. *Aḥāsin al-maḥāsin*, containing extracts from the *Ṣifat al-ṣafwa* of Ibn al-Jawzī, and an abstract of the *Ḥilyat al-awliyāʾ* by Abū Nuʿaym, see I, 445.—2. See Suppl. (Wüst. *Gesch.* 378).

| 2. Kamāl al-Dīn Abu ʾl-Faḍl Jaʿfar b. Thaʿlab[2] b. Jaʿfar al-Adfuwī al-Shāfiʿī was 39
born in 685/1286. A linguist and *faqīh*, he was a student of Ibn Daqīq al-ʿĪd and Abū Ḥayyān, with whom he stayed until the latter's death, after which he lived independently in a mansion in Cairo, dying on 10 Ṣafar 748/23 May 1347 (ḤKh mistakenly states 749).

DK I, 535, no. 1452, *RA* 93r, *Orient.* II, 391, Wüst. *Gesch.* 413. 1. *al-Ṭāliʿ al-saʿīd al-jāmiʿ li-asmāʾ nujabāʾ al-Ṣaʿīd*, a history of learned men, originally completed in 738/1337 but then continued up to the year 740/1339, Paris 2148, Bodl. I, 716, II, 592, Lee 95, Alex. Taʾr. 83, Cairo V ^{1}77, ^{2}246, print. C. 1914, 1919, cf. de Sacy, *Chrest.* ^{2}II, 32; used by Muḥammad b. Afḍal al-Dīn b. Badr al-Dīn b. Maḥmūd al-Qudsī al-Makhzūmī al-Shāfiʿī in his *Kitāb al-maqāl al-makhṣūṣ wal-maqām al-manṣūṣ fī madḥ madīnat Qūṣ* (in Upper Egypt), Gotha 1687 (which goes up to the year 989/1581).—2. *al-Badr al-sāfir wa-tuḥfat al-musāfir*, biographies, focussed on poets of the fifth to seventh centuries, Vienna 1169.—3. *al-Imtāʿ bi-aḥkām al-samāʿ*, on the permissibility of singing and instrumental music, Gotha 105,$_1$, Esc. ^{1}1240, Cairo ^{1}II, 67, *Nashra* 4.—Abstracts: a. *Mutʿat al-asmāʿ bi-aḥkām al-samāʿ* by Muḥammad b. ʿUmar b. Mubārak Baḥraq al-Ḥimyarī, d. 930/1524 (Suppl. II, 554), Berl. 5508.—b. *Tashnīf al-asmāʿ bi-aḥkām al-samāʿ* by Aḥmad Ḥāmid al-Maqdisī, Alex. Fun. 160,$_2$.—4. *Kitāb farāʾid wa-maqāṣid al-qawāʿid*, on duties, *al-farḍ*, as the basis of the *furūʿ*, as an explanation of an unknown *Muqaddima* by al-Nawawī, d. 676/1277 (I, 496), Gotha 105,$_2$.—5. *al-Mūfī bi-maʿrifat al-taṣawwuf wal-ṣūfī*, Fātiḥ 2876, 741 AH (Ritter).

3. Ṣalāḥ al-Dīn Abu ʾl-Ṣafāʾ Khalīl b. ʿAbdallāh Aybak al-Ṣafadī was born in 696/1296 in Safad. He studied in Damascus with the poet Ibn Nubāta (p. 11),

1 For the *Ṭabaqāt al-fuqahāʾ*, see the respective *madhhabs*, and for works on *ḥadīth*-scholars see the section on *ḥadīth*.

2 Thus in *DK*, *RA*, and the Cairo MSS'; Pertsch and Wüst. have between parentheses Taghlib, as do al-Subkī, al-Shawkānī, and ḤKh (see Suppl.).

the linguist Abū Ḥayyān, and the *fuqahāʾ* Ibn Jamāʿa and al-Mizzī. He worked
32 as a secretary in | Safad, Cairo, Aleppo, and al-Raḥba, and was a treasurer (*wakīl bayt al-māl*) when he died of the plague in Damascus on 10 Shawwāl 764/24 July 1363.

40 | *DK* II, 87, no. 1654, *RA* 118v, *ḤS* III, 2, 9, Wüst. *Gesch.* 423, Hartmann, *Muw.* $81_{,1}$, Hoogvliet, *Divers. script. loci* 152/8. 1. *al-Wāfī bil-wafayāt*, see Suppl. (with G. Gabrieli, *Rend. Lincei* XXIV, 551/615, vol. 13/4, Garr. 682, another volume of the autograph AS 4036, Ritter. Edition of vol. II by S. Dedering in preparation).—2. *Aʿyān al-ʿaṣr wa-aʿwān al-naṣr*, biographies of famous men and women of the eighth cent., Berl. 9864/5 (?), Cairo ^{2}V, 35 (photograph of ʿĀšir Ef,. see Suppl.).[3]—3. *Tuḥfat dhawi ʾl-albāb fī-man ḥākama bi-Dimashq min al-khulafāʾ wal-mulūk wal-nuwwāb*, a versification (*urjūza*) of a work by Ibn ʿAsākir (I, 403), Pet. AM 166, Paris 5827, see M. Kurd ʿAlī, *RAAD* V, 445/56.—4. *Nakt al-himyān fī nukat al-ʿumyān*, on famous blind people, Berl. 9866, Pet. AM 218, ʿĀṭif Ef. ḤKh VII, 219, no. 694, Patna II, $299_{,2385}$.—5. *al-Shuʿūr bil-ʿūr*, on one-eyed people, as a supplement to the previous work, Berl. 9867.—6. *Alḥān al-sawājiʿ min al-nādī wal-rājiʿ*, a collection of letters from the year 760/1359, Berl. 8631 (autograph), individual letters ibid. 8632, Pet. AM 288, Upps. 87, Paris 2067, Br. Mus. Suppl. 1016, Bodl. I, 380, Esc. ^{2}326, Qilič ʿA. ḤKh VII, 104, no. 667, Garr. 88/9, Patna I, 194; poems in praise thereof, Berl. $65_{,40}$.—7. *Munshaʾāt*, Cairo ^{1}IV, 334.—8. *al-Tadhkira al-Ṣalāḥiyya* (*Ṣafadiyya*), abstracts of various works, in 30 vols., individual vols. Gotha 2140/1, Br. Mus. 765, Suppl. 1017/8, Bodl. II, 335, Esc. ^{2}483 (?), Cairo ^{1}IV, 216, ^{2}III, 59, Mosul *RAAD* IX, 105/6, Ind. Off. 3829 (*Juzʾ* 1–3), 3799 (*Juzʾ* 48/9), see Krenkow, ibid. 687/93, see ibid. XIII, 405, XIV, 38/40.—9. *Dīwān al-fuṣaḥāʾ wa-tarjumān al-bulaghāʾ*, an anthology in prose and verse composed for Sultan Āqbughā al-Khāṣṣakī, the lālā of al-Malik al-Ashraf (*DK* I, 391, no. 1003), autograph Vienna 389.—10. *Lawʿat al-shākī wa-damʿat al-bākī*, tales of a pederast and his lover, with many poems, Gotha 2046/7 (where other MSS are listed), Heid. *ZDMG* 91, 308, Paris 3074, $3658_{,12}$, 4642, Algiers 1895, Esʿad 2884, Cairo ^{1}VI, 231, print. C. 1274, 1302, 1307, Tunis 1281, Istanbul 1291, 1301, attributed by ḤKh V, $344_{,11336}$ to Zayn al-Dīn Manṣūr b. ʿAbd al-Raḥmān al-Shāfiʿī, p. $335_{,10}$, see Suppl. 463, in MS Sarkis 1213 attributed to ʿAlāʾ al-Dīn b. Sharīf al-Māridīnī,
41 and in | a MS of A. Taymūr to Ṣafī al-Dīn al-Ḥillī.[4]—11. *al-Ḥusn al-ṣarīḥ fī miʾat*

3 Mainly on the basis of this work, Mūsā b. Khālid b. Yūsuf b. Ayyūb Sharaf al-Dīn wrote an anthology of exceptional ʿAbbāsid poets, *Mukhtaṣar tadhkira* part I, autograph ʿĀšir I, 625. (Ritter).

4 Similarly, the *Khalʿ al-ʿidhār fī waṣf al-ʿidhār* of al-Nawājī, p. 56, is attributed to him in Munich 598.

malīḥ, selected verses about beautiful youngsters, | Br. Mus. Suppl. 1112, AS 33
3177, Cairo ^{2}III, 15.—12. *Kashf al-ḥāl fī waṣf al-ḥāl*, a collection of poems whose words have a different sense if pronounced differently, Copenhagen 293/4.—13. *Ladhdhat al-samʿ fī ṣifat al-damʿ*, an anthology of poems referring to tears, in 37 chapters, each of which ends with a poem by the author, Copenhagen 297, with the title *Tashnīf al-samʿ fī waṣf al-damʿ*, Munich 597.—Abstracts with additions by ʿAlī b. Muḥammad al-Balāṭunsī, d. 936/1529 (p. 320), Leid. 519.—14. *al-Rawḍ al-nāsim wal-thaghr al-bāsim*, epigrams, Esc. ^{2}1848.—16. *Rashf al-zulāl fī waṣf al-hilāl*, from which a *qaṣīda* by al-Ḥaṣkafī, d. 551/1156, on the various meanings of the word *al-hilāl*, Berl. 7064,$_{1}$—17. *Rashf al-raḥīq fī waṣf al-ḥarīq*, a *maqāma*, Esc. ^{2}564,$_{3}$.—18. A *qaṣīda*, Berl. 7860.—19. A *ṭāʾiyya* with a commentary by ʿUmar b. Abī Bakr al-ʿAlawānī, Leipz. 475.—20. A *muwashshaḥ*, Gotha 26,$_{i}$.—21. *Nuṣrat al-thāʾir ʿala ʾl-mathal al-sāʾir*, against Ibn al-Athīr (I, 358), Cairo ^{1}IV, 339, ^{2}III, 413.—22. *Jinān al-jinās*, paronomasias, Leid. 320, Pet. AM, Esc. ^{2}429,$_{2}$, NO 3761, Istanbul 1299; abstract *Nuzhat al-khalāṣ fī ʿilm al-jinās*, Berl. 7333.—23. *Faḍḍ al-khitām ʿani ʾl-tawriya wal-istikhdām*, Esc. ^{2}219, 429, 430, Köpr. 1351, Cairo ^{1}IV, 144, ^{2}II, 214, see p. 1925, 17.—24. *Ikhtirāʿ al-khurāʿ*, a lengthy explanation of two obscure verses in derision of the pedantism of various commentators (see Rosen and Kračkovsky, *Zap Koll. Vost.* 1925, 291/303), Leid. 321.—25. *Sharḥ Lāmiyyat al-ʿajam* I, 285.—26. *Ṭawq al-ḥamāma, mukhtaṣar Sharḥ qaṣīdat b. ʿAbdūn li-Ibn Badrūn* I, 321.—27. *Sharḥ Risālat b. Zaydūn* I, 325.—28. *Kitāb ghawāmiḍ al-Ṣaḥāḥ* I, 134.—29. *Ṣarf al-ʿayn ʿan ṣarf al-ʿayn fī waṣf al-ʿayn*, autograph in Berlin Ms. or. oct. 3806 (just some leaves), continuation in a MS from Istanbul (photograph in Ritter's possession).—31.–41. see Suppl.

4. Abu ʾl-Maʿālī Muḥammad b. Rāfiʿ b. Hijris Taqī al-Dīn al-Sallāmī al-Ṣamīdī al-Shāfiʿī was born in Cairo in Dhu ʾl-Qaʿda 704/June 1305 and began his studies
there, | before continuing them in Damascus in 714/1314. Soon after his return 42
to Cairo in 721/1321 his father passed away. Having revisited Damascus following his pilgrimage in 723/1323 and again in 729/1329, this time with a side trip to Hama and Aleppo, he moved permanently to that city in 739/1339, where he lectured at the Nūriyya and Fāḍiliyya *ḥadīth* schools. He died in 18 Jumādā I 774/14 October 1372.

DK III, 439, no. 1176, *Ḥuff.* XXII, 10, *Orient.* II, 433, Wüst. *Gesch.* 433. *Kitāb al-wafayāt*, a continuation of the work with the same title, which had been written by his teacher al-Birzālī (p. 45), covering the years 738–74/1338–72, Gotha 1758, Cairo V ^{1}175, ^{2}406.—2. *al-Mukhtār al-mudhayyal bihi ʿalā Taʾrīkh b. al-Najjār* (I, 433), from which a *Muntakhab* by Taqī al-Dīn al-Fāsī (p. 222), ed. ʿAbbās al-ʿAzzāwī, Baghdad 1357/1938 (Maṭbaʿat al-Ahālī).

34 | 5. Muwaffaq al-Dīn Abū Muḥammad ʿAbd al-Raḥmān b. al-Faqīh ʿUthmān b. Abi ʾl-Ḥazm Makkī b. Tāj al-Dīn Abu ʾl-ʿAbbās b. Sharaf al-Dīn Muḥammad al-Shāfiʿī al-Khazrajī al-Anṣārī wrote, between 771/1369 and 780/1378:

Murshid al-zuwwār ilā qubūr al-abrār, on the Muqaṭṭam mountain near Cairo and those buried there, Br. Mus. Suppl. 662/3, Gotha 1091, Cairo ^{1}V 146 (see Suppl.).

5a. Muḥammad b. al-Ḥasan b. ʿAbdallāh al-Ḥusaynī al-Wāsiṭī, d. 776/1373.

1.–3. see Suppl.—4. *Sharḥ al-Mukhtaṣar fi ʾl-uṣūl*, vols. 3 and 4, Dam. ʿUm. $37_{,114}$.

6. Abu ʾl-Fidāʾ Ismāʿīl b. Muḥammad b. Bardīs al-Baʿlī al-Ḥanbalī Kātib al-Dhahabī (p. 46), who died in Baalbek in 786/1384 or 785 (see Suppl.).

1. *al-Iʿlām fī wafayāt al-aʿlām*, in verse.—2. *al-Intikhāb fi ʾkhtiṣār Kashf al-alqāb*, AS 2961.—3. see Suppl.

7. ʿAlāʾ al-Dīn Abu ʾl-Ḥasan ʿAlī b. Muḥammad b. Saʿd b. Khaṭīb al-Nāṣiriyya, who was born in Jibrīn near Aleppo in 774/1372, was *qāḍī* in Aleppo and Tripoli, and died in 843/1439.

43 | Wüst. *Gesch.* 480. 1. *Kitāb al-durr al-muntakhab fī takmilat taʾrīkh Ḥalab*, alphabetically ordered biographies of famous men with some connection to Aleppo, with an introduction on the topography of the town, individual volumes Berl. 9791, Gotha 1772, Br. Mus. $436_{,2}$; an abstract by his son Muḥammad, ca. 860/1456, Berl. 9875.—2. *Muntakhabāt min Kitāb al-kawākib al-waḍīʾa fi ʾl-Dhayl ʿalā Taʾrīkh b. Khaṭīb al-Nāṣiriyya*, Alex. Taʾr. 115.

8. Ḥamza b. Aḥmad al-Dimashqī al-Ḥusaynī ʿIzz al-Dīn, who died in 874/1469 (see Suppl.).

Ibn al-Shammāʿ, *al-Qabas al-ḥāwī* I, f. 67a, Wüst. *Gesch.* 492. *Kitāb al-muntahā fī wafayāt uli ʾl-nuhā*, autograph Leipz. 678.

9. Shams al-Dīn Abu ʾl-Khayr Muḥammad b. ʿAbd al-Raḥmān b. Muḥammad b. Abī Bakr b. ʿUthmān al-Sakhāwī al-Shāfiʿī was born in Rabīʿ I 830/January 1427 and died in Medina in Shaʿbān 902/April 1497 (see Suppl.).

RA 228v, al-Kattānī, *Fihris* II, 335/8, Wüst. *Gesch.* 504. 1. *al-Ḍawʾ al-lāmiʿ fī aʿyān al-qarn al-tāsiʿ*, biographies of famous men of the ninth cent., but in which he also included a son of the Nuwayrī family who only reached two months of age (VII, 209), alphabetically arranged in 5 vols. (see Suppl.), cf. ZDMG VI, 411, VII, 578.—Abstracts: a. *al-Badr al-ṭāliʿ min al-Ḍawʾ al-lāmiʿ* by Aḥmad b. Muḥammad b. ʿAbd al-Salām al-Manūfī, d. 931/1525, Vienna 1179, Leid. 872, Paris 2078.—b. *al-Qabas al-ḥāwī li-ghurar al-Ḍ. al-l.* by Zayn al-Dīn ʿUmar b. al-Shammāʿ al-Ḥalabī, d. 936/1529 (p. 304), Bodl. I, 855, Patna I, 298,$_{2379/80}$.—2. *al-Kawkab al-muḍīʾ*, on scholars of the ninth cent., Berl. 9878.—3. *Wajīh al-kalām, dhayl Duwal al-islām*, a continuation of al-Dhahabī's world history (p. 46), | covering the years 745–898/1344–1493, Berl. 9463, Vienna 809, Br. 35
Mus. 1232, 1, Bodl. I, 843, 853.—4. *Dhayl Rafʿ al-iṣr ʿan quḍāt Miṣr*, a continuation of the work of Ibn Ḥajar (p. 70), Paris 2150, Leid. 905, Patna II, 321,$_{2428}$.—5. *al-Iʿlān bil-tawbīkh li-man dhamma ahl al-tawārīkh,* a defence of historiography, followed by a list of historians and their works, a description of chronology, and an overview of biographical collections, ordered alphabetically by country and city, Berl. 9364, Leid. 746.—6. *al-Jawāhir al-majmūʿa wal-nawādir al-masmūʿa*, traditions | praising generosity and condemning greed, Esc. ^{2}502, 44
Patna I, 147,$_{1415}$.—7. *al-Maqāṣid al-ḥasana fī kathīr min al-aḥādīth al-mashhūra ʿala ʾl-alsina*, NO 1271, Yeni 297, Cairo ^{1}I, 427, ^{2}I, 150, Alex. Ḥad. 55,$_{2}$, 64, Mosul 195,$_{90}$.—Abstract, *Tamyīz al-ṭayyib min al-khabīth fī-mā warada ʿalā alsinat al-nās min al-ḥadīth,* by ʿAbd al-Raḥmān b. ʿAlī b. Muḥammad al-Zabīdī Abu ʾl-Faraj b. al-Daybaʿ, d. 897/1492 (p. 401), Berl. 1631, Heid. ZDMG 91, 381, Garr. 1499, from which *Aḥādīth multaqaṭa min al-T.* or *Ikhtiṣār Mukhtaṣar al-M. al-ḥ* by Muḥammad b. ʿAbd al-Bāqī al-Zurqānī, d. 1122/1710 (p. 328), Berl. 1631, Garr. 1409, Cairo ^{1}I, 259, a further abstract Berl. 1632, Ms. or. oct. 3897.—8. *al-Qanāʿa fī-mā yaḥsun al-iḥāṭa bihi min ashrāṭ al-sāʿa*, on the signs of the Last Judgement, Berl. 2752, Asʿad 1446,$_{2}$.—9. *al-Qawl al-munabbiʾ ʿan tarjamat b. ʿArabī*, especially against his *Kitāb al-futūḥāt* and *Kitāb al-fuṣūṣ* (I, 572), Berl. 2849.—10. *al-Tawajjuh lil-rabb bi-daʿawāt al-karab*, AS 1743.—11. *al-Iṣṭifāʾ fī asmāʾ al-Muṣṭafā*, Qawala II, 227.—12. *al-Qawl al-badīʿ fi ʾl-ṣalāt ʿala ʾl-ḥabīb al-shafīʿ*, composed in Ramaḍān 861/July–Aug. 1457, Berl. 3921, Köpr. 385, Cairo ^{1}II, 209, Alex. Ḥad. 54,$_{1}$, Faw. 15, Indian printing Patna I, 149,$_{1427}$; *al-Ḥirz al-manīʿ etc.* see Suppl.—13. *Istijlāb irtiqāʾ al-ghuraf etc.* see Suppl.—14. *al-Sirr al-maktūm fi ʾl-farq bayna ʾl-maʾālayn al-maḥmūd wal-madhmūm*, AS 1849.—15. *Tuḥfat al-aḥbāb wa-bughyat al-ṭullāb fi ʾl-khiṭaṭ wal-mazārāt wal-tarājim wal-biqāʿ*, on visiting graves, Alex. Taʾr. 44, Cairo ^{1}V, 29, ^{2}V, 125, Qawala II, 231, C. 1937.—16. *al-Qawl al-tāmm fi ʾl-ramy bil-sihām*, Cairo ^{1}VI, 177.—17. *Fatḥ al-mughīth bi-sharḥ*

Alfiyyat al-ḥadīth (I, 442), Lucknow 1886.—18. *Sharḥ al-Hidāya lil-Jazarī*, see p. 203.—19. A continuation of Maqrīzī's *al-Sulūk*, p. 39$_{,3}$.—20.–36. see Suppl. (25. Garr. 1916).

C Local and National History

1. Al-Ḥasan b. Abī Muḥammad ʿAbdallāh al-ʿAbbāsī al-Hāshimī al-Ṣafadī, see Suppl.

1a. Shams al-Dīn Abū ʿAbdallāh Muḥammad b. Majd al-Dīn Abū Isḥāq Ibrāhīm b. Abī Bakr b. ʿAbd al-ʿAzīz al-Jazarī al-Dimashqī, who died in 739/1338, see Suppl. I, 589, II, 33, 45, 3a.

2. Muḥammad b. Qāsim b. Muḥammad al-Nuwayrī al-Mālikī al-Iskandarī, see Suppl.

45 | *Al-Ilmām etc.* Berl. 9815, Patna I, 286$_{,2355}$, P. Herzsohn, *Der Überfall Alexandriens*
36 *durch Peter I,* | Diss. Bonn 1886, see Kahle, *Mél. Maspéro* III, 1935, 141/54.

3. Abū Muḥammad al-Qāsim b. Muḥammad b. Yūsuf ʿAlam al-Dīn al-Birzālī al-Shāfiʿī, who was of Berber stock, was born in Seville in Jumādā I 665/February 1267. After completing his studies there he went to Aleppo in 685/1285, and made the pilgrimage to Mecca in 688/1289. In Damascus he became a professor at the Ashrafiyya school for *ḥadīth*—which merged with the Ẓāhiriyya in 713/1313—and finally was senior professor at the Nūriyya and Nafīsiyya. He made the pilgrimage four more times, but during the last one he died at Khulayṣ springs, between Mecca and Medina, on 4 Dhu ʾl-Ḥijja 739/14 June 1339.

Ḥuff. XXI, 15, *Fawāt* II, 130, Wüst. *Gesch.* 403. 1. *Kitāb al-wafayāt*, see Suppl.—2. *Mukhtaṣar al-miʾa al-sābiʿa*, a chronicle of the years 601–736/1204–1335, with particular emphasis on obituaries, Berl. 9448.—3.–4. see Suppl.—5. *al-ʿAwāli ʾl-musnada*, Patna II, 364$_{,2547,5}$.

4. Badr al-Dīn Abū Muḥammad al-Ḥasan (Ḥusayn) b. ʿUmar (ʿAmr) b. Ḥabīb al-Dimashqī al-Ḥalabī al-Shāfiʿī was born in Damascus in Jumādā II 710/November 1310. Having started his studies in Damascus, he continued these in Aleppo where his father had become a professor of *ḥadīth* and a *muḥtasib*, but who had died in 726/1326 on a trip to Marāgha. In 733/1332 he made the pilgrimage, then stayed in Cairo, spent five months in Alexandria, and visited Jerusalem and Hebron in 738/1337, before making his second pilgrimage in

739/1338. In 745/1344 he travelled with the emir Sharaf al-Dīn through Syria. In 755–6/1354–5 he was a guest of | the governor Sayf al-Dīn Manjak in Tripoli, 37
and of the same person in Damascus in 759–61/1358–60. He spent his final years in Aleppo, where he died on 21 Rabīʿ II 779/28 August 1377.

| DK II, 29, no. 1543, RA 103v, Ṭabbākh, *Taʾr. Ḥalab* V, 66/71, *Orient.* II, 197, 343, 46
Quatremère, *Hist. des Sultans Maml.* I, 204, Wüst. *Gesch.* 440. 1. *Durrat al-aslāk fī mulk* (*dawlat*) *al-Atrāk*, a history of the Mamlūk sultans of Egypt, in rhymed prose, covering the years 648–777/1250–1375, arranged by year, with asides on neighbouring countries and detailed obituaries, Berl. 9723/4, Paris 1719/20, 4680 (autograph), Bodl. I, 819 (up to 708), Assemani, BO I, 627$_{,xiv}$, Yeni 849, 850, vol. III, with a continuation by his son Zayn al-Dīn Ṭāhir for the years 778/801, Bodl. I, 739.—Abstract *Muntakhab* by Ibn Qāḍī Shuhba, d. 851/1448 (p. 51), Paris 1721 (a draft in his own hand).—2. *Juhaynat*[1] *al-akhbār fī mulūk al-amṣār*, Vat. V. 277, Köpr. 1069, Cairo ^{1}V, 42, ^{2}V, 152, Alex. Taʾr. 56.—3. *Tadhkirat al-nabīh fī ayyām al-Manṣūr wa-banīhi*, a history of Sultan Qalāʾūn and his sons, Berl. 9816, Br. Mus. 315.—4. *al-Najm al-thāqib fī ashraf al-manāqib*, on the character of the Prophet, Berl. 2572/3, Brill M. 316, Algiers 1680, Alex. Taʾr. 16.—5. *al-Muqtafā fī sīrat al-Muṣṭafā*, Esc. ^{2}1745$_{,8}$, Cairo V ^{1}156, ^{2}355.—6. *Nasīm al-ṣabā*, descriptions of nature and the life of man in rhymed prose and verse, composed in 756/1355, Berl. 8380/1, Brill M. 315$_{,3}$, Gotha 2775, Leid. 499, Paris 3244$_{,2}$, 3206$_{,3}$, 3361/4, 6240, 6707, Bodl. I, 1283$_{,2}$, Esc. ^{2}306$_{,3}$, 474$_{,2}$, 551$_{,3}$, 552, AS 4332, Cairo ^{1}IV, 307, 338, print. Alex. 1289, C. 1307, 1320/1902; a commendation of it in verse and prose, Berl. 31.—7. Praise of God in rhymed prose, Berl. 2285.—8. *Kashf al-murūṭ ʿan maḥāsin al-shurūṭ*, forms for legal deeds, Berl. 4964, Cairo ^{1}III, 266.—9. A collection of *dūbayt* verses, Paris 3362$_{,4}$.—10.–11. see Suppl.—12. *Qaṣīda tāʾiyya*, Alex. Adab 129 = Ṭabbākh, op. cit., 69/70.—13. *Taʾrīkh* until Abū Saʿīd, Bursa, Haraccizade Taʾr. 18 (Ritter).

5. Muḥammad b. Ḥasan al-Banbī al-Shāfiʿī wrote, around 826/1423:

Al-ʿUqūd al-durriyya fi ʾl-umarāʾ al-Miṣriyya (see I, 409$_{,4}$), organised by century from the year 1 until the accession to the throne of Barsbāy in 825/1422, | with 38
death notices of scholars up to Ibn al-ʿIrāqī, d. 826/1423, which was continued by al-Nuʿaimī (d. 927/1521) up to the year of his death, Br. Mus. Suppl. 487$_{,iv}$.

1 See al-Maydānī, *Amth.* I, 304, al-ʿAskarī, ibid., in the margin of 1310, II, 65, Ps.-Jāḥiẓ, *Kitāb al-maḥāsin* 271, 14, TA IX, 169.

47 | 6. Sāliḥ b. Yaḥyā b. Buḥtur was of the Banū Buḥtur, which had controlled the al-Gharb district near Beirut as an emirate since 542/1147. He died after 840/1436.

Wüst. *Gesch.* 479. *Taʾrīkh Bayrūt* (*āl Tanūkh*) sketches the history of Beirut and the Buḥtur family under Egyptian, Damascene, and Frankish rule, with charters from the family archives, Paris 1670, continued by his son Muḥammad, ed. L. Cheikho, *al-Mashriq* I, 11, Beirut 1898.

7. Abu ʾl-ʿAbbās Aḥmad b. ʿAlī b. ʿAbd al-Qādir b. Muḥammad al-Ḥusaynī Taqī al-Dīn al-Maqrīzī, who was born in Cairo in 766/1364, was raised as a Ḥanafī by his maternal grandfather Ibn al-Ṣāʾigh (p. 32). However, in 786/1384 he moved to the Shāfiʿīs, fought his former *madhhab*, and even seemed to have acquired Ẓāhirī leanings. He made the pilgrimage the following year, after which he became acting *qāḍī* and *kātib*. From 801–2/1399 onward he worked for a few months as *muḥtasib*, and then became a preacher at the ʿAmr b. al-ʿĀṣ mosque and at the madrasa of Sultan Ḥasan, *qayyim* of the mosque of al-Ḥākim, and teacher of *ḥadīth* at the Muʾayyadiyya. In 811/1408 he went to Damascus as the custodian of the Qalānisiyya Endowment and the Nūrī hospital, as well as being a professor at the Ashrafiyya and Iqbāliyya madrasas. In the 820s he retired to become a private citizen in Cairo, devoting himself entirely to his literary work. In 834/1430 he made the pilgrimage, along with his whole family, and did not return to Cairo until 839/1435. He died there, after a long illness, on 27 Ramaḍān 845/9 February 1442.

39 | Al-Suyūṭī, *Ḥusn al-muḥ.* I, 321, de Sacy, *Chrest.* ^{2}I, 112, Hamaker, *Spec. Cat.* 207, Wüst. *Gesch.* 482, Goldziher, *Ẓāhir.* 196/202. 1. *al-Mawāʿiẓ wal-iʿtibār fī dhikr*
48 *al-khiṭaṭ wal-āthār*,[2] a geography and history of Egypt with | special emphasis on the topography of al-Fusṭāṭ and Cairo, Berl. 6108/9, Gotha 1675/82 (where other MSS are listed), Paris 1729/64, 2265 (see E. Galtier, *Bull. de l'Inst. franç. d'Arch. or.* V, 117), 5865, Algiers 1601, Garr. 595, NO. 3289/91, Yeni 902/4, AS 3475 (830 H), 3476/7, 3478/9, 3480 (part IV, a copy of the autograph), 3481 (part IV), 3482/3 (part II, from the autograph), 3484, Cairo V ^{1}162, print. Būlāq 1270, 2 vols.

2 Al-Sakhāwī, *al-Ḍawʾ al-l.* II, $22,_{18}$, accuses him of simply having appropriated the work of his predecessor al-Awḥadī in his *Khiṭaṭ* (Quatremère, *Hist. des sultans Mamlouks* I, xii), and this accusation becomes all the more credible when it is discovered that the same al-Maqrīzī also copied Ibn Ḥazm verbatim, without mentioning him even once; Goldziher, *Ẓāh.* 202, *M. St.* II, 269. For a modern imitation by ʿAlī Bāshā Mubārak, d. 1893, see p. 482.—On the translation of the title see F. Galtier, *Bull. de l'Inst. franç. d'Arch. or.* V, 156ff.

Excerpts in Langlès, *Not. et Extr.* VI, 320, de Sacy, *Chrest.* ^{2}I, 93/369, II, 88/190, v. Tiesenhausen, *Goldene Horde* I, 417. *Takyoddini Ahmedis al-Makrisii Narratio de expeditionibus adversus Dimyatham*, ed. H.A. Hamaker, Amsterdam 1824. *M. s. Geschichte der Copten v.* F. Wüstenfeld, Göttingen 1845. The same text in *al-Qawl al-ibrīzī lil-ʿallāma al-M.* by Mīnā Efendi Iskander, C. 1898.—Abstracts: a. *al-Rawḍa al-bahiyya* by Aḥmad al-Ḥanafī, Gotha 1683.—b. *Qaṭf al-azhār* by Abu ʾl-Surūr b. Muḥammad b. Abi ʾl-Surūr al-Bakrī al-Ṣiddīqī, Leid. 974, Paris 1765/6, Pet. AM 237; cf. C. Vollers, Note sur un ms. ar. abrevié de M., *Bull. Soc. Khéd. Géogr.* III s. 2, 131/9.—2. *Ittiʿāẓ al-ḥunafāʾ bi-akhbār al-aʾimma al-khulafāʾ*, a history of the Fāṭimids, Gotha 1652 (autograph), cf. Kosegarten, *Chrest. Ar.* p. XVII, no. 115.—3. *al-Sulūk li-maʿrifat duwal al-mulūk*, a history of Egypt covering the period 577–840/1181–1436, Gotha 1620/1 (where other MSS are listed), Paris 1726/8, Br. Mus. Suppl. 480, Yeni 887, Köpr. 1137, Patna I, $266_{,2223}$, cf. de Sacy, *Chrest. Ar.* ^{2}I, 484/98. *Histoire des Sultans Mamlouks par Makrizi, trad. par* Quatremère, 2 vols. Paris 1837/44.—Continuations: a. *al-Tibr al-masbūk fī dhayl al-Sulūk*, Continuation de l'Hist. des Mamlouks par El-Sakhaoui (p. 43) texte ar. d'après le ms. unique conservé à la Bibl. Khéd. (^{2}V, 121), revue et corr. par A. Zeki Bey, *Rev. d'Ég.* II, III, Būlāq 1896/7.—b. Ibn Taghrībirdī, see no. 9, 6.—4. *Kitāb al-muqaffā*, descriptions of the lives of all rulers and famous men who ever lived in Egypt, alphabetically listed, planned to be 80 volumes, of which he only finished 16 in clean copy, 3 vols. Leid. $1032_{,1}$, 1 vol. Paris 2144 (all 4 autographs), cf. Dozy, *Notices sur quelques Mss.* | *ar. Leyde* 1847/51, ZDMG 52, 224.— 49
5. *Durar al-ʿuqūd al-farīda fī tarājim al-aʿyān al-mufīda*, biographies of famous contemporaries, alphabetically listed, vol. I, *alif* and a part of *ʿayn*, Gotha 1771 (autograph).—6. *al-Durar al-muḍīʾa fī taʾrīkh al-duwal al-islāmiyya*, which runs from the death of ʿUthmān until al-Muʿtaṣim, the last ʿAbbāsid caliph, Cambr. p. 365.—7. *Imtāʿ al-asmāʿ bi-mā lil-nabī ṣlʿm min al-aḥwāl wal-ḥafada wal-matāʿ*, on the relatives and the household utensils of the Prophet, based on lectures held in | Mecca, 6 vols., Gotha 1830, Köpr. 1004.—8. A collection of 40
smaller works of mixed content, Paris 4657, ʿĀṭif 2814, Welīeddin 3195, ed. M. Ṣādiq ʿAbdallāh, Najaf 1356, following the order in Leid. 2408 (partly autograph, partly revised by the author, see Dozy, *Not.* p. 17): a. *Shudhūr* (*Nubdhat*) *al-ʿuqūd fī dhikr* (*umūr*) *al-nuqūd*, also Berl. 6024, Leid. 1012/3, Esc. ^{2}1771. *Almakrizii hist. monetae Arab. e cod. Esc. ed. ab* O.G. Tychsen, Rostock 1787. *Traité des monnaies musulmanes*, transl. S. de Sacy in *Mag. enc. par* Millin, 2nd year, IV, 1797, $472_{,13}$, year I, p. 38, augmented special edition, Paris 1797, print. in *Thalāth rasāʾil*, al-Jawāʾib, Istanbul 1298, no. 1.—b. *Risālat al-Makāyīl wal-mawāzīn al-sharʿiyya*, only Leid. 1014, and Cairo ^{1}V, 186. *Takieddin Almakrizii track. de legalibus Arab. ponderibus et mensuris*, ed. O.G. Tychsen, Rostock 1800.—c. *Maqāla laṭīfa wa-tuḥfa saniyya sharīfa fī ḥirṣ al-nufūs al-fāḍila ʿalā baqāʾ*

al-dhikr.—d. *Ḍawʾ al-sārī fī maʿrifat akhbār Tamīm al-Dārī*, see Br. Mus. 669.—e. *Risāla fī dhikr al-naḥl wa-mā fīhi min gharīb al-ḥikma*.—f. *al-Ṭurfa al-gharība min akhbār Ḥaḍramawt al-ʿajība*, written in Mecca, based on information gleaned from pilgrims from Hadramawt, *Maqrizii de valle Hadhramaut libellus, ar. ed. et illustr. a* P. Berlin Noskowyj, Bonn 1866.—g. *al-Bayān wal-iʿrāb ʿammā bi-arḍ Miṣr min al-Aʿrāb*, additionally Vienna 910, Paris 1725, Cairo V, ^{1}21, ^{2}64. *El-Macrizis Abh. über die in Ägypten eingewanderten arab. Stämme, hsg. v.* F. Wüstenfeld, Göttingen 1847.—h. On the statement by the Prophet: *Ṣalāt al-layl mathnā mathnā*, written as a result of a dispute with a Ḥanafī *faqīh*.—i. *Ḥuṣūl al-inʿām wal-mayr bi-khātimat al-khayr*, on sura $12_{,102}$.—k. *al-Maqāṣid al-saniyya li-maʿrifat al-ajsām al-madaniyya*.—l. *al-Ilmām bi-akhbār man bi-arḍ al-Ḥabasha min mulūk al-Islām*, *Macrizii hist. regum Islam, in Abyssinia*, ed. Fr. Th. Rink, Leiden 1790, print. C. 1895 (Maṭbaʿat al-Taʾlīf).—m. *Maʿrifat*
50 *mā yajibu li-āl al-bayt al-sharīf min al-ḥaqq ʿalā man ʿadāhum*, | also Vienna 890.—n. *al-Dhahab al-masbūk fī dhikr man ḥajja min al-khulafāʾ wal-mulūk*, an abstract of a larger work in 5 volumes, completed in 841/1437, see ḤKh ^{1}III, 5831, ^{2}I, 828, also Cambr. 442/3.—o. *al-Nizāʿ wal-takhāṣum fī-mā bayna Banī Umayya wa-Hāshim*, also Vienna 886, see S. de Sacy in *Mag. enc.* 1806, III, 282, F. Wüstenfeld, ZDMG VII, 35. *Die Kämpfe u. Streitigkeiten zwischen den B. U. und dem B. H. hsg. v.* G. Vos, Leiden 1888, C. 1937.—p. *Dhikr mā warada fī binyān al-Kaʿba al-muʿaẓẓama*, Leid. 942.—q. *al-Ishāra wal-īmāʾ ilā ḥall laghz al-māʾ*, Cairo ^{1}VI, 111, ^{2}III, 12.—r. *Tajrīd al-tawḥīd* (*al-mufīd*), only Paris 12, Garr. 1496, Alex. Fun. $99_{,6}$.—s. *Izālat al-taʿab wal-ʿanāʾ fī maʿrifat ḥāl al-ghināʾ*, in Paris instead *Ighāthat al-umma etc.*, see Suppl. Cairo ^{1}VII, 564.—t. *Tarājim mulūk al-gharb*, on the Ziyānid ruler Abū Ḥammū Mūsā II and his successors in Tlemcen; as conjectured by Dozy, a lemma from no. 5.—9. *Dhikr mā warada fī Banī Umayya wa-Bani ʾl-ʿAbbās*, on that which had been transmitted in praise or blame of these two houses, and which one of the two deserves our pref-
41 erence, Vienna 887.—10. *Kitāb al-khabar ʿani ʾl-bashar*, see Suppl. |—11. *Jany al-azhār min al-Rawḍ al-miʿṭār*, Berl. 6049, Cairo ^{1}V, 40 ^{2}VI, 25 is an abstract of *al-Rawḍ al-miʿṭār fī khabar al-aqṭār*, written around 800/1397 by Abū ʿAbdallāh Muḥammad b. ʿAbd al-Munʿim al-Ḥimyarī, and which was revised around 900/1494 by one of his descendants, see Suppl. III, 1279.—12. *al-Bayān al-mufīd fi ʾl-farq bayna ʾl-tawḥīd wal-talḥīd*, an autograph dated to 813/1410, Leid. Amīn 188, Cairo ^{1}VII, 565.—13. *Muntakhab al-tadhkira fi ʾl-taʾrīkh*, a brief account of history from the Creation until the year 270/883, from the *Tadhkira* of Ibn Ḥamdūn I, 330? Paris 1514, photograph Cairo ^{2}V, 368 (which has, however, *Taʾrīkh Abī Bakr al-Maqrīzī*?).—13.–16. see Suppl.

8. Shams (Burhān) al-Dīn Abū ʿAbdallāh Muḥammad b. Shihāb al-Dīn Abu ʾl-ʿAbbās Aḥmad b. Nāṣir al-Bāʿūnī al-Shāfiʿī, who was born in 776/1374 and died in 871/1465.

Al-Sakhāwī, *al-Ḍawʾ* III, 114. 1. *Tuḥfat al-ẓurafāʾ fī taʾrīkh al-khulafāʾ* or *Farāʾid al-sulūk fī taʾrīkh al-khulafāʾ wal-mulūk*, ḤKh IV, 391, 8954, 578 *rajaz* verses on the rulers of Egypt from Abū Bakr until al-Malik al-Ashraf Barsbāy, d. 841/1437, dedicated to the latter's vizier ʿAbd al-Bāsiṭ, Berl. 9712/3, Gotha 1866,$_2$, Leipz. 296, f. 50, Br. Mus. Suppl. 487,$_{ii}$ (where other MSS are listed).—2. *Minḥat al-labīb fī sīrat al-ḥabīb*, a versification of the *sīra* of al-ʿAlāʾ Mughalṭāʾi (p. 60), | Gotha 51
1866,$_1$, Cairo ^{2}V, 370.—4. *Mulakhkhaṣ taḍmīn al-Mulḥa*, a humorous poem that employs verses from the *Mulḥat al-iʿrāb* of al-Ḥarīrī (I, 328), Copenhagen 217,$_2$.—5. *Takhmīs qaṣīdat b. Zurayq* (Suppl. II, 157,$_{5a,4}$), Heid. *ZDMG* 91, 388.—6. A collection of poems, Berl. 7911.—7. A sermon, ibid. 3953,$_5$.

9. Abu ʾl-Maḥāsin Jamāl al-Dīn Yūsuf b. Taghrībirdī b. ʿAbdallāh al-Ẓāhirī al-Juwaynī was born in Cairo in Shawwāl 813/February 1411. He was the son of a Greek slave whom his master, Sultan al-Malik al-Ẓāhir[3] Barqūq, had made governor of Aleppo and Damascus, where he died in 815/1412 (or 814, MT 48v). Raised by his two brother-in-laws, | he studied in Cairo under al-Maqrīzī and 42
others. In 863/1458 he made the pilgrimage, and died in 874/1469 (or, according to others, in 870).

RA 293r, al-Bustānī, *Dāʾirat al-maʿārif* II, 344, Wüst. *Gesch.* 490. 1. *al-Nujūm al-zāhira fī mulūk Miṣr wal-Qāhira*, a history of Egypt from the Arab conquest until the year 857/1453, with excursions on neighbouring countries and death notices for each year, in a clean copy completed in 860–2/1456–8, Berl. 9820, Gotha 1627 (a continuation covering the years 865–72), Paris 1171–89, 4948, 6065, Br. Mus. 178, Upps. 262, Pet. AM 178, Garr. 596, Köpr. 1811, fragm. Munich 391. *Abu ʾl-M. T. Annales*, ed. F.G. Juynboll and Matthes, 2 vols. (up to the year 365), Leiden 1855/61. *Extraits rél. au Maghreb.*, trad. par Fagnan, *Recueil de Notices et Mém. de la Soc. Arch. de Constantine* XXX, 1906.—An abstract, *al-Kawākib al-bāhira fi ʾl-nujūm al-zāhira*, which is limited to Egypt and the necrologies until the year 856/1452, Leid 976/7, a continuation until 867/1462, Paris 1790.—2. *Mawrid al-laṭāfa fī-man waliya ʾl-salṭana wal-khilāfa*, a short history of the life of the Prophet, with a list of his companions and of the rulers of Egypt and their viziers up to the year 842/1438, Gotha 1624 (continued until 906/1500), ʾ5, Paris

3 It is from him that he derived his *nisba*, and not from the village of Ẓāhir near al-Fusṭāṭ, Yāqūt *GW* III, 572, as believed by Derenbourg, Esc.^{2} no. 367.

1606, Bodl. I, 691, 778, Cambr. Prest 3_2, 207, 11, 280, Tunis, *Bull. de Corr. Afr.* 1884,
52 p. 25, no. 77, Garr. 597. *Maured al latafet Jamaleddini* | *Togri-Bardii*, see *Annales*, ed. J.E. Carlyle, Cambridge 1792. Abstract with major alterations, Gotha 1626.—Appendix, *Manhal al-ẓarāfa bi-dhayl Mawrid al-laṭāfa*, the rulers of Egypt up to the year 884/1479, by Muḥammad b. ʿAbd al-ʿAzīz Fahd, d. 954/1547 (p. 393), Berl. 9827.—3. *Mansha' al-laṭāfa fī dhikr man waliya 'l-khilāfa*, a history of Egypt from the earliest times until 842/1438, with a continuation until 932/1526, Paris 1770.—4. *al-Manhal al-ṣāfī wal-mustawfī baʿd al-Wāfī*, biographies of sultans, emirs, and some other people from the year 650/1252 until his own time, using al-Ṣafadī's *al-Wāfī* (p. 40) as the basis, Vienna 1174, Paris 2068/73, Cairo V, ^{1}162, ^{2}372.—5. *Nuzhat al-rāya*, a large historical work ordered by year, month, and day, vol. 9, the years 678–747/1279–1346, Bodl. I, 733.—6. *Ḥawādith al-duhūr fī mada 'l-ayyām wal-shuhūr*, a continuation of al-Maqrīzī's *al-Sulūk* (p. 48) for the years 840–60/1436–56, Berl. 9462, Br. Mus. 1244.—7. *al-Baḥr al-zākhir fī ʿilm al-awwal wal-ākhir*, a large historical work, from which the years 32–71/652–90, Paris 1551, photograph Cairo ^{2}V, 53, an abstract by ʿAlī b. Muḥammad al-Ḥalabī, Daḥdāḥ 45 = Berl. Brill M. 181.—8. *al-Sukkar al-qādiḥ wal-ʿitr al-fāʾiḥ*, mystical poems, Esc. ^{2}367.—9., 10. see Suppl. (9. *Zap.* XXI, 1912, 16/22).

10. Muḥammad b. Maḥmūd b. Khalīl Shams al-Dīn b. Ajā al-Ḥalabī al-Ḥanafī was born in Aleppo in 820/1417. In 843/1439 he went with his uncle to Cairo, where he gained the favour of Yashbak, the *dawādār kabīr*. At the order of the latter and of Sultan Qāʾītbāy he led several missions to Uzun Ḥasan in Tabriz and to Rūm, before becoming *qāḍi 'l-ʿaskar*. He died in Aleppo in Jumādā II 841/December 1437.

Al-Sakhāwī, *al-Ḍaw'* X, 43, no. 146. *Riḥlat al-amīr Yashbak*, a history of the campaign against the emperor Shāh Siwār in 875/1470, MS A. Taymūr, see M. Kurd ʿAlī, *RAAD* V, 316/8. His Turkish translation of the *Futūḥ al-Shām*, in 12,000 verses, is lost.

10a. Muḥammad b. Muḥammad b. ʿAlī b. Ẓāhira al-Qudsī, d. 888/1483.

Al-Faḍāʾil al-bāhira etc. (see Suppl), Istanbul MSS in Tauer, *Arch. Or.* VI, 99, Patna I, $85_{,2332}$.

53 | 11. Abu 'l-Faḍl Muḥammad b. Muḥammad b. Muḥammad b. al-Shiḥna Muḥibb al-Dīn al-Ḥalabī was born on 12 Rajab 804/16 February 1402, the son of the Ḥanafī *qāḍī* of Aleppo (p. 141, 5). He was, with some interruptions, the chief Ḥanafī *qāḍī* of Cairo between Shawwāl 866/July 1463 and 876/1471, and then became Shaykh al-Islām. He died in Ramaḍān 890/September 1485.

| Al-Suyūṭī, *Ḥusn al-muḥ.* II, 111, *Naẓm* 171, Wüst. *Gesch.* 461. 1. *Nuzhat al-nawāẓir* 43
fī rawḍ al-manāẓir, see p. 332, Suppl. I, 568, II, 40.—2.–4. see Suppl.—5. *Taʾrīkh* running up to the year 806/1404, composed for Muḥammad b. Mūsā al-Shahrī, the *nāʾib al-salṭana* in Aleppo, Bursa, Haraccizade tar. 18, (Ritter, 100ff).

12. ʿAlī b. Dāʾūd b. Ibrāhīm al-Khaṭīb al-Jawharī b. al-Ṣayrafī al-Ḥamawī al-Ḥanafī Nūr al-Dīn was, at first, a jeweller like his father. He then became a copyist of the works of Ibn Taghrībirdī, replaced Ibn al-Shiḥna as *qāḍī* in 871/1466, and died in 900/1495.

Al-Sakhāwī, *al-Ḍawʾ* V, 217, no. 738 (an account filled with bile), Ibn Ayās II, 286, Wüst. *Gesch.* 499. 1. *al-Durr* (*al-thamīn*) *al-manẓūm fī-mā warada fī Miṣr wa-ahlihā* (*wa-ʿamalihā*) *min mawjūd wa-maʿdūm* (*bil-khuṣūṣ wal-ʿumūm*), see Suppl., Garr. 614.—2.–3. see Suppl.

13. Abu ʾl-Yumn ʿAbd al-Raḥmān b. Muḥammad Mujīr al-Dīn al-ʿUlaymī al-ʿUmarī al-Ḥanbalī al-Maqdisī, d. 927/1521 (see Suppl.).

Wüst. *Gesch.* 512. 1. *al-Ins* (*Anīs*) *al-jalīl bi-taʾrīkh al-Quds wal-Khalīl*, a history of Jerusalem and Hebron, started on 25 Dhu ʾl-Ḥijja 900/17 September 1494, collected in about three months, and completed on 17 Ramaḍān 901/31 May 1495, Berl. 9795/7, Gotha 1716/7 (where other MSS are listed), Paris 1671/82, 4922, 5759/60, 5999, 6303, Algiers 1611, Br. Mus. Suppl. 573, Pet. AM 180, Ros. 45, Yeni 821, Beirut 170, Cairo V ^{1}16, ^{2}46, Tunis, Zaytūna, *Bull. de Corr. Afr.* 1884, p. 18, no. 54, Patna I, $289_{,2336}$, II, $536_{,5885}$, print. C. 1283. Abstract, Berl. 9797. Abstracts in v. Hammer, *Fundgr. der Or.* II–V, *Journal des étrangers*, 1754, April 2/45. *Histoire de Jérusalem et d'Hébron depuis Abraham jusqu'à la fin du XVème siècle, Fragments de la chronique de Moudjiraddin par* H. Sauvaire, Paris 1876.—2. The continuation for the years 902–14/1496–1508 that is promised at the end
is preserved in Leid. 953 and | Bodl. I, $853_{,2}$.—3. A general history, with particu- 54
lar emphasis on Jerusalem, running up to the year 896/1491, Br. Mus. Suppl. 488 = *al-Taʾrīkh al-muʿtabar fī anbāʾ man ʿabar*, ḤKh II, 150, V, 619, ^{2}I, 305 ?—4. *al-Manhaj al-aḥmad fī tarājim aṣḥāb al-imām Aḥmad*, a continuation of the *Ṭabaqāt al-Ḥanābila* of Ibn Rajab (p. 107), Berl. 10043, see Suppl.

14. Aḥmad b. Zunbul al-Maḥallī wrote, in the first half of the tenth century:

A history of the conquest of Egypt by the Ottoman sultan Selīm I, and a history of that country up to the latter's death in 926/1520, Gotha 1669 (where other MSS are listed).

15. Ḥamza b. Aḥmad b. Asbāṭ al-Gharbī al-Faqīh al-Darazī, was a talented poet and a productive writer who died in 926/1520.

Ṣāliḥ b. Yaḥyā, ed. Cheikho, 1927, 230/2, *ZDMG* 1849, p. 122, Wüst. *Gesch.* 511, see Suppl.

D Universal History

1. Shihāb al-Dīn Maḥmūd b. Salmān b. Fahd al-Ḥalabī al-Ḥanbalī Abu 'l-Thanā', who died in 725/1325 (see Suppl.).

1. *Ta'rīkh*, an appendix to *al-Kāmil* by Ibn al-Athīr (I, 422), of which some excerpts are preserved in Berl. 9441.—2. *Manāzil al-aḥbāb wa-manāzih al-albāb*, love stories involving poets, and love poems, Br. Mus. 771.—3. *Ḥusn al-tawassul*, see Suppl., also Garr. 2194.—4. *Ahna 'l-manā'iḥ etc.* ibid., with AS 3794, Alex. Adab 15.—5.–8. see Suppl.

2. Al-Amīr Rukn al-Dīn Baybars al-Manṣūrī al-Dawādār was a Mamlūk of Sultan al-Manṣūr Qalā'ūn. The latter made him to governor of Karak, a position from which he was later removed by al-Ashraf. After a time he was appointed as secretary of state, but was again deposed by Sallār in 704/1304. When al-Nāṣir assumed power for the third time in 709/1310, he reinstated him, then appointed him as custodian of the religious endowments[1] and as *nā'ib dār*
55 *al-'adl* and finally, | in 711/1311, as *nā'ib al-salṭana*. But as early as the following year he was incarcerated in Alexandria, being released only in Jumādā II 717/August 1317, following the intercession of his successor Arghūn. After making a final pilgrimage in 723/1323 he died, aged 80, in Ramaḍān 725/August 1325.[2]

DK I, 509, no. 1384, al-Suyūṭī, *Ḥusn al-muḥ.* I, 320, *Orient* II, 341. 1. *Zubdat al-fikra fī ta'rīkh al-hijra*, a general history of Islam until 724/1324 in 11 volumes (or, according to others, 25), written with the help of his secretary, the Christian Shams al-Riyāsa b. Bakr, vol. IV, a history of the 'Abbāsids up to 252/866, Upps. 231; vol. V, the years 252–322/866–934, Paris 1572; vol. VI, the year 400/1009 Bodl. I, 711,$_2$; vol. VII, 400–89/1009–1096, Faiẓ. 1459; vol. IX, 599–744/1164–1343, Bodl. I, 704; vol. X, 655–709/1257–1309, Br. Mus. 1233.—2. *al-Tuḥfa al-mulūkiyya*

1 See Strauss, *WZKM* 43, 194.

2 Wüst., *Gesch.* 390 confuses the author with Sultan Baybars, which explains the apparent contradictions of his sources with regard to his last fortunes; see Weil, *Gesch. der Chal.* IV, 337, n. 2, with which *DK* is in agreement on all major points.

fi 'l-dawla al-Turkiyya, a history of the Mamlūks covering 647–721/1249–1321, Vienna 904.—3. *Mawāʿiẓ al-abrār*, Patna I, 151,$_{1440}$.

2a. Abū Bakr b. ʿAbdallāh b. Aybak al-Dawādārī, d. 732/1333.

1. See Suppl. *Durar al-tījān etc.* also Alex. Taʾr. 67, abstract *Kanz al-Durar etc.* Top Kapu 2932.

3. Abu 'l-Fidāʾ Ismāʿīl b. ʿAlī b. Maḥmūd b. Muḥammad b. ʿUmar b. Shāhānshāh b. Ayyūb ʿImād al-Dīn al-Ayyūbī, a scion of the line of the Egyptian Ayyūbids who ruled at Hama, | was born in Damascus in Jumādā I 672/November 1273. It was 45
to this city that his father al-Malik al-Afḍal—brother of the ruler of Hama al-Malik al-Manṣūr—had fled from the Mongols. Even as a youth he participated in campaigns against the crusaders. Following the death of his childless cousin Maḥmūd II on 21 Dhu 'l-Qaʿda 698/20 August 1299, the kingdom of Hama | was 56
transferred to the emir Qārā Sonqor and, at this time, Abu 'l-Fidāʾ entered the service of al-Malik al-Nāṣir. After 12 years of service, the latter appointed him as governor in the kingdom of his ancestors on 18 Jumādā I 710/14 October 1310. During a visit to Cairo he was awarded the title al-Malik al-Ṣāliḥ, on 25 Rabīʿ II 712/31 August 1312; finally, on 17 Muḥarram 720/1 March 1320, he received the heriditary dignity of sultan, through the title al-Malik al-Muʾayyad. He served his hometown of Hama through the construction of public buildings, while also finding the energy to engage in extensive literary activities. He died at the age of 60 in Hama, on 23 Muḥarram 732/27 October 1331.

Fawāt I, 70, al-Bustānī, *Dāʾirat al-maʿārif* II, 298, *Orient.* II, 354. A. Jourdain in *Ann. des voy. publ. par* Malte Brun, XIV, 180/230, de Slane, *Rec. des hist. d. crois.* I, 166/86, Wüst., *Gesch.* 398, Leclerc II, 277, Hartmann, *Muw.* 10.—1. *Mukhtaṣar taʾrīkh al-bashar*, a broad universal history in 2 parts: a. pre-Islamic history, b. a history of Islam until 729/1329, Istanbul 1287, 2 vols.—a. *Abulfedae historia anteislamica ar. ed. vers. lat. auxit* H.O. Fleischer, Leipzig 1831.—b. *Ismail Abulfedae de vita et rebus gestis Mohammedis, text. ar. ed. lat. vert.* J. Gagnier, Oxford 1723. *Vie de Mohammed, texte ar. d'Aboulfeda accomp. d'une trad. franç. et des notes par* Noël des Vergers, Paris 1837. *Life of Mohammed transl. from the Ar. of Abulfeda by* W. Murray, London n.d.—c. *Abulfedae Annales moslemici ar. et lat. op. et studio* I.J. Reiske, *sumt. atque auct.* P. Fr. Suhm *ed.* J.G. Chr. Adler, i–vi, Copenhagen 1789/94.—*Annales moslemici, lat. ex. ar. fecit* I.J. Reiske, Leipzig 1754 (1778), | run- 46
ning to the year 406. F.W.C. Umbreit, *Historia Emirorum al Omrah ex Abulfeda*, Göttingen 1816.—Urdu translation, supplemented with other sources, 3 vols., Delhi 1846.—Abstracts: a. *Tatimmat al-Mukhtaṣar*, by Ibn al-Wardī, d. 749/1348,

see p 140.—b. *Lubb al-lubāb al-mukhtaṣar fī akhbār al-bashar,* by Muḥammad b. Ibrāhīm b. Muḥammad b. ʿAlī b. Abi ʾl-Riḍā, Pet. 115, see Gottwaldt, *JA* s. IV, v. 8 (1846), 510.—c. *Rawḍat al-manāẓir,* by Ibn al-Shiḥna, d. 815/1412, see p. 142.—d. See Suppl.—2. *Taqwīm al-buldān,* a general geography, completed in
57 721/1321, a copy revised by the author is preserved in Leid. 802, Basle | M VII, 6, Ğārullāh 1581,$_{2}$ (721 AH); with the title *Aqālīm al-buldān wa-taqwīmihā* Mosul 28,$_{86}$. *Abulfedae Chorasmiae et Mawaralnahrae descriptio ed.* J. Gravius, London 1650. *A. Tabulae Syriae c. excerpto geogr. ex Ibn ol Wardi geographia et hist. nat. ar. et lat. ed. notis explan.* I.B. Koehler, Leipzig 1766. *A. Descriptio Aegypti ar. lat. ed. ill.* J.D. Michaelis, Göttingen 1776. *A. Tabulae geogr. et alia specimina ed.* F. Th. Rinck, Leipz. 1791. *A. Africa* ed. J.G. Eichhorn, Gött. 1791. *ΠεριγραΦὴ Χορασμίας Μαουαραλνάκρης ἤτου τῶν πέραν τοῦ ποταμοῦ Ὤξου τόπων Ἀραβίας Αἰγύπτου Πέρσιδος κτλ. Ἐκδ. ἀραβιστὶ καὶ μεταΦρασθ. ὑπὸ Δ. Ἀλεξανδρίδου. Ἐν Βίεννῃ* 1807. Im Anhang *Δύο πίνακκες γεωγραΦικοὶ ὁ μὲν Νασσιρ Εδδινου Πέραου ὁ δὲ Ουλουγ Μπει Τατάρου, ἐπιμελέιᾳ Δ.Α. A. Tabulae quaedam geogr. ed. lat. vert. notis illustr.* F. Wüstenfeld, Gott. 1835. *A. description des pays du Maghreb, texte ar., avec trad. ar. par* Reinaud *et* Mac Guckin de Slane, Paris 1840, *autographié par* Ch. Schier, Dresden 1846, *trad. de l'Ar. en Franç. par* Reinaud I (*Introduction générale à la géographie des Orientaux*), II, 1. Paris 1848, II, 2. *par* St. Guyard, ibid. 1883.—Anon. abstract Br. Mus. 379, relinquishing the tabular form and omitting the information on longitudes and latitudes, Munich 460.—Alphabetically arranged with some additions by Muḥammad Sipāhīzāde, d. 997/1589, Br. Mus. 378, see p. 443.—3. *al-Kunnāsh fi ʾl-naḥw wal-ṣarf,* grammar, Cairo ^{1}IV, 90, ^{2}II, 154.—5. See Suppl.

4. Abū ʿAbdallāh Muḥammad b. Aḥmad b. ʿUthmān b. Qāymāz Shams al-Dīn al-Dhahabī al-Turkumānī al-Fāriqī al-Shāfiʿī, who was born in Damascus on 3 Rabīʿ II 673/7 October 1274, lived for a long time in Cairo in order to study. After his return, he became a teacher of *ḥadīth* at the Umm al-Ṣāliḥ shrine in Damascus. When al-Mizzī died in 742/1341, he tried to succeed him as professor at the Ashrafiyya school of *ḥadīth* but, in compliance with a stipulation by the school's founder, he had to be excluded on the grounds of his *madhhab*. He died on 3 Dhu ʾl-Qaʿda 748/5 February 1348.

Ḥuff. XXI, 9, *Fawāt* II, 183, *DK* III, 336, no. 894, *RA* 22r, *Orient.* II, 388, Wüst.
58 *Gesch.* 410, al-Kattānī, | *Fihris* I, 312/4. 1. *Taʾrīkh al-islām,* a political history and history of learned men, from Muḥammad until ca. 700 (715) in 12 (or 20, or more) volumes in 70 segments, each spanning 10 years, with those who died in the course of a decade listed alphabetically, MSS: years 1–40 Paris 1580, Lee 71,
47 years 41–130 Bodl. I, 652, years 143–5 (from a copy of volume III, 131–90) | Gotha

1563, 181–200 Cairo ^{1}v, 21, years 191–240 Bodl. I, 659, years 241–350, in draft, Leid. 863, 301–400 Paris 1581, 261–70, 546–650 Cairo ^{2}v, 411, 301–400, Paris 1581, 351–400 Gotha 1564, Br. Mus. 1636, 401–50 Br. Mus. 1637, 451–90 ibid. 1638, biographies for the years 487–500 and 501/50 Munich 378, 531–80 Bodl. I, 649, 561–80 Br. Mus. 1639, 581–620 Paris 1582, 581–610 Br. Mus. 1640, 621–60 Bodl. I, 654, 661–700 ibid. 656, 681–90 Br. Mus. 1641, Suppl. 468, up to the year 744 Mosul $233_{,134}$, unspecified Pet. AM 77, Köpr. 1015/21.—Abstracts: a. By the author himself, see Suppl.—b. Ibn ʿAbd al-Bāsiṭ, see no. 17.—c. Muḥammad b. Muḥammad al-Jazarī, d. 833/1430 (p. 201), completed in 793/1391, Alex. Taʾr. 132. Cf. Reinaud in Michaud, *Bibl. des crois.* IV, p. XXIII, v. Tiesenhausen, *Goldene Horde* I, 272.—2. A biographical supplement to the previous title covering the years 701–40 with a continuation by the editor up to the year 750, Leid. 866; see Weijers, *Orient.* II, 179ff.—The author subdivided both works into several more: a. *al-Duwal al-islāmiyya*, a political history, with a continuation for the years 716–40, Vienna 809, Leid. 864/5, Br. Mus. Suppl. 471, Köpr. 1079, Cairo V, ^{1}56, ^{2}184 (see Suppl.), also with the title *al-ʿIbar fī akhbār al-bashar mimman ʿabar*, completed on 17 Dhu ʾl-Ḥijja 715/15 March 1316, Vienna 810, Paris 1584/6, 5819, Br. Mus. 1231, Alex. Taʾr. 86, a supplement of which is the *Dhayl* by ʿAbd al-Raḥīm al-ʿIrāqī (p. 77) and his son Aḥmad (p. 79).—A second edition, runnning to the year 744, Bodl. I, 647, II, 590 (with the wrong title, and with a continuation until the year 764/1362 by Abu ʾl-Maḥāsin Muḥammad al-Ḥusaynī, d. 763/1363, see no. 7).—Abstracts: *α Mukhtaṣar al-ʿIbar* by Ibn Qāḍī Shuhba, d. 851/1447, no. 13, Br. Mus. Suppl. 470 (autograph).—*β Safīnat Nūḥ*, ḤKh III, 600, 7185 by ʿUmar b. Aḥmad b. al-Shammāʿ, d. 936/1529, composed in 927/1521 in Mecca, Gotha 1566, vol. 21/2, autograph Cairo ^{2}v, 217.—b. *Siyar al-nubalāʾ*, ḤKh ^{1}III, $639_{,7319}$, a supplement of which is *Taʿrīf dhawi ʾl-ʿalāʾ li-man lam yadhkurhu ʾl-Dhahabī min al-nubalāʾ* by Taqī al-Dīn Muḥammad b. Aḥmad al-Fāsī, d. 832/1429 (see p. 172), covering from 741/1340 until his own time, Berl. 9873.—c. *Tadhkirat al-ḥuffāẓ*, see Suppl., enlarged and abridged by al-Suyūṭī, d. 911/1505, Gotha 1760/1, Yeni 861, Garr. 699. *Liber classium | virorum qui Korani et traditionum cognitione* 59
excelluerunt, auctore Dhahabio ed. F. Wüstenfeld, *pars 1/3*, Göttingen 1833/4.—d. *Ṭabaqāt al-qurrāʾ al-mashhūrīn*, see Suppl., Köpr. 1116 = *Maʿrifat al-qurrāʾ al-kibār ʿala ʾl-ṭabaqāt wal-aʿṣār*, Berl. 9943.—3. *al-Iṣāba fī tajrīd asmāʾ al-ṣaḥāba*, alphabetical, Paris 2013 (draft, autograph), Br. Mus. 356, Qawala I, 87, II, 227.—4. *Mukhtaṣar Taʾrīkh Baghdād li-Ibn al-Dubaythī*, see I, 403.—5. *Mukhtaṣar Akhbār al-naḥwiyyīn li-Ibn al-Qifṭī*, see I, 397.—6. *Kitāb al-mushtabih fī asmāʾ al-rijāl*, composed in 723/1323, see Suppl., Patna II, $308_{,2428}$, II, $438_{,2614,2}$, ed. P. de Jong, Leiden 1881.—7. *Tadhhīb Tahdhīb al-Kamāl fī asmāʾ al-rijāl*, see Suppl. I, 606.—8. *al-Kāshif fī maʿrifat asmāʾ al-rijāl*, abstract of 7, ibid.—9. *Mīzān al-iʿtidāl fī tarājim al-rijāl*, Berl. 9939, AS 3488, Köpr. 1178/80, Cairo ^{1}I, 254, print. Lucknow

1301/1884.—Abstracts: a. *Lisān al-mīzān* by Ibn Ḥajar al-ʿAsqalānī, d. 852/1448, p. 80, see Suppl. Alex. Muṣṭ. al-ḥad. 14.—b. Ibrāhīm b. Aḥmad al-ʿAjlūnī, Gotha
48 1867,$_4$.—c. see Suppl. |—10. *al-Muqtanā fī sard al-kunā*, see Suppl., abstract by Aḥmad b. Ismāʿīl b. Khalīfa al-Ḥasbānī, d. 815/1412, Berl. 9942.—11. *al-Mustarjal fī 'l-kunā*, Lee 68,$_2$.—12. *Muʿjam* of his teachers, Cairo ^{1}I, 252.—13. *Manẓūma fī asmāʾ al-ḥuffāẓ*, Cairo ^{1}V, 162.—14. *al-Muhadhdhab, mukhtaṣar asānīd al-Sunan al-kubrā*, Cairo ^{2}I, 153.—15. *al-Mūqiẓa*, on the different kinds of traditions, Paris 4577,$_8$.—16. *Kitāb al-ʿuluww*, on the majesty of God, very detailed, commenced in 693/1294, Berl. 2313, Patna I, 125,$_{1252}$, II, 512,$_{2754}$.—17. *Kitāb al-kabāʾir wa-bayān al-maḥārim*, Cairo ^{1}II, 168, VII, 658 = (?) *al-Nāfiʿ bi-maʿrifat al-kabāʾir ijmāʿan wa-tafṣīlan*, Heid. ZDMG 91, 385.—18. *al-Mughnī fī 'l-ḍuʿafāʾ wal-matrūkīn*, see Suppl.—19. *Taṣḥīḥ al-khasīs bi-ahl al-khamīs*, Cairo ^{1}VI, 124.—20. *Risāla fīmā yudhamm wa-yuʿāb fī kulli ṭāʾifa*, on good and bad aspects of different social classes, published by Khalīl b. Kaykaldī al-ʿAlāʾī, d. 761/1360 (p. 76), Berl. 5570.—21. *Mufākharat al-mishmish wal-tūt*, a battle of words between the apricot and the mulberry, Berl. 8592,$_2$.—22. *Mukhtaṣar al-Mustadrak*, see I, 175.—23.–33. see Suppl.—34. *Rijāl al-kutub al-sitta*, Patna II, 307,$_{2423}$.—35. *Risāla fī 'l-adʿiya al-ḥadīthiyya*, perhaps an abstract of *Silāḥ al-muʾmin* by Muḥammad al-Miṣrī al-Gharnāṭī, d. 745/1344, p. 86, Br. Mus. Suppl. 249, Alex. Fun. 159, 12, Cairo ^{1}I, 349.—36. *Kitāb fī maʿrifat al-anghām*, Paris 2480, Bodl. Marsh 82, Ous. 106 (*Kitāb al-ṭarab*), Arab. C. 40, Cairo f. j. 340, 342 (*al-Inʿām fī maʿrifat al-anghām*),
60 see Farmer, *Sources*, 53.—37. His | *Mukhtaṣar Kitāb al-muḥallā li-Ibn Ḥazm*, ḤKh V. 429, is lost; see Asín Palacios, *Abenhazam* I, 322.

4a. Shams al-Dīn Muḥammad b. Muḥammad b. Nubāta, see Suppl. *Kitāb al-iktifāʾ*, also Qawala II, 228.

5. Nāṣir al-Dīn Abū ʿAbdallāh Mughalṭāy b. Qilič b. ʿAbdallāh ʿAlāʾ al-Dīn al-Bakjarī al-Ḥikrī al-Ḥanafī, who was born in 689 or 690/1291 of Turkish stock, became, following the death of Ibn Sayyid al-Nās (p. 71) in 734/1333, lecturer of *ḥadīth* at the Ẓāhiriyya in Cairo, dying on 24 Shaʿbān 762/30 June 1361.

DK IV, 352, no. 963, Ibn Quṭlūbughā no. 236, *Ḥuff.* XII, 9, al-Suyūṭī, *Ḥusn al-muḥ.* I, 202, *Orient.* II, 409, Wüst. *Gesch.* 420. 1. *al-Zahr al-bāsim fī sīrat Abi 'l-Qāsim*, a history of the Prophet, ḤKh III, 6881, *Dībāja*, Gotha 2, 4, see Suppl.—2. *al-Ishāra ilā sīrat al-Muṣṭafā wa-āthār* (*taʾrīkh*) *man baʿdahu min al-khulafāʾ*, an abstract of 1, with an appendix on the history of the caliphs, Berl. 9582 (on which glosses, ibid. '3), Munich 448, Br. Mus. Suppl. 513, Alex. Taʾr. 3, Cairo ^{1}V, 9, anon. abstract Alex. Taʾr. 15.—3. *al-Iʿlām bi-sunnatihi, sharḥ Sunan b. Māja*, see I, 171.—4.–7. see Suppl.—8. *al-Sīra al-sariyya fī manāqib khayr al-bariyya*, Alex. Taʾr 8.

6. Abū ʿAbdallāh Muḥammad b. Shākir b. Aḥmad b. ʿAbd al-Raḥmān Ṣalāḥ (Fakhr) al-Dīn al-Ḥalabī al-Dārānī al-Dimashqī al-Kutubī studied in Aleppo and Damascus, acquired a large fortune through the booktrade, and died in Ramaḍān 764/June–July 1363.

DK III, 451, no. 1218, Wüst. *Gesch.* 422. 1. *ʿUyūn al-tawārīkh*, a history of caliphs and men of learning, with particular emphasis on Damascus, individual volumes Gotha 1567 (the years 297–337/909–48), Paris 1586/8, Br. Mus. Suppl. 472, Lee, 72, Garr. 589 (vol. 6).—2. *Fawāt al-wafayāt*, a continuation of Ibn Khallikān (I, 399), Berl. 9868/9, Garr. 681 (fragm.), print. Būlāq 1283, 1299.

| 7. Abu 'l-Fidā' Ismāʿīl b. ʿUmar b. Kathīr ʿImād al-Dīn b. al-Khaṭīb al-Qurashī 49
al-Buṣrawī al-Shāfiʿī was born in Damascus in 701/1301, studied with Yūsuf al-Mizzī (p. 75) and the Ḥanbalī Ibn Taymiyya (p. 100), and suffered persecu-
tion | just as the latter did. In 748/1347 he became senior lecturer of *ḥadīth* at 61
the shrine of Umm al-Ṣāliḥ in Damascus and lectured at the Ashrafiyya for a brief period as well. He died in Shaʿbān 774/February 1373.

DK I, 373, no. 944, *RA* 60r, *Ḥuff.* XXII, 3, *Orient.* II, 433, Wüst. *Gesch.* 434. 1. *al-Bidāya wal-nihāya*, a voluminous historical work from the Creation up to the final years of his life, which, up to the year 738/1337, follows on al-Birzālī (p. 45), complete in 4 vols., Welīeddīn 2347/50 (photograph Cairo ^{2}V, 54), AS 2991/2002, Spies 78/9. The most complete version from among the remaining copies, Vienna 813, consisted of 8 vols., of which the following are missing: vol. II, from the marrriage of Muḥammad's parents until the year 7; vol. VI, the years 289–614; and vol. VIII, from the year 747 to the end. Vol. I, Berl. 9455, Gotha 1568, Br. Mus. 575/6, Bodl. I, 734, Cairo V, ^{1}19, ^{2}54, Bodl. II, 122 (from Jesus until Muḥammad's *miʿrāj*), Br. Mus. 277 (from the first ʿAqaba until the year 7), Suppl. 474 (years 3/9), Gotha 1569 (years 680/738), Bodl. II, 121 (years 600/737), with many additions by Aḥmad b. Abī Bakr al-Ṭabarānī, d. 835/1431 (p. 63), Paris 1515/6, Garr. 592 (vols. VI, VII, years 96/241, 278/465), print. vols. I–VII, C. 1348/51. From this work, J.F.L. George, *De Aethiopum imperio in Arabia felici*, Berlin 1833. Turkish translation Leipz. 274/5 (from Joseph until Muḥammad's death), Paris 97, Ibr. P. 892/6.—2. *Tafsīr al-Qurʾān*, AS 122/4, Cairo ^{1}I, 140, ^{2}I, 37 (see Suppl.), print. 4 vols., C. 1356/1937.—Abstract, *al-Badr al-munīr*, by ʿAfīf al-Dīn b. Saʿīd al-Dīn b. Masʿūd al-Kāzarūnī (p. 195), NO 383.—3. *Jāmiʿ al-masānīd wal-sunan al-hādī li-aqwam al-sanan*, alphabetically ordered by the last authority, Berl. 1344, Cairo I, ^{1}323, ^{2}105.—2. *al-Ijtihād fī ṭalab al-jihād*, Köpr. 234, Cairo ^{1}V, 4.—5.–8. see Suppl. (8. sec. ed. print. C. 1937).

8. Aḥmad al-Bayrūtī wrote:

50 | A history of the years 768–80/1366–78, with necrologies, Bodl. I, 712, Wüst. *Gesch.* 442.

9. Muḥammad b. ʿAbd al-Raḥīm (p. 20) b. ʿAlī b. al-Furāt Nāṣir al-Dīn al-Miṣrī al-Ḥanafī was born in 735/1334 in Cairo into a respected family, studied *ḥadīth* and *fiqh*, and died on 1 Shawwāl 807/2 April 1405.

62 | Al-Sakhāwī, *al-Ḍawʾ al-lāmiʿ* VIII, 51, no. 58, Jourdain in *Fundgr. des Or.* IV, 308, Wüst. *Gesch.* 454. *Taʾrīkh al-duwal wal-mulūk*, which is written in highly colloquial language, commences with the year 799 and then continues in reverse order until the fourth century, in a draft version comprising 100 *kurrāsas*, of which he had only written the last 20 or so volumes in clean copy at the time of his death, ḤKh ^{1}II, 104,$_{2104}$, ^{2}I, 279, 9 vols. for the years 501–799/1107–1396 with many lacunae, and with a whole volume missing, Vienna 814 (autograph), Paris 1596 (abstracts by Jourdain), Br. Mus. Suppl. 476 (the patriarchs from Seth to Isaac), vols. 9, 10, 11, Bursa Ḥü. Čelebī, Ta'r. 22/4, vol. IX, 3 (p. 245/596), Beirut 1938. Cf. Michaud, *Hist. d. crois.* VII, *Bibliogr. des crois.* v. II, *Bibliothèque d. crois.* p. IV, Reinaud *JA* 1826, VIII, 18/39, 149/68.

10. Ibrāhīm b. Muḥammad b. Aydamur al-ʿAlāʾī b. Duqmāq[3] Ṣārim al-Dīn al-Miṣrī, who was born around 750/1349, was the governor of Damietta under al-Nāṣir, and died in Dhu ʾl-Ḥijja 809/beginning of June 1407.

Al-Suyūṭī, *Ḥusn al-muḥ.* I, 320 (with the incorrect statement "d. 790/1388," which is also found in several places in ḤKh), *MT* 12r, Wüst. *Gesch.* 457. 1. *Nuzhat al-anām fī taʾrīkh al-islām*, a mostly Egyptian history, in chronological order up to 779/1377, in 12 vols., completed in 784/1382, autograph, covering the years 436–552, 565–6, Gotha 1570, the years 628–59, Paris 1597 (photograph Cairo ^{2}V, 396), the years 710–2, 742–3, Gotha 1571, the years 768–79, ibid. 1572. Cf. v. Tiesenhausen, *Goldene Horde*, 315, *Rec. d. hist. d. crois.* I, LI.—2. *al-Jawhar al-thamīn fī siyar al-khulafāʾ wal-salāṭīn*, a history of the rulers of Egypt, composed on the order of Sultan Barqūq (d. 801/1398) and continued until the year 805/1402, Berl. 9711, Bodl. I, 648, Br. Mus. 1492, Serāi A. III, 2903 (until 813 AH), with an anonymous continuation up to 906/1500, Bodl. I, 680, AS 3172 (the name of the person continuing the account being Ghars al-Dīn al-Miʿrājī?).—

3 Actually: *Doqimaq* (Turkish, "the hammer," *Uig.* I, 43,$_{1}$, *toqimaq*, "fuller's baton," *al-Kashgharī* III, 133,$_{12}$).

3. *al-Intiṣār li-wāsiṭat ʿiqd al-amṣār* (only vols. 4 and 5), Cairo ^{2}V, 41, print. Būlāq 1309, on which is based the *Fihrist al-asmāʾ wal-aʿlām* of Muḥammad al-Bīblāwī and ʿAlī Efendi Ṣubḥī, ibid. 1314.—4. *Naẓm al-jumān fī ṭabaqāt aṣḥāb imāmina ʾl-Nuʿmān*, on the classes of Ḥanafīs, Berl. 10022, Munich 437/9, Paris 2096.

| 11. Abu ʾl-ʿAbbās Aḥmad b. ʿAlāʾ al-Dīn b. Ḥijjī Shihāb al-Dīn al-Saʿdī al-Dimashqī 63
al-Shāfiʿī, d. 816/1413, see Suppl.

JA s. IX, v. 3, p. 449, Wüst. *Gesch.* 462. 1. A continuation of the chronicle of Ibn Kathīr (no. 8) for the years 741–60 and from 769 until shortly before his death, arranged by month. At the request of the author, Ibn Qāḍī Shuhba added the
missing years 760–68, then added the latest events | that had occurred in 51
Egypt and other countries, increasing the work by 7 hefty volumes, which he then abbreviated again until they were half their length, ḤKh ^{1}II, 100,$_{2083}$, IV, 180,$_{8036}$, ^{2}I, 277, Berl. 9458.[4]

12. Aḥmad b. Abī Bakr b. Khalīl al-Ṭabarānī al-Kāmilī Abu ʾl-ʿAbbās, who died in Ṣafar 835/October 1431.

Wüst. *Gesch.* 477. 1. Additions to the chronicle of Ibn Kathīr (p. 61).—2. On the merit of prayer and punishments for those neglecting it, Berl. 3521.—3. On the prohibition of drinking wine and the punishment for those who do, ibid. 5482.

13. Abū Bakr b. Aḥmad b. Muḥammad b. ʿUmar Taqī al-Dīn b. Qāḍī Shuhba al-Asadī al-Dimashqī al-Shāfiʿī, who was born in Rabīʿ I 779/July 1377, was a professor at the Amīniyya and Iqbāliyya and, in the years 820–35/1417–31, acting *qāḍī*. Soon after his pilgrimage in 837/1433 he became chief *qāḍī*, and also held professorships at all the important madrasas, the position of inspector of the Nūrī hospital, and other offices. He died on 11 Dhu ʾl-Qaʿda 851/19 January 1448.

RA 83r, Wüst. *Gesch.* 486, a biography with a list of his writings, compiled by his son Abu ʾl-Faḍl Muḥammad, d. 874/1469, Berl. 10130. 1. *al-Iʿlām bi-taʾrīkh al-islām*, a continuation of the chronicle of al-Dhahabī (no. 4), reports about famous people, alphabetically ordered by decade, ḤKh ^{1}I, 362,$_{951}$, II, 103,$_{2098}$,

4 The continuaton of the chronicle of al-Dhahabī in Paris a. f. 642 that is attributed to him by Wüstenfeld is actually the 23rd volume of the encyclopaedia *Masālik al-abṣār* by ʿUmarī, d. 749/1348 (p. 141); cf. Cat. de Slane 2328.

64 ^{2}I, 127, 279, the years 691/740 Bodl. | I, 721, the years 741/780, Paris 1598/1600.[5]—2. *Mukhtaṣar al-ʿIbar lil-Dhahabī*, p. 58.—3. *Manāqib al-imām al-Shāfiʿī*, Berl. 10010.—4. *Ṭabaqāt al-Shāfiʿiyya* in 29 chapters of 20 years each, ordered chronologically until the year 840/1436, and with each chapter alphabetically arranged, Berl. 10040, Gotha 1763, Pet. AM 209, Br. Mus. 370, 1298, Suppl. 644, Garr. 694, Cairo V, ^{1}36, ^{2}249, Patna II $315_{,2455}$, $561_{,2549/50}$, abstracts Gotha $1867_{,3}$, Br. Mus. $1240_{,2}$.—5. *Muntakhab Durrat al-aslāk li-Ibn Ḥabīb*, see p. 46.—6.–8. see Suppl.—9. *Sanad*, Garr. 1465.

52 | 14. Abū Muḥammad Maḥmūd b. Aḥmad b. Mūsā b. Aḥmad b. Ḥusayn b. Yūsuf Badr al-Dīn al-ʿAynī (ʿAnṭābī) al-Ḥanafī was born on 17 Ramaḍān 762/22 July 1360, the son of the *qāḍī* of ʿAynṭāb, a town between Aleppo and Antioch. At the age of 20 he was already able to represent his father, who had educated him in *fiqh*. After his return from a study trip to Aleppo in 783/1381 his father passed away. In 788/1386, he befriended the Sufi ʿAlāʾ al-Dīn Aḥmad in Jerusalem, who took him with him to Cairo, where he put him up at the newly-founded al-Barqūqiyya monastery in 789/1387. Having devoted himself to scholarship there for a number of years he returned to a normal life and, on the first of Dhu ʾl-Ḥijja 801/4 August 1399, replaced al-Maqrīzī as *muḥtasib* of Cairo, then became administrator of religious endowments and professor at various madrasas. When al-Malik al-Muʾayyad Shaykh acceded to power in 815/1412, he was tortured and lost all his property. He was compensated for this with a professorship at the newly-founded Muʾayyadiyya madrasa. However, his knowledge of Turkish soon restored his popularity in courtly circles and once even led to him being despatched on a mission to Istanbul. Through his historical and religious lectures in Turkish, he greatly influenced al-Malik al-Ashraf Barsbāy (r. 825–42/1422–
65 38). | The latter appointed him Ḥanafī chief *qāḍī* in Rabīʿ I 829/January 1426.
53 | Even though Barsbāy's successor al-ʿAzīz Yūsuf dismissed him to once again assume his chair at the Muʾayyadiyya in Muḥarram 842/July 1438, he became the Ḥanafī chief *qāḍī* again under al-Ẓāhir Čaqmaq in Shawwāl 846/February 1443. In addition, he also acquired the offices of *muḥtasib* and administrator of religious endowments. After he had lost the latter—extremely profitable—office on 16 Rajab 853/5 September 1449 he retired from public life, dying on 4 Dhu ʾl-Ḥijja 855/29 December 1451.

---

5 Among which a. f. 687, attributed wrongly in Wüst. *Gesch.* 44, to the older Yaḥyā b. Qāḍī Shuhba, d. 789/1387, see Cat. de Slane, loc. cit.

MT 84v, al-Suyūṭī, *Ḥusn al-muḥ.* I, 270, *al-Khiṭaṭ al-jadīda* VI 10, Quatremère, *Hist. des Mamlouks* I, 2, 219, de Slane, *Hist. des Crois.* XLIV/V, Wüst. *Gesch.* 489.
1. *ʿIqd al-jumān fī taʾrīkh ahl al-zamān*, from the Creation up to 850/1446, in 19 parts or 4 hefty volumes, wrongly attributed to a certain Ḥasan b. Ibrāhīm al-Yāfiʿī (cf. Defrémery, *JA*, s. IV, v. 8, p. 535), vol. 1 until Muḥammad, composed in 825/1422, Cambr. Pr. 1; vols. 2/4, years 16/850, Pet. AM 177; other parts Paris 1542/4, 5761, Cairo V ^{1}88, ^{2}267, Istanbul MSS in ʿĀdile ʿĀbidīn, *Istanbul Ün. Taʾr. Semineri Dergisi* I (1938), 150ff, *Bull. de Corr. Afr.* 1884, p. 28, no. 98.—2. *Taʾrīkh al-badr fī awṣāf ahl al-ʿaṣr*, an abbreviation of 1 in 10 parts, part 8, 144/99, Upps. 254, 717/98, Br. Mus. 935.—3. *al-Jawhara al-saniyya fī taʾrīkh al-dawla al-Muʾayyadiyya*, a biography of the sultan al-Malik al-Muʾayyad (see above) in verse, Munich 410. Eulogy (*taqrīẓ*) by Badr al-Dīn Muḥammad al-Bashtakī, d. 830/1427, and Ibn Ḥijja al-Ḥamawī (p. 18), Berl. 41. Biting criticism of the bad verses in *Qadha ʾl-ʿayn min naẓm gharīb al-bayn* by Ibn Ḥajar al-ʿAsqalānī, d. 852/1449 (p. 67), ḤKh IV, 506,$_{9384}$.—4. *al-Sayf al-muhannad fī sīrat al-Malik al-Muʾayyad*, which glorifies the same, running up to the year 819/1416, Paris 1723.—5. *al-Durar al-zāhira* and *al-Durar al-fākhira*, see p. 98.—6. *al-Masāʾil al-Badriyya al-muntakhaba min al-fatāwi ʾl-Ẓahīriyya* (I, 472), Cairo ^{1}III, 129.—7. *al-Muqaddima al-Sūdāniyya fi ʾl-aḥkām al-dīniyya*, AS 1439.—8. *Maghāni ʾl-akhyār fī rijāl Maʿāni ʾl-āthār* (see I, 181,$_{7,2}$, mistakenly associated with no. 10 in Suppl.), Cairo ^{1}I, 253.—9. *al-Maqāṣid al-naḥwiyya fī sharḥ shawāhid shurūḥ al-Alfiyya* I, 361.—10. *Sharḥ al-Kalim al-ṭayyib li-Ibn* | *Taymiyya*, see 66
p. 105.—11. *al-Nihāya fī sharḥ al-Hidāya*, see I, 467.—12. *Sharḥ Majmaʿ al-baḥrayn*, see I, 477.—13. *Sharḥ Tuḥfat al-mulūk*, ibid.—14. *Ramz al-ḥaqāʾiq, sharḥ Kanz al-daqāʾiq*, p. 197.—15. *ʿUmdat al-qāriʾ fī sharḥ al-Bukhārī*, I, 165.—17.–19. see Suppl.

15. Nāṣir al-Dīn Muḥammad b. Muḥammad b. Muḥammad al-Jaʿfarī, who flourished around 900/1494.

1. *Bahjat al-sālik fī taʾrīkh al-khulafāʾ wal-salāṭīn wal-mulūk*, covering the period from Muḥammad until 886/1481, Paris 1607.—2. *Anhaj al-ṭarāʾiq wal-manāhij wal-sulūk ilā tawārīkh al-anbiyāʾ wal-khulafāʾ wal-mulūk*, composed in 875/1470, ibid. 1815, 3/5.—5. *al-Waraqa al-marḍiyya fi ʾl-wathāʾiq wal-taʿlīqāt al-sharʿiyya*, composed in Egypt, ibid. 1041.

16. Muḥammad b. Maḥmūd b. Abi ʾl-Saʿādāt b. Abi ʾl-Jūd al-Salmūnī, who flourished around 900/1494 (see Suppl.).

Tāj al-maʿārif wa-taʾrīkh al-khalāʾif, which goes up to Qāʾītbāy's accession to power in 872/1467, Paris 1608, Fir. Ricc. 12, 1.

17. ʿAbd al-Bāsiṭ b. Khalīl b. Shahīn al-Malaṭī al-Qāḍī al-Ḥanafī, d. 920/1514 (see Suppl.).

1. *Taʾrīkh ʿAbd al-Bāsiṭ* or *Nayl al-amal*, a continuation of al-Dhahabī's work for the years 744–896/1343–1490, Bodl. I, 803, 812, Nicholson, *JRAS* 1899, 909, no. 9.—2.–10. see Suppl. (9. to be excised).—11. *Risāla fi ʾl-taʾrīkh* Patna I, 268,$_{2232}$.—12. *Risāla fī man waliya Miṣr min al-salāṭīn* ibid. 283,$_{2322}$, with the title of 4, also AS 4793,$_{6}$, where we find a wrong *Nuzhat al-salāṭīn*.—13. *al-Majmaʿ al-mufattan* (*mufannan?*) *bil-muʿjam al-muʿanwan*, reports on learned men, poets, caliphs, kings, and sultans in alphabetical order, Alex. Taʾr. 107.—14. *Majmūʿ al-bustān al-nūrī li-ḥaḍrat mawlāna ʾl-sulṭān al-Ghūrī* AS 4793 (15 treatises, among which 3 see Suppl. 2, 6 = 4, 14 = 5, 11. *al-Manfaʿa fī sirr kawn al-wuḍūʾ makhsūṣan bil-aʿḍāʾ al-arbaʿa*, probably = 6, further 4. *al-Qawl al-jazm fī taʾrīkh al-anbiyāʾ uli ʾl-ʿazm*, 5. *al-Rawḍa al-murabbaʿa fī sīrat khulafāʾ al-arbaʿa*, the rest is Qurʾānic exegesis, 1, 2, prayers, 7, 8, 9, philology 12. *al-Zahr al-maqṭūf fī makhārij al-ḥurūf*, 15. *Risāla fi ʾl-ashʿār al-rakīka* and others).—15. *Sharḥ al-funūn*, see p. 198.

18. Muḥammad b. Yūsuf b. Aḥmad al-Bāʿūnī al-Dimashqī Bahāʾ al-Dīn, who was born in 850/1446 in al-Ṣālihiyya near Damascus and died on 11 Ramaḍān 910/16 February 1505.

67 | *RA* 227v, 279r. 1. *Tuḥfat al-ẓurafāʾ fī tawārīkh al-mulūk wal-khulafāʾ*, in *rajaz*, until the ascension to the throne of Qāʾitbāy, composed in 901/1495, Paris 3412,$_{7}$.—2. *al-Qawl al-sadīd al-aẓraf fī sīrat al-Malik al-Saʿīd al-Ashraf*, 557 *rajaz* verses on the governments from Barsbāy until Qāʾitbāy, Berl. 9821, appendix up to 908/1502, ibid. ʾ2.—3. *al-Lamḥa al-Ashrafiyya wal-bahja al-saniyya*, a eulogy on Qāʾitbāy, Paris 1615,$_{2}$.—4. *Bahjat al-khalad fī nuṣḥ al-walad*, 203 *kāmil* verses on one's duties towards God and fellow-men, Berl. 5400.—5. A prayer in 14 *kāmil* verses, ibid. 3937,$_{7}$.—6. *al-Ishāra al-wafiyya ila ʾl-khuṣūṣiyyāt al-Ashrafiyya*, *urjūza* as an appendix to that of his uncle Abu ʾl-Faḍl Muḥammad al-Bāʿūnī, d. 871/1466, from Yūsuf b. Barsbāy until Qāʾitbāy, Alex. Taʾr. 12.

4 *Popular Literature in Prose, Anthologies, and Folk Tales*

Muḥammad Jād al-Mawlā Bek, Muḥammad al-Baghdādī, Muḥammad Abu ʾl-Faḍl Ibrāhīm, *Qiṣaṣ al-ʿArab*, I, C. 1939.

1. Muḥammad b. Ibrāhīm b. Yaḥyā b. ʿAlī al-Anṣārī Jamāl al-Dīn al-Waṭwāṭ al-Kutubī al-Warrāq, who was born in Dhu ʾl-Ḥijja 632/August 1235 and died in Ramaḍān 718/November 1318.

DK II, 298, no. 799, Ṣafadī, *al-Wāfī*, AS 2968_{112}. 1. *Ghurar al-khaṣāʾiṣ al-wāḍiḥa wa-ʿurar al-naqāʾiṣ al-fāḍiḥa*, an anthology, in 16 chapters, on 8 virtues and 8 vices, Gotha 1220/3 (where other MSS are listed), Paris 1300/4, Br. Mus. Suppl. 747/9, Cairo ^{1}IV, 287, ^{2}III, 263, Tunis, Zaytūna, *Bull. de Corr. Afr.* 1884, p. 11, no. 21, print. Būlāq 1284, C. 1299 among others—Abstracts: a. *Maḥāsin al-ghurar wa-masāwi ʾl-ʿurar* by Muḥammad b. Jānībek al-Sayfī Āqbāy (see Suppl.), dedicated to the sultan Qāʾitbāy, Gotha 1224.—b. *Khaṣāʾiṣ al-ghurar wa-naqāʾiṣ al-ʿurar*, anon. Vienna 388, cf. Lee 37, II, Alex. Adab 133/4 without title.—c. see Suppl.—2. *Mabāhij al-fikar wa-manāhij al-ʿibar*, an encyclopaedia of the natural sciences and geography, part II, Berl. 6045, part IV, ibid. 6307, abstracts Gotha $28_{,3}$ (where other MSS are listed), Köpr. 1170/1, Tunis, Zaytūna, *Bull. de Corr. Afr.* 1884, p. 11. no. 18, Cairo ^{1}V, 388.

2. Muḥammad b. Muḥammad b. Sharaf al-Zaraʿī al-Shāfiʿī completed, in 744/1343:

| *Jawāhir al-kalām*, an anthology in prose and verse, Paris 3342/3. 68

3. Muḥammad b. Muḥammad b. ʿAlī al-Bilbaysī wrote, in 746/1345:

Kitāb al-mulaḥ wal-ṭuraf min munādamāt arbāb al-ḥiraf, table-talk of ca. 50 representatives of various professions, mixed with verses, at times in colloquial Arabic, Br. Mus. $1128_{,6}$, Esc. ^{2}499, print. C. 1866.

4. Muḥammad b. ʿAlī b. Maḥmūd al-Kātib al-Dimashqī wrote, in 753/1352:

Al-Durr al-multaqaṭ min kulli baḥr wa-safaṭ, poems, tales, and aphorisms, Br. Mus. 1100, Paris $4435_{,2}$, see Quatremère, *Hist. des sultans Mamlouks* I, p. xviii.

5. Muḥammad b. Najm al-Ṣāliḥī al-Ḥallālī al-Arīnī compiled, sometime after the eighth century:

1. *Safīnat al-Ṣāliḥī* or *Safīnat al-durar*, an anthology of verse and prose, Paris $4236_{,2}$, Br. Mus. Suppl. 1147, Köpr. 1289/90, AS 4234, Cairo ^{2}III, 186, Mosul $49_{,34}$ (fragm.), anon. under the title *Safīnat al-bulaghāʾ* Vienna 420 (with the same beginning).—2. *al-Mukhtār fī maḥāsin al-ashʿār wa-nawādir al-akhbār* Garr. 222.

6. ʿAlāʾ al-Dīn ʿAlī b. ʿAbdallāh al-Bahāʾī al-Juzūlī al-Dimashqī was of Berber stock and a student of Damāmīnī (p. 32), and died in 815/1412.

Maṭāliʿ al-budūr fī manāzil al-surūr, an anthology of rich cultural historical content, Vienna 397, Garr. 208, Cairo ^{1}IV, 325, ^{2}III, 358, print. C. 1299, 1300, 2 vols.

7. Muḥammad b. Bakr al-Suyūṭī, ca. 818/1415.

Al-Marj al-naḍir wal-araj al-ʿaṭir, an anthology of prose and verse, a completion of his *Riyāḍ al-albāb wa-maḥāsin al-ādāb* Paris 3429 (ḤKh III, 516, without author), Paris 3385 (autograph, dated 818), 3386, Alex. Adab 158, Cairo ^{2}III, 350.

56 | 8. Muḥammad b. Aḥmad al-Khaṭīb al-Ibshīhī, who was born ca. 790/1388 and died around 850/1446.

69 | I. *al-Mustaṭraf fī kulli fann mustaẓraf*, an anthology, Berl. 8387/8, Gotha 2142/51 (where other MSS are listed), Paris 3369/82, 6235/9, Esc. ^{2}718,$_{1}$, Algiers 1877/8, BDMG 117, Garr. 210/1, AS 4264/8, Qawala II, 215, Patna I, 206,$_{1835}$, print. Būlāq 1268, 1272, 1285, 1292, C. 1279, 1300, 1302, 1304, 1305, 1306, 1308, 1320/1. Cf. G. Crolla, *Muséon* 1886, 605/9, G. Rat in *Bull. de l'Ac. du Var*, N. S. XVI, 210/22. *Trad. franç. par* G. Rat, Paris-Toulon 1899. Turkish translation by Asʿad Efendi, Istanbul 1263, cf. Hammer, *SBWA*, *phil.-hist. Cl.* III, 225, anon. abstract Paris 3383/4, anon. imitation, *al-Mustaẓraf min zubd al-Mustaṭraf*, Esc. ^{2}568.—II. see Suppl.

9. Qaraṭāy al-Ghazzī al-Khazandārī wrote, around 806/1403:

Majmūʿ (*Taʾrīkh*) *al-nawādir mimmā jarā lil-awāʾil wal-awākhir*, episodes from sacred and secular history, with varia from poets at the end, Berl. 9445/6, Rāmpūr I, 632,$_{35}$.

10. Shihāb al-Dīn Aḥmad b. al-Ḥusayn al-ʿAzāzī wrote, before 793/1391:

Rawḍat al-nāẓir wa-nuzhat al-khāṭir, popular prose works, which ḤKh III, 6692 attributes to ʿAbd al-ʿAzīz al-Kāshī, abstract by the author in Berl. 8403, see Suppl. II, 58,$_{14}$.

11. Muḥammad b. Ḥasan b. ʿAlī b. ʿUthmān al-Nawājī al-Qāhirī al-Shāfiʿī Shams al-Dīn was born in Cairo around 785/1383, studied with al-Damīrī (p. 138), and

was, being a poet himself, a friend of Ibn Ḥijja al-Ḥamawī (p. 18). Being a professor of *ḥadīth* at the Ḥusayniyya and Jamāliyya madrasas, he also organised Sufi gatherings. He made the pilgrimage in 820/1417 and again around the year 833/1429, dying on 25 Jumādā I 859/14 May 1455.

RA 222r, *MT* 30r (year of death 849), al-Suyūṭī, *Ḥusn al-muḥ.* I, 330, *al-Khiṭaṭ al-jadīda* XVII, 13 (following al-Sakhāwī), Kračkovsky, *EI*, Erg. 181/2.—1. *Ḥalbat al-kumayt*, an anthology of wine poetry, which incurred a number of hostile
responses to him,[1] Berl. 8392/3, Gotha 2157/8 (where other MSS | are listed), 70
Paris 3393/3400, Br. Mus. Suppl. 117/8, Garr. 101. AS 3847/9, NO 859, Cairo ^{1}IV, 227, ^{2}III, 343, Patna I, 205$_{,1833}$, print. Būlāq 1276, C. 1299, anon. abstracts Berl. 8394/5, Cairo ^{1}IV, 321.—2. *Marātiʿ al-ghizlān fi ʾl-ḥisān min al-jawārī wal-ghilmān*, an anthology of love poems on pretty girls and boys, completed in 828/1425, Berl. 8397/8, Gotha 2314, Leid. 508, Paris 3402/3, Esc. ^{2}339, 426/7, Cairo ^{1}IV, 322, ^{2}III, 348.—3. *Khalʿ al-ʿidhār fī waṣf al-ʿidhār*, a collection of erotic poems, Vienna 1850, Munich 598 (wrongly attributed to al-Ṣafadī, see ḤKh ^{1}II, 4787, ^{2}I, 721. see p. 41, n. 1), Paris 3401$_{,1}$, Esc. ^{2}341$_{,1}$, 428$_{,1}$.—4. *Ṣaḥāʾif al-ḥasanāt*, a collection of poetic fragments on moles on the cheek, Berl. 8186, Paris 3401$_{,2}$, Esc. ^{2}340$_{,2}$, 428$_{,2}$.—5. *Kitāb al-ṣabūḥ*, anecdotes and verses on morning drinks at the time of the ʿAbbāsids, Berl. 8396.—6. *al-Tadhkira*, popular prose, Berl. 8400.—7. *Nuzhat al-albāb fī akhbār dhawi ʾl-albāb*, anecdotes about generous people, misers, smartasses, smooth-talkers, and idiots, Berl. 8401.—8. *Tuḥfat al-adīb*, proverbs in verse, ordered by the final letter, autograph Berl. 8701.—9. *Taʾhīl al-gharīb*, a collection of verses by various poets, excluding the pagan and early Islamic ones, ordered alphabetically by the rhyme, Paris 3392.—10. *ʿUqūd
al-laʾāl fi ʾl-muwashshaḥāt wal-azjāl* Esc. ^{2}434. |—11. A *qaṣīda* on the Prophet, 57
Esc. ^{2}442.—12. Two *qaṣīdas*, Berl. 7907.—13. *Muqaddima fī ṣināʿat al-naẓm wal-nathr*, on stylistics, Paris 4453.—14. *al-Shifāʾ fī badīʿ al-iktifāʾ*, on rhetoric, Gotha 2823$_{,3}$, Leid. 328, Paris 3401$_{,3}$, Esc. ^{2}340$_{,3}$, 428$_{,3}$, 433, Garr. 554.—15. *Rawḍat al-mujālasa wa-ghayḍat al-mujānasa*, on paronomasia, Esc. ^{2}424.—16. *al-Ḥujja (Maḥajja) fī sariqāt b. Ḥijja*, on the poetic borrowings of his aforementioned friend, Leid. 509, Patna I, 196$_{,1757}$.—17.–20. see Suppl.—21. *Risāla fī ḥukm ḥarf al-muḍāraʿa* Alex. Fun. 188$_{,6}$.

12. Abu ʾl-ʿAbbās Aḥmad b. Qāḍi ʾl-qudāt Abū Isḥāq Ibrāhīm b. Qāḍī Naṣrallāh al-Kinānī al-ʿAsqalānī al-Ḥanbalī was born in Cairo in Dhu ʾl-Qaʿda 800/July 1397. He became acting *qāḍī* at the age of just twenty, then a Ḥanbalī professor

---

1 See *MT* and ḤKh III, 106, W. Jones, *Comment. poes. as.* London 1774, 430.

and, following the death of al-Badr al-Baghdādī, chief *qāḍī.* He died on 11 Jumādā I 876/27 October 1471.

71 | Al-Suyūṭī, *Ḥusn al-muḥ.* I, 276. 1. *Tanbīh al-akhyār ilā mā qīla fi 'l-manām min al-ash'ār* Cairo [1]VII, 94, [2]III, 68.—2., 3. see Suppl.

13. After a long voyage, Abu 'l-Fatḥ Muḥammad b. Badr al-Dīn b. Abi 'l-Ḥasan 'Alī al-'Awfī al-Iskandarī arrived in Damascus in 879/1474. There he wrote, in 883/1478:

1 *Tuḥfat al-labīb wa-bughyat al-ka'īb*, an anthology, vols. I, III, autograph Leid. 511, vol. II, Paris 3404.—2., 3. see Suppl. (ad 2. Sul. 873 vol. 1. of the autograph).

14. Aḥmad b. Maḥmūd al-Maḥallī al-Shāfi'ī.

A fictional work about King Jardāmāh, his son Tāj al-Mulk, and Nūr al-'Uyūn, AS 4029 (MS ninth cent. Ritter).

15. Muḥammad b. Abī Bakr al-Sakhāwī, ca. 900/1494.

Bahjat al-nāẓir fi 'l-ḥikāyāt wal-nawādir, anecdotes, aphorisms, and proverbs, vol. I, Berl. 8406.

16. Abū Isḥāq Ibrāhīm b. Mufarrij (Faraj) al-Ṣūrī (Ṣūlī) wrote, around 900/1495:

Sīrat (Akhbār) al-Malik al-Iskandar, see Suppl. 58, 17a, 909, 41 (Garr. 734/5).

17. In Ḥiṣn al-Akrād, Uways al-Ḥamawī wrote, in 901/1496:

Sukkardān al-'ushshāq wa-manāziḥ al-asmā' wal-arfāq (Paris 3405: *wa-manārāt al-asmā' wal-āmāq*), anecdotes, verses, and sayings, collected by the author far from his native Tripoli, as a consolation in difficult times, concluded with tales of ascetics, censure of the world, reminders of death, and repentance, Berl. 8407.

18. Al-Mamlūk Tānībek al-Khazindār was punished at the accession to power of al-Malik al-Ashraf Jānbalāṭ in 905/1499.

58 | Ibn Ayās III, 431,$_{9}$, *Tadhkirat al-'ulamā' wal-shu'arā'*, poems and tales, Br. Mus. 1108.

19. Ibrāhīm b. ʿUmar b. Ibrāhīm al-Samadīsī wrote, in 916/1510:

| *Tāj al-akhbār wa-nitāj al-afkār*, an anthology, Br. Mus. 1107. 72

20. Saʿdī b. Tājī al-Dimashqī, who died in 922/1516.

1. *Tuḥfat arbāb al-kamāl*, belletristic causeries with many verses by the author and other writers, Berl. 8416.—2. See Suppl.—3. *Khayr al-aḥlām*, in the form of a *maqāma*, dated 895, Istanbul, Ün. H 7168 (*ZS* III, 252).

21. *Alf layla wa-layla*, see Suppl.

M.J. de Goeje, De Ar. nachtvertellingen, *De Gids* 1886 III, 385 ff, idem, *Enc. Brit.* 9. v. XXIII. A. Müller, Zu den Märchen der 1001 Nacht, *Bezzenbergers Beitr.* XIII, 222/44, idem, *Deutsche Rundschau*, July 1887, 77/96, J. Östrup, *Studier over Tusind og en nat*, Copenhagen 1891. R. Basset, Notes sur les 1001 nuits, *Rev. des trad. pop.* XIII, 37/87, 303/8. | Aḥmad Ḥasan al-Zayyāt, *Alf wal. taʾrīkh* 61
ḥayātihā, *RAAD* XII, 129/42, 204/15, 282/91. D.B. Macdonald, A bibliographical and literary study of the first appearance of the Arabian Nights in Europe, *The Lit. Quart.* II, 2 Oct. 1932, 387/420. A. Abel, *Les enseignements des Mille et une nuits*, Brussels 1939. MSS in Leningrad, see M. Sallier (Sale), *Izv. Ak. Nauk*, 1928, 185/6, 299/300. *Tausend und eine Nacht arabisch, nach einer Hds. aus Tunis hsg. v.* Maximilian Habicht, I–VIII, *fortgesetzt v.* H.L. Fleischer, IX–XII, Breslau 1825/43. *The Alf Laila or Book of the thousand nights and one night, publ. from an Egypt. Ms. by* W.H. Macnaghten, 4 vols. Calcutta 1839/42, print. Lucknow 1869, Būlāq 1251, 1279, 1297, C. 1305, 1339 (illustr.), ed. Aḥmad Ṣālḥānī, 5 vols., Beirut 1888/92 (truncated), 1926. Persian translation on the order of Prince Bahman of Azerbaijan, the grandson of Fatḥ ʿAlī, by ʿAbd al-Laṭīf Tabrīzī, Tehran 1315, old Trübner Cat. 1869, 104. Turkish *Terjemeʾi Alf L. u. l.* 6 vols., Istanbul, n.d.—*Les Mille et une nuits, contes ar. trad. en franç. par* M. Galland, Paris 1704/17, I–XII, *continués par* M. Caussin de Perceval, Paris 1806. *The Thousand and One Nights, commonly called in England The Arabian nights Entertainments, transl. by* E.W. Lane 3 vols., London 1841, other editions by Edw. Stanley Poole, London, lastly in 1882 (additionally, E.W. Lane, *Arabian Society in the Middle Ages, Studies from the 1001 Nights*, ed. by St. Lane-Poole, London 1883). *Burton's Translation of the 1001 Nights*, ed. | by J.H. McCarthy, 6 vols. London 1887, *Supplemental nights etc.* 73
(transl. from the Breslau edition, from Galland, from the Wortley Montague Cod. in the Bodl. Libr. and the "New Arabian Nights" by Dom Chavis and Cazotte, etc.), with anthrop. and explanatory notes by R.F. Burton, 6 vols,. Varanasi 1886/8. *1001 Nacht, zum ersten Mal aus dem ar. Urtext übers. v.* G. Weil, *hsg. v.*

G. Lewald, *mit 200 Bildern u. Vignetten v.* J. Gross, 4 vols. Stuttgart-Pforzheim, 1838/41, 3rd ed. Stuttgart 1889, 4th printing Bonn 1897. German by Habicht, v. d. Hagen and C. Schall, 5th ed. 15 vols., Breslau and Stuttgart 1840 ff. *Der 1001 N. noch nicht übers. Märchen, Erzählungen u. Anekdoten, zum ersten Mal aus dem Ar. ins Franz. übers. v.* J. v. Hammer *und ins Deutsche v.* E. Zinserling, 2 vols., Stuttgart 1823/4. *1001 N. übers. v.* M. Henning, Reclams Univ.-Bibl. 3692 ff, 3721 ff. Russian translation by M. Sallier, I–VIII, Moscow 1929/36, by Kračkovsky, *Bibl. Vostoka*, I–IV 1934. Danish translation by J. Östrup, Copenhagen 1937/8. *The Thousand and One Nights, new and revised edition, completed and unabridged translation from the French of Dr. J. Mardrus by* E. Pawys Mathois, 4 vols. London 1937 ff.—Supplements: *Ṭarāʾif al-fukāhāt, Contes ar. publ. par* A. Ṣālḥānī, Beirut 1890. *Enis el Djelis ou histoire de la belle Persane, conte des 1001 Nuits, publ. en ar. et trad. avec des notes par* A. de Biberstein-Kazimirski, Paris 1846. *Qiṣṣat Qamar al-zamān b. al-malik Shahramānshāh bi-jazāʾir Khālidān wa-mā jarā lahu maʿa
62 *ʾl-sayyida Budūr bint al-malik al-ghayūr*, C. 1287, 1324. | *Histoire de calife le pécheur et du calife Haroun Er Rechid, conte inédit des Mille et une nuits, texte turc avec trad. franç. et des notes publ. par* Ch. Clermont Ganneau, Jerusalem 1869. *Voyages de Sindbad le Marin, texte ar. extr. des 1001 Nuits, publ. avec vocab. et des notes par* L. Machuel, 2nd ed. Algiers 1884, 3rd ed. 1910. Histoire de Jalʿād et de Chimas, (Berl. Brill M. 156) publ. par H. Zotenberg, *JA* 1886, I, 97/123. *Histoire d'ʿAlāʾ aldīn ou la lampe merveilleuse, texte ar. publ. avec une notice sur quelques mss. des Mille et une nuits par* H. Zotenberg, Paris 1889. *Zein el Aṣnām, Conte des 1001 nuits, extr. des mss. de la Bibl. Nat. texte ar. vocalisé et vocab. ar. ang. et franç. par* Fl. Groff, Paris 1889. *Bāsim le forgeron et Hārūn er-Rachīd, texte ar. en dialecte d'Égypte et de Syrie, publ. d'après les mss. de Leyde, de Gotha et du
74 Caire et accompagné d'une trad. et d'un gloss. par le Comte* | C. de Landberg, I, Leiden 1888. *Tawaddud al-jāriya*, ed. M. Brugsch, Heidelberg 1924.

22. From among the many romances, *Sīrat ʿAntar* seems to have received its current form by the time of the Crusades. Nevertheless, it has been modified and augmented by professional storytellers right up to the present day, just like the related *Sīrat Abī Zayd wa-Banī Hilāl, Sīrat Dhi ʾl-Himma, Sayf Dhi ʾl-Yazan*, and the romanesque history of sultan al-Ẓāhir Bāybars, the *Sīrat al-Ẓāhir*.

1. *Sīrat ʿAntar b. Shaddād* (MSS also Patna II, 537,2887/94), in 32 vols., C. 1283, 1286, 1307/11, 1331, another recension in 10 vols. Beirut 1869/71. *Antar a bedoueen romance transl. from the Ar. by* T. Hamilton, P. I/LV London 1820. *Antar poème héroique ar. d'après la traduction de* M. Dévic, 2 vols. Paris 1878.

2. *Sīrat Abī Zayd wa-Banī Hilāl*, 4 vols., Beirut n.d. (cf. R. Basset, *Bull. de Corr. Afr.* 1885, 136/48, M. Hartmann, *Zeitschr. f. afrik. u. ocean. Sprachen* IV, part 4,

290 ff). Individual parts, with different titles C. 1282 ff, Beirut 1866 ff. *Taghrībat Banī Hilāl* Damascus 1922, *Qiṣṣat Banī Hilāl* ibid. 1927.

3. *Kitāb Bakr wa-Taghlib* and *Kitāb ḥarb Banī Shaybān wa-Kisrā Anūsharwān*, 2 vols., Bombay 1305.

4. *Sīrat al-Ẓāhir Bāybars*, see Suppl., with Garr. 730, where Muḥyi ʾl-Dīn Abu ʾl-Faḍl ʿAbdallāh b. ʿAbd al-Ẓāhir b. Najda al-Ḥizāmī al-Miṣrī is named as the author.

5. *Sīrat Sayf (b.) Dhi ʾl-Yazan etc.* see Suppl. Berl. Ms. or. oct. 3860.—6., 7. see Suppl.—8. *Sīrat al-mujāhidīn wa-abṭāl al-muwaḥḥidīn* Berl. Ms. or. oct. 3820 (40 vols.), BDMG 120.—9.–14. see Suppl.—15. *Qiṣṣat al-malik Jayʿād wa-wazīrihi Shīmān* Berl. Brill M. 156.

Table of contents of other romances in Lane, *An Account of the Manners and Customs of the Modern Egyptians*, II, 117/63, in greater detail in Ahlwardt's catalogue VIII, 69 ff. Chauvin, *Bibliographie des ouvrages ar. Livr.* III, Liège, 1898, see Suppl.

23. Luqmān, see Suppl.

| R. Basset, *Loqmān Berbère, avec quatre glossaires et une étude sur la légende* 63
de Loqmān, Paris 1890 (with comprehensive bibliography). *Naẓm al-jumān fī amthāl Luqmān* by ʿAbdallāh Efendi Furayj, C. 1311.

| 5 *Ḥadīth* 75

A *ʿIlm al-ḥadīth wa-ʿilm al-rijāl*

1. Taqī al-Dīn Abu ʾl-Fatḥ Muḥammad b. ʿAlī b. Wahb al-Qushayrī b. Daqīq al-ʿĪd al-Manfalūṭī was born in Yanbūʿ in Lower Egypt in Shaʿbān 625/July 1228. He grew up in Qūṣ, studied in Cairo, lived for some time in Damascus, and then became a professor of Mālikī, and subsequently Shāfiʿī, *fiqh* at al-Madrasa al-Fāḍiliyya in Cairo. He died there in Ṣafar 702/October 1302.

Fawāt II, 244, *DK* IV, 91/6, Ṣafadī, *al-Wāfī* AS $2968_{,11,2}$, *Khiṭ. jad.* XIV, 135. 1. *al-Iqtirāḥ fī bayān al-iṣṭilāḥ*, a compendium of the science of *ḥadīth* in 9 chapters and a *khātima* in 7 sections, each with 40 genuine traditions from Bukhārī and Muslim, Berl. 1063.—2. *al-Ilmām fī aḥādīth al-aḥkām* Köpr. 250, Alex. Ḥad. 6, self-commentary Qawala I, 126. An abstract, *al-Ihtimām*, by ʿAbd al-Karīm b. ʿAbd al-Nūr b. Munayyir, d. 735/1334 (Ibn al-Qāḍī, *Durrat al-ḥijāl* II, 389, al-Kattānī, *Fihris* II, 313), Cairo ^{1}I, 274, ^{2}I, 93.—3. *Nubdha fī ʿulūm al-ḥadīth* Br. Mus. 876.—4. A letter to his representative Mukhliṣ al-Dīn in Ikhmīm, Berl. $8003_{,4}$.—5. *Tuḥfat al-labīb fī sharḥ al-Taqrīb* I, 492.—6.–8. see Suppl.

64 | 2. Abu 'l-Ḥajjāj Yūsuf b. al-Zakī ʿAbd al-Raḥmān b. Yūsuf Jamāl al-Dīn al-Mizzī al-Quḍāʿī al-Kalbī al-Shāfiʿī was born in Aleppo on 10 Rabīʿ II 654/8 May 1256. He grew up in al-Mizza near Damascus. From *fiqh*, he moved to studying *ḥadīth*, which he started on his own and then continued while travelling, from the age of 20. On his return, he became senior lecturer at the Ashrafiyya school of *ḥadīth* in Damascus, which he directed for 23½ years until he passed away on 12 Ṣafar 742/29 July 1341.

Ḥuff. XXXI, 9, al-Kattānī, *Fihris* I, 107, Orient. II, 377, Wüst. *Gesch.* 406. 1. *Tahdhīb al-kamāl fī asmāʾ al-rijāl*, Suppl. I, 606.—2. *Tuḥfat al-ashrāf bi-maʿrifat al-aṭrāf*,
76 names of the transmitters of the six works with brief specifications | of the *ḥadīth*, Berl. 1374/5, Algiers 499, 500.—3. *al-Muntaqā min al-aḥādīth* Cairo [1]I, 429, [2]I, 152.

3. Abū ʿAbdallāh (Abū Muḥammad) al-Ḥusayn b. ʿAbdallāh b. Muḥammad al-Ṭībī, d. 743/1342, see Suppl.

1. *al-Khulāṣa fī uṣūl maʿrifat al-ḥadīth*, from the works of Ibn al-Ṣalāḥ, al-Nawawī, and Ibn Jamāʿa, with additions from the *Kitāb jāmiʿ al-uṣūl* and others, Berl. 1064/8, AS 453, Köpr. 230, Cairo [1]VII, 217, 456,7, [2]I, 73, Garr. 1456.—2. *Asmāʾ rijāl al-Mishkāt* I, 449.—3. *Sharḥ asmāʾ Allāh al-ḥusnā* Cairo [1]VII, 215.—4. *Kitāb al-tibyān fi 'l-maʿānī wal-bayān*, on rhetoric, completed in 725/1325, with a self-commentary, completed in 737/1337, Berl. 7250/1, Paris 4422, Br. Mus. 558, 1692, Esc. [2]217, NO 4378, Alex. Bal. 3, with a commentary by his student ʿAlī b. ʿĪsā, completed in 737/1336, Br. Mus. 559, Esc. [2]224.—5.–7. see Suppl.

4. Abu 'l-Ḥasan ʿAlī b. ʿUthmān b. Ibrāhīm ʿAlāʾ al-Dīn al-Māridīnī b. al-Turkumānī was born in 683/1284. In Shawwāl 748/1348 he became Ḥanafī *qāḍī* in Cairo, where he died on 10 Muḥarram 750/1 April 1349.

RA 193v, Ibn Quṭlūb. 130, Wüst. *Gesch.* 416. 1. *Mukhtaṣar Talkhīṣ al-mutashābih lil-Khaṭīb al-Baghdādī*, I, 401.—2. *al-Tanbīh ʿalā aḥādīth al-Hidāya* (I, 466) *wal-Khulāṣa* (*t al-Nihāya fī qawāʿid* [*fawāʾid*] *al-Hidāya* of Maḥmūd b. Aḥmad al-Qūnawī, d. 770/1369, ḤKh VI, 481,3, p. 97, I, 466) Paris 924.—3. *Manẓūma fi 'l-kabāʾir*, a poem about the 70 mortal sins, Berl. 2039/40.—4. *Bahjat al-arīb* (*adīb*) *fi 'l-kitāb al-ʿazīz al-gharīb* Berl. 7026.—5., 6. see Suppl.

5. Khalīl b. Kaykaldī b. ʿAbdallāh al-ʿAlāʾī al-Dimashqī al-Shāfiʿī Ṣalāḥ al-Dīn was born in Rabīʿ (I or II) 694/February—March 1295 (or, according to others, in
65 691 or 693). The son of a Turkish soldier, | he studied *ḥadīth* in Damascus from

703/1303, then travelled to Jerusalem, Mecca, and Cairo, during which period he studied with more than 700 teachers. In 719/1318, he became a teacher of *ḥadīth* at al-Madrasa al-Nāṣiriyya in Damascus, in 723 at the Asadiyya, in 728 at the Ḥalqa in Homs,[1] and in 731 at the Ṣalāḥiyya in Jerusalem, where he died on 13 Muḥarram 761/6 December 1359.

| *DK* II, 90/2, *JA* s. IX, v. 3, p. 297, al-Kattānī, *Fihris* II, 117/8. 1. *al-Tahdhīb fī* 77
uṣūl al-sitta Yeni 179.—2. *Ithārat al-fawāʾid al-majmūʿa fi ʾl-ishāra ila ʾl-fawāʾid al-masmūʿa* Cairo ¹I, 224, ²I, 67.—3. *Rafʿ al-ishkāl ʿan ḥadīth ṣiyām sittat ayyām fī ʾl-Shawwāl* ibid. VII, 187, ²I, 120.—4. *al-Majmūʿ al-mudhahhab fī qawāʿid al-madhhab* Cairo ¹I, 259. III, 261 (see Suppl).—5. *Kitāb al-ʿidda ʿinda* (*fī adʿiyat*) *al-karab wal-shidda*, prayers using the names of God, Berl. 4148, Cairo ¹VII, 573, ²I, 331.—6.–18. see Suppl. (8. Garr. 1457; 17. Ibid. 1438).

6. Muḥammad b. ʿAlī b. al-Ḥasan b. Ḥamza al-Ḥusaynī al-Dimashqī, who was born in 715/1315, became a professor at the Dār al-ḥadīth al-Bahāʾiyya in Cairo, and died on the last day of Shaʿbān or the first of Ramaḍān of 765/1 or 2 June 1364.

DK IV, 61, no. 171. 1. *al-Ikmāl fī dhikr man lahu riwāya fī Musnad al-imām Abī b. Ḥanbal* (I, 193) Berl. 9945.—2.–4. see Suppl.

7. Abu ʾl-Faḍl ʿAbd al-Raḥīm b. al-Ḥusayn b. ʿAbd al-Raḥmān Zayn al-Dīn al-ʿIrāqī al-Kurdī was born in Jumādā I 725/April 1325 in Rāziyān near Arbela (or, according to others, in Manshaʾat al-Mihrānī near Cairo). He began his studies with *fiqh* in Cairo, but in 752/1351 he let himself be talked into the science of *ḥadīth* by ʿIzz al-Dīn b. Jamāʿa. Study tours through Egypt, Syria, and the Hijaz brought him to Mecca in 768/1366, and in 771/1369 back to Cairo. Having worked for three years as a *qāḍī* in Medina, starting in 788/1386, he then became a teacher of *ḥadīth* at various institutions in Cairo, and finally became a professor there, at the Fāḍiliyya. He is credited with having reintroduced *imlāʾ*, by which he gave new life to the study of *ḥadīth*. He died on 8 (or, according to others, 27) Shaʿbān 806/21 February or 10 March 1404.

| *Ḥuff.* XXIII, 6, al-Suyūṭī, *Ḥusn al-muḥ.* I, 209, RA 149 v, Ibn al-Qāḍī, *Durrat* 66
al-ḥijāl II, 369, no. 1032, al-Kattānī, *Fihris* II, 197/9, Wüst. *Gesch.* 453. 1. *al-Tabṣira*
| *wal-tadhkira* or *al-Alfiyya fī uṣūl al-ḥadīth*, a versification of the *Kitāb ʿulūm* 78
al-ḥadīth by Ibn al-Ṣalāḥ, d. 643/1245, vol. I, 442.—2. (*Naẓm*) *al-Durar al-saniyya*

1 See Quatremère, *Mamlouks* I, 2, p. 199.

fī 'l-siyar al-zakiyya or, shorter, *al-Alfiyya fī 'l-siyar,* a biography of the Prophet in 1000 *rajaz* verses, Berl. 9594/5, Gotha 1794, Cairo ^{1}I, 444, ^{2}I, 158, Alex. Taʾr. 17, Fun. 103$_{,3}$, 158$_{,i}$, Qawala II, 249, Garr. 643. Commentaries: a. Ibn al-Hāʾim, d. 795/1393, Cairo ^{1}I, 373.—b. ʿAbd al-Raʾūf al-Munāwī, d. 1031/1622 (p. 306), Berl. Brill M. 218, Esc. ^{2}446, Algiers 1683, Cairo ^{1}I, 355, ^{2}I, 128, 134, Alex. Taʾr. 12.—c. al-Ujhūrī, d. 1066/1656 (p. 317), Berl. 9587, Algiers 1682, Cairo ^{1}I, 355, ^{2}I, 125.—d. Anon. Berl. 9586.—e., f. see Suppl.—g. Muḥammad b. Aḥmad al-Sakhāwī, d. 902/1496, Alex. Taʾr 11.—h. *al-Badr al-munīr* by Muḥammad al-Rashīdī al-Burullusī al-Awsī al-Anṣārī, composed in 1102/1690, ibid. 5.—Didactic letter thereon to his son in the year 792/1390, and to somebody else in the year 795/1393, Berl. 157$_{,4}$.—3. *Taqrīb al-asānīd wa-tartīb al-masānīd,* a collection of *ḥadīth,* written for his son Abū Zurʿa, arranged according to the plan of legal works, Berl. 1347, AS 473, Garr. 1458.—*Dībāja* Gotha 2$_{,102}$, self-commentary *Ṭarḥ al-tathrīb, Dībāja* ibid. 13., on which a *takhrīj* Cairo ^{1}I, 283.—4. *al-Taqyīd wal-īḍāḥ fī uṣūl al-ḥadīth* Berl. Ms. or. oct. 3976, Yeni 165.—5. *al-Mughnī ʿan ḥaml al-asfār fī 'l-asfār,* see Suppl. I, 749$_{,19}$.—6. *Maḥajjat al-qurab fī maḥabbat* (*faḍl, faḍāʾil*) *al-ʿArab,* on love felt for the Prophet, according to genuine traditions, Berl. 1391/2, Garr. 1519/20, Qawala I, 256, Cairo ^{1}VI, 194, VII, 262, 312, print. in *Majmūʿa,* starting with Ibn Ḥayyān's *al-Muqābasāt,* Alexandria 1299 (Alex. Fun. 135).—7. *Alfiyya fī gharīb al-Qurʾān,* in alphabetical order, which he commenced while on the way to Mecca, and which was completed by the time of his arrival in Suez, Berl. 700, Cairo ^{1}I, 127, ^{2}I, 33, printed in the margin of the *Tafsīr* by ʿAbd al-ʿAzīz b. Aḥmad al-Dīrīnī, C. 1310.—8. *al-ʿAdad al-muʿtabar fī 'l-awjuh allatī bayna 'l-suwar* Cairo ^{1}I, 102.—9. *al-Bāʿith ʿala 'l-khalāṣ min ḥawādith al-qiṣāṣ,* written against the Sufis Ibn al-Muḥāsibī (I, 213), Ibn ʿArabī, and ʿAbd al-Qādir al-Jīlānī; against which an anonymous defence of the Sufis: *al-Bāʿith ʿala 'l-khalāṣ min sūʾ al-ẓann bil-khawāṣṣ* Br. Mus. Suppl. 239.—10. *Fatwā fī anna mā uʿtīda yawm ʿĀshūrāʾ*[2] *min akl al-dajāj wal-ḥubūb mubāḥ* Cairo ^{1}VII, 187.—13. *Istiḥbāb al-wuḍūʾ,* in 10 *ṭawīl* verses, with a commentary by his son Aḥmad, Gotha 107.—13.–22. see Suppl. (16. See al-Kattānī, *Fihris* II, 249$_{,19}$, Alex. Fun. 170$_{,5}$).

79 | 8. Nūr al-Dīn Abu 'l-Thanāʾ Maḥmūd b. Aḥmad b. Muḥammad b. Khaṭīb al-Dahsha al-Ḥamawī, d. 834/1431, see Suppl.

1. *Tuḥfat dhawi 'l-arab fī mushkil al-asmāʾ wal-nasab,* the names of the transmitters in the *Muwaṭṭaʾ* (I, 185) and both of the *Ṣaḥīḥs,* apparently an abstract of *Tahdhīb al-maṭāliʿ* on the *Maṭāliʿ al-anwār ʿalā ṣiḥāḥ al-āthār* by Ibrāhīm b. Yūsuf b. Qurqūl, d. 569/1173 (see I, 457), ḤKh, V, 594, composed in 804/1401, Berl. 1563, Br. Mus. 541$_{,2}$.—2. *Wasīlat al-iṣāba fī ṣunʿat al-kitāba,* a poem with

2 Lane, *Manners and Customs* II, 168 ff.

a commentary, Cairo ^{1}VI, 152.—3. *al-Taqrīb fī ʿilm al-gharīb* Alex. Lugha 9, Cairo ^{1}I, 286, ^{2}IV. 62.—4. see Suppl.

9. Aḥmad b. ʿAbd al-Raḥīm (no. 7) al-Wazīr al-ʿIrāqī al-Shāfiʿī was born in 762/1360, studied in Cairo and Damascus and succeeded his father in his offices. In Shaʿbān 824/August 1421 he replaced Jalāl al-Dīn al-Bulqīnī as chief *qāḍī* of Egypt, but in Dhu 'l-Ḥijja/November of the following year he had been dismissed. He died on 27 Shaʿbān 826/6 September 1423.

Ḥuff. XXIV, 7, al-Suyūṭī, *Ḥusn al-muḥ.* I, 167, II, 107, RA 21r, al-Kattānī, *Fihris* II, 435/6, Wüst. *Gesch.* 469. 1. *al-Mustafād min mubhamāt al-matn wal-isnād*, after Ibn Bashkuwāl, al-Khaṭīb al-Baghdādī, and al-Nawawī, completed in four days in 786/1384, Berl. 1676/7.—2. *Amālī* Köpr. 251.—3. *al-Aḥādīth al-ʿushāriyyāt* ibid. 371.—4. *Risāla fi 'l-ḥukm bil-ṣiḥḥa wal-mūjib* Gotha $58_{,1}$, Cairo ^{1}VII, 565, Garr. 1851.—5. *Taḥrīr al-fatāwī ʿala 'l-Tanbīh* (I, 485) *wal-Minhāj* (ibid., 496) *wal-Ḥāwī* (ibid., 494) Cairo ^{1}III, 202.—6. *Sharḥ al-Bahja al-Wardiyya* I, 495.—7. *Sharḥ al-Urjūza al-Yasāmīniyya* I, 621.—8.–17. see Suppl. (12. Alex. Taʾr. 70, 14. Garr. 1218).

10. Aḥmad b. Abī Bakr b. Ismāʿīl b. Qaymāz al-Būṣīrī was born in Muḥarram 762/November 1360 and died on 28 Muḥarram 840/13 September 1436 in the madrasa of Sultan Ḥasan in Cairo.

1. *Itḥāf al-khiyara* (*al-sāda*) *bi-zawāʾid al-masānīd al-ʿashara, Mukhtaṣar* by the author himself, completed in 832/1428, Algiers 501 (vol. II), | Cairo ^{1}I, 411.—2. 80
Miṣbāḥ al-zajāja fī zawāʾid b. Māja (I, 171) Cairo ^{1}I, 423.—5. See Suppl.

11. Abū Isḥāq Ibrāhīm b. Muḥammad b. Khalīl Burhān al-Dīn al-Ḥalabī Sibṭ b. al-ʿAjamī was regarded as the foremost *ḥadīth*-expert of his time in the Aleppo region. He died in Cairo of the plague on 26 Shawwāl 841/21 April 1438 (see Suppl.).

MT 32, v, *Ḥuff.* XXIV, 9, al-Kattānī *Fihris* I, 158, Wüst. *Gesch.* 478. 1. *al-Tabyīn fī asmāʾ al-mudallisīn*, on the names of *ḥadīth* falsifiers, Berl. 9946, Bodl. II, 379.—2. *al-Ightibāṭ bi-man rawā* (*rumiya*) *bil-ikhtilāṭ*, on *ḥadīth*-scholars who became unreliable towards the end of their lives, Berl. 9947.—3. *Nūr al-nibrās ʿalā Sīrat b. Sayyid al-Nās*, see p. 71.—4.–9. see Suppl.

13. Abu 'l-Faḍl Aḥmad b. ʿAlī b. Muḥammad b. Ḥajar b. Shihāb al-Dīn al-ʿAsqalānī al-Kinānī al-Shāfiʿī was born in Old Cairo on 22 Shaʿbān 773/7 March 1372. After his father's premature death, he was raised by a relative.

In 784/1382, before he was even 11 years old, he arrived in Mecca on the pil-
68 grimage, remaining there for another year. | He was dissatisfied with com-
merce, which he had engaged in first. This is why he devoted himself to the
study of *ḥadith* instead, initially in Cairo and after that, in 793/1391, in Upper
Egypt and Palestine. After his marriage—in Shaʿbān 798/July 1396—to the
daughter of the inspector of the army, Karīm al-Dīn b. ʿAbd al-ʿAzīz, he first
travelled to Yemen where he made the acquaintance of Zabīd al-Fīrūzābādī
(p. 181) and then—in 800/1398—again went on the pilgrimage to Mecca. On
the way back, he went in 802/1399 to Damascus via Cairo, where he stayed
until the end of that year. However, after another brief sojourn in Cairo, he
returned to Aden and Zabīd, via Mecca. From 806/1403 he was a teacher of
fiqh and *ḥadīth* in Cairo. In 824/1421 be became the representative of the chief
qāḍī Jalāl al-Dīn al-Bulqīnī, whom he replaced in Muḥarram 827/January
81 1424. | However, in 833/1429 he had to make way for him again. In 834, he
was reinstated, this time remaining in office—with just one interruption in
840/1—until he was forced to relinquish his position for health reasons on
30 Jumādā II 852/30 August 1448. Soon after he died in Cairo, on 18 Dhu 'l-Qaʿda
852/21 February 1449.

The biography *al-Jawāhir wal-durar fī tarjamat shaykh al-islām b. Ḥajar* by
Shams al-Dīn Abu 'l-Khayr Muḥammad b. ʿAlī al-Sakhāwī (see Suppl.), Paris
2105. *Fihrist muṣannafāt shaykh al-islām b. Ḥajar* by al-Biqāʿī, d. 885/1480
(p. 142), Leid. 22, cf. v. Rosen, *Mél. As.* VIII, 691 ff. Extremely detailed university
course Berl. 10213. *Ḥuff.* XXIV, 12, al-Suyūṭī, *Ḥusn al-muḥ.* I, 206, II, 105, *RA* 21v,
al-Khiṭaṭ al-jadīda VI, 37, al-Kattānī, *Fihris* I, 236/50, Quatremère, *Hist. des
Mamlouks* I, 2, 209, Wüst. *Gesch.* 487, Hartmann, *Muw.* 36. 1. *al-Iṣāba fī tamyīz
al-ṣaḥāba*, on Muḥammad's contemporaries and their successors, Berl.
9948/53, Brill M. 286, Algiers 1721/3, Yeni 817, AS 2955/9; ed. by Mowlawies M.
Wajyh Abdalhaqq and Gholám Qádir and A. Sprenger, Bibl. Ind. Calcutta
1856/93.—2. *Nuzhat al-albāb fi 'l-alqāb*, on the nicknames of the transmitters,
Br. Mus. 541.—3. *Tahdhīb Tadhhīb al-Kamāl fī maʿrifat al-rijāl*, see suppl. I, 606.
Taqrīb al-Tahdhīb Alex. Muṣṭ Ḥad. 7, Mosul 54_{101}.—4. *Lisān al-Mīzān* p. 59.—5.
Taʿlīq al-taʿlīq Rāġib 247, AS 472.—6. *Tabṣīr al-muntabih bi-taḥrīr al-mushtabih*
Br. Mus. Suppl. 632.—7. *Nukhabat al-fikar fī muṣṭalaḥ ahl al-athar*, I, 441.—8.
69 *al-Dirāya fī takhrīj aḥādīth al-Hidāya* I, 467. |—9. *Fatāwī ('l-ḥadīth)* de Jong
108_{2}, AS 1564, Qawala I, 138.—10. *Takhrīj aḥādīth al-Mukhtaṣar*, extracts of traditions from the legal work of Ibn Ḥājib (I, 373) and *Muwāfaqat al-ḥubr al-
khabar fī takhrīj aḥādīth al-Mukhtaṣar*, both dictated in Aleppo, Esc. $^{2}705_{1,2}$,
with the title *al-Amāli 'l-Ḥalabiyya* Alex. Ḥad. 7.—12. *Taʿjīl al-manfaʿa bi-riwāyat
rijāl al-aʾimma al-arbaʿa*, Cairo ^{1}I, 231, ^{2}I, 71, V, 141.—13. *Kitāb al-mashyakha*

al-bāsima lil-Qibābī (ʿAbd al-Raḥmān b. ʿUmar, d. 838/1434, al-Sakhāwī *Ḍaw'*, IV, 133/4), *wal-Fāṭima* (bint Khalīl, d. 833/1429), Berl. 158, see al-Kattānī, *Fihris* II, 59, 451.—14. *al-Muʿjam al-mufahras* Cairo ^{1}I, 252.—15. *al-Majmaʿ al-mu'assas lil-Muʿjam al-mufahras*, a revision of the previous work by Muḥammad b. ʿAbd al-Raḥmān al-Sakhāwī (p. 43), ibid. 245.—16. *Taʿrīf ahl al-taqdīs bi-marātib al-mawṣūfīn bil-tadlīs*, on falsifiers of traditions, Cairo ^{1}I, 231, 247, VII, 630.—17. | *Musnad al-bazzāz* Köpr. 426/8.—18. *Zahr al-firdaws*, a collection of traditions, 82
Yeni 199/201.—19. *Bulūgh al-marām min adillat al-aḥkām* Br. Mus. Suppl. $1217_{,9}$ (fragm.), AS 1038, Alex. Ḥad. 8, Fun. $133_{,11}$, Cairo ^{1}I, 277, Patna I, $40_{,410}$, *Dībāja* Gotha $92_{,105}$, print. Lucknow 1253, Lahore 1888.—Commentaries: a.–c. see Suppl. (b. Indian printing 1311, Alex. Ḥad. 26).—d. *Ifhām al-afhām min sharḥ B. al-m.* by Yūsuf b. Muḥammad b. Yaḥyā al-Baṭṭāḥ al-Zabīdī, ca. 1243, library of Aḥmad b. Ismāʿīl al-Barzanjī in Medina, al-Kattānī, *Fihris* II, 458.—20. *Badhl al-maʿān fī akhbār* (*faḍl*) *al-ṭāʿūn*, on the plague, Leid. 203, Esc. ^{2}I, 1510, Köpr. 255, AS 880, Cairo ^{1}VI, 117, ^{2}I, 272, with the title *Khulāṣat mā rawāhu 'l-wāʿūn fī 'l-akhbār al-wārida ʿani 'l-ṭāʿūn*, with an anonymous continuation until 1050–51/1643 Alex. Fun. 85.—Abstracts: a. By one of his students *Tuḥfat al-rāghibīn fī bayān amr al-ṭawāʿīn* Alex. Fun. 18, Cairo ^{1}VII, 521.—b. al-Suyūṭī, see p. $146_{,32}$.—c. Anon. Berl. 6370.—21. *al-Basīṭ al-mabthūth fī khabar al-burghūth*, on flees, Land.-Br. 98 (*al-Basṭ*), revised by al-Suyūṭī, p. $154_{,218}$.—22. *al-As'ila al-fā'iqa wal-ajwiba al-lā'iqa*, some questions on *ḥadīth*, Berl. 1116.—23. *Natā'ij al-afkār fī takhrīj aḥādīth al-adhkār*, dictates from the years 825/31 and 828/45, Berl. 1349.—24. *al-Khiṣāl al-mukaffira lil-dhunūb al-muqaddama wal-mu'akhkhara*, which employs the work on *ḥadīth* by al-Mundhirī, d. 656/1258 (I, 452), Berl. 1394/6, Alex. Fun. $20_{,3}$, Cairo ^{1}VII, 176, 586, ^{2}I, 114, 150.—25. *al-Imtāʿ bil-arbaʿīn al-mutabāyina bi-sharḥ al-samāʿ* Berl. 1510, Alex. Ḥad. 7 = (?) *Arbaʿūn* Patna I $38_{,382}$.—26. *Jawāb as'ila tataʿallaq bil-ḥadīth fī waqf balad al-Khalīl*, on the *ḥadīth* that Muhammad would have promised Tamīn al-Dārī a piece of land in Hebron, Berl. 1589, Br. Mus. $1468_{,2}$.—27. *Fī ḥall mushkilāt ḥaḍarat fī su'ālāt*, questions concerning the dead, how they are interrogated in the grave, whether punishment is corporeal or spiritual, where the soul resides after death, and how resurrection takes place, etc. Berl. 2662.—28. Other questions along the same lines, ibid. 2663, Paris $1176_{,24}$ = ? *Risāla tataʿallaq bi-baʿḍ as'ila fī aḥwāl al-mayyit* Alex. Mawāʿiẓ 17.—29. *al-Istiʿdād qabl al-fawt fī nuṣrat malak al-mawt*, written answers to various persons on the angel of death, the event of dying, and immortality, Berl. 2664.—30. *al-Jawāb al-shāfī min al-su'āl al-khāfī*, questions about things pertaining to the End, ibid. 2751.—31. *al-As'ila al-mufīda wal-ajwiba al-ʿadīda*, 28 questions on the situation of believers between death
| and resurrection, Gotha 757/8, Paris $744_{,8}$.—32. *al-Durar al-zāhira fī bayān* 83
aḥwāl al-ākhira Gotha 754 (fragm.), Cairo ^{1}VII, 123, 149, ^{2}I, $178_{,2}$.—33. *Risāla*

fī suʾāl al-mayyit fi ʾl-qabr Cairo ^{1}VII, 623, ^{2}I, 181.—34. *Kitāb al-munabbihāt ʿala ʾl-istiʿdād li-yawm al-maʿād* Ind. Off. 186/7, Pet. 233, Berl. Pers. 14, no. 44, print. also Istanbul 1315 (see Suppl.).—35. *Kashf al-sitr ʿan ḥukm al-ṣalāt baʿd al-witr* Cairo ^{1}VII, 631, ^{2}I, 139.—36. *Tabyīn al-ʿajab bi-mā warada fī faḍl Rajab* ibid.—37. *Risāla,* answers to legal questions, ibid. 58.—38. *Fī adab al-ḍayf wal-muḍayyif,* a piece from a further unidentified work, Berl. 5469.—38. *al-Zahr al-naḍr fī nabaʾ al-Khiḍr* Cairo ^{1}VII, 662, ^{2}V, 213.—39. *Mawlid al-nabī,* a commentary by Muḥammad b. Muḥammad al-Khayyāṭ, composed in 1166/1753, Cairo ^{1}I, 270, glosses by Muḥammad b. ʿUbāda b. Barrī al-ʿIdwī, d. 1193/1779, Makram 22.—40. *al-Durar al-kāmina fī aʿyān al-miʾa al-thāmina,* biographies of famous men of the eighth century, mostly from Syria and Egypt, Vienna 1172, Paris 2077, Br. Mus. Suppl. 613/4, Cairo V^1 53, ^{2}180, abstract *al-Multaqaṭ* by al-Suyūṭī, end Gotha 109, f. 105/8, anon. *Muntakhab* Köpr. $1112_{,2}$.—41. *Inbāʾ al-ghumr bi-abnāʾ al-ʿumr,* a political and literary history of Syria and Egypt for the years 773–850/1371–1446, which is an appendix to the compendium of the chronicle of Ibn Kathīr (p. 61), Berl. 9460/1, Gotha 1622/3 (where other MSS are listed), Paris 1601/4, Algiers 1597/1600, Yeni 814, Köpr. 1005/9, NO 3056, AS 2974, cf. Quatremère, *Maml.* I, 2, 219, v. Tiesenhausen, *Gold. Horde* I, 449 ff. Abstract by al-Damīrī (p. 138) draft Paris $1605_{,1}$.—42. *Ṭawāliʿ al-taʾsīs fī maʿālī b. Idrīs,* on al-Shāfiʿī and his students, completed in 835/1431, Paris 2098, AS 3508, Cairo V^1, 138, ^{2}148, print. C. 1301.—43. *Rafʿ al-iṣr ʿan quḍāt Miṣr,* a continuation of the history of Ibn Zūlāq (I, 156), Paris 2149, Cairo V^1, 60, ^{2}202, to which a *Dhayl* by Shams al-Dīn Muḥammad b. ʿAbd al-Raḥmān al-Sakhāwī (p. 43), Leid. 1118, Paris 2150, under the title *Bughyat al-ʿulamāʾ wal-ruwāt,* ḤKh ^{1}II, $60_{,1880}$, III, $473_{,6487}$, an abstract of the *Dhayl* by ʿAlī b. Abi ʾl-Luṭf, Paris 2131.—Abstract and revision with a continuation until the year 871/1466 by his grandson Jamāl al-Dīn Yūsuf b. Shāhīn, d. 828/1425 (Suppl. II, 76), *al-Nujūm al-zāhira bi-talkhīṣ akhbār quḍāt Miṣr wal-Qāhira* Berl. 9819, Paris 2152, Br. Mus. 1299.—44. *Tarjamat Aḥmad al-Badawī,* d. 675/1276 (I, 586), Berl. 10101.—45. *al-Marḥama al-ghaythiyya bil-tarjama al-Laythiyya,* on the life of Faqīh al-Layth b. Saʿd b.
84 ʿAbd al-Raḥmān al-Fahmī al-Fāris Abu ʾl-Ḥārith, d. 175/791, Berl. 10121.—| 46. *Dīwān* Paris 3219, Esc. $^2345_{,2}$, 444, Cairo ^{1}IV, 232, ^{2}III, 106, print. 1301 as part 1 of no. 42.—Selection *Manẓūm al-durar* or *al-Sabʿa al-sayyāra al-nayyirāt,* Berl. 790, Leid. 743, Esc. $^2345_{,2}$, further selection Berl. 7902.—47. Individual poems, Berl. 7903.—48. 3 *basīṭ* verses on the ten pronunciations of the word *al-khātam,* ibid. $7069_{,1}$.—49. *Rajaz* on the various kinds of the divine, ibid. $8159_{,4}$.—50. A *qaṣīda* on al-Malik al-Ashraf Ismāʿīl of Yemen (r. 842–5/1438–41), Cairo ^{1}VII, 443.—51. *Mukhtaṣar al-Asās* I, 348.—52.–90. see Suppl. (64. Garr. 1466, Alex. Ḥad. $55_{,1}$, Patna I, $56_{,567}$. Garr. 1405 by al-Haytamī [p. 387, 72], Patna I, $41_{,424}$, which has *Tasdīd,* 78, Garr. $1439_{,79}$. *Riyāḍ al-azhār fī jalāʾ al-abṣār* ḤKh III,

545/6, anon. Garr. 2076, 80. Mosul $52_{,18}$, attributed to al-Haytamī |, Garr. 84
$2076_{,1}$.)—91. *al-Durr al-manẓūm aw al-Muʿashsharāt* Alex. Ḥad. 23.—92. *Sharḥ al-manāsik* Mosul $111_{,172}$.

14. Abū Dharr Aḥmad b. Ibrāhīm b. Muḥammad b. Khalīl al-Ḥalabī Muwaffaq al-Dīn was born in Ṣafar 818/April 1415 and died in Dhu ʾl-Qaʿda 884/January–February 1479.

MT 13v. 1. *Qurrat al-ʿayn fī faḍl al-shaykhayn wal-ṣihrayn wal-sibṭayn* Cairo ^{1}VII, 588, ^{2}V, 294.—2.–4. see Suppl.

B Biographies of the Prophet

1. Muḥammad b. Ayyūb b. ʿAbd al-Qāhir al-Tādhifī Badr al-Dīn al-Ḥanafī al-Ḥalabī, d. 705/1305.

| 1. *al-Durra al-fākhira*, a commentary on a biography of Muḥammad in verse, 71
al-Rawḍa al-nāḍira, Paris 1965.—2. See Suppl.

2. Muḥammad b. ʿAlī b. ʿAbd al-Wāḥid (I, 528) al-Zamlakānī was born in Shawwāl 667/June 1269, worked in Damascus in the *Dīwān al-inshāʾ*, became a hospital inspector in 707/1307, and taught at the Shāmiyya, Ẓāhiriyya, and Rawāḥiyya madrasas. In 724/1324 he became a *qāḍī* in Aleppo, but for only three years. In 727/1327 al-Malik al-Nāṣir wanted to appoint him as chief *qāḍī*, but he died on the way from Damascus to Cairo, reportedly of poison, in Bilbays, on 16 Ramaḍān 727/7 August 1327.

| *Fawāt* II, 250, *DK* IV, 74, no. 210. 1. *ʿUjālat al-rākib fī dhikr ashraf al-manāqib* 85
Cairo ^{1}VII, 659, ^{2}I, 130.—2. *Mawlid al-nabī* Berl. 9527.—3. *Taḥqīq al-awlā min ahl al-rifq al-aʿlā* Qawala I, 223.

3. Abu ʾl-Fatḥ Muḥammad b. Muḥammad b. Muḥammad b. Aḥmad b. ʿAbdallāh b. Muḥammad Fatḥ al-Dīn al-Yaʿmarī al-Andalusī al-Shāfiʿī b. Sayyid al-Nās was born in Cairo on 14 Dhu ʾl-Qaʿda 661/20 September 1263 (or, according to others, 671/3 June 1273), to parents who originally came from Seville. He started his studies there and then continued them, from 690/1291, in Damascus. He later became a teacher of *ḥadīth* in the Shāfiʿī section of al-Madrasa al-Ẓāhiriyya in Cairo and died in Shaʿbān 734/April 1334.

Fawāt II, 169, *Ḥuff.* XXI, 11, *DK* IV, 208/13, Wüst. *Gesch.* 400. 1. *ʿUyūn al-athar fī ghazawāt sayyid Rabīʿa wa-Muḍar wa-fī shamāʾilihi idh hiya ashraf shamāʾil*

al-bashar, a detailed biography of the Prophet, Berl. 9577/8, Brill, M. 292, Gotha 1784/7 (where other MSS are listed), Strasb. 18, Pet. Ros. 40, Paris 1967, 5374, 5411, Algiers 1657, Br. Mus. 355, Suppl. 512, *Bull. de Corr. Afr.* 1885, 214, no. 3, Garr. 640, AS 3315/6, Köpr. 1089, 1120, Alex. Ta'r. 11, Cairo V, ^{1}91, ^{2}274, Makram 47, print. C. 1356, 2 vols.—Commentary *Nūr al-nibrās ʿalā sīrat b. Sayyid al-Nās* by Sibṭ b. al-ʿAjamī, d. 841/1437 (p. 80), Berl. 9579, Leid. 868, Paris 1968/9, Cairo V, ^{1}172, ^{2}400.—Abstracts: a. By the author himself *Nūr al-ʿuyūn* Br. Mus. Suppl. 1277, 10, Pet. AM 1469 (fragm.), Garr. 641, Alex. Ta'r. 18, Cairo ^{1}V, 172, VII, 666, ^{2}V, 400.—b. Sibṭ b. al-ʿAjamī, Berl. 9580/1.—*Naẓm ʿUyūn al-a.* by Muḥammad b. Yūsuf, Alex. Ta'r. 17.—2. Didactic letter to Ṣalāḥ al-Dīn al-Ṣafadī, d. 764/1362, Berl. 153$_{,2}$.—3. *Bushra 'l-labīb bi-dhikra 'l-ḥabīb, qaṣīda*s in praise of the Prophet, ordered by rhyme and by poet, Gotha 2297, one of them in the *Fawāt*, shortened to half its size in *Carminum Orientalium triga, Arabicum M. Ebn Seid-Ennas*, ed. Kosegarten, Stralsund 1815, see R. Basset, Une élégie d'Ibn Said en Nās in *le*
72 *Muséon*, 1886, 247/55 | (also in *Mélanges d'hist. et de lit. or.* I, Louvain 1886).—4. *al-Maqāmāt al-ʿaliyya fi 'l-karāmāt al-jaliyya*, in praise of the Prophet and the *aṣḥāb*, Pet. AM 146$_{,10}$.—5. *Sharḥ Jāmiʿ al-Tirmidhī* I, 169.—6.–9. see Suppl. (9. also in the library of Yāsīn b. Bāshayān al-ʿAbbāsī in Basra).

86 | 4. Abū ʿUmar ʿAbd al-ʿAzīz b. Badr al-Dīn Abū ʿAbdallāh Muḥammad b. Ibrāhīm ʿIzz al-Dīn b. Jamāʿa al-Kinānī al-Shāfiʿī was born in Damascus on 19 Muḥarram 694/10 December 1294. He was educated by his father, who was the chief *qāḍī*, and worked as a teacher from 714/1314. In 738/1337 he was appointed chief *qāḍī* in Egypt and, after losing his office under Ṣarghitmish for a brief period in 740/1348, he gave it up it for good in Jumādā I 766/February 1365, limiting himself to his professorship at the mosque of Ibn Ṭūlūn. He then went on pilgrimage and died in Mecca, on 10 Jumādā II 767/15 February 1366.

Ḥuff. XXII, 6, *RA* 159v, *Orient.* II, 418, Wüst. *Gesch.* 428. 1. *Mukhtaṣar sīrat al-nabī*, composed in 735/1335 in Cairo, Ind. Off. 1038$_{,7}$, Esc. ^{2}1744, Cairo ^{1}VII, 181, ^{2}V, 335, Garr. 642.—2. *Kitāb al-arbaʿīn al-wusṭā al-mukhtaṣar min al-Arbaʿīn al-kubrā* Berl. 1508.—3. *Hidāyat al-sālik fi 'l-manāsik* (*ilā maʿrifat al-madhāhib al-arbaʿa fi 'l-manāsik*), Cairo ^{1}III, 291, abstract Br. Mus. 259$_{,3}$.—4. *Qaṣīda taḍammanat muṣṭalaḥ al-ḥadīth* Br. Mus. 169$_{,2}$.—5. Draft of the third volume of the *Nuzhat al-alibbā'* (Maqq. I, 910), on the poets of the fifth to seventh centuries, Paris 3342.—6.–8. see Suppl. (6. Garr. 663 is rather by ʿAlī al-ʿImrīṭī).

5. ʿAbdallāh b. ʿAlā' al-Dīn ʿAlī b. Aḥmad b. ʿAbd al-Raḥmān b. Ḥadīda al-Anṣārī al-Khazrajī al-Maqdisī al-Miṣrī completed, on 4 Dhu 'l-Ḥijja 779/3 April 1378:

Al-Miṣbāḥ al-muḍīʾ fī kuttāb al-nabī al-ummī wa-rusulihi ilā mulūk al-arḍ min ʿArabī wa-ʿAjamī, Paris 1971, Esc. ^{2}1742 (Wüst. *Gesch*. 441).

6. Ärkmäs al-Ṭawīl al-Yashbakī enjoyed the confidence of the Mamlūk sultans al-Ẓāhir Čaqmaq (r. 842–57/1438–53) and Īnāl (r. 857—65/1453—60), and in 868/1464 he wrote a copy of the *Tadhkirat b. Ḥamdūn* in Cairo.

Al-Sakhāwī, *Ḍawʾ* II, 267, no. 835 (with a mistaken 'd. 844'). *Al-Durr al-thamīn fī-mā warada fī ummahāt* | *al-muʾminīn*, Fez, library of the sultan, al-Kattānī 87
Fihris II, 441, n. 1.

7. Following a successful career as a military man and an administrator, Yashbak b. Mahdī al-Ẓāhirī Čaqmaq al-Ṣaghīr al-Maqarr al-Ashraf al-Amīr al-Sayfī al-Dawādār fell into the hands of one of the emirs of sultan Yaʿqūb b. Uzun in a campaign against him, and was executed in al-Ruhā in Ramaḍān 885/November 1481.

Al-Sakhāwī, *Ḍawʾ* X, 272/4, see p. 52. *Shajarat al-nasab al-sharīf al-nabawī* Alex. Taʾr. 117, Cairo ^{2}V, 229, lith. in *Majmūʿa*, C. n.d., print. in *Majmūʿa*, Būlāq 1292.

| 8. Abu ʾl-ʿAbbās Aḥmad b. Muḥammmad b. Abī Bakr al-Khaṭīb Shihāb al-Dīn 73
al-Qasṭallānī al-Shāfiʿī lived as a preacher in Cairo where he was born on 12 Dhu ʾl-Qaʿda 851/20 January 1448, visited Mecca twice, and died on 7 Muḥarram 923/31 January 1517.

Wüst. *Gesch*. 509, *al-Khiṭaṭ al-jadīda* VI, 11, al-Kattānī, *Fihris* II, 318/20. 1. *al-Mawāhib al-laduniyya fi ʾl-minaḥ al-Muḥammadiyya*, a history of the Prophet,[1] in a draft version dated 2 Shawwāl 898/18 July 1493, completed in clean copy on 15 Shaʿbān 899/22 May 1494, Berl. 9591/3, Gotha 1795 (where other MSS are listed), Munich 454/5, Ind. Off. 179/80, Garr. 650, NO 3432/41, Yeni 905/6, AS 3489, Köpr. 1176/7, Algiers 1689/91, Alex. Ḥad. 65, Cairo I^1, 434, ^{2}153, App. 18, Makram 60, print. C. 1281, among others. Commentaries: a. al-Shawbarī, d. 1069/1659, Berl. 9594, Cairo ^{1}I, 334.—b. al-Shabrāmallisī, d. 1087/1676, Berl. 9595/8, Cairo ^{1}I, 332.—c. al-Suḥaymī, d. 1078/1669, Cairo ^{1}I, 369.—d. al-Zurqānī, d. 1122/1710 (p. 318), Cairo ^{1}I, 356, Qawala I, 128, print. Būlāq 1278, 1291, 8 vols.—e. Anon. Berl. 9599/600.—2. *Irshād al-sārī fī sharḥ al-Bukhārī*, I, 165.—3. *al-Fatḥ*

1 Because of this work, al-Suyūṭī reported him to the Shaykh al-Islām on charges of plagiarism. The author must have felt guilty, since he vainly tried to settle the dispute amicably.

al-Mawāhibī fi 'l-imām Abi 'l-Qāsim al-Shāṭibī (I, 520) Berl. 10123. Abstracts:
88 a. By the author himself *Minḥa min minaḥ al-fatḥ* Cairo V, | ^{1}161, ^{2}370.—b. Anon. Br. Mus. $88_{,ii}$.—4. *Laṭā'if al-ishārāt li-funūn al-qirā'āt* Garr. 1230, Köpr. 24/6, NO 89, Cairo ^{1}I, 105, Qawala I, 29, a part of which, on sura $6_{,138}$, Berl. 993.—5. *Masālik al-ḥunafā' ilā mashāri' al-ṣalāt 'ala 'l-nabī al-muṣṭafā* Yeni 278, AS 895, Cairo ^{1}II, 248.—6. *Maqāmāt al-'ārifīn* Köpr. 784.—7. *Sharḥ al-Muqaddima al-Jazariyya*, see p. 202.—8. *al-Muqaddima fi 'l-ḥadīth* with a commentary, *Nayl al-amānī*, by 'Abd al-Hādī al-Abyārī (p. 487), C. n.d.—9.–12. (Garr. 108) see Suppl.—13. *Zahr al-riyāḍ wa-shifā' al-qulūb al-mirāḍ* Alex. Mawā'iẓ 20.

C Collections of *Ḥadīth* and Edifying Works[1]

1. Abū Muḥammad 'Abd al-Mu'min b. Abi 'l-Ḥasan b. Sharaf b. al-Khiḍr Sharaf al-Dīn al-Tūnī al-Dimyāṭī al-Shāfi'ī was born towards the end of 613/1217 on the
74 island of Tūna between Tinnīs and Damietta, | where he also studied. After extensive travels, he became senior professor at the Manṣūriyya academy in Cairo that had been founded by al-Malik al-Nāṣir Qalawūn, and also taught *ḥadīth* at the Ẓāhiriyya. He died on 10 (15) Dhu 'l-Qa'da 705/25(30) June 1306.

Al-Subkī, *Ṭab.* VI, 132/41, *Ḥuff.* XXI, 7, Ibn al-Qāḍī, *Durrat al-ḥijāl* II, 396, no. 1115, al-Kattānī, *Fihris* I, 304/6, Quatremère, *Maml.* II, 2, 259, *Orient.* II, 308, Wüst. *Gesch.* 379. 1. *Faḍl al-khayl*, traditions about horses, Paris 2816, Bodl. I, 384, II, 173n. 2, Lee 139. Turkish translation by Ḥusayn Naẓmīzāde for Ḥasan Pāshā in Baghdad, Es'ad 1824. Abstracts: a. see Suppl.—b. *Qaṭr al-sayl fī amr al-khayl* by 'Umar b. Raslān b. Naṣr al-Bulqīnī, d. 805/1402 (p. 114), Gotha 2081, Bodl. II, 199, shorter adaptation AS 4158.—2. *Kashf al-mughaṭṭā fī faḍl al-ṣalāt al-wusṭā* Garr. 1952, Cairo ^{1}I, 388, ^{2}I, 140.—3. *al-Tasallī wal-ightibāṭ bi-thawāb man taqaddama min al-infirāṭ* Cairo I, ^{1}285, ^{2}96.—4. *al-Matjar al-rābiḥ fī thawāb al-'amal al-ṣāliḥ* Cairo I, ^{1}396, ^{2}143.—5.–9. see Suppl.

89 | 2. Fakhr al-Dīn 'Abd al-Raḥmān al-Ba'labakkī wrote, in 729/1329:

1. *Sirāj al-mudhakkirīn wa-nūr al-muqtabisīn fī tanbīh al-ghāfilīn* Cairo ^{1}VII, 653.—2. *Mukhtaṣar Kitāb al-thabāt 'inda 'l-mamāt li-Ibn al-Jawzī* see I, 664.—3. *Mukhtaṣar Kitāb al-ma'shūq lahu* ibid. 665.

3. Badr al-Dīn Abū 'Abdallāh Muḥammad b. Burhān al-Dīn Abū Isḥāq Ibrāhīm b. Sa'dallāh b. Jamā'a al-Kinānī al-Ḥamawī al-Shāfi'ī, who was born in Hama

1 Which are not always easy to distinguish from the popular works discussed in § 4.

in Rabīʿ II 639/October 1241, studied philology, among other things, with Ibn Mālik in Damascus, and later became a professor there. In 687/1288 he became *qāḍī* in Jerusalem, in Ramaḍān 690/September 1291 chief *qāḍī* in Egypt, and three years later in Damascus, where he also assumed the office of sermoniser at the Umayyad mosque, together with a number of other clerical functions. After the death of Ibn Daqīq al-ʿĪd (p. 75) he had to go to Cairo, was dismissed in 709/1309, but reinstated again the following year. There he also taught at the mosque of Ibn Ṭūlūn and other madrasas. After he had been dismissed for a second time in 727/1327, he limited himself to teaching and writing. He died on 21 Jumādā I 733/8 February 1333.

Fawāt II, 174 (with the mistaken 'd. 773', see Sauvaire, *JA* s. IX, v. 5, 302), DK III, 280/3, al-Ṣafadī, *al-Wāfī* AS $2968_{,116/7}$. 1. *al-Aḥādīth al-arbaʿūn al-tusāʿiyyāt al-isnād*, 40 traditions documented ninefold, Berl. 1622, his lessons from the years 718/9, ibid. $153_{,1}$.—2. *Mukhtaṣar fī munāsabat tarājim al-Bukhārī li-aḥādīth al-abwāb*, on the relation between titles and contents of chapters in al-Bukhārī, Cairo [1]VII, 260.—3. *Mukhtaṣar Aqṣa ʾl-amal wal-shawq fī ʿulūm ḥadīth al-rasūl li-Ibn al-Ṣalāḥ* see I, 441.—4. *Taḥrīr al-aḥkām fī tadbīr millat al-islām*, a compendium of Islamic constitutional and administrative law, Qara Muṣṭafā P. 401 (copy of Vienna 1830!), Alex. Taʾr. 43, ed. H. Kofler, *Islca* VI, 349/414, VII, 1/64, *AKM* XXIII, 6, 18/129, abstract by the author himself at the order of al-Malik al-Ashraf, d. 693/1294, Berl. 5613.—5. *al-Fawāʾid al-lāʾiḥa min maʿāni ʾl-Fātiḥa* Leid. 1636.—6. *Tadhkirat al-sāmiʿ wal-mutakallim fī ādāb al-ʿālim wal-mutaʿallim*, composed in 672/1273, | Berl. 142/3, used in ibid. 103, Gotha 162, Garr. 787.—7. 90
An admonishing *qaṣīda* Berl. $7846_{,3}$.—8. (Mosul $103_{,57}$).—11. see Suppl.

4. Jamāl al-Dīn ʿAbdallāh b. ʿAlī b. Muḥammad b. Sulaymān b. Ghānim, who was born in 711/1311 and died in 744/1343.

Al-Fāʾiq fi ʾl-kalām al-rāʾiq, a collection of traditions, Cairo I, [1]373, [2]133, Mosul $94_{,21,2}$, $156_{,92}$.

5. ʿAbdallāh b. Muḥammad b. Muḥammad b. Muḥammad b. ʿAbd al-Qādir al-Anṣārī al-Shāfiʿī, *qāḍī* of Sarmīn near Aleppo, ca. 749/1348.

Arbaʿūn Berl. 1506.

6. Sharaf al-Dīn Yūnus al-Mālikī, a student of al-Dhahabī (p. 57), wrote, ca. 750/1349:

Al-Kanz al-madfūn wal-fulk al-mashḥūn, a collection of the ethical maxims of great men, print. Būlāq 1288, C. 1303, 1321. Abstract *al-Jawhar al-maṣūn al-multaqaṭ min al-K. al-m.* by ʿUmar b. Ibrāhīm al-ʿAbbādī, ninth cent. (al-Sakhāwī, *Ḍawʾ*, VI, 67, no. 223), Vienna 1846.

7. Jamāl al-Dīn Muḥammad b. ʿAbd al-Hādī al-Fuwwī al-Shāfiʿī, who died in 766/1364 (see Suppl.).

Tanqīḥ al-taḥqīq fī aḥādīth al-taʿlīq Köpr. II, 43.

8. Badr al-Dīn Abū ʿAbdallāh Muḥammad b. Taqī al-Dīn Abū Muḥammad ʿAbdallāh al-Dimashqī al-Shiblī b. Qayyim al-Shibliyya al-Ḥanafī was born in 712/1312 in al-Shibliyya, a quarter of al-Ṣāliḥiyya, near Damascus, where his father was a *qayyim*, or dean of the mosque. He studied in Cairo and Damascus, became a *qāḍī* in Tripoli in 755/1354, and died there in 769/1367.

Ibn Quṭlūb. no. 189, Orient. I, 422. 1. *Ākām al-marjān fī aḥkām al-jānn*, a work on jinns, Berl. 10327, Gotha 747, Paris 1388, 5864, Calcutta 897, Cairo ^{1}VI, 107, ^{2}I, App. 36, V, 3, AS 2183, Köpr. 237, Mosul 145, 67, print. C. 1326, 1356.—Abstracts *Laqṭ al-marjān*, with additions, by al-Suyūṭī, d. 911/1505, Berl. 2512, Leid. 2029,
91 Ind. Off. 177, Algiers 854, Alex. Fun. 59, $164_{,2}$, Cairo ^{1}VI, 189, | ^{2}I, App. 47, from which again a. *Iltiqāṭ al-marjān* perhaps by al-Suyūṭī himself, Berl. 2513, Qawala I, 411.—b. *ʿIqd al-marjān fī-mā yataʿallaq bil-jānn* by ʿAlī b. Ibrāhīm
76 al-Ḥalabī, d. 1044/1634 (p. 307), de Sacy $31_{,2}$, Alex. Fun. $155_{,4}$ (see Suppl.). |—2. *Maḥāsin al-wasāʾil ilā maʿrifat al-awāʾil*, composed in 742/1341, Br. Mus. Suppl. $604_{,1}$, abstract *Unmūdhaj M. al-w.* by Ibrāhīm b. ʿUmar al-Shirbīnī al-Khaṭīb (in Aleppo), composed in 850/1446, in the library of Muḥammad ʿAlī Hibat al-Dīn al-Shahrastānī, and another abstract of this abstract by Abū Muḥammad al-Ḥasan b. Abi ʾl-Ḥasan al-Hādī al-Mūsawī al-ʿĀmilī al-Kāẓimī, d. 1354/1935, composed in 1334/1916, *Dharīʿa* II, $408_{,1630}$ (where al-Shiblī is corrupted to al-Subkī, and with 747 as the year of his death).

9. Muḥammad b. Muḥammad b. Muḥammad b Muḥammad al-Manbijī wrote, on the occasion of the plague of 775/1373:

Tasliyat ahl al-maṣāʾib fī mawt al-awlād wal-aqārib Gotha 1230, Paris 952, C. 1348.

10. Muḥammad b. Aḥmad b. ʿAlī al-Ḥalabī b. al-Rukn, d. 803/1400.

Rawḍ al-afkār wa-ghurar al-ḥikāyāt wal-akhbār, an edifying work, Berl. 8812/3.

11. Nūr al-Dīn Abu ʾl-Ḥasan ʿAlī b. Abī Bakr b. Sulaymān b. Ḥajar al-Haytamī, who was born in 735/1334, was a student of al-Zayn al-ʿIrāqī, whom he accompanied on his travels. He died in Cairo, on 15 Ramaḍān 807/18 March 1405.

Al-Suyūṭī, *Ḥusn al-muḥ.* I, 205. 1. *Majmaʿ al-zawāʾid wa-manbaʿ al-fawāʾid*, addenda to the 6 *ḥadīth* collections, Garr. 1393, Cairo [1]I, 399, Patna I, $59_{,595}$, print. Delhi 1308, *Dībāja* Gotha $2_{,106}$.—2. *Taqrīb al-bughya fī tartīb aḥādīth al-Ḥilya* I, 445.—3.–6. see Suppl.[2]

12. Shams al-Dīn Aḥmad b. Ibrāhīm b. Muḥammad b. al-Naḥḥās al-Dimashqī al-Dimyāṭī, d. 814/1411 (see Suppl.).

1. *Mashāriʿ al-ashwāq ilā maṣāriʿ al-ʿushshāq wa-muthīr al-gharām ilā dār al-islām*, a call to jihad, Leid. 1853, Esc. [1]1112, Algiers 1301/2, Cairo [1]IV, 324, [2]I, 358, App. 48, Leningrad, collection Smogorzewski, Patna | I, $206_{,1837}$.—Abstracts: 92
a. By the author himself *Mashāriq al-ashwāq* (see Suppl.), Turkish translation *Faḍāʾil al-jihād* by Bāqī, d. 1008/1599, completed in 975/1567, Vienna 1414, Dresden 410, Algiers 1303, print. Būlāq 1251, following this J. v. Hammer, *Die Posaune des hl. Krieges*, Vienna 1805.—b. *Fukāhat al-adhwāq etc.* see Suppl.—2. *Bayān al-maghnam fī ʾl-wird al-aʿẓam*, a collection of prayers, ḤKh [1]$79_{,1994}$, [2]I, 262, Cairo [1]VII, 107, Alex. Fawāʾid 5.—3. See Suppl.

13. Shams al-Dīn Muḥammad b. ʿAbdallāh b. Muḥammad al-Qaysī al-Dimashqī b. Nāṣir al-Dīn, d. 842/1438 (see Suppl.).

Ḥuff. XXIV, 17, *al-Qabas al-ḥāwī* II, 79b, *Dustūr al-aʿlām* 146, *Tāj al-ṭabaqāt* II, 1909, *JA* S. IX, V. 3, 294. 1. *al-Aḥādīth al-arbaʿūn al-mutabāyinat al-asānīd wal-mutūn* Berl. 1509.—2. *Bard al-akbād ʿan(ʿinda) faqd al-awlād* Leid. 2167, Paris 1312, Bodl. I, $157_{,5}$, Alex. Fun. $99_{,3}$, an abstract *Multaqaṭ* (see Suppl.) Garr. $2025_{,4}$.—3. *Badīʿat al-bayān ʿan mawt al-aʿyān ʿala ʾl-zamān*, a *rajaz* poem on the names of Muḥammad's companions, successors, and traditionists, in 25 classes, Br. Mus. 369.—4. A list of the ʿAbbāsid caliphs and 5 death notices of *ḥadīth*-scholars from the years 720–8/1320–8, Br. Mus. Suppl. 487_{iii}.—5. *al-Radd al-wāfir ʿalā man zaʿama anna man sammā Ibn Taymiyya shaykh al-islām kāfir*, | 77
which lists scholars who do not regard Ibn Taymiyya (p. 125) as an heretic, Berl.

2 Sometimes works by his younger namesake Aḥmad (d. 973/1565, p. 387) are attributed to him.

10129, Patna I, $125_{,1250}$.—6. See Suppl.—7. *Jāmiʿ al-āthār fī mawlid al-Mukhtār*, in 3 vols., ḤKh, [1]II, $499_{,3559}$, [2]I, 533, Dam. Z. $74_{,42}$.

14. Aḥmad b. Abī Bakr b. al-Rassām al-Ḥamawī, d. 842/1438 (see Suppl.).

ʿIqd al-durar wal-laʾālīʾ fī faḍl al-shuhūr wal-ayyām wal-layālī, composed in 816/1413, Cairo [1]VI, 156.

15. Zayn al-Dīn Abu ʾl-Naʿīm Riḍwān b. Muḥammad b. Yūsuf b. Salāma b. al-Bahāʾ b. Saʿīd al-ʿUqbī al-Mustamlī al-Miṣrī was born in 769/1367 in the village of Minyat al-ʿUqba near Giza and died on 3 Rajab 853/23 August 1449 (see Suppl.).

Al-Arbaʿūn al-mutabāyina bi-sharṭ al-samāʿ al-muttasiʿ, Cairo [1]I, 263, [2]I, 287.

16. ʿAlī b. Muḥammad b. Aḥmad b. Yūsuf al-Haythamī al-Makkī al-Ṭubnāwī Nūr al-Dīn Abu ʾl-Ḥasan, d. 888/1483 (see Suppl.).

93 | 1. *Rāḥat al-qulūb min taʿab al-iṭnāb fī ʾl-juyūb*, composed in Cairo in 854/1450, Cairo [1]V, 247.—2. *Wasīlat al-khadam ilā ahl al-ḥill wal-ḥaram*, an edifying work based on sayings of the Prophet, his companions and later persons, which also covers the spiritual gifts of saints, based on accounts by his contemporaries, Berl. 8821.

17. Muḥammad b. Khalīl b. Ghars al-Dīn b. Aḥmad b. Jumʿa al-Ḥusaynī al-Shāfiʿī, a student of Ibn Ḥajar (p. 80), wrote, around 870/1465:

Iʿlām al-sāda al-amājid bi-faḍl bināʾ al-masājid Cairo [1]VII, 586, [2]I, 90.

18. Yaḥyā b. Saʿd al-Dīn al-Munāwī al-Ḥaddādī Sharaf al-Dīn was born in 798/1395, became a Shāfiʿī *qāḍī* in Cairo, and died in 871/1466 (see Suppl.):

Al-Suyūṭī *Ḥusn al-muḥ.* I, 253. *Al-Ihtimām bi-takhrīj arbaʿīn ḥadīthan min marwiyy shaykh al-islām* Berl. 1511. Is he the author of the *Taḥqīq al-wuṣūl ilā sharḥ al-Fuṣūl* (of Hippocrates), Esc. [2]878?

19. Muḥammad b. Muḥammad al-Qāhirī Imām al-Kāmiliyya Kamāl al-Dīn, who died in Cairo in 874/1469.

1. *Risāla fī ʾl-Khiḍr wa-ḥayātihi* Ind. Off. 668.—2.–4. see Suppl.

20. Abū Ḥāmid Muḥammad al-Qudsī, d. 912/1506?

| 1. *Bushrā bi-ḥuṣūl al-ajr al-matīn wal-naṣr al-mubīn fī tasliyat al-ḥazīn*, written for sultan Qāʾitbāy as consolation for the defeat of his army in Syria in Shawwāl 885/December 1480 (see p. 87, 7), Cairo ^{1}VII, 199.—2. *al-Jawāb al-murhaf ʿan suʾāl al-Malik al-Ashraf*, composed in Ramaḍān of the same year, ibid.—3. *Kanz al-akhbār* NO 4207. 78

21. ʿAlī b. Muḥammad b. Abī Qaṣība al-Ghazzālī al-Ḥusaynī, ca. 910/1504.

1. *Khāliṣat ʿiqd al-durar min khulāṣat ʿiqd al-ghurar*, an ethical work that follows the example of Muḥammad b. Ibrāhīm al-Kutubī Waṭwāṭ's (p. 67) *Ghurar al-khaṣāʾiṣ*, dedicated to a certain "Qānṣūh", one of the court of the sultan of Egypt (the al-Ghūrī who reigned as sultan from 920/1514 onwards, p. 24?), Paris 4594.—2. *al-Qawāʿid al-wāqiya al-wāfiya bil-ʿaqāʾid al-kāfila al-kāfiya* Cairo ^{1}VII, 655.—3. | *Maṣābīḥ al-fuhūm wa-mafātīḥ al-ʿulūm* ibid. 656, ^{2}VI, 191.— 94
4. *Istiʿṭāf al-marāḥim wastisʿāf al-makārim*, composed in 878/1473, Cairo ^{1}VII, 656, ^{2}III, 11, Landb. Br. 345.—5. See Suppl.

22. Ibrāhīm b. ʿAlī b. Aḥmad al-Qalqashandī al-Maqdisī Burhān (Jamāl) al-Dīn Abu 'l-Fatḥ, who died in Cairo in 922/1516.

Al-Kattānī, *Fihris* II, 314/6. 1. *al-ʿUshāriyyāt*, 22 tenfold-confirmed traditions, Berl. 1624/5.—2. 30 traditions, AS 335.—3. *Tathbīt al-mulk bi-tafsīr qawlihi qul allāhumma mālik al-mulk* (sura $3_{,25}$), Esc. $^{2}739_{,4}$.

6 *Fiqh*

A The Ḥanafīs

1a. ʿAlī b. Muḥammad b. al-Ḥasan al-Khilāṭī al-Ḥanafī, d. 708/1308 (see Suppl.).

Kitāb al-ḥudūd Garr. 1630, Cairo ^{2}IV, 163.

1b. Abu 'l-Makārim Ẓahīr al-Dīn Isḥāq b. Abī Bakr al-Ḥanafī al-Walwālijī, who died in 710/1310.

Fatāwī NO 2043/5, Yeni 664/5, Cairo ^{1}III, 94.

2. Fakhr al-Dīn ʿUthmān b. ʿAlī b. Miḥjan al-Bāriʿī al-Zaylaʿī came from Zaylaʿ in Abyssinia, arrived in Cairo in 705/1305, where he became a *muftī* and a professor, and died in 743/1342.

ʿAlī Mubārak, *al-Khiṭaṭ al-jadīda* V, 57, VIII, 7, 14. *Sharḥ Kanz al-daqāʾiq* see p. 196.

3. Aḥmad b. ʿAlī b. Aḥmad al-Hamdānī al-Kūfī Fakhr al-Dīn b. al-Faṣīḥ al-Qayṣarī, who was born in 680/1281 in Iraq, became a professor in Damascus and died on 26 Shaʿbān 755/16 September 1354.

DK I, 204, no. 528, Ibn Quṭlūb. no. 31. *Naẓm al-Sirājiyya fi ʾl-farāʾiḍ* I, 471.

79 | 4. Ibrāhīm b. ʿImād al-Dīn Abu ʾl-Ḥasan ʿAlī b. Aḥmad Najm (Burhān) al-Dīn Abū Isḥāq al-Ṭarasūsī, born in 721/1321, was chief *qāḍī* in Damascus, and died in 758/1358 (see Suppl.).

95 | DK I, 43, al-Ṣafadī, *al-Wāfī*, AS 2962$_{26/7}$. Ibn Quṭlūb. no. 5, *Orient.* II, 383, Wüst. *Gesch.* 419. 1. *Anfaʿ al-wasāʾil ilā taḥrīr al-masāʾil* (*fi ʾl-furūʿ*), Munich 311, Paris 925/6, Yeni 358, 366/8, Alex. Fiqh Ḥan. 7, Cairo ^{1}IV, 8, Mosul 146$_{91}$.—2. *al-Fawāʾid al-fiqhiyya al-Badriyya*, in 1000 verses, composed in 754/1352, Berl. 4595, Alex. Fiqh Ḥan. 26, Cairo ^{1}III, 118.—3. *Tuḥfat al-Turk fī-mā yajibu an yuʿmala fi ʾl-mulk*, chapter I, demonstration of the fact that a sultanate can also be ruled by a Turk, chapters II ff, on the art of government, composed in 753/1351, Berl. 5614, Paris 2445/6 (but where the author is Aḥmad b. al-ʿIzz al-Ḥanafī), AS 2854.—4. *al-Nūr al-lāmiʿ fī-mā yuʿmal bihi fi ʾl-jāmiʿ*, on the administration of the main mosque of Damascus, Berl. 6078 (ḤKh VI, 14042, author al-ʿIzz).—5. Suppl.—6. *ʿUmdat al-ḥukkām* ḤKh IV, 258, Ind. Off. 1878 (?).

5. Qiwām al-Dīn Luṭfallāh Amīr Kātib b. Amīr ʿUmar b. Amīr Ghāzī Abū Ḥanīfa al-Itqānī, d. 758/1357 (see Suppl.).

DK I, 414, no. 1078, Ibn Quṭlūb. no. 47, al-Suyūṭī, *Ḥusn al-muḥ.* I, 268. 1. *al-Risāla* (*al-Dimashqiyya*) *fī* (*tark*) *rafʿ al-yad fi ʾl-ṣalāt wa-ʿadam jawāzihi ʿinda ʾl-Ḥanafiyya* Leid. 1839, Garr. 1723.—2. *al-Risāla raddādat al-bidaʿ* Leid. 2027.—3. *Ghāyat al-bayān fī sharḥ al-Hidāya* I, 466.—4. *al-Tabyīn, sharḥ al-Ḥusāmī* I, 474.—5. *al-Laʾālīʾ al-maṣūna wa-sharḥuhā*, 292 verses on grammar, *Cat. Ital.* 276, no. 39.—6., 7. see Suppl.

6. Amīn al-Dīn ʿAbd al-Wahhāb b. Aḥmad b. Wahbān al-Humāmī al-Ḥārithī al-Muzanī al-Ḥanafī, who was born sometime before 730/1330, became a *qāḍī* in Hama in 760/1358, was relieved of this position and reinstated several times, and died in 768/1366.

DK III, 423, no. 2540. I. *Qayd al-sharāʾid wa-naẓm al-farāʾiḍ*, 400 *ṭawīl* verses on Ḥanafī law, Berl. 4596, Munich 318, Garr. 1724.—Commentaries: 1. Self-commentary, see Suppl., abstract by ʿIzz al-Dīn ʿAbd al-Raḥmān b. al-Furāt, d. 851/1447 (p. 20), Cairo ^{1}III, 142, ^{2}I, 469.—2. *Tafṣīl ʿiqd al-fawāʾid* by ʿAbd al-Barr b. Muḥammad b. al-Shiḥna al-Ḥalabī, d. 921/1515 (p. 100), Gotha 1026, Paris 4572, Ibr. P. 569, Yeni 475, Alex. Fiqh Ḥan. 13, Cairo ^{1}III, 27, ^{2}I, 411, Qawala I, 312.—2. Ḥasan b. ʿAmmār al-Shurunbulālī, d. 1069/1658 (p. 313), Garr. 1725, Yeni 476/7, Cairo ^{1}III, 30.—II. See Suppl.

| | 7. Muḥammad b. Ismāʿīl b. Maḥmūd b. Muḥammad Badr al-Rashīd, d. 96 80
768/1366.

Kitāb alfāẓ al-kufr Berl. 2138, Leid. 1842, AS 2262, Alex. Faw. $25_{,12}$, Fun. $68_{,9}$, Qawala I, 186, commentary by al-Qāriʾ al-Harawī (p. 395), Berl. 2139, BDMG 30.

8. Abū Saʿīd (Saʿd) Ṭāhir b. Islām b. Qāsim al-Anṣārī al-Khwārizmī wrote, in 771/1369 in Cairo:

1. *Kitāb jawāhir al-fiqh*, on Ḥanafī *furūʿ*, on the basis of 105 works, Gotha 1027/8 (where other MSS are listed), Munich 314, Pet. Ros. 20, $224_{,1}$, Yeni 394, Um. 2484, Garr. 1726/7, BDMG 37, Alex. Fiqh Ḥan. 18, Cairo ^{1}III, 36, Qawala I, 319, abstract Pet. Ros. $224_{,1}$.—2. See Suppl.

9. Sirāj al-Dīn ʿUmar b. Isḥāq b. Aḥmad al-Hindī al-Ghaznawī al-Shiblī was born in 714/1314, studied in Mecca, moved to Egypt in 740/1339, became *qāḍi ʾl-ʿaskar* in 769/1367, and died on 4 Rajab 773/12 January 1372.

DK III, 154, no. 366, Ibn Quṭlūb. 144, al-Suyūṭī, *Ḥusn al-muḥ*. I, 268. 1. *Zubdat al-aḥkām fi ʾkhtilāf al-aʾimma al-aʿlām*, an explanation of the shared and differing views of the four major imams, Berl. 4862, Ind. Off. 1875, Cairo ^{1}III, 62, VII, 510, ^{2}I, 436, 483, 549.—2. *Fatāwī*, collected by al-Timūrṭāshī, d. 1004/1595 (p. 311), Alex. Fiqh Ḥan. 61, Cairo ^{1}III, 112, VII, 69, Mosul $37_{,199}$, Patna I, $98_{,990}$, rearranged under the title *al-Fawākih al-Ṭūriyya fi ʾl-ḥawādith al-Miṣriyya* by Muḥammad b. al-Ḥusayn al-Ṭūrī al-Qādirī, Alex. Fiqh Ḥan. 44.—3. *Mukhtaṣar al-Talkhīṣ* I, 178.—4. *Lawāʾiḥ al-anwār fi ʾl-radd ʿalā man ankara ʿala ʾl-ʿārifīn laṭāʾif al-asrār*, on the nature of divine revelation, awareness of it, its grounds, objectives, and modalities, on the occasion of two verses by ʿAbdallāh al-Yāfiʿī, d. 768/1366 (p. 176), in which *laylat al-qadr* had been said to be insignifcant in comparison with the night during which God reveals Himself to the inner eye of the Sufi, in rhymed prose, Berl. 3322.—5.–7. see Suppl.

10. ʿAbd al-Qādir b. Muḥammad b. Muḥammad b. Naṣrallāh b. Sālim b. Abi ʾl-Wafāʾ al-Qurashī Muḥyi ʾl-Dīn al-Ḥanafī, born in Shaʿbān 696/June 1297, studied in Cairo and Mecca and died in Rabīʿ I 775/September 1373.

97 | *DK* II, 392, no. 2472, Ibn Quṭlūb. 111, al-Suyūṭī, *Ḥusn al-muḥ.* I, 268, Wüst. *Gesch.* 429. 1. *al-Jawāhir al-muḍīʾa fī ṭabaqāt al-Ḥanafiyya*, Berl. 10020/1, Garr. 689, Yeni 840, Cairo V, ^{1}42, ^{2}154, Alex. Taʾr. 57, *Intikhāb*, restricted to authors and their authorities, by Ibrāhīm b. M. al-Ḥalabī, d. 956/1549 (p. 432), Vienna 1171, AS 3103, Köpr. 1110/2, Alex. Taʾr. 132 (anon.).—2. *Takhrīj aḥādīth al-Hidāya* I, 467.—3. See Suppl.—4. *Mukhtaṣar fī ʿilm al-athar* Alex. Muṣṭ. Ḥad. 21.—5. *al-Anwār al-sāṭiʿa fī aḥkām al-jumla al-jāmiʿa* Qawala I, 306.

11. In Cairo, Jamāl al-Dīn Maḥmūd b. Mursal al-Rūmī wrote, in 775/1375:

A *Sharḥ* on a *Manẓūma fī ʾl-fatāwī* Cairo ^{1}III, 68.

12. Muḥammad b. Maḥmūd Akmal al-Dīn al-Bābartī al-Ḥanafī al-Dimashqī, a student of Ibn Ḥajar and Shams al-Dīn al-Iṣfahānī, who died in 786/1384 (see Suppl.).

81 | *DK* IV, 250, no. 686, Ibn Quṭlūb. 199. 1. 13 treatises on *fiqh*, *farāʾiḍ*, and *tafsīr*, AS 1384 (p. 344).—2. *al-Maqṣad*, a compendium on the principles of religion, AS 1384$_{,10}$, with a self-commentary, Berl. 1813, AS 1384$_{,1}$.—3. *ʿAqīda* Cairo ^{1}II, 34.—4. *Risāla fī ʾqtidāʾ al-Ḥanafiyya bil-Shāfiʿiyya*, ibid. VII, 292.—5. *al-ʿInāya* I, 466.—6. *Tuḥfat al-abrār, sharḥ Mashāriq al-anwār* I, 443.—7. *Sharḥ Manār al-anwār* see p. 196.—8. *al-Ḥikam al-nabawiyya* Suppl. I, 285, *Mukhtaṣar* Sarajevo 127$_{,1}$.—9.–13. see Suppl. (12. Alex. Fun. 66$_{,3}$, 13. read: Suppl. I, 538$_{,147}$).

13. Shams al-Dīn Abū ʿAbdallāh Yūsuf b. Ilyās al-Dimashqī al-Qūnawī al-Safarī al-Ḥanafī, d. 788/1386.

Ibn Quṭlūb. no. 206. 1. *Durar al-biḥār*, a compendium of Ḥanafī law, composed in 749/1348, Berl. 4603 (fragm.), Leid. 1849, Cairo ^{1}III, 48.—2. See Suppl.

14. Abu ʾl-Maḥāsin Maḥmūd b. Aḥmad b. Masʿūd al-Qūnawī al-Ḥanafī, who died in 771/1369 in Damascus (see Suppl.).

1. *Bughyat al-qunya*, legal questions from the collection of fatwas entitled *al-Qunya*, by Najm al-Dīn al-Zāhidī (I, 475), Cairo ^{1}III, 13.—2., 3. see Suppl.—4. *Sharḥ ʿAqīdat ahl al-sunna wal-jamāʿa* I, 182.—5. *Khulāṣat al-Nihāya fī fawāʾid (qawāʿid) al-Hidāya* I, 466, ḤKh VI, 481$_{,3}$.

| 15. Abu ʾl-Maḥāsin Ḥusām al-Dīn al-Ruhawī, who flourished towards the end 98
of the eighth century.

1. *al-Biḥār al-zākhira*, a versification of *Majmaʿ al-baḥrayn* (I, 477) and other works on the teachings of all four *madhhabs*; commentaries: a. *al-Durar al-fākhira* by al-ʿAynī, d. 855/1451 (p. 65), composed in 778/1376 after he had studied the book with the author, Berl. 4863.—b. *al-Durar al-zāhira* Cairo [1]III, 50.—2. *ʿUqūd al-jawāhir wa-durar al-mafākhir*, on the advantages of education and scholarship, the conduct of teachers etc., densely written, commentary *al-Durr al-fākhir* by Yūsuf b. Ibrāhīm al-Wannūghī, ninth cent., Berl. 103, Paris 644,$_{2}$, AS 4071.

16. Qāḍī al-quḍāt Muḥammad b. Ibrāhīm b. Aḥmad al-Imām al-Samadīsī, who flourished at the beginning of the ninth century.

Fatḥ al-mudabbir lil-ʿājiz al-muqṣir ʿUm. 224, 1741, Cairo [1]III, 96.

17. Ṭāhir b. al-Ḥasan b. ʿUmar al-Ḥanafī Zayn al-Dīn Abu ʾl-ʿIzz b. Ḥabīb, who was born in 742/1341 and died in 807/1405 (see Suppl.).

1. *al-Muqtabas al-mukhtār min nūr al-manār fī uṣūl al-fiqh*, after al-Nasafī (p. 196), Berl. 4411, abstract by the author ibid. 4412, with commentaries by a. Ibn Quṭlūbughā, d. 879/1474 (no. 21), Gotha 932, Paris 5055, Cairo [1]II, 252, Qawala I, 287.—b., c. see Suppl.—d. *Tanqīḥ al-muʿtabar* by al-Qāriʾ al-Harawī, d. 1014/1605 (p. 394), Lālelī 763, Cairo [2]I, 382.—e. *Jawāhir al-afkār* by Manṣūr b. Abi ʾl-Khayr al-Bilbaysī al-Ḥanafī, Qawala I, 279.—2. *Nāsim al-ṣabā*, approved by al-Subkī, among others, Paris 3244,$_{2}$.

18. ʿUmar b. ʿAlī b. Fāris al-Qaṭṭānī al-Ḥanafī Sirāj al-Dīn Abū Ḥafṣ Qāriʾ al-Hidāya, d. 829/1426 (see Suppl.).

1. *al-Fatāwi ʾl-Sirājiyya*, published by his student Kamāl al-Dīn b. al-Humām al-Ḥanafī, d. 861/1457 (no. 19a), Berl. 4824 Mosul 37,$_{99}$.—2. Answers to questions, Mosul 112, 180,$_{2}$.

| 19. ʿAlī b. Khalīl al-Ṭarābulusī ʿAlāʾ (Ḥusām) al-Dīn Abu ʾl-Ḥasan al-Ḥanafī, 82
d. 844/1440.

| *Muʿīn al-ḥukkām fī-mā yataraddad bayna ʾl-khaṣmayn min al-aḥkām*, Berl. 99
4794, Yeni 572/4, NO 2066, Cairo [1]III, 111, 133, [2]I, 464, Qawala I, 396, print. Būlāq 1300.

19a. Kamāl al-Dīn Muḥammad b. Humād al-Dīn ʿAbd al-Wāḥid b. ʿAbd al-Ḥāmid b. al-Humām al-Sīwāsī al-Iskandarī al-Ḥanafī, d. 861/1457 (see Suppl.).

Ibn Quṭlūb. p. 75, Flügel. *Classen* 338. 1. *al-Taḥrīr fī uṣūl al-dīn*, an abstract of a larger, unfinished work, Berl. 4416, Ind. Off. 331, 1461, Köpr. 471, Cairo ^{1}II, 241, print. Būlāq 1316/7.—Commentary *al-Taqrīr wal-taḥbīr* or *al-taysīr* by Muḥammad b. Muḥammad b. Amīr al-Ḥājj al-Ḥalabī, d. 879/1474, Cairo ^{1}II, 243 ^{2}I, 382, Qawala I, 275, a passage from which is preserved in Gotha 1000.—Abstract *Lubb al-uṣūl* by Zayn al-ʿĀbidīn b. Nujaym al-Miṣrī, d. 970/1562 (p. 310), Ibr. P. 429, Cairo ^{1}II, 258, ^{2}I, 395.—2. *Zād al-faqīr fī 'l-furūʿ* Berl. Ms. or. qu. 2079,$_2$.—Commentaries: a. *Iʿānat al-ḥaqīr* by Muḥammad b. ʿAbdallāh al-Tīmūrtāshī, d. 1004/1595 (p. 311), Berl. 4609, Cairo ^{1}III, 6.—b. Tāj al-Dīn ʿAbd al-Wahhāb al-Humāmī, entitled *Fatḥ al-qadīr lil-ʿājiz al-faqīr* Berl. Ms. or. qu. 2109, under the title *Māʾ al-masīr li-Zād al-faqīr* Gotha 1029, *zād al-faqr li-fatḥ zād al-fuqarāʾ* ḤKh III 527,$_{6767}$, with *Natāʾij al-afkār fī kashf al-rumūz wal-asrār* by Shams al-Dīn Aḥmad b. Badr al-Dīn Rāḍīzāde, d. 988/1580, Tunis, Zayt. IV, 260,$_{2429}$, Cairo ^{1}III, 141, Qawala I, 403.—c. *Nuzhat al-baṣīr* by ʿAbd al-Raḥīm al-Mashnāwī, Paris 944 (ḤKh Manshawī).—3. *al-Musāyara fī 'l-ʿaqāʾid al-munjiya fī 'l-ākhira*, an abbreviation of *al-Risāla al-Qudsiyya* by al-Ghazzālī I, 538,$_8$.—Commentaries: a. Self-commentary, see Suppl.—b. *al-Musāmara* by Muḥammad b. Abi 'l-Sharīf al-Ashʿarī al-Shāfiʿī, d. 906/1500, Leid. 2038, Algiers 559, Alex. Tawḥīd 43, Cairo ^{1}II, 53, ^{2}I, 207, Qawala I, 209, Patna I, 126,$_{1257}$.—4. *Fawātiḥ al-afkār fī Sharḥ Lumaʿāt al-anwār*, on anatomy, with a commentary, Berl. 6252.—5. *Fatḥ al-qadīr* I, 467.—6.–8. see Suppl.

20. Aḥmad b. Muḥammad b. Muḥammad b. Ḥasan b. ʿAlī b. Yaḥyā Tāj al-Dīn Abu 'l-ʿAbbās al-Tamīmī al-Dārī al-Qusanṭīnī al-Shumunnī, d. 872/1468 (see Suppl.).

MT 18r/19v. 1. *Sharḥ al-Nuqāya* I, 469.—2. *Sharḥ al-Shifāʾ* ibid. 455.

21. Abu 'l-Faḍl Zayn al-Milla wal-Dīn al-Qāsim b. ʿAbdallāh b. Quṭlūbughā al-Ḥanafī al-Sūdūnī was born in 802/1399, became a student of Ibn Ḥajar, and died in Cairo in 879/1474.

100 | Al-Kattānī, *Fihris* II, 321, Wüst. *Gesch.* 494. 1. *Tāj al-tarājim fī ṭabaqāt al-Ḥanafiyya*, ed. G. Flügel, AKM II, 3, Leipzig 1862.—2. *Musnad sayyidī ʿUqba b. ʿĀmir al-Juhanī*, d. 58/678, at whose grave he had buried his father and sons, Berl. 1396.—3. Some traditions of the Sufi Dhu 'l-Nūn (I, 214) and some from

the *Arbaʿūn* of Saʿd Aḥmad b. Muḥammad al-Mālīnī, d. 409/1018 or 412 (Subkī *Ṭab.* III, 24, Ibn Taghr. 632,$_{13}$, C. IV, 256), Berl. 1347.—4. *ʿAwālī ḥadīth al-Ṭaḥāwī*, d. 321/933 (I, 181), Berl. 1398.—5. *ʿAwālī ḥadīth al-Layth*, of Ibn Layth b. Saʿd b. ʿAbd al-Raḥmān al-Fahmī, d. 175/791, Berl. 1399.—6. Abstract of *al-Muntaqā* by Abū Muḥammad ʿAbdallāh b. ʿAlī al-Jārūd al-Nīshābūrī, ibid. 1400.—7. *al-ʿIṣma ʿani ʾl-khaṭaʾ fī naqd al-qisma*, on the law of inheritance, ibid. 4724.—8. *Fatāwī* ibid. 4826, Leid. 1862, Cairo [1]III, 118, VII, 166.—9. *Mūjibāt al-ahkām* Yeni 582, Cairo [2]I, App. 57.—10. *Rafʿ al-ishtibāh ʿan masʾalat al-miyāh* Cairo [1]VII, 167, [2]I, 435.—11. *Risāla fi ʾl-ṣalāt baʿd al-witr hal hiya min al-nawāfil aw lā* ibid. VII, 165.—12. *Risāla fī waṣl al-taṭawwuʿ* ibid.—13. *Jawāb* ibid.—14. *Sharḥ al-Muqtabas* see no. 17, 1.—17.–25. see Suppl. (20. Garr. 1561/2).

22. Muẓaffar al-Dīn Abu ʾl-Thanāʾ Maḥmūd b. Aḥmad al-ʿAyntābī al-Amshāṭī al-Ḥanafī, who died in Cairo in 902/1496 (see Suppl.).

1. *al-Qawl al-sadīd fi ʾkhtiyār al-imāʾ wal-ʿabīd* see 136, (Suppl. 169$_3$), Cairo [1]VII, 565.—2.–4. see Suppl. (2. *fī* 1. *ʿan*, 3. Garr. 1110, Paris 3025/6).

23. Muḥammad b. Mūsā b. ʿUmar b. Mūsā b. Sulaymān b. Yūsuf al-Ghazzī al-Maqdisī al-Ḥanafī wrote, in 890/1485:

Mukhtaṣar fi ʾl-manāsik Cairo [1]III, 127.

| 24. Aḥmad b. Muḥammad b. Ḥasan b. ʿAlī b. Muḥammad al-ʿAbbāsī al-Ḥanafī, 83
a contemporary of al-Malik al-Ashraf Qāʾitbāy (r. 872–901/1467–95), wrote:

Tuḥfat al-sāʾil fī ajwibat al-masāʾil, 300 questions on *fiqh*, Gotha 1141, Br. Mus. 868, Alex. Fun. 99, 4 (see Suppl.).

25. Sarī al-Dīn ʿAbd al-Barr b. Muḥammad b. Muḥammad b. al-Shiḥna al-Ḥanafī died in 921/1515, see Suppl.

1. *al-Dhakhāʾir al-Ashrafiyya fī alghāz al-Ḥanafiyya*, legal problems in the form of riddles, following Ḥanafī and Shāfiʿī authors, | explicitly intended for 101
all schools, Gotha 1031, Garr. 1733, Alex. Fiqh Ḥan. 26, Cairo [1]III, 50.—2. *Zahr al-riyāḍ fī masʾalat al-tawaḍḍuʾ min al-ḥiyāḍ* Cairo [1]III. 117.—3. *Fatāwī* ibid. VII, 165.—4. *Qaṭʿ al-mujādala ʿinda taghyīr al-muʿāmala* ibid. 167.—5. *ʿUqūd al-laʾālīʾ wal-marjān li-mā yataʿallaq bi-fawāʾid al-Qurʾān* ibid. 295, [2]I, 55.—6.–8. see Suppl.—9. *al-Kalām fī tanfīdh mā thabata bil-shahāda ʿala ʾl-khaṭṭ* Garr. 1731.

26. Ibrāhīm b. Mūsā al-Ṭarābulusī al-Ḥanafī Burhān al-Dīn, born in Tripoli in 843/1439, studied in Damascus and died in 922/1516.

MT 13r. 1. *Mawāhib al-raḥmān fi 'l-furūʿ*, Alex. Fiqh Ḥan. 68, on which the commentary *al-Burhān* is preserved in Yeni 478.—2. *al-Isʿāf fī aḥkām al-awqāf* Berl. 4766, Cairo ^{1}III, 5, VII, 10 Garr. 1878/9.—3. See Suppl.

27. Ibrāhīm b. ʿAbd al-Raḥmān al-Karakī al-Ḥanafī, who was born in Cairo on 6 Ramaḍān 834/19 May 1431, was the imam to sultan Qāʾitbāy and a professor at various madrasas. He died in 922/1516.

MT 11r. 1. *Fayḍ al-mawla 'l-karīm ʿalā ʿabdihi Ibrāhīm*, a collection of fatwas, Cairo ^{1}III, 98, ^{2}I, 453.—2. A history of Abraham, Paris $1931_{,1}$ (sic ! = 1.?).

B The Mālikīs

1. Muḥammad b. Muḥammad b. Muḥammad b. al-Ḥājj al-Fāsī al-ʿAbdarī al-Qayrawānī al-Tilimsānī al-Maghribī al-Mālikī studied in Fez, went as a pilgrim to Cairo where he became a professor, and died in Jumādā I 737/December 1336.

DK IV, 237, no. 627, ʿAbdallāh Gannūn, *al-Nubūgh al-Maghribī* I, 137. 1. *Mudkhal al-sharʿ al-sharīf*, against innovations (*bidaʿ*), Berl. 3519 (vol. 2), Garr. 1517, Cairo ^{1}II, 313, print. Alexandria 1293, 3 vols., see Goldziher, ZDPV XVII, 115/22.—2. *Shumūs al-anwār wa-kunūz al-asrār*, on the secrets of letters, Cairo ^{1}V, 346 (in print Ibn al-Ḥājj al-Tilimsānī al-Maghribī, probably another author, likewise in *al-Azhār fi 'qtiṣār Sh. al-a.*, Mosul $236_{,155,5}$).—3. See Suppl.

102 2. Khalīl b. Isḥāq b. Mūsā Ghars (Ḍiyāʾ) al-Dīn | Abu 'l-Ṣafāʾ al-Jundī al-Mālikī
84 al-Miṣrī studied in Cairo, | was appointed a *muftī* and professor at the Shaykhūniyya, and died in Rabīʿ I 767/November 1365.

DK II, 86, no. 1653, RA 117v, al-Suyūṭī, *Ḥusn al-muḥ.* I, 362. 1. *al-Mukhtaṣar* (on the MSS see Suppl., and also Makram 55), *Précis de jurisprudence musulmane ou principes de législation musulmane civile et religieuse selon le rite malékite par Khalil, trad. de l'Ar. par* Perron, 1st ed. in *Exploration scientifique de l'Algérie, Sciences hist. et géogr.* X–XVI, Paris 1844/52, 2. ed. 1877, prints see Suppl., Constantine 1878. E. Fagnan, *Concordances du Manuel de droit de Sidi Khalil*, Algiers 1889.—Commentaries: a. Tāj al-Dīn Bahrām b. ʿAbdallāh al-Damīrī, d. 815/1412 (Suppl. II, 99), completed in 776/1374, Munich 350, Br. Mus. 233/4, Paris 4552/3, 5354, 6119, Algiers 1121/30, Alex. Fiqh Māl. 11, *al-Awsaṭ* by the same,

completed in 779/1377, Algiers 1131/5.—b. Abu 'l-Faḍl Muḥammad b. Aḥmad b. Marzūq al-Tilimsānī, d. 842/1438 (p. 246), Algiers 1136.—bb. Shams al-Dīn Muḥammad b. Muḥammad al-Bisāṭī, d. 842/1439, see Suppl., Br. Mus. 236.—c. Dā'ūd b. Muḥammad al-Mālikī, ninth cent., Cairo ^{1}III, 169.—d. *al-Tāj wal-iklīl* by Abū ʿAbdallāh Muḥammad b. Yūsuf al-Mawwāq al-ʿAbdarī al-Gharnāṭī, d. 897/1492, Algiers 1165, Alex. Fiqh Māl. 5.—dd. see Suppl. and also Alex. Fiqh Māl. 14, with glosses by ʿAbd al-Raḥmān al-Ujhūrī, d. 957/1550.—e. *Fatḥ al-jalīl* by Muḥammad b. Ibrāhīm al-Tatā'ī, d. 942/1535 (p. 316), Munich 351, Br. Mus. 237/8, Paris 4555, Algiers 1137/42, glosses by al-Kharāshī, d. 1101/1689 (p. 318), Algiers 1230.—f. *Jawāhir al-durar*, shorter, by the same, Algiers 1143/54, Cairo ^{1}III, 159, ^{2}I, 478, Makram 14.—ff. al-Suyūṭī, d. 911/1505, *ḥabs* in Riwāq Sayyidinā ʿUthmān in Medina, al-Kattānī *Fihris* II, 359.—g. *Mawāhib al-jalīl* by Abū ʿAbdallāh Muḥammad b. Muḥammad al-Khaṭṭāb, d. 953/1546, Algiers 1155/61, Cairo ^{1}III, 87, print. C. 1329, 6 vols.—h. On the *khuṭba*, by Nāṣir al-Dīn al-Laqānī, d. 958/1551, Paris 4554, 5350, Cairo ^{1}III, 169, glosses thereon by al-Zurqānī, d. 1099/1687 (p. 318), Br. Mus. $902_{,1}$, Cairo loc. cit.—i. *Taysīr al-malik al-jalīl* by Abu 'l-Najm Sālim al-Sanhūrī, d. 1011/1602 (p. 316), Algiers 1162/4.—j. on the *muqaddima*, by Badr al-Dīn al-Mālikī, ca. 1010/1601, Cairo ^{1}III, 181.—k. Aḥmad b. Muḥammad al-Zurqānī, d. before 1061/1651, Paris 1079, Algiers 1166/7, Cairo ^{1}III, 170.—l. *Jawāhir* (*Mawāhib*) *al-jalīl* by ʿAlī al-Ujhūrī, d. 1066/1656 (p. 317), Munich 346/9, Paris 1080/1, Algiers 1168/75, Cairo ^{1}III, 168, 187.—m. | *Natā'ij* 103
al-fikar fī kashf asrār al-M. by ʿAbd al-Bāqī b. Yūsuf al-Zurqānī, d. 1099/1688 (p. 318), abstract of l., Br. Mus. 239/40, Paris 1082/91, Algiers 1176/89, Hamel 1, glosses thereon *al-Fatḥ al-rabbānī* by Muḥammad Ḥasan al-Bannānī, d. 1163/1749, see Suppl., Algiers 1245/8, by Muḥammad b. Aḥmad b. Muḥammad b. Yūsuf al-Rahūnī, ca. 1229/1814, print. Būlāq 1309/7, 8 volumes.—n. *al-Mawāhib al-jalīla* by Abū ʿAbdallāh Muḥammad al-Kharāshī, d. 1101/1689 (p. 318), Br. Mus. Suppl. 303, Algiers 1190/1, Makram 59, print. Būlāq 1299, C. 1307/8, 5 vols. with glosses by ʿAlī al-ʿAdawī, d. 1189/1775 (p. 319), Algiers 1231/8 in the margin, glosses by Muṣṭafā al-Ramāṣī, Br. Mus. $902_{,6-8}$.—o. The smaller commentary by the same, Gotha 1056/7, de Sacy 60, Paris 1093/6, 4556/9, Algiers 1192/1229.—p. Ibrāhīm b. Marʿī al-Shabrakhītī, d. 1106/1694.—*α* The large one, Paris 4560, Algiers 1239/41, Cairo ^{1}III, 171.—*β* The medium one, Algiers 1242/3.—*γ* The small one, Algiers 1244.—q. ʿAlī b. Khiḍr al-ʿAmrūsī, d. 1173/1759 (p. 319), Algiers 1249/50, Cairo ^{1}III, 172.—r. Aḥmad b. Muḥammad al-Dardīr, d. 1201/1786 (p. 353), Algiers 1251/3, Cairo ^{1}III, 169, Makram 36, print. Būlāq 1282, 1287, C. 1301, glosses thereon Muḥammad b. ʿArafa al-Dasūqī, d. 1230/1815 (p. 485), Algiers 1254/7, Makram 19, print. 4 vols. C. 1305, 1309, 1310, by Muḥammad b. ʿAlī ʿUllaysh, d. 1299/1881 (p. 486), Cairo ^{1}III, 188.—s. *al-Iklīl* by Muḥammad b. Muḥammad al-Amīr al-Kabīr al-Sunbāwī, d. 1232/1817 (p. 486), Makram 5.—t. Muḥammad

ʿUllaysh, d. 1299/1881, Cairo [1]III, 185, print. with glosses by the author, 4 vols., Būlāq (*Khiṭaṭ jadīda* IV, $42_{,17}$).—u. Anon., Munich 352, Paris 1092/8, 4561/2, Br. Mus. 235, Algiers 1258/65, Rabat 201/4.—v. *Mawāhib al-jalīl* by ʿAlī b. Sulaymān al-Jīzī al-Shādhilī, Alex. Fiqh Māl. 20.—w–oo. see Suppl.—Abstract *al-Muqaddima, mulakhkhaṣ Mukhtaṣar al-shaykh Khalīl* by ʿAlī b. Khiḍr al-ʿAmrūsī (see q.) Alex. Fiqh Māl. 11.—2. *al-Manāsik* Br. Mus. $258_{,2}$, Algiers 1088/1120,
85 Alex. Fiqh Māl. 16, | Cairo [1]III, 184, [2]I, 493.—3. *Manāqib al-shaykh ʿAbdallāh al-Manūfī*, his teacher, Cairo V, [1]159, [2]365.

3. Abū ʿAbdallāh Muḥammad b. Muḥammad al-Andalusī al-Gharnāṭī al-Rāʿī died in Cairo in 853/1449 (see Suppl.).

1. *Intiṣār al-faqīr al-sālik li-tarjīḥ madhhab al-imām al-kabīr Mālik* Algiers 1354.—2. *al-Ajwiba al-marḍiyya ʿani ʾl-asʾila al-naḥwiyya* Cairo [1]IV, 196, VII, 631, [2]II, 74.—3. *Sharḥ al-Ājurrūmiyya* see p. 238.—4. See Suppl.

104 | C The Shāfiʿīs[1]

1. Ibn al-Naẓẓār al-Shāfiʿī wrote, in 710/1310:

Aḥkām al-nisāʾ Cairo [1]III, 190.

2. ʿAlāʾ al-Dīn ʿAlī b. Muḥammad b. ʿAbd al-Raḥīm b. Muḥammad al-Hindī al-Bājī al-Shāfiʿī was born in 631/1233, studied in Damascus, became a treasurer in Karak, then a professor at the Sayfiyyya in Cairo, before dying in Dhu ʾl-Qaʿda 714/February 1315.

DK cod. Vienna II, 285v, Dr. III, 105, no. 238 (corrupted). 1. *Ghāyat al-suʾūl fi ʾl-uṣūl* Cairo [1]VII, 258.—2. See Suppl.

3. Quṭb al-Dīn Muḥammad b. ʿAbd al-Ṣamad b. ʿAbd al-Qādir al-Sanbāṭī al-Shāfiʿī, born in Sanbāṭ in 653/1255, became a professor and *nāʾib al-ḥukm* in Cairo, and died in Dhu ʾl-Ḥijja 722/December 1321.

1. *Aḥkām al-mubaʿʿaḍ*, special cases of manumission (Sachau, *Muḥ. Recht*, 132) Br. Mus. Suppl. 1203.—2. See Suppl.

4. Abu ʾl-Ḥasan ʿAlī b. Ibrāhīm b. Dāʾūd b. al-ʿAṭṭār, one of the most famous students of al-Nawawī (I, 496), was born on the final day of Ramaḍān 654/21

1 On the dominance of the Shāfiʿī *madhhab* in Egypt, see al-Suyūṭī, *Ḥusn al-muḥ.* II, 133.

October 1256. In 694/1295, he became a Shāfiʿī professor at the Nūriyya school for *ḥadīth* in Damascus, lecturing at the Qūsiyya as well. Having lived with the effects of a stroke for 20 years, he died on the first of Dhu ʾl-Ḥijja 724/19 November 1324.

DK III, 61, 1. *Orient.* II, 339, Wüst. *Gesch.* 389, *JA* s. IX, v. 3 p. 297. 1. *Risāla fī aḥkām al-mawtā wa-ghaslihim wa-takfīnihim* Cairo [1]II, 172.—2. A biography of al-Nawawī, see Suppl. I, 680.—3.–6. see Suppl.

| 5. Najm al-Dīn Abu ʾl-ʿAbbās Aḥmad b. Muḥammad b. al-Ḥazm Makkī 86
al-Makhzūmī al-Qamūlī al-Shāfiʿī, d. 727/1327, see Suppl.

| *DK* I, 304, no. 796, al-Ṣafadī, *al-Wāfī* AS 2617$_{,127}$, al-Suyūṭī, *Ḥusn al-muḥ.* I. 239, 105
ʿAlī Mubārak, *al-Khiṭaṭ al-jadīda* XIV, 120. 1. *al-Baḥr al-muḥīṭ fī sharḥ al-Wasīṭ* I, 543.—2. *Sharḥ al-Kāfiya* I, 368$_{,10}$.—3. See Suppl.

5a. Muḥammad b. Muḥammad b. Fakhr al-Dīn al-Ṣaqalī, a student of al-Ṣanbāṭī (no. 3), was a *qāḍī* in Cairo, and died on 15 Dhu ʾl-Qaʿda 727/3 October 1327.

Al-Subkī *Ṭab.* VI, 31. *Sirāj al-maʿrifa fi ʾl-tanbīh ʿalā nakth al-mutaṣawwifa* Dam. Z. 36$_{,101}$.

6. Sharaf al-Dīn Abu ʾl-Qāsim Hibatallāh b. Qāḍi ʾl-quḍāt Najm al-Dīn b. ʿAbd al-Raḥīm b. Qāḍi ʾl-quḍāt Shams al-Dīn Ibrāhīm b. al-Bārizī al-Juhanī al-Ḥamawī al-Shāfiʿī was born in 645/1247 and died on 15 Dhu ʾl-Qaʿda 738/5 June 1338.

1. *Iẓhār al-fatāwī min asrār al-Ḥāwī* Cairo [1]III, 193.—2. *Kitāb kanz al-zubad*, see no. 29, 1.—3.–5. see Suppl.[2]

7. ʿAlāʾ al-Dīn Abu ʾl-Ḥasan ʿAlī b. Ismāʿīl b. Yūsuf al-Qūnawī was born in Konya in Asia Minor in 668/1269, and went to Damacus in 693/1294, where he became a professor at the Iqbāliyya. In 700/1300 he was appointed a professor at the mosque of Ibn Ṭūlūn in Cairo and provost of a Sufi monastery there. In 727/1327 he returned to Damascus as its chief *qāḍī*, dying there on 14 Dhu ʾl-Qaʿda of that same year (or, according to others, in 729).

---

2 On 3. Aḥmad b. ʿUmar ʿUthmān b. Qara, see Suppl. III, 1254, an abstract of *al-Masālik* by Muḥammad al-Kirmānī, Berl. Or. qu. 2076 (Suppl. II, 1023$_{,66}$).

DK III, 248, no. 54, Ibn Baṭṭūṭa I, 214, Ibn al-Qāḍī, *Durrat al-ḥijāl* II, $427_{,1216}$, *Orient.* II, 348, Wüst. *Gesch.* 395. 1. The beginning of an answer—dated 701/1301—to someone from Damascus on the contradiction between free will and predestination, Berl. 2824.—2., 3. See Suppl.—4. *Risāla jāmiʿa li-zubdat ʿaqāʾid ahl al-sunna wal-jamāʿa* Garr. $2091_{,1}$.

8. Taqī al-Dīn Muḥammad b. Muḥammad b. ʿAlī b. Humām b. al-Imām al-Gharnāṭī al-ʿAsqalānī al-Miṣrī, born in Shaʿbān of 677/December 1278, was imam at the al-Ṣāliḥ mosque in Cairo, and died in Rabīʿ I 745/July 1344.

106 | *DK* IV, 203, no. 549. *Silāḥ al-muʾmin fī ʾl-duʿāʾ*, on prayer, Gotha 763, Yenī 702 (see Suppl.)—Abstracts: 1. al-Dhahabī, d. 748/1347 (p. 57), Br. Mus. Suppl. 249, Cairo ^{1}I, 349, ^{2}I, 356.—2. Ibn Jamāʿa, d. 767/1365 (p. 72), Berl. 705.

9. Taqī al-Dīn ʿAlī b. ʿAbd al-Kāfī al-Subkī was born on 1 Ṣafar 683/19 April 1284 in Subk al-Thalāth in Lower Egypt, in the province of al-Manūfiyya. He studied
87 in Cairo under Ibn Ḥayyān and | the Sufi ʿAṭāʾallāh al-Iskandarī. In 707/1307 he went to Damascus, visited Jerualem and Hebron, and then performed the pilgrimage to Mecca. After that he became a professor at al-Madrasa al-Manṣūriyya, which was part of the mosque of Ibn Ṭūlūn. After the death of Jalāl al-Dīn al-Qazwīnī (p. 26) he succeeded him as chief *qāḍī* of Syria on 19 Jumādā II 739/3 January 1339, and was, for a brief time, preacher at the Umayyad mosque as well. He was also in charge of the Dār al-ḥadīth al-Ashrafiyya and later of the Dār al-ḥadīth al-Shāmiyya. After the death of his son al-Ḥusayn, he fell ill in Ramaḍān of 755/September 1354. For this reason he relinquished his position as judge in Rabīʿ I of the following year to his son Tāj al-Dīn. He died in Cairo, where he had hoped to recover in his villa on the Nile, just 20 days after his arrival there, on 4 Jumādā II 756/16 June 1355 (or, according to others, in 755).

DK III, 63, no. 148, RA 189_r. *Ḥuff.* XXI, 13, Ibn al-Qāḍī, *Durrat al-ḥijāl* II, 466, al-Kattānī, *Fihris* II, 369/71, *al-Khiṭ. al-jad.* XII, 7, *JA* s. IX. v. 3, p. 448. 1. *al-Taʿẓīm wal-minna fī taḥqīq la-tuʾminunna bihi wa-la-tanṣurunnahu* (sura 3, 81), Cairo ^{1}VII, 346.—2. *al-Sayf al-maslūl ʿalā man sabba ʾl-rasūl*, on whether unbelievers defaming the Prophet should receive the death penalty, and which concludes with praise of his qualities, based on the Qurʾān and *ḥadīth*, and with man's duties towards him, Berl. 2571, Leid. 1838, Yeni 209, Cairo ^{1}II, 234, ^{2}V, 133.—3. *al-Tuḥfa fī ʾl-kalām ʿalā ahl al-ṣuffa*, on those sitting on the benches
107 in the mosque of the Prophet as the precursors of the Sufis, Berl. 3478.—| 4. A *qaṣīda*, in admonition of his son Muḥammad, Berl. 4003.—5. *Shifāʾ al-saqām*

(*al-asqām*) *fī ziyārat khayr al-anām*, Yeni 264, print. Būlāq 1319, abbreviation with additions by Muḥammad b. al-Ḥasan b. ʿAbdallāh al-Wāsiṭī, d. 776/1374 (p. 42), completed in 765/1363, Berl. 4048.—6. *al-Mawāhib al-ṣamadiyya fi ʾl-mawārith al-Ṣafadiyya*, on whether the inheritance of a Jew under protection should, in part, go to the state, Berl. 4714.—7. *al-Nuqūl wal-mabāḥith al-mushriqa fī ḥukm al-waqf ʿalā ṭabaqa baʿda ṭabaqa*, Berl. 4762.—8. *al-Tamhīd fī-mā yajibu fīhi ʾl-taḥdīd*, on exemption clauses in court forms, Berl. 4963.—9. *al-Qawl al-mūʿib fi ʾl-qaḍāʾ al-mūjib*, on a special kind of judicial ruling, | draw- 88
ing on a fictional case in which a woman has reserved the supervision of a *waqf* founded by her to herself and her family, Gotha 979.—10. *Aṣl al-manāfiʿ fī ibdāʿ al-dāfiʿ maʿa Risālat al-fawāʾid al-fiqhiyya fī aṭrāf al-qaḍāyā al-ḥukmiyya* AS 1025.—11. *Kitāb al-fatāwī*, completed in 753/1352 (according to ḤKh IV, 8766 collected by his son), with an appendix, *al-Iʿmāl fī maʿna ʾl-ibdāl* Gotha $_{1}$137, Cairo ^{1}III, 249, ^{2}I, 524, print. C. 1356, 2 vols.—12. *Ibrāz al-ḥikam min ḥadīth rufiʿa ʾl-qalam*, Berl. 1588 (beginning), 9399.—13. *Risāla fī rafʿ al-yadayn ʿinda ʾl-rukūʿ wal-sujūd* (author ?) Cairo ^{1}III, 228.—14. *Risāla fī birr al-wālidayn* Berl. 5599.—15. *Nayl al-ʿulā fi ʾl-ʿaṭf bi-lā* Berl. 6899, Esc. ^{2}107,$_{5}$.—16. Two *qaṣīdas* Berl. 7589.—17. *Tāʾiyya* Br. Mus. 616,$_{3}$, with a commentary by Jalāl al-Dīn Muḥammad b. Aḥmad al-Samannūdī (ca. 838/1434, p. 150), Garr. 104, Cairo ^{1}VI, 267, ^{2}III, 197.—18.–48. see Suppl. (27. Garr. 2003,$_{24}$, 47 AS read: Āṣaf.).—49. *al-Sayf al-ṣaqīl fi ʾl-radd ʿalā b. Zafīl* (i.e. the *Nūniyya* by Ibn Qayyim al-Jawziyya, p. 166) C. 1937.—50. *al-Masāʾil al-Ḥalabiyya wa-ajwibatuhā* Alex. Fiqh Shāf. 40.—51. *Fatwā fī qawl al-nabī kullu mawlūd yūlad ʿala ʾl-fiṭra* Alex. Fun. 67,$_{15}$, 95,$_{4}$.—52. *Risāla fi ʾl-farq bayna ṣarīḥ al-maṣdar wa-an wal-fiʿl* ibid. 95,$_{4}$.—53. *Risāla manẓūma fi ʾl-ḥajj* Patna II, 451,$_{2628,3}$.—54. *Gharyat al-īmān al-jalī bi-Abī Bakr wa-ʿUmar wa-ʿUthmān wa-ʿAlī* Berl. Ms. or. oct. 3087.

10. ʿUmar b. ʿĪsā b. ʿUmar al-Bārīnī al-Ḥalabī al-Shāfiʿī Zayn al-Dīn was born in 710/1310 and died in Aleppo in Shawwāl 764/July 1363.

Daqāʾiq al-ghawāmiḍ fī ʿilmay al-īṣāʾ wal-farāʾiḍ, with a commentary by Yaḥyā b. Taqī al-Dīn b. Ismāʿīl b. ʿUbāda al-Ḥalabī al-Shāfiʿī, born in 953/1546, composed in 1031/1622, Berl. 4715.

| 11. ʿAbdallāh b. ʿAbd al-Raḥmān b. ʿAbdallāh al-Hāshimī b. ʿAqīl al-Shāfiʿī 108
al-Qurashī al-Bālisī was born in Muḥarram 694/November 1294 (or, according to others, in 698 or 700), and studied in Cairo under Abū Ḥayyān. The *qāḍī* ʿIzz al-Dīn b. Jamāʿa (p. 72) appointed him as his representative, before Emir Ṣarghatmish appointed him as a *qāḍī* in his own right for a period of eighty days, starting on 28 Jumādā II 756/11 July 1355. As well as this, he also taught at

the mosque of Ibn Ṭūlūn and in various madrasas. He died on 23 Rabīʿ I 769/18 November 1367.

DK II, 266, no. 2157, Ibn al-Qāḍī, *Durrat al-ḥijāl* II, 347/8. RA 147r, al-Suyūṭī, *Ḥusn al-muḥ.* I, 310. 1. *Taysīr al-istiʿdād li-rutbat al-ijtihād,* Cairo [1]III, 212, [2]I, 507.—2. *Sharḥ Alfiyyat b. Mālik* I, 360.

12. Shams al-Dīn Muḥammad b. Khalaf b. Kāmil b. ʿAṭāʾallāh al-Ghazzī al-Dimashqī al-Shāfiʿī was born in Gaza in 716/1316, studied in Damascus and became the representative of the *qāḍī* Tāj al-Dīn al-Subkī (no. 13). When the latter was deposed he shared that misfortune, something for which he was rewarded once the *qāḍī* had returned to power. He died in Rajab 770/February 1369.

DK III, 432, no. 1162. *Maydān al-fursān fī 'l-fiqh* Cairo [1]III, 283.

89 | 13. Abū Naṣr ʿAbd al-Wahhāb b. ʿAlī b. ʿAbd al-Kāfī Tāj al-Dīn al-Subkī al-Shāfiʿī was born in 727/1327 in Cairo, and studied both there and in Damascus, where his father (p. 106) had been transferred in 739/1338. While still a young man he held various professorships as well as the position of preacher at the Umayyad mosque, and in 756/1354 his father appointed him as *qāḍī.* He lost this office in 759/1357, then held it again, a situation that was repeated several times. In Jumādā I 769/January 1368 he was indicted for embezzlement of trust money
109 and spent 80 days in prison. It was only then that his friends | succeeded in exculpating him and in getting him reinstated. He died of the plague, on 7 Dhu 'l-Ḥijja 771/3 July 1370.

DK IV, 425, no. 2547, RA 163v, *Khit. jad.* VII, 8, al-Kattānī, *Fihris* II, 372, *Orient.* II, 427, Wüst. *Ac. der Ar.* 51, *Gesch.* 431. 1. *Kitāb jamʿ al-jawāmiʿ fī 'l-uṣūl,* on legal principles, completed in 760/1358 in Nayrāb near Damascus, an autograph of 762 Berl. 4400/1, Esc. [2]653, Alex. Uṣūl 7, Tawḥīd 42$_{,4}$, Cairo [1]II, 243.—Commentaries: a. A self-commentary, completed in 770/1368, Algiers 958.—b. *Tashnīf al-masāmiʿ,* by Badr al-Dīn al-Zarkashī, d. 794/1392 (p. 112), Gotha 926.—c. *al-Badr al-ṭāliʿ fī ḥall J. al-j.*, in some manuscripts incorrectly titled as b., by Muḥammad b. Aḥmad al-Maḥallī, d. 864/1460 (p. 114), completed in 827/1424, Berl. 4403, Munich 360, Leid. 1844, Paris 803/4, 5343, Br. Mus. Suppl. 265, Ambros. 67$_{,2}$, Algiers 951/2, Alex. Uṣūl 10, Cairo [1]II, 250, Qaw. I, 258, Makr. 41/2, Garr. 1811.—Glosses: *α al-Durar al-lawāmiʿ* by Muḥammad b. Muḥammad b. al-Sharīf al-Kawrānī al-Maqdisī, d. 906/1500, completed in 886/1482 in Cairo, Berl. 4404/5, Garr. 1812, Alex. Uṣūl 9, Cairo [1]II, 247.—*β* Zakariyyāʾ al-Anṣārī, d. 926/1520 (p. 99), Br. Mus.

259, Algiers 953/5, Cairo ^{1}II, 260.—*γ al-Āyāt al-bayyināt etc.* on the original work and on c., by Aḥmad b. Qāsim al-ʿIbādī al-Shāfiʿī al-Ṣabbāgh, d. 992/1584 (p. 320), Leid. 1845, Paris 805, Algiers 956, Cairo ^{1}II, 235, Qaw. I, 273, print. Būlāq 1289, 4 vols.—*δ* Nāṣir al-Dīn al-Laqānī, d. 959/1551, Paris 807/8, Cairo ^{1}I, 246.—*ε* ʿAlī b. Aḥmad al-Najjārī al-Shaʿrānī, Berl. 4406, Garr. 1813, Cairo ^{1}II, 260.—*ζ* ʿĪsā b. Muḥammad al-Barāwī, Paris 806.—*η* Muḥammad al-Barrī al-ʿAdawī, d. 1193/1779, Cairo ^{1}II, 246.—*ϑ* ʿAbd al-Raḥmān al-Bannānī, d. 1198/1784, Garr. 1814, Cairo ^{1}II, 244, Makr. 16, print. Būlāq 1285, 1297, C. 1308/9, 2 vols. 1913.—*ι* Anon. Berl. 4407.—*κ, λ,* d–h (Garr. 1815), see Suppl.—i. Ḥasan b. Muḥammad al-ʿAṭṭār, d. 1250/1834 (p. 473), C. 1316.—Versifications: a. *al-Kawkab al-sāṭiʿ* by al-Suyūṭī, d. 911/1505, Esc. ^{2}218, with a commentary Br. Mus. $893_{,8}$, Algiers 957, Dam. Z. $48_{,61}$, Alex. Uṣūl 11.—b–d. see Suppl.—Abstracts: a. *Lubb al-uṣūl* by Zakariyyāʾ al-Anṣārī, d. 926/1520, Cairo ^{2}II, 258.—Commentaries: *α* Self-commentary *Ghāyat al-wuṣūl ilā L. al-u.* Marseille 1631.—*β* Anon. Paris $809_{,1}$.—A didactic letter, handwritten by the author in 767/1365 in Damascus, Berl. $157_{,2}$.—2. *Manʿ al-mawāniʿ ʿan Jamʿ al-jawāmiʿ*, answers | to 33 questions, raised by Shams 110 al-Dīn Muḥammad al-Ghazzī, d. 808/1405, in his *al-Burūq al-lawāmiʿ fī-mā ūrida ʿalā J. al-j.*, Gotha 927, Paris 810.—3. *Tawshīḥ al-taṣḥīḥ fī uṣūl al-fiqh* Suppl. I, 670, 682.—4. *Tarshīḥ al-Tawshīḥ* ibid.—5. *Tarjīḥ taṣḥīḥ al-khilāf*, ca. 1600 *rajaz* verses, a rectification of oversights by al-Nawawī (I, 496) | in one of his juridical 90 works, following drafts by his father, Berl. 4597.—6. *Kitāb al-ashbāh wal-naẓāʾir* Leid. 1843, Alex. Fiqh Shāf. 5.—7. *Muʿīd al-niʿam wa-mubīd al-niqam*, on how to regain divine mercy, explained by 110 (or 112) examples, and on how each social class, from caliph to beggar, has to live up to his duties, Berl. 5571/2, Gotha 848, Paris 2447, Br. Mus. Suppl. 750, Esc. ^{2}II, 773, Leningrad Un. 767, 847, Garr. 923, AS $4276_{,11}$, Cairo ^{2}VI, 199, VII, 233, 661 (see Suppl.).—8. *Ṭabaqāt al-Shāfiʿiyya* in 3 recensions: a. the large one, Berl. 10037 (fragm.), Paris 2100/1, Esc. ^{2}1669, Yeni 870/1, Köpr. 1108/9, AS 3299/3301, Cairo V ^{1}78, ^{2}250.—b. the medium one, completed in 754/1353, Berl. 10035, Br. Mus. 1297, Cambr. 16, Bodl. I 667, 747, Pet. AM 208, Cairo V ^{1}79, ^{2}251.—c. the small one, Berl. 10036, Gotha 1762, Bodl. I 727, Br. Mus. Suppl. 642, Cairo V ^{1}78, ^{2}250.—9. *Manāqib al-shaykh Abī Bakr b. Qawwām*, d. 658/1260, Berl. 10099, Garr. 688.—10. A long *qaṣīda* on al-Ashʿarī (I, 207) and his teachings, with an appendix on his deviations from Abū Ḥanīfa, Berl. 2098, cf. ibid. 941, 4861.—11. 22 *basīṭ* verses addressed to al-Ṣafadī (p. 39), ibid. $7865_{,1}$.—12. A *qaṣīda* with riddles, partly of a grammatical kind, Leid. 735.—13. A Sufi prayer, composed in 764/1363 in Cairo, published by Tāj al-Dīn al-Malīḥī, Esc. $^2772_{,2}$.—14. *Adʿiya manthūra*, from the end of his large *Ṭabaqāt*, ibid. 3.—15. *Awḍaḥ al-masālik fi ʾl-manāsik* Dam. ʿUm. $47_{,275/81}$.—16.–23. see Suppl. (21. C. 1356/1937, 2 vols.).—24. *al-Dalāla ʿan ʿumūm al-risāla jawāban ʿan asʾilat ahl Ṭarābulus* ʿUm. 2888.

14. Abū Muḥammad ʿAbd al-Raḥīm b. al-Ḥasan b. ʿAlī Jamāl al-Dīn al-Asnawī al-Qurashī al-Umawī al-Shāfiʿī was born in Dhu ʾl-Ḥijja 704/July 1305 in Asnā in Upper Egypt, and commenced his studies in Cairo under Abū Ḥayyān and others in the year 721/1321. He first worked for the fiscal authorities and then became a professor at various madrasas. In Ramaḍān 759/August 1358 he also
111 assumed the *ḥisba*, but | relinquished all his posts three years later, following a dispute with the vizier. From then on he devoted himself to scholarship, until he passed away on 18 Jumādā I 772/9 December 1370.

91 | *DK* II, 254, no. 2376, *RA* 150r, al-Suyūṭī *Ḥusn al-muḥ.* I, 243, Ibn al-Qāḍī, *Durrat al-ḥijāl* II, 376, no. 1133, *al-Khiṭ. al-jad.* VIII, 63, *Orient.* II, 429, Wüst. *Ac.* 155, *Gesch.* 432. 1. *al-Tamhīd fī tanzīl al-furūʿ ʿalā uṣūl al-fiqh* (*fi ʾstikhrāj al-masāʾil al-furūʿiyya min al-qawāʿid al-uṣūliyya*), Berl. 4409, Ind. Off. 329, Garr. 1816, Alex. Fiqh Shāf. 40,$_1$ (*Tamhīd al-wuṣūl ilā maqām istikhrāj al-furūʿ min qawāʿid al-uṣūl*), Cairo [1]II, 242, 260, VII, 31.—2. *al-Kawkab al-durrī fī ʿilm al-uṣūl al-Shāfiʿiyya*, with particular emphasis on linguistic aspects, Berl. 4410, Ind. Off. 330, Garr. 1817, Alex. Fiqh Shāf. 40,$_2$, Cairo [1]VII, 31.—3. *Majmaʿ* (*jawāhir*) *al-baḥrayn fī tanāquḍ al-ḥabrayn fī uṣūl al-fiqh* Leid. 1837, Vat. V. 418, Cairo [1]IV, 215, 269, [2]I, 508.—4. *Maṭāliʿ al-daqāʾiq fi ʾl-jawāmiʿ wal-fawāriq* Cairo [1]III, 275, Alex. Fiqh Shāf. 41.—5. *Aḥkām al-khunthā*, on hermaphrodites according to the *Taḥqīq al-mawhūm wa-sulālat al-ʿulūm* by Abu ʾl-Futūḥ ʿAbdallāh b. Muḥammad b. Abī ʿAqāma, ca. 500/1106 (Subkī, *Ṭab.* IV, 237), and according to Abu ʾl-Ḥasan ʿAlī al-Shahrazūrī, d. 533/1138, Berl. 4790.—6. *Ṭirāz al-maḥāfil fī alghāz al-masāʾil*, completed in 770/1368, his final work, which is a book of legal questions, Alex. Fiqh Shāf. 28, Cairo [1]III, 242.—Abstract: *Nafāʾis al-aḥkām* by ʿAlī b. Abī Bakr al-Yamanī al-Azraq, d. 859/1455, in 5 parts: a. from no. 2.—b. from no. 1.—c. on the contradictory legal opinions of al-Rāfiʿī (I, 493) and al-Nawawī (I, 496).—d. from no. 6.—e. interesting legal problems, from the same work; a selection from c. and e. Berl. 4989.—7. *Ṭabaqāt al-Shāfiʿiyya*, commenced sometime before 750/1349 and completed on 21 Shawwāl 769/10 June 1368, Ind. Off. 709, Br Mus. Suppl. 643.—8. *al-Naṣīḥa al-jāmiʿa wal-ḥujja al-qāṭiʿa* Cairo [1]VII, 355, 409.—9. *al-Muhimmāt fi ʾl-furūʿ fī sharḥ al-Rāfiʿī wal-Rawḍa* I, 543.—10. *Sharḥ Minhāj al-wuṣūl lil-Bayḍāwī* I, 533.—11. *Sharḥ Minhāj al-Nawawī* I, 496.—12. An unfinished, extensive legal work, Cairo [1]III, 265.

15. In Ṣafad, Abū ʿAbdallāh Muḥammad b. ʿAbd al-Raḥmān b. al-Ḥusayn al-Qurashī al-ʿUthmānī al-Shāfiʿī al-Dimashqī al-Ṣafadī Ṣadr al-Dīn wrote, in 780/1378:

| 1. *Raḥmat al-umma fi ʾkhtilāf al-aʾimma* Berl. 4864, Qilič ʿA. 375, Qawala I, 112
415, Patna I, $88,_{895}$, Bat. 142 (part 2), print. Būlāq 1300, 1302, in the margin *OB* III, 1032, Cat. Cairo ^{1}III, 238.—2. *Ṭabaqāt al-fuqahāʾ al-kubrā* (see Suppl.), Paris 2093, Garr. 692.

16. ʿUmar b. Muslim b. Saʿīd b. ʿUmar al-Qurashī Abū Ḥafṣ Zayn al-Dīn, who was born in 724/1324 and died in 792/1390.

Al-Masʾala al-Nuṣayriyya, on the Nuṣayriyya sect, Berl. 2100.

17. Badr al-Dīn Abū ʿAbdallāh Muḥammad b. Bahādur b. ʿAbdallāh al-Turkī al-Miṣrī al-Zarkashī was born in 745/1344, studied in Cairo under al-Asnawī and Mughalṭāy, in Damascus under Ibn Kathīr, and in Aleppo. He then moved to Cairo where he lived purely on his writings. He died on 3 Rajab 794/27 May 1392.

DK III, 397, no. 1059, al-Suyūṭī, *Ḥusn al-muḥ.* I, 248. 1. *al-Baḥr al-muḥīṭ fī uṣūl al-fiqh*, with additional consideration of the Ẓāhirīs, Muʿtazilīs, and Shīʿīs, composed in 777/1375 in Cairo, Paris 811.—2. *al-Manthūr fī tartīb al-qawāʿid al-fiqhiyya*, in alphabetical order, | Berl. 4605, Gotha 978/80, Cairo ^{1}II, 266, glosses 92
thereon by Sirāj al-Dīn b. ʿUmar al-Ḥalabī, composed in 924–5/1518–9, Cairo ^{1}II, 245.—3. *Khabāya ʾl-zawāyā fi ʾl-furūʿ* Gotha 981, Bodl. I, 277.—4. *Luqṭat al-ʿajlān wa-bullat al-ẓamʾān*, general questions of biology, Berl. 5798, Munich $893,_{13}$. Commentary, *Fatḥ al-raḥmān*, by Zakariyyāʾ al-Anṣārī, d. 926/1520, Berl. 5099, anon. glosses, ibid. 5100.—5. *Fī khulāṣat al-funūn al-arbaʿa*, on the art of disputation, completed in 769/1367, Berl. 5320.—6. *Fī aḥkām al-tamannī*, on the conditions under which wishes are permitted or prohibited, Berl. $5410,_{2}$.—7. *Iʿlām al-sājid bi-aḥkām al-masājid*, of which a part, ibid. 5466, used in ibid. 6098.—8. *Mā lā yasaʿu ʾl-mukallaf jahluhu*, from which a discourse on prayer, Esc. $^2707,_{7}$.—9. *Zahr al-ʿarīsh fī aḥkām (taḥrīm) al-ḥashīsh*, Berl. 5486/7, Gotha $2096,_{1}$, Alex. Fun. $154,_{1}$, Cairo ^{1}VII, 639, Qaw. I, 419.—10. *al-Tanqīḥ li-alfāẓ al-Jāmiʿ al-ṣaḥīḥ* I, 164.—11. *Khādim al-Rāfiʿī wal-Rawḍa* I, 543.—12. *Sharḥ Jamʿ al-jawāmiʿ* p. 109.—13. *Tawḍīḥ al-Minhāj* I, 497.—14. *Sharḥ Tanbīh al-Shīrāzī* I, 485.—16.–21. see Suppl.—22. *Risāla fī kalimat al-tawḥīd* Alex. Fun. $87/8,_{2}$.

| 18. Sharaf al-Dīn Abu ʾl-Rūḥ ʿĪsā b. ʿUthmān b. ʿĪsā al-Ghazzī al-Shāfiʿī went to 113
Damascus when he was about 20 years old, where he studied under Ibn Qāḍī Shuhba and Tāj al-Dīn al-Subkī. He then went to Tripoli, and to see al-Asnawī in Cairo. He later became a professor and acting *qāḍī* in Damascus, and died in Ramaḍān 799/June 1397.

DK III, 205, no. 499, *RA* 171 v. 1. *Adab al-ḥukkām fī sulūk ṭuruq al-aḥkām* Cairo ^{1}III, 190, ^{2}I, 496, as *Adab al-qaḍāʾ* Alex Fiqh Shāf. 3, Rāmpūr I, $167_{,10}$.—2. *Sharḥ Minhāj al-Nawawī* I, 497.

19. Al-Qāḍī Sharaf al-Dīn Abū ʿAbdallāh Muḥammad b. al-Shaykh Quṭb al-Dīn ʿAbd al-Raḥmān b. Muḥammad b. ʿAlī b. Ismāʿīl al-Anṣārī al-Khazrajī al-Bahnasī al-Shāfiʿī was born in 736/1336 and died in 800/1397.

1. *al-Kāfī fī maʿrifat ʿulamāʾ madhhab al-Shāfiʿī*, alphabetically listed and divided into 2 groups: 1. Those who are known by their *ism*, *nasab*, *kunya*, nickname, and tribal name; 2. Those who are named after their father, Cairo V, ^{1}136, ^{2}301.—2. See Suppl.

20. Abū Ḥafṣ ʿUmar b. Nūr al-Dīn Abu ʾl-Ḥasan ʿAlī b. Aḥmad b. Muḥammad Sirāj al-Dīn b. al-Mulaqqin al-Anṣārī al-Andalusī al-Shāfiʿī was born in Rabīʿ I 732/March 1332 in Cairo, the son of a grammarian originally from Spain. His father died before he was even a year old, and he was then brought up by his stepfather ʿĪsā al-Maghribī, who was an elementary teacher (*mulaqqin*) at the mosque of Ibn Ṭūlūn, which is how he got his rather unpleasant nickname. He
93 studied in Cairo and, from 770/1368, in Damascus. | There and in Jerusalem he also worked as a teacher. Having returned to Cairo, he died on 6 Rabīʿ 804/15 October 1401.

Ḥuff. XXIII, 4, al-Suyūṭī *Ḥusn al-muḥ.* I, 249, *al-Khiṭ. al-jad.* IV, 105/6, Wüst. *Gesch.* 452. 1. *al-Tadhkira fī ʿulūm al-ḥadīth* Cairo ^{1}I, 274.—2. *Īḍāḥ al-irtiyāb* ibid. I, 274.—3. *Khaṣāʾiṣ afḍal al-makhlūqīn*, composed in 758/1356, Paris $1667_{,1}$.—
114 4. *Ghāyat al-suʾūl fī khaṣāʾiṣ al-rasūl* Yeni 273, Cairo ^{1}VII, | 630, ^{2}I, 132.—5. *Nuzhat al-nuẓẓār fī quḍāt al-amṣār*, abstract Gotha $1532_{,2}$.—6. *al-ʿIqd al-mudhahhab fī ṭabaqāt ḥamalat al-madhhab*, Berl. 10039, Leid. 1102, Bodl. II, 129, Cairo V, ^{1}89, ^{2}270.—7. 3 commentaries on Nawawī's *Minhāj* I, 497.—8. *Sharḥ Tanbīh al-Shīrāzī* I, 485.—9. *Sharḥ Mukhtaṣar al-Tabrīzī* ibid. 493.—10. *Sharḥ al-Ḥāwi ʾl-ṣaghīr* ibid. 494.—11. *Sharḥ ʿUmdat al-aḥkām* ibid. 438.[3]

21. Sirāj al-Dīn ʿUmar b. Raslān al-Bulqīnī al-Kinānī al-ʿAsqalānī was born in Bulqīna in Egypt on 12 Shaʿbān 724/5 August 1324, went to Cairo in 736, and took up residence there in 738/1338. He made the pilgrimage in 740 and 747/1346. In

3 According to al-Sakhāwī *Ḍawʾ* VI, 103/4, the greater part of his 300 works was stolen from others; Goldziher, *M.St.* II, 269.

742/1351 he became the brother-in-law of Ibn ʿAqīl and, when the latter became *qāḍī* in Damascus in 769/1367, he was made his representative and, as early as 765/1363, he had become a *muftī* at the Dār al-ʿadl. Following the death of al-Asnawī he became a professor at the Mālikiyya and at the mosque of Ibn Ṭūlūn, and finally was appointed *qāḍi 'l-ʿaskar*. Having relinquished some of his posts in favour of his sons, he died on 10 Dhu 'l-Qaʿda 805/2 June 1403.

RA 183r, Ibn al-Qāḍī, *Durrat al-ḥijāl* II, 415, no. 1176, *al-Khiṭ. al-jad.* IX, 80. 1. *al-Tadrīb fi 'l-fiqh ʿalā madhhab al-imām al-Shāfiʿī* Berl. 4606, Br. Mus. 900, Cairo ^{1}III, 206.—An appendix, *Tatimmat al-Tadrīb*, by his son Ṣāliḥ (no. 32), Berl. 4607.—2. *al-Fatḥ al-mūhab fi 'l-ḥukm bil-ṣiḥḥa wal-mūjab* Algiers 1360,$_{1}$.—3. *Tartīb al-aqsām fi 'l-fiqh* AS 1055.—4. *al-Mulimmāt bi-radd al-Muhimmāt* I, 543.—5.–10. see Suppl.

22. Shihāb al-Dīn Abu 'l-ʿAbbās Aḥmad b. ʿImād al-Dīn b. Muḥammad al-Aqfahsī al-Miṣrī al-Shāfiʿī, a student of al-Asnawī, died in 808/1405.

Al-Suyūṭī, *Ḥusn al-muḥ.* I, 249. 1. *Kashf al-asrār ʿammā khafiya ʿani 'l-afkār*, pedantic and nit-picking theologico-ethical questions, Berl. 1816/9, Munich 214, Br. Mus. Suppl.

| 196, Algiers 854,$_{3}$, Garr. 1494/5, ʿĀšir I, 493/5, Köpr. II, 130, AS 2012/4, NO 2526, 115
4116, Cairo VI ^{1}180, ^{2}209, VII, 90. | Printed with glosses by Abū ʿAlī Aḥmad 94
al-Azharī, Alexandria 1315.—2. *Tashīl al-maqāṣid li-zuwwār al-masājid*, composed in 786/1384, Leid. 1848, de Jong 130,$_{1}$, Garr. 1823, a part therefrom Berl. 5466, used in 6098.—3. *al-Qawl al-tamām fī aḥkām al-maʾmūm wal-imām* Berl. 3578.—4. *Manẓūma fi 'l-maʿfuwwāt*, on pardonable impurities, Alex. Fun. 77,$_{1}$.—Commentaries: a. Self-commentary, Gotha 1153, Alex. Fun. 77,$_{2}$.—b. *Fatḥ al-jawād* by Aḥmad b. ʿAlī b. Ḥamza Shihāb al-Dīn al-Dimashqī, d. 957/1550 (see Suppl.), Berl. 3632/3, Alex. Fiqh Shāf. 39,$_{2}$. —c. *Fatḥ al-mubīn* by Muḥammad Shams al-Dīn b. Abi 'l-ʿAbbās Aḥmad al-Ramlī, d. 1004/1596 (p. 321), Gotha 1080, legal questions from which Berl. 4991.—d. See Suppl.—e. *Fatḥ al-mubīn* by Aḥmad b. Khalīl al-Subkī al-Shāfiʿī, d. 1032/1623, Alex. Fiqh Shāf. 31.—f. Aḥmad al-Azharī al-Tarmamīnī, ca. 1281/1864, ibid. 26.—5. *al-Farq bayna 'l-ḥayāt al-mustamarra wal-ḥayāt al-mustaqarra wa-ḥayāt ʿaysh al-madhbūḥ*, on the act of slaughtering and permitted foodstuffs, Berl. 4990, Gotha 19,$_{3}$.—6. *Dīwān al-ḥayawān* (see Suppl.), abstract *Tajrīd* by Yūsuf b. ʿAbdallāh al-Ḥasanī, Gotha 94,$_{2}$.—7. *Aḥkām al-awānī wal-ẓurūf wa-mā fīhā min al-maẓrūf* Cairo ^{1}III, 190, VII, 470.—8. *Rafʿ al-ilbās ʿan wahm al-waswās* Cairo ^{1}III, 229, ^{2}I, 517.—9. *Rafʿ al-janāḥ ʿammā*

huwa min al-mirʾāt mubāḥ ibid.—10. *al-Sirr al-mustabāḥ mim-mā awdaʿahu ʾllāh min al-khawāṣṣ fī ajzāʾ al-ḥayawān* Cairo [1]VI, 149.—11. *al-Durra al-ḍawʾiyya fi ʾl-aḥkām al-sunniyya etc.* (see Suppl.), with an anonymous commentary, Cairo [1]VII, 157.—12. *Ikrām man yaʿīsh bi-taḥrīm* (*bijtinābihi*) *al-khamr wal-ḥashīsh* Garr. 1822, Alex. Fun. 157,$_{8}$, Cairo [1]VII, 157, [2]I, 499.—13. *al-Qawl al-tamām fī ādāb dukhūl al-ḥammām*, medical and religious guidelines for bathing, Berl. 3635.—14. *Dalāʾil al-ḥukkām ilā maʿrifat ghawāmiḍ al-aḥkām wal-intiqāl ʿalā ṭāʾifatay al-shuhūd wal-ʿuqūd*, questions on marital law, Berl. 4666.—15. *al-Manẓūma* (*al-ʿImādiyya*) *fī ādāb al-akl wal-shurb wal-nawm wal-yaqaẓa wal-duʿāʾ*, rules of etiquette in 340 *basīṭ* verses, with a self-commentary, Berl. 5466, Garr. 92/3, Cairo [1]VII, 256, 521, [2]I, 326.—16. *al-Wajīz fī-mā yuqaddam ʿalā muʿīn al-tajhīz*, a *rajaz* on the question of whether gifts brought by guests on the occason of the circumcision of a boy belong to the father or to the child; a commentary by al-Ḥasan al-Ḥusaynī, a fragment from which Berl. 5467.—18. On the miracles
116 of the Nile (author?), Berl. 6115 = (?) *Risāla* | *fī ʾl-Nīl* Alex. Taʾr. 112 (p. 28, 29).—19. Guidelines concerning things to be considered regarding a marriage, which qualities are appreciated in a woman, and which ones are objectionable, Berl. 8159,$_{1}$, 8529 (a part of 14 ?).—20. *al-Qawl fī tafsīr al-kalimāt al-ṭayyibāt* Leid. 2032, de Jong 130,$_{2}$.—21. A *lāmiyya* in ca. 300 verses, with a commentary, Munich 568 = (?) *Lāmiyya fī ādāb al-mawāʿiẓ*, with a commentary, Alex. Fun. 116,$_{4}$.—22.–26. see Suppl.—27. *Urjūza fī ṭabaqāt al-anbiyāʾ* Alex. Fun. 98,$_{1}$.—28. *Risāla fi ʾl-Nīl wa-ahrāmihā* ibid. 77,$_{3}$.—29. *Risāla fī manbaʿ al-Nīl*, composed in 780/1378, ibid. 4.—30. *Majmūʿ fī aḥkām al-najāsāt wa-anwāʿihā* Alex. Fiqh Shāf. 38,$_{1}$.

23. Abū ʿAbdallāh Muḥammad b. Abī Bakr b. ʿAbd al-ʿAzīz b. Jamāʿa ʿIzz al-Dīn al-Kinānī al-Shāfiʿī was born in Yanbūʿ in the Hijaz in 759/1357, lived as a physician and teacher of medicine and philosophy in Cairo, and died of the plague in Rabīʿ II 819/June 1416.

Al-Suyūṭī, *Ḥusn al-muḥ.* I, 317, Wüst. *Gesch.* 465. 1. *Zawāl al-taraḥ* I, 459.—2. *Sharḥ al-Arbaʿīn al-Nawawiyyāt* I, 499.—3. *al-Nafaḥāt al-sirriyya wa-laṭāʾif al-ʿulūm al-khafiyya*, on sympathetic drugs, Berl. 4162/4, Cairo [1]V, 374.—4. Glosses on the maxims of Hippocrates, Ber. 6226.—5.–12. See Suppl.—13. *Lamaʿāt al-anwār wa-nafaḥāt al-azhār fi ʾl-tashrīḥ* Dam. Z, 88,$_{44}$.

95 | 24. Abu ʾl-ʿAbbās Aḥmad b. Muḥammad b. Sulaymān al-Qāhirī Shihāb al-Dīn al-Zāhid al-Shāfiʿī, d. 819/1416.

1. *Hadiyyat al-nāṣiḥ wa-ḥizb al-falāḥ al-nājiḥ fī maʿrifat al-ṭarīq al-wāḍiḥ*, on the foundations of religion, Berl. 1821, Paris $665_{,2}$, commentary *ʿUmdat al-rābiḥ* by Muḥammad b. Aḥmad al-Ramlī, d. 1004/1595 (p. 321), Garr. 1826, Alex. Fiqh Shāf. 28, Cairo ^{1}III, 245, ^{1}I, 525, Dam. Z. $61_{,144}$, glosses by Muḥammad b. Dāʾūd al-ʿInānī, composed in 1075/1664, Cairo ^{1}III, 221.—2. *Muqaddimat al-Zāhid* or *al-Sittūn masʾala fi ʾl-fiqh*, on prayer, alms, fasting, and pilgrimage (see Suppl.).—Commentaries: a. *Isʿāf al-qāṣid li-tafhīm masāʾil al-Shihāb al-Z.* by Abu ʾl-Ḥasan ʿAlī b. Muḥammad b. Muḥammad al-Maḥallī al-Shāfiʿī, Alex. Fiqh Shāf. 4 (also attributed to al-Suyūṭī, see Suppl.).—b. Muḥammad b. Aḥmad al-Ramlī, Cairo ^{1}III, 245, glosses: α *al-Futūḥāt* see Suppl. Garr. 1827, Alex Fiqh Shāf. $16_{,32}$.—β Aḥmad al-Mayhī al-Shībīnī, composed in 1246/1830, Cairo ^{1}III, 222.—γ ʿAbd al-Raḥmān al-Makkāwī, ibid. 227.—c. | *Tadhkirat al-ʿābid* by Shihāb al-Dīn 117
Aḥmad b. Muḥammad b. ʿAbd al-Salām, d. 931/1525, Alex Fiqh Shāf 11.—d. See Suppl.—e. Anon., Berl. 3579.—3. *Tuḥfat al-sālik wal-mubtadiʾ wa-lumʿat al-muntahī* Cairo ^{1}VII 687.—4. *al-Manāsik*, on the pilgrimage, Berl. 4049.—5. *Mukhtaṣar fi ʾl-fiqh* ibid. 4608.—6. *Tuḥfat al-sullāk fī faḍl al-siwāk*, on the toothpick, ibid. 5440/1, Cairo ^{1}VI, 121.

25. Taqī al-Dīn Abū Bakr b. Muḥammad b. ʿAbd al-Muʾmin al-Ḥiṣnī al-Ḥusaynī al-Shāfiʿī al-Dimashqī was born in 752/1351, studied in Damascus, and was an Ashʿarī activist and enemy of the Ḥanbalīs. He died in Jumādā II 829/April 1426.

RA 85r. 1. *Fatwā fī Ibn Taymiyya*, on his heretical views, endorsed by a *qāḍī* and a chief *qāḍī*, Berl. 2014.—2. *Dafʿ shubah man sabbaha wa-tamarrada wa-nasaba dhālika ila ʾl-imām A.*, polemics against those who discredit the views of Ibn Ḥanbal, especially Ibn Taymiyya, ibid. 4866.—3. Decorum and moderation in food and drinks, based on the Qurʾān and *ḥadīth*, ibid. 5468.—4. *Siyar al-sālik fī asna ʾl-masālik*, on pious men, Leipz. 693, Paris $4596_{,8}$, abstract Paris $2042_{,2}$, a fragment therefrom, on the permissibility of music, Berl. 5513, on the abuse of music by some Sufis, Paris 4591.—5. *al-Niswa al-ʿābidāt wal-umūr al-mufsidāt* or *Siyar al-ṣāliḥāt al-muʾmināt al-khayrāt*, a counterpart to 4, Paris $2042_{,1}$.—6. *Qamʿ al-nufūs wa-ruqyat al-maʾyūs*, anecdotes from the life of the Prophet, the first 4 caliphs, and the Umayyyads, Berl. 8816/7, Gotha 1590, Bodl. I, 767, Garr. 1913, Alex. Mawāʿiẓ 30, $39_{,2}$, Patna I, $149_{,1426}$.—7. *Kifāyat al-akhyār fī sharḥ al-Taqrīb* I, 492.—8., 9. See Suppl.—10. *al-Asbāb al-muhlikāt wal-ishārāt al-wāḍiḥāt fī manāqib al-muʾminīn wal-muʾmināt wa-mā lahum min al-karāmāt* Qawala I, 217, II, 216.

26. Aḥmad b. ʿAbd al-Raḥmān b. ʿIwaḍ al-Ṭunbudhāʾī al-Qāhirī al-Shāfiʿī Shihāb al-Dīn was born in 751/1349 and died in 831/1428.

Tuḥfat al-amīn fī-mā yuqbal fīhi qawluhu bi-lā yamīn Berl. 4960 (attributed in ḤKh [1]II, 2549, [2]I, 363 to Ṣāliḥ al-Bulqīnī, no. 32).

118 27. Muḥammad b. ʿAbd al-Dāʾim b. Mūsā al-Nuʿaymī al-ʿAsqalānī | al-Miṣrī
al-Birmāwī al-Shāfiʿī Shams al-Dīn Abū ʿAbdallāh was born on 15 Dhu ʾl-Qaʿda
763/6 September 1361, studied under al-Bulqīnī and represented him as *qāḍī*,
96 then became a *muftī* at the Dār al-ʿadl and | a professor at the Rawāḥiyya and
Amīniyya in Damascus. Following the death of his son Muḥammad he returned to Cairo. During the years 828—30 he lived in Mecca, then became a professor at the Ṣalāḥiyya in Jerusalem, where he died in 831/1427.

Al-Khiṭ. al-jad. IX, 34. 1. *al-Nubdha al-zakiyya fi ʾl-qawāʿid al-aṣliyya*, turned into 1031 verses by the author in *al-Nubdha al-alfiyya fi ʾl-uṣūl al-fiqhiyya* Berl. 4414, Alex. Uṣūl 21, Cairo [1]II, 267, [2]I App. 52, a self-commentary on which, *al-Fawāʾid al-saniyya*, composed in 826/1423 in al-Ṣāliḥiyya, Cairo [1]II, 256, Garr. 1647, glosses thereon by Abū ʿAbdallāh Muḥammad b. Aḥmad b. ʿAbdallāh, Ind. Off. 1487.—2. *al-Lāmiʿ al-ṣabīḥ* I, 165.—3.–5. See Suppl.

28. Jamāl al-Dīn ʿAbdallāh b. ʿAlī b. Ayyūb al-Shāfiʿī al-Qādirī al-Makhzūmī, fl. ca. 840/1436.

1. *Siyāsat al-khalq bi-taḥsīn al-khulq*, on ethics, Berl. 5398, Leid. 1945.—2., 3., see Suppl. (II, 1027$_{,3}$).

29. Shihāb al-Dīn Aḥmad b. al-Ḥusayn b. Ḥasan b. Raslān al-Ramlī al-Qudsī al-Shāfiʿī, who died in Jerusalem in 844/1440, see Suppl.

1. (*Ṣafwat*) *al-Zubad fī-mā ʿalayhi ʾl-muʿtamad* (*fi ʾl-tawḥīd wal-fiqh wal-taṣawwuf*), a versification of the *Kitāb al-zubad* by al-Bārizī, d. 738/1337 (p. 105$_{,6}$), in ca. 1000 *rajaz* verses, Berl. 1822/3, Gotha 919, Br. Mus. 1487, Leid, 1858, Bodl. I, 270, II, 575, Cairo [1]III, 232, VII, 523, print. Būlāq 1285, Bombay 1312.—Commentaries: a. Self-commentary on the final part Berl. 1824.—b. Shihāb al-Dīn al-Ramlī, d. 957/1550: α *Fatḥ al-raḥmān* Gotha 920, Leid. 1859, Cairo [1]III, 250.—β *Ghāyat al-bayān* Berl. 1824, Br. Mus. Suppl. 318, Cairo [1]III, 246, [2]I, 526 (attributed to his son Muḥammad, d. 1004/1595), print. Būlāq 1291, C. 1305.—c. *Ṣahwat al-Zubad* by Shams al-Dīn Muḥammad b. al-Ṭaḥḥān, abstract by the author himself,

Gotha 921.—d.–g. see Suppl. (f. in the margin of Būlāq 1291).—2. *Tahdhīb al-adhkār*, on silent prayers, based on al-Nawawī, Ibn Humām, and others, Berl. 3706, Patna I, 152$_{,1447}$.

| 30. Aḥmad b. Yūsuf al-Sharjī al-Shāfiʿī, d. 862/1458. 119

Al-Ṭirāz al-mudhahhab li-aḥkām al-madhhab, ḤKh IV, 156$_{,7945}$, Mosul 199$_{,17,19}$.

31. Muḥammad b. Aḥmad (no. 22) b. ʿImād al-Aqfahsī al-Shāfiʿī Shams al-Dīn was born in 780/1378 and died in 867/1462 (see Suppl.).

Al-Dharīʿa ilā aʿdād al-sharīʿa, on the use of numbers in legal issues, Berl. 4992, Cairo ^{1}III, 227, ^{2}I, 515.

32. Ṣāliḥ b. ʿUmar (no. 21) b. Raslān al-Bulqīnī ʿAlam al-Dīn, d. 868/1463, see Suppl.

Al-Suyūṭī, *Ḥusn al-muḥ*. I, 253, *al-Khiṭ. al-jad.* IX, 81. 1. *al-Jawhar al-fard fī-mā yukhālif fīhi 'l-ḥurr al-ʿabd* Berl. 4993, Alex. Fun. 121$_{,8}$.—2. *al-Qawl al-maqbūl fī-mā yuddaʿā fīhi bil-majhūl* Garr. 1828.—3. See Suppl.

32a. Aḥmad b. ʿUmar b. ʿUthmān b. ʿAlī al-Shihāb al-Khwārizmī al-Dimashqī al-Shāfiʿī b. Qara, a student of al-Taqī al-Ḥiṣnī, constructed a *zāwiya* for dervishes behind the Bustān al-Ṣāḥib in Damascus, made the pilgrimage to Mecca via Jerusalem and Hebron in 864/1460, and died on 10 Jumādā I 868/21 January 1464.

Al-Sakhāwī, *Ḍawʾ* II, 54. 1. *al-Rawḍ al-bāsim fi 'l-takannī bi-Abi 'l-Qāsim* Dam. Z. 38$_{,127,1}$.—2. *al-Durr al-naẓīm fī faḍl bismillāh al-raḥmān al-raḥīm*, abstract, ibid. 73$_{,37}$.—3. *Mukhtaṣar al-Masālik fi 'l-manāsik*, by Abū Manṣūr al-Kirmānī (ḤKh V, 508$_{,1}$, Suppl. 1023, 66), ibid. 38$_{,27,3}$.—4. *Mukhtaṣar Tawthīq ʿura 'l-īmān* Suppl. II, 10$_{,6}$.—5. *al-Muntaqā min al-Madārik* Suppl. I, 632$_{,5}$.

| 33. ʿAbd al-Raḥmān b. Khalīl al-Qābūnī al-Adhraʿī Zayn al-Dīn, d. 869/1464 97
(see Suppl.).

1. *al-Naṣīḥa lil-ḥurr wal-ʿabd bijtināb al-shiṭranj wal-nard* Berl. 5498.—2. *Bishārat al-maḥbūb bi-ghufrān al-dhunūb* Dam. Z. 52, 87, ʿUm. 66, 87.—3., 4. see Suppl. II, 932, 23.

34. Ismāʿīl b. ʿAlī b. Ḥasan b. Hilāl b. Muʿallā al-Ṣaʿīdī al-Qāhirī al-Shāfiʿī, who was born in 828/1425, wrote, in 871/1466:

120 | *Al-Layth al-ʿābith fī ṣadamāt al-majālis fī uṣūl al-fiqh*, definitions, Berl. 4417, Cairo [1]IV. 81.

35. Taqī al-Dīn Abū Bakr b. Walī al-Dīn b. Qāḍī ʿAjlūn al-Shāfiʿī, d. 876/1471.

Iʿlām al-nabīh bi-mā zāda ʿala ʾl-Minhāj wal-Ḥāwī wal-Bahja wal-Tanbīh Alex. Fiqh Shāf. 6.

36. Muḥibb al-Dīn Abu ʾl-Walīd Ibrāhīm b. Muḥammad al-Ḥalabī b. al-Shiḥna, d. 882/1477.

Lisān al-ḥukkām fī maʿrifat al-aḥkām, in 30 chapters, the last 9 of which were completed in 1027/1618 by Burhān al-Dīn Ibrāhīm al-Khāliʿī al-ʿAdawī under the title *Ghāyat al-marām*, Berl. 4796, Ms. or. oct. 3799, Gotha 1030 (only chapter 25), Vienna 1789, Paris 935, Esc. [2]304,3, Garr. 2092,1, Köpr. 641, II, 102, Yeni 537/9, Cairo [1]III, 112/4, VII, 622, [2]I, 458.

36a. Ibrāhīm b. Ibrāhīm b. Muḥammad b. Aḥmad b. Nāṣir al-Nawawī, who died around 885/1480 in Damascus.

Al-Sakhāwī, *Ḍawʾ* I, 8. *Manẓūma fī ʿilm al-farāʾiḍ wal-jabr wal-muqābala*, completed in 854/1450, Berl. 5993.

37. Muḥammad b. ʿAbd al-Munʿim b. Nabīh al-Dīn al-Jawharī arrived in Cairo at the age of 7 in 821/1418, later became an acting *qāḍī* and professor at al-Azhar, and died in 889/1484.

Al-Khiṭ. al-jad. X, 70. 1. *Tarjamat al-imām al-Shāfiʿī* Berl. 10011, cf. 4514.—2. *Sharḥ Hamziyyat al-Būṣīrī* I, 363.—3. *Sharḥ al-Irshād* ibid. 495.—4., 5. See Suppl.

38. Quṭb al-Dīn Abu ʾl-Khayr Muḥammad b. Muḥammad b. ʿAbdallāh b. Ḥayḍir al-Ḥayḍarī al-Dimashqī al-Shāfiʿī was born on 16 Ramaḍān 821/18 October 1418 in Damascus, and studied there, in Baalbek and, from 843/1439, in Cairo. After making the pilgrimage, during which he also visited Jerusalem, he became Chancellor of the Exchequer (*wakīl bayt al-māl*) in Damascus and, on 1 Muḥarram 859/22 December 1454, privy secretary. After he had lost this

position four years later, he became a professor at the Dār al-ḥadīth al-Ashrafi-
yyya in Dhu 'l-Qaʿda 865/August 1461 | and, in the following year, *qāḍī* for the 121
Shāfiʿīs. He died in Damascus in 888/1483 (or, according to others, not until 894/1489).

RA 217r, *JA* S IX, v. 3, p. 258, Wüst. *Gesch.* 501. 1. *al-Rawḍ al-naḍr fī ḥāl al-Khiḍr*,
on whether he should be regarded as a *walī* or as a *nabī*, | and whether he is still 98
alive, Berl. 2529, fragm. Cairo ^{1}VII, 565; on which notes, *Iftirāḍ dafʿ al-iʿtirāḍ*, by Abu 'l-Ghayth al-Kamrānī, Berl. 2530.—2. *al-Lafẓ al-mukarram bi-khaṣāʾiṣ al-nabī al-ʿaẓam* Cairo I, ^{1}394, ^{2}142.—3. *Zahr al-riyāḍ fī radd man shanaʿahu 'l-Qāḍī ʿIyāḍ* (I, 455) *ʿalā man awjaba 'l-ṣalāt ʿala 'l-bashīr fi 'l-tashahhud al-akhīr*, a rebuttal of attacks on al-Shāfiʿī by al-Qāḍī ʿIyāḍ, Br. Mus. Suppl. 323.—4. See Suppl.

39. Sirāj al-Dīn al-Makhzūmī al-Ḥimṣī al-Shāfiʿī wrote, in the ninth or tenth century:

Al-Irshād min al-murshid ilā rabb al-ʿibād, on the *furūʿ*, with particular emphasis on al-Bulqīnī (p. 114) and al-Nawawī (I, 496), Gotha 988.

40. Burhān al-Dīn Abū Isḥāq Ibrāhīm b. Muḥammad b. Maḥmūd al-Nājī al-Dimashqī al-Shāfiʿī, who died in Ramaḍān 900/June 1495.

Biography Berl. $297_{,82}$, al-Kattānī, *Fihris* II, 81/2. 1. *Kanz al-rāghibīn al-ʿufāt fi 'l-ramz fi 'l-mawlūd al-Muḥammadī wal-wafāt*, a series of questions concerning the Prophet, Berl. 2574, Alex. Fun. $88_{,1}$.—2. *Ḥuṣūl al-bughya lil-sāʾil hal li-aḥad min ahl al-janna liḥya*, on whether the inhabitants of paradise have beards, Berl. 2698.—3. *al-Jawāb al-mujallī li-lafẓ tashwīsh al-qāriʾ ʿala 'l-muṣallī*, on whether the rule that readers should not disturb those who are praying originated with Muḥammad or not, ibid. 3582.—4. Against the rule, propagated by modern jurists (Sachau, *Muḥ. Recht* 55): "Whoever repudiates his wife three times with a single word has only repudiated her once," composed in 834/1430, ibid. 4667.—5. *al-Amr bil-muḥāfaẓa ʿala 'l-kitāb wal-sunna* Cairo ^{1}VIII, 140.—6. *al-Ḥiṣāl al-mukaffira* ibid.—7. *Taḥḍīr al-ikhwān mim-mā yūrith al-fuqr wal-nisyān*, also under the title *Qalāʾid al-ʿiqyān fī mūrithāt al-fuqr wal-nisyān* Gotha 80, Upps. $225_{,17}$. Alex. Mawāʿiẓ 9, Cairo ^{1}II, 173, VII, 9, ^{2}I, 275, Patna II, $418_{,25,89,2}$, versified by Abū ʿAbdallāh al-Ghazzī, Gotha $81_{,1}$, Alex. Fun. $167_{,23}$, Cairo ^{1}II, 173.—8. A fatwā regarding the question whether Jaʿfar b. Abī Ṭālib al-Ṭayyār has descendants until that very day, which he answered in the affirmative,

122 published by his | student Shams al-Dīn b. Bizza, ca. 920/1514, Berl. 9400.—9. On the *muʾadhdhins* of the Prophet, Berl. 9956.—10., 11. (Garr. 771) see Suppl.

41. Abu ʾl-Maʿālī Muḥammad b. Aḥmad b. Abī Bakr al-Maqdisī Kamāl al-Dīn b. Abī Sharīf al-Shāfiʿī al-Ashʿarī, who died in 906/1500.

1. *Risāla fī bayān ḥadīth ḥabbib ilayya min dunyākum* Berl. 1590.—2. *Fi ʾl-istithnāʾ*, on exceptions in legal issues, ibid. 4994.—3 *Ṣawb al-ghamāma fī irsāl al-ʿimāma*, on the custom of letting the tip of the turban hang free, ibid. 5433.—4. *al-Musāmara fī sharḥ al-Musāyara* p. 226.—5. See Suppl.

99 | 42. Muḥammad b. ʿUmar b. Aḥmad al-Safīrī al-Shāfiʿī, a student of al-Suyūṭī, who flourished around 920/1514.

Tuḥfat al-akhyār fī ḥukm aṭfāl al-muslimīn wal-kuffār Cairo ^{1}VII, 588.

43. Muḥammad b. Dāʾūd al-Bāzilī al-Kurdī al-ʿImādī al-Ḥamawi al-Shāfiʿī Shams al-Dīn, who was born in 845/1441, is believed to have died in 925/1519 (? See Suppl.).

Wüst. *Gesch.* 510. 1. *Muqaddimat al-ʿājil li-dhakhīrat al-ājil*, on faith and the manner of its confession, Berl. 1834.—2. *Tuḥfat dhawi ʾl-arab fī-mā warada ʿalaynā min istishkāl Ḥalab*, removes the exception taken by a learned man from Aleppo to al-Taftāzānī's interpretation of *Lā ilāha illa ʾllāh* in his *al-Talwīḥ* and *al-Muṭawwal* (I, 354), Berl. 2443.—3. On the order of the 47 parts of the *al-Ḥāwī al-ṣaghīr* and, more particularly, on the treatment of *al-ḥadath* and *al-khabath*, which both come under the notion of impurity, ibid. 4996.—4. *Ghāyat al-marām*, on the transmitters in al-Bukhārī's *Ṣaḥīḥ*, *Br. Mus. Quart.* VI, 97 (MS dated 888 AH), Rāġib 345/6, Köpr. 374.

44. Zayn al-Dīn Abū Yaḥyā Zakariyyāʾ b. Muḥammad al-Anṣārī al-Sumaykī al-Shafiʿī, born in 826/1422 in Sumayka, east of Cairo, was a professor in Cairo and, from Rajab 886/September 1481, Shāfiʿī chief *qāḍī*. After some years he lost
123 this position because he had unlawfully declared a man | insane and had him locked up in hospital. He died in Dhu ʾl-Ḥijja 926/December 1520.

RA 129v, al-Ṣafadī, *al-Wāfī* AS 2962f 41/63 (with an extensive listing of his writings), al-Kattānī, *Fihris* I, 344. 1. *al-Luʾluʾ al-naẓīm fī rawm al-taʿallum wal-taʿlīm*, on the drawbacks and advantages of the different sciences, Berl. 79/81, Garr. 788, $2034_{,4}$, Cairo ^{1}VII, 57, 158, 605, ^{2}I, 350, Patna II, $439_{,2615,1}$.—2. *al-Maqṣad li-takhlīṣ* (*li-talkhīṣ*) *mā fi ʾl-Murshid fi ʾl-waqf wal-ibtidāʾ*, on pausas

in the Qurʾān, from the *Murshid* of al-Ḥasan b. ʿAlī b. Saʿīd al-ʿUmānī,before 669/1270 (*Gesch. des Qor*, III, 236), with additions, mostly following al-Dānī (I, 516), Berl. 564, Leid. 1645, Fātiḥ Waqf Ibr. 151,$_{2}$, print. Būlāq 1282, C. 1305, among others, see Cairo ^{1}I, 110, 114.—3. *Fatḥ al-raḥmān bi-kashf mā yalbas* (*labis, yaltabis*) *fī ʾl-Qurʾān*, Basle, M. III, 23, Paris 600, Pet. Ros. 15, AS 429, NO 589, Cairo ^{1}I, 186,$_{207}$, ^{2}I, 56, Qawala I, 74, perhaps identical with Suppl. no. 51 (F. Meier; incipit: *hādhā mukhtaṣar fī āyāt al-Qurʾān al-mutashābihāt*).—4. *Fatḥ al-jalīl bi-bayān khafī Anwār al-tanzīl lil-Bayḍāwī* I, 531.—5. *Hidāyat al-mutanassik wa-kifāyat al-mutamassik*, a work on *ḥadīth*, Berl 1369, cf. 1591.—6. *al-Iʿlām bi-aḥādīth al-aḥkām* with a commentary, *Fatḥ al-ʿallām*, completed in 910/1504, Br. Mus. 195, Cairo ^{1}I, 377, ^{2}I, 134.—7. *Risāla fī ʾl-basmala wal-ḥamdala* Berl. 2274/5, Br. Mus. 902,$_{3}$, Yeni 355.—Commentaries: a. Aḥmad b. ʿAbd al-Ḥaqq al-Sanbāṭī, d. 990/1582, composed in 972/1564, Berl. 2276, Alex. Fun. 40, Patna I, 30,$_{295}$, glosses thereon by ʿAlī b. ʿAlī b. Mukarram al-Ṣaʿīdī al-ʿIdwī al-Mansafīsī, d. 1189/1775 (p. 319), Garr. 1310, Makram 22.—b. *Qurrat ʿuyūn dhawi ʾl-afhām* by Aḥmad b. Ismāʿīl al-Shanawānī, d. 1019/1610 (p. 285), Garr. 1964.—c. *Khayr al-kalām* by ʿAlī al-Ḥalabī, Qawala II, 255.—d. Anon., ibid. 257.—8. *Taḥrīr tanqīḥ al-Lubāb* I, 192 (see Suppl.), with a commentary, *Tuḥfat al-ṭullāb*, and glosses by ʿAbdallāh b. Ḥijāzī al-Sharqāwī, d. 1227/1812 (p. 479), 2 vols. C. 1306, 1309.—9. *Manhaj al-ṭullāb fī ʾl-fiqh* I, 498.—10. *Nahj al-ṭālib li-ashraf al-maṭālib*, with a commentary, *Tuḥfāt al-rāghib*, Paris 1049.—11. *Adab al-qāḍī* Yeni 355.—12. *Manhaj al-wuṣūl ilā taḥrīr al-fuṣūl fī ʾl-farāʾiḍ* see p. 125.—13. *Taʿrīfāt*, short defnitions of technical terms | from *uṣūl al-dīn wal-fiqh*, Berl. 100
3463.—14. *al-Iʿlām wal-ihtimām li-jamʿ fatāwī shaykh al-islām*, ordered by the *furūʿ* by an unidentified individual, Gotha 1145, Paris 950, Alex. Fiqh Shāf. 6.—15. *al-Futūḥāt al-ilāhiyya fī nafʿ arwāḥ al-dhāt al-insāniyya*, a short exposition | 124
of mysticism, Berl. 3035/6, Alex. Fun. 150,$_{15}$, Cairo ^{1}II, 99, VII, 605, ^{2}I, 337, App. 45.—16. *Risāla fī taʿrīf al-alfāẓ allatī yatadāwaluhā muḥaqqiqu ʾl-Ṣūfiyya* Cairo ^{1}II, 84.—17. *al-Tuḥfa al-ʿaliyya fī ʾl-khuṭab al-minbariyya* ibid. 149.—18. *al-Aḍwāʾ al-bahija fī ibrāz daqāʾiq al-Munfarija* I, 316.—19. *al-Muṭṭalaʿ ʿala ʾl-Isāghūjī* I, 610.—20. *Aqṣa ʾl-maʿānī* (*amānī*), on rhetoric with a commentary, *Fatḥ manāzil al-mabānī*, Cairo ^{1}IV, 143.—21. *Tuḥfat nujabāʾ al-ʿaṣr fī aḥkām al-nūn al-sākina wal-tanwīn wal-madd wal-qaṣr* Cairo ^{1}VII, 60.—22. *Nihāyat al-Hidāya* see p. 126.—23. *Sharḥ Shudhūr al-dhahab li-Ibn Hishām* p. 30.—24. *Lubb al-uṣūl mukhtaṣar Jamʿ al-jawāmiʿ lil-Subkī* p. 109.—25. *Fatḥ al-raḥmān sharḥ Luqṭat al-ʿajlān lil-Zarkashī* p. 112.—26. *Sharḥ al-Bahja al-Wardiyya* I, 495.—27. *Sharḥ Minhāj al-Nawawī* I, 497.—28. *Sharḥ al-Arbaʿīn al-Nawawiyya* I, 497.—29. *Asna ʾl-maṭālib* p. 191,$_{10}$.—30. *al-Mulakhkhaṣ min Talkhīṣ al-Miftāḥ* I, 355.—31. *Sharḥ al-Shāfiya* I, 371.—32. *Sharḥ al-Qaṣīda al-Khazrajiyya* I, 380.—33. *Mukhtaṣar Adāb al-Bayhaqī* I, 447.—34. *Sharḥ al-Muqaddima al-Jazariyya* p. 202.—35. *Sharḥ Risālat al-tawḥīd* I, 589.—36.–52. see Suppl. (2. After the *Adab al-qaḍāʾ* of

al-Ghazzī, p. $91_{,19}$, also Garr. 1818.—45. With the title *Nubdha fī bayān al-alfāẓ al-muṣṭalaḥ ʿalayhā inda ʾl-uṣūliyyīn* Qawala I, 300, excise *Qurrat etc.* see above). 53. *al-Daqāʾiq al-muḥkama* Alex. Fun. $174_{,20}$, $190_{,2}$.—54. *Tuḥfat al-rāghibīn fī bayān amr al-ṭawwāʿīn* ibid. 144, I.

D The Ḥanbalīs

1. Shams al-Dīn Muḥammad b. Abi ʾl-Fatḥ b. Abi ʾl-Faḍl al-Baʿlī al-Naḥwī al-Ḥanbalī, who was born in 645/1247 and was student of Ibn Mālik, went from Damascus to Jerusalem, before dying in a hospital in Cairo in Muḥarram 709/June 1309.

DK Vienna, III, 301 v. 1. *al-Muṭliʿ ʿalā abwāb al-Muqniʿ* I, 503.—2. *al-Muthallath bi-maʿnan wāḥid min al-asmāʾ wal-afʿāl* Berl. 7089.—3., 4. See Suppl.

2. Abu ʾl-Ṣafāʾ ʿAbd al-Raḥmān b. Taqī al-Dīn b. Abī Bakr b. Dāʾūd al-Ṣāliḥī al-Ḥanbalī, d. 711/1311.

Al-Kanz al-akbar fi ʾl-amr bil-maʿrūf wal-nahy ʿani ʾl-munkar Cairo [1]II, 169.

125 | 3. Abu ʾl-ʿAbbās Aḥmad b. ʿAbd al-Ḥalīm b. ʿAbd al-Salām (I, 504) b. ʿAbdallāh b. Muḥammad b. Taymiyya Taqī al-Dīn al-Ḥarrānī al-Ḥanbalī was born in Ḥarrān
101 near Damascus on 10 Rabīʿ I 661/23 January 1263. | He studied in the capital, where his father had fled with his family from the Mongols, early in 667/1268. Following his father's death in 681/1282 he succeeded him as a teacher of the Ḥanbalīs, and ten years later, when he made the pilgrimage, he was regarded as their highest authority. When in Rabīʿ I 699/December 1298 he answered a question from Hama on God's attributes (below, no. 3) in a way that contradicted the Shāfiʿīs, he was dismissed from his teaching position, summoned to a Shāfiʿī court in Cairo in 705/1305, and sentenced to jail. After 1½ years he was sent back to Damascus, but remained in custody. After a second hearing in Cairo, he was detained under slightly better conditions in Alexandria. After his former patron al-Malik al-Nāṣir had returned to power he was released unconditionally in 709/1309. The sultan appointed him senior professor at the madrasa that he had founded in Cairo, and took him with him to Damascus on 1 Dhu ʾl-Qaʿda 712/28 February 1313, where Ibn Taymiyya resumed his teaching activities. But a fatwa on divorce pronounced in 718/1318 resulted in another prosecution. When, in spite of a ban, he continued to teach, he was detained in the citadel for five months and 18 days. In Shaʿbān 726/July 1326 he was arrested once again, this time for a treatise on visiting the graves of prophets and saints, which he had written in 710/1310. Even though mildly treated, he was

hard-hit by a two-year ban on ink and paper. He died soon after, in the night of Tuesday 22 Dhu ʾl-Qaʿda 728/29 September 1328, his funeral drawing massive crowds.

| As a teacher of theology he went his own way, independent from estab- 102
lished school opinions. And in the same way | in which he forbade the invoca- 126
tion of the Prophet and making a pilgrimage to his grave, he also did not shrink from rejecting the decisions of the caliph. He opposed al-Ghazzālī and the Ashʿarīs, as well as Ibn ʿArabī and the mystics in general. Being dogmatic, he advocated *tajsīm*, i.e. the literal interpretation of anthropomorphic passages in the Qurʾān. As a *faqīh*, he claimed *ijtihād*. But although he derived his rulings straight from the *ḥadīth*, he did recognise *qiyās*. He opposed Aristotelian philosophy in his *Naṣīḥat ahl al-bayān fi ʾl-radd ʿalā manṭiq al-Yūnān*, of which al-Suyūṭī published an abstract. His influence lent a new prestige to the otherwise rather neglected school of Aḥmad b. Ḥanbal. The founder of modern Wahhābism, Muḥammad b. ʿAbd al-Wahhāb (p. 390), drew his initial motivation from, and even copied the works of, Ibn Taymiyya and his student Ibn Qayyim al-Jawziyya (Cod. Amīn 217, 638, Landb. Br. 35, 176); as such, his opponents are always against Ibn Taymiyya.

Fawāt I, 35, Ibn Baṭṭūṭa I, 215 ff, DK I, 144/60, *Ḥuff.* XXI, 7, biography by Marʿī al-Karmī, d. 1033/1624 (p. 369, no. 20), anon. *Dhikr aḥwāl Abi ʾl-ʿAbbās Aḥmad b. Taymiyya al-Ḥarrānī* Paris 2104, al-Kattānī, *Fihris* I, 199/202, Abū ʿAbdallāh Muḥammad b. ʿAbd al-Hādī, *al-ʿUqūd al-durriyya min manāqib shaykh al-islām b. Taymiyya* C. 1938 (with a list of his works, 38 ff), *Büschings Magazin* V, 413, *Orient.* II, 347, Wüst. *Gesch.* 393, Steinschneider, *Polem. u. apol. Lit.* 442, Schreiner, ZDMG 52, 540 ff, Goldziher, *Die Ẓāhiriten* 188, 190, ZDMG 52, 156. Ghulam Jilani Barque, *Ibni Teimiyya*, Thesis, Lahore 1940 (?). H. Laoust, *Essai sur les doctrines sociales et politiques d'Ibn T., Rech. d'Arch. de Phil. et d'Hist.* IFAO, Cairo 1939. His works were purportedly stylistically revised by his student Ibn Qayyim al-Jawziyya (no. 4), DK Vienna III, 134_r. Listing, Suppl. II, 120/6.

I. 2. Patna I, $126_{,1264}$.—5a. *al-Muntaqā min akhbār al-Muṣṭafā*, 2 vols., C. 1933.

II A. 11. Printed in *Majmūʿa* Ind. 1296.—13a. *Tafsīr* | *qawlihi taʿālā wa-kallama* 127
ʾllāhu Mūsā taklīman (p. $4_{,162}$) ibid.—13b. *Muqaddima fī uṣūl al-tafsīr* Damascus 1936.—13c. *Risāla fi ʾl-Qurʾān wa-mā waqaʿa fīhi min al-nizāʿ hal huwa qadīm aw muḥdath* Qawala I, 189.—13d. with the title *Risāla fī-mā waqaʿa fi ʾl-Qurʾān bayna ʾl-ʿulamāʾ hal huwa makhlūq aw ghayr makhlūq wa-bayān al-ḥaqq fī dhālik wa-mā dalla ʿalayhi ʾl-kitāb wal-sunna wal-jamāʿa* ibid. 67.

B. 24b. *Taʾwīl mukhtalaf al-ḥadīth fi ʾl-radd ʿalā ahl al-ḥadīth wal-jamʿ bayna ʾl-akhbār allatī iddaʿaw ʿalayha ʾl-tanāquḍ wal-ikhtilāf* C. n.d.—25. *Sharḥ al-ʿAqīda al-Iṣfahāniyya* by Muḥammad b. Maḥmūd Shams al-Dīn al-Iṣfahānī, d. 688/1289.—29. Fātiḥ 2565, Qawala I, 206, Patna II, 514,$_{2765}$.—30. *Kitāb al-īmān* Berl. Brill M. 232, *Sharḥ al-īmān* Patna II, 512,$_{2730}$.—70a. *Risāla fi ʾl-munāẓara fī ṣifāt al-bāriʾ* ibid. 557,$_{2935,2}$.

D. b. 84a. al-Radd ʿala ʾl-Ikhnāʾī (the Mālikī qāḍī of Damascus), written in the margin of the Kitāb al-istiyāh (?) = al-Radd ʿala ʾl-Bakrī C. 1346 (Laoust, loc. cit.).—d. 93 see Isl. Culture I, 1927, p. 91.

E. 109, 110 = *al-Ijtimāʿ wal-firāq* (*iftirāq*) *fī masāʾil al-aymān wal-ṭalāq* (*fi ʾl-ḥilf bil-ṭalāq*) Dam. Z. 35,$_{99,8}$, print. C. 1342, see H. Laoust, Une r. d' i. T. sur le serment de répudiation, *Bull. d. Ét. or. de l'Inst. franç. de Damas* VI/VII, 1937/8, 215/36.—114. Mosul 62,$_{18}$ = *al-Siyāsa al-sharʿiyya fī aḥkām al-sulṭān ʿala ʾl-raʿiyya* ibid. 157,$_{107}$ (anon.).—131. C. 1318.—140a. *al-Masāʾil wal-ajwiba* Alex. Fiqh Ḥanb. 7.—140b. *Risāla fi ʾl-nusk* Patna II, 449,$_{2625,1}$.—140c. *Faṣl fi ʾl-mujtahidīn hal kullu mujtahid muṣīb aw al-muṣīb wāḥid wal-bāqūn mukhṭiʾūn* Dam. Z. 36,$_{99,12}$.
105 |—140d. *Kalām ʿalā masʾalat al-shitranj wa-faṣl fī anwāʿ al-istiftāḥ fi ʾl-ṣalāt wa-jawāb ʿan suʾāl ulqiya ʿalayhi ʿani ʾl-qiyām baʿd al-adhān al-awwal yawm al-jumʿa* ibid. 86,$_{3}$.

4. Shams al-Dīn Abū ʿAbdallāh Muḥammad b. Abī Bakr b. Ayyūb b. Qayyim al-Jawziyya al-Zarʿī al-Dimashqī al-Ḥanbalī was born in 691/1292. His father was the headmaster of al-Madrasa al-Jawziyya in Damascus. When Ibn Taymiyya returned from Cairo in 712/1312, he became one of his most diligent and devoted students. He shared his honours as well as his persecutions, and even
106 after his master's death | he was still subjected to great difficulties. He died on 13 Rajab 751/17 September 1350.

128 | *DK* Vienna 134r/136v. Schreiner, *ZDMG* 53, 59 ff. 1. *Kitāb al-manār*, on the hallmarks of the credibility and genuineness of the sayings of the Prophet, Berl. 1069.—2. *Ijtimāʿ al-juyūsh al-islāmiyya ʿalā ḥarb* (*fi ʾl-radd ʿala ʾl-firqa*) *al-Muʿaṭṭila wal-Jahmiyya* Berl. 2090/1. Leid. 2022.—3. *al-Kāfiya al-shāfiya fi ʾl-intiṣār fi ʾl-firqa al-nājiya*, on the points of contention regarding the qualities and the sublimeness of God, Berl. 2092/3.—4. *al-Ṣawāʿiq al-mursala ʿalā firaq al-Muʿtazila wal-Jahmiyya wal-Muʿaṭṭila* Berl. 2094, abstract ibid. 2095.—5. *Hidāyat al-ḥayārā fī ajwibat al-Yahūd wal-Naṣārā* Leid. 2024, Yeni 761, AS 2243, Garr. 1518.—6. *Iʿlām al-muwaqqiʿīn fī* (*ʿan*) *rabb al-ʿālamīn* (*fi ʾl-uṣūl*) Cairo ^{1}II, 237, ^{2}I, 378, App. 50, the closing remarks Berl. 4819 (see Suppl.), some passages ibid. 4820.—7. *al-Ṭuruq al-ḥikmiyya fi ʾl-siyāsa al-sharʿiyya*, on physiognomy and its value for princes, Gotha 1235, Alex. Mawāʿiẓ 26, Cairo ^{1}V, 81, ^{2}VI, 181.—8. *Badāʾiʿ al-fawāʾid* Cairo ^{1}II, 117, ^{2}IV, 81, print. Damascus n.d., 4 vols.—9. *Akhbār al-nisāʾ* C. 1307 and others.—10. *Risāla fi ʾkhtiyārāt Taqī*

al-Dīn b. Taymiyya, author? Berl. 2096.—11. *Zād al-maʿād fī hady khayr al-ʿibād*, vol. 2. *Br. Mus. Quart.* XI 84, vol. 3. Alex. Fun. 133,$_5$, Cairo I, ^{1}346, ^{2}121, *Dībāja* Gotha 2,$_3$.—12. *Shifāʾ al-ʿalīl fī 'l-qaḍāʾ wal-ḥikma wal-taʿlīl* Cairo ^{1}II, 32, ^{2}I, 194.—13. *Tabʿīd al-shayṭān bi-taqrīb ighāthat al-lahfān* (*fī maṣāʾid al-shayṭān*), against the veneration of tombs, Garr. 1905. Abstracts: a. Rūmī Ef., Berl. 2657/9.—b. Anon., Cairo ^{1}VII, 519.—14. *Miftāḥ dār al-saʿāda wa-manshūr alwiyat al-ʿilm wal-irāda*, on mysticism, AS 2085, ed. Maḥmūd Ḥ. Rabīʿ, C. 1939.—15. *Ṭarīq al-hijratayn wa-bāb al-maʿādatayn* Berl. 3276, 8795, Fātiḥ 2737.—16. *al-Kalim al-ṭayyib fī 'l-ʿamal al-ṣāliḥ*, on prayer, Berl. 3697.—17. *Jilāʾ al-afhām fī faḍl al-ṣalāt ʿalā khayr al-anām*, on prayer for the Prophet, Berl. 3915/6, Algiers 796,$_1$, Bursa, Ulu Cami Taş. 56,$_1$.—18. *al-Dāʾ wal-dawāʾ*, on the secret powers of the Qurʾān as a cure, Berl. 6295/6, Br. Mus. Suppl. 238, Cairo ^{1}III, 519, ^{2}I, 345.—19. *al-Ṭibb al-nabawī* Paris 3045, Upps. 348.—20. *Ṭibb al-qulūb*, on the effects of supernatural cures, extracted from a larger work, Berl. 4161.—21. *Tuḥfat al-mawdūd bi-aḥkām al-mawlūd*, on the ritual handling of newborns, Paris 2094.—22. *Kitāb al-rūḥ*, answers to 21 questions on the destiny of man after death, Vienna 1533, Ind. Off. 172, Esc. ^{2}699, 1590, 1592, Cairo | ^{1}II, 104, 168, abstract by Ismāʿīl b. Muḥammad 129
b. Bardis (p. 34) entitled *Asʾila ʿadīda wa-ajwiba mufīda*, Heid. ZDMG 91, 381.—23. 105 verses on bliss in paradise, Berl. 7859.—24. *Ḥādi 'l-arwāḥ ilā bilād al-afrāḥ*, a depiction of paradise to strengthen the true faith and as a proper preparation for the life to come, Berl. 8798, Leid. 2023, Br. Mus. Or. 8090, 9259, Paris 1387, Esc. ^{2}1591, AS 2259, Cairo ^{1}VI, 133, ^{2}I, 285, print. C. 1938, see F. Cooke, *The Moslem World* 1937, p. 1/18.—25. *Kitāb al-furūsiyya etc.* see Suppl.—26. *al-Shāfiya lil-amrāḍ al-fāshiya*, a paraenesis inspired by a sojourn in Egypt, where he had seen preachers and reciters of the Qurʾān go astray, so that instead of serving their religion, they only brought it harm, Berl. 8800.—27. *Ḥadīth*, taken from one of his works, Gotha 864,$_8$.—28. *Madārij al-sālikīn* see Suppl. I, 774,$_6$.—30.–52. see Suppl. (35. Patna II, 556,$_{2932,1}$. 40. Br. Mus. Or. 9219, 47. C. 1344).

5. Muḥammad b. Mufliḥ b. Muḥammad b. Mufarraj al-Qāqūnī al-Maqdisī al-Ḥanbalī, d. 763/1361, see Suppl.

1. *Uṣūl al-fiqh* Berl. 4399.—2. *Kitāb al-furūʿ* Cairo ^{1}III, 295, ^{2}I, 550.—3. *al-Ādāb al-sharʿiyya wal-maṣāliḥ al-marʿiyya* Cairo ^{1}II, 107, ^{2}I, 260.—4. See Suppl.

6. Zayn al-Dīn Abu 'l-Faraj ʿAbd al-Raḥmān b. Aḥmad b. Rajab al-Sālimī al-Baghdādī al-Ḥanbalī was born in Baghdad in Rabīʿ I 709/August 1309, moved with his father to Damascus where he became a preacher, and died in Rajab 795/May 1393.

DK II, 321 no. 2276, *Ḥuff.* XXIV, 1, Wüst. *Gesch.* 441. 1. See Suppl.—2. *Kitāb al-tawḥīd* Gotha 702.—3. *Aḥwāl al-qubūr*, on the condition of the dead between death and resurrection, Berl. 2661. Alex. Mawāʿiẓ 6.—4. *al-Takhwīf min al-nār wal-taʿrīf bi-ḥāl dār al-bawār* ibid. 2697.—5. *Laṭāʾif al-maʿārif li-mawāsim al-ʿāmm min al-waẓāʾif*, on religious duties in the different months, Berl. 3816/7, Leid. 2166, Alex. Mawāʿiẓ 34, Cairo ^{1}II, 171, VI, 188, ^{2}I, 331, App. 197, Patna I, $150_{,1433}$, print. C. 1924, abstract Berl. 3818.—6. *Kitāb al-istikhrāj li-aḥkām al-kharāj* Paris 2454.—7. *Ṭabaqāt al-Ḥanābila* see Suppl. *Dhayl* by Muḥammad b. ʿAlī b. ʿAlī b. ʿUthmān b. Jamāʿa al-Najdī (see Suppl. II, 812), Patna II, $317_{,2468}$.—8. *Ikhtiyār*
130 *al-abrār* | a section from which on the merits of the first four caliphs, of Fāṭima and of Fiḍḍa, Berl. 9690.—9. *Sharḥ khamsīna ḥadīthan min Jawāmiʿ al-kalim* (Suppl. $125_{,141}$) AS 571.—9a. *Jāmiʿ al-ʿulūm* I, $499_{,6}$.—10.–16. see Suppl. (13. Alex. Fun. $160_{,6}$).—17. *Faḍāʾil al-Shām* Alex. Taʾr. 108.—18. *Mashyakha*, see al-Kattānī, *Fihris* II, 60.—19. See I, $663_{,29a}$.

7. Aḥmad b. Abī Bakr b. Aḥmad b. ʿAlī al-Qādirī al-Ḥanbalī wrote, in 831/1428 in Aleppo:

Tanbīh al-ghāfilīn al-ḥayārā ʿalā mā warada min al-nahy ʿani ʾl-tashabbuh bil-Naṣārā, against innovations that resemble Christian teachings, Berl. 2105.—2. *Dhamm al-kāfir al-jaḥūd min al-umma al-ghaḍabiyya wal-Yahūd* ibid. 2016.—3. *Tuḥfat al-ʿābid fī faḍl bināʾ al-masājid* 3581.—4. *Waʿẓ fī taḥdhīr man ʿamila ʿamal qawm Lūṭ*, against sodomy, ibid. 5592.—5. *Kashf al-sirr ʿan masʾalat al-rūḥ kayfa taṣʿad wa-tanzil wa-taghdū wa-tarūḥ* ibid. 5362.—b. *Arbaʿūn* Patna I, $37_{,381}$.

8. Jamāl al-Dīn Abu ʾl-Maḥāsin Yūsuf b. Badr al-Dīn Abū Muḥammad al-Ḥasan b. Aḥmad al-Dimashqī al-Maqdisī al-Ḥanbalī b. ʿAbd al-Hādī b. al-Mibrad, d. 909/1503.

Al-Kattānī, *Fihris* II, 453, Wüst. *Gesch.* 495. 1. *Bulghat al-ḥathīth ilā ʿilm al-ḥadīth* Berl. 1119.—2. *Tuḥfat al-wuṣūl ilā ʿilm al-uṣūl*, autograph dated 865/1461, ibid. 1828.—3. *al-Radd ʿalā man shaddada wa-ʿassara fī jawāz al-uḍḥiyya bi-mā tayassara*, a refutation of those who maintain that on the occasion of festive offerings it is inadmissible to slaughter any animals other than the *bahīmat al-anʿām*, i.e. camels, cows, and sheep, ibid. 4051.—4. *Ghāyat al-suʾūl ilā ʿilm al-uṣūl*, autograph dated 865/1461, ibid. 4418.—5. *Maqbūl al-manqūl min ʿilmay al-jadal wal-uṣūl* ibid. 4419, commentary *al-Zuhūr al-bahiyya fī sharḥ al-Fiqhiyya*, an abstract of a commentary by Muḥammad b. ʿĪsā b. Kinnān al-Ḥanafī, d. 1153/1740 (p. 299), but this may be on *ʿUmdat al-mubtadiʾ*, ḤKh

IV, 8350, ibid. 4420.—6. *al-Thamara al-rāʾiqa fī ʿilm al-ʿarabiyya* ibid. 6768. |— 108
7. *Maḥḍ al-ṣawāb fī faḍāʾil amīr al-muʾminīn ʿUmar b. al-Khaṭṭāb* ibid. 9704.—8. *Taʾrīkh al-Ṣāliḥiyya*, corrected and supplemented by Muḥammad b. Kinnān (see above), with the title *al-Murūj al-sandaliyya al-fayḥiyya bi-taʾrīkh al-Ṣāliḥiyya* ibid. 9789.—9. *Baḥr al-dam fī-man takallama fī-hi Aḥmad b. Ḥanbal bi-madḥ aw dhamm*, Aḥmad b. Ḥanbal's views on the transmitters, ibid.
9957.—10. *al-Durra al-muḍīʾa wal-ʿarūs al-marḍiyya wal-shajara* | *al-nabawiyya* 131
AS 1450, Cairo V, ^{1}54, ^{2}181, lith. Būlāq 1285, Bombay 1289.—11. *Nuzhat al-sāmir bi-akhbār Majnūn b. ʿĀmir* (I, 43) Gotha 1836.—12. *Marāqi ʾl-jinān bil-sakhāʾ wa-qaḍāʾ ḥawāʾij al-ikhwān wa-idrāk al-suʿūd bil-karam wal-jūd* Esc. ^{2}770.—13.–47. see Suppl.—48.–82. ibid. $947_{,151}$.

E The Shīʿa

1. Jamāl (Shams) al-Dīn Abū ʿAbdallāh Muḥammad b. Makkī al-ʿĀmilī al-Jizzīnī al-Shahīd al-Awwal al-ʿAllāma al-Thānī was imprisoned by Baydamur, the governor of Damascus, because of his Shīʿī sympathies. After being held for one year, he was put to death on 19 Jumādā I 782/22 August 1380.[1]

RAAD IX 273/6. 1. *al-Lumʿa al-Dimashqiyya*, on the legal views of the Imāmīs, see Suppl. Patna I, $89_{,908,12}$.—Commentaries: a. *al-Rawḍa al-bahiyya* by Zayn al-Dīn b. ʿAlī al-Shāmī al-ʿĀmilī al-Shahīd al-Thānī, d. 966/1559 (p. 325), Berl. 4602, Br. Mus. Suppl. 334, glosses thereon by ʿAlī b. Muḥammad b. Ḥasan b. Zayn al-Dīn al-ʿĀmilī, d. 1103/1692, Ind. Off. 1839, another 1536, by Shaykh Jaʿfar, *qāḍī* in Isfahan 12th/18th cent., ibid. 1838 (see Suppl. b. c.), another *Ḥāshiya* ibid. 1837.—b–i. See Suppl. (i. read: al-Gharawiyya, see p. 498).—k. *al-Anwār al-Gharawiyya* in 10 vols. by Muḥammad al-Jawād b. Taqī b. Muḥammad Mollā Kitāb al-Aḥmadī al-Bayātī al-Najafī, d. 1267/1851, MS *Dharīʿa* II, $435_{,1700}$.—2.–7. See Suppl. (4. also Ind. Off. 1804/6, 31 commentaries *Dharīʿa* II, 296/7; as a supplement thereto *Bayān al-mustaḥabbāt fī ʾl-ṣalāt* Ind. Off. 1807).—8. *al-Asʾila al-Miqdādiyya*, questions asked by Miqdād b. ʿAbdallāh b. Muḥammad al-Suyūrī, d. 826/1423 (Suppl. II, $209_{,4}$), in *Majmūʿat Rasāʾil Aḥmad b. Fahd al-Ḥillī* in Mashhad, *Dharīʿa* II, $92_{,365}$.—9. *Arbaʿūna ḥadīthan fī ʾl-ʿibādāt*, MSS *Dharīʿa* I, $427_{,2185}$, printed together with *Ghaybat al-Nuʿmānī* Pers. 1378.—10. *al-Arbaʿūn masaʾla fī ʾl-kalām* or *al-Masāʾil al-arbaʿīniyya*, contained in the *Mukhtaṣar Taʾrīkh al-Shīʿa* of Aḥmad ʿĀrif al-Zayn al-ʿĀmilī, print. in Sidon, ibid. $436_{,2206}$.

1 This and no other is the correct date, and not 786 as stated in Ahlw. loc. cit., since the governor who had put him to death was himself ousted in 782, see Rieu loc. cit.

2. His student Ḥasan b. Sulaymān b. Khālid al-Ḥillī.

132 | 1. *Ithbāt al-rajʿa*, in the library of the Rājā of Fayḍābād and the Madrasat Fāḍil Khān in Mashhad, *Dharīʿa* I, $91,_{1039}$.—2a–6. see Suppl. (4. *RAAD* IX, 341.—3. *Nūr ḥadaq al-badīʿ* Qawala II, 178).

7 Sciences of the Qurʾān

1. Sulaymān b. ʿAbd al-Qawī b. ʿAbd al-Karīm b. Abi ʾl-ʿAbbās Najm al-Dīn al-Ṭawfī al-Ḥanbalī, who was born in Ṭawf near Baghdad in 657/1259, moved, via Damascus, to Cairo. There, he became embroiled in a controversy with Saʿd al-Dīn al-Ḥārithī, was accused of being a Shīʿī, and expelled. He took up residence in the house of a Christian in Qūṣ, and died in Hebron in Rajab 716/ September–October 1316.

109 | *DK* II, 154, no. 1850. 1. On numbers in the Qurʾān, Berl. 436.—2. *Īḍāḥ al-bayān ʿan maʿnā umm al-Qurʾān*, on the meaning of the name of sura three, in three sections, the third of which explains the text, composed in Rajab 711/November 1311 in Cairo, Berl. 940.—3. *Tafsīr sūrat Qāf* (no. 50), written in that same month, ibid. 956.—4. *Tafsīr sūrat al-Nabaʾ* (no. 78), composed the same month, ibid. 964.—5. *Qudwat al-muhtadīn ilā maqāṣid al-dīn* or *Ḥallāl al-ʿuqad fī bayān aḥkām al-muʿtaqad*, a short treatise on dogmatics, composed in 711/1311 in Cairo, ibid. 1795.—6. *al-Ṣaʿqa al-ghaḍabiyya fi ʾl-radd ʿalā munkir al-ʿarabiyya* Cairo ^{1}VII, 275.—7.–13. see Suppl.—14. *Ibṭāl al-ḥiyal* quoted by Ibn Ḥajar, *DK* I, $153,_{15}$.

2. Shihāb al-Dīn Abu ʾl-ʿAbbās Aḥmad b. Muḥammad b. Yaḥyā al-Nābulusī al-Dimashqī Sibṭ al-Sulʿūs, who was born in 687/1288 and died in 732/1333.

DK I, 305, no. 775, al-Jazarī *Ṭab*. 621. *Al-Ikhtiyār al-Khalafī*, 66 verses on the reading of Khalaf, AS $39,_{4}$, (Ritter).

2a. Burhān al-Dīn Abu ʾl-ʿAbbās Ibrāhīm b. ʿUmar b. Ibrāhīm b. Khalīl b. al-Sarrāj al-Jaʿbarī, d. 732/1333, see Suppl.

5. *al-Wāḍiḥa etc.* Berl. 542, Garr. 1211, Köpr II, 2, Fātiḥ Waqf Ibr. $28,_{8}$.—Commentaries: b. Garr. 1212, Fātiḥ $42,_{3}$.—c. Anon., Garr. 1213/4, Fātiḥ Waqf Ibr. 65, to, 1.–20. *Ḥusn al-madad etc.* Fātiḥ Waqf Ibr. $14,_{1}$, Qawala I, $13,_{20}$.—
133 25. *Dīwān* C. 1324.—26. *Iʿlām al-ẓurafāʾ fī ayyām | al-khulafāʾ*, a *qaṣīda* with a commentary written for the Cairene caliph al-Mustakfī (701–41/1301–39), AS $39,_{5}$.—27. *al-Ijzāʾ fī maʿrifat al-ajzāʾ* Fātiḥ Waqf Ibr. $14,_{2}$ (Ritter).

3. ʿImād al-Dīn al-Ḥusayn b. Abī Bakr b. al-Ḥusayn Qāḍi ʾl-Iskandariyya al-Kindī al-Naḥwī al-Mālikī, d. 741/1340.

Al-Kafīl bi-maʿāni ʾl-tanzīl Cairo ^{1}I, 193, ^{2}I, 59.

4. ʿAlāʾ al-Dīn ʿAlī b. Muḥammad b. Ibrāhīm al-Khāzin al-Shīḥī al-Baghdādī, whose family hailed from Shīḥa near Aleppo, was born in Baghdad in 678/1279. He studied there and in Damascus, and became a librarian in the Sumaysāṭiyya in Aleppo, where he died at the end of Rajab or the beginning of Shaʿbān of the year 741/1340—1.

DK III, $97_{,221}$. 1. *Lubāb al-taʾwīl fī maʿāni ʾl-tanzīl*, mostly following the *Maʿālim al-tanzīl* of al-Baghawī (I, 449), completed in 725/1325, Berl. 878/80, Paris 639/42, 5750, Algiers 342/6, *Giorn. Soc. As. It.* X, 53, AS 260/8, Sarajevo 62, NO 425/43, Köpr. 60/2, Garr. 1266, Qawala I, 78/9, Makr. 53, printings Cairo I, 194, *OB* VI, 4863, Sarkis 809. Abstract Paris $659_{,7}$.—2. *Maqbūl al-manqūl*, in 10 books from the *Musnad* of al-Shāfiʿī and Aḥmad b. Ḥanbal, the 6 books, the *Muwaṭṭaʾ*, and al-Dāraquṭnī, Garr. 1392, Cairo I, ^{1}428, ^{2}150, ḤKh ^{1}VI, 12729, *Dībāja* Gotha $2_{,14}$.

4a. Abu ʾl-Ḥasan ʿAlī b. Abī Muḥammad b. Saʿd al-Qurashī al-Wāsiṭī al-Dīwānī was born in 636/1238 and died in 743/1342.

Ibn al-Jazarī, *Ṭab.* 2352. A *qaṣīda* on the 10 readers, AS $39_{,6}$ (Ritter).

5. Abū Ḥayyān Muḥammad b. Yūsuf b. ʿAlī b. Yūsuf b. Ḥayyān al-Gharnāṭī al-Jayyānī al-Nafzī Athīr al-Dīn was born towards the end of Shawwāl 654/November 1256 in Matakhshāras, near Granada. His family originated in Jaén and belonged to the Berber tribe of Nafza. From 670/1272 onward, he studied the Qurʾān and linguistics in Malaga. After a conflict with his teacher Abū Jaʿfar b. al-Zubayr, he was forced to leave Spain. After extensive travels through Egypt, the Hijaz, and Syria | he took up residence in Cairo, in time to follow 134
the lectures of Bahāʾ al-Dīn Muḥammad b. al-Naḥḥās. After the latter's death, he took over his chair of grammar in 698/1298 and taught *tafsīr* and *ḥadīth* at al-Qubba al-Manṣūriyya and the art of reading the Qurʾān at the al-Aqmar mosque. In 735/1335 he accepted a professorship at the Ṣāliḥiyya. After initially having sided with the Ẓāhirīs, he joined Ibn Taymiyya after he was restored to honour in Cairo. Later he became one of the strictest of Shāfiʿīs, | accusing Ibn 110
Taymiyya of *tajsīm* (anthropomorphism) in his Qurʾān commentary. He died on 28 Ṣafar 745/11 July 1345.

DK IV, 302, no. 832, al-Ṣāfadī, *al-Wāfī* AS 2969$_{,110/24}$, Maqqarī I, 823ff, 862, *Fawāt* II, 282, al-Suyūṭī, *Ḥusn al-muḥ.* I, 307, al-Zarkashī, *Taʾrīkh al-dawlatayn*, Tunis 1289, 63/4, al-Kattānī, *Fihris* I, 108, *Orient.* II, 382, Wüst. *Gesch.* 409, Goldziher, *Ẓāhir.* 187/93, Hartmann, *Muw.* 11, Pons Boigues no. 268. 1. *al-Baḥr al-muḥīṭ fī tafsīr al-Qurʾān*, AS 126/34, Rāġib 58/61, Yeni 31/2, NO 191/201.—Abstracts: a. *al-Nahr al-mādd*, by the author himself, Berl. 882 (fragm.), Esc. ^{2}1261, Algiers 347, Köpr. 67, Cairo ^{1}I, 220, ^{2}I, 65.—b. *al-Durr al-laqīṭ* by Ibn Maktūm (no. 6), Yeni 44/7, Köpr. 96, Cairo ^{1}I, 171, ^{2}I, 48.—2. *Tuḥfat al-arīb* (*adīb*) *fī mā fi ʾl-Qurʾān min al-gharīb* Paris 644$_{,1}$, print. C. 1926.—3. *Ghāyat al-iḥsān* with a commentary, *al-Nukat al-ḥisān*, Berl. 6697.—4. *Irtishāf al-ḍarab min lisān al-ʿArab* NO 4526/7, Cairo ^{1}IV, 21, ^{2}171.—5. *al-Lumḥa fi ʾl-naḥw*, a commentary by Muḥammad b. ʿAbd al-Salām al-Birmāwī, d. 831/1427, Br. Mus. 514$_{,1}$.—6. Two panegyrical *qaṣīdas* on al-Zamakhsharī and on syntax, Berl. 7848$_{,2}$.—7. *Sharḥ al-Tashīl li-Ibn Mālik* I, 359.—8. *Sharḥ Alfiyyat Ibn Mālik* ibid. 360.—9. *al-Shadhā fī aḥkām kadhā*, revised by his student Ibn Hishām, p. 31.—10.–20. see Suppl. (14. *ʿIqd al-laʾālīʾ etc.* after the example of *Ḥirz al-amānī* I, 520, commentary *Nukat al-amānī*, Patna I, 21$_{,185}$).—21. *Hidāyat al-naḥw*, on which anonymous glosses *Dirāyat al-hidāya*, Indian print n.d. (Alex. Naḥw 16).

6. Tāj al-Dīn Abū Muḥammad b. ʿAbd al-Qādir b. Maktūm al-Qaysī al-Ḥanafī,
135 who was born towards the end of Dhu ʾl-Ḥijja 682/March | 1284, was an acting judge and died during the great plague in Ramaḍān 749/December 1348.

DK I, 175, no. 451, Ibn Quṭl. no. 28, al-Suyūṭī, *Ḥusn al-muḥ.* I, 268. 1. *al-Durr al-laqīṭ* see no. 5. 1. a.—2. 9 *rajaz* verses in praise of learning, Berl. 8158$_{,2}$.

7. Shams al-Dīn Abu ʾl-Thanāʾ Maḥmūd b. ʿAbd al-Raḥmān al-Iṣfahānī al-Shāfiʿī, d. 749/1348 in Cairo, see Suppl.

Al-Ṣafadī, *al-Wāfī*, AS 2969$_{,154/6}$, Al-Yāfiʿī, *Mirʾāt al-jin.* (places his death in the year 746) followed by Khwandamīr, *HS* III, 1, 132. 1. *Anwār al-ḥaqāʾiq al-rabbāniyya fi ʾl-tafsīr* Köpr. 45, AS 176/7, Rāġib 62/5, Cairo ^{1}I, 142.—2. *Sharḥ Minhāj al-Bayḍāwī* I, 533.—3. *Maṭāliʿ al-anẓār fī sharḥ Ṭawāliʿ al-anwār* ibid.—4.–7. see Suppl.—8. *Bayān mushkil al-Badīʿ* Suppl. I, 658.

111 | 8. Muḥammad b. Aḥmad b. ʿAbd al-Muʾmin b. al-Labbān al-Miṣrī died of the plague in Cairo in Shawwāl 749/January 1349, see Suppl.

Al-Suyūṭī, *Ḥusn al-muḥ.* I, 242, Khwandamīr *ḤS* III, 2, 9. 1. *Tafsīr al-Qurʾān* Cairo I, ^{1}14, ^{2}37.—2. *Mutashābihāt al-Qurʾān* Paris 645$_{,1}$, Cairo ^{1}VII, 137.—

3. *Radd maʿāni 'l-āyāt al-mutashābihāt* Berl. 716, Garr. 1292, by Ibn ʿArrāq, d. 933/1527, prefixed to his *Jawharat al-ghawwāṣ*, Berl. 427.—4. See Suppl.

9. Shihāb al-Dīn Abu 'l-ʿAbbās Aḥmad b. Yūsuf b. ʿAbd al-Dāʾim b. Muḥammad b. Masʿūd b. Ibrāhīm b. al-Samīn al-Naḥwī al-Shāfiʿī was a student of Abū Ḥayyān and acting judge in Cairo, and died in Jumādā II 756/June 1355.

RA 149v, al-Suyūṭī, *Ḥusn al-muḥ.* I, 309. 1. *al-Durr al-maṣūn fī ʿulūm al-kitāb al-maknūn*, especially on matters of grammar, which is why it is also called *Iʿrāb Ibn al-Samīn*, criticised by al-Suyūṭī in his *Itqān* for being too long-winded (ḤKh, [1]I, 354, [2]I, 122) Gotha 533, AS 75/7, Rāġib 24/8, Yeni 48/50, Köpr. 99, Cairo I, [1]171, [2]48, Algiers 348.—2. *ʿUmdat al-ḥuffāẓ fī tafsīr ashraf al-alfāẓ* AS 431, Rāġib 199, 200, NO 584, Cairo I, 181, [2]55.—3. *al-Qawl al-wajīz fī aḥkām al-kitāb al-ʿazīz* Cairo I, [1]189, [2]58.

10. Khiḍr b. ʿAbd al-Raḥmān al-Azdī, who died in 773/1371.

Al-Tibyān fī tafsīr al-Qurʾān NO 244.

| 11. Aḥmad b. ʿAlī b. ʿAbd al-Raḥmān al-Bilbaysī, d. 779/1377. 136

Muʿīn al-muqriʾ al-niḥrīr ʿalā ma 'khtuṣṣa bihi 'l-ʿUnwān wal-Qaṣīda wal-Taysīr, an abstract of the *ʿUnwān* of Ismāʿīl, d. 455/1063, from the *Shāṭibiyya* and the *Taysīr* (I, 517, 520), Berl. 621.

12. Shihāb al-Dīn Abū Jaʿfar Aḥmad b. Yūsuf b. Mālik al-Ruʿaynī al-Gharnāṭī al-Mālikī studied together with his compatriot Ibn Jābir (p. 14) in Cairo under Ibn Ḥayyān and, after their joint pilgrimage, in Damascus under al-Mizzī. They then lived for some years in Aleppo and finally in al-Bīra on the Euphrates, where he died in 779/1377.

RA 19r. 1. *Tuḥfat al-aqrān fī-mā quriʾa bil-tathlīth min ḥurūf al-Qurʾān*, composed in 745/1344 in al-Bīra, Paris 4452,$_1$. |—2. *Iqtiṭāf al-azāhir waltiqāṭ al-jawāhir*, a 112
compilation of all Arabic verbs of which the second radical has an a in the perfect, and a u or an i in the imperfect tense, Gotha 398 (V, 14).—3. *Sharḥ Badīʿiyyat al-ʿimyān* of his friend Ibn Jābir, p. 14.—4. *Sharḥ qaṣīdat al-ẓāʾ* by the same, ibid.—5. See Suppl.

13. Qāḍi 'al-quḍāt Burhān al-Dīn Ibrāhīm b. ʿAbd al-Raḥīm b. Muḥammad b. Jamāʿa al-Kinānī al-Shāfiʿī was born in Cairo in Rabīʿ II 725/March–April 1325

and studied there and in Damascus. Before he took on a position as a preacher in Jerusalem, he let himself be represented by a deputy. In Jumādā II 773/December 1371 he became chief judge of Egypt and a professor at the Ṣalāḥiyya in Cairo, but returned to Jerusalem the next year. Having again been appointed chief judge of Egypt in 781/1379, he went as *qāḍī* to Damascus in 785/1383, where he died in 790/1388.

DK I, 38, no. 95, *RA* 113 v. 1. *Tafsīr* in 10 vols., lost.—2. *al-Fawāʾid al-Qudsiyya wal-farāʾid al-ʿitriyya*, separate remarks on passages from the Qurʾān and *ḥadīth*, Berl. 1439.—3. *Naṣīḥa fī dhamm al-ghināʾ wastimāʿihi* ibid. 5510.—4. A prohibition of music in the form of a fatwa from the year 772/1370, when he was still a preacher in Jerusalem, ibid. 5511.

137 | 14. Abu ʾl-ʿAbbās Aḥmad b. ʿAlī b. Muḥammad al-Maqdisī al-Ḥanafī b. al-Naqīb, who was born in 771/1369 and died in 816/1413.

1. *Kitāb al-muwāfaqāt allatī waqaʿat fi ʾl-Qurʾān al-ʿaẓīm li-amīr al-muʾminīn Abī Ḥafṣ ʿUmar b. al-Khaṭṭāb al-ʿAdawī al-Qurashī*, on the basis of an unidentified source, following the order of the suras and augmented with *isnād*s from the *Kitāb faḍāʾil al-ṣaḥāba*, Berl. 468.—2. See Suppl.

15. Ṣadaqa b. Sallām b. al-Ḥusayn al-Maṣḥarānī, who came from Maṣḥara near Damascus, studied in Cairo in 784/1382 and wrote, around 816/1413:

Kitāb al-tatimma fi ʾl-qirāʾāt al-thalāth, following the last 3 of the 10 canonical readers: al-Qaʿqāʿ, d. 130/747, Yaʿqūb al-Ḥaḍramī, d. 205/820, and Khalaf al-Bazzār, d. 229/843, Br. Mus. Suppl. 90, Cairo ^{2}I, 16.

16. ʿAbd al-Raḥmān b. ʿUmar (p. 114) b. Raslān b. Nuṣayr b. Ṣāliḥ al-Bulqīnī (Bulqaynī) Jalāl al-Dīn was born in Cairo in Jumādā I 762/March 1361 (or, according to others, in Ramaḍān 763/July 1363). In 767 he went to Damascus when his father became a *qāḍī* there, but then returned with him to Cairo. In
113 804/1401 he became *qāḍi ʾl-ʿaskar* in Cairo, | and after he had gained and lost this office several times, he died on 11 Shawwāl 824/9 September 1421.

RA 153r. 1. *Nahr al-ḥayāt*, a Qurʾān commentary composed in 789/1387, Br. Mus. 1553/7.—2. *al-Naṣīḥa fī dafʿ al-faḍīḥa*, on prerequisites for *qāḍī*s, Berl. 5615.

17. ʿAlāʾ al-Dīn ʿAlī b. Mūsā al-Rūmī, d. 841/1438, see Suppl.

Al-Suyūṭī, *Ḥusn al-muḥ.* I, 307. Answers to questions on the Qur'ān, *fiqh*, and *kalām*, Esc. $^{2}547_{,1}$.

18. Muḥammad b. Khalīl al-Qabāqibī, d. 849/1445, see Suppl.

1. *Majmaʿ al-surūr wa-maṭlaʿ al-shams wal-budūr*, on the readings of the Qur'ān, with a commentary entitled *Īḍāḥ al-rumūz wa-miftāḥ al-kunūz*, Berl. 669, Köpr.
27, Cairo I, $^{1}105$, $^{2}26$, Qawala I, 7, | Bank. XVIII, 1250.—2. *al-Mawāhib*, a poem 138
about the readings of the Qur'ān, Rāġib 15.—3. *Urjūzat al-tajwīd* Bank. XVIII, $1291_{,iii}$.—4. See Suppl.

19. Shams al-Dīn Muḥammad al-Nuwayrī was born in al-Maymūn, between Nuwayra and Cairo, in 801/1398, studied in Cairo and then, in 828/1425, under al-Jazarī in Mecca. He then lived in Gaza, Jerusalem, and Damascus, and died in 857/1453 in Mecca.

Khiṭ. jad. XVII, 16 (after al-Sakhāwī, not in the *Ḍaw'*). 1. *al-Qawl al-jādhdh li-man qara'a bil-shādhdh*, against the use of abnormal readings, Br. Mus. Suppl. 91.—2. *Sharḥ Ṭayyibat al-nashr lil-Jazarī* (p. 202) Bodl. I, 660.

20. Muḥammad b. Aḥmad b. Muḥammad b. Ibrāhīm Abū ʿAbdallāh al-Anṣārī al-Maḥallī al-Shāfiʿī Jalāl al-Dīn, born in 791/1389, was a professor of *fiqh* at al-Mu'ayyadiyya and al-Barqūqiyya in Cairo, and died on 1 Muḥarram 864/28 October 1459.

RA 323v, al-Suyūṭī, *Ḥusn al-muḥ.* I, 232, *Khiṭ. jad.* XV, 21. 1. *Tafsīr al-Jalālayn*, completed by his student al-Suyūṭī, p. 145.—2. *al-Qawl al-mufīd fi 'l-Nīl al-saʿīd*, a collection of verses from the Qur'ān, *ḥadīth*, and passages from Masʿūdī and other writers, about the Nile, Paris 2259/60, Cairo ^{1}V, 156, ^{2}VI, 51.—3. *al-Ṭibb al-nabawī* Paris $2800_{,16}$,—4. *Sharḥ al-Burda* I, $308_{,14}$.—5. *Sharḥ Kitāb al-waraqāt* I, 487.—6. *Sharḥ Minhāj al-Nawawī* I, 497.—7. *Sharḥ Jamʿ al-jawāmiʿ lil-Subkī* p. 109.

21. Muḥammad b. Aḥmad b. Yūsuf al-shahīr wāliduhu bi-Ibn akhī ʿAbd al-Ḥamīd al-Mālikī al-Azharī wrote, in 874/1469:

Fawātiḥ al-raḥmān fī tajwīd al-Qur'ān AS $4825_{,2}$.

22. Sirāj al-Dīn Abū Ḥafṣ ʿUmar (ʿAmr) b. ʿAlī b. ʿĀdil al-Ḥanbalī al-Dimashqī wrote, in 880/1475:

Al-Lubāb fī ʿulūm al-kitāb Algiers 360, Garr. 1275, AS 254/6, Cairo I, [1]197, [2]60, fragm. Esc. [2]II, 744.

23. Abū ʿAbdallāh Muḥammad b. Sulaymān al-Muḥyawī al-Kāfiyajī, who was
139 born in 788/1386 or just after in Kökjākī in Ṣarukhān, | studied in Tabriz and Cairo, became a professor at the Shaykhūniyya there, and died on 4 Jumādā I 879/17 September 1474.

Al-Suyūṭī, *Ḥusn al-muḥ.* I, 317, Ṭāshköprīzāde, *ShN*I, 123. 1. *al-Taysīr fī qawāʿid al-tafsīr*, composed in 856/1452, NO 476, Cairo [1]VII, 445, [2]I, 43.—2. *Tafsīr āyāt mutashābihāt* AS 178.—3. *Nuzhat al-ikhwān fī tafsīr qawlihi taʿālā yā Lūṭ innā rusulu rabbika* (p. 11, 83) AS 413.—4. *al-Bishāra fī qawlihi taʿālā faʾtū bi-sūratin min mithlihi* (p. 2, 21), composed on 7 Rabīʿ I 870/29 October 1465, Cairo [1]VII, 448.—5. *Nayl al-marām*, on the same verse, completed on 27 Ṣafar 870/19 October 1465, ibid.—6. *Risāla fī ʿilm al-tafsīr wa-wujūh al-qirāʾāt* Cairo [1]VII, 448.—7. *Kashf al-niqāb lil-aṣḥāb wal-aḥbāb*, completed on 27 Rabīʿ I 870/18 October 1465, ibid. [2]I, 58.—8. *Anwār al-saʿāda fī sharḥ kalimatay al-shahāda*, Berl. 2473/8, Cairo [1]II, 5, VII, 547, 579, [2]I, 165.—9. *al-Faraḥ wal-surūr fī ʾl-madhāhib*, on the 4 orthodox schools of *fiqh* in Islam, Berl. 2808, Br. Mus. Suppl. 322$_{,1}$, anon. comm. dated 869/1465, ibid. 2.—10. *Zayn al-faraḥ bi-mīlād al-nabī* Cairo [1]II, 447.—11. *Khulāṣat al-aqwāl fī ḥadīth Innama ʾl-aʿmāl*
115 *bil-niyyāt* AS 525. |—12. *al-Kāfī fī bayān al-ṣaff al-ṭawīl al-mustaqīm al-nāʾī ʿani ʾl-Kaʿba fī ʾl-shamāl wal-janūb aw al-sharq wal-gharb* Cairo [1]VII, 315, 447.—13. *al-Iḥkām fī maʿrifat al-īmān wal-aḥkām*, completed on 5 Jumādā I 866/6 February 1462, ibid. 446, [2]I, 455.—14. *al-Durra al-ghāliya al-ʿāliya al-nūrāniyya wal-alṭāf al-sharīfa al-rabbāniyya*, completed on 25 Jumādā I 877/29 October 1472, Cairo [1]VII, 446.—15. A question on *waqf*, ibid. 663.—16. *Qalāʾid al-ʿiqyān fī baḥr faḍāʾil shahr Rajab wa-Shaʿbān* ibid. 175.—17. *al-Hidāya li-bayān al-khalq wal-takwīn*, completed on 20 Jumādā I 870/9 January 1466, ibid. 175.—18. *Banāt al-afkār fī shaʾn al-iʿtibār*, completed on 22 Jumādā I 870/11 January 1466, ibid.—19. *Ramz al-khiṭāb bi-rashḥ al-ʿabāb*, completed on 10 Rabiʿ I 878/6 August 1473, ibid. [2]I, 187.—20. *Qarār al-wajd fī sharḥ al-ḥamd* Cairo [1]VII, 445.—21. *Ḥall al-ishkāl fī mabāḥith al-ashkāl* ibid. 446.—22. *Risāla fī ʾl-maḥabba* Berl. 5410$_{,3}$.—23. *al-Rawḍa al-zāhira al-nāfiʿa fī ʾl-dunyā wal-ākhira*, on the merits of Friday prayer, Paris 1126$_{,3}$.—24. *al-Nuzha fī rawḍat al-rūḥ wal-nafs* Berl. Ms. or. fol. 4249, Br. Mus. 433, Cairo [1]VII, 569.—25. *al-Ins al-anīs fī maʿrifat shaʾn al-nafs al-nafīs* Br. Mus. 433$_{,3}$, Cairo [1]VII, 569, [2]I, 245.—26. *Manāzil al-arwāḥ*
140 on Sufi eschatology, | Esc. [2]750$_{,1}$, Cairo [1]II, 137, [2]I, 363.—27. *Miʿrāj al-ṭabaqāt wa-rafʿ al-darajāt li-ahl al-fahm wal-thiqāt* (see Suppl.) Cairo [1]VII, 443.—28. *Qiblat al-arwāḥ* ibid. 445, 448.—29. *al-Kāfī ʾl-shāfī* ibid. 445.—30. *Mukhtaṣar*

fī ʿilm al-irshād ibid. 446.—31. *al-Mukhtaṣar al-mufīd fī ʾl-taʾrīkh*, completed on 8 Rajab 867/30 March 1463, ibid. V. 145, ^{2}V, 335, AS 3402/3.—32. *al-Ishrāq fī marātib al-ṭibāq* Cairo ^{1}VII, 446, ^{2}II, 176.—33. *al-Taḥrīr li-mā dhukira fī ʾl-Durr al-manẓūm wal-Washy al-marqūm* (I, 358) *min al-umūr al-thalātha allatī hiyaʾl-ghalaṭ wal-sahw wal-nisyān* Br. Mus. 433,$_{2}$.—34. *Nuzhat al-muʿrib fī ʾl-mashriq wal-maghrib* (*fī awjuh rafʿ wa-naṣb wa-jarr lafẓ akmal fī qawl ʿAbd al-Wahhāb b. Muḥammad b. Sharaf al-ḥamd wa-atammuhu*) Esc. ^{2}107,$_{8}$, Cairo ^{1}VII, 310, ^{2}II, 70.—35. *Ramz al-asrār fī masʾalat akmal* (*fī afʿal al-tafḍīl*), composed on 26 Ramaḍān 874/9 April 1470, Esc. ^{2}107,$_{7}$ (wrongly *al-kuḥl*), Cairo ^{1}VII, 311, ^{2}II, 115. Abstract by al-Suyūṭī, *Fajr al-thamd fī iʿrāb akmal al-ḥamd*, Berl. 6885, Patna II, 401,$_{2571,35}$.—36. *al-Mukhtār fī masʾalat akmal* Esc. ^{2}107,$_{6}$.—37. *Sharḥ Tahdhīb al-manṭiq* p. 215.—38.–50. see Suppl. (49. Berl. Ms. or. oct. 3745).—51. *Lawāmiʿ al-anwār fī ʾl-taṣawwuf* (according to others this was by Sirāj al-Dīn ʿUmar al-Hindī, d. 773/1371), Alex. Fun. 159,$_{4}$.

24. Zayn al-Dīn Abu ʾl-Fatḥ Jaʿfar b. Ibrāhīm b. Jaʿfar al-Sanhūrī al-Dihnī, born in Sanhūr around 810/1407, studied at the al-Azhar and became a reciter of the Qurʾān at the Muʾayyadiyya. In addition, he later received a professorship at the Ḥanafī Barqūqiyya, even though he was a Shāfiʿī. He died in Dhu ʾl-Qaʿda 894/October 1489.

Khiṭ. jad. XII, 60 (after al-Sakhāwī). *Al-Jāmiʿ al-mufīd fī ṣināʿat al-tajwīd*, completed in Ṣafar 847/June 1443, Berl. 527/8.

25. Abū Ḥafṣ ʿUmar b. Zayn al-Dīn Qāsim b. Shams al-Dīn Muḥammad al-Anṣārī al-Miṣrī al-Nashshār, ca. 900/1495.

| 1. *al-Mukarrar fī-mā tawātara fī* (*min*) *al-qirāʾāt al-sabʿ wa-taḥarrara*, a detailed 116
exposition of the 7 readings of the Qurʾān, Berl. 623, Fātiḥ Waqf Ibr. 33.—2. *al-Qaṭar al-Miṣrī fī qirāʾat Abī ʿAmr b. ʿAlāʾ al-Baṣrī*, in the *riwāya* of Ḥafṣ b. ʿUmar, d. 246/860 and of Ṣāliḥ b. Ziyād, d. 261/874, Berl. 639, Garr. 1226.—3.–5. See Suppl.—26. See Suppl. 28, 984,$_{14}$.

| 8 *Dogmatics and uṣūl al-dīn* 141

1. Muḥammad b. Muḥammad b. al-Muʿallim wrote, around 703/1303, after the victory of sultan Nāṣir b. Qalawūn over the Mongols:

1. *Najm al-muhtadī wa-rajm al-muʿtadī*, against the interpretation of the Qurʾān by a certain Ḥanbalī, citing various authorities from Abū Bakr up to the year 706, mostly Ashʿarīs, Paris 638.—2. *al-Irshād fī aḥwāl al-aʿmā* Patna I,

276,$_{2293}$ (which has Muḥammad b. Muḥammad b. Luqmān b. al-Muqayyad b. al-Muʿallim).

2. Ḥusām al-Dīn al-Ḥusayn b. ʿAlī b. Ḥajjāj al-Sighnāqī from Sighnāq[1] died, after 710/1310, in Aleppo.

1. *al-Tasdīd fī Sharḥ al-Tamhīd lil-Nasafī* (I, 547) Cairo ^{1}II, 11.—2. *Dāmighat al-mubtadiʾīn wa-nāṣirat al-muhtadīn* (according to others by Ḥusām al-Dīn al-Ḥasan b. Sharaf al-Ḥusaynī, d. 715/1315), Patna II, 429,$_{2603,3}$, a part of which Berl. 1390.

3. Muḥammad b. ʿAbd al-Raḥīm b. Muḥammad al-Hindī al-Urmawī Ṣafī al-Dīn al-Shāfiʿī was born in India in Rabīʿ I 644/July–August 1246, and left Delhi in Rajab 667/March 1269 on the pilgrimage to Mecca. From there he went to Yemen and Egypt, where he lived for four years. By way of Antioch, he then went to Konya and Sīwās, where he remained about five years in all. Then he spent another year in Qayṣariyya. In 685/1286 he went to Damascus where he became a professor at the Ẓāhiriyya and several other madrasas. He died on 29 Ṣafar 715/3 June 1315.

DK IV, 14/5, no. 29, al-Suyūṭī, *Ḥuṣn al-muḥ.* I, 314, *JA* S. IX, v. 3, p. 446. 1. *al-Fāʾiq fī uṣūl al-dīn* Cairo ^{1}II, 255.—2. *Nihāyat al-wuṣūl fī ʿilm al-uṣūl* ibid. 269.—3. See Suppl.

4. Abū Firās ʿUbaydallāh b. Shibl b. Firās b. Jamīl wrote, on 17 Rajab 725/30 June 1325:

142 | *Kitāb al-radd ʿala ʾl-Rāfiḍa wal-Yazīdiyya* Köpr. Majmūʿ 1717, see ʿAbbās al-ʿAzzāwī, *Taʾrīkh al-Yazīdiyya* 81 ff.

5. Raslān b. Sībawayh b. ʿAbdallāh b. ʿAbd al-Qādir al-Dimashqī, a contemporary of Taqī al-Dīn al-Subkī, died in 711/1370 (p. 106).

Risāla fi ʾl-tawḥīd, with a commentary by Ḥasan b. Mūsā al-Bānī al-Kurdī al-Dimashqī, d. 1148/1735 (p. 345), Alex. Tawḥīd 21.

---

1 The capital of the pagan Qipčāq people, not far from Otrār on the Syr Daryā, in al-Kāshgharī, *Dīwān lughāt al-Turk* I, 392. Sughnāq is today the archeological site of Sunak or Saganaq, see Barthold, *Turkestan*, 179, Abulghazi Romanzoff 60/1.

| 6. ʿIzz al-Dīn Muḥammad b. ʿAbd al-Hādī b. Ibrāhīm, ca. 830/1427. 117

Taḥrīr al-kalām fī masʾalat al-ruʾyā wa-tajwīdihi, on the teachings of the Muʿtazilis and the Ashʿaris with regard to the question of whether God can been seen by man, Berl. 2107.

7. ʿUmar b. Mūsā b. al-Ḥasan al-Ḥimṣī Sirāj al-Dīn, d. 861/1457, see Suppl.

Suṭūr al-iʿlām fī mabāni ʾl-īmān wal-islām Berl. 1825.

7a. ʿAlī b. Muḥammad b. ʿAbdallāh al-Fakhrī, ninth cent.

Talkhīṣ al-bayān fi dhikr firaq ahl al-adyān Pet. AM 94.

9 *Mysticism*

1. ʿAbd al-Ghaffār b. Aḥmad b. ʿAbd al-Ḥamīd (ʿAbd al-Majīd) b. Nūḥ al-Qūṣī al-Anṣārī al-Khazrajī had built a beautiful monastery for the Sufis in front of the gates of his hometown of Qūṣ. On a Friday in the year 700/1300, he misused the prestige that he had won through this to stir up violence against the Christians, during which six churches were laid in ruin. As a result of this Sultan al-Nāṣir had him brought to Cairo where he was kept in custody until his death in Dhu ʾl-Qaʿda[1] 708/April 1309.

DK II, 385, no. 2454, al-Suyūṭī, *Ḥusn al-muḥ.* I, 306. *Kitāb al-waḥīd fī sulūk ahl al-tawḥīd*, a collection of legends and edifying stories on famous Sufis, following the example of *Risālat al-Qushayrī* (I, 556), completed in Rabīʿ I 708/August-September 1308 in Alexandria, Paris 3525, Bursa Ulu Cami Taş. $163_{,1}$, Cairo [1]II, 143.

| 2. Tāj al-Dīn Abu ʾl-Faḍl Aḥmad b. Muḥammad b. ʿAṭāʾallāh al-Iskandarī al-Shādhili, one of the most famous mystics of his time and a sworn enemy of Ibn Taymiyya (p. 125), died in al-Madrasa al-Manṣūriyya in Cairo on 16 Jumādā II 709/21 November 1309. 143

DK I, 273, no. 700, al-Ṣafadī, *al-Wāfī*, AS $2617_{,119}$, al-Suyūṭī, *Ḥusn al-muḥ.* I, 301, *al-Khiṭ. al-jad.* VII, 70, Wüst. *Gesch.* 382. 1. *Risāla*, an incitement to piety and the fulfilment of one's religious duties, | Berl. 1794, Cairo [1]II, 84.—2. *Risālat al-qaṣd* (*ʿiqd*) *al-mujarrad fī maʿrifat al-ism al-mufrad* Munich 140.—3. *Miftāḥ* 118

1 Thus in DK, according to Cat. Cairo on 19 Shawwāl/2 April.

al-falāḥ wa-miṣbāḥ al-arwāḥ, on *dhikr*, Berl. 3696, Br. Mus. 755,$_{6}$, Suppl. 238,$_{7}$, Esc. ^{2}780,$_{1}$, under the title *Miftāḥ al-ghayb* Bursa Ulu Cami 156,$_{2}$.—4. *Munājāt*, prayer, Berl. 3904.—5. Religious prescripts, Br. Mus. Suppl. 237,$_{2}$.—6. *Qaṣīdas*, Berl. 7846.—7. *Mawāʿiẓ* Paris 1299.—8. *al-Tanwīr fī isqāṭ al-tadbīr*, on surrender to God and unification with Him, commenced in Mecca and completed in Damascus in 695/1296, Berl. 3089, Gotha 891 (where other MSS are listed), Paris 1348, Algiers 881,$_{2}$, 1349,$_{3}$, Köpr. II, 117, Yeni 700, Alex. Faw. 20, Makram 13, Cairo ^{1}II, 117, 171, VII, 7, ^{2}I, 282.—9. *al-Ṭarīq al-jādda fī nayl al-saʿāda*, on how to gain knowledge of God, Berl. 321.—10. An admonition to his friends in Alexandria, Berl. 3997.—11. *al-Ḥikam al-ʿAṭāʾiyya*, theological reflections, Berl. 8689/90, Gotha 890 (where other MSS are listed), Paris 1349, 3971,$_{2}$, Garr. 2003,$_{17}$, Alex. Adab 134,$_{2}$, Mawāʿiẓ 36,$_{1}$, Cairo ^{1}II, 80, VII, 7, 38, 76, 521, ^{2}I, 290, print. in *Saʿādat al-dārayn*, together with *al-Manẓūma al-Mawṣiliyya al-ʿUthmāniyya fī asmāʾ al-suwar al-Qurʾāniyya* C. (?) 1318, Sarkis 1791.—Commentaries: a. *Ghayth al-mawāhib al-ʿaliyya* by Muḥammad b. Ibrāhīm b. ʿAbbād al-Nafzī al-Rondī, d. 796/1394 (p. 252), Berl. 8691/2, Munich 138, Leid. 2261, Paris 1350, 2450,$_{4}$, Br. Mus. 889, Ind. Off. 696, Esc. ^{2}740,$_{1}$, Algiers 917/9, Dügümlü Bābā 302, ʿĀšir 474,$_{2}$, 475,$_{1}$, Cairo ^{1}II, 97, Qawala I, 254/5, print. Būlāq 1285, C. 1303, 1306 (with the commentary by ʿAbdallāh al-Sharqāwī, Pet. AMK 921, in the margin).—b. *Tanbīh dhawi ʾl-himam* by Aḥmad b. Muḥammad b. Zarrūq, d. 899/1493 (p. 253), Berl. 8693, Munich 139, Br. Mus. 755,$_{7}$, Algiers 916, 920, ʿĀšir I, 473, Alex. Taṣ. 20.—c. Ibrāhīm b. Maḥmūd al-Aqsarāʾī, completed in Mecca in 903/1497, Berl. 8694/5, Gotha 890.—d. ʿAlī b. Ḥusām al-Dīn al-Hindī
144 al-Muttaqī, d. | 977/1569 (p. 384), Berl. 8696.—e. ʿAbd al-Raʾūf al-Munāwī, d. 1031/1622 (p. 306), Berl. 8697/8, Cairo ^{1}II, 114.—f. Muḥammad Ḥayāt al-Sindī (Suppl. II, 522), composed in 1145/1732 in Medina, Algiers 532,$_{5}$.—g. *al-Hidāya lil-insān* by ʿAlī b. Ḥijāzī al-Bayyūmī, d. 1183/1769 (p. 351), Cairo ^{2}II, 117, ^{2}I, 374.—h. Sīdī Muḥammad Zakrī, d. 1144/1731, Paris 1351.—i. ʿAbd al-Majīd al-Sharnūbī (who was alive in 1322/1904, Sarkis 1119) see *OB* I, 901, VII, 2437.—k. *Īqāẓ al-himam* by Aḥmad b. Muḥammad b. ʿAjība al-Ḥusaynī al-Maghribī, composed in 1211/1796, print. in *Majmūʿa* C. 1324.—l. Anon. Malay commentary, printed in Mecca, Snouck Hurgronje, Mekka II, 387,$_{1}$.—Versification *Fayḍ al-karam* by Kamāl al-Dīn b. ʿAlī Sharīf, d. 906/1500, Berl. 8699, cf. Ahlw. 8700.—12. *Tāj al-ʿarūs wa-qamʿ al-nufūs*, an edifying work, Berl. 8792, Paris, 1298, Br. Mus. Suppl. 237, Esc. ^{2}143,$_{5}$, Algiers 881,$_{2}$, Cairo ^{1}II, 72, VII, 7, ʿĀšir I, 452, Alex. Taṣ. 35,$_{10}$, 41,$_{1}$.—13. *al-Tuḥfa fi ʾl-taṣawwuf* Cairo ^{1}VII, 205.—15. *Laṭāʾif al-minan fī manāqib al-shaykh Abi ʾl-ʿAbbās wa-shaykhihi Abi ʾl-Ḥasan*, a biography of the Sufi Shihāb al-Dīn Abū ʿAbbās Aḥmad b. ʿUmar al-Anṣārī al-Mursī, d. 686/1287, and of his teacher Taqī al-Dīn Abu ʾl-Ḥasan ʿAlī b. ʿAbdallāh b. ʿAbd al-Jabbār al-Shādhilī, d. 656/1258 (I, 583), Berl. 10105, Gotha 1848 (where other MSS are

listed), Algiers 1714, Köpr. 772/3, AS 2028/9, Cairo V, [1]122, [2]317, [1]VII, 2, Makram 53.—14.–17. see Suppl.—18. *Uns al-ʿarūs* Alex. Taṣ. 7.—19. *Qaṣīdas* and smaller treatises, Fātiḥ 5375.—20. *Waṣiyyat shuhbat* (?) *al-samāʿ*, with a commentary, *Kashf al-qināʿ*, by ʿAlī b. Muḥammad al-Miṣrī, tenth cent., Alex. Taṣ. 29.

3. Nūr al-Dīn Abu ʾl-Ḥasan ʿAlī b. Yūsuf b. Jarīr al-Lakhmī al-Shaṭṭanawfī, d. 713/1314, see Suppl.

DK III, 141, no. 323, al-Suyūṭī *Ḥuṣn al-muḥ*. I, 290. 1. *Bahjat al-asrār wa-maʿdin al-anwār fī baʿḍ manāqib sayyidī ʿAbd al-Qādir al-Kīlānī* (I, 560) or *al-Sāda al-akhyār min al-mashāyikh al-abrār*, | Berl. 10072/6, Garr. 683/4, AS 4340, Alex. 119
Taʾr. 23, Cairo [1]II, 71, V, 20, VII, 37, [2]I, 273, V, 62, Makram 7.—Abstracts: 1. By the author himself, Berl. 10077.—2. ʿAbd al-ʿAzīz al-Dīrīnī, d. 694/1295 (I, 588), ibid. 10079.—3. al-Fīrūzābādī, d. 817/1414 (p. 181), ibid. 10080/1.—4.–6. see Suppl.

4. Muḥammad b. ʿAlī b. ʿAbd al-Raḥmān al-Qurashī al-Dimashqī b. al-Sarrāj, ca. 714/1314.

| *Tuffāḥ al-arwāḥ wa-miftāḥ al-arbāḥ*, a part of *Tashwīq al-arwāḥ wal-qulūb ilā dhikr ʿallām al-ghuyūb*, edifying anecdotes, Berl. 8794. 145

5. ʿĪsā b. Muḥammad b. Muḥammad b. Qarājā b. Sulaymān b. Baraka b. Yārūq al-Suhrawardī al-Miṣrī al-Saljūqī, who died in Cairo on 28 Rabīʿ II 729/2 March 1329.

DK III, 209, no. 507. *Muʿlam al-ṭarafayn bi-mā ḥawathu sādātuna ʾl-ʿulamāʾ min al-sharafayn* Gotha 845, Bursa Haraccizade Taṣ. 16. Lost are the following of his works: *Khalīl al-akhillāʾ wa-jalīl al-ajillāʾ, Karīm al-nudamāʾ wa-nadīm al-kuramāʾ, Kanz al-qanāʿa fī man lahu fī ʾl-waʿẓ ṣināʿa, Muʿīn al-aʿyān ʿalā firaq al-ikhwān, Izālat al-qaṣaṣ fī aḥwāl āthār al-qiṣaṣ* (Ritter).

6. Shams al-Dīn Abu ʾl-Fatḥ Muḥammad b. Muḥammad Wafāʾ al-Iskandarī al-Shādhilī, who was born in 702/1302 and died in 760/1358.

On his family, see Goldziher, *ZDMG* 50, 468. 1. *Dīwān*, Sufi, Leid. 733 (where other MSS are listed), Paris 3208, Algiers 1823,$_1$, Garr. 87, Alex. Adab 132, Cairo [1]IV, 237.—2. *Ḥizb al-sādāt fī jamīʿ al-ʿādāt* Paris 1200,$_1$, Cairo [1]II, 191.—3. *Ḥizb al-fardāniyya* Cairo [2]I, 289, a commentary, *al-Futūḥāt al-rabbāniyya*, by ʿAbd al-Qādir al-Mawāhibī, composed in 887/1482, Cairo [1]II, 207, [2]I, 337.—4. *al-Azal*

Cairo ^{1}II, 65.—5. *Nafāʾis al-ʿirfān fī anfās al-raḥmān* ibid. 141.—6. *Shaʿāʾir al-ʿirfān fī alwāḥ al-kitmān* ibid. 112, Esʿad 1324 (by ʿAlī b. Wafāʾ al-Anṣārī al-Shādhilī, Suppl. II, 900, 26? Ritter).—7. *al-ʿUrūsh* Alex. Taṣ. 24, Cairo ^{1}II, 117.—8. *al-Shaʿāʾir al-insāniyya li-ʿayn al-ʿināya al-rabbāniyya* Cairo ^{1}II, 5.—9., 10. See Suppl.—11. *al-Tāʾiyya al-kubrā* Alex. Adab 132.—12. *Ḥizb al-fatḥ* Alex. Taṣ. $35_{,13}$.

7. Muḥammad b. al-Ḥasan b. ʿAlī al-Asnāwī al-Shāfiʿī ʿImād al-Dīn, born in 695/1296, studied in Cairo and Damascus, lived for a time as a professor in Hama, then became an acting judge and professor in Cairo, dying in Rajab 74/April 1363.

DK III, 421, no. 1124. *Ḥayāt al-qulūb fī kayfiyyat al-wuṣūl ila ʾl-maḥbūb*, Alex. Taṣ. 16, Cairo ^{1}II, 81, ^{2}I, 292, printed in the margin of al-Wāʿiẓ al-Makkī, *Qūt al-qulūb*, C. 1310.

146 | 8. Muḥammad b. ʿAbd al-Dāʾim b. bint Maylaq Abu ʾl-Maʿālī Nāṣir al-Dīn, born in 731/1330, was a preacher at the madrasa of al-Nāṣir Ḥasan, and *qāḍi ʾl-quḍāt* under Barqūq for a brief time. He died in 797/1395.

DK III, 494, no. 1331, Ibn al-ʿImād, *ShDh* VI, 351. 1. *Sharḥ al-ṣudūr ʿalā fahm mā yuʿbar ʿan qawl Allāh yahabu li-man shāʾa ināthan wa-yahabu li-man shāʾa ʾl-dhukūr* (p. $42_{,48,49}$), admonitions not to regard the birth of daughters as a misfortune but to raise them with | the same care as boys, with consolations on the loss of children, Berl. 8805.—2. *Ḥādi ʾl-qulūb ilā liqāʾ al-maḥbūb* Esc. ^{2}787, Garr. 1577, Cairo ^{1}II, 79, ^{2}I, 286.—3. A *qaṣīda* with a commentary by Muḥammad b. ʿAlī b. ʿAllān, d. 1057/1647 (p. 390), Cairo ^{1}IV, 265, ^{2}III, 191.—4.–6. see Suppl. (5. AS 79, Köpr. $46_{,1}$).—7. *Mawārid dhawi ʾl-ikhtiṣāṣ ilā maqāṣid sūrat al-ikhlāṣ* (ḤKh VI, $230_{,13335}$, attributed to al-Qūnawī) AS $79_{,2}$ (Ritter). 120

9. Abu ʾl-Fatḥ Muḥammad Shams al-Dīn al-Fuwwī al-Azharī, who flourished in the middle of the eighth century.

Silāḥ al-sālik wa-sadd al-mahālik Cairo ^{1}VII, 176.

10. Abū Bakr b. Dāʾūd b. ʿĪsā al-Ṣāliḥī Taqī al-Dīn Abu ʾl-Ṣafāʾ, who died in 806/1403.

1. *al-Durr al-muntaqā al-marfūʿ fī awrād al-yawm wal-layl wal-usbūʿ* Berl. 3776.—2. See Suppl.

11. Abu 'l-Ḥasan ʿAlī b. Muḥammad (p. 145) b. Muḥammad b. Wafāʾ al-Shādhilī al-Iskandarī al-Wafāʾī, a famous Sufi who was born in Cairo in 759/1357 and died there, on Rawḍa, in 807/1404.

MT 58r, al-Suyūṭī *Ḥusn al-muḥ.* I, 304, *al-Khiṭ. al-jad.* V. 142ff (with the dates: b. 11 Muḥarram 761/4 December 1359, d. 801/1398, following al-Shaʿrānī, *Ṭab.* not in print), Hartmann *Muw.* 14. 1. *Dīwān*, mostly short poems, often modern in form, alphabetically arranged, Berl. 7580/1, Copenhagen 27 (also contains poems by his relatives), Br. Mus. 625, Esc. ^{2}445, Garr. 94, Patna I, 198$_{,1774}$.—2. Panegyric poem in the form of a *muwashshaḥ*, Berl. 8172$_{,5}$.—3. A mystical poem, with a commentary, *Istinzāl al-laṭāʾif al-riḍwāniyya bi-sharḥ al-qaṣīda al-ḥamdiyya al-ʿirfāniyya* by Abū ʿAbdallāh Muḥammad b. Muḥammad al-Miknāsī | 147
b. al-Sakkāk, Esc. ^{2}384$_{,1}$.—4. *al-Masāmiʿ al-rabbāniyya* Esc. ^{2}780$_{,3}$, Cairo ^{1}II, 135, VII, 5.—5. *Mafātīḥ al-khazāʾin al-ʿaliyya* Cairo ^{1}II, 36, VII, 5.—6. *al-Waṣāyā* Paris 1359$_{,1}$, Cairo ^{1}VII, 6, 108$_{,1}$.—7. *Risālat al-taṣawwuf* Cairo ^{1}II, 85.

12. Badr (Shams) al-Dīn Muḥammad b. Aḥmad b. al-Shaykh Muḥammad al-Ḥalabī al-Aṭʿānī (Iẓʿānī?) al-Bisṭāmī, who died in 807/1404.

1. *Tadhkirat al-murīd al-ṭālib al-mazīd*, on all kinds of things important for a Sufi, completed in 797/1395, Berl. 3020.—2. *Risāla fī naṣīḥat aṣḥāb al-nufūs al-zakiyya fī ḥukm al-samāʿ ʿala 'l-ṭarīqa*, against music, ibid. 5512.—3. See Suppl.

12a, b. See Suppl. (12a. Patna I, 197$_{,1770}$).

12c. ʿAbdallāh Makhdūm al-Malik collected, in 809/1406 in Jerusalem:

Kashf al-ghumma ʿan baṣāʾir al-aʾimma Alex. Mawāʿiẓ 32.

12d. Jamāl al-Dīn Muḥammad b. Muḥammad al-Mizjājī al-Ḥanafī al-Ṣūfī al-mulaqqab Ibn al-Baḥr wrote, from Dhu 'l-Ḥijja 820/January 1418 until Jumādā I 821/June 1418:

Hidāyat al-hālik ilā ahda 'l-masālik wal-naṣāʾiḥ bil-ʿulūm al-nāfiʿa wal-adilla al-wāḍiḥa wal-barāhīn al-sāṭiʿa wal-ḥujaj al-qāṭiʿa, on the permissibility of enjoying music, Wehbi 646 (Ritter).

13. Abu 'l-Laṭāʾif b. Fāris, ca. 830/1427.

Al-Minaḥ al-ilāhiyya min manāqib al-sādāt al-Wafāʾiyya, on the followers of ʿAlī b. Wafāʾ (no. 11), Cairo V, [1]161, [2]369.

14. Aḥmad b. ʿUmar b. Aḥmad al-Shādhilī al-Anṣārī al-Shābb al-Tāʾib, who was
121 born in Dhu ʾl-Ḥijja 767/26 August 1366, went, as a wandering dervish, | to Yemen twice (in 804/1401 he was in Zabīd), several times to Iraq, to Baghdad, Mosul, Diyār Bakr and Ḥiṣn Kayfā. Upon his return to Cairo he constructed a Zāwiya right near the gates of the city. Having completed the pilgrimage on a number of occasions, he moved to Damascus, where he died (however, according to *MT*, this occurred in Jerusalem) on 18 Rajab 832/24 April 1429.

148 | *RA* 50r, *MT* 50v. 1. An interpretation of sura 20_{119}, with some poems as a postscript, Berl. 1003.—2., 3. See Suppl.

15. Abu ʾl-Ṭayyyib Muḥammad b. ʿAlī b. Abi ʾl-ʿAbbās Aḥmad al-Shādhilī al-Maḥallī wrote, in 838/1434:

Maḥāsin al-niẓām min jawāhir al-kalām fī dhikr Allāh al-malik al-ʿallām Cairo [1]VII, 227, see Suppl.

16. Abū ʿAbdallāh Muḥammad b. ʿUmar b. Aḥmad al-Ghamrī, d. 849/1445, see Suppl.

3. *Nūr al-iqtibās etc.* Bursa Ulu Cami Taş. $169_{,3}$, Dam. ʿUm. $89_{,98}$.—8. *al-Ḥukm al-maḍbūṭ fī taḥrīm fiʿl qawm Lūṭ* Alex. Fun. $159_{,1}$.—9. *al-Intiṣār fi ʾl-dhabb ʿan ṭarīq al-akhyār* Bursa Ulu Cami Taş. $169_{,1}$, (Ritter).

17. Quṭb al-ʿĀrifīn Shams al-Dīn Abū ʿAbdallāh Muḥammad b. al-Ḥasan b. ʿAlī al-Ḥanafī al-Ṣūfī al-Shādhilī al-Taymī (Tamīmī), who was born in 775/1373 (or, according to others, in 767/1365) and died in Rabīʿ I 847/August 1443.

Al-Suyūṭī, *Ḥusn al-muḥ.* I, 305. *al-Sirr al-ṣafī fī manāqib sayyidī (ʾl-sulṭān) Muḥammad al-Ḥanafī*, biography by his student al-Batanūnī, ca. 900/1494 (no. 31), Gotha 1853, Cairo V, [1]67, [2]216, VII, 396, print. C. 1306.—1. *al-Rawḍ al-nashīq fī ʿilm al-ṭarīq*, a commentary on a statement by his teacher Muḥammad al-ʿAjjām, Cairo [1]II 87.—2. *Ḥizb al-nūr* ibid. VII, 397.—3. See Suppl.

18. ʿUmar al-Tirmidhī al-Ṣūfī wrote for al-Malik al-Ẓāhir, d. 858/1454:

1. *Tafsīr sūrat al-Ikhlāṣ* Cairo [1]II, 173.—2. *Kitāb al-niyya* ibid.

19. Sharaf al-Dīn Muḥammad b. Ṣadaqa b. ʿUmar b. Muḥammad al-ʿĀdilī, who died in 854/1450 in Cairo.

Minhāj al-ṭarīq wa-sharḥ al-taḥqīq Cairo [1]II, 138.

20. ʿAbd al-Raḥmān b. Abi ʾl-Ṣafāʾ Abū Bakr b. Dāʾūd al-Ḥanbalī al-Ṣāliḥī al-Qādirī al-Dimashqī, who died in 856/1452.

Tuḥfat al-ʿibād wa-adillat (bi-natījat) al-awrād NO 716, Selīm Āġā 473, Cairo [1]II, 74, [2]I, 277.

| 21. Muḥammad b. Mūsā b. Muḥammad b. ʿUthmān al-Hudhbānī Nāṣir al-Dīn 149
Abu ʾl-Faḍl, who was born in 780/1378 and died in 858/1454.

| *Futūḥ al-wahhāb wa-dalāʾil al-ṭullāb ilā manāzil al-aḥbāb*, a biography of his 122
maternal grandfather, the Sufi Abū Bakr b. ʿAlī al-Shaybānī, d. 797/1395, Berl. 10108.

22. Abu ʾl-Fatḥ Muḥammad b. Badr al-Dīn Muḥammad b. Aḥmad b. Ṣāliḥ b. Abi ʾl-Wafāʾ al-ʿAwfī al-Iskandarī, ca. 880/1475.

1. *Irtiqāʾ al-rutba bil-libās wal-ṣuḥba*, different from ḤKh I, 447, the first section Berl. 3026.—2. *Nuzhat al-nāẓir fī waḍʿ khuṭūṭ faḍl al-dāʾir*, composed in 878/1473, Cairo [1]V, 326.—3. *al-Ḥujja al-rājiḥa* Dam. ʿUm. 68_{125}.—4. *Sharḥ Ghunyat al-bāḥith* (I, 490), composed in 883/1478, lost, ḤKh IV, 336.

23. Al-ʿĀrif billāh Abū Isḥāq Ibrāhīm b. ʿAlī b. ʿUmar al-Anṣārī al-Matbūlī al-Aḥmadī, d. 877/1472, see Suppl.

Al-Shaʿrānī *Ṭab.* II, 75 (see A. Schmidt, *al-Sh.* Petersburg 1914, Index), followed by *Khit. jad.* IX, 18. A *waṣiyya* with a commentary by al-Shaʿrānī, d. 973/1565, Cairo [1]II, 120.

23a. ʿAbdallāh b. Muḥammad b. Maḥmūd Raḍī al-Dīn Khaṭīb Qaḍāʾ wrote, in 845/1441:

Kitāb al-khuṭab Garr. 1914.

24. Ibrāhīm b. ʿAlī b. Aḥmad b. Burayd al-Qādirī, who died in 880/1475.

Mafātīḥ al-maṭālib wa-ṭabaqāt al-ṭālib, on being admitted into the ranks of the Sufis, Berl. $3361_{,2}$.

25. Majd al-Dīn b. Muḥammad al-Ḥalwaʾī al-Khūnajī al-Tabrīzī wrote, in Cairo in 884/1479:

Taʾdīb al-nafs wa-taṣḥīḥ al-istinād li-ahl al-ṣafāʾ wal-wadād, on the errors of the soul, Šehīd ʿA. $1151_{,2}$, Cairo ^{1}II, 73.

26. Ibrāhīm b. ʿAlī b. Tāj al-ʿĀrifīn Abu ʾl-Wafāʾ Ibrāhīm b. Yūsuf al-Ḥusaynī al-Maqdisī al-ʿIrāqī Abu ʾl-Ṣafāʾ b. Abi ʾl-Wafāʾ, who was born in 810/1407 and died in 887/1482.

150 | Hartmann, *Muw.* 24. 1. *Adab al-dukhūl fī ʾl-ṭarīq*, a manual on mysticism, Berl. 3282.—2. A *waṣiyya* to a younger Sufi friend, ibid. 4007.—3. Mystical *dīwān* ibid. 7917.

27. ʿAbd al-Qādir b. Ḥusayn b. ʿAlī b. Mughayzil al-Shādhilī wrote, in 894/1489 (see Suppl.):

Al-Fatḥ al-mubīn fī maʿrifat maqām al-ṣādiqīn or *al-Kawākib al-ẓāhira fī ʾjtimāʿ al-awliyāʾ bi-sayyid al-dunyā wal-ākhira*, a history of Abu ʾl-Ḥasan al-Shādhilī and his followers, ḤKh 10964, MS in the Abbey of St. Boniface in Munich (ZDMG VI, 14, Wüst. *Gesch.* 502), Esc. ^{2}1750, abstract Paris $1605_{,2}$.

28. Ibrāhīm b. Ḥasan b. ʿAlī b. Isḥāq al-Faraḍī, who died in 880/1475.

Minhāj al-mudhakkirīn wa-miʿrāj al-muḥadhdhirīn Alex. Mawāʿiẓ 46.

29. Yūnus b. Ḥasan al-Miṣrī wrote, in 896/1490:

Ghāyat al-sarāʾir wa-āyat al-baṣāʾir Cairo ^{1}II, 97.

30. Jamāl (Ṣafī) al-Dīn Abu ʾl-Mawāhib Muḥammad b. Aḥmad b. Muḥammad al-Tūnisī al-Wafāʾī al-Shādhilī b. Zaghdūn b. al-Ḥājj al-Yazaltīnī, d. 882/1477, see Suppl.

Al-Shaʿrānī *Ṭab.* II, 60/72, al-Nabhānī, *Jāmiʿ karāmāt al-awliyāʾ*, C. 1329, I, 170. 1. *Qawānīn ḥikam al-ishrāq etc.* also Berl. Brill M. $316_{,4}$, Leid. 2285, Garr. 1583, print. Damascus 1309, see E. Jabra Jurji, *Illumination or Islamic Mysticism, a Transl. with an Introd. and Notes based on a Critical Edition of... al-Shadilis Treatise entitled* Q. ḥ. al-i., Princeton 1938, see Brockelmann, *Orient.* IX 176/8.—3. *Faraḥ al-asmāʿ etc.* also AS $4296_{,11}$, Fātiḥ $2625_{,2}$, Cairo m. 225 *Nashra* 21 (*Qarʿ etc.* as in ḤKh IV, 513, Farmer, *Sources*, 58).—5. Under the title *Maʿārif al-mawāhib* Fez Qar. 1493, Cairo ^{2}III, 360.

31. Abū Isḥāq b. Ibrāhīm b. Muḥammad b. Maḥmūd al-Tājī al-Dimashqī, who died in 900/1495.

Taḥdhīr al-ikhwān mimmā yūrith al-faqr wal-nisyān Alex. Mawāʿiẓ 9.

| 32. Zayn al-Dīn ʿAbd al-Ṣamad wrote, around 900/1494: 151

| *Al-Jawāhir al-saniyya fi ʾl-karāmāt wal-nisba al-Aḥmadiyya*, a biography of the 123
Sufi Aḥmad al-Badawī, see I, 586.

33. ʿAlī b. ʿUmar al-Batanūnī al-Būṣīrī al-Shādhilī al-Ḥanafī, ca. 900/1494.

1. *al-Sirr al-ṣafī fī manāqib al-sulṭān Muḥammad al-Ḥanafī*, see p. 148.—2. *al-ʿUnwān fi ʾl-iḥtirāz min* (*makāyid*) *al-niswān*, on the ruinous influence of women, Gotha 1233, Paris Suppl. $1149_{,i}$, Garr. 1915.

34. Al-Malik al-Ashraf Abu ʾl-Naṣr Qāʾitbāy, d. 901/1495.

Weil, *Gesch. d. Chal.* V, 325 ff. *Adhkār*, Sufi prayers and *muwashshaḥāt*, Cairo ^{1}II, 183, ^{2}I, 344 (lacking in Hartmann, *Muw.*).

35. Burhān al-Dīn Abu ʾl-Ṭayyib Ibrāhīm b. Maḥmūd b. Aḥmad b. Ḥasan al-Āqsarāʾī al-Ḥanafī al-Shādhilī al-Mawāhibī, who studied in Cairo under Ibn Zaghdūn (no. 30), stayed in Mecca and Medina a number of times, and died in 909/1503.

MT 13r, *al-Khit. al-jad.* II, $128_{,15}$, following the *Ṭabaqāt al-Munāwī*, p. $307_{,23}$ (with the date: d. 914/1508). 1. *al-Fatḥ al-qarīb fi ʾl-istighfār baʿd shamm al-ṭīb* Gotha 916, Esc. $^{2}1607_{,7}$.—2. *Hidāyat al-rabb li-man aḥabb* ibid. 2 and 3.—3. *al-Tafrīd fī maʿnā kalimat al-tawḥīd* Gotha $916_{,2}$ = *al-Tafrīd bi-dawābiṭ al-tawḥīd*, composed in 905/1499, Leid. 2278, Esc. ^{2}1607,$_{8}$.—4. *Uṣūl muqaddamat al-uṣūl*, composed in 903/1497, Cairo ^{1}VII, 178, Esc. ^{2}1687,$_{6}$, Cairo ^{1}VII, 178, a commentary thereon, *al-Ṣafāʾ bil-suʾūl*, composed in 905/1499, ibid. VI, 143.—5. *Sharḥ al-Ḥikam al-ʿAṭāʾiyya* p. 143.—6.–10. see Suppl.—In some MSS he is credited with the *Risālat qawānīn ḥikam al-ishrāq* of his teacher.

36. Abu ʾl-Najāʾib ʿAbd al-Qādir b. Muḥammad b. ʿUmar b. Ḥabīb al-Ṣafadī, who died in 915/1509.

Biography Berl. 10137. 1. *Silk al-ʿayn li-idhhāb al-ghayn*, a Sufi *qaṣīda* in 283 *basīṭ* verses, Berl. 3414/5, 7929, Garr. 2003,$_{22}$, commentary *Nūr al-ʿayn* by ʿAlī
152 b. ʿAṭiyya ʿAlawān, | d. 936/1529 (p. 333), ibid. 3416/7, Paris 3225.—2. A mystical *qaṣīda* in 29 verses, Krafft 493.

37. ʿAlī b. Maymūn b. Abī Bakr al-Idrīsī al-Maghribī, who was born around 854/1450, passed himself off as an ʿAlid, even though he was of Berber stock. As a young man he is said to have to have relinquished the dignity of emir of a *qabīla* of the Banū Rāshid on Jabal Ghumāra because he was unable to enforce
124 the prohibition of wine-drinking among his people. | In 901/1495 he went from Fez to Damascus, Mecca, Aleppo, and Bursa. He then took up permanent residence in Damascus, and died there in 917/1511.

1. *Risālat al-ikhwān fī (min) ahl al-fiqh wa-ḥamalat al-Qurʾān*, addressed to his friends in Fez, from whom he received word through a social call in the vicinity of Damascus in 915, on the mystical sense of some passages from the Qurʾān, Paris 1372 (de Slane), Berl. 2545 (origin of Adam, the genesis of his offspring, behaviour towards God), 3033, 3713 (*tawḥīd*, liturgy, struggle against passions and lust as the duty of every believer, thus in Ahlw. Are these then different treatises?), Cairo ^{1}VII, 543.—2. *Bayān ghurbat al-islām bi-wāsiṭat ṣinfay al-mutafaqqiha wal-mutafaqqira min ahl Miṣr wal-Shām wa-mā yalīhā min bilād al-Aʿjām*, against self-styled jurists and mendicant devishes, Berl. 2119/21, Cairo ^{1}VII, 543, see I. Goldziher, ʿA. b. M. al-M.'s Sittenspiegel des östl. Islāms, *ZDMG* 28, 293 ff.—3. *al-Risāla al-Maymūniyya fī tawḥīd al-Ājurrūmiyya*, a commentary on this grammatical work (p. 237) which aims to demonstrate the unity of God, Berl. 2442, Cairo ^{1}VII, 543.—4. *Bayān faḍl khiyār al-nās wal-kashf ʿan makr al-waswās*, Berl. 3522, cf. Goldziher, op. cit. 301.—5. *Risāla fī ʾl-radd ʿalā munkiri ʾl-shaykh al-akbar b. al-ʿArabī* I, 582.—6. *Mabādiʾ al-sālikīn ilā maqāmāt al-ʿārifīn* Berl. 3034.—7. *Bayān al-aḥkām fī ʾl-sajjāda wal-khirqa wal-aʿlām*, on the emblems of the Sufis and their meanings, ibid. 3098, Rāġib 1476.—8. A Sufi work on the tasks and duties of teachers and students, following the rules of his teacher Aḥmad b. Muḥammad al-Tūnisī Abu ʾl-ʿAbbās, d. 930/1524, Berl. 3180.

| 38. Ibrāhīm b. Muḥammad b. ʿAbd al-Raḥmān al-Dasūqī al-Ṣūfī, who was born 153
in 833/1429, and died on 5 (or, according to others, 9) Shaʿbān 919/5 October 1514.

RA 37v. Prayer pericopes, Berl. 3778.

39. Muḥammad al-Dimyāṭī, d. 921/1515.

Lāmiyya fi ʾl-tawassul bi-asmāʾ Allāh al-ḥusnā with a commentary, *Bulūgh al-qaṣd wal-munā fī khawāṣṣ asmāʾ Allāh al-ḥusnā* Alex. Faw. 5.

40. Aḥmad b. al-Ḥājjī wrote, at the time of Qānṣūh al-Ghūrī:

Al-Munabbihāt, paraenesis, AS 2108/9.

41. Shams al-Dīn Muḥammad Dimirdāsh al-Muḥammadī al-Khalwatī al-Jarkasī was admitted into the ranks of the Sufis by Aḥmad b. ʿUqba. He then went to Tabriz to study with ʿUmar Rūshānī. Back in Egypt, he settled in a *zāwiya* near Cairo and planted a palmgrove that was to become famous. He died in 929/1523.

| 1. *al-Qawl al-farīd fī maʿrifat al-tawḥīd* Berl. 3229, Br. Mus. Suppl. 242, Alex. 125
Faw. $150_{,9}$, Cairo ^{1}VI, 109.—2. *Majmaʿ al-asrār wa-kashf al-astār*, a Sufi interpretation of a tale from the *Manṭiq al-ṭayr* of the Persian poet ʿAṭṭār, Berl. 3486.—3. *Risāla fī maʿrifat al-ḥaqāʾiq al-sabʿ al-kulliyya al-aṣliyya wa-fī maʿrifat ḥaqīqat al-ḥaqāʾiq wa-fī maʿnā qawlihi taʿālā wa-laqad ataynāka etc.* (p. 5, 67) Berl. 5103.—4. *Tuḥfat al-ṭullāb al-rāʾimīn ḥaḍrat al-wahhāb* Cairo ^{2}II, 74.

10 *Mathematics*

Shihāb al-Dīn Abu ʾl-ʿAbbās Aḥmad b. Muḥammad b. ʿAbbād b. ʿAlī b. al-Ḥāʾim al-Faraḍī al-Maʿarrī al-Maqdisī was born in 753/1352 (according to others in 756) and died in Jerusalem in 815/1412.

1. *Murshidat al-ṭālib ilā asna ʾl-maṭālib*, on arithmetic, Berl. 5978, Br. Mus. $420_{,5}$, Alex. Ḥisāb 18.—Commentaries: a. al-Azharī, d. 926/1520, Cairo ^{1}V, 183.—b. Ibn
al-Ḥanbalī, d. 971/1563, Berl. 5981.—c. al-Ghazzī, | d. 983/1575, Berl. 5982.— 154
d. *Bughyat al-rāghib* by Bahāʾ al-Dīn Muḥammad al-Shinshawrī, d. 999/1590 (p. 320), completed in 995/1587, Gotha 1478, Alex. Ḥisāb 4.—e. *al-Lumʿa* by ʿAbd al-Qādir b. Muḥammad b. Aḥmad al-Fayyūmī, d. 1022/1614 (p. 358), Gotha 1482. Abbreviations see Suppl. α. Garr. 1033, $2084_{,1}$.—β Garr. $2145_{,2}$.—ζ Abu ʾl-Faḍl Muḥammad b. Aḥmad b. Ayyūb al-Shāfiʿī b. Imām al-Naḥḥāsīn, Br. Mus. Suppl.

752 (889/90 AH).—*η al-Nubha* by Muḥammad b. Fakhr al-Dīn b. Qays al-ʿUrḍī (Suter 505), Bodl. I, 966,$_5$.—*ϑ* Aḥmad b. Muḥammad b. Muḥammad al-Ghazzī Shihāb al-Dīn, d. 983/1575, Garr. 1042.—An anonymous commentary on a versification, Garr. 2084,$_4$.—2. *al-Lumaʿ al-yasīra fī ʿilm al-ḥisāb*, on arithmetic, with particular emphasis on the division of estates, Berl. 5986/7, Paris 2471, 4162,$_2$, 4585,$_5$ (cf. Woepcke, *Sur l'introduction de l'arithmétique indienne en occident*, Rome 1859, p. 53), Algiers 1447, Br. Mus. 421,$_1$, Bodl. I, 971,$_6$, Garr. 1035/6, 2111,$_3$, 2145,$_1$, Lālelī 2723,$_9$, Cairo ^{1}V, 186, VII, 127.—Commentaries: a. Muḥammad b. Muḥammad Sibṭ al-Māridīnī (p. 167), composed in 893/1488, Berl. 5988, Gotha 1483 (where other MSS are listed), Alex. Ḥisāb 11, 15,$_2$, Fun. 142, 186,$_1$.—b. Aḥmad b. Mūsā b. ʿAbd al-Ghaffār, composed in 910/1504 in Mecca, Berl. 5989, Paris 2472, Garr. 1038.—c. Zayn al-Dīn b. Sarī al-Dīn b. Aḥmad al-Durrī, Berl. 5990.—An abstract, *al-Wasīla*, completed in 792/1390, Lālelī 2714,$_1$.—3. *al-Muqniʿ fī ʿilm al-jabr wal-muqābala*, a didactic poem on algebra in 57 or 60 verses, Berl. 5991, Gotha 1484/5, Alex. Fun. 82,$_9$.—Commentaries: a. Self-commentary, *al-Musmiʿ* (see Suppl.), Alex. Ḥisāb 24 (where: *al-Musriʿ*), abstract *al-Mumtiʿ* Makram 58.—b. *al-Qawl al-mubdiʿ* by Sibṭ al-Māridīnī, d. 912/1506 (p. 167), Gotha 1491,$_3$, Garr. 1048.—c. *Fatḥ al-mubdiʿ* by Zakariyyāʾ al-Anṣārī (p. 122), Garr. 1049, Alex. Ḥisāb 23.—4. *Targhīb al-rāʾiḍ fī ʿilm al-farāʾiḍ* Berl. 4719, autograph dated 800, Garr. 1876.—Commentaries: a. *al-Fuṣūl al-mulimma* (*muhimma*) by Sibṭ al-Māridīnī, Berl. 4720, Garr. 1877, Alex. Far. 11, Cairo ^{1}III, 313.—Super-commentary *Manhaj al-wuṣūl ilā taḥrīr al-fuṣūl* by Zakariyyāʾ al-Anṣārī, d. 926/1520, Berl. 4721, Cairo ^{1}III, 118, author's abstract Berl. 4722, with the title *Ghāyat al-wuṣūl*, Cairo ^{1}III, 310.—5. *al-Tuḥfa al-Qudsiyya fi 'l-farāʾiḍ*, 76 *mathnawī* verses on the law of inheritance following the *Raḥbiyya* of Ibn al-Mutaqqina (I, 490), Gotha 1104 (where other MSS are listed), Alex. Far. 4.—Commentaries: a. *al-Lumʿa al-shamsiyya* by Sibṭ al-Māridīnī the Younger, d. 934/1527, Gotha 1105, 1115, Cairo ^{1}VII, 198.—b. See Suppl.—6. *Kifāyat al-ḥuffāẓ*, a didactic poem on the divi-
155 sion of estates, Gotha | 1106 (where other MSS are listed), Cairo ^{1}III, 314/5, ^{2}I, 561.—Commentaries: a. Self-commentary, Gotha 1107/8, 1479,$_1$, Garr. 1825.—
126 b. *Nihāyat al-hidāya ilā taḥrīr al-K.* | by Zakariyyāʾ al-Anṣārī, d. 926/1520, Paris 1034, Cairo ^{1}III, 318.—c. Muḥammad Abu 'l-Barakāt al-Wafāʾī al-Dalajūnī, composed in 1079/1668, Algiers 1322.—d. see Suppl.—7. *al-Maʿūna fī ʿilm al-hawāʾī*, a manual for mental arithmetic, Berl. 5984, Alex. Ḥisāb 19, Cairo ^{1}V 190.—Commentaries, see Suppl. (a. Cairo ^{1}I, 180).—Author's abstract *al-Wasīla* Berl. 5985, Garr. 1034, Alex. Ḥisāb 16, 20, Cairo ^{1}V. 192.—8. *Risāla fi 'l-munāsakhāt* Paris 2475,$_4$, Alex. Far. 16, Ḥisāb 15,$_2$, Cairo ^{1}VII, 599, as *Shubbāk fī aʿmāl al-munāsakhāt* (see Suppl.) Alex. Far. 8.—9. *Risāla fi 'l-ḥisāb* Paris 2475,$_5$, commentary *Muntaha 'l-irādāt li-jadwal al-munāsakhāt* by Ḥusayn b. Aḥmad al-Maḥallī, d. 1170/1756 (p. 323), Alex. Far. 15, Cairo ^{1}VII, 317, ^{2}I, 562.—10. *Ghāyat*

al-suʾūl fī ʾl-iqrār bil-majhūl Cairo ^{1}V, 212, VII, 54, Dam. Z. $89_{,3,2}$, Patna I, $96_{,975}$, two questions regarding it Cairo ^{1}VII, 54.—11. *Mukhtaṣar wajīz fī ʿilm al-ḥisāb* Cairo ^{1}V, 215.—12. *al-Tibyān fī tafsīr gharīb al-Qurʾān* Cairo ^{1}I, 136.—13.–18. see Suppl.

11 *Astronomy*

1. Shihāb al-Dīn Aḥmad b. Abī Bakr ʿAlī b. al-Sarrāj al-Ḥamawī, who died around 726/1326 in Aleppo.

Suter 508. 1. *Risālat al-asṭurlāb wal-jayb al-ghāʾib* Berl. $5799_{,1}$.—2. *Risālat al-ʿamal bi-rubʿ al-muqanṭarāt* ibid. 5859.—3. *al-Durr al-gharīb fi ʾl-ʿamal bi-rubʿ al-mujayyab* Leid. 1142 (with the mistaken information that it was dedicated to Bāyezīd II).—4. *Masāʾil handasiyya* Cairo ^{1}V, 205.—5. *Riṣala fī rubʿ al-mujannaḥ* Cairo ^{1}V, 274. In the year 714 AH he copied MS AS 1719 (Krause, St. Hdss. 506) and at one point owned AS 2762.

2. Nāṣir al-Dīn Muḥammad b. Samʿūn al-Muwaqqit, who died in 737/1336.

1. *al-Tuḥfa al-malakiyya fi ʾl-asʾila wal-ajwiba al-falakiyya* Cairo ^{1}V, 232.—2. *al-Uṣūl al-thamira fī ʾl-ʿamal bi-rubʿ al-mashāṭara* Qawala II, 275.—3. *Kanz al-ṭullāb fī ʾl-ʿamal bil-asṭurlāb* Paris $2524_{,3}$.

3. Zayn al-Dīn Muḥammad b. Aḥmad b. ʿAbd al-Raḥmān al-Mizzī al-Ḥanafī, born in 690/1291, studied in Cairo, lived subsequently in Damascus, where he died in 750/1349.

| *DK* III, 325, no. 873, see Schmalzl, *Zur Gesch. des Quadranten* 33/7. 1. *al-Risāla* 156
al-asṭurlābiyya Paris $2547_{,6}$, Br. Mus. $977_{,1}$.—2. *Kashf al-rayb fī ʾl-ʿamal bil-jayb* Br. Mus. Suppl. $764_{,4}$ (where other MSS are listed), Serāi $3483_{,18}$, (747h).

4. ʿAlāʾ al-Dīn ʿAlī b. Ibrāhīm b. Muḥammad b. al-Shāṭir al-Muwaqqit bil-Jāmiʿ al-Umawī, who died in 777/1375.

Sánchez Péres, *Los matemáticos en la Bibl. del Esc.* Madrid 1928, p. 8. 1. *al-Zīj al-jadīd*, astronomical tables, Leid. 113/4 (photograph *Qu. u. St.* VII, 33, ii, 23), Paris 2522, Bodl. I, 876, II, 278, Pet. Ros. 189, Garr. 973.—Commentary *al-Misk al-ʿāṭir* by Yūsuf b. Aḥmad al-Nābulusī, composed in 998/1589 following the example of Shihāb al-Dīn al-Ḥalabī's commentary on the *Zīj al-Ilkhānī* and his abstract of the *Zīj b. al-Shāṭir*, Bank. XXII, $54_{,2464}$.—Abbreviations: a. *Nuzhat al-nāẓir* by al-Kūm al-Rishī no. 8.—b. *al-Rawḍ al-ʿāṭir* by Muḥammad b. ʿAlī

b. Ibrāhīm b. Zurayq al-Khayrī, d. 803/1400 (Suppl. no. 5a), Gotha 1403.—
127 c. *Nuzhat al-nāẓir* by Muḥammad al-Mukhallalātī, | d. 1140/1727, Cairo ^{1}VII, 513, glosses *Tuḥfat al-nāẓir fī ḥall Zīj Ibn al-Shāṭir* by the same, a table therefrom Berl. 5876.—2. *Nihāyat al-suʾūl fī tashīl al-uṣūl* Leid. 1116, Bodl. I, 920,$_{2}$, 934, 938, 979.—3. *Risālat al-rubʿ al-tāmm*, on the perfect quadrant, an abstract of *al-Nafʿ al-ʿāmm fī ʾl-ʿamal bil-rubʿ al-tāmm* (ḤKh VI, 13940) Berl. 5816, Leid. 1115, Vat. V, 318,$_{6}$, Qawala II, 277.—4. *Nuzhat al-sāmiʿ fī ʾl-ʿamal bil-rubʿal-jāmiʿ* Cairo V, 281, 316 (photograph *Qu. u. St.* VII, 20, ii, 4).—5. *Jadwal li-ʿarḍ shamāl fī maʿrifat al-ghāya wa-niṣf al-qaws wal-ḥaḍīḍ* Leid. 1111.—6. *Urjūza fī ʾl-kawākib* ibid. 1112.—7. *Risāla fī ʾstikhrāj al-taʾrīkh*, Cambr. Palmer p. 28, n. 1.—8. *Risālat al-asṭurlāb* Br. Mus. 407, 408,$_{5}$.—9. *Mukhtaṣar fī ʾl-ʿamal bil-asṭurlāb wa-rubʿ al-muqanṭarāt wal-rubʿ al-mujayyab* ibid. 977,$_{2}$.—10. *Īḍāḥ al-mujayyab fī ʾl-ʿamal bil-rubʿ al-mujayyab* Cairo ^{1}V, 273, Bursa Haraccizade, Heyet wa Hikmet 12, l. see ibid. 2.—11. *Risāla fī ʾl-ʿamal bi-daqāʾiq ikhtilāf al-āfāq al-marʾiyya* Cairo ^{1}V, 306.—12., 13. See Suppl.

5. Muḥammad b. Muḥammad b. Muḥammad al-Khalīlī Shams al-Dīn, ca. 800/1397.

1. Tables for finding the zenith and the *qibla*, following the method of Abū
157 ʿAlī al-Marrākushī (I, 625), Berl. | 5754.—2. *al-Jadwal al-āfāqī* ibid. 5755.—3. Astronomical tables and overviews, ibid. 5756.—4.–8. See Suppl. (4. Mosul 179,$_{129}$).

6. Mūsā b. Muḥammad b. ʿUthmān al-Khalīlī Sharaf al-Dīn Abū ʿImrān, who was *muwaqqit* at the Umayyad mosque in 805/1402.

1. *Talkhīṣ fī maʿrifat awqāt al-ṣalāt wa-jihāt al-qibla ʿinda ʿadam al-ālāt* Berl. 5684, Paris 2574,$_{12}$ (without title).—2. *Risāla fī ʾl-rubʿ al-mushaṭṭar bi-arḍ Dimashq* Paris 2547,$_{8}$.—3. See Suppl.

7. Ibrāhīm al-Ḥalabī wrote, around 814/1411:

Risāla fī masʾalat al-jabl min awāʾil sharḥ Qāḍīzāde ʿalā Mulakhkhaṣ al-Jaghmīnī (I, 624) Cairo ^{1}V, 224.

8. Shihāb al-Dīn Aḥmad b. Ghulāmallāh b. Aḥmad al-Kūm al-Rīshī[1] was *muwaqqit* at the mosque of al-Malik al-Muʾayyad (815—24/1412—21), which had been constructed in 818/1415, and died in 836/1432.

---

1 See Maqrīzī, *Khitaṭ* II, 325.

1. *al-Lumʿa fī ḥall al-sabʿa*, 60 astronomical tables, abbreviated from his larger work *Nuzhat al-nāẓir fī talkhīṣ Zīj Ibn al-Shāṭir* (no. 4), Berl. 5685/6, Gotha 1389, Lee 55, Bodl. II, 243, Paris 2526/7, Alex. Ḥisāb 52, Cairo ^{1}V, 272 (see *Qu. u. St.* VII, 51, ii, 44, 51, where mistakenly Kawm). Abstract Gotha $1379_{,3}$.—Commentaries: a. see Suppl.—b. Shams al-Dīn Muḥammad b. Aḥmad Khiḍrī b. al-Ḥājj Muṣṭafā al-Khiḍrī al-Dimyāṭī, d. 1288/1871, Alex. Ḥisāb 51, Berl. 5687 (*Qu. u. St.* VII, 55, II, 53).—2. *Kitāb al-taʿlīm fī waḍʿ al-taqwīm*, on making calendars, Cairo ^{1}V, 284.

9. Abū ʿAbdallāh Muḥammad b. Muḥammad b. Muḥammad b. Muḥammad b. al-ʿAṭṭār al-Bakrī (al-Bayṭār) al-Shāfiʿī wrote, in 830/1426, after lectures by Nūr al-Dīn b. al-Naqqāsh b. ʿAbd al-Qādir:

1. *Kashf al-qināʿ fī rasm al-arbāʿ* Br. Mus. Suppl. $753_{,5}$, Paris $2546_{,1}$, (*JA* 1862, I, 124), Cairo ^{1}V, 269, 275, 286, Dam. Z. 90, 14.—2. *al-Riyy wal-ishbāʿ* by al-Urmayūnī,
Cairo ^{1}V, 260, 310.—2., 3. See Suppl.—4. *Risāla fī khiṣāl al-miyāh* | *al-jāriya* 158
Patna II, 556, 2930/1.—5. *Risāla fī ʿurūḍ al-bilād wa-aṭwālihā* ibid. II, $336_{,2520,2}$.—6. *Risālat al-hay'a* ibid. 3.—7. *al-Jadwal* ibid. 5.—8. *Fī maʿrifat ikhrāj al-qibla* ibid. $336_{,2520,11}$.

| 10. Shihāb (Jamāl) al-Dīn Abu 'l-ʿAbbās Aḥmad b. Rajab b. Ṭaybughā b. al- 128
Majdi al-Qāhirī al-Shāfiʿī was born in Dhu 'l-Ḥijja 767/August–September 1365 and died on 10 Dhu 'l-Qaʿda 850/28 January 1447.

1. *Khulāṣat al-aqwāl fī maʿrifat al-waqt wa-ru'yat al-hilāl*, Leid. 1126, Bodl. I, $1023_{,4}$, Pet. Ros. $190_{,2}$, Cairo ^{1}V, 292, 310.—2. *Irshād al-ḥā'ir ilā takhṭīṭ faḍl al-dā'ir* Berl. 5688, Leid. 1130, Cairo ^{1}V, 227, fragm. ibid. 311, commentary by Ibn al-ʿAṭṭār Patna II, $336_{,4520,7}$.—abstract Berl. 5689.—3. *Tuḥfat al-aḥbāb fī naṣb al-bādhahanj wal-miḥrāb*, on the direction of prayer, Berl. 5690, Cairo ^{1}V, 280, 292, 304.—4. *Risāla (Natīja) fi 'l-ʿamal bi-rubʿ al-muqanṭarāt al-maqṭūʿ* Berl. 5846, Gotha 1417, Munich 856/8, Copenhagen $87_{,19}$, Leid. 1128/9, Br. Mus. Suppl. $765_{,4}$. Bodl. I, $1023_{,8}$, Paris $2547_{,3}$, Alex. Ḥisāb $56_{,1}$, Cairo ^{1}V, 248, 302, 306, VII, 148, Garr. 980, $2006_{,5}$.—Commentaries: a. Yūnus b. ʿAbd al-Qādir al-Rashīdī, Munich 859, Copenhagen $87_{,3}$.—b. Anon. Berl. 5847.—5. *al-Fuṣūl al-ʿashara*, commentary *Ghāyat al-sūl* by Yūnus b. ʿAbd al-Qādir al-Rashīdī, Alex. Ḥisāb $60_{,3}$, *Qu. u. St.* VII, 25, ii, 8.—6. *al-Jāmiʿ al-mufīd fi 'l-kashf ʿan uṣūl masā'il al-taqwīm wal-mawālīd* de Jong 112.—7. On shadows and solar altitude, Berl. 6021.—8. *al-Durr al-yatīm fī tashīl ṣināʿat al-taqwīm* see Suppl., thereon *Risāla fī ʿamal kitābihi 'l-musammā al-Durr etc.* Leid. 1127, Esc. ^{1}956, Cairo ^{1}V, 282.—9. *Taʿdīl zuḥal min al-Durr al-yatīm* Cairo ^{1}V, 233.—10. *Kashf al-ḥaqā'iq fī ḥisāb al-daraj wal-daqā'iq* Bodl. I, $1023_{,1}$, Algiers 1456, adapted in *Raqā'iq fī ḥisāb al-daraj wal-daqā'iq* by Muḥammad Sibṭ al-Māridīnī (Suter $176_{,4}$), *Qu. u. St.* VII, 54_{11}, 49 MSS.—11. *Zād*

al-musāfir fī (maʿrifat) rasm khuṭūṭ faḍl al-dāʾir Paris $2541_{,4}$, Algiers $1457_{,2}$, AS $2673_{,4}$, Cairo ^{1}v, 260, 287, 296, 312, *Dhayl* by Ibn al-ʿAṭṭār Patna II, $337_{,2520/6}$.—Commentary by Muḥammad b. Abi ʾl-Khayr al-Ḥasanī al-Mālikī, tenth cent. (p. 358), Cairo ^{1}v, 287.—12. (*al-Tashīl w*) *al-Taqrīb fī* (*bayān*) *ṭuruq al-ḥall wal-tarkīb* Munich 855, Bodl. I, $967_{,3}$, Cairo ^{1}v, 278.—13. *Ghunyat al-fahīm wal-ṭarīq ilā*
159 *ḥall al-taqwīm* Paris $2531_{,3}$, Bodl. I, $982_{,1}$.—14. *al-Kawākib al-muḍīʾa* | *fi ʾl-ʿamal bil-masāʾil al-dawriyya* Cairo ^{1}III, 268.—15. *Risālat dustūr al-nayyirayn* ibid. V, 246.—16. *Zīj al-shams wal-qamar* ibid. 295.—17. *al-Manhal al-ʿadhb al-zulāl fī taqwīm al-kawākib wa-ruʾyat al-hilāl* ibid. 307, see Suppl.—18. *ʿIqd al-durar fi ʾl-ʿamal bil-qamar* Cairo ^{1}v, 310.—19. *Irshād al-sāʾil ilā uṣūl al-masāʾil* see p. 169.—20. *Ibrāz laṭāʾif al-ghawāmiḍ wa-iḥrāz ṣināʿat al-farāʾiḍ*, on the law of inheritance, abstract of his *al-Kāfī fī mīrāth al-umma*, composed in 838/1434, Paris 1031, Cairo ^{1}III, 316, VII, 395, Alex. Far. 3, Fun. $82_{,1}$.—Commentary *al-Īḍāḥ al-fāʾiḍ* by Ibrāhīm b. Zayn al-Dīn ʿUbayd al-Ghazzī, ca. 1000/1591 (or 1050/1640?), Berl. 4723.—21. *Sharḥ Naẓm al-laʾālī* see p. 163.—22. *Bahjat al-albāb fī ʿilm al-asṭurlāb* Alex. Ḥisāb 44.—23.–26. see Suppl. (25, photograph *Qu. u. St.* VII, 37, II, 32, 26. Bodl. I, $1023_{,3}$).—27. *al-Muftakarāt al-ḥisābiyya*, with a commentary by Nūr al-Dīn ʿAlī al-Faraḍī, composed in 868/1464, Esc. $^1948_{,3}$.

11. ʿAbd al-Ghanī b. Ḥusām al-Dīn Aḥmad b. al-ʿArabānī al-Miṣrī, d. 854/1450.

129 | *Gharāʾib al-funūn wa-mulaḥ al-ʿuyūn wa-nuzhat al-ʿushshāq lil-ṭālib al-mushtāq fi ʾl-falak wal-aqālīm*, a cosmography, Algiers 1554, see Suppl.

12. Abu ʾl-ʿAbbās Aḥmad b. Burhān al-Dīn Ibrāhīm b. Khalīl b. Aḥmad al-Ḥalabī, d. 859/1455.

Suter $77_{,434}$. 1. *Bughyat al-ṭullāb fi ʾl-ʿamal bi-rubʿ al-asṭurlāb* Leid. 1133 (photograph *Qu. u. St.* VII, 31, II, 19), Paris $2524_{,10}$.—2. *Nubdha*, on sexagesimal tables, Bodl. I, 1035 (or by the translator of the *Zīj Ilkhānī*, Shihāb al-Dīn al-Ḥalabī?).

13. ʿAbd al-Raḥmān ʿAlī b. Muḥammad al-Aqfahsī al-Ṣūfī, a student of Ibn al-Majdī, ca. 860/1456.

Al-Jawhar al-maknūn fi ʾl-ḥisāb al-maṣūn, a manual for astronomical calculations with the help of tables, Berl. 5692.

14. ʿIzz al-Dīn ʿAbd al-ʿAzīz b. Muḥammad al-Wafāʾī al-Muwaqqit bil-Jāmiʿ al-Muʾayyadī, who died in 874/1469 (or, according to others, in 876 or 879).

1. *al-Nujūm al-zāhirāt fī 'l-ʿamal bi-rubʿ al-muqanṭarāt* (see Suppl.) Leid. 1123, Paris 2531, Cairo ^{1}V, 260, 276, 304, | 325.—2. *Quṭb al-zāhirāt etc.* Turin $64_{,8}$, 160
Cairo ^{1}V, 267.—3. *al-Durr al-muntathirāt fī 'l-ʿamal bi-rubʿ al-muqanṭarāt* Paris $2544_{,16}$, 4825, Cairo ^{1}V, 279.—4. *Nuzhat al-naẓar fī 'l-ʿamal bil-shams wal-qamar* Paris $2531_{,2}$, abstract Berl. 5824, Leid. 1125.—5. *Risāla fī dā'irat al-muʿaddil* Leid. 1124, Paris $2521_{,10}$, $32_{,1}$, '$32_{,1}$, '$44_{,7}$, AS 2626, Lālelī $2726_{,2}$, Cairo ^{1}V, 312,—Garr. 982.—Commentary *al-Mufaṣṣal fī 'l-ʿamal bi-ṣūrat al-muʿaddil* by Muḥammad b. Abi 'l-Fatḥ al-Ṣūfī, Alex. Ḥisāb 53.—6. *al-Lu'lu'a al-muḍī'a fī 'l-ʿamal bil-nisba al-sittīniyya* Cairo ^{1}V, 275, 285.—7. *Naẓm al-ʿuqūd fī ʿamal al-sāʿāt ʿala 'l-ʿumūd* ibid. 296.—8. *Fā'ida fī ḥisāb al-munḥarifāt* Gotha $1381_{,3}$.—9.–12. See Suppl.

15. Shams (Badr) al-Dīn Abū Muḥammad al-Ḥasan b. Khalīl b. Mazrūʿ al-Ṭubnī al-Muwaqqit al-Karādīsī, born in 823/1429, was *mu'adhdhin* at the Sharafiyya in Cairo, and died in 887/1482.

1. *Ashkāl al-wasā'iṭ fī rasm al-munḥarifāt wal-basā'iṭ* Cairo ^{1}V, 228, 272, Garr. 983 (see Suppl.).—2. *Kifāyat al-muḥtāj min al-ṭullāb ilā maʿrifat al-masā'il al-falakiyya bil-ḥisāb* Gotha 1391, Cairo ^{1}V, 270.—3., 4. See Suppl.

16. Shams al-Dīn Muḥammad b. Shams al-Dīn b. Taqī al-Dīn al-Ḥalabī al-Tīzīnī (Tīzā'ī), *muwaqqit* at the great mosque of Damascus, ca. 896/1490.

1. Suter, 450 1. *Jadwal al-kawākib al-thābita li-ākhir sanat 940 min al-hijra*, table of the fixed stars, ed. Hyde *The Appendix to Ulughbeg* see p. 212.—2. Tables: a. Concordances between solar and lunar years, b. Position of the sun up to the year 1000 AH, Paris 2521.—3. *Risāla mukhtaṣara fī 'l-ʿamal bi-rubʿ al-dā'ira al-mawḍūʿ ʿala (yhi) l-muqanṭarāt al-maṭwiyya* Berl. 5803, Gotha $1421_{,1}$, Paris $2547_{,9}$, Bodl. I, $967_{,9}$, Cairo ^{1}V, 308.—4. *Fī ʿilm al-waqt* Berl. 5804.—5. *Risāla fī maʿrifat rubʿ al-shakāziyya (?) lil-aʿmāl al-falakiyya* Paris $2547_{,16}$.—6. *Fī ʿamal al-rubʿ al-mujayyab* Paris $2547_{,22}$, Cairo ^{1}V, 315.—7. *al-Rubʿ al-kāmil* Bodl. I, 967.—8. Tables of sines from the year 896/1491, Bodl. I, $1035_{,2}$.—9. *Risāla mukhtasara fī 'l-ʿamal bi-rubʿ al-dā'ira etc.* Paris $2547_{,9}$.—10. *Risāla fī 'l-ʿamal bil-ṣaḥīfa al-Zarqāliyya* ibid. 10 (anon.).—11. Tables for the eras of the Arabs, the Greeks, and the Copts, Bodl. 1. $1039_{,1}$.

17. ʿAbd al-Raḥmān b. Banafsha al-Jawharī al-Ṣāliḥī, ca. 900/1494.

| | 1. *al-Durr al-naẓīm fī tashīl al-taqwīm*, short astronomical tables following 161 130
Ulughbeg, Berl. 5757.—2. See Suppl.

12 *Geography and Cosmography*

1. Shams al-Dīn Abū ʿAbdallāh Muḥammad b. Ibrāhīm b. Abī Ṭālib al-Anṣārī al-Ṣūfī al-Dimashqī, an imam in Rabwa in Syria, who died in 727/1327.

1. *Nukhabat al-dahr fī ʿajāʾib al-barr wal-baḥr*, Berl. 6042, Copenhagen 96, Br. Mus. 384. *Cosmographie*, ed. A.F. Mehren, St. Petersburg 1866, French transl. Copenhagen 1874, cf. Mehren, *Annaler for nord. Oldk.* 1857, p. 54, no. 25, Reinaud, *Aboulféda Trad.* I, p. CL. Chwolson, *Die Ssabier*, II, xxviii, no. 647. H. Déherain, *Quid Schemseddin ad-Dimaschqui geographus de Africa cognitum habuerit*, Paris 1898 (see Suppl.).—2. *al-Siyāsa fī ʿilm al-firāsa* AS 3782, Köpr. 1601,$_{18a/248b}$, Bursa Ḥu. Čelebi Edeb. 36,$_{1}$, Alex. Fun. 53, Cairo ^{1}VI, 150, Patna II, 551/2,$_{2925,1-4}$., under the title *Aḥkām al-firāsa* Heid. ZDMG 91, 384.—3.–5. see Suppl.—6. *Maḥāsin al-tijāra* C. 1318.

2. Burhān al-Dīn Abū Isḥāq Ibrāhīm b. ʿAbd al-Raḥmān b. Ibrāhīm b. al-Firkāḥ al-Fazārī al-Badrī, who was born in Rabīʿ I 660/February 1262, became a lecturer under his father (I, 502) and the latter's successor as a professor at the Bādarāʾiyya. He was also preacher at the Umayyad mosque for a time. He died in Jumādā I 729/March 1329.

DK I, 34, no. 88, *Orient* II, 348, Wüst. *Gesch.* 394. 1. *Bāʿith al-nufūs ilā ziyārat al-maḥrūs* (see Suppl.), an abstract of the *Kitāb al-jāmiʿ al-mustaqṣā fī faḍāʾil al-masjid al-aqṣā* of Ibn ʿAsākir, d. 600/1203 (I, 403), and to a lesser extent of the *Kitāb faḍāʾil al-Quds wal-Shām* of Abu ʾl-Maʿālī al-Musharraf b. al-Murajjā b. Ibrāhīm al-Maqdisī (Suppl. I, 567), Berl. 6093/4, Leid. 947/8, Paris 5941, Alex. Taʾr. 116, Jaghr. 5; cf. de Guignes, *Not. et Extr.* III, 605, ed. C.D. Matthews, *JPOS* 1935, 51/87, transl. 284/93.—2. *al-Iʿlām bi-faḍāʾil al-Shām*, from the *Faḍāʾil al-Shām wa-Dimashq* by al-Rabaʿī, d. 435/1043, I, 403.—3. *al-Manāʾiḥ li-ṭālib al-ṣayd wal-dhabāʾiḥ*, on the killing and slaughter of animals, Gotha 2095.—4. *Kitāb al-manṭiq* Garr. 810.—5. *al-Miṣbāḥ fi ʾl-inshāʾ* AS 4270.

162 | 3. Najm al-Dīn Aḥmad b. Ḥamdān b. Shabīb al-Ḥarrānī al-Ḥanbalī was in Egypt in 732/1332.

Jāmiʿ al-funūn (*ʿulūm*) *wa-salwat al-maḥzūn*, a cosmography (see Suppl.), Gotha 1513, Pet. AM 224, ʿĀšir I, 780, cf. B. Dorn, *Bull. de St. Pétersbourg* XVI, 17 ff, Frähn, *Ibn Foszlan* p. 184.

4. ʿAbdallāh b. Hishām, d. 761/1360.

Taḥṣīl al-uns li-zāʾir al-Quds Alex. Taʾr. 108.

| 5. Shihāb al-Dīn Abū Maḥmūd Aḥmad b. Muḥammad b. Ibrāhīm b. Hilāl al-Maqdisī al-Shāfiʿī was born in 714/1314, became a professor at al-Madrasa al-Tankīziyya in Jerusalem, and died in Cairo in Rabīʿ II 765/January 1364. 131

Wüst. *Gesch.* 425. 1. *Muthīr al-gharām ilā ziyārat al-Quds wal-Shām*, on the blessings of the pilgrimage to Jerusalem, completed on 23 Shaʿbān 752/16 October 1351, Berl. 6095/6, Gotha 1715 (where other MSS are listed), Paris 1667/9, Cairo ^{1}V, 125, ^{2}V, 322, cf. C. König, *Der* Kitāb al-muthīr etc. Diss. Leipzig 1896.—Abstract *Muntaha 'l-marām fī taḥṣīl M. al-gh.* by Muḥammad b. ʿAmmār b. Muḥammad b. Aḥmad al-Mālikī Abū Shākir, born in 768/1366 and died in 844/1440, composed, in 803/1400 (see Suppl.), Berl. 6097.—2. *al-Miṣbāḥ fi 'l-jamʿ bayna 'l-Adhkār wal-Silāḥ*, after the works of al-Nawawī (I, 501) and Ibn Humām (p. 106), used in Berl. 3705.

6. Shams (Nāṣir) al-Dīn Muḥammad b. Jalāl al-Dīn ʿAbdallāh b. Abī Ḥafṣ Sirāj al-Dīn ʿUmar al-Anṣārī al-ʿAbbāsī al-Suʿūdī b. al-Zayyāt wrote, in 804/1401:

Al-Kawākib al-sayyāra fī tartīb al-ziyāra fi 'l-Qarāfatayn al-kubrā wal-ṣughrā Cairo ^{1}V, 119, ^{2}V, 312, VI, 8, print. Būlāq 1325 (see Suppl.).

7. Isḥāq b. Ibrāhīm b. Aḥmad b. Muḥammad b. Kāmil al-Tadmurī al-Shāfiʿī al-Khaṭīb al-Khalīlī, who died in 833/1429.

Muthīr al-gharām fī ziyārat al-Khalīl ʿam., on the pilgrimage to Hebron, composed in 814/1411, Paris 1667,$_{2}$, 1668,$_{2}$, 1929/30, Br. Mus. Suppl. 500, Alex. Taʾr. 107, Garr. 590, used in Berl. 6098.

| 8. Sirāj al-Dīn Abū Ḥafṣ ʿUmar b. al-Muẓaffar b. al-Wardī al-Qurashī al-Bakrī al-Maʿarrī al-Ḥalabī, ca. 850/1446. 163

Wüst. *Gesch.* 412. *Kharīdat al-ʿajāʾib wa-farīdat al-gharāʾib*, a cosmography, for the most part copied from the works of Najm al-Dīn al-Ḥarrānī (no. 3) and the *Badʾ al-khalq* of al-Maqdisī,[1] Berl. 6046/8, Ms. or. oct. 3938/9, Gotha 1514/7 (where other MSS are listed), Paris 2188/2206, 6010, 6476, 6727, 6737, Algiers

1 Attributed by many, e.g. in *RA* 197v, to the famous Zayn al-Dīn b. al-Wardī, d. 749/1348 (p. 175), which is why Ahlw. believed that it must have been falsly attributed to him by a later writer.

1553, Br. Mus. Suppl. 761/2, AS 2611, NO 3020, Alex. Jaghr. 20, Cairo ^{1}V, 46, ^{2}VI, 26, Garr. 767/70, 2112, print. C. 1276, 1280, 1289, 1298, 1303, 1309, cf. Wüst. in *Lüddes Ztschr.* 155, no. 95, Mehren, *Ann. f. nord. Oldk.* 1857, p. 57, *Journal des Sçavans* (Amsterdam) 1758, 267/91, de Guignes, *Not. et Extr.* II (1787) 19/59, Ch. M. Frähn, *Ägyptus auctore Ibn al-Vardi*, Halle 1804. *A καὶ Ω Operis cosmographici Ibn el Vardi caput primum de regionibus, ex. cod. Ups. ed. lat. vert.* Andr. Hylander, *lect. nonnullas var. et ind. geogr. adjecit* Sven Hylander, London-Gotha 1823. *Fragmentum libri Margarita mirabilium prooemium caput 2. 3. 4. 5. continens*,
132 ed. C.J. Tornberg, Uppsala 1835/9. | S. Freund, *de rebus die resurrectionis eventuris*, Wroclaw 1853, p. 7 ff.—Turkish translation by Maḥmūd Efendi al-Khaṭīb al-Rūmī, Upps. 315, Paris 151, *Pet. Bull. sc.* VII, 368, phil. X, 80, NO 3021, As'ad 2040, another Br. Mus. Rieu 789.

9. Tāj al-Dīn ʿAbd al-Wahhāb b. Muḥammad al-Ḥusaynī, who died in 875/1470.

1. *al-Rawḍ al-mugharras fī faḍā'il al-Bayt al-muqaddas*, composed in 871/1466 following a visit to Jerusalem, Berl. 6098.—2. *Nafā'is al-marjān* see I, 449, 4b.

10. Sharaf al-Dīn Yaḥyā b. al-Maqarr Shākir b. al-Jīʿān Mustawfī Dīwān al-jaysh died in Jumādā II 885/August 1480.

Al-Sakhāwī, *Ḍaw'* X, 226/9, (on his family), see Wiet in *Mél. H. Basset* I (1923), 311. See Suppl.

164 | 11. Taqī al-Dīn Abu 'l-Baqā' ʿAbdallāh (Abū Bakr) b. ʿAbdallāh b. Muḥammad al-Badrī al-Dimashqī al-Wafā'ī died around 909/1503 (see Suppl.).

1. *Nuzhat al-anām fī maḥāsin al-Shām*, Berl. 6079/80, Paris $2253_{,2}$, Br. Mus. Suppl. 705, Cairo V, ^{1}165, ^{2}387, cf. de Sacy, *Abdollatiph* p. 574, Quatremère, *Mamlouks* II, 277, Sauvaire JA s. IX, vv. 3 and 4.—2. *Rāḥat al-arwāḥ fi 'l-ḥashīsh wal-rāḥ*, a collection of anecdotes and verses, written in 869/1464 in Cairo, Paris 3544.—3. *Ghurrat al-ṣabāḥ fī waṣf al-wujūh al-ṣibāḥ*, an anthology composed in 871/1466, Br. Mus. 1423.—4. *al-Maṭāliʿ al-Badriyya fi 'l-manāzil al-qamariyya*, composed in 880/1475, Bodl. I, 999, II, 300 (autograph).—5. *Siḥr al-ʿuyūn* (see Suppl.), Leningr. AM A. 327.—6. see Suppl.

12. Muḥammad Abū Ḥāmid al-Qudsī al-Miṣrī al-Shāfiʿī was born in Jerusalem in 820/1417, lived in Cairo, and died in 888/1483.

Wüst. *Gesch.* 498. *al-Faḍāʾil fī maḥāsin Miṣr wal-Qāhira*, a brief description of the history of Egypt and Cairo, completed in 861/1457, Gotha 1428 (autograph), Ind. Off. 718 (without author), Br. Mus. Suppl. 563.

13. Abū ʿAbdallāh Muḥammad b. Shihāb al-Dīn Aḥmad b. ʿAlī b. ʿAbd al-Khāliq al-Minhājī Shams al-Dīn al-Suyūṭī was born in 810/1407 and went with his family to Mecca in 848/1444. In 857/1453 he returned to Cairo, where entered into the service of a high official. In 874/1469, he went to Jerusalem as a member of the latter's retinue, and it is there that he completed the journal of his pilgrimage, on 13 Ṣafar 875/12 August 1470. He released a second edition in 880/1475.

Wüst. *Gesch.* 496. 1. *Itḥāf al-akhiṣṣāʾ bi-faḍāʾil al-Masjid al-Aqṣā*, Berl. 6099/100, Munich 386, Gotha 1718/9, Leid. 950, Copenhagen 143, Pet. Ros. 42, | Br. Mus. 133
386, 1245, Suppl. 572, Cambr. Prest. 20, 11,[2] Paris 2255/7, 6035, 6054, Köpr. | 165
998, AS 2446, Alex. Taʾr. 5. Garr. 598. *Commentatio philologica exhibens specimen (cap. 9) libri* Itḥāf etc., *auctore Kemaladdino etc. quem obtulit* P. Lemming, Copenhagen 1817. *The History of the Temple of Jerusalem, transl. from the Ar. Ms. of the Imam Jalálal-addin al-Siúti,*[3] *with Notes and Dissert. by* Reynolds, London 1836. Suyuti, Description of the noble Sanctuary at Jerusalem, extracts retransl. by Guy Le Strange, *JRAS* XIX, 247/305; cf. Steinschneider, *Pol. u. apol. Lit.* 169/76.—2. *Jawāhir al-ʿuqūd wa-muʿīn al-quḍāt wal-muwaqqiʿīn wal-shuhūd* Alex. Fiqh Shāf. 14, Garr. 1829.

14. ʿImād al-Dīn b. Muḥammad b. Shams al-Dīn b. Muḥibb al-Dīn b. ʿImād al-Dīn al-Ḥanafī, ca. 920/1514.

Fī faḍāʾil al-Shām Berl. 6081/2 (autograph), Cambr. Suppl. 301/2, abstract Berl. 6083.

15. Abu ʾl-Mafākhir Muḥyi ʾl-Dīn ʿAbd al-Qādir b. Muḥammad b. ʿUmar al-Nuʿaymī, born on 12 Shawwāl 845/24 February 1442, was an acting judge in Damascus, and died on 3 Jumādā I 927/12 April 1521.

---

2 In this MS and in ḤKh [1]I, 148, 42, [2]I, 5, whom Lemming follows, it is wrongly attributed to the Shāfiʿī Kamāl al-Dīn b. al-Sharīf, d. 906/1500 (cf. Wüst.).

3 Sic, a result of confusion with the famous polymath.

RA 167r. 1. *Tanbīh al-ṭālib wa-irshād al-dāris fī-mā fī Dimashq min al-jawāmiʿ wal-madāris*, Munich 387, Paris 5912, Dam. Z. 1, n. 1. Abstract by ʿAbd al-Bāsiṭ al-Dimashqī al-ʿAlmāwī, d. 981/1573, Berl. 6084/5, Paris 4943, Br. Mus. 970, Suppl. 706, cf. Sauvaire *JA* s. IX, v. 3, 250/318, 385/501, and 4, 242/331, 460/503, 6, 221/313, 401/84, 7, 185/285, 369/460. A. v. Kremer, ZDMG IX, 267.—2. *al-ʿUnwān fī ḍabṭ mawālīd wa-wafayāt ahl al-zamān* Leipz. $847_{,1}$ (draft).—8. Historical tables and excerpts, Br. Mus. Suppl. 487 (autograph).

13 *Politics and Public Administration*

1. Najm al-Dīn Aḥmad b. Muḥammad b. ʿAlī b. al-Rafʿa al-Miṣrī al-Shāfiʿī, who was born in 645/1247, was *muḥtasib* and acting judge in Cairo, and died on 18 Rajab 710/12 December 1310.

166 | DK I, 284/7. *Badhl al-naṣāʾiḥ al-sharʿiyya fī-mā ʿala ʾl-sulṭān wa-wulāt al-umūr
134 wa-sāʾir al-raʿiyya*, on good behaviour and proper conduct | in the different
classes, Gotha 1219, see Oestrup, *Or. Höflichkeit*, Leipzig 1929, 68/9.—2. *al-Īḍāḥ wal-tibyān fī maʿrifat al-mikyāl wal-mīzān* Cairo ^{1}V, 178.—3. *Sharḥ al-Tanbīh lil-Shīrāzī* I, 485.—4. *Sharḥ Wasīṭ al-Ghazzālī* I, 543.

2. Shihāb al-Dīn Abu ʾl-ʿAbbās Aḥmad b. ʿAlī b. ʿAbdallāh al-Qalqashandī al-Miṣrī b. Abī Ghudda hailed from a family of scholars from Qalqashanda, near Qalyūb, and died on 10 Jumādā II 821/16 July 1418.

1. *Ṣubḥ al-aʿshā fī ṣināʿat al-inshāʾ*, a manual for the professional writing of papers and reports, especially for Egyptian administrative officials, at the same time covering geography, history, and the local cultures of Egypt and Syria, 10 divisions in 7 volumes, ḤKh IV, 7710; vols. I, II, VII Bodl. I, 365/6, 390, IV Cambr. p. 54 no. 36, III–VI, Cairo ^{1}IV, 278, ^{2}III, 238 (ZDMG 30, 315), vol. I, Garr. 209; Second division, chapter 3 in abstract in Gotha 1619, from this: *Die Geographie und Verwaltung von Ägypten nach dem Arab. des Abu ʾl-Abbas el-Calcaschandi von* F. Wüstenfeld, Göttingen 1879. W. v. Tiesenhausen, *Zap. Vost. otd.* I, 208, *Goldene Horde* I, 395. H. Sauvaire, *Extraits de l'ouvrage de Q. intitulé Lumière de l'aurore pour l'écriture des hommes* (*Ms. ar. de la Bibl. Bodl.*) *trad.* Mém. de l'Académie de Marseille 1886/7. H. Lammens, La Chine d'après C., *al-Mashriq* IV, 406/11, 446/51, O. Spies, *An Arab account of India in the 14th Century*, Stuttgart 1936 (Bonner, *Or. St.* 14).—2. *Nihāyat al-arab fī maʿrifat qabāʾil al-ʿArab*, a genealogy and history of the Arab tribes before Muḥammad, with an alphabetical register, composed in 812/1409, Berl. 9382/33 Br. Mus. 341/2, Cairo V, ^{1}170, ^{2}297. The alphabetical register was reworked into a genealogical overview and

extended to include the caliphs and the sultans, by Abu 'l-Fawz Muḥammad Amīn al-Suwaydī (II, 498) in 1229/1814 under the title *Sabāʾik al-dhahab fī maʿrifat qabāʾil al-ʿArab* Berl. Ms. or. qu. 2092, Br. Mus. 957, 1267, Suppl. 596, lith. Baghdad 1280, print. ibid, 1332, Bombay 1296.—3. *Qalāʾid al-jumān fi 'l-taʿrīf bi-qabāʾil ʿArab al-zamān*, a supplement on the previous work running to his own time, composed after | 818/1415, Berl. 9384, Br. Mus. Suppl. 595, abstract by 167
al-Suyūṭī Berl. 9385.—4. *Ḥilyat al-faḍl wa-zīnat al-karam bil-mufākhara bayna 'l-sayf wal-qalam* Cairo ^{1}VII, 554, ^{2}III, 89.—5. Poem in praise of the Prophet, Berl. 7889$_{,2}$.

3. His son Najm al-Dīn Muḥammad wrote imitations of both of his major works:

1. *Qalāʾid al-jumān fī muṣṭalaḥ mukātabat ahl al-zamān* Br. Mus. Suppl. 1020.—2. *Nihāyat al-arab fī maʿrifat ansāb al-ʿArab*, for Zayn al-Dīn Abu 'l-Jūd Baqar b. Rāshid al-Zaynī, Grand Emir of the Arabs, East and West (al-Sakhāwī, *Ḍawʾ* I, 17, no. 75), Paris 2049 (autograph dated 846/1442).

4. Muḥammad b. Aḥmad al-Ṣaydānī.

Al-Kiyāsa fī aḥkām al-siyāsa, MS dated 884/1479, Jer. Khāll. 49, 1.

5. Muḥammad al-Maqdisī Muḥibb al-Dīn Abū Ḥāmid wrote, in 868/1463:

Badhl al-naṣāʾiḥ al-sharʿiyya fī-mā ʿala 'l-sulṭān wa-wulāt al-umūr wa-sāʾir al-raʿiyya, an imitation of 1, 1, Berl. 5618.

| 6. Khalīl b. Shāhīn al-Ẓāhirī Ghars al-Dīn, born in 813/1410, received a robe 135
of honour as *ḥakīm* of Alexandria in 839/1435, was nominated vizier and *amīr al-ḥajj* in 840/1436, *ḥakīm* of Karak in 841, of Safad in 842, and colonel in Damascus in 843, before dying in 872/1468.

ʿAlī Mubārak, *al-Khiṭaṭ al-jadīda* VIII, 86. 1. *Zubdat kashf al-mamālik fī bayān al-ṭuruq wal-masālik*, a kind of state almanac for the Mamlūk empire, Berl. 9818, Paris 1724$_{,1}$, 2258, Bodl. I, 753$_{,3}$, ed. P. Ravaisse, Paris 1894, Garr. 752. Cf. Wüstenfeld in *Lüddes Ztschr.* I, 61, no. 113, Volney, *Voyage* ^{3}I, 247 ff.—Abstract *al-Ṣafwa* by Muḥammad b. Abi 'l-Fatḥ Muḥammad al-Ṣūfī al-Shāfiʿī, composed in 904/1498, Br. Mus. Suppl. 704.—2. *al-Ishārāt fī ʿilm al-ʿibārāt*, on dream interpretation, Berl. 4274$_{,3}$, Munich 878, Paris 2752, Br. Mus. 763, cf. N. Bland, *JRAS*

XVI, 125, printed in the margin of ʿAbd al-Ghanī al-Nābulusī's *Taʿṭīr al-anām*, C. 1301, 1306.

7. Aḥmad Ṭūghān al-Muḥammadī al-Ashrafī al-Ḥanafī Shihāb al-Dīn, ca. 880/1475.

168 | 1. *al-Burhān fī faḍl al-sulṭān*, on royal priviliges, Berl. 5619.—2. *Manhaj al-sulūk fī sīrat al-mulūk*, composed in 875/1470, AS 2905.—3. *al-Muqaddima al-sulṭāniyya fī 'l-siyāsa al-sharʿiyya*, composed in 878/1473, Cairo ^{1}V, 156, VII, 10, the end, historical overview from 872/1467 until Qāytbāy, Berl. 9838.

8. ʿAbd al-Ṣamad b. Yaḥyā b. Aḥmad b. Yaḥyā al-Ṣāliḥī wrote, around 902/1496:

Hadiyyat al-ʿabd al-qāṣir ila 'l-Malik al-Nāṣir (901–4/1495–8), on politics, Copenhagen 147$_{,2}$.

9. Nūr al-Dīn ʿAlī b. Abi 'l-Fatḥ wrote, before 947/1540 (the date of the MS):

Manhaj al-ṣawāb fī qubḥ istiktāb ahl al-kitāb Qawala I, 267.

14 *Militaria, Hunting, and Agriculture*

1. Badr al-Dīn Baktūt al-Rammāḥ al-Khāzindārī al-Mālikī al-Ẓāhirī was the *nāʾib* of Alexandria. He died in 711/1311.

Kitāb fī ʿilm al-furūsiyya Br. Mus. Suppl. 820$_{,2}$, AS 4826$_{,1}$, from which *Fawāʾid jalīla fī maʿrifat al-dawābb allatī lā taṣluḥ lil-qany wa-lā lil-jihād wa-ʿādātihā*, Garr. 2083$_{,4}$.

2. Al-Ḥusayn b. Muḥammad al-Ḥusaynī wrote, in 729/1329:

Idrāk al-sūl fī musābaqat al-khuyūl Garr. 1066 (see Suppl. II, 986, 14?).

3. Lājin b. ʿAbdallāh al-Dhahabī Ḥusām al-Dīn al-Ṭarābulusī, who died in 738/1337.

Tuḥfat al-mujāhidīn fī 'l-ʿamal bil-mayādīn, on tactics, Ber. 5522 (see Suppl.).

4. An anonymous author wrote, for al-Malik al-Nāṣir:

Tafrīj al-kurūb fī taʿbīr al-ḥurūb Fātiḥ 3483 (Ritter).

5. Ṭaybughā al-Ashrafī al-Baklamishī al-Yūnānī, who died in 797/1394 (?).

| 1. *Bughyat al-marām wa-ghāyat al-gharām*, a *qaṣida* on archery, dedicated to Sultan al-Malik al-Ashraf | Shaʿbān (r. 764–78/1362–76), Leid. 1417 or *Ghunyat al-ṭullāb fī maʿrifat al-ramy bil-nushshāb* Gotha 1341/2 (fragm.), Leid. III, 296, Paris 2833, Br. Mus. 1464, Suppl. 821, Cambr. Burckh. 55, no. 16, Cairo ^{1}VI, 178; on the as-yet unclarified relation between these two, see Suppl.—2. *Kitāb fi ʾl-jihād wal-furūsiyya wa-funūn al-ādāb al-ḥarbiyya* Alex. Fun. ḥarb. 78, Cairo ^{1}VI, 178. 136 169

6. Muḥammad b. Mänglī al-Nāṣirī, who was colonel in the guard of Sultan al-Malik al-Ashraf Shaʿbān (r. 764–78/1362–76).

1. *Uns al-mala' bi-waḥsh al-fala'*, on hunting, Paris $3832_{,1}$.—2.–4. See Suppl. (3. copy of Pet. Ros. 213 Leningr. 762, see Kračkovsky, *Shaykh Ṭanṭāwī* 108, no. 19; Alex. Fun. ḥarb. 76).—5. *al-Aḥkām al-mulūkiyya wal-ḍawābiṭ al-nāmūsiyya fī fann al-qitāl fi ʾl-baḥr* A. Taymūr, see G. Zaydān, *Taʾrīkh al-adab* III, 254/5, *al-Muqtaṭaf* May 1932, p. 88.

7. Muḥammad b. Lājīn (no. 2) al-Ḥusāmī al-Ṭarābulusī al-Rammāḥ wrote, in Ramaḍān 780/January 1379:

1. *Bughyat al-qāṣidīn bil-ʿamal fi ʾl-mayādīn*, in particular on cavalry tactics, for the emir Ashyktimur[1] Sayf al-Dīn al-Māridīnī, the governor of Aleppo, Leid. 1418.—2. *Tuḥfat al-mujāhidīn fi ʾl-ʿamal bil-mayādīn* Bodl. I, $368_{,2}$.—3. *Ghāyat al-maqṣūd fi ʾl-ilm al-ʿamal bil-bunūd*, following Najm al-Dīn al-Aḥdab (Suppl. I, 905), Paris $2827_{,2}$.—4. *Kitāb mubārak yashtamil ʿalā bunūd al-rimāḥ wa-ghayrihā min al-fawāʾid wal-mayādīn* (author?) Leid. 1419 (see V, 249).

7a. Muḥammad b. ʿĪsā b. Ismāʿīl al-Ḥanafī (see Suppl.).

2. *Surūr al-muhaj wal-albāb fī rasāʾil al-aḥbāb*, love letters to boys with poems, riddles etc., AS $4033_{,1}$ (with illegible *nisba*, Ritter).

7b. Ṣafī al-Dīn Idrīs b. Bīdkīn b. ʿAbdallāh al-Turkumānī al-Ḥanafī, ca. 800/1397 (see Suppl.).

3. *al-Lumaʿ fi ʾl-ḥawādith wal-bidaʿ* Berl. ms. or. qu. 1681, Cairo ^{1}I, 351, ḤKh V, $332_{,11180}$.

---

1 I.e. 'helmet-steel', see Houtsma, *Türk. ar. Glossar*, p. 34, Cat. Leid. Ošaktimor.

170 | 8. Abū Bakr al-Ḥalabī Minqār wrote, around 887/1482:

Al-Urjūza al-Ḥalabiyya fī ramy al-sihām ʿani ʾl-qusiyy al-ʿArabiyya, ca. 400 *rajaz* verses, Berl. 5540.

9. Abū Isḥāq Ibrāhīm b. ʿAbd al-Jabbār b. Aḥmad al-Fajījī, a younger contemporary of al-Suyūṭī, ca. 920/1514.

Al-Farīd fī taqyīd al-sharīd wa-tarṣīd al-walīd or *Rawḍat al-sulwān*, 213 *ṭawīl* verses on falconry, with a commentary by his nephew Abu ʾl-Qāsim b. Muḥammad b. ʿAbd al-Jabbār b. Aḥmad al-Fajījī, completed in 986/1578, Berl. 5541, Munich $571_{,3}$, Paris 3236, Algiers 1509, Fez, Qar. 1332.

10. Ḥasan b. ʿAbd al-Raḥmān b. ʿAbdallāh al-Yūnānī.

Al-Qaṣīda al-Yūnāniyya fi ʾl-ramy ʿani ʾl-qaws Alex. Fun. ḥarb. 81 (MS dated 942).

11. Yūsuf al-Ḥaṣibānī.

Sirāj al-layl fī surūj al-khayl Beirut 1060.

12. Ṭaybughā al-Čeriklemishī al-Timārtamarī, eighth cent.

Al-Filāḥa al-muntakhaba Paris 2807/8, Cairo ^{1}V, 385.

15 *Medicine and Veterinary Science*

1. Abū Bakr b. al-Mundhir al-Bayṭār, horse veterinarian of Sultan al-Nāṣir b. Qalāwūn, who died in 741/1340, wrote for the same:

Kāshif (*Kashf*) *al-wayl fī maʿrifat amrāḍ al-khayl* or *Kāmil al-ṣināʿatayn al-bayṭara wal-zardaqa* (*zarṭaqa*), commonly called *al-Nāṣirī*, Gotha 2082/3, Vienna $1481_{,1}$, Br. Mus. 994, Bodl. I, 376, Alex. Ṭibb 36. Beginning of the first
137 *maqāla*, adapted by an unidentified author, | Berl, 6183. *La perfection des deux arts ou traité complet d'hippologie et d'hippiatrie, trad. de l'Ar. par* M. Perron, 3 vols. Paris 1852/60.

2. Shihāb al-Dīn Aḥmad b. Yūsuf b. Hilāl al-Ṣafadī, who was born in 661/1263, was a physician at the Bīmāristān Manṣūrī in Cairo, and was also known as a poet. He died in 737/1337.

| Al-Ṣafadī, *al-Wāfī* AS 2617, 156. *Al-Wajīz al-muntaqā wal-ʿazīz al-multaqā*, an account in rhymed prose of a conversation on medicine between a sultan and a philosopher, Paris 3110 (autograph), Glasgow 60, 11. 171

3. Abū ʿAbdallāh Shams al-Dīn Muḥammad b. Burhān al-Dīn Ibrāhīm b. Ṣāʿid al-Sinjārī al-Miṣrī al-Akfānī al-Anṣārī al-Sakhāwī was born in Sinjār, settled as a physician in Cairo, and died of the plague in 749/1348.

DK III, 279, no. 744, al-Ṣafadī, *al-Wāfī*, AS 2968, 124/7. 1. *Kashf al-rayn fī aḥwāl al-ʿayn*, a handbook on ophthalmology, Cairo [1]VI, 30; author's abstract *Tajrīd* (see Suppl.), a commentary thereon *Wiqāyat al-ʿayn* by Nūr al-Dīn ʿAlī al-Munāwī, ninth cent., Pet. Ros. 176, Sbath 16.—2. *Ghunyat al-labīb fī ghaybat* (*ḥaythu lā yūjad*) *al-ṭabīb*, on household remedies, Cairo [1]VII, 184, abstract Gotha $2034,_3$.—3. *Nihāyat al-qaṣd fī ṣināʿat al-faṣd*, on bloodletting, Cairo [1]VI, 48.—4. *al-Naẓar wal-taḥqīq fī taqlīb al-raqīq*, tips on buying slaves, Paris $2234,_3$.—5. *Nukhab al-dhakhāʾir fī aḥwāl al-jawāhir*, gemmology, Cairo [1]VII, 640, ed. P. Anastase Marie de St. Elie, C. 1939.—6. *Irshād al-qāṣid ilā asna ʾl-maqāṣid*, an encyclopaedic overview of 60 sciences, Gotha 163, Paris 2231/3, Esc. [1]944, Bonon. 457, Cairo [1]VII, 21, 253, 528, 618, [2]VI, 180, Garr. 1129, b, c. Cf. ZDMG VII, 413, ed. A. Sprenger, *Bibl. Ind.* no. 21, 1849.—7. *al-Durr al-naẓīm fī aḥwāl al-ʿulūm wal-taʿlīm*, possibly revised by an unidentified person (attributed to Ibn Sīnā in ḤKh [1]III, $197,_{4903}$, [2]I, 736), Vienna 2, f. 42/4, Leid. 17, a part in Hebrew characters ed. Gottheil in *JQR* XXIII, 1932, 176/80, translation ibid. 174/75, see Farmer, *Sources* 52.

4. Abū Manṣūr al-Ḥusayn b. Nūḥ al-Qamarī wrote, before 788/1386 (the date of the MS):

Mukhtaṣar fī ʾl-ṭibb Bursa Haraccizade Tibb 213 (Ritter).

5. Ṣadaqa b. Ibrāhīm al-Miṣrī al-Ḥanafī al-Shādhilī wrote, in the second half of the eighth century:

Al-ʿUmda al-kuḥliyya fī ʾl-amrāḍ al-bashariyya Munich 834, Pet. Ros. 175, see M. Meyerhof, *The History of the Trachoma Treatment*, C. 1936, p. 46/7.

6. Ibrāhīm b. ʿAbd al-Raḥmān b. Abī Bakr al-Azraqī wrote, after 815/1412:

| *Tashīl al-manāfiʿ fī ʾl-ṭibb wal-ḥikam*, see Suppl. Meshh. XVI, $6,_{20}$. 172

7. ʿAbd al-Raḥmān al-Munajjim b. Abī Yūsuf al-Ḥāfiẓ wrote, in 907/1501:

Kitāb al-jawhar fī ḥifẓ al-ṣiḥḥa AS 3635.

8. ʿAbd al-Qādir b. Muḥammad b. Aḥmad al-Shādhilī, a student of al-Suyūṭī, ca. 920/1514.

1. *Shifāʾ al-mutaʿāll bi-adwiyat al-suʿāl*, on the treatment of coughs, Berl. 6363.—2. *Mawāʾid al-afrāḥ fī fawāʾid al-nikāḥ* Cairo [1]VII, 538.

16 *Zoology*

1. Kamāl al-Dīn Muḥammad b. Mūsā al-Damīrī was born in 745/1344 and died in Cairo in 808/1405, see Suppl.

ʿAlī Mubārak, *al-Khiṭaṭ al-jadīda* XI, 59, Wüst. *Ärzte* 265, Leclerc, II, 278. I. *Ḥayāt al-ḥayawān*, arranged alphabetically, etymologies of animal names, the meaning of animals in the Qurʾān, *ḥadīth*, ancient poetry, and proverbs, and their effectiveness in medicine and role in superstition; in 3 recensions: 1. *al-Kubrā*, completed in 773/1371, Berl. 6168/71, Gotha 2068/9 (fragm.), Vienna 1441/3, Copenhagen 105/6, Lee 132, BDMG 61, Garr. 1067/8, Meshh. XVI, 12,$_{38/9}$, print. C. 1274, 1284, 1292, 1305, 1309, 1311, 1314, 1319, 1330, see J. de Somogyi, *Biblical Figures in Damiris Ḥ. al-Ḥ. Jub. Vol. Mahler*, Budapest 1937, 262/99.—2. *al-Wusṭā* Berl. 6172, BDMG 62 (?), Gotha 2070 (where other MSS are listed), Paris 2783/4, ’8/9, Algiers 1506/7, Br. Mus. Suppl. 779.—3 *al-Ṣughrā* Paris 2798.—Abstracts: 1. *ʿAyn al-ḥayāt* by Muḥammad b. Abī Bakr al-Damāmīnī, d. 827/1424 (p. 32), Berl. 6173, Bat. 157, Garr. 1069.—2. Ibn Qāḍī Shuhba, see p. 37.—3. *Dīwān al-ḥayawān* by al-Suyūṭī, d. 911/1505, Gotha 2071 (fragm.), Paris 2800,$_{1}$, Cairo [1]VI, 141, *lat. ab Abr. Ecchellensi*, Paris 1667 (Ellis I, 62), abstract by al-Maydānī, autograph Leipz. 748,$_{5}$.—3a. Muḥammad ʿIsā b. Kannān, d. 1153/1740 (p. 299), Berl. 6174.—4. *Ḥāwi ’l-ḥisān* by Muḥammad b. ʿAbd al-Qādir al-Damīrī al-Ḥanafī, Ind. Off. 1004, Paris 2799.—4a. Ibrāhīm b. Muḥammad b. ʿAlāʾ al-Dīn al-Ṭarābulusī, Leipz. 749.—5. Anon. Berl. 6175, Paris 2801, Alex. Fun. 201.—6. The same,
173 under the title *Khawāṣṣ al-ḥayawān*, | Br. Mus. Suppl. 780, Cairo [1]VI, 137 (attributed to al-Damīrī himself).—7. A Persian translation *Khawāṣṣ al-ḥayawān* by Muḥammad b. Taqī Tabrīzī, made during the reign of Shāh ʿAbbās II? (r. 1052–77/1642–66), Br. Mus. Pers. II, 842 b, Cambr. Suppl. 422.—8. Turkish translation by ʿAbd al-Raḥmān Efendi al-Sīwāsī, Istanbul 1272.—Augmented imitation by Ibn Ḥijja, see p. 19.—II. *Sharḥ Minhāj al-Nawawī* I, 497.—III. *Mulakhkhaṣ sharḥ al-Ṣafadī li-Lāmiyyat al-ʿAjam* I, 287,$_{1}$.—IV. See Suppl. (Garr. 1819).

2. Muḥammad b. ʿAbd al-Karīm al-Ṣafadī wrote, in 896/1490:

Al-Multaqaṭ min ʿAjāʾib al-makhlūqāt (I, 633) *wa-Ḥayāt al-ḥayawān* NO 3023.

17 *Music*

1. Muḥammad b. Muḥammad b. Aḥmad al-Dhahabī b. al-Ṣabbāḥ, 14th cent.

Kitāb fī ʿilm al-mūsīqī wa-maʿrifat al-anghām Bodl. Ous. 102f. 1/11v, Cairo f. j. 506 (photograph), Farmer, *Sources* 54 = *Urjūza fī ʾl-naghamāt al-mūsīqiyya* photograph Cairo, *Nashra* 3 with a commentary.

2. Abu ʾl-Ḥasan Muḥammad b. al-Ḥasan al-Ṭaḥḥān, 14th cent.

Ḥāwi ʾl-funūn wa-salwat al-maḥzūn, Cairo f. j. 539, see Farmer, *Studies on Oriental Musical Instruments*, Glasgow 1939, *Sources* 55.

3. Muḥammad b. ʿĪsā b. ʿAlī b. Kurr, see Suppl. p. 173, 8.

4. Muḥammad b. ʿAbd al-Ḥamīd al-Lādhiqī, d. 849/1445.

Al-Risāla al-fatḥiyya fī ʾl-mūsīqī, Br. Mus. or. 6629, Cairo f. j. 364, Farmer, *Sources* 57.—2. *Zayn al-alḥān fī ʿilm taʾlīf al-awzān* Cairo, *Nashra* 71, Farmer, ibid.

18 *Occult Sciences*

1. Aydamur b. ʿAlī b. Aydamur al-Jildakī ʿIzz al-Dīn died in Cairo in 743/1342 or, according to others, in 762.

S. de Sacy, *Not. et Extr.* IV, 108, Wüst. *Ärzte* 254, Leclerc II, 280, E.J. Holmyard, *Iraq* IV, 47/53. 1. *al-Burhān* | *fī asrār ʿilm al-mīzān*, on alchemy, Berl. 4185 174
(5. vol.), Leid. III, 209, Paris 1355, Br. Mus. 1657, Pet. Ros. 199, NO 3618, Patna I, 209$_{,1861}$, II, 525$_{,2823/4}$, abstracts Gotha 1295/7, 1769. |—2. *al-Miṣbāḥ fī asrār ʿilm* 139
al-miftāḥ Gotha 1285 (fragm.), Leid. 1274, Paris 2615/6 (see de. Sacy, op. cit. 108), 6560, Pet. Ros. 200, 203$_{,1}$, Cairo ^{1}V, 396, lith. Bombay 1302.—3. *Anwār al-durar fī īḍāḥ al-ḥajar* Berl. 4187, Br. Mus. 1002, 1371$_{,3}$, Pet. Ros. 205$_{,1}$, Cairo Ṭab. 318, 413.—4. *Bughyat al-khabīr fī qānūn ṭalab al-iksīr*, composed in Damascus in 740/1339, Pet. Ros. 205$_{,2}$.—5. *al-Shams al-munīr fī taḥqīq al-iksīr* Pet. Ros. 205$_{,4}$, Br. Mus. 1002$_{,21}$.—6. *Sharḥ al-Shams al-akbar li-Bālīnūs* Berl. 4188.—7. *Natāʾij al-fikar fī aḥwāl al-ḥajar* Alex. Kīm. 12$_{,1}$, Cairo ^{1}V, 397, print. Būlāq n.d.—8. *al-Taqrīb fī asrār al-tarkīb*, on alchemy, Paris 2617/8, NO 3620, Cairo, Ṭab. 566, Patna II,

532,$_{2867}$.—9. *Risāla fī 'l-ṭabā'iʿ al-arbaʿ* Cairo [1]v, 391.—10. (*Kanz*) *al-Ikhtiṣāṣ wa-durrat al-ghawwāṣ fī asrār al-khawāṣṣ*, on the healing powers of animals and stones and their use in the making of talismans, composed in Damascus in 743/1342, Berl. 4186, Gotha 2117 (part 2), Br. Mus. 987, Cambr. Prest. no. 60, p. 13, Cairo [1]vi, 182, Ṭab. 417.—11. *Sharḥ Risālat al-shams ila 'l-hilāl, mukhammas min al-Mā' al-waraqī* vol. i, 279, Vienna 1496, Cairo [1]v, 393.—12. *Nihāyat al-ṭalab fī sharḥ al-Muktasab fī zirāʿat al-dhahab* i, 654.—14. *al-Durr al-maknūn fī sharḥ qaṣīdat Dhi 'l-Nūn* i, 214, composed in 743/1342 in Cairo, Cairo [1]v, 393.—15. *Sharḥ qaṣīdat Abi 'l-Iṣbaʿ* Suppl. i, 432.—16.–20. See Suppl. (16. Garr. 940; Taymūr, Ṭab. 95; AS 4914 f. 19r/52v).—21. *Thamarāt al-irshād wa-tamzīj al-arwāḥ wal-ajsād* see *Qu. u. St.* vii, 109, vi, 43.—22. *Ghāyat al-surūr*, composed in 742, print. C. 1881.

2. Muḥammad b. Abī Bakr al-Zarkhūrī al-Miṣrī was in Aleppo in 852/1448.

Zahr al-basātīn fī ʿilm al-mashātīn (see Dozy, Suppl. ii, 594), on juggler's tricks, Br. Mus. Suppl. 1210,$_3$.

3. Nāṣir al-Dīn Muḥammad b. ʿAbdallāh b. Qurqmās was born in 802/1399 and died in 882/1477.

1. *Kitāb fatḥ al-khallāq fī ʿilm al-ḥurūf wal-awfāq*, on occult sciences, Esc. [2]127.—2. *al-Maqālāt al-falsafiyya wal-tarjumānāt al-ṣūfiyya* Cairo [1]ii, 137.—3. *Qabs*
175 *al-mujtadī wa-tawqiyat al-mubtadi'* Cairo [1]v, 350.—| 4. *Ṭarīqat al-ma'mūm fī maʿjūn al-balādhur*, in 52 *rajaz* verses, a manual for the preparation of the universal remedy *balādhur* and information on what it is good for in each month, Berl. 6430.—5. *Zahr al-rabīʿ fī shawāhid al-badīʿ*, a compendium on rhetoric in 42 chapters, Berl. 7279/80, Gotha 2797, Leid. 329/30, Paris 2502,$_9$, Esc. [2]245/6, AS 4031, Alex. Bal. 12, Cairo [1]iv, 137. Commentary *al-Ghayth al-murīʿ* vol. ii, Leid. 331.

5. Abu 'l-ʿAbbās Aḥmad b. Muḥammad al-Ghamrī, d. 905/1499, see Suppl.

1. *Ḥall al-ṭilasm etc.* Garr. 941.—3. *Sharḥ bayt min manẓūmat Kashf al-rān li-Ibn ʿArabī* (i, 581) ibid. 942.

19 *Encyclopaedias and Polyhistors*

1. Abu 'l-ʿAbbās Aḥmad b. ʿAbd al-Wahhāb b. Aḥmad Shihāb al-Dīn al-Nuwayrī al-Bakrī al-Taymī al-Kindī al-Shāfiʿī, a protégé of al-Malik al-Nāṣir, and *nāẓir al-jaysh* in Tripoli, died, at the age of about 50, on 21 Ramaḍān 732/17 June 1332.

| *DK* I, 197, no. 506, al-Ṣafadī, *al-Wāfī*, AS 2962, 94, al-Suyūṭī, *Ḥusn al-muḥ.* I, 140
320, *Orient.* II, 358, Wüst. *Gesch.* 399, Kračkovsky, *EI* III, 1045 ff. *Nihāyat al-arab fī funūn al-adab*, an encyclopaedia in 10 (or 30) volumes: 1. heaven and earth (geography); 2. Man; 3. the animal kingdom; 4. the world of plants; 5. history. Detailed table of contents in J.J. Reiske, *Prodidagmata ad Hadgi Khalfae tabulas, after Abulfedae Tab. Syriae*, ed. Köhler and Cat. Leid. ^{2}no. 5 (partly autograph). Individual parts Berl. 6202, 9804/6, Vienna 900, Paris 1573/9, 5050, Br. Mus. Suppl. 714. Cairo ^{1}V, 170, ^{2}VI, 192, AS 3511/37, NO 3451/2, Köpr. II, 221/4. A listing of sections published earlier in Wüst. loc. cit.; add no. 5 E. Mittwoch, *Proelia Arabum paganorum*, Berlin 1899, 26/30. Corrections to the edition of Dār al-kutub by al-Maghribī, *RAAD* V/VII, IX, X, XII, XIV.

2. Abū Ḥafṣ ʿUmar b. al-Muẓaffar b. ʿUmar al-Qurashī al-Bakrī al-Maʿarrī Zayn al-Dīn b. al-Wardī al-Shāfiʿī was born sometime before 689/1290 in Maʿarrat
al-Nuʿmān and studied in Hama, Damascus, and Aleppo. In this city, | he was 176
for a certain period of time the representative of the *qāḍī* Muḥammad b. al-Naqīb, d. 745/1343. He dedicated the final years of his life to writing. On 27 Dhu ʾl-Ḥijja 749/19 March 1349 he died of the plague in Aleppo.

DK III, 195, no. 472, *RA* 179, v, *Fawāt* II, 116, *Orient.* II 390, Wüst. *Gesch.* 412, Abicht, loc. cit., Hartmann *Muw.* 60. I. Poetry. 1. *Dīwān* Berl. 7849/50, Leid. 731, print. Istanbul 1300 (*Majmūʿat al-jawāʾib*).—2 *Maqāma fī ʾl-ṭāʿūn al-ʿāmm*, included by al-Suyūṭī in his work on the plague, = *al-Nabaʾ ʿani ʾl-wabaʾ*, a *maqāma* on the plague of the year 749/1349, Berl. 8550,$_{3}$?—3. *Lāmiyya* or *Waṣiyya* or *Naṣīḥat al-ikhwān wa-murshidat al-khillān*, an admonition to his son in 77 *ramal* verses, Berl. 5998/9, Gotha 26, 1 (where other MSS are listed), Heid. *ZDMG* 9, 389, Garr. 81, 2003,$_{23}$, Qawala II, 222.—Commentaries: a. ʿAbd al-Wahhāb al-Khaṭīb al-Ghumrī, composed in 1031/1622, Berl. 4000/1, Ms. or. oct. 3836, Vienna 437, Br. Mus. Suppl. 1084, Paris 3202/4, Garr. 82, 1810, Alex. Mawāʿiẓ 26, Fun. 127,$_{1}$, Cairo ^{1}II, 64, IV, 339, ^{2}III, 249.—b. Muḥammad b. Muḥammad al-Ghazzī al-ʿĀmirī, d. 1061/1651, composed in 1047/1637, Berl. 4002.—c. Yāsīn, Algiers 882.—d. Masʿūd b. Ḥasan b. Abī Bakr al-Ḥusaynī al-Qīnawī, print. C. 1307, 1310, among others.—e. Anon., Algiers 1829,$_{2}$.—f.–i. see Suppl.—*Takhmīs*: a. Yūsuf al-Maghribī, d. 1019/1611 (p. 305), Paris 3200.—b. Aḥmad b. Marzūq al-Rushdī, print. C. 1310.—c. Anon., Paris 3199.—d.–g. See Suppl.—4. *Mufākharat* (*Munāẓarat*) *al-sayf wal-qalam*, also included in the *Dīwān*, Copenhagen 217,$_{3}$, 231,$_{9}$, Br. Mus. 623, Esc. ^{2}524,$_{2}$.—5. *Ṣafw al-raḥīq fī waṣf al-ḥarīq*, imputes a story to Moisture, son of the sea, depicting an all-consuming blaze, Berl. 8371.—6. Poem for a special occasion, Berl. 8158,$_{3}$.—II. Grammar.—7. *Taḥrīr al-khaṣāṣā fī taysīr al-khulāṣa*, an transposition of the *Alfiyya* (I, 359) into prose, Cairo ^{1}IV,

96, [2]II, 83.—8. *al-Tuḥfa al-wardiyya*, a short didactic poem, ed. R. Abicht,
Diss. Breslau 1891. Commentaries, see Suppl. (c. ʿUm. 6289).—III. History.—9.
Tatimmat al-mukhtaṣar fī akhbār al-bashar, an abstract of the chronicle of
Abu ʾl-Fidāʾ, with a continuation up to 749/1357, Vienna 811, Yeni 834, print.
141 C. 1285. |—IV. *Fiqh*.—10. *al-Bahja al-Wardiyya*, a versification of *al-Ḥāwī* by
al-Qazwīnī, d. 665/1266, I, 495.—11. *al-Masāʾil al-mulaqqabāt al-Wardiyya fi*
177 *ʾl-farāʾiḍ*, *rajaz* on 24 questions on the law of | inheritance, Berl. 4713, Cairo [1]III,
316.—Commentary by al-Shinshawrī, d. 999/1590 (p. 320), Alex. Far. 13, Cairo
[1]III, 316, 21, 561.—12. *Manẓūma fī shuhūd al-sawʾ* (author?) Cairo [1]VII, 145.—V.
Mysticism.—13. *al-Shihāb al-thāqib wal-ʿatāb al-wāṣib al-wāqiʿ bi-dhawi ʾl-niḥal
al-kawādhib*, against the *Futuwwa*, AS 1943.—14. *al-Muqaddima* (*al-alfiyya*) *al-
wardiyya*, a juvenile work on the interpretation of dreams, Berl. 4278/9, Paris
2582, Cairo VI, [1]165, [2]174, Garr. 938,$_{19}$.—15. *al-Minaḥ* Alex. Mawāʿiẓ 45.

3. Abu ʾl-ʿAbbās Aḥmad b. Yaḥyā b. Faḍlallāh Shihāb al-Dīn al-ʿUmarī al-ʿAdawī al-Qurashī al-Kirmānī al-Shāfiʿī was born in Damascus on 3 Shawwāl 700/12 June 1301, and studied there, as well as in Cairo, Alexandria, and the Hijaz. When his father became privy secretary he was given the task of reporting to the sultan on incoming mail. However, in Dhu ʾl-Ḥijja 740/June 1340 he fell into disgrace and was transferred to Damascus. Having met with further vicissitudes in his career, he died there on 9 Dhu ʾl-Ḥijja 749/1 March 1349.

RA 241r, *Fawāt* II, 17, *Orient.* II, 389, Wüst. *Gesch.* 411, Hartmann *Muw.* 49. 1.
Masālik al-abṣār fī mamālik al-amṣār, 27 (or 22) volumes on geography, history, and biography, vol. I, on geography and natural history, Bodl. II, 900,
heavily used ibid. I, 454, vol. III (Asia) Paris 2325, vol. 1/2, geography, Paris
5867/8, biographies of musicians ibid. 5870, abstracts on the population of the
earth ibid. 5962, vol. 1/2, geography and natural history Alex. Taʾr. 125, entitled
title *al-Masālik wal-mamālik* Fez, Qar. 1324, history of the Arabs, Bodl. I, 128,
cf. Pococke *Spec. hist. Ar.* and de Sacy's additions, vol. 14 on the poets of the
Jāhiliyya Paris 2326, vol. 15 the poets of Islam up to and including the third century, completed in 745/1343, Br. Mus. 373, Esc. [2]287, vol. 16 the poets of the West,
Br. Mus. 1293, vol. 17 the poets of the fourth/seventh century, Paris 2327, vol. 23
the history of the years 541/744 ibid. 2328; cf. AS 3415/39, geographical abstract
Pet. AM 228, see Dorn, *Mél. As.* VI, 672 ff, Deguignes, *Journal des savants* 1758,
354, Quatremère, *Not. et Extr.* XIII, 1838, 151/384, *I. F. al ʿO. ʾs. Bericht über Indien
in s. Werke* M. al a. fī m. al. a. *hsg. u. übers. v.* O. Spies (Sammlg. or. Arbeiten 14),
178 Leipzig 1943.—2. *al-Taʿrīf bil-muṣṭalaḥ al-sharīf*, | a collection of sample letters,
important as a source on relations between the sultans of Egypt and outside
powers, composed in 741/1340, Berl. 8639, Gotha 1657 (fragm.), Leid. 350 (where

other MSS are listed), AS 3160, 3823, Cairo [1]V, 219, [2]III, 65, print. C. 1312, cf. v. Tiesenhausen, *Goldene Horde* 301 ff.—3. *al-Shatawiyyāt,* letters from the snowy winter of 744/5, from Damascus to various scholars, with their answers, Leid. 351, Istanbul Un. R. 3104 (*ZS* III, 249).—4.–6. See Suppl.

4. Shihāb al-Dīn Aḥmad b. ʿUmar b. Hilāl al-Mālikī al-Iskandarānī al-Dimashqī was a student of Ibn al-Ḥājib al-Furūʿī who died in 795/1393.

DK I, 232, no. 589. 1. *Risāla fī aʿdād al-ʿulūm* Berl. 68.—2. *al-Risāla al-musammāt bil-Durr al-manẓūm fī bayān ḥashr al-ʿulūm* ibid. 69.

5. Abu ʾl-Walīd Muḥammad b. Kamāl al-Dīn Muḥammad b. Maḥmūd b. al-Shiḥna Zayn al-Dīn al-Ḥalabī, d. 815/1412, see Suppl.

| Wüst. *Gesch.* 460. 1. *Manẓūma fī uṣūl al-dīn,* 100 *rajaz* verses, Berl. 1820.— 142
2. *Manẓūma fī ʿilm al-taṣawwuf,* 102 *rajaz* verses, ibid. 3022.—3. *Manẓūma fī uṣūl al-fiqh,* 103 *rajaz* verses, ibid. 4413, Br. Mus. $421_{,18}$.—4. *Lisān al-ḥukkām fī maʿrifat al-aḥkām* Paris 935.—5. *Manẓūma fi ʾl-farāʾiḍ* Berl. 4718, Br. Mus. $421_{,16}$.—6. *Manẓūma fi ʾl-ijmāʿ,* on the agreements between the four major imams, Berl. 4865.—7. *ʿAqīda* Alex. Tawḥīd 38, 41, with commentaries by: a. Ḥasan b. ʿAbd al-Muḥsin, composed soon after 1125/1713, Cairo [1]II, 7.— b. Sharīf Aḥmad al-Ḥamawī Alex. Tawḥīd 41.—8. *Manẓūma fī ʿilm al-manṭiq* Berl. $5186_{,14}$.—9. *Manẓūma fī ʿilm al-ṭibb* ibid. 6307.—10. *Manẓūma fī ʿilm al-naḥw* ibid. 6759.—11. *al-Urjūza al-bayāniyya,* a didactic poem on rhetoric, Berl. 7254/5, Gotha 2788,[2], Bodl. I, 534, II, $586_{,q}$, Br. Mus. $421_{,16}$,—Commentaries: a. Muḥibb al-Dīn Muḥammad b. Abī Bakr Taqī al-Dīn al-Ḥanafī al-ʿUlwānī al-Ḥamawī, completed in 969/1561, Berl. 7256/7, Gotha 2789.—b. Muḥammad b. ʿAbd al-Ḥaqq al-Ṭarābulusī, composed in 1009/1600, Berl. 7258.—c. al-Azharī, d. 1066/1655, ibid. 7259.—d, e. See Suppl.—12. *Rawḍat al-manāẓir fī ʿilm al-awāʾil wal-awākhir,* an abstract of the annals of Abu ʾl-Fidāʾ (p. 56), with a continuation up to the year 806/1403, Berl. 9456/7, | Gotha 1573 (where other MSS are 179
listed), Br. Mus. 283, 1239, Suppl. 478/9, Nicholson *JRAS* 1899, 909, no. 8, printed in the margin of the edition of Ibn al-Athīr, C. 1290, vol. 7, 8, 1303, vol. 11/2, individual parts in the Beirut magazine *Ḥadīqat al-akhbār* (see Fleischer, *ZDMG* 12, 332, *SBSGW phil. hist. Cl.* XI, 13), cf. J. Gottwaldt, *JA* s. IV, v. 8, p. 510.—Abstract by Zayn al-Dīn b. Aḥmad b. ʿAlī b. al-Ḥusayn b. ʿAlī al-Shuʿaybī, from the abstract by Ibn al-Manlā (Muḥammad b. Aḥmad b. Muḥammad al-Ḥaṣkafī, S II, 407?), Alex. Taʾr. 122.—13. *Manẓūma fī sīrat al-rasūl,* 99 *rajaz* verses, Berl. 9588.— 14. See Suppl.

6. Burhān al-Dīn Abu 'l-Ḥasan Ibrāhīm b. ʿUmar al-Biqāʿī al-Shāfiʿī, born around 809/1406 in Khirbat Ruhā in the Biqāʿ, between Baalbek, Homs, and Damascus, participated in 844/1440 in a *ghazwa* against Cyprus and Rhodes, studied under Ibn Ḥajar (p. 80) in Cairo in 846/1442, and died in 885/1480 in Damascus.

Wüst. *Gesch.* 497. Listing of his writings Leid. 23. 1. *al-Aqwāl al-qawīma fī ḥukm al-naql min al-kutub al-qadīma* Esc. [2]1539/40, Cairo [1]I, 126, [2]33.—2. *Naẓm al-durar fī tanāsub al-āy wal-suwar* Yeni 160/3, NO 241/3, Köpr. 83, Cairo I, [1]218, [2]142.—3. *Masāʾil al-naẓar lil-ishrāf ʿalā maqāṣid al-suwar* NO 598, Dāmādzāde 309, Garr. 1224.—4. *al-Fatḥ al-Qudsī fī āyat al-kursī* (p. 2, 250) AS 387.—5. *al-Īdhān bi-fatḥ asrār al-tashahhud wal-adhān*, on the secret powers of the profession of faith and the call to prayer, composed in 873/1468 in Cairo, Berl. 4149, Paris 1139.—6. *Tanbīh al-ghabī ʿalā takfīr b. al-ʿArabī* I, 582.—7. *al-Nāṭiq bil-ṣawāb al-fāriḍ li-takfīr Ibn al-Fāriḍ* I, 307.—8. *Aswāq al-ashwāq fī maṣāriʿ al-ʿushshāq* I, 431.—9. *ʿUnwān al-zamān fī tarājim al-shuyūkh wal-aqrān*, an alphabetical list of his teachers, contemporaries, and students, with information on the orthography of their names, genealogies, and years of death, Köpr. 1119. ḤKh 8387 explains al-Sakhāwī's (*Ḍawʾ* I, 105) reproaches as based on jealousy of a fellow-student.—An abstract therefrom Bodl. I, 858.—110. *Taʾrīkh*, a brief survey of the life of Muḥammad and the first three caliphs, completed in 876/1471 in Cairo,
143 Berl. 9694. |—11. *Badhl al-nuṣḥ wal-shafaqa lil-taʿrīf bi-ṣuḥbat al-sayyid Waraqa*, a demonstration that Muḥammad b. Nawfal belongs to the Ṣaḥāba, *Khiz.* II,
180 38 ff.—12. *al-Iʿlām bi-sann al-hijra ila 'l-Shām*, completed on 5 Rabīʿ | II, 880/9 August 1475 in Cairo, Alex. Ḥad. 6., Cairo [1]VII, 586, [2]I, 90.—13. *Muqaddimat Īsāghūjī*, on dialectic, *ʿilm al-mīzān*, Esc. [2]636,$_{6}$, 653,$_{4}$, 697,$_{5}$, a commentary by Muḥammad b. Yūsuf al-Sanūsī, d. 895/1490 (p. 250), ibid. 697,$_{3}$.—14. *al-Bahāʾ fī ʿilmay al-ḥisāb wal-misāḥa*, an *urjūza* with a commentary, *al-Ibāḥa*, Cairo [1]V, 177.—16.–21. see Suppl. (20. Garr. 798).

7. Abu 'l-Faḍl ʿAbd al-Raḥmān b. Abī Bakr b. Muḥammad b. Abī Bakr Jalāl al-Dīn al-Suyūṭī al-Khuḍayrī al-Shāfiʿī was born on 1 Rajab 849/3 October 1445. His father (d. Ṣafar 855/1451) was a professor at the Shaykhūniyya and a preacher at the mosque of Ibn Ṭūlūn, while his mother was a Turkish slave. His ancestors came from Persia; the *nisba* al-Khuḍayrī they traced back to the Khuḍayriyya quarter of Baghdad where one of them had lived. They were called al-Suyūṭī after his grandfather of nine generations back who had lived as a Sufi in Suyūṭ and whose descendants were officials and traders there. After his father's premature death he was raised by a friend of his who lived as a Sufi near the shrine of al-Nāfisa. He began his studies in 864/1460, and after two years he was officially active as a teacher and author. He then went to other cities in Egypt and,

in Rabīʿ II of 869/December 1464, to Mecca. From the year 871/1466 onward he
issued legal opinions in Cairo, | became professor of *ḥadīth* in 872 and then, 144
thanks to the intercession of his teacher al-Bulqīnī (p. 119), succeeded his own
father as a profesor of Islamic law at the Shaykhūniyya. After his transfer to the
more prestigious al-Baybarsiyya in 891/1486, he made a lot of enemies because
of his arrogance. On 12 Rajab 906/2 February 1501 his students stood up against
him because of his backhanded management of trust money, and on the 26th
of that month they obtained his removal from office. He then retired from
public life to the island of al-Rawḍa on the River Nile. After the death of his
successor Layshīn b. al-Ballān al-Bilbaysī | on 25 Dhu 'l-Ḥijja 909/10 June 1503 181
he refused to assume his earlier professorship once again. Thus, he died in solitude, on 18 Jumādā I 911/17 October 1505.

In his productivity, al-Suyūṭī is unrivalled in Arabic literature. Apart from
countless smaller writings, whose numbers were ever increasing, he also composed a series of larger works which, because they contain material otherwise
lost, are useful even today. He had just as little concern for intellectual property
as did his predecessors and contemporaries, which did not, however, keep him
from officially prosecuting his rival al-Sakhāwī for plagiarism.

Autobiography *Ḥusn al-muḥ.* I, 153, 203, II, 65, Biography *Bahjat al-ʿābidīn*, by
his student ʿAbd al-Qādir b. Muḥammad b. Aḥmad al-Shādhilī (p. 304), after
a lost autobiography *al-Taḥadduth bi-niʿmat Allāh* Ind. Off. 4574,$_2$ (*JRAS* 1939,
366), anon. *Manāqib al-S.* Qawala II, 248, Biography by Muḥammad al-Dāʾūdī,
d. 945/1538, Berl. 10134, cf. '5, '6, *RA* 154r, *MT* 34v, *Fihrist muʾallafāt al-S. wa-sīrat
b. al-Jawzī* Garr. 2198, ʿAlī Mubārak, *al-Khiṭaṭ al-jadīda* XII, 105, al-Kattānī, *Fihris*
II, 353/6 (mentions under no. 359 a list of 538 writings in al-Suyūṭī's own hand,
dated 904, and which he had seen himself), Meursinge, *Prolegomena*, Wüst.
Gesch. 506, Goldziher, *SBWA* LXIX (1871) 1–28, | Hartmann, *Muw.* 82. A list of 145
300 writings dated 901/1495 *Ḥusn* ^{2}I, 190/5, printed in Meursinge p. 6 ff.[1] 503
titles Paris 4472 (see Leid. ^{2}24, Cambr. Prest. p. 51, Cairo ^{1}VI, 48) in Flügel, ḤKh
VI, 616, 561 titles in the same, *Wien. Jahrb.* 1832, vol. 58/60, *majmūʿa* of 43 works
Mosul 240,$_{230}$, of 20 works Garr. 2007.

I *Fann al-tafsīr wa-taʿalluqātuhu wal-qirāʾāt*

1. *al-Itqān fī ʿulūm al-Qurʾān*, completed 13 Shaʿbān 878/24 March 1474, Berl.
423/4, Leid. 1096, Paris 656/8, 6489, Br. Mus. 93, Algiers 314, Garr. 1227/9, AS
63, Cairo ^{1}I, 120, Mosul 27,$_{60}$, | 230,$_{60}$; ed. by Mowlawies Basheeroodeen and 182

1 This one lies at the basis of the list that will follow presently, and in which works still lacking in the former have been marked with an asterisk.

Noorool-Haqq with an Analysis by A. Sprenger, Calcutta 1852/4, C. 1278, 1306.—Abstract, somewhat abbreviated, by Ismāʿīl b. Muḥammad al-Ḥusaynī al-Mawṣilī, composed in 1216/1801, Berl. 425.—Notes to the Cairo edition by Naṣr al-Hūrīnī (Supp. II, 488), Berl. 426.—2. *Tarjumān al-Qurʾān fi ʾl-tafsīr al-musnad*, mostly *ḥadīth*, abbreviated *al-Durr al-manthūr fi ʾl-tafsīr al-maʾthūr* Berl. 896/7, Br. Mus. Suppl. 125, Ind. Off. 101, AS 199/201, 204/7, 208/10, 211, Yeni 51/6, Köpr. 15/21, II, 31/2, Cairo I, ^{1}172, ^{2}48, print. C. 1314, 6 vols.—3. *Lubāb al-nuqūl fī asbāb al-nuzūl* Cairo I, ^{1}197, ^{2}60, printed in the margin of *Tafsīr al-Jalālayn* C. 1313 (OB VI, 2418).—4. *Mufḥamāt al-aqrān fī mubhamāt al-Qurʾān* Cairo I, ^{1}207, ^{2}63, Qawala I, 82 print. Būlāq 1284, C. 1310.—5. *al-Mudhahhab fī-mā waqaʿa fi ʾl-Qurʾān min al-muʿarrab* Cairo ^{1}VII, 541, 608.—6. *Tafsīr al-Jalālayn*, commenced by al-Maḥallī (p. 138), completed by al-Suyūṭī in 870/1465 in 40 days, Berl. 885/95, Paris 652/5, 6135, Upps. 385, Leid. 1693/6, de Jong 126/7, Br. Mus. 78/80, 823, Suppl. 121/4, Ind. Off. 99, 100, Algiers 350, Hamb. Or. Sem. 11, Garr. 1295/6, Sarajevo 63, AS 181/7, Cairo I, ^{1}71, ^{2}38/9, Mosul $65_{,235}$, $125_{,63/4}$, $193_{,45}$, print. Bombay 1869, Lucknow 1869, Calcutta 1257, Delhi 1884, C. 1305, ʾ8, ʾ13. Glosses: a. *Majmaʿ al-baḥrayn wa-maṭāliʿ al-badrayn* by al-Karkhī, d. 1006/1597, AS 299, 300 Cairo ^{1}I, 198, ^{2}61.—b. *Kitāb al-Jamālayn* by al-Qāriʾ al-Harawī, d. 1014/1605 (p. 394), Berl. 894, Cairo I, ^{1}163, ^{2}44, Patna II, $27_{,255}$.—c. *al-Kawkabayn al-nayyirayn* by ʿAṭiyya al-Ujhūrī, d. 1190/1776 (p. 328), Cairo I, ^{1}194.—d. *al-Futūḥāt al-ilāhiyya* by Sulaymān al-Jamal, d. 1204/1790 (p. 353), Cairo I, ^{1}186, ^{2}57, 59, Qawala I, 75, print. Būlāq 1275, 1282, C. 1308, from which *Tuḥfat al-Mukhtār, Talkhīṣ ḥāshiyat al-Jamal ʿalā Tafsīr al-Jalālayn* by Aḥmad Mukhtār Bek Khafīd Qojā Yūsuf Pāshā, Ṭarābulus al-Gharb 1317.—e. *Kashf al-mahjūbayn* by Muḥammad Saʿdallāh al-Qandahārī, Bombay 1307.—f. ʿAlī Aṣghar b. ʿAbd al-Jabbār al-Iṣfahānī, lith. Tehran(?) 1272.—g–q. see Suppl.—7. *al-Takhbīr fī ʿulūm al-tafsīr*, composed in 872/1367, later included in the *Itqān* (no. 1), Leid. 1693.—8. *al-Fatḥ al-jalīl lil-ʿabd al-dhalīl*, a demonstration of the presence of 120 rhetorical figures in sura 2, 258, Vienna 1640, Alex. Bal. 16, Fun. $130_{,2}$.—9. *Ḥāshiya ʿalā tafsīr al-Bayḍāwī* I, 531.—10. *al-Qawl al-faṣīḥ fī taʿyīn al-dhabīḥ*, on whether with *al-dhabīḥ* Isḥāq or Ismāʿīl is meant, Berl. 2535, Paris
183 4588, | Qawala II, 243.—11. *al-Yad al-busṭā fi ʾl-ṣalāt al-wusṭā* Berl. 3584.—12. * *Muqaddima fi ʾl-alfāẓ al-muʿarraba fi ʾl-Qurʾān* Berl. 724, Patna II, $394_{,2570,23}$.—13. * *al-Mutawakkalī fī-mā warada fi ʾl-Qurʾān bil-lughāt, mukhtaṣar fī muʿarrab*
146 *al-Qurʾān* Cairo ^{1}VII, 578, ^{2}I, 61, Patna II, $407_{,2577}$. |—14. * *Itḥāf al-wafd bi-nabaʾ sūratay al-khalʿ wal-ḥafd*, on the authenticity of two suras recited by Ubayy b. Kaʿb, Berl. 438 Patna II, $392_{,2570,7}$; cf. Nöldeke, *Gesch. d. Qorʾāns* I 208.—15. * *al-Ḥabl al-wathīq fī nuṣrat al-ṣiddīq* Cairo ^{1}VII, 163, ^{2}I, 47, Qawala II, 233.—16. *Qaṭf al-thamar (thimār) fī muwāfaqat sayyidinā ʿUmar*, a *rajaz* enumerating

the passages that had been revealed to Muḥammad after having been triggered thereto by ʿUmar during a conversation, with a commentary by Badr al-Dīn al-Baysabīnī woven into it, Berl. 469.—17. *Discussion on sura 48,$_{2}$ Berl. 1008.—18. *The same on sura 92, ibid. 1012.—19. * *al-Qawl al-muḥarrar*, an exegesis of sura 48,$_{2}$, Paris 659,$_{1}$, 5316, Cairo ^{1}VII, 63, 165.—20. * *Dafʿ* (*Rafʿ*) *al-taʿassuf ʿan* (*fī*) *ikhwān sayyidinā Yūsuf*, on whether Joseph's brother had been a prophet as well, Berl. 2537/8, Cairo ^{1}VII, 425, 587, 620, Qawala I, 183.—21. * A *qaṣīda* on the value of reading the Qurʾān, even if nothing should come to mind while doing it, Berl. 7926,$_{2}$.—21a. * *al-Iklīl fī ʾstinbāṭ al-tanzīl*, Qawala I, 29, print. Delhi 1296 in the margin of Muʿīn al-Dīn al-Ṣafawī's *Jāmiʿ al-tibyān fī tafsīr al-Qurʾān* (p. 203).—21b–k. see Suppl.—21l. * *al-Naḍāda fī taḥqīq maḥall al-istiʿāda* Qawala I, 84.—21m. * *Risāla fī bayān al-basmala hal hiya min al-Qurʾān am lā* Qawala I, 63.—21n. * *Risāla fī tafsīr qawlihi taʿālā*, on sura 20, 123, ibid. I, 66.—21o. * *Risāla fī tafsīr qawlihi taʿālā*, on sura 7, 52, ibid. I, 64.—21p. * *Risāla fī tafsīr qawlihi taʿālā*, on sura 48, 2, ibid. 65.—21q. * *Risāla fī tafsīr qawlihi taʿālā*, on sura 74, 37, ibid. 66.—21r. *Risāla fī tafsīr qawlihi taʿālā*, on sura 78, 6, ibid. 64, II, 271.—21s. *Risāla fī qawlihi taʿālā*, on sura 13, 39, Patna II, 392,$_{2579,2}$.

II *Fann al-ḥadīth wa-taʿalluqātuhu*

22. *Isʿāf al-mubaṭṭaʾ bi-rijāl al-Muwaṭṭaʾ* (I, 185) Berl. 9958.—23. *al-Tawshīḥ ʿala ʾl-Jāmiʿ al-ṣaḥīḥ* I, 165.—24. *Tadrīb al-rāwī fī sharḥ Taqrīb al-Nawāwī* I, 441.—25. * *Mawāhib al-mujīb fī khaṣāʾiṣ al-ḥabīb*, *urjūza* with a commentary by Aḥmad b. ʿAlī al-Manīnī al-ʿAdawī, d. 1172/1759, Alex. Ḥad. 38.—26. *al-Laʾāliʾ al-maṣnūʿa fī ʾl-aḥādīth al-mawḍūʿa* NO 1281, Alex. Muṣṭ. Ḥad. 19, Cairo I, ^{1}393, ^{2}141, *Dhayl* Patna I, 50,$_{493}$.—27. *Lubb al-lubāb fī taḥrīr al-ansāb* I, 402.—28. *Muntaha ʾl-āmāl fī sharḥ ḥadīth inna-ma ʾl-aʿmāl etc.* Berl. | 1592, Cairo I, ^{1}430, ^{2}150, 184
abstract Berl. 1593, Qawala I, 98.—29. (*al-Muʿjizāt w*) *al-Khaṣāʾiṣ al-nabawiyya* Berl. 2576, Paris 1978, Algiers 1687, Köpr. 283, Alex. Ḥad. 27, Cairo I, ^{1}338, ^{2}91, under the title *Kifāyat al-ṭālib etc.* Berl. Ms. or. qu. 2085.—Abstract *Unmūdhaj al-labīb fī khaṣāʾiṣ al-ḥabīb* Berl. 2577/85, Paris 4608,$_{5}$, Br. Mus. Suppl. 992,$_{3}$, Cairo I, ^{1}158, 273, 296, 406, VII, 53, 233, 396, Mosul 240,$_{230}$.—Commentaries: a. al-Munāwī, d. 1031/1622 (p. 306), Br. Mus. 186, Cairo I, ^{1}290, ^{2}93, 125, Bank. XV, 1020.—b. Anon., Cairo ^{1}I, 356, VII, 111.—c. Persian by Aḥmad b. Muḥammad b. Murshid al-Naqshbandī, Br. Mus. Pers. I, 16.—*Mukhtaṣar* by ʿAbd al-Wahhāb al-Shaʿrānī, d. 972/1564 (p. 335), Alex. Taʾr. 14.—Versifications: a, b. see Suppl.—c. *Durar al-ghāʾiṣ* by Umm ʿAbd al-Wahhāb al-Bāʿūniyya, d. 922/1516 (p. 271), Cairo I, ^{1}340, ^{2}115.—30. *Sharḥ al-ṣudūr fī sharḥ ḥāl al-mawtā fi ʾl-qubūr*, after the *Tadhkira* of al-Qurṭubī, d. 672/1273 (I, 529), also entitled *Kitāb al-barzakh*, Berl. 2665/8, Ms. or. oct. 3926, Leid. 2056, Paris 4587, 5979, Br. Mus. 1615, Algiers 852,

Yeni 712/3, Garr. 1503/4 Alex. Ḥad. 31, Mawāʿiẓ 36,$_5$, Cairo II, 361, II, 163, ^{2}I, 127, Calcutta 432, Patna I, 53,$_{534/5}$, Bat. 22, print. C. 1309, Persian translation Lahore 1871.—Abstracts: a. By the author himself ∗ *Bushra ʾl-kaʾīb bi-liqāʾ al-ḥabīb*, Berl. 2669/70, Leid. 1755, Paris 1390,$_1$, Alex. Mawāʿiẓ 8, Fun. 183,$_1$, Cairo ^{1}III, 233, VII, 54, I, 93, 273, App. 38, Qawala I, 162, print. C. 1309 in the margin.—b. Anon., Gotha 755, Munich 331.—31. *al-Budūr al-sāfira fī umūr al-ākhira*, composed in 884/1479, Ind. Off. 176, Algiers 853, AS 1676, Cairo ^{1}II, 146, Alex. Mawāʿiẓ 7, Fun. 65,$_3$, Garr. 1502, abbreviation ∗ *al-Laṭāʾif al-fākhira fī mawāqif al-ākhira* Fātiḥ 2802.—32. *Mā rawāhu ʾl-wāʿūn fī akhbār al-ṭāʿūn*, an abbreviation of *Badhl al-māʿūn* by Ibn Ḥajar (p. 82), Berl. 1429/30, Gotha 52,$_1$, 58,$_3$, shorter ibid. 1977, Leid. 203, Br. Mus. Suppl. 160, Garr. 1423, AS 4296,$_7$, Alex. Mawāʿiẓ 36, Fun. 85,$_2$, 130,$_1$, Cairo ^{1}VII, 589, ^{2}I, 142. Main source for A. v. Kremer, Über die grossen Seuchen des Orients, *SBWA, phil.-hist. Cl.* 1880, p. 69/156.—32a. ∗ *Fāʾida fī ʾl-wiqāya min al-ṭāʿūn* Alex. Fun. 130,$_5$.—33. (*Ḍawʾ al-shamʿa*) *Fī khaṣāʾiṣ yawm*
147 *al-jumʿa*, | Berl. 3809/10, Munich 134, Paris 2800,$_1$, AS 1149, Alex. Taṣ. 41, Cairo ^{1}VII, 82, 247, ^{2}I, 130, 513, whence *al-Lumʿa fī khuṣūṣiyyat yawm al-jumʿa* Garr. 1854.—34. ∗ *Ḍawʾ al-shamʿa fī ʿadad rijāl al-jumʿa* Cairo ^{1}VII, 347.—35. *Buzūgh*
185 *al-hilāl fi ʾl-khiṣāl al-mūjiba lil-ẓilāl*, an abstract of the | *Tamhīd al-farsh fi ʾl-khiṣāl al-mūjiba li-ẓill al-ʿarsh*, on the 70 qualities that one must have in order to stand in the shadow of the throne of the Divine, Berl. 1831/2, Gotha 628, Paris 2700,$_{18}$, Cairo ^{1}VII, 9, 465, 541, ^{2}I, 92, Qawala I, 102.—36. *Miftāḥ al-janna fi ʾl-iʿtiṣām* (*iḥtijāj*) *bil-sunna* Cairo ^{1}VII, 541, ^{2}I, 150.—37. *Sihām al-iṣāba fi ʾl-daʿawāt al-mujāba* Cairo ^{1}VII, 54, 331.—38. *Maṭlaʿ al-badrayn fī man yuʿṭā ajrayn* Berl. 5587/8, AS 4828,$_2$, Cairo ^{1}VII, 53, 273, 331, 465, Qawala I, 120.—39. *al-Kalim al-ṭayyib wal-qawl al-mukhtār fi ʾl-maʾthūr min al-daʿawāt wal-adhkār* Cairo ^{1}I, 409, VII, 610.—40. *Adhkār al-Adhkār lil-Nawawī* I, 501.—41. *al-Manhaj al-sawī wal-manhal al-rawī fi ʾl-ṭibb al-nabawī*, Berl. 6302, Bodl. I, 646, Pet. Ros. 224,$_3$, cf. Leclerc II, 300.—Abstract by Muḥammad b. Muḥammad Najm al-Dīn al-Ghazzī, d. 1061/1651 (p. 291), Berl. 6031.—42. *Kashf al-ṣalṣala ʿan waṣf al-zalzala* Berl. 1433, Gotha 661,$_9$, Paris 4658,$_1$.—43. *al-Taʿẓīm wal-minna* (*taʿẓīm al-minna*) *fī anna abaway al-nabī fi ʾl-janna* or *al-Fawāʾid al-kāmina fī īmān al-sayyida Āmina* Berl. 2703, Qawala I, 164.—44. ∗ *Masālik al-ḥunafāʾ fī wāliday al-Muṣṭafā*, on whether Muḥammad's parents went to Hell, Berl. 2699/700, Ind. Off. 1035,$_2$, Alex. Taʾr. 113, Fun. 83,$_2$ (attributed to Ibn Kamālpāshā), 164,$_1$, 166,$_1$, Cairo ^{1}VII, 11, 52/3, 216, ^{2}I, 146, 257, Dam. Z. 38, 126,$_{31}$, Patna II, 400,$_{2571,28}$ = *Risāla fī wāliday al-nabī?* Alex. Fun. 83,$_1$.—45. ∗ *al-Maqāma al-sundusiyya fī khabar wāliday khayr al-bariyya* Berl. 2701, Cairo ^{1}IV, 331, print. C. n.d., in the edition of the *Maqāmāt*, Constantinople 1298, p. 84 ff.—46. ∗ *al-Daraj al-munīfa fi ʾl-ābāʾ al-sharīfa*, on whether Muḥammad's parents are in Hell, the shortest of his four tracts on the matter, Berl. 2702, Munich 135, Alex. Taʾr

113.—47. ∗ *Nashr al-ʿalamayn al-munīfayn fī iḥyāʾ al-abawayn al-sharīfayn*
Cairo ^{1}VII, 233, 469, ^{2}I, 158, 211.—48. ∗ *Subul al-najāh*, the sixth work on the
same question, Berl. 10341.—49. *Risāla fī ʾl-aḥādīth al-musalsalāt* Cairo ^{1}VII, 11
= *Jiyād al-musalsalāt* A. Taymūr Ḥadīth 114 (see al-Kattānī, *Fihris* IV, 360 *Manār
al-musalsalāt* Patna II, 394,$_{2570}$).—50. *Abwāb al-saʿāda fī asbāb al-shahāda*,
Berl. 1406/9, Paris 659,$_{2}$, Cairo ^{1}I, 404, VII, 51, 580, 687.—51. (*al-Ḥabāʾik*) *Fī
akhbār al-malāʾik*, Berl. 2506, Paris 1389, NO 2360, AS 1758, Alex. Ḥad. 19, Cairo
^{1}VI, 133, VII, 37, ^{2}I, 110, 286.—51a. *Fī sīmāʾ al-malāʾika* Qawala I, 418.—52. *al-
Thughūr al-bāsima fī manāqib al-sayyida Fāṭima* Berl. 9685, Cairo ^{1}VII, 605, ^{2}I,
99, | Qawala II, 232.—53. *Manāhil al-ṣafāʾ fī takhrīj aḥādīth al-Shifāʾ* (I, 455) 186
Berl. 1434, Alex. Fun. 85,$_{1}$.—54. *al-Asās fī manāqib Bani ʾl-ʿAbbās*, composed on
the order of the Egyptian caliph ʿAbd al-ʿAzīz b. Yaʿqūb, d. 903/1497, Berl. 1518,
Cairo ^{1}VII, 464, ^{2}I, 88, Qawala II, 226.—55. *Darr al-saḥāba fī man dakhala Miṣr
min al-ṣaḥāba* Paris 2016,$_{2}$, Cairo ^{1}V, 52, ^{2}176.—56. *Jāmiʿ al-masānīd* or *Jamʿ
al-jawāmiʿ* or *Jāmiʿ al-kabīr*, supposedly containing all Muḥammad's sayings,
Berl. 1350/2, Alex. Ḥad. 16, Cairo I, ^{1}325, Qawala I, 112, Mosul 28,$_{91}$, 231,$_{77/8}$. Patna
I, 47,$_{475/9}$.—Abbreviation *al-Jāmiʿ al-ṣaghīr min ḥadīth al-bashīr al-nadhīr* Berl.
1353/60, Paris 766, 5421, 6324, Yeni 194/7, Cairo ^{1}I, 321, Qawala I, 111, print. C.
1321.—Appendix *Ziyāda* (*Dhayl*) Berl. 1361, Yeni 203, Alex. Ḥad. 26, Cairo ^{1}I, 347,
^{2}I, 122, Qawala I, 121.—Commentaries: a. *al-Kawkab al-munīr* by Shams al-Dīn
Muḥammad b. ʿAbd al-Raḥmān al-Kawkabī, d. after 978/1570 (see Suppl.), | 148
Berl. 1362, Paris 770/2, Garr. 1398, Alex. Ḥad. 43, Cairo ^{1}I, 393.—b. Aḥmad b.
Muḥammad al-Matbūlī, vol. 3., Paris 767.—c. al-Mundhirī, abstract, ibid.
768/9.—d. *al-Sirāj al-munīr* by ʿAlī b. Aḥmad al-ʿAzīzī al-Būlāqī al-Shāfiʿī, d.
1070/1659, Cairo ^{1}I, 347, print. C. 1271, 1278, 1304/5 (4 vols. with, in the margin,
glosses by Muḥammad al-Ḥifnī, d. 1181/1767), 1324.—Abstract Gotha 849 (on
the 71 sects of the Jews). *Sharḥ duʿāʾ al-Jāmiʿ al-ṣaghīr* Garr. 1399.—e. *Fayḍ
al-qadīr* by ʿAbd al-Raʾūf al-Munāwī, d. 1032/1623 (p. 305), Pet. AM 59, Algiers
1507/9, Yeni 223/34, Alex. Ḥad. 40, Cairo I, ^{1}291, 383, ^{2}99, 137, print. 1286, C. 1938
(6 vols.), Qawala I, 142.—f. *Taysīr al-wuṣūl* by ʿAbd al-Raḥmān b. ʿAlī b. al-Rabīʿ
al-Shaybānī al-Yamanī, Patna I, 42,$_{434}$.—g. ʿĪsā b. Aḥmad al-Zubayrī al-Barrāwī
al-Azharī, d. 1182/1768, Cairo I, ^{1}292, ^{2}99.—h–m. see Suppl. (1. m. Garr. 1400).—
Rearrangement: a. *Fatḥ al-qadīr* by Ibrāhīm b. Muḥammad al-Mālikī, Gotha
598.—b. *F. al-q. bi-tartīb al-Jāmiʿ al-ṣaghīr* by Amīr al-Ḥājj Aḥmad Katkhudā
Ṣāliḥ Mustaḥfiẓān, MS dated 1179/1765, Qawala I, 139.—Abstracts: a. *al-Badr
al-munīr*, anonymous, containing only the beautiful and undisputed *ḥadīth*,
Berl. 1363.—b. *Manhaj al-ʿummāl* by ʿAlī b. Ḥusām al-Dīn al-Hindī, d. 975/1567
(p. 384), Ind. Off. 188, NO 1278, Cairo ^{1}I, 271.—c. ʿAbd al-Ghanī al-Nābulusī, d.
1143/1730 (S. 345), Berl. 1364.—d. with additions from the *Kitāb al-maqāṣid
al-ḥasana* of al-Sakhāwī, d. 902/1496, Berl. 1365.—e. 128 traditions, by Abū Bakr

187 Bey Ef., ibid. 1366.—f. Anon., with a rather | longwinded commentary, ibid.
1367.—g–n. see Suppl. (k. self-commentary *Fatḥ al-sattār wa-kashf al-asrār*
Alex. Ḥad. 37; m. Garr. 1402/3).—o. *Mukhtaṣar al-Jāmiʿ al-ṣaghīr* by ʿAbd
al-Laṭīf b. Qaḍībalbān, composed in 1050/1640, Alex. Ḥad. 58.—57. *al-Fawāʾid*
(Jawāhir) al-mutakāthira fī ʾl-akhbār al-mutawātira, Köpr. 383.—58. *al-Azhār*
al-mutanāthira fī ʾl-akhbār al-mutawātira Cairo ^{1}VII, 607.—59. *al-Durar al-*
muntathira fī ʾl-aḥādīth al-mushtahira, an abstract of a work by Badr al-Dīn
al-Zarkashī, d. 794/1392 (p. 112), augmented by supplementary material, Berl.
1401/4, Cairo ^{1}I, 340, VII, 26, 179, 388, ^{2}I, 116, Dam. Z. $38_{,23,13}$, Mosul $31_{,116}$, Patna
I, $49_{,493}$, (with the title of 61), Garr. 1395.—60. *al-Ḥaṣr wal-ishāʿa li-ashrāṭ*
al-sāʿa Paris $2800_{,24}$.—61. *al-Durr al-munaẓẓam fī ʾl-ism al-muʿaẓẓam* Berl.
2241/3, Gotha $52_{,2}$, $94_{,2}$, Paris $4585_{,6}$, $4588_{,31}$, Alex. Fun. $78_{,11}$, Cairo ^{1}II, 193, VII,
52, 465, 608, Qawala I, 232, Patna II, $391_{,2509,20}$, $396_{,2571,4}$.—62. *Risāla fī asmāʾ*
al-mudallisīn Cairo ^{1}VII, 608.—63. *al-Riyāḍ al-anīqa fī sharḥ asmāʾ khayr*
al-khalīqa, composed in Muḥarram 879/May 1474, Berl. 9514.—64. *Dhikr al-isrāʾ*
wal-miʿrāj al-sharīf Berl. 2602.—65. *Arbaʿūna ḥadīthan min riwāyat Mālik ʿan*
Nāfiʿ b. ʿUmar Cairo ^{1}VII, 48, 608.—66. *al-Hīʾa al-saniyya fī ʾl-hayʾa al-sunniyya*,
on astronomy in the Qurʾān, *ḥadīth*, and history, Berl. 5697/8, Gotha $52_{,4}$, 1383
(where other MSS are listed), Ind. Off. 1037, Br. Mus. Suppl. $1226_{,31}$, Algiers 1556,
Cairo ^{1}I, 337, 448, VII, 146, ^{2}I, 160, Hamb. Or. Sem. $15_{,1}$, Alex. Fun. $41_{,3}$, Patna II.
$392_{,2579,1}$, $492_{,2652,1}$.—Abstract: a. Anon., Munich 133.—b. Ibrāhīm al-Qaramānī
(see Suppl.) Qawala II, 271 (commentary by the same, ibid. 273).—67. *Takhrīj*
aḥādīth sharḥ al-ʿAqāʾid al-Nasafiyya I, 549.—68. *Faḍl al-jalad fī faqd al-walad*,
Berl. 2673/4 (with a similar, though different, content, and without a title, ibid.
ʾ5), Paris $2800_{,9}$, Alex. Mawāʿiẓ 29 (*Faḍāʾil*), Cairo ^{1}VII, 162, ^{2}I, 135.[2]—
69. *Arbaʿūna ḥadīthan* Cairo ^{1}VII, 347.—70. *al-Taʿrīf bi-ādāb al-taʾlīf* Alex. Fun.
$76_{,3}$, Cairo ^{1}VII, 51, ^{2}III, 65.—71. *Risāla fī ʿushāriyyāt al-Bukhārī* Cairo ^{1}VII,
587.—71a. * *Nādiriyyāt min al-ʿushāriyyāt* Qawala I, 156, s. 164.—72. *al-Qawl al-*
ashbah fī ḥadīth man ʿarafa nafsahu faqad ʿarafa rabbahu Berl. 1830, Paris 773,
Cairo ^{1}VII, 545, ^{2}I, 120, Qawala I, 143, Garr. $2003_{,13}$, Patna II, $400_{,2571,30}$.—72a. *
188 *Zahr al-rubā* I, 171.—72b. *Miṣbāḥ al-zajāja ʿalā sunan b. Māja* | I, 171, in the mar-
gin of Delhi 1282.—Abstract by al-Bajmaʿwī, *Nūr Miṣbāḥ al-Zajājā*, C. 1299.—
149 73. * *al-Ḥikam al-mushtahira min ʿadad al-ḥadīth min al-wāḥid ila ʾl-ʿashara*, |
wise sayings by various people, Berl. 1405.—74. * *al-Riyāḍ al-naḍra fī aḥādīth*
al-māʾ wal-riyāḍ wal-khuḍra Berl. 1410/1, Qawala I, 121.—75. * *al-Fānīd fī ḥalāwat*
al-masānīd, on whether Abū Ḥanīfa or Mālik preserved and submitted better
traditions, Berl. 1413/5, Paris $2800_{,3}$, $4588_{,7}$, Cairo ^{1}VII, 463.—76. * *Itḥāf al-firqa*

2 Wrongly attributed to him is *Bard al-akbād ʿinda faqd al-awlād*, C. 1304 and others, in *Majmūʿat rasāʾil thamāniya*, Lahore 1893 (see Suppl.).

bi-rafw al-khirqa, on al-Ḥasan al-Baṣrī's transmissions from ʿAlī, Berl. 1416, Paris 2800$_{,7}$, Cairo [1]VII, 608, [2]I, 261, Qawala I, 216, Patna II, 398$_{,2514/7}$.—77. * *al-Qawl al-jalī fī ḥadīth al-walī* on the privileged position of the pious with God, Berl. 1417, Cairo [1]VII, 459, [2]I, 138, Qawala I, 143, 257, Patna II, 396$_{,2871,2}$. Abbreviation Berl. 1418.—78. * *Naṣb maydān jadalī,* a discussion of some points of contention, Berl. 1418.—79. * *Risāla fī anna 'l-maʿānī tujassam,* on the fact that pictorial expressions in the traditions are to be understood corporeally, Berl. 1419.—80. * *al-Izdihār fī-mā ʿaqadahu 'l-shuʿarāʾ min al-āthār,* a collection of poetical fragments with *ḥadīth,* ibid. 1420/1.—81. * *Dāʿī 'l-falāḥ fī adhkār al-masāʾ wal-ṣabāḥ,* Berl. 1422, Gotha 764, Alex. Fun. 134$_{,6}$, Cairo [1]II, 192, VII, 610, [2]I, 118, Patna II, 407$_{,2574,26}$.—82. * *Mā rawāhu 'l-asāṭīn fī ʿadam al-majīʾ ila 'l-salāṭīn,* Berl. 1423/4, Alex. Mawāʿiẓ 36$_{,2}$, Cairo I, [1]395, [2]142, Patna II, 393$_{,257020}$.—83. * *Faḍḍ al-wiʿāʾ fī aḥādīth fī rafʿ al-aydī,* on raising the hands during prayer, Berl. 1425, Cairo I, [2]135, Patna II, 393$_{,2570,10}$.—84. * *Bulūgh al-maʾārib fī qaṣṣ al-shārib,* on shaving the moustache, Berl. 1426/7, Cairo [1]VII, 464, [2]I, 193, Qawala I, 413, Patna II, 395$_{,2570,27}$, 466$_{,2635,35}$.—85. * *al-Ajr al-jazl fi 'l-ghazl,* on spinning by women, Berl. 1428, Cairo [1]VII, 50, Alex. Fun. 120$_{,4}$.—86. * *Ḥuṣūl al-rifq bi-uṣūl al-rizq,* Berl. 1431, 3711, Paris 748$_{,3}$, 4588$_{,25}$, 4658$_{,2}$, Alex. Faw. 7, Fun. 85$_{,10}$, 133$_{,1}$, 155$_{,3}$, Cairo [1]VII, 305, 331, 465, [2]I, 111, App. 15.—87. * *Iḥyāʾ al-mayt fī faḍl al-bayt,* 60 *ḥadīth,* Berl. 1451/3, Cairo [1]VII, 37, 426, [2]I, 184, Qawala I, 97, Dam. Z. 61$_{,153,5}$, Garr. 2007$_{,13}$.—88. * *al-Rawḍ al-anīq fī faḍl al-Ṣiddīq,* 40 *ḥadīth,* Berl. 1513.—89. * *al-Durar fī faḍāʾil ʿUmar* 40 *ḥadīth,* ibid. 1514.—90. * *Tuḥfat al-ʿajlān fī fadl ʿUthmān,* 40 *ḥadīth,* ibid. 1515.—91. * *al-Qawl al-jalī fī faḍāʾil ʿAlī,* 40 *ḥadīth,* ibid. 1516.—92. * *Taḥrīr ahl al-ākhira min dhamm al-dunya 'l-dāthira,* 40 *ḥadīth,* ibid. 1517.—93. * *Rafʿ al-ṣawt bi-dhabḥ al-mawt* Berl. 1594, Cairo [1]VII, | 305, 608, [2]I, 121, Qawala I, 190, Patna II, 398$_{,2571,16}$.—94. * 189
Ḥadīth al-salām min al-nabī ʿalā ummatihi Berl. 1595, Qawala I, 118.—95. * *Fī ḥadīth al-bādhinjān* 1596.—96. * *Kashf al-labs fī ḥadīth radd al-shams* Cairo [1]VII, 51.—97. * *Tuḥfat dhawi 'l-adab fī mushkil al-asmāʾ wal-nasab,* on the *Muwaṭṭaʾ* and the two *Ṣaḥīḥs* after Ibn Qurqūl, d. 569/1173 (I, 457), *Maṭāliʿ al-anwār,* Berl. 1665.—98. * *al-Taṭrīf fi 'l-taṣḥīf* Berl. 1664.—99. * *al-Mulāḥin fī maʿna 'l-mashāḥin* Berl. 1669/70, Cairo [1]VII, 587, [2]I, 151, Qawala I, 9.—100. * *Shuʿab al-īmān* Berl. 1829, Garr. 2003$_{,12}$. *Mukhtaṣar* by Abū Ḥafṣ ʿUmar al-Qazwīnī, Patna I, 59$_{,598}$.—101. * *Manẓūma fi 'l-mujtahidīn* or *Irshād* (*Tuḥfat*) *al-muhtadīn ilā asmāʾ al-mujaddidīn,* 27 *rajaz* verses on the *ḥadīth* that at the beginning of every century one must expect a religious reformer, Berl. 1833, 8160$_{,2}$, 9464, Alex. Fun. 120$_{,6}$, Cairo [1]VII, 409, [2]V, 130.—102. * *Itmām al-niʿma fi 'khtiṣāṣ al-islām bi-hādhihi 'l-umma,* on the fact that the Arabs were the first to receive the true religion, composed in 888/1483, Berl. 2116, Cairo [1]VII, 307, [2]I, 82, 495, Patna II, 398$_{,2501,1}$, 404$_{,2574,3}$.—103. * *al-Ḥaẓẓ al-wāfir fi 'istidrāk al-kāfir*

idhā aslama, on whether an unbeliever can catch up on neglected religious acts of worship after conversion, Berl. 2217, Qawala I, 415.—104. * *Nuzūl al-raḥma bil-taḥadduth bil-niʿma*, on one's duty to thank God for His benefac-
150 tions, | Berl. 2118, Cairo ^{1}VII, 587, ^{2}I, 157, Qawala I, 422.—105. * *Risāla* on the question of whether the Basmala is part of the Qurʾān or not, with an excursus on the orthography of *bism*, Berl. 2257 = *Muqaddima fi 'l-Basmala* Makram 58, Patna II, $403_{,2572,3}$.—106. * *Riyāḍ al-ṭālibīn fī sharḥ al-istiʿādha wal-basmala* Berl. 2258, Cairo ^{1}VII, 54, ^{2}II, 108, 115.—107. * *Fatāwi 'l-nidhāra fī ahl al-ishāra*, on whether *baʿd* can come before *aʿūdhu billāh* or not, Berl. 2259.—108. * *Mabḥath al-mīʿād*, questions and answers on the Resurrection and the Afterlife, Gotha 52, Patna II, $399_{,237,24}$, (*maʿād*).—109. * *Nūr al-shaqīq fi 'l-ʿaqīq*, 14 *ḥadīth* on carnelian, Gotha 66, 7, Leid. $2409_{,34}$, Cairo ^{1}VII, 609.—110. * *al-Durra al-tājiyya ʿala 'l-asʾila al-Nājiyya*, traditions received in Damascus from Ibrāhīm b. Muḥammad Burhān al-Dīn al-Nājī, d. 900/1494, Gotha $94_{,3}$, Patna II, $397_{,2571,11}$.—111. * *al-ʿUjāla* (*ʿAjāja*) *al-Zarnabiyya fi 'l-zulāla al-Zaynabiyya*, on the Zaynabids being sharifs Berl. 9401, Gotha $91_{,1}$, Paris $4261_{,16}$, $4588_{,22}$, $4659_{,2}$,
190 Cairo ^{1}VII, 245, ^{2}V, | 264, Qawala, II, 240, Patna II, $397_{,2571,9}$, Garr. $2007_{,2}$.—112. * *Waẓāʾif al-yawm wal-layla*, on ceremonies, especially prayers and blessings on the occasion of events in daily life, shortened from *al-Kalim al-ṭayyib* (no. 39) and *Minhāj al-sunna* Gotha 774, Cairo ^{1}VII, 610, Garr. 1852 = (?).—113. * *ʿAmal al-yawm wal-layla* Paris ^{2}I, 376, $665_{,3}$, Cairo ^{1}VII, 410, ^{2}I, 132.—114. * *Ifāḍat al-khabar bi-naṣṣihi fī ziyādat al-ʿumr wa-naqṣihi*, Berl. 2487, Gotha 743, Upps. $225_{,10}$, Garr. 1523, Alex. Fun. $121_{,2}$, $133_{,2}$, Cairo ^{1}VII, 49, ^{2}I, 33, 90, Mosul $240_{,230}$.—115. * Answer to a question asked of him on the free will of man, in connection with sura $28_{,68}$, which would oppose it, Berl. 2488.—116. * *al-Fawāʾid al-bāriza wal-kāmina fi 'l-niʿam al-ẓāhira wal-bāṭina*, in connection with sura $31_{,19}$, Berl. 2489.—117. * *Lubs al-yalab fi 'l-jawāb ʿan īrād Ḥalab*, on whether Gabriel was an intermediary between God and the prophet or another angel, Berl. 2507/8, Cairo ^{1}VII, 165, 587, ^{2}I, 142, Qawala I, 141, Garr. $2007_{,12}$, $2038_{,6}$, Patna II, $399_{,2571,33}$.—118. * *Jawāb*: a. *fī sīmat al-malāʾika*, b. *fi 'l-ʿadhaba*, c. *wa-hal yajūzu an yuqāl lil-aḥādīth kalām Allāh*, d. on whether the turban of the Prophet had a tip or not (Qawala I, 418), Berl. 2509.—119. * *Inbāh* (*Inbāʾ*) *al-adhkiyāʾ li-ḥayāt al-anbiyāʾ*, on whether prophets live on after death, Berl. 2533/4, Ind. Off. 178, Cairo ^{1}I, 273, Qawala I, 161.—120. * *Fī nubuwwat al-sayyid Ibrāhīm* Berl. 2536.—121. * *al-Iʿlām bi-ḥukm ʿĪsā ʿam*, on the return of Christ, composed in 888/1483, Berl. 2539/44, Gotha 725/6, Leid. 2055, Alex. Fun. $67_{,18}$, Cairo ^{1}VI, 113, VII, 165, 395, 587, 610, ^{2}I, 267, Qawala I, 160, Patna II, $399_{,2581,22}$.—122. * *Laqṭ al-marjān fī akhbār al-jānn* see p. 90.—123. * *Tazyīn al-arāʾik fī irsāl al-nabī ila 'l-malāʾik* Berl. $2586_{,17}$, Alex. Mawāʿiẓ 38 (without *Tazyīn*), Fun. $67_{,18}$, Cairo ^{1}II, 53, Qawala I, 164, Patna II, $399_{,2511,321}$.—124. * *al-Bāhir fī ḥukm al-nabī*

bil-bāṭin wal-ẓāhir, on the superiority of the Prophet over everyone else and on
his capacity for passing judgments on the basis of external indicators and inner
logic, Berl. 2588, Paris 2800,$_5$, Qawala I, 257 (*al-Qawl al-bāhir*).—125. * *Shuʿlat
nār*, on the fact that Muḥammad reunited within himself the law and the
quintessential, that is, a binding authority that is both external and internal, on
which occasion he discusses some aspects of Sufism, Berl. 2589, Gotha 742,
Cairo ^{1}VII, 463.—126. * *Ṭulūʿ al-thurayyā bi-iẓhār mā kāna khafiyyā*, | on the 191
interrogation in the grave, Berl. 2671, Qawala I, 203, Patna II, 400,$_{2571}$, 405,$_{2574,16}$.
|—127. * *al-Lumʿa fī ajwibat al-asʾila al-sabʿa*, on the state of the deceased in the 151
grave, Berl. 2672, Gotha 94,$_6$, Paris 4659,$_7$, Cairo ^{1}VII, 53, ^{2}I, 205, Qawala I, 209,
Alex. Fun. 164,$_3$, Garr. 1522.—127a. * *Risāla fī aḥwāl al-mawtā* Patna II,
466,$_{2635,30}$.—127b. * *al-Durra al-fākhira fī nūr al-ākhira* Berl. Ms. or. oct.
3906,$_3$.—127c. * *Tabṣirat al-akhyār fī khulūd al-kāfir fi ʾl-nār* ibid. Ms. or. oct.
3980.—128. * *al-Maqāma al-wardiyya*, on the death of infants, Berl. 2676.—129.
* *al-Iḥtifāl fī suʾāl al-aṭfāl*, on whether infants are also interrogated by Munkar
and Nakīr in their graves, Berl. 2677/8, Gotha 94,$_4$, Garr. 2093,$_3$, Alex. Fun. 134,$_1$,
164,$_4$, Qawala I, 159, Patna II, 399,$_{2571,25}$, 407,$_{2574,15}$, also included in his collection of fatwas *al-Ḥāwī lil-fatāwī* Suppl. 169c.—130. * *al-Tathbīt fī ʿilm* (*ʿinda*)
l-tabyīt, 176 *rajaz* verses on the questioning of the dead in their graves, Berl.
2679/80, Gotha 34,$_1$, Munich 215,$_1$, Paris 4588,$_1$, Esc. ^{2}636,$_2$, Nicholson, *JRAS*
1899, 907, Cairo ^{1}VII, 253, 433, 485, 587, ^{2}I, 167, 275 Alex. Mawāʿiẓ 36,$_3$, Fun. 155
(*Urjūza fī suʾāl al-malʾakayn fi ʾl-qabr*), Mosul 25,$_{29,3}$, 199,$_{96,3}$, Patna II,
393,$_{2570,15}$.—Commentaries: *Fatḥ al-ghafūr fī manẓūmat al-qubūr* by Aḥmad b.
Khalīl al-Subkī Sharaf al-Dīn, d. 1032/1623, Berl. 2681, Munich 215,$_2$, Paris 3224,
Algiers 855, Garr. 1505, Alex. Mawāʿiẓ 28, 36,$_4$, Cairo ^{1}II, 167, VII, 10, 149, 462, ^{2}I,
335, Makram 48.—b. *Fatḥ al-muqīt*, by the same, Algiers 1830,$_6$.—c. Yūsuf b.
Muḥammad Bū ʿAṣriyya, Fez 1314.—131. * *Risāla fī ḥukm al-shahīd wa-ghaslihi
wa-dafnihi*, on the burial of martyrs, Berl. 2682.—132. * *Risāla fī dhabḥ al-mawt*,
on death appearing in the shape of a ram that gets killed, Berl. 2685 Qawala I,
189 (with another title) (= 93? p. 267).—133. * *Tuḥfat al-julasāʾ bi-ruʾyā Allāh
al-nisāʾ*, on whether women see God in Paradise, Berl. 2704, Alex. Mawāʿiẓ 9,
Patna II, 400,$_{2571,27}$ (*Itḥāf*).—134. * *Kayfiyyat al-malāḥim*, on the struggles that
will take place on the appearance of the Mahdī, Berl. 2724.—135. * *al-Kashf ʿan
mujāwazat hādhihi ʾl-umma al-alf*, composed in 898/1492, against the view that
the Last Judgment will take place at the end of the first millennium after
Muḥammad, the author asserts that while the world will pass this deadline, it
will not last for another 500 years, Berl. 2753/60, Gotha 721, Vienna 1660,$_6$, Leid.
2051/4, Paris 1546,$_3$, 3502,$_4$, 5350, Algiers 533, 596,$_2$, 613, 1549,$_2$, 1568,$_2$, BDMG 46,
Heid. *ZDMG* 91, 384,$_{317,3}$, Garr. 2001,$_2$, Alex. Ḥad. 41, Cairo ^{1}VII, 11, 13, 53, 178, 212,
216, 235, 254, 262, 467, 599, ^{2}I, 139, 348, | App. 16.—136. *5 fatwas, four on 192

chronology, one on the interpretation of dreams, Berl. 2761.—137. * *Miftāḥ al-janna fī ādāb al-sunna*, directives on prayer and fasting, Berl. 3521, Patna II, 397, 2571$_{,13}$.—138. * *al-Awj fī khabar ʿAwj*, on the giant Og, Munich 286, f. 128/9, Cairo ^{1}VII, 609, ^{2}V, 49, Qawala II, 229, Patna II, 402$_{,2571,14}$.—139. * *al-Musāraʿa ila 'l-muṣāraʿa* Upps. 225$_{,8}$.—140. * *Fī faḍl al-qiyām bil-salṭana* ibid. 4.—141. * *al-Durar al-ḥisān fi 'l-baʿth wa-naʿīm al-jinān*, on eschatology, 4 printings, Cairo ^{1}II, 146, cf. *OB* I, 921, IV, 1481.—142. * *Taʾkhīr al-ẓalāma ilā yawm al-qiyāma* Paris 659$_{,3}$, 4588$_3$ Cairo ^{1}VII, 49, Qawala I, 222, Alex. Fun. 191$_{,2}$.—143. * *al-Fawz al-ʿaẓīm fī liqāʾ al-rabb al-karīm* Cairo ^{1}II, 168, ^{2}I, 339, Patna I, 56$_{,560}$.—144. * *al-Naṣīḥa fī-mā warada min al-adʿiya al-ṣaḥīḥa* NO 1283.—145. * *Tuḥfat al-āthār fi 'l-adʿiya wal-adhkār* Köpr. 258.—146. * *Zād al-masīr fi 'l-fihrist al-ṣaghīr* Cairo ^{1}I, 237, ^{2}I, 74, Garr. 2025$_{,1}$.—147. * *al-Aḥādīth (al-Rutab) al-munīfa fī faḍl al-salṭana al-sharīfa* Cairo ^{1}I, 259, VII, 307, ^{2}I, 116, Patna II, 406$_{,2574,7}$.—148. * *Kitāb fī faḍl al-aghawāt alladhīnaʾstuʾminū ʿala 'l-ḥarīm*, on eunuchs, Cairo ^{1}VI, 179.—149. * *Ākām al-ʿiqyān fī aḥkām al-khiṣyān* Paris 2800$_{,11}$, Cairo ^{1}VII, 464, 528, ^{2}I, 82, 499.—150. * *Kitāb al-khaḍrāwāt al-sabʿa* Cairo ^{1}VII, 534.—151. * *Risāla fi 'l-raml* ibid.—152. * *al-Durr al-khāliṣ fi 'l-muʿjizāt wal-khaṣāʾiṣ* ibid. 396.—153. * *Kanz al-ʿummāl fī sunan al-aqwāl wal-afʿāl* abstract by ʿAlāʾ al-Dīn al-Muttaqī al-Hindī, p. 384.—154. * *Bard al-ẓalāl fī takrīr al-suʾāl* Cairo ^{1}VII, 52, 64, ^{2}I, 92.—155. * *Tanzīh al-iʿtiqād ʿani 'l-ḥulūl wal-ittiḥād* Cairo ^{1}VII, 53, ^{2}I, 176, Alex. Fun. 67$_{,7}$, Patna II, 399$_{,2571,20}$, 404$_{,2574,4}$.—156. * *Kifāyat al-muḥtāj fī*
152 *maʿrifat al-ikhtilāj* Cairo ^{1}VII, 53. |—157. * *al-ʿArf al-wardī fī akhbār al-Mahdī* Cairo ^{1}VII, 54, ^{2}I, 196. Abstract of *Talkhīṣ al-bayān fī ʿalāmāt al-Mahdī ākhir al-zamān* by ʿAlī al-Muttaqī (p. 384), Qawala I, 413$_{,3}$, see Suppl. 169, k.—158. * *al-Lumʿa fī asbāb al-ḥadīth* Cairo ^{1}VII, 62, ^{2}I, 78.—159. * *Ṭarḥ al-saqaṭ wa-naẓm al-luqaṭ* ibid. ^{1}VII, 62, ^{2}I, 130, Patna II, 395$_{,2570,24}$, 406.—160., $_{2574,20}$. * *Juzʾ fī ṭuruq man ḥafiẓa ʿalā ummatī arbaʿīna ḥadīthan* Cairo ^{1}VII, 63.—161. * *al-Faḍl al-ʿamīm fī iqṭāʿ Tamīm al-Dārī* ibid. ^{2}I, 135.—162. * *Ḍawʾ al-badr fī iḥyāʾ Laylat ʿArafa wal-ʿīdayn wa-niṣf Shaʿbān wa-Laylat al-Qadr* Cairo ^{1}VII, 63.—163. *
193 *Aḥādīth al-shitāʾ* ibid. 586.—164. * *al-Kawākib al-sāriyāt fi 'l-aḥādīth* | *al-ʿushāriyyāt* ibid. 246, see 71, Kattānī *Fihris* II, 95/7.—165. * *Ḥusn al-taʿahhud bi-aḥādīth al-tasmiya fi 'l-tashahhud* ibid. 247.—166. * *al-Ṣawāʿiq ʿala 'l-nawāʿiq* ibid. 462, Patna II, 406$_{,2574,23}$.—167. * *Kitāb al-baʿth* Cairo VII, 466, ^{2}I, 345.—168. * *ʿUqūd al-zabarjad* AS 876.—169. * *Qalāʾid al-farāʾid wa-shawārid al-fawāʾid* Paris 1160$_{,5}$, 2800$_{,4}$.—169a.–bbbb. see Suppl. (c. BDMG 46, Alex. Fiqh Shāf. 21, Patna II, 396$_{,2571}$.—e. C. 1351.—g. Patna II, 402$_{,2571,41}$.—i. *Risāla laṭīfa fī bayān asmāʾ al-sinnawr* Garr. 2041.$_3$, thereon *Naẓm al-billawr fī asāmi 'l-sinnawr* Patna II, 395$_{,2570,26}$.—n. Qawala I, 97, II, 255.—o. ibid. I, 411.—v. Patna II, 392$_{,2570,4}$., Garr. 647.—dd. Patna II, 392$_{,2570,6}$, 406$_{,2574,18}$.—ff. Alex. Fun. 177$_{,2}$.—gg. Qawala I, 420, Patna II, 392$_{,2570,8}$.—hh. Garr. 1422.—rr. Qawala I, 101 (*A. al-mafāʿil*),

Patna II, 397,$_{2571,6}$.—vv. Patna II, 391,$_{2509,18}$).—169cccc. *Bāb al-ḥadīth* Makram 60.—169dddd. ∗ *Risāla tataʿallaq bil-shams wa-ilā ayna tadhhab baʿda ghurūbihā* Qawala II, 276.—169eeee. *Risāla fī kusūf al-shams wa-asbābihi* ibid. 278.—169ffff. *Risāla fi ʾl-kalām ʿala ʾl-shams wal-qamar* ibid.—169gggg. *Mulakhkhaṣ Kitāb irsāl al-kisāʾ ʿala ʾl-nisāʾ* Patna II, 482,$_{2643,3}$.—169hhhh. *Risāla fī faḍl Makka* Patna II, 405,$_{2574,9}$.—169iiii. *Risāla fi ʾl-asmāʾ al-mukhtalifa li-Makka* ibid. 10.—169kkkk. *al-Bahja al-saniyya fi ʾl-asmāʾ al-nabawiyya* Alex. Ḥad. 8.—169llll. *Asmāʾ al-muhājirīn* Patna II, 466,$_{2635,22}$.—169mmmm. *Fī faḍl al-dhikr baʿd al-ṣalawāt al-khams* Qawala I, 237, 411.—169nnnn. *Risāla fī lubs al-sarāwīl* Qawala II, 235.—169oooo. *Risāla fi ʾl-bayān hal yuktafā bil-fiqh ʿani ʾl-taṣawwuf* Qawala I, 235.—169pppp. *Risāla fi ʾl-tafḍīl bayna ʾl-mashriq wal-maghrib wa-bayna ʾl-arḍ wal-shams* ibid. 236.—169qqqq. *Risāla fī faḍl al-tawsiʿa ʿalā yawm al-ʿĀshūrāʾ* ibid. 238.—169rrrr. *Risāla fi ʾl-aḥādīth al-wārida fī ithm man ightaṣaba shayʾan min al-arḍ wa-ṭarīq al-muslimīn* ibid. I, 416.—169ssss. *Risāla fī aḥkām al-libās wa-hayʾat ʿimāmat al-nabī ṣlʿm wa-mā kāna taḥta ʿimāmatihi* ibid.—169tttt. *Risāla fī bayān iṭlāq al-ukht ʿala ʾl-zawja wa-bayān al-sabab alladhī ḥamala sayyidanā Ibrāhīm al-Khalīl ʿam. ʿalā qawlihi fī zawjatihi innahā ukhtī* ibid. 417.—169uuuu. *Risāla fī tashbīk al-aṣābiʿ fi ʾl-masjid wa-ghayrihi* ibid.—169vvvv. *Risāla fi ʾl-jinn wa-mā yataʿallaq bihā mina ʾl-aḥkām* ibid.—169wwww. *Taʿlīq ʿalā ākhir ḥadīth al-Bukhārī* Patna II, 403,$_{2573,2}$.—169xxxx. *Risāla fī Laylat al-Qadr* ibid. 406,$_{2574,162}$.—169zzzz. *al-Muʿtaṣar min al-mukhtaṣar fī taḥqīq ḥadīth ṣadaqatāni ʿalā āl al-nabī* ibid. 21.—169aaaaa. *Bughyat al-ṭālib fī īmām Abī Ṭālib* Qawala I, 162.—169bbbbb. *Risāla fī aṭfāl al-mushrikīn* Qawala I, | 185.—169ccccc. *Risāla fī idkhāl al-muʾminīn al-ʿāṣīn* 194
al-nār li-yaʿrifū qadr al-janna ibid. 188.—169ddddd. *Risāla fī ḥawādith ayyām al-dajjāl* ibid.—169eeeee. *al-Ḍāʿa fi ʾshtirāṭ al-sāʿa* Patna II, 406,$_{2574,25}$.—169fffff. *Risāla fī bayān anna ʾl-imām Abā Ḥanīfa hal rawā ʿani ʾl-imām Mālik b. Anas shayʾan am lā* Qawala I, 118.—169hhhhh. *Sharḥ qawl al-nabī ṣlʿm li-bnihi Ibrāhīm law ʿāsha Ibrāhīm la-kāna ṣiddīqan nabiyyan etc.* 119.—169iiiii. *Fi ʾl-kalām ʿalā qawl al-nabī ṣlʿm sayakūnu rajulun min Quraysh etc.* ibid.—169kkkkk. *Risāla fī maʿnā qawlihi ṣlʿm al-ṣabiyyu ʾlladhī lahu ab etc.* ibid.—169lllll. *Risāla fī khalq al-ṣuwar baʿda khalq al-samāwāt wal-arḍ* ibid. 188.

III *Fann al-fiqh wa-taʿalluqātuhu*

170. *al-Ashbāh wal-naẓāʾir*, a compendium on *fiqh*, Berl. 410/1, Ind. Off. 977, ZDMG 32, 5/7, Cairo ^{1}III, 192, ed. M. Ḥāmid al-Faqqī, C. 1356/1938.—171. *al-Wajh al-nāḍir fī-mā yaqbiḍuhu ʾl-nāẓir*, on who, other than the trustees of pious endowments, are entitled to take control of their earnings at their due date, Gotha 1128, Cairo ^{1}VII, 589.—172. ∗ *Masāʾil tataʿallaq bi-ḥukm al-ṣayd* Berl. 4995.—173. ∗ *al-Fatāwa ʾl-uṣūliyya wal-dīniyya* Dam. Z. 38,$_{126,2}$, Patna II,

$404_{,2574,2}$.—174. * *Fī dhamm al-maks*, on the reprehensibility of tolls, Berl. 5620.—175. * *Badhl al-majhūd fī khizānat Maḥmūd*, on the lending of books which Jamāl al-Dīn Maḥmūd had bequeathed as a *waqf*, so that these could only be consulted on the spot, Algiers 1295, Cairo ^{1}VII, 64, ^{2}I, 50.—176. * *Risāla fī jawāz iqṭāʿ al-sulṭān al-shāriʿ* or *al-Bāriʿ fi 'l-shāriʿ*, on whether a king can enfeoff a public road, Paris $4591_{,11}$.—177. * *Kashf al-ḍabāba fī masʾalat al-istināba* Cairo ^{1}VII, 52, ^{2}I, 524, 535 (which has *Fatḥ al-ṣabāba*), Garr. $2007_{,16}$.—178. * *Nathl al-kattān fi 'l-khushknān* Berl. 8568, Cairo ^{1}VII, 247, ^{2}I, App. 45, Qawala II, 221.—178a–m. see Suppl.—(178c. Garr. 1853).—178n. *Sharḥ Mukhtaṣar Khalīl* see p. 102.—178o. *al-Farāʾiḍ* Patna II, $404_{,2574,6}$.—178p. *Ādāb al-fatyā* ibid. $393_{,2570,9}$.

IV *al-Ajzāʾ al-mufrada fī masāʾil makhṣūṣa ʿalā tartīb al-abwāb*

179. *al-Ẓafar bi-qalm al-ẓufr*, on clipping of nails, Berl. 5438, Upps. $225_{,11}$, Cairo ^{1}VII, 48, ^{2}I, 525, Patna II, $404_{,2574,5}$, Garr. $2007_{,14}$.—180. * *al-Isfār ʿan qalm*
195 *al-aẓfār* | Cairo ^{1}VII, 51. 241, ^{2}I, 89.—181. *Badhl al-ʿasjad li-suʾāl al-masjid*, on whether begging inside mosques is allowed, Berl. 3590, Cairo ^{1}VII, 49, 466, ^{2}I, 92, 500, Qawala I, 412.—182. *al-Jawāb al-jazm ʿan ḥadīth al-takbīr jazm*, on the tradition that the *takbīr* should be pronounced without the final vowels, its origin and bindingness, and al-Shāfiʿī's opinion concerning it, Berl. 2288.—183. *al-Muʿaddila fī shaʾn al-basmala* Gotha $66_{,3}$.—184. *Juzʾ fī ṣalāt al-ḍuḥā* Berl. 3583, Paris $4659_{,5}$, Alex. Fun. $85_{,4}$, Qawala I, 411.—185. *al-Maṣābīḥ fī ṣalāt al-tarāwīḥ* Garr. $2027_{,2}$, Cairo ^{1}VII, 305, Alex. Fun. $85_{,5}$, Patna II, $407_{,2635,43}$.—186. *Basṭ al-kaff fī itmām al-ṣaff*, on that the rows of those who pray must be complete and uninterrupted before a new row is formed, Berl. 3588, Cairo ^{1}VII, 326, Qawala I, 413, Patna II, $403_{,2572,2}$.—187. * *al-Minḥa fi 'l-sabḥa*, on whether the use of the rosary has a foundation in the Sunna, Berl. 3585/6, Cairo ^{1}VII, 425, ^{2}I, 152, Alex. Fun $85_{,8}$, Qawala I, 266, 421, Patna II, $396_{,2571,5}$, as *Mukhtaṣar al-Tanqīḥ fī mashrūʿiyyat al-tasbīḥ* Qawala I, 226, 414.—188. * *Fi 'l-taḥmīd*, on when the imam has to pronounce the formula *samiʿa 'llāh li-man ḥamidahu*,
153 Berl. 3587. |—189. * *Ḥusn al-taslīk fī ḥukm al-tashbīk*, on women entering houses of prayer, Berl. 3589, Gotha $639_{,1}$, Cairo ^{1}VII, 609, ^{2}I, 110, Patna II, $397_{,2374/7}$.—190. * *al-Taṣḥīḥ li-ṣalāt al-tasbīḥ* Cairo ^{1}VII, 463, Alex. Fun. $85_{,3}$, Patna II, $405_{,2574,11}$.—191. *Wuṣūl al-amānī bi-uṣūl al-tahānī*, on the custom of congratulation having a foundation in *ḥadīth*, Berl. 5576, Leid. 1948, Cairo ^{1}I, 402, VII, 49, 331, 620, Qawala II, 223, Garr. $2025_{,6}$, $2027_{,1}$.—192. *Shadd al-athwāb fī sadd al-abwāb* (*fi 'l-masjid al-nabawī*), an explanation of two *ḥadīth*, also included in *al-Ḥāwī lil-fatāwī* (Suppl. 169c), Gotha $629_{,2}$, Patna II, $397_{,2571,8}$.—193. *Badhl al-himma fī barāʾat al-dhimma*, on whether slander and deceit towards relatives are expiated by remorse, or whether one must also ask for forgiveness, Berl. 5427, Cairo ^{1}VII, 149, ^{2}I, 501, Qawala I, 412.—194. *al-Inṣāf fī*

tamyīz al-awqāf Berl. 4765, Cairo ^{1}VII, 52, ^{2}I, 499.—195. *Jazīl al-mawāhib fī 'khtilāf al-madhāhib*, that the diversity of sects has good aspects, Berl. 2809, Gotha 66$_{,8}$, Leid. 2409$_{,35}$, Cairo ^{1}II, 63, 463, 608, ^{2}I, 382, App. 61, Alex. Fun. 66$_{,7}$, Patna II, 393$_{,2570,2}$, 467$_{,2635,38}$.—196. *al-Zahr al-bāsim fī-mā yuzawwij fīhi*
'l-ḥākim, Alex. Fiqh Shāf. 37$_{,2}$, Cairo ^{1}VII, 235, 327, 465.—197. *Tanzīh* | *al-anbiyā'* 196
'an tashbīh (*tas'iyat*) *al-aghbiyā'*, on the prophets being too highly placed to allow for their being cited in comparisons involving human things, Berl. 2532, Qawala, I, 165, Patna II, 396$_{,2571,3}$.—198. (*Risāla fī*) *Dhamm al-qaḍā'* (*wa-taqallud al-aḥkām wa-mā warada fī dhālika min al-aḥādīth wal-akhbār*), Berl. 1412, Qawala I, 417.—199. *Faḍl al-kalām fī ḥukm al-salām* = *Masā'il tata'allaq bil-ziyādā 'alā radd al-salām*, on Turkish words and phrases used by ordinary people in addition to the greeting formulas demanded by religion, Berl. 5575.—200. *Natījat al-fikr fī 'l-ijhār bil-dhikr*, traditions on *dhikr*, Berl. 3710, Cairo ^{1}VII, 465, Qawala I, 268, Garr. 2007$_{,6}$, 2093$_{,1}$.—200a. *I'māl al-fikr fī tafḍīl al-dhikr* or *Faḍl al-dhikr 'ala 'l-ṣadaqa* Qawala I, 218, Dam. Z. 126$_{,11}$.—201. *Tanwīr al-ḥalak fī imkān ru'yat al-nabī wal-malak* Berl. 4276/7, Leid. 2050, Paris 4659$_{,4}$, Bodl. I, 117, Cairo ^{1}VII, 52, 666, 680, 685, ^{2}I, 98, Qawala I, 226, Alex. Fun. 67$_{,12}$, Patna I, 146$_{,1406}$, II, 400$_{,2571,32}$, Garr. 2038$_{,2}$.—202. *Ilqām al-ḥajar li-man zakkā sābb Abī Bakr wa-'Umar*, against the admissibility of the testimony of those who defame the first two caliphs, Berl. 4957, Cairo ^{1}VII, 49, 463, Alex. Fun. 121$_{,3}$, 130$_{,3}$.—203. *al-Jawāb al-khātim 'an su'āl al-khātim*, on signet rings, Berl. 5458, Qawala I, 414.—204. *al-Ḥujaj al-mubīna fī 'l-tafḍīl bayna Makka wal-Madīna* Copenhagen 231$_{,3}$, Cairo ^{1}VII, 11, 48, Alex. Ta'r. 57, Patna II, 393$_{,2570,13}$.—205. * *Sāji'at al-ḥarām*, a *maqāma* on Mecca and Medina, Berl. 8551a, Cairo ^{1}IV, 261.—206. *Aqwāl al-'ulamā' fī 'l-ism al-a'ẓam* Alex. Fun. 85$_{,9}$.—207. * *Shaqā'iq al-utrunj fī daqā'iq al-ghunj*, on flirtatiousness, Berl. 8414, 8475, f. 165, Gotha 52$_{,5}$, 53$_{,2}$, Munich 215, Tüb. 80, Br. Mus. 988$_{,2}$, 1404$_{,12}$, 1466$_{,2}$, Esc. ^{2}707$_{,14}$, Cairo ^{1}VII, 466, 580, Qawala II, 257, Alex. Adab 141.—208. * *al-Wishāḥ fī fawā'id al-nikāḥ*, with a lexical section, Gotha 2048/9 (where other MSS are listed), Paris 3066/7, Algiers 1784; as an appendix thereto; 209. * *Nawāḍir al-ayk fī nawādir al-nayk*, depicts the pleasures of lawful intercourse, so as to control perversions, Berl. 6384, Paris 3068.—210. * *al-Īḍāḥ fī 'ilm al-nikāḥ* (an abstract of the previous
work?) Paris 3060$_{,3}$, 3571$_{,2}$, 5180, lith. C. n.d. 1279. |—211. * *Nuzhat al-muta'ammil* 154
wa-murshid al-muta'ahhil, on marriage, Gotha 2052/3, Cairo ^{1}II, 178.—212. * *Mu'akkid al-maḥabba bayna 'l-muḥibb wa-man aḥabbahu*, on aphrodisiacs,
Gotha 2054, Paris 3039$_{,16}$, Garr. 1111.—213. * *Bulūgh* | *al-ma'mūl fī khidmat* 197
al-rasūl, on sodomy being worthy of the death penalty, Berl. 5593, Qawala I, 102, Patna II, 398$_{,2571,18}$, 404$_{,2574,1}$.—214. * *Rashf al-zulāl min al-siḥr al-ḥalāl*, a *maqāma* in which 20 representatives of as many sciences describe their wedding night in the technical language proper to their own profession, Gotha

2049,$_{2}$ (where other MSS are listed), Cairo ^{1}IV, 257, ^{2}III, 170.—215. * *al-Yawāqīt al-thamīna fī ṣifāt al-samīna*, Leid. 514, Alex. Adab 141.—216. * *Itḥāf al-nubalāʾ bi-akhbār al-thuqalāʾ*, Berl. 5579, Leid. 516/7, Garr. 2007,$_{9}$, Köpr. 1579, Qawala II, 185, Patna II, 405,$_{2574,15}$.—217. * *Hamziyya*, an answer to a question about the plague, Gotha 34,$_{2}$.—218. * *al-Ṭurthūth fī fawāʾid al-burghūth* Gotha 37,$_{1}$, 66,$_{6}$, Leid. 2409,$_{33}$, Cairo ^{1}VII, 326, Patna II, 395,$_{2570,28}$.—219. * *Tashnīf al-samʿ bi-taʿdīd al-sabʿ*, on the number 7 in the Qurʾān and *ḥadīth*, Gotha 66,$_{1}$, Upps. 225,$_{4}$, Leid. 2409,$_{6}$.—220. * *Musāmarat al-sumūʿ fī ḍawʾ al-shumūʿ*, on whether one should light candles for the prophet, Berl. 5577, Gotha 66,$_{2}$, Leid. 2409,$_{7}$, Cairo ^{1}VII, 410, ^{2}I, 145, Qawala II, 215.—221. * *Iʿlām (Bughyat) al-arīb bi-ḥudūth bidʿat al-maḥārīb*, Gotha 737/8, Vienna 1640,$_{5}$, Paris 2800,$_{10}$, 4589,$_{12}$, Qilič ʿA. 1024,$_{3}$, Garr. 2027,$_{6}$, 2030,$_{3}$, Cairo ^{1}VII, 49, ^{2}V, 32, Patna II, 392,$_{2570,5}$.—222. *Tuḥfat al-anjāb bi-masʾalat al-sinjāb*, on whether the skin of squirrels and other animals is soiled by tanning, Berl. 3636, Garr. 2038,$_{4}$.—222a. *Risāla fi ʾl-nahy ʿan ittikhādh julūd al-sibāʿ wal-namir* Qawala I, 419.—223. *al-Thubūt fī ḍabṭ al-qunūt*, on whether *yaʿizz* is to be pronounced differently in prayer, Berl. 3921, 8412,$_{49}$, Cairo ^{1}VII, 305, 633.—224. *al-Zajr lil-hajr*, on that one may only break for good with those who want to introduce religious innovations, Berl. 5411, Paris 4588,$_{19}$, 4659,$_{10}$, Alex. Fun. 120,$_{2}$, Cairo ^{1}II, 160, VII, 245, ^{1}I, 121, 315, Qawala I, 419.—225. * *al-Maradd fī karāhiyyat (ḥukm) al-suʾāl wal-radd*, on whether one should be apprehensive about begging and on whether one should refuse an offering that one is given without begging, Berl. 5412, Leid. 1949, Cairo ^{1}VII, 307, ^{2}I, 146, Qawala I, 421, Patna II, 406,$_{2574,22}$.—226. * *Kashf al-rayb ʿan al-jayb*, on the "chest" in the mantle of the Prophet, Berl. 5454, Qawala I, 420, II, 245, Patna II, 406,$_{2574,22}$.—227. * *Risāla fi ʾl-sarāwīl*, on whether the Prophet wore trousers, Berl. 5455, Qawala II, 235.—228. * *Thalj al-fuʾād fī aḥādīth lubs al-sawād* Berl. 5457, Qawala I, 414.—229. * *Khādim al-naʿl al-sharīf*, on the shoe of the Prophet, Berl. 9644.—230. * *al-Akhbār al-maʾthūra fi ʾl-iṭlāʾ bil-nūra*, on
198 the depilatory called | *al-nūra*, Berl. 5444, Cairo ^{1}VII, 246, ^{2}I, 84, Qawala I, 411.—231. * *Risāla fi ʾl-ghāliya*, on a certain perfume, Berl. 8412,$_{2}$, 8569, Cairo ^{1}VII, 50, 232, ^{2}III, 167.—232. * *Mā rawāhu ʾl-sāda fi ʾl-ittikāʾ ʿala ʾl-wisāda*, on how the Prophet rested, Berl. 5451, Vienna 1640,$_{6}$, Garr. 1424, Alex. Mawāʿiẓ 41,$_{2}$, Qawala I, 420.—233. * *Ghars al-anṣāb fi ʾl-ramy bil-nushshāb*, on the bow and arrow, Berl. 5440.—234. * *al-Simāḥ fī akhbār al-rimāḥ*, Cairo ^{1}VII, 64.—235. * *al-Wāḍiḥ fī taʿlīm al-ramy*, NO 4098.—236. * *al-Bāḥa fi ʾl-sibāḥa*, on the uses of swimming, Berl. 5559, Upps. 225,$_{11}$, Cairo ^{1}VII, 305, Patna II, 392,$_{2570,3}$.—237. * *al-Maqāma wal-maqāla al-dhahabiyya fi ʾl-ḥummā*, an interpretation of sura 19,$_{72}$, on fever as a cure from sins and some superstitious remedies against it,
155 Berl. 6361/2, printed in the *Maqāmāt*, Constantinople 1298, p. 56. |—238. * *al-Khadam* Patna II, 405,$_{2574,13}$.—239. * *al-Lafẓ al-rāʾiq wal-maʿna ʾl-fāʾiq fī*

'l-ḥaqāʾiq wal-ṭarāʾiq, on the duties of man in various circumstances, with citation of witnesses from the Qurʾān, *ḥadīth*, sayings by others, and many verses, Berl. 8409.—240. * Discourse on the horse, ibid. 8412$_{,1}$.—241. * *al-Jahr bi-manʿ al-burūz ʿalā shāṭiʾ al-nahr*, against squatting on the banks of the Nile, ibid. 8415$_{,2}$.—242. * *Waqʿ al-asal fī ḍarb al-mathal*, on that one may also use passages like sura 3$_{,189}$ with regard to matters other than those for which they were originally conceived, ibid. 8722, Qawala II, 223.—243. * *Rafʿ al-khidr ʿan qaṭʿ al-sidr*, Cairo ^{1}VII, 609, Patna II, 397$_{,2571,12}$.—244. * *al-Nujūm al-ẓawāhir fī 'stikhārat al-musāfir*, pious counsels for the way, Berl. 5578, Garr. 1959.—245. * *al-Wadīk fī faḍl al-dīk*, following a booklet of *ḥadīth* composed by Abū Nuʿaym (I, 445), Berl. 6201, Gotha 66$_{,4}$, 2072, Leid. 2049$_{,17}$, Patna II, 395$_{,2570,31}$.—245a. * *Qaṭʿ al-mujādala ʿinda taghyīr al-muʿāmala*, on coins, Leid. Amin 586, Alex. Fun. 110$_{,3}$.—245b–z. see Suppl. (d. Patna II, 403$_{,2572,4}$.).—245aa. *al-Naqd al-masṭūr (fi 'l-waqf)*, Patna II, 405$_{,2574,14}$.—245bb. *Marr al-nasīm ilā Ibn ʿAbd al-Karīm*, ibid. 393$_{,2570,4}$.—245cc. *Risāla fī 'l-aʿmāl wal-āthār baʿd al-mawt*, ibid. 394$_{,2570,18}$.—245dd. *Risāla fī anna iqāmat al-sulṭān ʿala 'l-raʿiyya aʿẓam niʿam Allāh*, ibid. 393$_{,2570,19}$.—245ee. *Risāla fi 'l-khilāfa al-kubrā*, ibid. 21.—*al-Asʾila al-wazīriyya wa-ajwibatuhā*, Alex. Fun. 134$_{,1}$.—245ff. *al-Ajwiba al-zakiyya ʿani 'l-alghāz al-Subkiyya*, ibid. 2, Patna II, 402$_{,2571,4}$.—245gg. *Rafʿ al-sina fī naṣb al-zina*, Patna II, 401$_{,2571,1}$.—245hh. (*Faḍl*) *al-Zand al-warī fi 'l-jawāb ʿan | suʾāl* 199
al-Sikandarī, ibid. 401$_{,2571,37}$.—245jj. *Ghāyat al-raghba fī ādāb al-ṣuḥba*, Alex. Mawāʿiẓ 27, Garr. 2007$_{,8}$.—245kk. *al-Kawkab al-sāṭiʿ naẓm Jamʿ al-jawāmiʿ* p. 109.

V *Fann al-ʿarabiyya wa-taʿalluqātuhu*

246. *al-Bahja al-marḍiyya fī sharḥ al-Alfiyya* I, 362$_{,15}$.—247. *al-Farīda fi 'l-naḥw wal-taṣrīf wal-khaṭṭ*, with a commentary, *al-Maṭāliʿ al-saʿīda*, completed in 885/1480, Paris 527, 893$_{,10}$, Alex. Naḥw 28, Garr. 463.—248. *al-Nukat ʿala 'l-Alfiyya wal-Kāfiya wal-Shāfiya wa-Nuzhat al-ṭuraf wa-Shudhūr al-dhahab*, begun in 867, continued in 876 and 885, and completed in 895, Leid. 237, Esc. ^{2}41, 81, ^{2}270$_{,3}$.—249. *Sharḥ shawāhid al-Mughnī* p. 29.—250. *Jamʿ al-jawāmi*,ʿ on grammar, Munich 745, Berl. Ms. or. oct. 3879$_{,5}$, Patna I, 169$_{,1535}$, commentary *Hamʿ al-hawāmiʿ* Munich 745, Esc. ^{2}38/9, 105/6, Algiers 179, Mosul 199$_{,95}$.—251. *al-Akhbār al-marwiyya fī sabab waḍʿ al-ʿarabiyya* Berl. 6851/2, Upps. 225$_{,2}$, Cairo ^{1}VII, 609, ^{2}V, 17, 115, Patna II, 394$_{,2579,22}$, printed in *al-Tuḥfa al-bahiyya*, Constantinople 1302, p. 49/53.—252. *al-Iqtirāḥ fī ʿilm uṣūl al-naḥw wa-jadalihi* Br. Mus. 526, Esc. ^{2}107$_{,1}$, 186$_{,1}$, Cairo ^{1}IV, 24, ^{2}II, 79, see A. Sprenger, *ZDMG* 32$_{,7}$, A. Schmidt in *al-Muẓaffariyya*, St. Petersburg 1897, 309 ff.—253. *al-Shamʿa al-muḍīʾa fī ʿilm al-ʿarabiyya*, a précis on grammar, Berl. 6769, Ms. or. oct. 3878.—Commentaries: a. Muḥammad b. Muḥammad al-Dimyāṭī, d. 1140/1727,

Cairo ^{1}IV, 110, ^{2}II, 159.—b. Muḥammad b. ʿĪsā b. Kannān, d. 1153/1740 (p. 299), Berl. 6770/1.—254. *Sharḥ al-Qaṣīda al-kāfiyya fī ʾl-taṣrīf* (anon. Esc. ^{2}86$_{,4}$, ḤKh IV, 551$_{,9506}$), completed on 17 Muḥarram 884/11 April 1479, Esc. ^{2}86$_{,5}$.—255. *Durrat al-tāj fī iʿrāb mushkil al-Minhāj* I, 395.—256. (*al-Silsila*) *al-muwashshaḥa* Cairo ^{1}IV, 331, a commentary, *al-Munaqqaḥ*, by Shihāb al-Dīn Aḥmad b. ʿAbd al-Ghaffār (p. 387), Paris 4195.—257. *Fajr al-thamd fī iʿrāb akmal al-ḥamd*, abstract of a work by his teacher al-Kāfiyajī, p. 139.—258. * *al-Muzhir fī ʿulūm al-lugha*, Berl. 6772, Ms. or. oct. 3887, Leid. 95/7 (where other MSS are listed), BDMG 87, Paris 3984/6, 4859, 6503/4, Br. Mus. Suppl. 879, Mosul 183, 238, print. Būlāq 1282.—260. * *Ghāyat al-iḥsān fī khalq al-insān*, following older works,
156 Berl. 7038, Leid. 38, used by Peñuela, *Die Goldene des b. Munāṣif.* |—261. * *Zubdat al-laban*, from the standpoint of language, *ḥadīth*, and medicine, Berl.
200 7053, Munich 883$_{,2}$, Leid. 99.—262. * *al-Tabarrī* | *min maʿarrat al-Maʿarrī*, 37 *rajaz* verses with 70 names for the dog, Berl. 7056, Alex. Fun. 120$_{,3}$, Patna II, 395$_{,2570,30}$, anon. in *Majmūʿa* Taymūr 201$_{,3}$ (*Orient.* VIII, 285).—263. * *al-Ashbāh wal-naẓāʾir al-naḥwiyya* Leid. 238 (where other MSS are listed), BDMG 88 (fragm.), Algiers 178, Cairo ^{1}IV, 22, ^{2}II, 76, 140, Alex. Naḥw 2, Mosul 198, 2. see A. Schmidt, loc. cit.—263a–s. see Suppl. (a. Patna II, 400$_{,2571,33}$, c. ibid. 36, e. Alex. Fun. 134$_{,3}$, 177$_{,1}$, Patna II, 402$_{,2571,39}$, n. ibid. 396$_{,2570}$, 85$_{,4}$ (which has *Taʿrīf*)).—263t. *al-Tahdhīb fī asmāʾ al-dhiʾb* Patna II, 395$_{,2570,30}$.—263u. *al-Jawāb al-muṣīb ʿan iʿtirāḍāt al-khaṭīb* (*fī ʾl-naḥw*) ibid. 402$_{,2571,40}$.—263v. *ʿUnwān al-dīwān fī asmāʾ al-ḥayawān* ibid. I, 265$_{,2216}$.—263w. *Jarr al-dhayl fī ʿilm al-khayl* ibid. II, 396$_{,2570,34}$, AS 2983$_{,2}$.

VI *Fann al-uṣūl wal-bayān wal-taṣawwuf*

264. *Taʾyīd al-ḥaqīqa al-ʿaliyya wa-tashyīd al-ṭarīqa al-Shādhiliyya*, on mysticism as a system, Berl. 3032, print. C. 1934, abstract Upps. 4675.—265. *Tashyīd al-arkān min Laysa fī ʾl-imkān abdaʿ mimmā kān*, defence of an assertion by al-Ghazzālī, Cairo ^{1}II, 11, VII, 52, 607, ^{2}I, 163, 169.—266. *al-Khabar al-dāll ʿalā wujūd al-quṭb wal-awtād wal-nujabāʾ wal-abdāl* Cairo ^{1}VII, 188, 406, Qawala I, 231, Patna II, 400$_{,2571,31}$, 403$_{,2472,1}$.—267. *al-Maʿānī wal-daqīqa fī idrāk al-ḥaqīqa*, 1. that the acts of man are essentially constituted in faith, prayer, fasting etc., 2. that death appears in the shape of a ram that will be slaughtered (see no. 132), composed in 883 or 888/1478, Berl. 2683/4, Gotha 91$_{,3}$, Qawala I, 81, 263.—268. *al-Nuqāya*, encyclopaedia of 14 sciences, also with the title *al-Uṣūl al-muhimma fī ʿulūm jāmma*: a. *al-tafsīr*, b. *uṣūl al-dīn*, c. *tashrīḥ*, d. *badīʿ*, e. *bayān*, f. *maʿānī*, g. *khaṭṭ*, printed in *al-Tuḥfat al-bahiyya*, Constantinople 1302 154/6, h. *taṣrīf*, i. *naḥw*, k. *farāʾiḍ*, l. *uṣūl al-fiqh*, m. *ḥadīth*, n. *taṣawwuf*, Berl. 75, Garr. 1133, 2096$_{,1}$, Patna II, 496$_{,2651,4}$.—a self-commentary, *Itmām al-dirāya*, composed in 873/1468, Berl. 76/8, Leid. 11/2 (where other MSS are listed), Garr. 1133, Alex. Fun. 5, Cairo ^{1}V,

108, print. Bombay 1309.—versification *Rawḍat al-fuhūm* by Aḥmad b. Aḥmad
al-Sunbāṭī, d. 990/1582 (p. 368), Berl. 89, Gotha 169, Leid. 13, Br. Mus. $893_{,7}$,
Algiers $67_{,2}$, Zāwiya d'El-Hamel, *Giorn. Soc. As. It.* X, 51, on which a commentary, *Fatḥ al-ḥayy al-qayyūm*, Leid. 14.—269. * *ʿUqūd al-jumān fī ʿilm al-maʿānī
wal-bayān* I, 356, also Berl. Brill M. 203, | Alex. Fun. $198_{,7}$, Mosul $162_{,224}$.—270. * 201
Jany al-jinās, paronomasia, Berl. 7534, Upps. 62, Esc. $^2328_{,6}$, 335/7, Cairo ^{1}IV, 126,
^{2}II, 185, Alex. Bal. 5.—271. * *al-Munjalī fī taṭawwur al-walī*, on whether a friend
of God can be in two places at once, also under the title *al-Muʿtalī fī taʿaddud
ṣuwar al-walī* Berl. 3363, Alex. Fun. $76_{,2}$, $166_{,3}$, Qawala I, 265, 421 (also in *al-Ḥāwī
lil-fatāwī* 169c), Patna II, $403_{,2573,1}$. Against this Aḥmad b. Ḥajar al-Haytamī, d.
973/1565 (p. 387), wrote *al-Fiqh al-jalī fi 'l-radd ʿala 'l-khalī* Berl. 3364.—272. *
al-Barq al-wāmiḍ fī sharḥ Yāʾiyyat b. al-Fāriḍ I, 307.—273. * *Qamʿ al-muʿāriḍ fī
nuṣrat b. al-Fāriḍ*, a *maqāma*, Vienna $1640_{,3}$, Cairo ^{1}VII, 141, Alex. Fun. $83_{,3}$.—
274. *Isʿāf al-qāṣid li-tafahhum masāʾil al-Shihāb al-Zāhid* Paris $2800_{,15}$.—274a–e.
see Suppl. (a. Dam. Z. $38_{,126}$, 32, Alex. Fun. $67_{,19}$, Patna II, $400_{,2571,29}$).

VII *Fann al-taʾrīkh wal-adab*

275. *Ṭabaqāt al-ḥuffāẓ* p. 58.—276. *Ṭabaqāt al-mufassirīn*, *S. Liber de inter-
pretibus Korani*, ed. A. Meursinge, Leiden 1839.—277. * *Ṭabaqāt al-naḥwiyyīn
wal-lughawiyyīn*: a. *al-kubrā*, lost, b. *al-wusṭā* autograph Paris 2119, c. *al-ṣughrā*,
also with the title *Bughyat al-wuʿāt*, completed in 871/1466, Berl. 10062
(abstract), Strassburg, ZDMG XL, 310, Vienna 1175, Garr. 698, Pet. AM 215, Br.
Mus. 1644, Suppl. 649, Yeni 873/4, Köpr. 1117, Cairo ^{1}VI, 19, ^{2}V, 60, anonymous
revision entitled *Sirāj al-ruwāt*, dated 1037/1627, Algiers 1724, abstract Pet. AM
216, entitled *al-Khulāṣa* Cairo V, ^{1}20, ^{2}278.—278. *Manāhil al-ṣafāʾ bi-tawārīkh
al-aʾimma wal-khulafāʾ* Berl. Qu. 1200, Paris 1614, abstract *Taʾrīkh al-khulafāʾ*,
Berl. 9714/5, Gotha 1584/6 (where other MSS are listed), Paris 1609/11, 4713,
6027, Algiers 1576, Yeni 828/9, Cairo V, ^{1}22, ^{2}85, Garr. 602/3, Mosul $209_{,30}$,
ed. Lees and Maulawi Abdalhaqq, Calcutta 1857, print. C. 1305, Lahore 1887,
Dehli 1306, abstract Paris 1612/3. English translation by H.S. Jarrett, Calcutta
1880/1, Bibl. Ind. Abstract by Aḥad b. Ḥajar al-Haytamī, d. 973/1565 (p. 389),
Itḥāf ikhwān al-ṣafāʾ bi-nubadh min akhbār al-khulafāʾ, with a continuation by
Muḥammad b. al-Ḥusayn al-Ḥasanī al-Samarqandī up to the year 982/1574,
Gotha 1587.—279. *Ḥusn al-muḥāḍara fī akhbār Miṣr wal-Qāhira*, Berl. 9823/4,
Ms. or. qu. 2104, Gotha 1630 (where other MSS are listed), Paris 1794/1810, 5871,
Algiers 1602 Yeni 844/6, Cairo V, ^{1}43, ^{2}161, Mosul $173_{,23}$, $264_{,4}$, lith. C. (1860?),
print. C. 1299, | 2 vols.—An abstract, *al-Anwār al-saniyya fī taʾrīkh al-khulafāʾ* 202
wal-mulūk al-sunniyya, Berl. 9825, Paris 1811, Turkish translation by Maḥmud
b. ʿAbdallāh b. Muḥammad al-Baghdādī, Vienna 916.—280. * *Muqaddima fī Nīl
Miṣr wa-maḥāsinihā wa-faḍlihā*, Gotha $34_{,3}$.—281. * *Bahjat al-nāẓir wa-nuzhat*

al-khāṭir, verses on the Nile and the sights near Cairo, Cairo ^{1}VII, 50, ^{2}III, 40.—282. * *Kawkab al-Rawḍa*, description and poetical glorification of the island of al-Rawḍa, near Cairo, composed in 895/1490, Berl. 1611, Ms. or. oct. 3941, Gotha 1530/1, Altona 7, Munich 416, Vienna 913, Paris 2266/72, Algiers 1603, Upps. 313/4, Cambr. Prest. 21, no. 138, Pet. AM 236, Garr. 601, Cairo ^{1}VII, 120, ^{2}V, 313, entitled *Bulbul al-Rawḍa* Alex. Fun. $85_{,2}$.—283. *Tuḥfat al-kirām bi-akhbār (khabar) al-ahrām*, on the pyramids, Berl. 6112, Gotha 1688.—284. *al-Munajjam fī 'l-muʿjam*, a list of his teachers, Cairo V, ^{1}161, ^{2}369, (autograph), see al-Kattānī, *Fihris* II, 29.—285. * *Ḥusn al-maqṣid fī ʿamal al-mawlid*, Berl. 9544, Qawala I, 415, II, 234, Patna II, $369_{,2553,3}$.—286. * *Tabyīḍ al-ṣaḥīfa fī manāqib Abī Ḥanīfa*, Berl. 10002, Paris 2094, Algiers $1359_{,7}$, Cairo V, ^{1}563, ^{2}122, Heid. ZDMG 91, 383, Alex. Fun. $85_{,1}$.—287. *al-Minhāj al-sawī fī tarjamat al-imām al-Nawawī* Suppl. I, 680.—288. * *Badāʾiʿ al-zuhūr fī waqāʾiʿ al-duhūr*, a universal history, Paris 1552, Yeni 822/4, AS 2987, Qawala II, 189, print. C. 1282 and others.—289. * *al-Darārī fī abnāʾ al-sarārī*, a list of slave women who had been mothers of caliphs, Berl. 9396, Munich $893_{,1}$, Cairo ^{1}VII, 51, Qawala II, 236.—290. *al-Sharaf al-muḥattam fī-mā manna 'llāh bihi ʿalā waliyyihi sīdī Aḥmad al-Rifāʿī min taqbīl yad al-nabī* Cairo V, ^{1}140, ^{2}233, printed in *Majmūʿa* Būlāq 1301.—290a–d. see Suppl. (a. Alex. Taʾr. 50, d. Yeni 872, 2).—291. *al-Nafḥa al-miskiyya*, following the example of the *ʿUnwān al-sharaf* of Ibn Muqriʾ al-Yamanī, d. 837/1433 (p. 190), in 3 black and wide (2, 4, 6), and 4 red and narrow, columns (1, 3, 5, 7). The first narrow one, read from the top to the bottom, contains comments on metrics; the third, part of the first part of rhetoric, *ʿilm al-maʿānī*; the fifth, part of *ʿilm al-badīʿ*; the seventh, which is only composed of the last letter of the last word of the preceeding ones, gives a short note on the author, while all the columns, read from right to left, give the actual treatise on syntax, written in one day in Mecca, Vienna $13_{,2}$, Algiers $1865_{,2}$, Alex. Fun. $127_{,1}$.—292. *Durar al-kalim wa-ghurar*
158 203 *al-ḥikam*, a collection of maxims, | Berl. 8555, Paris $3972_{,1}$, | Garr. 215, Cairo ^{1}VII, 247, 464, Qawala II, 192.—293. *Manhal al-laṭāʾif fī 'l-kināfa wal-qaṭāʾif*, Berl. 8537, Cairo ^{1}VII, 50.—294. * *al-Muḥāḍarāt wal-muḥāwarāt*, anthology, Paris 3406/7.—295. * *Saqṭ al-jawāhir al-manẓūma fī 'l-ashʿār al-maḥkūma* ibid. 3408.—296. * *Rasf al-laʾāl fī waṣf al-hilāl*, compilation of verses by Khalīl al-Ṣafadī (p. 39) on the new moon, ibid. $3972_{,4}$, $4588_{,24}$, print. in *al-Tuḥfa al-bahiyya* Constantinople 1302, 67/78.—297. * *al-Marj al-naḍir wal-araj al-ʿaṭir*, anthology, print. Damascus 1350, abstract Berl. $8415_{,3}$, see Kosegarten, *Chrest. ar.* 151/76, Grangerie de la Grange, *Anthologie ar.*, Paris 1828, no. 11, 16, 19, 20, and others.—298. * *al-Araj fī intiẓār al-faraj* I, 160, with Patna II, $407_{,2676,1}$.—299. *Mushtaha 'l-ʿuqūl fī muntaha 'l-nuqūl*, on the most productive writer, the greatest flood, etc., Br. Mus. Suppl. 1198, Cairo ^{1}VII, 524, ^{2}III, 357, IV, 199, Rāmpūr I, 729, 89 (which has *Muntahā etc.*), lith. C. 1276, s. RAAD IX, 638, 8, abstract

Berl. 8410/1, Vienna 824 (*Majmūʿ*), Cairo ^{1}VII, 252.—300. ⁎ *Qūt al-nadīm wa-nuzhat al-musāfir wal-muqīm*, a collection of poems by various authors, Gotha 2318, *Nuzhat al-nadīm* ḤKh VI, 678.—301. ⁎ *Fākihat al-ṣayf wa-anīs al-ḍayf*, some tales, Gotha 2699.—302. *al-Maqāmāt* Leid. 435/6 (where other MSS are listed), AS 4296$_{,2}$, Mosul 42$_{,4}$, 50$_{,61}$, Patna II, 458$_{,2632,12}$, lith. n.p. 1275, print. Constantinople 1298 (only 12 *maqāmas*), individual ones Berl. 8555/71, Paris 3521$_{,2}$, 3949/51, 3972, 4588, 6596, Cairo ^{1}VII, 50 Qawala II, 217/9, Mawāʿiẓ, 36$_{,13}$, *Maqāmāt fī jamīʿ al-wuḥūsh* Patna II, 396$_{,2570,35}$.—303. *Kitāb al-wasāʾil ilā maʿrifat al-awāʾil*, following the work of al-ʿAskarī (I, 132), Berl. 9369/79, Ms. or. oct. 3958, Munich 467, Gotha 1551 (where other MSS are listed), Garr. 599/600, see Gosche in Pott and Gosche, *Festgruss zur XXV. Philologenvers.* Halle 1867.—304. *al-Shamārīkh fī ʿilm al-taʾrīkh* Garr. 2027$_{,3}$, Alex. Fun. 85$_{,7}$, Patna II, 393$_{,2570,11}$, ed. C.F. Seybold, Leiden 1896.—305. *al-Qawl al-mujmil fi ʾl-radd ʿala ʾl-muhmil*, Paris 2800$_{,13}$, Cairo ^{1}VII, 165 see Suppl.—306. *al-Munā fi ʾl-kunā*, ed. Seybold, ZDMG 49, 231/43.—307. *Rafʿ shaʾn al-Ḥubshān*, an elaboration of Ibn al-Jawzī's *Tanwīr al-ghabash* (I, 665), Paris 659$_{,5}$, Br. Mus. Suppl. 602, see de Sacy, *Chrest. ar.* I, 458.—308. ⁎ *Azhār al-ʿurūsh fī akhbār al-Ḥubūsh* Gotha 1693 (?).—309. ⁎ *Nuzhat al-ʿumr fi ʾl-tafḍīl bayna ʾl-bīḍ wal-sūd wal-sumr* Berl. 8413, 9846, Leid. 515, Qawala II, 221.—310. *Sharḥ Bānat Suʿād* Suppl. I, 69.—311. *Tuḥfat al-ẓurafāʾ* | *fī asmāʾ al-khulafāʾ*, in verse Paris 3972$_{,6}$, Cairo V, 204
^{1}140, ^{2}131, Mosul 136$_{,90,5}$.—312. ⁎ *Dīwān al-ḥayawān* p. 172.—313. ⁎ *Naẓm al-badīʿ fī madḥ al-shafīʿ*, imitation of the *Badīʿiyya* by Ibn Ḥijja (p. 18), Berl. 7373, Gotha 59$_{,1}$, 2798 (fragm.), Vienna 1640$_{,2}$, Paris 1160$_{,8}$, 3207$_{,3}$, 3432$_{,2}$, 4124$_{,7}$, Garr. 107$_{,567}$, Qawala II, 177, with a self-commentary Berl. 7374/5, Cairo ^{1}VII, 464, ^{2}II, 206.—314. *al-Munaqqaḥ al-ẓarīf ʿala ʾl-muwashshaḥ al-sharīf* p. 24.—315. *al-Risāla al-sulṭāniyya*, to Qāʾitbāy, when the latter had summoned him to reappear at court, Cairo ^{1}VII, 465.—316. *Risāla ilā malik al-Takrūr* (see Ibn Khald. *Prol.* 95$_{,8}$), a call to piety, Paris 4588$_{,10}$, Cairo ^{1}VII, 466.—317.–333. see Suppl. (325, Patna II, 395$_{,2570,32}$, 327, Qawala I, 219, Istanbul 1311).—334. *al-Lumaʿ al-saniyya fī madḥ khayr al-bariyya* Berl. Brill. M. 161$_{,3}$.—335. *Risāla fī faḍl al-shitāʾ* Patna II, 406$_{,2574,24}$.—336. *al-Shihāb al-thāqib fī dhamm al-khalīl al-ṣāḥib* Alex. Fun. 191$_{,2}$, Patna II, 393$_{,2570,16}$ (*al-khalīl wal-muṣāḥib*).

Chapter 2. Iraq and al-Jazīra

Under the yoke of Turkish and Mongol regionalism both countries, which during the heydays of the caliphate had been the real home of Arabic literature, now sank to an unprecedented low. In Baghdad, which had been thoroughly destroyed by the Mongols under the command of Hūlāgū, there were not many people who were able to elevate themselves above the miseries of daily life by engaging in intellectual pursuits. And things were hardly any better in Arbela and Mosul. Princes appreciative of the arts had been replaced by foreign gang leaders who hardly knew Arabic and who took no interest in Arabic poetry or in the sciences of Islam. This is why there are so few poets and scholars worth mentioning from these two countries, and then their names were for the most part only known locally.

205 | 1 *Poetry and Rhymed Prose*

1. Shams al-Dīn Maʿadd b. Muḥammad Naṣrallāh b. Rajab al-Jazarī b. al-Ṣayqal, who died in 701/1301.

Al-Maqāmāt al-Zayniyya al-Jazariyya, 50 in number, for his son Zayn al-Dīn Abu 'l-Fatḥ Naṣrallāh, Br. Mus. 669, 1403, NO 4273, Patna I, 206,$_{1841}$.

2. Muḥammad b. al-Qāsim b. Abī Badr al-Milḥī Shams al-Dīn al-Wāʿiẓ al-Wāsiṭī died, at the age of almost 70, in Ramaḍān 744/June 1344.

Fawāt II, 295/303 (samples of his poetry). A *muwashshaḥ*, Berl. 8176, cf. Hartmann p. 70.

3. Ṣafī al-Dīn Abu 'l-Faḍl ʿAbd al-ʿAzīz b. Sarāyā al-Ḥillī al-Ṭāʾī al-Sinbisī, born on 5 Rabīʿ II 677/27 August 1278, lived as a poet at the court of the Artuqids in Mārdīn, the place to which he returned after his visit to al-Malik al-Nāṣir in Cairo in 726/1326. He died in Baghdad on 30 Dhu 'l-Ḥijja 749/21 March 1349 (or, according to some, in 750/1349, according to al-Ṣafadī in 752/1351, according to yet others not until 757). His contemporaries considered him the best
160 poet, | even though he did not embark on any new paths but just continued the well-known themes of ancient times. His fame continued for centuries and continues even today.

Fawāt I, 279/87, *RA* 160r, Ibn al-Qāḍī, *Durrat al-ḥijāl* II, 372,$_{332}$, *Orient.* II, 293, Hartmann *Muw.* 79 (with an unfair appreciation), *RAAD* XII, 243/9. 1. *Dīwān*

Berl. 7851/8, Ms. or. oct. 3838, Gotha 2300 (where other MSS are listed), Paris 3205, 5786, Br. Mus. 624, Suppl. 1085, Cairo [1]IV, 248, [2]III, 136, Garr. 84, print. Damascus 1297/1300, Beirut 1300. Selection, Gotha 2301/2, Cambr. Palmer 31, no. 17. 2. *Durar al-buḥūr fī madāʾiḥ al-Malik al-Manṣūr* or *al-Qaṣāʾid al-Artuqiyyāt*, 29 poems of 29 distiches each, which each start with the same letter, in alphabetical order, in praise of al-Malik al-Manṣūr Abu ʾl-Fatḥ Ghāzī al-Artuqī, ruler of Mārdīn (r.693—| 712/1294–1312), Leid. 732 (where other 206
MSS are listed), Paris 3953,$_4$, Esc. [2]498,$_2$, 1. (*D. Ṣafwat al-shuʿarāʾ wa-khulāṣat al-bulaghāʾ*), Garr. 85/6, Cairo [1]V, 291, 306, [2]III, 279, print. C. 1283, 1322.—3. *al-Kāfiya* (*Kifāya*) *al-badīʿiyya*, a poem in praise of the Prophet that employs 151 rhetorical figures, with the self-commentary *al-Natāʾij al-ilāhiyya*, Berl. 7349/52, Ms. or. oct. 3779,$_2$ (Burch. Fischer 31), commentary ibid. 3846, Gotha 2793 (where other MSS are listed), Paris 3206/7, 3248, Esc. [2]240,$_2$, 390,$_1$. Br. Mus. Suppl. 985/6, Cairo [1]IV, 262, [2]II, 179, 225, Qawala II, 177, Alex. Adab 87, Patna II, 524,$_{2828}$, Garr. 565, 2146/1.—4. Individual poems and fragments in *Nufhat ool-Yumun* 515 ff., *Hudeekat ool Ufrah* 280 ff.—5. *Szafieddini Hellensis ad Sulthanum Elmelik Asz-szaleh Schemseddin Abulmekarem Ortokidam carmen, ar. ed. interpr. et lat. et germ. annotationibusque illustr.* G.H. Bernstein, Leipzig 1816.—6. 16 *sarīʿ* verses, ending in identically shaped but differently vocalized words rhyming in *mā*, Berl. 7030,$_2$.—7. *Qaṣīda rāʾiyya* Cairo [1]VII, 32.—8. *al-ʿĀṭil al-ḥalī wal-murakhkhaṣ al-ghalī*, a treatise on the modern verse forms of the *zajal, mawālī, kānkān*, and *qūmā*, as an appendix to his *Dīwān*, Munich 528.—9. *al-Khidma al-jaliyya fi ʾl-qidma al-Afḍaliyya*, on shooting with the musket (*bunduq*) and a description of birds that one can shoot with it, with verses cited, Berl. 5537.—10. *Risālat al-faʾr wal-dār* Br. Mus. 624,$_1$.—11. *ʿIddat abḥur al-shiʿr*, a précis on metrics, Gotha 1350,$_7$, Leipz. 327,$_2$, f. 38.—12. *al-Aghlāṭī*, a lexicon of solecisms, Esc. [2]123.—13. *Fāʾida fī tawallud al-anghām baʿḍihā ʿan baʿḍ wa-tartībihā ʿala ʾl-burūj* Cairo, *Nashra* 19, Farmer, *Sources* 53.—14.–21. see Suppl.—22. *Tasmīṭ Miftāḥ al-tawba ilā ahl Ṭība* with a commentary, *al-Badīʿ fī aṣnāf al-badīʿ*, by al-Ḥasan b. ʿAlī Abū Ṣāliḥ al-ʿAdawī al-Bukurī (see Suppl. I, 462, 7), ninth cent., Alex. Adab 98.—23. *Tasmīṭ* on the *urjūza* of Mudrik b. ʿAlī al-Shaybānī (Suppl. I, 438) on a Christian boy Heid. *ZDMG* 91, 388.

4. Al-Khalīl b. Aḥmad b. Sulaymān b. Ghāzī al-Ayyūbī Sayf al-Dīn Abu ʾl-Makārim al-Malik al-Kāmil, ruler of Ḥiṣn Kayfā, came to power in 836/1432 and was executed on the order of his son in Rabīʿ I 846/July 1442.

| *MT* 57v, al-Sakhāwī, *al-Tibr al-masbūk fī dhayl al-Sulūk*, Būlāq 1896, 399/400, 161
Weil, *Gesch. d. Chal.* V, 192, n. 3.

207 | 1. *al-Durr al-munaḍḍad*, a collection of poems in ten sections with special titles, with the tenth in Turkish, Berl. 7898.—2. See Suppl.—3. *al-Qaṣd al-jalīl min naẓm al-Khalīl*: 1. in praise of the Prophet, 2. in praise of his father al-Ashraf and his grandfather al-ʿĀdil (d. 827/1424, who had been a poet himself, *MT* 58r), 3. sermons, 4. on love, 5. *muwashshaḥ* and *zajal*, 5. varia, Garr. 646.

5. His court poet was ʿAlāʾ al-Dīn Abu ʾl-Ḥasan ʿAlī b. al-Musharraf al-Māridīnī.

1. *Ithbāt al-dalīl fī ṣifāt al-Khalīl*, poems in honour of this prince from the years 834/7, Br. Mus. 626.—2. *al-Jawhar al-fard fī munāẓarat al-narjis wal-ward*, a battle of words between the daffodil and the rose, Leid. 428.—3. *Ladhdhat al-samʿ fi ʾl-munāẓara bayna ʾl-sulāf wal-shamʿ*, Pet. Ros. 108$_{,3}$.

2 *Philology*

1. Shams al-Dīn Abū ʿAbdallāh Muḥammad b. Ḥusayn (ʿAbdallāh) al-Mawṣilī al-Khalīlī al-Ḥanbalī, who died in 735/1335.

Al-ʿUqūd fī naẓm al-ʿunqūd, a grammar in verse, Berl. 6832, Mosul 169$_{,8,3}$, commentary by ʿUmar b. Ibrāhīm b. ʿAbd al-Ghanī, Garr. 442, anon. Alex. Naḥw 23.

2. Shams al-Dīn Muḥammad b. Sharaf b. ʿAlawī al-Kallāʾī al-Shāfiʿī al-Faraḍī al-Zubayrī, who died in 777/1375.

1. *al-Jāmiʿ al-ṣaghīr fi ʾl-naḥw*, composed in 772/1370, Leid. 224.—2. *al-Majmūʿ fi ʾl-farāʾiḍ*, Leid. 1847, Paris 1025$_{,1}$, Br. Mus. Suppl. 437, Pet. AM 137, Cairo ^{1}III, 315, ^{2}I, 562. Commentary by Dāʾūd b. Sulaymān Abu ʾl-Jūd al-Burhānī, d. 863/1459, Alex. Far. 11. *Tartīb* by Sibṭ al-Māridīnī, Cairo ^{1}III, 304, 316, VII, 197.—3. *al-Qawāʿid al-kubrā fi ʾl-farāʾiḍ* Cairo ^{1}III, 313, ^{2}I, 561.

3 *Historiography*

1. Ṣafī al-Dīn Muḥammad b. ʿAlī b. Ṭabāṭabā b. al-Ṭiqṭaqā was writing in 701/1301 (see Suppl.).

Al-Kitāb al-Fakhrī fi ʾl-ādāb al-sulṭāniyya wal-duwal al-islāmiyya, a mirror for princes and history of the Islamic empire from its beginnings until the end
208 of the caliphate, one of the most brilliant | works of Arabic literature, Paris 2441, ed. W. Ahlwardt, Gotha 1860, H. Derenbourg, Paris 1895, *Bibl. de l'École des Hautes Ét.* fs. 105.—Abstract by the author Paris 2442, cf. Cherbonneau, *JA* s. IV, v. 7, 8, 9.

2. Al-Ḥasan b. ʿAbdallāh b. Muḥammad b. ʿUmar al-ʿAbbāsī commenced, in 708/1308:

Āthār al-uwal fī tartīb al-duwal Cairo v, ^{1}2, ^{2}1, see Suppl.

| 3. ʿAlī b. Muḥammad b. al-Muḥayyā al-ʿAbbāsī ʿImād al-Dīn Abu ʾl-Ḥasan, who 162
was born in Shawwāl 720/November 1320.

Nuzhat dhawi ʾl-ʿuqūl fī nasab al-rasūl, Berl. 9839.

3a. Kamāl al-Dīn Abu ʾl-Faḍāʾil ʿAbd al-Razzāq b. Aḥmad b. Muḥammad b. ʿUmar b. al-Fuwaṭī, d. 723/1323, see Suppl.

Al-Kattānī, *Fihris* II, 275, M. Iqbal in *Isl. Culture* XI, 516/22.

4. In 812/1409 an anonymous author wrote, for al-Malik al-Ashraf Aḥmad of Ḥiṣn Kayfā (827–36/1424–32), the father of the poet (§ 1, 4):

Shifāʾ al-qulūb fī manāqib Banī Ayyūb Br. Mus. 314.

4 *Ḥadīth*

1. Aḥmad b. Ibrāhīm b. ʿAbd al-Raḥmān al-Wāsiṭī al-Ḥanbalī ʿImād al-Dīn Abu ʾl-ʿAbbās b. al-ʿArīf al-Ḥizāmī, who died in 711/1311 (see Suppl.).

1. *Mukhtaṣar al-sīra al-nabawiyya*, an abstract of Ibn Hishām (I, 141), Berl. 9566/7.—2. *Miftāḥ ṭarīq al-muḥibbīn wa-bāb al-uns bi-rabb al-ʿālamīn al-muʾaddī ilā aḥwāl al-muqarrabīn*, on mysticism, Cairo ^{1}II, 177.—3. An answer to a theological question, Gotha 892.—4.–7. see Suppl. (6. Garr. 1903).

2. Ḥusayn b. al-Mubārak b. al-Thiqa Yūsuf al-Mawṣilī, who died in 742/1341.

1. *al-Fatāwi ʾl-nabawiyya fi ʾl-masāʾil al-dīniyya wal-dunyawiyya* Cairo ^{1}VI, 160.—2. See Suppl.

3. ʿAbd al-Raḥmān b. al-Muʿammar al-Wāsiṭī wrote, in 755/1354:

| *Tuḥfat dhawi ʾl-rushd fi ʾl-aḥādīth al-thunāʾiyyāt al-sanad* Paris 4577,5. 209

4. Ghiyāth al-Dīn Abu ʾl-ʿAbbās Muḥammad b. Muḥammad b. ʿAbdallāh al-Rabbānī al-ʿĀqūlī, who died in 797/1394 (see Suppl.).

1. *Kitāb al-dirāya fī maʿrifat al-riwāya*: a. theory of the science of *ḥadīth*, in 10 chapters.—b. a list of his 82 teachers, Leid. 1751.—2. *Kifāyat al-nāsik fī maʿrifat al-manāsik* ibid. 1846.

5. Jamāl al-Dīn Abu ʾl-Muẓaffar Yūsuf b. Muḥammad b. Masʿūd al-Surramarrī, who died in 736/1335 (or, according to others, in 776/1374), see Suppl.

Al-Suyūṭī, *Bughya* 423. 1. *Kitāb al-arbaʿīn al-ṣaḥīḥa fī-mā dūna ajr al-manīḥa* Berl. 1587.—2. 149 *basīṭ* verses in defence of Ibn Taymiyya (p. 125), against Taqī al-Dīn al-Subkī (p. 106), ibid. 2009.—3. *Shifāʾ al-ālām fī ṭibb ahl al-islām*, two fragments, Gotha 2008.—4.–7. see Suppl. (5. *Manẓūma fi ʾl-naḥw Luʾluʾat al-nuḥāt*, with a commentary, Garr. 483, anon. Bodl. I, 157, 9).—8. *al-Fawāʾid al-Surramarriyya min al-Mashyakha al-Badriyya* see al-Kattānī, *Fihris* II, 214.

163 | 5 *Fiqh*

A The Ḥanafīs

Al-Ḥusayn b. Muḥammad al-Samʿānī al-Ḥanafī, ca. 740/1339.

Khizānat al-muftīn Ind. Off. 1598/1600, Yeni 608/9, see Suppl.

B The Mālikīs

ʿAbd al-Raḥmān b. Muḥammad b. ʿAbd al-Raḥmān al-Baghdādī al-Mālikī b. ʿAskar was born in Baghdad in Muḥarram 644/May 1246, studied in Mecca and Yemen, taught at al-Madrasa al-Mustanṣiriyya in Baghdad, and died in Shawwāl 732/June 1332.

DK II, 344, no. 2353. *Irshād al-sālik*, a compendium of Mālikī law, with a commentary by Abū ʿAbdallāh Sulaymān b. Shuʿayb al-Buḥayrī al-Mālikī, who was born in 836/1432 and died in 900/1494; an abstract of both works: *Talkhīṣ*
210 *Irshād al-sālik ilā fiqh al-imām* | *Mālik* by ʿAlī b. Saʿīd b. ʿAbdallāh al-Baghdādī al-Suwaydī Abu ʾl-Maʿālī, ca. 1206/1791, Berl. 4593.

C The Shāfiʿīs

1. Tāj al-Dīn Abū Muḥammad Abu ʾl-Faḍl Ṣāliḥ b. Thāmir al-Jaʿbarī al-Shāfʿī, d. 706/1306 (see Suppl.).

Naẓm al-laʾālīʾ fi ʾl-farāʾiḍ, 488 (in another recension 700) *ṭawīl* verses with a commentary by Aḥmad b. Rajab b. al-Majdī, d. 851/1446 (p. 158), completed in 844/1440, Berl. 4711, Br. Mus. Suppl. 436, Garr. 1875.

2. Al-Ḥusayn b. Yūsuf b. Muḥammad b. Abi ʾl-Sarī al-Dujaylī al-Baghdādī, who was born in 664/1265 and died in 732/1331.

Al-Kāfiya fī naẓm al-farāʾiḍ Cairo [1]III, 314.

3. Muḥammad b. Muḥammad b. Muḥammad (Aḥmad) b. Zankī al-Shuʿaybī al-Isfarāʾinī al-ʿIrāqī al-Shāfiʿī, who was born in 670/1271 and died in 747/1346.

1. *Yanābīʿ al-aḥkām fī maʿrifat al-ḥalāl wal-ḥarām* AS 1526, Cairo [1]III, 291.—2. *Sarḥ al-Ḥāwi ʾl-ṣaghīr* I, 494.—3. See Suppl.

4. Muḥammad b. Abī Bakr b. ʿAbbās al-Shāfiʿī Ṣadr al-Dīn b. al-Khābūrī, who was born in 693/1294 and died in 763/1361.

Fawāʾid, various legal digressions, Berl. 4988.

5. Sarīja b. Muḥammad al-Malaṭī al-Māridīnī, who died in 788/1386.

1. *Bayān lahjat al-furrāḍ wa-tibyān lahjat al-murtāḍ*, a *rajaz* poem, with a commentary, Leid. 1840.—2. A *qaṣīda* in 19 *sarīʿ* verses, Berl. $7872_{,1}$.—3. See Suppl.—4. *Taqwīm al-adhhān fī ʿilm al-mīzān* Alex. Manṭiq 5.

6. Muḥammad b. Abī Bakr al-Dayrī al-Shāfiʿī, ca. 820/1417.

Naṣāʾiḥ, polemics, directed particularly against the Shīʿīs, Berl. 2103.

7. Ibrāhīm b. Mūsā al-Karakī, d. 853/1449, see Suppl.

1. *Fatāwī Fayḍiyya* Yeni 649/52, AS 1574.—2. See Suppl.

| D The Ḥanbalīs 211

Naṣrallāh b. Aḥmad al-Baghdādī al-Ḥanbalī Jalāl al-Dīn, ca. 790/1388.

Manẓūmat al-farāʾiḍ, 103 *ṭawīl* verses, composed in 767/1365, revised by his son Muḥibb al-Dīn, d. 844/1440, and published by Muḥammad Sibṭ al-Mārdīnī, ca. 863/1459, Berl. 4717, commentary by the same, ibid. 4718.—2. Suppl.

E The Shīʿa

Jamāl al-Dīn Ḥasan b. Yūsuf b. ʿAlī b. al-Muṭahhar al-Ḥillī al-Shīʿī al-ʿAllāma Āyatallāh, a student of al-Ṭūsī (I, 670), was head of the Imāmīs of Iraq under sultan Khudābanda, and died in 726/1326.

Khwandamīr *HS* III, I, 112. 1. A didactic letter on his own writings in the field of philosophy and on those writings on which he himself possessed didactic letters, Berl. 152.—2. *Naẓm al-barāhīn fī uṣūl al-dīn*, with the self-commentary *Maʿārij al-fahm fī sharḥ al-Naẓm*, Berl. 1796, Ind. Off. 471$_{,6}$.—3. *Irshād al-adhhān ilā aḥkām al-īmān* (author?) Berl. 4590/1, Pet. 76, Ind. Off. 1794/6. 8 commentaries thereon *Dharīʿa* I, 511/2 (see Suppl.), *Kitāb al-iqtiṣād* by ʿAbd al-Nabī b. Saʿd al-Jazāʾirī, d. 1021/1612, *Dharīʿa* II, 268$_{,1088}$.—4. *Qāwāʿid al-aḥkām fī maʿrifat al-ḥalāl wal-ḥarām*, with an anonymous commentary, Berl. 4789, Leid. IV, 162, Pet. AM 135, Br. Mus. Suppl. 333, Ind. Off. 1798/1800. Commentaries: see Suppl. (a. Ind. Off. 1801, *Dharīʿa* II, 495$_{,1950}$; d. Ind. Off. 1802/3).—5. *Nahj al-ḥaqq wa-kashf al-ṣidq*, a refutation of Sunnī dogma, with particular emphasis on the Ashʿaris, Ind. Off. 437, 471$_{,2}$, *Dharīʿa* I, 291, see Goldziher, *SBWA* 1878, p. 469.—6. *Minhāj al-karāma fī maʿrifat al-imāma* Ind. Off. 471$_{,3}$, see Suppl.—7. *Kashf al-yaqīn*, on the merits of ʿAlī, ibid. 471$_{,4}$.—8. *Manāhij al-yaqīn fī uṣūl al-dīn* ibid. 5, commentary, *Īḍāḥ al-tabyīn*, by Kamāl al-Dīn ʿAbd al-Raḥmān b. Muḥammad b. Ibrāhīm b. Muḥammad b. Yūsuf b. al-ʿAtāʾiqī al-Ḥillī, completed in 787/1385, with *al-Risāla al-kāmila* or *Zubdat Risālat al-ʿilm* on questions asked of Nāṣir al-Dīn al-Ṭūsī by Kamāl al-Dīn Mītham, autograph in al-Khizāna al-Gharawiyya, *Dharīʿa* II, 502$_{,1965}$.—9. *Irshād al-ṭālibīn* Ind. Off. 471$_{,7}$.—10. *Tahdhīb al-wuṣūl ilā ʿilm al-uṣūl* Br. Mus. 1608 (?), Suppl. 263. Commentaries: see Suppl.
212 (a. Ind. Off. 1502, c. by Jamāl al-Dīn | b. ʿAbdallāh al-Ḥusaynī al-Jurjānī, Ind. Off. 1501).—11. *Taḥrīr al-aḥkām al-sharʿiyya ʿalā madhhab al-Imāmiyya* Munich 372, Br. Mus. 280, Or. 8328 (autograph).—12. *Khulāṣat al-aqwāl fī maʿrifat al-rijāl*, Berl. 9926/7, Paris 1108$_{,2}$.—13. *Īḍāḥ al-intibāh fī asmāʾ al-ruwāh* Berl. 10164.—14. *al-Abyāt al-fakhriyya*, 34 verses in praise of the relatives of Muḥammad, ibid. 9667.—15. *Sharḥ Tajrīd al-ʿaqāʾid* I, 671.—16. *Sharḥ Tajrīd al-manṭiq* ibid. 673.—17.–39. see Suppl. (18. *Dharīʿa* II, 444$_{,1725}$; 19. Ind. Off. 1791/2; 21. in 2 vols., composed in 709 and 712 for his son Fakhr al-Muḥaqqiqīn Muḥammad, who rearranged it in 754, only partly preserved, *Dharīʿa* II, 298$_{,1199}$; 23. the commentary *Irshād al-ṭālibīn* by Jamāl al-Dīn b. ʿAbdallāh al-Miqdād b. ʿAbdallāh b. Muḥammad b. Ḥusayn b. Muḥammad al-Asadī al-Suyūrī al-Ḥillī, d. 826/1423 (no. 4), completed in 792, MSS *Dharīʿa* I, 515$_{,1520}$; 25. Ind. Off. 1793, Tehran 1329; 27. commentary see *Dharīʿa* I, 63$_{,310}$; 28. *Istiqṣāʾ al-naẓar etc.* or *Istiqṣāʾ al-baḥth wal-naẓar* MSS *Dharīʿa* II, 31$_{,122}$; 29. See *Dharīʿa* 501$_{,1961}$, Suppl. I, 847, to II; 30 other MSS *Dharīʿa* II, 498, 1954$_{,34}$. Berl. 4427, Ind. Off. 1500, Alex. Uṣūl 18$_{,1}$, anon. comm. ibid. 2; 39. autograph in al-Khizāna al-Gharawiyya *Dharīʿa* II, 45$_{,175}$; 37.

Ind. Off. 1790, lith. Pers. 1324).—40. *Wājib al-iʿtiqād fī ʾl-uṣūl wal-furūʿ*, commentary *al-Iʿtimād* by Jamāl al-Dīn al-Miqdād (no. 4), printed in *Majmūʿat kalimāt al-muḥaqqiqīn*, Persia 1315.—41. *Masāʾil Muhannā b. Sinān b. ʿAbd al-Wahhāb al-Ḥusaynī*, who had come from Medina to Baghdad to ask him some questions, composed in 719 (Kentūrī 2886), Ind. Off. 1797.—42. *al-Arbaʿūn masʾala fī uṣūl al-dīn*, library of the Rājā of Fayḍābād, *Dharīʿa* I, 435,$_{2205}$.—43. *Ithbāt al-rajʿa* library of the Madrasa Fāḍil Khān in Mashhad, ibid. I, 92,$_{442}$.—44. *Ādāb al-baḥth* in *Majmūʿa* in the library of Muḥammad ʿAlī al-Khwānsārī al-Najafī, ibid. I, 13, 60.—45. *Risāla fī ʾl-waṣiyya* Patna II, 349,$_{2536,2}$.

2. His son Fakhr al-Muḥaqqiqīn, d. 771/1369, see Suppl.

4. *Irshād al-mustarshidīn wa-hidāyat al-ṭālibīn fī uṣūl al-dīn*, MSS in Najaf and Tabriz, *Dharīʿa* I, 521,$_{2531}$.

3a. Rukn al-Dīn Muḥammad b. ʿAlī al-Jurjānī al-Gharawī wrote, in 728/1328 in Gharī:

Al-Abḥāth fī taqwīm al-ḥadīth, against the Zaydīs, a demonstration of the theory behind Twelver Shīʿism, MS with al-Ḥājj Muḥammad Sulṭān al-Mutakallimīn in Tehran *Dharīʿa* I, 63,$_{308}$.

| 3b. Ḥaydar b. ʿAlī b. Ḥaydar al-ʿAlawī al-Ḥusaynī al-Āmulī wrote, in 759/1358 213
in al-Ḥilla:

Al-Asʾila al-Āmuliyya, asked by Fakhr al-Muḥaqqiqīn (no. 2), MS with ʿAbd al-Ḥusayn al-Ṭihrānī in Karbala, *Dharīʿa* II, 72, 190.

3c. Raḍī al-Dīn Rajab b. Muḥammad b. Rajab al-Ḥāfiẓ al-Birsī al-Ḥillī wrote, in 773/1371:

Mashāriq al-anwār and, in 811/1408, *Mashāriq al-amān; Kitāb al-alfayn fī waṣf sādāt al-kawnayn* MS *Dharīʿa* II, 299,$_{1200}$.

3d. Bahāʾ al-Dīn ʿAlī b. Ghiyāth al-Dīn ʿAbd al-Karīm b. ʿAbd al-Ḥamīd al-Ḥusaynī al-Nīlī al-Najafī wrote, between 772–7/1370–5:

Al-Anwār al-ilāhiyya fī ʾl-ḥikma al-sharʿiyya, vol. I in al-Khizāna al-sharīfa al-Gharawiyya *Dharīʿa* II, 415/8,$_{1654}$.—2. *al-Inṣāf, al-radd ʿalā ṣāḥib al-Kashshāf*, lost, ibid. 379,$_{1594}$.

4. Sharaf al-Dīn al-Miqdād b. ʿAbdallāh b. Muḥammad al-Suyūrī al-Asadī al-Ḥillī, who died on 26 Jumādā II 826/7 June 1423, see Suppl.

Dharīʿa II, 92, 365.

5. Jamāl al-Dīn Aḥmad b. Muḥammad b. Fahd al-Asadī al-Ḥillī, who died in 841/1437, see Suppl.

11. *Miṣbāḥ al-mubtadiʾ etc.* additionally Ind. Off. 1873.—13. *al-Mūjiz al-ḥāwī li-taḥrīr al-fatāwī* (Kentūrī 3212), Ind. Off. 1808, commentary by (?) Muflis b. Ḥusayn al-Ṣammīrī, a contemporary of ʿAbd al-Nabī al-Karakī, d. 944/1537 (Kentūri 2000), ibid. 1809.

5a. His student ʿAbd al-Ṣamad al-Fayyāḍ wrote:

Kifāyat al-ṭālibīn Meshh. V. 102,$_{928}$.

6a. Aḥmad b. Muḥammad b. ʿAbdallāh b. ʿAlī b. Ḥasan b. ʿAlī b. Muḥammad b. Subaʿī b. Rifāʿa al-Baḥrānī al-Subaʿī wrote, in 853/1449:

Al-Anwār al-ʿAlawiyya fī sharḥ al-Risāla al-alfiyya for a friend in India, MS in Najaf, *Dharīʿa* II, 434,$_{1698}$.

214 | 7. (On Yūsuf b. Makhzūm al-Aʿwar al-Maqṣūdī al-Wāsiṭī, ca. 700, see *Dharīʿa* II, 419,$_{1657}$).

6 *Sciences of the Qurʾān*

1. ʿAbdallāh b. Aḥmad b. ʿAlī al-Kūfī al-Hamadhānī, d. 745/1344, see Suppl.

1. *Manẓūma fi ʾl-farq bayna ʾl-ḍād wal-ẓāʾ fi ʾl-Qurʾān maʿa sharḥihā* Berl. 10326.—2. *ʿUmdat al-qurrāʾ* Garr. 1253,$_{4}$.

2. ʿAbd al-Aḥad b. Muḥammad b. ʿAbd al-Aḥad al-Ḥanbalī al-Ḥarrānī wrote, in 787/1385:

1. *Nuzhat al-ʿālim fī qirāʾat ʿĀṣim* Leid. 1639.—2. Another work on the art of reciting the Qurʾān, without a title, ibid. 1640.

3. Abu ʾl-Baqāʾ ʿAlī b. ʿUthmān b. Muḥammad b. al-Qāṣiḥ al-ʿUdhrī al-Baghdādī, d. 801/1399, see Suppl.

1. *Qurrat al-ʿayn fi ʾl-fatḥ wal-imāla wa-bayna ʾl-lafẓayn*, arranged according to sura, Berl. 549/50, Heid. ZDMG 91, 393, Leid. 1641, Paris 2677,$_{8}$, Garr. 1215, Fātiḥ 40,$_{5}$, 59, Waqf Ibr. 68, Cairo ^{1}I, 109, ^{2}I, 25, Qawala I, 226.—2. *Sharḥ al-Shāṭibiyya* I, 521.—3. *Durrat al-afkār fī maʿrifat awqāt al-layl wal-nahār*, in verse, Br. Mus. Suppl. 764,$_{5}$.—4. *Tuḥfat al-ṭullāb fi ʾl-ʿamal bi-rubʿ al-asṭurlāb* Cairo ^{1}V, 232 (photograph in *Qu. u. St.* VII, 39, II, 34), Garr. 1024 (anon.).—5.–9. see Suppl. (7. Köpr. 30,$_{1}$, 31,$_{9}$, 8. Garr. 1216/7).

4. Muḥammad b. Ḥasan b. Muḥammad al-Najafī, see Suppl.

Maʿārij al-suʾūl wa-mashāriq al-maʾmūl, a Qurʾān commentary, Ind. Off. 1810, Meshh. III, 67,$_{215}$.

7 Dogmatics

1. Aḥmad b. Ibrāhīm b. Aḥmad al-Sinjārī, who died in 742/1341, see Suppl.

Al-Qaṣīda al-saniyya fi ʾl-ʿaqīda al-sunniyya Berl. 1997.

2. Tāj al-Dīn ʿAlī b. Muḥammad al-Mawṣilī al-Shāfiʿī b. al-Durayhim, who died in 762/1361, see Suppl.

Ghāyat al-maghnam fi ʾl-ism al-aʿẓam Berl. 2235/6, Cairo ^{1}VII, 542, ^{2}I, 334.

| | 8 Mysticism 215 166

1. Abu ʾl-Ḥasan ʿAlī b. al-Ḥasan b. Aḥmad al-Wāsiṭī, who died in 733/1333, see Suppl.

2. Taqī al-Dīn Abu ʾl-Faraj ʿAbd al-Raḥmān b. ʿAbd al-Muḥsin al-Wāsiṭī al-Anṣārī, d. 744/1343, see Suppl.

3. Al-Ḥasan b. Abi ʾl-Qāsim b. Bādis, d. 787/1385, see Suppl.

Commentary *Ins al-jalīs*, also Berl. Ms. or. oct. 3835,$_{2}$.

4. Taqī al-Dīn Abū Bakr b. Aḥmad b. ʿAbdallāh al-Shaybānī al-Mawṣilī al-Ṣūfī, d. 797/1395, see Suppl.

1. A *maqāla*, on the relation between a student or *murīd* and his first teacher, Berl. 144.—2. *Futūḥ al-raḥmān*, on questions from various sciences, ibid. 295.—3. *al-Risāla al-anīsa al-muntakhaba min kalām ahl al-qulūb al-ṭāhira*

al-nafīsa, a manual aimed at a true knowledge of God and one's religious duties, ibid. 1814/5, Leipz. $247_{,2}$.—4. *Muḥdhirat al-ikhwān mimmā yaqaʿ min qawl aw fiʿl aw iʿtiqād yalzam fīhi ʾl-kufrān*, a warning against Ḥanafī views, composed in 794/1392 in Jerusalem, Berl. 2101/2.—5. *al-Ādāb fi ʾl-taṣawwuf* ibid. 3094/5.—6. *Mukhtaṣar maʿārif al-qulūb sammāhu Sitr al-sirr*, a part of which ibid.—7. *Tuḥfat al-abrār al-jāmiʿa fi ʾl-adhkār* ibid. 3698.—8. *al-Durar al-muḍīʾa fi ʾl-waṣāyā al-ḥikmiyya*, collected from various works for his son, ibid. 4005.—9. *Ikhtiṣār al-waṣāyā*, written to his friends, ibid. 4006.—10. *al-Muthallatha fi ʾl-lugha al-musammāt bil-Ḥibāla*, after Quṭrub (I, 102), ibid. 7090.—11.–14. see Suppl.

167 | 5. Shihāb al-Dīn Abu ʾl-ʿAbbās Aḥmad b. Abī Bakr al-Qurashī al-Hāshimī al-Baghdādī.

Al-Majmūʿ al-sharīf al-muḥtawī ʿalā kulli maʿnā laṭīf, on Shaykh Abu ʾl-Ḥasan ʿAlī b. ʿUmar al-Qurashī al-Shādhilī al-ʿUmānī, who died in 828/1425, AS 3244 (Ritter).

6. Aḥmad b. Muḥammad al-Karakī Jalāl al-Dīn, ca. 900/1494.

1. *Nūr al-ḥadaq fī lubs al-khiraq*, Berl. 3335.—2. *al-Fatḥ al-dhawqī fi ʾl-kalām ʿalā baʿḍ karāmāt Sayyidī Ibrāhīm al-Dasūqī*, d. 696/1296, based on sura $10_{,63/5}$,
216 which is | regarded as the key point of faith, treats of the nature of the *wālī*, his relation to God and his tasks and duties, illustrated through the person of al-Dasūqī and various other Sufis, completed in 912/1506, Berl. 3362, Cairo ^{1}V, 121.—3., 4. See Suppl. (4. Cairo ^{2}V, 112).

9 *Mathematics*

1. ʿAbdallāh b. Muḥammad al-Baghdādī al-Khaddām ʿImād al-Dīn, ca. 736/1335, see Suppl.

1. *al-Fawāʾid al-Bahāʾiyya fi ʾl-qawāʿid al-ḥisābiyya*, on arithmetic and geometry, dedicated to Bahāʾ al-Dīn al-Juwaynī, Berl. 5976, Books 2–5 Ind. Off. $771_{,2}$, Garr. $2106_{,3}$, commentaries see Suppl. (a. Köpr. $941_{,1}$, Qawala II, 261, Patna I, $229_{,2012}$; b. ʿUm. 4528, Krause, *St. Hdss.* 518).—2. See Suppl.—3. *al-Tadhkira al-Saʿdiyya fi ʾl-qawānīn al-ṭibbiyya* Mosul $33_{,152,6}$.

2. Badr al-Dīn Muḥammad b. Muḥammad b. Aḥmad Sibṭ al-Mārdīnī The Elder, who was born in 826/1422 and was a student of Ibn al-Majdī (p. 158), was still alive in 891/1486.

1. *Tuḥfat al-aḥbāb fī ʿilm al-ḥisāb*, on arithmetic, Berl. 5994, AS 2752,$_{2}$, Alex. Ḥisāb 5, Cairo ^{1}V, 179.—Commentary by Bahāʾ al-Dīn Muḥammad b. ʿAbdallāh al-Shinshawrī, d. 982/1574, *Tuḥfat uli ʾl-albāb* Gotha 1486, *Bull. de Corr. Afr.* 1884, p. 373, no. 46, Alex. Ḥisāb 10.—2. *Kashf al-ghawāmiḍ fī ʿilm al-farāʾiḍ*, with a commentary, *Irshād al-fāriḍ*, completed in 891/1486 after 14 days of work, Berl. 4726, Gotha 1109 (attributed to The Younger), Paris 870, Algiers 1329, Alex. Far. 3, Makram 3.—3. *al-Mawāhib al-saniyya fī aḥkām al-waṣiyya*, on the principles that are to be followed when drawing up a testament, Berl. 4764, Cairo ^{1}VII, 197.—4. *Jadāwil fī rasm al-munḥarifāt ʿala ʾl-ḥīṭān bi-ṭarīq sahl ḥasan lam yusbaq ilayhi* Bodl. Uri 434, Cairo ^{1}V, 238 (see Suppl. 20) Berl. *Qu. u. St.* VII, 4, II, 40, 55, II, 52, translation by C. Schoy, *Isis* VI, 1924, 44 ff.—5. *Laqṭ al-jawāhir fī (taḥdīd) al-khuṭūṭ wal-dawāʾir*, on prayer times, for beginners, Berl. 5693, Garr. 984, print. C. 1293 (Cat. V, 271/2, 284, 292, VII, 323); commentary by Aḥmad b. Muḥammad al-Sijāʿī, d. 1197/1783 (p. 323), Garr. 1008, Cairo ^{1}VII, 269.—6. *Wasīlat al-ṭullāb fī maʿrifat al-awqāt bil-ḥisāb* Munich 683, Kap. 26. Paris 2560,$_{6}$.—7. *al-Risāla* | *al-Fatḥiyya* (*Shihābiyya*) *fi ʾl-aʿmāl al-jaybiyya*, | on the sine quadrant, 217 168
Berl. 5918/9, Munich 861, Br. Mus. 407,$_{2}$, Algiers 1457,$_{5}$, 1460/1, Garr. 2006,$_{11}$, Alex. Ḥisāb 51, Cairo ^{1}V, 266, 271, 289, Qawala II, 276.—Commentaries: (see add Suppl. 16) a. ʿAbd al-Raḥmān b. Muḥammad b. Aḥmad al-Maghribī al-Ṭarābulusī, completed in 944/1537, Berl. 5820, Br. Mus. 408,$_{8}$, Algiers 1462.—b. Aḥmad b. Aḥmad b. ʿAbd al-Ḥaqq al-Sunbāṭī, d. 995/1587, Berl. 5821, Vienna 1420,$_{2}$, Br. Mus. 407,$_{2}$, Copenhagen 86,$_{5}$, Alex Ḥisāb 69, Cairo V, 260, 301.—c. Jamāl al-Dīn Muḥammad b. Ibrāhīm al-Mārdīnī (see Suppl.), glosses thereon Br. Mus. 407,$_{3,6}$, versified by ʿAbd al-Raḥmān b. ʿAṣr, ibid. 4.—d. ʿAlī b. Muḥammad b. Ghānim, ibid. 5.—e. ʿAlī b. ʿAbd al-Qādir al-Nabtītī, d. 1062/1652, Berl. 5822 (photograph *Qu. u. St.* VII, 22, ii, 6).—f–h. see Suppl. (g. Makram 36, *Qu. u. St.* VII, 28, II, 14).—i. *al-Shams al muḍīʾa* by Yūsuf b. Muḥammad b. Manṣūr al-Masdī (Suppl. II, 1025, 83), Cairo ^{2}V, 263, Alex. Ḥisāb 53 (*Qu. u. St.* VII, 26,$_{ii}$, 9).—8. *Iẓhār al-sirr al-mawḍūʿ fi ʾl-ʿamal bil-rubʿ al-maqṭūʿ* Leid. 1143, Bodl. I, 1041,$_{4}$, Esc. ^{1}965,$_{2}$, Sarajevo 137,$_{10}$, Alex. Ḥisāb 53,$_{4}$, abstract *Kifāyat al-qunūʿ fi ʾl-ʿamal bil-rubʿ al-maqṭūʿ* Berl. 5848/9, Paris 2521,$_{17}$, 2542, Copenhagen 86,$_{6}$, Cambr. Palmer 33/4, Garr. 2006,$_{7}$, Alex. Ḥisāb 55, 61, Fun. 65,$_{6}$, Cairo ^{1}V, 270, 299, 302, VII, 197, 361, Qawala II, 281.—9. *Ḥāwi ʾl-mukhtaṣarāt fi ʾl-ʿamal bi-rubʿ al-muqanṭarāt* Berl. 5850, Copenhagen 86,$_{1}$, Br. Mus. Suppl. 776, Garr. 985, Cairo ^{1}I, 243, 302.—10. *Quṭb al-zāhirāt fi ʾl-ʿamal bi-rubʿ al-muqanṭarāt*, an abstract of *al-Nujūm al-zāhirāt* Berl. 5851, abstract by Muḥammad al-Ṣakhrī, ibid. 5852.—11. *Daqāʾiq* (*Raqāʾiq*) *al-ḥaqāʾiq* (*al-daqāʾiq*) *fī maʿrifat ḥisāb al-daraj wal-daqāʾiq*, a manual for the calculation of the movements of celestial bodies with arcminute precision, following the *Muqaddima* of his teacher Ibn al-Majdī, Berl. 5694/5, Paris 2541,$_{1}$, 2560,$_{15}$, Algiers 1463, Br. Mus. Suppl. 767, Alex. Ḥisāb 48, Cairo ^{1}V, 247;

glosses thereon *Ḥaqaʾiq al-daqāʾiq* by Ḥasan al-Jabartī, d. 1188/1774 (p. 359), Cairo ^{1}V, 294, abstract *Zubd* ibid. 278.—12. *Sharḥ al-gharām fī sharḥ al-ghulām*, on how he came to decide, when in Damascus, to write his *Dāʾirat al-najm* (Vat. V. 476,$_3$), Berl. 5696.—13. *Hidāyat al-ʿāmil* (*al-sāʾil*) *bil-rubʿ al-kāmil* (*fi ʾl-ʿamal ila ʾl-rubʿ al-kāmil*), Berl. 5853/4, (according to Ahlw. two different, if very similar, works), Gotha 1417,$_2$, 1428, Leid. 1146, Bodl. I, 1041,$_4$, Cambr. Palmer p. 37, no. 36, Cairo ^{1}V, 328, VII, 350, Alex. Ḥisāb 59, 65, 10, Garr. 2006,$_{15}$.—14. *al-Rawḍāt*
218 *al-zāhirāt fi ʾl-ʿamal bi-rubʿ al-muqanṭarāt* Algiers 1457,$_4$, Cairo | ^{1}V, 248.—15. *Muqaddima fī ḥisāb al-masāʾil al-jaybiyya wal-aʿmāl al-falakiyya*, with a commentary by Aḥmad b. ʿĪsā al-ʿAjabī, Munich 862 (Suter 183, 445, for his *Risāla fī ḥisāb al-masāʾil al-jaybiyya etc.* see *Qu. u. St.* VII, 29, II, 15).—16. *al-Ṭuruq al-saniyya fī ḥisāb al-nisba al-sīniyya* Cambr. Palmer p. 35, no. 30, Cairo ^{1}V, 264.—17. *Laṭāʾif al-ikhtirāʿ fi ʾl-rubʿ alladhī quṭbuhu min ṭaraf qaws al-irtifāʿ* Paris 2547,$_{18}$.—18. *al-Istīʿāb lil-ʿamal bi-ṣadr al-iwazza wa-janāḥ al-ghurāb* Cairo ^{1}V, 280.—19. *Risāla fi ʾl-munḥarifa wal-shākhiṣ* ibid. 300.—20. *al-Waraqāt fi ʾl-ʿamal bi-rubʿ al-dāʾira al-mawḍūʿ ʿalayhi ʾl-muqanṭarāt* see § 10, 2, 2a.—21. *Naẓm al-jawhar al-ghālī fi ʾl-ʿamal bil-rubʿ al-shamālī* Cairo ^{1}V, 327.—22. *Sharḥ al-Muqniʿ li-Ibn al-Hāʾim* p. 154.—26.–42. see Suppl. (28, Garr. 1960; 33. Patna I, 111,$_{1122}$).

3. Kamāl al-Dīn ʿAbd al-Raḥmān b. Muḥammad b. Ibrāhīm b. Muḥammad b. Yūsuf b. al-ʿAtāʾiqī al-Ḥillī, a student of al-ʿAllāma al-Ḥillī and Naṣīr al-Dīn ʿAlī b. Muḥammad al-Kāshānī, d. 755/1354, wrote:

Al-Irshād fī maʿrifat maqādīr al-abʿād fi ʾl-handasa and other works, autograph dated 732–88/1331–86 in the Khizāna al-Gharawiyya, *Dharīʿa* I, 510,$_{2507}$.

169 | **10** ***Astronomy***

1. ʿAbdallāh b. Khalīl b. Yūsuf al-Māridīnī Jamāl al-Dīn al-Qāhirī, who died in 809/1406.

1. *al-Durr* (*al-Luʾluʾ*) *al-manthūr fi ʾl-ʿamal bi-rubʿ al-dustūr*, on calculating time with the aid of the sine quadrant, for any region, Berl. 5840, Paris 2519,$_2$, Cambr. Palmer 31, no. 18, Cairo ^{1}VII, 287, 296, 299.—commentary *Irshād al-sāʾil ilā uṣūl al-masāʾil* by Ibn al-Majdī, d. 850/1446, Paris 2533, Makram 3.—2. *al-Waraqāt* or *Risāla fi ʾl-ʿamal bi-rubʿ al-dāʾira al-mawḍūʿ fīhi ʾl-muqanṭarāt*, on quadrants with parallels, Berl. 5841/2, Leid. 1121, Cairo ^{1}V, 305.—a commentary by al-Ḥasan b. Khalīl al-Karādīsī (p. 160, 15), *al-Nukat al-zāhirāt*, Leid. 1122, Cambr. Palmer p. 32, no. 21.—Abstracts: a. Sibṭ al-Māridīnī, Berl. 5843, Cairo ^{1}V, 243, 302.—b. ʿAbd al-Raḥmān b. Muḥammad, Algiers 613,$_5$.—c. Anon., Paris 2547,$_{17}$.—3. *Risāla fi ʾl-ʿamal bi-rubʿ al-mujayyab* Leid. 119/20, Bodl. I, 1041,$_4$, abstract

Dresd. 23,$_2$, cf. Esc. ^{1}963,$_1$.—4. *al-Shabaka*, trigonometric tables, Paris 2525.—5. A *qaṣīda* Berl. 7882,$_1$.

| 11 *Music* 219

Muḥammad b. ʿAlī al-Khaṭīb al-Irbilī wrote, in 729/1329:

Al-Qaṣīda fi ʾl-anghām, 102 *rajaz* verses on melodies, with a commentary, Berl. 5515.—2. See Suppl.

12 *Medicine*

1. Yūsuf b. Ismāʿīl b. Ilyās al-Juwaynī (Khuwayyī?) al-Baghdādī b. al-Kutubī wrote, in 710/1310 or 711:

Mā lā yasaʿu ʾl-ṭabīb jahluhu, on remedies, taken from Ibn al-Bayṭār, Berl. 6427/8, Leid. 1361/3, Paris 3005/65, 108, Br. Mus. 1362, Bodl. I, 563, 568, 618, II, 174, 184/9, Glasgow 40, 430 (*JRAS* 1899, 749), Upps. 355, Garr. 1106/7, AS 3718, Köpr. II, 193 (incorrectly in Ibn al-Kathīr "d. 826"), NO 3586/8 (Ibn al-Kathīr), Cairo ^{1}VI, 131, abstract of part I, on simple remedies and foodstuffs, Leid. 1364, by Dāʾūd b. ʿUmar al-Anṭākī (see Suppl.), Alex. Ṭibb 40.

2. Dāʾūd b. Nāṣir al-Aghbarī, who was born in Mosul, lived in Ḥiṣn Kayfā around 820/1417.

| 1. *Nihāyat al-idrāk wal-aghrād min aqrābādhīn al-aqrābādhīnāt*, also *al-Kitāb* 170
al-ʿĀdilī, on pharmacy, for Fakhr al-Dīn Sulaymān b. Shihāb al-Dīn Ghāzī b. Muḥammad al-Ayyūbī, the grandfather of the poet in § 1. 4 (who was still in power in 823/1420, Weil, *Chal.* V, 149, n. 3), Paris 2970 (in part copied by the author's brother in 826/1421), Leclerc II, 48 is mistaken.

Chapter 3. North Arabia

The Mongol onslaught never reached Arabia, and the lives of the herdsmen and bandits who made up the Bedouins of Najd remained undisturbed. Only rarely was the peace of the holy places of Mecca and Medina disturbed by disputes, usually between the ruling families of sharifs or as a result of attempts by Egyptian or Yemeni rulers to bring the area under their control. As such,
220 many foreign scholars, having carried out their duties as pilgrims, | could not resist the temptation to enjoy Allah's hospitality on sacred soil somewhat longer. Consequently, in the Hijaz belles lettres were completely overshadowed by theological and historiographical works.

171 | 1 *Poetry and Rhymed Prose*

1. Al-Shaykh ʿAlī b. Nāṣir al-Ḥijāzī, mudarris al-ʿilm al-sharīf bil-ḥarām al-Makkī, wrote, at the beginning of the tenth century:

1. *al-Maqāma al-Ghūriyya wal-tuḥfa al-Makkiyya*, in honour of the penultimate Mamlūk sultan, Qānṣūh al-Ghūrī (r. 906–22/1500–16), Gotha 2773.—2. See Suppl.

2. Aḥmad b. al-Ḥusayn (who was also a well-known poet, *MT* 56v) b. Muḥammad al-ʿAkkī al-Makkī Shihāb al-Dīn Abu 'l-ʿAbbās al-ʿUlayyif Shāʿir al-Baṭḥā', who was born in 852/1448 and died in 922/1516.

Dīwān, which was compiled by Muḥammad b. al-Ḥusayn al-Samarqandī al-Makkī al-Madanī in 1008/1591. For the most part this consisted of panegyrics on the Prophet and the notables of Baṭḥā', Berl. 7931, individual poems ibid. '2.

2 *Historiography*

1. Abū ʿAbdallāh Muḥammad b. Aḥmad b. Khalaf al-Maṭarī Jamāl al-Dīn al-Khazrajī al-ʿIbādī, who came from Maṭar in Yemen and who died in 741/1340, see Suppl.

Wüst. *Gesch.* 405. *Al-Taʿrīf bi-mā assasat al-hijra min maʿālim dār al-hijra*, Cairo V, [1]36, [2]141.

2. Abu 'l-Maḥāsin ʿAbd al-Bāqī b. ʿAbd al-Majīd b. ʿAbdallāh Tāj al-Dīn al-Makhzūmī al-Yamanī al-Shāfiʿī, who died in 743/1342, see Suppl.

Wüst. *Gesch.* 408. 1. *Luqṭat al-ʿajlān*, an abstract of Ibn Khallikān's (I, 399) *Kitāb al-wafayāt*, with an appendix containing 32 new biographies, written at the request of ʿAbdallāh b. Muḥammad al-Maṭarī, d. 765/1363, Bodl. II, 120.

| | 3. Abu 'l-Ḥasan ʿAlī b. Naṣr Saʿd al-Dīn al-Isfarāʾinī al-Makkī al-Shāfiʿī wrote, in 762/1361: 221 172

Zubdat al-aʿmāl wa-khulāṣat al-afʿāl, containing: 1. An abstract of al-Azraqī's history of Mecca (I, 143).—2. The life of Muḥammad, a description of his grave, and the privileges of the city of Medina, Paris 1631/2, Br. Mus. Suppl. 575.—Wüst. *Gesch.* 421.

4. Abū Bakr b. al-Ḥusayn b. Muḥammad b. Ṭūlūn Zayn al-Dīn al-Qurashī al-ʿUthmānī al-Marāghī al-Shāfiʿī was born in 727/1327, studied in Cairo, before settling in Medina where, in his old age, he was *qāḍī* for a short period. He died in Dhu 'l-Ḥijja 816/February–March 1413.

RA 83r. Biographical note, Ind. Off. 4576 (*QRAS* 1938, 368). *Taḥqīq al-nuṣra bi-talkhīṣ maʿālim dār al-hijra*, a history of Medina after Ibn al-Najjār, completed on 12 Rajab 766/5 April 1365 (see I, 443).

4a. Najm al-Dīn Muḥammad b. ʿUmar b. Fahd al-Shāfiʿī al-ʿAlawī al-Makkī, who died in 835/1431 (see Suppl.).

Muʿjam Patna II, $318{,}_{2429}$.

5. Taqī al-Dīn Abu 'l-Ṭayyib Muḥammad b. Aḥmad b. ʿAlī al-Fāsī al-Makkī al-Mālikī was born on 10 Rabīʿ 775/31 August 1373, went with his mother to Medina in 779/1377, and then, in 785/1386, with her back to Mecca. In 797/1395 he travelled to Cairo, to Damascus and Jerusalem the following year, in 802/1399 to Alexandria, and in 806 to Yemen. In Shawwāl 807/April 1405 he became *qāḍī* in Mecca and in 814/1412 a Mālikī professor there. In Shawwāl 817/December 1413 he lost both positions, but was reinstated in Dhu 'l-Qaʿda/January 1415. From 10 Dhu 'l-Qaʿda 819/30 January 1417 until Rabīʿ II 820/May 1417 he was suspended again, and in 828/1425 was forced to resign from his office because he had supposedly lost his eyesight. Consequently, he went to Cairo to have his continued suitability for the post confirmed by the Mālikī *muftī* there. Having | 222
received a clean a bill of health, he returned to his post in Mecca, although he was deposed once more in 830/1427, dying on 3 Shawwāl 832/7 July 1429.

RA 215r, *Ḥuff.* XXIV, 6, Wüst. *Gesch.* 473. 1. *al-ʿIqd al-thamīn fī taʾrīkh* (*faḍāʾil*) *al-balad al-amīn*, a historico-topographical description of Mecca, Paris 2123/6, Tunis, Zaytūna, *Bull. de Corr. Afr.* 1884, p. 17, no. 47, Cairo V, ^{1}87, ^{2}266, Qawala II, 240, biographical abstract, Berl. 9874; abbreviated therefrom:—2. *Ujālat al-qurāʾ fī taʾrīkh umm al-qurā*; and abbreviated therefrom, in turn:—3. the
173 first edition of the *Tuḥfat al-kirām bi-akhbār al-balad al-ḥarām*, | Paris 1668,$_{3}$, Tunis, Zaytūna, *Bull. de Corr. Afr.* 1884 p. 17, no. 48.—4. Second edition *Shifāʾ al-gharām bi-akhbār al-balad al-ḥarām*, completed in 819/1416, Berl. 9753, Kap. 8., Gotha 1706, Paris 1633, Köpr. 1097, Cairo V, ^{1}74, ^{2}234; individual chapters in Wüstenfeld, *Die Chron. der Stadt Mekka* II, 55 ff.; abbreviated therefrom:—5. *Taḥṣīl al-marām fī taʾrīkh al-balad al-ḥarām*, Berl. 9754, Garr. 594, positive opinions on it from the year 820/1417, Berl. 37 (according to *RA* he wrote a total of five abstracts of the *Shifāʾ*; one of those abstracts was probably *al-Zuhūr al-muqtaṭafa mīn taʾrīkh Makka al-musharrafa*; words of praise for which by various people, Berl. 36).—6. *al-Muntakhab al-mukhtār*, see I, 443.—7.–9. see Suppl.

6. Muḥammad b. ʿAlī b. Muḥammad b. Abī Bakr al-Qurashī al-ʿAbdarī al-Shaybī Jamāl al-Dīn, d. 837/1433, see Suppl.

1. *al-Sharaf al-aʿlā fī dhikr qubūr maqburat bāb al-Muʿallā*, a list of the memorial stones in al-Muʿallā cemetery in Mecca, with the text of the inscriptions and further notes, Berl. 6124.—2. See Suppl.

7. Muḥammad b. ʿUmar b. Muḥammad b. Aḥmad al-Tamīmī al-Tūnisī al-Makkī al-Mālikī Shams (Jamāl) al-Dīn Abū ʿAbdallāh b. ʿAzm al-Khaṭīb al-Wazīrī, d. 891/1486, see Suppl.

Wüst. *Gesch.* 500. 1. *Dustūr al-iʿlām bi-maʿārif al-aʿlām*, a biographical dictionary listing, in alphabetical order, the names, surnames, and nicknames of various notables from the beginning of Islam until the author's own lifetime, Berl. 9876/7.—2. *al-Manhal al-ʿadhb fī sharḥ asmāʾ al-rabb*, composed in 883/1478 in Mecca for Qāʾitbāy, Cairo ^{1}II, 233.—3. See Suppl.

223 | 8. Abū ʿAbdallāh Muḥammad al-Maḥjūb wrote, in the ninth century:

Qurrat al-ʿayn fī awṣāf al-ḥaramayn, a topographical description and history of Mecca and Medina from the beginning of time until the ninth century, Paris 1204,$_{4}$.

9. Abu ’l-Ḥasan ʿAlī b. ʿAbdallāh b. Aḥmad al-Ḥasanī Nūr al-Dīn al-Samhūdī al-Shāfiʿī, who came from Samhūd in Upper Egypt, began his studies in Cairo in 853/1449 under Ibn Quṭlūbughā (p. 99). After making the pilgrimage he settled down in 870/1465 in Medina. In 879/1474, he induced Sultan Qāʾitbāy to have restoration works undertaken on the mosque of the Prophet which, after the fire of 654/1256, had only been repaired in a rudimentary manner. When the latter arrived to inspect the new constructions in 884/1479, al-Samhūdī prompted him to suppress the trade in false relics, which was booming at the time. While he was in Mecca for the ʿUmra in Ramaḍān 886/November 1481, both the mosque in Medina and his own house behind it were burned to the ground. | As a result of this event he lost his precious library, and so he trav- 174
elled to Egypt to try to repair the damage and, in addition, to visit his aged mother. Since she died only ten days after his arrival in Samhūd, he returned to Medina in 887/1482, making a detour to Jerusalem on the way. In Medina, he was appointed Shaykh al-Islām, before dying on 18 Dhu ’l-Qaʿda 911/6 April 1506.

MT 70v, Wüst. *Gesch.* 507. 1. *Tabiʿat wafāʾ fī taʾrīkh al-bayt al-muṣṭafā*, was to contain everything that he had come to know regarding the history of Medina, but was lost in the aforementioned fire before it was entirely finished. Yet before that he had already made the following abstracts: 2. *Wafāʾ al-wafāʾ*, a draft version of which was completed on 24 Jumādā I 886/22 July 1481, and a clean copy that was finished in Mecca in Shawwāl/December888/1483, after his return from Egypt, and which was supplemented by the account of the fire, along with various other matters, Munich 381, Leid. 804, Br. Mus. 828, Bodl. I, 731, from this: F. Wüstenfeld, *Geschichte der Stadt Medina im Auszug aus dem Ar. des S. Göttingen* | 1864 (Gött. Abh. IX, 1/56). A second abstract of it was: 224
3. *Khulāṣat al-wafāʾ* Berl. 9759/61, Munich 382, Vienna 892, Paris 1634/6, $2252_{,2}$, Br. Mus. $329_{,2}$, Suppl. 1284, Rāġib 974, Yeni 848, Köpr. 1077, Cairo V, ^{1}50, ^{2}173, VII, 611, print. Būlāq 1285, Persian translation Berl. Pers. 532a, Bodl. 138/9.—4. *Jawāhir al-ʿiqdayn fī faḍl al-sharafayn sharaf al-ʿilm al-jalī wal-nasab al-ʿalī*, composed in 897/1492, Leid. 2043, a piece of which ibid. $909_{,4}$, Esc. ^{2}702, AS 3171, Qawala II, 232, Patna I, $147_{,1414}$.—5. *al-Maqālāt al-musfira ʿan dalāʾil al-maghfira*, on the pardoning of sins, Berl. 2641.—6. *Risālat al-iḥrāʾ fī ḥukm al-ṭalāq bil-ibrāʾ*, on divorce, on the condition that the bridal dowry should not be returned, Berl. 4669/70.—An abstract, *al-Talkhīṣ al-aḥrā fī ḥukm taʿlīq al-ṭalāq wal-ibrāʾ*, by Ibn Ḥajar al-Haytamī (p. 389), Alex. Fun. $120_{,1}$, Fiqh Shāf. 36, $37_{,2}$, Cairo ^{1}V, II, 195, 426.—7. *Īḍāḥ al-bayān li-mā arādahu l-ḥujja min “laysa fī ’l-imkān abdaʿ mimmā kān”*, on this statement by al-Ghazzālī that had

been criticised by Ibn al-ʿArabī, by Ibn al-Munayyir (d. 683/1284, in his *al-Ḍiyāʾ al-mutalaʾliʾ fī taʿaqqub al-Iḥyāʾ lil-Ghazzālī*), and by Ibn al-Biqāʿī (d. 885/1480, see p. 179), in his *Dalālat al-burhān* and *Tahdīm al-arkān*, Berl. 5102, AS 2187, Rabat 520,4.—8. *Ṭayyib al-kalām bi-fawāʾid al-salām*, answers to ca. 30 questions on correct greeting, which were collected by Ibn Quṭlūbughā, composed in 892/1487, Berl. 5574.—9. *Durar al-sumūṭ fī-mā lil-wuḍūʾ min al-shurūṭ*, Leid. 1864, Cairo ^{1}III, 226, ^{2}I, 514.—10. *Arbaʿūna ḥadīthan fī faḍl al-ramy bil-sihām* Cairo ^{1}I, 262.—11. *Sharḥ al-Ājurrūmiyya*, p. 237.—12. *Ḥāshiya ʿalā sharḥ Jamʿ ʿal-jawāmiʿ*, Suppl. p. 105.—13.–21. see Suppl. (21. Alex. Uṣūl 13).

175 | 10. ʿAbd al-ʿAzīz b. ʿUmar b. Muḥammad b. Muḥammad b. Fahd al-Makkī al-Hāshimī al-Ḥāfiẓ ʿIzz al-Dīn, d. 921/1515, see Suppl.

1. *Ghāyat al-marām bi-akhbār salṭanat al-balad al-ḥarām*, history of the emirs of Mecca, from the earliest times until the author's own lifetime, mostly after both of the chronicles by his father Najm al-Dīn ʿUmar (§ 3, 3), *Itḥāf al-warā bi-akhbār Umm al-qurā* and *al-Kamīn bi-dhayl al-ʿIqd al-thamīn*, Berl. 9755.—2., 3. See Suppl.

225 | 3 *Ḥadīth*

1. Muḥammad b. Aḥmad Shams (ʿIzz) al-Dīn al-Makkī al-Maqdisī al-Ḥanbalī, Qāḍi ʾl-quḍāt, was born in 771/1369 in Kafr al-Labad near Nablus, became *qāḍī* in Mecca, and died in 855/1451.

Safīnat al-abrār al-jāmiʿa lil-āthār Cairo ^{1}VI, 149.

2. Taqī al-Dīn Abu ʾl-Faḍl Muḥammad b. Muḥammad b. Fahd al-Hāshimī al-ʿAlawī al-Makkī al-Shāfiʿī, d. 871/1466, see Suppl.

5. *Bughyat al-ṭālib al-fāliḥ min mashyakhat qāḍī Ṭība Abi ʾl-Fatḥ Ṣāliḥ*. Alex. Muṣṭ. Ḥad. 5, Taʾr. 21.

3. His son ʿUmar b. Muḥammad b. Muḥammad b. Fahd al-Makkī al-Atharī al-Shāfiʿī Najm al-Dīn, who died in 885/1480, see Suppl.

Wüst. *Gesch.* 476. *Muʿjam* of his male and female teachers, Berl. 10131; a supplement, *Dhayl*, by Abu ʾl-Futūḥ ʿAlī, ibid. 10132.

4. Abū Bakr ʿAlī b. Abi ʾl-Barakāt Muḥammad b. Abi ʾl-Suʿūd Muḥammad b. Ḥusayn al-Qurashī al-Makhzūmī b. Zuhayra, d. 889/1484, see Suppl.

1. *Kifāyat al-muḥtāj ilā 'l-dimā' al-wājiba ʿalā 'l-muʿtamir wal-ḥājj*, Berl. 4050, Cairo [1]III, 266 (cf. Wüst. *Gesch.* 524/5).—2. See Suppl.

5. ʿImād al-Dīn Abū Zakariyyā' Yaḥyā b. Abī Bakr al-Āmirī, d. 893/1488, see Suppl.

1. *Bahjat al-maḥāfil etc.* also Alex. Ta'r. 5; commentary by Muḥammad b. Abī Bakr Ashkhar al-Yamanī, ibid. 10.—3. *al-Tuḥfa al-jāmiʿa etc.* also Patna II, 531$_{,2858/9}$.

4 *Fiqh*

A The Ḥanafīs

Abu 'l-Baqā' b. Muḥammad b. Aḥmad al-ʿUmarī al-Ṣāghānī al-Makkī al-Ḥanafī, was born in 759/1358, and who died in 854/1450 in Mecca.

1. *Mukhtaṣar Tanzīh al-masjid al-ḥarām ʿan bidaʿ jahalat al-ʿawāmm*, Esc. [2]707$_{,5}$.—2. *al-Baḥr al-ʿamīq fī manāsik al-muʿtamir wal-ḥājj ila 'l-bayt al-ʿatīq*, Leid. 1860.

| B The Mālikīs 226

1. Burhān al-Dīn Ibrāhīm b. ʿAlī b. Muḥammad b. Farḥūn al-Mālikī al-Yaʿmarī al-Andalusī was born in Medina, became a *qāḍī* there, and died in Dhu 'l-Ḥijja 799/September 1397.

| DK I, 48, no. 124, Wüst. *Gesch.* 448, Pons Boigues 298. 1. *Tabṣirat al-ḥukkām* 176
fī uṣūl al-aqḍiya wa-manāhij al-aḥkām, Leid. 1850, Br. Mus. 261, Algiers 1367, Cairo [1]III, 156, print. C. 1301/2.—2. *al-Dībāj al-mudhahhab fī maʿrifat aʿyān ʿulamā' al-madhhab* Algiers p. 12 (237), p. 10 (136), Garr. 690, Cairo V, [1]56, [2]186.—Supplement *Tawshīḥ al-Dībāj wa-ḥilyat al-ibtihāj* by Badr al-Dīn Muḥammad b. Yaḥyā al-Qarāfī (see JA, 1859, I, 94), Paris 4614$_{,2}$, 4627, and *Nayl al-ibtihāj bi-taṭrīz al-dībāj* by Aḥmad Babā b. Aḥmad al-Timbuktī, d. 1032/1623, Suppl. 466.—An abstract, *Kifāyat al-muḥtāj li-maʿrifat man laysa fī 'l-Dībāj*, by the same.—3. *Durrat* (*Durar*) *al-ghawwāṣ fī muḥāḍarat al-khawāṣṣ*, on juridical riddles, Cairo [1]III, 187, [2]I, 512, Garr. 1835.—4., 5., see Suppl.

5 *Sciences of the Qur'ān*

1. Zayn al-Dīn ʿAbd al-Raḥmān b. Shihāb al-Dīn Aḥmad b. Yūsuf b. ʿAlī b. ʿAyyāsh al-Makkī, who was born in 772/1370 and died in 853/1449.

Naẓm al-ʿiqyān 123. *Ghāyat al-maṭlūb fī qirā'at Abī Jaʿfar wa-Khalaf wa-Yaʿqūb*, Garr. 1222.

2. Muʿīn al-Dīn Muḥammad b. ʿAbd al-Raḥmān b. Muḥammad b. ʿAbdallāh b. Muḥammad b. ʿAbdallāh al-Ījī al-Ṣafawī, who died in 905/1500.

Jāmiʿ al-bayān fī tafsīr al-Qurʾān, completed in Mecca in 870/1465, Patna I, 26,$_{250}$/$_{1}$, print. in *Majmūʿa* Ind. 1296.

6 *Mysticism*

1. ʿAfīf al-Dīn ʿAbdallāh b. Asʿad b. ʿAlī b. Sulaymān al-Yāfiʿī al-Shāfiʿī al-Tamīmī was born in Yemen around 698/1298 and began his studies in Aden. From 718/1318 he lived alternately in Mecca and Medina, travelled to Jerusalem, Damascus, and Cairo in 724/1324, as well as staying in Yemen for a period in
227 738. After that | he lived once more in Mecca, where he died on 20 Jumādā II 768/22 February 1367.

177 | Biography: Berl. 297,$_{12}$, *DK* I, 247/9, no. 202, *RA* 146r, Ibn Baṭṭūṭa I, 356, Jāmī, *Nafaḥāt* 681, Khwandamīr *ḤS* II, 2, 9, *Orient.* II, 419. Wüst. *Gesch.* 429. 1. *Mukhtaṣar al-Durr al-naẓīm fī faḍāʾil al-Qurʾān al-ʿaẓīm wal-āyāt wal-dhikr al-ḥakīm* Suppl. I, 913,$_{7a}$, print. C. 1315.—2. *Shams al-īmān wa-tawḥīd al-raḥmān wa-ʿaqīdat al-ḥaqq wal-itqān*, for Sufis, in 160 *ṭawīl* verses, Berl. 2000, Algiers 581,$_{2}$.—3. *Marham al-ʿilal al-muʿaṭṭila fī ʾl-radd ʿalā aʾimmat al-Muʿtazila*, an abbreviation of the second section and the closing part in Berl. 2806, an introduction thereto, consisting of the biographies of various Ashʿarīs, following Ibn ʿAsākir (I, 403), Leid. 902.—4. *Nashr al-maḥāsin al-ʿaliyya fī faḍl al-mashāyikh uli ʾl-maqāmāt al-ʿaliyya* Garr. 1908, 2123,$_{4}$, AS 2133, ʿĀšir I, 514, II, 175, Cairo [1]II, 141, [2]I, 370.—5. *Nūr al-yaqīn wa-ishārat ahl al-tamkīn*, abstract Gotha 914,$_{4}$.—6. Calendar poem, fragment Gotha 8,$_{6}$.—7. *Qaṣīdas*, mostly of Sufi content, Berl. 7864.—8. *al-Risāla al-Makkiyya fī ṭarīq al-sāda al-Ṣūfiyya* Cairo [1]VII, 72.—9. *al-Irshād wal-taṭrīz fī faḍl dhikr Allāh wa-tilāwat kitābihi ʾl-ʿazīz*, an edifying work, Berl. 8801/2, ʿĀšir I, 807.—10. *al-Wāridāt*, Sufi sayings with a Persian paraphrase by Shāh Niʿmatallāh, Br. Mus. 885,$_{3}$.—11. *Rawḍ al-rayāḥīn fī ḥikāyāt al-ṣāliḥīn*, 500 edifying tales, Berl. 8804, Leid. 1076/7, (where other MSS are listed), Paris 2040/1, Ind. Off. 708, Pet. AM 211/2, Bat. 89, Cairo [1]V, 62, 143, print. Būlāq 1286, C. 1301/2, 1307 (*OB* IV, 3905, in the margin ibid. 4856), abstract print. C. 1281, 1315, 1322, in the margin of Thaʿlabī ibid. 1314, anon. Gotha 2712, Pet. AM 213.—12. Appendix of the former, *Asna ʾl-mafākhir fī manāqib al-shaykh ʿAbd al-Qādir* (*al-Jīlānī*), a supplement to a Persian revision of it, Berl. Pers. 19,$_{1}$.—Abstract, *Khulāṣat al-mafākhir fi ʾkhtiṣār manāqib al-shaykh ʿAbd al-Qādir wa-jamāʿa mimman ʿaẓẓamahu min al-shuyūkh al-akābir* or *ʿAjāʾib al-āyāt wal-barāhīn wa-irdāf gharāʾib ḥikāyāt rawḍ al-rayāḥīn*, 200 edifying stories about ʿAbd al-Qādir al-Jīlānī (see I, 560) and around 40 other Sufis esteemed by him,

Berl. 8804, Ind. Off. 708,$_2$.—Javanese translation by S.W.S. Drewer in R. Mg. A. Poerbatjaraka, *De mirakelen van Abdoolkadir Djeelani*, Bibl. Javan. 8, Bandung 1938.—13. *Mirʾāt al-janān wa-ʿibrat al-yaqẓān fī maʿrifat ḥawādith al-zamān*
wa-taqallub aḥwāl al-insān wa-taʾrīkh mawt baʿḍ al-mashhūrīn | *al-aʿyān*, run- 228
ning up to the year 750, Berl. 9452/3, Vienna 812, Paris 1589/92, 5952, Br. Mus. 932, Suppl. 473, Ind. Off. 706/7, Bodl. I, 725, Garr. 591, Köpr. 1144, Tunis, *Bull. de Corr. Afr.* 1884, p. 23, no. 71.—Abstracts: a. *Ghirbāl al-zamān* by Abū ʿAbdallāh Ḥusayn b. ʿAbd al-Raḥmān al-Ahdal, d. 855/1451 (p. 235), Vienna 1170, Paris 1593, 4727, Bodl. I, 672, Br. Mus. 933.—b. ʿAlī al-Qurashī al-Shushtarī, ca. 1010/1601, Berl. 9454.—c. Yaʿqūb b. Sayyid ʿAlī al-Burūsawī, d. 930/1524 in Egypt, Cambr. Suppl. 1179, Qawala II, 246.—14.–22. see Suppl. (16. Alex. Faw. 8, author?).—23. *Baḥth al-samāʿ* Berl. 5509, see Farmer, *Sources*, 55.—24. *Manẓūma fī ʾl-ṭibb* Alex. Ṭibb 49, Patna II, 488,$_{2649,8}$.—25. *Fakhr al-ṭawāf, al-ʿUnwān al-ʿazīz* AS 79,$_3$.

2. Abū Madyan Shuʿayb ʿAbdallāh b. Saʿd b. ʿAbd al-Kāfī al-Miṣrī al-Makkī al-ʿImrāwī al-Qafṣī al-Ḥurayfīsh was born in Egypt and lived in Mecca. He died in 801/1398.

Wüst. *Gesch.* 450. 1. *al-Rawḍ al-fāʾiq fī ʾl-mawāʿiẓ wal-raqāʾiq*, which contains anecdotes, biographical notes on pious men and women, *ḥadīth*, poems, examples of conversions of the unpious, and of Muḥammad himself, his relatives, and his followers, the spiritual gifts of saints, and the Last Judgement, | 178
Berl. 8806/11, BDMG 27, Paris 1305/9, Algiers 577,$_2$, 579, Br. Mus. 1439, Pet. Ros. 24, Cairo [1]II, 59, Qawala I, 241, print. Būlāq 1280, C. 1300, 1304, 1308, 1315, 1321.—abstract Paris 743,$_2$, 782,$_2$.—2. 28 *munsariḥ* verses rhyming on *lā ilāha illāhu* Berl. 434.—3. *Qaṣīda* ibid. 7879,$_2$.—4. *Tatimmat al-riyāḍ al-naḍira* I, 444.—5., 6. See Suppl.

3. ʿAlī b. Aḥmad b. Ibrāhīm al-Ḥijāzī al-Shāfiʿī al-Saqaṭī, ca. 800/1398.

Risāla li-man yasluk ṭarīq Allāh Berl. 3277.

4. ʿAlī b. Muḥammad b. Aḥmad al-Ḥijāzī al-Saqaṭī, ca. 880/1475, see Suppl.

Kashf ṭarīq al-wafāʾ ilā qadm ahl al-ṣafāʾ, on attaining God, illustrated by the example of Abraham, Berl. 3281.

5. ʿAfīf al-Dīn ʿAbdallāh b. Muḥammad b. al-Ṣafāʾ Muḥibb al-Dīn Khalīl b. al-Faraj b. Saʿīd al-Maqdisī al-Dimashqī, who was born in Mecca in 810/1407.

229 | *Tuḥfat al-mutahajjid wa-ʿutbat al-mutaʿabbid*, on weekly prayer-gatherings, Köpr. 712 (Ritter).

6. Muḥyi ʾl-Dīn Yaḥyā b. ʿAbd al-Raḥmān al-Maqdisī al-Shāfiʿī al-Qādirī wrote, in Medina in 838/1478:

Kīmiyyāʾ al-saʿāda li-man arāda ʾl-ḥusn wal-ziyāda Cairo [1]II, 209, [2]I, 350 (see Suppl.).

7. ʿAbd al-Raḥmān b. ʿAbd al-Salām al-Ṣaffūrī al-Shāfiʿī wrote, in Mecca in 884/1479:

1. *Nuzhat al-majālis wa-muntakhab al-nafāʾis*, a work on general and religious ethics, interspersed with many tales and examples, Berl. 8827/31, Gotha 846/7, Paris 3554/5, AS 2132, Cairo [1]II, 179, *Hespéris* XII, 128,$_{1039}$, printed in 2 volumes, C. 1281, 1300, 1305, 1307, 1322, among others. Abstract Br. Mus. Suppl. 447,$_{2}$.—2. He may also have been the author of *al-Maḥāsin al-mujtamiʿa wal-anwār al-multamiʿa fī faḍāʾil al-khulafāʾ*, on the merits of the first four caliphs, Berl. 9695/6, Garr. 695/6, Alex. Taʾr. 120.

8. Muḥammad b. Sharaf al-Dīn al-Shāfiʿī al-Madanī wrote, in 895/1490:

Hibat al-fattāḥ lil-murīd, for the Ottoman sultan, Bāyezīd II, AS 1803.

7 *Mathematics*

ʿAlī b. Muḥammad b. Ismāʿīl al-Zamzamī al-Makkī wrote, in 878/1473:

1. *Fatḥ al-wahhāb manẓūma fi ʾl-ḥisāb*, a commentary thereon by ʿArafa b. Muḥammad al-Urmawī, d. 931/1524, which was composed in 918/1512, Cairo [1]V, 183, anon. commentary Alex. Ḥisāb 11.—2., 3. See Suppl.

179 | 8 *Geography*

Shihāb al-Dīn Aḥmad (Muḥammad) b. Mājid b. Muḥammad (ʿUmar) b. Muʿallaq al-Saʿdī b. Abi ʾl-Rakāʾib al-Najdī wrote, in 895/1490 (see Suppl.).

1. *Kitāb al-fawāʾid fī uṣūl ʿilm al-baḥr wal-qawāʿid*, on the origins of navigation,
230 its progress since the time of Noah, the lunar | mansions, constellations, major stars, navigation in the Persian Gulf, the Indian Ocean, along the coast of the Arabian peninsula, around Sumatra, Ceylon, and Zanzibar, on the winds, typhoons, the monsoon, etc., Paris 2292,$_{1}$.—2. *Ḥāwiyat al-ikhtiṣār fī uṣūl ʿilm*

al-biḥār, in *rajaz*, ibid. 2.—3. *al-Urjūza al-muʿriba fī ʾl-Khalīj al-Barbarī* ibid. 3.—4. *Urjūza* on the determination of the *qibla*, ibid. 4.—5. Description of the Arabian coast of the Persian Gulf, in *rajaz*, ibid. 5.—6. Various other poems, ibid. 6.—7., 8. See Suppl.—9. *Urjūza* on navigation routes, AM Leningrad B 992, ff. 83/105, see Kračkovsky, *Nachr. der Geogr. Ges. in Leningrad* 1937, no. 5, 758/60 with facsimile.

180 | **Chapter 4. South Arabia**

The peace that reigned in Yemen under the Rasūlids (626–858/1229–1454) and the Ṭāhirids (850–923/1446–1517) allowed a lively literary culture, whose focal point was the academies in Zabīd. In spite of its isolation, the country enjoyed close relations with the other lands of Islam. Only the Zaydīs, who produced a rich literary heritage, primarily in defence of their own particular interpretation of Islam, remained apart from this.

1 *Poetry*

1. ʿAbd al-Raḥmān b. Muḥammad b. Yūsuf al-ʿAlawī al-Yamanī Wajīh al-Dīn, who flourished at the beginning of the ninth century.

Dīwān Leid. 740 (on the *Badīʿiyya* mentioned there see no. 8).

1c. Al-Wāthiq billāh, see Suppl.

3. Commentary *al-Washy al-marqūm ʿala ʾl-Durr al-manẓūm* by Shihāb al-Dīn Aḥmad b. Muḥammad b. al-Ḥasan b. Aḥmad al-Kawkabānī, composed in 1123/1711, Alex. Adab 186.

2. Al-Sharīf al-Murtaḍā wrote, around 820/1417:

A *Qaṣīda*, as an intercession with Sultan Aḥmad b. Ismāʿīl (803–28/1400–26) on behalf of Ḥasan b. ʿAjlān, Berl. 7889.

231 | 4. Al-Mutawakkil ʿala ʾllāh al-Muṭahhar b. Muḥammad b. Sulaymān b. Yaḥyā b. al-Ḥusayn b. Ḥamza b. ʿAlī b. Muḥammad b. al-Ḥusayn b. ʿAbd al-Raḥmān b. Yaḥyā b. ʿAbdallāh b. al-Ḥusayn b. al-Qāsim b. Ibrāhīm, a Zaydī imam who died in Dumār in Ṣafar 879/July 1474.

1. *Dīwān*, compiled by his son Yaḥyā, Br. Mus. 1672,$_{1}$.—2. Two letters, ibid. 3.—3. Poems in praise of Muḥammad, Berl. 7912,$_{3}$.—4. Answers to legal problems, Br. Mus. Suppl. 423,$_{1}$.—5., 6. See Suppl.

181 | 5. ʿImād al-Dīn Yaḥyā b. al-Mukhtār b. Amīr al-Muʾminīn Muṭahhar b. Muḥammad b. Sulaymān al-Ḥamzī, the former's grandson, lived in Taʿizz during the reign of al-Ẓāfir Ṣalāḥ al-Dīn ʿĀmir (894–923/1488–1517).

Poems in praise of Muḥammad, written in al-Jawf, Br. Mus. 1672,$_{2}$.

6. Ḍiyā' al-Dīn Jarrāḥ b. Shājir wrote, in the first half of the tenth century:

A poem in praise of Jamāl al-Dīn al-Mahdī b. Aḥmad b. Khālid, the prince of Jāzān, Br. Mus. 1673 (see Suppl.).

7. Abū Bakr b. ʿAbdallāh b. Abī Bakr Bāʿalawī al-ʿAydarūs al-Yamanī Fakhr al-Dīn, who died in 909/1503.

1. *Dīwān* Berl. 7928, selection *Majmūʿat ashʿār mukhtalifa* Garr. 103.—2. *Waṣiyya*, 20 verses with a commentary by ʿAbd al-Qādir b. Shaykh al-ʿAydarūs, who died in 1038/1628, composed in 999/1591, ibid. 4012, Buhār 433.

8. ʿAbd al-Raḥmān b. Ibrāhīm b. Ismāʿīl b. ʿAbdallāh al-ʿAlawī al-Yamanī al-Zabīdī Wajīh al-Dīn, who was born around 860/1456 and died around 920/1514.

Al-Jawhar al-rafīʿ wa-wajh al-maʿānī fī maʿrifat anwāʿ al-badīʿ, an imitation of the *Badīʿiyyya* of al-Ḥillī (p. 205), Berl. 7376, Br. Mus. Suppl. 985v. (see Suppl.).

2 *Philology*

Abu 'l-Ṭāhir Muḥammad b. Yaʿqūb b. Muḥammad b. Ibrāhīm Majd al-Dīn al-Shīrāzī al-Fīrūzābādī al-Shīrāzī was born in | Kāzarūn near Shiraz in Rabīʿ 232
II or Jumādā II 729/February or April 1329. He passed himself off as a descendant of Abū Isḥāq al-Shīrāzī (I, 484), even though the latter supposedly died childless, and later in Yemen pretended to be a descendant of the caliph Abū Bakr, which is why he called himself al-Ṣiddīqī. From the age of eight he studied in Shiraz, then in Wāsiṭ, and, in 745/1344, in Baghdad. In the year 750 AH he studied under Taqī al-Dīn al-Subkī (p. 106) in Damascus, and then accompanied him to Jerusalem. Having worked there as a professor for ten years, he then went to Asia Minor and Cairo.[1] From the year 770/1368 he lived in
Mecca, as well as spending five years in Delhi at some point. | In 794/1392 he 182

1 According to *ShN* and al-Suyūṭī he visited Bāyezīd (782–805/1390–1402), although his sojourn in Asia Minor must have taken place in the years 765–70. The report on his wandering years in RA which we follow here deviates in several instances from the *Ṭabaqāt* by Qāḍī Shuhba in Wüstenfeld. According to this source he was in Asia Minor and India sometime after 760, while it was as a pilgrim that he founded schools in Mecca and Medina. After a visit to Tīmūr in Shirāz in 790 he supposedly went to India again, while the sultan of Yemen, al-Malik al-Ashraf Ismāʿīl, appointed him as the successor to *qāḍī* Jamāl al-Dīn Aḥmad al-Raymī in 791, and, in 795, following the death of Abū Bakr b. al-ʿĀjil, as chief *qāḍī* of Yemen, with his base in Zabīd. However, he can only have met Tīmūr after the conquest of Shiraz by the Mongols in 795/1393 (Khwandamīr, *ḤS* III, 3, 34, Müller, *Der Islam* II, 296), and it is less likely that he

accepted an invitation of Sultan Aḥmad b. Uways (794–813/1392–1410) to come to Baghdad, and then visited Tīmūr in Shiraz. By way of Hormuz he arrrived in Yemen in Rabīʿ I 796/January 1394, where he stayed with Sultan al-Malik al-Ashraf in Taʿizz for 14 months. The latter appointed him chief *qāḍī* of Yemen on 1 Dhu ʾl-Ḥijja 797/17 September 1395 and gave him his daughter as a wife. During the pilgrimage he made in 802/1400 he founded a Mālikī madrasa in
233 Mecca, endowed with three professorships. He | learned of the death of al-Ashraf in 803, while he was in Medina. In Ramaḍān 805/April 1403 he again stayed in Mecca, but soon returned to Zabīd, where he died on 20 Shawwāl 817/3 January 1415.

RA 218v, *ShN* I, 92 (Rescher 16), Wüst. *Gesch.* 464. 1. *al-Qāmūs al-muḥīṭ wal-qabas al-wasīṭ al-jāmiʿ li-mā dhahaba min lughat al-ʿArab shamāṭīṭ*, an abstract of his lost 60 volume (or, according to others, 100 volume) work *al-Lāmiʿ al-muʿallam al-ʿujāb al-jāmiʿ bayna ʾl-Muḥkam* (of Ibn Sīda I, 376) *wal-ʿUbāb* (of Ṣaghānī, ibid. 443), in which he also included a considerable amount of lexical material from Yemen, MSS in almost every library (see Gotha 395, Leid. 88/91), print. Calcutta 1230–2/1817, 2 vols. Būlāq 1274, 4 vols., 1289, 1301/3, C. 1280/1, Lucknow 1885, Bombay 1272, 1884, Istanbul 1250, 1304, with Turkish translation ibid. 1272, this alone Būlāq 1250, Istanbul 1305, among others, Persian translation by Muḥammad Ḥabīballāh Br. Mus. 1016/7.—Commentaries and glosses: a. *al-Qawl al-maʾnūs* by ʿAbd al-Bāsiṭ b. Khalīl al-Ḥanafī, composed in 920/1514, AS 4731.—b. *al-Qawl al-maʾnūs bi-taḥrīr mā fī ʾl-Qāmūs* (*bi-sharḥ mughlaq al-Qāmūs*) by Muḥammad Badr al-Dīn b. Yaḥyā al-Qarāfī, d. 1008/1599 (p. 316), composed in 977/1569, Berl. Ms. or. oct. 3886, Esc. [2]594/5, Garr. 282, Cairo [1]IV, 179, [2]II, 26.—c. On the *Khuṭba* by al-Munāwī (d. 1031/1622, p. 306), Cairo [1]IV, 174, [2]II, 18.—d. Nūr al-Dīn ʿAlī b. Ghānim al-Maqdisī (d. 1036/1626, p. 306), compiled by his son, Gotha 397.—e. Anon., Berl. 6975.—f. *Tāj al-ʿarūs* by Sayyid Murtaḍā al-Zabīdī (d. 1206/1791, p. 288), 10 vols., Būlāq 1307/8.—g. *Iḍāʾat al-udmūs wa-riyāḍat al-shamūs min iṣṭilāḥ ṣāḥib al-Qāmūs* by Aḥmad b. ʿAbd al-ʿAzīz al-Hilālī, Paris 5298, Algiers 248.—h.–n. see Suppl.—o. Amīr Muḥammad Hāshim, on the *hamza* and the *wāw*, Patna I, 185$_{,1693}$.—addendum by the author (?) *Ibtihāj al-nufūs bi-dhikr mā fāta ʾl-Qāmūs*, Cairo [1]IV, 162, [2]II, 2, 1.—Abstract *Nāmūs al-maʾnūs etc.* by al-Qāriʾ al-Harawī (p. 394) (see Suppl.), BDMG 92 (?). Critique: *al-Jāsūs ʿala ʾl-Qāmūs* by Aḥmad Fāris al-Shidyāq (p. 505), Constantinople 1299.—2. *Majmaʿ al-suʾālāt min Ṣaḥāḥ al-Jawharī*, Köpr. 1517.—3. *Taḥbīr al-muwashshīn*

---

would have founded schools in Mecca and India during his wandering years than just a small school in Mecca when he was chief *qāḍī* of Yemen.

fī-mā yuqāl bil-sīn wal-shīn Br. Mus. 526,$_3$, Algiers 246,$_4$.—4. *al-Jalīs al-anīs fī asmāʾ al-khandarīs* Alex. Adab 32, Cairo ^{1}IV, 223, ^{2}II, 11, III, 75.—5. *al-Ghurar al-muthallatha wal-durar al-mubaththatha* Algiers 246,$_3$, Garr. 284.—6. *Fatwā fī ʾl-shaykh b.* | *ʿArabī* Fātiḥ 5376,$_3$ (= 19?).—7. *al-Bulgha fī taʾrīkh aʾimmat al-lugha* 234
Berl. 10060/1.—8. *Tuḥfat al-abīh fī-man nusiba ilā ghayr abīhi* Algiers 246,$_{10}$.—9. *Risāla fī ḥukm al-qanādīl al-nabawiyya* ibid. 1360,$_3$.—10. *Sufar al-saʿāda*, tales from the life of the Prophet, originally written in Persian (Gotha Pers. 33), translated into Arabic in 814/1401 by Abu ʾl-Jūd Muḥammad b. Maḥmūd al-Makhzūmī al-Ḥanafī al-Miṣrī, Algiers 1681, Cairo ^{1}I, 348, ^{2}I, 123, *khātima* AS 524.—11.–23. see Suppl. (20. Garr. 1954).

3 *Historiography*

1. Isḥāq b. Jarīr al-Ṣanʿānī, the teacher of al-Janadī (no. 3).

Taʾrīkh Ṣanʿāʾ al-Yaman Alex. Taʾr. 35.

2. Al-Amīr al-Kabīr al-Sharīf Abū Muḥammad Idrīs b. ʿAlī b. ʿAbdallāh b. Sulaymān ʿImād al-Dīn was granted—by the Rasūlid al-Malik al-Muʾayyad (r.696–721/1297–1321)—the emirate of his father with the fortresses of al-Qaḥma and Lahj in fiefdom and he submitted to the Jaḥāfil tribe.

Kay, *Yaman* XXVI. *Kanz al-akhyār fī maʿrifat al-siyar wal-akhbār*, an abstract of the *Kāmil* of Ibn al-Athīr (I, 422), with an appendix on events in Iraq, Egypt, and Syria up to the year 713, and then a history of Yemen up to 714, Br. Mus. Suppl. 469.

3. Abū ʿAbdallāh Muḥammad b. Yaʿqūb b. Yūsuf Bahāʾ al-Dīn al-Janadī, who died in 732/1332.

Wüst. *Gesch.* 399a. *Al-Sulūk fī ṭabaqāt al-ʿulamāʾ wal-mulūk*, a history of Yemen and its scholars to the year 724/1324, Berl. Ms. or. oct. 2090, Paris 2127 (with a continuation until 736/1336), *Ṭabaqāt fuqahāʾ al-Yaman*, Cairo ^{1}V, 80, whence *al-Qarāmiṭa fī ʾl-Yaman* as no. 3 of the *Majmūʿa*, Alexandria 1899, An Account of the Karmathians of Yaman by al-Janadi, in H.C. Kay, *Yaman by Omara* (I, 407).—Abstract and continuation *Tuḥfat al-zaman fī sādat ahl al-Yaman* by Abū ʿAbdallāh al-Ḥusayn b. ʿAbd al-Raḥmān al-Ahdal, d. 855/1451 (no. 7), Br. Mus. Suppl. 670, Patna II, 322,$_{2485}$, see Flügel, ZDMG XIV, 527/34 (based on a codex owned by the Honourable Charles Murray, in which it is wrongly stated that Muḥammad b. Muḥammad b. Manṣūr b. Asīr was the author).

235 | 4. Al-Malik al-Afḍal ʿAbbās b. al-Mālik al-Mujāhid ʿAlī b. Dāʾūd b. Yaḥyā b. ʿUmar b. Abī Rasūl came to power in Zabīd in Jumādā I 764/February 1363 and died in 778/1376.

C. Th. Johannsen, *Hist. Jemanae*, Bonn 1828, 165/8, Wüst. *Gesch.* 439a. 1. *Bughyat dhawi ʾl-himam fī maʿrifat ansāb al-ʿArab wal-ʿAjam* Berl. 9381(?).—2. *al-ʿAṭāya ʾl-saniyya wal-mawāhib al-haniyya fi ʾl-manāqib al-Yamaniyya* Cairo V, ^{1}129, ^{2}265.—3. *Nuzhat al-ʿuyūn fī taʾrīkh ṭawāʾif al-qurūn*, an appendix to 2, Cairo V, ^{1}129, ^{2}389.—4. See Suppl.

5. In the eighth century AH an unidentified author wrote:

Taʾrīkh al-Ḥusayn or *al-Iʿtibār fī dhikr al-tawārīkh wal-akhbār*, vol. I being a history of the Ziyādids and the Ṣulayḥids until Ibn al-Mahdī, mostly taken from ʿUmāra (I, 407), vol. II being a history of the princes and castles of Waṣāb, including biographies of various scholars, Cairo V, ^{1}139, ^{2}31.

6. Abu ʾl-Ḥasan ʿAlī b. al-Ḥasan b. Wahhās al-Khazrajī al-Nassāba, who died in 812/1409.

Wüst. *Gesch.* 459. According to ḤKh II, 159,$_{2344}$, ^{2}I, 310, he wrote three histories of Yemen: 1. by year, which may have been *al-ʿAsjad al-masbūk fī man waliya l-Yaman min al-mulūk* (see Suppl.), Alex. Taʾr. 89.—2. by dynasty, *al-Kifāya wal-iʿlām fī man waliya l-Yaman wa-sakanahā fi ʾl-Islām* Leid. 942, whence, separately, the history of the Rasūlids known as *al-ʿUqūd al-luʾluʾiyya fī akhbār al-dawla al-Rasūliyya* Ind. Off. 710, Patna II, 535,$_{2883}$, translation by J.W. Redhouse
185 (see Suppl.). |—3. alphabetically by name, *Ṭirāz aʿlām al-zaman fī ṭabaqāt aʿyān al-Yaman*, much of which is taken from the work written by his teacher al-Janadī (no. 3), also including an introduction focussing on the lives of the Prophet and the caliphs, Leid. 1031, Br. Mus. Suppl. 671.

7. Al-Ḥusayn b. ʿAbd al-Raḥmān b. Muḥammad al-Ḥasanī Badr al-Dīn Abū Muḥammad, or Abū ʿAlī or Abū ʿAbdallāh b. al-Ahdal, who died in 855/1451 (see Suppl.).

Al-Muḥibbī I, 6, 7, on his family. 1. *Ghirbāl al-zamān mukhtaṣar Mirʾāt al-janān lil-Yāfiʿī* see p. 227.—2. *Mukhtaṣar taʾrīkh al-Janadī*, no. 3.—3. *Kashf ghiṭāʾ ʿan ḥaqāʾiq al-tawḥīd wal-ʿaqāʾid*, a defence of orthodoxy and a response to unbelief, Berl. 2019, see Schreiner, *ZDMG* 52, 478 f.

| 8. ʿUmar b. Zayd al-Dawʿanī al-Ḥaḍramī wrote, around 900/1494: 236

Al-Durr al-nafīs fī manāqib al-imām Aḥmad b. Idrīs (*al-Shāfiʿī*) Berl. 10012, Alex. Taʾr. 66.

9. Muḥammad b. Aḥmad b. Muḥammad al-Zamlakānī wrote, in 831/1427 in Zabīd:

1. *Mukhtaṣar Ithārat al-targhīb etc.* see Suppl. II, 39.—2. *ʿUqūd al-jumān fī taʾrīkh al-zamān* I, autograph AS 3310.

10. Abū Makhrama, see Suppl.

Taʾrīkh thaghr ʿAdan also Alex. Taʾr. 29.

4 *Fiqh*

A The Ḥanafīs

Abū Bakr b. ʿAlī b. Mūsā al-Hāmilī al-Yamanī al-Ḥanafī Sirāj al-Dīn, who died in 769/1367.

1. *Durr al-muhtadī wa-dhukhr al-muqtadī fī naẓm Bidāyat al-mubtadiʾ* I, 469.—2. *Maʿūnat al-ṭullāb fī maʿrifat al-ḥisāb*, arithmetic based on the *Mukhtaṣar al-Hindī* of al-Ṣardafī, d. 500/1106, Berl. 5977.—3. A *qaṣīda* ibid. 7847,3.—4., 5. See Suppl.

B The Shāfiʿīs

Jamāl al-Dīn Muḥammad b. Aḥmad b. Sufyān al-Ghassānī al-Shāfiʿī wrote, for the Rasūlid ruler al-Malik al-Mujāhid Sayf al-Dīn ʿAlī b. Dāʾūd (721–64/1321–63):

Maʿdin al-fiqh wal-fatwā wa-ʿumdat ahl al-tadrīs wal-taqwā Hamb. Or. Sem. 69.

C. Independent from the dominant schools, but with a strong liking for the Ẓāhirīs and Ḥanbalīs, the true teachings of the *sunna* were defended by the Zaydī-born Sayyid Muḥammad b. Ibrāhīm b. ʿAlī b. al-Murtaḍā b. al-Mufaḍḍal b. al-Hādī b. al-Wazīr, in opposition to his own Zaydī relatives. Born in Ḥajr al-Ẓahrawayn in 775/1373, he studied in Mecca under Ibn | Ẓāhira, and died in 237
840/1436 in Ṣanʿāʾ (see Suppl. 249, 12).

1. *Mukhtaṣar fī ʿilm al-ḥadīth*, a short revision of an appendix to the compendium by Ibn Ḥajar (p. 81), written in 817/1414 on the way to Mecca, Berl. 1117.—2. *Tanqīḥ al-anẓār fī ʿilm al-āthār*, a introduction to the science of *ḥadīth*, ibid. 1118.—3. *Jawāb man saʾala ʿani ʾkhtilāf al-Muʿtazila wal-Ashʿariyya fī ḥamd Allāh taʿalā ʿala ʾl-īmān* ibid. 2280.—4. *Īthār al-ḥaqq ʿala ʾl-khulq*, on right belief, especially concerning predestination and free will, ibid. 2484.—6.–16. see Suppl. (12. Garr. 1497).

186 | D The Zaydīs

1. ʿAbdallāh b. Zayd b. Aḥmad al-ʿAnsī al-Madhḥijī, ca. 748/1347.

1. *Kitāb māʾ al-yaqīn fī maʿrifat rabb al-ʿālamīn* Berl. 10323.—2. Answers to various theological questions, ibid. 10325

1a. Muḥammad b. al-Muṭahhar b. Yaḥyā Amīr al-Muʾminīn, d. 729/1329, see Suppl.

2. *al-Manhaj al-jalī etc.* Berl. Ms. or. qu. 2037 (Burch. Fischer 36).

2. Al-Muʾayyad billāh Yaḥyā b. Hamza b. ʿAlī b. Ibrāhīm b. Rasūlallāh, who was born in 669/1270 and died in 747/1346 (or, according to others, in 749).

1. *al-Intiṣār*, the largest Zaydī legal work, vol. 2 Br. Mus. Suppl. 347, vol. 3 ibid. 348, vol. 5 ibid. 349, vol. 6 ibid. 350, vol. 8 ibid. 351, vols. 16/7, ibid. 353.—2. *al-Ikhtiyārāt al-Muʾayyadiyya*, a legal work, Berl. 4879.—3. *al-Daʿwa al-ʿāmma*, a call to jihad, ibid. 2175,$_5$.—4.–11. see Suppl.—12. *Mukhtaṣar al-Anwār al-muḍīʾa* Hamb. Or. Sem. 117.

3. Al-Ḥasan b. Muḥammad b. al-Ḥasan al-Naḥwī Sharaf al-Dīn, who died in 791/1389 in Ṣanʿāʾ.

Al-Tadhkira al-fākhira fī fiqh al-ʿitra al-ṭāhira, on Zaydī law, Berl. 4880/1, Br. Mus. Suppl. 354/5.—Commentaries: 1. His student Najm al-Dīn Yūsuf b. Aḥmad b. Muḥammad b. ʿUthmān, completed in 796/1394, Br. Mus. Suppl. 356.—2.
238 *al-Kawākib al-nayyira al-kāshifa li-maʿāni ʾl-Tadhkira*, by the latter's student | ʿImād al-Dīn Yaḥyā b. Aḥmad b. Muẓaffar, Berl. 4884.—3. *al-Barāhīn al-zāhira* by Sulaymān b. Yaḥyā b. Muḥammad b. Manṣūr al-Suʿayṭirī Humām al-Dīn, d. 815/1412 (a nephew of the author, by his sister), ibid. 4882/3.—4. *al-Tibyān fī tahdhīb maʿāni ʾl-Tadhkira wal-bayān*, by Muḥammad b. Aḥmad b. Yaḥyā b. Muẓaffar, composed in 889/1383, Br. Mus. Suppl. 363.

4. ʿAlī b. Sulaymān al-Dawwārī al-Najrānī ʿAfīf al-Dīn, ca. 800/1397.

Miṣbāḥ al-sharīʿa al-Muḥammadiyya, a Zaydī legal work following the structure of the *Kitāb al-nukat wal-jumal* of Shams al-Dīn Jaʿfar b. Aḥmad, d. 573/1177, Berl. 4886 (see Suppl.).

5. Jamāl (Ḍiyāʾ, Ṣafī) al-Dīn al-Hādī Muḥammad b. Ibrāhīm b. ʿAbd al-Raḥmān b. al-Murtaḍā b. al-Hādī ila ʾl-Ḥaqq Yaḥyā b. al-Ḥusayn b. al-Qāsim b. Rasūlallāh b. al-Wazīr, who died in 822/1420, see Suppl.

1. *Riyāḍ al-abṣār fī dhikr al-aʾimma al-aqmār wal-ʿulamāʾ al-abrār wal-shīʿa al-ʿārifīn al-aḥyāʾ*, a theological *qaṣīda* in the form of a list, drawn up by a Shāfiʿī, of the representatives of his sect, in juxtaposition to important ʿAlids, Zaydīs, and Muʿtazilīs, Berl. 9669.—2.–10. see Suppl.—11. *Manẓūma fī uṣūl al-dīn*, with the anonymous commentary *al-Irshād al-hādī ilā manẓūmat al-Sayyid al-Hādī*, Hamb. Or. Sem. 133.

6. Al-Qāḍī ʿImād al-Dīn Yaḥyā b. Aḥmad b. Muẓaffar, a second-generation student of al-Ḥasan Sharaf al-Dīn (no. 3) who flourished in the first half of the ninth century.

1. *al-Bayān al-shāfī ʿani ʾl-burhān al-kāfī*, a work on Zaydī law, Br. Mus. 1609, on which a commentary by his grandson Badr al-Dīn Muḥammad b. Aḥmad al-Bustān, with a prologue and additions, entitled *al-Tarjumān al-mufattiḥ li-thamarāt kamāʾim al-Bustān* ibid. 907.—2. *al-Kawākib al-nayyira* see no. 3, 2.—3. See Suppl.

| 7. Aḥmad b. Yaḥyā b. al-Murtaḍā al-Mahdī li-Dīn Allāh was born in 764/1363[1] 187
in Anīs, was proclaimed to be Imam in 793/1391, and incarcerated by his opponents in Ṣanʿāʾ during the years 794–801/1392–8. He died of the plague in 840/1437, in Ẓafār.

| 1. *al-Azhār fī fiqh al-aʾimma al-aṭhār*, written during his time in prison, Berl. 239
4919, Ms. or. oct. 3759 (Burch.-Fischer 2), Br. Mus. Suppl. 365/7, Alex. Firaq 3. Commentaries: 1. Self-commentary *al-Ghayth al-midrār al-mufattiḥ li-kamāʾim al-Azhār* Berl. 4920, Br. Mus. Suppl. 368/73, abstract Berl. 4920.—2. Abstract of 1, *al-Anwār wa-jana ʾl-athmār etc.* (see Suppl.) or *al-Muntazaʿ al-mukhtār min al-Ghayth al-midrār etc.*, by ʿAlī b. Muḥammad al-Najrī b. Miftāḥ Fakhr al-Dīn,

1 According to Rieu, but see Ahlwardt, who places it in 775/1373.

d. 877/1472, Berl. 4922/6, Br. Mus. Suppl. 377/8, 381, Vat. v. 1002, 1007, 1052, print. 4 vols., Maṭb. Shirkat al-Tamaddun 1332 (Sarkis 247). Gloss Br. Mus. Suppl. 379.—Completion of 1, *Takmīl*, by Aḥmad b. Yaḥyā b. Ḥābis al-Ṣaʿdī Shams al-Dīn al-Dawwārī, d. 1061/1651, Berl. 4927/9, Br. Mus. Suppl. 374/6.—3. ʿAbd al-Qādir b. ʿAlī b. Yaḥyā b. ʿAbd al-Raḥmān al-Muḥayrisī Wajīh al-Dīn, Berl. 4930.—4. Jamāl al-Dīn ʿAbd al-Raḥmān b. Hādī b. Muḥammad Samūja al-Ithnay ʿAsharī, MS dated 1075/1664, Rāmpūr I, 220.—5. Ibn Qamar, Br. Mus. Suppl. 380.—6. *Hidāyat al-afkār* by Ṣārim al-Dīn Ibrāhīm b. Yaḥyā al-Suḥūlī, d. 1060/1650 (p. 406), ibid. 382/3, 385/7, glosses ibid. 384.—7. al-Ḥasan b. Aḥmad al-Jalāl, d. 1079/1668, ibid. 389/92, glosses ibid. 393.—7a. On the *muqaddima* by Yaḥyā b. Ḥumayd al-Miqrāʾī (Muqrānī), ca. 960/1553, Berl. 4931/2, Br. Mus. Suppl. 1216$_{,i}$.—8. *Riyāḍat al-afkār etc.* the same, by al-Imām al-Nāṣir al-Ḥasan b. ʿAlī, d. 1024/1615 (p. 400), composed in 994/1586, Berl. 4933.—12.–15. see Suppl. Abstract with a commentary, Br. Mus. Suppl. 424/8.

II. *al-Baḥr al-zakhkhār al-jāmiʿ li-madhāhib ʿulamāʾ al-amṣār*, on *fiqh* and dogmatics, Berl. 4894/4907, Br. Mus. Suppl. 395/407.—parts of the Introduction: 1. *al-Taḥqīqa fī ʾl-ikfār wal-tafsīr*, on heresy, Berl. 2108.—2. *al-Qalāʾid fī taṣḥīḥ al-ʿaqāʾid*, on the attributes of God and the prophets, ibid. 2323.—3. *al-Munya wal-amal fī sharḥ Kitāb al-milal wal-niḥal* ibid. 2807.—4. *al-Imāma*, together with 1 and 2, Vat. v. 984$_{,5}$.—5. *Miʿyār al-ʿuqūl fī ʿilm al-uṣūl*, self-commentary *al-Minhāj*, Garr. 1620.—Commentaries: a. self-commentary *Ghāyāt al-afkār wa-nihāyat al-anẓār al-muḥīṭa bi-ʿajāʾib al-Baḥr al-zakhkhār* Berl. 4908/9, Br. Mus. Suppl. 408/22, of which abstracts Berl. 4912/4, from the introduction *Mirqāt al-anẓār al-muntazaʿa min Ghāyat al-afkār* by ʿAbdallāh b. Muḥammad b. Abi ʾl-Qāsim al-Najrī Fakhr al-Dīn (see I, 2), Berl. 4911/2—2. On the final part, *al-Takmila lil-aḥkām*, Patna II, 450$_{,2626,2}$, a. *al-Iḥkām* by Badr al-Dīn Muḥammad b. ʿIzz al-Dīn b. Muḥammad al-Muftī, d. 1049/1639 (al-Shawkānī II,
240 203/4), Vat. v. 984$_{,6}$, Patna I, 74$_{,750}$.—b. *Shifāʾ al-asqām* | *fī tawḍīḥ al-Takmila* by Aḥmad b. Yaḥyā b. Ḥābis al-Dawwārī al-Ṣaʿdī, d. 1061/1651 (al-Shawkānī I, 127), Berl. 4908$_{,9}$, Ambr. NF 355$_{iii}$, Vat. v. 984$_{,3}$ (different from Berl. 4913), Ambr. NF 248$_{,vi}$.—3 other commentaries in Berl. 4913/8.—Abstracts: a. *al-Manār fī ʾl-mukhtār min jawāhir al-Baḥr al-zakhkhār* by Ṣāliḥ b. Ḥamdallāh b. Mahdī al-Yamanī al-Maqbalī, completed in 1102/1690 in Mecca, Berl. 4917, Ambr. B 89$_{,iii}$.—b. of the second part, *al-Qalāʾid al-muntazaʿa min al-durar al-farāʾid*, by Dāʾūd b. Aḥmad Ṣārim al-Dīn, Berl. 4910.

III. *Ḥayāt al-qulūb fī maʿrifat ʿibādat ʿallām al-ghuyūb*, on the duty of prayer, Berl. 3522/3.

IV. A collection of sermons, poems, epistles, admonitions etc., ibid. 8536.

V. *Yawāqīt al-siyar fī sharḥ Kitāb al-jawāhir wal-durar min sīrat khayr al-bashar wa-aṣḥābihi ʾl-ʿashara al-ghurar wa-ʿitratihi ʾl-muntakhabīn al-zuhar*:

a. *Riyāḍ al-fikar fī sharḥ sīrat ʿitratihi 'l-muntakhabīn al-zuhar*; b. *Tuḥfat al-akyās fī sharḥ taʿyīn āl Umayya wal-ʿAbbās*, composed in 836/1432; c. *Khātima: Risālat tazyīn al-majālis bi-dhikr al-tuḥaf al-nafāʾis wa-maknūn ḥisān al-ʿarāʾis*, 60 saints' tales from Ibn al-Jawzī's *Tuḥfat al-wuʿʿāẓ* (Suppl. I, 920,$_{75a}$), Leid. 898/9 (Amin 271), see Goldziher, ZDMG 66, 140, under the title *Dhayl*: 1. *ʿAjāʾib al-malakūt*, 2. *Salwat al-awliyāʾ*, 3. *Dhikr al-amjād*, 4. *Ḍiyāʾ al-qahhār*, 5. *Riyāḍ al-iftikār*, 6. *Tuḥfat al-akyās* Patna II, 509,$_{2739}$.

va.–IX. See Suppl., 31 works in Ahlw. 495,$_{oxv}$.

8. a.–d. see Suppl.

8e. ʿAbdallāh b. Amīr al-Muʾminīn al-Mutawakkil ʿala 'llāh al-Muṭahhar (8d) b. Muḥammad b. Sulaymān al-Yamanī wrote:

Al-Masāʾil al-mukhtāra Cairo ^{2}VI, 212.

9. Al-Hādī ila 'l-Ḥaqq ʿIzz al-Dīn b. al-Ḥusayn b. al-Muʾayyad, an imam of the Zaydīs who was born in 845/1441 and died in 900/1494.

1. *Nubadh shāfiya wa-nukat bil-murād wāfiya*, a text on preparing oneself for the Hereafter, Berl. 10338, Hamb. Or. Sem. 3, Ambr. C 33,$_{vii}$.—2. Answers to legal questions, Br. Mus. Suppl. 423,$_{2}$.—3. A treatise on the manumission of slaves in compensation for bodily harm, ibid. 1241,$_{2}$.—4.–7. see Suppl.

| 10. Ṣārim al-Dīn Ibrāhīm b. Muḥammad b. ʿAbdallāh al-Hādawī al-Wazīr, who died in 914/1508 (see Suppl.). 241

1. *Hidāyat al-afkār ilā maʿāni 'l-Azhār fī fiqh al-ʿitra al-aṭhār* (6. 1) Berl. 4934.—Commentaries, see Suppl.—2. *al-Fuṣūl al-luʾluʾiyya al-jāmiʿa li-aqwāl āl al-rasūl fi 'l-uṣūl* Br. Mus. Suppl. 267,$_{1}$.—Commentaries: a. Luṭfallāh b. Muḥammad Abū Ghiyāth al-Ẓāfirī (d. 1035/1625), ibid. 2.—b. al-Ḥasan b. Aḥmad b. Muḥammad al-Jalāl, ibid. 268.—c. see Suppl.—3. *Maḥajjat al-inṣāf fi 'l-radd ʿalā dhawi 'l-bidaʿ wal-iʿtisāf*, a rebuttal of a Shāfiʿī, Berl. 10302.—4. *al-Maqāma al-manẓariyya wal-fākiha al-khabariyya wal-ḥadīqa al-ʿanbariyya* Leid. 438, Garr. 172.—5. *Qaṣīda fī āl al-bayt*, in praise of Muḥammad and the imams and preachers of Yemen, Br. Mus. 907.—6. See Suppl.

| 5 *Sciences of the Qurʾān* 189

1. Raḍī al-Dīn Abū Bakr b. ʿAlī b. Muḥammad al-Ḥaddād al-ʿAbbādī al-Miṣrī al-Ḥanafī, who died in 808/1397 in Zabīd.

1. *Kashf al-tanzīl fī taḥqīq al-mabāḥith wal-taʾwīl* AS 188/91, Köpr. 89, NO 280/1, whence a commentary on sura 78, Berl. 985.—2. *al-Sirāj al-wahhāj* see I, 183.—3. *al-Jawhara al-nayyira* ibid.

2. Muḥammad b. Ibrāhīm al-Shāwarī al-Ṣanʿānī wrote, in 836/1432:

Fukāhat al-bashar wal-samʿ fi ʾl-qirāʾāt al-sabʿ, on the lives and significance of the seven readers of the Qurʾān and all the questions pertaining to reading it, dedicated to Abū Muḥammad ʿAlī b. Muḥammad, Berl. 622.

3. ʿAfīf al-Dīn Abu ʾl-Tawfīq ʿUthmān b. ʿUmar b. Abī Bakr al-Nāshirī al-Zabīdī al-ʿAdnānī, ca. 860/1456.

1. *al-Durr al-nāẓim fī qirāʾat ʿĀṣim*, in the *riwāya* of Ḥafṣ b. Sulaymān, d. 128/745, Berl. 646, Algiers 376,$_7$.—2., 3. See Suppl. 250, 278/9.

6 *Mysticism*

1. Jamāl al-Dīn Muḥammad b. ʿAbdallāh b. ʿUmar b. Muḥammad al-Ḥabashī (Ḥubayshī) al-Yamanī died in 782/1382.

242 | 1. *al-Baraka fī madḥ (faḍl) al-saʿy wal-ḥaraka* Munich 175,$_2$ (incomplete), Br. Mus. 749, Cairo ^{1}VI, 117, ^{2}II, 272, App. 38, Makram 6, Alex. Mawāʿiẓ 7, Garr. 1910/2.—2. *Kitāb al-nūrayn fī iṣlāḥ al-dārayn* see Suppl., Garr. 1909.—3. *al-Tadhkira bi-mā ilayhi ʾl-masīr* Makram 10.—4. *ʿUmdat al-ṭālib fi ʾl-iʿtiqād al-wājib* ibid. 47.—5. *Kitāb fī tarājim al-Ṣūfiyya wa-akhbārihim wa-ḥikāyātihim wa-manāqibihim* see I, 560.

2. Abu ʾl-Surā Aḥmad Muḥyi ʾl-Dīn b. Abī Bakr al-Raddād al-Zabīdī, who died in 821/1418.

1. *ʿUddat al-murshidīn wa-ʿumdat al-mustarshidīn*, an abstract on various matters relating to the transfer of the *khirqa* of this Sufi to his students, Paris 2677,$_{13}$.—2. See Suppl.

7 *Medicine*

Muḥammad al-Mahdawī b. ʿAlī b. Ibrāhīm al-Ṣanawbarī (Ṣuburī?) al-Yamanī al-Hindī, who died in 815/1412.

Kitāb al-raḥma fi ʾl-ṭibb wal-ḥikma, Berl. 6305/6, Munich 807,$_2$, Leid. 1371, Paris 2700,$_2$, 3016/8, Br. Mus. 977 (fragm.), Bodl. II, 193, Garr. 1109, 2169,$_1$, Alex. Fun. 146,$_2$, Cairo ^{1}VI, 16, VII, 145, 517.

| 8 *Horse Breeding* 190

Al-Malik al-Mujāhid ʿAlī b. Dāʾūd b. Yūsuf b. ʿUmar b. ʿAlī b. Rasūl al-Rasūlī, who ruled in the period 721–64/1321–63.

Johannsen, *Hist. Jemanae* 159. 1. *al-Aqwāl al-kāfiya wal-fuṣūl al-shāfiya*, on horse breeding, Br. Mus. Suppl. 816; Persian translation by Aḥmad b. Khiḍr al-Rūdbārī, Br. Mus. Pers. Suppl. 161.—2., 3. See Suppl.

9 *Occult Sciences*

Shihāb al-Dīn Aḥmad b. Aḥmad b. ʿAbd al-Laṭīf al-Sarjī al-Zabīdī al-Ḥanafī, who was born on 22 Ramaḍān 812/29 January 1410 in Zabīd, studied in Mecca in 834/1431, and died in Zabīd in Rabīʿ I 893/March 1488 (or, according to others, in 898).

MT 14v. 1 *Kitāb al-fawāʾid fi ʾl-ṣilāt* (*ṣila*) *wal-ʿawāʾid*, 100 pieces of advice, for talismans, magic tricks, prayers, | etc., using Qurʾānic verses, Gotha 1271, Paris 243
$765_{,2}$, $955_{,2}$ (attributed to Abu ʾl-Ḥasan ʿAlī al-ʿAlawī al-Yamanī), Esc. [2]II, 779, Alex. Fun. $186_{,4}$, Cairo [1]II, 207, V, 349, print. C. 1297 and others.—2. *Ṭabaqāt al-khawāṣṣ ahl al-ṣidq wal-ikhlāṣ* Br. Mus. Suppl. 672.—3. See Suppl.—4. *Nuzhat al-aḥbāb fī gharāʾib al-ittifāq wa-nawādir dhawi ʾl-albāb* ḤKh [1]VI, 320, [2]II, 1938, Garr. 726.

10 *Encyclopaedias*

Sharaf al-Dīn Ismāʿīl b. Abī Bakr b. al-Muqriʾ al-Shāwarī al-Yamanī, who was born in 765/1363 in Abyāt Ḥusayn, in the Surdad region of Yemen, lectured at al-Madrasa al-Mujāhidiyya in Taʿizz, and then at the Niẓāmiyya in Zabīd, where he also held the office of *qāḍī*, and where he died in 837/1433.

RA 59r, MT 47v. 1. *ʿUnwān al-sharaf al-wāfī fi ʾl-fiqh wal-naḥw wal-taʾrīkh wal-ʿarūḍ wal-qawāfī*, in 4 narrow (1, 3, 5, 7) and 3 wide (2, 4, 6) columns. The first narrow one is on metrics, the three wide ones, together with the middle narrow ones (3 and 5), which deal with the history of the Rasūlids and with grammar, represent the main part of the work, a theory of law, while the last, narrow column is related to the theory of rhyme. The first and the final columns consist almost exclusively of single letters, which form the first letters of each line of the second and the last ones of those of the sixth column at one and the same time, | and again of the third and the fifth when these are read 191
as independent treatises but which are otherwise incomprehensible, while the last two together contain whole words and syllables of the text, which runs horizontally over the three wide columns (see Hammer, *Wiener Jahrb.* 61, Anz.-Bl. 11ff.), Gotha 164/5 (where other MSS are listed), Berl. or. qu. 2057,

Paris 4652/6, Br. Mus. 899, Suppl. 716, AS 1334/8, 4826,$_{3}$, Köpr. 637, Cairo ^{1}III, 191, VI, 159, Patna I, 95,$_{967}$, lith. Calcutta, print. Aleppo 1294. Imitated by al-Suyūṭī, p. 202, no. 291.—2. *Dīwān* Köpr. II, 266, with the title *al-Jazl al-muʿtamad al-mufīd* Garr. 100.—3. A *qaṣīda* for his son, which is an admonition to study, Berl. 104.—4. *al-Dharīʿa ilā naṣr al-sharīʿa*, 162 *basīṭ* verses against the Sufis and their practises, especially dancing and playing music, ibid. 3382.—5. *al-Ḥujja*
244 | *al-dāmigha li-rijāl al-fuṣūṣ al-rāʾigha*, 241 verses against Ibn ʿArabī, 41 verses against the same, and other *qaṣīdas*, ibid. 7896/7.—6. A religious poem, ibid. 7929,$_{6}$, 7986,$_{3}$.—7. *Lāmiyyat al-ʿAjam*, an imitation of the poem by al-Ṭughrāʾī (I, 286), Leid. 757.—8. *Badīʿiyya*, Berl. 7370, with the title *al-Jumānāt al-badīʿa fī madḥ ʿalam al-sharīʿa* Garr. 99, 2146, Alex. Fun. 187,$_{7}$, with a self-commentary Berl. 7371/2, Gotha 2794, Leipz. 480, Cairo ^{1}IV, 212, VII, 562, ^{2}II, 203.—9. *al-Rikāz al-mukhammas* (see Suppl.) Cairo ^{1}III, 60, ^{2}I, 518.—10. *Rawḍ al-ṭālib fī ʾl-fiqh*, with the commentary *Asna ʾl-maṭālib* by Abū Zakariyyāʾ Yaḥyā al-Anṣārī, d. 926/1520 (p. 122), Cairo ^{1}III, 192, Alex. Fiqh Shāf. 7, Garr. 1868/9.—11. *Kitāb al-irshād* I, 495.—12.–22. see Suppl. (12. Alex. Adab 140.—13. A commentary by ʿAbd al-Malik b. Jamāl al-Dīn al-ʿIṣmānī, Suppl. p. 513, Patna II, 451,$_{2628,2}$, by ʿAlī b. Abī Bakr al-Jamāl al-Anṣārī, ibid. 4.—14. see 8). He is occasionaly wrongly credited with a *qaṣīda* actually written by Imām al-Ḥaramayn (I, 487).

Chapter 5. Iran and Tūrān

The old centres of Islamic culture in Iran and its neighbouring regions, in particularly Bukhara, Samarqand, and Herat, had suffered much more under the Mongol onslaught and its aftermath than Iraq. One emphemeral dynasty
quickly followed another, and it was only at the end of this period that | the 192
Safavid ruler Shāh Ismāʿīl was at least able to bring the whole of Iran under his sway. Even though some of the smaller dynasties had tended to the intellectual interests of their subjects, there was nevertheless an ever-increasing tendency to express oneself in the local tongue; Persian reigned supreme in poetry and historiography, and the Sufis, too, made use of it at a steadily increasing rate. It was only in *fiqh* and Qurʾānic exegesis that Arabic maintained its previous position. Philosophy was fostered more diligently in this region than elsewhere, although this was only in the field of logic. In spite of their political separation,
| there was a lively connection between the cultural life of Transoxiana and 245
Iran. As such, these two regions must be considered together.

1 *Poetry and Rhymed Prose*

1. Aḥmad b. Muḥammad b. al-Muʿaẓzam al-Rāzī, see Suppl.

2. Faḍlallāh b. al-Ḥamīd al-Zawzānī al-aṣl al-Ṣīnī al-mawlūd al-Fāḍil wrote, in 740/1339:

1. *al-Ṣīniyyāt*, an imitation of the *Najdiyyāt* of Abīwardī (I, 293), Cairo ^{1}VII, 614, ^{2}III, 241.—2. *al-Kifāya al-kāfiya*, an adaptation of Ibn Ḥājib's (I, 367) *Kāfiya*, ibid. ^{2}II, 154.

3. Hindūshāh b. Sanjar b. ʿAbdallāh al-Ṣāḥibī al-Jayrānī wrote, in the first half of the eighth century:

1. *Mawārid al-adab*, an anthology, Br. Mus. 1420.—2. See Suppl.

4. In 790/1388 Junayd b. Maḥmūd al-ʿUmarī wrote, for the Muẓaffarid ruler Abū Naṣr Shāh Yaḥyā, the sultan of Kirman, before he was executed in 795/1393 on the orders of Tīmūr (see Suppl.):

1. *Ḥadāʾiq al-anwār wa-badāʾiʿ al-ashʿār*, an anthology, Paris 3368.—2.–4. see Suppl.

193 | 5. Ikhtiyār al-Dīn b. Ghiyāth al-Dīn al-Ḥusaynī studied in Herat, became a *qāḍī* there, and died in 928/1522.

Khwandamīr, *ḤS* III, 3, 347. 1. *Asās al-iqtibās*, a collection of verses from the Qur'ān, *ḥadīth*, maxims, proverbs, and highlights from prose writers and poets, which concludes with guidance on bibliography and terminology in various sciences, meant as a source of information for secretaries and public speakers so they could stand out in social gatherings. It was composed in 897/1492 on the orders of Sultan Ḥusayn Bayqarā,[1] Gotha 2825, Vienna 346/7, Bodl. I, 428, Algiers 1359$_{10}$, NO 3670/1, AS 3772/3, NO 4272 (under the title *Maqāmāt al-Ḥusaynī*), Alex. Adab 8, Cairo ^{1}IV, 202, VII, 113, 164, Garr. 1135, print. Istanbul 1298.

246 | 2 **Philology**

1. Muṣṭafā b. Qubādh al-Lādhiqī, who died in 722/1322.

Mishkāt al-maṣābīḥ, an Arabic-Persian dictionary, Upps. 14.

1a. Ḥamīd al-Dīn Abū ʿAbdallāh Maḥmūd b. ʿUmar al-Najātī, see Suppl.

Al-Risāla al-Qalamiyya by ʿAbd al-ʿAzīz b. Abi 'l-Ghanā'im al-Kāshī, see Suppl. II, 905,2, translated into Persian in 701 AH, Köpr. 1589, 197a/171a, in the margin, and the *Risāla-yi sayfiyya* ibid. 171a, 174a, in the margin (Ritter).

2. Aḥmad b. al-Ḥasan (Ḥusayn) b. Yūsuf b. Ibrāhīm al-Jārabardī al-Shāfiʿī Fakhr al-Dīn, a student of al-Bayḍāwī, was regarded as the greatest scholar of Tabriz in his lifetime. He died in Ramaḍān 746/January 1346.

Khwandamīr, *ḤS* III, 1. 132. 1. *al-Mughnī fī ʿilm al-naḥw*, almost entirely a copy of the *Unmūdhaj* by al-Zamakhsharī (I, 347), Berl. 6698, Bodl. I, 1136, 1159.—Commentaries: a. Muḥammad b. ʿAbd al-Raḥīm b. Muḥammad al-ʿUmarī, d. 811/1408, Berl. 6699/700, Ms. or. oct. 3872, Pet. 190, Br. Mus. Suppl. 970, Ind. Off. 1033, Bodl. II, 1136,$_2$, 1159,$_2$, Paris 4143, Garr. 443/4, 2105,$_1$.—b. ʿAbdallāh b. al-Sayyid Fakhr al-Dīn al-Ḥusaynī, Garr. 2130,$_2$.—2. *Sharḥ al-Shāfiya li-Ibn al-Ḥājib* I, 371.—3. *Sharḥ al-Kashshāf* ibid. 345.—4., 5. See Suppl.

3. Abū Naṣr al-Farāhī wrote, sometime in the eighth century AH:

---

1 See *ḤS*. 5 III, 3, 102ff., H. Terté, *La vie du sulṭān Hossain Baikara trad. de Khondemir*, Paris 1898.

Niṣāb al-ṣibyān, an Arabic-Persian vocabulary in verse, Leid. 112/3 and almost every other library, print. Calcutta 1819.

3a. ʿAlāʾ al-Dīn Aḥmad al-Khujandī, d. ca. 830/1427, see Suppl.

Al-Quṣārā fi ʾl-ṣarf, a commentary by Aḥmad b. Aḥmad b. Muḥammad al-Sijistānī, Pet. AM Buch. 844.

4. Jamāl al-Dīn Muḥammad b. ʿUthmān b. ʿUmar al-Balkhī wrote, around 800/1397 (?):

Al-Wāfī fi ʾl-naḥw Ind. Off. 970/1, the commentary *al-Manhal al-ṣāfī* by al-Damāmīnī, d. 827/1424 (p. 32), ibid. 972/3, Stewart $127_{,xxxiv}$.—2. See Suppl.

| 5. Abu ʾl-Ḥasan Naṣr b. al-Ḥasan al-Marghīnānī wrote, at the beginning of the ninth century AH: 247

1. *Kitāb al-badīʿ* Esc. $^{2}264_{,1}$.—2. *Kitāb al-maḥāsin fi ʾl-naẓm wal-nathr* ibid. 2.

| 6. ʿAlī b. Nuṣra b. Dāʾūd wrote, in 843/1439: 194

Al-Tarjumān, an Arabic-Persian dictionary, autograph Garr. 285, Leid. 114, Bodl. I, 1050.

7. Abu ʾl-Qāsim b. Abī Bakr al-Laythī al-Samarqandī wrote, ca. 888/1483:

I. *Farāʾid al-fawāʾid* (*ʿawāʾid*) *li-taḥqīq maʿāni ʾl-istiʿāra*, more commonly known as *al-Risāla al-Samarqandiyya*, on metaphors based on comparisons (Mehren, *Rhet.* 57), Berl. 7297/8, Gotha 2799 (where other MSS are listed), BDMG 95, b, Hamb. Or. Sem. 75, Sarajevo $22_{,1}$, Qawala II, 156/7, Garr. 901.—Commentaries and glosses: 1. ʿIṣām al-Dīn Ibrāhīm b. Muḥammad b. ʿArabshāh al-Isfarāʾinī, d. 942/1535 (p. 410), Berl. 7299/300, Gotha 2800/2 (where other MSS are listed), Sarajevo $22_{,2}$, Qawala II, 160/1, Garr. 555/7, $2138_{,2}$, print. Istanbul 1837 (with glosses by Muḥammad al-Arzanjānī, *BO* I, 332).—Glosses: a. By his grandson Jamāl al-Dīn ʿAlī b. Ismāʿīl al-Isfarāʾinī, d. 1007/1598, Berl. 7301/2, Garr. 558, Qawala II, 143, Alex. Bal 4, 20, Fun. 111, 6, anon. supergl. Qawala II, 150.—b. Ibn al-Maymūnī, d. 1079/1668, Berl. 7303.—c. Mollā Ḥasan al-Kurdī al-Zībarī, ibid. 7304/5, Gotha 2803, Qawala II, 145, Garr. 559, print. Istanbul 1276.—d. al-Ghunaymī, d. 1044/1634, Berl. 7306.—e. Muḥammad b. al-Shawbarī, d. 1069/1659, ibid. 7307.—f. Ilyās b. Ibrāhīm al-Kūrānī, d. 1138/1725, ibid.

7308.—g. Muḥammad b. ʿAlī al-Ṣabbān, d. 1206/1791 (p. 288), ibid. 7309, Leid. 335, Alex. Fun. 111,7, print. C. 1286, 1299.—h. Ismāʿīl al-Mawṣilī, Berl. 7310.—i. Ibrāhīm b. Muḥammad al-Bājūrī, d. 1276/1860 (p. 487), print. Būlāq 1865 and others.—k.–w. see Suppl. (k. Garr. 562, l. ibid. 560, w. Alex. Balʿ. 22).—x. Aḥmad b. ʿUmar al-Asqāṭī, d. 1159/1746 (p. 327), Alex. Bal. 7.—y. Aḥmad Efendi al-Ḥalabī, MS dated 1134/1722, Garr. 561.—z. Aḥmad Efendi Khalīl al-Fawzī b. Muṣṭafā al-Qilbāwī, completed in 1282/1865, Istanbul 1282 (Qaw. II, 141/2), 1308.—aa. Aḥmad b. Ismāʿīl al-Nafrāwī al-Mālikī, completed in 1183/1769, Alex. Bal. 22.—Abbreviation of the self-commentary, Gotha 2804/5,
248 Algiers 22/3.—2. Ḥafīd | al-ʿIṣām Aḥmad b. Ismāʿīl al-Isfarāʾinī, Paris 4425,5.—3. Qul Aḥmad b. Muḥammad b. Khaḍir, completed in 1038/1620, Berl. 7311/2, Garr. 902/4, Qawala II, 164.—4. Aḥmad b. ʿAbd al-Fattāḥ al-Mollawī, d. 1181/1767 (p. 355), Berl. Br. M. 314,3, Paris 4426, Alex. Bal. 13, 20 (*al-kabīr*), Qawala II, 160.—Glosses: a. His student Aḥmad b. Yūnus al-Khalīfī, d. 1209/1794, Leid. 336, Garr. 574, Alex. Bal. 19,2, 23/4, Fun. 108,5, Makram 61 (on *al-ṣaghīr*).—b. Muḥammad b. Muḥammad al-Amīr, d. 1232/1817 (p. 328), Alex. Bal. 21, Fun. 128/9, on which *Taqrīrāt* by Muḥammad al-Shabīnī, ibid. 4, by Aḥmad al-Ujhūrī (see Suppl.), d. 1276/1859, ibid.—c.–h. see Suppl. (d. Alex. Bal. 8, on h. *Taqrīr* by Sayyid al-Sharshīmī al-Sharqāwī, ibid. 4).—Abstract, Berl. 7314.—5. Muḥammad al-Amīr, completed in 1185/1771, ibid. 7315 (no. 4c?).—6. Aḥmad al-Damanhūrī, d. 1192/1778 (p. 371), Gotha 2816, Algiers 220, Alex. Bal. 2, Fun. 108,4.—7. Ḥasan b. Muḥammad al-Zībarī (see 1c), Gotha 2807.—8. Ḥasan b. Muḥammad al-ʿAṭṭār, d. 1250/1834 (p. 473), C. 1309 (with glosses by Zaynī Daḥlān, d. 1886, in the margin, *OB* VI, 4880).—9.–23. see Suppl. (9. Alex. Bal. 17, 15. Garr. 905, Qawala II, 16, 18, see. ix).—24. *al-Mawāhib al-ṣamadiyya li-kashf lithām al-Samarqandiyya* by Ṭāhir b. Masʿūd Khalīfat Imām al-Jāmiʿ al-Zaytūnī, Tunis 1298.—Abstracts: 1. *Bulūgh al-arab min taḥqīq istiʿārāt al-ʿArab*, with a commentary by Ibn ʿIṣām (?), Berl. 7316.—2., 3. See Suppl.—Versifications: 1. Manṣūr Sibṭ Nāṣir al-Dīn al-Ṭablāwī, d. 1014/1606 (p. 321), Berl. 737/8, with commentary.—2.–5. see Suppl.

II. *Ḥāshiya ʿala ʾl-Sharḥ al-muṭawwal* I, 354, lith. Istanbul 1307.

III., IV., see Suppl.

8. Ibrāhīm b. ʿAlī al-Shirwānī wrote, in 892/1487:

Risāla shāfiya fī maʿrifat al-ʿarūḍ wal-qawāfī NO 3899.

9. Muḥammad b. ʿAbd al-Khāliq b. Maʿrūf wrote, in the ninth century:

Kanz al-lughāt, an Arabic-Persian dictionary, Leid. 115 (where other MSS are listed), lith. Persia 1283.

10. Ibrāhīm al-Shabistarī al-Naqshbandī Sībawayh al-Thānī, d. 917/1511 (see Suppl.).

Nihāyat al-bahja or *al-Ṭāʾiyya fi ʾl-naḥw*, with a self-commentary, Paris 4196, Cairo [1]IV, 77, [2]II, 138, 172, Qawala II, 97.

| | 3 Historiography 249 193

1. Ismāʿīl b. Muḥammad Sharīf, a *mudarris* in Āqsarāy, wrote, in 756/1355:

Tadhkirat al-ʿibar fī baḥth al-umam wal-amṣār, see Zeki Validi Togan, ZDMG 95, 367.

2. Abū Muḥammad al-Ḥasan b. Abi ʾl-Ḥasan b. Muḥammad al-Daylamī, a contemporary of Fakhr al-Muḥaqqiqīn (p. 212).

Rawḍāt al-jannāt 177/8. *Irshād al-qulūb etc.* (see Suppl.); MSS *Dharīʿa* I, 517,$_{2527}$, Patna I, 144,$_{1396/7}$.

4 Ḥadīth

1. Abū Bakr b. Mūsā al-Khwārazmī, who died in 710/1310, wrote:

Al-Nāsikh wal-mansūkh fi ʾl-ḥadīth AS 872.

2. Shams al-Dīn Muḥammad b. ʿAbdallāh al-Khaṭīb al-Tabrīzī wrote, in 737/1336:

Mishkāt al-maṣābīḥ I, 448, on which *Asmāʾ al-rijāl* Berl. 9928/9, NO 656, Garr. 685, by ʿAbd al-Ḥaqq al-Muḥaddith al-Dihlawī, Patna II, 304,$_{2409}$.

3. Abu ʾl-Faḍl al-Ḥasan b. Maḥmūd al-Rajāʾinī, ca. 750/1350.

Arbaʿūn Berl. 1505.

4. Saʿd al-Dīn Muḥammad b. Masʿūd al-Kāzarūnī, who died in Jumādā II 758/June 1357 (see Suppl.).

DK IV, 255, no. 706. 1. *Mawlūd al-nabī* or *al-Muntaqā fī sīrat al-nabī al-muṣṭafā* Br. Mus. 920, Persian translation Yeni 857.—2. *Musalsalāt* Cairo [1]VII, 455, [2]I, 146.—3., 4. see Suppl.

5. Ibrāhīm b. ʿAbd al-Karīm al-Ṭūsiyawī Ḥājjī Bābā, ca. 840/1436.

Risālat al-lahw, on games, Munich 884,$_2$. On his son Ḥājjī Bābā b. Ibrāhīm, see p. 223.

250 196 | | 5 ***Fiqh***

A The Ḥanafīs

1. Ḥāfiẓ al-Dīn Abu ʾl-Barakāt ʿAbdallāh b. Aḥmad b. Maḥmūd al-Nasafī, who died in 710/1310 (see Suppl.).

Ibn Quṭlūbughā 86, *DK* II, 247, no. 2118 (which places his death in 701). I. *Manār al-anwār fī uṣūl al-fiqh* Berl. 4385, Gotha 930/1 (where other MSS are listed), Ind. Off. 312, 1447/8, Garr. 1631/2, Qawala I, 298, Bank. XIX, 2, 1502/3.—Commentaries: 1. Self-commentaries a. *al-Munawwir* Ind. Off. 313.—b. *Kashf al-asrār* ibid. 314, 1449, 4572 (*JRAS* 1939, 364), Cairo [1]II, 258, Qawala I, 293.—2. Ṣadr al-Dīn al-Thānī al-Maḥbūbī, d. 747/1346 (p. 214), Br. Mus. 205, 270.—2a. *Jāmiʿ al-asrār* by Muḥammad b. Muḥammad b. Aḥmad al-Sakhāwī al-Kākī, d. 749/1348 (see Suppl.), also Alex. Uṣūl 7, Qawala I, 278.—3. Muḥammad b. Maḥmūd al-Bābartī, d. 786/1384 (p. 97), Yeni 337, Qawala I, 274.—4. ʿAbd al-Laṭīf b. ʿAbd al-ʿAzīz b. Firishte b. al-Malak, d. 797/1395 (see Suppl. 315), Berl. 4386/7, Munich 298, Paris 794/5, Glasgow 19 (*JRAS* 1899, 742), Garr. 1633/6, Yeni 338, Cairo [1]II, 238, [2]II, 388, Qawala I, 288/9.—Glosses: a. Abū Zakariyyāʾ Yaḥyā al-Ruhāwī, Yeni 318, Cairo [1]II, 246, Alex. Uṣūl 8, Qawala I, 181.—b. Muṣṭafā b. Muḥammad ʿAzmīzāde, ca. 1040/1630, Berl. 4388, BDMG 39, Cairo [1]II, 287, Alex. Uṣūl 21.—c., d. see Suppl.—5. Saʿd al-Dīn Abu ʾl-Faḍāʾil al-Dihlawī, d. 891/1486, Yeni 308/9, Cairo [1]II, 238.—6. ʿAbd al-Raḥmān b. Abī Bakr al-ʿAynī Zayn al-Dīn, d. 893/1488, completed in 868/1463, Berl. 4389, Algiers 970/1, Cairo [1]II, 253, Qawala I, 291.—7. al-Āqsarāʾī, with glosses by Abū Suʿūd, completed in 936/1530, Pet. 81,$_{17}$.—8. *Fatḥ al-ghaffār* by Zayn al-ʿĀbidīn b. Nujaym, d. 970/1562 (p. 310), completed in 965/1357, Berl. 4390, Cairo [1]II, 265, with the title *Mishkāt al-anwār fī uṣūl al-Manār* Garr. 1637.—9. Aḥmad b. Muḥammad b. ʿAbd al-ʿAzīz al-Marʿashī, ca. 1000/1591, dedicated to Sultan Murād III, beginning Berl. 4391.—10. *al-Ishrāḥāt al-Maʿāliyya* see Suppl.—11. *Ifāḍat al-anwār* by Muḥammad b. ʿAlī al-Ḥaṣkafī, d. 1088/1677, Patna I, 68,$_{635}$, on which glosses entitled *Nasamāt al-asḥār*, by Muḥammad Amīn b. ʿUmar b. ʿĀbidīn al-Shams, d. 1258/1842 (see Suppl. II, 773), Cairo [1]II, 268, Alex. Uṣūl 21, print. Istanbul 1300.—12. Abū Bakr b. Isḥāq, Krafft 457 (incomplete).—13. *Dāʾirat al-wuṣūl* by Muḥammad b. Mubārakshāh al-Harawī, Ind. Off. 315, on which anonymous glosses Ind. Off. 1454, Pers. ibid.
251 1455.—| 14. *Nūr al-anwār* by Shaykh Jīwan, d. 1130/1711 (p. 417), composed in 1105/1794 in Medina, Ind. Off. 316, 1456/9, print. Calcutta 1819, Lucknow 1266,

Kanpur 1886, among others.—15.–24. see Suppl.—Abstracts: 1. Muḥammad b. Aḥmad al-Qūnawī, d. 747/1346, with a commentary, Cairo ^{1}II, 251.—2. Ḥabīb al-Ḥalabī, d. 807/1405, p. 98.—3.–5. see Suppl.—Versifications: 1. Ghars al-Dīn b. al-Ḥalabī, d. 1057/1647, Br. Mus. 893.—2. *Manẓūmat al-kawākib* Alex. Fiqh Ḥan. 67, print. C. 1317, with the commentary *Irshād al-ṭālib*, by Muḥammad b. Ḥasan al-Kawākibī, d. 1096/1685, Cairo ^{1}II, 236.—3. Anon., Paris 4542.—4. see Suppl. and also Ahlw. 4392.

II. *al-Wāfī fi ʾl-furūʿ*, with the commentary *al-Kāfī*, completed in Bukhārā on 22 Ramaḍān 684/21 November 1275, Berl. 4574, Paris 890, Ind. Off. 250/4, 1610, Yeni 484/6, 592, Alex. Fiqh Ḥan. 47, 72, Cairo ^{1}III, 101, 147, ^{2}I, 455. Abbreviation:

III. *Kanz al-daqāʾiq fi ʾl-furūʿ* Gotha 1013/9 (where other MSS are listed), Ind. Off. 1611/22, Garr. 1719/20, Alex. Fiqh Ḥan. 48, Qawala I, 384/5, print. Delhi 1870, 1883, Lucknow 1874, 1877, Bombay 1882, C. 1309, among others. Persian translation by Nāṣir b. Muḥammad al-Kirmānī, Berl. Pers. 200, Cambr. Pers. 22. Commentaries: 1. *Tabyīn al-ḥaqāʾiq* by Fakhr al-Dīn ʿUthmān b. ʿAlī al-Zaylaʿī, d. 743/1342, Berl. 4577/8, Ms. or. qu. 2075, Munich 304/5, Paris 897/8, 902, Algiers 1004/6, Ind. Off. 264, 1623/5, Yeni 445/51, Qawala I, 309, Mosul 226,$_{20}$; his attacks on the main work are rebutted in *al-ʿAqāʾiq ʿalā Tabyīn al-ḥaqāʾiq* by Muḥammad b. Muḥammad al-Ḥasanī, which he composed after remarks made by his teacher Shams al-Dīn al-Maghribī, d. 1004/1692, Gotha 1023. |— 197
Glosses by Karīmallāh b. Luṭfallāh al-Fārūqī al-Dihlawī, d. 1291/1874 (*ʿUlamā i Hind* 172), Ind. Off. 1627.—2. *Kashf al-ḥaqāʾiq* (*raqāʾiq*) by Yūsuf b. Maḥmūd al-Rāzī al-Ẓahrānī, d. 794/1392, completed in 773/1371, Cairo ^{1}III, 103, ^{2}I, 457.—3. *Ramz al-ḥaqāʾiq* by Badr al-Dīn Maḥmūd al-ʿAynī, d. 855/1451 (p. 64), composed in 818/1415, Berl. 4579/80, Paris 899, 900, Ind. Off. 265,$_1$, 1628/30, Yeni 452/3, Qawala I, 353, print. Būlāq 1285, lith. Bombay 1302, Delhi 1884.—3a. *Maʿdin al-ḥaqāʾiq* by Muḥammad b. Ḥājjī b. Muḥammad al-Samarqandī, the author of *al-Fatāwi ʾl-Kāfūriyya*, eighth century AH, Ind. Off. 1626, Rāmpūr 251,$_{557/8}$, As. Soc. Beng. 19.—4. Muḥammad Efendi b. Muṣṭafā al-Ḥamīdī Qirq Emre al-Ḥanafī, d. 860/1456, Cairo ^{1}III, 75, Alex. Fiqh Ḥan. 53.—5. *Mustakhlaṣ al-ḥaqāʾiq* by Ibrāhīm b. Muḥammad al-Samarqandī, d. 907/1501 (p. 259), Paris 901, print. Bombay | 1882, Lucknow 1884, Delhi 1884.—6. *Tabyīn al-ḥaqāʾiq* 252
by Muʿīn al-Dīn Muḥammad b. Ibrāhīm al-Farāhī Mollā Miskīn al-Harawī, ca. 811/1408, Berl. 4582/3, Gotha 1020/1, Ind. Off. 269/70, Algiers 1000/3, Garr. 1721, Qawala I, 366.—Glosses: a. *Kashf al-ramz* by Aḥmad b. Muḥammad al-Ḥamawī al-Ḥanafī, d. 1098/1687, Gotha 1022;—aa.–c. see Suppl.—d. Anon. Munich 306.—7. *al-Baḥr al-rāʾiq* by Zayn al-ʿĀbidīn b. Nujaym al-Miṣrī, d. 970/1562 (p. 310), Leid. 1832, Paris 903, Algiers 1007/9, Ind. Off. 266/8, 1631/6, Yeni 242/4, Qawala I, 307/8 (c = ? Muḥammad Abu ʾl-Suʿūd b. ʿAlī b. ʿAlī al-Ḥusaynī,

completed in 1155/1742, Qawala I, 380/1) print. C. 1311, 8 vols. Glosses: a. *Maẓhar al-ḥaqāʾiq al-khafiyya* by Khayr al-Dīn al-Ramlī, d. 1081/1670, compiled by his son Najm al-Dīn in the year 1089/1678, Berl. 4584, Cairo ^{1}III, 132.—b. *Takmila* by Muḥammad Ḥusayn b. ʿAlī al-Miṣrī al-Ṭūrī al-Qādirī, d. 1004/1595, Qawala I, 313.—8. *al-Nahr al-fāʾiq* by Sirāj al-Dīn ʿUmar b. Nujaym Abu ʾl-Barakāt, d. 1005/1596, Ind. Off. 1637/8, Alex. Fiqh Ḥan. 70, Cairo ^{1}III, 146, ^{2}I, 471.—9. *Fatḥ masālik al-ramz fī manāsik al-Kanz* by ʿAbd al-Raḥmān b. ʿĪsā al-Murshidī, d. 1037/1627 (p. 380), completed in 1012/1603 in Mecca, Berl. 4585.—10. *Kashf al-ramz ʿan khabāya ʾl-Kanz* by Aḥmad b. Muḥammad al-Ḥamawī, d. 1142/1729, Cairo ^{1}III, 103, ^{2}I, 457.—11. *Tawfīq al-raḥmān* by Muṣṭafā b. Muḥammad al-Ṭāʾī, d. 1192/1778, Cairo ^{1}III, 73, ^{2}I, 440, print. 1291, abstract *Kanz al-bayān* C. 1282, 1306.—12. *Kashf al-ḥaqāʾiq* by Muḥammad b. Sulṭān al-Dimashqī al-Ḥanafī, see Suppl.—13. *al-Īḍāḥ* by Yaḥyā al-Qujḥiṣārī, Leid. 1831, Paris 902.—14. Bākir, Berl. 4581.—15. Anon., Ind. Off. 1639, Mosul $198,_{162}$.—17.–33. see Suppl. (23 see 3a).—34. *Kashf al-ḥaqāʾiq* by Abū Bakr b. Isḥāq, Krafft 457, Alex. Fiqh Ḥan. 48.—Versifications: a. *Mustaḥsan al-ṭarāʾiq fī naẓm Kanz al-daqāʾiq* by Aḥmad b. ʿAlī b. al-Faṣīḥ, d. 755/1354, Berl. 4596, Paris 904. Commentary by ʿAlī b. Ghānim al-Maqdisī, d. 1004/1595, Berl. 4587/8.—b. see Suppl. and also Ahlw. 4589.

IV. *al-Qunya fī ʾl-fiqh* AS 1355 (? = I, 550, ii?).—V. A treatise on the foundations of the law according to the orthodox, with comparisons with heterodox views, Berl. 2163.—VI. *Miʿyār al-naẓar* Köpr. 530.—VII. *al-Mustaṣfā fī sharḥ al-Nāfiʿ fī ʾl-furūʿ* I, 475, 43, 1.—VIII. A treatise on taking hashish, Gotha $2096,_{2}$.—IX. *Madārik al-tanzīl wa-ḥaqāʾiq al-taʾwīl*, a Qurʾān commentary, Br. Mus. 68/9, Ind. Off. 95/6, AS 280/4, Yeni 94, Köpr. 138/9, Rāġib 228/9, Cairo ^{1}I, 209, printed
253 in the margin | of *OB* IV, 4863.—Abstracts: a. Aḥmad b. Aybak al-ʿImādī, d. 893/1488, Cairo I, ^{1}149, ^{2} 140, a part of which is *fī bayān al-madhāhib* Gotha $98,_{7}$.—X. *al-ʿUmda fī ʾl-ʿaqāʾid* or *al-ʿUmda al-Ḥāfiẓiyya*, a defence of the *ʿAqāʾid* of al-Nasafī (I, 548) against heretical opinions about it, Berl. 1988/90, Leid. 2017, Paris $784,_{3}$, Br. Mus. 1485, Ind. Off. 434/6, 465, Garr. $2091,_{3}$, Alex. Fun. $190,_{1}$ (*ʿUmdat al-muwaḥḥidīn fī uṣūl al-dīn*)—*The Pillar of the Creed*, ed. W. Cureton, London 1843.—Commentaries: 1. Self-commentary *al-Iʿtimād fī ʾl-iʿtiqād* Berl. 1991, Paris $1261,_{1}$, abstracts in the margin of Ind. Off. 434.—2. Anon., Berl. 1992.—3.–6. see Suppl.—7. Rafīʿ al-Dīn and Zakariyyāʾ, in the margin of Ind. Off. 434.—Versification by al-Marʿashī, d. 872/1467, Berl. 1993.—11. *al-Laʾālīʾ al-fākhira fī ʿulūm al-ākhira* Berl. 2750.—12.–15. see Suppl.—16. *Faḍāʾil al-aʿmāl* ḤKh ^{1}IV, 446, ^{2}II, 1274, Garr. 922.

2. Maḥmud b. ʿUbaydallāh (p. 214) al-Maḥbūbī, d. 745/1344.

Al-Kifāya I, 466.

| 3. Qiwām al-Dīn Muḥammad b. Muḥammad b. Aḥmad al-Kākī al-Khujandī 198
al-Sinjārī, who died in 749/1348, see Suppl.

ʿUyūn al-madhāhib al-Kāmilī Berl. MS. or. oct. 3187, Garr. 1644, Yeni 519, Köpr. 638, Alex. Fiqh Ḥan. 39, Cairo [1]III, 82.—Commentaries: a., b. see Suppl. c. *Sharḥ al-funūn* by ʿAbd al-Bāsiṭ b. Khalīl b. al-Wazīr al-Ḥanafī, d. 920/1514 (p. 66), Alex. Fiqh Ḥan. 30.

4. Ḥusām al-Dīn al-Ḥasan b. Sharaf al-Tabrīzī, who died in 770/1368.

Durar al-biḥār, a work of Ḥanafī law in verse form, Paris 928.—Commentaries: 1. Zayn al-Dīn Abū Muḥammad ʿAbd al-Raḥmān b. Abī Bakr al-ʿAynī, d. 893/1488, Yeni 425.—2. Shams al-Dīn Maḥmūd b. Muḥammad al-Bukhārī, ibid. 439.

5. Luṭfallāh al-Nasafī al-Fāḍil al-Kaydānī, ca. 750/1349, see Suppl.

1. *Maṭālib al-muṣallī* or *Muqaddimat al-ṣalāt* (according to ḤKh [1]VI, 8384, [2]II, 1802, this was by al-Fanārī, d. 833/1429, and according to others it was by Kamāl, d. 983/1575), Berl. 3524, Munich 162, Br. Mus. 1200,$_2$, Ind. Off. 1672/5, Qawala I, 329, Sarajevo 123,$_3$.—Commentaries: a.–c. see Suppl.—d. Muḥammad al-Qūhistānī al-Ṣamadānī Shams al-Dīn, composed in 947/1540, Berl. 3525, Garr. 1958, *Mukhtaṣar* | Qawala I, 393.—e.–k. see Suppl. (k. with the title *al-ʿAlaq al-shamsī* 254
al-thānī, composed in 1296/1879, Ind. 1302).—l. Ibn Kamālpāsha, d. 940/1533 (p. 449), Gotha 936, Ind. Off. 1676.—m. Anon. Ind. Off. 1677/80. Abstracts: a. al-Zanjānī, ca. 1095/1684, Berl. 3526.—b. Anon. *Khulāṣat al-Kaydānī*, Arabic-Persian, Tashkent 1893 (*OB* VII, 5535/6).—2. *Risāla fī anwāʿ al-mashrūʿāt* Cairo [1]VII, 421, 424.—3., 4. See Suppl.

6. Muḥammad b. Maḥmūd b. Aḥmad al-Tabrīzī ʿImād Ṣadr b. Rashīd b. Ṣadr Qāḍī Khwāja wrote, in 772/1370:

Dustūr al-quḍāh Ind. Off. 1045, VII, 1601/2, Garr. 1645, see Suppl.

7. Muḥammad b. Abi ʾl-Qāsim Maḥmūd b. Tāj al-Dīn Abu ʾl-Mafākhir al-Sharīdī (Shadīdī) al-Zawzānī, who died in 801/1398.

1. *Niṣāb al-dharāʾiʿ fī taʿlīm al-sharāʾiʿ* Yeni 591.—2., 3. See Suppl.

8. Sharaf al-Dīn al-Qāsim b. Ḥusayn al-Damrāghī al-Ghaznawī, who died in 854/1459.

Al-Nutaf al-ḥisān fi 'l-fatāwī Yeni 586/90, Cairo ^{1}III, 142 (see Suppl.).

9. Muḥammad al-Rūyānī al-Ḥasanī al-Ḥanafī, who died in 925/1519.

Zād al-gharīb al-ḍā'i' fī badā'i' al-ṣanā'i' fī tartīb al-sharā'i' AS 1209.

B The Shāfiʿīs

1. Burhān al-Dīn ʿAbdallāh b. Muḥammad al-ʿUbaydī al-Farghānī al-Shāfiʿī was a *qāḍī* in Tabriz and died in 743/1342.

199 | Khwandamīr, *HS* III, 1, 131. 1. *Sharḥ Minhāj al-wuṣūl* I, 533.—2. *Sharḥ Ṭawāliʿ al-maṭāliʿ* ibid.—3. See Suppl.

2. Aḥmad b. ʿUmar b. Aḥmad al-Nasāʾī al-Madlijī al-Shāfiʿī Kamāl al-Dīn, who was born in 691/1292 and died in 757/1355.

1. *Jāmiʿ al-mukhtaṣarāt wa-mukhtaṣar al-jawāmiʿ*, a legal compendium, Berl. 4594, Cairo ^{1}III, 214, ^{2}I, 508.—2. *Muntaqa 'l-jawāmiʿ* ibid. ^{1}III, 278, ^{2}I, 540.—3. See Suppl.

255 | 3. Jamāl (ʿIzz) al-Dīn Yūsuf b. Ibrāhīm al-Ardabīlī al-Shāfiʿī, who died in 776/1374 (or, according to others, in 799/1396).

Al-Anwār li-aʿmāl al-barara, on Shāfiʿī law, Berl. 4598, Paris 1027 (?), Ind. Off. 268, 1773, Br. Mus. Suppl. 317, print. C. 1310, 1328. Abstracts Gotha $87,_{6}$, perhaps also 989. Persian translation and commentary by Fatḥallāh b. Abī Yazīd, Berl. Ms. or. qu. 2029, Burch.-Fischer 8.

4. Muḥammad b. ʿAbdallāh b. ʿAbd al-Munʿim al-Ḥasanī al-Jurwaʿānī al-Shāfiʿī, ca. 788/1386.

1. *al-As'ila al-qādiḥa wal-ajwiba al-wāḍiḥa wal-khātima al-nāṣiḥa taḥwī ʿuyūnan ṭāfiḥa*, 50 questions, some of which he had included previously in *al-Mawāhib al-ilāhiyya fī muṣṭalaḥ al-diyār al-Miṣriyya*, which was written during a stay in Mecca in 788, Cairo ^{1}III, 192.—2. See Suppl. (1. Berl. Qu. 2011).

C The Shīʿa

1. Jamāl al-Dīn Aḥmad b. ʿAlī b. al-Ḥusayn b. Muhannā b. ʿInaba b. al-Ḥusayn b. ʿAlī b. Abī Ṭālib, who died in 828/1424 (see Suppl.).

Wüst. *Gesch.* 470. 1. *Baḥr al-ansāb* Cairo V, ^{1}17, ^{2}52.—2. *ʿUmdat al-ṭālib fī nasab āl Abī Ṭālib*, completed in 814/1411 and dedicated to Tīmūr, Gotha 1755, Br. Mus. 346,$_5$, Garr. 693, Ibr. Pāshā 385, part of an abstract in Berl. 9399,$_2$.

2. Khiḍr b. Muḥammad al-Rāzī al-Hawalarūdhī wrote, in 840/1436 in Mashhad:

Al-Tawḍīḥ al-anwar li-dafʿ shibh al-aʿwar, written in response to the work of an unknown person from Wāsiṭ who rejected the merits of the family of the Prophet, which he composed in 839/1435 while on the way to al-Ḥilla, Berl. 9668 (see Suppl.).

| 3. Muḥammad b. ʿAlī b. Ibrāhīm b. Abī Jumhūr al-Aḥsāʾī, ca. 880/1478 (see 200
Suppl.).

1. *Kashf al-barāhīn*, a commentary on his *Zād al-musāfirīn*, which he had written in 877/8 AH while on the way to Mashhad; the former work was composed in the house of Ghiyāth al-Dīn Muḥsin b. Muḥammad, a descendant of ʿAlī Riḍā, in Mashhad, Ind. Off. 471,$_{11}$.—2. *Munāẓarāt* | *Ibn Jumhūr maʿa l-Harawī*, 256
an account of his three debates with a Sunni Mollā from Herat that had taken place in 787/1473 in the house of Muḥsin b. Ḥasan al-Qummī in Mashhad, Berl. 2110, Ind. Off. 471,$_{18}$, Br. Mus. 433,$_{33}$.—3. *Risālat al-ʿAqāʾid*, composed in 889/1484 in Mashhad, Ind. Off. 471,$_{12}$.—4.–7. see Suppl.—8. *Asrār al-ḥajj*, composed in 901/1496, *Dharīʿa* II, 43,$_{170}$.—9. *al-Aqṭāb al-fiqhiyya wal-waẓāʾif al-dīniyya ʿalā madhhab al-Imāmiyya*, MSS in Najaf and Tehran, ibid. II, 273,$_{1106}$.

6 *Sciences of the Qurʾān*

1. Faḍlallāh b. Abi 'l-Khayr ʿAlī Rashīd al-Dīn al-Ṭabīb al-Hamadhānī, who was born around 645/1247 in Hamadan and may have been of Jewish stock, worked for Sultan Abaqa as a physician and was appointed vizier by Ghāzān Khān in 697/1297. The latter's brother and successor Uljaytu confirmed him in this office. Sultan Abū Saʿīd, however, had him executed in Tabriz in 718/1318 because he suspected him of having poisoned Uljaytu.

Hist. des Mongols, ed. Quatremère (Coll. Or. Paris, 1836), I/CLXXV, Elliot, *Hist. of India* III, 1/23, I, 42, II, 550. 1. *Mafātīḥ (Miftāḥ) al-tafāsīr* Cairo ^{1}VI, 200, ^{2}I, App. 71.—2. *Laṭāʾif al-ḥaqāʾiq*, 3. *al-Tawḍīḥāt fi 'l-mukātabāt*, 4. *al-Sulṭāniyya*, begun in Ramaḍān 706/March 1307, together in *al-Majmūʿa al-Rashīdiyya* Paris 2324 (see Quatremère, op. cit., CXIVff.).—5., 6. See Suppl. Also, a collection of 86 *taqrīẓ* by contemporary writers, for whose completion he instituted a private endowment at the school of Tabriz, Krafft 148.

2. Niẓām al-Dīn al-Ḥasan b. Muḥammad (Maḥmūd) b. al-Ḥusayn al-Aʿraj al-Qummī al-Nīsābūrī, fl. eighth century (see Suppl.).

Suter, *Math.* 395. 1. *Gharāʾib al-Qurʾān wa-raghāʾib al-furqān* also Berl. 871, Ind. Off. 1138, Garr. 1291, Qawala I, 73, Patna I, $30,_{300/1}$.—2. *al-Risāla al-Shamsiyya fī ʾl-ḥisāb*, dedicated to Shams al-Dīn ʿAbd al-Laṭīf, a son of Rashīd al-Dīn (no. 1), also Munich Pers. $346,_{3}$.—3.–5. see Suppl. (3. completed in 704, 4. in 711).—6. *Sharḥ Zīji Ilkhānī* Persian, Suppl. I, 931.—6. *Sharḥ Sī faṣl* ibid., Leid. 1176, AS 2664.

257 201 | | 3. Shihāb al-Dīn Abū Saʿīd Aḥmad b. Aḥmad b. Aḥmad b. al-Ḥusayn b. Mūsā b. Mūsak al-Kurdī al-Hakkārī, who was born in 702/1302, was a teacher of Qurʾānic recitation at the Madrasat al-Manṣūr and of *ḥadīth* at the Manṣūriyya, both in Cairo. He died on 8 Jumādā II 763/6 April 1362 (or, according to Ṣafadī, 12 Jumādā I 750).

DK I, 98, no. 2661, al-Ṣafadī, *Wāf.* AS 2962, 52. *Tafsīr al-Qurʾān*, mostly based on al-Thaʿlabī (I, 429) and al-Wāḥidī (ibid. 524), Cairo I, ^{1}153, ^{2}40.—2. *Rijāl al-sunan al-arbaʿ* Cairo ^{1}I, 237.—3. See Suppl.

4. ʿUthmān b. Muḥammad b. Muḥammad al-Ghaznawī, fl. eighth century.

Al-Maḍbūṭ fī bayān al-qirāʾāt al-sabʿ Leid. 1637, Ind. Off. 1186, Bank. XVIII, 1241, Rāmpūr 54.—Abstract of *Maqālīd al-ḥurūf*, with a commentary, *Maqālīd al-rumūz*, Leid. 1638.

5. Zayn al-Dīn ʿUmar b. Ḥajjāj b. Aḥmad al-Ḥanafī al-Ṣūfī al-Waḥshī, ca. 800/1397 (?).

Explanatory note to sura $2,_{195}$, with due consideration of al-Zamakhsharī, Berl. 982.

6. Shams al-Dīn Abu ʾl-Khayr Muḥammad b. Muḥammad b. al-Jazarī al-Qurashī al-Dimashqī al-Shīrāzī was born in Damascus on 25 Ramaḍān 751/27 November 1350. After completing his studies in the Qurʾānic sciences and *ḥadīth* in 768/1367 he went on the pilgrimage and then, in 769, to Cairo for further schooling. After a second trip to that city in 774 he became a *qāḍī* in Damascus in 793/1391. Having lost all his possessions—they were probably confiscated—in Egypt in 798/1395, he went to Sultan Bāyezīd I in Bursa. However, in 805/1402 they were both captured by Tīmūr and deported, first to Kashsh and then to

Samarqand. After Tīmūr's death in 807/1404 he went to Iran and became a *qāḍī* in Shiraz. Having made another fortune there he went to Basra, was to be found in Mecca and Medina in 823/1420, and, in 828/1425, in Zabīd and Mecca again. He died in Shiraz on 5 Rabīʿ I 833/3 December 1429.

| Autobiography in *Ṭabaqāt* no. 3433, *Ḥuff.* XXIV, 5, Ṭāshköprīzāde, *ShN* 98/101, 258
Wüst. *Gesch.* 474, *JA* s. IX, vol. 3, p. 259.—1. *Kitāb al-nashr fī 'l-qirā'āt al-ʿashr*, composed in 2 volumes in Medina in 825/1420, Berl. 657, Esc. ^{2}129, Garr. 1219, Sarajevo 25, NO 97, Fātiḥ 58/60, Waqf Ibr. 2, Qawala I, 35, Cairo ^{1}I, 117, ^{2}I, 29. | 202
The additions of the *Nashr* to the *Ḥirz al-amānī* (I, 520) and *al-Taysīr* (ibid. 517) were versified by Aḥmad al-Ṭībī, d. 951/1541, in *al-Tanwīr*, to which he made his own additions, Berl. 665.—An abstract by the author, *Taqrīb al-nashr*, Berl. 658, Basle M III, 22, Paris $4532_{,4}$, Garr. 1219a, Fātiḥ 37, Waqf Ibr. 46, Qawala I, 30.—2. *Taḥbīr al-Taysīr fī 'l-qirā'āt*, on whose author see I, 517.—3. *Ṭayyibat al-nashr fī 'l-qirā'āt al-ʿashr*, in ca. 1000 *rajaz* verses, completed in Shaʿbān 799/May 1396 in Anatolia, Berl. 659, Paris $4532_{,6}$, Algiers $376_{,6}$, Br. Mus. $88_{,3}$, Sarajevo 29, Garr. $1253_{,1}$ (Suppl. 391), Cairo I, ^{1}101, ^{2}23, lith. C. 1282, print. C. 1296.—Commentaries: a. His son Abū Bakr Aḥmad (see Suppl.), abstract Gotha $857_{,13}$.—b. Muḥammad b. Muḥammad al-ʿAqīlī al-Nuwayrī, d. 837/1433, who had studied the work in 828/1425 with its author in Mecca, Berl. 660/1, Fātiḥ 53, Waqf Ibr. 25, Qawala I, 21.—c.–f. see Suppl. (e. has the title *Saṭaʿāt lamaʿān anwār ḍiyā' al-fajr fī sharḥ al-Nashr*, Fātiḥ Waqf Ibr. 50; f. Qawala I, 6).—4. *al-Durra al-muḍī'a (bahiyya) fī qirā'āt al-a'imma al-thalātha al-marḍiyya*, 241 *ṭawīl* verses, composed in 823/1420 (see I, 517), Berl. 662/3, Gotha 558, Munich $893_{,18}$, Vienna $1632_{,1}$, Algiers $376_{,4}$, Sarajevo $20_{,2}$, Garr. $2067_{,1}$, Köpr. $17_{,1}$, AS $60_{,2}$, Fātiḥ $40_{,2}$, Waqf Ibr. $48_{,2}$, Cairo I, ^{1}108, ^{2}19, Qawala I, 14.—Commentaries: a. by his son Abū Bakr Aḥmad, Qawala I, 20.—b. *al-Ghurra*, an anonymous work completed in 919/1513, possibly by Jamāl al-Dīn Ḥusayn b. ʿAlī al-Ḥiṣnī, d. 952/1546, Berl. 664.—c. *al-Ghurra al-bahiyya* by Aḥmad b. ʿAbd al-Jawād al-Wā'ī, Cairo I, ^{1}108, ^{2}24, Makram 47.—d.–k. see Suppl. (e. ʿUthmān b. ʿUmar al-Nāshirī, Köpr. $17_{,2}$, Patna I, $16_{,137/8}$; the same *al-Durr al-naẓīm li-riwāyat Ḥafṣ b. Sulaymān* Patna I, $4_{,20}$.—f. Fātiḥ Waqf Ibr. $51_{,3}$.—h. Cairo ^{1}I, 108.—i. Fātiḥ Waqf Ibr. 23).—l. Khālid b. ʿAbdallāh al-Azharī (p. 34), Patna II, $367_{,2549,7}$.—m. *Taḥrīr al-ṭuruq wal-riwāyāt min ṭarīq Ṭayyibat al-nashr*, by ʿAlī al-Manṣūrī, 11th cent., Qawala I, 8.—5. *Hidāyat* (*ShN Ghāyat*) *al-mahara fī taʿlīm al-qirā'āt al-ʿashara* AS 39 (783 A.H.).—6. *Munjid al-muqri'īn wa-murshid al-ṭālibīn*, on reading the Qur'ān, Berl. 656 (with the title *Munjid al-muqarrabīn*, listed as a Sufi work in Ahlw. $3080_{,28}$).—7. 41 *ṭawīl* verses on difficult questions | surrounding reading the 259
Qur'ān, Berl. 526.—8. *al-Muqaddima al-Jazariyya fī 'l-tajwīd*, a didactic poem, Berl. 500/10, Gotha 562 (where other MSS are listed), Garr. 1220/1, Sarajevo $20_{,4}$,

AS 41$_{,2}$, 60$_{,2}$, 61, Köpr. II, 3, III, 5$_{,2}$, Fātiḥ 69$_{,1}$, Waqf Ibr. 48$_{,3}$, 62$_{,4}$, Alex. Fun. 146$_{,2}$, 195$_{,19}$, Qawala I, 32/3, lith. C. 1282.—Commentaries: a. *al-Ḥawāshi 'l-mufahhima* by his son Abū Bakr Aḥmad, completed in Laranda in Qaramān in Ramaḍān 806/March 1404 (*ShN* I, 39), Berl. 511/2, Gotha 563/4, Leipz. 100$_{,4}$, Br. Mus. Suppl. 93, Bodl. I, 1290, Algiers 390$_{,3}$, 409, Sarajevo 27$_{,1}$, Fātiḥ Waqf Ibr. 65$_{,2}$, Qawala I, 13, 2 (*Sharḥ*), print. C. 1309, with marginal glosses Kazan 1893.—b. ʿAbd al-Dāʾim b. ʿAlī al-Ḥadīdī, d. 870/1465, Berl. 514, Sarajevo 30$_{,9}$, Br. Mus. Suppl. 96$_{,ii}$.—c. Khālid b. ʿAbdallāh al-Azharī, d. 905/1499 (p. 34), Berl. 515, Gotha 565/6, Leid. 1642, Bodl. II, 232$_{,4}$, Esc. ^{2}521$_{,5}$, Fātiḥ 70, Waqf Ibr. 58.—d. *al-Laʾālīʾ al-saniyya* by Aḥmad b. Muḥammad al-Qasṭallānī, d. 923/1517 (p. 87), Cairo I, ^{1}104, ^{2}26.—e. *al-Daqāʾiq al-muḥkama* by Zakariyyāʾ al-Anṣārī, d. 926/1520 (p. 122), Berl. 516/21, Hamb. Or. Sem. 15$_{,2}$, Vienna 1636, Br. Mus. Suppl. 94$_{,ii}$, Esc. ^{2}139$_{,4}$, 521$_{,3}$, Algiers 407, Garr. 1231/2, Köpr. III, 5$_{,2}$, Cairo ^{1}I, 97, 109, 112/3, VII, 213, 495, ^{2}I, 20, App. 1, Makram 27, Qawala I, 15, print. C. 1308.—Glosses: α His grandson Zayn al-ʿĀbidīn Yūsuf, d. 1068/1657, Leid. 1643/4, Bodl. I, 1214, II, 232$_{,2}$.—β Abu 'l-Naṣr ʿAbd al-Raḥmān al-Nahrāwī, Garr. 1245.—γ *al-Nukat al-lawdhaʿiyya* by ʿAlī al-Shabrāmallisī, d. 1087/1676 (p. 322), Garr. 1233.—f. Ṭāshköprīzāde, d. 968/1560 (p. 425), Br. Mus. Suppl. 94$_{,i}$, Köpr. III, 5, 1, Fātiḥ 113, Waqf Ibr. 6, Cairo ^{1}I, 117, Qawala I, 22, print. Kazan 1887.—g. Muḥammad b. Ibrāhīm al-Ḥalabī al-Ḥanbalī, d. 971/1563 (p. 368), Vienna 1631, Sarajevo 30 (?), Paris 4531, Br. Mus. Suppl. 94$_{,iv}$.—h. al-Qāriʾ al-Harawī, d. 1014/1605 (p. 394), Berl. 522, Br. Mus. Suppl. 95$_{,i}$, Ind. Off. 49, Fātiḥ 40$_{,4}$, 55, Waqf Ibr. 55, Cairo I, 116, VII, 426, ^{2}I, 23, print. C. 1308 and others.—i. Muḥammad Ḥijāzīzāde al-Makkī, composed in 1072/1661, Berl. 523.—k. Khalīl b. Badr al-Dīn al-Ṣafadī (10th cent. AH?), ibid. 524, Pet. 54$_{,3}$.—l. ʿAlī b. Ḥasan al-Sanhūrī, Gotha 567.—m. Anon., Berl. 525, Vienna 1630/1.—n.–t. see Suppl. Cf. Ahlw. 526, Turkish translation Fātiḥ Waqf Ibr. 65, another Ḥamīd. 16$_{,1}$.—9. *al-Tamhīd fī ʿilm al-tajwīd*, composed in 769/1367, Paris 592$_{,2}$, Fātiḥ Waqf Ibr. 56, Turkish translation by Maghnīsī in *Majmūʿa* (starting with al-Birkawī's *al-Durr al-yatīm*), Istanbul
260 1280, | 98/148 (Ritter).—10. *Kifāyat al-almaʿī fī āyat Yā arḍu 'blaʿī* (sura 11$_{,44}$) Cairo ^{1}VII, 578.—11. *Ghāyat al-nihāya fī asmāʾ rijāl al-qirāʾāt etc.* (see Suppl.) NO 85.—12. *Muqaddimat ʿilm al-ḥadīth* Berl. 1084.—13. *al-Hidāya ilā maʿālim (ʿilm)*
203 *al-riwāya*, a didactic poem in 370 verses, see Suppl.—| Commentaries: a. Self-commentary *Tadhkirat al-ʿulamāʾ*, composed in 806/1403 in Kashsh, Berl. 1085, Leid. 1753.—b. *al-Ghāya* by Shams al-Dīn Abu 'l-Khayr Muḥammad al-Sakhāwī al-Shāfiʿī, d. 902/1497 (p. 43), Alex. Ḥad. 36.—14. *ʿIqd al-laʾālīʾ fi 'l-aḥādīth al-musalsala wal-ʿawālī*, compiled in 808/1405 in Shiraz, Paris 4577$_{,3}$.—15. Another collection of traditions, ibid. 4.—16. *al-Risāla al-bayāniyya fī ḥaqq abaway al-nabī*, on whether the parents of the Prophet went to Paradise, Berl. 10343.—17. *al-Mawlid al-kabīr* Br. Mus. Suppl. 515.—18. *Dhāt al-shifāʾ fī sīrat al-nabī*

wal-khulafā', a poem in *rajaz*, written at the behest of Sultan Muḥammad of Shiraz on 25 Dhu 'l-Ḥijja 798/1 October 1396, three days after the battle of Nicopolis, thereby fixing its date (Hammer, *Gesch. des Osm. Reiches* I, 240, 616), a brief account of the life of the Prophet and his first four successors, with an overview of Islamic history up to Sultan Bāyezīd and the conquest of Constantinople, Berl. 9692, Garr. 645, a commentary by Ibn al-Ḥājj, completed in 1187/1773, in Berl. 9693, Br. Mus. Suppl. 516.—19. *al-Ḥiṣn al-ḥaṣīn min kalām sayyid al-mursalīn*, prayers (cf. Flügel, *Wien. Jahrb.* 47, p. 104), Vienna 1705, Br. Mus. 127, 143, Garr. 1955, Alex. Ḥad. 20, Cairo [1]I, 336, [2]I, 111, 290, Patna I, 153$_{,1453/5}$, lith. C. 1279, printed in the margin of C. 1315.—Commentaries: a. Self-commentary *Miftāḥ al-Ḥiṣn al-ḥasīn* or *al-Manhiyya* (see Suppl.) Alex. Ḥad. 64, Patna I, 157$_{,1496}$.—b. *al-Ḥirz al-thamīn* by al-Qārī' al-Harawī, d. 1014/1605 (p. 394), Berl. 3701, Ind. Off. 348, Alex. Ḥad. 20, Cairo I, [1]335, [2]110, Qawala I, 115, Patna I, 152$_{,1450}$.—c.–i. see Suppl. (e. Muḥammad b. 'Abd al-Qādir al-Fāsī, d. 1116/1704, Alex. Ḥad. 31).—Abstracts: a. *'Uddat al-ḥiṣn* Br. Mus. Suppl. 250 (where other MSS are listed), Ind. Off. 4591 (*JRAS* 1939, 375), Garr. 1956/7, print. Calcutta 1229, C. 1303.—Commentaries: *α* Muḥammad b. 'Abd al-Qādir al-Fāsī, Cairo [1]I, 281, [2]130.—*β* see Suppl.—b., c. see Suppl.—d. *Muntakhab*, by the author himself, Alex. Ḥad. 55$_{,3}$.—20. *Mukhtaṣar al-naṣīḥa bil-adilla al-ṣaḥīḥa* Alex. Mawā'iẓ 42, Cairo [1]VII, 564.—22. *al-Zahr al-fā'iḥ*, paraenesis, under another title also attributed to al-Ghazzālī, Br. Mus. 337, print. C. 1305, 1310.—22. *al-Iṣāba fī lawāzim al-kitāba*, | on the art of writing, containing brief sam- 261
ples from letters (by the author?), Berl. 6.–23. *Rajaz* poem on astronomy (author?), ibid. 8159$_{,3}$.—24.–28. see Suppl.—29. *Risāla fī arba'īn su'ālan min al-masā'il al-mushkila wal-jawāb 'anhā* Alex. Fun. 167$_{,26}$.—30. *Lāmiyya fī 'l-qirā'āt al-shādhdha* Qawala I, 26, on which *al-Zawā'id al-mufīda fī ridf al-qaṣīda fī 'l-qirā'āt al-shādhdha* Alex. Fun. 165$_{,24}$.

7. Sa'dallāh b. Ḥusayn al-Salamāsī, ca. 847/1443 (?).

Baḥth al-ma'rūf fī ma'rifat al-wuqūf, on pausas in the Qur'ān, Paris 650 (dated 847, autograph?), cf. de Sacy, *Not. et Extr.* VIII, 360.

8. 'Alā' al-Dīn 'Alī b. Yaḥyā al-Samarqandī, ca. 850/1446.

Baḥr al-'ulūm, a Qur'ān commentary running up to sura 58, ḤKh [1]II, 1764, [2]I, 225, vol. 4. Berl. 883, fragm. ibid. 884.

9. Mu'īn al-Dīn Muḥammad b. Ṣafī al-Dīn 'Abd al-Raḥmān al-Ījī al-Ṣafawī, who was born in 832/1428 and died in 905/1500.

1. *Jawāmiʿ al-tibyān fī tafsīr al-Qurʾān*, completed in 870/1465 in Mecca, Garr. 1294, Köpr. 93, Cairo ^{1}I, 159, ^{2}43.—2. see Suppl.

10. Shams al-Dīn Aḥmad b. Nuṣayr al-Maydānī al-Muqriʾ al-Ḍarīr, who died in 923/1517.

Qawāʿid al-tajwīd, Berl. 529, Leipz. 877$_{,\mathrm{vii}}$.

7 *Dogmatics*

1. ʿAlāʾ al-Dīn ʿAlī al-Ṭūsī studied in Persia and was given a professorship in Bursa by Sultan Murād II. After the conquest of Constantinople, the latter's son Meḥmed made him responsible for one of the eight madrasas that he subsequently founded in the city but then transferred him to his father's madrasa in Adrianople. When he lost out to Khujāzāde (p. 230) in a literary competition organised by the sultan he resigned from his post and retired first to Tabriz
262 and then to Khurāsān, | where he consoled himself with mystical fantasies surrounding his failed career.

ShN I, 158/62. 1. *Ḥawāshī ʿalā sharḥ al-Mawāqif* see p. 269.—2. *Ḥawāshī ʿala ʾl-Talwīḥ* p. 214.—3. *Ḥawāshī ʿalā sharḥ Lawāmiʿ al-asrār* I, 467.—4. A poem in an anonymous anthology, Esc. ^{2}481.—5., 6. see Suppl. (5. Garr. 1498).

2. Mīr Ṣadr al-Dīn Muḥammad b. Mīr Ghiyāth al-Dīn Manṣūr al-Ḥusaynī al-Shīrāzī, who was born in 828/1425 in Shiraz, was murdered by Bayandari Turkmens in 903/1497.

1. *Risāla fī ithbāt al-bāriʾ taʿālā wa-ṣifātihi ʾl-ḥusnā* Ind. Off. 468, Alex. Fun. 88$_{,7}$.—2. *Masʾalat khalq al-aʿmāl* Br. Mus. 980$_{,4}$.—3. *Risāla fī taḥqīq al-taṣawwur wal-taṣdīq* ibid. 981$_{,20}$.—4. see Suppl.—Various smaller treatises A. Taymūr, Ḥikma 55.

8 *Mysticism*

1. Jamāl al-Dīn ʿAbd al-Razzāq al-Kāshānī (Qāshānī, Kāshī), who died in 730/1330 in Kāshān (see Suppl.).

Jāmī, *Nafaḥāt* 357/68. 1. *Iṣṭilāḥāt al-Ṣūfiyya* a. technical terms, b. on the ways of the Sufis, Berl. 3460/1, Gotha 76$_{,2}$ (where other MSS are listed), Alex. Taṣ. 33$_{,1}$, Persian paraphrase in Br. Mus. Pers. II, 832a, commentary ibid. b. part 1 Pers. *Abdurrazzaq's Dictionary of the Technical Terms of the Sufies*, ed. A. Sprenger, Calcutta 1845.—2. *Laṭāʾif al-iʿlām fī ishārāt ahl al-ilhām*, similar to no. 1, Leid.

81/2, Ind. Off. 663, Köpr. 770, | used and partly edited by Tholuck, *Die specula-* 205
tive Trinitätslehre des späteren Orients, 13/22, 28ff.—3. *Taʾwīlāt al-Qurʾān* see Suppl. 1; AS 81, on sura 108 and 112, Berl. 971 (with regard to *ʿArāʾis al-bayān etc.* see I, 527).—3a. *Ḥaqāʾiq al-taʾwīl wa-daqāʾiq al-tanzīl* AS 198, Patna I, $28_{,280}$, with the title *Ḥaqāʾiq al-Qurʾān* Berl. Qu. 3719.—4. *Taʾwīlāt bi-smillāh al-raḥmān al-raḥīm*, with a supercommentary by al-Qayṣarī, d. 751/1350, Cairo ^{1}II, 137.—5. *al-Risāla al-sarmadiyya*, on the notion of eternity, Berl. 2312.—6. *Risāla fi ʾl-qaḍāʾ wal-qadar*, ibid. 2483; Traité de la prédestination et du libre arbitre, transl. St. Guyard, *JA* s. VII, v. 1, 125ff; also rev. transl. with additions, Nogent-le-Rotrou 1875.—7. *Risāla fī bayān al-ḥaqīqa maʿa sharḥihā* Berl. 3462.—8. *al-Risāla al-Kumayliyya*, on an answer given by ʿAlī to Kumayl b. Ziyād, | Br. 263
Mus. $980_{,13}$, $981_{,17}$, Cairo ^{1}VII, 383.—9. *al-Tadhkira al-ṣāḥibiyya* Cairo ^{1}II, 556.—10. Metaphysical questions from several of his works, Br. Mus. $981_{,13}$.—11. *Sharḥ Manāzil al-sāʾirīn* I, 558.—12. *Sharḥ Mawāqiʿ al-nujūm* ibid. 574.—13.–19. see Suppl.

1a. Aḥmad b. Muḥammad b. Aḥmad al-Samnānī, who died in 736/1366, see Suppl.

1. *Tafsīr* also Basle Univ., without shelfmark.—2. *Ṣafwat al-ʿUrwa* Laleli 1432.—4. Entitled *Iṣṭilāḥāt al-Ṣūfiyya*, Šehīd ʿAli 1119.—6. *Mashāriʿ abwāb al-quds wa-marātiʿ abwāb al-uns* ibid. 1328.—8. *Faḍl al-sharīʿa* Faiẓ. 2133.—9. *Risālat al-wārid al-shārid al-ṭārid li-subḥat al-māriḍ* Hekīm Oğlū 933.—10. *Tuḥfat al-sālikīn* Fātiḥ 2567.—11. *Risāla mā lā budd fi ʾl-dīn* Asʿad 1431 (Ritter).

1b. Abu ʾl-Ghanāʾim ʿAbd al-Razzāq al-Sijistānī.

Tazkiyat al-arwāḥ ʿan mawāniʿ al-falāḥ, on ethics, based on the example of *Akhlāq-i Nāṣirī*, ḤKh ^{1}II, 286, ^{2}I, 402 (anonymous) Garr. 1936 (MS copied in 746 in Irbil).

2. Jamāl al-Dīn Abu ʾl-Maḥāsin Yūsuf b. ʿAbdallāh b. ʿUmar b. Khiḍr al-Kūrānī al-Tamlījī al-Kurdī, who died in 768/1366.

1. *Rayḥān al-qulūb fi ʾl-tawassul ila ʾl-qulūb*, on how students are accepted into the ranks of the Sufis, Berl. 3351/2, Cairo ^{1}II, 131, VII, 227 (see Suppl.).—2. *Ḥizb*, ejaculatory prayer, Berl. 3885.

3. Bahāʾ al-Dīn Pīr Muḥammad b. Muḥammad b. Muḥammad Naqshband al-Bukhārī was born in Bukhārā, went to the Sufi emir Kalāl in Nasaf following

a dream, founded the dervish order named after him, and died in Rabīʿ I 791/1 March 1389.

Manāqib Naqshband (see Suppl.) Šehīd ʿA. 1188$_{,2}$, Jāmī, *Nafaḥāt* 439/45, Khwāndamīr, *ḤS* II, 3, 87, *ShN* I, 378/80. Gordlewski in *Festschrift Oldenburg*, Leningrad 1934, 147/69. 1. *al-Awrād al-Bahāʾiyya*, prayers, with the anonymous commentary *Manbaʿ al-asrār fī bayān khawāṣṣ al-Awrād al-Bahāʾiyya*, cited Ahlw. 3797$_{,2}$, on which is the commentary *al-Fuyūḍāt al-iḥsāniyya*, by ʿAbd al-Qādir b. Muḥammad b. Abi ʾl-Nūr b. Abi ʾl-Suʿūd al-Kayyālī, written in 1268/1851, Alexandria 1289 (see Suppl.).

264 | 3b. ʿAbdallāh b. Muḥammad b. Amīn al-Iṣfahbadhī, see Suppl.

Al-Risāla al-Makkiyya fi ʾl-khalwa al-ṣūfiyya Alex. Taṣ. 18, copied in 755 AH, apparently during the lifetime of the author.

3c. Muḥammad b. Muḥammad b. Maḥmūd al-Ḥāfiẓī al-Bukhārī Khwāja Pāshā Muḥammad Pāshā, who died in 822/1420, see Suppl.

8. *al-Ghurra al-gharrāʾ wal-durra al-bayḍāʾ fī ʿilm al-miftāḥ*, on logic, with a commentary by ʿAbd al-Ḥalīm b. Luṭfallāh, AS 3841$_{,2}$.—9. A definition of *iʿjāz* based on al-Taftāzānī's *Muṭawwal*, ibid. 3, ff. 138b/141b.—10. *Taḥqīq al-arkān al-arbaʿa li-dīn al-Islām wa-hiya ʾl-tawḥīd wal-maʿrifa wal-īmān wal-islām* Garr. 2003$_{,14}$.

4. Quṭb al-Dīn ʿAbd al-Karīm b. Ibrāhīm b. Sibṭ ʿAbd al-Qādir (I, 560) al-Jīlānī (Kīlānī) al-Ṣūfī, who was born in 767/1365 and died in 832/1428.

An (incomplete) inventory of his works is in Ind. Off. p. 183/4. 1. *al-Insān al-kāmil fī maʿrifat al-awākhir wal-awāʾil* Berl. 2314/7, Gotha 893/5 (where other MSS are listed), BDMG 20, Paris 1356/8, 6596, Br. Mus. 1298, Garr. 1579, Halet 205, Nāfiz 487/8, Riẓā P. 860, Asʿad 1325, Cairo ^{1}II, 67, 145, print. 1301, 1304.—Commentaries: a. Aḥmad b. Muḥammad al-Madanī, d. 1071/1660, completed in 1056/1646 in Medina, Berl. 2318, Ind. Off. 667 (whose *Mūḍiḥat al-ḥāl etc.* is preserved in Garr. 1528); this is a mostly polemical work against the author. Against this: b. ʿAbd al-Ghanī al-Nābulusī, d. 1143/1730 (p. 345), Berl. 2319.—2. *al-Ghāyāt fī maʿrifat maʿāni ʾl-āyāt wal-aḥādīth al-mutashābihāt*, on the nature of God, Berl. 2320.—3. The beginning of a treatise on knowing God, ibid. 2321.—4. *al-Nāmūs al-aʿẓam wal-qāmūs al-aqdam*, on the secrets of the word of God as revealed to Muḥammad, in 40 volumes, vol. 9 Ind. Off. 664$_{,1}$, vol. 10
206 Cairo ^{1}II, 45, | vol. 11 (with the title *Sirr al-nūr al-mutamakkin*) Berl. 3024,

Cairo ^{1}II, 45, VII, 277, vol. 12 Cairo ^{1}VII, 100; another volume Ind. Off. 664,$_5$.—5. *Marātib al-wujūd wa-bayān ḥaqīqat ibtidāʾ kulli mawjūd* Berl. 3219/20, Ind. Off. 665, 1032,$_6$, Alex. Fun. 135/6, 151,$_{19}$, Cairo ^{1}II, 125, 134, ^{2}I, 206, 357.—6. *Zulfat al-tamkīn*, on the difficulty of grasping the nature of God, Berl. 3221, with the title *Ḥaqīqat al-yaqīn wa-zulfat al-tamkīn* Alex. Taṣ. 32, Patna II, 409,$_{2579,9}$.—7. *Lawāmiʿ al-barq al-mūhin fī maʿnā mā wasaʿanī etc.*, an abstract of *Qabs al-lawāmiʿ*, Cairo ^{1}VII, 6, | 108.—8. *al-Safar al-qarīb natījat al-safar al-gharīb*, an 265
extensive treatment of the content of Ibn ʿArabī's *Kitāb al-asfār* (I, 571), Berl. 3278.—9. *Kitāb al-asfār*, on the journey of man from and to God, ibid. 3279.—10. *Munāẓara ʿaliyya* (*ilāhiyya*), on the 100 levels at which man contemplates God, Berl. 3306, Pers. 54,$_2$, Ind. Off. 666,$_3$, 1038,$_2$, Cairo ^{1}VII, 386, Patna II, 409,$_{2579,12}$, 416,$_{2584,4}$.—11. *Risālat arbaʿīn mawāṭin*, on the different states of being of the Sufi, Berl. 3307.—12. *al-Kahf wal-raqīm fī sharḥ bismillāh al-raḥmān al-raḥīm*, on the various connotations of *bismillāh* in relation to the majesty of God, composed in 789/1396 in Zabīd, Berl. 3445, Ind. Off. 606,$_2$, Alex. Taṣ. 30, Fun. 136,$_3$, 152,$_{28}$, Cairo ^{1}II, 207, VII, 108, 277, ^{2}I, 59, 347, Patna II, 409,$_{2579,6}$.—13. *al-Kamālāt al-ilāhiyya wal-ṣifāt al-Muḥammadiyya*, composed in 803/1400 (according to Algiers, see Suppl.) in Ghazza, Paris 1338,$_6$, Algiers 921/2, autograph Cairo ^{1}II, 127, ^{2}I, 349.—14. *Ḥaqīqat al-ḥaqāʾiq* Ind. Off. 608, Cairo ^{1}VII, 5.—15. *Ghunyat arbāb al-samāʿ fī kashf al-qināʿ ʿan wujūh al-istimāʿ* Ind. Off. 1038,$_{23}$, Cairo ^{1}II, 127.—16. *al-Asrār* Patna II, 455,$_{2630,9}$.—17. *Lisān al-qadar bi-kitāb Nasīm al-saḥar* (see no. 28), Cairo ^{1}VII, 277.—18. A *qaṣīda*, Berl. 7889,$_2$.—19. *al-Nawādir al-ʿayniyya fi ʾl-bawādir al-ghaybiyya*, a Sufi poem, Berl. 3411, Gotha 2316/7, Paris 3171,$_2$, 3222, Bodl. I, 45,$_2$. The commentary *al-Maʿārif al-ghaybiyya* by ʿAbd al-Ghanī al-Nābulusī (d. 1143/1731, see p. 324), composed in 1086/1675, is preserved in Berl. 3412/3, Paris 3223,$_2$, Cairo ^{1}VII, 312, ^{2}I, 360, Alex. Taṣ. 39, 40, Fun. 90,$_3$,—a *takhmīs* by Abu ʾl-Fatḥ Sirḥān al-Samarjī al-Sharnūbī al-Dimyāṭī, Paris 3223,$_1$, Alex. Taṣ. 39.—20. *Sharḥ al-Futūḥāt al-Makkiyya* I, 572.—21.–27. see Suppl.—28. *Nasīm al-saḥar* (p. 17) Patna II, 409,$_{2579,8}$.—29. *Sabab al-asbāb wal-kanz li-man ayqana wastajāb* Alex. Fun. 152,$_{24}$.

5. Abū Bakr Muḥammad b. Muḥammad al-Khawāfī[1] Zayn al-Dīn was born on 15 Rabīʿ I 757/19 March 1356 in Khawāf in Khurāsān, joined the Sufi Nūr al-Dīn ʿAbd al-Raḥmān al-Miṣrī in Cairo, before later returning to Khurāsān where he died on 2 Shawwāl 838/1 May 1435.

Jāmī, *Nafaḥāt* 569, *ShN* I, 132/4. 1. *Risālat al-waṣāya ʾl-Qudsiyya*, a work of advice for ascetics and prospective mystics | composed in Jerusalem in 825/1422, Berl. 266

1 Several times corrupted to Khāfī, or, in *ShN*, to Khāqī.

3023 (with incorrect name and date), Pet. AM 146,$_2$, Paris 762,$_3$, AS 37,$_3$, Alex. Mawāʿiẓ 50.—2. A treatise explaining that the pious man must desist from earthly desires in order for the darkness to vanish from his heart and that he must chasten himself in order to attain knowledge of God, composed in 825/1422, Berl. 3096, 3280.—3. *al-Awrād al-Zayniyya*, a book of prayers, abstract Paris 1176,$_1$.—4. See Suppl.

207 | 6. Bābā Ṭāhir al-Hamadhānī wrote, in 889/1484:

A mystical treatise, on which a commentary, *al-Futūḥāt al-rabbāniyya fī mazj al-ishārāt al-Hamadhāniyya*, is in Paris 1903,$_2$; see Bābar, *Mem.* ed. Beveridge 177v, 222/3.

7. ʿAbd al-Raḥmān b. Aḥmad al-Jāmī al-Naqshbandī Qiwām al-Dīn, the famous Persian poet, was born on 23 Shaʿbān 817/8 November 1414 and died in Herat on 18 Muḥarram 898/10 November 1492.

Khwandamīr, *ḤS* III, 2, 337, *ShN* I, 389/93, Nawāʾī, *Khamsat al-mutaḥayyirīn*, in Bersine, *Chrest. turque*, Kazan 1857, 168/79, de Sacy, *Not. et Extr.* XII, 287, Jourdain, *Biogr. univ.* XI, 431, Ouseley, *Biographical Notices* 131, V. v. Rosenzweig, *Biographische Notizen über Dschami*, Vienna 1840, W. Nassau Lee, *Biographical Sketch of Jami*, Calcutta 1859. 1. *Tafsīr al-Qurʾān* AS 405 (with a personal dedication to Yaʿqūb Bey, Tabriz 883), 412, Cairo ^{1}I, 143, 203, ^{2}I, 38, whence *Tafsīr al-Fātiḥa* NO 344/5.—2. *al-Durra al-fākhira fī ḥaqāʾiq madhhab al-Ṣūfiyya*, on the nature and properties of God, Berl. 2324/5, Gotha 87,$_2$ (where other MSS are listed), Ind. Off. 670, Cairo ^{1}III, 124, ^{2}I, 295, with the title *Risālat muḥākamat al-mutakallimīn etc.* (see Suppl.) Garr. 1584, entitled *Taḥqīq madhhab al-ṣūfiyya wal-mutakallimīn wal-ḥukamāʾ al-mutaqaddimīn* Vienna 1930,$_2$.—Commentary by Mollā Ibrāhīm b. Ḥaydar al-Kurdī b. al-Ḥusaynābādhī, Alex. Fun. 96,$_2$.—3. *Sharḥ al-asmāʾ al-ḥusnā* Berl. 2237/8.—4. *Risālat al-wujūd* ibid. 2326/7.—5. *Fī waḥdat al-wujūd*, on the unity of God, with a commentary entitled *al-Ẓill al-mamdūd* by ʿAbd al-Ghanī al-Nābulusī, d. 1143/1731 (p. 345), ibid. 2440.—6. *Nafaḥāt al-uns wa-ḥaḍarāt al-quds*, biographies of Sufis based on the *Ṭabaqāt al-Ṣūfiyya* of al-Sulamī (I, 218, 558), Persian edition, based on the translation into the dialect of Herat by ʿAbdallāh b. Muḥammad Anṣārī Harawī, by W. Nassau Lees, Calcutta 1859, Lucknow 1323, translated into Arabic by:
267 | a. Taqī (Tāj) al-Dīn ʿUthmān al-Naqshbandī, Paris 1370, whence an excursus on miracles, gifts of grace, and witchcraft, Berl. 4096.—b. Tāj al-Dīn b. Sulṭān al-ʿAbshamī, d. 1050/1640 (p. 419), Cairo ^{1}II, 75.—7. *Risāla fī bayān kalimat al-shahāda* Alex. Tawḥīd 18.—8. *al-Tiryāq li-ahl al-istiḥqāq* Alex. Ḥikma 24,$_1$,

40 sayings of the Prophet, each of which is explained by a half-verse, Ind. Off. 697,3.—9. *Risāla fī kalimat al-tawḥīd* Cairo [1]VII, 78, 576 (= 7?).—10. *Marātib ahl al-sulūk wal-kamāl wal-takmīl*, translated from Persian by an unidentified person, Cairo [1]VII, 378.—11. *al-Fawāʾid al-Ḍiyāʾiyya* ibid. I, 369.—12. *Sharḥ al-risāla al-waḍʿiyya*, p. 268.—13. *Sharḥ Fūṣūṣ al-ḥikam* Cairo I, 573.—14. *Sharḥ Naqsh al-Fuṣūṣ* ibid.—15.–18. see Suppl.

9. Shams al-Dīn Abū Thābit Muḥammad b. ʿAbd al-Malik al-Daylamī wrote, in 899/1493:

1. *Mirʾāt al-arwāḥ wa-ṣūrat al-awjāh*, an explanation of a representation symbolising the order of the world based on the ideas of the Sufis, from the highest region, the *ʿĀlam al-ḥayra wal-ʿilm al-majhūl*, to the deepest, the *Maḥall al-shayṭān taḥt al-arḍ*, Gotha 70,6.—2. *al-Jamʿ bayna ʾl-tawḥīd wal-taʿẓīm* ḤKh II, 622, 4183, [2]I, 601 (where authored before 699?).

| 9 *Philosophy* 208

1. Shams al-Dīn Muḥammad b. Yūsuf al-Zarandī, who died in 750/1349.

Bughyat al-murtāḥ fī ṭalab al-arbāḥ fī nuṣḥ al-salāṭīn wa-wulāt al-muslimīn wal-ḥukkām min al-rāghibīn lil-falāḥ Alex. Mawāʿiẓ 8.

1a. ʿAḍud al-Dīn ʿAbd al-Raḥmān b. Aḥmad al-Ījī, who died in 756/1355 (see Suppl.).

Khwandamīr, *ḤS* III,1, 125, Wüst. *Gesch.* 417. I. *Taḥqīq al-tafsīr fī takthīr al-tanwīr* Köpr. 50, Yeni 38, NO 370.

II. *Risāla fī ādāb al-baḥth*, on dialectic, Berl. 5293/4, Leid. 1552, Ind. Off. 586,2, Alex. Fun. 156,2, Qawala II, 293.—Commentaries: 1. al-Jurjānī, d. 816/1413 (p. 216), Berl. 5295, Alex. Fun. 107,7, 156,6, Qawala II, 308.—2. *al-Risāla al-Ḥanafiyya* by Muḥammad al-Tabrīzī al-Ḥanafī, d. 900/1494, Berl. 5296/7, Gotha 2811,i (where other MSS are listed), Pet. 235,3, | 239,3, Garr. 889/91, 268
Alex. Fun. 106,5, Qawala II, 312/3, Patna I, 229,2011.—Glosses by: a. Abu ʾl-Fatḥ Muḥammad b. Amīn al-Saʿīdī al-Ardabīlī, d. 950/1543 (see Suppl.), Berl. 5298/9, Gotha 2811,3 (where other MSS are listed), Pet. Ros. 197,1, Garr. 895, Cairo [1]VII, 138, Qawala II, 301/2. Superglosses: *α* Yaḥyā b. ʿUmar Minqārīzāde, d. 1088/1667, Berl. 5300, Pet. Ros. 197,2.—*β* ʿUmar b. Aḥmad Čillī, composed in 1122/1710, Berl. 5301, Garr. 896.—*γ* Ḥamza Efendi, composed in 1124/1712, ibid. 5302.—*δ* Muḥammad b. al-Ḥusayn al-Kurdī, ca. 1150/1737, ibid. 5303.—*ε* ʿAbdallāh b. Ḥaydar al-Kurdī al-Ḥusaynābādhī, ibid. 5304.—*ζ* Qara Khalīl b. Ḥasan al-Tīrawī,

ca. 947/1540, Qawala II, 299.—η Muḥammad b. al-Ḥājj Ḥumayd al-Kaffawī, ibid. 300.—ϑ Ismāʿīl b. Muṣṭafā b. Maḥmūd al-Kalanbawī Shaykhzāde (Suppl. II, 302_{n}, 1015, 18_{a}), ibid.—b. Muḥammad al-Bāqir, d. 1101/1689 (p. 411), Gotha 2817.—c. Muḥammad b. ʿAlī al-Ṣabbān, d. 1206/1791 (p. 288), Garr. 898, print. C. 1310.—d.–k. see Suppl. (d. Garr. 892, Makram 17. f. Shāh Aḥmad, Qawala II, 297).—l. Muḥammad b. Ibrāhīm al-Dalajī, Makram 20.—2a. ʿAbd al-ʿĀlī b. Muḥammad al-Barjandī, d. 911/1505, Suppl. II, 591, Qawala II, 309.—3. Ibrāhīm b. Muḥammad b. ʿArabshāh al-Isfarāʾinī ʿIṣām al-Dīn, d. 944/1537 (p. 410), Berl. 5505, Paris $4424_{,5}$, Garr. 894, Alex. Fun. $107_{,6}$, Ādāb al-b. $9_{,2}$, $11_{,5}$, Qaw. II, 309.—4. Muḥammad b. Maḥmūd al-Shaykh al-Bukhārī, Paris $4253_{,2}$.—5. Aḥmad b. Muḥammad al-Dardīr, d. 1201/1786, Berl. 5306.—6. Aḥmad al-Janadī, Gotha 2818, Garr. 897, Qaw. II, 308.—7.–12. see Suppl.—13. al-Masʿūdī, glosses by Mīr Abu ʾl-Fatḥ Muḥammad al-Ardabīlī, Makram 25 (or 20a?).—14. Ghiyāth al-Dīn Manṣūr b. Ṣadr al-Dīn al-Dashtakī al-Shīrāzī, d. 949/1542 (p. 414), MS in Najaf, *Dharīʿa* I, 14, 649.—15. Murshid b. Imām al-Shīrāzī, Qawala II, 308. Cf. Ahlw. 5307.

III. *al-Risāla al-waḍʿiyya al-ʿAḍudiyya*, on concepts and their linguistic articulation (cf. Fleischer, *ZDMG* 30, 487), in 10 lines, Berl. 5309, Krafft 400, Leid. 1552, Pet. 238, Garr. 872/3, Alex. Waḍʿ 2, Ādāb al-b. 7, $8_{,3}$, $11_{,2}$.—Commentaries: 1. al-Jurjānī (p. 216), Garr. 874, Alex. Ādāb al-b. $11_{,1}$, on which glosses by Muḥammad al-Shīranāsī, composed in 1016/1607, Br. Mus. 540.—2. ʿAlāʾ al-Dīn ʿAlī al-Qushjī, d. 879/1474 (p. 234), Berl. 5310/1, Pet. $169_{,3}$, $239_{,6}$, Garr. 875/8.—Glosses: a. Abu ʾl-Baqāʾ ʿAbd al-Bāqī al-Ḥusaynī al-Ḥanafī, ca. 1050/1640, Berl. 5312, Pet. $238_{,6}$, Garr. 879.—b. Anon., Garr. 880.—3. Abu ʾl-Qāsim al-Laythī al-Samarqandī (p. 247), composed in 888/1483, Berl. 5314,
269 Gotha 1213, Paris $4424_{,4}$, Esc. $^{2}687_{,2}$, Pet. $234_{,5}$, $238_{,2}$, Garr. 883.—Glosses: a. | Abu ʾl-Baqāʾ ʿAbd al-Bāqī al-Ḥusaynī al-Ḥanafī, ca. 1050/1640, Paris $4425_{,9}$, Qawala III, 3.—b. Muḥammad b. ʿArafa al-Dasūqī, d. 1230/1815 (p. 485), Garr. 882, Makram 19, print. Istanbul 1275, 1320.—c. Muḥammad b. Sālim al-Ḥifnāwī, d. 1181/1767 (p. 323), see Suppl. Alex. Waḍʿ 2.—d.–i. see Suppl. (f. superglosses by Ḥāfiẓ Sayyid Efendi, Istanbul 1259, 1267, 1272, 1285, 1305, Qawala II, 11/2).—4. Jāmī, d. 898/1492, Pet. $91_{,2}$, $239_{,8}$, Garr. 885.—5. ʿIṣām al-Dīn al-Isfarāʾinī, d. 944/1537 (p. 410), Berl. 5515/6, Leid. 1553, Alex. Waḍʿ 3, Fun. $172_{,3}$.—Glosses: a.–f. see Suppl. (b. Garr. 887.—f. completed in 968/1581, Qawala II, 13).—g. Ḥāfiẓ Sayyid Efendi, Qawala II, 12.—h. Muḥammad b. ʿArafa al-Dasūqī, d. 1230/1815, Alex. Waḍʿ 3, print. C. 1322.—i. Ḥasan b. Muḥammad al-ʿAṭṭār, d. 1250/1834, Alex. Waḍʿ 2.—k. Muḥammad b. Sālim al-Ḥifnāwī, d. 1181/1767 (p. 323), Berl. 5315, Garr. 881.—l. Anon., Paris $4424_{,1}$, $4425_{,8}$,—6. Muḥammad Saʿīd b. Muḥammad Amīr, Berl. 5317.—7. ʿAbdallāh b. Muḥammad al-Shubrāwī, d. 1117/1758 (p. 281), Berl. 5315, Paris $4424_{,5}$.—8. Muẓaffar al-Dīn Muḥammad Yazdī, Br. Mus.

421,$_{12}$.—9. Mollā Ḥājjī, ibid. 12.—10. Anon., Paris 4423/4,$_{2}$, Algiers 1400, Qawala II, 309.—11.–17. see Suppl. (11. on which glosses by Yūsuf al-Ḥifnāwī, d. 1178/1764, Alex. Ādāb al-b. 3. Versifications: a. with commentary by Muḥammad b. Aḥmad al-Bahūtī, Paris 4424,$_{6}$.—b. see Suppl.—c. Muḥammad b. ʿAlī al-Ḥamawī al-Ḥanafī, completed in 969/1562, Alex. Fun. 198,$_{4}$.—Cf. Ahlw. 5318.

IV. *Kitāb al-mawāqif fī ʿilm al-kalām*, Berl. 1800, Dresd. 397, Leid. 1551, Paris 2932, Br. Mus. 1614. *Statio quinta et sexta et appendiz libri Mevakif auctore Adhadeddin el Īğī cum cmt. Ǧorǧanii*, ed. Th. Sörensen, Leipzig 1848, print. Istanbul 1239 and others. Commentaries: 1. al-Jurjānī, d. 816/1413 (p. 216), Berl. 1801/2, | Leid. 1548/50, Ind. Off. 438/45, Paris 2393/4, Garr. 1492/5, Yeni 209
741/53, Cairo ^{1}II, 29, ^{2}I, 191, Qawala I, 195, print. Istanbul 1239, and elsewhere. Glosses: a. *ʿala ʾl-umūr al-ʿāmma*, by Ḥasan b. Muḥammad al-Fanārī, d. 886/1481 (p. 229), Berl. 1807/9, Ind. Off. 446/7, Yeni 738/40.—b. ʿAlāʾ al-Dīn al-Ṭūsī, d. 887/1482 (p. 261), Paris 1262,$_{1}$, Esc. ^{2}547,$_{6}$.—c. Fatḥallāh al-Shirwānī, d. 891/1496, Munich 677,$_{4}$, Ind. Off. 448, Esc. ^{2}691, 1500,$_{2}$.—d. Qarabālī, completed in 898/1492, Esc. ^{2}547.—e. Muḥammad b. Ibrāhīm Khaṭībzāde, d. 901/1495, ibid. 5.—f. al-Dawwānī, d. 907/1501 (p. 217), Leid. 1551, Esc. ^{2}695,$_{3}$, 706,$_{6}$.—g. ʿAbd al-Ḥakīm al-Siyālkūtī, d. 1060/1650 (p. 417), Ind. Off. | 449/50.—h. On the second 270
book, *al-Umūr al-ʿāmma* by Mīr Muḥammad Zāhid al-Harawī, d. 1101/1689 (p. 421), Ind. Off. 451/2, part 1 print. Lucknow 1263.—Superglosses: *α* Qāḍī Mubārak Muḥammad Dāʾim al-Fārūqī, d. 1162/1748, Ind. Off. 453.—*β–ο* see Suppl.—i. On the beginning of the second book by Mollā Ṣādiq, Ind. Off. 454.—k.–n. see Suppl.—2. Luṭfallāh al-Tūqātī, d. 900/1494 (p. 235). Abstract Esc. ^{2}237,$_{7}$.—3. Muʾayyadzāde, d. 922/1516 (p. 209), ibid. 236,$_{3}$.—4. Sayf al-Dīn al-Abharī, Yeni 748.—5. ʿAlī b. Muḥammad al-Nabīhī, Br. Mus. Suppl. 188, abstract Cairo ^{1}II, 12.—6. Anon., Berl. 1803/6, Paris 2395, 5128, Algiers 625.—7.–12. see Suppl. (8. Qawala I, 169, 12. ibid. 176, cf. 849, 2), cf. Ahlw. 1812.

V. *al-Risāla al-shāhiyya fī ʿilm al-akhlāq*, on psychology and ethics, Berl. 5396, NO 2347, Cairo ^{1}VII, 556, on which a commentary by Mufaḍḍal b. Muḥammad b. ʿAbd al-Raḥīm, d. 1129/1713 in Allāhābād, Manch. 426.

VI. *Jawāhir al-kalām* AS 2281, on which the commentary *Silk al-niẓām*, by Ibrāhīm al-Ḥalabī al-Ḥanafī, Qawala I, 191.

VII. *al-ʿAqāʾid al-ʿAḍudiyya* Br. Mus. Suppl. 1206,$_{3}$, Sarajevo 137,$_{8}$, Cairo ^{1}VII, 555.—Commentaries: 1. al-Dawwānī, d. 907/1501 (p. 217), Berl. 1999, Leid. 2026, Ind. Off. 455/8, 466,$_{1}$, Esc. ^{2}706, Garr. 1560, Sarajevo 137,$_{9}$, 161, Qawala I, 196/7, Mosul 130,$_{139}$, 158,$_{137}$, 169,$_{19}$, print. C. 1322. Kazan 1888 (*OB* III, 991). Glosses by: a. al-Khalkhālī, d. 1014/1605 (p. 413), Pet. 240, Cairo ^{1}II, 16, ^{2}I, 173, Qawala I, 168.—b. Mollā Yūsuf b. Muḥammad Jān al-Qarabāghī, d. 1036/1621 (on whose *Risāla fī ithbāt al-wājib* see Patna II, 422,$_{2592,5}$), Ind. Off. 459, Patna I, 118,$_{190/1}$, II, 559,$_{2937,5}$.—c. *Taʿlīqāt*, by Aḥmad b. Ḥaydar al-Kurdī, ca. 1070/1659, Cairo ^{1}II,

111.—d.–ii. see Suppl. (f. with glosses by al-Marghanī, al-Āsitāna 1327, Qawala I, 182.—g. at the end read: al-Sihālawī.—hh. Iftikhār al-Dīn Muḥammad al-Dāmaghānī, Sarajevo 156.)—kk. Ḥakīmshāh Muḥammad b. Mubārak al-Qazwīnī, d. ca. 902/1496, Alex. Tawḥīd 14.—ll. Muḥammad al-Ḥifnī, d. 1181/1767, Alex. Fun. $110_{,2}$.—mm. Niẓām al-Dīn Wālid ʿAbd al-ʿAlī Baḥr al-ʿUlūm, Patna I, $119_{,1197}$.—nn. Muḥammad b. ʿAbd al-ʿAzīz Fakhr al-Dīn, ibid. I, $119_{,1195}$.—oo. Muḥammad Sharīf b. Muḥammad al-Ḥusaynī, ibid. II, $425_{,2596/3}$.—pp. on the *Dībāja* by Muḥammad Amīn b. Taqī al-Dīn b. Abī Ḥāmid b. ʿĪmād al-Dīn b. Muḥammad b. Ismāʿīl al-Mawṣilī, completed in 1140/1727, Qawala I, 182.—2. al-Jurjānī, see Suppl.—3. Anon., Berl. 1998, Paris 1263.—4.–10. see Suppl.

VIII. *al-Mudkhal fī ʿilm al-maʿānī wal-bayān wal-badāʾiʿ* Cairo ^{1}IV, 45, ^{2}II, 218, IV, b. 29.

271 | IX. *al-Fawāʾid al-Ghiyāthiyya*, an abstract of the third part of *Miftāḥ al-ʿulūm* (I, 353), dedicated to Ghiyāth al-Dīn, the vizier of Sultan Muḥammad Khudābanda, Berl. 7252, Leid. 314.—Commentaries: 1. Ṭāshköprīzāde, d. 968/1560 (p. 425), Berl. 7253.—2. Muḥammad Sharīf al-Ḥusaynī, Gotha $2788_{,4}$, Br. Mus. Suppl. 988.—3.–5. see Suppl. (4. also Patna I, $181_{,1663}$).

X. *Ishrāq al-tawārīkh*, a history of the patriarchs, Muḥammad, and his companions, translated into Turkish by ʿAlī Efendi Muṣṭafā b. Aḥmad Čelebī, d. 1008/1599, with the title *Zubdat al-tawārīkh*, Vienna 857.

XI. *Sharḥ mukhtaṣar al-uṣūl* I, 372.

XII. see Suppl.

XIII. *al-Risāla al-ʿAḍudiyya fī ʾl-istiʿārāt* Alex. Fun. $189_{,13}$.

XIV. *al-Maqāla al-muqarrara fī taḥqīq al-kalām al-nafsī*, with a commentary by Ibn Kamālpāsha (p. 449), Alex. Fun. $152_{,3}$.

2. Quṭb al-Dīn Muḥammad b. Muḥammad al-Rāzī al-Taḥtānī, d. 766/1364 (see Suppl.), wrote:

1. *Laṭāʾif al-asrār* Cairo ^{1}VI, 67.—2. *Risāla fī ʾl-kulliyyāt wa-taḥqīqihā* Munich $308_{,5}$, Leid. 1555/6, Ind. Off. $586_{,7}$, Esc. $^{2}677_{,2}$, Patna II, $457_{,2631,1}$ (see Suppl. 12), Alex. Fals. 11.—3. *Risālat al-taṣawwur(āt) wal-taṣdīq(āt)* Leid. 554, Esc. ^{2}695.—Commentaries: a. Mīr Zāhid al-Harawī, d. 1101/1689 (p. 420), Ind. Off. 533, print. Lucknow (?) 1264, 1287 (Cairo ^{1}VI, 83). Glosses and b.—d., see Suppl.—4. *Risāla fī ʾl-nafs al-nāṭiqa* Leid. 1557.—5. *al-Muḥākama bayna l-imām wal-Naṣīr* I, 593.—6. *Sharḥ al-Risāla al-Shamsiyya* ibid. 612.—7. *Sharḥ maṭāliʿ al-anwār*
210 ibid. 614.—8. *Sharḥ al-Kashshāf* ibid. 345.—10.–13. see Suppl. |

3. Nūr al-Dīn Muḥammad b. al-Sayyid al-Sharīf (p. 216) al-Jurjānī, who died in 838/1484 in Shiraz.

Khwandamīr, *ḤS* III, 3, 147. 1. *al-Ghurra* (*al-gharrā'*) *fi 'l-manṭiq*, with a commentary by al-Ṣafawī, d. 953/1546, Paris 2397.—2. *Sharḥ irshād al-hādī* p. 215, 3a.—3. *Sharḥ Risālat al-uṣūl* ibid. 3, 10.—4. See Suppl.

4. Abū ʿAbdallāh Maḥmūd b. al-Najrānī (?Cat. Njdātī) al-Nīsābūrī wrote, in 858/1454:

Risāla qawsiyya fi 'l-manṭiq NO 3913.

| 5. Abū Isḥāq Ibrāhīm b. Muḥammad b. ʿAbdallāh b. Muḥammad al-Fārisī 272
wrote, in 883/1478:

Taḥrīr al-ḥaqq fi 'l-markaz AS 2391.

6. Ḥusayn b. Muʿīn al-Dīn al-Maybūdī was put to death for defending the Sunna in 904/1498. This happened in the presence of an Ottoman delegation, on the orders of Shāh Ismāʿīl.

ḤKh II, [1]499, III, 297, [2]I, 533, 802, Browne, *Lit. Hist.* IV, 57. 1. *Mukhtaṣar maqāṣid ḥikmat falāsifat al-ʿArab al-musammā* Jāmī Gētī numā: *Synopsis propositorum sapientiae Arabum philosophorum inscripta Speculum mundum repraesentans, ex. ar. sermone lat. juris facta ab* Abr. Ecchellensi, Paris 1641 (with Arabic text).—2.–7. see Suppl. (5. see I. 39, Suppl. I, 74, Fātiḥ 3954/5).—8. *Sharḥ al-Risāla al-Shamsiyya* I, 612.

7. Abū Ḥafṣ ʿUmar b. Muḥammad al-Ghaznawī, ca. 900/1494.

Risāla fi 'l-munāẓara Berl. 5322.

10 *Politics*

1. Aḥmad b. Maḥmūd al-Jīlī al-Iṣfahbadhī wrote, in 729/1329:

Minhāj al-wuzarā' fi 'l-naṣīḥa AS 2907.

2. Muḥammad b. al-Kāshgharī wrote, in 764/1363:

Tāj al-saʿāda fi 'l-naṣā'iḥ al-malakiyya AS 1690.

3. During the reign of Jahānshāh b. Qarā Yūsuf of the Qarā Qoyunlu dynasty (841–72/1437–67) an anonymous author wrote, in 856/1452:

Kawkab al-mulk wa-mawkib al-Turk, a work of administrative geography, focussing on Syria and Egypt, Gotha 1885.

211 | **11** ***Mathematics***

1. Ṣāʿid b. Muḥammad b. Muṣaddaq al-Ṣughdī Jamāl al-Dīn al-Turkistānī wrote, in 712/1312:

273 | *Al-ʿAlāʾiyya*, on arithmetic, Upps. 321, on which perhaps a commentary by Abu ʾl-Ḥasan ʿAlī b. Muḥammad b. ʿAlī b. Kaykhusraw al-Bahmanī, dedicated to Sultan Ghiyāth al-Dīn Abu ʾl-Muẓaffar Muḥammad Khān (799/1397 in Kulbarga, Lane-Poole 316 ?), Pet. Ros. $225_{,1}$ (858 AH).

2. Amīn al-Dīn al-Abharī, who died in 733/1333.

Fuṣūl kāfiya fī ḥisāb al-takht wal-mīl, on arithmetic on a writing board, Berl. 5975.

3. Abu ʾl-ʿAlāʾ Muḥammad b. Aḥmad al-Bihishtī al-Isfarāʾinī Fakhr (Qamar) Khurasān, ca. 908/1502.

1. *Mā lā budda lil-faqīh min al-ḥisāb* Br. Mus. $1346_{,2}$, Suppl. 610.—2 *Sharḥ al-Farāʾiḍ al-Sirājiyya* I, $470_{,26,I,3}$.—3. *Sharḥ al-Qaṣīda al-tarjīʿiyya* I, 293.—4. *Sharḥ Ādāb al-baḥth lil-Samarqandī* ibid. 616.—5. See Suppl.

4. Ghiyāth al-Dīn Jamshīd b. Masʿūd b. Maḥmūd al-Kāshī, ca. 830/1427 (see Suppl.):[1]

Khwandamīr, *ḤS* III, 3, $159_{,2}$. 1. *Miftāḥ al-ḥussāb fi ʾl-ḥisāb*, composed for Ulugh Beg, Berl. 5992, Leid. 1036, Br. Mus. 419, Ind. Off. 756, Pet. 131, Yeni 804, Patna I, $232_{,2027}$, II, $530_{,2854}$ (see *Qu. u. St.* VII, 6, I, 2).—An abstract, *Talkhīṣ al-Miftāḥ*, Ind. Off. 757, Patna II, $442_{,2618,3}$.—2. *al-Risāla al-Kamāliyya* or *Sullam al-samāʾ fī ḥall ishkāl fi ʾl-abʿād wal-ajrām* Leid. 1141, Ind. Off. 755, Bodl. I, 881, 4.—3.–14. see Suppl. (4. fragm. Mashh. XVIII, $33_{,102}$.—5=9=12).—15. *Sharḥ-i ālat-i raṣad*, composed in 848/1444, Leid. V, 327, 12.

1 The date of his death is often wrongly given as 887 or even 919.

5. Kamāl al-Dīn Abu 'l-Ḥasan al-Fārisī, d. ca. 720/1320, see Suppl.

Suter, 389. For commentaries on the writings of Ibn al-Haytham (I, 617) see Krause, *St. Hdss.* 508.—6. *Fi 'l-hāla wa-qaws quzaḥ* in Zanjān, *Lughat al-ʿArab* VI (1928) 93/6.

6. ʿImād al-Dīn Yaḥyā b. Aḥmad al-Kāshānī (Kāshī), ca. 744/1343, see Suppl.

Krause, *St. Hdss.* 17/8. 1. *Lubāb al-ḥisāb* also Köpr. I, 151, AS 2757.—3. Read: *Ḥall al-iʿtirāḍāt etc.* see Suppl. I, | 516.—5. *Īḍāḥ al-maqāṣid* see 216 § 9, 11, Suppl. 274
215.—6. *Risāla fī burhān al-masʾalatayn*, on two geometrical problems, Berl. Oct. 2978,$_2$, 13r/21v (dated 817 in Samarqand), ʿĀṭif 1714, 21. f. 224/33.—7. A translation of ʿIzz al-Dīn al-Zanjānī's (I, 336) treatise *Fī maʿrifat al-waqf al-tāmm* is in Zanjān, *Lughat al-ʿArab* VI, 94.

7. Al-Ṣalāḥī wrote, in 735/1334 (see Suppl.):

Mukhtaṣar al-Ṣalāḥī fi 'l-misāḥa, also Vat. Barb. 31, Ğārullah 1506, Kamankash 321, Serāi 3133, the commentary *al-ʿImādiyya*, by Shams al-Dīn Muḥammad al-Khaṭībī (ḤKh V, 444,$_{11612}$), Vat. Barb. 31,$_2$, Serāi 3133,$_2$.

12 *Astronomy*

1. Quṭb al-Dīn Maḥmūd b. Masʿūd b. Muṣliḥ al-Shīrāzī was a student of Naṣīr al-Dīn al-Ṭūsī (I, 670) who died in Tabriz on 4 Ramaḍān 710/26 January 1311.

Khwandamīr *ḤS* III, I, 67, 112.[1] 1. *Nihāyat al-idrāk fī dirāyat al-aflāk* Berl. 5682, Leid. 1106, Paris 2517/8, Br. Mus. 399, Bodl. I, 924, Köpr. 956, Bursa, Hü. Celebi, Heyet 19.—On the basis of this an anonymous author wrote *Fī ḥarakat al-daḥraja wal-nisba bayna 'l-mustawī wal-munḥanī*, on which he himself again wrote explanatory notes, Gotha 1158,$_{18}$,—Abstract Ind. Off. 769,$_3$.—2. *al-Tuḥfa al-Shāhiyya fi 'l-hayʾa* Leid. 1105, Paris 2516, Br. Mus. 398, 1344, Bodl. I, 891, 924, 102,$_2$, AS 2584, Köpr. 928, Patna I, 234,$_{2039}$.—Commentary by ʿAlī al-Qūshjī, d. 879 (p. 305), AS 2643, Cairo ¹V, 223.—3. *Kitāb faʿaltu fa-lā talum fi 'l-hayʾa* AS 2668.—4. *al-Tabṣira fi 'l-hayʾa* NO 2890.—5. *Sharḥ al-Tadhkira al-Nāṣiriyya*, I, 675.—6. *al-Tuḥfa al-Saʿdiyya sharḥ kulliyyāt al-Qānūn* I, 597.—7. *Sharḥ al-Qānūn* ibid.—8. *Risāla fī bayān al-ḥāja ila 'l-ṭibb wa-ādāb al-aṭibbāʾ wa-waṣāyāhum* Cairo ¹VI, 35.—9. *Risāla fi 'l-baraṣ*, on leprosy, Berl. 6360.—10. *Sharḥ Ḥikmat al-ishrāq* I, 565.—11. *Durrat al-tāj li-ghurrat al-dubāj fi 'l-ḥikma* Köpr. 867 (see

1 Appears to take the authors of 6 and 9 to be different persons.

Suppl.), from which a single *juzʾ* is in Aligarh $3_{,1}$, $10_{,2}$.—12. *Fatḥ al-mannān fī*
275 *tafsīr al-Qurʾān* Cairo ^{1}I, 186.—13. *Fī mushkilāt* | *al-Qurʾān* Yeni 149.—14.–30. see Suppl. (22=30 completed in Shaʿbān 681, see Zanjān, *Lughat al-ʿArab* VI, 216).

1b. Muḥammad Ibrāhīm b. Mubārakshāh Shams al-Dīn Mīrak al-Bukhārī, d. ca. 840/1340, see Suppl.

1. *Sharḥ Ḥikmat al-ʿayn* Suppl. I, 847.—2. *Sharḥ al-Tabṣira lil-Kharaqī* ibid. I, 863.—3. *al-Zīj al-muḥaqqiq al-sulṭānī ilā raṣd al-Ilkhānī*, dedicated to the Ilkhānid Bahādur Khān, see Krause, *St. Hdss.* 518/9 (which has Abu ʾl-Ḥasan Shams al-Munajjim al-Wābiknawī, as does ḤKh III, $566_{,6950}$, ^{2}II$_{969}$).—7. *Maʿrifat-i asṭurlāb-i shimālī* Serāi $3327_{,4}$, composed in 703.

2. Mūsā b. Muḥammad b. Maḥmud al-Rūmī Qāḍīzāde, the youngest son of the *qāḍī* of Bursa, studied in Persia, Khurāsān, and Mā warāʾ al-nahr, succeeded Ghiyāth al-Dīn Jamshīd (§11, 4) at the observatory in Samarqand, and died in 815/1412.

Khwandamīr, *ḤS* III, 3, 159, *ShN* I, 78, Suter 430, *Nachtr.* 178, Ṣāliḥ Zaki Bey *Āthār-i bāqiye*, Istanbul 1910, I, 190 (see *Isis* 19, 1933, p. 506), Abdulhakk Adnan, *La science chez les Turcs ott.* 12/4, Ilim 4/5. 1. *Sharḥ Kitāb al-Jaghmīnī* I, 624.—2. *Sharḥ Ashkāl al-taʾsīs* ibid. 616.—3. *Sharḥ al-Tadhkira al-Nāṣiriyya* I, 675.—4. A mathematical treatise with a commentary, Berl. 5948.—5. *Sharḥ Taḥrīr al-Mijisṭī* I, 674.—6. *Sharḥ Ḥikmat al-ʿayn* Suppl. I, 847, II, 1f.

3. Ulughbeg b. Shāhrukh b. Tīmūr, the oldest son of Shāhrukh, was born in al-Sulṭāniyya in 796/1394. His father appointed him governor of Mā warāʾ al-nahr. He lived in Samarqand, where he ordered the construction of a large observatory. After the death of his father and his victory over his nephew and rival ʿAlāʾ al-Dawla he acceded to the throne in Herat in 852/1448, but was executed the following year by his son Mirzā ʿAbd al-Laṭīf.

Khwandamīr, *ḤS* III, 3, 151, Burckhardt in *Zachs Ephem*, 1799, III, 179, Quatremère, *Journal des Sav.* 1847, 562.

276 | Audiffret, *Biogr. univ.* XXXII, 26ff., Delambre, *Hist. de l'astr.* 204, Price,
213 *Retrospect* III, 566/73, A. Müller, *Der Islam* II, 316. | 1. *Zīj-i jadīd-i sulṭānī*, a work on astronomical tables he started on the order of Jamshīd (§ 11, 4), continued under Qāḍīzāde (§ 12, 2), and completed under Ibn al-Qūshjī (p. 305), Berl. Pers. 387/8, Br. Mus. II, 455b, translated into Arabic by Yaḥyā b. ʿAlī al-Zamāʿī

(Rifāʿī?), Paris 2534/6, AS 2693, Pertew P. 376, Faiẓ. 1340, Rāġib 920, Yaḥyā Ef. 246, Ḥamīd. 844, ʿĀšir Reʾīs 571, ʿĀšir Ḥafīd 195, Welīeddīn 2284,$_3$, Yeni 783, Bešīr Āġā (Sül.) 427, ʿĀṭif 1705, NO 2932, Serāi Revān Köshk 1714, Ğārullāh 1478, Asʿad 993, ʿUm. 4612, Alex. Ḥurūf 14 (*Faṣl* 4), Cairo ^{1}V, 261, Qawala II, 279, Garr. 981; ed. L. Sédillot, *Prolégomènes des Tables astronomiques d'Ouloug Beg*, Paris 1847, transl. and comm. 1853.—Commentaries: a. Persian by ʿAbd al-ʿĀlī b. Muḥammad b. Ḥusayn al-Barjandī, d. after 930/1524 (Suppl. 591), Br. Mus. Pers. II, 457.—b.–d. see Suppl.—e. ʿAlī Qūshjī, d. 879/1474 (p. 234), Rāġib 928, Rasadhanekütüb 113.—a. *Nahj al-bulūgh* by Aḥmad Miṣrī, composed in 1158/1745, Smyrna Milli Kütüb ph. 50/726, 21/672, Adnan, Ilim 167.—Adaptations: a. *Tashīl al-Ṣāliḥī* or *al-Durr al-naẓīm fī tashīl al-taqwīm* by Zayn al-Dīn ʿAbd al-Raḥmān al-Ṣāliḥī al-Dimashqī (see Suppl.), Garr. 995.—b. *Tashīl Zīj Ulughbeg* by Shams al-Dīn Muḥammad b. Abi ʾl-Fatḥ al-Miṣrī al-Ṣūfī, ninth cent., Alex. Ḥisāb 45, with the title *Taqwīm al-kawākib al-sabʿa* ibid. 46.—Turkish translation by ʿAbd al-Raḥmān b. ʿUthmān, which was made in Cairo, Istanbul (Univ. Heyet 19, Adnan 167).

13 *Medicine*

1. Abu ʾl-Faḍl al-Ḥusayn b. Ibrāhīm al-Mutaṭabbib al-Tiflīsī wrote, before 738/9 (1337/8), the date of the manuscript:

Majmūʿat al-rasāʾil al-ṭibbiyya, totalling nine, Garr. 1108.

2. Nafīs b. ʿIwaḍ al-Kirmānī, the personal physician of Ulughbeg.

Khwandamīr, *ḤS* III, 3, 159,$_5$, Wüst., *Ärzte* 106. 1. *Sharḥ al-Asbāb wal-ʿalāmāt*, composed in 827/1424, see Suppl. I, 895.—2.–4. see Suppl.

3. ʿAlāʾ al-Dīn ʿAlī b. al-Ḥusayn b. ʿAlī al-Bayhaqī wrote, in 912/1506:

| 1. *Tarwīḥ al-arwāḥ li-taṣḥīḥ al-ashbāḥ*, on dietetics, Berl. 6403.—2. *Maʿdin* 277
al-nawādir fī maʿrifat al-jawāhir, composed in 915/1508, AS 3743.

14 *Encyclopaedias and Polyhistors*

1. ʿUbaydallāh b. Masʿūd b. Tāj al-Sharīʿa Maḥmūd b. Ṣadr al-Sharīʿa Aḥmad (I, 473) b. Jamāl al-Dīn b. ʿUbaydallāh b. Ibrāhīm b. Aḥmad al-Maḥbūbī al-Bukhārī al-Ḥanafī, who died in 747/1347 (see Suppl.).

Ibn Quṭl. 118, Flügel, *Classen* 277, 324, Krafft, *Wien. Jahrb.* 90, p. 27. 1. *Taʿdīl al-ʿulūm*, an encyclopaedia of philosophy and the natural sciences, with a

self-commentary, Berl. 5096, Vienna 7, Ind. Off. 522, AS 2198/9, NO 2657/9, Cairo ^{1}VI, 161, whence *Risāla fī 'l-jabr wal-qadar* Alex. Fiqh Ḥan. 59$_{,6}$.—2. *Taʿdīl hayʾat al-aflāk*, an astronomical compendium with a self-commentary, Berl. 5683 (where it is wrongly referred to as *Taʿdil al-ʿulūm*), Br. Mus. 400.—3. *Tanqīḥ al-uṣūl*, Berl. 4393, Gotha 933 (where other MSS are listed).—Commentaries: a. Self-commentary, *Tawḍīḥ fī ḥall ghawāmiḍ al-Tanqīḥ*, Gotha 933 (where other MSS are listed), Paris 796, 6345/6, Algiers 973, Ind. Off. 319/21, Br. Mus. Suppl. 264, Garr. 1638/41, AS 954/8, 1463/6, Alex. Uṣūl 6, Cairo ^{1}II, 243, 261, ^{2}I, 381, Mosul 24$_{,26}$, 61$_{,164}$, 93$_{,7}$, 121$_{,4}$, 167$_{,38}$, 208$_{,19}$, 226$_{,17/8}$.—b. *al-Talwīḥ fī kashf ḥaqāʾiq al-Tanqīḥ* by al-Taftāzīnī (no. 2), Berl. 4394/5, Gotha loc. cit., Paris 797, Ind. Off. 1367/72, Garr. 1642/3, 1722, Yeni 311/6, NO 1297/1302, Cairo ^{1}II, 242, 261, ^{2}I, 381, Qawala I, 276, Mosul 61$_{,162}$, 121$_{,273}$, 197$_{,121}$, 241$_{,253}$, printed together with the *Tanqīḥ* and the *Tawḍīḥ* Delhi 1267, Lucknow 1281, 1287, with the *Tawḍīḥ* Kazan 1301, 1311.—Glosses by: *α* His great-grandson Sayf al-Dīn (p. 284), Ind. Off. 1476, Rāġib 374, Bank. XIX, 1523, Rāmpūr I, 269/30.—*αα* Mawlānāzāde ʿUthmān al-Khiṭāʾī, d. 917/1511 (ḤKh I, 407), Berl. 4396, Basle M. III, 31$_{,2}$, Ind. Off. 1473.—*β* Mollā Khusraw, d. 885/1490 (p. 292), Cairo ^{1}II, 263.—*γ* Ḥasan al-Fanārī, d. 884/1481 (p. 297), Berl. 4397, Ind. Off. 325, 1474, Algiers 974, Yeni 319/20, Cairo ^{1}II, 245, Qawala I, 284, print. Istanbul 1284.—*δ* al-Ṭūsī (ʿAlāʾ al-Dīn, d. 887/1282?), Esc. ^{2}547$_{,9}$.—*ε* Zakariyyāʾ al-Anṣārī, d. 926/1520 (p. 122), Cairo ^{2}II, 263.—*ζ* Anonymous, dedicated to Sultan Sulaymān b. Selīm, d. 975/ 1567, Berl. 4398.—*η* ʿIṣām al-Dīn al-Isfarāʾinī, d. 944/1537 (p. 410), Basle M
278 III, 31$_{,3}$, with superglosses by | Muḥammad Sayrīzāde, dedicated to Aḥmad Pāshā, the vizier of Sultan Meḥmed III (r. 1003–12/1594–1603), Gotha 70$_{,9}$.—*ϑ* ʿAbd al-Ḥakīm al-Siyālkūtī (p. 417), d. 1067/1656, Ind. Off. 326, Cairo ^{1}II, 261.—*ι* ʿAbdallāh Labīb, Ind. Off. 327.—*ϰ* Anon. ibid. 328, under the title *Kulliyyāt Tanqīḥ al-uṣūl*, Qawala I, 294.—*λ–Φ* see Suppl. (*ρ*=*Φ*=*α*).—*χ* Aḥmad b. ʿAbdallāh al-Qrīmī, d. 850/1446, or, according to others, 862/1458, Alex. Uṣūl 7.—c. *al-Tawḍīḥ* by al-Jurjānī, d. 816/1413 (no. 3), only on the beginning of the *Talwīḥ*, ḤKh ^{1}II, 445$_{,3074}$, Basle M, III, 31$_{,1}$, Cairo ^{1}II, 243.—d. See Suppl. (e. delete see I, 646).—f. al-Dawwānī (p. 281), Mosul 226$_{,256}$.—g. An adaptation, *Taghyīr al-Tanqīḥ*, by Ibn Kamālpāshā, d. 940/1533 (p. 449), Paris 798, AS 950, Qawala I, 275.—Supplement by Abu 'l-Suʿūd, d. 982/1574 (p. 439), composed in 939/1532, Pet. 81$_{,18}$.—4. *al-Muqaddimāt al-arbaʿ*, a section from the *Tanqīḥ* against the Ashʿaris, commentaries: a. Ismāʿīl b. Muḥammad b. Muṣṭafā al-Qūnawī, d. 1195/1781, Vienna 1539.—b. *Ḥāshiyat al-uṣūl wa-ghāshiyat al-fuṣūl* by Abu 'l-Nāfiʿ Aḥmad b. Muḥammad b. Isḥāq al-Qāzābādī, Qawala I, 280.—5. *Arbaʿūna ḥadīthan* Cairo ^{1}VII, 601.—6. *Sharḥ al-Wiqāya* I, 468.—7. *al-Nuqāya* I, 469.—8. See Suppl.—9. *al-Ḥawāshī wal-nikāt wal-fawāʾid al-muḥarrarāt ʿalā Mukhtaṣar al-maʿānī* Mosul 115$_{,236}$.—10. *al-Wishāḥ fī ḍabṭ maʿāqid al-Miftāḥ*,

on which a commentary, *Ḥall al-Wishāḥ*, by ʿAbd al-Raḥmān b. Abī Bakr b. Muḥammad b. al-ʿAynī, d. 893/1488 (p. 250, 253), Garr. 553.—11. *Fī ʿilm al-ṣarf* Mosul $107_{,22}$, $138_{,76}$.—For his son, see below p. 253.

| 2. Saʿd al-Dīn Masʿūd (Maḥmūd) b. ʿUmar al-Taftāzānī, who was born in 215
Taftāzān near Nasā in Ṣafar 722/March 1322, was a professor in Sarakhs, before being moved to Samarqand by Tīmūr. He died in 791/1389, 792, or perhaps as late as 797.

Khwandamīr, *ḤS* III, 3, 87. An inventory of his writings is in Berl. $17_{,1}$, 1959 (including dates of composition). 1. *Tahdhīb al-manṭiq wal-kalām* Berl. 5174/5, Gotha 1193 (where other MSS are listed), Paris $1013_{,6}$, $1396_{,4}$, 6293, Ind. Off. $582_{,10}$, 588, NO 2720, Alex. Fun. $107_{,8}$, Cairo ^{1}VI, 78, VII, 67, ^{2}I, 225, Patna I, $217_{,1929,39}$, lith. Lucknow n.d., with a Persian commentary ibid. 1869.—Commentaries and glosses: a. al-Kāfiyajī, d. 879/1474, Munich $673_{,2}$, Ind. Off. 538.—b. His great-grandson, Aḥmad b. Yaḥyā (p. 284), Gotha $87_{,1}$, 88.—c. al-Dawwānī, d. 907/1401 (p. 281), Berl. 5176/7, Gotha 1194 (something else), where other MSS are listed, Alex. Manṭiq 17, | Cairo ^{1}VI, 61, 73, Qawala II, 362/3, print. Lucknow (?) 279
1264.—Glosses: *α* Mīr Abu ʾl-Fatḥ Saʿīdī (under Dawlat Girāy from the Crimea, 958–85/1551–77), Ind. Off. 543, 553, Pet. $84_{,2}$, Yeni 778, Garr. 851, $2080_{,1}$, Qawala II, 351/2, on which *Taʿlīqāt* by al-Kalanbuwī (see Suppl.), al-Āsitāna 1300, 1313, Qawala II, 348/9.—*β* Mīr Zāhid al-Harawī, d. 1101/1689 (Suppl. 621), Ind. Off. 544.—Superglosses (see Suppl.) by: *αα* Faḍl Imām b. Muḥammad Arshad, Patna II, $528_{,2841}$.—*γ* ʿAbdallāh b. al-Ḥusayn al-Yazdī, d. 1015/1606, Ind. Off. 545/6, 589, Br. Mus. Suppl. 735.—*δ* al-Khalkhālī, Pet. $240_{,3}$, Qawala II, 332/3.—d. ʿAlī b. Muḥammad al-Shīrāzī, d. 922/1522, Br. Mus. $1583_{,2}$.—e. ʿAbdallāh b. al-Ḥusayn Najm al-Dīn b. Shihāb al-Dīn al-Yazdī, d. 1015/1606, completed in 967/1559, Berl. 5179/80, Ind. Off. 547/51, Pet. $94_{,3}$, Garr. 852, Qawala II, 367, print. Calcutta 1243, n.p. 1292.—Glosses by ʿAbd al-Raḥmān al-Hindī, ca. 1100/1688, Berl. 5181, Leningr. AM 1926, no. 3.—f. *Tahdhīb al-manṭiq al-shāfī* by ʿUbaydallāh b. Faḍlallāh al-Khabīṣī Fakhr al-Dīn, ca. 1050/1640, Berl. 5182/3, Paris $1396_{,5}$, 2396, Algiers 1406, Leid. 1558, Qawala II, 326, Makram 10.—Glosses (see Suppl.) by: (*α* Qawala II, 341, *δ* C. 1328).—g. al-Ujhūrī, d. 1066/1655 (p. 328), Algiers 1405.—h. al-Kalanbuwī (see above), Istanbul 1234.—i. Pīr ʿAlī b. Ḥasan al-Tūnī, Pet. Ros. $225_{,3}$.—k. ʿAbd al-Ḥayy b. ʿAbd al-Wahhāb al-Ḥusaynī, ca. 930/1524, Leid. 1561.—l. al-Marʿashī Walījānī, Algiers $1047_{,1}$.—m. Shāh Fatḥallāh Shirwānī, Ind. Off. $553_{,4}$.—n. Sayyid Shāh Mīr, ibid. 5.—o. Aḥmad b. Sulaymān, ibid. 8, $558_{,3}$.—p. ʿImād al-Dīn, ibid. $553_{,7}$, $588_{,4}$.—q. Zayn al-ʿĀbidīn b. Yūsuf al-Kūrānī, Paris $2351_{,3}$.—r. Persian by Jamāl al-Dīn Muḥammad al-Ḥusaynī al-Shahrastānī, Leid. 1560.—s.-ee. See Suppl.—ff. *Tahdhīb al-Tahdhīb* by Muḥammad Yaʿqūb

al-Banbānī, d. after 1081/1670, Patna I, $115_{,1154}$.—gg. *Tuḥfat al-labīb*, on the *kalām* part, by Ḥāfiẓ b. ʿAlī al-ʿImādī, Qawala I, 163.—hh. ʿAlī b. Aḥmad al-Qustanṭīnī, eleventh cent., Qawala I, 193.—ii. *Sharḥ qism al-kalām* by Burhān al-Dīn Lār Muḥammad al-Ḥusaynī al-Pattanī al-Hindī, completed in 1015/1606, Indian print 1312.—kk. *Takhrīj aḥādīth sharḥ ʿAqāʾid al-Taftāzānī* by al-Suyūṭī, Alex. Fun. $155_{,2}$.—Versification see Suppl. *Sharḥ Naẓm muwajjahāt T. al-m.* by Ibn Manṣūr al-Manūfī al-Azharī, completed in 1090/1679, Alex. Manṭiq 17.—2. *Sharḥ Taṣrīf al-Zangānī* I, 336.—4. *al-Tarkīb al-jalīl*, on syntax, with a commentary entitled *Tartīb jamāl*, by Dabbāghzāde Muḥammad Efendi, ca. 280 1100/1688, Berl. 6757, Vienna 208.—5. *Tarkīb gharīb wa-tartīb ʿajīb*, on the | main points of syntax, in one sentence, Berl. 6880.—6. *Baḥth al-mushtarak* Paris $4187_{,1}$.—7. *Sharḥ Talkhīṣ al-Miftāḥ*, completed in Ṣafar 748/May 1347 in Herat, 216 with an abstract that was completed in 756/1355 in Ghujduwān, see I, 354. |—8. *Sharḥ al-qism al-thālith min al-Miftāḥ*, completed in Shawwāl 789/October–November 1387, ibid. 353.—9. *Sharḥ al-Risāla al-Shamsiyya*, completed in Jumādā II 762/April 1360 in Mazārjām, I, 612.—10. *Maqāṣid al-ṭālibīn fī uṣūl al-dīn* (*fi ʾl-kalām*), completed in Dhu ʾl-Qaʿda 784/January 1383 in Samarqand, with a self-commentary, Ind. Off. 461, Garr. 2150, NO 2215, AS 2364/5, Köpr. 854/5, Algiers 626, Cairo [1]II, 26, 2 I, 191, Qawala I, 201, Makram 57, print. Istanbul 1277, 1305. Anonymous commentary, Paris 1265.—11. *Sharḥ ʿAqāʾid al-Nasafī*, completed in Shaʿbān 768/April 1367 in Khwārizm, I, 548.—12. *Sharḥ al-Kashshāf*, completed in Samarqand, I, 346.—13. *al-Miftāḥ*, a compendium on Shāfiʿī law, Berl. 4604.—14. *Sharḥ Sharḥ al-Mukhtaṣar fi ʾl-uṣūl*, completed in Dhu ʾl-Ḥijja 770/July 1369 in Khwārizm, I, 372.—15. *al-Talwīḥ*, completed in Dhu ʾl-Qaʿda 758/November 1357 in Gulistāni Turkistān, p. 277.—16. *al-Radd wal-tashnīʿ* I, 573.—17. *Sharḥ Nawābigh al-kalim* I, 349.—18.–21. see Suppl.—22. *Dalālāt*(?) Alex. Manṭiq 13.

3. ʿAlī b. Muḥammad al-Jurjānī al-Sayyid al-Sharīf, d. 816/1413, see Suppl.

Khwandamīr, *ḤS* II, 3, 89, de Sacy, *Not. et Extr.* X, 4ff, Suter 424, ʿAbd al-Qādir Sarfarāz, Cat. Bombay 78. An inventory of his writings is given in Berl. $17_{,2}$. 1. *Risāla fī taqsīm al-ʿulūm* Ind. Off. $585_{,1}$.—2. *Taʿrīfāt*, on definitions, Berl. 5378/9, Leid. 84/7 (where other MSS are listed), Garr. 1578, $235_{,141}$, AS 3823 ter (not in the defter), Qawala I, 1/2, Mosul $25_{,48}$, ed. Flügel, Leipzig 1845, print. Istanbul 1253, 1265, C. 1283, 1306, among others, St. Petersburg 1897.—A supplement, *al-Tawqīf ʿalā muhimmāt al-Taʿārīf*, was written by ʿAbd al-Raʾūf al-Munāwī, d. 1031/1622 (p. 306), Paris 4262.—3. *Maqālīd al-ʿulūm fi ʾl-ḥudūd wal-rusūm*, definitions of technical terms from 21 sciences, Br. Mus. Suppl. 715.—4. *Taḥqīq al-kulliyyāt*,

definitions of the universal, Berl. 5134.—5. *Marātib al-mawjūdāt*, stations in
the chain of creatures, ibid. 5135.—6. *Risāla fī taḥqīq nafs al-amr*, definitions of the nature of a thing and how this differs from its external appearance, ibid. 5185.—7. *Risāla fī qawāʿid al-baḥth* (*ʿilm ādāb al-munāẓara*) Alex.
| Fun. $86,_{11}$, Patna I, $228,_{2008}$.—Commentaries: a. *al-Ādāb al-bāqiya* by ʿAbd 281
al-Bāqī b. Ghawth al-Islām al-Ṣiddīqī, d. 1084/1673, composed in 1060/1650,
Berl. 5321, Ind. Off. 554/7.—b. see Suppl.—c. *al-Rashīdiyya* by ʿAbd al-Rashīd
al-Jawnfūrī, d. 1083/1672 (p. 420), Ind. Off. 558.—8. *al-Risāla al-waladiyya fi
'l-manṭiq*, originally in Persian, Bodl. Pers. 1455, translated by his son Muḥammad
(p. 271), Gotha 1195, Munich $608,_{2}$, Pet. $106,_{7}$, Cairo ^{1}VII, 106.—9. *al-Risāla
al-ḥarfiyya fī maʿāni 'l-ḥarf* Munich $308,_{6}$, Ind. Off. $586,_{9}$, Garr. 900, Cairo ^{1}VII,
590, 600.—10. *Riṣala fi 'l-uṣūl*, with a commentary by his son Muḥammad, Esc.
$^{2}673,_{2}$.—11. *Fī taḥqīq al-mabāḥith al-mawjūdiyya wal-maqāṣid al-uṣūliyya*,
Persian Munich Ar. 659, f. 107, Pers. 61, Arabic by Kamāl al-Dīn al-Nīsābūrī,
translated in 876/1471, Gotha $1930,_{2}$, Munich 659.—12. *al-Shāfī fi 'l-fiqh* AS
1200/1. |—13. *Mukhtaṣar uṣūl al-ḥadīth* Patna I, $36,_{367}$.—14. Two treatises, on 217
free will and on cause and effect, Br. Mus. $909,_{5}$.—15. 24 verses in praise of
virtuous self-sufficiency, Berl. 7883.—16. *Sharḥ al-Kashshāf* I, 346.—17. *Sharḥ
al-qism al-thālith min al-Miftāḥ* I, 353.—18. *Sharḥ al-Sharḥ al-Muṭawwal* I,
354.—19. *Sharḥ Sharḥ Mukhtaṣar al-uṣūl* I, 372.—20. *Sharḥ Mishkāt al-maṣābīḥ*
I, 449.—21. *Sharḥ al-Farāʾiḍ al-Sirājiyya* I, 379.—22. *al-Tawḍīḥ, sharḥ al-Tanqīḥ*
p. 277.—23. *Sharḥ Ādāb al-baḥth lil-Ījī* p. 268.—24. *Sharḥ al-Risāla al-waḍʿiyya*
ibid.—25. *Sharḥ Kitāb al-Jaghmīnī* I, 624.—26. *Sharḥ Sharḥ al-Risāla al-Shamsiyya* I, 612.—27. *Sharḥ Sharḥ Ḥikmat al-ʿayn* I, 613.—28. *Sharḥ Sharḥ Maṭāliʿ
al-anwār* ibid. 614.—29. *Sharḥ Jawāhir al-farāʾiḍ al-Nāṣiriyya* I, 670.—30. *Sharḥ
al-Sharḥ al-qadīm* ibid.—31. *Sharḥ al-Tadhkira al-Naṣīriyya* I, 675.—32.–44. See
Suppl.—45. *Dalāʾil al-iʿjāz* Qawala II, 155.—46. *Risāla fī ʿadam kawn afʿāl Allāh
subḥānahu wa-taʿālā muʿallala bil-aghrāḍ* Alex. Fun. $86,_{9}$.—47. *Risāla fī taḥqīq
al-wāqiʿ etc.* Qawala II, 385.

4. Jalāl al-Dīn Muḥammad b. Asʿad al-Dawwānī al-Ṣiddīqī, who was born in
830/1427 in Dawwān, in the district of Kāzarūn, where his father was a *qāḍī*,
passed himself off as a descendant of the caliph Abū Bakr while at the same
time professing twelver Shīʿism. In Shiraz he worked as the *qāḍī* of Fārs and as
a professor at the Madrasat al-Aytām. | He died near Kāzarūn in 907/1501 (or, 282
according to others, in 908).

Khwandamīr, *ḤS* II, 4, 111, Rieu, *Pers. Cat.* II, 442b, *Thabt* Alex. Fun. $88,_{5}$. 1.
Unmūdhaj al-ʿulūm, on problems in all kinds of sciences, and which contains

a list of his teachers, dedicated to the Ottoman Sultan Maḥmūd, Berl. 72/4, Cairo ^{1}VII, 617, ^{2}VI, 181, *Dharīʿa* II, 406/7,$_{1627}$, Patna II, 421,$_{2592}$. A discussion of the geometrical problem set out in the *Unmūdhaj*, Berl. 5950.—2. *Taʿrīf al-ʿilm* Cairo ^{1}VII, 73.—3. Treatise on 3 questions concerning *ḥadīth* and the principles of law, Berl. 296.—4. *Risāla fī masāʾil al-funūn* (*al-masāʾil al-ʿashr*) Vienna 12, Leid, 1572.—5. *Risāla fi ʾl-taṣawwuf* Patna II, 489,$_{2650,10}$.—6. *Tafsīr sūrat al-Fātiḥa* Berl. 944, Sarajevo 28,$_{1}$.—7. *Risāla fī īmān Firʿawn Mūsā*, after sura 10,$_{90}$, Berl. 2111, 2391,$_{1}$, Leid. 2049, Alex. Fun. 86,$_{7}$, Garr. 2197, Cairo ^{1}VII, 632.—A commentary, *Farr al-ʿawn mimman yaddaʿī īmān Firʿawn*, by al-Qāriʾ al-Harawī, d. 1014/1605 (p. 394), Berl. 2112/3, Munich 886 f. 181, Rāmpūr I, 303,$_{211}$, Āṣaf. I, 610,$_{269}$, to which an addition in Berl. 2114/5.—8. *Sharḥ ʿalā qawl al-shaykh al-akbar etc.* Alex. Fun. 126,$_{3}$.—9. *al-Tashbīh fi ʾllāhumma ṣalli ʿalā Muḥammad* Berl. 2291, Vienna 1791,$_{21}$.—10. *Risāla fī tawjīh al-tashbīh alladhī taḍammanahu lafẓ kamā taṣallayta ʿalā Ibrāhīm* Leid. 2048, Alex. Fun. 64,$_{3}$.—11. *Risālat ithbāt al-wājib* (*al-wāḥid*) *al-qadīma*, a proof of the necessary existence of God, Berl. 2328/30, Leid. 1575, Esc. ^{2}1839,$_{1}$, AS 2275, NO 2089/90, Alex. Tawḥīd 35, Cairo ^{1}VII, 377, ^{2}I, App. 21, Qawala I, 184, II, 379, Najaf *Dharīʿa* I, 106/7,$_{521}$, Mosul 96,$_{59}$, 109,$_{133,1}$.—Commentaries and glosses: a. Muḥammad b. ʿAlī al-Qarabāghī, d. 942/1535, Vienna 1791,$_{16}$.—b. Muḥammad al-Mollā al-Ḥanafī, d. ca. 900/1494, Berl. 2331/2, Alex. Tawḥīd 35, Qawala I, 201, superglosses by Ḥabīballāh Mīrzājān al-Shīrāzī, d. 994/1586 (p. 414), Berl. 2333, NO 2102/4, Alex. Tawḥīd 35, Qawala I, 182.—c. Anonymous, dedicated to Rustan Pāshā, d. 968/1560, Berl. 2334.—d. Anonymous, dedicated to Sultan Murād III, 982–1003/1574–94, Leid. 1576 (see Suppl.), another anonymous one, Mosul 158,$_{131}$.—12. *Risālat ithbāt al-wājib al-jadīda*, written ten years later, Berl. 2335, Leid. 1577, Ind. Off. 468,$_{2}$, 1040,$_{13}$, *Dharīʿa* I, 107,$_{522}$, 109,$_{530}$.—Commentaries: a.–d. Suppl. (a. see *Dharīʿa* I, 103/4,$_{509}$, 108,$_{527}$, where we read Maḥmūd b. Muḥammad b. Maḥmūd
218 al-Nayrīzī (instead of Tabrīzī as in the catalogue), | a student of Ṣadr al-Dīn al-Dashtakī, composed in 921/1515.—12a. *Risāla fi ʾl-wujūd* Patna II, 421,$_{2591,4}$.—
283 | 13. *al-Risāla al-Jalāliyya fī tawjīh al-wujūd al-ilāhiyya* Berl. 2396.—14. *Tafsīr al-kalima al-ṭayyiba*, on the meaning and phrasing of the profession of unity, Berl. 2441 = *kalima-i shahādat*, Persian (?), Esc. ^{2}607,$_{3}$.—15. *Khalq al-aʿmāl*, on free will, Berl. 2485/6, Gotha 103,$_{3}$, 1158,$_{32}$, Leid. 1574, 2649/50, Garr. 1501, 2005,$_{3}$, Alex. Fun. 152,$_{8}$, Mosul 104,$_{73,24}$, of which a selection dedicated to Sultan Qāʾitbāy is in AS 399,$_{4}$.—16. *Risāla fī afʿāl al-ʿibād*, on the duties of the believer, Esc. ^{2}701, Sarajevo 137,$_{6}$, Taymūr, Majāmīʿ 1,$_{7}$, printed in *Majmūʿat kalimāt al-muḥaqqiqīn* 1315 (*Dharīʿa* II, 260,$_{1058}$).—17. *Risāla ʿala ʾl-Muḥākamāt* Esc. ^{2}706,$_{7}$, Garr. 795, Mosul 180,$_{154}$.—18. *al-Arbaʿūn al-sulṭāniyya fi ʾl-aḥkām al-rabbāniyya* Cairo ^{1}VII, 185, ^{2}I, 87.—19. *Bustān al-qulūb*, on mysticism, NO 2288.—20. *Risālat al-zawrāʾ*, a treatise on various questions in philosophy and

mysticism, completed in 870/1465[1] after an appearance by ʿAlī on the banks of the Tigris (or al-Zawrāʾ), Berl. 3223/4, Gotha 87,$_{8}$ (where other MSS are listed), Alex. Taṣ. 42,$_{6}$, Ḥikma 242, Fun. 126,$_{2}$, Taymūr Ḥikma 145.—Commentaries: a. Self-commentary, *al-Ḥawrāʾ*, completed on 17 Shawwāl 871/23 May 1467 in Hamadan, Berl. 3225, Gotha 87,$_{9}$ (where other MSS are listed), Garr. 2005,$_{i}$, Alex. Ḥikma 24,$_{4}$.—b. Kamāl al-Dīn Muḥammad b. Fakhr al-Dīn al-Lārī, completed 918/1512, Berl. 3226.—c. al-Kurdī al-Asnawī, completed in 1018/1609, Berl. 3227 = (?) Mollā Ilyās Shaykhī al-Kurdī, completed in 1025/1616, Cairo ^{1}VI, 98, Garr. 1611, after Dam. Z. 47,$_{53}$, glosses on *al-Ḥawrāʾ*, after ḤKh III, 393,$_{1}$, by Shaykham al-Kurdawī.—d. al-Ardabīlī, Berl. 3228.—Rebuttal of the *Zawrāʾ* and the *Ḥawrāʾ* by Ghiyāth al-Dīn al-Shīrāzī, d. 949/1542 (p. 414), Leid. 1587.—21. *Risāla fī taqaddum al-ʿilla al-tāmma*, on the assertion by later philosphers that causes do not precede their effects, Berl. 5136.—22. *al-Risāla al-Burhāniyya* Esc. ^{2}236,$_{11}$.—23. Some remarks on sophisms, Berl. 5190.—24. *Risālat khawāṣṣ al-jism al-laṭīf*, on the properties and nature of man, ibid. 5399.—25. *Risāla fī māhiyyat al-ṭabīʿa* Leid. 1569.—26. *Risāla fi ʾl-taṣawwurāt* Leid. 1570, Ind. Off. 1040,$_{4}$.—Glosses by Qāḍīkhān, Esc. ^{2}405,$_{5}$.—27. *Risāla fī anna ithbāt al-ṣāniʿ bi-ḥudūth al-ʿālam bi-imkānihi* Leid. 1573.—28. *Risālat al-yarāʿa* or *al-Risāla al-qalamiyya* Leid. 433/4, Garr. 214, Vienna 2003,$_{40}$, Copenhagen 231,$_{5}$.—29. *Sharḥ Hayākil al-nūr* I, 565.—30. *Lawāmiʿ al-ishrāq* ibid. 673.—31. *Sharḥ al-ʿAqāʾid al-ʿAḍudiyya* | 284
p. 270.—32. *Sharḥ Sharḥ al-Jurjānī ʿala ʾl-Mawāqif* p. 269.—33. *Sharḥ Tahdhīb al-manṭiq* p. 278.—34. *Sharḥ Sharḥ al-Risāla al-Shamsiyya* I, 612.—35. *Sharḥ Sharḥ Maṭāliʿ al-anwār* ibid. 614.—36. *Sharḥ Ādāb al-baḥth* ibid. 616.—37. *Sharḥ al-Sharḥ al-jadīd* ibid. 671.—38. *Sharḥ Ithbāt al-jawhar al-mufāriq* ibid. 673.—39. Persian letter in verse to Sultan Bāyezīd II (886–918/1481–1512), Esc. ^{2}687,$_{4}$.—40.–70. see Suppl. (43. Patna II, 461,$_{2634,12}$, 57. read: Asʿad 1185,$_{67}$, Rāġib 1457,$_{11}$).—71. *Ishtikākāt al-ḥurūf wa-ṭabāʾiʿihā wa-aʿdādihā wa-mā yataʿallaq bi aʿdād al-ḥurūf min al-masāʾil al-mawsūma li-arithmāṭīqī* Bibl. Hādī Āl Kāshif al-ghiṭāʾ, *Dharīʿa* II, 33,$_{129}$.—72. *Risāla fi ʾl-ʿaqāʾid wa-ṣifāti ʾllāh* Alex. Fun. 88,$_{6}$, Patna II, 457,$_{2631,13}$.—73. *Risāla fī ʿilm al-nafs* Taymūr Ḥikma 44, Patna II, 453,$_{2629,4}$.—74. *Risālat al-ʿawālim al-thalātha* Taymūr Ḥikma 44.—75. *Sharḥ al-Risāla al-musammāt bi-ʿAql al-kull* Patna II, 453,$_{2629,5}$.—76. *Risāla fī tashrīḥ qawlihi al-Taṣawwurāt lā yashtamil ʿadam al-muṭābaqa bi-khilāf al-taṣdīqāt* ibid. II, 420,$_{2891,3}$, 421,$_{2592,1}$.

5. Sayf al-Dīn Aḥmad b. Yaḥyā b. Muḥammad b. Saʿd al-Dīn Ḥafīd al-Taftazānī al-Harawī succeeded his father as Shaykh al-Islām in Herat before being

1 Ahlw., op. cit., 872; however, see the date of the *Ḥawrāʾ*.

executed on the orders of the Safavid shah Ismāʿīl in Ramaḍān 916/December 1510 (or, according to others, in 906/1500).

Khwandamīr, *ḤS* III, 3, 198, 343, Bābar, *Mem.* ed. Beveridge 177v, transl. Pavet de Courteille I, 401. 1. *Majmūʿa nafīsa,* an encyclopaedia of philosophy and traditional Islamic sciences, Br. Mus. Suppl. 717, abstract *al-Durr al-naḍīd min Majmūʿat al-Ḥafīd* Cairo ²I, 294, VI, 183, Qawala II, 258, print. C. 1322.—2. *al-Fawāʾid wal-farāʾid majmūʿa fī ʿiddat funūn* Cairo VI, ¹164, ²186.—3. Small philosophical treatise in two parts on the Divine Word in the Qurʾān and *ḥadīth,* Berl. 488.—4. 34 treatises from various sciences, AS 4799.—5. *Sharḥ al-Sharḥ al-mukhtaṣar* I, 355.—6. *Sharḥ Tahdhīb al-manṭiq* p. 277.—7., 8. See Suppl.—9. *al-Talwīḥ* p. 278.

Chapter 6. India

From the very beginning, Islamic culture in India was entirely under Persian influence. | In the same way in which Arabic was supplanted more and more 285
by Persian in literary use in Iran, Persian Muslims moving to India with their Turkish or Mongol sovereigns imposed their language on the newly converted local populations. Even though individual travelling scholars such as Ibn Baṭṭūṭa and al-Fīrūzābādī were received with honour at the courts of Muslim India, occasionally even finding a place where they could work for a significant period of time, their influence did not extend far enough to be able to give Arabic literature any real significance compared to Persian. Similarly, relations between the Muslim theologians of India and the cultural centres of South Arabia and Mecca have left almost no evidence. Thus, the contribution of Indian Muslims to Arabic literature remained very limited.

1 *Philology*

Shihāb al-Dīn Aḥmad b. Shams al-Dīn ʿUmar al-Ghaznawī al-Dawlatābādī, d. 849/1455, see Suppl.

1. *al-Irshād fi ʾl-naḥw* Leid. 232, Br. Mus. 525, Ind. Off. 974/5, Calc. p. 1. Patna I, $160_{,1596}$, II, $560_{,2942}$.—Commentaries: a. Wajīh al-Dīn al-ʿAlawī, Ind. Off. 976.—b. Muḥammad (Aḥmad) b. Sharīf al-Ḥusaynī, Calc. p. 15c, see Suppl.—2.–5. see Suppl.

2 *Historiography*

Muḥammad b. ʿAbd al-ʿAzīz al-Kalīkūtī al-Shāfiʿī wrote:

Al-Fatḥ al-mubīn lil-Samurī alladhī yuḥibb al-muslimīn, ca. 500 *rajaz* verses on the battles between Zamori and the Portuguese under Vasco da Gama, ca. 903/1497, Ind. Off. $1044_{,6}$.

3 *Fiqh, Ḥanafī*

1. Abū Bakr Isḥāq b. Tāj al-Dīn ʿAlī b. Abi ʾl-Ḥasan ʿAlī b. Abī Bakr al-Ṣūfī al-Bakrī al-Multānī al-Ḥanafī Abū Bakr b. al-Tāj, ca. 736/1335.

| 1. *Khulāṣat jawāhir al-Qurʾān fī bayān maʿāni ʾl-furqān,* composed in 717/1317 286
in Multān, which begins with the *Fātiḥa* but then continues in reverse order from the last until the second sura, starting with a particular word in each case, often from the beginning of a sura, explaining the idea it means to convey, often adding some saying of Muḥammad. The explanatory notes to the

text are consistently written in Persian, and those regarding the *ḥadīth* more often in Persian than not, Berl. 876.—2. *Khulāṣat al-aḥkām bi-sharāʾiṭ al-islām*, Arabic and Persian, later abbreviated, an extract from this abbreviation is in Berl. 1798, part of the original work, ibid. 1799.—3. *al-Ḥajj wa-manāsikuhu* ibid. 4046.

2. Muḥammad b. Ḥājjī b. Muḥammad al-Samarqandī wrote, for Khwājā Kāfūr, governor of Ẓafarābād under Sultan Fīrūz Shāh (Ṭughluq 752–99/1351–97?):

1. *al-Fatāwi ʾl-Kāfūriyya* Ind. Off. 1670.—2. *Maʿdin al-ḥaqāʾiq* p. 251.

3. ʿUmar b. Isḥāq al-Ghaznawī al-Dawlatābādī, who died in 773/1371.

Sharḥ al-Mughnī I, 477.

4. Abu ʾl-Faḍāʾil Saʿd al-Dīn ʿAbdallāh b. ʿAbd al-Karīm al-Dihlawī, who died in 891/1486.

Sharḥ al-Manār p. 250.

221 | 5. Qāḍī Čakān (Čukān) al-Hindī, who died in 920/1514 in Qiraw, in Gujārāt.

Khizānat al-riwāyāt Ind. Off. 276, 1603/4, Yeni 605, Patna I, 86,$_{845/8}$.

4 *Qurʾānic Exegesis*

ʿAlāʾ (Zayn) al-Dīn ʿAlī b. Aḥmad al-Mahāʾimī al-Hindī, who died in 835/1432 (see Suppl.).

1. *Tabṣīr al-raḥmān wa-taysīr al-mannān al-mashhūr bil-Tafsīr al-Raḥmānī*, an allegorical commentary, Berl. 870, Köpr. 84/7, II, 14, Cairo ^{1}I, 135, ^{2}357, Qawala I, 44, Patna I, 23,$_{214}$, 24,$_{215}$.—2.–4. see Suppl.

287 | 5 *Mysticism*

1. ʿAlī b. Shihāb al-Dīn al-Ḥusaynī al-Hamadhānī al-Amīr al-Kabīr, who died in 786/1383 (see Suppl.).

Jāmī, *Nafaḥāt* 518, Khwandamīr, *ḤS* II, 3, 87, Newall, Hist. of Cashmere, *JRAS Beng.* XXIII, 414, XXXIII, 278, Rieu, *Pers. Cat.* 4478, *Grundr. d. ir. Phil.* II, 349. 1. *Awrād fatḥiyya* Leid. 2196, Ind. Off. 368/9, Patna I, 152,$_{1446}$, print.

Lucknow 1257.—2. *al-Risāla al-qudsiyya fī asrār al-nuqṭa al-ḥissiyya ilā asrār al-huwiyya al-ghaybiyya* Ind. Off. 693,ii, 1, Br. Mus. 406, Cairo ¹VII, 548.—3. *Kitāb al-mawadda fi 'l-qurba* Br. Mus. 980,1.—4. *Kitāb al-sabʿīn fī faḍāʾil amīr al-muʾminīn* ibid. 2.—5. *Arbaʿīn amriyya* ibid. 3.—6. *Manāzil al-sālikīn* ibid. 5.—7. *Sharḥ al-Fuṣūṣ*, in Arabic and Persian, see I, 572.—8.–11. see Suppl. (8. Pet. AM 1381.—10. Dresd. 152, see. Steinschneider, *AKM* VI, 3, 182,5).—12. *Mashārib al-adhwāq etc.* see Suppl. I, 464, 4, 1.

2. Zayn al-Dīn b. ʿAlī b. Aḥmad al-Maʿbarī al-Malībārī, who was born in 872/1467 in Kushān and died in Fanān in 928/1522.

1. *Hidāyat al-adhkiyāʾ ilā ṭarīq al-awliyāʾ* in verse.—Commentaries: a. *Maslak al-atqiyāʾ*, by his son ʿAbd al-ʿAzīz, Cairo ¹II, 135, III, 258, ²I, 358.—b. Abū Bakr b. Muḥammad Shaṭṭāʾ al-Dimyāṭī, completed in 1302/1855, print. C. 1304 (Cat. II, 106).—c. See Suppl.—2.–4. See Suppl.—An eschatological work without a title, printed in the margin of *al-Rawḍ al-fāʾiq* by al-Ḥurayfīsh (p. 228), C. 1315.

222 |
Chapter 7. The Turks of Rūm and the Ottoman Empire

The Ottoman empire, which from a small polity struggling against the dominion of the Byzantines in Asia Minor had risen to a world power in little over two hundred years, completed its 'internal' development through the capture of Constantinople in 856/1453, while crowning its successes abroad by the conquests of Syria and Egypt in 923/1517. Despite the military focus being predominant in almost all of the sciences, Ottoman sultans did not entirely neglect the pursuit of the sciences from the ninth/fifteenth century onwards.
288 | Meḥmed, the conquerer of Constantinople, occupied himself extensively with matters related to the sciences, seeking guidance from the very best scholars of his time. He had a particular interest in learned debates. Like his predecessors, he founded madrasas for the pursuit and dissemination of the Islamic sciences in all the major cities of the empire, and in particular in Bursa, Constantinople, and Adrianople.[1] Nevertheless, in belles lettres[2] and historiography Persian was initially predominant as it had been under the Saljūqs, although this soon gave way to Turkish. However, in theology and related areas Arabic asserted its primary position. Yet any new ideas were absent here, just as was the case in Cairo or Damascus, where people turned for their ideas.
223 | Byzantine science, itself also petrified, could no longer influence anybody's writings, even though Meḥmed the Conqueror did take an interest in collecting Greek manuscripts.[3]

1 *Philology*

1. Ḥājjī Bābā b. Ibrāhīm (p. 249) al-Ṭūsiyawī, who flourished under Meḥmed II (r. 855–86/1451–81).

ShN I, 319. 1. *Sharḥ al-ʿAwāmil* I, 341.—2. *Sharḥ al-Miṣbāḥ* I, 351.—3. *Sharḥ al-Kāfiya* I, 368.—4. *Sharḥ Anwār al-tanzīl* I, 530.—5. See Suppl.—6. *al-Wasāʾil wal-wasāʾiṭ*, selected questions from various sciences, AS 4347.

---

1 The history of public education in Turkey up to and including the seventeenth century could already be written in relative detail on the basis of information contained in Ṭāšköprīzāde and his successors.

2 Only Muṣliḥ al-Dīn Muṣṭafā b. Wafāʾ al-Qūnawī (d. 896/1491, Brussali, *Osm. Müell.* I, 181) also left an Arabic *Dīwān*, AS 3925.

3 See A. Deissmann, *Forschungen und Funde im Serai*, Berlin and Leipzig 1933. On Meḥmed's intellectual aspirations cf. Abdulhak Adnan, *La science chez les Turcs Ottomans*, Paris 1939, 31 ff., *Ilim* 29.

| 2. Ḥusām al-Dīn b. al-Maddās Naʿlbandzāde al-Tūqātī, who died in Istanbul 289
in 860/1456.

ShN I, 164 (Rescher 61), Brussali, *Osm. Müell.* I, 272. 1. *Sharḥ ʿAwāmil al-Jurjānī* I, 341, lost.—2. *Risāla fī qaws quzaḥ*, on the rainbow, Berl. 5791, Beirut 213, print. *al-Mashriq* XV (1912) 742/4.—See Suppl. II, 323, 3, 2, see I, 368, 12a.

3. Al-Sayyid Muḥammad b. al-Sayyid Ḥasan b. al-Sayyid ʿAlī, who died in 866/1462.

Jāmiʿ al-lugha, a lexicon, written in 854/1450 in Adrianople, Leid. 92, Bodl. I, 1071, II, 608, with the title *al-Rāmūz fī ʾl-lugha al-ʿArabiyya* Garr. 281, Yeni 1126/7, see ḤKh III, 341/2, ^{2}I, 831.

4. Luṭfallāh b. Abī Yūsuf Mollā Čelebī, a student of al-Taftazānī, ca. 886/1481.

1. *Muṣarriḥat al-asmāʾ* Cairo ^{1}IV, 188, ^{2}II, 38.—2. See Suppl.

2 *Historiography*

1. Yaʿqūb b. Idrīs al-Qaramānī Qara Yaʿqūb, who was born in Nakīdā in Qaramān, studied in Damascus and Cairo, and lived in Laranda until his death in 833/1429.

ShN I, 123. *Ishrāq al-tawārīkh*, a history of Muḥammad, his relatives and main companions, the founders of the major sects, and the most famous *ḥadīth*-scholars and Qurʾān experts, including information on their age and year of death, Gotha 1744, Paris 2014, AS 2954, 3023, 3509, Alex. Taʾr. 13 (see Suppl.), an abstract or adaptation entitled *Ashraf al-tawārīkh* by Sary Yaʿqūb b. ʿAṭāʾallāh al-Qaramānī, ca. 820/1417, Berl. 9589. The relationship between these two works separately and, jointly, between them and the one by al-Ījī (see p. 271), remains to be clarified. The beginning of the Berlin MS is the same as the others and with ḤKh I, $^{1}319_{788}$, ^{2}I, 103; have the title and the author in the Berlin text been distorted?

2. An otherwise unidentified al-Āqshahrī, from whose *Riḥla* Ibn Ḥajar, *DK* I, 153_{101}, citing a description of Ibn Taymiyya, wrote:

| *Al-Rawḍa al-firdawsiyya*, a history of Medina, library of Daḥdāḥ 268 = Berl. 290
Ms. or. qu. 2082.

224 | 3 *Fiqh, Ḥanafī*

1. Maḥmūd b. Aḥmad b. Ẓāhir al-Dīn b. Shams al-Dīn al-Rūmī al-Lārandī al-Ḥanafī died before 720/1320.

DK IV, 321, no. 879. *Irshād al-rājī li-maʿrifat al-farāʾiḍ al-Sirājiyya* (I, 470), with an anonymous commentary, Berl. 4712.

2. ʿĪsā b. Muḥammad b. Īnanj al-Qarashahrī al-Ḥanafī, ca. 734/1334.

Al-Mubtaghī fi ʾl-furūʿ Cairo [1]III, 108, [2]I, 459.

3. Fakhr al-Dīn al-Rūmī lived under Bāyezīd I (792–805/1389–1402) in Mudurnu.[1]

ShN I, 110 (Rescher, 26) 1. *Mushtamil al-aḥkām* Berl. 4795, NO 2024/5, Alex. Fiqh Ḥan. 64, Cairo [1]III, 119; in two editions: a. *al-kabīr* Yeni 576.—b. *al-ṣaghīr* ibid. 569.—2. *al-Daʿawāt al-maʾthūra* Br. Mus. 143$_{,2}$, cf. Add. 765a.

4. Shihāb al-Dīn Abu ʾl-Ḥāmid Aḥmad b. Maḥmūd b. ʿAlī b. Abī Ṭālib al-Sīwāsī, who died in 803/1400.

1. *al-Farāʾiḍ*, with a commentary by ʿAbd al-Ḥalīm al-Sukkarī (d. ca. 900/1494), Alex. Far. 16.—2. *Sharḥ al-Sirājiyya* I, 470.

5. Muṣṭafā al-Qaramānī, who died in 809/1406.

Risāla fī ḥukm al-laʿib bil-nard wal-shiṭranj Cairo [1]VII, 428.

6. Badr al-Dīn Maḥmūd b. Isrāʾīl b. Qāḍī Samawna, from Samauna near Demotika in Thrace, who died in 819/1416, see Suppl.

225 | *ShN* I, 112, MT 97v (entirely invented), on Babinger, loc. cit., see Köprülüzade M. Fuat, *MOG* I, 203/22; on his place of birth and year of death, see Babinger, *Südost forsch.* VIII (1943), 259/61. 1. *Jāmiʿ al-fuṣūlayn*, a practical handbook for
291 judges, composed in 814/1411, Leipz. 206, Barb. Hammer, *Lettere* V, 3, Leid. | 1855, AS 1531/5, Yeni 386/91, NO 1936/41, Köpr. 547/8, Fātiḥ 2288, Bursa, Haraccizade, *Fiqh* 17, Cairo [1]III, 33, [2]I, 413, Qawala I, 317, print. Būlāq 1300/1.—Glosses: a. Ibn Nujaym, d. 970/1562 (p. 310), Leid. 1855$_{,1}$, Qawala I, 320, *Mukhtaṣar* anon.

1 Ahlw., loc. cit., wrongly ca. 880, Cairo 879, due to a confusion with Bāyezīd II.

Berl. 4792, Qawala I, 392.—b. *al-La'āli' al-durriyya fi 'l-fawā'id al-Khayriyya* by Khayr al-Dīn al-Ramlī, d. 1081/1670 (p. 314), Alex. Fiqh Ḥan. 49, Qawala I, 385, in the margin of the printing of Būlāq 1300/1.—c. *Nūr al-ʿayn fī iṣlāḥ Jāmiʿ al-f.* by Muḥammad Nishānjīzāde, d. 1031/1622 (p. 434), Ind. Off. 1692, NO 2078, Alex. Fiqh Ḥan. 71.—2. *Laṭā'if al-ishārāt*, with the commentary *Tashīl al-fatāwī*, begun on 8 Shawwāl 816/2 January 1414 and completed on 27 Jumādā II 818/4 September 1415 in Iznik, Yeni 540, 598, Cairo [1]III, 26, 106, [2]I, 410, 459.—3. *al-Wāridāt*, a Sufi work, Cairo [1]II, 143, [2]I, 375.—4. See Suppl.

7. Muḥammad b. Muḥammad al-Iznīqī Quṭb al-Dīn was born in Iznik and died there in 821/1418.

ShN II, 87, Rescher 18/9 (with an invented account of his meeting with Tīmūr). *Murshid al-muta'ahhil*, on the duties of spouses and children towards each other, Gotha 2052, Algiers 1785, Br. Mus. $420_{,4}$, Alex. Ṭibb 44, Qawala I, 395.

8. Ḥāfiẓ al-Dīn Muḥammad b. Muḥammad b. al-Bazzāzī al-Kardarī moved from Sarāi on the Volga river to the Crimea and thence to Asia Minor, where he died in Ramaḍān 827/August 1414.

ShN I, 92. 1. *al-Jāmiʿ al-wajīz* or *Fatāwi 'l-Kardarī* or *al-Fatāwi 'l-Bazzāziyya*, Berl. 4823, Munich 315, Vienna 1809, Ind. Off. 271, Pet. AM 126, Yeni 630, 663, AS 1548/50, NO 1983/8, Köpr. 667/8, Alex. Fiqh. Ḥan. 18, Cairo [1]III, 35, Qawala I, 318, print. Kazan 1308.—Glosses by Najm al-Dīn b. Khayr al-Dīn al-Ramlī, ca. 1089/1678, Qawala I, 325.—Abstract by al-Qāri' al-Harawī, d. 1014/1605 (p. 394), Alex. Fiqh. Ḥan. 24.—2. *Manāqib Abī Ḥanīfa*, together with a history of his followers, Berl. 10001, Köpr. 1168, Cairo V, [1]158.—3. *Mas'ala*, on whether someone can perform a meritorious act such as praying, fasting, or going on the pilgrimage, for someone else, Berl. 3580.—4., 5. See Suppl.—6. *Mukhtaṣar fī bayān taʿrīfāt al-aḥkām* Garr. 1665.—7. *Ādāb al-qaḍā'* Alex. Fiqh Ḥan. 5.

| | 9. Qyrq Emre al-Ḥamīdī (Ḥumaidī?) al-Ḥanafī, ca. 880/1475. 292 226

Jāmiʿ al-fatāwī Berl. Brill M. 186, Br. Mus. 214, Pet. AM 128, Yeni 599, 600, AS 1529/30, NO 1935, Qawala I, 316.

10. Muḥammad b. Farāmurz b. ʿAlī Mollā Khusraw, the son of a Greek convert to Islam, was a professor in Adrianople and, under Meḥmed, *qāḍi 'l-ʿaskar*. When the latter was ousted by his son Murād, he pledged allegiance to him but reaped the fruit of this when Meḥmed returned to power after Murād's

death. After the death of Khiḍrbeg (§ 5.1) he became a *qāḍī* in Istanbul, Galata, and Skutari, as well as a professor at the Aya Sofia. When one day he saw himself neglected for al-Kūrānī (§ 4.4) in a banquet he went to Bursa and constructed a madrasa there. However, Meḥmed soon called him back to Istanbul and appointed him as a *muftī*. He died in 885/1480 and was buried in Bursa.

ShN I, 182/7, Rescher 69/72. 1. *Ghurar al-aḥkām* (see Suppl.), with a commentary, *Durar al-ḥukkām*, composed in 877–83/1472–7 following his recovery from the plague that he had caught in 872/1467, autograph Köpr. 639, Berl. 4797/8, Leipz. $109_{,8}$, Dresd. 227, 403, Munich 316, Leid. 1863, Paris 936/42, 6193, Algiers 1018, Bodl. I, 228, 271, Br. Mus. 215/6, Suppl. 295/6, Pet. Ros. 21, AM 129/32, Ambr. 77, Yeni 417/22, NO 152/63, 1771, AS 1151/66, Cairo [1]III, 48, [2]I, 421, Qawala I, 331/3, 371, Garr. 1728/30, print. C. 1294, 1305.—Commentaries and glosses: a. *Risāla fī iṣlāḥ al-ghalaṭāt al-wāqiʿa fī kitāb Durar al-ḥukkām* by Ibrāhīm b. Muḥammad al-Ḥalabī, d. 953/1549 (p. 432), Qawala I, 338.—b. Qinālīzāde, d. 979/1571 (p. 433), Yeni 377.—c. Muḥammad b. Muṣṭafā al-Wānqulī, d. 1000/1591 (p. 444), Berl. 1799, Yeni 408, Cairo [1]III, 144.—d. ʿAzmīzāde, d. 1040/1630, Yeni 398/9, Cairo [1]III, 39.—e. *Kashf rumūz Ghurar al-aḥkām wa-tanwīr Durar al-ḥukkām* by ʿAbd al-Ḥalīm b. Pīr Qadam b. Naṣūḥ b. Mūsā b. Muṣṭafā b. ʿAbd al-Karīm b. Ḥamza, completed in 1060/1650, Cairo [1]III, 103, Qawala I, 383/4, print. Istanbul 1270.—f.
293 Ḥasan al-Shurunbulālī, d. 1069/1658 | (p. 313), Algiers 1019, Garr. 1763, Yeni 520, Cairo [1]III, 85, Qawala I, 372/3, print. Istanbul 1301; words of praise about it, Berl. 55.—g. Nūḥ Efendi, d. 1070/1659 (p. 314), Cairo [1]III, 141.—h. Muṣṭafā b. ʿUthmān al-Khādimī, ibid. 38, Qawala I, 321.—i. *Risāla fī baʿḍ maʾākhidh ʿalā kitāb Durar al-ḥukkām* by ʿUmar Muḥyi ʾl-Dīn Qāḍī bi-Edirne, Qawala I, 339.—k. On the
227 preface by Yaʿqūb b. Ibrāhīm al-Jirkāshī, C. 1307. | Cf. Ahlw. 4800.—2. *Mirqāt al-wuṣūl ilā ʿilm al-uṣūl* Cairo [1]II, 204, Qawala I, 297, print. Istanbul 1291, self-commentary *Mirʾāt al-uṣūl* Garr. 1648/9 Yeni 336, Alex. Uṣūl 19, Qawala I, 295/6, print. Istanbul 1217, 1272, 1273, 1282, 1310, 1321.—Glosses: a. Sulaymān al-Izmīrī, d. 1102/1690, Cairo [1]II, 244, print. Būlāq 1262, Istanbul 1304.—b. Muḥammad b. Aḥmad b. Muḥammad al-Ṭarasūsī, Garr. 1650, Qawala I, 283, Istanbul 1317.—c. *Miftāḥ al-uṣūl* by ʿAbd al-Razzāq b. Muṣṭafā al-Anṭākī (Suppl. II, $973_{,12}$), printed together with b., Istanbul 1279.—d.–k. see Suppl. (g. Qawala I, 338.—i. *Taqrīr al-M.* Istanbul 1297, 1311).—3. *al-Risāla al-walāʾiyya*, on the rights of a master towards the freedman, composed in 873/1468, Gotha $1095_{,1}$, Munich 893 f. 152, Cairo [1]III, 115, VII, 611, 681, with a rebuttal by Aḥmad b. Ismāʿīl al-Kūrānī (§ 4, 4), Cairo [1]VII, 681, on which notes by Qāḍīzāde, Gotha $1095_{,2}$.—4. *Ḥāshiya ʿala ʾl-Talwīḥ* p. 277.—5.–9. see Suppl.

11. Yūsuf b. Junayd Akhī Čelebī al-Tūqātī, d. 904/1499, see Suppl.

1. See Suppl.—2. Ibid. Istanbul 1285.—3. *Hadiyyat al-muhtadīn fī 'l-masā'il al-fiqhiyya wal-tawḥīdiyya* Qawala I, 407.

12. ʿAbd al-Raḥmān b. ʿAlī Mu'ayyadzāde al-Amāsī, who was born in Amasia in 860/1456, was, as a young man, part of the retinue of Bāyezīd II, at that time governor of Amasia. When his father wanted to have him killed as a result of some slander, Bāyezīd helped him escape to Aleppo. He then spent seven years with al-Dawwānī (p. 281) in Shiraz. After Bāyezīd came to power he went to Istanbul, in 888/1483, and there he was given the Qalandarkhāne madrasa and, following his marriage to the daughter of Muṣliḥ al-Dīn al-Qasṭallānī in
891/1486, | he was given eight large madrasas. In 899/1484 he became *qāḍī* 294
of Adrianople, in 907/1501 *qāḍi 'l-ʿaskar* for Anatolia, and in 911/1505 that for Rumelia. He was deposed in 917/1511 following the ransacking of his *qonaq* by supporters of Prince Selīm because of his sympathy for Prince Aḥmad. However, when Selīm came to power the following year the first thing he did was compensate him by means of the proceeds of a judgeship in Qara Ferī'e, while he also reinstated him as *qāḍi 'l-ʿaskar* in 918/1513. But the following year he had to be removed from this post because of mental health problems that developed after his return from the military campaign against Shāh Ismāʿīl. He died on 15 Shaʿbān 922/14 September 1516.

| *ShN* I, 430/7 (Rescher 191/4). 1. *Majmūʿat masā'il*, on individual sections of 228
legal works, Berl. 4828, Paris 948, Garr. 1734/5.—2. *Majmūʿat fatāwī* Berl. 4829, AS 1593, Yeni 660/2, NO 2038/9, Cairo ^{1}III, 92, 110, Alex. Fiqh Ḥan. 42.—3. *Risāla fī 'l-subḥa* Esc. ^{2}236,$_{4}$.—4. *Sharḥ al-Mawāqif lil-Ījī* p. 270.—5. *Targhīb al-labīb* Qawala I, 312, which has an incorrect date.

4 *Sciences of the Qur'ān*

1. Mu'min b. ʿAlī b. Muḥammad al-Rūmī al-Falakābādī, who died in 799/1397.

Jāmiʿ al-kalām fī rasm muṣḥaf al-imām Fātiḥ, Waqf Ibr. 31,$_{11}$, see Bergsträsser, *Gesch. des Qor'āntextes* 26.

2. Ṣafarshāh al-Ḥanafī, ca. 800/1397.

ShN I, 93. *Risāla fī tafsīr sūrat al-takāthur* (no. 102), Cairo ^{1}VII, 557 (with an incorrect date: "composed in 919").

2a. Aḥmad b. ʿImād al-Dīn Mawlānāzāde al-Rūmī.

Risālat al-khalāṣ fī tafsīr sūrat al-ikhlāṣ (p. 112), MS dated 832/1428, Esc. ^{2}1602$_{,1}$.

295 3. Aḥmad b. Muḥammad al-Sīwāsī was born as a slave in Sīwās, | where he joined a Sufi order and wandered with his teachers to Ayatholūgh (Ephesus), where he died in the eighties of the eighth century (according to *ShN*, but according to others in 803).

ShN I, 94. 1. *ʿUyūn al-tafāsīr lil-fuḍalāʾ al-samāsīr*, usually called *Tafsīr al-Shaykh*, Garr. 1293, Sarajevo 59$_{,1}$, AS 171, 219/20, Rāġib 202/3, NO 329/32, Yeni 59, Köpr. 110, Cairo ^{1}I, 182, ^{2}I, 55, ḤKh IV, 289$_{,8462}$.—An abstract from this, on the ca. 500 verses of legal content based on Shīʿī *fiqh*, and composed at the instigation of Miqdād b. ʿAbdallāh al-Suyūrī (p. 213), *Maʿārij al-masʾūl wa-madārij al-maʾmūl* Ind. Off. 1810.—2. *Risālat al-najāt min sharr al-ṣifāt*, on the ten conditions of salvation, Krafft 431.—3. See Suppl. (also 974$_{,20}$).

4. Muḥammad b. Aḥmad al-Kirmānī al-Kūyabānī wrote under Bāyezīd:

Zubdat al-bayān fī rusūm maṣāḥif ʿUthmān Garr. 1244, Hyderabad, Niẓām, *JRAS* 1917, XCI, 7.

5. Aḥmad b. Ismāʿīl b. ʿUthmān al-Kūrānī, who was born in 813/1416, studied in his homeland and in Cairo. After he was banished from there (see Suppl.) Shaykh Yegān (*ShN* I, 138) took him to Anatolia with him and introduced him to Sultan Murād. The latter appointed him professor at the madrasa in Bursa that had been founded by his grandfather, then at the one of Bāyezīd, before finally entrusting him with the education of his son Meḥmed in Magnesia. When the latter had risen to power, he appointed him as *qāḍi ʾl-ʿaskar*. However, because he acted too independently in that position, Meḥmed instead made him *qāḍī* with responsibility for the supervision of pious endowments in Bursa. Yet in this office, too, he had the temerity to go against the orders of the sultan, so, having been relieved of his post, he went to Egypt, where Qāʾitbāy received him with full honours. In 861/1457 Meḥmed called him back and appointed him a
229 296 *muftī* in Istanbul, where he died in 893/1488. | In spite | of his large income he left significant debts, which Sultan Bāyezīd quietly paid on his behalf.

ShN I, 143/51 (Rescher 48/53, where Gūrānī?), *MT* 20r. 1. *Kashf al-asrār ʿan qirāʾat al-aʾimma al-akhyār* NO 84.—2. *Ghāyat al-amānī fī tafsīr al-kalām al-rabbānī*, composed in 868/1463, ibid. 421/4, AS 253, Selīm Āġā 95, Qawala I, 72.—3. *Risālat al-walāʾ*, p. 293.—4.–7. see Suppl.

5. His student Yūsuf b. Gündil, who was imam at the Aya Sofia, wrote for Bāyezīd II:

Kashf al-asrār, explanations to a Qurʾān executed by himself following the rules of the *Shāṭibiyya*, AS 414 (Ritter).

6. Muḥammad b. Najīb al-Qaraḥiṣārī, ninth cent. (?)

Rawnaq al-tafāsir fī ḥaqq al-anbiyāʾ, a history of the prophets in the Qurʾān, Berl. 1028, Garr. 2076,$_4$ (anon.), with the life of Muḥammad Berl. 1029.

7. Muḥyi ʾl-Dīn b. Ibrāhīm Tāj (Shams) al-Dīn Khaṭībzāde al-Rūmī was a professor in Iznik and then at one of the eight madrasas of Istanbul. In this capacity he was also the teacher of Sultan Meḥmed. He was, however, dismissed when, in a state of hubris caused by his position, he wanted to engage in a debate with Khājazāde (§ 5, 3). He died in 901/1495.

ShN I, 231/6, MT 95r. 1. *Ḥawāshī ʿalā ḥāshiyat al-Kashshāf lil-Sayyid al-Sharīf* I, 346.—2. *Ḥāshiya ʿalā awāʾil sharḥ al-Mawāqif* p. 269.—3. *Ḥāshiya ʿalā sharḥ al-Wiqāya* I, 468.—4.–6. see Suppl.

8. Aḥmad b. ʿAbd al-Laṭīf al-Burlawī wrote, around the middle of the tenth century:

Al-Durr al-naḍīd fi ʾl-masāʾil al-mutaʿalliqa bil-tajwīd Sarajevo 31.

5 *Dogmatics*

1. The son of a *qāḍī*, Khiḍrbeg b. Jalāl al-Dīn b. Aḥmad Pāshā al-Māturīdī was born in Siwriḥiṣār on 1 Rabīʿ I 810/6 September 1407. | He married the daughter 297
of his teacher Yegān (see p. 295 above) and became a professor in his hometown. Having performed well in a debate in front of Sultan Meḥmed I, he was given a professorship in Bursa, then a judgeship in Āinegöl, and then another professorship, this time in Adrianople. After the conquest of Constantinople he became a *qāḍī* there, continuing to hold that office until he died in 863/1459.

ShN I, 151/5, MT 55v. 1. *al-Nūniyya fi ʾl-ʿaqāʾid*, in 103 (or 105) *basīṭ* verses, Berl. 2001, Pet. 239,$_2$, Garr. 2011,$_{14}$, Sarajevo 157/9, Alex. Tawḥīd 14, printed in *Majmūʿa* Istanbul 1318.—Commentaries: a. Aḥmad b. Mūsā al-Khayālī, d. 863/1459 (Suppl. 318), Berl. 2002, AS 2318, Cairo ^{1}VII, 83, ^{2}I, 190, Qawala I, 193.—Glosses see Suppl. (ϑ Berl. 2003, Br. Mus. 869,$_1$, Cairo ^{1}II, 31, Turkish Br. Mus. 869,$_2$,

Istanbul 1318).—b. ʿUthmān b. Abdallāh al-ʿUryānī, d. 1168/1754, Berl. 2004, Sarajevo 1601, print. Istanbul 1300.—c. Muḥammad Nāfiʿ b. Aḥmad b. Muḥammad al-Qāzābādī, Cairo ^{1}II, 13.—d. Muḥammad b. al-Ḥājj Ḥasan al-Ḥāfiẓ al-Kabīr, Qawala I, 200.—e. Ḥāfiẓ al-Dīn Muḥammad Amīn b. Taqī al-Dīn Abū Ḥāmid Aḥmad b. ʿImād al-Dīn Muḥammad b. Ismāʿīl al-Mawṣilī, completed on 2 Ramaḍān 1215/28 January 1800, ibid. 202.—2. A poem, Berl. 7908,$_2$.

2. While a professor in Adrianople, Ḥasan Čelebī b. Muḥammad Shāh (§ 9, 2) b. al-Fanārī (b. 840/1436) went for a second time to Cairo to study the *Mughni
230 ʾl-labīb* (p. 28) under someone from the Maghreb. | After his return he became a professor in Iznik, and then at one of the eight madrasas[2] in Istanbul. He ended his life as a pensioner in Bursa, where he died in 886/1481.

ShN I, 287/90, MT 53v. 1. *Risāla fi ʾl-mabdaʾ al-awwal* Leid. 1532.—2. *Sharḥ al-Mawāqif* 269.—3. *Sharḥ al-Talwīḥ* p. 277.—4. *Sharḥ al-Sharḥ al-muṭawwal* I, 354.—5. See Suppl.

3. Muṣliḥ al-Dīn Muṣṭafā b. Yūsuf Khājazāde, the son of a merchant, studied in
298 Bursa under | Khiḍrbeg and became a lecturer there. Sultan Murād II appointed him a *qāḍī* in Kastal and then a professor in Bursa. When Sultan Meḥmed II acceded to the throne, he accompanied him on his trip from Istanbul to Adrianople, during which time he won his trust, so that he appointed him his teacher. However, the vizier Maḥmūd tried to remove him from the court by appointing him *qāḍi ʾl-ʿaskar*. Time and again he tried to regain the favour of the sultan, as a professor at the Sulṭāniyya in Bursa, then in Istanbul, as a *qāḍī* in Adrianople and Istanbul, until Maḥmūd finally limited him to a professorship in Iznik. Nevertheless, the next sultan, Bāyezīd II, transferred him to the Sulṭāniyya and promoted him to being a *muftī* in Bursa. He died in 893/1488.

1. *Tahāfut al-falāsifa*, a critical assessment of the work of al-Ghazzālī (I, 544) and of philosophy, composed together with the treatise by ʿAlī al-Ṭūsī (p. 261) in a competition instigated by Sultan Meḥmed, from which he emerged victorious, Paris 2398, Naples Cat. It. 217, no. 41, Garr. 799, AS 2204/5, Köpr. 798, Laleli 2488, Cairo ^{1}VI, 90, print. C. 1303 (together with al-Ghazzālī's *Tahāfut*), on which are glosses by Ibn Kamālpāshā, d. 944/1537 (p. 449), Paris 2399,$_1$, Vienna 1791,$_{17}$.

2 Which had been founded by Muḥammad Fātiḥ; see Adnan, *Ilim* 307.

4. Muḥyi ’l-Dīn Muḥammad b. Qāsim Akhawayn was a professor at one of the eight madrasas in Istanbul, and died towards the end of the ninth century.

ShN I, 291, ḤKh ^{1}I, 478 u, ^{2}I, 192 (who fixes his death in 904/1498). 1. *al-Sayf al-mashhūr ʿala ’l-zindīq wa-sābb al-rasūl* Cairo ^{1}III, 107.—2., 3. See Suppl.

| 5. Yūsuf b. Ḥasan (Ḥusayn) al-Kirmāstī, a student of Khājazāde, was a profes- 231
sor in Istanbul and then a *qāḍī* in Bursa and Istanbul. He died in 906/1500.

ShN I, 316/7. 1. *Risāla fī ʿaqāʾid al-firaq al-nājiya min al-firaq al-islāmiyya* AS 2261.—2. *al-Wajīz fī uṣūl al-dīn* Tüb. 105, Algiers $560,_{2}$, Garr. 1732, Alex. Uṣūl 22, Fun. $64,_{5}$.—3. *Risāla fi ’l-waqf* Vienna 1798.—4.–9. see Suppl.

| 6. Ḥusayn b. ʿAbd al-Raḥmān Ḥusām Čelebī, a student of Khājazāde, was a 299
professor in Kutāhya, Bursa, Amasia, and Istanbul, then a *qāḍī* in Adrianople and Bursa, and then a professor at one of the eight madrasas in Istanbul. He died in that city in 926/1520.

ShN I, 610/2. 1. *Risāla fī sabb al-nabī* ḤKh ^{1}III, 408, ^{2}I, 871, Leid. 1865.—2. See Suppl.

6 *Mysticism*

1. Dāʾūd b. Maḥmūd al-Rūmī al-Qayṣarī was born in Qaramān and studied both there and, later, in Cairo. After his return to his hometown, Sultan Orkhān built the first madrasa in his kingdom for him. He died in 751/1350.

ShN I, 70. 1. *Risāla fi ’l-taṣawwuf*, Cairo ^{1}II, 86.—2. *Sharḥ Fuṣūṣ al-ḥikam* I, 622.—3. *Sharḥ Taʾwīlāt bismillāh* p. 257.—3.–11. see Suppl. (4. Garr. 588.—8. *Taḥqīq māʾ al-ḥayāt wa-kashf astār al-ẓulumāt*, on Khiḍr, Garr. 731, Taymūr, Majāmīʿ 1, 3.—10. Mashhad, *Dharīʿa* II, $7,_{18}$).—12. *Risāla fī taḥqīq al-zamān* Patna II, $454,_{2629,6}$.

1a. Qāḍī Aḥmad Burhān al-Dīn, the ruler of Sīwās, died in 800 or 801/between 1397 and 1399. He is particularly famous as one of the earliest Turkish lyricists.

Cl. Huart, *EI* I, 832, Brussali *Osm. Müʾell.* I, 396. *Iksīr al-saʿādāt fī asrār al-ʿibādāt* AS 1658 (Ritter).

2. Muḥammad b. Muḥammad al-Āqshahrī wrote, in 839/1435:

Tuḥfat al-murīd wa-nuzhat al-mustafīd, autograph, As'ad 1437,$_{12}$, (Ritter).

3. Ṣā'in al-Dīn 'Alī b. Muḥammad b. Muḥammad al-Turkī, who wrote between 823–8/1420–4.

1. *al-Mafāḥiṣ* Nāfiz 695.—2. *Bayān al-marātib al-thalāth fī 'l-taṣawwuf* AS 1914, 2.—3. *Sharḥ al-Fuṣūṣ* Suppl. I, 793, y, z.

4. Zayn al-Dīn Abu 'l-Waqt 'Abd al-Laṭīf b. 'Abd al-Raḥmān b. Aḥmad b. 'Alī b. Ghānim al-Maqdisī (Qudsī) al-Anṣārī, who was born in 786/1384 in Jerusalem,
300 went with his teacher, | the Sufi Zayn al-Dīn al-Khawāfī (p. 265), to Khurāsān, then, via Damascus, to Konya and Bursa, where he died in 856/1452.

ShN I, 126 (Rescher 37). 1. *Tuḥfat wāhib al-mawāhib fī bayān al-maqāmāt wal-marātib*, on the stages of the mystic, Berl. 3308/9, AS 4802,$_{1}$, Alex. Taṣ. 11, Cairo ^{1}VII, 585.—2. See Suppl.—3. *Ḥāwi 'l-qulūb* Bursa Ulu Cami, Taṣ. 183,$_{2}$.

5. 'Abd al-Raḥmān b. Muḥammad b. 'Alī b. Aḥmad al-Bisṭāmī al-Ḥanafī al-Ḥurūfī, who was born in Antioch, studied in Cairo and then went to Bursa, where he gained the favour of Sultan Murād II. He died in 858/1454.

ShN I, 108, Wüst. *Gesch.* 481 (where it is wrongly stated that he died in 845). 1. *al-Fawā'iḥ al-miskiyya fī 'l-fawātiḥ al-Makkiyya*, an encyclopaedia of 100 sci-
232 ences, composed in 795–844/1392–1440 and dedicated to Sultan Murād II | (see Hammer, *Vienna. Jahrb.* 83, Anz.-Bl. 1, 2/5), Berl. Ms. or. oct. 3931, Leipz. p. 530, Vienna 9, 10, Leid. 10, AS 4160, Cairo ^{1}II, 137.—2. *Durrat al-'ulūm wa-jawharat al-fuhūm*, on the division of the sciences, Gotha 90,$_{1}$.—3. *Rashḥ 'uyūn al-dhawq fī sharḥ funūn al-shawq*, Sufi tales and poems, composed in 842/1438, Gotha 90,$_{2}$.—4. *Rashḥ 'uyūn al-ḥayāt fī sharḥ funūn al-mamāt*, a work similar to the previous, Leid. 2269.—5. *Awrāq al-ḥikma al-rabbāniyya fī sharḥ al-Lum'a al-nūrāniyya* (I, 656,$_{7}$), Yeni 785.—6. *Manāhij al-tawassul fī mabāhij al-tarassul*, on Sufi letter-writing, Berl. 8818/9, Paris 1363,$_{16}$, Algiers 1900, Esc. ^{2}523,$_{1}$, Cairo ^{1}IV, 332, ^{2}III, 383.—7. *Mabāhij al-a'lām fī manāhij al-aqlām* Cairo ^{1}V, 353, Alex. Adab 167 (*Manāhij al-a'lām fī manāhij al-aqlām*).—8. *al-Zahr al-fā'iḥ wal-nūr al-lā'iḥ* Cairo ^{1}V, 343.—9. *al-Sirr al-afkhar wal-kibrīt al-aḥmar* ibid.—10. *Durrat man ẓahara bi-ghurrat al-fawā'id wa-atā min baḥr futūḥātihi bi-durrat al-farā'id* Leid. 1234.—11. *Irtiyāḍ al-arwāḥ fī riyāḍ al-afrāḥ*, composed in 844/1440, Leid. 2268.—12. *Qiblat ḥudūd al-bawānī fī qublat khudūd al-ghawānī*, on the location of the Ka'ba and the Qibla, composed in 845/1441, ibid. 2270.—13. *Kashf asrār al-ḥurūf ma-waṣf ma'āni 'l-ẓurūf*, on the mystical significance of letters,

Paris 2686.—14. *Kanz al-asrār al-abjadiyya wa-laṭāʾif al-anwār al-Aḥmadiyya* ibid. 2687$_{,1}$.—15. *Waṣf al-dawāʾ fī kashf āfāt al-wabāʾ* ibid. 2.—16. *Mafātīḥ asrār al-ḥurūf wa-maṣābīḥ anwār al-ẓurūf* Gotha 1511/2 (where it is mistakenly stated
| that it was composed in 899), Leid. 1131, Paris 2660, 2688, Cairo ^{1}VII, 213, ^{2}V, 301
354.—17. A treatise on prayer, Paris 2690$_{,1}$.—18. *al-Adʿiya al-muntakhaba fī ʾl-adwiya al-mujarraba* ibid. 2691, AS 377$_{,3}$.—19. *al-Durra al-lāmiʿa fī ʾl-adwiya al-jāmiʿa* on cures, prayers, talismans etc., Paris 2690$_{,1}$.—20. *Baḥr al-wuqūf fī ʿilm al-ḥurūf* Vienna 1497.—21. *Shams al-āfāq fī ʿilm al-ḥurūf wal-awfāq* Leid. 1224, Paris 2689, Br. Mus. 760, Ind. Off. 349 (? Attributed to al-Būnī, I, 655).—22. *Miftāḥ al-jafr al-jāmiʿ* or *al-Durr al-munaẓẓam fī ʾl-sirr al-aʿẓam*, on the wars and events that will precede the Last Judgement, Nicholson, *JRAS* 1899, p. 907, Köpr. II, 166.—Abstract by ʿAbd al-Ḥāfiẓ b. Shams al-Dīn al-ʿUmarī al-Marṣafī, Br. Mus. Suppl. 198.—23. *Tawḍīḥ manāhij al-anwār wa-tanqīḥ mabāhij al-azhār*, a chronicle whose words all take on different meanings depending on the way in which they are dotted, Br. Mus. Suppl. 481.—24. *Durar fī ʾl-ḥawādith wal-siyar* ḤKh ^{1}III, 221$_{,5032}$, ^{2}I, 750, called in Leid. 852 *Wafayāt ʿalā tartīb al-aʿwām*, biographies of famous men from the past, from Muḥammad until 700/1300 and dedicated to Sultan Murād II in 835/1431 in Bursa.—25. Biographies of learned men, beginning with the supposed author of *Kalila and Dimna* and ending with al-Ṭabarī and al-Jawharī, composed in 840/1436, Gotha 1738.—26.–34. see Suppl.—35. *Lumʿat al-ishrāq fī maʿrifat ṣanʿat al-awfāq* Alex. Ḥurūf 8 (author only al-Bisṭāmī).—36. *al-Risāla al-waḍʿiyya* Alex. Fun. 152, 9 (author only ʿAbd al-Raḥmān al-Bisṭāmī).

5a. Āq Shams al-Dīn Muḥammad b. Ḥamza, d. 863/1459, see Suppl.

1. *al-Risāla al-nūriyya* also Ğārullah 1084$_{,2}$.

6. Muḥammad b. Maḥmūd Jamāl al-Milla wal-Dīn al-Āqsarāʾī, who wrote at the time of Bāyezīd II 886–918/1481–1512.

1. *Arbaʿūna ḥadīthan*, selected from *al-Aḥādīth al-Qudsiyya wal-āthār al-Muṣṭafawiyya* by Ibn ʿArabī (I, 572$_{,7}$), with Sufi explanations, Berl. 1512, Gotha 3$_{,3}$, Qawala I, 124/5, 243.—2. *Kitāb al-asʾila wal-ajwiba* AS 69/72. 3.–4. See Suppl.—5. *al-Ḥiṣn al-akbar, sharḥ qawlihi ṣlʿm fī-mā yarwīhi ʿan rabbihi ʿazza wa-jalla lā ilāha illa ʾl-lāhu ḥiṣnī fa-man dakhala ḥiṣnī amina min ʿadhābī*, Qawala I, 115, 229 (also attributed to al-Ghazzālī).—6. *Anwār al-qulūb li-ṭalab
ruʾyat al-maḥbūb* ibid. 219.—7. *Risāla fī ḥaqīqat al-adhkār* | ibid. 236.—8. 302
al-Mawʿiẓa al-ḥasana ibid. 267.—9. *Asrār al-wuḍūʾ* ibid. 304.

233 | 7. Idrīs b. Ḥusām al-Dīn al-Bidlīsī, d. 926/1520, see Suppl.

ShN I, 470/1. Brussali, *Osm. Mü'ell.* III, 6. 1. *al-Ibā' 'an mawāqi' al-wabā'*, dedicated to Sultan Selīm I, a defence against the accusation that he lacked trust in God because, on his way back from Mecca in 917/1511, he had avoided Egypt because at the time it was being ravaged by the plague, Berl. 6371.

8. Muḥammad b. 'Abd al-Wahhāb, who was imam and *khaṭīb* at the Murādkhāniyya madrasa, wrote, in 906/1500:

Uṣūl al-khuṭab fī 'ilm al-adab Fātiḥ 3667 (Ritter).

7 *Medicine*

1. 'Abdallāh b. 'Abd al-'Azīz b. Mūsā al-Sīwāsī, who flourished at the beginning of the eighth/fourteenth century.

'Umdat al-fuḥūl fī sharḥ al-Fuṣūl, see Suppl., also Alex. Ṭibb 30.

2. Ḥājjī Pāshā Khiḍr b. 'Alī al-Āydīnī, d. 820/1417, see Suppl.

Abdulhakk Adnān, *La science chez les Turcs Ottomans*, Paris 1939, 15/7, *Ilim* 81/2. 1. *Shifā' al-asqām wa-dawā' al-ālām* autograph Serāi A. III, 2070, Berl. 6356, Leid. 1370, Paris 3102/4, Med. 236, Bodl. I, 524, 528, Yeni 920/1, NO 3543, Köpr. 974, Ibr. P. 933, Garr. Suppl. 2, abstract by the author himself Gotha 1938, Turkish Dresd. 51.—2.–6. see Suppl.—(3. Also under the title *Kumm al-jalālī* Welīaddīn 2536, Manisa Küt. 1788) Turkish translation, *Muntakhab al-shifā'*, Istanbul, Ün. Yildiz Tip 877.—7. *Kitāb al-ta'līm*, on medicine, Turhan Valide 258, see Adnan, *Ilim* 9.

3. Muḥammad b. Maḥmūd b. Ḥājjī Shirwānī, see Suppl.

Rawḍat al-'iṭr also Qawala II, 288.

7a *Mathematics and Astronomy*

1. Muḥammad b. Kātib Sinān, who flourished during the reign of Bāyezīd, see Suppl.

303 | Suter 455. Abdulhakk Adnan, *Ilim* 34/5. 1. *Mūḍiḥ al-awqāt etc.* also Garr. 2006,$_{14}$.—2. *Mīzān al-kawākib* AS 2710.—3. A *risāla* on sharp angles, Köpr. 721 *Majm.*

2. In 905/1500, Muṣliḥ al-Dīn b. Sinān dedicated to Sultan Bāyezīd II:

Risāla Aflāṭūniyya, a treatise on "specific weight" going back to an unknown Greek original, in several Cairene manuscripts, translated as an abstract by E. Wiedemann, *Beitr. z. Gesch. d. Nat.* VIII (1906) 173/80, cf. Abdulhakk Adnān, *Ilim* 49, 204/5.

8 *Occult Sciences*

Muḥammad b. Quṭb al-Dīn al-Rūmī al-Iznīqī Quṭb al-Dīn-zāde, d. 885/1480, see Suppl.

1. *al-Taʿbīr al-munīf wal-taʾwīl al-sharīf* also Paris 2753.—2. *Sharḥ al-Awrād* also Bursa Ulu Cami Taş. $183_{,1}$.

9 *Encyclopaedias and Polyhistors*

1. Shams al-Dīn Muḥammad b. Ḥamza al-Fanārī al-Ḥanafī was born in Ṣafar 751/April 1350, studied in Asia Minor and Egypt and became a *qāḍī* in Bursa, before being captured during the invasion of Tīmūr. He died upon his return from a pilgrimage, on 1 Rajab 834/15 March 1431.

ShN I, 84/92. Abdulhakk Adnān, *La science chez les Turcs Ottomans* 11/2, *Ilim* 3/4. 1. *ʿAwīṣat al-afkār fī ʾkhtibār uli ʾl-abṣār*, on difficult questions concerning the rational sciences, Cairo ^{1}VII, 615, ^{2}I, 254.—Commentary by Muṣṭafā al-Muʿīd, Gotha 1169, Cairo ^{1}VII, 616.—2. *Tafsīr al-Fātiḥa* Leid. 1689, Yeni 61, Köpr. 111, NO 338, Alex. Fun. $152_{,1}$, Cairo ^{1}I, 147, ^{2}I, 39, Qawala I, 51.—3. *Fuṣūl al-badāʾiʿ fī uṣūl al-sharāʾiʿ*, Berl. 4415, Yeni 343/4, AS 999, Cairo ^{1}II, 255, ^{2}I, 378, Qawala I, 292; glosses by his son Muḥammad Shāh (no. 2), Cairo ^{1}II, 245. | 234
Abstract *Ghāyat al-taḥrīr al-jāmiʿ* by Yūsuf b. Ibrāhīm al-Maghribī, composed in 832/1428 with a commentary, Leid. 1857.—4. *Muqaddimat al-ṣalāt* see $253_{,5}$, Suppl. 269, 5a, 1.–5. *al-Risāla al-qudsiyya fī bayān al-maʿārif al-ṣūfiyya* | Berl. 304
3222.—6. *Muqaddimāt ʿashr*, on the names and properties of God and the nature of His unity, Berl. 2322.—7. *Risāla fī māhiyyat al-shayāṭīn wal-jinn* Leid. 1690.—8. *Kitāb al-manṭiq* print. Istanbul 1304.—9. *Sharḥ al-Miṣbāḥ* I, 351.—10. *Ḥāshiya ʿalā Sharḥ al-Miftāḥ lil-Sayyid al-Sharīf* I, 353.—11. *Sharḥ Miftāḥ al-ghayb* I, 580.—12. *Baḥth fī ʾl-nāsikh wal-mansūkh min tafsīr al-Fātiḥa* Alex. Fun. $153_{,10}$.—12.–20. see Suppl. (12. Alex. Fun. $69_{,6}$, attributed to his son Muḥammad Shāh, completed in 824/1421.—20. With the title *Miftāḥ al-uns bayna ʾl-maʿqūl wal-mashhūd fī sharḥ Miftāḥ al-ghayb al-jamʿ wal-wujūd* Patna I, $142_{,1379}$, see I, 807).—21. *Risāla fī ādāb al-baḥth*, a commentary by Darwīsh Aḥmad b. Muḥammad al-Tūqātī, Garr. 917.

2. His son Muḥammad Shāh Čelebī b. Muḥammad al-Fanārī, who was a professor at the Sulṭāniyya madrasa in Bursa. He died in 839/1435 (or, according to others, in 859).

ShN I, 96. 1. *Unmūdhaj al-ʿulūm ṭibāqan li-mafhūm*, an overview of more than 100 sciences, following the example of *Ḥadāʾiq al-anwār* by Fakhr al-Dīn al-Rāzī (I, 666), Berl. 71, Vienna 11. —2. *Risālat al-bayān* Cairo ^{1}VII, 160, ^{2}II, 199.

3. ʿAlāʾ al-Dīn ʿAlī b. Majd al-Dīn Muḥammad b. Masʿūd al-Harawī Muṣannifak al-Shāhrūdī al-Bisṭāmī was a descendant of Fakhr al-Dīn al-Rāzī who was born in 803/1400. He went with his brother to Herat in 812/1409, and then in 846/1442 to Asia Minor. Because of his deafness he had to resign from his post as a professor in Konya. He then moved to Istanbul, where he died in 875/1470.

ShN I, 255/62 (with a chronological inventory of his writings before the age of 58, of which the majority has been lost, based on the preface to his Persian *al-Tuḥfat al-Maḥmadiyya*, no. 8, from which the dates below have been taken), *ShDh* VII, 319. 1. *Sharḥ al-Sharḥ al-muṭawwal*, composed in 832/1429, I, 354.—2. *Sharḥ al-Burda*, composed in 835, ibid. 310.—3. *Sharḥ Sharḥ al-Miftāḥ lil-Sayyid al-Sharīf*, composed in 850/1446, ibid. 354.—4. *Mukhtaṣar al-Muntaẓam* ibid. 661.—5. *Ḥall al-rumūz wa-mafātīḥ al-kunūz* Cairo ^{1}II, 81.—6.–11. see Suppl. (6, see p. 424,$_8$, Garr. 2092,$_3$.—8., with the title *Tuḥfat al-wuzarāʾ*, autograph AS 2855).

305 | 4. ʿAlāʾ al-Dīn ʿAlī b. Muḥammad al-Qūshjī, the son of a falconer of Ulughbeg, studied under Qāḍīzāde in Samarqand and also in Kirman, where he had travelled in secret. Returning to the court of Ulughbeg, he completed the astronomical map named after the ruler (p. 276). After the death of Ulughbeg he
235 went on the pilgrimage, and then travelled to | Uzun Ḥasan, the emir of Tabriz, who sent him as an emissary to Sultan Meḥmed II. Having completed his mission, he returned to the latter and became a professor at the Aya Sofia. He died there on 5 Shaʿbān 879/16 December 1474.

Khwandamīr, *ḤS* III, 3, 160, *ShN* I, 250/5, *MT* 94v (relates the honorable reception that he was given—at the order of the sultan—by the scholars of Istanbul when he entered Skutari, in the biography of Khājazāde), Salih Zeki Bey, *Āsāri Baqiya* I, 198, Abdulhakk Adnān, *Science* 33, *Ilim* 32/4. 1. *al-Risāla al-Muḥammadiyya fi ʾl-ḥisāb*, dedicated to Sultan Meḥmed upon his return to his court, Dresd. 116 (abstract?), Leid. 1034, Pers. AS 2723 Majm. Abstract Leid. 1035, Bodl. I, 73, 85,$_4$.—2. *al-Risāla al-fatḥiyya*, on astronomy, dedicated to the same on the occasion of the conquest of Persian Iraq, Persian original see

Suppl., additionally AS 2670, Yildiz, *Riyāḍ* 370, Istanbul Univ.; Arabic translation Paris 2504,4, AS 2733, Rasath. Kütüp. 65/8.—Commentaries: a. His grandson Maḥmūd b. Muḥammad Mīram Čelebī, d. 931/1524 (p. 447), Paris 2504,5, Garr. 990, Persian translation see Suppl.—b. ibid.—c. *Mir'āt ül-ʿālam* by Sayyid ʿAlī Pāshā, d. 1845, Adnān, *Ilim* 34, n. 1.—3. *al-Risāla al-mufradiyya*, on simple and complex notions, Berl. 5101.—4. *ʿUnqūd al-zawāhir*, on the theory of forms, Garr. 460, commentary by ʿAbd al-Raḥīm, under Selīm, Berl. Oct. 3662, print. Istanbul (? 1866, Alex. Taṣrīf 7).—5. *ʿUqūd al-jawāhir*, on syntax in verse, Cambr. Palmer p. 100.—6. *al-Istiʿārāt*, on metaphors, Berl. 7319, on which a commentary by Ismāʿīl al-Aywālī, completed in 1194/1780, ibid. 7320.—7. *Sharḥ al-Risāla al-ʿAḍudiyya* see p. 268.—8. *Sharḥ al-Tajrīd al-jadīd* I, 671.—9. *Sharḥ al-Tuḥfa al-Shāhiyya* p. 274.—10.–14. see Suppl.—15. *Sharḥ Zīj Ulugh Beg* p. 276.

5. Mollā Luṭfī Luṭfallāh b. Ḥasan al-Tūqātī, a student | of Sinānpāshā[3] and Qūshjī, was appointed by Sultan Meḥmed as librarian at the Fātiḥ mosque on the recommendation of the aforementioned Sinānpāshā. When the latter was banished to Siwriḥiṣār, al-Tūqātī accompanied him there. After his accession to the throne Bāyezīd appointed him as a professor in Bursa, then in Adrianople, Istanbul and, once more, Bursa. His arrogance earned him many enemies and, suspected of heresy, he was beheaded in 900/1494, such in compliance with a fatwa issued by Khaṭībzāde (p. 296). 306

ShN I, 413/9, *MT* 95r, Brussali, *Osm. Müell.* II, 11. Abdulhakk Adnān, *Science* 43, 78, *Ilim* 44/6. 1. *al-Maṭālib al-ilāhiyya fī mawḍūʿāt al-ʿulūm*, dedicated to Bāyezīd, Vienna 15,1, Br. Mus. 430,1, Garr. 1130/1, self-commentary Vienna 15,2, Br. Mus. 430,2.—2. *Risāla fi 'l-sabʿ al-shidād*, answers to seven questions by al-Jurjānī (p. 280), Leid. 1564.—3. *Risāla wujūdiyya* ibid. 1563.—4. *Marātib al-mawjūdāt* ibid. 1565, Ind. Off. 586,6.—5. *Risāla fī nafs al-amr* ibid. 1566.—6. *Mabāḥith al-burhān* ibid. 1567.—7. *Risāla fi 'l-wujūd al-dhihnī* ibid. 568.—8. *Risāla fi 'l-farq bayna 'l-ḥamd wal-shukr* ibid. 294.—9. A short treatise on the letters of the alphabet, ibid. 235.—*Risāla fī taḍʿīf al-madhbaḥ*, on the Delic problem,[4] ibid. 1229. | *Mollā Luṭfi 'l-Maqtūl, La Duplication de l'autel, Platon et le problème de Delos, texte ar. publié par* Serefettin Yaltkaya, *traduction franç. et introduction par* Abdulhakk Adnan et H. Corbin, Paris 1940 (Études or. publiés par l'Institut franç. d'archéologie de Stamboul sous la direction de M.A. Gabriel VI).—11. *Sharḥ al-Mawāqif* p. 270.—12. *Sharḥ Sharḥ Lawāmiʿ al-maṭāliʿ* I, 614.—13. See Suppl. 236

3 See Suppl. 327, § 7a, 3, Abdulhakk Adnan 35.

4 See A. Sturm, Das Delische Problem, *Prog. Gymn. von Seitenstetten 1895/7*, *Bl. f. gymn. Schulwes.* 34, 494ff.

Chapter 8. North Africa

North Africa faced the eastern lands of Islam as one united bloc, even though Tunis and Morocco, and, before 796/1393, Algeria as well, under the Ziyānids, 307 were independent states. | Through the movement of the Almohads, the Berbers, who had always outnumbered the Arabs, had finally also got the better of them politically and culturally, even though they were unable to assert their own language in literature. However, their contributions to intellectual culture did not turn out to be very fruitful. Popular poetry as pursued in Arab circles is entirely overshadowed by conventional court poetry and edifying doggerel. The great historian Ibn Khaldūn and the globe-trotter Ibn Baṭṭūṭa stand alone among their contemporaries, with no-one to follow in their footsteps. The dominance of two rather insignificant schoolbooks, the *Ājurrūmiyya* and the *Sanūsiyya*, is indicative of this.

237 | Zark. *Taʾrīkh al-dawlatayn al-Muwaḥḥidiyya wal-Ḥafṣiyya lil-faqīh Abī ʿAbdallāh Muḥammad b. Ibrāhīm al-Luʾluʾī al-Zarkashī* (p. 456), Tunis 1289.

1 *Poetry*

1. ʿAlī b. ʿAbd al-Ḥamīd al-Maghribī, fl. ca. 830/1427.

Al-Durra al-maknūza, a poem in *rajaz*, Berl. 8159,$_2$.

2. Shihāb al-Dīn Abu ʾl-ʿAbbās Aḥmad b. Abi ʾl-Qāsim b. Muḥammad b. ʿAbd al-Raḥmān al-Fāsī al-Tūnisī b. al-Khallūf, who was born on 3 Muḥarram 828/16 November 1425, lived in Tunis as a poet at the court of the Ḥafṣid sultan ʿUthmān b. Muḥammad (839–93/1435–88), and died in 899/1494.

MT 50v, Hartmann, *Muw.* 33. 1. *Dīwān*, arranged alphabeticaly, Berl. 7919, Tüb. 49, Leid. 774, Garr. 105, Copenhagen 284, Paris 3098,$_3$, Pet. AM 5, selection Berl. 7920, individual poems ibid. 7921, print. Damascus 1291, Beirut 1873.—2. *Muwashshaḥ* Berl. 8172,$_{26}$.—3. *Madāʾiḥ nabawiyya* Alex. Adab 157, Br. Mus. 406,$_{3b}$, 1081,$_3$.

3. Shihāb al-Dīn Aḥmad al-Qusanṭīnī, who flourished around 898/1493.

308 | *Dīwān*, including a vision in a dream of the year 881 and a prayer of the year 898, Copenhagen 279.

2 *Philology*

1. Abū ʿAbdallāh Muḥammad b. Muḥammad b. Dāʾūd al-Ṣanhājī b. Ājurrūm, who lectured in Fez and died in Ṣafar of 723/February 1323.

Al-Muqaddina al-Ājurrūmiyya, a précis on grammar, extremely widespread and still in use; consequently, manuscripts are to be found in every library and it has been printed innumerable times, e.g. by Erpenius, Leiden 1617, Obicini, Rome 1631, Combarel, Paris 1844, Bresnier, Algiers 1846, 1866, Perowne, Cambridge 1852, Trumpp, Munich 1876, Brünnow-Fischer, *Chrest.*; see Cairo IV, 20, 50/8.—Commentaries: 1. Muḥammad b. Aḥmad b. Yaʿlā al-Ḥasanī, born in 672/1273 in Fez, where he died in 723/1322, Paris 4127, Algiers 145/54, Esc. ^{2}88, on which *Sharḥ al-shawāhid* by Aḥmad b. Muḥammad b. Mūsā al-Asilsilī, Algiers 168,$_{2}$.—2. ʿAbd al-Raḥmān b. ʿAlī b. Ṣāliḥ al-Makkūdī, d. 804/1401 (no. 5), Munich 726, Paris 4128, Esc. ^{2}896,$_{2}$, Garr. 433, print. C. 1309, 1345. |—3. Muḥammad b. 238
Muḥammad al-Gharnāṭī al-Rāʿī, d. 853/1449, completed in 824/1421, Munich 733, Esc. ^{2}161.—4. Muḥammad b. Muḥammad al-Ḥalāwī al-Maqdisī, completed in 873/1468, Berl. 6672.—5. ʿAlī b. ʿAbdallāh al-Sanhūrī, d. 889/1484, ibid. 6673.—6. Khālid b. ʿAbdallāh al-Azharī, d. 905/1499 (p. 34), completed in 887/1482, ibid. 6674/5, Gotha 287/93 (where other MSS are listed), BDMG 68, 86, Garr. 434, ed. Schnabel, Amsterdam 1756 (cf. Fraehn, *Leipz. Litztg.* 1830, p. 732), print. Būlāq 1251, 1259, 1274, 1290.—Glosses: a. Yūsuf al-Fayshī al-Mālikī, d. 1052/1642, Leid. 219, Algiers 159, 1324,$_{2}$.—b. ʿAbd al-Raḥmān b. al-ʿĀrī (p. 286), composed in 1107/1696, Munich 732.—c. Aḥmad b. Aḥmad al-Qalyūbī, d. 1069/1658 (p. 364), Berl. 6670, Alex. Naḥw 28.—d. ʿAbd al-Muʿṭī al-Azharī al-Wafāʾī, published by one of his students in 1080/1669, Berl. 6687, Alex. Naḥw 17.—e. Abu ʾl-Najāʾ Muḥammad Mujāhid al-Ṭantidāʾī, completed in 1233/1818, Būlāq 1284, C. 1305, 1306, 1320, among others, ed. V.P. Carletti, Tunis 1290; on which *Taqrīrāt sharīfa wa-tadqīqāt munīfa* by Muḥammad b. Muḥammad al-Anbābī, lith. C. 1281, 1302, 1319.—f. Aḥmad b. Muḥammad b. al-Ḥājj, completed in 1269/1853, Fez 1315.—g.–p. see Suppl. (g. completed in 1223/1808, Alex. Naḥw 32, n. Makram 48).—q. Yūsuf b. Muḥammad b. Yūsuf | al-Qurashī al-Maḥallī al-Aḥmadī (Suppl. 309
II, 926, 120), Alex. Naḥw 29, MS dated 1190.—7. ʿAlī b. ʿAbdallāh al-Samhūdī, d. 911/1505 (p. 223), Berl. 6677.—8. Burhān al-Dīn Ibrāhīm al-Buḥayrī al-Azharī, d. 916/1510, Esc. ^{2}102,$_{6}$, Cairo ^{2}II, 119.—9. ʿAlī b. Maymūn al-Maghribī, d. 917/1511, Sufi see p. 152.—10. Muḥammad b. Muḥammad al-Shirbīnī, d. 977/1569, Berl. 6679.—11. Najm al-Dīn al-Ghaythī, d. 894/1576 (p. 320), ibid. 6680, abstract ibid. 6681.—12. Abu ʾl-Ḥasan al-Shādhilī al-Mālikī, d. 939/1532, Esc. ^{2}93.—13. Rayḥān Āghā, d. 1015/1606, Berl. 6082/3, Leid. 210, Garr. 436.—14. Abū Bakr b. Ismāʿīl al-Shanawānī, d. 1019/1610 (p. 285), Vienna 186, Paris 4137, Algiers 68,$_{2}$, shorter

Paris 1194, Algiers 167.—15. Zayn al-Dīn Muḥammad Jibrīl, ca. 1054/1644, Berl. 6684/5, Paris 4135/6, Algiers 160/2,$673_{,6}$, Alex. Naḥw 34, ed. G. Delphin, Paris 1885, 2nd ed. 1886.—16. Muḥammad b. Muḥammad b. Amīr, ca. 1073/1662, Berl. 6686.—17. Najm al-Dīn al-Faraḍī, d. 1090/1679, ibid. 6686, Garr. 437, Alex. Naḥw $34_{,2}$.—18. Ḥasan b. ʿAlī al-Kafrāwī, d. 1202/1787 (p. 324), Berl. 6689/90, Paris 4138/9, 5339, see Suppl.—19. ʿAbd al-Muʿṭī al-Burnusī, Berl. 6691.—20. Ibrāhīm b. ʿAbd al-Raḥmān, ibid. 6692.—21. Jamāl al-Dīn Yūsuf, Leid. 211.—22. Maḥmūd Pāshā al-Bārūdī (Suppl. III, 7), ibid. 212.—23. Muḥammad b. Aḥmad b. Qadd, Algiers 163/4.—24. Muḥammad b. Muḥammad b. Aḥmad b. al-Ṣabbāgh, ibid. $165_{,1}$, Garr. 434.—25. ʿAbdallāh al-Thaʿlabī, ibid. $168_{,1}$.—26. Aḥmad b. ʿAjība, ibid. 169.—27. Shihāb al-Dīn Aḥmad al-Ramlī, d. 957/1550 (p. 319), ibid. $173_{,2}$, Alex. Naḥw 20, Cairo ^{2}II, 119. —28. ʿAbdallāh b. al-Fāḍil al-ʿAshmāwī, print. C. 1306 and others.—29. Aḥmad b. Aḥmad al-Bijāʾī, Paris 4140, Algiers $166_{,1}$ (which mistakenly has al-Bājī), $1307_{,5}$, 1308.—30. Aḥmad b. Aḥmad al-Sūdānī, Paris 4141.—31. Abu ʾl-Khayr b. Abi ʾl-Suʿūd, ibid. $4151_{,2}$.—32. Aḥmad b. Zaynī Daḥlān, d. 1886 (p. 499), C. 1301, and others.—33. Muḥammad al-Nawawī (p. 501), ibid. 1281.—34.–57. see Suppl. (35. Alex. Naḥw 2; 36. ibid. 17; 51. ibid. 17).—58. ʿAlī b. Muḥammad b. Muḥammad b. Jibrīl al-Manūfī, d. 939/1552 (p. 316), Makram 31.—59. Muḥammad Abu ʾl-Khayr al-Khaṭīb, Alex. Naḥw 2.—60. A Sufi work, by Ismāʿīl al-Bībīdī, Alex. Naḥw 20.—61. Muḥammad b. Mubārak al-Mkdsī, ibid. 32.—*Tatimmat al-Ā.* by Muḥammad b. Muḥammad al-Ruʿaynī, d. 954/1547, with a commentary by ʿAbdallāh al-Fākihī, ca. 924/1518, Leid. 213, BDMG 89, Ind. Off. 980, Paris $4123_{,3}$, 4142, Garr. 435, print. C. 1306, Būlāq 1309.—
310 Versifications: 1. *al-Tuḥfa al-bahiyya* | by ʿAlī b. al-Ḥasan al-Shāfiʿī al-Sanhūrī, completed in 901/1495, Esc. ^{2}162.—2. *al-Durra al-bahiyya* by al-Sharīf al-ʿAmrīṭī (p. 320), composed in 976/1568, Berl. 6693, Ind. Off. 965, Alex. Adab $135_{,6}$, with a commentary by Ibrāhīm al-Bājūrī, d. 1277/1861 (p. 487), print. C. 1309.—3. *al-Manẓūma al-Sunniyya*, by ʿAlī al-Sunnī al-Masarrātī al-Ṭarābulusī, print. C. 1307.—*Miftāḥ al-masāʾil al-naḥwiyya ʿalā naẓm al-Ājurrūmiyya* by al-Shaykh al-Rasmūkī, completed in 1264/1848, Alex. Fun. $80_{,3}$.—Cf. Ahlw. 6696.

2. Abū Isḥāq Ibrāhīm b. Abī Muḥammad ʿAbd al-Salām al-Ṣanhājī b. al-ʿAṭṭār wrote, around 705/1305:

Al-Mishkāt wal-nibrās, a commentary on an anonymous work of grammar, the *Kitāb al-kurrāsa* (autograph dated 642/1244, Esc. ^{2}198), ibid. 128.

239 | 3. Abū ʿAbdallāh Muḥammad b. Aḥmad al-Ḥasanī,who died on 4 Dhu ʾl-Ḥijja 770/11 July 1368 in Tlemcen.

Zark. p. 92. *Sharḥ Jumal al-Khūnajī* I, 607.

4. Abū ʿAbdallāh Muḥammad b. Aḥmad b. Muḥammad b. Abī Bakr b. Marzūq al-Tilimsānī, d. 781/1379, see. Suppl.[1]

Zark. 96, Ibn Farḥūn, *Dībāj*, C. 305. 1. *al-Mafātīḥ al-Marzūqiyya li-ḥall aqfāl wastikhrāj khabāya 'l-Khazrajiyya* I, 380.—2. *Sharḥ ʿUmdat al-aḥkām ʿan sayyid al-anām* I, 438.—3.–5. see Suppl.

5. Abū Zayd ʿAbd al-Raḥmān b. ʿAlī b. Ṣāliḥ al-Makkūdī al-Muṭarrizī, d. 807/1405, see Suppl.

ʿAbdallāh Gannūn I, 141. 2. c. *Sharḥ Maqṣūrat al-M.* by ʿAbdallāh Gannūn al-Ḥasanī, C. 1357.

3 *Historiography*

A Local History

1. Aḥmad b. Aḥmad b. ʿAbdallāh b. Muḥammad al-Ghubrīnī, of the Berber Ghubra tribe, was born in 644/1246 in Bijāyā where he became a *qāḍī*, and was killed on 12 Dhu 'l-Qaʿda 714/18 February 1315.

| 1. *ʿUnwān al-dirāya fī man ʿurifa min ʿulamāʾ al-miʾa al-sābiʿa fī Bijāya* Paris 311
2155, Algiers 1734, Tunis, *Bull. de Corr. Afr.* 1884, p. 32, no. 125, see Cherbonneau, *JA* s. V, vol. 7, p. 475.—2. See Suppl.

2. ʿAbdallāh Qāsim b. ʿĪsā b. al-Nājī hailed from a famous family of the Tanūkh, and became a preacher at the Zaytūna mosque in Kairouan when he was 21 years old. Four years later he went to Tunis where he studied for 14 years, before becoming a preacher and judge on the island of Jerba, in Bijāya three years after that, and then in Qābīs, al-Urbus, and Tabissa. He died in the latter in 837/1433.

Ibn Maryam, *Bustān* 149. *Maʿālim al-īmān*: a. Description of the old mosques and history of the foundation of Kairouan, b. biographies of famous people from there, based on Abū Zayd al-Dabbāgh (see Suppl., *Mashāriq anwār al-qulūb etc.* also Wehbi, 1113/4), *Bull. de Corr. Afr.* 1884, 40/65, 97/136, a volume of

1 Wrongly identified by Derenbourg, Esc. ^{2}II, XIX, with the person mentioned in vol. I, 607$_{,21,4}$, see Suppl. II, 345.

biographies, Garr. 691.—Abstract, *Ghāyat al-taḥṣīl wa-tark al-taʿlīl wal-tazwīl*, by al-Barādhiʿī, vol. I in Kairouan, *Bull. de Corr. Afr.* 183, no. 16.

240 | 3. Abū ʿAbdallāh Muḥammad b. Aḥmad b. Muḥammad b. Muḥammad b. ʿAlī b. Ghāzī ʿUthmān al-Miknāsī, d. 919/1513, see Suppl.

ʿAbdallāh Gannūn I, 139. 1. *al-Rawḍ al-haṭūn fī akhbār Miknāsat al-Zaytūn*, up to the year 919, Br. Mus. Suppl. 597ii, see O. Houdas, *JA* $1885_{,1}$, 101/147.—2. *al-Fihrista al-mubāraka*, an inventory of the *ḥadīth*-scholars of Fez and their writings, Upps. 392.—3. *Inshād al-sharīd fī ḍawāll al-qaṣīd* (*fī rasm al-Qurʾān*) Algiers 375, on which a commentary by Masʿūd Jamūʿ al-Maghribī, ibid. $374_{,5}$.—5. On the metrical particularities of the *qaṣīda* and the *dūbayt* ibid. $241_{,2}$.—6. *Munyat al-ḥussāb*, on arithmatic, Br. Mus. 420, Suppl. 1303, Esc. $^{1}928_{,1}$, Algiers 1459. Glosses by Muḥammad b. ʿAbdallāh b. Aḥmad al-Qāsim al-Ghāzī al-Jazūlī, ibid.—7. *Kulliyyāt* Cairo ^{1}III, 180.—8.–11. see Suppl. (10. Commentary also Alex. Fun. 17).—12. *al-Majālis al-Miknāsiyyāt* Fez Qar. 1120.

B History of the Ibāḍīs

1. Abu ʾl-Faḍl Abu ʾl-Qāsim b. Ibrāhīm al-Barrādī al-Dammarī, a student of the Ibāḍī Abū Sakan ʿĀmir al-Shammākhī, d. 792/1391, wrote, around 810/1407:

312 | *Al-Jawāhir al-muntaqāt min itmām mā akhlā bihi Kitāb al-Ṭabaqāt*, a supplement to the Ibāḍī biographies of al-Darjīnī (I, 410), *Bull. de Corr. Afr.* 1885, 43/6, lith. C. 1302.

2. Abu ʾl-ʿAbbās Aḥmad b. Abī ʿUthmān Saʿīd b. ʿAbd al-Wāḥid al-Shammākhī al-Yafranī al-ʿĀmirī, who died in Jumādā I 928/April 1522 on Jabal Nafūsa.

1. *Kitāb al-siyar*, abstracts of and supplements to the *Siyar* of Abū Zakariyyāʾ (I, 410), the *Ṭabaqāt* of Darjīnī, ibid., and the *Jawāhir* (no. 1), lith. C. n.d. (1854?), 1301 (577 pp.), cf. *Bull. de Corr. Afr.* 1885, 57/71, Basset, *JA* s. IX, vol. 13, 434ff, T. Lewicki, *REI* 1934, 59/78.—2. See Suppl.—3. *Sard al-ḥijja ʿalā ahl al-ghafla*, Alexandria 1309.

C Histories of Dynasties

1. Abu ʾl-Ḥasan ʿAlī b. ʿAbdallāh b. Abī Zarʿ al-Fāsī, who died after 726/1326.

Wüst. *Gesch.* 392. *Al-Anīs al-muṭrib* (*bi-rawḍ*[*at*] *al-qirṭās*) *fī akhbār mulūk al-maghrib wa-taʾrīkh madīnat Fās*, a history of the Idrīsids, the Banū Zanāta, the Almoravids, the Almohads, and the Marīnids, Gotha 1696 (where other MSS

are listed), Paris 1868/70, Marseille 1638, Algiers 1615$_{,1}$, 1616$_{,1}$, Tunis, *Bull. de Corr. Afr.* 1884, 26, no. 84, Br. Mus. Suppl. 597$_{,1}$, lith. Fez 1303, 1307, 1313. *Annales regum Mauretaniae a condito Idrisidarum imperio ad annum 726 ab a. l-Ḥ. A. b. a. Z. Fesano vel, | ut alii malunt, ab a. M. Ṣāliḥ b. ʿAbdalḥalīm Granatensi conscriptos,* 241
ed. C.J. Tornberg, 2 vols. Uppsala 1843/6. *Geschichte der mauretanischen Könige, verf. von Ebul H. A. b. E. Zeraa aus dem Ar. übers. v.* F. v. Dombay, Zagreb 1794/7. *Historia dos Soberanos Mahometanos das primeiras quatro dynastias et de parte da quinta, que reinarão na Mauritania, traduz. por* Fr. Jozé de Santo Antonio Moura, Lisbon 1824. *Roudh el Kartas, Histoire des souverains du Maghreb et annales de la ville de Fès, trad. par* A. Beaumier, Paris 1860.

2. Abū Zakariyyāʾ Yaḥyā b. Muḥammad b. Khaldūn, who died in 788/1387, see Suppl.

A. Bel, *EI* II, 420/1. *Bughyat al-ruwwād fī dhikr al-mulūk min ʿAbdalwād*, a history of the Ziyānids up to 777/1376, Algiers | 1619, see *JA* 1841, 2, 483, 1842, I, 460. 313
Bargès, *Complément de l'histoire des Beni Zeiyan*, Paris 1887, VIII ff.

3. Abu ʾl-Walīd Ismāʿīl b. Yūsuf b. Muḥammad b. al-Aḥmar al-Naṣrī, who died in 807/1404 in Fez, or, according to others, in 810/1407.

Wüst. *Gesch.* 451, see Suppl. 1. *Rawḍat al-nisrīn* Krafft 254, Algiers 1737, translation by Mirante in *Mobacher* (E. Doutté, *Bull. bibl. de l'Islam maghr.* I, 58, n. 5).—2. See Suppl.

4. ʿAbdallāh b. Ibrāhīm al-Asīlī, who came from Arzilla near Tangiers, died in 792/1390.

ʿUmdat al-ṭālib fī nasab āl Abī Ṭālib, a genealogy of the ʿAlids, Berl. 9399, Paris 2021.

5. Abu ʾl-ʿAbbās Aḥmad b. al-Ḥusayn (Ḥasan) b. ʿAlī b. al-Khaṭīb b. Qunfūdh al-Qusanṭīnī[1] al-Jibrītī was a *qāḍī* in Constantine and died in 810/1407.

1. *al-Fārisiyya fī mabādiʾ al-dawla al-Ḥafṣiyya*, a history of the Banū Ḥafṣ from 461 to 804 (6), dedicated to the ruling emir Abū Fāris ʿAbd al-ʿAzīz al-Marīnī,

1 In the manuscript in Vienna we find the vulgar form Qsamṭīnī, see Cherbonneau op. cit. 12, p. 256

Paris 4616, Esc. ^{2}1727, 2, see Cherbonneau, *JA* s. IV, vol. 12, 237/79, 13, 185/212, 17, 51/84, 20, 208/57 (based on a manuscript in Constantine).—2. *Sharaf al-ṭālib fī asna 'l-maṭālib*, biographies of famous men from all the branches of the sciences, running to the year 807, arranged by the year in which they died, and in sections arranged by century, Krafft 310, Paris 1546,$_{2}$, 4629, see *JA* 1852, 2, 208ff.—3. *Uns al-faqīr wa-ʿizz al-ḥaqīr* Cairo ^{1}VII, 344, ^{2}V, 45.—4.–7. see Suppl.

6. Muḥammad b. ʿAbdallāh b. ʿAbd al-Jalīl al-Tanasī, who died in 899/1493.

1. *Naẓm al-durar wal-ʿiqyān fī bayān sharaf Banī Ziyān*, 1. A genealogy of the
242 Ziyānids, 2. the qualities needed in a prince, 3. anecdotes, | 4. an anthology of verse and prose, 5. an ethical treatise, Paris 1875/6, Tunis, *Bull. de Corr. Afr.* 1884, 26, no. 85, see *JA* 1851, 585/91; transl. of chapter 7 of Part 1 in *Histoire des B. Zeiyan, rois de Tlemcen, trad. par* Bargès, Paris 1852.

314 | D Universal History

Abū Zayd ʿAbd al-Raḥmān b. Muḥammad b. Muḥammad b. Khaldūn Walī al-Dīn al-Tūnisī al-Ḥaḍramī al-Ishbīlī al-Mālikī came from a family of the Kinda tribe that had moved from Seville to Africa in the middle of the seventh century. He was born in Tunis on 1 Ramaḍān 732/27 May 1322. After completing his studies he became the secretary to the Ḥafṣid sultan Abū Isḥāq Ibrāhīm II al-Mustanṣir in Tunis. Because the latter was unable to keep control over his lands, Ibn Khaldūn fled in 753/1352 to his brother Yaḥyā (C. 2) in Biskra, which was ruled by the sovereigns of the Zāb, the Banū Muznī. He had already developed relations with the Marīnids in 748/1347, when Abu 'l-Ḥasan had occupied Tunis, so when Abū ʿInān Fāris laid siege to Bijāya after the capture of Tlemcen, he joined the latter and was appointed secretary in Fez in 755/1354. Because he had secret dealings with the deposed emir of Bijāya, Abū ʿAbdallāh Muḥammad, who was detained in Fez, Ibn Khaldūn was incarcerated together with the latter, and only released and given back his post when the sultan died in 759/1358. After the murder of Sultan Abū Salīm, who had appointed him chief *qāḍī*, in 764/1362 he went to Granada, where he assisted Abū ʿAbdallāh b. al-Aḥmar in the struggle for power against his brother. However, as he did not get along with the vizier Ibn al-Khaṭīb (p. 260) he went to Bijāya in 766/1364, where his old friend the Ḥafṣid Abū ʿAbdallāh had acceded to the throne again, and where he was appointed *ḥājib*. But when, in the following year, his master lost a battle and his life to his cousin Abu 'l-ʿAbbās of Constantine, Ibn
243 Khaldūn returned to Biskra | where he promoted the cause of ʿAbd al-Wādid Abū Ḥammū II among the Bedouins, to whom he recommended his brother Yaḥyā as *ḥājib*.

| When the Marīnid ʿAbd al-ʿAzīz had ousted Abū Ḥammū, Ibn Khaldūn 315
offered his services to the former, although he had first gone to Muḥammad III al-Saʿīd of Fez in 774/1372. When, after the latter's death, a struggle for his succession broke out between the two rivals Abu ʾl-ʿAbbās and ʿAbd al-Raḥmān, he was deported to Spain after a brief spell in jail. From there he was soon sent back to Tlemcen, where Abū Ḥammū was ruling again. The latter sent him as an emissary to his old friends the Arab nomads, and Ibn Khaldūn spent four years at Qalʿat b. Salāma, where he worked on his universal history. In order to complete this work in a place that was more favorable to literary pursuits, he went to Tunis in 780/1378, where he also wrote his history of the Berbers. In 784/1382 he went on the pilgrimage, but got no further than Cairo where he started lecturing. In Jumādā II 786/August 1384 Barqūq al-Malik al-Ẓāhir appointed him chief Mālikī *qāḍī*. When he wanted to bring his family over from Fez, he lost them all in a shipwreck and, since his job at the court had taken a downturn as well, he retired to his estate in the Fayyūm and finally accomplished the pilgrimage in 789/1387. On 15 Ramaḍān 801/22 March 1399 he was again appointed chief *qāḍī*, before being deposed once more in Muḥarram 803/September 1400. In Rabīʿ II 803/November–December 1400
he accompanied the Egyptian army | on a military campaign against Tīmūr. 244
He supposedly took part in a mission sent by the city of Damascus, led by the Ḥanbalī chief *qāḍī* Taqī al-Dīn Ibrāhīm b. Mufliḥ, which went to plead for mercy for their city from Tīmūr. After his return to Cairo on 1 Shaʿbān 803/17 March 1401 he was reinstated in office on 15 Ramaḍān/30 April. He lost his post a further four more times during his life and died, as chief *qāḍī*, on 25 Ramaḍān 808/17 March 1406.

| As a man, Ibn Khaldūn possessed an indestructable power to survive and 316
a pliability that fitted all circumstances rather than moral backbone and loyalty. Similarly, his literary achievements stand out by a number of brilliant observations on the processes behind the formation of states on the borderline between the desert and the civilised world—observations for which he could draw on his rich political experience in the muddled circumstances of his native country and which lent his *Muqaddima* its attractiveness as a modern conception of history—but enlightening accounts of history itself they are not. Nevertheless, in his otherwise carelessly written universal history, his history of the Berbers and the parts related to the Maghrib, too, are invaluable sources of information.

Autobiography *ʿIbar* VII, 379/98, transl. de Slane, *JA* s. IV, vol. 3, p. 5ff., 187ff., 291ff., 325ff., ʿA. Mubārak, *al-Khiṭ. al-Jad.* XIV, 5, Wüst. *Gesch.* 456, A. Müller, *Der Islam* II, 668ff., Fereiro, *Un sociologo arabe del sec. XIV in Riforma sociale*

245 1897, no. 3, A. Iskandarī, *RAAD* IX, 421/32, 461/71. |—(*ʿUnwān*) *al-ʿIbar wa-dīwān
al-mubtadaʾ wal-khabar fī ayyām al-ʿArab wal-ʿAjam wal-Barbar wa-man ʿāṣara-
hum min dhawi ʾl-sulṭān al-akbar* Tub. 3/5, Paris 1517/35, Br. Mus. 1237/8, NO
3065/70, Yeni 888, print. Būlāq 1284, 7 vols. Jac. Gråberg di Hemsö, *Notizia
intorno alla famosa opera istorica d'Ibnu Kaldun*, Florence 1834. Vol. I, *al-
Muqaddima*, drafted in the first five months of 779/1377 and re-edited later,[1]
Berl. 9362/9, Munich 373, Vienna 815/6, Br. Mus. 934, 279, Suppl. 477, Garr.
593, Prolégomènes d'Ebn Khaldoun, ed. Quatremère I/III, *Not. et Extr. 16/8*,
Beirut 1886 and others. *I. Kh. ʿAr. A selection from the Prolegomena with notes
and an English-German glossary by* D.B. Macdonald, Leiden 1905 (*Sem. Study
Series* IX). Transl. M.G. de Slane, *Not. et Extr.* 19/21. A. v. Kremer, I. Ch. und seine
Culturgeschichte der islamischen Reiche, *SBWA* 93 (1879), 581/634.—Turkish
translation, see Suppl.—Vols. II/VI, history of the Arabs, Nabateans, Syrians,
317 Persians, Israelites, Copts, | Greeks, Romans, Turks, and the Franks, from this:
I. Kh. Narratio de expeditionibus Francorum in terras Islamismo subjectas, ed. C.J.
Tornberg, Upps. 1840 (*Acta Reg. Soc. Sc. Ups.* XII).—Vol. VII: *Histoire des Berbères
et des dynasties Musulmanes de l'Afrique septentrionale par I. Kh. Texte ar. i, 2,
publié par* de Slane, Algiers 1857/51,t. ibid, I–IV, Algiers 1852. I. Kh. Histoire des
Benou ʾl-Ahmar rois de Grenade, transl. M. Gaudefroy-Demombynes, *JA* s. IX,
vol. 12, 309/40, 407/62.

4 *Ḥadīth*

1. Abū ʿAbdallāh Muḥammad b. ʿUmar b. Muḥammad al-Sabtī Muḥibb al-Dīn
b. Rushayd al-Fihrī al-Andalusī was born in Ceuta in Jumādā I 657/March 1259.
He studied there and in Fez. After making the pilgrimage in 683/1284 he spent
some time in Egypt and Syria. When his travelling companion Muḥammad b.
ʿAbd al-Raḥmān b. al-Ḥakam al-Zubaydī al-Lakhmī became undersecretary
in Granada, the latter appointed him as a professor of *ḥadīth* there. After the
murder of his patron in Shawwāl 708/March 1309, he returned to his native
246 country | where he received a position at the court of the Marīnid ʿUthmān
(710–31/1310–31) in Fez, dying there in Muḥarram 721/March 1321.

DK IV, 111, no. 308, Sanchez Pérès, *Biogr.* 117. 1. *Milʾ al-ʿayba fī-mā jamaʿa bi-ṭūl
al-ghayba fi ʾl-riḥla ilā Makka wa-Ṭayba*, accounts of the scholars living in Cairo
and Alexandria around the year 700/1300, 5 vols., Esc. ²1680, 1735/7 (autograph),
1739.—2., 3. See Suppl.

---

1 The fact that he still worked on it in Egypt is, for instance, borne out by the passages of Paris i, 326ff. ii, 200.

2. Abū ʿAbdallāh Muḥammad b. Saʿīd b. ʿĪsā b. ʿUmar b. Saʿīd al-Ṣanhājī Amghshāb,[1] *qāḍī* of Azammūr, wrote, in the first half of the eighth century:

1. *Kanz al-asrār wa-lawāqiḥ al-afkār*, on Muḥammadan mythology, Berl. Ms. or. oct. 3920 (which has *wa-lawāmiʿ*), Gotha 774, Vienna 1924, Leid. 2025, Paris 1400/1, Algiers 859/60, | Pet. Ros. 25, Ibr. Pāshā 774, Cairo [1]VI, 183, [2]I, 349, App. 17, 318
Alex, Mawāʿiẓ 22, 33, Bursa, Haraccizade Taṣ. 22.—Abstracts Munich 133, Cairo [1]VII, 115, table of contents in Hammer, *Wien. Jahrb.* 83, 6, no. 327.—2. *al-Tuḥfa al-ẓarīfa fī 'l-asrār al-sharīfa* Fez Qar. 1494.

3. Yaḥyā b. Aḥmad b. Muḥammad al-Nafzī al-Ḥimyarī al-Sarrāj al-Maghribī, who died in 805/1403.

Taqyīd or *Mashyakha*, a collection of *ḥadīth* and biographical notes, Paris $758_{,1}$.

4. Aḥmad b. Zakariyyāʾ al-Maghribī wrote, in 875/1470:

Muʿallim al-ṭullāb bi-mā lil-aḥādīth min al-alqāb (such as *ṣaḥīḥ, ḥasan*, etc.), Cairo [1]VII, 285.

5. Abū ʿAbdallāh Muḥammad b. al-Qāsim al-Faḍl al-Raṣṣāʿ al-Tūnisī al-Anṣārī, who died in 894/1489, see Suppl.

Tuḥfat al-akhyār fī faḍl al-ṣalāt ʿala 'l-nabī al-mukhtār, completed in Ramaḍān 869/May 1465, Br. Mus. $872_{,6}$ (fragm.)—2. *Tadhkirat al-muḥibbīn fī asmāʾ sayyid al-mursalīn*, an explanation of the names of the Prophet occurring in the *Shifāʾ* of Ibn ʿIyāḍ (I, 455), with special emphasis on their paraenetic content, Berl. 9513.—3. *al-Hidāya al-kāfiya* p. 319.

5 *Fiqh, Mālikī*

1a. Abū ʿAbdallāh Muḥammad b. ʿAbdallāh b. Rāshid al-Bakrī al-Qafṣī al-Mālikī, d. 736/1335, see Suppl.

1. *Lubāb al-lubāb fī bayān mā taḍammanathu abwāb al-kitāb min al-arkān wal-shurūṭ wal-mawāniʿ wal-asbāb* additionally Alex. Fiqh Māl. 14.—2. *al-Martaba al-ʿulyā fī taʿbīr al-ruʾyā* ibid. Fun. 202.

1 According to H. Stumme, from the many variants of this name mentioned in Ros., loc. cit., (Anmashāyad etc. Nqshābu Fez Qar.) only this one looks Berber in its morphology and might have been formed out of the Arabic Khashshāb.

1b. ʿIzz al-Dīn Abū ʿAbdallāh Muḥammad b. ʿAbd al-Salām al-Mālikī, who died in 749/1348.

Fatāwī Algiers 1360$_{,2}$.

247 | 2. Abū ʿAbdallāh Muḥammad b. Aḥmad al-Sharīf, who died in 760/1358.

Mukhtaṣar fi ʾl-uṣūl, dedicated to the Marīnid Abū ʿInān (749–59/1348–58), Algiers 976.

3. Abu ʾl-Rūḥ ʿĪsā b. Abī Masʿūd b. Manṣūr al-Naklātī al-Ḥimyarī al-Zawawī, who died in 774/1372.

319 | *Manāqib al-imām Mālik* Alex. Taʾr. 133, Cairo ^{2}V, 366, printed in the margin of al-Suyūṭī's *Tazyīn al-mamālik* C. 1325.

4. ʿAlī b. Masʿūd al-Khuzāʿī, d. 789/1387, see Suppl. III, 1276/7.

5. Abū ʿImrān Mūsā b. ʿĪsā al-Maghīlī al-Māzūnī, of the Maghīla tribe, died in 791/1389.

1. *al-Muhadhdhab al-rāʾiq fī tadbīr al-nāshī min al-quḍāt wa-ahl al-wathāʾiq* Br. Mus. 242$_{,1}$.—2. *Qilādat al-tasjīlāt wal-ʿuqūd wa-taṣarruf al-qāḍī wal-shuhūd* ibid. 2.

6. Abū ʿAbdallāh Muḥammad b. Abī Zayd (Yazīd) ʿAbd al-Raḥmān al-Marrākushī al-Ghumārī, who was born in 726/1326, wrote, in 801/1399:

Kitāb ismāʿ al-ṣumm fī ithbāt al-sharaf min qibal al-umm Br. Mus. 134$_{,3}$.

7. Abū ʿAbdallāh Muḥammad b. Muḥammad b. ʿArafa al-Warghamī al-Tūnisī, who died in 803/1400, see Suppl.

Zark. 105, *Hist. des Berbères* I, 52, Vincent, *Études* 43. 1. *al-Mabsūṭ fī uṣūl al-fiqh*, vol. II, Algiers 1273/4.—2. *al-Mukhtaṣar fi ʾl-fiqh*, commenced in 772/1370, Cairo ^{1}III, 181, ^{2}I, 491.—3. *al-Ḥudūd al-fiqhiyya*, with the commentary *al-Hidāya al-kāfiya* by Muḥammad b. al-Qāsim al-Raṣṣāʿ, d. 894/1489 (§ 4, 5), Algiers 1275/6.—4. *Sharḥ al-Farāʾiḍ al-Ḥawfiyya* I, 480, no. 5.—5. *Tafsīr* NO 184.—6. Some short definitions of theological terms, Berl. 2788.

8. Abu 'l-Qāsim Aḥmad b. Muḥammad b. Abi 'l-Muʿtall al-Burzulī al-Mālikī was imam at the Zaytūna mosque, and a preacher and professor in Tunis. He died on 25 Dhu 'l-Qaʿda 841/22 May 1438.

Zark. 122. *Jāmiʿ masāʾil al-aḥkām mimmā nazala min al-qaḍāyā bil-muftīn wal-ḥukkām*, Br. Mus. 244/6, Algiers 1333/4. Abstract (?) by the author himself, Br. Mus. 247. Selected *masāʾil* by Abu 'l-ʿAbbās Aḥmad b. ʿAbd al-Raḥmān Ḥalūlū, first half of the ninth century, from which an abstract by Abū Muḥammad b. Akrīsh from the year 1149/1736, Algiers 1337.

9. Abū Zakariyyāʾ Yaḥyā b. Mūsā (no. 5) b. ʿĪsā al-Maghīlī, who died in 883/1478.

| *Al-Durar al-maknūna fī nawāzil Māzūna*, on legal rulings, Algiers 1335/6. 248

| 10. Aḥmad b. Yaḥyā b. Muḥammad al-Tilimsānī al-Wansharīshī was born in 834/1430 in Tlemcen, where he also studied. After a dispute with an officer of the Ziyānī emir Ḥammū Mūsā b. Yūsuf he had to flee to Fez in 874/1469, where he died in 914/1508. 320

Bargès, *Complément à l'hist. des B. Zeiyan* 420, Delpech, *Rev. Afr.* XXVII (1883), 337, Basset, *Giorn. d. Soc. As. Ital.* X, 49. 1. *Īḍāh al-masālik ilā qawāʿid al-imām Abī ʿAbdallāh Mālik* Algiers 975$_{,2}$.—2. *al-Manhaj al-fāʾiq wal-manhal al-rāʾiq fī aḥkām al-wathāʾiq* (*ādāb al-muwaththiq*) Kairouan, *Bull. de Corr. Afr.* 1884, 185, no. 39.—3. *al-Miʿyār al-mughrib ʿan fatāwī ʿulamāʾ Ifrīqiya wal-Andalus wal-Maghrib*, composed in 901/1495, Madr. 474/5, 537, Algiers 1338/41, Zaouiyah d'El Hamel, see *Giorn. d. Soc. As. It.* X, 48, no. 15, Cairo ^{1}III, 183, ^{2}I, 492, print. Fez 1314/5, 12 vols.—4., 5. See Suppl.—6. *Le Livre des magistratures, texte ar. publié et trad. par* H. Brunot et Gaudefroy Demombynes, *Coll. de textes ar. publieé par l'Inst. des Hautes Étutes Maroc.* VIII, Rabat 1937.

6 *Sciences of the Qur'ān*

1. Abū ʿAbdallāh Muḥammad b. Muḥammad b. Ibrāhīm b. ʿAbdallāh al-Umawī al-Sharīshī al-Kharrāzī wrote, around 703/1303:

A poem on *ḍabṭ* (see Suppl.), commentaries: a. *al-Ṭirāz fī sharḥ Ḍabṭ al-Kharrāz* by Muḥammmad b. Yūsuf b. ʿAbdallāh b. ʿAbd al-Jalīl al-Tanasī (§ 3, C. 6), Algiers 390$_{,2}$.—b. see Suppl.—2. *Mawrid al-ẓamʾān fī rasm al-Qurʾān*, in *rajaz*, ibid. 386/9$_{,3}$, 394$_{,1}$, 411$_{,3}$, Paris 3264/6 (anon.), Alex. Fun. 146$_{,9}$, Fātiḥ Waqf Ibr. 28$_{,3}$.—Commentaries: a. Abū ʿAbdallāh Muḥammad b. ʿUmar al-Ṣanhājī, composed in 744/1343, ibid. 389,$_{15}$, abbreviated by Muḥammad b. Khalīfa b. Ṣalāḥ al-Sijilmāsī in 825/1422 in Sfax, ibid. 389,$_{2}$, Munich 890, Paris 1061,$_{5}$, Br. Mus. 92.—b. *Fatḥ al-mannān* by ʿAbd al-Wāḥid b. Aḥmad b. ʿĀshir al-Anṣārī, d. 1040/1630 (p. 461, § 8, 2), Br. Mus. 92 (cf. Add. 764), Algiers 390.—c. *Tanbīh al-ʿaṭshān*, by Ḥusayn b. ʿAlī b. Ṭalḥa al-Rajrājī al-Shawshāwī, d. 899/1493, Algiers 391.—d. al-Ḥasan, ibid. 392,$_{1}$.—e. Anon., ibid. 393.—f. see Suppl. A supplement, *Bayān al-ikhtilāf wal-istiḥsān wa-mā aghfalahu Mawrid etc.*, by Abū Zayd ʿAbd al-Raḥmān b. al-Qāḍī, Algiers 392,$_{2}$.

321 | 2. ʿAlī b. Muḥammad b. ʿAlī b. al-Barrī al-Ribāṭī, who died in 730/1330.

1. 30 *rajaz* verses entitled *Fī makhārij al-ḥurūf*, Berl. 548.—2. *al-Durar al-lawāmiʿ fī aṣl maqraʾ al-imām Nāfiʿ*, 242 *rajaz* verses in 17 sections, all of whose titles are in verse, composed in 697/1297, Berl. 643, Paris 1077,$_{5}$, 3264 (anon.), Algiers 389,$_{4}$, 394,$_{2}$, Br. Mus. 91.—commentaries: a. Abū ʿAbdallāh Muḥammad b. ʿAbd al-Malik al-Qaysī al-Mintawrī, composed in 733–4/1371–3, Paris 1077,$_{5}$, Algiers 380, Br. Mus. 91.—b. Yaḥyā b. Saʿīd al-Simlālī, composed in 793/1391, Algiers 377,$_{1}$.—c. ʿAbd al-Raḥmān b. Muḥammad b. Makhlūf al-Thaʿālibī, composed in 842/1438, ibid. 405, 2.—d. Ḥusayn b. ʿAlī b. Ṭalḥa al-Rajrājī al-Shawshāwī, d. ca. 899/1493 (no. 6.), ibid. 379.—e. ʿAbdallāh Muḥammad b. Saʿīd al-Anṣārī, ibid. 381.—f. Anon. fragm., ibid. 378.—h., i. 3. See Suppl.

3. Ibrāhīm b. Muḥammad b. Ibrāhīm al-Safāqusī al-Naḥwī Burhān al-Dīn was born in 697/1298, studied in Bijāya and in Cairo under Ibn Ḥayyān (p. 133), and in Damascus under al-Mizzī (p. 75). He died on 18 Dhu ʾl-Qaʿda 742/26 April 1342.

DK I, 55, no. 146. 1. *al-Mujīd fī iʿrāb al-Qurʾān al-majīd*, 2 vols., Berl. 881, Br. Mus. Suppl. 118, Köpr. 42/3, Cairo ^{1}I, 207, ^{2}I, 61.—2. *Tuḥfa wafiyya fī maʿānī ḥurūf al-ʿarabiyya* Garr. 274.

4. Aḥmad b. Muḥammad b. Aḥmad al-Basīlī, who died in 830/1427.

ḤKh ^{1}II, 348, ^{2}I, 438. A Qurʾān commentary based on the lectures of his teacher Abū ʿAbdallāh Muḥammad b. ʿArafa (al-Warghamī? § 4, 6), Algiers 349.

5. ʿAbd al-Raḥmān b. Muḥammad al-Thaʿālibī, who died in 873/1468[1] in Algiers, see Suppl.

1 This is according to his epitaph, see Fagnan, *Cat.* 244, Basset, op. cit., 55, no. 3; 875 or 876 is wrong.

A. Devoux, *Les édifices religieux de l'ancien Alger*, 1870, 37/48, Bargès, *Compl.* 394/6, Cherbonneau, *Essai sur la littérature arabe au Soudan* (Annuaire de la Soc. Arch. de Constantine, II, 1855) 45/6, Basset, *Giorn. d. Soc. As. It.* X, 54. 1. *al-Jawāhir al-ḥisān fī tafsīr al-Qurʾān*, completed on 25 Rabīʿ I 833/23 December 1429, Paris 646/8, 5283, 5379, | Esc. ^{2}1324, *Bull. de Corr. Afr.* 1885, 469, no. 2, 322
Zaouiyah d'El Hamel, *Giorn. de Soc. As. It.* X, 55, Cairo I, ^{1}163, ^{2}44.—2. *Sharḥ al-Durar al-lawāmiʿ* no. 2, 2, c.—3. *Jāmiʿ al-ummahāt fī aḥkām al-ʿibādāt* Algiers 583.—4. *al-ʿUlūm al-fākhira fi 'l-naẓar fī umūr al-ākhira* ibid. 850, another edition completed in 847, ibid. 851.—5. *Riyāḍ al-ṣāliḥīn wa-tuḥfat al-muttaqīn* Br. Mus. 1438, Algiers 883, Alex. Mawāʿiẓ 20, Cairo ^{2}I, App. 41.—6. *Rawḍat al-anwār wa-nuzhat al-akhyār*, Algiers 884; a tradition on the *miʿrāj* taken from it, Br. Mus. 126,$_5$.—7. A story of a vision in which the Prophet appeared to him in a dream, Br. Mus. 124,$_2$.—8.–12. see Suppl. (12. Berl. Brill, M. 303).

6. Abū ʿAbdallāh Ḥasan (Ḥusayn) b. ʿAlī b. Ṭalḥa al-Rajrājī al-Shawshāwī al-Simlālī, who died around 899/1493.

1. *al-Fawāʾid al-jamīla fi 'l-āyāt al-jalīla*, a general and specific introduction to the Qurʾān, Berl. 421/2, Algiers 313, Alex. Fawāʾid 14.—2. *Sharḥ Mawrid al-ẓamʾān* see no. 1, 2c.—3. *Sharḥ al-Durar al-lawāmiʿ* see no. 2, d.—4. *Qurrat al-abṣār ʿala 'l-thalātha al-adhkār*, on the merits of the three forms of *dhikr*, Algiers 761/3.—5., 6. See Suppl.

7 *Dogmatics*

1. Sirāj al-Dīn Abū ʿAlī Muḥammad b. Khalīl al-Tūnisī al-Sukūnī, who died in 716/1316.

Laḥn al-ʿawāmm fī-mā yataʿallaq bi-ʿilm al-kalām Berl. 2037.

2. Abū Zayd ʿAbd al-Raḥmān b. Aḥmad al-Waghlīsī al-Maghribī, who died in 786/1384.

1. *al-Muqaddima*, or *al-ʿAqīqa al-Waghlīsiyya*, Br. Mus. 126, xiii, Algiers 590/1.—Commentaries: a. Abū Zayd ʿAbd al-Raḥmān al-Ṣabbāgh, Algiers 392/7,$_3$, Garr. 924.—b. Ibn Zarrūq, d. 899/1493 (p. 328), Br. Mus. 126,$_4$.—2. *Risāla fi 'l-īmān wal-islām*, Kairouan, *Bull. de Corr. Afr.* 1884, 184, no. 35.

3. ʿAbdallāh b. ʿAbdallāh al-Tarjumān al-Mayurqī was born in Morocco to Christian parents. He studied in Lerida and Bologna. On the advice of bishop

323 Nicholas Martell, who was secretly a Muslim himself, | he went to Tunis, converted to Islam and wrote, in 823/1420:

Tuḥfat al-arīb fi 'l-radd ʿalā ahl al-ṣalīb, a polemical tract against Christianity, which Abu 'l-Ghayth Muḥammad al-Qashshāsh provided with an introduction and a new title, *Taḥiyyat al-asrār, taʾlīf al-akhyār al-anṣār fi 'l-radd ʿala 'l-Naṣāra 'l-kuffār*, and dedicated to Sultan Aḥmad I, 1012–26/1603–17, Berl. Ms. or. oct. 3917, Gotha 860, Leid. 2033, Upps. $406,_{1}$, Paris 1464, 6051/2, Algiers 720, Cairo ^{1}VI, 120, ^{2}I, App. 19 (with Turkish translation), Garr. 1521, $2167,_{1}$, print. C. 1904 and others; cf. Steinschneider, *Polem. u. apol. Lit.* 34, no. 15, *Rev. Afr.* V, 266, *Rev. de l'hist. des rel.* XII, 68/89, 179/201, 278/301.

3a. ʿAlī b. ʿĪsā b. Salāma b. ʿĪsā al-Biskrī wrote, in 860/1456 in Biskra:

Al-Lawāmiʿ wal-asrār fī manāfiʿ al-Qurʾān wal-akhbār Algiers $828,_{2}$, $1767,_{4}$, Tunis Zayt. III, $223,_{1687/8}$, Alex. Faw. 17.

4. Abū ʿAbdallāh Muḥammad b. Yūsuf b. ʿUmar al-Ḥasanī al-Sanūsī, a student of al-Qalaṣādī (p. 343), lived as a Sufi in Tlemcen and died in 892/1486 or, according to others, in 895.

Biography: *al-Mawāhib al-quddūsiyya fi 'l-manāqib al-Sanūsiyya* by Muḥammad b. ʿUmar al-Tilimsānī al-Mallālī, composed in 897/1492, Algiers 1706, cf. *Rev. Afr.* V, 264, Cherbonneau, *JA* 1854, I, 175. I. *ʿAqīdat ahl al-tawḥīd wal-tasdīd al-mukhrija min ẓulumāt al-jahl wa-rabqat al-taqlīd* or *al-ʿAqīda al-kubrā* Berl. 2023, Alex. Fun. $77,_{3}$, $147,_{9}$, Cairo ^{1}II, 34, Patna II, $431,_{2606,5}$.—Self-commentary *ʿUmdat ahl al-tawfīq wal-tasdīd* Berl. 2024/5, Paris 1271/2, Algiers 630/3, Sarajevo 164/5, Makram 46.—Glosses: a. al-Ḥasan b. Masʿūd al-Yūsī, d. 1111/1699 (p. 455), Paris 1273, Patna II, $450,_{2627,1}$.—b. Ramaḍān al-ʿAkkārī, ibid. 1274.—c.–f. see Suppl.—g. Muḥammad b. Qāsim Jassūs al-Fāsī, twelfth cent., Alex. Tawḥīd 11.—II. *ʿAqīdat ahl al-tawḥīd al-ṣughrā* or *Umm al-barāhīn*, Berl. 2006/7, Gotha 682, Paris $1141,_{2}$, 1270, 5320, Br. Mus. $140,_{2}$, $146,_{3}$, $872,_{4}$, Esc. $^{2}248,_{3}$, $636,_{8}$, Garr. 1499, $2003,_{16}$, Qawala I, 160. *El Senusis Begriffsentwicklung des muhammedan-*
251 *ischen Glaubensbekentnisses,* | *ar. u. deutsch mit Anmm. v.* Ph. Wolff, Leipzig 1848, *Petit Traité de théologie musulmane par Senousi, texte ar, publié par ordre*
324 *de M. Jules Cambon, gouverneur général de l'Algérie, avec* | *une trad. franç. et des notes par* J.D. Luciani, Algiers 1896. La philosophie du cheikh Sennousi d'après son aqida es soʾra par G. Delphin, *JA* s. IX, vol. 10, 356/70.—Commentaries: 1. Self-commentary, Berl. 2008/9, Gotha 1159, Paris 1271/2, 4584, Br. Mus. 154,

159,$_3$, 160/1,$_2$, Alex. Tawḥīd 19, Makram 38.—Glosses: a. Dāʾūd b. Sulaymān al-Raḥmānī, d. 1078/1667, composed in 1065/1655, Berl. 2012/3, Alex. Tawḥīd 6.—b. ʿĪsā b. ʿAbd al-Raḥmān al-Saktānī, d. 1062/1652, Berl. 2014.—c. Aḥmad al-Dardīr, d. 1201/1786 (p. 353), Gotha 678.—d. al-Dasūqī, d. 1230/1815 (p. 485), Makram 18/9, print. Būlāq 1281, 1297, C. 1295, 1305, 1306, 1314.—e. al-Bājūrī, d. 1277/1861 (p. 487), Būlāq 1287, C. 1307, among others.—f. Muḥammad b. Abi ʾl-Qāsim al-Fajījī, composed in 1048/1638, Br. Mus. 154,$_2$, 156, Algiers 668/75,$_2$, 758.—g. ʿAlī b. Muḥammad al-Majdūlī, composed in 1104/1692, ibid. 694.—h. Abū Zakariyyāʾ Yaḥyā al-Zawāwī, ibid. 696.—i. al-Jawd b. Ḥājj Yaʿlawī (sic?), ibid. 1426,$_3$.—k. Ḥasan b. Yūsuf al-Zayyātī, d. 1023/1685, ibid. 5.—l., m. see Suppl.—2. Muḥammad b. ʿAmr (ʿUmar) b. Ibrāhīm al-Tilimsānī al-Mallālī, ca. 1000/1591, Berl. 2015/6, Br. Mus. 871,$_1$, Ind. Off. 470,$_6$, Algiers 676/9, 1300,$_2$, Alex. Tawḥīd 20.—3. ʿAbd al-Raḥmān b. al-ʿĀrī al-Arīḥawī, eleventh century, Gotha 679.—4. Aḥmad b. ʿAbdallāh al-Ghadāmiṣī al-Miṣrī, composed in 1064/ 1654, Algiers 682/5.—5. ʿAbd al-Ghanī al-Nābulusī, d. 1143/1730 (p. 441), Berl. 2017.—6. Muḥammad b. ʿAbdallāh al-Raṣāṣī, composed in 1154/1741, ibid. 2018.—7. Muḥammad b. Manṣūr al-Hudhudī, eleventh century, ibid. 2019, BDMG 31c, Alex. Fun. 185,$_2$, Makram 44, 102/3. Glosses: a. ʿAlī b. Aḥmad al-Saʿīdī al-ʿAdawī, d. 1189/1775 (p. 319), Algiers 1431,$_2$, Alex. Tawḥīd 31, Makram 23.—b. ʿAbdallāh al-Sharqāwī, d. 1227/1808, Makram 20, print. C. 1292, 1310.—c.–e. see Suppl.—(c. Alex. Tawḥīd 11, Fun. 111,$_5$, Makram 18; d. Alex. Tawḥīd 45, *Talkhīs* by Muṣṭafā al-Saqqā al-Maḥallī, ibid. 38).—f. Muḥammad b. ʿUbāda b. Barrī al-ʿAdawī al-Mālikī, d. 1193/1779, Makram 22.—g. *al-Aqwāl al-mufīda* by ʿAlī b. Muḥammad b. Qāsim al-Sharanqāshī al-Khaṭīb, completed in 1145/1732, Alex. Tawḥīd 5.–8. Muḥammad al-Maʾmūn b. Muḥammad al-Ḥafṣī, d. 1114/1702, Paris 1276, Algiers 632,$_6$, 680/1.–9. Aḥmad b. ʿAbd al-Ghanī al-Khazrajī, Br. Mus. 155.—10. Saʿd b. ʿAbdallāh al-Wajahānī, ibid. 158/9.–11. Aḥmad b. ʿAṭiyya al-Ṣafatī, Munich 144.—12. ʿAbd al-Raḥmān al-Akhḍarī (p. 355), Algiers 1426,$_7$.—13. (= 1, e) al-Bājūrī (p. 487), Būlāq 1302, with a *taqrīr* by Aḥmad al-Ujhūrī, d. 1293/1876, in the margin, on which a *taqrīr* by Muḥammad al-Anbābī, d. 1313/1895, | Alex. Tawḥīd 8, by Sayyid al-Sharqāwī al-Sharshīmī, ibid.— 325
14. *Bidāyat al-hidāya*, by Muḥammad Zayn, Istanbul 1302.—15. *Dharīʿat al-yaqīn*, by Muḥammad al-Nawawī (p. 501), C. 1303, Mecca 1317.—16. *Sirāj al-hudā*, a Malay work by Zayn al-Dīn Sumbāwa, Mecca 1303.—17.–36. see Suppl. (35 = 15).—37. *Ḥāshiya* by Abū Muḥammad Manṣūr b. Abi ʾl-Qāsim b. Naṣr al-Saʿīdī al-Thawrī, Alex. Tawḥīd 41 (whose *ʿAqīda* ibid. 3).—38. *Tawkīd al-ʿaqd fī-mā akhadha ʾllāhu ʿalaynā min al-ʿahd* by Yaḥyā b. Muḥammad b. Abi ʾl-Barakāt al-Jazāʾirī, ibid. 8.—Versifications: 1. ʿAlī b. Aḥmad b. ʿAlī al-Fāsī al-Saqqāṭ, d. 1183/1769, Berl 2021. Commentary by Muḥammad b. Muḥammad al-Amīr

al-Kabīr, d. 1232/1817 (p. 486), ibid. 2022.—2. Muḥammad al-Ḥusaynī al-Madanī al-Ghammāzī, Gotha 680/1.—3. Anon. *Wāsiṭat al-sulūk* Br. Mus. 872.—4., 5. See Suppl.—6. Sīdī ʿAbdallāh b. Ḥamza, *Hesp.* XVIII, $97_{,27,9}$.

III. *al-Jumal* or *al-Murshida* or *al-Sanūsiyya al-wuṣṭā*, with a self-commentary from the year 875/1470, Berl. 2026, Esc. ^{2}697, Algiers $632_{,7}$, 634, Cairo ^{1}II, 28, ^{2}I, 191, Alex. Tawḥīd 21. Glosses a.–d., see Suppl.—e. Ibrāhīm al-Andalusī, Alex. Tawḥīd 12.

IIIa. *al-ʿAqīda al-ṣughrā* see Suppl. IIIa. Commentaries by Aḥmad b. ʿAbd al-Fattāḥ al-Mallawī al-Shāfiʿī, d. 1181/1767 (Suppl. II, 482), Alex. Tawḥīd 21, by Abū Muḥammad b. Muḥammad Khazrajī al-Darʿī, d. 1006/1598 in Fez, ibid. 38.

IV. *Sharḥ al-Manẓūma al-Jazāʾiriyya* or *al-ʿIqd al-farīd fī ḥall mushkilāt al-tawḥīd* see no. 5.

V. *Sharḥ al-Farāʾiḍ al-Ḥawfiyya* I, 480.

VI. *al-Muqaddima*, on the basic concepts of philosophy, Dresd. $216_{,5}$, Vienna 1536, Paris 4583, Esc. $^{2}636_{,12}$, Algiers $149_{,3}$, $632_{,8}$, Alex. Tawḥīd 38.—Commentaries: a.–d. see Suppl. (a. Garr. 1500, Alex. Tawḥīd 29, $42_{,7}$).—3. *al-Anwār al-bahiyya* by ʿAbd al-Ghanī al-Nābulusī (p. 345), Alex. Fun. $90_{,11}$.

VII. Proof that the formula expressing the *tawḥīd* comprises all the qualities of God and the Prophet, Br. Mus. 101, Stockh. 190.

VIII. *Mukhtaṣar al-manṭiq*, including a self-commentary, Berl. 5189, Gotha 1196/7, Pet. 160, Paris 2400/1, Br. Mus. $156_{,2}$, Esc. $^{2}636_{,7}$, $653_{,3}$, Garr. 820, Alex. Tawḥīd 38, Manṭiq 31.—Commentaries: 1. al-Ḥasan b. Masʿūd al-Yūsī, d. 1102/1691 (p. 455), Paris 2400, Alex. Manṭiq $31_{,2}$, 35, Garr. 857.—2. Based on his lectures, by Aḥmad b. Muḥammad al-Sūsī, Algiers 1410.—3. Anon., ibid. $2100_{,2}$.—4. Glosses on the author's self-commentary by Muḥammad b. Ḥasan al-Bannāʾī, d. 1194/1780, Fez 1302.—5.–10. see Suppl. (8. Muḥammad b. Yaʿqūb al-Miknāsī al-Mālikī, Makram 54, Patna I, $228_{,2003}$).—11. ʿAṭiyya, Alex. Manṭiq 12.

326 | IX. *Nuṣrat al-faqīr* or *Nuṣrat ahl al-dīn wa-ahl al-yaqīn ʿalā man taʿarraḍa*
252 *fī 'l-ṭarīq fī 'l-radd ʿalā Abi 'l-Ḥasan al-Ṣaghīr al-Miknāsī* | (see Suppl.), Br. Mus.
$228_{,5}$, Cairo ^{1}II, 172, ^{2}I, 370.

X. *al-Ṭibb al-nabawī* or *Tafsīr mā taḍammanathu etc.* (see Suppl.), Br. Mus. 460/1, Leid. 1375, Cairo ^{1}VII, 145, 381, Alex. Ḥad. $47_{,1}$ (in which XXVII, read: *al-maʿidatu*), cf. Berl. 6402.

XI. *Kitāb al-ḥaqāʾiq* Cairo ^{1}VII, 620.

XII. *al-Mujarrabāt*, on sympathic cures, Berl. 4164, Cairo ^{1}II, 210, Patna I, $157_{,1492}$, print. C. 1279.

XIII. *Ṣalawāt* Cairo VII, ^{1}68, ^{2}I, 329.

XIV. *ʿUmdat dhawi 'l-albāb* see p. 332.

XV. *Sharḥ Kitāb al-Īsāghūjī* I, 610, above p. $180_{,13}$.

XVIII–XXXI. See Suppl.

5. Aḥmad b. ʿAbdallāh al-Jazāʾirī, who died in 898/1497.

Al-Manẓūma al-Jazāʾiriyya fī ʾl-tawḥīd Algiers 687, 1440,3, Alex. Fun. 147,11, Garr. 2031,6.—Commentaries: 1. Muḥammad b. Yūsuf al-Sanūsī, Berl. Ms. or. oct. 3911, Bodl. I, 66/7, Br. Mus. 628,1, 901, 1617, iii, Paris 1268, 5338, Cairo [1]I, 28, [2]I, 191, Qawala I, 194.—2. Abstract: Bodl. I, 152, II, 570, Br. Mus. Suppl. 189.—3. ʿAbd al-Salām al-Laqānī, d. 1078/1667 (p. 307), Cairo [1]I, 35, Alex. Tawḥīd 20, abbreviated by Abū Hurayra ʿAbd al-Salām b. ʿAbd al-Raḥmān b. ʿUthmān b. Nabhān al-Ṣaffūrī al-Shāfiʿī, ibid.—3. Muḥammad al-Jawharī al-Khālidī, d. 1215/1800, Paris 1269, Cairo [1]I, 26.

8 *Mysticism*

1. Shams al-Dīn Abu ʾl-Faḍl al-Qāsim b. Saʿd b. Muḥammad b. ʿAbd al-Bāriʾ al-ʿUdhrī al-Bustī al-Sabṭī al-Tūnisī al-Ṣūfī al-Raqqām, who died in 705/1305.

1. *Iṣṭilāḥ al-Ṣūfiyya wal-tanbīh ʿalā maqāṣidihim al-juzʾiyya wal-kulliyya* Berl. 3459.—2. *Takmilat al-anwār min ʿulūm al-mujarrabīn wal-abrār* Bursa Ulu Cami Taş. 142.

1a. Abū ʿAbdallāh Muḥammad b. Muḥammad b. al-Ḥājj al-ʿAbdarī al-Maghribī al-Fāsī, who died in 737/1336.

Ibn Farḥūn 327/8. 1. *al-Mudkhal* Fez Qar. 1508/10, Alexandria 1291, C. 1320.—2. *Shumūs al-anwār wa-kunūz al-asrār* C. 1297, 1329.—3. *Bulūgh al-qaṣd wal-munā fī khawāṣṣ asmāʾ Allāh al-ḥusnā* Berl. 3757, Vat. V. 1251.

| 1b. Muḥammad b. Abi ʾl-Qāsim al-Ḥimyarī b. al-Ṣabbāgh, who flourished at the beginning of the eighth century. 327

Durrat al-asrār wa-tuḥfat al-abrār fī manāqib sayyidī Abi ʾl-Ḥasan al-Shādhilī, Tunis 1304.

1c. ʿUmar b. ʿAlī al-Jazāʾirī al-Rashīdī moved to Tunis in 757/1356, where he wrote:

1. *Ibtisām al-ʿarūs etc.* see Suppl.—2. *Qamʿ al-nufūs min kalām b. ʿArūs* Gotha 2362, Frank 427 (different from Gotha 2363, which is another collection of poems with the same title).—3. *Dīwān*, lith. C. 1880.

2. Jamāl al-Dīn Abu 'l-Maḥāsin Yūsuf b. ʿAlī b. Aḥmad b. Muḥammad al-Nadrumī (i.e. from Nadruma, near Oran) al-Gharnāṭī wrote, in 786/1384:

1. *Qabs al-anwār wa-jāmiʿ al-asrār*, on the mystical properties of letters and of the names of plants and animals, Gotha 1283 (fragm.), Paris 2681/3, Glasgow 45 (*JRAS* 1899, 750), 173, Ambr. 249, Esc. [1]975, NO 2837/8, Berl. 4128.

3. While on the pilgrimage in Mecca, Ibrāhīm b. Muḥammad al-Tāzī al-Wahrānī joined a Sufi order. He died on 9 Shaʿbān 866/9 May 1462.

Al-Ḥifnāwī, *Taʿrīf al-khalaf* II, 7/11. *Al-Murādiyya* Algiers 1846,$_3$, commentary by Abū Zakariyyāʾ Yaḥyā al-Madyūnī, ibid. 497,$_4$, and by Abū ʿAbdallāh Muḥammad b. Aḥmad b. ʿAlī al-Ṣabbāgh al-Qalʿī, ibid. 1856.

4. Abū ʿAbdallāh Muḥammad b. Sulaymān (ʿAbd al-Raḥmān) b. Abī Bakr al-Jazūlī[1] al-Simlālī, from the Berber tribe of Simlāla, a branch of the Jazūla, was poisoned in Sūs al-Aqṣā on 16 Rabīʿ I 870/7 November 1472. His body was laid to rest in Marrakesh that year.

1. *Dalāʾil al-khayrāt wa-shawāriq al-anwār fī dhikr al-ṣalāt ʿala 'l-nabī al-mukhtār*,
253 | a series of prayers and litanies in praise of the Prophet, a devotional work that was widely used in the European part of the Ottoman Empire, Berl.
328 3919/20, Dresd. 288, Munich | 173, Vienna 1706, Krafft 442, Basle M. II, 1, IV, 30, Copenhagen 49, 50, Upps. 400/1, Pet. 81, Ros. 13, AM 73/4, Paris 1180/96, 5258, 6246, 6675, 1270,$_2$, 4578,$_1$, Millau (Aveyron, Galtier *Bull. Inst. fr. d'Arch. or.* V, 136), Leid. 2198/9, de Jong 131/2, Br. Mus. 94/101, Suppl. 251, Ind. Off. 350/3, Glasgow 22 (*JRAS* 1899, 743), Algiers 807/21, Rāġib 255/9, Cairo [1]II, 4/8, 18, 235, VII, 339, [2]I, 297, Qawala I, 233, Garr. 2046,$_1$, 2047/8, Patna I, 153,$_{1460/1}$, II, 518,$_{2780}$, print. St. Petersburg 1842, C. 1287, 1291, 1304, 1305, 1307, 1308, among others—Commentaries: 1. *Maṭāliʿ al-masarrāt* by Ibn Aḥmad b. ʿAlī Muḥammad al-Mahdī al-Fāsī, d. 1063/1653, Br. Mus. 102, Ind. Off. 354, Algiers 823, Constantine, *JA* 1854, ii, 441, no. 86, Ibr. Pasha 355, Rāġib 271/2, Qawala I, 263, Makram 56, Calcutta 61, no. 505, Patna I, 157,$_{1495}$, print. C. 1278, 1301, 1309; Glosses entitled *al-Anwār al-lāmiʿāt*, by his son ʿAbd al-Raḥmān, Leipz. 853, Tetouan 71,$_5$.—2. Muḥammad Fāḍil al-Dihlawī, Calcutta 64, no. 441.—3. Muḥammad b. Sulaymān al-Arīḥawī, d. 1158/1745, Br. Mus. Suppl. 252,$_2$, Alex. Faw. 28.—4. Ḥasan al-ʿIdwī al-Ḥamzāwī, d. 1303/1885, C. 1289.—5. Sulaymān b. ʿUmar al-ʿUjaylī al-Jamal, d. 1204/1789, Algiers 822, Alex. Faw. 29, Cairo [1]II, 233.—6. Turkish by Dāʾūdzāde Muḥammad

1 The Berber G is now represented by a jīm, then by a ghayn, and at other times by a qāf.

Efendi, Istanbul 1254.—7.–13. see Suppl. (13 = 3, see Alex.).—14. *Munawwir al-sarīrāt* by ʿAbdallāh al-Ḥamdūnī al-Azharī, completed in 1142/1729, Alex. Faw. 10, 29.—15. Glosses by Abū ʿAbdallāh Muḥammad al-Ṣaghīr al-Suhaylī, MS dated 1174/1761, Alex. Faw. 7.–16. Anon., Hamb. or. Sem. 16.—Abstract see Suppl.—II. *Ḥizb al-falāḥ*, prayer, Berl. 3886, Gotha 820, Leid. 2200, 1, Copenhagen $49,_5$.—III, IV. (Garr. 1581), see Suppl.

5. Muḥammad b. Muḥammad b. Yaʿqūb al-Kūmī al-Tūnisī, who died after 880/1475.

1. *Taysīr al-maṭālib wa-raghbat al-ṭālib*, on the secret properties of the names of the letters of the alphabet, Paris 2707, Cairo ^{1}V, 333, 361.—2. *al-Īmāʾ ilā ʿilm al-asmāʾ*, completed in 880, Alex. Faw. 5.

5a. Barakāt b. Aḥmad b. Muḥammad al-ʿArūsī, see Suppl. and 247, 9.

6. Shihāb al-Dīn Abu ʾl-ʿAbbās (Abu ʾl-Faḍl) Aḥmad b. Aḥmad b. Muḥammad b. ʿĪsā b. Zarrūq al-Burnusī al-Fāsī was born in 846/1442 and died in Tripoli in Ṣafar 899/November 1493.

ʿAbdallāh Gannūn, *Nubūgh* I, 138, Berbrugger, *Voyage dans* | *le sud de l'Algérie* X, 329
Rinn, *Marabouts et Khouan* 270. 1. *al-Kunnāsh*, an autobiography, Br. Mus. $888,_3$, Algiers $581,_{10}$, after which Aḥmad Bābā, *Nayl* 71, in the margin of Ibn Farḥūn 84.—2. *Sharḥ al-Muqaddima al-Qurṭubiyya* I, 551.—3. *Tamhīd* (*Taʾsīs*) *ʿaqāʾid al-taṣawwuf wa-uṣūlihi*, adapted with the title *Qawāʿid al-ṭarīqa fi ʾl-jamʿ bayna ʾl-sharīʿa wal-ḥaqīqa* by ʿAlī b. Ḥusām al-Dīn al-Muttaqī al-Hindī, d. 977/1569 (p. 384), Berl. 3031, Esc. $^2741,_4$. A commentary on the original work by ʿAbdallāh b. Muḥammad b. ʿAlī al-Kharrūfī al-Ṭarābulusī, Algiers $916,_3$.—4. *Mukātaba ilā kāffat al-fuqarāʾ*, a message to the Sufis concerning the five qualities that are required for being adopted into their ranks, Berl. 3354.—5. On the right way of performing the *dhikr*, ibid. 3707.—6. The morning and evening prayer, ibid. 3708.—7. *al-Naṣīḥa al-kāfiya li-man khaṣṣahu ʾllāh bil-ʿāfiya*, composed in 877/1472, ibid. 4008/9, Leid. 2169, Br. Mus. $126,_8$, $461,_5$, Algiers 885, Alex. Mawāʿiẓ $41,_2$, 49, Cairo ^{1}II, 181, ^{2}I, 371. |—8. *al-Maqṣad al-asmā* 254
(*asnā*) *fī mā yataʿallaq bi-maqāṣid al-asmāʾ* Berl. 2239, Leid. 2043, Cairo ^{1}VII, 427.—9. *al-Maqṣad al-asmā al-asnā fī sharḥ al-asmāʾ al-ḥusnā* Berl. 2240, Br. Mus. $872,_3$, $99,_3$, NO 2873, Alex. Faw. 23, Cairo ^{1}II, 201, VII, 532.—10. *al-Waẓīfa* or *Safīnat al-najāʾ li-man ila ʾllāh intajā* Br. Mus. 867, Cairo ^{1}VII, 58, 322, 378, 686, ^{2}I, 362.—Commentaries: a. Aḥmad b. Muḥammad al-Būnī, Br. Mus. loc. cit.—b. Muḥammad al-Faṭnāsī, Algiers $366,_2$.—c. ʿAbd al-Raḥmān b. Muḥammad b.

ʿAbdallāh al-ʿAyyāshī, completed in 1135/1723, ibid. 826, Alex. Faw. 4, 19, 20, Cairo ^{1}II, 185, ^{2}I, 269.—d. Anon. *al-Fawāʾid al-laṭīfa*, Heid. ZDMG 91, 387, A. 333.—e. *al-Lawāqiḥ al-quddūsiyya*, by Aḥmad b. Muḥammad b. ʿAjība al-Ḥasanī, completed in 1196/1782, Alex. Faw. 19.—f. *al-Anwār al-qudsiyya*, by Muṣṭafā b. Kamāl al-Dīn al-Bakrī, d. 1162/1749, Būlāq (?) n.d. ibid. 4/5.—g. *Fatḥ dhi ʾl-ṣifāt al-saniyya*, by ʿAlī al-Suṭūḥī al-Baysūsī, twelfth cent., ibid. Fun. 91, 2.–11. *al-Durra (Durar) al-muntakhaba fī ʾl-adwiya al-mujarraba* Garr. 1126, Algiers 1322,$_{2}$, Alex. Ṭibb 17, Cairo ^{1}VI, 14, abstract ibid. VII, 33.—12. *Sirāj al-ḥikam* Cambr. p. 2.—13. *al-Jāmiʿ li-jumal min al-fawāʾid wal-manāfiʿ* Br. Mus. 126,$_{15}$.—14. *al-Naṣāʾiḥ* Cairo ^{1}II, 171.—15. (*al-Mawāhib al-saniyya*) *fī khawāṣṣ Manẓūmat Nūr al-Dīn al-Dimyāṭī* (*Naẓm asmāʾ Allāh al-ḥusnā*) Cairo ^{1}II, 233, V, 362, VII, 113, 255, 363, see Suppl.—16. *al-Kashf* ibid. V, 387.—17. *Mafātīḥ al-ʿizz wal-naṣr fī ʾl-tanbīh ʿalā baʿḍ mā yataʿallaq bi-Ḥizb al-baḥr* (I, 584), Cairo ^{1}II, 231.—18. *Sharḥ Ḥizb al-baḥr* I, 584.—19. *Sharḥ al-Ḥikam al-ʿAṭāʾiyya* p. 143.—20. *Sharḥ al-Muqaddima*
330 *al-Waghlīsiyya* | p. 322.—21. *Sharḥ al-Tadhkira al-Qurṭubiyya* Suppl. I, 737.—22.–31. see Suppl.

7. Abū ʿAbdallāh Muḥammad b. Muḥammad b. ʿAlī al-Ṣabbāgh Qāḍi ʾl-Qalʿa wrote, in the first half of the tenth century:

Bustān al-azhār fī manāqib Zamzam al-akhyār wa-maʿdin al-anwār Sayyidī Aḥmad b. Yūsuf al-Rāshidī, a student of Ibn Zarrūq buried in Milāna (see Suppl.), Algiers 1707/8, 1 (whose *Dictons* ed. Basset, *JA* s. VIII, vol. 16, 203ff., see also Suppl. II, 1001, 43).

8. Muḥammad b. ʿAlī b. Muḥammad al-Ḥamīnī al-Ṣiqillī al-Shuṭaybī wrote in the ninth century:

Miftāḥ al-janna ʿala ʾl-kitāb wal-sunna Alex. Faw. 27.

9 *Politics*

1. Abū Ḥammū Mūsā b. Yūsuf b. Ziyān al-ʿAbdwādī, the prince of Tlemcen 753–88/1352–86.

Wāsiṭat al-sulūk fī siyāsat al-mulūk Algiers 1374, Tlemcen *RAAD* XI (1931), 97/101, print. Tunis 1279, Istanbul 1295, cf. de Slane, *Hist. des Berbères*, transl. III, 436/8.

2. Ibrāhīm b. Abi ʾl-Nūr wrote, for the Ḥafṣid al-Mutawakkil ʿala ʾllāh, 718–47/1318–46:

Siyāsat al-umarāʾ wulāt al-junūd al-mutaḍammin li-thalāthat ʿuhūd Esc. ^{2}719.

| 10 *Mathematics* 255

Abu ʾl-ʿAbbās Aḥmad b. Muḥammad b. ʿUthmān al-Azdī b. al-Bannāʾ al-Marrākushī al-Saraqusṭī al-Fāsī, who was born in 649/1251 and died on 6 Rajab 721/2 August 1321.[1]

DK I, 278, no. 713, ʿAbdallāh Gannūn, *Nubūgh* I, 144, Sanchez Pérez, *Biogr.* 51, P.J. Renaud, Ibn al-Banna de Marrakech sufi et mathématicien du XIII/XIV s. J.C., *Hespéris* XXV | (1938) 13/42, idem, *Isis* XXVII, 216/8. Biography from the 331 *Takmilat al-Dībāj* of Aḥmad Bābā, d. 1036/1626, ed. and transl. by A. Marré, *Atti dell'Acc. dei Nuovi Lincei*, 3 December 1865. 1. *Talkhīṣ fī ʿamal al-ḥisāb* Br. Mus. 180, 417, Ind. Off. 770$_{,1}$, Bodl. I, 207$_{,4}$, Esc. ^{2}248$_{,11}$, 933, 953, Algiers 613$_{,3}$, Cairo ^{1}V, 179, 213, transl. by A. Marré in *Atti dell' Acc. Pontific. dei Nuovi Lincei* XVII, 5 June 1865.—Commentaries: a. al-Qalaṣādī, d. 891/1486 (p. 343), Gotha 1477, Paris 2464$_{,1}$, Tetouan 227, see Woepcke, *Ann. di Mat. pura ed applicata*, vol. V, no. 3 (1864).—aa. by the author himself (see Suppl.), Garr. 1032a.—b. ʿAbd al-ʿAzīz b. Dāʾūd al-Huwārī, Ind. Off. 770$_{,3}$, Bodl. I, 76$_{,3}$.—c. Anon., Paris 2464$_{,2}$.—d. *al-Tamḥīṣ* by Abu ʾl-Ḥasan ʿAlī b. Muḥammad b. ʿAbdallāh al-Tādilī, Alex. Ḥisāb 6.—e.–g. see Suppl.—h. Aḥmad b. al-Majdī, d. 850/1447 (p. 158), Br. Mus. 417.—2. *al-Maqālāt fī ʾl-ḥisāb* Berl. 5974.—3. *Tanbīh al-albāb ʿalā masāʾil al-ḥisāb* Br. Mus. 420$_{,8}$.—4. *Risāla fī ʿilm al-misāḥa*, a manual for calculating surfaces, Berl. 5945.—5. *Minhāj al-ṭālib li-taʿdīl al-kawākib* Bodl. I, 373, Algiers 1454$_{,1}$, Esc. ^{1}904.—6. *Qānūn li-tarḥīl al-shams wal-qamar fī ʾl-manāzil wa-maʿrifat awqāt al-layl wal-nahār* Br. Mus. 407$_{,2}$.—7. *al-Yasāra fī taqwīm al-kawākib al-sayyāra* Br. Mus. 977$_{,7}$, to which there is an anonymous supplement entitled *Tashīl al-ʿibāra fī takmīl mā naqaṣa ʿani ʾl-Yasāra*, ibid. 12.—8. *al-Manākh*, for calculating the beginning of the month, ibid. 11.—9. *Bidāyat al-taʿrīf*, a profession of faith (author?), ibid. 168.—10.–14. see Suppl. (13. *Urjūza*, commentary *al-Ishārāt al-saniyya fī baʿḍ maʿānī al-Mabāḥith al-aṣliyya* by Muḥammad b. ʿAbd al-Raḥmān al-Andalusī al-Shāṭibī, d. 963/1556, Alex. Taṣ. 5 and Suppl. p. 359, 3a).—15. *Mudkhil fī tasyīr wa-maṭāriḥ al-shuʿāʿāt* Berl. Oct. 2592$_{,9}$.—16. *Muwashshaḥ kāfil lil-muṭṭalib* Ambr. 246.—17. *Fī ʿamal al-ṭilasm* Berl. Oct. 2592$_{,11}$.

---

1 His surviving works are without exception scholarly texts on mathematics and astronomy; Ibn Khaldūn, *Prol.* I, 213, 6, calls him Shaykh al-Maghrib in the occult sciences, astrology, divination, and the interpretation of the letters of the alphabet.

11 *Astronomy*

1. Abū Miqraʿ Abī Muḥammad ʿAbd al-Ḥaqq b. ʿAlī al-Baṭṭiwī al-Warzīzī al-Mujmilī al-Marjūsī al-Sūsī, ca. 730/1330.

Colin and Renaud, *Hespéris* XXV, 1938, 94/6. A *rajaz* poem on calendars and astronomy, with a commentary by ʿAbd al-Raḥmān al-Ḥāfidī, Esc. ^{2}361$_{,3}$.

2. Shams al-Dīn Muḥammad al-Jazūlī, ca. 745/1344.

332 | 1. *Risāla fi ʾl-ʿamal bil-asṭurlāb* Berl. 5799$_{,2}$.—2. *Risāla fi ʾl-ʿamal bil-jayb al-ghāʾib* ibid. 5837, Paris 2519$_{,1}$, composed after 735 for Shams al-Dīn b. Saʿīd, chief muezzin of the Umayyad mosque in Damascus, see W.H. Murray, *Description of an Arabic Quadrant*, London 1860, P. Schmalzl, *Zur Gesch. des Quadranten bei den Arabern*, Munich 1929, 37/8.—3. *Risāla fī thumn al-dāʾira* ibid. 5838, composed in 736, Cairo ^{1}V, 258.—4. *Risāla fī rubʿ al-musātara* Cairo ^{1}V, 251.

3. Muḥammad b. Aḥmad b. Abī Yaḥyā al-Ḥabbāk Abū ʿAbdallāh, who died in 867/1462.

256 | 1. *Bughyat al-ṭullāb fī ʿilm al-asṭurlāb* in *rajaz*, Berl. 5800, Krafft 329, Algiers 1458$_{,1}$. Commentaries: a. *ʿUmdat dhawi ʾl-alqāb* by Muḥammad b. Yūsuf al-Sanūsī, d. 892/1486 (p. 250), Algiers 613$_{,8}$, 1458$_{,2}$, Garr. 986/7.—b. Anon., Krafft 344.—2. *Sharḥ Rawḍat al-azhār lil-Jādarī* Suppl. 217, § 10$_{,1,2}$, Br. Mus. 411$_{,2}$.—3. See Suppl.

12 *Travelogues*

Abū ʿAbdallāh Muḥammad b. ʿAbdallāh b. Muḥammad al-Lawāṭī al-Ṭanjī b. Baṭṭūṭa was born in Tangiers on 17 Rajab 703/24 February 1304. From there he set out on his first journey in 725/1325, one that took him through Africa and a large part of Asia. After completing the pilgrimage, he trekked through Syria, Iraq, Persia, Mesopotamia, Asia Minor, the Qipchāq regions, and southern Russia to Constantinople. Then he went to Delhi, by way of Asia Minor, Bukhara, and Afghanistan, where he was a *qāḍī* for two years. Entrusted with a mission to China by Sultan Ṭughluq, he got no further than the Maldives, where he worked again as a *qāḍī*, for one and a half years. After a visit to Ceylon and China, he returned to his native country by way of Sumatra and Arabia. In 751 he visited Granada and the next year he went to Melli and Timbuktu. He died in 779/1377 in Marrakesh.

Ibn Khald. *Prol.* I, 327/8, ʿAbdallāh Gannūn, *al-Nubūgh* II, 143. At the request
of the Marīnid ruler Abū ʿInān | Fāris he dictated a description of his travels 333
to Muḥammad b. Muḥammad b. Aḥmad b. Juzayy al-Kalbī, d. 757/1356 (see de
Slane, *JA*, 1843, I, 244ff.), who shortened it and published it under the title
Tuḥfat al-nuẓẓār fī gharāʾib al-amṣār wa-ʿajāʾib al-asfār, Paris 2287/91, ed. Defré-
mery and Sanguinetti, 4 vols. Paris 1853/8, 2nd ed. 1869/79, 3rd ed. 1893/5, print.
C. 1287/8, 1322. Cf. J.G. Kosegarten, *de M. Ebn Batuta Arabe Tingitano ejusque
itineribus*, Jena 1818, Wüstenfeld in *Lüddes Ztsch.* I, 56, no. 98, *Géographie
d'Aboulfeda*, transl. Reinaud, I, p. CLVI, Leclerc II, 282, Mehren, *Ann. f. Nord.
Oldk.* 1857, 67, no. 69, Almquist, *Ibn Batutas Rese genom Maghhrib*, Uppsala
1866, W. v. Tiesenhausen, *Sbornik mater. otn. hist. Zol. Ord. I*, St. Petersburg 1884,
278, P. Chaix, *Le Globe*, Feb.-Apr. 1887, 145/63, idem, *Geogr. Mag.* 1889, 575/9,
M.R. Haig, *JRAS* XIX, 393/412, St. Janiesek, I.B.'s journey to Bulghar. Is it a fabri-
cation? *JRAS* 1929, 791/800. |—Abstract by Muḥammad Fatḥallāh b. Maḥmūd 257
al-Baylūnī, eleventh cent.,[1] Berl. Ms. or. oct. 3974, Gotha 1541, Cambr. Prest. 23,
no. 203/5, Garr. 761; whence another anonymous abstract Gotha 1542. lith. C.
1278.—Turkish translation in the Ottoman state newspaper *Taqwīmi waqāʾiʿ*
(see *ZDMG* XVI, 756) by Dāmād Ḥaḍrat Shahriyār Muḥammad Sharīf, 2 vols.,
Istanbul 1335/7.

13 *Medicine*

In Tunis, Aḥmad b. ʿAbd al-Salām al-Sharīf al-Ṣaqalī wrote, for the Ḥafṣid Abu 'l-Fāris ʿAbd al-ʿAzīz, 796–837/1394–1433:

1. *Kitāb al-aṭibbāʾ*, an alphabetical listing of simple cures, Leid. 1372, BDMG 64; shortened and entitled *al-Ṭibb al-sharīf* in two MSS in Tunis, see Griffini, *Cent. Amari* II, 487/9.—2. See Suppl.

14 *Music*

Around 700/1300 Muḥammad b. Ibrāhīm al-Ṣalāḥī wrote, for the Marīnid Abū Yaʿqūb b. Yaḥyā b. ʿAbd al-Ḥaqq:

Al-Imtāʿ wal-intifāʿ, on music, Madr. 603, see G. Farmer, *Studies in Or. Mus. Instruments*, London 1939, 21/35, *Sources* 49.

---

1 For whose *Khulāṣat mā yaḥṣul ʿalayhi 'l-sāʿūn fī adwiyat dafʿ al-wabaʾ wal-ṭāʿūn*, Alex. Fun. 89,3.

334 | 15 *Alchemy and Occult Sciences*

1. In Tlemcen, Abū ʿAbdallāh Muḥammad b. Aḥmad b. ʿAbd al-Malik al-Ḥasanī al-Maṣmūdī wrote, in 897/1492:

1. *al-Wāfī fī tadbīr al-kāfī* Cairo [1]V, 398, and under the title *Kāfī ʾl-wāfī* Alex. Kīm. 9.—2. See Suppl.—3. *Tuḥfat man ṣabar ʿalā taṭhīr arkān al-ḥajar* Alex. Kīm. 9.

2. Muḥammad b. Jābir al-Miknāsī al-Ghassānī, d. 827/1424, was also known as a poet; see Suppl.

ʿAbdallāh Gannūn, *al-Nubūgh* I, 161.

3. ʿAbdallāh b. ʿAbdallāh b. ʿAlī al-Munajjim b. al-Makhfūf (sic Berl.), who died before 800/1397.

Kitāb fī ʿilm al-raml Berl. Qu. 1734, Mosul $236,_{153}$, Patna I, $242,_{2077}$.

16 *Eroticism*

1. Abū ʿAbdallāh Muḥammad b. Aḥmad (Abū Muḥammad ʿAbdallāh) b. Aḥmad al-Tījānī (Tijānī), ca. 710/1310, see Suppl.

1. *Tuḥfat al-ʿarūs wa-nuzhat al-nufūs*, on women and marriage, Berl. 6386/7, or. oct. 3949, Leid. 489/90, Br. Mus. 1465, Cambr. $246,_{2}$, Paris 3061/4, 5887, 5899, Copenhagen 288, Esc. [2]I, 527, 562, 1249/50, Algiers 1786, Cairo [1]VI, 121, [2]III, 47, AS 318, Patna I, $244,_{2087}$, Rāmpūr I, 581, print. C. 1301, cf. Dozy, *Script. ar. loci de Abbad.* II, 139ff. *Touhfat el arous ou le Cadeau des époux, trois chapitres, I, VII, VIII, sur les femmes et le mariage par le Chaikh M. b. A. el Tidjani*, Paris and Algiers 1848.—2. *Riḥla* from the year 706/8, Paris 2285, cf. Rousseau, *JA* s. IV. vol. 20, 57ff., s. v. vol. 1, 102ff.

2. Abū ʿAbdallāh b. ʿUmar al-Nafzāwī wrote, for Muḥammad b. ʿAwāna al-Zawāwī, the vizier of ʿAbd al-ʿAzīz of Tunis (§ 13):

Al-Rawḍ al-ʿāṭir fī nuzhat al-khāṭir, an extremely obscene work on love, Copenhagen 289, Paris $3669,_{7}$, lith. Fez 1310 (see Suppl.).

| Chapter 9. Spain 258 335

Due to the steady advance of the Christians, Islam in Spain was now almost totally limited to the kingdom of Granada. Thanks to skilful political manoeuvring amongst its various enemies, it was able to stand its ground for another two hundred years and to offer a safe haven for Arab trade and industry. At its court the traditions of a great literary past lived on until the very end. Poetry and prose flourished, as did historiography, although interest in scholastics waned. Unfortunately, we are even worse informed on this last period than on the preceding centuries of the literature of Spain; when the Christian conquerors of Granada started their hunt for and destruction of Arabic books, the monuments of this final literary era were the first victims. However, many and certainly not the least of Spain's sons had already left their native country; there being no more room for the unfolding of their talents, they had emigrated to Egypt and Syria, to where Spain thus lost its literary fame.

1 *Poetry and Belles Lettres*

1. Muhammad b. ʿAbdallāh b. Muḥammad Muqātil al-Mālaqī Abu ʾl-Qāsim, who died in 739/1338.

Zajal Berl. 7847$_{,2}$.

| 2. Abū Jaʿfar Aḥmad b. ʿAlī b. Muḥammad b. Khātima al-Anṣārī, who was born 259
in 724/1324 in Almeria and died around 770/1369.

Gayangos, *Moh. Dyn.* I, 359, following Ibn al-Khaṭīb. 1. *Dīwān* Esc. ^{2}381 (autograph from the year 738?).—2. *Rāʾiq al-taḥliya fī fāʾiq al-tawriya*, a collection of poems, ibid. 419$_{,1}$.—3. *Taḥṣīl* | *gharaḍ al-qāṣid fī tafṣīl al-maraḍ al-wāfid*, writ- 336
ten in Almeria on the occasion of the Great Plague of the year 749/1348–9, Berl. 6369, see Suppl.

3. Abū ʿUbaydallāh b. Zumruk, who was born in Granada in 733/1333, was killed in 795/1393, see Suppl.

Maqq. II, Kap. 7, Ibn Khald. *Hist. d. Berb.* IV, 412. Poems, Br. Mus. 108, I, iv. G. Gómez, Ibn Zamrak, *el poeta de la Alhambra*, Real Ac. de Hist. Madrid 1943.

4. For Yūsuf II, the prince of Granada, ʿAlī b. Āzim collected, in 793/1391:

A poetical anthology in 5 chapters, Leid. 738 (incomplete).

2 *Philology*

1. Abū Bakr Muḥammad b. Muḥammad b. Idrīs b. Saʿd b. Mālik b. ʿAbd al-Wāḥid al-Quḍāʿī al-Qallūsī lived in Granada and Malaga, and died in the Great Plague of 707/1307.

ḤKh ^{1}IV, 445, ^{2}II, 1273, Pons Boigues 266. 1. *al-Khitām al-mafḍūḍ ʿan khulāṣat ʿilm al-ʿarūḍ* Esc. ^{2}288,$_{6}$.—2. *Urjūza mawsūma bil-Nukat al-mustawʿaba mawḍūʿa fī nukat al-qawāfī*, composed in 686/1287, ibid. 7.—3. *Zahrat al-ẓurf wa-zuhrat al-ẓarf fī basṭ al-jumal min al-ʿarūḍ al-muhmal* ibid. 8, see M.M. Antuña, *al-Andalus* VI, 296.

2. Faraj b. Aḥmad b. Aḥmad al-Shāṭibī Abū Saʿīd b. Lubb (Layth) al-Thaʿlabī al-Gharnāṭī, born in 701/1301, was a preacher in Granada. He died in 783/1381.

Maqq. II, 265/70. 1. *Qaṣīda lāmiyya fī ʾl-naḥw* or *Manẓūma fī ʾl-alghāz al-naḥwiyya* Garr. 2031,$_{5}$.—Commentaries: a. Self-commentary, Cairo ^{2}II, 121.—b. Yaḥyā b. Muḥammad b. Muḥammad b. ʿAbdallāh b. ʿĪsā b. Shibl, Berl. 6753.—c. Anon., Cairo ^{1}VII, 309, ^{2}II, 137.—2. A collection of fatwas, Esc. ^{1}460, see Lopez Ortiz, *al-Andalus* VI, 84ff.

3 *Historiography*

1. Muḥammad b. Yaḥyā b. Muḥammad b. Yaḥyā b. Abī Bakr b. Saʿd al-Ashʿarī
337 al-Mālikī, who was born in 674/1275, became a *khaṭīb* and *qāḍī* | in Granada in 703/1303. He was killed on 7 Jumādā I 741/30 October 1340 in the battle against the Christians at the Rio Salado.

DK IV, 284, no. 801. *Al-Tamhīd wal-bayān fī faḍl al-shahīd ʿUthmān b. ʿAffān*, Cairo V, ^{1}37, ^{2}135.

2. Abū ʿAbdallāh Muḥammad b. ʿAbdallāh b. Saʿīd b. al-Khaṭīb Lisān al-Dīn was born on 25 Rajab 713/16 November 1313 in Loja, where his father held the office of vizier, as some of his ancestors had also done. He studied in Granada after his father had assumed charge of the administration of the army there. When death took his father away from him on 7 Jumādā II 741/29 November 1341, the vizier Abu ʾl-Ḥasan al-Jayyāb employed him as a secretary. When the latter died in the Great Plague of 749/1348, Sultan Yūsuf appointed him as his successor as vizier. He remained in office when Yūsuf's son Muhammad succeeded his father, who had been murdered in 755/1354. However, he had to share his power with the general Riḍwān, who was the guardian of the prince, who at that time was still under-age. While the sultan was out in the country in Ramaḍān 760/August

1360, the general Abū Saʿīd took possession of the Alhambra, proclaimed his brother Ismāʿīl ruler, and threw Ibn al-Khaṭīb into jail. The Marīnid sultan Abū Sālim Ibrāhīm, who had just acceded to the throne in Fez, obtained free passage for the deposed monarch out of Guadix where he had held out until then, and offered him and his vizier safe haven at his court. While Muḥammad was working on his reinstatement with the help of Ibn Khaldūn, his vizier lived a reclusive life in Salé. It was only after Muḥammad had re-entered Granada on 20 Jumādā II 763/17 April 1363 that he returned to his post there. The next year he dislodged the Marīnid ʿUthmān b. Yaḥyā, who had rendered invaluable
service in the recapture of Granada | but who was also curbing his influence. | 338 261
However, this abuse of power raised the suspicion of the sultan and so, while visiting the fortress of Gibraltar in 773/1371, he decided to escape to Ceuta. The Marīnid ʿAbd al-ʿAzīz received and accommodated him in Tlemcen, which he did because he had been in Ibn al-Khaṭīb's debt ever since 767/1366, when the latter had deposed his uncle who had been living in Granada as a pretender to the throne. He also did not hand him over when the *qāḍī* of Granada had sentenced him to death on grounds of sacrilege. However, when Ibn al-Khaṭīb's patron passed away in 774/1372, Muḥammad offered to help Abu 'l-ʿAbbās in his struggle for the throne on condition that he render Ibn al-Khaṭīb to him. When Fez was captured he fell into the hands of his enemies, and Muḥammad sent his vizier Ibn Zumrūk (p. 336) to lead the prosecution against him. However, while the procedure was still ongoing, the supposed heretic was killed in jail by a mob in 776/1374.

In spite of his eventful life, Ibn al-Khaṭīb still found time to compose a vast literary corpus, involving poetry, classical prose, and historiography, as well as mystical, philosophical, and medical texts.

Maqq. (ed. Būlāq) III/IV. Ibn Khaldūn, *Hist. d. Berb.* transl. de Slane IV, 390ff., DK III, 469, no. 1261, Gayangos, *Moh. Dyn.* I, 307, Dozy, *Loci de Abbad.* II, 156, Leclerc II, 285, Flügel in *Ersch. u. Grubers Enc. u. Ibn al-Chatib*, Wüst. *Gesch.* 439, A. v. Schack, *Poesie und Kunst* ^{2}I, 312/24, A. Müller, *der Islam* II, 666ff., Hartmann, *Muw.* 65, Pons Boigues no. 294.

1. *al-Ḥulal al-marqūma* or *Raqm al-ḥulal fī naẓm al-duwal*, a history of the caliphs in the Orient, Spain, and Africa, written in *rajaz* verse with a prose commentary at the end of each chapter, composed in 765/1364, Esc. ^{2}1776,$_1$, 1777,$_1$, Madrid 101, Paris 5026, Br. Mus. Suppl. 475, print. Tunis 1316/7.—Arabic-Latin excerpts in Casiri II, 177/246, print: *Regum Aglabidarum et Fatamidarum (sic) qui Africae et Siciliae imperarunt series in Rerum Ar. quae ad hist. Siciliae
spectant, ampla coll.* | *op. et studio* Rosarii Gregorio, Palermo 1790, 87/10.— 339
2. *al-Lamḥa al-badriyya fi 'l-dawla al-Naṣriyya*, a history of the princes of

Granada up to 765/1364, Esc. ^{2}1776,$_{2}$; excepts in Casiri II, 246/319.—3. *al-Iḥāṭa bi-ta'rīkh Gharnāṭa*, biographies of famous men from Granada, written in 15 volumes with an autobiography and the titles of 37 of his other works (the latter esp. Paris 3347,$_{2}$); individual volumes Br. Mus. Suppl. 666, Esc. ^{2}1673/4 (VIII, IX), copy Leid. 1082, Cairo V, ^{1}128, ^{2}V, 9 (II, photograph of BMS); abstracts in Casiri II, 71/121. Abstract *Markaz al-iḥāṭa bi-udabā' Gharnāṭa* Berl. 9871/2, Paris 3347,$_{1}$, Madr. see Codera, *Miss. hist.* 174/5.—4. *I'lām al-a'lām fī man būyi'a qabl al-iḥtilām min mulūk al-islām wa-mā yata'allaq bi-dhālika min al-kalām*: a. a history of the Prophet, of the Umayyads and 'Abbāsids, the oriental dynasties up to the Baḥrī Mamlūks, and the 'Alids in Mecca and Medina, b. a history of Muslim Spain until Muḥammad b. Yūsuf and the Christian empire, c. a history of the Maghreb, Algiers 1617, abstract 1618, cf. Fagnan, *Rev. Afr.* 34 (1890) 259/62.—5. *al-Tāj al-muḥallā fī musājalat al-qidḥ al-mu'allā*, a history of Spain starting with the accession to the throne of Ibn al-Aḥmar in Granada in 629/1232, written in stylish prose, abstract Esc. ^{2}554,$_{2}$; cf. Gayangos, *Moh. Dyn.* II, 532.—6. *Manẓūma fi 'l-ṭabā'i' wal-ṭubū' wal-uṣūl* (this work is also attributed to 'Abd al-Wāḥid al-Wansharīshī), Madr. 334 f. 15/9, Cairo, *Nashra* 27, see G. Farmer, *Coll. of Or. Writers on Music*, Glasgow 1933, *Sources* 54.—7. *Nufāḍat al-jirāb fī 'ulālat al-ightirāb*, his memoirs of his stay in Morocco and a description of cities in Spain, with special emphasis on its learned men and libraries, Esc. ^{2}1755.—8. *Khaṭrat al-ṭayf fī riḥlat al-shitā' wal-ṣayf*, a description of his trip to Africa composed in 748/1347, Maqq. I, 822, Esc. ^{2}470,$_{4}$, whence the description of a trip by Prince Abu 'l-Ḥajjāj through the eastern provinces of Granada in M.J. Müller, *Beitr. z. Gesch. d. westl. Araber* I, 14/41.—9. *Muqni'at al-sā'il 'an al-maraḍ al-hā'il*, on the plague in Granada of the year 749/1348, Esc. ^{2}1785,$_{2}$.
263 |—10. *Rayḥānat al-kuttāb wa-nuj'at al-muntāb*, a collection of sample letters, Leid. 352, Br. Mus. Suppl. 1019, Upps. 65, Esc. ^{2}1825.—11. *Mi'yār al-ikhtiyār fī dhikr al-ma'āhid wal-diyār*, an abstract of 10 *majālis* in praise of about 100 famous men and the most important cities of Spain, Esc. ^{2}554, 1777,$_{3}$, an
340 edition of the first *majlis* by D.F.X. Simonet, *Descripcion del reino de* | *Granada bajo la dominación de los Naseritas*, Madrid 1861, rev. ed. Granada 1872 (without the Arabic text).—12. Letter in the name of the sultan addressed to the Prophet's grave, Br. Mus. 367.—13. *al-Siḥr wal-shi'r*, an anthology, Esc. ^{2}455/6.–14. *Muwashshaḥ* Berl. 7886,$_{6}$, 8172,$_{29}$, Gotha 26, f. 214 b.—15. *Durrat al-tanzīl wa-ghurrat al-ta'wīl* Rāġib 181.—16. *Kitāb 'amal man ṭabba li-man ḥabba*, a medical handbook dedicated to the Marīnid ruler Abū Sālim Ibrāhīm, Leid. 1365, Paris 3011.[1]—17. *Manẓūma (Urjūza) fi 'l-ṭibb* Gotha 2032,$_{1}$, Leid. 1366.—18. *al-Wuṣūl*

1 = A. f. 1070, so not the *Kitāb al-Yūsufī fī ṣinā'at al-ṭibb*, as indicated by Wüstenfeld.

li-ḥifẓ al-ṣiḥḥa fī ʾl-fuṣūl, on dietetics according to the seasons, Berl. 6401.—20.–26. see Suppl.

3. Abu ʾl-Ḥasan ʿAlī b. Abī Muḥammad ʿAbdallāh al-Judhāmī al-Mālaqī, who wrote after 794/1392.

Nuzhat al-baṣāʾir wal-abṣār see Suppl. M.J. Müller, *Beitr.* I, 101/60, Wüst. *Gesch.* 443, Pons Boigues no. 297.

4. Muḥammad b. ʿAlī al-Shāṭibī al-Maghribī, who wrote in Tāza around 870/1465.[2]

Kitāb ʿuqūd al-jumān fī (mukhtaṣar) akhbār al-zamān, a universal history in 3 *faṣl*: 1. before Islam, 2. the life of Muḥammad, 3. Islam after the death of Muḥammad, Gotha 1575/6, Munich 379, Leid. 771, Paris 1545/9, 4608$_{,1}$, Copenhagen 126/7 (wrongly attributed to Shihāb al-Dīn Aḥmad b. Muḥammad al-Maqqarī al-Fāsī, d. 1041/1631, p. 296), Br. Mus. Suppl. 482, 518$_{,i}$, 1298, Nicholson, *JRAS* 1899, 909, no. 6, Algiers 1575, Alex. Taʾr. 56, cf. de Sacy, *Not. et Extr.* II, 124/63, Wüst. *Gesch.* 485, Pons Boigues 303.

| 4 *Fiqh, Mālikī* 264

1. Sirāj al-Dīn al-Qāsim b. ʿAbdallāh b. Muhammad b. al-Shāṭ al-Anṣārī al-Ishbīlī, who died in 725/1323 in Ceuta, aged over 80.

ʿAbdallāh Gannūn, *al-Nubūgh* I, 138/9, Wüst. *Gesch.* 388, Pons Boigues 271, see Suppl.

1a. ʿAbdallāh b. ʿAlī b. ʿAlī b. ʿAbd al-ʿAzīz b. Salmūn, d. 741/1340, see Suppl.

| *Al-Wathāʾiq*, see Lopez Ortiz, Algunos capítulos del Formulario de Aben Salmún 341
in *Anuario del Derecho Español* IV, 1928, 16f.

2. Abu ʾl-Qāsim b. Salmūn b. ʿAlī b. ʿAbdallāh al-Kinānī al-Bayyāsī al-Gharnāṭī, *qāḍi ʾl-jamāʿa* in Granada, who died in 767/1365.

Zark. 89. *Al-ʿIqd al-munaẓẓam lil-ḥukkām fī mā yajrī bayna aydīhim min al-wathāʾiq wal-aḥkām* Algiers 1366.

---

2 The Egyptian Sultan al-Malik al-Ẓāhir, r. 865—72/1460—7, is also referred to as being alive.

3. Abū Bakr Muḥammad b. Muḥammad b. ʿĀṣim al-Mālikī, who was born in 760/1358, was the vizier of Yūsuf II of Granada. He died in 829/1426.

1. *Tuḥfat al-ḥukkām fī nukat al-ʿuqūd wal-aḥkām*, a work in *rajaz* on the principles of the law, Paris 1100/1, 5330, Algiers 1281/3, Br. Mus. 248. *Traité de droit musulman, la Tohfat d'Ebn Acem, Texte ar. avec trad. franç. cmt. jur. et notes phil. par* O. Houdas et Fr. Martel, *fs 1/3*, Algiers 1883, 4/5, Paris 1888, 6/8, Algiers 1892/3.—Commentaries: a. Abū Yaḥyā, the son of the author, Esc. [1]1088, Alex. Fiqh Māl. 10.—b. Abū ʿAbdallāh Muḥammad b. Aḥmad Mayyāra, d. 1072/1662 (p. 461), Gotha 1058/9, Munich 354, Algiers 1284/5, print. C. 1314, and others. Glosses: Paris 1102, see *JA* 1842,$_{ii}$, 272.—c. ʿAlī b. ʿAbd al-Salām al-Tasūlī al-Sabrārī, Algiers 1286/7, Cairo [1]III, 155, print. Būlāq 1256, C. 1304/5, among others.—d.–f. see Suppl.—2. *Ḥadāʾiq al-azhār* (*Ḥadīqat al-azāhir*) *fī mustaḥsan al-ajwiba wal-muḍḥikāt wal-ḥikam wal-amthāl wal-ḥikāyāt wal-nawādir*, dedicated to Yūsuf II, Paris 3528, Br. Mus. Suppl. 1145, Alex. Adab, 35, print. Fez n.d. (Fulton 661).

4. Abū ʿAbdallāh Muḥammad b. Ibrāhīm b. al-Sharrān al-Andalusī al-Gharnāṭī al-Rammāl was *raʾīs al-kataba* in Granada around 837/1433.

A. Bābā, *Nayl*, Fez 1317, p. 323/8, C. 311. 1. *al-Urjūza al-manẓūma fi 'l-farāʾiḍ* Esc. [2]853,$_5$, commentary by al-Qalaṣādī, see Suppl. 379,$_2$.—2. *Badīʿ al-maqāl fī madḥ man nabaʿa bayna aṣābiʿihi 'l-zulāl* Būlāq 1319 (in Sarkis 570 anon.).

5. Abu 'l-Ḥasan ʿAlī b. Qāsim b. Muḥammad al-Tujībī al-Zaqqāq studied in Fez and Granada, became a preacher there, and died in 912/1506.

342 | Rieu, Add. 768b. 1. *al-Manhaj al-muntakhab ilā uṣūl al-madhhab* see Suppl.—2. ibid. (commentaries: d. *Tuḥfat al-ḥukkām fī masāʾil al-daʿāwī wal-aḥkām* by Abū ʿAbdallāh Muḥammad b. al-Ṭālib al-Murrī al-Fāsī al-Tāʾūdī, d. 1207/1793, Alex. Fiqh Māl. 9, as *taʿlīq* ibid. 15.—e. *Tuḥfat al-ḥukkām* by Muḥammad b. ʿAbd al-Salām al-Bannāʾī, composed in 1129/1717, ibid. 15.—f. anon., ibid. 12).

5 *Sciences of the Qurʾān*

1. Aḥmad b. Ibrāhīm b. al-Zubayr al-Thaqafī, see Suppl. (Ṣafadī, *Aʿyān al-ʿaṣr* AS 2962, 47b).

1a. Muḥammad b. Aḥmad b. Muḥammad b. ʿAbdallāh b. Yaḥyā al-Kalbī al-Gharnāṭī Abu 'l-Qāsim Abū ʿAbdallāh b. Juzayy, born in 693/1294, was a preacher in Granada who perished in the battle on the Rio Salado on 7 Jumādā I 741/30 October 1340.

| DK III, 356, no. 942, Maqq. III, 270/99. 1. *al-Tashīl li-ʿulūm al-tanzīl*, a mostly factual discussion of individual pasages, Berl. 877, Cairo [1]I, 138, [2]I, 36.—2. *al-Anwār al-saniyya fī 'l-alfāẓ al-sunniyya* Leid. 1750, Alex. Ḥad. 49, the commentary *Lubb al-azhār* by Abu 'l-Ḥasan ʿAlī b. Muḥammad b. ʿAlī al-Qurashī al-Basṭī al-Qalaṣādī, d. 891/1486 (§ 8), ibid. 44. 265

6 *Mysticism*

1. ʿAbd al-Ḥakīm b. Barrajān al-Andalusī, who died in 708/1308.

Sharḥ al-asmāʾ al-ḥusnā AS 1869.

2. Abū Isḥāq Ibrāhīm b. Muḥammad b. Yaḥyā b. Aḥmad b. Zakariyyāʾ b. ʿĪsā b. Muḥammad b. Zakariyyāʾ al-Anṣārī al-Awsī al-Mursī was born in Shaʿbān 687/September 1288. He lived in Granada, and died in Jumādā II 751/August 1350.

DK I, 77. *Zahr al-kimām (akmām) fī qiṣṣat Yūsuf ʿam*, in 27 sections, comprising Qurʾānic verses, *ḥadīth*, reflections on morals, and edifying anecdotes in verse and rhymed prose, Berl. Brill M. 197, 273, Paris 1933/8, Alex. Taʾr. 75, Patna I, 147,1418.

3. Abū ʿAbdallāh Muḥammad b. Muḥammad b. Aḥmad b. ʿAbd al-Raḥmān b. Ibrāhīm al-Anṣārī al-Sāḥilī al-Muʿammam al-Mālaqī was born in Dimellos, near Muntames, in 649/1251, | worked at a number of mosques, and eventually 343
became preacher at the main mosque in Malaga. He died in 754/1353.

DK IV, 161, no. 430. 1. *Bughyat al-sālik fī ashraf al-masālik*, on the Sufi grades and the duties of a scholar, Br. Mus. 758.—2. See Suppl. 3. Treatise on the *dhikr*, Berl. Brill M. 316, 2.

| 7 *Politics* 266

Muḥammad b. ʿAlī b. Muḥammad b. ʿAlī b. al-Qāsim b. al-Azraq al-Aṣbaḥī wrote, in 883/1478 in Wādī Āsh (Guadix):

Al-Ibrīz al-masbūk fī kayfiyyat ādāb al-mulūk Algiers 1375.

8 *Mathematics and Astronomy*

1., 2. see p. 379.

3. Abu 'l-Ḥasan ʿAlī b. Muḥammad b. Muḥammad b. ʿAlī al-Qurashī al-Qalaṣādī al-Basṭī was born in Basṭa, studied in Granada, in Tlemcen with Ibn Marzūq

(p. 310), and in Tunis. After the pilgrimage he took up residence in Granada but, during the turmoil preceding the capture of the city by the Christians, he first went to Tlemcen but then led a restless, wandering existence for the rest of his life. He died in Bāja in Africa, in the middle of Dhu 'l-Ḥijja 891/December 1486.

Maqq. I, 935, Hankel, *Zur Gesch. der Math.* 257. 1. *Kashf al-jilbāb ʿan ʿilm al-ḥisāb* Paris $2463_{,3}$ (cf. *JA* 1862, I, 110), Cairo ^{1}V, 178.—Abstract: 2. *Kashf al-asrār* (*astār*) *ʿan ʿilm* (*waḍʿ*) *ḥurūf al-ghubār* Krafft 323, Paris 2473, 5350, Algiers $399_{,7}$, 1448/9, entitled *Inkishāf al-jilbāb ʿan funūn al-ḥisāb* Alex. Ḥisāb 4, Pet. Ros. 193, Br. Mus. 418, $903_{,2}$, Esc. $^2853_{,4}$, commentary ibid. 5, Garr. 1039, Alex. Ḥisāb 17, Cairo ^{1}V, 185, VII, 570, see Woepcke, *JA* s. V, vol. 1, 1854, 358ff., Cherbonneau, ibid. $1859_{,ii}$, 437ff. M. b. Cheneb and E. Lévi-Provençal, *Revue d'Alep* 1922, SA 22.—3. *Qānūn al-ḥisāb wa-ghunyat dhawi 'l-albāb* Berl. 5995.—4. *Bughyat al-muhtadī wa-ghunyat al-muntahī*, on the law of inheritance, ibid. 4725, Alex. Far. 4, print. Fez n.d.—5. *Sharḥ Talkhīṣ b. al-Bannā'* p. 331.—6. *Sharḥ al-Urjūza al-Yāsamīniyya*
344 I, 621.—7. *Sharḥ* | *Mulḥat al-iʿrāb* I, 328.—9.–12. see Suppl.—13. *Sharḥ Lubb al-azhār* see § 5.

1. Abū Aḥmad Yaʿīsh b. Ibrāhīm b. Sammāk al-Umawī al-Andalusī, who wrote before 774/1372.

Suter 453, Sanchez Pérez, *Biografias de los mat.* 142. 1. *Rafʿ al-ishkāl fī misāḥat al-ashkāl*, a manual for calculating surfaces, Berl. 5949, Br. Mus. Suppl. $753_{,2}$, Alex. Ḥisāb 30.—2. *Marāsim al-intisāb fī maʿālim al-ḥisāb* Br. Mus. Suppl. $753_{,1}$, Ğārullāh 1509 (dated 774 AH).—3. *Risāla fī ʿilm al-qabbān*, on scales, Cairo ^{1}V, 218.

2. Al-Zubayr b. Aḥmad b. Ibrāhīm b. al-Zubayr al-Thaqafī al-Qāḍī Abu 'l-Qāsim, who died in 790/1388 in Granada.

Suter 513. *Tadhkirat dhawi 'l-albāb fī 'stīfā' al-ʿamal bil-asṭurlāb* Br. Mus. 407, 1, Algiers 1466 (where he is called Zubayr b. Jaʿfar b. Zubayr), Cairo ^{1}V, 232 (of which a photograph in *Qu. u. St.* VII, 38, II, 33), Mosul $103_{,66,2}$, Rāmpūr I, $422_{,11}$.

9 *Travelogues and Geographies*

1. Abu 'l-Baqā' Khālid b. ʿĪsā b. Aḥmad b. Ibrāhīm al-Balawī, who was a *qāḍī* in Qanṭūriyya, travelled through Africa and Jerusalem to Mecca in the years 736–40/1336–40, and wrote:

Tāj al-maʿārif bi(fī) taḥliyat ʿulamāʾ al-mashriq, in rhymed prose, relying heavily on Ibn Jubayr (I, 629, ed. Wright p. 11), Berl. 6133, Gotha 1540 (where the itinerary is given in detail), Fez Qar. 1296 (see *Bull. de Corr. Afr.* 1883, 375, no. 52), Tunis ibid. 1884, 35, no. 141, see Cherbonneau *JA* s. v. vol. 12, 449, Wüst. *Gesch.* 438, Pons Boigues 62, ʿA. Mubārak, *al-Khiṭ. al-jad.* XIV, 62.

2. See Suppl. III, 1279, 379.

10 *Medicine*

1. See Suppl. III, 366 § 13, 1.

2. See Suppl. III, 1279 and 379.

| 11 *Sports* 345

1. Muḥammad b. Riḍwān b. Muḥammad b. Aḥmad b. Ibrāhīm b. Arqam al-Numayrī came from Guadix and died in 757/1356.

Pons Boigues 329, no. 286. *Kitāb al-iḥtifāl fi ʾstīfāʾ taṣnīf mā lil-khayl min al-aḥwāl*, written for the emir Abū ʿAbdallāh Muḥammad b. Naṣr of Granada (r. 701–8/1302–9), Esc. [2]902.—Lost: 2. *Manẓūm fī ʿilm al-nujūm*.—3. *Risāla fi ʾl-asṭurlāb*.—4. *Shajara fī ansāb al-ʿArab*.

2. Abu ʾl-Ḥasan ʿAlī b. ʿAbd al-Raḥmān b. Hudhayl al-Fazārī al-Andalusī:

See Suppl. (5. read: C. 1303, 1318).

 267

From the Conquest of Egypt by Sultan Selīm I in 1517 to the Napoleonic Expedition to Egypt in 1798

Introduction

After the conquest of Syria and Egypt, the Ottoman Empire was complete. And it did not take long for a lively exchange between the various regions of the eastern Mediterranean to come about, an exchange that was good for trade and for scholarship. The capital Istanbul especially, from where the sultan in his mercy distributed all the benefices of the empire, was very attractive for scholars from all regions. But all this coming and going did not produce any fertile movement of the mind. While in the West the enlargement of
the geographical horizon, the revival of classical antiquity, and the | struggle 346
against the spiritual bonds of the Old Church led to a new worldview, the Orient persevered in its intellectual torpidity. Even though the new worldview that was brought on by the discovery of the Americas was closely monitored in learned circles in Istanbul and by the statesmen who kept a keen eye on the shifts of power in Europe, the only "benefit" from the New World that reached the Muslim masses was tobacco. Even though this was to lead to a lively debate among the *fuqahāʾ* that lasted several decades, tobacco itself seemed merely to aggravate the listlessness of the masses. It was only with Napoleon's invasion of Egypt that the Orient was opened to the influence of
European culture, | which gradually made itself felt in intellectual life as well. 268

Next to Istanbul, Cairo also asserted itself as a intellectual capital of Islam in this period, primarily through the al-Azhar academy, to which students from all parts of the Muslim world flocked together. Syria, on the other hand, fell into the background, immersing itself ever more deeply in an isolated provincial existence, lacking any internal urge to develop further. Even the emirates that came into being under Ottoman dominion in coastal cities like Tripoli and in Lebanon were unable to add new lustre to that existence. Despite their political hegemony, the Turks never fully disengaged themselves from the Arab school. In Iran, on the other hand, which had once given so many excellent contributors to Arabic literature, Arabic was more and more overshadowed by the national language. In contrast, Arabic was able to spread to the East, from South Arabia to India, all the way to the inhabitants of the Malay archipelago.

 | DOI 10.1163/9789004326323_003

In North Africa, Islamic intellectual life was even more fossilised than in the east, but here, too, its influence reached ever further into the Sudan.

347 | TA: *Tarājim al-aʿyān min abnāʾ al-zamān* by al-Ḥasan al-Būrīnī, d. 1024/1617 (p. 290), cod. Berl. Wetzst. I, 29 (Ahlw. 9889).

Muḥ: *Khulāṣat al-athar min aʿyān al-qarn al-ḥādī ʿashar* by Muḥammad al-Amīn al-Muḥibbī, d. 1111/1699 (p. 293), 4 vols., C. 1284.

Mur.: *Silk al-durar fī aʿyān al-qarn al-thānī ʿashar* by Muḥammad Khalīl al-Murādī, d. 1206/1791 (p. 294), 4 vols., C. 1291/1301.

Jab.: *ʿAjāʾib al-āthār fi ʾl-tarājim wal-akhbār* by al-Jabartī, d. 1236/1821 (p. 480), 4 vols., Būlāq 1297.

Khiṭ. jad.: al-Khiṭaṭ al-Tawfīqiyya al-jadīda by ʿAlī Bāshā Mubārak, d. 1893 (p. 482), 20 vols., Būlāq 1306.

Chapter 1. Egypt and Syria

The countries of the erstwhile Mamlūk Empire owed a debt of gratitude to the Ottoman conquerors whose administration put an end to political chaos, even though the resources of the people, especially of Syria, were more heavily solicited than ever before. | In Egypt, the Mamlūk Beys retained their former 269
feudal powers, which were not too strongly curbed by the sultan's governor. Nevertheless, subjects always had the possibility of directing themselves at the central government in Istanbul, which at times even moved against its own pashas, for instance when these, in their management of teaching posts, had the impudence to follow the example of the Mamlūk sultans. But Syria and Egypt, too, shared the fate of the empire as a whole, whose feudally-inspired organisation was unable to solve any other than military problems. The Levantine trade, of whose blessings they had once received an opulent share, took another direction with the discovery of the seaway to the East Indies and lost steadily in importance to trade with America. The lands of Islam thus sank into poverty, while its inhabitants gradually descended into a state of barbarism in comparison with the peoples | of Europe whose teachers they once were. 348

This general cultural situation is also reflected in literature. In none of its disciplines is there any progress of note. Poetry is dominated by the glorification of the Prophet as introduced by Ibn Fāriḍ in the form, and to the nauseatingly sweet tones, of earthly love.[1] There were but few poets who had the courage to express themselves in the language of the people. The *Hazz al-quḥūf* of al-Shirbīnī (p. 278), which is the most skilful in its handling of it, | only 270
embraces it for satirical purposes. The sciences are pursued according to the same old patterns, with very few scholars, such as ʿAbd al-Qādir al-Baghdādī (p. 286) and al-Murtaḍā al-Zabīdī (p. 288), trying to connect with the traditions of classical times, over and above the common kind of knowledge that was considered good enough by the majority of the compilers.

In theology and law, scholars were only able to summarise the opinions of the masters of previous times. The main work of this period is Ibn al-Ramlī's (p. 323) commentary on al-Nawawī's *Minhāj*.[2] Only mysticism saw a certain upswing. The two dervish orders of the Khalwatiyya and the Naqshbandiyya attracted ever more followers, and the Sufis al-Shaʿrānī (p. 335) and ʿAbd al-Ghanī al-Nābulusī (p. 345) tried to emulate the unsurpassed master Ibn ʿArabī in the temerity of their theosophical speculations. In the exact sciences no advances were made. Oblivious of the enlargement of

---

1 See Hartmann, *Muwashshaḥ* 236.

2 Snouck Hurgronje, *ZDMG* 53, 142ff.

the geographical image of the world, knowledge of which did not reach beyond
Istanbul, writers of travelogues still drew familiar pictures of the routes from
Damascus and Cairo to Istanbul and Mecca, more out of laziness than for the
349 instruction | of their readers. From among the discoveries in the natural sci-
ences in Europe, only the alchemistic fantasies of Paracelcus found their way
to the Orient (§ 18, 6).

1 *Poetry and Rhymed Prose*[1]

Heyworth Dunne, Arabic Literature in Egypt in the 18. Century with special reference to Poetry and Poets, *BSOS* I (1938) 675/90 (from Jab.).

1. ʿĀʾisha bint Yūsuf b. Aḥmad b. Nāṣir b. Khalīfa al-Bāʿūniyya al-Ṣāliḥiyya, who died in 922/1516, see Suppl.

1. *al-Fatḥ al-mubīn fī madḥ al-amīn*, a *badīʿiyya*, Berl. 7378, Brill M. $161_{,2}$, Br. Mus. Suppl. $985_{,\text{vi}}$, Garr. 109.—2. Some *qaṣīdas*, Berl. $7933_{,1-3}$.—see Suppl.

2. Nāṣir al-Dīn Muḥammad b. Qānṣūh b. Ṣādiq, who was a student of al-Suyūṭī, flourished in the first half of the tenth century.

Hartmann, *Muw.* 42 (not completely accurate). 1. *al-Siḥr al-ḥalāl min ibdāʾ al-jalāl*, with 1 introduction and 5 *maqāmāt*: a. on the intellect, b. on adab, c. on traditions, d. sample poems, only the *muqaddima* Ind. Off. 833, Baghdad, see *al-Muqtaṭaf*, Febr. 1928, 201/4.—2. *Marātiʿ al-albāb min marābiʿ al-ādāb*, a poetical anthology, Br. Mus. $770_{,1}$.—3. A panegyric on Malik al-Umarāʾ Khayrbeg, Berl. $8176_{,2}$.—4.–11. see Suppl.

2a. ʿAlāʾ al-Dīn b. Mulayk al-Ḥamawī, who died in 917/1511.

Al-Nafaḥāt al-adabiyya min al-riyāḍ al-Ḥamawiyya Beirut 1312.

3. ʿAlī b. Muḥammad b. Duqmāq al-Ḥusaynī, who died in 940/1533.

Badīʿiyya, with a commentary, Berl. 7379.

---

1 Poems by unidentified individuals, which have been transmitted in great numbers from this period, will not be considered here, similar to the poetry albums of the 18th century in German literary history.

| 4. Muḥammad b. Aḥmad b. ʿAbdallāh al-Rūmī Māmāya (Māmiyā) was born 350
in Istanbul in 930/1534, went as a young man to Damascus, and then joined the Janissaries, before making the pilgrimage with them in 960/1553. Later he dedicated himself to scholarship and became a dragoman at al-Maḥkama al-Ṣāliḥiyya. After he had been removed from office he had to make a living by writing panegyrics for a time, before he was granted a new post at the court dealing with inheritances, which earned him a large fortune. As a poet he preferred *taʾrīkh* and *muʿammayāt*, following the example of the Persians and the Turks. He did not include *hijāʾ* poetry in his *Dīwān*, which he compiled in 971/1563. He died in Dhu ʾl-Ḥijja 987/January 1580 or the following month, i.e. Muḥarram/February.

RA 250v, Hartmann, *Muw.* 66. 1. *Dīwān*, entitled *Rawḍat al-mushtāq*, including love songs, panegyrics on the sultans Süleymān I, Selīm II, Murād II, and important people surrounding them, a *Taʾrīkh* for the period 930–83/1523–75 (supplemented subsequently), at the end *muʿammayāt*, Berl. 7945/7, Ms. or. oct. 3837, Gotha 2350 (cf. 43,$_{19}$, 1435, f. 1a), Munich 552/3, Copenhagen 281, Paris 3235, Pet. Ros. 98, Br. Mus. 631, Bodl. I, 1234, Cairo [1]IV, 240, with the title *Rawḍat al-ʿushshāq wa-bahjat al-mushtāq* Patna I, 199,$_{1782}$. |—2. *Burhān al-burhān*, a 272
dīwān illustrating the different kinds of tropes, Berl. 7282.—3. Two poems in *Nufhat ool Yumun* 263.—(see Suppl.).

5. Abū Bakr al-Bakrī, ca. 1000/1591.

A *dīwān*, collected by himself at the request of his relative Zayn al-Dīn al-Bakrī, who was Shaykh al-Islām in Egypt in the period 994–1013/1586–1604, Br. Mus. 1529.

6. Shams al-Dīn Qāsim b. Muḥammad al-Dimashqī al-Ḥalabī al-Qawwās, ca. 1000/1591.

Riyāḍ al-azhār wa-nasīm al-asḥār, 9 *maqāmas*, Berl. 8574/5, Paris 3952, with a tenth that remains unfinished.

7. Zayn al-Dīn ʿAbd al-Raḥmān b. Aḥmad b. ʿAlī al-Ḥumaydī lived as a physician in Egypt and died on 17 Muḥarram 1005/11 September 1596 (or, according to others, in 995/1587).

| Muḥ. II, 376. 1. *al-Durr al-munaẓẓam fī madḥ al-ḥabīb al-aʿẓam*, a *dīwān* 351
ordered by the rhyme consonants, Gotha 2321, Upps. 146, Garr. 111, print. Būlāq

1313.—2. *Tamlīḥ al-badīʿ li-madḥ al-shafīʿ*, a rhetorical poem in praise of the Prophet, Paris 3248,$_{11}$, Garr. 566, printed in the *dīwān*. Commentary, *Fatḥ al-badīʿ*, abstract *Manḥ al-samīʿ*, completed in 993/1585, Berl. 7380, Leid. 338, Paris 3238, Esc. ^{2}354, 421/3.—3. A panegyric on Muḥammad in 49 verses, Berl. 7951.—4. A panegyric on Muḥammad rhyming on the single word *khāl*, each time in a different sense, ibid. 2.—5. *Manẓūma fi 'l-jinās* Berl. 7335.

8. Shams al-Dīn Muḥammad b. Najm al-Dīn b. Muḥammad al-Ṣāliḥī al-Hilālī was born in Damascus (according to *RA* in Mecca) in 956/1549, studied there and in Mecca, and returned to Damascus after his father died in 964/1557. He amassed a considerable fortune through his calligraphic copying of various works, notably al-Bayḍāwī's Qur'ān commentary, and following a sojourn in Egypt in 994/1586 he devoted himself entirely to writing poetry. During a visit to his married sister in Tripoli in 1008/1599 he made the acquaintance of the emir ʿAlī b. Sayfā, who entrusted him with the education of his son. He died in 1012/1603 in Damascus.

RA 266v, Muḥ. IV, 239/48. 1. *Sajʿ al-ḥamām fī madḥ khayr al-anām* Br. Mus. 1084, print. C. n.d., Istanbul 1298.—2. Poetic letters to a number of famous people who hailed from Damascus between the years 977–94/1569–86, Br. Mus. 1084,$_{2}$.—3.–5. see Suppl.

273 | 9. Shihāb al-Dīn Aḥmad b. Aḥmad b. ʿAbd al-Raḥmān b. Aḥmad b. Makkiyya al-Nābulusī al-ʿInāyatī came from Nablus.[2] After years of wandering, during which time he stayed in the Hijaz, Jerusalem, Aleppo, and other Syrian cities, he took up residence in Damascus in 988/1580, where he passed away in the Badharā'iyya madrasa in 1014/1605. His poems strictly follow the ancient Arabic schemes.

RA 58r, *TA* 19v, Muḥ. I, 166. 1. *Dīwān* Br. Mus. 1082, another collection ibid.
352 1083 = *Cat. Ital.* 234, no. 89, | Garr. 112, incomplete Gotha 1660, individual poems Berl. 7956, Br. Mus. 641.—2. *al-Durar al-muḍī'a fi 'l-akhlāq al-marḍiyya*, *mathnawī* of moral and contemplative content, Gotha 2322.

10. Shams al-Dīn Muḥammad al-Ṣaydāwī wrote, in 997/1589:

2 According to Muḥ. he was born in Mecca between 930/40. This would tally with the fact that throughout his life he retained the Meccan vernacular.

1. See Suppl.—2. *al-Inʿām fī maʿrifat al-anghām* Paris 2480, photograph Cairo *Nashra* 4.

11. Darwīsh Muḥammad b. Aḥmad b. Ṭālū al-Urtuqī al-Dimashqī, who was the son of a Turk who had been in Selīm's army, was born in Damascus in 955/1540. He joined a Sufi order and became a professor at the Ḥātimiyya as well as acting *qāḍī* for the Ḥanafīs at the Maḥkamat Maydān al-Ḥaṣā. In 992/1584, he went with the *qāḍi 'l-quḍāt* Muḥammad b. Bustān to Istanbul where he was granted a professorship. After four years he was removed from that office and returned to Damascus. Following a visit to his cousin Ibrāhīm al-Ṭālawī, who was emir of Nablus, and to Gaza where he sang the praises of the local notables, he went on pilgrimage in 998/1590. From then on he lived until his death in 1014/1605 in Damascus, with a fearsome reputation as a composer of *hijāʾ* poetry.

RA 123r, *TA* 113v, Muḥ. II, 149/55. *Ṣāniḥāt duma 'l-qaṣr fī muṭāraḥāt bani 'l-ʿaṣr*, poetic correspondence with other contemporaneous poets, compiled in 981/1573, Berl. 7954/5, Paris 4442, Br. Mus. 632/3, Alex. Adab 77, Cairo II, [1]261, [2]181, probably a *risāla* from Istanbul from it in Gotha 26i.

12. Muḥammad b. Abi 'l-Wafāʾ Maʿrūf al-Ḥamawī al-Maʿrūfī, who died in 1016/1607.

A collection of short poems, mostly in *rajaz*, containing health directives, astronomical and historical lore etc., Berl. 8205.

| 13. Ibrāhīm b. Aḥmad b. Muḥammad b. Aḥmad b. al-Mollā al-Ḥalabī al-Ḥaṣkafī 274
lived in Aleppo, made the pilgrimage in 1000/1596, and died after 1030/1621.

Muḥ. I, 11. 1. *Ḥalbat al-mufāḍala wa-ḥilyat al-munāḍala fi 'l-muṭāraḥa wal-murāsala wal-munājala*, a poetical | correspondence with his friends in Syria 353
and Istanbul, Gotha 2323, another version Berl. 7959.—2. *Abkār al-maʿāni 'l-mukhaddara wa-asrār al-mabāni 'l-mudhakhkhara*, poems from the years 987–1017/1579–1608, Paris 3239, AS 900,$_{34}$.—3. See Suppl.

14. Ḥusayn b. Aḥmad b. Ḥusayn b. al-Jazarī al-Ḥalabī was born in Aleppo and travelled extensively in Syria and Iraq, as well as through Anatolia in 1014/1605. He then took up residence in his hometown, but every now and then he would visit the court of the Banū Sayfā, the emirs of Tripoli. He died in 1034/1625.

Muḥ. II, 81. His *dīwān*, arranged by subject: praise of scholars and members of the upper class, admonition and counsel, love songs, poetical correspondence, jokes, dirty stories, elegies, and satires, Berl. 7962, Garr. 113, see Suppl.

15. Abu 'l-Wafā' wrote, in 1034/1625:

Al-Ṭirāz al-badīʿ fi 'mtidāḥ al-shafīʿ, an imitation of the *Burda* (I, 308) with a commentary indicating the rhetorical figures in each verse, Munich 549.

16. Muḥammad Fatḥallāh b. Maḥmūd b. Muḥammad al-Ḥalabī al-Baylūnī was born in Aleppo in 977/1569, visited Mecca, Medina, Jerusalem, Damascus, Tripoli, and al-Rūm, and died in Aleppo in 1042/1632.

Muḥ. III, 254/7. 1. *Dīwān*, alphabetically arranged by his nephew Muḥammad b. Muḥammad, Berl. 7967, Paris 3249, Garr. 116.—2. *Khulāṣat mā taḥṣul ʿalayhi 'l-sāʿūn fī adwiyat al-waba' wal-ṭāʿūn*, containing medical and spiritual cures against the plague, Berl. 6374, Köpr. II, 156, Cairo ^{1}VII, 4, 266.—3. *Mukhtaṣar Riḥlat b. Baṭṭūṭa* S.

16a. Muḥammad b. Muḥyi 'l-Dīn ʿAbd al-Qādir al-Ṣaydāwī al-Ḥādī, who was *muftī* of Sidon, died in 1042/1632.

Muḥ. IV, 11. *Dīwān* (*Alḥān*) *al-Ḥādī bayna l-murājiʿ wal-bādī* (*mubādī*) Garr. 117, Alex. Adab 11.

17. Ibrāhīm b. Muḥammad b. Muḥammad al-Dimashqī al-Ṣāliḥī b. al-Akram, who died in 1044/1635.

354 | *Dīwān*, containing panegyrical poems, poetical letters, wine and love songs, and finally songs of austerity and repentance, Berl. 7969.

18. ʿAbd al-Raḥmān b. Yaḥyā b. Muḥammad al-Miṣrī Zayn al-Dīn al-Maddāḥ, who died in 1044/1635.

Two *qaṣīda*s written in 1033/1624, Berl. $7970_{,1}$.

19. Aḥmad b. ʿAbd al-Raḥmān b. Muḥammad al-Bakrī al-Wārithī, who died in 1047/1637.

See Suppl. *Dīwān* on love, wine, nature's beauty, flowers, and gardens, Berl. 7971.

| 20. Aḥmad b. Zayn al-ʿĀbidīn b. Muḥammad al-Miṣrī al-Bakrī al-Ṣiddīqī, who 275
died in Cairo in 1048/1638.

Muḥ. I, 201, *Khiṭ. jad.* III, 129. *Dīwān*, with many *muwashshaḥāt*, Alex. Adab 52 (which mistakenly states that he died in 1087). A *qaṣīda* on love, Berl. 7972. More poems are found in Hartmann, *Muw.* 12.

21. Abū Ḥafṣ Aḥmad Efendi b. Shāhīn al-Qubrusī al-Dimashqī was born in 885/1587, the son of an Egyptian who had been forced to join the Turkish army. Aḥmad also joined the army but was captured when the Syrian troops were defeated by Aḥmad b. Jānbūlādh. After his release he went to study, became a *qāḍī* in the caravan of Syrian pilgrims in 1030/1621, and lectured at the Jaqmaqiyya madrasa. In his leisure time he practised alchemy. He died in 1053/1643.

Muḥ. I, 210/7. *Dīwān*, featuring songs in praise of contemporary notables, brought together after his death by ʿAbd al-Salām b. Aḥmad in 1053, Berl. 7978.

22. Muḥammad b. Aḥmad b. Qāsim al-Ḥalabī al-Qāsimī, who died in 1054/1644.

Dīwān, beginning in Berl. 7978.

23. Having gone to Istanbul several times, Muḥammad b. Jamāl al-Dīn b. Aḥmad b. Ḥāfiẓ al-Dīn al-Qudsī al-Ḥanafī b. al-ʿAjamī became a *qāḍī* in Cairo,
then a *muftī* and professor in Jerusalem, where he | did not get along with 355
his fellow citizens, and so moved to Damascus. Denounced for a homosexual affair, he went to Istanbul where he succeeded in getting himself nominated as *qāḍī* of Tripoli. When he was again removed from office there he returned to Damascus in 1044/1634, but was again able to secure a position for himself as a *qāḍī*, first in Bosnia, and then Sofia. He died in 1055/1645.

Muḥ. III, 41/4. 1. *al-Minan al-ẓāhira ʿala ʾl-sāda al-ṭāhira*, poems in praise of his patrons in Istanbul, Berl. 7980.—2. Individual *qaṣīda*s, ibid. 7981.

24. Yūsuf b. Abi ʾl-Fatḥ b. Manṣūr al-Suqayyifī al-Dimashqī was born in Damascus in 994/1586, became a preacher at the Salīmiyya, and then, in Istanbul, the imam of Sultan ʿUthmān (Osman) II (1027–31/1618–22). After the
murder of the latter he returned to Damascus | where he became a preacher 276
at the Umayyad mosque and a professor at the Salīmiyya. In 1044/1634 Sultan

Murād IV appointed him as his imam, he entered this office in Khuwayy (Khūy) in Azerbaijan, and remained in his post until his death in Istanbul in 1056/1646.

Muḥ. IV 493/500 (with sample poems). 1. A *qaṣīda*, Berl. 7982.—2. A prayer in *basīṭ*, ibid. 3639,$_{1}$.

25. ʿAbdallāh al-Ziftāwī al-Khaṭīb wrote, in 1059/1649:

Badīʿiyya Berl. 7382, on which the commentary *Ḥusn al-ṣanīʿ fī sharḥ Nūr al-rabīʿ* by ʿAbd al-Laṭīf al-ʿAshmāwī, d. 1067/1656 (p. 318, 8), Paris 4420,$_{2}$, Garr. 569.

26. ʿAbd al-Bāqī b. Muḥammad al-Isḥāqī al-Manūfī studied in his hometown of Manūf and in Cairo, became famous as a poet, and died soon after 1060/1650.

Muḥ. II, 289/91. *Dīwān sulāf al-inshāʾ fi ʾl-shiʿr wal-inshāʾ* Vienna 494.

27. Al-Ḥasan b. Aḥmad b. Muḥammad al-Dimashqī al-Usṭuwānī was an acting judge in Damascus, and died in 1062/1656.

356 | Muḥ. II, 16. *Dīwān*, compiled by himself, Berl. 7983.

28. Muḥammad b. Nūr al-Dīn b. Muḥammad al-Dimashqī b. al-Darrāʾ was born in Damascus in 1025/1619, studied in Cairo and Mecca, and died in his hometown in 1065/1655.

Muḥ. IV, 249/57 (with sample poems). *Dīwān* Berl. 7985, individual poems also in Garr. 148.

29. Muḥyi ʾl-Dīn b. Taqī al-Dīn Abū Bakr al-Salaṭī al-Dimashqī flourished around 1065/1655.

1. *Dīwān* Berl. 7984.—2. *Ṣabābat al-muʿānī wa-ṣabbābat al-maʿānī*, on love, following the example of the *Dīwān al-ṣabāba* of Ibn Abī Ḥajala (p. 13), ibid. 8431.

30. Muḥammad b. Yūsuf al-Karīmī al-Dimashqī, born in 1008/1599, went to Istanbul with his father in 1028/1619 and became a professor at the ʿIzziyya madrasa in Damascus after the latter's death. After a second trip to Istanbul he became *qāḍī* of the caravan of Syrian pilgrims. After his return from a third trip to Istanbul in 1043/1633 he retired from public life due to depression and died in 1068/1657.

Muḥ. IV, 273/80. *Dīwān*, containing letters and riddles, from the years 1029–1047/1620–1637, Berl. 7987/8, Br. Mus. 634, Or. 6296 (DL 58), Garr. 121, Patna I, 197$_{,1767}$.

30a. Ḥasan Čelebī b. Ḥusayn al-ʿAqqād al-Shāmī al-Dimashqī wrote, in 1069/1659:

Jalīs al-ẓurafāʾ wa-anīs al-aḥbāb wal-ḥulafāʾ Alex. Adab 32.

| 31. Ṣadr al-Dīn ʿAlī b. Aḥmad al-Ḥusaynī flourished around 1078/1667. 277

Al-Raḥīq al-makhtūm, his *dīwān*, Paris 3259,2, print. Damascus 1331.

32. Manjaq Pāshā b. Muḥammad b. Manjaq b. Abī Bakr | al-Yūsufī al-Dimashqī, 357
who was born in Damascus in 1005/1596, squandered his father's fortune after the latter's death and then vainly tried to make some money in Istanbul. As such, he was forced to live in solitude in Damascus until his death on 24 Jumādā II 1080/20 November 1669.

Muḥ. IV, 409/23. *Dīwān*, compiled by Faḍlallāh, the father of al-Muḥibbī, d. 1082/1671, in two editions: a. ordered chronologically, starting with a poem on Sultan Ibrāhīm I from the year 1055/1645, Berl. 7994/5, Br. Mus. 1055, Copenhagen 285; b. in alphabetical order, including poems from later times (the last one written in the year 1071/1660), Br. Mus. Suppl. 1093, print. Damascus 1301. Individual *qaṣīda*s, Berl. 7996.

33. Muṣṭafā Efendi b. ʿUthmān (ʿAbd al-Malik) al-Bābī was born in Aleppo and studied there and in Damascus. In 1051/1641 he went to Asia Minor, where he was active as a teacher and joined a Mawlawī order. Then he became *qāḍī* in Tripoli, Magnesia, Baghdad, and Medina. In 1091/1680 he made the pilgrimage, and died in Mecca.

Muḥ. IV, 377/85, al-Ṭabbākh, *Taʾrīkh Ḥalab* VI, 367/73. His *dīwān*, containing panegyrical poems and elegies on Turkish officials, Gotha 2324, Br. Mus. 1086$_{,1}$, Cambr. Pr. 32, no. 218, Garr. 123, print. Beirut 1872, 1326. A *qaṣīda* in 19 verses praising God's goodness, Berl. 8003$_{,3}$.

34. Mūsā Efendi al-Rāmḥamdānī was born in Rāmḥamdān near Aleppo in 1004/1595, studied in Aleppo, and died there in 1089/1678. He was a great admirer of Abu 'l-ʿAlāʾ al-Maʿarrī (I, 295).

Muḥ. IV, 435/42 (with sample poems). A *qaṣīda* on the Prophet, Berl. 8003$_{,2}$.

35. ʿAbdallāh b. Muḥammad Ḥijāzī b. ʿAbd al-Qādir al-Ḥalabī b. Qaḍībalbān studied in Aleppo and became a *qāḍī* in Diyarbakir. A close associate of the
358 vizier al-Fāḍil, he left his duties to his subordinate, | who abused his position to blackmail people. As a result, he was removed from office and then lived for five years in Istanbul. When he accompanied the sultan to Adrianople he was
278 granted the position of *qāḍī* in Jerusalem, | and ordered the levying of taxes on the ʿAlids in Arab lands to begin. In Cairo he met with fierce resistance, and so arranged for his transfer as a *qāḍī* to Aleppo, with Mecca as a stop on the way. During a famine in 1096/1685 he was killed by an angry mob after being bribed by grain speculators, while he was also under suspicion of poisoning the *mutasallim* who had tried to bring such profiteering under control.

Muḥ. III, 70/80. 1. A *qaṣīda*, based on the example of Abu ʾl-Ḥasan al-Kawkabānī, d. 1112/1700, Berl. 8003$_{,7}$.—2. A *qaṣīda* in praise of the Prophet, ibid. 8.—3. *Ḥall al-ʿiqāl*, a consolatory work, ibid. 8849, see Suppl.—4., 5.—ibid. (5. al-ʿUryānī, d. 1168/1754, Garr. 128).

36. Yūsuf b. Muḥammad b. ʿAbd al-Jawād b. Khiḍr al-Shirbīnī wrote, in 1098/1687:

Hazz al-quḥūf,[3] a song of mockery and mourning on the unkempt ways and coarse language of Egyptian farmers, including diatribes on the spiritual arrogance and narrow-mindedness of theologians, written in 52 verses in the vernacular, put into the mouth of a ficticious farmer called Abū Shādūf or Ibn ʿUjayl,[4] with a detailed self-commentary, Berl. 7973 (with a mistaken *kanz* instead of *hazz*), Gotha 2345/6, Leid. 466, Br. Mus. Suppl. 1094, Cambr. Pr. 31, no. 117, Paris 3267/70, print. Būlāq 1274, 1284, 1308, among others, lith. Alexandria 1289; cf. A. v. Kremer, *Ägypten* I, 58, v. Mehren, *Overs. over d. kgl. Danske Videnskab. Selsk. Forh. no. i*, Copenhagen 1872, Vollers, ZDMG 41, 370ff.

37. Muḥammad b. ʿAlī b. Ḥaydar al-Ḥusaynī flourished in the first half of the twelfth century.

359 | *Dīwān*, religious songs of praise, Paris 3259,1.

3 I.e. the rocking of the farmer's head while dancing on the threshing floor.

4 Vollers, loc. cit., has shown, contra Ahlw., that this name is also a fabrication.

37a. Naṣr al-Khalwatī al-Jalwatī al-Dimashqī.

Dīwān, manuscript dated 1101, Alex. Adab 142.

38. Yaḥyā b. Mūsā al-ʿĪdī al-Ḥabūrī ʿImād al-Dīn, who flourished ca. 1104/1692.

1. *al-Zahr fī ghayāhib al-dayjūrī dīwān Abī Mūsā al-Ḥibūrī*, prayers, praise of the Prophet, *muwashshaḥāt*, Berl. 8005.—2. A *maqāma*, ibid. 8567$_{,3}$.—3. *al-Faraj baʿd al-shidda*, based on the work by Tanūkhī (I, 162), Cambr. 726 = (?) *Tafrīḥ al-muhaj bi-talwīḥ al-faraj* C. 1317.

| 39. Ibrāhīm b. Muḥammad b. ʿAbd al-Karīm al-Safarjalānī was born in 279
1055/1645 and died in 1112/1700.

Mur. I, 15/9. His *dīwān*, alphabetically arranged, mostly shorter pieces, among which are a number of *takhmīs*, Berl. 8010, Garr. 126.

40. Muṣṭafā b. Ismāʿīl b. Aḥmad al-Khazāʾinī al-Sukkārī, ca. 1113/1701.

Mukhtaṣar al-dīwān al-tāsiʿ Berl. 8012.

41. ʿAbd al-Ḥayy b. ʿAlī b. Muḥammad b. Maḥmūd al-Dimashqī al-Ṭālawī b. al-Ṭawīl al-Ḥāl, who was the most celebrated poet of his time, died in 1117/1705.

Mur. II, 244/53. 1. *Dīwān* Berl. 8013/4.—2. see Suppl. (also Garr. 158, where he is named as ʿAbdī Bishr al-Khāl).

42. ʿAbd al-Karīm b. Muḥammad b. Muḥammad al-Ḥusaynī Kamāl al-Dīn b. Ḥamza al-Naqīb was born in Damascus in 1051/1641, became a professor at al-Madrasa al-Qaymariyya al-Barrāniyya, and was *naqīb* of the ʿAlids several times. He died in 1118/1706.

Mur. III, 65/81 (with sample poems), Hartmann, *Muw.* 37. A *muwashshaḥ* in praise of Damascus, Berl. 8074$_{,1}$.

43. ʿAbd al-Raḥmān b. Ibrāhīm b. ʿAbd al-Raḥmān b. al-Mawṣilī al-Shaybānī al-Maydānī al-Dimashqī came from a famous family of Sufis. He was born in 1031/1622 and passed away in 1118/1706 (or, according to others, in 1109/1697).

360 | Mur. II, 259/66. 1. *Dīwān*, compiled by his son, Berl. 8015, Gotha 2333, Garr. 125.—2. *Istighfāra* in 40 verses, Berl. 3940,$_{2}$.

44. Ḥusayn b. Rajab b. Ḥusayn b. ʿAlawān al-Shāfiʿī al-Shaṭṭārī, who died in 1121/1709.

Qaṣīdas, Berl. 8018,$_{2}$.

45. Aḥmad al-Dulanjawī, who died in 1123/1711.

Jab. I, 71. *Dīwān*, starting with a *tashṭīr* on the *Burda*, Paris 3260, only the latter ibid. 3185,$_{2}$ (see I, 312).

46. Suʿūdī (Abu ʾl-Suʿūd) Yaḥyā b. Muḥyi ʾl-Dīn al-Mutanabbiʾ died in 1127/1715 in Damascus.

Mur. I, 58/62 (with sample poems). *Muwashshaḥ* in praise of Damascus, Berl. 8174,$_{2}$.

47. ʿUmar b. ʿAlī b. ʿUmar b. ʿAlī b. al-Sukkārī al-Dimashqī, who died in Damascus in 1129/1717.

Mur. III, 183. 1. A *qaṣīda* describing love for God, Berl. 8019,$_{2}$.—2. *Naẓm al-futūḥ fī ṭarab al-nafs wal-rūḥ*, a *muwashshaḥ* in 22 *dawr*; in each of the first verses of the first 10 *dawr* he inserted his own name ʿUmar, ibid. 8174,$_{3}$.

280 | 48. Al-Ḥasan al-Badrī al-Ḥijāzī al-Azharī adapted the everyday occurrences of his time into poetry written in the common vernacular, which was used by al-Jabartī in his historical work. He died in 1131/1719.

Jab. I, 75/83 (with sample poems), see Goldziher, *MSt* II, 285, BSOS IX, 681. *Tanbīh al-afkār lil-nāfiʿ wal-ḍārr* or *Ijmāʿ al-iyās min al-wuthūq bil-nās*, Sufi poems, Cairo ^{1}IV, 221, ^{2}III, 69.

49. Muḥammad b. Ibrāhīm b. ʿAbd al-Raḥmān al-ʿImādī al-Dimashqī was born in Damascus in 1075/1664, succeeded his brother—who had raised him after their father's untimely death—in his professorship at the Sulaymāniyya, became a *qāḍī* for the Ḥanafīs in 1121/1709, and died in 1135/1723.

Mur. IV, 17/23. 7 *qaṣīdas*, Berl. 8021,$_{2}$.

| 50. Muṣṭafā Efendi b. Ḥasan Efendi b. Muḥammad al-Ṣimādī, who died in 361
1137/1725 in Damascus.

Mur. IV, 179/83 (with sample poems). *Dīwān*, compiled by ʿAbd al-Raḥmān b. Muḥammad b. ʿAlī al-Turkumānī al-Buhlūl al-Nakhlāwī al-Dimashqī, d. 1163/1750 (see no. 59), Berl. 8022.

51. ʿAbd al-Raḥmān b. Ibrāhīm b. Aḥmad al-Dimashqī b. ʿAbd al-Razzāq was born in Damascus in 1075/1664 and became a student of ʿAbd al-Ghanī al-Nābulusī (see below p. 345), before dying in 1128/1726.

Mur. III, 266/74. A *muwashshaḥ* in praise of Damascus, Berl. $8174_{,3}$, see Hartmann, 34.

52. Muḥammad Ṣādiq b. Muḥammad b. Ḥusayn b. Muḥammad al-Kharrāṭ was the son-in-law of ʿAbd al-Ghanī al-Nābulusī and a professor at the ʿUmariyya madrasa. He died in 1143/1731.

Mur. II, 192/8. A *muwashshaḥ* in praise of Damascus, Berl. $8175_{,2}$, see Hartmann, 34.

53. Jarmānūs Gabrāʾīl b. Farḥāt, who died in 1732, see Suppl.

1. *Dīwān*, also Berl. Ms. or. oct. 3957, printed as *Naẓm al-laʾālīʾ lil-baḥr al-shimālī*, Aleppo 1895.—5. entitled *Bulūgh al-arab fī ʿilm al-badīʿ fī lughat al-ʿArab* Berl. Ms. or. oct. 3851, Alex. Bal. 3.–7. *Mukhtaṣar al-ʿarūḍ wal-qawāfī* Alex. ʿArūḍ 5.

53a. Niqūlā al-Ṣāʾigh, d. 1756, see Suppl.

Dīwān also Berl. Ms. or. oct. 3958, Patna I, $198_{,1792}$.[5]

54. Muḥammad Saʿdī b. ʿAbd al-Qādir al-ʿUmarī b. ʿAbdallāh was born after 1080/1669, travelled to Istanbul in 1131/1719, and was appointed professor at the Dār al-ḥadīth in Damascus. He died there in 1147/1734.

Mur. II, 151/6. A *muwashshaḥ* in praise of Damascus, Berl. $8175_{,3}$, see Hartmann, 78.

---

5 On the upsurge of Christian literature thanks to the first printing house in Bucharest, founded by Partriarch Dabbās VI, see *DLZ* 1940, 902.

362 | 55. Aḥmad b. Muṣṭafā al-Ṭālib al-Khulāṣī wrote, between 1134/1721 and 1147/1734 in Damascus and Baalbek:

His *dīwān*, in praise of the emir Ismāʿīl b. Ḥarfūsh and his sons, Br. Mus. 1087.

281 | 56. Muḥammad b. ʿUthmān b. al-Shamʿa, ca. 1150/1737.

A *muwashshaḥ* in praise of Damascus, Berl. 8175$_{,4}$, see Hartmann, 58.

57. The son of an *amīr al-umarāʾ* who had passed away in 1089/1678, Muṣṭafā b. Aḥmad Pāshā b. Ḥusayn al-Tarzī al-Dimashqī lived as a private scholar in Damascus. During the turmoil in which the governor Asʿad Pāshā was murdered, he lost his son while his house was plundered. He died soon after, in 1155/1742.

Mur. IV, 166/78 (with sample poems). *Dīwān* Berl. 8034.

58. Muḥammad al-Ḥāfiẓ al-Najjār, who died in 1163/1750 in Damascus.

1. *al-Kashf wal-bayān ʿan awṣāf ḥiṣāl shirār ahl hādha 'l-zamān* Berl. 5431.—2. *Qaṣīda*s and *Mawāliyāt*, ibid. 8037.

59. ʿAbd al-Raḥmān b. Muḥammad al-Turkumānī al-Bahlūl al-Nakhlāwī, who died in 1163/1750.

1. A *muwashshaḥ* in praise of Damascus, Berl. 8175$_{,5}$, see Hartmann, 18.—2. See no. 50.

60. Muḥammad b. Muṣṭafā b. Khudāwirdī al-Dimashqī al-Rāʿī, who died after 1170/1756.

Al-Barq al-mutaʾalliq fī maḥāsin Jilliq, a poetic glorification of Damascus and its surroundings, completed in 1171/1757, Berl. 6490, Vienna 1268 (autograph), Cairo ^{2}V, 56, in which there is a longer *rajaz* in praise of Damascus, which is also found on its own in Berl. 8163$_{,2}$.

61. ʿAbdallāh b. Muḥammad b. Amīr b. Sharaf al-Dīn al-Qāhirī al-Shubrāwī
363 al-Azharī al-Shāfiʿī was born in 1091/1680, | and became a professor and then, in 1137/1724, principal of al-Azhar. He died in 1172/1758.

Mur. III, 107, Jab. I, 208, Hartmann, *Muw.* 83, BSOS IX, 681. 1. *Dīwān* or *Manīḥ al-alṭāf fī madāʾiḥ al-ashrāf*, poems in praise of important people and the Prophet, Berl. 8038, Gotha 2338, Paris 3266, Garr. 129/30, Lening. Un. Or. 858, Cairo ^{1}IV, 332, Qawala II, 207, print. Būlāq 1282, 1293, C. 1302, 1306.—2. *al-Istighātha al-Shubrāwiyya*, with an anonymous *takhmīs*, Gotha 2339, by Aḥmad Abu ʾl-Faḍl al-Zabūn al-Fuwwī, ibid. 2340.—3. *ʿArūs al-ādāb wa-furjat al-albāb*, on character traits, advice for rulers, histories of poets with poems, on generosity and meanness, | friendship and loneliness, forgiveness and revenge, 282
and reproof of contemporaries, Leid. 527 (incomplete).—4. *ʿUnwān al-bayān wa-bustān al-adhhān*, recreational prose, Berl. 8435, Paris 2120,$_2$ Cairo ^{1}IV, 285, print. C. 1282, 1287, 1305, 1313, among others.—5. *Nuzhat al-abṣār fī raqāʾiq al-ashʿār*, containing *qaṣīda*s and fragments and anecdotes in prose, completed in 1154/1741, Paris 3443.—6. *Ḥiml Zajal*, print. C. 1290 (15 p.).—7. *Mashyakha* Paris 2120,$_1$, 1, Āṣaf. II, 1708, 205.—8. *Asna ʾl-maṭālib li-hidāyat al-ṭālib*, 47 *ṭawīl* verses on declensions, with a commentary by ʿAlī Nidāʾ al-Barrānī composed in 1261/1845, Berl. 6793.—9. *al-Risāla* or *al-Manẓūma al-Shubrāwiyya fi ʾl-naḥw* Gotha 340, BDMG 67, c.—10. *Naẓm asmāʾ abḥur al-shiʿr wa-ajzāʾuhā* Cairo ^{1}VII, 62.—11. *Itḥāf bi-ḥubb al-ashrāf*, on the descendants of the Prophet, Paris 2120,$_3$.—12. Commentary on a *qaṣīda* by Aḥmad b. Masʿūd, sharif of Mecca, ibid. 4.—13. *Sharḥ al-ṣadr bi-ghazwat Badr*, on those who took part in the battle of Badr, ibid. 6, Cairo V, ^{1}73, 523, ^{2}231, lith. C. 1297, print. C. 1303.—14. *Talkhīṣ al-ʿaqīda* Paris 2120,$_5$.—15.–17. see Suppl. (15. Garr. 151, which has al-Bakhātī).

62. Muḥammad Saʿīd b. Muḥammad b. Aḥmad al-Shāfiʿī al-Dimashqī Shams al-Dīn b. al-Sammān was born in Damascus in 1118/1706, and travelled to Asia, Mecca, Egypt, Tripoli, and Baalbek. In 1156/1743 he became imam at the newly constructed madrasa of Fatḥallāh al-Daftarī, to whom he dedicated work no. 3. He died in 1172/1759 or, according to others, in 1189/1775.

Mur. II, 141/9, Jab. I, 242/8. 1. *Dīwān*, entitled *al-Falāqansī* | *min al-madāʾiḥ*, 364
Berl. 8040.—2. *Taʾrīkh*, an anthology of 69 poets of the twelfth century, Berl. 7428.—3. *al-Rawḍ al-nāfiḥ fī-mā warada ʿala ʾl-fatḥ al-Falāqansī*, on the same subject, abstract, ibid. 7429.—4., 5. See Suppl. (4. Attributed to his son, with a commentary, Alex. Taṣ. 14).

63. Abū ʾl-Najāḥ Aḥmad b. ʿAlī al-ʿUthmānī al-Manīnī, d. 1172/1759, see Suppl.

Mur. I, 133/45. 1. *Dīwān*, primarily directed at various notables, covering the years 1133–70/1721–57, Berl. 8039.—2. *al-Iʿlām bi-faḍāʾil al-Shām* Cairo V,

[1]137, [2]333.—3. *al-Fatḥ al-wahbī ʿalā taʾrīkh Abī Naṣr al-ʿUtbī* I, 383.—4.–6. see Suppl. (4. Garr. 1968/9, Qawala I, 246, C. 1281; 5. Qawala I, 139).—7. *al-Qawl al-sadīd fī ʾttiṣāl al-asānīd* Qawala II, 93.

64. Aḥmad Bek b. Ḥusayn Bāshā b. Muṣṭafā b. Ḥusayn al-Kaywānī al-Dimashqī was born in Damascus, where he became public scribe at the Darwīsh market after he had completed his studies in Cairo. Later he accompanied Mollā Sāmī ʿUthmān, the inspector of the *waqf*s in Damascus, to Istanbul. After the latter was murdered, he returned to his native country and died in 1173/1760.

Mur. I, 97/107, Hartmann, *Muw.* 64. *Dīwān*, in which there is a *rajaz* of ca. 2,000 verses on the art of social intercourse, Berl. 8041$_{,2}$, = 8163, print. Damascus 1301.—2. See Suppl.

283 | 65. Yūsuf b. Sālim b. Aḥmad al-Ḥifnī (Ḥifnāwī) al-Shāfiʿī Abu ʾl-Maḥāsin al-Miṣrī, who died in Ṣafar 1178/August 1764.

Jab. I, 263, whence *Khit. jad.* X, 75. 1. *Dīwān*, completed in 1157/1744, Cambr. Pr. 30, no. 49 (autograph dated 1175/1761), Algiers 1825.—2. A panegyrical poem, Berl. 8043$_{,3}$.—3. *Maqāmat al-muḥākama bayna ʾl-mudām wal-zuhūr*, a battle of words between wine and flowers, ibid. 8580.—4. *al-Maqāma al-Ḥifniyya*, in praise of Abu ʾl-ʿAbbās Aḥmad b. Muḥammad al-Bāhī and the madrasa that he founded in Tunis, and of his son Abu ʾl-Fidāʾ Ismāʿīl, with a commentary by Abū Muḥammad ʿAbd al-Wahhāb b. Muṣṭafā b. Ibrāhīm al-Dimashqī, Br. Mus.
365 1052$_{,i}$.—5. *Risāla fī ʾl-kalām ʿalā lafẓay al-wāḥid wal-aḥad* Cairo [1]VII, | 273, 371, [2]II, 15.—6.–10. see Suppl.—11. *Risāla fī ʾl-faṣd wal-ḥijāma* Alex. Ṭibb 20.

66. ʿAbdallāh b. ʿAbdallāh b. Salāma al-Idkāwī al-Miṣrī al-Shāfiʿī was born in Idkū near Rosetta in 1104/1692, studied in Cairo and went on the pilgrimage in 1147 with his patron ʿAlī Efendi Burhānzāde, the *naqīb* of the ʿAlids. After the latter's death he freeloaded from al-Shubrāwī (no. 61) and al-Ḥifnī (no. 65), before dying on 5 Jumādā I 1184/28 August 1770.

Jab. I, 352/63, BSOS IX, 683. 1. *Biḍāʿat al-arīb fī shiʿr al-gharīb*, a collection of his poems, Paris 3446, Br. Mus. Suppl. 1103.—2. *al-Durr al-munaẓẓam* (*muntaẓam*) *fī ʾl-shiʿr al-multazam* or *Badāʾiʿ al-iltizām bi-rawāʾiʿ al-niẓām*, poems in praise of Muḥammad, Paris 3444$_{,1,2}$, Garr. 133.—3. *al-Fawāʾiḥ al-jināniyya fī ʾl-madāʾiḥ al-Riḍwāniyya*, a collection of panegyrical poems by various authors, especially by the author himself, on the Egyptian emir Katkhudā Jalfī ʿAzabān, Paris 3445 (dedicated autograph, dated 1164/1751).—4. *al-Maqāma al-Iskandariyya wal-taṣḥīfiyya*, composed of words that only differ by their diacritical points, dedicated to Muḥammad b. Ismāʿīl al-Iskandarī, Berl. 8581$_{,2}$.—5. *al-Durr al-thamīn fī maḥāsin al-taḍmīn* (Mehren, *Rhet.* 138), Cairo ^{1}IV, 135, ^{2}II, 195.—6. *Hidāyat al-mutawahhimīn fī kadhib al-munajjimīn*, against astrology, Gotha 1455.—7., 8. See Suppl. (7. Garr. 1857).

67. Ismāʿīl b. Tāj al-Dīn b. Aḥmad al-Maḥāsinī al-Ḥanafī al-Dimashqī was born in 1139/1726 in Damascus and died in 1187/1773.

Mur. II, 162. *Dīwān*, see RAAD IV, 556/8.

68. Aḥmad b. ʿUmar b. ʿUthmān al-Shākir al-Ḥamawī al-Ḥakawātī Fāʾiq al-Dīn
Abū ʾl-Ṣafāʾ was born in 1121/1709. As a young man he travelled through Syria,
Mesopotamia, Egypt, and the Hijaz before settling down in Damascus, where
he dedicated himself to alchemy. Because of this, he sank into such poverty
that he had to make a living as a storyteller in a coffeehouse. Towards | the end 366
of his life he turned to mysticism. He died in 1193/1779.

Mur. I, 155/62. A lengthy poem in praise of Muḥammad, Berl. 8045$_{,5}$.

| 69. ʿAbdallāh b. Yūsuf b. ʿAbdallāh al-Yūsufī was born in Aleppo where he ran 284
a coffee trading business, and went to Tripoli, Latakia, and Damascus several
times. He died in 1194/1780.

Mur. III, 108/16. A collection of his poems from the years 1157–93/1744–79, including those in praise of the Prophet and his relatives, on ʿAbd al-Qādir al-Jilānī (I, 560) and his contemporaries, elegies, and other poems written for special occasions, Berl. 8046.—2. *Mawārid al-sālik li-ashal al-masālik* Būlāq 1308, Alex. Adab 131.—3. See Suppl. 1018, 10 (?).

70. ʿAbd al-Qādir Efendi al-Ḥusaynī al-Adhamī, ca. 1207/1792, see Suppl.

2. *Nuzhat al-ʿuqūl fī maʿālim Ṭāhā al-rasūl* C. 1319.

71. Muḥammad Mujāhid Abu ʾl-Najāʾ al-Ṣaghīr, who died after 1205/1790.

Majmūʿat ashʿār fī madḥ sayyidī Aḥmad al-Badawī Garr. 137.

2 *Philology*

1. Muḥammad b. Muḥammad b. Aḥmad b. ʿAbdallāh al-Ghazzī al-ʿĀmirī al-Shāfiʿī Raḍī al-Dīn Abu ʾl-Faḍl was born in Damascus in 862/1457, where he became an acting *qāḍī*. He died on 14 Shawwāl 935/22 June 1529.

RA 229r. 1. *al-Ifṣāḥ ʿan lubb al-fawāʾid wal-Talkhīṣ* (I, 353) *wal-Miṣbāḥ* (ibid.), on rhetoric, with a commentary entitled *Taḥrīr al-iṣlāḥ fī taqrīr al-Ifṣāḥ*, Paris $4427_{,1}$.—2. *Urjūza fi ʾl-ẓāʾāt*, with a commentary by his son, ibid. 2.–3. Commemorative verses in different metres, Berl. 7165 c.—4. *Jāmiʿ fawāʾid al-malāḥa fi ʾl-filāḥa*, see Suppl. Abstracts: a. *ʿAlam al-malāḥa fī ʿilm al-filāḥa* by ʿAbd al-Ghanī al-Nābulusī, d. 1143/1731 (below p. 345), composed in 1137/1715, Berl. 6209, Tüb. 136, print. Damascus 1299, Beirut 1299.—b. *ʿUmdat al-ṣināʿa fī*
367 *ʿilm al-zirāʿa* | by ʿAbd al-Qādir al-Khilāṣī, ca. 1200/1785, ibid. 5210.—c. *al-Bayān wal-ṣarāḥa bi-talkhīṣ Kitāb al-malāḥa* by Muḥammmad b. ʿĪsā b. Maḥmūd b. Kannān, d. 1153/1730 (below p. 299), ibid. 6211.—5. *al-Jawhar al-farīd fī ādāb al-ṣūfī wal-murīd*, written in 1238 *rajaz* verses, ibid. 3811, Garr. 1585.—6.–8. Suppl. (8., 9. in Alex. Ḥad. 1. attributed to Najm al-Dīn al-Ghazzī, below p. 291, see also Suppl. II, 416, 6a).

2. His son Muḥammad Badr al-Dīn Raḍī al-Dīn wrote:

Two glosses on Ibn Ḥazm's *al-Muḥallā*, ḤKh V, 429, see Asín Palacios, *Aben Ḥazm* I, 323.

3. ʿAlī b. ʿUmar al-ʿArabī al-Mudarris, ca. 980/1572, wrote:

Risāla fi ʾl-badīʿ, a short exposition on tropes with examples from the Qurʾān, *ḥadīth*, and proverbs, Berl. 7281.

4. Shams al-Dīn Muḥammad b. Abi ʾl-Luṭf wrote, in 992/1584:

Dafʿ al-iltibās ʿan munkar al-iqtibās Cairo ^{1}VII, 618, ^{2}II, 196.

285 | 5. Muḥammad al-Nuʿmān b. Muḥammad b. ʿArrāq wrote, towards the end of the tenth century:

1. *al-Jawāhir al-muftakhira min al-kināyāt al-muʿtabira*, based on al-Jurjānī (I, 341), al-Thaʿālibī (I, 338), al-Suyūṭī (p. 180), and his brother and teacher ʿAbd al-Nāfiʿ, Leid. 337.—2. *Kanz al-zinād wal-wārī fī dhikr abnāʾ al-sarārī*, autograph, ibid. 518.

6. Abū Bakr b. Ismāʿīl b. Aḥmad al-Shanawānī was born in Shanawān near Manūf, studied in Cairo, and died in 1019/1610.

Muḥ. I, 79/81, followed by *al-Khiṭ. al-jad.* XII, 142. 1. *Ḥilyat al-kamāl bi-ajwibat asʾilat al-Jalāl*, answers to 7 questions by al-Suyūṭī on the letters of the alphabet and the etymology of their names, Vienna 210, Cairo ^{1}VI, 135, ʿĀshir I, 457, Patna II, 557,$_{2934,1}$.—2.–7. see Suppl.—8. *al-Shihāb al-ḥāwī ʿalā ʿAbd al-Raʾūf al-ghāwī* Patna I, 123,$_{1236}$.

7. Yūsuf al-Maghribī, who died in 1019/1609 in Cairo, see Suppl.

| 1. *Rafʿ al-iṣr etc.*, abstracts in Kračkovsky, *Izvestiya Ak. Nauk* 1926, 279/99, other 368
works ibid. 286ff., 293/5.

8. Muḥammad b. ʿAlī b. Badr al-Dīn b. Muḥammad b. ʿAbd al-ʿAzīz al-Bisāṭī al-Shāfiʿī wrote, in 1044/1634:

Al-Tālid wal-ṭarīf fī jinās al-taṣḥīf Cairo ^{1}IV, 124, ^{2}II, 180 (see Suppl.).

9. Aḥmad b. Muḥammad b. ʿUmar Shihāb al-Dīn al-Khafājī al-Miṣrī al-Shāfiʿī was born in Siryāqūs near Cairo, studied first under his uncle al-Shanawānī (no. 6) in that town, and then in Cairo. After completing the pilgrimage with his father, he continued his studies in Istanbul and became a *qāḍī* in Rumelia, and then in Saloniki. Sultan Murād IV appointed him *qāḍi ʾl-ʿaskar* but he was soon deposed, whereupon he returned to Istanbul via Damascus and Aleppo. However, due to the fact that the *muftī* Yaḥyā b. Zakariyyāʾ and the vizier were both his enemies, he was transferred to Cairo where he turned to writing and giving talks. He died on 12 Ramaḍān 1069/23 May 1659.

Muḥ. I, 331/43, Wüst. *Gesch.* 571, J. Zaydān, *Taʾr. al-adab* IV, 126. 1. *Dīwān* Copenhagen 283.—2. *Qaṣīda*s, Berl. 7990,$_{3}$, Cairo ^{1}VII, 109.—3. A *ghazal* addressed to the Shaykh al-Islām Muḥammad al-Bakrī, Gotha 737.—4. *Rayḥānat al-nadd* or *Dhawāt al-amthāl*, a *qaṣīda* in which each verse contains a maxim, Paris 2350,$_{1}$.—5. Some *maqāma*s Berl. 8576,$_{1}$.—6. *Khabāyā ʾl-zawāyā fī-mā fi ʾl-rijāl min al-baqāyā*, on the scholars of his time, and his own and his father's teachers, in sections: Syria, the Hijaz, Egypt, the Maghreb and al-Rūm, in a very pompous style, Berl. 7414, Gotha 2164, Vienna 406, (see *Wien. Jahrb.* 86, *Anz.-Bl.* 32), Pet. AM 248, Köpr. 1239, NO 3772, Cairo ^{1}IV, 229, ^{2}III, 92.—7. *Rayḥānat al-alibbāʾ wa-nuzhat al-ḥayāt al-dunyā*, an adaptation of the previous work with particular emphasis on poets, Berl. 7465/6, Vienna 407/8, Leid. 524,

Paris 2134/6, Br. Mus. Suppl. 1123, Pet. AM 249/50, Garr. 218, AS 4021, Cairo [1]IV,
369 259, [2]III, | 176, print. Būlāq 1273, C. 1295, 1306.—Continuations: a. *Sulāfat al-ʿaṣr* by ʿAlī b. Maʿṣūm, d. 1104/1692, p. 421.—b. *Nafḥat al-rayḥāna* by Muḥammad Amīn b. Faḍlallāh al-Muḥibbī, d. 1111/1699, p. 294.—8. *Ṭirāz al-majālis*, all kinds of questions on poetry, lexicography, rhetoric, philosophy, Qurʾānic exegesis, etc., in 51 parts, Berl. 8429, Munich 601, Vienna 405, NO 4082/3, AS 4134, Cairo [2]III, 244, print. C. 1284.—9. *Shifāʾ al-ghalīl fī-mā fī kalām al-ʿArab min al-dakhīl* Cairo [1]IV, 182, [2]II, 19, print. C. 1282, 1325.—10. *Sharḥ Durrat al-ghawwāṣ* I, 328.—11. *Sharḥ Kitāb al-shifāʾ* I, 455.—12. *Ḥāshiya ʿala ʾl-Bayḍāwī* I, 532.—13.–16. see Suppl. (16. Patna I, 30,$_{297/8}$).

10. Yūsuf al-Badīʿī al-Dimashqī lived as a scholar and poet in Aleppo and was made a *qāḍī* in Mosul. He died in 1070/1662, before he was able to take up this position.

Muḥ. IV, 410, Wüst. *Gesch.* 576. 1. *al-Ḥadāʾiq al-badīʿiyya fi ʾl-anwāʿ al-adabiyya*, a detailed book on poetry and rhetoric, vol. I, Gotha 2792.—2. *al-Ṣubḥ al-munabbiʾ ʿan ḥaythiyyat al-Mutanabbiʾ* I, 88.—3. *Hibat al-ayyām fī-mā yataʿallaq bi-Abī Tammām* (I, 83), Cairo [1]IV, 342, [2]III, 429, print. C. 1934.

11. ʿAbd al-Qādir b. ʿUmar al-Baghdādī was born in 1030/1621 in Baghdad, studied in Damascus for a year, then in Cairo at al-Azhar under al-Khafājī (no. 8). In 1085/1674 he went to Damascus and from there, with Grand Vizier ʿAbdallāh Köprülü Pāshā,[1] to Adrianople, where he met up with al-Muḥibbī. He returned to Cairo plagued by illness, while on a second trip to Rūm he contracted an eye disease and so returned to Cairo almost blind, where he died in 1093/1682.

Muḥ. II, 451/4. 1. *Khizānat al-adab wa-lubb lubāb lisān al-ʿArab*, the famous commentary on the poetry quotations in al-Astarābādhī's commentary on the *Kāfiya* of al-Ḥājib (I, 368).—2. *Taʿrīb Tuḥfat al-Shahīdī* Cairo [1]IV, 166.—4.–9. see Suppl.—10. A biographical work without a title, ʿĀšir I, 627.—11.

370 | *Risāla fī maʿna ʾl-tilmīdh wa-waznihi wa-fiʿlihi wa-wajh istiʿmālihi* Pet. AM Buch. 46 (only ʿAbd al-Qādir Efendi).

12. ʿAbd al-Raḥmān b. Muḥammad al-ʿĀrī al-Arīḥawī, who died in 1128/1716.

1 See Zinkeisen, *Gesch. des Osm. Reiches* V, 275.

1. *Munyat al-rāghib wa-bughyat al-ṭālib*, a compendium on syntax, composed in 1079/1668, Gotha 339.—2. *Sharḥ al-Durra al-durriyya* I, 342.—3. *Sharḥ Umm al-barāhīn* p. 324.—4. *Ḥāshiya ʿalā sharḥ al-Azharī ʿalāʾ l-Ājurrūmiyya* Suppl. II, 333, 6. b.

| 13. Aḥmad b. ʿAṭāʾallāh b. Aḥmad al-Azharī wrote, in 1162/1748: 287

Nihāyat al-ījāz fi ʾl-ḥaqīqa wal-majāz, with a commentary by his son, Berl. 7289, Rabat 518,$_7$.

14. Qāsim Muḥammad b. ʿAlī al-Bakrajī al-Ḥalabī was a poet and scholar in Aleppo, and died in 1169/1756.

Mur. IV, 10/2, al-Ṭabbākh, *Taʾr. Ḥalab* VI, 535. 1. *al-Durr al-muntakhab min amthāl al-ʿArab* I, 289, Cairo [1]IV, 230.—2. See Suppl.

15. Ibrāhīm b. Muṣṭafā b. Ibrāhīm al-Ḥanafī al-Ḥalabī al-Mudārī was born in Aleppo, studied for a number of years in Cairo and then in Damascus, where he was won over to mysticism by ʿAbd al-Ghanī al-Nābulusī (p. 349). Returning to Cairo, he became the private tutor of ʿAlī al-Ḍarīr al-Ḥanafī, and gave talks on the commentary on *al-Durr al-mukhtār* (no. 2) for four years. Because the emir Sančaq ʿUthmān had robbed him of his possessions he joined a deputation that went to Istanbul to file a complaint. There he made the acquaintance of Rāghib Pāshā (p. 424) and, through him, he obtained a professorship that he retained until his death in 1190/1776.

Mur. I, 37/9. 1. *al-Ḥulla al-ḍāfiya fī ʿilmay al-ʿarūḍ wal-qāfiya* Cairo [1]IV, 198, [2]II, 231.—2. *Tuḥfat al-akhyār ʿala ʾl-Durr al-mukhtār* p. 311.

| 16. Abu ʾl-Fayḍ Muḥammad Murtaḍā b. Muḥammad b. Muḥammad b. ʿAbd al-Razzāq al-Ḥusaynī al-Zabīdī al-Ḥanafī was born in 1145/1732 in Bilghrām, near Qannawj (N.W. Territories) in India. After extensive travels in search of knowledge he settled in Cairo on 9 Ṣafar 1167/7 December 1733. From there he travelled to Upper Egypt, where he enjoyed high esteem from the shaykh of the Arabs, Humām, and also to Damietta, Rosetta, and al-Manṣūra. He succeeded in resuscitating a long-forgotten scholarly activity, viz. the dictation of traditions with their *isnād*s and the public reading of works on *ḥadīth* before large crowds of invitees. In 1191/1777 the government allotted him a considerable pension, while he also received large numbers of precious gifts, including 371

some from such distant places as Fazzān, Ṣanʿāʾ, and India. He died of the plague in Shaʿbān 1205/April 1791.

288 | *Khit. al-jad.* III, 94/6, based on Jab. II, 196/210. 1. *Tāj al-ʿarūs*, p. 233, completed in 1181/1767. The autograph was bought for 100,000 dirhams by Muḥammad Bey Abu ʾl-Dhahab for the library of the mosque that he constructed.—2. *Nashwat al-irtiyāḥ fī bayān ḥaqīqat al-maysir wal-qidāḥ* Berl. 5502, Cairo ^{2}VI, 206.—3. *al-Qawl al-mabtūt fī taḥqīq lafẓ al-tābūt* Cairo ^{1}IV, 179, ^{2}II, 26.—4. *Tuḥfat al-qamāʾil fī madḥ shaykh al-ʿArab Ismāʿīl* Cairo ^{1}IV, 214.—5. *Risāla fī aḥādīth yawm al-ʿAshūrāʾ* ibid. VII, 209.—6. *al-Amāli ʾl-Shaykhūniyya*, dictates on *ḥadīth*s that he had read aloud in the Jāmiʿ Shaykhū, Berl. 10253.—7. *Itḥāf al-sāda al-muttaqīn* I, 539.—8.–40. see Suppl. (9. Alex. Taʾr. 18.—18. Garr. 712.—22. ibid. 1858).

17. Abu ʾl-ʿIrfān Muḥammad b. ʿAlī al-Ṣabbān was originally a *muwaqqit* at the tomb of al-Shāfiʿī that had been restored by ʿAbd al-Raḥmān Katkhudā, and then at the mosque of Muḥammad Bey Abu ʾl-Dhahab. When his income had dwindled after the decline in *waqf*s, he lived for a time as a private person, until he became acquainted with the *qāḍī* ʿAbdallāh Efendi in Mecca, through whom he acquired great fortune and power. He died in Jumādā I 1206/January 1792.

372 | Jab. II, 227/33, followed by *Khiṭ. jad.* III, 84. 1 *Risāla fī ʿilm al-bayān* Cairo ^{1}IV, 136, ^{2}b, 27, on which glosses by ʿUllaysh, d. 1299/1882 (p. 486), C. 1281.—2. *Risāla fi ʾl-istiʿārāt*, autograph dated 1182/1768, Algiers 230.—3. *al-Shāfiya al-kāfiya* (*al-K. al-sh.*) *manẓūma fī ʿilm al-ʿarūḍ*, with a commentary, C. 1307, 1310, Alex. ʿArūḍ 2, Qawala II, 184.—4. *Ḥāshiyat sharḥ al-Ushmūnī ʿala ʾl-Alfiyya* I, 362.—5. *al-Risāla al-kubrā fi ʾl-basmala* Berl. 2267, Cairo ^{1}IV, 53, print. Būlāq 1291, C. 1297, 1301.—6. *Isʿāf al-rāghibīn fī siyar al-Muṣṭafā wa-faḍāʾil āl baytihi al-ṭāhirīn* Berl. Ms. or. oct. 3908, Alex. Taʾr. 3, print. C. 1290, 1307, 1315, 1317, in the margin of Ḥasan al-ʿIdwī al-Ḥamzāwī, *Mashāriq al-anwār* and others.—7. *Kitāb fī ʿilm al-hayʾa* Cairo ^{1}V, 223.—8. *Ḥāshiya ʿalā sharḥ al-Sullam* p. 355.—9. *Ḥāshiya ʿalā sharḥ al-Samarqandiyya* p. 247.—10. *Ḥāshiya ʿalā Sharḥ Ādāb al-baḥth* p. 268.—11.–15. see Suppl. (13. Alex. Adab 11.–14. *Makram* 28).—16. *Naẓm asmāʾ ahl al-Badr* with a commentary, *Rawḍat al-ṭālibīn*, by Muṣṭafā b. Muḥammad b. ʿAbd al-Khāliq al-Bannānī, composed in 1232/1817, Alex. Faw. 9.

18. Abū ʿAbdallāh Muḥammad b. ʿAbdallāh b. Muḥammad al-Baytūshī al-Shāfiʿī was born in 1161/1747 and died in 1211/1796 (or, according to others, in 1221/1806).

Al-Kifāya etc. see Suppl. Berl. 6704, Garr. 479, Istanbul 1289.

19. Aḥmad b. Mūsā b. Aḥmad b. Muḥammad al-Bīlī al-ʿAdawī al-Mālikī was born in 1141/1728. He succeeded al-Dardīr (p. 353) as Shaykh Riwāq al-Ṣaʿāʾida at al-Azhar, and died in 1218/1798.

Jab. III, 60, followed by *Khiṭ. jad.* IX, 96. 1. *al-Minaḥ al-mutakaffila bi-ḥall alfāẓ al-qaṣīda al-ʿarabiyya al-mawsūma bi-Mawrid al-ẓamʾān fī ṣināʿat al-bayān*, a commentary on a didactic poem on rhetoric, Berl. 7266.—2. *Fāʾidat al-ward fī ʾl-kalām ʿalā ammā baʿd* Cairo [1]IV, 80, [2]II, 143.—3. *Risālat al-bishāra li-qāriʾ al-Fātiḥa* Cairo [1]VII, 291.—4. *Manẓūma fī ʾl-ʿurf* ibid.—5.–7. see Suppl.—8. *Urjūzat Ḍabṭ al-masāʾil al-mustathnāt min qāʿidat kullu ṣalāt baṭilat ʿala ʾl-maʾmūm*, with a commentary, Alex. Fiqh Māl. 9.

| | 3 *Historiography* 373 289

A Individual Biographies

1. Muḥammad b. Muḥammad b. ʿUmar b. Sulṭān al-Dimashqī al-Ḥanafī Quṭb al-Dīn Abū ʿAbdallāh, who was born in 870/1465 and died in 950/1543.

1. *al-Jawāhir al-muḍīʾa fī ayyām al-dawla al-ʿUthmāniyya*, a short biography of Sultan Selīm I, d. 926/1520, Berl. 9725.—2. See Suppl.

2. Ramaḍān b. ʿĀmir b. ʿAlī wrote, around 980/1572:

Fatḥ al-wujūd wa-sharḥ al-jūd fī madḥ mawlāna ʾl-bāshā Maḥmūd, a panegyric on Muḥammad, the governor of Egypt under Sultan Selīm II (974–82/1566–74), Paris 2165.

3. Aḥmad b. Muḥammad b. Yūsuf al-Khālidī al-Ṣafadī was born in Ṣafad, studied in Cairo, then returned to his hometown where he became a professor and acting *qāḍī*, before dying in 1034/1625.

Muḥ. I, 297. *Taʾrīkh Fakhr al-Dīn b. Maʿn* (1021–33/1612–24) and his son ʿAlī, Munich 427, Garr. 606, see G. Mariti, *Istoria di Faccardino Grand-Emir dei Drusi*, Livorno 1787, German in Gotha 1790, Ritter, *Erdkunde* XVII, 1, 396, Wüstenfeld, *Abh. G. G. W.* 33, 2, (1886).—P. Paolo Carali, Fakhraddīn II al-Mani in Toscana, Sicilia, Napoli e la sua vista a Malta 1613/8, *Annali R. Ist. Or. Napoli* VII, 4, 1937.

4. Aḥmad b. Muḥammad b. Aḥmad b. ʿUthmān wrote, in 1157/1744:

Manāqib al-shaykh ʿAlī al-Yūnīnī, d. 617/1221, Garr. 711.

B Collective Biographical Works

1. Shams al-Dīn Muḥammad b. ʿAlī b. Aḥmad al-Dāʾūdī al-Mālikī was a student of al-Suyūṭī and died in 945/1538.

1. *Ṭabaqāt al-mufassirīn* Cairo V, ^{1}81, ^{2}254.—2. See Suppl.—3. See p. 144 below.

2. Mūsā b. Yūsuf b. Aḥmad b. Yūsuf Sharaf al-Dīn b. Ayyūb al-Anṣārī al-Dimashqī
374 al-Shāfiʿī, who was born in 946/1539. | On 1 Rajab 995/7 June 1587 he became acting *qāḍī* at al-Dīwān al-Ṣāliḥī in Damascus. On 24 Shawwāl 998/27 August 1590 he was transferred to Qanāt al-ʿAwnī, a post he still occupied when he wrote his autobiography on 11 Ṣafar 999/10 December 1590. He died in that very same year.

RA 264r, Wüst. *Gesch.* 539. 1. *al-Rawḍ al-ʿāṭir fī-mā tayassara fī akhbār ahl al-qarn al-sābiʿ ilā khitām al-qarn al-ʿāshir* Berl. 9886 (see p. 8).—2. *al-Tadhkira*
290 *al-Ayyūbiyya*, sketches of the lives of various notables | from across the ages, part I, composed in 998/1589 in Damascus, Berl. 9887.—3. *Mukhtaṣar Nuzhat al-khāṭir wa-bahjat al-nāẓir*, by an unidentified author, on the *qāḍīs* of Damascus, starting with Abu ʾl-Dardāʾ, d. 42/652, and going up to 998/1590, Pet. Ros. 51, Beirut 126.

3. Al-Ḥasan b. Muḥammad b. Muḥammad b. al-Ḥasan al-Būrīnī al-Dimashqī al-Ṣaffūrī Badr al-Dīn was born in Ṣaffūriyya in Galilee in the middle of Ramaḍān 963/July 1556. In 973/1566 he went with his father to Damascus, where he studied at the Ṣāliḥiyya. However, the next year he had to leave Damascus due to famine, and it was not until four years later, time he spent in Jerusalem, that he was able to return to the former city. Having completed his studies, he held lectures at al-Madrasa al-Nāṣiriyya al-Jawwāniyya al-Shāmiyya al-Barrāniyya, at the small ʿĀdiliyya, the Fārisiyya, and Kallāsa. In 1020/1611 he was *qāḍī* in the Syrian pilgrimage caravan. He died on 13 Jumādā I 1024/11 June 1615.

RA 112v, Muḥ. II, 51, Wüst. *Gesch.* 551. 1. *Tarājim al-aʿyān min abnāʾ al-zamān*, biographies of 205 people that were collected over a number of years and completed in 1023/1614, before being edited in 1078/1667 by Faḍlallāh b. Muḥibballāh and published with a postscript, Berl. 9889 (see p. 347), Vienna 1190, Cairo V, ^{1}33, ^{2}133.—2. *Dīwān* Köpr. 1287.—3. A poem, Br. Mus. 630,$_{2}$.—4. Elegies on the Sufi Muḥammad b. Abi ʾl-Barakāt al-Maydānī al-Qādirī, d. 1008/1600, Berl. 7958,$_{3}$.—5. Poetical letter to Asad b. Muʿīn al-Dīn al-Tabrīzī al-Dimashqī, with

a response, | Gotha $44_{,23}$.—6. *Sharḥ Dīwān ʿUmar b. al-Fāriḍ* I, 305.—7. *Sharḥ* 375
al-Tāʾiyya al-ṣughrā ibid. 306.—8.–11. see Suppl.

4. With the exception of a brief period, Maḥmūd b. Muḥammad b. Muḥammad b. Mūsā al-Ṣāliḥī al-ʿAdawī Nūr al-Dīn al-Zūkārī spent most of his life as a *nāʾib* in Damascus, until he passed away in 1032/1623.

Muḥ. IV, 322. *Al-Ishārāt fī amākin al-ziyārāt*, a list of the prophets, their companions and successors, scholars, saints, and pious men who are buried in and around Damascus, with biographical data, Berl. 6126/8, Rāmpūr I, $635_{,204}$.

| 5. ʿAbd al-Karīm Efendi b. Sinān studied from ca. 990/1582 onward in Cairo, 291
became a *qāḍī* in Aleppo in 1028/1619, and held the same position in Cairo from 24 Jumādā I 1030/17 April 1621, but was removed from office there less than six months later. He died around 1045/1635.

Muḥ. III, 2/8, Wüst. *Gesch.* 563. *Tarājim kibār al-ʿulamāʾ wal-wuzarāʾ*, 17 eulogies, Vienna 1188, used by al-Muḥibbī in his work.

6. ʿAbd al-Raḥmān b. Muḥammad b. Muḥammad al-ʿImādī al-Ḥanafī al-Dimashqī was born on 14 Rabīʿ II 978/16 September 1570, was a student of al-Būrīnī (no. 3), became a professor at the Shibliyya in 1017/1608, was appointed to the same position at the Salīmiyya in 1023/1614, and then at the Sulaymāniyyya in 1031/1622, while at the same time becoming *muftī* of Syria. In this capacity he was in charge of the pilgrim caravans to Mecca. He died on 17 Jumādā I 1051/24 August 1641.

Muḥ. II, 380, Wüst. *Gesch.* 564. 1. *al-Rawḍa al-rayyāʾ fī man dufina bi-Dārayyā* Berl. 6130, Gotha $93_{,2}$.—2. *Taḥrīr al-taʾwīl ʿalā mā fī maʿānī baʿḍ āy al-tanzīl*, notes to different allegorical passages from the Qurʾān, indiscriminately collected and mixed with glosses by other authors by an unidentified individual, at the order of al-ʿImādī's great-grandson Ḥāmid b. ʿAlī b. Ibrāhīm al-ʿImādī, d. 1171/1757, Berl. 1015.—3. *Hadiyya*, a compendium on the principles of religious service, ibid. 3532.—4. *Muqaddima fi ʾl-ṣalāt* Cairo ^{1}VII, 569.—5.
al-Mustaṭāʿ min al-zād li-afqar al-ʿibād b. al-ʿImād, Ḥanafī | rules concerning 376
the pilgrimage, written during his first pilgrimage in 1014/1605, Berl. 4067, NO 1823, Cairo ^{1}III, 130, VII, 156, ^{2}II, 463, Mosul $240_{,232}$, print. C. 1304.—6. Two *qaṣīdas*, Berl. 7974.—7. See Suppl.

7. Abu 'l-Makārim Muḥammad b. Muḥammad b. Muḥammad Najm al-Dīn al-Ghazzī al-ʿĀmirī al-Dimashqī al-Shāfiʿī was born in Damascus on 11 Shaʿbān 977/20 January 1570, the son of the Shaykh al-Islām, became a professor at the Shāmiyya Barrāniyya and the ʿUmariyya, as well as imam of the Umayyad mosque. When Bākir Muḥḍir Pāshā divested him in 1032/1623 of his professorship at the Barrāniyya, giving it to Shams al-Dīn Maydānī instead, he arranged in Istanbul for it to be guaranteed his for life. However, at the instigation of the Pāshā he had to share his income from it with the latter's protégé until the latter's death the following year. He himself died on 18 Jumādā I 1061/9 June 1651.

292 | Muḥ. IV, 189, Wüst. *Gesch.* 569. 1. *al-Kawākib al-sāʾira bi-manāqib ʿulamāʾ al-miʾa al-ʿāshira*, Br. Mus. 938, abstract Berl. 9891, one of the sources of al-Muḥibbī.—2. *al-Fawāʾid al-mujtamiʿa*, a *rajaz* poem on the merits of Friday, composed in 1004/1613, Berl. 3812.—3. Two *qaṣīdas*, ibid. $7982,_{2,3}$.—4. *Āyat al-tawfīq ilā maʿāni 'l-jamʿ wal-tafrīq* see p. 333.—5.–10. see Suppl.—11. *Itqān mā yaḥsun min al-akhbār al-dāʾira ʿala 'l-alsun* Alex. Ḥad. 1 (see Suppl. $394,_{1n}$, $416,_{6a,1}$).—12. *ʿIqd al-kalām li-ʿaqd al-kalām* ibid., Mawāʿiẓ 27.—13. *Taḥbīr al-ʿibārāt fī taḥrīr al-ʿimārāt* ʿĀšir I, 763 (MS dated 1053).

8. Abu 'l-Wafāʾ b. ʿUmar b. ʿAbd al-Wahhāb al-ʿUrdī al-Shāfiʿī, the son of a Shāfiʿī *muftī*, was born in Aleppo in 993/1585, lectured at the Ḥabashiyya, a Qurʾān academy affiliated with the Great Mosque, for his whole life, succeeded to his father's office, and died on 4 Muḥarram 1071/10 September 1660.

Muḥ. I, 148, Wüst. *Gesch.* 573. 1. *Maʿādin al-dhahab fī 'l-aʿyān al-musharrafa bi-*
377 *him Ḥalab*, written as a chronicle, | Berl. 9476, one of al-Muḥibbī's sources.—2. *Fatḥ al-badīʿ fī ḥall al-Ṭirāz al-badīʿ fi 'mtidāḥ al-shafīʿ*, a *badīʿiyya* with a commentary, Berl. 7383.—3. Various poems, Paris $3118,_{7}$.—4. A riddle, ibid. 22.—5. *Ṭarīq al-hudā wa-muzīḥ al-radā* Alex. Maw. 26.

9. ʿAbd al-Barr b. ʿAbd al-Qādir al-Fayyūmī al-ʿAwfī al-Ḥanafī was the son of a professor. He was born in Cairo, studied there and in Mecca, Damascus, Aleppo, and in Istanbul with al-Khafājī (p. 368). When the latter was appointed *qāḍī* of Cairo he accompanied him there and worked for him as a subsitute and as a private tutor. Even though he was a Ḥanafī, he arranged in Istanbul for him to be nominated as a Shāfiʿī *qāḍī* and as a professor at the Ṣāliḥiyya in Jerusalem, although he was unable to take up his positions there, not even two years after the previous holder of these posts had passed away. He thus returned to Istanbul, joined a dervish order, and died in 1071/1660.

Muḥ. II, 29, *Khit. jad.* XIV, 9, Wüst. *Gesch.* 574. 1. *Tadhkira*, a merging of the biographies of the poet al-Khafājī (p. 368) and Taqī al-Dīn Muḥammad al-Fāriskūrī, d. 1053/1643, adding older poets and some contemporaries, Berl. 7407, a source for al-Muḥibbī.—2. *Bulūgh al-arab wal-suʾāl bil-tashawwuq bi-dhikr nasab al-rasūl* Cairo [1]I, 276, [2]I, 93.—3. Two *qaṣīdas* following Abū Nuwās and Abu ʾl-Suʿūd, d. 982/1574, Ber. 7990$_{,5}$.—4. *Nafāʾis al-luʾluʾ wal-marjān fī iʿrāb al-maḥallāt min sūrat āl ʿImrān* Cairo [1]219, [2]65 (that wrongly states it was composed in 815). |—5. A *risāla* on sura 18$_{,48}$, 2$_{,32}$, on the question of whether Satan 293
should be counted among the angels or not, Berl. 2523.

10. ʿAbd al-Raḥmān Muḥammad b. Ḥamza al-Ḥusaynī commenced, around 1100/1689:

Al-Jawāhir wal-durar fī tarājim aʿyān al-ḥādī ʿashar, of which he completed only the first section, covering the years 1011–38/1592–1623, as well as the entries for names starting with the letter M of section two, Berl. 6892; Wüst. *Gesch.* 587.

11. Muḥammad al-Amīn b. Faḍlallāh b. Muḥibballāh b. Muḥibb al-Dīn
Muḥammad b. Abī Bakr al-Muḥibbī al-Shāmī | was born in Damascus in 378
1061/1651 and followed his father to Beirut in 1077/1666, where the latter had found a job after a four-year sojourn in Istanbul. He lived alternately there and in Damascus. His patron, Muḥammad b. Luṭfallāh b. Bayrām, who had previously been a *qāḍī* in Damascus and then in Anatolia, granted him the means by which he completed his studies in Istanbul. After a period spent in Damascus, he travelled to Bursa and Adrianople on 8 Ṣafar 1086/4 May 1675 with the *muftī* Muḥammad b. ʿAbd al-Ḥalīm, where the latter procured him a post as *qāḍi ʾl-ʿaskar*. When the *muftī* was deposed the following year, he followed him to Istanbul where he took care of him during an illness, before he passed away on 10 Shawwāl 1092/24 October 1681. The following day, al-Muḥibbī left for Damascus, where he was active in literature for a number of years. After making the pilgrimage in 1101/1690 he worked for a time in Mecca and then in Cairo as acting *qāḍī*. His last post was a professorship at the Amīniyya in Damascus, where he died on 18 Jumādā I 1111/11 November 1699.

Mur. IV, 86/91, Wüst. *Gesch.* 590 (until the year 1101, according to his own statements in no. 1), idem, *Die Gelehrtenfamilie al-Muḥibbī und ihre Zeitgenossen*, Abh. GGW 1884. 1. *Khulāṣat al-athar fī aʿyān al-qarn al-ḥādī ʿashar*, 1289 biographies, a draft of biographies of the Hijaz and Yemen, autograph Garr. 710, the first clean copy completed in 1096/1685, Berl. 9893/4, Leipz. 683, Vienna 1192/5,

Paris 2083, 5830, Br. Mus. 1304/5, 1648, print. C. 1284, 4 vols.; draft of an abstract,
294 Berl. 9895. |—3. *Nafḥat al-rayḥāna wa-rashḥat ṭilāʾ al-ḥāna*, a continuation of
the *Rayḥānat al-alibbāʾ* of Khafājī (p. 368), Berl. 7421, Tüb. 13, Cairo ^{1}IV, 340, ^{2}III,
419. A *dhayl* by Muḥammad b. Muḥammad b. Maḥmūd al-Suʾālātī al-ʿUthmānī,
completed in Shawwāl 1111/April 1700, Berl. 7422, Pet. AM 252, Copenhagen
170, Alex. Adab 179.—4. A *dīwān*, mostly *qaṣīda*s on friends and patrons who
are also mentioned in no. 1, Berl. 8007, fragment ibid. 8, cf. Flügel, *ZDMG* IX,
224.—5. *Barāḥat al-arwāḥ jālibat al-surūr wal-afrāḥ, rajaz* on aphorisms, Berl.
379 8162.—6. *Mā yuʿawwal ʿalayhi fi ʾl-muḍāf wal-muḍāf ilayhi* | see Suppl. As 4236,
Dāmād Ibr. 956, Cairo ^{1}IV, 299, ^{2}III, 285.—7. See Suppl., E. Galtier, *Bull. de l'Inst.
franç. d'archéologie or.* V, 121.

12. Al-Ḥasan b. al-Sayyid ʿAbd al-Laṭīf al-Qudsī Muftī al-Ḥanafiyya wrote, for al-Murādī (no. 15):

Biographies of 30 scholars living in Jerusalem in the twelfth century, Br. Mus. Suppl. 661.

13. ʿAbd al-Qādir b. ʿAbdallāh al-ʿAbd al-Ānī al-Kurdī Nazīl Dimashq, who died in 1178/1764.

Tuḥfat al-kirām fī dhikr baʿḍ al-khalāʾiq al-ʿiẓām Alex. Taʾr. 47.

14. ʿAbd al-Raḥmān b. Ḥasan b. ʿUmar Abu ʾl-Laṭāʾif al-Ujhūrī al-Mālikī al-Maghribī Sibṭ al-Quṭb al-Khuḍayrī studied in Cairo and Damascus, became a professor at al-Azhar and at the Sināniyya in Būlāq, before dying on 27 Rajab 1198/17 June 1784.

Jab. II, 85/9. 1. *Mashāriq al-anwār fī āl al-bayt al-akhyār*, on the unknown ʿAlids that lie buried in Cairo, Cairo V, ^{1}150, ^{2}345.—2.–4. see Suppl. (3. Garr. 1234).

15. Abu ʾl-Faḍl Muḥammad Khalīl b. ʿAlī b. Muḥammad b. Muḥammad Murād al-Murādī al-Ḥusaynī, d. 1206/1791, see Suppl.

1. *Silk al-durar fī aʿyān al-qarn al-thānī ʿashar*, following the model of al-Muḥibbī, but less precise about the facts, with many poems, 4 vols., Būlāq 1291/1301.—2. *Maṭmaḥ al-wājid fī tarjamat al-wālid al-mājid*, a biography of his father al-Sayyid ʿAlī (d. 1184/1770), his teachers, relatives, and contemporaries, Br. Mus. Suppl. 659.—3., 4. See Suppl.

16. Abu 'l-Faḍā'il Ḥasan b. ʿAlī al-ʿAwdī al-Badrī al-Muqri' b. al-Muqri', who died in Shaʿbān 1214/January 1800.

1. *Manāhil al-ṣafāʾ fī manāqib āl al-Wafāʾ*, panegyrical biographies of ʿAlids from the house of Wafā', Gotha 1754.—2. *Faṣl al-maqāl ʿalā naẓm b. Ghāzī fawāṣil al-mumāl*, on *imāla* in the Qur'ān, Cairo ^{1}I, 103.

| C Local and National History 380

1. Abu 'l-Barakāt Muḥammad b. Aḥmad b. Iyās Zayn (Shihāb) al-Dīn al-Nāṣirī al-Čerkesī al-Ḥanbalī, who was born on 6 Rabīʿ II 852/10 June 1448 and was a student of al-Suyūṭī, died around 930/1524 (see Suppl.).

Wüst. *Gesch.* 513. 1. *Marj al-zuhūr fī waqāʾiʿ al-duhūr*, a universal history, Gotha 1577 (up to Kisrā Anūsharwān), Vienna 823, Paris 1554 (up to Yazdagird).—2. *Badāʾiʿ al-zuhūr fī waqāʾiʿ al-duhūr* (see Suppl.), Vienna 923, Paris 1822/5, Br. Mus. 317, 941/3, Nicholson *JRAS* 1899, 909, no. 5. Pet. Ros. 46, Bursa Hü. Čelebī Ta'r. 42 (parts 1–3 until the year 84), print. C. 1299/1306, Būlāq 1311/2, *Fihrist* I/III by Muḥammad al-Biblāwī, Būlāq 1314. Cf. Weil, *Gesch. der Chal.* V, p. vi, Vollers, *Revue d'Égypte* I, 126ff., II, 545ff., III, 551, *ZDMG* 43, 104.—Abbreviation Br. Mus. 941.—3. *Nashq al-azhār fī ʿajāʾib al-aqṭār*, a cosmography with particular emphasis on Egypt, completed in 922/1517, Berl. 6050/1, Ms. or. oct. 3940, Gotha 1518/9, Paris 2207/11, 3513,3, Br. Mus. 385, Ind. Off. 728, Bodl. I, 914, Pet. Ros. 68, Kazan 109, Dorpat *Jahrb.* III, 252, Tunis Zaytūna, *Bull. de Corr. Afr.* 1884 p. 12, no. 6, Cairo ^{1}V, 168, ^{2}VI, 66; cf. Wüstenfeld, *Lüddes Ztschr.* I, 65, Mehren, *Ann. f. Nord. Oldk.* 1857, p. 71, Langlès, *Not. et extr.* VIII, I/131, de Sacy, *Mém. de l'Ac. des inscr.* 48, 618, 758, Uylenbroek, *Iracae pers. descriptio* p. 80, Quatremère, *Mém. sur l'Égypte* II, 6ff., Arnold, *Chr. ar.* 54/73, A. v. Kremer, *SBWA, hist. phil. Cl.* V, 77ff.—4. *Nuzhat al-umam fi 'l-ʿajāʾib wal-ḥikam* AS 3500.—5., 6. See Suppl.

2. Abu 'l-ʿAbbās Aḥmad b. Muḥammad b. Muḥammad b. ʿAbd al-Salām Shihāb al-Dīn al-Manūfī al-Shāfiʿī, who was born in Manūf on 14 Rabīʿ I 847/11 June 1443, studied in Cairo, and became a *qāḍī* in his hometown. He died in 931/1527.

Wüst. *Gesch.* 514. 1. *al-Fayḍ al-madīd fī akhbār al-Nīl al-sadīd* Marseille 1639, Alex. Ta'r. 97.—2. *al-Badr al-ṭāliʿ min al-Ḍaw' al-lāmiʿ* p. 43, no. 9, I. a.—3. See Suppl.

3. Nūr (Badr) al-Dīn Muḥammad b. Yūsuf Jamāl al-Dīn b. ʿAbd al-ʿAzīz al-Aqfahsī al-Minhājī (Ṣanhājī?) Khaṭīb al-Sayyida al-Nafīsa wrote, around 960/1553:

381 |1. *al-Budūr al-sāfira fī man waliya 'l-Qāhira*, which lists all the governors of Egypt from its conquest until the year 956/1549, in *rajaz* verse, Vienna 918,$_1$.—2. *al-Nujūm al-zāhira fī wulāt al-Qāhira*, the same, up to the year 961/1554, Berl. 9828, until 966/1669, Cairo V, ^{1}165, ^{2}384.—4.–6. see Suppl.[1]

3b. Muḥammad al-Ghazalī, see Suppl.

Tuḥfat al-jalīl etc. Garr. 616.

4. ʿAbd al-Wāḥid al-Burjī wrote, after 1017/1608:

Al-Riyāḍ al-zāhira fī akhbār Miṣr wal-Qāhira Algiers 1605.[2]

296 | 5. Muḥammad b. ʿAbd al-Muʿṭī b. Abi 'l-Fatḥ b. Aḥmad b. ʿAbd al-Ghanī b. ʿAlī al-Isḥāqī al-Manūfī al-Shāfiʿī wrote, around 1032/1623:[3]

1. *al-Rawḍ al-bāsim fī akhbār man maḍā min al-ʿawālim*, a history of the Prophet, the first caliphs, the Umayyads, ʿAbbāsids, Fāṭimids, Ayyūbids, and Egypt to the year 1032/1623, Paris 1562, Br. Mus. 1251.—2. *Dawḥat al-azhār fī man waliya 'l-diyār al-Miṣriyya* Bodl. I, 851, Pet. Ros. 56, mostly entitled *Laṭāʾif akhbār al-uwal fī man taṣarrafa fī Miṣr min arbāb al-duwal*, a history of Egypt from the Muslim conquest until Sultan Muṣṭafā I (d. 1032/1623), to whom the work is dedicated, Berl. Ms. or. qu. 2105, Gotha 1633/7, Munich 396/7, Vienna 924, Krafft 257, Leid. 983, Paris 1839/49, Upps. 265, Copenhagen 153, Cambr. p. 7, no. 208, Br. Mus. 1251, Suppl. 567, Cairo V, ^{1}121, ^{2}317, VII, 33, lith. C. 1276, 1296, print. C. 1304, 1310, 1311.

6. Abu 'l-ʿAbbās Aḥmad b. Muḥammad al-Maqqarī al-Tilimsānī al-Mālikī al-Ashʿarī was born in Tlemcen just before 1000/1591, and studied from 1009/1600 onward in Fez and Marrakesh. From there he went on the pilgrim-
382 age in 1027/1618, and got married in Cairo the following year, | but left for Jerusalem in Rabīʿ I 1029/February 1620. Before the year 1036/1626 he made the pilgrimage another five times and visited Medina seven times, where he held lectures. In Ṣafar 1037/October 1627 he again went to Cairo; then, in Rajab/March 1628 he went to Jerusalem, and then to Damascus in Shaʿbān/April of that year, where he took up quarters in al-Madrasa al-Jaqmaqiyya.

1 Muḥammad b. al-Ḥanbalī, d. 971/1564, see below, p. 368.

2 Marʿī b. Yūsuf al-Karmī, d. 1033/1624, see below, p. 369.

3 Wüst. *Gesch.* 568 identifies him, without sufficient reason, with the poet in § 1, 26.

Having lectured there with great success, he departed again for Cairo on 5 Shawwāl/9 June. He remained there until Shaʿbān 1040/March 1631, then went to Damascus again, thought of living there, but died suddenly of a fever in Jumādā I 1041/December 1631.

Muḥ. I, 382, Wüst. *Gesch.* 559. 1. *Nafḥ al-ṭīb min ghuṣn al-Andalus al-raṭīb wa-dhikr wazīrihā Lisān al-Dīn al-Khaṭīb* (p. 337), a political and intellectual history of Spain with a detailed biography of Lisān al-Dīn, written at the instigation of the intelligentia of Damascus after his return from that country to Cairo, in one year, | until 27 Ramaḍān 1038/21 May 1629, and completed on the last day 297
of 1039/9 August 1630, complete printing Būlāq 1279, C. 1302/5, 4 vols.; the first, main, part: *Analectes sur l'histoire et la littérature des Arabes d'Espagne par al-Makkari, publ. par* R. Dozy, G. Dugat, L. Krehl, & W. Wright, Leiden 1855/61, R. Dozy, *Lettre à. M. Fleischer contenant des remarques critiques et explicatives sur le texte d'Al-Makkari*, Leiden 1871, see Fleischer, *Kl. Schr.* II, 1, 1888. With the political history at the beginning as an abstract and with the order changed: *The History of the Mohammedan Dynasties in Spain, extracted from the Nafhu'ttib by Ahmad el-Makkari, transl. and illustr. by* Pascual de Gayangos, London 1840. MSS see Suppl. vol I, Garr. 608/9.—Abstract by al-Jazāʾirī, Br. Mus. 339/40.—2. *Nafaḥāt al-ʿanbar fī waṣf naʿl dhi 'l-ʿalāʾ wal-minbar*, a didactic poem on the sandals of the Prophet, Gotha $631_{,1}$.—3. *al-Nafaḥāt al-ʿanbariyya fī naʿl khayr al-bariyya*, the same subject in prose and verse, Tetouan no. 62, Alex. Taʾr. 17.—4. *Fatḥ al-mutaʿāl fī madḥ al-niʿāl* Leipz. 41, Basel M. III, 28, Sarajevo $80_{,2}$, Yeni 260, Cairo ^{1}I, 380, ^{2}I, 134, Qawala I, 141, Patna I, $148_{,1423/4}$; a part | thereof concerning 383
the question of whether Muḥammad's feet could leave traces on stones and remain without a trace in sand, Berl. 2595.—5. *Nayl al-marām al-mughtabaṭ li-ṭālib al-mukhammas al-khāli 'l-wasaṭ*, 313 *rajaz* verses on the preparation of talismanic squares of five by five, the middle of which is empty, Berl. 4119, Alex. Ḥurūf 17.—6. *Rafʿ al-ghalaṭ ʿani 'l-mukhammas al-khāli 'l-wasaṭ* Cairo ^{1}V, 342.—7. *Qawāʿid al-sariyya fī ḥall mushkilāt al-Shajara al-Nuʿmāniyya*, predictions for the years 1010–1110/1601–98, Berl. 4222.—8. *al-Qaṣīda al-Maqqariyya*, an elegy on the transitory nature of all earthly things, with a eulogy on Granada and the vizier Lisān al-Dīn (An. I, 6/8), Berl. 7965. Commentaries: a. Aḥmad b. ʿAlī al-Sandūbī al-Miṣrī, d. 1097/1686, ibid. 2, Paris 3244, Alex. Adab 155.—b. Aḥmad Efendi al-Adhamī, *muftī* of Damietta, Paris 3245.—c. See Suppl.—d. *al-Anwār al-qamariyya* by Abū Bakr b. ʿAbd al-Wahhāb b. Muḥammad Amīn al-Zurʿa, d. ca. 1236/1831, Garr. 140.—9. *Ḥusn al-thanāʾ fi 'l-ʿafw ʿamman janā*, lith. Cairo ^{1}VII, 227, ^{2}III, 84.—10. *Iḍāʾat al-dujunna fī ʿaqāʾid ahl al-sunna* Hamb. Or. Sem. $14_{,5}$, Garr. $2003_{,1}$, Alex. Tawhīd 38, Cairo ^{1}II, 52, VII, 288, 303, ^{2}I, 162.—Commentaries, see Suppl.—11. *Azhār al-riyāḍ fī akhbār ʿIyāḍ* Paris 2106

(beginning), 5027, Madr. Codera, Misión p. 176, (2 vols.) ed. Muṣṭafā al-Saqqā', Ibrāhīm al-Abyārī, ʿAbd al-Ḥāfiẓ Siltī, C. 1358/1938.—12.–14. See Suppl.—15. *Kitāb al-jumān min mukhtaṣar Akhbār al-zamān, Perles recueillies de l'Abrégé de l'Histoire des siècles*, transl. S. de Sacy, Paris A. f. 762, *Not. et Extr.* 1788.

7. Aḥmad b. Saʿd al-Dīn al-Ghumrī al-ʿUthmānī al-Shāfiʿī wrote, around 1050/1640:

Dhakhīrat al-iʿlām bi-taʾrīkh (tawārīkh) umarāʾ al-Miṣr fī 'l-islām, ca. 9,000 couplets on the history of Egypt from the Islamic conquest until 1040/1630, Berl. 9831, Gotha 1639/40, Paris 1851/1.

8. Shams al-Dīn Abū ʿAbdallāh Muḥammad b. Aḥmad b. Abi 'l-Surūr al-Bakrī al-Ṣiddīqī al-Miṣrī was born in 1005/1596 (?) in Cairo and died there around 1060/1650.

Wüst. *Gesch.* 565. 1. *al-Tuḥfa al-bahiyya fī tamalluk āl ʿUthmān al-diyār al-Miṣriyya* in 3 divisions: a. the conquest by Selīm, b. the Beglerbegs from the
384 conquest | until 1038/1625 (resp. 1045/1634), Vienna 925/6,[4] Copenhagen 158, see H. Jansky, MOG II, 173f.—2. *al-Rawḍa al-zahiyya fī wulāt Miṣr wal-Qāhira*
298 *al-Muʿizziyya*, | a history of Egypt from the earliest times until 1035/1625, Gotha 1638, up to 1041/1631 Bodl. I, 832, until 1061/1651 Vat. V, 734,$_4$.—3. *al-Kawākib al-sāʾira fī akhbār Miṣr wal-Qāhira*, a shortened version of no. 2, in 20 chapters, running up to 1053/1645 in Munich 398, 1060/1650 in Br. Mus. 324, 1063/1653 in Paris 1852, fragm. Gotha 1646, cf. de Sacy, *Not. et Extr.* I (1787), 165.—Anonymous continuation to 1168/1754, *al-Durra al-mudāna fī waqāʾiʿ al-Kināna* (see Suppl. III, 174), Munich 399, cf. J. Marcel, *Hist. de l'Égypte* XXV.—4. *Qaṭf al-azhār* see 48,$_{1b}$.—5. *Durar al-aʿāli 'l-jaliyya* NO 2378.—8.–9. see Suppl.

9. An unidentified author wrote, in eleventh-century Egypt:

Kitāb al-dhakhāʾir wal-tuḥaf fī biʾr al-ṣanāʾiʿ wal-ḥuraf, an explanation of a didactic poem on the guild system, Gotha 903, cf. Goldziher, *Abh.* II, LXXVII/LX.

10. Muḥammad b. Yūsuf al-Ḥallāq wrote, around 1128/1716:

Tuḥfat al-aḥbāb bi-man malaka Miṣr min al-mulūk wal-nuwwāb Pet. Ros. 58, from which is different a Turkish *Taʾrīkh Miṣr*, Vienna II, 161.

4 Attributed by Flügel, against the chronology, to al-Ṣiddīqī the elder, E no. 5, p. 301 below.

11–13. See Suppl. (13. Garr. 757).

D Chronicles

1. Aḥmad b. Abi 'l-Ḥasan ʿAlī b. Aḥmad Nūr al-Dīn al-Maḥallī al-Shāfiʿī b. Zunbul al-Rammāl witnessed the military campaigns that he describes during his time as an official in the war-office. He was still alive after 960/1653.

Wüst. *Gesch.* 531, Adnan, *Ilim* 88. 1. *Fatḥ Miṣr* (*Taʾrīkh akhdh Miṣr min al-Jarākisa*), a history of the conquest of Egypt by Sultan Selīm I, from Sultan Qānṣūh al-Ghūrī's departure on 16 Rabīʿ II 921/31 May 1515 until the submission of | the country in the year 923/1517,[1] Munich 411/4, Vienna 928/30, Leid. 980, 385
Paris 1832/8, 4612, Glasgow 60 (*JRAS* 1899, 754) = 155, Cairo V, ^{1}21, ^{2}404, 23, k. 173, (under the title *Wāqiʿāt al-sulṭān Selīm Khān* in a shorter version Vienna 929, Munich 412, Cambr. Pr. 7, 31, with a continuation until the death of Sultan Selīm I in 926/1520 in Gotha 1669, again continued until the conquest of Rhodes and siege of Malta, ibid. 1670/3, in the popular style of the ʿAntar romance, in two different versions Br. Mus. Suppl. 565/6,$_{1}$[2].—2. *Tuḥfat al-mulūk wal-raghāʾib li-mā fi 'l-barr wal-baḥr min al-ʿajāʾib wal-gharāʾib*, a work of general geography, Bodl. I, 892, Alex. Jagr. 5.—3. *al-Maqālāt fī ḥall al-mushkilāt*, on occult sciences, Cairo ^{1}V, 372. |—4. *al-Qānūn fi 'l-dunyā*, on geography, astronomy, divination, 299
maqāla 22/3 thereof astrological, Berl. 5889. Turkish translation Revan Köshk, NO 3000/1.

2. ʿAbd al-Qādir wrote, around 1053/1643:

Taʾrīkh, a chronicle of the years 1012–53/1603–43, from the reign of Sultan Aḥmad I until that of Ibrāhīm, Berl. 9729.

3. Ibrāhīm b. Abī Bakr al-Ṣāliḥī (Ṣawāliḥī) al-ʿAwfī completed, on 16 Rajab 1071/18 March 1661:

Tarājim al-ṣawāʿiq fī wāqiʿat al-Sanājiq, a history of the Egyptian Āghās and Sanjaqs from 17 Muḥarram 1071/13 September 1661 until 17 Rabīʿ II/21 December of the same year, followed by a detailed history of the uprising of Muḥammad Bey against the governor of Egypt in 1069/1658, Munich 415, Paris 1853 (cf. J. Marcel, *Hist. de l'Égypte* XXIV).—2. See Suppl. (also Alex. Maw. 14).

---

1 Written, according to de Goeje, after the death of ʿAlī Pāshā, the governor of Egypt, in 960/1553.

2 These or similar editions may also be contained in some of the MSS just mentioned.

4. Ibrāhīm b. Aḥmad Efendi al-Khaṭṭāṭ Shaykhzāde wrote, around 1133/1721:

1. *Mabdaʾ al-ʿajāʾib bi-mā jāʾa fī Miṣr min al-maṣāʾib* Cairo ^{1}VII, 414.—2. *Zād al-ashrāf fī wafq al-qāf* Garr. 944.

5. Muṣṭafā b. Ibrāhīm al-Maddāḥ al-Qinālī wrote, in 1152/1739:

386 A history of Egypt for the years 1100–52/1689–1739, mostly based on | his own experiences in the retinue of Ḥasan Pāshā, an officer of the ʿAzabs, Vienna 931, Copenhagen 159.

6. Muḥammad b. Zayn al-Tuqāt ʿĪsā b. Maḥmūd b. Kannān al-Dimashqī al-ʿAbbāsī al-Ḥanafī, who was born in 1074/1663, was a professor in Damascus and died in 1153/1740.

Mur. IV, 85. 1. *al-Ḥawādith al-yawmiyya min taʾrīkh iḥdā ʿashar wa-miʾa*, a diary from Muḥarram 1111/July 1699 until the end of 1134/October 1722, in which each year starts with information on the sultan in power and the pashas and *qāḍīs* of Syria, reporting subsequently on a day-by-day basis the events that took place, whether they were merely curious or really important, and especially his personal experiences and his contacts with prominent people, in particular poets and scholars, all the while including many poems by himself and others in his account, Berl. 9479/80.—2. *al-Risāla al-mufrada fī arbaʿīn ḥadīthan musnada*, based on a lecture by al-Kūrānī (d. 1101/1689) that occurred in the year 1092/1681, ibid. 1531.—3. *Makārim al-khallāq li-ahl makārim al-akhlāq fī sharḥ Risālat al-Ḥāfiẓ al-Muḥaddith Jamāl al-Dīn al-Maqdisī fi ʾl-taṣawwuf* ibid. 3515.—4. *Ḥadāʾiq al-yāsamīn fī dhikr qawānīn al-khulafāʾ wal-salāṭīn*, on etiquette for officials at the royal court, completed in 1122/1710, ibid. 5631.—5. *al-Iktifāʾ fī dhikr muṣṭalaḥ al-mulūk wal-khulafāʾ*, on the same, but shorter, ibid. 5632.—6. *al-Mawākib al-islāmiyya fi ʾl-mamālik wal-maḥāsin al-Shāmiyya*, a description of Syria, ibid. 6088.—7. A listing and history of the academies of Damascus, based on an earlier work and adapted in 1117/1705, ibid. 6089.—8. *Mukhtaṣar Ḥayāt al-ḥayawān* p. 172.—9. *al-Ilmām fī-mā yataʿallaq bil-ḥayawān min al-aḥkām*, an alphabetical list of animals with short descriptions and legal
300 judgements regarding them, Berl. 6177. |—10. Draft of a work on horses and their properties, ibid. 8184.—11. *al-Ishbāh bi-rafʿ al-ishtibāh*, 24 rules from morphology, ibid. 6853.—12. *al-Risāla al-mushtamila ʿalā anwāʿ al-badīʿ fi ʾl-basmala*, a demonstration of various tropes contained in the word bismillah, ibid. 7283.—13. Love songs, ibid. 8033.—14., 15. See Suppl.

7. Al-Amīr Aḥmad Katkhudā al-Damurdāshī ʿAzabān, who died after 1169/1755.

Al-Durra al-muṣāna fī akhbār al-Kināna, a diary covering the years 1099–1169/1668–1755, in colloquial language, Gotha 1684, Munich 399 (both anon.), Br. Mus. Suppl. 569/70, Cambr. 1012 (incomplete), see J. Marcel, *Hist. de l'Égypte* XXV.

| 8. Ḥasan b. al-Ṣādiq wrote, around 1186/1772: 387

Gharāʾib al-badāʾiʿ wa-ʿajāʾib al-waqāʾiʿ, on the events that took place between the rebels and vizier ʿUthmān Pāshā of Syria in the years 1184/1770 and 1185/1771, in 2 parts, Berl. 9832.

E Universal History

1. Darwīsh ʿAlī Efendi, who was a *muftī* in Aleppo ca. 988/1580.

Khulāṣat al-tawārīkh Berl. 9469/70, Vienna 925,2.

2. Abū Muḥammad Muṣṭafā b. Ḥasan b. Sinān b. Aḥmad al-Ḥusaynī al-Hāshimī al-Jannābī (from Jannāba in Iran), who died in 999/1590, see Suppl.

Wüst. *Gesch.* 538. 1. *al-ʿAylam al-ẓāhir fī aḥwāl al-awāʾil wal-awākhir*, usually called *Taʾrīkh al-Jannābī*, on 82 Muslim dynasties in as many chapters, in 2 parts, running to the year 997/1588, Bodl. I, 657/8, 785/6, Pet. AM 183, Ros. 50 (incomplete), Köpr. 1031/2, Yeni 831, NO 3097/3102.—Abstracts: a. Aḥmad b. Muḥammad b. ʿAlī b. al-Munlā, d. 1003/1595, Berl. 9726.—b. Abu 'l-ʿAbbās Aḥmad Čelebī al-Qaramānī al-Dīmashqī, no. 4.—c. Anonymous, in a manuscript from Lucknow, Br. Mus. Suppl. 4889/90. Turkish translation by the author himself, Vienna 853, an abstract from which, by the same, ibid. 854. From this *Mustaphae f. Hu. Algenabii de gestis Timurlenki s. Tamerlanis opusculum, Turc. Ar. Pers. lat. redd. a.* J. Bapt. Podestà, Vienna 1680.

3. Muḥammad b. Aḥmad b. ʿAlī al-Andalusī al-Mālikī Shams al-Dīn studied Mālikī law in Cairo, made the pilgrimage, then became an acting *qāḍī* and professor at the Umayyad mosque in Damascus, before dying sometime after 1004/1596.

RA 277v, Wüst. *Gesch.* 543. 1. *Dhakhāʾir al-āthār fī akhbār al-akhyār*, a history of Muḥammad and the caliphs until al-Maʾmūn, with biographies, most of which are from Ibn Khallikān, Leid. 1041.—2. See Suppl.

301 | 4. Abu 'l-ʿAbbās Aḥmad b. Yūsuf b. Aḥmad al-Dimashqī al-Qaramānī was born
388 in 938/1532. His father, an inspector at the Nūrī hospital and the | Umayyad mosque, was garroted because of misconduct in office on 14 Shawwāl 966/21 July 1559. Aḥmad then became a secretary and a board member in the Dīwān al-awqāf of the two Egyptian women's hospitals in Damascus. He died on 29 Shawwāl 1019/13 January 1611.

Muḥ I, 209, Wüst. *Gesch.* 550. 1 *Akhbār al-duwal wa-āthār al-uwal*, an abstract of al-Jannābī (no. 2), not without mistakes, and with some additions, composed in 1007/1598, Berl. 6052, 9471/2, Gotha 1579, Leid. 856/7, Bodl. I, 711, II, 595, Br. Mus. 284, 936, Suppl. 491, Nicholson *JRAS* 1899, 909, no. 4, Paris 1556/9, Pet. AM 185/6 1, Ros. 52/4, Köpr. 1002, NO 3042/3, 3155, Alex. Ta'r. 8, Cairo V, ^{1}6, ^{2}13, 409, lith. Baghdad 1282, printed in the margin of Ibn al-Athīr vol. 1–6, Būlāq 1290 (see Suppl.).—2. *al-Rawḍ al-nasīm wal-durr al-yatīm fī manāqib al-sulṭān Ibrāhīm*, an abstract of a translation of the Turkish *al-Ṭirāz al-muʿlam fī qiṣṣat al-sulṭān Ibrāhīm b. Adham*, d. 161/778, by Darwīsh Ḥasan al-Rūmī, composed in 973/1566, Berl. 9055/6, Rāmpūr I, 670, 14, as *Sīrat al-sulṭān Ibrāhīm b. Adham* by Ḥasan al-Rūmī al-Dimashqī, Dam., Ẓ $39_{30/2}$.

5. Muḥammad b. Muḥammad b. Abi 'l-Surūr Zayn al-Dīn al-Bakrī al-Ṣiddīqī al-Taymī al-Shāfiʿī, who died in Cairo on 20 Jumādā I 1028/6 May 1619.

Wüst. *Gesch.* 552. 1. *ʿUyūn al-akhbār wa-nuzhat al-abṣār*, a medium-sized work of universal history, from the Creation until his own time, Berl. 9473/4,[1] Paris 1560, Cairo V, ^{1}92, 2275.—2. *Nuzhat al-abṣār wa-juhaynat al-akhbār* Berl. 9475, Paris 1561.—3. *al-Minaḥ al-raḥmāniyya fi 'l-dawla al-ʿUthmāniyya*, an abstract of 1, with some additions and the history of the Turkish governors of Egypt, Paris 1623, and with a continuation until 1027/1618, entitled *al-Laṭāʾif al-rabbāniyya ʿala 'l-Minaḥ al-raḥmāniyya*, Vienna 978.—4. *Fayḍ al-mannān bi-dhikr dawlat āl ʿUthmān*, composed after no. 3, running to the year 1027/1618, with special emphasis on the *qāḍīs* of Egypt, Cairo ^{1}V, 103.—5. *Durar al-athmān fī aṣl manbaʿ āl ʿUthmān* Gotha 1614.[2]—6. *Tuḥfat al-ẓurafāʾ bi-dhikr al-mulūk wal-khulafāʾ* Alex. Ta'r. 119.—7. *al-Futūḥāt al-ʿUthmāniyya lil-diyār al-Miṣriyya* ibid. 2.

302 389 | | 6. Muḥammad b. Jumʿa al-Dimashqī, ca. 1156/1743.

---

1 Due to confusion with a younger namesake (see p. 383), Ahlwardt fixes his death at around 1050/1640.

2 On the date of this manuscript see Wüst., loc. cit.

Ta'rīkh, part of a larger historical work, chapter 74, on the pashas and *qāḍīs* of Damascus from 922/1516 until his own time (1156/1743), Berl. 9785.

7. Muḥammad b. Ibrāhīm b. Muḥammad b. Shaḥḥāda b. Ḥasan al-Khaṭīb wrote, in the years 1155–7/1742–4:

A brief overview of Islamic history until the Turkish Sultan Maḥmūd I (r. 1143–68–1730–54), Berl. 9481.

8. Aḥmad b. Muḥammad b. Muḥammad b. Muṣṭafā al-Ṣimādī al-Jarrāḥī al-Ḥasanī al-Dimashqī Kamāl al-Dīn Abu 'l-Ḥasan wrote, around 1209/1794:

Al-Barq al-lāmiʿ fi 'l-ta'rīkh al-jāmiʿ wal-kawkab al-sāṭiʿ, which was plagiarised from *Akhbār al-duwal* by al-Qaramānī (no. 4), Berl. 9483.

4 *Popular Works and Anthologies*

1. Muḥammad b. Ramaḍān b. Aḥmad al-Ghazzī al-Miṣrī al-Ḥanafī, a student of al-Suyūṭī, wrote, around 930/1524:

Maslāt al-ḥazan wal-tadhkira ʿinda maṣā'ib al-zamān, containing various anecdotes, sayings by Muḥammad, explanations of Qur'ānic verses, aphorisms, Sufi dicta, and wine- and love songs, Berl. 8418, Köpr. 781.

2. Zayn al-Dīn Abū Bakr ʿAlī b. Muḥammad b. Khālid al-Balāṭunisī al-Shāfiʿī al-Shāmī, who died in 936/1529.

1. *Nuzhat al-nāẓir wa-bahjat al-khāṭir*, an anthology in 45 *anwāʿ*, Esc. ²537.—2. Abstracts from al-Ṣafadī's *Ladhdhat al-samʿ*, p. 41.

3. Shaykh al-Islām al-ʿĀrif billāh Aḥmad Efendi, who was a *qāḍī* in Cairo, wrote, in 1030/1622:

Rawḍat al-mushtāq wa-bahjat al-ʿushshāq, on amorous ups and downs in verse and prose, Br. Mus. 776.

4. Muḥammad b. Abi 'l-Wafā' b. Maʿrūf al-Khalwatī al-Ḥamawī wrote, in 1031–3/1621–3:

Nuzhat al-akhyār wa-majmaʿ al-nawādir wal-akhbār, recreational prose, Berl. 8424, Nicholson *JRAS* 1899, 913.

303 390 || 5. Muḥammad b. Muḥammad al-Hurayrī al-Ḥalabī al-Dimashqī was born in Aleppo, lived as a poet in Damascus, and died in 1037/1627.

Muḥ. IV, 300. *Mufākhara bayn awlād al-khulafāʾ al-rāshidīn*, a contest between the sons of Abū Bakr, ʿUthmān, and ʿAlī; each of them enumerates five of their qualities, and Muḥammad decides in favour of ʿAlī, Berl. 9698/9.

6. ʿAlī b. Muḥammad b. Muḥammad b. ʿAlī al-Shirbīnī was born in 977/1569 and was still alive in 1044/1634.

Maṭāliʿ al-budūr al-ʿaliyya fī manāzil al-surūr al-adabiyya, recreational prose, Berl. 8422.

7. Ṣāliḥ b. Muḥammad b. ʿAbdallāh al-Tīmūrtāshī (see § 6, no. 5) was born in 980/1572, studied in Cairo, and died in 1055/1645.

Muḥ. II, 239. *Abkār al-afkār wa-fākihat al-akhyār*, following the example of the *Sulwān al-muṭāʿ* (I, 431), Berl. 8425.

8. Muḥammad b. Aḥmad b. al-Ilyās (Ilyās) al-Ḥanafī, fl. ca. 1060/1650.

1. *al-Jawāhir al-farīda fi ʾl-nawādir al-mufīda*, short stories about marvellous events, taken from nature and the life of man, Berl. 8426.—2. *Kitāb fi ʾl-nawādir al-muḍḥika wal-hazaliyyāt al-muṭriba*, amusing anecdotes, ibid. 8427.—3. *al-Durr al-maknūn fi ʾl-sabʿ al-funūn*, on the seven modern metres in poetry, completed in 1001/1592, Paris 3409.

9. Muḥammad b. ʿUmar al-Aḥdab wrote, in 1066/1655:

Nuzhat al-albāb wa-bughyat al-aḥbāb, a collection of stories, Gotha 2702.

10. Muḥammad Diyāb al-Itlīdī wrote, in 1100/1688:

Iʿlām al-nās bi-mā waqaʿa lil-Barāmika maʿa Banī ʿAbbās, mostly containing mythical tales, Munich 640, Pet. AM 184, Paris 2108/10, 5246, 6587, Br. Mus. 1502, Suppl. 1153, Cambr. Pr. 8, 42, Suppl. 73, Patna I, 275,2287, print. C. 1279, 1280, 1296, 1307, 1315 among others, Wüst. *Gesch.* 588.

11. Muṣṭafā b. ʿAbd al-Laṭīf al-ʿAwnī, fl. ca. 1150/1737.

| *Al-Nawādir wal-rawḍ al-anīq al-zāhir*, recreational prose, Berl. 8434. 391

12. Al-Shaykh Ibrāhīm wrote, in 1197/1783:

Kitāb al-sharḥ wal-faraḥ, a collection of tales, aphorisms, and poems, Gotha 2705.

| 13. Shihāb al-Dīn Aḥmad al-Ḥifnāwī al-Bishārī wrote, in 1183/1769: 304

Bughyat al-jalīs wal-musāmir wa-nuzhat al-arwāḥ wal-khawāṭir fi 'l-ashʿār wal-nawādir, anecdotes and poems, arranged in 21 sections, according to their main characters, among whom are: judges, grammarians, teachers, Bedouin, girls, boys, etc., Gotha 2716, Paris 3448/51. See *Fundgr. d. Or.* IV, 30.

14. Aḥmad al-Shaqīfātī al-Rabbāṭ al-Ḥalabī wrote, around 1202/1788:

Collections of poems and pieces of prose, *zajal, takhmīs*, and *mawālī*, entitled *Safīna*, Berl. 8188/94.

5 *Ḥadīth*

1. ʿAbd al-Qādir b. Muḥammad b. Aḥmad al-Shādhilī al-Mālikī al-Muʾadhdhin, fl. ca. 920/1514.

Radd al-ʿuqūl al-ṭāʾisha ilā maʿrifat ma 'khtaṣṣat bihi Khadīja wa-ʿĀʾisha Garr. 700.

2. Zayn al-Dīn Abū Khafṣ ʿUmar b. Aḥmad b. Maḥmūd al-Shammāʿ al-Ḥalabī al-Shāfiʿī al-Ṣāfī al-Atharī was born in 880(1)/1475(6) and died in Aleppo on 15 Ṣafar 936/20 October 1529.

Wüst. *Gesch.* 515. 1. *Tuḥfat al-thiqāt bi-asānīd mā li-ʿUmar al-Shammāʿ min al-masmūʿāt*, on his teachers and the works read in their presence, with *isnād*s, Berl. 171.—2. *al-Jawāhir wal-durar min sīrat sayyid al-bashar wa-aṣḥābihi al-ʿashara al-ghurar*, a biography of the prophet, ḤKh II, 4310, ^{2}I, 617, on which a commentary Berl. 9601.—3. *Tashnīf al-asmāʿ bi-fawāʾid al-tasmiya ʿinda l-jimāʿ* ḤKh II, 299$_{,3008}$, ^{2}I, 409 (*bi-sharḥ aḥkām al-jimāʿ*. Commentary on the *Majmūʿ* by Abū Bakr b. al-ʿArabī al-Māliki, a student of al-Ghazzālī), anon. Esc. ^{2}707$_{,13}$, Garr. 2214.—| 4. *al-Qabs al-ḥāwī li-ghurr al-Ḍawʾ al-lāmiʿ* p. 43.—5. 392
–9. see Suppl. (9. Alex. Ḥad. 7).

3. Shams al-Dīn Abū ʿAbdallāh Muḥammad b. Yūsuf b. ʿAlī b. Yūsuf al-Dimashqī al-Ṣāliḥī al-Shāfiʿī al-Shāmī went from Damascus to Cairo, lived in the Barqūqiyya monastery, and died on 14 Shaʿbān 942/7 February 1536.[1]

Wüst. *Gesch.* 517. 1. *Subul al-hudā wal-irshād* (*rashād*) *fī sīrat khayr al-ʿibād* or *al-Sīra al-Shāmiyya*, a biography of the Prophet, put together on the basis of more than 300 works, in more than 700 chapters, arranged and completed by the author's student Muḥammad b. Muḥammad b. Aḥmad al-Fayshī (?) al-Mālikī, and finished on 15 Rabīʿ II 971/3 December 1563,[2] individual parts Gotha 1796/7, Br. Mus. 1278, Paris 1987/96, Algiers 1692/3, Cairo V, [1]66, [2]215, Makram 33, with the title *Rabīʿ al-atqiyāʾ fī dhikr faḍāʾil sayyid al-aṣfiyāʾ* Garr. 651.—2. *al-Āyāt al-ʿaẓīma al-bāhira fī miʿrāj sayyid ahl al-dunyā wal-ākhira*,
305 composed after no. 1, Leid. 2069. |—3. *ʿUqūd al-jumān fī manāqib al-imām Abī Ḥanīfa al-Nuʿmān*, composed in 939/1532 on the occasion of the publication, at the end of the previous year, of a work disparaging the imam,[3] Vienna 1180, Yeni 870, AS 3309, Cairo V, [1]90, [2]270.—4. *Maṭlaʿ al-nūr fī faḍl al-Ṭūr wa-qamʿ al-muʿtadī al-kafūr*, composed in the wake of rumours that monks on Mount Sinai had seized a mosque, Cairo V, [1]152, [2]349.—5. *al-Faḍl al-mubīn fi ʾl-ṣabr ʿinda faqd al-banāt wal-banīn* Cairo VII, 102.—6., 7. See Suppl. (6. See p. 68 and Suppl. II, 55, 914_{99}).

4. Jalāl al-Dīn al-Samannūdī wrote, around 950/1543:

Al-Ghammāz ʿala ʾl-lammāz, badly or entirely unfounded traditions, listed alphabetically, Berl. 1633/4, Cairo [1]II, 408, [2]I, 133.

5. ʿUthmān b. Aḥmad b. Mūsā al-Ḍijāʿī wrote, in 986/1578:

393 | *Al-Naql al-matīn fī shaqq ṣadr al-nabī al-amīn* Berl. 6245.

6. Aḥmad b. Ḥijāzī al-Fashnī wrote, in the second half of the tenth century:

1. *Tuḥfat al-ikhwān fī qirāʾat al-miʿād fī shahr Rajab wa-Shaʿbān wa-Ramaḍān*, C. 1297.—2. *al-Majālis al-saniyya fi ʾl-kalām ʿala ʾl-arbaʿīn al-Nawawiyya*, I,

1 The second date in Wüst., 17. Muḥ. 974, from Casiri II, 152, contradicts the other dates.

2 This is according to the manuscript in Cairo; according to Paris 1996 completion took place in 999 (another edition?). Šehid ʿA. 1879/84 (*juzʾ* 1–6) are dated 943/955 A.H.; see Ritter.

3 This is according to Cairo; according to Wüstenfeld it is a defence of a work about Abū Ḥanīfa that he had published at the end of 936, to ward off attacks by ignorant people.

499.—3.–5. see Suppl. (3. Garr. 1974).—6. *Muzīl al-ʿanāʾ fī sharḥ asmāʾ allāh al-ḥusnā*, on a poem by Shaḥḥādha b. ʿAlī al-ʿIrāqī, Garr. 1308.

7. Sālim b. Muḥammad al-Sanhūrī was born in Sanhūr, went to Cairo at the age of eleven where he became a Mālikī *muftī*, and died on 3 Jumādā II 1015/7 October 1606.

Khit. jad. XII, 61. 1. *Faḍāʾil laylat al-niṣf min Shaʿbān* Alex. Ḥad. 47, 1, Cairo ^{1}VII, 136, 212, 513, ^{2}I, 135.—2. See Suppl.

8. Abu ʾl-Tawfīq Sālim al-Wafāʾ wrote, in 1015/1606:

Taklīl al-tāj bi-jawāhir al-miʿrāj Paris 1237,$_{2}$.

9. ʿAbd al-Nāfiʿ b. ʿUmar al-Ḥamawī, who was first a historian in Hama and then a *muftī* in Maʿarrat al-Nuʿmān, went to Tripoli because of some personal enmity, betrayed this city to the rebel ʿAlī b. Jānbūlādh (*EI*, 1057/8), had to flee to Aleppo after the withdrawal of the latter's troops, and died in Idlīb al-Ṣughrā in Jumādā I 1026/September 1607.

TA 144v, Muḥ. III, 90/3. *Taḥrīr al-abḥāth ʿalā ḥadīth Ḥubbiba ilayya min dunyākum thalāth* Cairo I, ^{1}280, ^{2}94.

10. ʿAbd al-Raʾūf Muḥammad b. Tāj al-ʿĀrifīn b. ʿAlī b. Zayn al-ʿĀbidīn al-Ḥaddādī al-Munāwī al-Shāfiʿī was born in Cairo in 952/1545. In his youth he studied the most important teachers of the Sufis | but remained faithful to his Shāfiʿī 306
school. Having worked for a brief spell as an acting | judge, he devoted the 394
remainder of his life entirely to scholarship until he was given a position at the Ṣāliḥiyya madrasa. Rumour had it that he was poisoned by people jealous of his successful teaching career, and he died, after suffering for a long time, on 13 Ṣafar 1031/2 December 1621.

Muḥ. II, 412/6, followed by *Khiṭ. jad.* XVI, 56, Wüst. *Gesch.* 553, his biography Berl. 10140, his eulogy ibid. ʾ41. 1. *Kunūz al-ḥaqāʾiq fī ḥadīth khayr al-khalāʾiq*, an alphabetical collection of 10,000 short *ḥadīth* from 44 works, Gotha 610, Paris 777, Algiers 517, AS 874/5, 947, Cairo I, ^{1}389, ^{2}140, Makram 50, lith. Istanbul 1285, print. Būlāq 1286, C. 1305. Abstract *Kanz al-ḥaqq al-mubīn fī aḥādīth sayyid al-mursalīn*, containing 3,800 *ḥadīth*, by ʿAbd al-Ghanī al-Nābulūsī, d. 1143/1730 (see below, p. 345), Berl. 1372, Garr. 1410, Cairo I, ^{1}389, ^{2}140.—2. *al-Jāmiʿ al-azhar min ḥadīth al-nabī al-anwar* Cairo I, ^{1}294, ^{2}100.—3. *Sharḥ*

Alfiyyat al-ʿIrāqī fi ʾl-siyar p. 77.—4. *Sharḥ al-Shamāʾil lil-Tirmidhī* I, 169.—5. *Sharḥ Kitāb al-shifāʾ* I, 455.—6. *al-Ithāfāt al-saniyya bil-aḥādīth al-Qudsiyya* Leid. 1761, Cairo I, [1]258, [2]82, print. Hyderabad 1323.—7. *al-Maṭālib al-ʿaliyya fi ʾl-adʿiya al-zahiyya al-muntakhaba bil-aḥādīth al-Qudsiyya*, a collection of Sufi prayers and *ḥadīth* as a complement to *al-Aḥādīth al-Qudsiyya* by Ibn ʿArabī (I, 572), Gotha 899, 900.—8. *al-Nuzha al-zahiyya fī aḥkām al-ḥammām al-sharʿiyya wal-ṭibbiyya*, on baths and their uses in the context of religon and medicine, Berl. 6409, Gotha 1985, Cairo [1]VI, 206, Garr. 1113.—9. *Taysīr al-wuqūf ʿalā ghawāmiḍ aḥkām al-wuqūf* Cairo [1]III, 203.—10. *al-Tawqīf ʿalā muhimmāt al-tāʿārīf* NO 4742, Cairo [1]IV, 170.—11. *al-Durr al-manḍūd fī dhamm al-bukhl wa-madḥ al-jūd* Cairo [1]IV, 230, [2]III, 98.—12. *al-Jawāhir al-muḍīʾa fi ʾl-aḥkām (bayān al-ādāb) al-sulṭāniyya* Leid. 1941.—13. *al-Kawākib al-durriyya fī tarājim al-sāda al-Ṣūfiyya*, including the four first caliphs, in eleven classes, according to the eleven centuries, Berl. 9984/7, Vienna 1168, Br. Mus. 1303, Algiers 1739, Tunis, *Bull. de Corr. Afr.* 1884, p. 33, no. 129, ʿĀšir I, 676, Cairo [1]V, 119, Makram 53, Alex. Taʾr. 104; from which a lemma on ʿUmar ʿAbd al-ʿAzīz in Berl. 9710,[4]
395 on ʿAbd al-Wahhāb al-Shaʿrāwī in ibid. 10112, abstract Gotha | 173.—14. *Irghām awliyāʾ al-shayṭān bi-dhikr manāqib awliyāʾ al-raḥmān* or *al-Ṭabaqāt al-ṣughrā* Cairo V, [1]8, [2]21.—15. *Nuzhat al-aṭibbāʾ Sharḥ al-Qaṣīda al-nafsiyya li-Ibn Sīnā*
307 (I, 594,$_{35}$), Bodl. I, 1258. |—16. *Ghāyat al-irshād ilā maʿrifat aḥkām al-ḥayawān wal-nabāt wal-jamād*, on omens from the three realms of nature, Gotha 2064, Paris 2768/9.–17. *Sharḥ Risālat al-Ṣiddīqī fī Faḍl laylat al-niṣf min Shaʿbān* p. 439, 5, 17.–18. *Sharḥ Manāzil al-sāʾirīn* I, 557.—19. *Sharḥ al-Lubāb fi ʾl-fiqh* I, 192.—20. *ʿImād al-balāgha* I, 339.—21.–34. see Suppl. (23., 24. Garr. 707/8, 30. Taymūr Ṭab. 59, 32. read: *Fatḥ* see Patna I, 99,$_{101}$).—35. *Sharḥ Asmāʾ Allāh al-ḥusnā wa-khawāṣṣihā* Alex. Faw. 10.–36. *Fatḥ al-raʾūf al-khabīr* p. 418.

11. Abu ʾl-Faraj ʿAlī b. Ibrāhīm b. Aḥmad b. ʿAlī b. ʿUmar Nūr al-Dīn al-Ḥalabī al-Qāhirī al-Shāfiʿī, who was born in Cairo in 975/1567, was a professor at the Ṣāliḥiyya there and died on 30 Shaʿbān 1044/19 February 1635.

Muḥ. III, 122, Wüst. *Gesch.* 560. 1. *Insān al-ʿuyūn fī sīrat al-amīn al-maʾmūn* or *al-Sīra al-Ḥalabiyya*, an abstract of *al-Sīra al-Shāmiyya* (no. 3) with additions, completed in 1043/1633, Berl. 9604/11, Gotha 1801/5, Munich 449/51, Paris 1999/2055, Br. Mus. 924/5, Suppl. 1274/6, Cambr. Pr. p. 11. no. 275, Nicholson, *JRAS* 1899, 908, Calcutta 2, no. 660, Kazan no. 21, Algiers 1695/6, Yeni 819, NO 3049/54, Qawala II, 228, print. C. 1280, 1308, among others—Abstracts:

4 Completing a fragment from the work by Ibn al-Jawzī (I, 662, no. 15), cf. C.H. Becker, *Ibn Jawzīs Manāqib ʿO. b. ʿA.* Leipz. 1890/3.

a. *Khulāṣat al-athar* by Aḥmad b. Abī Bakr al-Baṭḥīshī, d. 1147/1734, Berl. 9612, Cairo [1]II, 141.—b. Anonymous, dated 1104/1692, Paris 2006.—c.–e. see Suppl.—2. *al-Naṣīḥa al-ʿAlawiyya fī bayān ḥusn ṭarīqat al-sāda al-Aḥmadiyya*, on the followers of the Sufi Aḥmad al-Badawī, d. 675/1276 (I, 586), Berl. 10104, Alex. Taṣ. 50.—3. *ʿIqd al-marjān fī-mā yataʿallaq bil-jānn* Cairo VI, [1]157, [2]207, VII, 302.—4.–6. see Suppl.

12. Nāṣir al-Dīn ʿAbd al-Salām b. Ibrāhīm al-Laqānī, born in 971/1563, was a student and successor to his father (d. 1041/1631, p. 412) as a professor at al-Azhar. He died on 15 Shawwāl 1078/30 March 1668.

Muḥ. II, 416, followed by *Khiṭ. jad.* XV, 17, al-Afrānī, *Ṣafwa* 161. 1. *Tarwīḥ al-fuʾād bi-mawlid khayr al-ʿibād* Cairo I, [1]285, [2]96, V, [2]139, VII, [1]512.—2. *Sharḥ Jawharat al-tawḥīd* | *li-wālidihi* p. 412.—3. *Sharḥ al-Manẓūma al-Jazāʾiriyya fi ʾl-tawḥīd* 396
p. 326.—4.–8. see Suppl. (8. Br. Mus. 9118).

13. Ibrāhīm b. Muḥammad b. ʿĪsā al-Maymūnī al-Shāfiʿī died in Cairo on 12 Ramaḍān 1079/4 January 1670.

Muḥ. I, 45, followed by *Khit. jad.* XVI, 90. 1. *Kitāb al-isrāʾ wal-miʿrāj* Cairo I, [1]267, [2]89.—2.–5. see Suppl.—6. *Risāla fī tafsīr qawlihi*, on sura 42,$_{49}$, Qawala I, 65.

14. Ṭāhā b. Muḥammad b. Fattūḥ al-Dimashqī al-Bayqūnī wrote, before 1080/1669:

Al-Bayqūniyya, 34 *rajaz* verses on the technical terms of the science of *ḥadīth*, Berl. 1125/8, Cairo [1]VII, 335.—Commentaries: a. Muḥammad b. ʿAbd al-Bāqī al-Zurqānī, d. 1122/1710 (p. 415), Berl. 1129, Cairo I, [1]238, [2]75, on which glosses by ʿAṭiyya al-Ujhūrī al-Shāfiʿī, d. 1190/1776 (p. 431), print. C. 1305, 1310, among others.—b. Muḥammad b. Maʿdān al-Ḥājirī, d. 1814, Cairo [1]I, 238, [2]75.—c.–h. see Suppl. (d. Alex. Muṣṭ. al-Ḥad. 12; g. ibid. 11, 18).—i. ʿAbdallāh Suwaydān al-Damlījī, d. 1234/1819 (see below p. 485), ibid. 15.—k. Ḥasan al-Jiddāwī, completed in 1288, ibid. 11, 18.

15. Shams al-Dīn Abū ʿAbdallāh al-Bābilī al-Qāhirī, who died in 1077/1666.

Muntakhab al-asānīd fī waṣl al-muṣannafāt wal-ajzāʾ wal-masānīd, collected by his student ʿĪsā b. Muḥammad al-Maghribī al-Thaʿālibī al-Jazāʾirī, d. 1080/1669 (Suppl. 691, 1 c), Alex. Muṣṭ. ḥad. 17, Patna II, 538,$_{2890}$.

308 | 16. Aḥmad b. Aḥmad b. Muḥammad b. Aḥmad b. Ibrāhīm b. al-ʿAjamī al-Miṣrī al-Wafāʾī was born in Cairo on 13 Rajab 1014/28 November 1605 and died there on 19 Dhu ʾl-Qaʿda 1086/4 February 1676.

Muḥ. I, 176, Wüst. *Gesch.* 580. 1. *Tanzīh al-Muṣṭafā fi ʾl-mukhtār ʿammā lam yathbut fi ʾl-āthār* Berl. 2596/7, Cairo [1]VII, 13, [2]I, App. 12, V. 416.—2. *Sharḥ al-Thulāthiyyāt lil-Bukhārī* I, 166.—3. *Dhayl Lubb al-lubāb lil-Suyūṭī* (I, 402; II, 183), Pet. AM 1974.—6. See Suppl.

17. Muḥammad b. Aḥmad b. ʿAlī al-Bahūtī al-Khalwatī al-Ḥanbalī al-Miṣrī was born in Cairo, and died there on 19 Dhu ʾl-Ḥijja 1088/13 January 1678.

397 | Muḥ. III, 390, followed by *Khiṭ. jad.* IX, 99. 1. *al-Tuḥfa al-ẓarfiyya fi ʾl-sīra al-nabawiyya* Cairo V [1]30, [2]130.—2. See Suppl.

17b. ʿAbd al-Raḥīm b. Muḥammad al-Qāḍī, eleventh century (?), see Suppl.

Daqāʾiq al-akhbār etc. also Qawala I, 233. Turkish translation Kazan 1900, see E. Galtier, *Bull. de l'Inst. franç. d'arch. or.* V (1906) 311/2.

17d. See Suppl. 420, 487 16b, 945,$_{162}$.

Kitāb al-muʿjīzāt, MS Strasbourg, see Schwally on Bayhaqī, al-Maḥāsin 18. n. 8.

17e. Muḥammad b. al-ʿAtīq al-Ḥimṣī al-Shāfiʿī died in Egypt in 1088/1677.

Khulāṣat mā rawāhu ʾl-wāʿūn fi ʾl-akhbār al-wārida fi ʾl-ṭāʿūn Alex. Ḥad. 22, Fun. 85,$_{1}$ (attributed to Ibn Ḥajar al-ʿAsqalānī).

18. Muḥammad b. Muḥammad b. Muḥammad b. Aḥmad al-Bakfalūnī al-Ḥalabī, who died in 1093/1682 (or, according to others, in 1098/1687).

1. An introduction to his lectures on al-Bukhārī, one of which was written in Mecca, Berl. 1130.—2. *Risāla fī tafṣīr sabbiḥ isma rabbika ʾl-aʿlā* (sura 87), dedicated to Qara Muṣṭafā (d. 1095/1684), the grand vizier of Sultan Meḥmed IV, d. 1104/1692, ibid. 967.

19. ʿAbd al-Ḥalīm b. ʿAlī b. ʿAbd al-Hādī al-ʿUmarī al-Dimashqī, fl. ca. 1096/1685.

Durrat al-khawāṣṣ fī sharḥ Urjūzat al-ikhtiṣāṣ, commentary on a *rajaz* (by whom?) on the science of *ḥadīth*, Berl. 1138.

20. Muḥammad b. Yūsuf Abū Shāma al-Dimashqī, who died in 1101/1690.

1. *Muzīl al-labs ʿan ḥadīth radd al-shams* Alex. Fun. 166, 6.—2. *Ajwibat al-asʾila al-wāridāt ʿani ʾl-azwāj wal-banīn wal-banāt* ibid. 16.

21. Muḥammad b. Muḥammad b. ʿUmar al-Rawḍī al-Mālikī wrote, in 1103/1691:

Kashf al-lithām ʿammā jāʾa fi ʾl-aḥādīth al-nabawiyya fī shamāʾil al-Muṣṭafā wa-minhājihī ʿalayhi ʾl-ṣalāt wal-salām Cairo [1]I, 388.

| 22. ʿAlī b. Yaḥyā b. Aḥmad b. ʿAlī b. Qāsim al-Kaysalānī al-Qādirī al-Ḥamawī, who died in Hama in 1113/1701. 398

Naẓm al-durar fī ḥadīth khayr al-bashar, with the commentary *Bulūgh al-bughya fī sharḥ manẓūmat al-ḥilya*, Alex. Taʾr. 5.

23. Ibrāhīm b. Muḥammad Kamāl al-Dīn al-Ḥusaynī al-Ḥanafī al-Dimashqī, who died in 1120/1708.

Mur. 1, 22. *Al-Bayān wal-taʿrīf fī asbāb wurūd al-ḥadīth al-sharīf*, from the *Muṣannaf* of Abu ʾl-Baqāʾ al-ʿUkbarī, d. 616/1219, I, 335, cf. Suppl. II, 223,4.

24. Abu ʾl-Ṣafāʾ ʿAlī al-Shanawānī wrote, in 1142/1729:

Al-Fawāʾid al-saniyya fī dhikr al-ṣalāt ʿalā khayr al-bariyya Cairo [1]II, 213.

25. Aḥmad b. Muḥammad b. Abi ʾl-Qāsim b. Aḥmad b. ʿAbd al-Raḥmān b. Muḥammad al-ʿAshmāwī al-Makkī wrote, in ca. 1142/1729:

1. *al-Taḥqīq fi ʾl-nasab al-wathīq* Cairo V, [1]133, [2]32.—2. See Suppl.

26. Ismāʿīl al-Ilāhī al-Ṣūfī wrote, in ca. 1143/1730:

Al-Mushājara fī ḥadīth al-ghufrān li-ahl Badr fi ʾl-dunyā wal-ākhira Berl. 1597.

27. Ismāʿīl b. Ghunaym al-Jawharī, fl. ca. 1160/1717.

1.–8. see Suppl.—9. *al-Kalim al-jawāmiʿ fī bayān masʾalat al-uṣūlī li-Jamʿ al-jawāmiʿ*, completed in 1150/1737, Alex. Uṣūl 17 (5. See RAAD IX, 638, 7, which has *musaddala*).

28. Ismāʿīl b. Muḥammad Jarrāḥ b. ʿAbd al-Hādī al-ʿAjlūnī al-Jarrāḥī was born in ʿAjlūn around 1087/1676. Starting in 1100/1688, he studied for 13 years in
309 Damascus. | In 1119/1707 he travelled to Istanbul, and the following year, he obtained a professorship under the Dome of the Eagle in the Umayyad mosque, which he kept until his death in Muḥarram 1162/January 1749.

Mur. I, 259/72, *Tāj al-Ṭabaqāt* II, f. 73b. 1. *Kashf al-khafāt wa-muzīl al-ilbās ʿamma ʾshtahara min al-aḥādīth ʿalā alsinat al-nās*, after *al-Maqāṣid al-ḥasana*
399 by al-Sakhāwī (p. 44), | *al-Laʾālīʾ al-manthūra* by Ibn Ḥajar (p. 80), the *Tamyīz al-ṭayyib* by Ibn al-Daybaʿ (p. 44), and *al-Durar al-muntathira* by al-Suyūṭī (p. 187,$_{59}$), Berl. 1438.—2. *ʿIqd al-jawhar al-thamīn fī arbaʿīna ḥadīthan min aḥādīth sayyid al-mursalīn* ibid. 1532/4, BDMG 15, print. Alexandria 1301.—3. A collection of poems, Berl. 8036.—4. *al-Farāʾid wal-darārī fī tarjamat al-imām al-Bukhārī* Alex. Taʾr. 114.—5.–9. see Suppl. (6. Alex. Muṣṭ. Ḥad. 9).—10. *Shadha ʾl-rawḍ al-badīʿ al-mudrik fī ziyārat al-sayyida Zaynab wa-sayyidī Mudrik* Alex. Taʾr. 114.

29. Abu ʾl-Maʿālī Muḥammad b. ʿAbd al-Raḥmān b. Zayn al-ʿĀbidīn b. Zakariyyāʾ al-Ghazzī al-ʿĀmirī al-Qurashī al-Shāfiʿī was born in Damascus in 1096/1685, where he died as a Shāfiʿī *muftī* in 1167/1756.

Mur. IV, 53. 1. *Tashnīf al-masāmiʿ bi-tarājim rijāl Jamʿ al-jawāmiʿ* (p. 109), Br. Mus. Suppl. 646.—2. See Suppl.

30. Muḥammad b. Ḥasan b. Muḥammad b. Himmāt (zāde) al-Dimashqī, who died in 1175/1761, see Suppl.

1. *al-Fatḥ al-mubīn fī jawāz al-duʿāʾ wa-ihdāʾ thawāb al-aʿmāl li-sayyid al-mursalīn* Berl. 3929.—2. *Natījat al-naẓar fī ʿilm al-athar*, composed in 1161/1748, Cairo I, ^{1}348, ^{2}80, VII, 536.—3.–5. see Suppl. 423.

31. Muḥammad b. Muḥammad b. Muḥammad al-Ḥusaynī al-Ṭarābulusī al-Sandarūsī al-Ḥanafī, who died in 1176/1762.

1. *al-Kashf al-ilāhī ʿan sadīd al-ḍuʿf wal-mawḍūʿ wal-wāhī*, on weak *ḥadīth*, Cairo I, ^{1}387, ^{2}139.—2. The names of the participants in the Battle of Badr, Sbath 1165.

32. Ṭāhā b. Muhannā al-Jibrīnī al-Ḥalabī was born in 1084/1673. In 1131/1719 and 1161/1748 he travelled to the Hijaz and stayed in Mecca for two years before returning to his native country, where he died in 1178/1764.

Mur. II, 219. 1. *al-Qawl al-mukhtār fī ḥill al-ṣanṣār*, which is the same as a *dalaq* or weasel, not a *nims* or mongoose, which is also why one is allowed to eat it and to pray while covered by its fur, Berl. 3640.—2. *Ḍabṭ* (*Sharḥ*) *asmāʾ ahl Badr*, with some biographical information, composed in 1164 A.H., Munich 886f. 223b, Cairo [1]II, 222, Alex. Faw. 10, print. Būlāq 1294, see Suppl.

| 33. Abu ʾl-Ikhlāṣ Ḥasan b. ʿAbdallāh b. Muḥammad al-Bakhshī, who died in 1190/1776. 400

Al-Nūr al-jalī fi ʾl-nasab al-sharīf al-nabawī, completed in 1171/1758, Alex. Taʾr. 18, Cairo [2]V, 399 (which has al-Najāshī).

36. Nūr al-Dīn ʿAlī al-Mīqātī, who worked at the Umayyad mosque in Aleppo, died in 1192/1778.

Mawlid al-nabī Alex. Ḥad. 47, Taʾr. 18.

37. Yūsuf b. Saʿīd al-Safaṭī al-Mālikī wrote, in 1193/1779:

1. *Nuzhat al-arwāḥ fī baʿḍ awṣāf al-janna dār al-afrāḥ*, print. C. 1277, 1305.—2. See Suppl.—3. *Nuzhat al-ṭullāb fī-mā yataʿallaq bil-basmala min fann al-iʿrāb* Alex. Fun. 97,1.

| 38. Sulaymān b. Ṭāhā al-Akrāshī b. Abi ʾl-ʿAbbās Aḥmad b. Aḥmad b. Sulaymān al-Ḥuraythī al-Ḥusaynī al-Shāfiʿī studied at al-Azhar, lectured at various mosques, and then became a Qurʾān reciter at the *maqām* of Sayyida Nafīsa. He died in 1199/1785. 310

Jab. II, 97/8. *Ḥaẓīrat al-iʾtinās fī musalsalāt Sulaymān b. Ṭāhā b. Abi ʾl-ʿAbbās*, composed in 1189/1755, Cairo [1]II, 109.

39. Kamāl al-Dīn ʿAbd al-Karīm b. Aḥmad b. Nūḥ al-Ṭarābulusī wrote, in 1206/1792:

Fatḥ al-muʿīn ʿala ʾl-Durr al-thamīn fī naẓm asmāʾ al-Badriyyīn Qawala II, 242.

6 *Fiqh*

A The Ḥanafīs

1. Badr al-Dīn Abu ʾl-Yusr Muḥammad b. Muḥammad b. al-Ghars al-Miṣrī al-Ḥanafī, who died in 932/1525.

1. *al-Fawākih al-Badriyya fī 'l-aqḍiya al-ḥukmiyya* Cairo [1]III, 97, VII, 286, 669, 681, [2]I, 452, Garr. 1736, 2096,3, entitled *Adab al-qaḍā'* ibid. 2129,2.—2. *Risāla fī ḥukm al-mā' al-mustaʿmal* Garr. 1737.

2. Shihāb al-Dīn Abu 'l-ʿAbbās Aḥmad b. Yūnus al-Ḥanafī b. al-Shilbī (al-Shalabī), who died in 947/1540 in Cairo.

401 | 1. *Fatāwī*, collected by his grandson Nūr al-Dīn ʿAlī b. Muḥammad b. Aḥmad, d. 1010/1601, Garr. 1738, Cairo [1]VII, 10.—2. On a legal work left by him, his great-grandson Muḥammad (b. 7 Jumādā II 967/6 March 1560, d. in 1038/1628) wrote the commentary *Tajrīd fawā'id al-raqā'iq*, Gotha 1030 (which has a mistaken 'son' instead of 'great-grandson').—3. See Suppl.

3. Zayn al-ʿĀbidīn b. Ibrāhīm b. Nujaym al-Miṣrī al-Ḥanafī, who died on 8 Rajab 970/4 March 1563, see Suppl.

1. *Kitāb al-ashbāh wal-naẓā'ir*, on Ḥanafī law, Berl. 4616/7, Bonn 11, Munich 323, Leid. 1878, Paris 967/8, Br. Mus. 223, Ind. Off. 272, 1605/7, Algiers 1023, Garr. 1742/3, AS 1022/4, Yeni 360/4, NO 1387/1400, 1410, Köpr. 535/6, Alex. Fiqh Ḥan. 56, Cairo [1]IV, 5, [2]I, 401, Qawala I, 415, print. Calcutta 1240/1825.—Commentaries and glosses: a. Ibn Ḥabīb al-Ghazzī, d. 1005/1596, Yeni 380.—b. Muṣṭafā b. Khayr al-Dīn, d. 1022/1613, NO 1567.—c. Aḥmad b. Muḥammad al-Ḥamawī, d. 1090/1679, Yeni 396 (see below no. 19).—d. ʿAbd al-Ghanī al-Nābulusī, d. 1143/1731 (see below p. 345), Algiers 1024 (see Suppl.).—e. Muḥammad Abu 'l-Fatḥ al-Ḥanafī, Cairo [1]III, 2nd print. Alexandria 1289.—f.–p. see Suppl. (g. Qawala I, 314, Alex. Fiqh Ḥan. 14; i. Alex. Fiqh Ḥan. 14, 56; m. d. 1010/1601, Qawala I, 355; n. Alex. Fiqh Ḥan. 29; o. print. Istanbul 1920 [sic], Qawala I, 404, together with c., n.d. & n.p., Sarkis 953).—q. *Taḥqīq al-bāhir* by Muḥammad Hibatallāh b. Muḥammad b. Yaḥyā al-Tājī, tenth cent., Qawala I, 311.—r. Muḥammad b. Walī b. Rasūl Qarashahrī Nazīl Izmīr, Qawala I, 355.—*Tatimma fī 'l-furūq min al-Ashbāh wal-naẓā'ir* by the author himself in *Majmūʿa*, Istanbul 1290, Qawala I, 301.—2. a. *al-Fatāwī (Rasā'il) al-Zayniyya fī fiqh al-Ḥanafiyya*, compiled by his son after his death, Berl. 4831, M. or. oct. 3902, Gotha 1142, Algiers 1028, Garr. 1755, Yeni 638, Köpr. 665, AS 1568, Dam. Ibr. Pasha 531, Cairo [1]III, 52, 90.—b. *Tartīb fatāwi 'l-ʿallāma Zayn b. Nujaym al-Miṣrī* by Muḥammad b. ʿAbdallāh al-Tīmūrtāshī, d. 1004/1595 (see below no. 5), Cairo [1]III, 120, Qawala I, 337, print. Istanbul 1290, *Tartīb al-Fatāwī al-Zayniyya* by Muḥammad b. Aḥmad al-Khaṭīb, Alex. Fiqh Ḥan. 13, 59.—3. *al-Fawā'id al-Zayniyya fī fiqh al-Ḥanafiyya*, composed when he was a teacher at the Ṣarghitmishiyya, which is mentioned in the preface of no. 2a, AS 1183. |—4. *Bayān al-maʿāṣī*, brief listing of large and small
311

sins, Berl. 2642, Algiers 552, Alex. Fiqh Ḥan. 33, Patna II 547$_{,32}$. Commentary by Ismāʿīl b. Sinān al-Sīwāsī, | Garr. 1933, 2037$_{,5}$.—5. *Risāla fī rafʿ (dafʿ) al-ghishāʾ ʿan waqtay al-ʿaṣr wal-ʿishāʾ*, composed in 952/1545, Berl. 3592/3, Patna II, 355$_{,5422}$, 594$_{,2917,6}$.—6. *Risāla fī dhikr al-afʿāl allatī tufʿal fi ʾl-ṣalāt ʿalā qawāʿid al-madhāhib al-arbaʿa* Berl. 3594, Qawala I, 339, 543, Patna II, 354$_{,2542,2}$.—7. *al-Khayr al-bāqī fī jawāz al-wuḍūʾ min al-fasāqī*, composed in 951/1544 in less than half a day, Berl. 3637, Paris 976$_{,2}$, Alex. Fiqh Ḥan. 57, Cairo [1]III, 117, Qawala I, 329$_{,3}$, Patna II, 354$_{,2542,1}$, 543$_{,2917,2}$.—8. *Risāla fi ʾl-ṭalāq al-muṭlaq ʿala ʾl-ibrāʾ* Berl. 4668, Qawala I, 348, Patna II, 355$_{,341,10}$.—9. *Risāla fi ʾl-qawl al-naqī ʿala ʾl-muftarī*, on fixed duties of endowments and on the removal of their officials, Berl. 4771, Alex. Fiqh Ḥan. 57, Patna I, 355$_{,2542,4}$.—10. *Taḥrīr al-maqāl fī masʾalat al-istibdāl*, on whether endowments are permitted to swap property, Berl. 4771, Patna II, 353$_{,2511,9}$, 544$_{,2917,9}$.—11. *Risāla fī bayān al-iqṭāʿāt wa-maḥallihā*, on loans involving lands, Berl. 4832, Patna II, 545$_{,2917,10}$, Qawala I, 340.—12. *Risāla fī ṣūrat faskh al-ijāra al-ṭawīla*, on the annulment of rental contracts, Berl. 4833, Qawala I, 344, Patna II, 544$_{,2917,1}$, 547$_{,2917,2}$.—13. Two fatwas, Berl. 4834/5.–14. *Risāla fi ʾl-rushwa wa-aqsāmihā*, on bribing judges, ibid. 4956, Qawala I, 345, Patna II, 355$_{,2542,11}$, 544$_{,2917,11}$.—15. *Risāla fī ṭalab al-yamīn*, on the oath of purgation in court depositions, Berl. 4961, Qawala I, 348.—16. *al-Tuḥfa al-marḍiyya fi ʾl-arāḍi ʾl-Miṣriyya*, a fatwa on the conditions surrounding depositions in Egypt, Berl. 5623, Vienna 919$_{,2}$, no. 6 of his *Rasāʾil*, completed by his son Aḥmad, Qawala I, 310, Patna II, 355$_{,2542,5}$.—17. *Risāla fi ʾl-ṭaʿn wal-ṭāʿūn*, on the occasion of the plague ravaging Egypt in 950/1543, Berl. 6372, Qawala I, 347, Patna II, 355$_{,2541,11}$, 544$_{,2917,10}$.—18. *Risāla fī iqāmat al-qāḍī al-taʿzīr ʿalā ahl al-tazwīr* Cairo [1]VII, 67, Qawala I, 339, Patna II, 385$_{,2541,13}$, 545$_{,2917,10}$.—19. *Risāla fi ʾl-ḥukm bi-lā taqaddum daʿwā wa-khuṣūma* Cairo VII, 681, Patna II, 547$_{,2917,35}$.—20. *Fatḥ al-ghaffār, sharḥ Manār al-anwār* p. 250.—21. *al-Baḥr al-rāʾiq, sharḥ Kanz al-daqāʾiq* p. 252.—22. *Mukhtaṣar al-Taḥrīr li-Ibn al-Humām* p. 99.—23. *Ḥāshiyat Jāmiʿ al-fuṣūlayn*, collected by his son Aḥmad, p. 290.—24.–49. see Suppl. (24. Ind. Off. 1462, Qawala I, 300, commentary Patna I, 75$_{,771}$; 25. Qawala I, 343; 27. ibid. I, 343, Alex. Fiqh Ḥan. 28; 31. Patna II, 545$_{,2917,12}$; 35. ibid. 546$_{,2917,28}$; 36. Qawala I, 343$_{,37}$, ibid. I, 340; 38. ibid. 341, Patna II, 545$_{,2917,15}$; 39. Patna II, 545$_{,2917,17}$; 41. ibid. | 546$_{,2017,24}$; 42. ibid. $_{25}$; 47. ibid. 355$_{,2542,5}$, 545$_{,2917,5}$).—50. *Risāla fī ḥukm sharṭ al-waqf lil-wāqif al-ziyāda wal-nuqṣān li-nafsih* Patna II, 545$_{,2917,19}$.—51. *Risāla fī bayān al-ʿushr wal-kharāj* ibid. 356$_{,2542,12}$.—52. *Risāla fī ḥukm sharṭ waqf Qānṣūh Ghūrī* ibid. 14, 546$_{,2917,21}$, Qawala II, 346.—53. *Risālat waqf al-walad aw walad al-walad* Patna II, 356$_{,2542,15}$, 545$_{,2917,14,22}$.—54. *Risālat al-tamassuk bi-ṣarīḥ lafẓ al-waqf* ibid. 356$_{,2542,16}$.—55. *Risālat man qāla mā tazawwajtu ʿala ʾmraʾatī hādhihi fa-hiya ṭalāq* ibid. $_{17}$, 545$_{,2917,7}$, 546$_{,2917,27}$.—56. *Risālat fisq shahādat al-shuhūd alladhīna shahidū ʿala ʾl-riqq ʿinda l-ṭahāra*

402 403

ibid. 356,$_{2542,18}$.—57. Eleven further treatises, ibid. 357/819–29.—58. *Risāla fī-mā yubṭil daʿwā muddaʿin min qawl wa-fiʿl* ibid. 547,$_{279,30}$.—59. *Risāla fi ʾl-jināya* ibid. $_{37}$.—60. *Risāla fī masʾala min kitāb al-daʿwā* ibid. $_{38}$.—61. *Risāla fī ḥudūd al-fiqh* ibid. $_{39}$.—61. *Risāla fī isqāṭ al-ḥaqq* ibid. $_{50}$.—62. *Risāla fi ʾl-muḥāḍarāt* ibid. 545,$_{2917,20}$.—63. *Risāla fi ʾl-waqf* ibid. 546,$_{2917,23}$.—64. *Risāla fī qawlihim idhā rufiʿa ilayhi ḥukm ḥākim amḍāhu in lam yukhālif al-Kitāb wal-sunna* ibid. $_{26}$.—65. *Risāla fi ʾkhtilāf naẓar al-awqāf* ibid. 547,$_{30}$.—66. *Risāla fī bayān mabdaʾ al-waqf* ibid. $_{31}$.—67. *Risāla fi ʾl-istījāb wa-mā yatafarrad ʿalayhi min al-masāʾil* ibid. $_{33}$.—68. *Risāla fi ʾl-nadhr bil-taṣadduq* ibid. $_{34}$.—69. *Risāla fī sharṭ kitāb waqf Khāʾir Bek al-Nāṣirī* Qawala I, 346.—70. *Risāla fī masʾalat istiʾjār al-safīna* Patna II, 545,$_{2917,18}$.—71. *al-Wuṣūl ilā qawāʿid al-uṣūl* Qawala I, 301.—72. *Risāla fi ʾl-safīna idhā ghariqat etc.* ibid. 345 (= 70 ?).—73. *Risāla fi ʾstiʿdāl al-waqt* ibid. 338.—74. *Risāla fi ʾl-istiṣḥāb* ibid.—75. *Risāla fi ʾmraʾatin aqarrat ʿanhu ḥākim mālikī* (sic) *etc.* Patna II, 355,$_{2542,8}$.—His son wrote a *khuṭba* to his *Rasāʾil*, Patna II, 543,$_{2917,1}$.

4. His student Muḥammad b. ʿAbdallāh al-ʿArabī wrote, in 986/1577:

1. *Muʿīn al-muftī ʿalā jawāb al-mustaftī* Köpr. 692, Alex. Fiqh Ḥan. 65 (attributed to no. 5, likewise in Esad 2212), Cairo ^{1}III, 133, ^{2}I, 464.—2. See Suppl.

4a. ʿUmar b. Muḥammad b. ʿIwaḍ al-Shāmī, see Suppl.

Niṣāb al-iḥtisāb see Suppl., Ind. Off. 1693/5, Leningr. Un. Or. 260 (Krakčovsky, *Bibl. Vost.* 1934, 101/2), MS Massignon, see Gaudefroy Demombynes *JA* 230 (1938), 451, Alex. Fiqh Ḥan. 70, Fun. 186, Qawala I, 404, A. Taymūr, *RAAD* XII, 57.

404 5. Shams al-Dīn Muḥammad b. ʿAbdallāh b. Shihāb al-Dīn Aḥmad | al-Tīmūrtāshī al-Ghazzī al-Ḥanafī (see above p. 390) studied in his hometown of Gaza and in Cairo where he went four times, the last of which was in 998/1590. He died in 1004/1595.

Muḥ. IV, 18/20. 1. *Tanwīr al-abṣār wa-jāmiʿ al-biḥār*, a compendium on Ḥanafī *furūʿ* composed in 995/1587, Berl. 4620/1, Ms. or qu. 2078, Gotha 1034/6 (where other MSS are listed), Br. Mus. 221, Ind. Off. 273/4, 1687, Algiers 1029, 1325,$_3$, Yeni 379, NO 1570/6, Köpr. 544/5, Dam. Ibr. Pāshā 500, Garr. 1756, Alex. Fiqh Ḥan. 14, Cairo ^{1}III, 28, Calcutta 10, no. 1124, Patna II, 87,$_{884,8}$.—Commentaries: a. Self-commentary *Minaḥ al-ghaffār* Berl. 4622, Garr. 1757, Yeni 431, Cairo ^{1}III, 138, Alex. Fiqh Ḥan. 67.—Glosses: α *Lawāʾiḥ al-anwār ʿalā Minaḥ al-ghaffār* by Khayr al-Dīn al-Ramlī, d. 1081/1670, Qawala I, 386.—β *Natāʾij al-afkār ʿalā*

Minaḥ al-ghaffār by Najm al-Dīn b. Khayr al-Dīn al-Ramlī, ibid. 403.—b. *al-Durr al-mukhtār* by ʿAlāʾ al-Dīn b. ʿAlī b. Muḥammad al-Ḥaṣkafī, d. 1088/1677, an abbreviation of his *Khazāʾin al-asrār wa-badāʾiʿ al-afkār* or *al-Taḥrīr ʿala ʾl-Tanwīr* (this in Alex. Fun. 107, 4), Berl. 4623/5, Br. Mus. 222, Ind. Off. 4571 (*JRAS* 1939, 364), Garr. 1758/9, Algiers 1030/2, NO 1578/9, Cairo ^{1}III, 47.—Glosses: *α* on the *Dībāja* by Muḥammad b. ʿUmar b. ʿAbd al-Jalīl (see Suppl. II, 696, 9; 962, 40), Berl. 4626.—*β Iṣlāḥ al-isfār ʿan wujūh baʿḍ mukhaddarāt al-Durr al-mukhtār* by al-Jabartī, d. 1188/1774 (see below, p. 359), ibid. 4627 (fragment), Garr. 1760, Cairo ^{1}VII, 387.—*γ* Saʿdī Efendi (see below, p. 433), Berl. 4628.—*δ* Ibrāhīm al-Ḥalabī, d. 1190/1776, Algiers 1033, Cairo ^{1}III, 8.—*ε* Ibn ʿĀbidīn, d. 1252/1836, Cairo ^{1}III, 52.—*ζ*, *τ* see Suppl. (*ζ* Qawala I, 323, *η* ibid.). *ν* Aḥmad b. Muḥammad al-Ṭaḥṭāwī, d. 1231/1816, Ind. Off. 1715/6, Bank. XIX, 2, 50. |—2. *ʿUmdat al-ḥukkām* Berl. 4802.— 312
3. *al-Wāfī fi ʾl-uṣūl*, based on the example of the *Kitāb al-tamhīd* of al-Asnawī (p. 111), Cairo ^{1}II, 269, ^{2}I, 397.—4. *Tuḥfāt al-aqrān (fi ʾl-fiqh)*, an *urjūza*, Alex. Fiqh Ḥan. 9, with the commentary *Mawāhib al-mannān*, Alex. Fiqh Ḥan. 64, Cairo ^{1}II, 140, ^{2}I, 131.—5. *ʿIqd al-jawāhir al-nayyirāt fī bayān khaṣāʾiṣ al-kirām al-ʿashara al-thiqāt* Cairo ^{1}VII, 155.—6. *Fatāwī* ibid. III, 88, 119, Qawala I, 375, Alex. Fiqh Ḥan. 40, 55.—7.–11. see Suppl.—12. *Fayḍ al-mustafīḍ fī masāʾil al-tafwīḍ* Alex. Fiqh Ḥan. 45, Qawala I, 381.

6. ʿAlī b. Muḥammad b. ʿAlī b. Ghānim al-Maqdisī al-Khazrajī al-Ṭūrī Nūr al-Dīn was born in Cairo in 920/1514 | where he became a professor at the madrasa of 405
the vizier Süleymān Pāshā and Sultan Ḥasan. He was regarded as the head of the Ḥanafīs during his lifetime. He died on 18 Jumādā II 1004/19 February 1596.

Muḥ. III, 180/5, al-Khafājī, *Rayḥ.* 157. 1. *Nūr al-shamʿa fī bayān zuhr al-jumʿa* Berl. 3596, 3811, Leid. 1881, AS 1174, Alex. Fun. 173,$_{1}$, Cairo ^{1}III, 122 (wrongly attributed by von Gosche to al-Ghazzālī, no. 30).—2. *Bughyat al-murtād li-taṣḥīḥ al-ḍād* Berl. 7025, Fātiḥ, Waqf Ibr. 32,$_{4}$, ʿUm. 124, Alex. Lugha 5, Cairo ^{2}II, 5, Patna I, 11,$_{95}$, lith. at the end of Abū Ḥayyān's *Muqābasāt*, no place or date.—3. *Radʿ al-rāghib ʿan ṣalāt al-raghāʾib* Cairo ^{1}VI, 69, ^{2}I, 422.—4. *al-Badīʿa al-muhimma fī bayān naqḍ al-qisma maʿa ʾl-ishāra ila ʾl-taswiya bayna ʿibāratay al-Subkī wal-Khaṣṣāf wa-bayān al-radd ʿalā ṣāḥib al-Ashbāh wal-tanbīh ʿalā mā waqaʿa lahu min al-khaṭaʾ wal-ishtibāh* Gar. 2002,$_{3}$, Cairo ^{1}III, 112, ^{2}I, 405.—5. Expert opinion on three assertions by some *wāʿiẓ*: a. that Muḥammad did not die; b. that Abraham proved himself an infidel in the Qurʾānic verse *hādhā rabbī*; c. that the plague is the result of foul air and not a divine punishment, Cairo ^{1}VII, 68.—6. See Suppl.—7.–10. See Suppl. 395, 9a,$_{2/5}$.—11. *al-Nasama al-nafsiyya*, with a commentary, Makram 43.

7. Sharaf al-Dīn b. ʿAbd al-Qādir b. Ḥabīb al-Ghazzī, who died in 1005/1496.

Muḥ. II, 223. 1. *Ḥāshiya ʿala ʾl-Ashbāh wal-naẓāʾir*, see above no. 3, 1. a.—2., 3. See Suppl. (2. Garr. 2002, 10).

7a. Sirāj al-Dīn ʿUmar b. Luṭf al-Maqdisī, who died in 1003/1595.

Risālat irsāl al-ghamāma bi-mā ḥālla min al-ẓalāma Alex. Fun. 178,$_2$.

8. Taqī al-Dīn b. ʿAbd al-Qādir al-Tamīmī al-Dārī al-Ghazzī was a *qāḍī* in Fuwwa, near Rosetta, who died in the prime of life on 5 Jumādā II 1010/2 December 1601 (or, according others, in 1005/1596).

Muḥ. I, 479, Wüst. *Gesch.* 544. 1. *al-Ṭabaqāt al-saniyya fī tarājim al-Ḥanafiyya* Berl. 10029 (part 2), Vienna 1189, Yeni 862, Köpr. 1113, AS 3295, Ḥamīd. 969, Welīeddīn 1601.—2. See Suppl.

406 | 9. Muḥammad b. ʿUmar Shams al-Dīn b. Sirāj al-Dīn al-Ḥānūtī al-Miṣrī, born in 927/1521, was a Ḥanafī *muftī* in Cairo who died in 1010/1601.

Muḥ. IV, 76. 1. *Ijābat al-sāʾilīn bi-fatwa ʾl-mutaʾakhkhirīn* Cairo ^{1}III, 2.—2. *Majmaʿ al-fatāwī* Garr. 1761, Alex. Fiqh Ḥan. 41, Cairo ^{1}III, 88.

10. Ṣāliḥ b. Maḥmūd al-Ghazzī al-Ḥanafī wrote, in 1045/1635 (see Suppl. 9a):

2. *Ṣūrat suʾāl wa-jawābuhu* Qawala I, 368.

313 | 11. ʿAbd al-Karīm b. Walī al-Dīn Yūsuf b. Walī al-Dīn al-Ḥanafī wrote, in 1059/1649:

Tabyīn al-kalām fī ʾl-qiyām wal-ṣiyām Munich 171.

12. Abu ʾl-Ikhlāṣ Ḥasan b. ʿAmmār al-Wafāʾī al-Shurunbulālī al-Ḥanafī was a professor at al-Azhar in Cairo and died in 1069/1658.

Muḥ. II, 38, followed by *Khiṭ. jad.* XII, 117. 1. *Arbaʿūna ḥadīthan fī faḍl al-salāṭīn wal-ḥukkām al-muqsiṭīn*, completed in 1069/1658, Berl. 1530.—2. *al-Naẓm al-mustaṭāb li-ḥukm al-qirāʾa fī ṣalāt al-jināza bi-umm al-kitāb*, a detailed proof that it is permissible to read the *Fātiḥa* during a prayer over the corpse of a

deceased, composed in 1065/1655, Berl. 2692.—3. *Risāla fi 'l-shahāda*, completed on 3 Jumādā I 1058/27 May 1648, Gotha 16,$_1$.—4. *Nūr al-īḍāh wa-najāt al-arwāḥ*, on duties relating to religious worship, Berl. 3534, Paris 1158, 1230,$_6$, Alex. Fiqh Ḥan. 71, 128,$_4$, Cairo ^{1}III, 122, 144, VII, 145, 511, Qawala I, 415. Abstract Leid. 1895.—Commentaries: a. Self-commentary, *Imdād al-fattāḥ*, composed in 1046/1636, Garr. 1764, Alex. Fiqh Ḥan. 7, Cairo ^{1}III, 7, abstract *Marāqi 'l-falāḥ* Berl. 3535, Algiers 611, Cairo ^{1}III, 128, Qawala I, 394, Patna I, 78,$_{790}$, print. C. 1305, 1308, 1321.—Glosses: Aḥmad b. Muḥammad al-Ṭahṭāwī, d. 1231/1816, Cairo ^{1}III, 38, print. Būlāq 1269, 1279, C. 1304, 1318.—b. *Sullam al-falāḥ* by ʿUthmān b. Yaʿqūb al-Kumākhī, composed in 1160/1747, Alex. Fiqh Ḥan. 31 (see Suppl.).—5. *Durr al-kunūz lil-ʿabd al-rājī an yafūz*, a *qaṣīda* on prayer, with commentary, Gotha 768, Cairo ^{1}VII, 82.—6. *al-Masāʾil al-bahiyya al-zakiyya ʿala 'l-masāʾil al-ithnay ʿashariyya*, on cases in which prayers are invalid, completed in 1060/1650, Berl. 3608, Alex. Fiqh Ḥan. 67, 21 | (*Rasāʾil*).—7. *Saʿādat ahl al-Islām bil-muṣāfaḥa* 407
ʿaqiba 'l-ṣalāt wal-salām, on shaking hands after prayer, completed in 1060/1650, Berl. 3609, Cairo ^{1}III, 122.—8. *al-Aḥkām al-mukhiṣṣa* (*mulakhkhaṣa*) *fī ḥukm māʾ al-ḥimmiṣa*, composed in 1059/1649, on the fact that, if a chickpea is used as a headrest and liquid issues from it, the required ritual purity for prayer is not adversely affected, Berl. 3638, Cairo ^{1}III, Alex. Fun. 162,$_3$.—9. *al-Taḥqīqāt al-Qudsiyya wal-nafaḥāt al-Raḥmāniyya al-Ḥasaniyya*, 60 legal essays compiled at the instigation of his teacher al-Muḥibbī, d. 1041/1631, Berl. 5002, Algiers 9, AS 1184, Cairo ^{1}III, 20/6, Patna I, 81,$_{825}$.—10. *Ḥifẓ al-aṣgharayn ʿan itʿiqād man zaʿama anna 'l-ḥarām lā yataʿaddā ilā dhimmatayn*, against the claim that prohibition and punishment for a transgression apply just to one person and not to two, viz. also to the person who, for example, profited by such an act, Berl. 5003.—11. *Tuḥfat al-akmal wal-humām al-muṣaddar li-bayān jawāz lubs al-aḥmar* Berl. 5461, Garr. 1765, Cairo ^{1}III, 19, VII, 47.—12. *Minnat al-jalīl fī qabūl qawl al-wakīl* Paris 1160,$_3$.—13. *al-ʿIqd al-farīd bi-bayān al-rājiḥ min al-khilāf fī jawāz al-taqlīd* Alex. Fun. 185,$_3$, Cairo ^{1}III, 80.—14. *Aḥsan al-aqwāl fi 'l-takhalluṣ ʿan maḥẓūr al-fiʿāl* Cairo ^{1}III, 112.—15. *Qahr al-milla al-kufriyya bil-adilla al-Muḥammadiyya li-takhrīb dayr al-maḥalla al-Jawwāniyya*, an inflammatory pamphlet against the Christians, Cairo ^{1}VI, 681, Patna II, 359,$_{4544,2}$.—16. *Marāqi 'l-saʿādāt*, on which a commentary, *Jawāhir al-kalām fī ʿaqāʾid ahl al-ḥaqq min al-anām* by ʿAbdallāh al-Ḥanafī, Cairo ^{1}II, 12.—17.–49. see Suppl.—50. *al-Durra al-yatīma fi 'l-ghanīma* Patna II, 359,$_{2544,1}$.—51. *Saʿādat al-mājid bi-ʿimārat al-masjid* ibid. $_3$.—52. *Taḥqīq al-aʿlām al-wāqifīn* ibid. $_4$.—53. *Ḥusām al-ḥukkām* ibid. $_5$.—54. *Taḥqīq al-sūdad* (?) *bishtirāṭ al-rubʿ wal-suknā fi 'l-waqf lil-walad* ibid. $_6$. Further treatises, ibid. $_{7/19}$.

314 | 13. Nūḥ Efendi b. Muṣṭafā al-Rūmī al-Miṣrī was born in Asia Minor, took up residence in Cairo, and died there in 1070/1659.

Muḥ. IV, 458. A biography by Yūsuf Efendi, composed in 1154/1741, Cairo ^{1}VII, 364, ^{2}V, 139. 1. *al-Qawl al-dāll ʿalā ḥayāt al-Khiḍr wa-wujūd al-abdāl* Cairo ^{1}II, 104, VII, 410, ^{2}I, 343.—2. *Risāla fī taʿaddud al-jumʿa fī miṣr wāḥid* Cairo ^{1}VII, 119.—
408 | 3. *al-Kalām al-masūq li-bayān masāʾil al-masbūq* ibid. 424.—4. *al-Ṣalāt al-rabbāniyya fī ḥukm man adraka rakʿa min al-thulāthiyya wal-rubāʿiyya* ibid. 433, Alex. Fiqh Ḥan 164, Fun. $67_{,10}$.—5. Five treatises, Cairo ^{1}VII, 471.—6. 10 treatises, ibid. 421/4.—7. 63 treatises, ibid. III, 5/8.—8.–14. see Suppl.

14. Yaḥyā b. Aḥmad b. ʿAwwād wrote, around 1070/1659:

Al-Nūr al-sāṭiʿ fī nafy al-ḥaraj ʿala ʾl-jāmiʿ, on whether one may, without solid grounds, change one's times of prayer or perform two prayers in one, Berl. 3610.

15. ʿUmar b. ʿUmar al-Dafrī al-Zuhrī al-Azharī al-Ḥanafī, a professor at al-Azhar, was blind for forty years, then spontaneously regained his eyesight. He died in 1079/1668.

Muḥ. III, 220. *Al-Durar* (*Durra*) *al-munīfa fī fiqh Abī Ḥanīfa*, composed in 1036/1626, Dresd. 98, Cairo ^{1}III, 47, self-commentary *al-Jawāhir al-nafīsa*, composed in 1046/1636, Gotha 1037, Munich 326, Paris $976_{,1}$, Cairo ^{1}III, 36, Garr. 1766.

16. Khayr al-Dīn b. Aḥmad b. Nūr al-Dīn ʿAlī b. Zayn al-Dīn b. ʿAbd al-Wahhāb al-Ayyūbī al-ʿUlaymī al-Fārūqī al-Ramlī was born in Ramla in 993/1585, and studied, from 1007/1598 onward, at al-Azhar in Cairo, where he first learnt Shāfiʿī and then Ḥanafī law. In 1013/1604 he returned to Ramla where he made a living from gardening and growing fruits. He died on 27 Ramaḍān 1081/8 February 1671.

Muḥ. III, 34/9, Biography Berl. 10143. 1. *al-Fatāwi ʾl-Khayriyya li-nafʿ al-bariyya*, collected by his son Muḥyi ʾl-Dīn, who was born in 1071/1660, and completed by Ibrāhīm b. Sulaymān al-Jīnīnī, d. 1108/1696, Berl. Ms. or. oct. 3905, Leid. 1894, Garr. 1767/8, Yeni 636/7, NO 1989/93, Zaouiyah El-Hamel, *Giorn. Soc. As. It.* X, 52, Cairo ^{1}III, 89, print. Būlāq 1300, 2 vols.—2. *al-Fawz wal-ghunm fī masʾalat al-sharīf min al-umm*, on whether descent via the father or the mother is more important for children, especially for the descendants of al-Ḥasan and al-Ḥusayn, composed in 1073/1662, Berl. 4730, Munich $884_{,6}$,

Alex. Fun. 68,$_{2}$.—3. *Muẓhir al-ḥaqāʾiq al-khafiyya min al-Baḥr al-rāʾiq Sharḥ Kanz al-daqāʾiq* p. 252.—5. See Suppl.—6. *Risāla fī jawāb ʿan suʾāl Yaḥyā Efendi,* Qawala I, 337.—7. *Masʾalat* | *al-inṣāf fī ʿadam al-farq bayna masʾalatay al-Subkī* 409
wal-Ḥaṣṣāf ibid. 395.

16a. ʿAlī Efendi b. al-Shaykh ʿUthmān al-Ḥanafī al-Khalwatī al-Ḍarīr Nāẓim al-Durar, who was a *muftī* in Tripoli, wrote, in 1069/1659:

Al-Ḥūr al-ʿīn, urjūza fi ʾl-madhhab, Alex. Fiqh Ḥan. 23.

16b. Amīn al-Dīn Muḥammad b. ʿAlī b. ʿAbd al-ʿĀlī al-Ḥanafī wrote, before 1095/1684 (the date of the manuscript):

Fatāwī Qawala I, 374.

17. Yāsīn b. Muṣṭafā al-Faraḍī al-Māturīdī al-Biqāʿī al-Dimashqī al-Juʿfī al-Ḥanafī wrote, around 1095/1684:

| 1. *Nuṣrat al-mutagharribīn ʿani ʾl-awṭān ʿala ʾl-ẓalama wa-ahl al-ʿudwān*, on 315
the right to citizenship, in response to the oppression of foreign scholars in Damascus, Berl. 5629, ʿUm. 2746.—2.–4. see Suppl.

18. Muḥammad b. Ḥasan b. Aḥmad b. Abī Yaḥyā al-Kawākibī al-Ḥalabī was born in Aleppo in 1018/1609, studied there, became a *muftī*, and died in 1096/1685.

Muḥ. III, 437/9, Ṭabbākh, *Taʾrīkh Ḥalab* VI, 380. 1. *Irshād al-ṭālib, sharḥ Manẓūmat al-kawākib fi ʾl-uṣūl* p. 251.—2. *al-Fawāʾid al-samiyya, sharḥ al-Farāʾid (Fawāʾid) al-saniyya* I, 469.—3.–5. see Suppl. (4. See Ritter in *Türkiyat Mecmuasi* VII–VIII, 1945, p. 37 and 39).—6. *Risāla fī tafsīr qawlihi* sura 23,$_{53}$, Alex. Fun. 155,$_{4}$.—7. *Risāla fi ḥayāt al-nabī ṣlʿm fī qabrihi* ibid. Taʾr. 113.

19. Shihāb al-Dīn Abu ʾl-ʿAbbās Aḥmad b. Muḥammad Makkī al-Ḥamawī al-Ḥusaynī al-Ḥanafī, who died in 1098/1687.

Jab. I, 65, without a date. 1. *Ithbāt karāmāt al-awliyāʾ*, composed in 1091/1680, following a question by the grand vizier ʿAbd al-Raḥmān Pāshā, Berl. 3339, entitled *Nafaḥāt al-qurb wal-ittiṣāl bi-ithbāt al-taṣarruf li-awliyāʾ Allāh wal-karāma baʿd al-intiqāl* Garr. 1530, printed in *Majmūʿa* C. 1319[1] (Alex.

1 In Subkī, *Shifāʾ al-saqām fī ziyārat khayr al-anām*, C. 1318, p. 209/226 (Ritter).

410 Fun. 83, 3).—2. *al-Durr al-nafīs fī bayān nasab al-imām Muḥammad b. Idrīs*, | completed in 1089/1678, Berl. 10013, Cairo ^{1}VII, 597, ^{2}V, 178.—3. *Durar al-ʿibārāt wa-ghurar al-ishārāt fī taḥqīq maʿāni ʾl-istiʿārāt*, of which a *Dhayl* Cairo ^{1}IV, 136, ^{2}II, 196/7.—4. *Risāla fi ʾl-mabāḥith al-naḥwiyya wal-bayāniyya wal-fiqhiyya*, completed on 15 Shawwāl 1076/21 April 1666, Cairo ^{1}VII, 535.—5. *al-Durr al-manẓūm fī faḍl al-Rūm*, completed in 1095/1684, ibid. 597, ^{2}I, 115, entitled *Sharḥ al-ḥadīth fī faḍl al-Rūm* Garr. 611.—6. *Tanbīh al-ghabī ʿalā ḥukm kafālat al-ṣabī* Cairo ^{1}VII, 597.—7. *Sharḥ Kanz al-daqāʾiq* p. 252.—8.–17. see Suppl. (10. Garr. 1701).—18. *Ḥusn al-ibtihāj bi-ruʾyat al-nabī ṣlʿm rabbahu bi-ʿayn baṣarihi fī laylat al-miʿrāj wal-isrāʾ* Alex. Fun. 83,5.—19. *al-ʿUqūd al-ḥisān fī qawāʿid madhhab al-Nuʿmān*, with a commentary entitled *Farāʾid al-luʾluʾ wal-marjān*, Qawala I, 381.—20. *Naẓm al-ḍawābiṭ al-fiqhiyya* Alex. Fiqh Ḥan. 54.—21. *Sharḥ al-Ashbāh* p. 401.

20. Ibrāhīm b. Sulaymān al-Azharī al-Ḥanafī, fl. ca. 1100/1688.

1. *al-Risāla al-mukhtāra fī manāhi ʾl-ziyāra*, on the belief that, while visiting graves, one may not touch, kiss, or lie down on them, Berl. 2964.—2. *Raḥīq al-firdaws fī ḥukm al-rīq wal-baws*, on spittle, kissing, and hugging, ibid. 5596.

21. Ḥasan b. Maḥmūd al-Maqdisī al-Luddī al-Māturīdī al-Ḥanafī, fl. ca. 1100/1688.

1. *Rafʿ al-ishtibāh ʿan masʾalat al-muḥādhāh*, on how men and women should be placed in rows during prayer, Berl. 3612.—2. A *qaṣīda* in praise of al-Munāwī, d. 1031/1622 (p. 393), ibid. 7992,3.—4. *Qurrat al-ʿayn muqaddimat awṣāf al-Mollā Ḥusayn*, 16 panegyric poems in the 16 metres on Mollā Ḥusayn Akhīzāde, d. 1043/1633, ibid. 4.

21b. Aḥmad b. Ibrāhīm b. ʿAbd al-Ghanī al-Sarūjī, d. 710/1310, see Suppl.

Al-Ṣafadī, *Aʿyān al-ʿaṣr* AS 2968, 49/50.

22. Aḥmad al-Qalānisī, who died in 1132/1720.

Tahdhīb al-wāqiʿāt Yeni 381, AS 1078.

23. Muḥammad b. Muḥammad b. Maḥmūd al-Azharī al-Ḥanafī wrote, in 1164/1751:

1. *al-Jawāhir al-bahiyya fi ʾl-farāʾiḍ wal-waṣiyya* Cairo ^{1}III, 304.—2. *Risālatān fī irth dhawi ʾl-arḥām* Garr. 1850.

| 24. Abu ʾl-Suʿūd Aḥmad b. Muḥammad b. Ḥasan al-Kawākibī (see no. 18) was 411
a *muftī* in Aleppo and died in 1137/1725.

Al-Ṭabbākh, *Taʾrīkh Ḥalab* VI, 465 (which has Abu ʾl-Suʿūd b. Aḥmad). *Fatāwī* Alex. Fiqh Ḥan. 43.

25. Muḥammad b. Ibrāhīm b. Muḥammad al-Shahīr bi-Shaykh Muḥammad al-Fallāḥ wrote, in 1151/1738 in Aleppo:

Risāla fī ṣuwar masāʾil al-riḍāʿ ʿala ʾl-madhāhib al-arbaʿa Alex. Fiqh Ḥan. 28.

| B The Mālikīs 316

1. Abu ʾl-Ḥasan Aḥmad b. Nāṣir al-Dīn b. Muḥammad b. Muḥammad b. Muḥammad b. Khalaf b. Jibrīl al-Manūfī al-Miṣrī al-Shādhilī, who was born on 3 Ramaḍān 857/8 September 1453, was a student of both al-Sanhūrī and al-Suyūṭī. He died in Cairo on 14 Ṣafar 939/8 October 1530.

Galtier, *Bull. de l'Inst. fr. d'archéologie or.* V, 135 (following the *Ḥāshiya* of al-ʿAdawī). 1. *Manāsik b. Jibrīl* Cairo [1]III, 184, [2]I, 492.—2. *Tuḥfat al-muṣallī ʿalā madhhab al-imām Mālik* ibid. VII, 111.—3.–7. see Suppl. (3. Commentaries: a. C. 1319, on which *al-Ifāḍāt al-ilāhiyya li-ḥall al-Zurqānī ʿala ʾl-ʿIzziyya* by Muḥammad b. ʿAbd Rabbihi b. ʿAlī al-ʿAzīzī al-Shilbī al-Mālikī b. al-Sitt, completed in 1135/1723, Makram 4; b. ibid. 50; 7. Būlāq 1321, with the commentary *al-Kawākib al-durriyya* of ʿAbd al-Sayyid al-Sharnūbī al-Azharī in the margin (his works are listed in Galtier, op. cit., 136/7).

2. Muḥammad b. Ibrāhīm al-Tatāʾī al-Mālikī Abū ʿAbdallāh Shams al-Dīn was a student of Sibṭ al-Māridīnī (see below p. 357) who became chief *qāḍī* of Egypt, but subsequently left this post to devote himself entirely to writing. He died in 942/1535.

Khiṭ. jad. X, 31. *Sharḥ Mukhtaṣar al-Khalīl* p. 102.

3. Badr al-Dīn Muḥammad b. Yaḥyā b. ʿUmar al-Qarāfī al-Miṣrī al-Mālikī was born on 17 Ramaḍān 939/25 April 1532 and died on 22 Ramaḍān 1009/28 March 1601.

1. *Risāla fī jawāb suʾāl* Cairo [1]III, 166.—2. *Risāla fī makhraj ḥadīth Lawlāka mā khalaqtu ʾl-aflāk* ibid. VII, 58.—| 3. *al-Durar al-munīfa fi ʾl-farāgh ʿani ʾl-waẓīfa* 412
ibid. 247, [2]I, 482.—4. *al-Jawāhir al-muntathira fī hibat al-sayyid li-umm al-walad*

wal-mudabbara ibid. 248, Garr. 1836.—5. *Taḥqīq al-ibāna fī ṣiḥḥat isqāṭ mā lam yajib min al-ḥiḍāna*, completed 15 Shawwāl 975/14 April 1568, Cairo ^{1}VII, 248.—6. *Iḥkām al-taḥqīq bi-aḥkām al-taʿlīq* ibid.—7. *al-Durar al-nafāʾis fī shaʾn al-kanāʾis* ibid.—8.–11. see Suppl.

4. Abu ʾl-Nūr Badr al-Dīn b. ʿAbd al-Raḥmān al-Mālikī wrote, in 1010/1601:

1. *al-Qawl al-murtaḍā fī aḥkām al-qaḍā* Cairo ^{1}III, 180 (autograph).—2. *al-Abwāb wal-fuṣūl fī aḥkām shahādat al-ʿudūl* ibid.—3. *al-Qawl al-muʿtabar ʿalā muqaddimat al-Mukhtaṣar* p. 102.

5. Abu ʾl-Imdād Burhān al-Dīn Ibrāhīm b. Ibrāhīm b. Ḥasan b. ʿAlī al-Laqānī (see p. 395) al-Mālikī, a professor at al-Azhar in Cairo, died in 1041/1631 on the way back from Mecca.[1]

Muḥ. I, 6/9, Afrānī, *Ṣafwa* 59. 1. *Jawharat al-tawḥīd*, in *rajaz* verse, Berl. 2044/5, Gotha 693, Br. Mus. 169$_{,1}$, Algiers 596$_{,6}$, 701/2, Garr. 1565, Alex. Fun. 147$_{,10}$, Cairo ^{1}II, 13, ^{2}I, 171, Qawala I, 166, Patna II, 379$_{,2564,2}$.—Commentaries: a. Self-commentary *Hidāyat al-murīd* Berl. 2046, Ms. or. oct. 3914, Gotha 694/5, Algiers
317 701$_{,3}$, 704, Alex. Tawḥīd 47, Qawala I, 212. |—Glosses by his son ʿAbd al-Salām, d. 1078/1668 (p. 395), *Hadiyyat al-murīd* Berl. 2047, Gotha 696, Alex. Tawḥīd 3, 14, 40, Makram 1.—b. his son ʿAbd al-Salām: *α* the larger commentary *Itḥāf al-murīd* Berl. 2048/9, Brill M. 117, BDMG 31, Munich 148/9, Hamb. Or. Sem. 62, Upps. 399, Paris 1281/2, Algiers 705/7, Constantine *JA* 1854 II, 441, no. 93, Sarajevo 172 (?); Glosses: *αα* ʿAlī b. Aḥmad al-ʿAdawī (no. 18), *Taqyīdāt*, Berl. Ms. or. oct. 3916, Algiers 1431$_{,3}$, Makram 23, print. Būlāq 1282.—*ββ* Aḥmad b. Muḥammad al-Suḥaymī, Algiers 708/9.—*γγ* Muḥammad al-Amīr, d. 1232/1816, Gotha 700, Makram 15, print. C. 1282, 1304, 1305, 1309.—*δδ* Ibrāhīm al-Bājūrī, d. 1277/1861 (see below p. 487), Būlāq 1281, C. 1306, 1310, 1314.—*εε, ζζ* see Suppl. (*ζζ* anon. *Fatḥ al-waṣīd* Alex. Tawḥīd 26, without title Brill. M. 243).—*ηη* Aḥmad b.
413 Muḥammad | al-Ṣāwī al-Mālikī, d. 1241/1825, Alex. Tawḥīd 12.—*β* the smaller commentary *Irshād al-murīd*, written before the larger, Yeni 743, Cairo ^{1}II, 3.—c. *Fatḥ al-qarīb* by ʿAbd al-Raḥmān al-Ujhūrī, ca. 1080/1669 (p. 428), Berl. 2050.—d., with a commentary in Malay, C. 1309; a (-nother?) commentary in Malay, printed in Mecca (Snouck Hurgronje II, 387).—e.–g. see Suppl.—h. *al-Manhaj al-ḥamīd* by Muḥammad b. ʿAbd al-Raḥīm b. Ibrāhīm al-Ḥanafī, Alex. Tawḥ. 46.—i. *al-Minhāj al-sadīd* by Muḥammad al-Ḥanīfī, d. 1342/1923 (al-Ṭabbākh

1 Snouck Hurgronje, *Mekka* II, 387 mistakenly described him as an Indian; in Mecca he is considered holy and is called, after his major work, Walī Jawhar (ibid. 66).

Ta'r. Ḥalab VII, 681).—2. *al-Fuṣūl fi 'l-fiqh* Cairo [1]VII, 110.—3. *Naṣīḥat al-ikhwān bijtināb al-dukhān*, against the smoking of tobacco, completed in 1025/1616, Gotha 2102,$_{3}$, Alex. Mawāʿiẓ 41, Fun. 157,$_{2}$, Cairo [1]III, 178, 187, VII, 123.—5. *Bahjat al-maḥāfil sharḥ al-Shamā'il* I, 170.—6. *Sharḥ al-Taqrīb wal-taysīr* ibid. 441.

6. ʿAbd al-Mutaʿālī b. ʿAbd al-Malik b. Abī Ḥafs ʿUmar al-Qurashī al-Jaʿfarī al-Qādirī al-Būtījī al-Mālikī wrote, in 1065/1655:

Qalā'id al-durr wal-jawhar fī farḍ al-jumʿa wattikhādh al-minbar Cairo [1]VII, 686, [2]I, 489.

7. Nūr al-Dīn Abu 'l-Irshād ʿAlī b. Muḥammad Zayn al-ʿĀbidīn b. ʿAbd al-Raḥmān al-Ujhūrī al-Mālikī, who was born in Ujhūr, north of Cairo, in 967/1559, became a Mālikī Shaykh al-Azhar. He lost his eyesight towards the end of his life as a result of a headwound inflicted by a student after he had refused to pronounce a fatwa on the latter's re-marriage to a divorcée. He died on 1 Jumādā I 1066/26 February 1656.

Muḥ. III, 157/60, Afrānī, *Ṣafwa* 126, *Khiṭ. jad.* VIII, 83. 1. *Manẓūma fī uṣūl al-dīn*, with a commentary, Berl. 1845, Paris 1283/4, Cairo [1]II, 25, [2]I, 189.—2. *al-Nūr al-wahhāj fi 'l-kalām ʿala 'l-isrā' wal-miʿrāj* Berl. 2610, Garr. 665, Cairo I, 447.—3. *Risāla fī faḍā'il shahr Ramaḍān* Cairo [2]II, 207, VI, 161, [2]I, 338, print. C. 1277.—4. *Risāla fī faḍl yawm al-ʿĀshūrā'* Paris 3244,$_{7}$, Alex Fun. 216, Cairo [1]VI, 201.—5. *Hidāyat al-mannān fī faḍā'il laylat al-niṣf min Shaʿbān* Cairo [1]VI, 216, VII, 435, [2]I, App. 49.—6. *Aḥkām al-khunthā*, legal opinions on hermaphrodites in 45 *rajaz* verses, Berl. 5001.—7. *Risāla fi 'l-mughārasa wa-aḥkāmihā*, on lease contracts, | Cairo [1]III, 166.—8. *Ghāyat al-bayān li-ḥill shurb mā lā yughayyib* 414
al-ʿaql min al-dukhān Gotha 2100/2, Cairo [1]III, 174.—9. *Risāla fī faḍā'il al-qahwa wa-manāfiʿihā* Gotha 2101,$_{2}$, = *Muqaddima fī faḍl al-bunn* Cairo [1]VII, 107.—10. *Risāla fī-mā yajūzu ṭarḥuhu min al-safīna ʿinda khawf al-gharaq* ibid. 305.
|—11. *al-Ajwiba al-muḥarrara li-as'ilat al-barara* Cairo [1]III, 153.—12. Verses on 318
the seven causes of ageing, Berl. 7986,$_{2}$.—13. *Sharḥ al-Risāla* I, 187.—14. *Sharḥ Alfiyyat al-ʿIraqī* p. 78.—15. *Sharḥ al-Mukhtaṣar* p. 102.—16.–20. see Suppl.

8. ʿAbd al-Laṭīf b. Sharaf al-Dīn al-ʿAshmāwī al-Mālikī wrote, in 1067/1653:

1. *al-Minaḥ al-samāwiyya* (*Manẓūma fi 'l-fiqh*), with a commentary, composed in 1086/1675, Cairo [1]III, 172.—2. See Suppl.—3. *Ḥusn al-ṣanīʿ bi-sharḥ Nūr al-rabīʿ* p. 355.

9. Aḥmad b. Aḥmad al-Fayyūmī al-Gharqāwī (Gharqī) al-Mālikī, fl. ca. 1084/1673.

1. *Ḥusn al-sulūk fī maʿrifat ādāb al-mulk wal-mulūk* Berl. 5630, Garr. 2041,$_2$, Alex. Adab 36.—2. *Risāla fī masʾalat al-khuluww al-maʿmūl bihā ʿinda ʾl-Mālikiyya*, composed in 1084/1673, Garr. 1837 Cairo ^{1}III, 166.—3. *Kashf al-niqāb wal-rān ʿan wujūh mukhaddarāt asʾila taqaʿu fī baʿḍ suwar al-Qurʾān*, composed in 1061/1651, Cairo ^{1}I, 193, ^{2}I, 59.—4. *al-Qawl al-tāmm fī bayān aṭwār sayyidinā Ādam ʿam* Garr. 1507, Cairo V, ^{1}114, ^{2}298, print. C. 1278.

10. ʿAbd al-Bāqī b. Yūsuf al-Zurqānī, who was born in Cairo in 1020/1611, was a reciter of the Qurʾān at al-Azhar, and died on 24 Ramaḍān 1099/23 July 1688.

Al-Afrānī, *Ṣafwa* 204, Jab. I, 66, followed by *Khiṭ. jad.* XI, 93. 1. *Sharḥ Mukhtaṣar al-Khalīl* see p. 102.—2. *Sharḥ ʿalā sharḥ khuṭbat al-Khalīl* ibid.—3. *Risāla fi ʾl-kalām ʿalā idhā* Cairo ^{1}VII, 60, ^{2}II, 113.—4., 5. See Suppl.

11. Abū ʿAbdallāh Muḥammad al-Kharāshī (Khirshī), who died in 1101/1689.

Al-Afrānī, *Ṣafwa* 205, Jab. I, 65. *Khiṭ. jad.* VII, 22. *Sharḥ al-Mukhtaṣar* p. 102.

415 12. ʿAbd al-Qādir b. ʿAbd al-Hādī al-ʿUmarī, who died in 1100/1688. | 1. *Sharḥ Muntaha ʾl-suʾāl* I, 373.—2. *Khulāṣat al-tawḥīd lil-mustafīd wal-mufīd* Garr. 2165.

13. In 1106/1697 Burhān al-Dīn Ibrāhīm b. Marʿī al-Shabrakhītī al-Mālikī was drowned in the Nile on his way to Rosetta.

Jab. I, 67, followed by *Khiṭ. jad.* XII, 119. 1. *Sharḥ al-Mukhtaṣar* p. 102.—2. *Sharḥ al-Arbaʿīn al-Nawawiyya* I, 500.

14. Nāṣir al-Dīn Muḥammad al-Nashratī al-Mālikī was a professor at al-Azhar and died in 1120/1708.

Jab. I, 70, followed by *Khiṭ. jad.* XVII, 7. *Al-Anwār al-wāḍiḥa fi ʾl-salām wal-muṣāfaḥa* Cairo ^{1}VI, 116.

15. Abū ʿAbdallāh Shams al-Dīn Muḥammad b. ʿAbd al-Bāqī b. Yūsuf b. Muḥammad al-Zurqānī (no. 10) al-Mālikī was born in Cairo in 1055/1645, became a private tutor to al-Shabrāmallisī (p. 419), and died in 1122/1710.

| Jab. I, 69. 1. *Wuṣūl al-amānī bi-uṣūl al-tahānī* Cairo [1]I, 449, [2]I, 161.—2. *Sharḥ* 319
al-Muwaṭṭaʾ I, 185.—3. *Sharḥ al-Mawāhib al-laduniyya lil-Qasṭallānī* p. 87.—4. *al-Ajwiba al-Miṣriyya* see Suppl., Vienna 1665,[1] Alex. Fiqh Māl. 15.—5. *Sharḥ al-Bayqūniyya* p. 396.

16. Muḥammad b. Sulaymān b. Muḥammad b. Zayd al-Kaffūrī wrote, in 1170/1756:

Fatāwī Alex. Fiqh Māl. 12, Cairo [1]III, 179, 180.

17. ʿAlī b. Khiḍr al-ʿAmrūsī died in 1173/1759.

1., 2. See Suppl. 960, 14.—3. *Risāla fī faḍāʾil laylat al-niṣf min Shaʿbān* Alex. Fun. 33.—4. *Ḥāshiya ʿala ʾl-Muṭṭalaʿ* I, 610.—5. *al-Muqaddima, mulakhkhaṣ Mukhtaṣar Khalīl* p. 103.

18. Abu ʾl-Ḥasan ʿAlī b. Aḥmad al-Ṣaʿīdī al-ʿAdawī (ʿIdwī) al-Mansafīsī al-Mālikī was born in Banū ʿAdī near Asyūṭ in 1112/1700, became a professor in Cairo, and died on 10 Rajab 1189/6 September 1775.

Mur. III, 206, Jab. I, 415. 1. *Risāla fī-mā tafaʿluhu firqat al-Muṭāwiʿa min al-mutaṣawwifa min al-bidaʿ* Cairo [1]VII, | 385.—2. *Ḥāshiya ʿala ʾl-Sullam* see 416
p. 355.—3. *Ḥāshiya ʿala ʾl-Sanūsiyya* p. 324.—4. *Ḥāshiya ʿalā Sharḥ al-Kharāshī ʿala ʾl-Mukhtaṣar* p. 102.—5.–7. see Suppl.

C The Shāfiʿīs

1. ʿAbd al-Bāsiṭ b. Muḥammad b. Aḥmad b. Muḥammad b. ʿAbd al-Raḥmān b. ʿUmar b. Raslān b. Naṣr b. Ṣāliḥ b. ʿAbd al-Khāliq al-Bulqīnī al-Shāfiʿī was born in Dhu ʾl-Qaʿda 870/June 1466, studied in Cairo and Mecca, and wrote, in Muḥarram 899/October 1493:

Al-Wafāʾ bi-sharḥ al-Istīfāʾ on his *Qaṣīdat al-istīfāʾ min asmāʾ al-Muṣṭafā*, on 400 names of Muḥammad, Ind. Off. 4630, *JRAS* 1939, 394, autograph, see al-Sakhāwī, *al-Ḍawʾ al-lāmiʿ* IV, 28/9.

2. Shams al-Dīn Muḥammad b. Muḥammad b. Muḥammad b. Aḥmad al-Dalajī, d. 947/1544, see Suppl.

1 Where his father's (no. 10) year of death is given as his.

1. *Darʾ al-naḥs ʿan ahl al-maks*, on whether a *qāḍī* who hires many assistants and who charges a fee for every lawsuit or legal document can be removed from office, Berl. 5621.—2.–4. see Suppl.

3. Shihāb al-Dīn Abu ʾl-ʿAbbās Aḥmad b. Aḥmad b. Ḥamza al-Ramlī al-Anṣārī al-Shāfiʿī was a professor at al-Azhar and died on 1 Jumādā II 957/17 June 1550.

Khiṭ. jad. IV, 119. 1. *Fatāwā* see Suppl. Cairo ^{1}III, 249, ^{2}I, 527, two of these Berl. 4836 (with wrong dates).—2. *Shurūṭ al-maʾmūm wal-imām*, commentaries: a. *Ghāyat al-marām*, by his son Shams al-Dīn Muḥammad, d. 1004/1595 (no. 13), Berl. 3595, Cairo ^{1}III, 247, VII, 256, ^{2}I, 526, Alex. Fun. $114_{,2}$.—b., c. see Suppl.—3.–11. ibid. (7. read: 897).

4. ʿAbd al-Wahhāb b. Ibrāhīm al-ʿUrdī, who died in 967/1559.

1. *Miṣbāḥ al-mishkāt fī ʿadam al-ḥaraj fi ʾl-zakāt*, on whether the division of alms is restricted to the eight classes of recipients mentioned in sura $9_{,60}$, as believed by al-Shāfiʿī, or not, Berl. 4038, Alex. Faw. 24.—2. See Suppl.

320 | 5. Shams al-Dīn Muḥammad b. Muḥammad b. Aḥmad al-Shirbīnī al-Qādirī al-Khaṭīb, who died on 2 Shaʿbān 977/11 January 1570.

417 | *Khiṭ. jad.* XII, 127. 1. *Sharḥ Minhāj al-ṭālibīn* I, 498.—1a. See Suppl.—2. *al-Sirāj al-munīr fi ʾl-iʿāna ʿalā maʿrifat baʿḍ maʿānī kitāb rabbina ʾl-ʿalīm al-khabīr*, composed after 961/1554 and after no. 1, Berl. 900/1, Zaouiyah El Hamel, *Giorn. Soc. As. It.* X, 53, Garr. 1301, Cairo I, ^{1}171, ^{2}253, print. C. 1311.—3. *Manāsik al-ḥajj* Cairo ^{1}III, 278, ^{2}I, 540, printed with glosses by Muḥammad al-Nawāwī, C. 1298; by Muḥammad b. Sulaymān Ḥasaballāh al-Makkī, C. 1310.—4. *Risāla fi ʾl-basmala wal-ḥamdala* Berl. 2978.—5. *Risāla fī birr al-wālidayn wa-ṣilat al-raḥim* Cairo ^{1}VII, 4.—6.–13. see Suppl. (11. read: *al-shāfiya* Garr. 1920).

6. Yūnus b. ʿAbd al-Wahhāb b. Aḥmad b. Abī Bakr al-ʿAythāwī al-Shāfiʿī al-Dimashqī, who was an imam and preacher at the new mosque near the Paradise Gate and professor at the Madrasat Abī ʿUmar, died in 978/1570.

RA 299r. 1 *al-Jāmiʿ al-mughnī li-uli ʾl-raghabāt fi ʾl-fiqh*, composed in 958/1551, Cairo ^{1}III, 214, ^{2}I, 508.—2. *Qawl ahl al-sunna fī taḥrīm al-qahwa*, against the drinking of coffee, Berl. 5477, abstracts RA 300r/3r, where further literature on the subject is also listed; laudatory reviews of it Berl. 43.—3. *Radd al-ḍāll fī-mā qāl wa-takdhībuhu bi-aṣdaq al-maqāl*, against a *muftī* who had spoken in favour of drinking coffee, ibid. 5478.—4. *Zubdat al-mukhtaṣarāt* I, 487/8.

7. Aḥmad b. Aḥmad b. Badr b. Ibrāhīm b. al-Ṭayyibī al-Shāfiʿī Shihāb al-Dīn was born in 910/1504. He was a professor at al-ʿĀdiliyya al-Ṣughrā in Damascus, and during the holy months he held sermons under the Dome of the Eagle in the Umayyad mosque. He died in 979/1571.

RA 42v. 1. *Jawāz taqlīd al-Shafiʿī ʿalā madhhab al-imām Abī Hanīfa*, 56 *rajaz* verses on the extent to which a Shāfiʿī may follow the rite of Abū Ḥanīfa, Berl. 4867.—2. 20 *munsariḥ* verses on verbs that are transitive in the first declension and intransitive in the fourth, ibid. 6873.—3. See Suppl.

8. Abū 'l-Faḍl Abi 'l-Qāsim b. Muḥammad Marzūq wrote, in 988/1580:

Barnāmaj al-shawārid, a legal work, Br. Mus. 243.

9. Aḥmad b. Muḥammad b. Qāsim al-ʿUbādī al-Qāhirī al-Shāfiʿī Shihāb al-Dīn died in 994/1586.

| 1. On the meaning of the word *al-futyā*, Berl. 4837.—2.–8. see Suppl.—9. *al-Ḥawāshī wal-nikāt wal-fawāʾid al-muḥarrarāt* Qawala II, 154.—10. *Ḥāshiya ʿalā sharḥ al-Alfiyya* Suppl. I, 522. 418

10. Shihāb al-Dīn Yaḥyā al-ʿImrīṭī al-Azharī, fl. ca. 989/1581, see Suppl.

3. *al-Taysīr, naẓm al-Taḥrīr*, a commentary on *Fatḥ al-raʾūf al-khabīr* by ʿAbd al-Raʾūf al-Munāwī, d. 1031/1622 (p. 395), Alex. Fiqh Shāf. 30.

11. ʿAbdallāh b. Bahāʾ al-Dīn Muḥammad b. Jamāl al-Dīn ʿAbdallāh b. Nūr al-Dīn ʿAlī al-ʿAjamī al-Shinshawrī al-Shāfiʿī was a preacher at al-Azhar in Cairo, and died in 999/1590.

| 1. *al-Mukhtaṣar fī muṣṭalaḥ ahl al-athar*, composed for his son ʿAbd al-Wahhāb,[2] with a commentary, *Khulāṣat al-fikar* Berl. 1122/4, Gotha 584, Paris 321

2 Who himself wrote 1. *al-Murshid fi 'l-ḥisāb*, abstract by the author, Berl. 5996.—2. A manual for calculating a camel's load (*wasq*) for the *zakāt*, as well as for the conversion of Baghdadi to Damascene weights and vice versa, Gotha 1078,2.

759, Algiers 549, Alex. Muṣṭ. Ḥad. 10.—2. *Qurrat al-ʿayn fī misāḥat al-qullatayn*, on the calculation of both measuring vessels for the minimum quantity of still water needed for the accomplishment of a legal cleansing, according to Shāfiʿī teaching, with the help of geometrical figures, Berl. 5951/2, Gotha 1078/9, Cairo [1]III, 260.—3. *al-Fawāʾid al-Shinshawriyya fī sharḥ al-Manẓūma al-Raḥbiyya* I, 491, Berl. 4697, Algiers $7_{,2}$, Cairo [1]III, 312, Patna I, $112_{,1123}$. Abstract by the author, Cairo [1]III, 310.—Glosses: a. *al-Luʾluʾa al-saniyya* by Muḥammad b. ʿAlī al-Adfīnī al-Buḥayrī, composed in 1081/1609, Berl. 4698, Cairo [1]III, 315.—b. Yūsuf al-Zayyāt, Berl. 46–99.—c. al-Bājūrī, d. 1267/1859 (see below p. 487), C. 1282, 1310; on which is based J.D. Luciani, *Traité des successions musulmanes, extrait du cmt. de la Rahbia par Chenchouri, de la glose d'El Badjouri et d'autres auteurs arabes*, Paris 1890.

12. Aḥmad b. Muḥammad b. Aḥmad al-Maghribī al-Būṣīrī al-Shāfiʿī wrote, in 1003/1594:

Al-Kawkab al-waḍḍāḥ fī manʿ al-sifāḥ wa-taʿlīm ʿāqid al-nīkāḥ, in verse form, Cairo [1]VII, 462, [2]I, 536.

13. Shams al-Dīn Muḥammad b. Abi ʾl-ʿAbbās Shihāb al-Dīn Aḥmad b. Aḥmad
419 b. Ḥamza al-Ramlī succeeded his father | (no. 3) as a professor and the Shāfiʿī *muftī* at al-Azhar, before dying on 13 Jumādā I 1004/15 January 1596.

Muḥ. III, 342/8, *Khiṭ. jad.* IV, 129/30. 1. *Ghāyat al-marām, sharḥ Shurūṭ al-maʾmūm wal-imām* p. 416.—2. *Nihāyat al-muḥtāj li-sharḥ al-Minhāj* I, 498, additionally Cairo [1]III, 287.—Together with the *Tuḥfa* of Ibn Ḥajar al-Haythamī (see below p. 389) this commentary has been regarded as one of the main authorities for Shāfiʿī *fiqh* from the sixteenth century onwards; see Snouck Hurgronje, ZDMG 53, 142.—3., 4. See Suppl.—5. *Risāla fī qawāʿid al-īmān* Alex. Fun. $114_{,5}$.

14. Manṣūr Sibṭ Nāṣir al-Dīn al-Ṭablāwī al-Shāfiʿī, d. 1014/1606, see Suppl.

1. *al-Sirr al-Qudsī etc.* AS 392, Ritter, *Türkiyat Mecm.* VII/VIII (1945), p. 84.—4. *Manẓūma fi ʾl-istiʿārāt* also Qawala II, 176.—5. *Risāla fi ʾl-taqsīm etc.* Garr. 856, Cairo [1]VII, 567.—6. *Bidāyat al-qāriʾ etc.* Garr. 1353.

15. ʿUmar b. Muḥammad b. Abī Bakr al-Fāriskūrī al-Shāfiʿī, who died in Damietta on 17 Muḥarram 1018/23 April 1609.

Muḥ. III, 221, followed by *Khiṭ. jad.* XIV, 66. 1. *al-Bahja al-jaḍīda wal-nahja al-rashīda*, in *rajaz* based on the *Bahjat al-ḥāwī* of Zakariyyāʾ al-Anṣārī, d. 926/1520 (p. 122), Berl. 4630/1.—2. *al-Suyūf al-murhafa fī ʾl-radd ʿalā zanādiqat al-mutaṣawwifa* ibid. 2182. |—3. *Majmūʿ*, a collection of poems in praise of the 322
qāḍi ʾl-quḍāt of Rūmelī, Yaḥyā Efendi, Vienna 499.

15a. Muḥammad b. ʿUmar b. ʿAbd al-Wahhāb al-ʿUrḍī al-Ḥalabī was a *muftī* in Aleppo and died in Ṣafar 1071/October 1660.

Al-Ṭabbākh, *Taʾr. Ḥalab* VI, 318/36. *Risāla fī faskh al-ṭalāq wa-ilghāʾihi* Alex. Fiqh Shāf. 36,$_6$.

16. ʿAlī b. ʿAlī al-Shabrāmallisī Nūr al-Dīn Abu ʾl-Ḍiyāʾ, born in Shabrāmallis in 997/1598, studied in Cairo from 1008/1599, became imam at the al-Azhar mosque, and died on 18 Shawwāl 1087/25 February 1677.

Al-Afrānī, *Ṣafwa* 148/9, *Tāj al-ṭab.* XI, f. 224r, *ʿIqd al-jawāhir wal-durar* f. 218v, Muḥ. III, 174, followed by *Khiṭ. jad.* XII, 124, Wüst. *Gesch.* 581. 1. *al-Muqaddima fī ṣalāt* | *al-ẓuhr baʿd al-jumʿa* Berl. 3813, Alex. Fiqh Shāf. 36,$_5$.—2. *al-Durra al-* 420
bahiyya fī waḍʾ basāʾiṭ faḍl al-dāʾir bil-ṭarīq al-handasiyya Bodl. II, 284, Ind. Off. 772,$_3$, Algiers 1467.—3. *Sharḥ al-Mawāhib al-laduniyya* p. 87.—4. *Ḥāshiya ʿalā Sharḥ al-Minhāj* I, 497.—5.–8. see Suppl.—9. *Risāla fī ṣalāt al-ẓuhr baʿd al-ʿaṣr* Patna II, 452,$_{2628,5}$.

17. Shams al-Dīn Muḥammad b. Ibrāhīm al-Ḥimṣī al-Shāfiʿī b. al-Quṣayr was born in Homs in Rabīʿ II 1011/September 1602, issued fatwas for 47 years, and died in Damascus on 13 Rabīʿ II 1093/22 April 1682.

Muḥ. III, 321. *Sharḥ ʿAqīdat Taqī al-Dīn Abī Bakr al-Qāriʾ* Gotha 690.

18. Aḥmad b. ʿAbd al-Laṭīf b. Aḥmad b. Shams al-Dīn b. ʿAlī al-Miṣrī al-Bishbīshī al-Shāfiʿī was born in Bishbīsh in 1041/1631, studied in Cairo, became a professor at al-Azhar, taught for a time in Mecca, and died in 1096/1685.

Khit. jad. IX, 66. 1. *al-ʿUqūd al-jawhariyya bil-juyūd al-mashrafiyya*, answers to questions posed by the vizier ʿAbd al-Raḥmān Pāshā, Cairo ^{1}VI, 157, ^{2}I, 332.—2. *al-Tuḥfa al-saniyyya bi-ajwibat al-asʾila al-marḍiyya* ibid. ^{1}VII, 406, ^{2}VI, 203, Alex. Fun. 171,$_3$, Berl. Ms. or. oct. 3913, Ğārullāh 980.

19. Ibrāhīm b. Muḥammad b. Shihāb al-Dīn al-Birmāwī was a professor at al-Azhar. He died in 1106/1694.

Jab. I, 68. 1. *Fī ithbāt karāmāt al-awliyāʾ* Berl. 3340.

19a. His son Aḥmad wrote, in 1096/1685:

Al-Mīthāq wal-ʿahd fī sharḥ man takallama fi ʾl-mahd, a commentary on a poem about children who spoke in the cradle, based on history and *ḥadīth*, Cairo ^{1}V, 1163, ^{2}378, *RAAD* IX, 638,$_{4}$, Landb.-Br. 619.

19b. ʿAbd al-Muʿṭī b. Sālim b. ʿUmar al-Shiblī al-Simillāwī, ca. 1110/1698, see Suppl.

2. *Laqṭ al-masāʾil etc.* Garr. 1831.—4. *al-Riyāḍāt etc.* ibid. 657.—6. *Iḥkām al-qawl etc.* ibid. 1881.—16. *al-Tuffāḥa al-wardiyya* Berl. Ms. or. oct. 3824.—17. *Kanz al-inʿām fī faḍāʾil shahr al-ṣiyām* Alex. Ḥad. 59,$_{3}$.

421 | 19c. Jamāl al-Dīn Abū ʿUmar Maḥmūd b. Muḥammad b. ʿAlī al-Qādirī al-Shaykhānī al-Shāfiʿī, who died in 1119/1707.

1. *Birr walīday khayr al-warā* Alex. Fun. 122,$_{1}$.—2. *Najāt al-qāriʾ min faḍl al-bāriʾ* ibid. Faw. 18.—3. See Suppl. II, 940,$_{104}$.

20. Shams al-Dīn Abū Ḥāmid Muḥammad b. Muḥammad b. Muḥammad b. Shihāb al-Dīn Aḥmad al-Budayrī al-Shāfiʿī al-Dimyāṭī studied in al-Thaghr, in Cairo at al-Azhar, and in 1091/2 in Mecca, under, among others, the daughter of Imam ʿAbd al-Qādir al-Ṭāhirī. He died in al-Thaghr in 1140/1727.

Jab. I, 881. *Irshād al-ʿummāl ilā mā yanbaghī fī yawm ʿĀshūrāʾ min al-aʿmāl* Cairo ^{1}VII, 110, ^{2}I, 264, App. 37.—2. *Bulghat al-murād fi ʾl-taḥdhīr ʿani ʾl-iftitān bil-amwāl wal-awlād* Cairo ^{1}VII, 118.—3. *Taḥrīr al-afhām fī kayfiyyat tawrīth dhawi ʾl-arḥām* Pet. AM 139.—4.–11. see Suppl.—12. *Iẓhār al-surūr bi-mawlid al-nabī al-masrūr* Alex. Taʾr. 3.

323 | 21. Aḥmad b. ʿUmar al-Dayrabī al-Shāfiʿī al-Azharī died in Cairo on 27 Shaʿbān 1151/11 December 1738.

Jab. I, 161, followed by *Khiṭ. jad.* XI, 72. 1. *Ghāyat al-maqṣūd li-man yataʿāṭa ʾl-ʿuqūq*, on marital law, composed in 1123/1711, Berl. 4675, Cairo ^{1}III, 247, VII, 278, ^{2}I, 526, 550, print. C. 1297 and others; glosses by the author Cairo ^{1}III,

271.—2. *Ghāyat al-marām fī-mā yataʿallaq bi-ankiḥat al-anām*, on the same subject, Berl. 4732, Alex. Fiqh Shāf. 29, Fun. 174,$_2$, Cairo ^{1}III, 246, I^2, 526.—3. *Fatḥ al-malik al-jawād li-tashīl qismat al-tarikāt ʿalā baʿḍ al-ʿibād*, on the law of inheritance, Alex. Fiqh Shāf. 36,$_4$, Cairo ^{1}III, 311, ^{2}I, 560.—4. *Kitāb al-mujarrabāt* Qawala II, 289, C. 1287 see Suppl., C.H. Becker, *Islamst.* II, 103; whence (?) a section on the *ḥabbat al-mulūk* Berl. 6203.—5. *Manāsik al-ḥajj* Alex. Fiqh Shāf. 39,$_4$.—6. *Risāla fī farāʾiḍ al-ḥajj wa-shurūṭihi wa-ādābihi* ibid. 2.

22. Ḥusayn b. Aḥmad (Muḥammad) al-Maḥallī al-Shāfiʿī, who died in 1170/1756.

Khiṭ. jad. XV, 25. 1. *Kashf al-lithām ʿan asʾilat al-anām* Alex. Taʾr. 14, 35, Cairo ^{1}III, 265.—2. *Mazīd al-niʿma li-jamʿ aqwāl al-aʾimma* Cairo ^{1}III, 274.—3. *al-Kashf al-tāmm* | *ʿan irth dhawi ʾl-arḥām* ibid. 314.—4. *Kashf al-astār ʿan masʾalat* 422
al-iqrār ibid.—5. *Muntaha ʾl-irādāt li-jadwal al-munāsakhāt*, a commentary on the *Jadwal* (*Risāla fi ʾl-munāsakhāt*) by Aḥmad b. Muḥammad b. al-Hāʾim, p. 155.—6. *al-Ifṣāḥ ʿan ʿaqd al-nikāḥ ʿala ʾl-madhāhib al-arbaʿa* Alex. Fiqh Shāf. 6, Cairo ^{1}VII, 81 (where it is mistakenly stated that it was composed on 7 Ramaḍān 1193/5 January 1770).—7. *Kashf al-asrār bil-majhūl* Dam. Ẓ. 89, 3. 2.

23. Najm al-Dīn Muḥammad b. Sālim b. Aḥmad al-Shāfiʿī al-Miṣrī al-Ḥifnī al-Ḥusaynī, who was born in Ḥifna near Bilbis in 1101/1689, studied in Cairo and made a living as a copyist until an admirer made it possible for him to enter the Khalwatiyya order. He died in Rabīʿ I 1181/August 1767.

Jab. I, 289/304 (with an account of the history of his order) followed by *Khiṭ. jad.* X, 74. 1. *al-Thamarāt al-bahiyya fī asmāʾ al-ṣaḥāba al-Badriyya* Garr. 2036,$_1$, Cairo ^{1}VII, 215, ^{2}V, 449, *Risāla fī dhikr asmāʾ ahl Badr* ibid. ^{1}II, 199.—2. *Risāla tataʿallaq bi-buṭlān al-masʾala al-mulaffaqa wa-buṭlān al-ʿaqd al-awwal baʿd wuqūʿ al-ṭalāq al-thalāth bi-qaṣd isqāṭ al-muḥallil* Garr. 2036,$_4$, Alex. Fiqh Shāf. 36,$_1$, 37,$_1$, Cairo ^{1}III, 271, ^{2}I, 471.—3. *Risāla tataʿallaq bil-taqlīd fi ʾl-furūʿ* Garr. 2036,$_7$, Alex. Fiqh Shāf. 37,$_2$, Cairo ^{1}III, 271.—4. *Risāla fi bayān al-tasbīḥ wal-tahlīl* Garr. 2036,$_2$, Alex. Fiqh Shāf. 36,$_2$, Cairo ^{1}VII, 20.—5. *Ḥāshiya ʿalā Sharḥ al-Jāmiʿ al-ṣaghīr* p. 186.—6.–9. see Suppl. (6. Garr. 2036,$_3$).—10. *Mukhtaṣar Risālat al-Nawawī fī-mā yataʿallaq bil-qiyām li-ahl al-faḍl wa-ghayr dhālik* (Suppl. I, 685,^{xx}), Garr. 2036,$_6$.—11. *Farāʾid ʿawāʾid jabriyya* see I, 621.—12. *Ḥāshiya ʿalā Sharḥ al-Risāla al-ʿAḍudiyya* p. 269.

24. ʿĪsā b. Aḥmad b. ʿĪsā al-Barrāwī al-Shāfiʿī studied at al-Azhar, became a private tutor and professor there, and died in 1182/1768.

Jab. I, 312. 1. *Risāla fī muṣāḥabat al-kuffār wa-maḥabbatihim wa-khidmatihim lil-umarāʾ* Cairo ^{1}VII, 60.—2. *Sharḥ al-Jāmiʿ al-ṣaghīr* p. 148.—3. See Suppl.

25. Aḥmad b. Muḥammad b. Muḥammad al-Sijāʿī al-Shāfiʿī died on 28 Dhu ʾl-Qaʿda 1190/9 January 1777.

423 Jab. II, 3, followed by *Khiṭ. Jad.* XII, 10 f. 1. *al-Qawl* | *al-nafīs fī-mā yataʿallaq bil-khalʿ ʿalā madhhab al-Shafiʿī b. Idrīs* Cairo ^{1}III, 262, IV, 87, ^{2}I, 534, ^{2}150.—
324 2. *Manẓūmat dhawi ʾl-arḥām fi ʾl-farāʾiḍ,* | with the commentary *Tuḥfat al-anām,* ibid. ^{1}III, 303, ^{2}I, 554.—3. *Risāla fī aḥkām lā siyyamā* ibid. ^{1}IV, 52.—4. *al-Iḥrāz fī anwāʿ al-majāz,* in *rajaz,* with a commentary, Berl. 7290, Cairo ^{1}IV, 122. Commentary by Abu ʾl-Jūd Muḥammad b. Shaʿbān al-Ghazzī, ca. 1180/1767, Berl. 7291.[3]—5. *Hidāyat uli ʾl-baṣāʾir wal-abṣār ilā maʿrifat ajzāʾ al-layl wal-nahār* Alex. Ḥisāb 68, Cairo ^{1}V, 291, 327, VII, 325.—6. *Naẓm uṣūl al-awfāq,* with a commentary entitled *Fatḥ al-malik al-razzāq,* ibid. ^{1}V, 348.—7. *ʿUqūd al-maqūlāt,* with the commentary *al-Jawāhir al-muntaẓimāt,* Garr. 800 and glosses by Muḥammad b. Ḥasan al-ʿAṭṭār, d. 1250/1834, Garr. 803, Cairo ^{1}VI, 91.—8. *Naẓm al-maqūlāt,* with a self-commentary, Cairo ^{1}VI, 98.—9. *Naẓm fī bayān al-rusul allatī fi ʾl-Qurʾān,* with the commentary *Fatḥ al-mannān,* ibid. ^{1}VI, 60, ^{2}I, 56.—10. *al-Rawḍ al-naḍīr* see Suppl., Cairo ^{1}VII, 204, 457.—11. *Manẓūmat ʿilm al-ādāb fi ʾl-baḥth,* with the commentary *Fatḥ al-malik al-wahhāb,* ibid. 254.—12.–30. see Suppl. (14. glosses by Muḥammad Mujāhid Abu ʾl-Najāʾ, Alex. Fun. 129,4).—31. *Mukhtaṣar Sharḥ qaṣīdat Imraʾ al-Qays Qifā nabki* Garr. 3, Alex. Adab 157.—32. *Sharḥ Dīwān al-Samawʾal* C. 1324.—33. *Risāla fī ithbāt karāmāt al-awliyāʾ* in *Majmūʿa,* Būlāq 1319.—34. *Fatḥ al-mālik fī-mā yataʿallaq bi-qawl al-nās wa-huwa ka-dhālik* Alex. Ṣarf 11,3.—35. *Manẓūma fi ʾl-ʿarūḍ,* with glosses by Muḥammad b. Muḥammad al-Amīr, ibid. ʿArūḍ 3.—36. Glosses on the *Mukhtaṣar Bahjat al-sāmiʿīn* p. 430, 19, 2a.

26. ʿAbd al-Jawād b. Aḥmad b. ʿAbd al-Karīm al-Kayyālī al-Shāfiʿī was born in Sarmīn in 1009/1697 and went to Aleppo after his father's death, where he lived as a scholar until his own passing in 1192/1778.

Mur. II, 239. 1. *Risāla* on the *ḥadīth,* mentioned by al-Munāwī and going back to al-Daylamī: "He who says 'I am a believer' is a heretic, and he who says 'I really am a believer' is both a heretic and a hypocrite," Berl. 1598.—2. *al-Iṣāgha lil-taṣrīḥ bil-mushṭ al-baghā,* against the view that combing the hair with a comb made from a tortoise shell would cause impurity, ibid. 5449.

3 See Suppl. II, 446, n. 1, not in Garr.

27. Aḥmad b. Aḥmad b. Jumʿa al-Bajīramī al-Shāfiʿī died on 2 Ramaḍān 1007/1 September 1793.

| Jab. II, 78. 1. *Ighbāṭ al-karīm al-ghaffār li-muḥājjat al-janna wal-nār* Cairo [1]VI, 108, [2]I, 261.—2. *al-Laṭāʾif al-dhawqiyya fī alghāz fiqhiyya wa-asʾila naḥwiyya* ibid. [1]VI, 56, [2]I, 536. 424

28. Ḥasan b. ʿAlī al-Kafrāwī al-Shāfiʿī studied at al-Azhar and became a *qāḍī* and professor at the madrasa built by Muḥammad Bek. He was removed from office by Yūsuf Bek because of his connections with the sorcerer and soothsayer Ṣādūma (Jab. II, 17), who had written an erotic spell on the belly of a female slave of Yūsuf Bek, addressed to her master, and was killed for this. But after Yūsuf Bek was himself killed the same year, he was reinstated. He died on 20 Shaʿbān 1202/27 May 1788.

Jab. II, 165/7, followed by *Khiṭ. jad.* XV, 7.—1. *al-Durr al-manẓūm bi-ḥall al-mubhamāt fi ʾl-khutūm*, composed in 1173/1759, Cairo [1]III, 227.—2. *Iʿrāb al-Ājurrūmiyya* p. 309.—3., 4. See Suppl.

| D The Ḥanbalīs 325

1. Zayn al-Dīn ʿAbd al-Qādir b. Muḥammad b. ʿAbd al-Qādir b. Muḥammad al-Anṣārī al-Jazīrī wrote, in 966/1558:

1. *ʿUmdat al-ṣafwa fī ḥill al-qahwa*, Gotha 2106, Paris 4590, Esc. [2]1170, Alex. Fiqh Ḥanb. 5, cf. de Sacy, *Chr. ar.* [2]I, 138/69, Galland, *De l'origine et du progrès du café*, Caen-Paris 1699, rev. ed. 1836.—2., 3. See Suppl.

2. Manṣūr b. Yūnus b. Ṣalāḥ al-Dīn al-Bahūtī al-Ḥanbalī, who died in 1051/1641, see Suppl.

1.–5. see Suppl.—6. *Dalīl al-ṭālib li-nayl al-maṭālib* Alex. Fiqh Ḥanb. 4.–7. *Kashshāf al-qināʿ* see Suppl. I, 688.

3. Muḥammad Abu ʾl-Mawāhib was the Ḥanbalī *muftī* in Damascus in the eleventh century.

Mashyakha, Alex. Fun. 122, 4.

4a. See Suppl. (Garr. 1408).

425 | 5. See Suppl.

(For 3., read: Ibn Ḥamdān, Berlin 2051; 5. Commentary, Garr. 1849).

5a. Ibrāhīm b. Bakr al-Danābī al-ʿAwfī al-Dimashqī al-Ṣāliḥī, who died in Cairo in 1094/1683.

Al-Rawḍ al-murbiʿ fī manāsik al-ḥajj, with a commentary entitled *Bughyat al-mutatabbiʿ*, Alex. Fiqh Ḥan. 3, Cairo ^{1}III, 293.

8. Shams al-Dīn Abū ʿAbdallāh Muḥammad b. Muḥammad b. Aḥmad b. Sālim al-Saffarīnī, who died in 1188/1774, see Suppl.

2. *al-Durra al-muḍīʾa etc.*, Alex. Tawḥīd 29, self-commentary *Lawāmiʿ al-anwār al-bahiyya wa-sawāṭiʿ al-asrār al-athariyya*, C. 1324.

9. His contemporary ʿAbdallāh b. ʿAwda b. ʿĪsā b. Salāma b. al-Ḥājj ʿUbayd al-Qudūmī al-Nābulusī al-Ḥanbalī, who was *khādim al-ʿilm bil-Ḥaram al-nabawī*, wrote:

Al-Riḥla al-Ḥijāziyya wal-riyāḍ al-unsiyya fi ʾl-ḥawādith wal-masāʾil al-ʿilmiyya, Nablus 1324 (Sarkis 1498).

E The Shīʿa

1. Zayn al-Dīn b. ʿAlī b. Aḥmad al-Jabaʿī al-ʿĀmilī al-Shahīd al-Thānī, who died in 966/1558, see Suppl.

RAAD X, 344/6. 1. *al-Tanbīhāt al-ʿaliyya ʿalā waẓāʾif al-ṣalāt al-qalbiyya*, composed in 951, Gotha $771_{,2}$.—2. *Tamhīd al-qawāʿid al-uṣūliyya wal-ʿarabiyya li-tafsīr qawāʿid al-aḥkām al-sharʿiyya*, on the legal opinions of the Imāmīs, composed in 958/1551, Berl. 4801.—3. *Musakkin al-fuʾād ʿinda faqd al-aḥibbāʾ wal-awlād*, consoling thoughts on the loss of friends and children, ibid. 8834.—4. *Kashf al-rayba ʿan aḥkām al-ghayba*, completed on 13 Ṣafar 949/30 May 1542, Leid. 2174.—5. *Masālik al-afhām* I, 515.—6.–25. see Suppl. (13. on al-Sammākī see *Dharīʿa* II, $86_{,38}$; 17. ibid. $267_{,1087}$).—26. *Ādāb al-ṣalāt*, in the al-Khwānsārī library in Najaf, *Dharīʿa* I, $22_{,10}$).—27. *Risāla fi ʾl-ḥajj* Ind. Off. 1812.—28. *al-Asʾila al-Māziḥiyya*, questions posed by Aḥmad al-ʿĀmilī al-Māziḥī, in the library of Muḥammad al-Ṭihrānī al-ʿAskarī, *Dharīʿa* II, $91_{,261}$.—28. *al-Īmān wal-Islām wa-bayān ḥaqīqatihimā wa-ajzāʾihimā wa-shurūṭihimā*, print. 1305, ibid. 514,$_{2019}$.

2. His son Abū Manṣūr Ḥasan b. Zayn al-Dīn al-ʿĀmilī, d. 1011/1602, see Suppl.

| RAAD IX, 347. 1. *Maʿālim al-dīn etc.* Ind. Off. 1503/4.—Commentaries: b. Ind. 426
Off. 1506, Rāmpūr 48.—e. Patna I, 76,$_{877}$.—g. Mollā Ṣāliḥ b. Aḥmad (Suppl. II, 578, 2a), Ind. Off. 1505.—6. *al-Asʾila al-Madaniyyāt*, questions asked by Muḥammad b. Juwaybir al-Madanī, in the library of ʿAlī Akbar al-Kirmānī in Mashhad, *Dharīʿa* II, 91,$_{363}$.

3a. His grandson Abū Jaʿfar Muḥammad b. Abī Manṣūr al-Ḥasan Zayn al-Dīn al-ʿĀmilī al-Shaʾmī, who died in Mecca in 1030/1621.

Istiqṣād al-iʿtibār fī sharḥ al-Istibṣār (Suppl. I, 707), in the library of al-Ṭihrānī in Najaf, *Dharīʿa* II, 30,$_{120}$.

3b. His great-grandson ʿAlī b. Muḥammad b. Ḥasan b. Zayn al-Dīn, d. 1103/1692, see Suppl.

Rawḍāt al-jannāt 411.

4. Muḥammad b. Muḥammad b. Ḥasan b. Qāsim al-Ḥusaynī al-ʿĀmilī wrote, in 1068/1657:

Al-Ithnay ʿashariyya etc. Patna I, 144,$_{1393}$ (see Suppl.).

5. Ḥusayn b. Shihāb al-Dīn Ḥusayn b. Jandār al-Biqāʿī al-ʿĀmilī al-Karakī, who died in 1076/1665.

Muḥ. II, 92/4, *Sulāfat al-ʿaṣr* 355. *Hidāyat al-abrār* Bank. XIX, 1, 1585.

6. Muḥammad b. ʿAlī b. Ḥaydar al-Mūsawī al-ʿĀmilī al-Makkī was born in 1071/1661 and died in 1139/1727.

Inās sulṭān al-muʾminīn (i.e. Shāhānshāh Ḥusayn) *biqtibās ʿulūm al-dīn min al-nibrās al-muʿjiz al-mubīn fī tafsīr al-āyāt al-Qurʾāniyya allatī hiya fi ʾl-āḥkām al-aṣliyya wal-farʿiyya wa-āyāt al-aḥkām*, manuscript in Isfahan, *Dharīʿa* I, 41,$_{194}$, II, 517,$_{2034}$.

7 Sciences of the Qurʾān

1. Yūsuf b. Jamāl al-Dīn ʿAbdallāh[1] b. Sulaymān al-Ḥusaynī al-Urmayūnī, fl. ca. 990/1553.

1. *Kitāb al-muʿtamad fī tafsīr Qul huwa allāhu aḥad*, a detailed commentary on sura 112, Berl. 973.—2. *Arbaʿūna ḥadīthan tataʿallaq bi-sūrat al-Ikhlāṣ*, ibid.
427 1522, Paris 744,$_3$, Garr. 2072,$_1$, | AS 515.—3. *Arbaʿūna ḥadīthan tataʿallaq bi-āyat al-kursī* Paris 744,$_4$, Garr. 2072,$_2$.—4. *Arbaʿūna ḥadīthan fī manāqib Muḥammad* Paris 744,$_5$.—4.–6. see Suppl.—7. *Risāla fī tajwīd al-basmala* Br. H. ^{1}325, ^{2}620, 7 (not mentioned Garr. 1253).

2. ʿAlāʾ al-Dīn b. Nāṣir al-Dīn al-Ṭarābulusī, ca. 1009/1600, see Suppl.

2. *al-Muqaddima al-ʿAlāʾiyya fī ʾl-tajwīd* Fātiḥ 69,$_2$.

2a. Jamāl al-Dīn Muḥammad b. Ḥamdān al-Qurashī wrote, in 1011/1603:

Tafsīr baʿḍ al-āyāt Garr. 1306 (autograph).

3. Muḥammad b. Maḥmūd al-Manāsīrī al-Ṣāliḥī was born in Rabīʿ II 981/August 1573 and died in Damascus on 11 Rajab 1039/25 February 1630.

Muḥ. IV, 214. 1. *al-Fulk al-mashḥūn fī tafsīr baʿḍ maʿānī Kitāb Allāh al-maknūn*, a very detailed follow-up to al-Baghawī (I, 449), Berl. 908.—2. *Nafḥat al-misk al-khitām wa-minḥat al-mutanassik min al-anām* Cairo ^{1}V, 293.—3. *Kitāb al-falak al-dawwār lil-shams al-munīr wal-qamar al-sayyār*, on astronomy, ibid.

4. Muḥammad b. Aḥmad al-ʿAwfī, ca. 1050/1640.

Suter, 514. 1. *al-Jawāhir al-mukallala li-man rāma ʾl-ṭuruq al-mukammala*, on the art of Qurʾānic recitation, composed in 1049/1639 as an abstract of *Baḥr al-maʿānī wa-kanz al-sabʿ al-mathānī*, Fātiḥ Waqf Ibr. 36,$_1$, Cairo I, ^{1}95, ^{2}18, Qawala I, 11.—2. *Durr al-afkār li-man kāna fī qirāʾat al-aʾimma al-ʿashara sayyār*, composed ca. 1046/1636, Cairo I, ^{1}97, ^{2}19, Qawala I, 13.—3. *al-Durr al-manthūr (nathīr) fī ʾl-nahj al-mashhūr*, on the ten readings Fāṭiḥ Waqf Ibr. 28,$_{16}$, Cairo I, ^{1}97, ^{2}19.—4. See Suppl.—5. *Kayfiyyat istikhrāj al-taqwīm* Berl. 5778, Gotha 1430, AS 2690.

1 The author of *al-Badr al-munīr fī ʾl-ṣalāt ʿala ʾl-bashīr al-nadhīr*, AS 461.

5. Muḥammad b. Aḥmad b. ʿAbbās Abu 'l-Surūr, fl. ca. 1050/1640.

Detailed commentary on sura $48,_{28/9}$, Berl. 1009.

6. Abu 'l-ʿAzāʾim Zayn al-Dīn Sulṭān b. Aḥmad b. Salāma b. Ismāʿīl al-Mazzāḥī, d. 1075/1665, see Suppl.

3. *Risāla fīhā fawāʾid etc.* Fātiḥ Waqf Ibr. $51,_{4}$, Qawala I, 16. | —4. *Risāla fī bayān al-awjuh allatī bayna 'l-suwar lil-qurrāʾ al-ʿashara min ṭarīq al-Durra li-Ibn al-Jazarī* Qawala I, 17.—5. *Risāla fi 'l-qirāʾa* (= 4 ?), autograph dated 1038/1629, Patna I, $15,_{123}$.—6. *al-Jawhar al-fard al-maṣūn fī jamīʿ al-wujūh min al-dakhāʾil fī qawlihi Ulāʾika humu 'l-mufliḥūn* (sura $2,_{5}$), composed in 1048/1638, Fātiḥ Waqf Ibr. $28,_{20}$. 428

7. Muḥammad b. ʿAlāʾ al-Dīn al-Qāhirī al-Shāfiʿī was born in Bābil in 1000/1591, moved to Cairo at the age of 4 where he later became a professor, before dying on 25 Jumādā I 1077/24 November 1666.

Muḥ. IV, 39/42. 1. *Risāla fi 'l-kalām ʿalā qawlihi taʿālā inna ʿiddat al-shuhūr ʿinda 'llāh etc.* (sura 9_{36}), completed at the beginning of Muḥarram 1077/July 1666, Cairo ¹VII, 560.—2. *Risāla fi 'l-jihād wa-faḍāʾilihi* Berl. 4093.—3. See Suppl., Garr. 1316, Cairo ¹I, 151/2.

8. Abu 'l-Fayḍ ʿAbd al-Raḥmān b. Yūsuf al-Shāfiʿī al-Ujhūrī wrote, in 1084/1673:

1. *al-Qawl al-muṣān ʿani 'l-buhtān fī gharaq Firʿawn wa-mā kāna ʿalayhi min al-ṭighyān* Alex. Faw. 112, Cairo ¹VI, 177, ²V, 299.—2., 3. See Suppl.—4. *Mablagh al-amānī fī-mā ṣanaʿahu Ibn al-Jazarī min Ḥirz al-amānī wa-wajh al-tahānī lil-Shāṭibī* (I, 520) Qawala I, 30.

9. Zakī al-Dīn Manṣūr b. ʿĪsā b. Ghāzī al-Anṣārī al-Miṣrī al-Samannūdī wrote, in 1084/1673:

Tuḥfat al-ṭālibīn fī tajwīd kitāb rabb al-ʿālamīn Cairo I, ¹93, 217.

10. ʿAbd al-Raḥmān b. ʿAbd al-Ḥalīm al-Marʿashī, fl. mid-eleventh century.

Risāla fī tafsīr qawlihi sura 4_{51}, Qawala I, 64.

11. ʿAbdallāh b. Muḥammad al-Ḥimṣī al-Ṣiddīqī al-Shāfiʿī b. al-ʿAtīq, who was born in Homs in 1020/1611 and died in Cairo in 1088/1677.

1. *Natījat al-fikar fī iʿrāb awāʾil al-suwar*, composed in 1050/1640, Cairo [1]VII, 579.—2. *Nukhabat al-adhhān fī-mā waqaʿa min al-takrīr fi ʾl-Qurʾān* ibid. I, 218.

327 | 12. Muḥammad b. Tāj al-ʿĀrifīn wrote, in 1094/1693:

429 | *Rajaz* on the times and circumstances of the revelation of the individual suras, Berl. 471.

13. Muḥammad b. al-Qāsim b. Ismāʿīl al-Baqarī, born in 1018/1609, was a teacher of Qurʾānic recitation at al-Azhar who died on 20 Jumādā II 1111/14 December 1699 (or, according to others, on 21 Rajab 1107/2 February 1696).

Jab. I, 66, Mur. IV, 121/2. 1. *al-Qawāʿid al-muqarrara wal-fawāʾid al-muḥarrara*, on the principles behind the seven readings of the Qurʾān, based on the lectures of ʿAbd al-Raḥmān al-Yamanī, d. 1050/1640 (Muḥ. II, 358), Berl. 624/6.—2. *Ghunyat al-ṭālibīn wa-munyat al-rāghibīn* (*fi ʾl-tajwīd*) Alex. Fun. 146, 189,$_{21}$. Cairo I, [1]III, [2]24.—3. See Suppl.

14. Aḥmad b. Muḥammad b. Aḥmad al-Dimyāṭī al-Bannāʾ was born in Damietta and studied in Cairo and Mecca. After making the pilgrimage he visited Yemen where he joined the Naqshbandiyya order. From then on he lived as a dervish in ʿAzbat al-Burj on the salt-lake, and died on 3 Muḥarram 1117/28 April 1705 in Medina while on pilgrimage.

Khiṭ. jad. XI, based on Jab. 1. *Itḥāf fuḍalāʾ al-bashar fī qirāʾāt al-arbaʿa ʿashar*, written in Medina, Garr. 1235, AS 32, Rāġib 4, Fātiḥ Waqf Ibr. 17, Cairo I, [1]91, [2]15, Qawala I, 5.—2.–10. see Suppl.—11. *Riyāḍ al-nayyirayn fī ʿamal al-kusūfayn* Garr. 1003.

15. Muḥammad b. ʿAbd al-Bāqī al-Ḥanbalī al-Baʿlī al-Dimashqī Abu ʾl-Mawāhib was born in Damascus in 1044/1634. From 1072/1661 he studied in Cairo, Mecca, and Medina. After the death of his father he succeeded him as a professor at the Miḥrāb al-Shāfiʿiyya in the Umayyad mosque. To the people he had an air of holiness, and his fearless behaviour in front of the Turkish pasha Muḥammad b. Kurd Bayrām inspired them with confidence. He died in 1126/1714.

Mur. I, 67/9. 1. *Risāla fī qirā'at Ḥafṣ 'an 'Āṣim*, Berl. 648, augmented by his student Ibrāhīm b. Ismā'īl al-'Adawī around 1140/1727, ibid. 649.—2. See Suppl.

| 16. Ḥasan b. 'Alī b. Khāṭir wrote, in 1126/1714: 430

A treatise on methods of Qur'ānic recitation, Gotha 559.

17. Maḥmūd b. 'Abbās b. Sulaymān al-Kindī wrote, in 1158/1745:

Zubdat al-anfās fī tafsīr sūrat al-Ikhlāṣ (sura 112), Berl. 975.

18. Abu 'l-Su'ūd Aḥmad b. 'Umar al-Asqāṭī al-Ḥanafī, who died on 12 Dhu 'l-Qa'da 1159/16 November 1746.

| Jab. I, 165. 1. *Risāla fi 'l-qirā'āt* Cairo ^{1}I, 98.—2. *Risāla* on the division of the Qur'ān into quarters, eighths etc., ibid. 106.—3. Answers to questions asked by the vizier 'Abdallāh Pāshā Köprülü on the art of Qur'ānic recitation, ibid., Fātiḥ Waqf Ibr. $28_{,7}$.—4.–6. see Suppl. (4. Qawala I, 18). 328

18a. 'Abd al-Raḥmān al-Biqā'ī al-Shāmī, who died after 1162/1749.

Risāla fi tafsīr ba'ḍ āyāt min al-Qur'ān (suras 6_{102-3}; 10_{63-5}), Garr. 1309.

19. Al-Ḥasan b. 'Alī b. Aḥmad b. 'Abdallāh al-Shāfi'ī al-Azharī al-Manṭawī al-Madābighī was a professor at al-Azhar who died towards the end of Ṣafar 1170/beginning of November 1757.

Jab. I, 209. 1. *Itḥāf fuḍalā' al-umma al-Muḥammadiyya bi-bayān jam' al-qirā'āt al-sab' min ṭarīq al-Taysīr* (I, 517) *wal-Shāṭibiyya* (I, 520), Cairo I, ^{1}91, 215.—2. *Mukhtaṣar Bahjat al-sāmi'īn fī mawlid al-nabī* (p. 445), Cairo ^{1}I, 405, Alex. Ta'r. $14_{,1}$, Rāmpūr $661_{,94}$. Glosses: a. al-Sijā'ī, d. 1190/1777 (p. 422), Cairo ^{1}I, 405.—b. Muḥammad b. 'Alī al-Shanawānī, d. 1233/1818, ibid. 328, Alex. Ta'r. $14_{,2}$.—3. *Mukhtaṣar Qiṣṣat al-isrā' wal-mi'rāj* p. 446.—5., 6. See Suppl.

20. 'Abdallāh b. Ibrāhīm Četteği was born in Jirmek in Diyarbakir in 1115/1703. In 1170/1756 he became a pasha in Tripoli and was given the same position in Aleppo in 1172/1758, before being transferred to Damascus due to famine. From there he made the pilgrimage, during which he replaced the incumbent sharif

of Mecca with another person, but following a complaint by the deposed sharif
431 Četteğī was transferred to Diyarbakir. He died there soon after | his arrival in 1174/1760, but not before he had suppressed an uprising, as described by Jaʿfar al-Barzanjī in his book *al-Fatḥ al-farajī fi 'l-fatḥ al-Jattajī.*

Mur. III, 81. *Anhār al-jinān min yanābīʿ āyāt al-Qurʾān* Cairo I, ^{1}129, 233; see Suppl.

21. Saʿd al-Dīn wrote, in 1177/1763:

Fayḍ al-raḥmān bi-tajwīd al-Qurʾān in 17 tables, *ṣaḥāʾif,* in the second of which there is a pictorial representation of the speech organs similar to the one in Tychsen, *Elem. ar.* 58, Gotha 568.

22. Aḥmad b. Muḥammad al-Suḥaymī al-Qalʿawī al-Ḥasanī al-ʿArshī al-Shāfiʿī al-Azharī, who died in 1178/1764.

1. *Manāhij al-kalām ʿalā āyat al-ṣiyām* Cairo I, ^{1}217, ^{2}63.—2. *Hidāyat al-muḥtāj fi 'l-miʿrāj,* with the commentary *al-Tāj,* ibid. I, 278.—3. *al-Yāqūt fī faḍāʾil Ramaḍān,* with the commentary *al-Qūt,* Garr. 1860, Alex. Fun. 13, Cairo ^{1}VI, 177.—4. *Sharḥ al-Mawāhib* p. 87.—5., 6. See Suppl.—7. *al-Zahr al-fāʾiq fī mawlid ashraf al-khalāʾiq* Garr. 660.

23. Hāshim b. Muḥammad al-Maghribī al-Mālikī, see Suppl. 16a.

A panegyric poem by his student Sayyid Aḥmad Yemiščīzāde, Fātiḥ Waqf Ibr. 28,$_{12}$. 1.–3. see Suppl. (2. Garr. 1239; 3. ibid. 1238).—4. *Hidāyat al-qurrāʾ,* composed in 1185/1771, Fātiḥ Waqf Ibr. 28, 10.—5. A treatise on Qurʾān reciters, ibid. $_{13}$.

23a. ʿAlī ʿAṭiyya Abū Muṣliḥ al-Ghamrīnī, see Suppl.

2. *Qurrat al-ʿayn fī marʿifat al-qullatayn* Garr. App. 5.

24. ʿAṭiyyatallāh b. ʿAṭiyya al-Burhānī al-Ujhūrī studied in Cairo, lived there
329 near the mosque of ʿAbd al-Raḥmān Katkhudā (Jab. II, 5), | which the latter had put at his disposal, and died at the end of Ramaḍān 1190/November 1776.

Mur. III, 260/73, Jab. II, 4, followed by *Khiṭ. jad.* VIII, 39. 1. *Irshād al-raḥmān li-asbāb al-nuzūl wal-naskh wal-mutashābih wa-tajwīd al-Qurʾān* Cairo I, ^{1}122, ^{2}31.—2. *Ḥāshiya ʿala 'l-Jalālayn* p. 182.—3. *Ḥāshiya ʿalā Sharḥ al-Zurqānī ʿala 'l-Bayqūniyya* p. 396.—4. See Suppl.

| 25. ʿAlī al-Manshalīlī, who died after 1211/1797, see Suppl. 432

3. *Ashrāṭ al-sāʿa* Garr. 1509.

8 *Dogmatics*

1. Abu ʾl-Faḍl al-Mālikī al-Suʿūdī wrote, in 942/1535.

Muntakhab takhjīl man ḥarrafa ʾl-injīl, Disputatio pro religione Muhammedanorum adversus Christianos, Text. ar. cum var. lect, ed. T.J. van den Hamm, Leiden 1877.

2. Muḥyi ʾl-Dīn b. Bahāʾ al-Dīn wrote, in 953/1541:

Risāla fi ʾl-wujūd wa-waḥdatihi Leid. 1599.

3. Ibrāhīm b. Aḥmad b. ʿAlī al-Ḥalabī, who died in 956/1549.

Al-Lumʿa fi ʾl-qaḍāʾ wal-qadar Alex. Tawḥīd 29.

4. Shihāb al-Dīn Aḥmad b. Muḥammad b. ʿAlī al-Junaymī was born in Cairo. At first he was a Shāfiʿī, but when in Asia Minor he converted to be a Ḥanafī. Having lost the fortune that he had made there in a shipwreck off Alexandria he moved back to Cairo, where he remained until his death in 1044/1634.

Muḥ. I, 312/5. 1. *al-Tasdīd fī bayān al-tawḥīd*, drawing on a verse by Abu ʾl-ʿAtāhiya (I, 76), Cairo [1]II, 10, [2]I 169.—2. *Risāla fī baʿḍ ṣifāt Allāh* ibid. [1]II, 23.—3. *Irshād al-ikhwān fi ʾl-farq bayna ʾl-qidam bil-dhāt wal-qidam bil-zamān*, an answer to a question posed by a man from Rosetta on the beginning of his gloss on a commentary on the *Sanūsiyya* (p. 323), Cairo [1]II, 2, [2]I, 163.—4. *Ibtihāj al-ṣudūr fī bayān kayfiyyat al-tathniya wal-jamʿ wal-iḍāfa lil-manqūṣ wal-maqṣūr*, written in Ramaḍān—Shawwāl 1038/May–June 1629, ibid. [1]VII, 120, [2]II, 73.—5. Six small treatises on grammar, rhetoric, Qurʾānic exegesis etc., ibid. 6.–12. see Suppl. (10. Garr. 475); II. p. 444.

4a. Nūr al-Dīn ʿAlī al-Ḥalabī, who died in 1044/1634.

Taʿrīf ahl al-Islām wal-īmān bi-anna Muḥammadan ṣlʿm lā yakhlū minhu makān wa-lā zamān Alex. Fun. 19.

5. Abū Bakr b. Ṣāliḥ al-Kutāmī, who died of the plague in Cairo in 1051/1641.

433 | Muḥ. I, 85. 1. *al-Manhaj (Minhāj) al-ḥanīf fī maʿna ʾsmihi taʿālā al-laṭīf* Cairo [1]VI$_{1}$, 6, 153, 243.—2., 3. See Suppl.

6. Muḥammad b. Abī Aḥmad Ṣafī al-Dīn al-Ḥanafī wrote, in 1061/1660:

Al-Ṣāʿiqa al-muḥriqa ʿala ʾl-mutaṣawwifa al-rāqiṣa al-mutazandiqa Pet. AMK 934, Cairo [1]II, 93, [2]I, 327.

330 | 7. ʿAbd al-Wahhāb b. Abī ʿAbdallāh b. Abi ʾl-Ḥasan b. Abi ʾl-Shihāb al-Janjāwī nazīl Dimashq wrote, in 1062/1652:

Al-Nibrās li-kashf al-iltibās al-wāqiʿ fi ʾl-asās li-ʿaqāʾid qawm sammā anfusahum bil-akyās Cairo [1]II, 57.

8. Muḥammad Amīn al-Ṣiddīqī al-Bakrī al-Lārī al-Baṣīr, the son of the sultan of Lār, fled to Baghdad when Shah ʿAbbās I conquered his father's kingdom. He went on pilgrimage, settled first in Mosul, then in Aleppo, and finally in Damascus, where he became famous as a Sufi. He died in 1066/1655.

Muḥ. IV, 308. 1. *Risāla fi ithbāt wājib al-wujūd*, Berl. 2345.—2. See Suppl.

9. Muḥammad b. Aḥmad al-Khaṭīb al-Shawbarī Shams al-Dīn, who was born in 977/1569, was a Shāfiʿī *muftī* and a professor at al-Azhar. He died in 1069/1659.

Muḥ. III, 385, followed by *Khiṭ. jad.* XII, 144. 1. *al-Ajwiba ʿani ʾl-asʾila fī karāmāt al-awliyāʾ* Berl. 3338, Garr. 2013$_{,4}$, print. in *Majmūʿa* Būlāq 1319.—2. *Jawāb ʿan suʾāl yataʿallaq bil-awliyāʾ* Cairo [1]VII, 406 (= 1?).—3. See Suppl.—4. *Taʿlīqāt ẓarīfa wa-taḥqīqāt laṭīfa ʿalā Sharḥ al-Arbaʿīn al-Nawawiyya* I, 499.

10. Ibrāhīm al-Ghamrī al-Khaṭīb al-Shāfiʿī wrote, in 1092/1681:

Risāla fi ʾl-firaq al-islāmiyya Alex. Fun. 33.

11. Aḥmad b. Muḥammad b. Muḥammad al-Ṣafadī al-Dimashqī, born in Safad, was imam at the Darwīsh Bābā mosque in Damascus and died in 1100/1688.

434 Muḥ. I, 356/9. 1. *al-Farāʾid al-saniyya fi ʾl-ʿaqāʾid al-sunniyya*, | in 353 *rajaz* verses, Berl. 2053, Munich 146 (autograph dated 1087/1676). Self-commentary, *al-Darārī al-muḍīʾa*, Berl. 2054.—2. *Bahjat al-anwār ʿala ʾl-Durr al-mukhtār*, prayer (*istighfāra*) in 73 verses with *takhmīs*, Berl. 3937$_{,1}$.—3. *al-Dīwān*

al-thālith, 2 *takhmīs* on poems in praise of Muḥammad by Ayyūb al-Khalwatī and al-Zamzamī, d. 1072/1661 (see below p. 379), Berl. 7991.—4. See Suppl.

12. Sulaymān b. ʿAbdallāh al-Baḥrānī, fl. ca. 1120/1708.

1. *Risāla* on whether someone born out of wedlock can enter Paradise if they have lived as a devout and law-abiding person, Berl. 2708.—2. *Dharīʿat al-muʾminīn wa-wasīlat al-ʿārifīn*, on knowledge of God, composed in 1101/1669, ibid. 3241.

| 13. ʿĪsā b. ʿĪsā al-Safaṭī al-Ḥanafī al-Buḥayrī al-Fuḥaylī wrote, in Jumādā I 1131/ 331
April 1719:

1. *al-Qawl al-sadīd fī wuṣūl thawāb fiʿl al-khayrāt lil-aḥyāʾ wal-amwāt bi-lā shakk wa-lā tardīd* Cairo [1]VII, 141.—2., 3. See Suppl.

14. ʿAlī b. Khalīfa al-Ḥusaynī al-Mālikī wrote, in 1131/1719:

Al-Riyāḍ al-Khalīfiyya, a metrical treatise on *uṣūl al-dīn* with a commentary by Aḥmad b. ʿAbd al-Muʾmin al-Damanhūrī, d. 1192/1778, completed in 1143/1730, Gotha 651.

15. Ziyād b. Yaḥyā al-Naṣb al-Raʾsī, fl. twelfth century, see Suppl.

1. *Kitāb al-baḥth al-ṣarīḥ etc.* manuscript Kračkovsky, see Schmidt, *Zap. Koll. Vost.* V, 774/9.—2. *al-Ajwiba al-jaliyya li-daḥḍ al-daʿawāt al-Naṣrāniyya* manuscript Kr. ibid. 780/97.

16. Muḥammad b. al-Najjār, who died in 1163/1750.

1. *Luʾluʾat al-tanzīh lil-rabb al-nazīh*, a profession of faith in 185 *rajaz* verses, Berl. 2055.—2. See Suppl.

17. Muḥammad b. Muḥammad al-Bulaydī al-Mālikī al-Ashʿarī al-Andalusī al-Tūnisī was a professor at al-Azhar who was held in high esteem by the Maghrebis of Cairo, who bought him a house there. He died in 1176/1750.

Jab. I, 259. 1. *Risāla fī dalālat al-ʿāmm ʿalā baʿḍ afrādihi*, | Cairo [1]II, 262, VII, 435
498.—2. *Nayl al-saʿādāt fī ʿilm al-maqūlāt wa-huwa risāla fi ʾl-maqūlāt al-ʿashr* ibid. VI, 106, [2]I, 258, App. 136, Alex. Manṭiq 20,4, Fun. 97,2, Garr. 801/2. Gloss

by ʿArafa al-Daṣūqī, d. 1230/1815, abbreviated in the *Taqyīdāt* by Muḥammad al-Dimyāṭī, Alex. Fals. 5.—3. *Fawāʾid fi ʾl-fiqh* Cairo [1]VII, 56.—4. *al-Māʾ al-zulāl fī ithbāt karāmāt al-awliyāʾ badʿ al-intiqāl* ibid. 298.—5.–9. see Suppl. (9 = 2?).

18. Aḥmad b. Ḥasan b. ʿAbd al-Karīm al-Jawharī al-Khālidī al-Shāfiʿī al-Karīmī al-Azharī was born in Cairo in 1096/1685, became a *muftī* there and a professor at al-Azhar, before dying in 1182/1768.

Jab. I, 309/12, followed by *Khiṭ. jad.* IV, 78/9. 1. *Khāliṣ al-nafʿ fī bayān al-maṭālib al-sabʿ* Cairo [1]II, 21, [2]I, 178.—2. *Risāla fī taʿalluqāt al-ṣifāt al-ilāhiyya* ibid. VII, 568.—3. *al-Mabāḥith al-marḍiyya fī nazāhat al-anbiyāʾ ʿan kulli mā yanquṣ maqāmatahum al-ʿaliyya al-zakiyya* ibid. [1]I, 198.—4.–15. see Suppl. (4. Garr. 1531, 6. ibid. 1140).—16. *Munqidh al-ʿabīd*, an *ʿaqīda* with a commentary by his son Muḥammad entitled *Laṭāʾif al-tawḥīd*, written in 1192/1778, Alex. Tawḥīd 29.

19. Muḥammad Taqī al-Dīn, ca. 1183/1769.

1. *ʿAqīdat al-ghayb*, with the commentary *al-Fatḥ al-mubīn* by Aḥmad b. ʿAbd al-Ghanī al-Tamīmī al-Khalīlī, composed in 1193/1779, Berl. 2057/8.—2. See Suppl.

20. Abu ʾl-Ḥasan ʿAlī b. Abī ʿAbdallāh Muḥammad b. ʿAlī al-Maghribī al-Saqqāt was born in Fez. He first studied there under his father, then in Mecca, and finally in Cairo, where he lived a secluded life until his death in 1183/1769.

Mur. III, 229, III, 41 following *Jab.* and *Khiṭ. jad. Urjūza* (*Manẓūma*) *fi ʾl-tawḥīd*, with a commentary by Muḥammad b. Muḥammad al-Sunbāwī, d. 1232/1817, Cairo [1]II, 25. Gloss by Ibrāhīm b. Muḥammad al-Jārim al-Rashīdī, d. 1265/1849, Alex. Tawḥīd 10.

21. Aḥmad Zayn al-Manūfī al-Shāfiʿī wrote, in 1184/1770:

Al-Qawl al-asnā bi-sharḥ asmāʾ Allāh al-ḥusnā Cairo [1]VII, 284.

22. ʿAbdallāh al-ʿUmarī al-Ḥanafī al-Ṭarābulusī, who died after 1186/1772 (see Suppl.).

436 | 1. *Qabs al-anwār fi ʾl-radd ʿala ʾl-Naṣāra ʾl-kuffār* Cairo [1]VII, 271.—2. *al-Kalim al-wāḥida fī ḥukm al-firaq al-malāḥida*, composed in 1180/1766, ibid.

23. ʿAbbās b. Aḥmad b. ʿAbd al-Karīm al-Ḥaddād al-Marḥūmī al-Shāfiʿī wrote, in 1187/1773:

Rayḥānat al-mushtāqīn ilā dhikr muʿjizāt al-mursalīn, on miracles performed by the prophets, the first four caliphs, the heads of the four religious schools, and the founders of dervish orders, Paris 2008 (autograph).

9 *Mysticism*

1. ʿAlī b. Khalīl al-Marṣafī Nūr al-Dīn, who died after 930/1524.

Khiṭ. jad. XV, 40. 1. *Manhaj al-sālik ilā ashraf al-masālik al-mutaḍammina li-Risālat al-Qushayrī* (I, 556), abstract by the author, Berl. 3037.—2. *al-Muqniʿ wal-mawrid al-ʿadhb li-man yashrab wa-yakraʿ* ibid. 3038.—3. See Suppl.

2. Muḥammad b. ʿAlī b. ʿAbd al-Raḥmān al-Dimashqī Abū ʿAlī al-ʿArrāq al-Kinānī al-Muhājirī was the son of a Circassian emir from Damascus. He renounced the splendour of a position in the army that he had inherited from his father in order to become a student of the Sufi ʿAlī b. Maymūn al-Maghribī, d. 917/1511. He then lived in his hometown, where he was regarded as a saint, and it was because of this that he received the visit of Sultan Selīm I,[1] who accorded him and his descendants a yearly pension. He died in Mecca on 14 Ṣafar 933/21 November 1526.

RA 231v, *ShN* I, 542/4. 1. *Jawharat al-ghawwāṣ wa-tuḥfat ahl al-ikhtiṣāṣ*, preceded by the *Risāla fī ʿilm al-mawāʿiẓ* of Ibn al-Jawzī (Suppl. I, 919,$_{75a}$). After a Sufi interpretation of syntactical expressions he gives an overview of the life of | the 437
Prophet, accompanied by reflections on one's love for him. He treats, in greater detail, the Prophet's Companions, whom he divides, like the planets, into seven classes. Finally, he explains remarkable phrases from the Qurʾān, basing his ideas on al-Silafī (I, 450) and 100 phrases from the Qurʾān in a Sufi manner, based on al-Būnī (I, 655), Berl. 427. |—2. *Kashf al-ḥijāb bi-ruʾyat al-janāb*, 333
a prayer for Muḥammad, ibid. 3921.

1 According to *ShN*, he lived in Medina following the death of his teacher. However, RA, whose author was from Damascus, is more reliable, especially because he reports that al-Muhājirī's descendants were still receiving their pensions in his lifetime.

3. ʿAlawān ʿAlī b. ʿAṭiyya b. Ḥasan al-Ḥamawī al-Haythamī, who was praised by his followers as a renewer of religion, died at over eighty years old in Hama in Jumādā I 936/January 1530.

RA 175r. 1. *Tuḥfat al-ikhwān fī masāʾil al-īmān*, on the conditions of faith, Berl. 1835/6.—2. *ʿAqīda* ibid. 2028, Gotha $79_{,2}$. Commentaries: a. Self-commentary Berl. 2029/33, Gotha $102_{,5}$, 684.—b. Anon., completed in 1028/1619, Berl. 2034/5.—c. Fatḥallāh b. Maḥmūd b. Muḥammad al-Baylūnī, d. 1042/1632 (p. 353), ibid. 2036.—3. *ʿAqīda* for boys and common folk, ibid. 2037.—4. Dogmatic reflections, ibid. 2038.—5. *al-Amr al-dāris fi ʾl-aḥkām al-mutaʿalliqa bil-madāris*, a defence of Sufism composed in 917/1511, ibid. 3182.—6. *al-Jawhar (al-Durr) al-maḥbūk (bil-ḥaly al-masbūk) fī ṭarīq al-sulūk*, a *basīṭ* poem on the deterioration of morals in his own time, ibid. 3283/4, partial ibid. 7936, Gotha 709/10, Munich 365, f. 78, Leid. 613, Alex. Maw. 15, Cairo ^{1}II, 155, VII, 521, ^{2}I, 287, 294.—7. *Nasamāt al-asḥār fī karāmāt al-awliyāʾ al-akhyār*, Berl. 3336.—8. 18 *ramal* verses of Sufi content, ibid. 3418.—9. *Asna ʾl-maqāṣid fī taʿẓīn al-masājid (wa-faḍlihā)*, ibid. 3591, Cairo ^{1}VII, 636.—10. Prayers, Berl. 3779.—11. *Miṣbāḥ al-hidāya wa-miftāḥ al-wilāya*, on Shāfiʿī law, Alex. Fun. $188_{,2}$, abstract by the author *Taqrīb al-fawāʾid wa-tashīl al-maqāṣid* Berl. 4612, Munich 365, cf. 366, Alex. Fiqh Shāf. 12.—11a. *Mukhtaṣar al-Hidāya wa-miftāḥ al-wilāya* Alex. Fiqh Ḥan. 62.—12. *Risāla fī faḍāʾil al-Shām wa-akhbārihā* Berl. 6085.—13. (*Nuzhat al-asrār fī*) *Muḥāwarat al-layl wal-nahār* in rhymed prose, Berl. 8589.—14. *al-Naṣāʾiḥ al-muhimma lil-mulūk wal-aʾimma* Berl. $8981_{,52}$, Alex. Maw. 48.—15. Four mystical verses, with a commentary entitled *Āyat al-tawfīq ilā maʿāni ʾl-jamʿ wal-tafrīq* by Najm al-Dīn Muḥammad b. Muḥammad al-Ghazzī al-ʿĀmirī, d. 1061/1651, Paris 3226.—16. *al-Sirr al-maknūn fī faḍāʾil al-qahwa wal-bunn* Cairo ^{1}VI, 149.—17. *Mujli ʾl-ḥazan ʿan il-maḥzūn fī manāqib al-shaykh
438 Abi ʾl-Ḥasan | ʿAlī b. Maymūn* Cairo ^{1}VII, 635, ^{2}V, 324.—18. *Tuḥfat al-ikhwān al-Ṣūfiyya bil-kashf ʿan ḥāl man yaddaʿi ʾl-quṭbiyya* ibid. ^{1}II, 636, ^{2}I, 276.—19.–26. see Suppl.—27. *ʿArāʾis al-ghurar* Alex. Fun. $160_{,2}$.—28. *Qaṣīda īmāniyya fi ʾl-ādāb al-sharʿiyya* ibid. Taṣ. 37.—29. *Risāla fi ʾl-waswasa* ibid. Faw. $24_{,5}$.—30. *Urjūza fi ʾl-mīqāt* ibid. Fun. $118_{,1}$.—31. *Khulāṣat Rawḍat al-abṣār wa-lubāb Sharḥ Ghāyat al-ikhtiṣār (fi ʾl-qirāʾāt)* from the commentary of his shaykh ʿAbd al-Raḥmān al-Muqriʾ al-Ḥanbalī on his *Manẓūma*, completed in 920/1514.—32. *Nathr al-durar fī farsh al-ḥurūf fi ʾl-qirāʾāt* ibid. $119_{,3}$.—33. *Mukhtaṣar min Khulāṣat sīrat sayyid al-bashar* ibid. $141_{,2}$.

4. ʿAlī al-Shūnī was born in Shūna, settled in Tanta, where the shrine of shaykh Aḥmad al-Badawī is located, and then moved to al-Azhar in Cairo. Later he was

appointed the guardian of the *turba* of Sultan Ṭūmān al-Dīn Bay al-ʿĀdil. He saw out his life living in al-Madrasa al-Ṣūfiyya, but not before he had married at the unlikely age of 90. He died in 944/1537.

Khiṭ. jad. XII, 145 (following al-Sharʿāwī, who was his student and servant for 35 years). 1. *al-Ṣalawāt al-Ibrāhīmiyya*, prayers for Muḥammad and Ibrāhīm, with a commentary by al-Bulqīnī (Ṣāliḥ b. Aḥmad, d. 1015/1606, or Yūsuf b. Muḥammad, d. 1045/1635), Berl. 3932.—2. *Miṣbāḥ al-ẓalām bil-ṣalāt wal-salām ʿalā khayr al-anām* Cairo ^{1}II, 229.

| 5. Abu ʾl-Makārim Shams al-Dīn Muḥammad b. ʿAbd al-Raḥmān al-Bakrī 334
al-Ṣiddīqī al-Shāfiʿī al-Ashʿarī was born in 898/1492, lived alternately one year in Cairo and one year in Mecca, and died in 952/1545.

Khiṭ. jad. III, 127, Wüst. *Gesch.* 520. 1. *Dīwān* of mystical content, Paris 3223/33, Cambr. Palmer 55/7, AS 4164 (*katabahā nāẓimuhā Muḥammad b. Abī Ḥasan al-Ṣiddīqī* 13 Ramaḍān 967/8 June 1560!).—2. *Tarjumān al-asrār wa-tajalliyyāt al-akhyār*, mystical poems, Esc. ^{2}439.—3. *Ṣūrat ruʾūs mukātābāt wa-murāsalāt*, mystical works in prose and verse, ibid. 532$_{,1}$.—4. *Kitāb al-inshāʾ*, letters, ibid. $_2$.—5. *Tashīl al-sabīl fī fahm maʿāni ʾl-tanzīl*, completed in Jumādā II 926/May 1520, Leid. 1697, Paris 661/2, Esc. ^{2}1397, AS 89, Cairo ^{1}I, 143, ^{2}36.—6. *Hidāyat al-murīd lil-sabīl al-ḥamīd* Gotha 865$_{,1}$.—| 7. *Tarkīb al-ṣuwar wa-tartīb al-* 439
suwar ibid. $_2$.—8. *al-Jawāb al-mujīd ʿani ʾl-madīḥ al-ḥamīd* ibid. $_3$.—9. *al-Jawāb al-ajall ʿan karab Muṣṭafā ʿinda ḥulūl al-ajal* ibid. $_4$.—10. On the meaning of the dictum attributed to ʿAlī: *Man lānat asāfiluhu ṣalubat aʿālīhi*, ibid. $_5$.—11. *Nafaḥāt min kalām Muḥammad al-Bakrī* ibid. $_6$.—12. *al-Risāla al-Nāṣiriyya* ibid. $_7$.—13. *Waṣiyyat al-shaykh Muḥammad Bakrī* ibid. $_8$.—14. *Tuḥfat al-sālik li-ashraf al-masālik* ibid. $_9$.—15. *al-Fāqa ila ʾl-fāqa* in 3 *maqṣad*, the last of which contains, among other things, 40 *ḥadīth*, completed in 922/1516, ibid. $_{10}$.—16. *Risāla fī faḍāʾil Ramaḍān* Paris 781.—17. *Risāla fī faḍl laylat al-niṣf min Shabʿān*, with a commentary by al-Munāwī, p. 395, Berl. 3823.—18. *ʿIqd al-jawāhir al-bahiyya fi ʾl-ṣalāt ʿalā khayr al-bariyya* Cairo ^{1}I, 1369.—19. *al-Rawḍ al-anīq fi faḍāʾil Abī Bakr al-Ṣiddīq* ibid. VII, 101, ^{2}I, 121.—20. *Tafsīr wāḍiḥ al-majāz*, ḤKh, VI, 416$_{,14149}$, Sulaim. 144.—21. *Kifāyat al-muḥsin fī waṣf al-muʾmin* Qawala I, 145, 208.—22.–24. see Suppl. (24. Garr. 1918).—25. *Bushrā kulli karīm bi-thawāb al-malik al-karīm*, 40 *ḥadīth*, Qawala I, 102.—26. *Tuḥfat al-kirām fī faḍāʾil iṭʿām al-ṭaʿām* ibid. 103.

6. Muhammad b. ʿAlī (no. 3) b. ʿAṭiyya al-Ḥamawī Shams al-Dīn died in 954/1547.

1. *Tuḥfat al-ḥabīb fī-mā yubhijuhu fī riyāḍ al-shuhūd wal-taqrīb*, on the fundamental notions of Sufism, Berl. 3039, Alex. Taṣ. 11.—2. See Suppl.

7. ʿAlī b. Aḥmad b. Muḥammad al-Kīzawānī (Kāzuwānī) al-Ḥamawī al-Shādhilī Abu 'l-Ḥasan, who died in 955/1548.

1. *Izālat al-ishkāl fī maʿrifat al-jalāl wal-jamāl*, on the fact that in God's quiddity, majesty and beauty are one, Berl. 2796, 3230.—2. *Ādāb al-aqṭāb*, an overview of Sufism, ibid. 3040.—3. *Nathr al-jawāhir fi 'l-mufākhara bayna 'l-bāṭin wal-ẓāhir*, a Sufi treatise, ibid. 3144.—4. *Tanbīh al-ṭālibīn ʿalā maqāṣid al-ʿārifīn*, on the censure of others and self-praise, ibid. 3149.—5. *Zād al-masākīn ilā manāzil al-sālikīn*, Berl. 3310/11, Paris $1337_{,13}$.—5. *Kashf al-qināʿ ʿan wajh al-samāʿ*, on the spiritual concerts of the Sufis, Berl. 5516, see Farmer, *Sources* 60.—7. *Dīwān* Berl. 7937.

335 | 8. Muḥammad b. Muḥammad b. Bilāl al-Ḥalabī al-Ḥanafī, who died in 957/1550.

440 | *Risāla fi 'l-masāʾil al-iʿtiqādiyya* AS 2278.—2. See Suppl.—3. A treatise on dogmatics for the *Defterdār bi-diyār al-ʿArab wal-ʿAjam*, dated 957/1550, Gotha 1240.—4. *Wāridāt* on Bayḍāwī, for the *Defterdār* Iskender Čelebi (who was killed under Süleymān the Magnificent in 942/1535, *Sijilli ʿUthmānī* II, 345), AS 406, Ritter, *Türkiyat Mecm.* VII/VIII (1945), p. 41.

9. Muḥammad b. Yaḥyā al-Tādhifī al-Rabaʿī al-Ḥalabī al-Ḥanbalī, d. 963/1556, see Suppl.

1. *Qalāʾid al-jawāhir fī manāqib al-shaykh ʿAbd al-Qādir* (I, 560), Garr. 703, Cairo ^{1}V, 113.—2. See Suppl.

10. Zayn al-Dīn Manṣūr b. ʿAbd al-Raḥmān al-Shāfiʿī al-Ḥarīrī Khaṭīb al-Saqīfa was born in Damascus in 914/1508, moved to Istanbul with Sultan Süleymān, and died in 967/1559.

TA 177r. 1. *Dīwān* Pet. Ros. 97, Esc. 2387, 431.—2. *al-Fanāʾ*, on whether there is an end to existence which would then be followed by eternal life, Berl. 2686.—3. *al-Bayān fī iẓhār al-tibyān*, on *ittiḥād* and *ḥulūl*, ibid. 3465.—4. Rules for good health in 67 verses, ibid. 6404.—5. *Lawʿat al-shākī wa-damʿat al-bākī*, a *maqāma* on lovesickness, Br. Mus. $1442_{,2}$, Patna II, 448, $2624_{,1}$.

11. Muḥammad b. Sibṭ al-Rajīḥī wrote, in 967/1562:

1. *Hadiyyat al-fuqarā'*, on the six core virtues of the Sufi (*'adl, sakhā', wara', ṣabr, tawba, ḥayā'*), dedicated to Aḥmad Pāshā, vizier of Sultan Süleymān I, Gotha $70_{,8}$.—2. See Suppl. (= Dam. Ẓāh. $84_{,88}$, which has Muḥammad al-Rukhkhajī al-Ḥanbalī al-Shaybānī!).

12. Muḥammad b. Muḥammad al-Ghumrī Zayn al-'Ābidīn Sibṭ al-Marṣafī (no. 1) was living in Mecca in 952/1545 and died in Cairo soon after 970/1562.

1. *Kīmiyyā' al-sa'āda fī ibṭāl kīmiyyā' al-'āda* Gotha $39_{,2}$, Ṭaymūr Ṭab. 75.—2. *al-Bahja al-insiyya fi 'l-firāsa al-insāniyya* Cairo ^{1}VI, 118.—3. *Hidāyat al-mushtāq al-mustahām ilā ru'yat al-nabī 'alayhi 'l-ṣalāt wal-salām* Paris 1546.—4.–13. see Suppl. (4. Alex. Ta'r. 112, Maw. $38_{,2}$; 5. Garr. 1586, *RAAD* IX, $638_{,2}$; 10. ibid. $_{3}$).—14. *Ghāyat al-ta'arruf fī 'ilmay al-uṣūl wal-taṣawwuf*, a didactic poem with the commentary *Baḥr al-anwār al-muḥīṭ*, completed 968/1561 (sic), Alex. Taṣ. 8, from which *al-Durar al-multaqaṭa bil-talaṭṭuf min Baḥr al-anwār*, composed in 958/1551 | (sic), Fātiḥ 3086.—15. *al-Ajwiba al-muskita 'an masā'il al-samā'* 441
al-mubhita Cairo, *Nashra* 1.

13. Ḍiyā' al-Dīn Abū Muḥammad Aḥmad b. Muḥammad al-Waṭarī al-Mawṣilī al-Baghdādī al-Shāfi'ī al-Rifā'ī, who died in Cairo soon after 970/1562, see Suppl.

13a. Nūr al-Dīn 'Alī al-Khawwāṣ al-Burullusī, the teacher of al-Sha'rānī, died in 939/1532 (or, according to others, in 961/1554).

'Imād al-Dīn, *ShDh* VIII, 233, 330, al-Sha'rānī, *Ṭab.* II, 130ff., al-Nabhānī, *Jāmi' karāmāt al-awliyā'*, C. 1329, II, 193 (Heffening), see Suppl.

14. Abu 'l-Mawāhib 'Abd al-Wahhāb b. Aḥmad b. 'Alī al-Sha'rānī (Sha'rāwī) al-Anṣārī al-Shāfi'ī al-Zughlī lived the life of a Sufi in al-Fusṭāṭ. In his writings he drew on the traditions of the boldests mystics of ancient times: "Under the cover of humble thankfulness for God having set him apart with wondrous powers of spirit and holiness, he relates the most preposterous things on his amazing qualities, his intercourse with God and the angels, his powers to work miracles and to penetrate into the secrets of the universe, etc".[2] | This 336
often caused dissent among his contemporaries, while one of his enemies,

2 Goldziher, *Muḥ. St.* II, 290.

by falsifying his works, even tried to raise suspicions against him that he was going against the Qurʾān and the Sunna. But he succeeded in convincing the most reputable shaykhs of his innocence, thus forestalling public riots. His supporters, the Shaʿrāniyya, considered themselves as an independent sect. He died in 973/1565.

Biography Br. Mus. 755, 8, *Khiṭ. jad.* XIV, 109/12, Flügel, *ZDMG* XX, 9f., XXI, 271, Wüst. *Gesch.* 530, A. v. Kremer, *JA* s. VI, vol. 11. 253ff., Vollers, *ZDMG* 44, 390,
442 M. Smith, *The Moslem World* XXIX, 240/7. 1. *al-Durar* | *al-manthūra fī bayān zubd al-ʿulūm al-mashhūra*, a concise encyclopaedia of Qurʾānic exegesis, the art of reciting the Qurʾān, *fiqh, uṣūl al-fiqh, uṣūl al-dīn*, syntax, rhetoric, and mysticism, Berl. 86/7, Gotha 170/1, Alex. Fun. 149,$_{7}$, Cairo VI, ^{1}39, ^{2}184, VII, 37, 153, 490.—2. *al-Yawāqīt wal-jawāhir fī bayān ʿaqāʾid al-akābir*, on Sufi dogmatics, completed on 17 Rajab 955/3 September 1548, Berl. 1837, Gotha 898 (incomplete), Vienna 1922, Br. Mus. 167, Ind. Off. 675, Calcutta p. 66, no. 1085, Bat. 23,$_{3}$, Algiers 926, Constantine, *JA* 1860 II, 438, Alex. Taṣ. 51, Cairo ^{1}II, 120, 144, ^{2}I, 376, Yeni 731, print. C. 1277, 1305, 1306, 1308, among others.—3. *Farāʾid al-qalāʾid fī ʿilm al-ʿaqāʾid* Berl. 2039.—4. *Kashf al-ḥijāb wal-rān ʿan wajh asʾilat al-jānn*, theosophical questions from jinns, composed in 955/1548, Berl. 2123/5, Leid. 2075, Paris 2348,$_{3}$, 2405,$_{1}$, Bodl. II, 256,$_{1}$, Garr. 1591, Algiers 856,$_{1}$, NO 2528/9, Alex. Fun. 54, Cairo ^{1}VI, 180, VII, 36, 135.—5. *al-Fatḥ al-mubīn fī jumla min asrār al-dīn*, on the five pillars of Islam, Berl. 3043, Alex. Fun. 174,$_{16}$.—6. *Irshād al-ṭālibīn ilā marātib ʿulamāʾ al-ʿāmilīn*, a manual on the stages of the Sufis, Berl. 3044, Cairo ^{1}II, 65.—7a. *al-Mīzān al-ṣughrā* or *al-Khiḍriyya* (see Suppl.), an amalgamation of the teachings of the four imams, based on the teaching of his mystical master Khiḍr, who had appeared to him in a vision in 933/1526 with the aim of fortifying the true faith, Berl. 3045, Vienna 1793/4, Paris 814/5, Br. Mus. Suppl. 324, Algiers 1357/8, NO 1874/8, Köpr II. 107, Yeni 583/5, Cairo ^{1}III, 283, 383 ^{2}I, 543, print. C. 1272, 1279, 1300, 1302, 1306, among others. *Balance de la loi musulmane ou esprit de la législation islamique et divergences de ses quatre rites jurisprudentiels par le cheikh ech-Chârâni, trad. de l'ar. par le Dr.* Perron, Algiers 1870, 1898.—7b. *al-Mīzān al-Shaʿrāniyya al-kubrā*, composed in 966/1158, Br. Mus. Suppl. 325, Cairo ^{1}III, 284, ^{2}I, 543, print. C. 1275 and others.—8. *Lawāqiḥ al-anwār al-Qudsiyya fī bayān qawāʿid al-Ṣūfiyya*, an abstract of Ibn ʿArabī's *al-Futūḥāt al-Makkiyya* (I, 572), Berl. 3046, Leipz. 229, cf. Gotha 885, NO 2495/9.—9. *Sawāṭiʿ*
337 *al-anwār al-Qudsiyya fī-mā ṣadarat bihi 'l-Futūḥāt al-Makkiyya*, | an explanation of the verses in this work, based on a dream he had in 937/1530, Cairo ^{1}II, 88, ^{2}I, 319.—10. *al-Qawl al-mubīn fi 'l-radd ʿan Muḥyi 'l-Dīn* (I, 571), Cairo ^{1}VII, 14, ^{2}I, 253, 343.—11. *al-Kibrīt al-aḥmar fī bayān ʿulūm al-shaykh al-akbar*, abstract

of no. 8 by the author, composed in 942/1535, Berl. 3047, Algiers 925, Cairo ^{1}II, 104, 113, ^{2}I, 344, lith. C. 1277, 1307; anon. abstract Berl. 3048.— | 12. *Tanbīh* 443
al-mughtarrīn fi 'l-qarn al-ʿāshir ʿalā mā khālafū fīhi salafahum al-ṭāhir, which is aimed at holding a mirror up to his contemporaries, and particularly how they should live, following the example of the Sufis of old, Berl. 3099, 3100, Alex. Maw. 12, print. C. 1278, 1318, etc.—An abstract, *Tanqīḥ*, by ʿAlawī b. ʿAbdallāh, completed in 1133/1721, Ind. Off. 679.—13. *al-Anwār al-Qudsiyya fī bayān* (*maʿrifat*) *ādāb al-ʿubūdiyya*, based on a vision that he had in 931/1524 in al-Fusṭāṭ, Berl. 3101, Cairo ^{1}II, 69.—14. *Mashāriq al-anwār al-Qudsiyya fī bayān al-ʿuhūd al-Muḥammadiyya*, which aims to highlight to worldly-oriented people the ways in which they fall short in meeting their religious duties, and offer them an opportunity to test, by examining the concrete duties listed in this treatise, the extent to which they do or do not satisfy Muḥammad's requirements, so they can work on bettering themselves, Berl. 3102/3, Vienna 1921, print. C. 1287, under the title *Lawāqiḥ al-anwār al-Qudsiyya* Patna II, 312,$_{2446}$.—Commentary by Ibn Mālik, Istanbul 1287.—15. *Madārij al-sālikīn ilā rusūm ṭarīq al-ʿārifīn*, on the behaviour of the Sufis, Berl. 3104, Gotha 896, Vienna 1923, Garr. 1587, Cairo ^{1}II, 133 (lith).—16. *al-Baḥr al-mawrūd fi 'l-mawāthīq wal-ʿuhūd*, on the duties of students towards their teachers, based on the principle of absolute obedience, composed in 974/1566 in Cairo, Berl. 3183/5, Munich 607, Br. Mus. 343, 756, Ind. Off. 676, Garr. 1588, Köpr. II, 113, Cairo ^{1}II, 69 (autograph), print. C. 1278, 1287 1321. Cf. v. Kremer, *JA* 1868, 268ff., a didactic letter thereon Berl. 173,$_4$.—17. *Mawāzīn al-qāṣirīn min al-rijāl*, against fake Sufis, composed in 973/1565, Berl. 3186/7, 3367 (incomplete, with the wrong date of 933, see Rieu, Br. Mus. Suppl. 245,$_4$), Gotha 736,$_2$, Leid. 2074, Br. Mus. Suppl. 245,$_4$ (different from Paris 369), print. C. 1297 (Cat. II, 86).—18. Seven short prayers for each day of the week, with detailed explanations, Berl. 3780.—19. *Mukhtaṣar Tadhkirat al-Qurṭubī* (I, 529), Alex. Ta'r. 8. Riza P. 456, print. Būlāq 1300, C. 1303, 1304, 1308, 1310, among others.—20. *Irshād al-mughaffalīn min al-fuqahāʾ wal-fuqarāʾ ilā shurūṭ ṣuḥbat al-umarāʾ* Berl. 5624, Ms. oct. 3933.—21. *Kashf al-ghumma ʿan jamīʿ al-umma* NO 1197, Cairo I, ^{1}387, ^{2}139, print. C. 1281, 1303, 2 vols., *Dībāja* Gotha 2,$_{129}$.—22. *Durar al-ghāwwāṣ ʿalā fatāwī* (*manāqib*) *sayyidī ʿAlī al-Khawwāṣ*, sayings by his teacher (13a), compiled in 955/1548, Br. Mus. Suppl. 243, Ind. Off. 676,$_2$, Alex. Fun. 161,$_5$, print. C. 1277 (Cat. II, 83).—23. *al-Jawāhir wal-durar*, sayings by the same, in three editions: a. *al-Kubrā*, compiled in 940/1533, | Berl. Ms. or. oct. 3934, Br. Mus. 755,$_1$, Bol.-Mars. 239,$_1$, Alex. 444
Taṣ. 15, Cairo ^{1}II, 78, ^{2}I, 287.—b. *al-Wusṭā*, compiled in 942/1535, Cairo ^{1}II, 120, VII, 36, ^{1}II, 78.—c. *al-Ṣughrā* Pet. AM 70.—24. *al-Mawāzīn al-durriyya al-mubayyina li-ʿaqāʾid al-firaq al-ʿaliyya*, sayings by famous Sufis, Ind. Off.

677.—25. *al-Nafaḥāt al-Qudsiyya fī bayān qawāʿid al-Ṣūfiyya* Leipz. 268.—26.
338 *Risālat al-murīd al-ṣādiq maʿa farīd al-khāliq* Algiers $924_{,1}$. |—27. *al-Badr al-munīr fī gharīb aḥādīth al-bashīr al-nadhīr* Köpr. 284, Alex. Ḥad. 8, Cairo I, 275, 402.—28. *al-Ajwiba al-marḍiyya ʿan aʾimmat al-fuqahāʾ wal-Ṣūfiyya* Cairo ^{1}II, 61, 113.—29. *Bahjat al-nufūs wal-aḥdāq fīmā tamayyaza bihi ʾl-qawm min al-ādāb wal-akhlāq* Cairo ^{1}II, 72.—30. *Ḥudūq ikhwat al-Islām*, on the mutual duties of Muslims, Paris $1248_{,4}$, Alex. Maw. 14, Cairo ^{1}II, 154.—31. *Miftāḥ al-sirr al-Qudsī fī tafsīr āyat al-kursī* NO 233.—32. *al-Jawhar al-maṣūn* (*al-maknūz*) *wal-sirr al-marqūm fī-mā tuntijuhu ʾl-khalwa min al-asrār wal-ʿulūm* Vienna 1920, Cairo ^{1}VII, 2, 136.—33. *Risāla fi ʾl-qawāʿid al-kashfiyya al-mūḍiḥa li-maʿāni ʾl-ṣifāt al-ilāhiyya* Garr. 1590, Algiers 731, 4, Cairo ^{1}II, 103, VII, 36, ^{2}I, 343.—34. *al-Kashf wal-tabyīn* Cairo ^{1}VI, 12.—35. *al-Jawhar al-maṣūn fī ʿilm Kitāb Allāh al-maknūn* ibid. 36.—36. *Sirr al-masīr wal-tazawwud li-yawm al-maṣīr* ibid.—37. *Minaḥ al-minna fi ʾl-talabbus bil-sunna* ibid. 152.—38. *Risāla fī ahl al-ʿaqāʾid al-zāʾigha wa-umūr tanfaʿ man yurīd al-khawḍ fī ʿilm al-kalām* ibid. 283.—39. *Radʿ al-fuqarāʾ ʿan daʿwa ʾl-walāya al-kubrā* ibid. 460.—40. *al-Minaḥ al-saniyya ʿala ʾl-waṣiyya al-Matbūliyya* see p. 149.—41. *al-Akhlāq al-Matbūliyya wal-mufāda min al-ḥaḍra al-Muḥammadiyya ʿalā sayyidinā Aḥmad al-Matbūlī* Bodl. I, 768.—42. *Dīwān* Paris 3234.—43. *Lawāqiḥ al-anwār fī ṭabaqāt* (*al-sādat*) *al-akhyār*, completed in Cairo in 952/1543, Berl. 9982/3, Gotha 1767, Munich 446, Vienna 1185, Br. Mus. 371/2, 964, Ind. Off. 713, Paris 2045 (autograph), Pet. AM 214, Köpr. 1112, III, 393, Yeni 863, Cairo ^{1}II, 108, ^{2}V, 319, Makram 54, Calc. p. 51, no. 271, print. C. 1305, 1308, among others.—44. *Laṭāʾif al-minan wal-akhlāq fī bayān wujūb al-taḥadduth bi-niʿmati ʾllāh ʿala ʾl-iṭlāq*, autobiography, Berl. 10111 Dresd. 392, Budapest, Ung. Nationalmuseum (Goldziher) 15, AS 2030, Cairo ^{1}II, 107, ^{2}V, 192, print. Būlāq 1287, C. 1311.—45. *al-Muqaddima al-naḥwiyya fī ʿilm al-ʿarabiyya*, with a commentary by Aḥmad al-Ghunaymī, d. 1044/1634 (p. 432),
445 Paris $4111_{,2}$, Garr. 474.—46. *Mukhtaṣar Tadhkirat al-Suwaydī* | *fi ʾl-ṭibb* I, 650.—47.–64. see Suppl. (60. with the title *Sabīl al-murīd al-ṣādiq maʿa man yurīd al-khāliq* Alex. Fun. $174_{,18}$).—65. *Asʾila* Alex. Fun. $174_{,15}$.—66. *Wird aqṭāb al-aqṭāb* ibid. $161_{,6}$.—67. *Mīzān al-qāṣirīn wa-hiya Risāla fī ḥāl baʿḍ al-mutaṣawwifa mimman yaddaʿūna ʾl-walāya* ibid. $127_{,2}$. (= 17 ?).

15. ʿAlāʾ al-Dīn ʿAlī b. Ṣadaqa al-Shāmī al-Dimashqī studied Shāfiʿī law and was a professor at the Ṣābūniyya. He gave public readings from al-Bukhārī in luxury mansions, and in the holy months he held small religious gatherings for laypeople in the Umayyad mosque. From an early age he devoted himself to Sufism and was an accomplished Sufi poet.

RA 202r. 1. A longer *Rāʾiyya*, Gotha $44_{,3}$.—2. A Sufi poem on friendship. Berl. $7939_{,5}$.

16. Najm al-Dīn Muḥammad b. Aḥmad b. ʿAlī al-Ghayṭī al-Iskandarī al-Shāfiʿī, who was born between 900–10/1494–1504, was Principal of al-Ṣalāḥiyya and al-Siryāqūsiyya Sufi convents in Cairo. | His influence was so great that he once 339 quelled an uprising against the government using it. He died on 17 Ṣafar 981/19 June 1573.

Khiṭ. jad. VIII, 20. 1. *Mashyakha* Cairo ^{1}I, 248. 2. *al-Farāʾid al-munaẓẓama wal-fawāʾid al-muḥakkama fī-mā yuqāl fi ʾbtidāʾ tadrīs al-ḥadīth al-sharīf* ibid. 246.—3. *Bahjat* (*Tuḥfat*) *al-sāmiʿīn wal-nāẓirīn bi-mawlid sayyid al-awwalīn wal-ākhirīn* Berl. 9532, Algiers $729_{,1}$, abstract by Ḥasan b. ʿAlī al-Madābighī, d. 1170/1756 (p. 430), Berl. 9533, Alex. Ḥad. $47_{,2}$.—Commentaries: a. ʿAlī b. ʿAbd al-Qādir al-Nabtītī, d. after 1070/1659, Garr. 654, Cairo ^{1}I, 264, ^{2}I, 88.—b. ʿAbdallāh Suwaydān, ca. 1200/1785 (for whose *Risāla* see Suppl., Garr. 1137), Berl. 9534.—4. *al-Ibtihāj bil-kalām ʿala ʾl-isrāʾ wal-miʿrāj* Berl. 2603, Paris 1985, Br. Mus. 152, $250_{,6}$, Garr. $2177_{,1}$, Alex. Ḥad. $147_{,8}$, $147_{,2}$, Cairo I, 257, VII, 513, ^{2}V, 335.—Commentary by Aḥmad b. Muḥammad b. Naṣr al-Andalusī al-Salāwī, composed in 1243/1827, Alex. Fun. $93_{,2}$.—5. *Qiṣṣat miʿrāj al-nabī*, a shorter work, Berl. 2608, Cairo ^{1}I, 384, VII, 65, 207, ^{2}V, 82, V, 295.—Glosses by Aḥmad al-Dardīr, d. 1201/1786 (see below, p. 353), Alex. Ḥad. $47_{,3}$, Makram. 18; Būlāq 1284, 1289, C. 1298, 1305, 1306, 1312, | 1315, 1322, 1341, 1344.—c. Aḥmad 446 al-Qalyūbī, d. 1069/1658 (see below, p. 364), Berl. Ms. or. oct. 3915, Garr. 656, 664, Tüb. 103. Alex. Ḥad. 40, Dam. 74 (ʿUm. $82_{,40}$).—Abstract by al-Madābighī, d. 1170/1756 (p. 430), Cairo ^{1}I, 405, on which was based the *Taqrīrāt* of Abū Naṣr ʿAbd al-Raḥmān al-Naḥrāwī Muqriʾ al-Shaykh ʿAṭiyya al-Ujhūrī, d. 1210/1796, Alex. Ḥad. 11, Cairo ^{1}I, 287, 2403, ^{2}I, 97.—6. *al-Ajwiba al-mufīda* (*al-sadīda*) *ʿala ʾl-asʾila al-ʿadīda* (*al-ʿaliyya*), 8 questions on what happens after death, composed in 974/1566, Berl. 2687/8, Ms. or. oct. 3921, Gotha 756, Paris 5316, Algiers 864 (?), Alex. Fun. $134_{,2}$, Cairo ^{1}VII, 13.—7. *Risāla fi ʾl-kalām ʿalā Khiḍr* Alex. Fun. $120_{,5}$, $166_{,2}$.—8. *Fawāʾid* (*Faḍāʾil*) *laylat al-niṣf min Shaʿbān* Cairo ^{1}VI, 163, VII, 135, 513.—9. *Mawāhib al-karīm al-mannān fi ʾl-kalām ʿalā laylat al-niṣf wa-fātiḥat sūrat al-dukhān* Cairo ^{1}VI, 203, VII, 169, Alex. Fun. $167_{,20}$, entitled *al-Imtinān fi ʾl-kalām ʿalā awāʾil sūrat al-dukhān* Garr. $2177_{,2}$.—10. Some answers concerning ʿŪj b. ʿUnq, i.e. Og of Bāshān, Gotha $91_{,3}$, Hamb. Or. Sem. $14_{,7}$.—11. *Fi ʾl-quṭb wal-awtād wal-nujabāʾ*, on the hierarchy of the saints, Berl. 3366.—12.–21. see Suppl.—22. *Asʾila wa-ajwiba fī aḥwāl al-mawtā* Alex. Fun. $135_{,1}$.—23. *Risāla fi ʾl-Islām wal-īmān* ibid. $121_{,1}$.

17. Karīm al-Dīn Abu ʾl-Tuqā Muḥammad b. Aḥmad b. Muḥammad al-Khalwatī was born in 896/1491. He became the leader of the Khalwatiyya order in Cairo and died in Jumādā II 986/August 1578.

Khiṭ. jad. IV, 110. 1. *Radd al-mutawaqqif bil-maḥāla fi 'l-ibtidā' bil-dhikr bil-jalāla* Cairo II, 83, VII, 47, 268.—2. *al-Ṭirāz al-dhahabī ʿalā abyāt b. ʿArabī* ibid. II, 14.—3. See Suppl.

17a. Muḥammad b. Muḥammad al-Dibsiyāwī.

Al-Zahr al-zāhir see Suppl., Garr. 1926, Alex. Maw. 20 (which says it was completed in 904/1499).

18. Aḥmad b. ʿUthmān al-Sharnūbī died in 994/1586 on a trip in Asia Minor.

1. *al-ʿAqā'id* Garr. 1564, Cairo [1]II, 34.—2. *Fatḥ al-mawāhib wa-manhaj al-ṭālib al-rāghib wa-kanz al-wāṣilīn min khawāṣṣ aḥbābihi* Alex. Taṣ. 26, Cairo [1]II, 99, [2]I, 336.—3. *al-Kashf al-ghuyūbī* or *Kitāb al-ṭabaqāt*, Sufi discussions with his
447 student Muḥammad al-Bulqīnī on the miracles of | the Egyptian poles (*aqṭāb*) and his own, Berl. 3371, Tüb. 15, 232, Paris 1361/3, print. C. 1281, 1305, cf. de Sacy, *Journ. des sav.* 1831, 158, entitled *al-Kashf al-ghuyūbī fī ṭabaqāt al-Sharnūbī* as a work by al-Būlqīnī, Alex. Ta'r. 103.—4. *Tā'iyyat al-sulūk ilā malik al-mulūk*, with a commentary by ʿAbd al-Majīd al-Sharnūbī (see Suppl.), C. 1310.

19. Shams al-Dīn Muḥammad b. ʿAlī b. Muḥammad al-Bakrī al-Ṣiddīqī, who was born on 13 Dhu 'l-Ḥijja 930/12 October 1525 and died in 994/1586.

Khiṭ. jad. III, 126. 1. *Tanbīh al-awwāh li-faḍl Lā ilāha illa 'llāh*, 107 *ḥadīth*, Berl. 1435.—2. *Urjūza fī ʿilm al-taṣawwuf*, in 135 verses, ibid. 3052.—3. *al-Iqtiṣād fī bayān marātib al-ijtihād* ibid. 3466.—4. *Ṣalawāt ʿala 'l-nabī* ibid. 1310.

340 | 20. Muḥammad b. Muḥammad b. ʿAbd al-Raḥmān al-Bahnasī al-ʿUqaylī al-Shāfiʿī al-Naqshbandī al-Khalwatī, who died around 1001/1592.

1. *Bulūgh al-arab bi-sulūk al-adab*, lessons in Sufism, Berl. 3188.—2. *al-Funūn al-ʿirfāniyya wal-hibāt al-malkāniyya* Cairo [1]II, 101, [2]I, App. 46.—3., 4. See Suppl. (4. Garr. 10. *Qaṣīdat b. ʿArūs*, in colloquial language, C. 1880).

21. Aḥmad b. Muḥammad b. Aḥmad al-Matbūlī was a preacher at al-Madrasa al-Mu'ayyadiyya in Cairo who died in 1003/1594.

Muḥ. I, 274/7. 1. *Najāḥ al-āmāl bi-īḍāḥ ʿarḍ al-aʿmāl*, on the reward in the Hereafter for one's actions, Berl. 2644.—2. *Nayl al-ihtidā' fī faḍl al-irtidā'* on the

Sufi's cloak, excerpts in Muḥ. I, 275.—3. *Rashf al-raḥīq fī waṣf al-nabī bil-ṣiddīq*, composed in 1001/1592, Cairo ^{1}VII, 572.

22. Muḥammad Ḥijāzī al-Jīzī al-Khalwatī al-Sandiyūnī, who died after 1003/1594.

1. *Mafātīḥ al-ghuyūb wa-taʿmīr al-qulūb fī tathlīth al-maḥbūb*, composed in 999/1590, Algiers 856,$_2$ = *al-Thulāthiyya* ḤKh. II, 492.—2. *Shaqq al-juyūb ʿan asrār māʿāni ʾl-ghuyūb wa-tajalli ʾl-maḥbūb fī ufq samāʾ al-qulūb*, composed in 1003/1594, ibid. 3.—3. *al-Bidāyāt wal-tawassuṭ wal-nihāyāt* Cairo ^{1}II, 118.—4. See Suppl.

| 23. Fāʾid b. Mubārak al-Abyārī, a Sufi from Cairo who died in 1016/1607 (or, 448
according to Berl. 1014, sometime after 1086/1680).

Muḥ. III, 254. 1. *Muqaddima*, on the reading of the Qurʾān by Ḥafṣ, *ʿan* ʿĀṣim, Berl. 647.—2. *Mawrid al-ẓamʾān ilā sīrat al-mabʿūth min ʿAdnān*, a biography of the Prophet, ibid. 9603.—3. *al-Qawl al-mukhtār fī dhikr al-rijāl al-akhyār*, a list of his teachers and other contemporaries, especially Sufis, with biographical data, ibid. 10114.—4., 5. See Suppl.

24. Aḥmad b. ʿUmar al-Ḥammāmī al-ʿAlawānī al-Ghūlī al-Ḥamawī al-Khalwatī al-Shāfiʿī was born in Hama, lived in Aleppo, and died in 1017/1608.

Muḥ. I, 257/9. 1. *al-Uṣūl al-ʿAlawāniyya fī ʾl-ādāb wal-akhlāq al-ṣūfiyya* Cairo ^{1}II, 117.—2. *Kitāb al-arwāḥ* ibid.—3. *Risāla fī ʾl-taṣawwuf* ibid.—4. *Aʿdhab al-mashārib fī ʾl-sulūk wal-manāqib* Alex. Taṣ. 6.

25. Muḥammad b. ʿAlī al-Qudsī al-Ḥanafī al-ʿAlamī al-Rifāʿī Shams al-Dīn studied in Jerusalem, Cairo, and Damascus, where he lived, and became a professor at the Ḥanafī al-Qudāʿiyya mosque. He died in 1018/1609.

Muḥ. IV, 43, TA 170r. *Al-Naṣīḥa al-marḍiyya ila ʾl-ṭarīqa al-Muḥammadiyya*, a manual on Sufism, Berl. 3390; anonymous commentary, Copenhagen 72.

26. Muḥammad al-Ṣiddīq b. Muḥammad al-Ḥanafī, ca. 1024/1615.

1. *Manāqib sayyidinā Uways al-Qaranī*, a proto-Sufi, d. 37/657, Berl. 10065/6.—2.–4. see Suppl.

341 | 27. ʿUmar b. ʿAbd al-Wahhāb b. Ibrāhīm b. Maḥmūd al-ʿUrdī al-Qādirī was born in Aleppo in 950/1543, became a *muftī* there, and died in 1024/1615.

Muḥ. III, 215/8. 1. *Lāmiyyat al-sharaf*, a mystical *qaṣīda*, with the commentary *Nahj al-saʿāda wa-nasj al-iʿāda*, Ind. Off. 697$_{,1}$.—2. Another *qaṣīda*, rhyming on *dāl*, in which each verse begins with a different letter of the alphabet, ibid.—3. *Fatḥ al-mutaʿālī fī taḥqīq fawāʾid mabāḥith al-Khayālī*, superglosses on Khayālī's (Suppl. II, 318) glosses on Taftazānī's commentary on Nasafī's *ʿAqāʾid* (I, 548), completed on 10 Dhu 'l-Ḥijja 1019/24 February 1611, Yeni 754.—4. See Suppl.

449 | 28. Muḥammad b. Abi 'l-Wafāʾ b. Maʿrūf al-Ḥamawī al-Khalwatī wrote, in 1034/1624:

Al-Tuḥfa al-mukmala fī sharḥ al-basmala, with regard to each of its letters, Berl. 3446.

29. Muḥammad b. ʿUmar b. Muḥammad al-Qudsī al-ʿAlamī moved to Damascus, but after the pilgrimage he took up residence in his hometown of Jerusalem, and died in 1038/1628.

Muḥ. IV, 78. *Tāʾiyya*, a Sufi work, with a commentary, Br. Mus. Suppl. 1090, see Suppl.—2. *Fayḍ fatḥ al-raḥmān fī waṣāyā wa-ḥikam lil-abnāʾ wal-muḥibbīn wal-ikhwān* Berl. 4016.—3., 4. See Suppl.

30. Shams al-Dīn Muḥammad b. Shuʿayb b. ʿAlī al-Shuʿaybī al-Aḥmadī al-Abshīhī al-Shāfiʿī, who died after 1040/1630.

1. *al-Maʿāni 'l-daqīqa al-wafiyya fī mā yalzam nuqabāʾ al-sāda al-Ṣūfiyya*, composed in 1021/1612, Cairo ^{1}II, 136, ^{2}I, 360.—2. *al-Jawhar al-farīd wal-ʿiqd al-waḥīd (mufīd) fī tarjamat ahl al-tawḥīd* ibid. ^{1}VII, 276, ^{2}I, 287.—3., 4. See Suppl. (4. Garr. 1972).

31. Aḥmad b. ʿAlī al-ʿUsālī al-Ḥarīrī was born in ʿUsāl near Damascus, to where his father, a Kurd from Ḥarīr, had emigrated. He studied in Damascus, Aleppo, and ʿAyntāb, and lived in Damascus. In 1045/1635 Aḥmad Pāshā Küčük, the governor of Syria, built him a monastery. He died in 1048/1638.

Muḥ. I, 248. 1. A prayer, Berl. 3655.—2. *Waṣiyya* ibid. 4017.—3. *Wird al-wasāʾil li-kulli sāʾil* Alex. Faw. 18$_{,3}$, Fun. 144$_{,2}$, 158$_{,5}$.

33. Ayyūb b. Aḥmad al-Qurashī al-Khalwatī al-Ṣāliḥī was born in Damascus in 994/1586, lectured there at the Ṣāliḥiyya and died in 1071/1660.

Muḥ. I, 428/33. A list of his *rasāʾil*, by his son Ismāʿīl, Berl. 241. 1. Didactic letters and educational program, ibid. $185_{,2}$.—2. *Dhakhīrat qawlihi ṣlʿm Yāsīn qalb al-Qurʾān* (sura 36), ibid. 953.—3. Sufi discussion around sura $3,_{25}$, ibid. 985.—4. *ʿAqīdat al-tafrīd wa-khamīlat al-tawḥīd* ibid. 2447/8.—5. *Dhakhīra* on
the profession of unity, ibid. 2449. |—6. Discussion of God's forgiveness in con- 342
nection with the | saying of the Prophet *Law lam tudhnibū la-dhahaba ʾllāhu* 450
bi-kum wa la-jāʾa ʾllāhu bi-qawmin yudhnibūn etc., ibid. 2645.—7. *Jawharat al-ʿulūm wa-durrat al-fuhūm* ibid. 3110.—8. A treatise on the states and tasks of the Sufi, on the occasion of a poem, ibid. 3111.—9. *Dhakhīrat ahl al-malāma*, ibid. 3112.—10. A Sufi treatise, ibid. 3113.—11. *Dhakhīrat al-ʿibāda wal-ʿubūdiyya wal-ʿubūda* ibid. 3114.—12. *Dhakhīrat al-danaf*, on lovesickness for God and His glorification, ibid. 3115.—13. *Dhakhīrat al-ghayra fi ʾl-maḥabba ʿala ʾl-maḥbūb*, on jealousy in one's love of God, ibid. 3116.—14. *Mukhāṭabat al-nafs al-ammāra bil-sūʾ ʿinda irādat al-tawajjuh bil-maḥabba al-dhātiyya ilā ʾllāh*, ibid. 3136.—15. *Dhakhīrat al-maraḍ* ibid.—16. *Dhakhīrat qawlihi ṣlʿm ʿan il-dunyā, annahu mā naẓara ilayhā mundhu khalaqahā… wa-mā yudhammu minhā wa-mā yumdaḥ* ibid. 3146.—17. *Dhakhīrat al-faraḥ bi-faḍl Allāh wa-raḥmatihi* ibid. 3153.—18. *Dhakhīrat al-shukr* ibid. 3154.—19. *Dhakhīrat qawl baʿḍihim: al-riḍā jannat al-dunyā* ibid. 3155.—20. *Dhakhīrat jumdān* on *al-tafrīd*, ibid. 3157.—21. *Dhakhīrat qawlihī ṣlʿm: baynamā Ayyūbu yaghtasilu ʿuryānan*, on the plagues inflicted by God, ibid. 3169.—22. *Dhakhīrat qawlihi ṣlʿm: kullu laḥmin nabata ʿan ḥarāmin fal-nāru awlā bihi* ibid. 3170.—23. *Dhakhīrat al-tawba* ibid. 3171.—24. On penance, in connection with sura $2,_{54}$, ibid. 3172.—25. *Dhakhīrat man jarradahu ʾl-ḥubb ʿani ʾl-khawf* ibid. 3173.—26. *Dhakīra* on the fear of men, ibid. 3174.—27. *Dhakhīra* on the *khalwa* (retreat), ibid. 3191.—28. *Dhakhīrat al-ʿaṭf*, on divine affection, ibid. 3234.—29. *Dhakhīrat al-iksīr*, on the inner grasp of God as a result of one's love for Him, ibid. 3235.—30. On *ḥusn al-khuluq* ibid. 3236.—31. *Dhakhīrat al-makr al-ilāhī* ibid. 3237.—32. *Dhakhīrat qawlihi ṣlʿm: inna ʾllāha amaranī bil-mudārāh* ibid. 3238.—35. *Dhakhīrat al-wujūd al-muṭlaq wal-muqayyad wal-waḥda wal-kathra* ibid. 3239.—34. *Dhakhīrat duʿāʾ Yūsuf… wa-bihi takhallaṣa min al-sijn* ibid. 3240.—35. *Dhakhīrat al-futūḥ*, on divine inspiration, ibid. 3323.—36. *Kashf al-rayb ʿani ʾl-istimdād min al-ghayb*, on the need for enlightenment in order to know the hidden nature of God, ibid. 3324.—37. The beginning of a treatise on miracles, ibid. 3325.—38. *Dhakhīrat qul aʿūdhu bi-rabbi ʾl-falaq*, on *wujūd* and *ʿadam* in the context of sura 113, ibid. 3326.—39. *Dhakhīrat tarassum ahl al-daʿwā*, against someone

who pretended to have experienced special enlightenment following 40 days of retreat, ibid. 3327.—40. *Dhakhīrat al-iṭlāq fi 'l-mushāhada wa-ʿayn al-shuhūd etc.*, ibid. 3328.—41. *Risālat al-qurba wal-wuṣūl ilā ḥaḍrat al-rasūl*, ibid. 3329.—
451 42. Four Sufi poems, ibid. 3423.—43. *Dhakhīrat al-anwār wa-samīrat* | *al-afkār*, on the deeper meaning of the letter *bāʾ*, ibid. 3448.—44. *al-Sirr al-muṭlaq wal-amr al-muḥaqqaq* ibid. 3467.—45. *al-Taḥqīq li-sulālat al-Ṣiddīq*, with several longer poems, ibid. 3487.—46. *Risālat kanz al-ghinā*, on the *dhikr*, ibid. 3720.—47. *Dhakhīrat qurbat al-ḥamd*, on the merits of praising God, ibid. 3721.—48. *Dhakhīrat al-tafrīd* ibid. 3722.—49. *Dhakhīrat suʾāl, saʾalahu ... min ahl al-Rūm al-Atrāk*, on why the *witr* is performed together in Ramaḍān, ibid. 3829.—50. *Raqīqat qalb al-ʿiyān fī qalb ḥaqīqat al-insān*, on the secret powers of letters,
343 ibid. 4129. |—51. Explanation of an uprising in Damascus in 1067/1656, based on information taken from the *Kitāb al-jafr*, ibid. 4223,$_{1}$.—52. A prophecy regarding the year 1070/1659 and the rest of the century, ibid. $_{2}$.—53. A promise of victory to Sultan Meḥmed, ibid. $_{3}$.—54. A prophecy on the second century of the second millenium, ibid. $_{4}$.—55. Some poems on the deeper meaning of the names of the letters of the alphabet, in particular *bāʾ*, ibid. 7990,$_{6}$.—56. A letter to Muṣṭafā Pāshā, Sultan Murād's vizier, in which he wishes both him and the sultan divine protection, ibid. 8616,$_{2}$.—57. See Suppl.

34. ʿUthmān b. Walī al-Būlawī wrote, in 1073/1662:

Bahjat al-dhākirīn wa-tuḥfat al-ʿābidīn Cairo ^{1}VI, 118.

35. ʿAlī b. ʿAbdallāh al-Miṣrī, ca. 1075/1664.

1. *Tuḥfat al-abrār fī dhikr shayʾ min faḍl ṣuḥbat al-akhyār*, on associating with pious people, Berl. 3117.—2. *Tuḥfat al-akyās fī ḥusn al-ẓann bil-nās* Leipz. 260.—3.–4. see Suppl.

36. Shāhīn b. Abi 'l-Yumn al-ʿĀtikī, ca. 1075/1664.

ʿUjālat al-ẓamʾān fī taʿdād shuʿab al-īmān, a Sufi guide on the path to God, Berl. 3286.

37. Tāj (Zayn) al-ʿĀrifīn Muḥammad b. Abi 'l-Ḥasan ʿAbbās al-Bakrī al-Ṣiddīqī al-Ghumrī al-Ṭabarkhazī al-Khwārizmī al-Ṣūfī al-Ashʿarī, who died in 1087/1676.

M. Hartmann, *Muwashshaḥ* 68. 1. Sufi *dīwān*, alphabetically ordered, Berl. 7997, Gotha 2326/7, Cambr. Palmer 55, other collections Berl. 7998/8000, Gotha

2329, Leipz. 573.—2. *Jumān al-tarjūman*, a collection of poems selected from his larger work *Tarjūmān al-asrār* Gotha 2328,$_{1}$.—3. *Lāmiyya* with a *takhmīs* by Muḥammad al-ʿAlamī (no. 29), ibid. 93,$_{9}$.—5. *al-Naṣīḥa* ibid. 2328,$_{2}$.—6. *al-Nāfiʿa* ibid. $_{3}$.—7. *Ṣādiḥat al-azal* | ibid. $_{4}$, see Suppl. 462, 5,$_{12}$.—8. *al-Sirr* 452
al-maktūm wal-durr al-manẓūm ibid. $_{5}$.—9. *Tarkīb al-ṣuwar wa-tartīb al-suwar*, an analogy between the composition of essences and the order of the suras of the Qurʾān, requiring a sound understanding of microcosm, Berl. 461.—10. *ʿAqīda* in rhymed prose, ibid. 2052.—11. *Maqṣad al-ṭullāb fī-mā yalzam al-shaykh wal-murīd min al-ādāb* ibid. 3193.—12., 13. See Suppl.

38. Muḥammad b. Aḥmad al-Anṣārī al-Burullusī wrote, in 1097/1686:

Al-Āyāt al-bayyināt fī thubūt karāmāt al-awliyāʾ fi ʾl-ḥayāt wa-baʿd al-mamāt Cairo ^{1}II, 126, ^{2}I, 260.[3]

39. Abū Bakr Ṣāliḥ al-Khālidī wrote, around 1100/1688:

Hadiyyat al-mulūk fi ʾl-ikhlāṣ wal-sulūk, dedicated to ʿAlī Pāshā, Berl. 3066.

| 40. Qāsim b. Ṣalāḥ al-Dīn al-Khānī al-Ḥalabī al-Ṣūfī al-Qādirī was born in 344
Aleppo in 1028/1619 and moved to Baghdad in 1050/1640, where he stayed for two years. After a two-month stay in Aleppo he went to Basra for 10 months, then, via Aleppo, to Mecca and then Istanbul, where he remained for one year and seven months. For the next seven years he lived as an ascetic in Aleppo, began his studies in 1066/1655, and, two years later, became a teacher. Finally, he became a *muftī* in Aleppo, where he died in 1109/1697.

Mur. IV, 9. 1. *al-Sayr wal-sulūk ilā malik al-mulūk*, a manual on how to reach God, Berl. 3287/8, Garr. 1593, Bursa Ulu Cami Taṣ. 13, Alex. Taṣ. 19, anonymous commentary Berl. 3289.—2. *Risāla fī ʿilm al-manṭiq* Tüb. 110,$_{2}$, Berl. 5208, Alex. Manṭiq 20,$_{2}$.—3. *Risāla fi ʾl-ridda wa-aḥkāmihā* Alex. Fun. 160,$_{3}$.—4. *Mukhtaṣar al-Sirājiyya* (I, 470) *wa-sharḥ al-Sayyid ʿalayhā* ibid. 161,$_{4}$.—5. *Risāla fi ʾl-tawḥīd* ibid. Tawḥīd 35.—6. *al-Taḥqīq fi ʾl-radd ʿala ʾl-zindīq* ibid. Taṣ. 33,$_{4}$.—7. *Majālis* ibid. Mawāʿiẓ 34.—8. *al-Ṭarīq al-wāḍiḥ ilā ʿaqīdat al-salaf al-ṣāliḥ* ibid. Fun. 67,$_{20}$.

---

3 Aḥmad al-Shaykh ʿAmīra al-Burullusī, the author of *Sharḥ al-basmala wal-ḥamdala* cannot have been his father because, according to Alex. Fun. 100,$_{5}$ (which has *Nukat wa-fawāʾid ʿala ʾl-b. wal-ḥ. min khuṭbat sharḥ al-Minhāj*), he died in 957/1550; see also the commentary *al-Ṭawāliʿ al-munīra ʿalā basmalat ʿAmīra* by Abū Bakr b. Ismāʿīl al-Shanawānī, d. 1026/1617 (p. 367), ibid. 100,$_{6}$.

453 | 41. Manṣūr b. Muḥammad al-Ḥalabī al-Ḥakīm, ca. 1110/1698.

ʿIlm al-anwār al-raqīqa bil-kashf ilā manāzil al-ṭarīqa wal-ḥaqīqa, a Sufi work, Berl. 3242.

42. Muṣṭafā b. Muḥammad al-Ḥamawī al-Laṭīfī, who was born in 1004/1595, lived as a dervish in Aleppo and died in 1126/1714.

Siyāḥa, an autobiography written at the suggestion of his son Muḥammad, focussed particularly on his pilgrimages in the years 1030–1110/1621–89, Berl. 6138/40.

43. ʿAlāʾ al-Dīn ʿAlī b. Muḥammad al-Miṣrī, ca. 1127/1715.

1. *al-Taʿlīq ʿalā waṣiyyat al-adab al-musammā bi-Kashf al-qināʿ ʿan wajh alfāẓ shubhat al-samāʿ*, a commentary on a Sufi work, Berl. 3067.—2.–5. see Suppl.

43a. ʿAlī al-Ḥalabī al-Nūrbakhshī wrote, in 1118/1706:

Jāmiʿ al-asmāʾ wal-adʿiya wa-ḥāmiʿ al-āthār wal-athniya Alex. Fawāʾid 6.

45. Aḥmad b. al-Ḥusayn b. Muḥammad b. al-Ḥasan al-Sharīf al-Ḥamūmī wrote, in 1132/1720:

Risāla fī ḥukm rafʿ al-ṣawt bil-dhikr Cairo [1]VII, 273.

46. Tāj al-Dīn al-Ghazzālī wrote, in 1144/1731:

Al-Nafaḥāt al-rabbāniyya wal-fuyūḍāt al-ilāhiyya al-ṣamdāniyya Cairo [1]II, 142.

345 | 48. Ḥasan b. Mūsā al-Kurdī al-Qādirī al-Bānī al-ʿAlawānī al-Naqshbandī, who lived in Damascus and died in 1148/1735.

Mur. II, 35. 1. *Risāla fī qawl al-Shaykh al-akbar wa-qawl al-Jīlī*, a. on the statement by Ibn al-ʿArabī that knowledge comes from what is known and the opposing view of al-Jīlī, between which he tries to mediate; b. on whether the angels were created from the same light as Muḥammad; c. on the boundaries and nature of knowledge, Berl. 1853.—2. *Risāla fī anna ʿilm allāh muḥīṭ bi-*
454 *nafsihi am lā*, on whether God has knowledge of Himself | or not, ibid. 2351.—3.

On God's nature, ibid. 2352.—4. On the nature and properties of God, ibid. 2353.—5. See Suppl.

49. ʿAbd al-Ghanī b. Ismāʿīl al-Nābulusī was born on 5 Dhu 'l-Ḥijja 1050/19 March 1641, lost his father in 1062/1652, and then joined the Sufi orders of the Qādiriyya and Naqshbandiyya. He studied the works of Ibn al-ʿArabī and ʿAfīf al-Dīn al-Tilimsānī (I, 300) for seven years. In this period he did not leave his house in the Anbra market near the Umayyad mosque, and let his hair and nails grow without restraint. In 1075/1664 he spent a short time in Istanbul (Dār al-khilāfa). In 1100/1688 he travelled to Lebanon, in 1101 to Jerusalem and Hebron, in 1108/1696 to Egypt and the Hijaz, and in 1112/1700 to Tripoli. In 1114/1702 he returned to Damacus, where he took up residence at the Ṣāliḥiyya in 1119/1707, before dying on 24 Shaʿbān 1143/5 March 1731.

Mur. III, 31/8, Jabartī I, 154/6, Hartmann, *Muwashshaḥ* 6. An inventory of his works from the year 1105/1693 is given in Flügel *ZDMG* XVI, 664 ff., another in Gotha 1860, by his grandson Muṣṭafā containing over 209 works BDMG 23. 1. Treatise on a passage in Jāmī's (d. 898/1492, p. 266) commentary on the *Fātiḥa*, composed on the order of ʿUthmān Pāshā, the vizier in Sidon, Berl. 943.—2. *Mukhtaṣar Ḍiyāʾ al-qulūb (fi 'l-tafsīr)* AS 430.—3. A short treatise on religious doctrines, Berl. 1852.—4. *Manẓūmat asmāʾ Allāh al-ḥusnā* ibid. 2244/5.—5. *Īḍāḥ al-maqṣūd min maʿnā waḥdat al-wujūd* ibid. 2348/50, 3468, Alex. Taṣ. $42_{,9}$, Fun. $90_{,13}$, 92, Mosul $123_{,48,\ 4}$, $143_{,35,\ 6}$.—A commentary, *al-Mawrid al-ʿadhb*, Leipz. 266 (fragment).—6. A treatise on free will, Berl. 2500.—7. *Fatḥ al-bārī fī taḥrīr masʾalat al-jazʾ al-ikhtiyārī*, on Creation, written after 1105/1693, Gotha $103_{,2}$.—8. *al-Kawkab al-sārī fī ḥaqīqat al-jazʾ al-ikhtiyārī*, a work of dogmatics concerning free will, ibid. 872, Alex. Taṣ. $42_{,11}$, Fun. $151_{,3}$, Cairo [1]II, 48.—9. *al-Ḥāmil fi 'l-falak wal-maḥmūl fi 'l-fulk*, composed in 1104/1692, on whether ʿAlī's two sons are to be considered as messengers of God, Berl. 2552.—10. A treatise on who will certainly go to Paradise and who will surely go to Hell, ibid. 2709.—11. *Hidāyat al-murīd wa-nihāyat al-saʿīd*, | on the bond with God and an 346
explanation of | the expressions *qalb, nafs*, and *rūḥ*, ibid. 3137, Cairo [1]II, 138.— 455
12. *al-Rusūkh fī maqām al-shuyūkh*, on the relationship between a shaykh and his novices, with special consideration of the practices of ancient times and the abuses in the lifetime of the author, Berl. 3194.—13. *ʿUdhr al-aʾimma fī nuṣḥ al-umma*, on the relationship between *ḥaqīqa* and *sharīʿa*, which begins and ends with a prayer of thanks for healing from a fever, composed in Dhu 'l-Qaʿda 1128/October 1716, Berl. 3243.—14. *Iṭlāq al-quyūd fī sharḥ Mirʾāt al-wujūd li-ʿAbd al-Aḥad al-Khalwatī al-Nūrī Awḥad al-Dīn*, d. 1061/1651 (see below p. 445), ibid.

3244, Cairo ^{1}II, 66.—15. *Hatk al-astār fī ʿilm al-asrār*, on the monism of Ibn ʿArabī, Berl. 3245, Paris 1374$_{,4}$.—16. *Qaṭrat al-samāʾ wa-naẓrat al-ʿulamāʾ*, on the nature of God and the properties of the Hereafter, Berl. 3246.—17. *Jamʿ al-asrār fī manʿ al-ashrār*, on the dancing and swirling of dervishes, Berl. 3384, Alex. Taṣ. 42, Cairo ^{1}II, 125.—18. *al-ʿUqūd al-luʾluʾiyya fī ṭarīqat al-sāda al-Mawlawiyya*, a defence of the Mawlawī dervishes, composed in three days in Shaʿbān 1096/July 1685, Berl. 3385, Tüb. 133.—19. *Anwār al-sulūk fī asrār al-mulūk*, in praise of Islam, comparing it with other religions, with a description of its three schools, Berl. 3392, Alex. Taṣ. 42$_{,12}$.—20. *Baqiyyat Allāh khayr baʿd al-fanāʾ fi ʾl-sayr*, a commentary on 5 Sufi verses, Berl. 3426.—21. *Natījat al-ʿulūm wa-naṣīḥat ʿulamāʾ al-rusūm*, an explanation of various issues concerning faith, ibid. 3480.—22. *al-Nafaḥāt al-muntashira fi ʾl-jawāb ʿani ʾl-asʾila al-ʿashara*, 10 theological questions, ibid. 3481, Alex. Fun. 90$_{,18}$, Cairo ^{1}II, 128.—23. *Munāghāt al-qadīm wa-munājāt al-ḥakīm*, a colloquy with God, in the form of a prayer, Berl. 3905, Cairo ^{1}II, 137, VII, 137.—24. *Istighfāra* in 99 verses, Berl. 3941$_{,2}$.—25. *al-Istighātha al-istighfāriyya* Cairo ^{1}VII, 125.—26. *Rafʿ al-ʿinād ʿan ḥukm al-tafwīḍ wal-isnād*, on the execution of testamentary dispositions, composed in 1113/1701, Berl. 4776, Cairo ^{1}VII, 366.—27. *Radd al-jāhil ila ʾl-ṣawāb fī jawāz iḍāfat al-taʾthīr ila ʾl-asbāb*, Berl. 5109, Cairo ^{1}II, 129.—28. *Taʿṭīr al-anām fī taʿbīr al-manām*, a book on dreams, Cairo ^{1}VI, 128, ^{2}VI, 176, print. C. 1287, 1301, 1304, 1306 2 vols., among others.—28a. *al-ʿAbīr fī ʿilm al-taʿbīr*, see Suppl., also Alex. Fun. 42$_{,1}$, 161$_{,7}$.—29. *al-Kashf wal-bayān fī-mā yataʿallaq bil-nisyān*, completed in 1106/1664 after his return from the pilgrimage, Berl. 5430.—30. *al-Qawl al-muʿtabar fī bayna ʾl-naẓar*, against the claim that it is forbidden to look at beardless young men, ibid. 5447.—31. *Ibānat al-naṣṣ fī masʾalat al-qaṣṣ*, on
456 whether and to what extent one should cut one's beard, | ibid. 5448, Cairo ^{1}VII, 368.—32. *al-Ṣulḥ bayna ʾl-ikhwān fī ḥukm ibāḥat al-dukhān*, on the lawful use of
347 tobacco, Berl. 5494/5, Vienna 1661$_{,13}$, 1662, Br. Mus. 1158, Algiers 1306$_{,2}$, | Garr. 1856, NO 2404, Alex. Fiqh Ḥan. 37, Fun. 157$_{,6}$, Cairo ^{1}II, 129, III, 77, Köpr. III, 103.—33. *Īḍāḥ al-dalālāt fī samāʿ al-ālāt*, on the use of musical instruments, Berl. 5522, Cairo *Nashra* 4.[4]—34. *al-Maqāṣid al-mumaḥḥaṣa fī kayy al-ḥimmaṣa*, on the fontanel, Berl. 6364, Cairo ^{1}VII, 558, 601, Alex. Fun. 162$_{,3}$ (*al-Aḥkām al-mulakhkhaṣa*).—35. *Kifāyat al-ghulām fī jumlat arkān al-Islām ʿalā madhhab al-imām Abī Ḥanīfa al-Numʿān* Cairo ^{1}VII, 349, print. Alexandria 1281, C. 1308. Self-commentary *Rashaḥāt al-aqlām* Garr. 1771 (see Suppl.).—36. *Jawāhir al-nuṣūṣ fī ḥall kalimāt al-Fuṣūṣ* I, 572.—37. *Ward al-wurūd wa-fayḍ al-baḥr al-mawrūd*, a commentary on the *Ṣalawāt Muḥammadiyya* of Ibn

4 Defended by Muḥammad b. Maḥmūd b. ʿAlī al-Dāmūnī in *al-Shihāb al-qabasī fi ʾl-radd ʿalā man radda ʿalā ʿAbd al-Ghanī* Leipz. 269 (autograph, dated 1215 A.H.).

al-ʿArabī, Vienna 1708.—38. *al-Radd al-matīn ʿalā muntaqiṣ al-ʿārif Muḥyi ʾl-Dīn* Br. Mus. Suppl. 1257, Alex. Fun. 90,$_2$, Cairo ^{1}II, 83, 128, ^{2}I, 300.—39. *Nafḥat al-qabūl fī midḥat al-rasūl* Tüb. 50.—39a. *Ghāyat al-maṭlūb fī maḥabbat al-maḥbūb* ibid. 83.—40. *Zubdat al-fāʾida fi ʾl-jawāb ʿan il-abyāt al-wārida* Alex. Fun. 90,$_{16}$, Cairo ^{1}II, 126, 128.—41. *Ziyādat al-basṭa fī bayān ʿilm al-nuqta*, completed on 21 Ramaḍān 1088/17 November 1677, Alex. Fun. 90,$_{17}$, Cairo ^{1}II, 126, 129.—42. *al-Tanbīh min al-nawm fī ḥukm mawājīd al-qawm* Alex. Fun. 90,$_8$, Cairo ^{1}II, 128.—43. *al-Sirr al-mukhtabī fī ḍarīḥ Ibn al-ʿArabī* Alex. Fun. 90,$_9$, Cairo ^{1}II, 128.—44. *Dafʿ (Rafʿ) al-rayb ʿan ḥaḍrat al-ghayb* Alex. Fun. 90,$_{19}$, Cairo ^{1}II, 128.—45. *al-Maʿārif al-ghaybiyya fī sharḥ al-ʿAyniyya* Cairo ^{1}II, 128.—46. *Ishtibāk al-asinna fi ʾl-jawāb ʿan il-farḍ wal-sunna*, composed in 1080/1675, Leid. 1898, Cairo ^{1}II, 129.—47. *Radd al-muftarī ʿani ʾl-ṭaʿn fi ʾl-Tustarī* Cairo ^{1}II, 129, ^{1}VII, 21.—48. *Nabwat al-qadamayn fī suʾāl al-malakayn* ibid. ^{1}II, 128.—49. *Rafʿ al-ishtibāh ʿan ʿalamiyyat ism Allāh* Alex. Fun. 90,$_2$, Cairo ^{1}II, 129.—50. *Miftāḥ al-maʿiyya fī ṭarīq al-Naqshbandiyya* see below p. 419.—51. *al-Tawfīq al-jalī bayna ʾl-Ashʿarī wal-Ḥanbalī* Cairo ^{1}VII, 293.—52. *Risāla fī ajwiba ʿan asʾila waradat min baʿḍ al-bilād al-nāʾiya*, composed in 1089/1678, ibid. 365.—53. *Risāla fī jawāb suʾāl warada min al-Quds al-sharīf*, completed on 5 Jumādā I 1114/28
September 1702, ibid.—54. *Risāla fī ḥukm al-tasʿīr*, completed in Dhū | ʾl-Qaʿda 457
1103/August 1692, ibid. 366.—55. *Risāla fī khams masāʾil waradat ilayhi min Bayt al-Maqdis*, composed in Ramaḍān 1101/June 1689, ibid. 366.—56. *al-Nasīm al-rabīʿī fi ʾl-tajādhub al-badīʿī*, composed in Rabīʿ I 1095/March 1684, ibid. 366, ^{2}II, 226.—57. *Kashf al-sitr ʿan farḍiyyat al-witr*, completed on 12 Dhu ʾl-Qaʿda 1089/27 December 1678, ibid. Cairo ^{1}VII, 366.—58. *Bughyat al-muktafī fī jawāz al-masḥ ʿala ʾl-khuff al-Ḥanafī* ibid.—59. *Nuqūd al-ṣurar fī sharḥ ʿUqūd al-durar fī-mā yuftā bihi min aqwāl al-imām Zufar b. Aḥmad al-Ḥamawī al-Miṣrī*, completed on 14 Dhu ʾl-Ḥijja 1112/25 May 1701, ibid. 367.—60. *Taḥqīq al-qaḍiyya fi ʾl-farq bayna ʾl-rishwa wal-hadiyya*, composed in Jumādā I 1106/December 1694, ibid.—61. *Taḥṣīl al-ajr fī ḥukm adhān al-fajr* ibid.—62. *Ghāyat al-wijazā fī takrār al-ṣalāt ʿala ʾl-jināza* ibid.—63. *Nuzhat al-wājid fī ḥukm al-ṣalāt ʿala ʾl-janāʾiz fi ʾl-masājid* ibid.—64. *al-Radd al-wafī ʿalā jawāb al-Ḥaskafī* ibid. 368.—65. *Itḥāf man bādara ilā ḥukm al-nūshādīr* ibid.—66. *Kanz al-ḥaqq al-mubīn fī aḥādīth sayyid al-mursalīn* p. 394.—67. *Ṣaḥīfa fī mā yaḥtāj al-Shāfiʿī*
ila ʾl-taqlīd fīhi li-Abī Ḥanīfa, | in *rajaz* verse, Berl. 8162,$_3$.—68. *al-Fatḥ al-rābbānī* 348
wal-fayḍ al-raḥmānī, an edifying work, Berl. 8880/1, Alex. Taṣ. 24, Fun. 90,$_4$.—69. *ʿAlam al-malāḥa fī ʿilm al-filāḥa* p. 366.—70. *al-Ḥaqīqa wal-majāz fī riḥlat al-Shām wa-Miṣr wal-Ḥijāz* Berl. 6146, Tüb. 28, Vienna 1269, Algiers 1561/3, Cairo ^{1}V, 43, ^{2}VI, 26, see Flügel, *ZDMG* XVI, 659ff., A. v. Kremer, *SBWA* V, 1850, 31ff.—71. *al-Ḥaḍra al-unsiyya (anīsiyya) fi ʾl-riḥla al-Qudsiyya*, on a trip from Damascus to Jerusalem and back, from 17 Jumādā II until 1 Shaʿbān

1101/29 March—10 May 1690, completed on 9 Dhu 'l-Ḥijja of that year/14 September, Berl. 6145, Gotha 1547, BDMG 59, cf. v. Kremer, op. cit. 316, Gildemeister, *ZDMG* 36, 385/400, Schefer, *Sefernameh*, $58_{,9\ \text{v.u.}}$.—72. *Ḥullat al-dhahab al-ibrīz fī riḥlat Baʿlabakk wal-Biqāʿ al-ʿazīz* Berl. 6143/4, Br. Mus. Suppl. 681, Lee 107, Garr. 758, MS Hartmann (where?).—73. *al-Riḥla al-Ṭarābulusiyya*, composed in 1112/1700, Br. Mus. 973.—74. *Nafaḥāt al-azhār ʿalā nasamāt al-asḥār fī madḥ al-nabī al-mukhtār, badīʿiyya* with a commentary, completed on 10 Jumādā I 1076/19 November 1665, Berl. 7385/6, Cairo ^{1}IV, 156, ^{2}II, 227, Istbl. Univ. A $1057_{,1}$, $1566_{,5}$, Jaḥyā $5850_{,1}$, Ḥamīdiyye $1239_{,1}$, Laleli 1388, Hüseyn Pasha Eyyub 991, print. Damascus 1299 (see Hartmann, *Or. Litbl.* I, 233), about which a letter of recommendation by Shihāb al-Dīn al-ʿImādī, d. 1078/1667, and Muḥammad Efendi al-Ḥusaynī, Berl. 56.—75. *Dīwān al-dawāwīn wa-rayḥān al-rayāḥīn fī tajalliyāt al-ḥaqq al-mubīn*, Berl. 8023/8, Vienna 498, Br. Mus. 636,
458 1416, Suppl. | 1097/8, Paris 3256, Alex. Adab 57, Qawala II, 193, Mosul $151_{,12}$, Bāb I, *Dīwān al-ḥaqāʾiq wa-majmūʿ al-rafāʾiq* Būlāq 1270, C. 1302, 1306.—76. Individual *qaṣīdas*, Berl. $3424_{,9}$/5, 8029/30, Gotha 26, f. 107a, $103_{,1}$.—77. *Muwashshaḥ* in praise of Damascus, Berl. $8175_{,1}$.—78. *al-Abyāt al-nūrāniyya fī mulūk al-dawla al-ʿUthmāniyya*, a *rajaz* on the Ottoman rulers up to Aḥmad b. Muḥammad (r. after 1115/1703), ibid. 9727.—79. *al-Kashf al-shāfī wal-bayān al-wāfī fī maʿrifat ḥawādith al-zamān fī dawlat āl ʿUthmān*, prophecies on famine, the plague etc., determined with the help of the letters of the alphabet, following the *Ishārāt* of Ibn ʿArabī, for the years 1107–59/1695–1746, Paris 1626.—80. *Fakk ṭilasm al-rumūz al-jafriyya ʿan bayān ḥawādith al-zamān fī dawlat āl ʿUthmān*, on the same, for the years 1139–1284/1726–1868, ibid. 1627.—81. *Fatḥ man lā yurā fī ḥall rumūz al-dāʾira al-kubrā*, on the same, following *al-Shajara al-Nuʿmāniyya* (I, 580), ibid.—82. *Mukhtaṣar al-Jāmiʿ al-ṣaghīr* p. 186.—83. *Taḥrīk al-iqlīd fī fatḥ bāb al-tawḥīd* see below p. 391.—84. *Nukhabat al-masʾala sharḥ al-Tuḥfa al-mursala* see below p. 418.—85. *Sharḥ al-Ṭarīqa al-Muḥammadiyya* see below p. 441.—86.–145. see Suppl. (93. Alex. Fun. $152_{,23}$, Taṣ. $42_{,9}$; 109, ibid. Fun. $90_{,6}$; 112. See I, 589, Suppl. 811; 117. on which *Kashf al-mukhaddarāt fī khibāʾ al-muʿashsharāt* by ʿAlī al-Qādirī b. ʿAbd al-Wahhāb b. al-Ḥājj ʿAlī al-Jafaʿtarī, completed in 1163/1750, Mosul $26_{,54,1}$; 119. *Badīʿiyya*, Istbl. Univ. A $1057_{,2}$, $1566_{,7}$, Jaḥyā $5820_{,2}$, Ḥamīdiyye $1239_{,2}$; 121. Alex. Fun. $90_{,5}$; 127. Garr. 946).—145a. A commentary on the *dīwān* of ʿUmar b. al-Fāriḍ, I 305.—146.–158. see Suppl. III, 1289.—159. *Risāla fī masʾalat al-tawḥīd* Patna II, $417_{,2587,2}$.—39 treatises in Kayseri, Rasāʾil 610.

50. ʿAbd al-Wahhāb al-Dikdikī, who was a student of ʿAbd al-Ghanī al-Nābulusī ca. 1160/1747.

Raf ʿ al-mushkilāt fī ḥukm ibāḥat samāʿ al-ālāt bil-naghamāt al-ṭayyibāt, on music being forbidden, e.g. during drinking bouts, but permitted for Sufis, Berl. 5524.

51. Muḥyi ʾl-Dīn Abū Muḥammad Muṣṭafā b. Kamāl al-Dīn b. ʿAlī al-Bakrī al-Ṣiddīqī al-Khalwatī al-Ḥanafī was born in Damascus in Dhu ʾl-Qaʿda 1099/September 1688. | He lost his father when he was 6 months old and was raised 349
by his cousin Aḥmad b. Kamāl al-Dīn. He joined the Khalwatiyya order and in 1122/1710 made a pilgrimage to Jerusalem, where he | wrote his prayer book 459
al-Fatḥ al-Qudsī (no. 14). When one of his enemies declared the reading of this work at the end of night to be *bidʿa*, ʿAlī Qarabāsh from Edirne defended him. In Shaʿbān 1122/October 1710 he returned to Damascus. In 1126/1714 he lived for a time in the al-Aqṣā mosque in Jerusalem, before going, by way of Aleppo, to Baghdad, where he stayed for two months. On his way back to Jerusalem he visited various saintly tombs in Syria. In Ramaḍān 1129/1717 he started out on the pilgrimage with his uncle Muḥammad al-Bakrī, but when the latter refused to give him his daughter in marriage he left him and got married in Jerusalem. From there he accompanied the vizier Rajab Jamīl Bek to Cairo. At the beginning of the year 1135/October 1722 he went, by way of Tripoli, Homs, Hama, and Aleppo, to Istanbul, where he arrived on 17 Shaʿbān/24 May 1723. It was only in 1139/1726 that he returned to Jerusalem again, this time by way of Aleppo, Baghdad, and Damascus. He made the pilgrimage in 1145/1732. In 1148/1735 he again went to Istanbul, where he arrived in Jumādā I/September. Taking a boat to Alexandria, he then returned to Jerusalem via Cairo. In 1149/1736 he made his second pilgrimage, and then went to Diyarbakir where he remained for eight months. Then, after having also stayed for 11 months in Nablus, he returned to Jerusalem in Shawwāl 1152/January 1740. He wanted to undertake the pilgrimage once more, starting from Cairo, but he passed away on 18 Rabīʿ II 1162/8 April 1749.

Mur. IV, 190/200, Jab. I, 125/6, *Khiṭ jad.* III, 129. 1. *Alfiyyat al-taṣawwuf*, a *rajaz* poem in ca. 1200 verses on the main aspects of mysticism, Berl. 3053.—2. *Bulghat al-murīd wa-mushtahā muwaffaq (al-) saʿīd*, | 214 *rajaz* verses on the same sub- 350
ject, ibid. 3054, 8035$_{,4}$, 8162$_{,1}$, Gotha 901, Br. Mus. 176, Cairo ^{1}II, 71, a commentary, *al-Jawhar al-farīd*, by his son Kamāl al-Dīn, Alex. Taṣ. 15, Cairo ^{2}I, 287.—3. *al-Basṭa al-tāmma fī naẓm Risālat al-Suyūṭī*, 105 *rajaz* verses, Berl. | 3055.—4. 460
al-Kaʾs al-rāʾiq fī sabab ikhtilāf al-ṭarāʾiq, on the different schools of thought in Sufism, ibid. 3056.—5. *Tasliyat al-aḥzān wa-taṣliyat al-ashjān*, which was begun in Qaryat al-malāḥa, on the occasion of a pilgrimage to Jerusalem in 1126/7,

and completed in Jumādā I 1128/May 1716, on love of God, its origin, stages,
and effects, ibid. 3118.—6. *Naẓm al-qilāda fī kayfiyyat al-julūs ʿala ʾl-sajjāda*,
on the properties and obligations of shaykhs and novices in mysticism, ibid.
3195.—7. *al-Kalimāt al-khawāṭir ʿala ʾl-ḍamīr wal-khāṭir*, ibid. 3247, Alex. Taṣ.
$39_{,2}$.—8. *al-Naṣīḥa al-saniyya fī maʿrifat ādāb kiswat al-Khalwatiyya*, on customs regarding the investiture of those who join the Khalwatiyya order,
Berl. 3357.—9. *al-Jawāb al-shāfī wal-lubāb al-kāfī*, a *rajaz* on mysticism, ibid.
3429.—10. *al-ʿArāʾis al-Qudsiyya al-mufṣiḥa ʿani ʾl-dasāʾis al-nafsiyya* Alex. Taṣ.
23, Cairo ^{1}II, 95, a part of which in Berl. 3488.—11. *al-Manhal al-ʿadhb al-sāʾigh
li-wurrādihi fī dhikr ṣalawāt al-ṭarīq wa-awrādihi* Berl. 3536, Alex. Faw. 17,
Cairo ^{1}II, 213, VII, 20, 249.—12. *al-Mawrid al-ʿadhb li-dhawi ʾl-wurūd fī kashf
maʿnā waḥdat al-wujūd* Cairo ^{1}II 125, VII, 224.—13. *al-Durr al-fāʾiq fi ʾl-ṣalāt ʿalā
ashraf al-khalāʾiq* Cairo ^{1}II, 193, 213, VII, 323.—14. *al-Fatḥ al-Qudsī wal-kashf
al-unsī* or *Wird al-saḥar* (see above p. 459), Berl. 3874/6, Alex. Faw. $25_{,6}$, Cairo ^{1}II,
213, VII, 267, 511. Commentaries: a. Self-commentary, *al-Ḍiyāʾ al-shamsī*, started
in 1123/1711, completed in 1138/1725, Cairo ^{1}II, 205, 217, ^{2}I, 330, Patna I, $156_{,1482}$;
abstract: *al-Lamḥ al-nadsī* Hamb. Or. Sem. $14_{,11}$, Dam. Ẓ. $61_{,165}$, Alex. Faw. 16,
Patna I, $157_{,1490}$.—b., c. see Suppl.—d. *Irshād al-murīdīn fī marʿifat kalām
al-ʿārifīn* by Jaʿfar al-Shubrāwī al-Shāfiʿī, completed in 1270/1854, Būlāq 1292.—
15. *Ḥizb al-ḥimāya wal-iʿtiṣām* Cairo ^{1}II, 217, VII, 20.—16. *al-Ṣalawāt al-hāmiʿa
bi-maḥabbat al-khulafāʾ al-jāmiʿa li-baʿḍ mā warada fī faḍāʾil al-khulafāʾ* ibid. II,
224, C. 1310.—17. *al-Awrād* Br. Mus. Suppl. 253.—18. *al-Suyūf al-ḥidād fī aʿnāq
ahl al-zandaqa wal-ilḥād* Alex. Faw. 19, Cairo ^{1}VII, 82.—19. *Ḥizb al-ḥifẓ wal-
ḥirāsa min al-humūm* Cairo ^{1}VII, 19, no. 49.—20. *Shifāʾ al-tabārīḥ bi-wird ṣalāt
al-tasābīḥ* ibid. no. 50.—21. *Intiẓār fatḥ al-furaj wastimṭār manḥ al-faraj*, in
verse, ibid. no. 51.—22. *al-Tawassul al-asnā bil-asmāʾ al-ḥusnā* ibid. no. 52.—23.
al-ʿUdda al-ʿumda al-mukhliṣa min kulli shidda ibid. no. 53.—24. *al-Damgha
al-naḍriyya al-Muḥammadiyya wal-ṣibgha al-naẓariyya al-Aḥmadiyya*, in
461 verse, ibid. | no. 54.—25. *al-Manḥ al-ʿujāb wal-nafḥ al-rāfiʿ al-ḥijāb*, on the
same, ibid. no. 55.—26. *Midḥat al-bayt rāfiʿ ghiṭāʾī wa-nāfiʿ dāʾī bi-rafʿ burquʿ
adwāʾī* ibid. no. 56.—27. *al-Lawāʾiḥ al-mulmiḥa dahrā fī fawāʾiḥ laylat al-zahrāʾ*
ibid. 20, no. 58.—28. *Awrād layāli ʾl-usbūʿ wa-ayyāmihi* ibid. no. 59.—29.
al-Maṭlab al-tāmm al-sawī ʿalā ḥizb al-imām al-Nawawī ibid. no. 61.—30.
Sādiḥat al-azal ibid. ^{1}VII, 327.—31. *al-Jawhara*, a prayer, Berl. 3656.—32. *Jarīdat
al-maʾārib wa-kharīdat kulli shārib*, the same, ibid. 3661.—33. Other prayers, ibid.
3662.—34. *al-Mudām al-bikr fī bayān baʿḍ aqsām al-dhikr wa-tark al-dhikr* ibid.
3727.—35. *Asmāʾ Allāh al-ḥusnā*, in verse, ibid. 3759.—36. A prayer in 26
verses, ibid. $3939_{,6}$.—37. *Qaṣīda ibtihāliyya*, a prayer, instigated by Muḥammad
al-Tāfilātī, d. 1191/1777 (no. 57a), written in verse in Istanbul in 1136/1723,

ibid. 3942$_{,2}$.—38. *al-Waṣiyya al-jaliyya lil-sālikīn ṭarīqat al-Khalwatiyya* | ibid. 351
4022, Garr. 2166$_{,2}$, Alex. Taṣ. 32, Cairo ^{1}II, 144, ^{2}I, 375.—39. *Hadiyyat al-aḥbāb fī-mā lil-khalwa min al-shurūṭ wal-ādāb* Cairo ^{1}II, 249, ^{2}I, 373.—40. *al-Mudāma al-Shāmiyya fī 'l-maqāma al-Shāmiyya*, on a trip to and stay in Damascus, Berl. 6148.—41. *al-Khamra al-ḥasiyya fī 'l-riḥla al-Qudsiyya*, on a trip from Damascus to Jerusalem in 1122/1710, ibid. 6149.—42. *Minḥat al-wuṣūl fī midḥat al-rasūl* or *Rashḥat al-ṣafā fī 'mtidāḥ al-Muṣṭafā*, a collection of poems in praise of the Prophet, ibid. 8035$_{,2}$.—43. 23 poems, Br. Mus. 176.—44. *al-Qaṣīda al-munbahija* Paris 743$_{,16}$.—45.–62. see Suppl.—63. *al-Ḥawāshi 'l-rāfiʿāt al-ghawāshī ʿalā baʿḍ kalimāt al-waṣiyya dhāt al-sirr al-fāshī* Alex. Taṣ. 39$_{,1}$.

53. Manṣūr al-Sarmīnī wrote, around 1170/1756:

Kashf al-lithām wal-sutūr ʿan mukhaddarāt arbāb al-ṣudūr, a commentary on three Sufi verses, Berl. 3431.

54. Ḥusayn b. Ṭuʿma b. Muḥammad al-Ḥusaynī al-Baytimānī al-Maydānī al-Qādirī al-Khalwatī lived for 15 years as a student with the Sufi Ilyās al-Kurdī, and even longer with ʿAbd al-Ghanī al-Nābulusī and other Sufi masters. Later he lectured in a Zāwiya in Maydān al-Ḥasā and in the madrasa of the vizier Ismāʿīl Pāshā, both in Damascus. He died in 1175/1761.

Mur. II, 52/5. 1. *Hawāmiʿ al-barq al-mūhin fī maʿnā Mā wasiʿanī samawātī wa-lā arḍī wa-wasiʿanī qalb ʿabdī* | *al-muʾmin*, a translation of an anonymous Persian 462
work on the various stages in one's progression towards God, Berl. 3312 (incomplete).—2. *Fayḍ al-khallāq al-ʿālim ʿalā qalb ʿabdihi 'l-muʾmin al-sālim*, composed after a meeting with the Sufi Sulaymān Efendi Zuhrāb Āghā in Damascus in 1170/1756, ibid. 3313.—3. *ʿArūs al-jalwa fī faḍl iʿtikāf al-khalwa* ibid. 3738.—4. *al-Mawāʿiẓ al-nabawiyya al-ṣūfiyya* ibid. 3729.—5. *Silsilat talqīn al-dhikr* ibid. 3730.—6. *Dīwān* Br. Mus. Suppl. 1102.—7. *al-Hidāya wal-tawfīq fī ādāb sulūk al-ṭarīq* Alex. Fun. 148$_{,1}$.

54a. Muḥammad b. ʿAbdallāh al-Dimashqī al-Ḥanbalī wrote, in 1155/1742:

1. *ʿArūs al-jalwa fī faḍl iʿtikāf al-khalwa* (p. 54, 3), Alex. Fun. 158$_{,2}$.—2. *al-Shamʿa al-muḍīʾa fī sayr ṭarīq al-Ṣūfiyya* ibid. $_{3}$.—3. *Khirqat al-dāliyya fī 'l-kiswa al-Khalwatiyya* ibid. $_{4}$.

54b. ʿAbd al-Karīm al-Sharābātī, who died in 1178/1764.

1. *Adʿiya mubāraka fi 'l-asfār al-ṣāliḥa* Alex. Fun. 122,$_{6}$.—2. *Sanad ijāza li-ṣalāt sayyidī ʿAbd al-Sālam al-Mashīshī* (I, 569), ibid. $_{7}$.—3. *Ṣalawāt Muḥyi 'l-Dīn b. al-ʿArabī* ibid. $_{8}$.—4. *al-Ḥadīth al-musalsal* ibid. $_{9}$.—5. *Ijāza ḥadīthiyya* ibid. $_{10}$.

56. ʿAlī b. Ḥijāzī al-Bayyūmī al-Dimirdāshī, who was born in 1108/1696 and died in 1183/1769.

Jab. I, 337/81. 1. *Ṭarīqat al-Dimirdāshiyya*, the profession of faith of this sub-
352 division of the Khalwatiyya, Berl. 3393. |—2. *al-Asrār al-khafiyya al-mūṣila ila 'l-ḥaḍra al-ʿaliyya*, on the *Ḥikam* of Abū Madyan al-Tilimsānī (I, 566), Cairo ^{1}II, 66, VII, 91.—3. *Sharḥ al-Ḥikam al-ʿAṭāʾiyya* p. 143.—4. *Risāla tashtamil ʿalā sanadihi wa-khawāṣṣ al-Fātiḥa wa-faḍl al-ṣalāt ʿala 'l-nabī wa-faḍl al-dhikr*, composed in 1144/1731, Cairo ^{1}II, 84.—5. *Ḥizb* ibid. 214.—6. *Khawāṣṣ al-asmāʾ al-Idrīsiyya* ibid. ^{1}VII, 91.—7. *Risāla fi 'l-ulfa wal-ukhuwwa* ibid.—8. *Fayḍ al-raḥmān ʿalā Risālat al-mawlā Raslān* (Suppl. III 1257), ibid.—9. *Risāla fi 'l-waḥdāniyya* ibid. 92.—10.–12. see Suppl.

57. ʿAbdallāh b. Muḥammad b. ʿAlī b. Shihāb al-Ḥalabī was born in Aleppo in 1116/1704 and moved with his father to Damascus in 1131/1719, where he
463 attended the classes of ʿAbd al-Ghanī al-Nābulusī | and studied of the works of Ibn ʿArabī. He died in 1186/1772.

Mur. III, 104/6. *Dīwān* Berl. 8044.

57a. Muḥammad b. Muḥammad b. al-Ṭayyib al-Tāfilātī al-Maghribī was *muftī* of the Ḥanafīs in Jerusalem and died in 1191/1777.

1. *al-Durr al-aʿlā*, with the commentary *al-Dawr al-aghlā*, Alex. Faw. 7.—2. *Ḥusn al-istiqṣāʾ bi-mā ṣaḥḥa wa-thabata fi 'l-Masjid al-Aqṣā* ibid. Taʾr. 111.

58. ʿAbd al-Raḥmān b. Muṣṭafā al-Ḥusaynī al-ʿAydarūsī Wajīh al-Dīn was born in Yemen in 1135/1722, and was introduced to mysticism by his father and grandfather. In 1153/1740 he went with his father via al-Shiḥr to India, where they stayed in Sūrat, Barūj, Fazāra, and in Sūrat again. When his father returned to Tarīm, he left him with his uncle. Some years later he returned to Tarīm and then, in 1158/1745, went to Cairo, passing by al-Ṭāʾif and Mecca on the way. A year later he returned to Mecca, married a cousin there and took up residence in al-Ṭāʾif. In 1162/1749 he accompanied the Egyptian pilgrimage caravan on its way back to Cairo and stayed there for a significant period of time.

Having concluded a second marriage in 1172/1758 he settled in Cairo in 1174/1760, but was to make numerous journeys through Egypt, Gaza, Nablus, Jerusalem, and Damascus. In 1191/1777 he visited Istanbul, and died soon after his return in 1192/1778.

Mur. II, 328, Jab. II, 27/34, *Khiṭ. jad.* V, 11/4. 1. *al-Nafḥa al-ʿAydarūsiyya fi 'l-ṭarīqa al-Naqshbandiyya* Berl. 2198/9.—2. *al-Nafḥa al-Madaniyya fi 'l-adhkār al-qalbiyya wal-rūḥiyya wal-sirriyya* ibid. 2200/3, Cairo ^{1}II, 142, VII, 685.—3. *Laṭāʾif al-jūd fī masʾalat waḥdat al-wujūd* Berl. 2355; a commentary by ʿAbd al-Raḥmān b. Ḥasan al-Kurdī of Damascus, which he had requested from him from Cairo in 1189/1775, entitled *Sharḥ Khuṭbat al-Risāla al-ʿAydarūsiyya*, ibid. 2356.—4. *al-ʿUrf al-wardī fī dalāʾil al-Mahdī* ibid. 2733.—5. *Ithḥāf al-khalīl bil-mashrab al-jalīl al-jamīl* Cairo ^{1}II, | 118, VII, 361, ^{2}I, 260.—6. *Risāla fī fann al-istiʿāra*, 464
with a commentary by Muḥammad b. Aḥmad al-Jawharī, | d. 1215/1800, Berl. 353
7326.—7. A *qaṣīda* on the glory of his lineage, with a list of his ancestors, ibid. $8045_{,3}$.—8. *al-Taraqqī ila 'l-ghuraf min kalām al-salaf wal-khalaf* ibid. $8729_{,36}$.—9. *Tamshiyat al-qalam bi-baʿḍ anwāʿ al-ḥikam* ibid. $_{37}$.—10. a. *Tanmīq al-asfār, dīwān*, b. *Tanmīq al-safar*, on his experiences in Egypt, c. *Dhayl al-Tanmīq*, letters from Egypt, print. C. 1304.—11. Two collections of poems, Gotha $15_{,1,2}$.—12. *Tarwīḥ al-bāl wa-tahyīj al-bilbāl*, a collection of poems, Paris 3262, Cairo ^{1}V, 217.—13.–17. see Suppl. (15. Cairo, *Nashra* 7).—18. *Risāla fi 'l-waḍʿ*, commentary *Tashnīf al-samʿ bi-baʿḍ laṭāʾif al-waḍʿ* by ʿAbd al-Raḥmān al-Ujhūri, Alex. Waḍʿ 3.

59. Muḥammad b. Ḥasan b. Muḥammad al-Samannūdī al-Azharī al-Munayyar Jamāl al-Dīn was born in Samannūd in 1099/1688, studied at al-Azhar, and joined the Khalwatiyya order. Later he worked as a reciter of the Qurʾān at al-Azhar, while also dedicating himself to the occult sciences. He died on 11 Rajab 1199/21 May 1785.

Khiṭ. jad. XII, 51. 1. *Tuḥfat al-sālikīn wa-dalālat al-sāʾirin li-nahj al-muqarrabīn*, a manual on Sufism composed with the help of his teacher al-Shams al-Ḥanafī, d. 1181/1767, Berl. 3057, Alex. Taṣ. 11, Cairo ^{1}II, 74, ^{2}I, 276, print. C. 1287, 1305, 1315.—2., 3. See Suppl. (3. Zāh. ʿIsh, Taʾrīkh 31).—4. *al-Ādāb al-saniyya al-Ḥifniyya wal-afʿāl al-sharīfa al-ʿaliyya li-murīd sulūk al-ṭarīqa al-Khalwatiyya* Alex. Tas. $40_{,1}$.—5. *Sharḥ al-basmala* ibid. 20.

60. Abu 'l-Barakāt Aḥmad b. Muḥammad b. Aḥmad al-Dardīr al-Mālikī al-ʿAdawī al-Azharī al-Khalwatī was born in Banī ʿAdī in 1127/1715 and studied at al-Azhar. After the death of his teacher, al-Shaykh al-Ṣaʿīdī, he became a Mālikī

shaykh, *muftī*, and *nāẓir* of the Ṣaʿāʾida *waqf*, as well as the shaykh of the Riwāq al-Ṣaʿāʾida at al-Azhar. He died on 6 Rabīʿ I 1201/18 December 1786.

Jab. II, 147/50, *Khiṭ. jad.* IX, 95. 1. *al-Kharīda al-bahiyya fi 'l-ʿaqāʾid al-tawḥīdiyya*, with commentaries: a. Self-commentary Berl. 2454, Gotha 692, print. Alexandria 1281, in *Majmūʿa* C. 1297 (Cat. ^{1}VII, 451), on which glosses: α Aḥmad b. Muḥammad
465 al-Ṣāwī, | d. 1241/1825, C. 1307, 1310.—β ʿAbd al-Muʿṭī b. ʿAbd al-Karīm b. Aḥmad b. Muḥammad al-ʿAdawī al-Mālikī, Makram 24.—b. Muṣṭafā al-ʿAqabāwī, d. 1221/1806, Cairo ^{1}II, 50.—2. *Ḥizb* Cairo ^{1}VII, 174.—3. *al-Mawrid al-rāʾiq fi 'l-ṣalāt ʿalā ashraf al-khalāʾiq*, with a commentary by Aḥmad b. ʿAbd al-Barr al-Shāfiʿī al-Wanāʾī al-Khalwatī, Gotha 732.—4. *al-Ṣalawāt al-Dardīriyya* Cairo ^{1}VII, 267; commentary by Aḥmad b. Muḥammad al-Ṣāwī, d. 1241/1825, ibid. ^{1}II, 214.—5. *Manẓūma fī asmāʾ Allāh al-ḥusnā*, with a commentary by the same, ibid. Alex. Faw. 11.—6. *Risāla fī bayān al-sayr ila 'llāh* Cairo ^{1}VII, 20.—7. *Tuḥfat al-ikhwān fī bayān ṭarīq ahl al-ʿirfān* Cairo ^{1}II, 74, VII, 179, 225, Makram 9, print. C. 1281, 1332.—8. *Mawlid al-nabī* Cairo ^{1}VII, 65, ^{2}I, 155, the commentary *Ishrāq maṣābīḥ al-anwār* by Aḥmad b. Muḥammad b. Naṣr al-Salāwī, composed in 1235/1820, Alex. Fun. $93_{,1}$; gloss *al-Rawḍ al-naḍir* by Aḥmad b. ʿAbd al-Ḥaqq al-Ḥajjājī al-Qūṣī al-Mālikī, Alex. Taʾr. 8.—9. *Aqrab al-masālik li-madhhab al-imām Mālik* Cairo ^{1}III, 154; self-commentary with glosses by Aḥmad b. Muḥammad al-Ṣāwī, d. 1241/1825, ibid. 135, Makram 7, by Ullays C. 1285, Makr. 61.—10. *Sharḥ Mukhtaṣar Khalīl* p. 102.—11. *Ḥāshiya ʿalā Qiṣṣat al-miʿrāj lil-Ghayṭī* p. 445.—12. *Sharḥ Ādāb al-baḥth* p. 268.—13.–18. see Suppl. (14. Garr. 1471, 15; 18. *Tuḥfat al-ikhwān fī ʿilm al-bayān*, with a self-commentary, Alex. Balāgha 13, Fun. $108_{,3}$, Makr. 35.—Glosses: a. Aḥmad al-Ṣāwī, Alex. Balāgha 6 (see Suppl. $480_{,7}$, $260_{,23,\,2}$).—b. Ḥijāzī b. ʿAbd al-Muṭṭalib al-ʿAdawī al-Mālikī, Makram 16).—19. *Risālat al-majāz wal-tashbīh wal-kināya* Alex. Balāgha 23.

61. Sulaymān b. ʿUmar b. Manṣūr al-ʿUjaylī al-Shāfʿī al-Azharī al-Jamāl was born in Minyat al-ʿUjayl, studied in Cairo, and joined a dervish order. Later he
354 became a preacher at the mosque | next to the house of his teacher al-Ḥifnī and a professor at the Ashrafiyya. He died on 11 Dhu 'l-Qaʿda 1204/26 June 1790.

Jab. II, 183, *Khiṭ. jad.* XVI, 70. 1. *al-Qawl al-munīr fī sharḥ al-Ḥizb al-kabīr lil-Shādhilī* (I, 583), Cairo ^{1}VII, 154.—2. *Ḥāshiya ʿalā tafsīr al-Jālālayn* p. 182.—3. (= 4.) *Ḥāshiya ʿalā Fatḥ al-wahhāb sharḥ Manhaj al-ṭullāb li-Zakariyyāʾ al-Anṣārī* I, 498.—5.–8. see Suppl.—9. *al-Futūḥāt al-ilāhiyya* p. 182.—10. *al-Fatḥ al-jawād* Suppl. III, 1192 p. 69.

| 10 *Homilies and Paraenesis* 466

2. Nūr al-Dīn Abu 'l-Ḥasan Aḥmad b. Muḥammad al-Jazzār wrote, at the time of an earthquake in Egypt in 984/1576:

Taḥṣīn al-manāzil min hawl al-zalāzil Cairo ¹VI, 119 ²I, App. 39, Taymūr Ṭab. 93.—2. See Suppl.

3. Muḥammad b. Tāj al-Dīn b. Aḥmad al-Maḥāsinī was born in 1012/1603, studied in Damascus and, after a trip to Istanbul, became a professor at the Umayyad mosque as well as a preacher in the mosque of Sultan Selīm. After a second trip to Istanbul he became imam at the Umayyad mosque and a professor at al-Madrasa al-Jawhariyya. He also lectured on *ḥadīth* under the Dome of the Eagle in the aforementioned mosque. He died in 1072/1661.

Muḥ. III, 408/11. *Dīwān khuṭab*, 4 sermons on each month, Berl. 3947, Dam. Ẓ. 61,146.

3a. Naṣr b. Aḥmad al-Ḥuṣrī wrote, in 1089/1678:

Al-Kanz al-maqṣūd etc. (see Suppl.) Garr. 1967.

3b. ʿAbd al-Qādir b. Muṣṭafā al-Ṣaffūrī al-Dimashqī, who died in 1081/1670.

1. *Nuzhat al-nufūs* Alex. Maw. 48.—2. Glosses on Bayḍāwī's *Anwār al-tanzīl* I, 532,31.

4. Ḥusayn b. Fakhr al-Dīn b. Qurqmās b. Maʿn al-Shāmī, a son of the famous leader of the Druzes (p. 373), was brought up in Galatasaray in Istanbul after both his father and his oldest brother, Manṣūr, had been executed there following their subjugation by Aḥmad Küčük Pāshā in 1043/1633. He then became a page in the palace and a treasurer. In this capacity he was entrusted with a mission to India, during which he visited his relatives in Lebanon, | whose offer to 355
assume the lordship of his father he declined. He died in Istanbul in 1109/1697.

Mur. II, 59/60. *Al-Tamyīz*, admonitions, Cairo ¹II, 151, ²I, 180, Damad Ibr. 495/6 (see Suppl.).

| 5. Aḥmad b. ʿAbd al-Fattāḥ b. Yūsuf al-Mujīrī al-Mollawī was born on 2 467
Ramaḍān 1088/30 October 1677, studied at al-Azhar, and died in 1181/1767.

Mur. I, 116, Jab. I, 286/7. 1 *Dīwān khuṭab jamʿiyya* Cairo ^{1}II, 157.—2. *Fatḥ al-salām*, with a commentary, *Miṣbāḥ al-ẓalām*, by Ibrāhīm b. Ṣāliḥ al-Dimirdāshī, twelfth century, ibid. 176, ^{2}I, 359.—3. *Naẓm al-mukhtaliṭāt*, with the commentary *Asrār al-maʿqūlāt*, on logic, Algiers 1411,$_2$.—4. *Sharḥ al-sullam* by Akhḍarī, see below p. 463.—5.–10. see Suppl.—11. *al-Laʾālī al-manthūrāt ʿalā Naẓm al-muwajjahāt* Alex. Tawḥīd 37,$_1$.—12. *Sharḥ al-ṣudūr bil-ṣalāt wal-salām ala ʾl-nāṣir al-manṣūr* Alex. Faw. 21.

6. Khalīl (ʿAlī) b. Shams al-Dīn b. Muḥammad al-Khuḍarī al-Shāfiʿī al-Rashīdī, who died in 1186/1772.

Jab. I, 374. *Al-Durar al-yatīma al-kāmila al-mutaʿalliqa bil-shuhūr al-thalātha al-fāḍila*, edifying reflections in 59 sessions for the months of Rajab, Shabʿān, and Ramaḍān, completed in 1159/1746, Berl. 8852, Alex. Fun. 30.

7. Maḥmūd b. Muḥammad b. Yazīd al-Kurdī al-Kūrānī, who died in 1195/1781.

Naṣīḥat al-aḥbāb Cairo ^{1}II, 180.

11 *Philosophy*

356 | 2. Manṣūr b. Muḥammad al-Arīḥāwī wrote, in 1014/1605:

Al-Jawhara al-saniyya fi ʾl-ḥikma al-ʿaliyya Cairo ^{1}VI, 91, with a self-commentary ibid. 97.

2a. Manṣūr al-Manūfī al-Shāfiʿī wrote, in 1090/1679:

Manẓūmat al-muwajjahāt fi ʾl-manṭiq, with a commentary, Alex. Fun. 128 (see § 10, no. 5, 11).

3.–5. See Suppl. (4. *al-Risāla al-Ḥusayniyya* Garr. 914, Qawala II, 302, print. in *Majmūʿa*, Istanbul n.d.—Commentaries: a. Garr. 916.—b. ibid. 2099, Qawala II, 296.—c. Garr. 915.—f. Muḥammad b. Muṣṭafā al-Āqkirmānī, ca. 1150/1737, Qawala II, 295.—g. Muḥammad Ṣādiq b. ʿAbd al-Raḥīm al-Arzinjānī Muftīzāde, ibid. 301.)

468 | 12 *Politics*

Manṣūr b. Baʿra al-Dhahabī al-Kāmilī wrote, in 1135/1722:

Kashf al-asrār al-ʿilmiyya bi-dār al-ḍarb al-Miṣriyya, on the coinage of Egypt, Cairo ^{1}V, 390.

13 *Mathematics*

2. ʿAbd al-Qādir b. Aḥmad al-Sakhāwī wrote, around 1000/1591 (see Suter 476).

1. *al-Risāla al-Sakhāwiyya* see Suppl., with the commentary *Fatḥ rabb al-bariyya*, also Alex. Ḥisāb 11/2, Rāmpūr I, 418,$_{87}$.—2. *Mukhtaṣar fī ḥisāb al-jumal* Alex. Ḥisāb 17.

3. ʿUthmān b. ʿAlāʾ al-Dīn b. Yūnus b. Muḥammad b. al-Malik al-Dimashqī wrote, in 1002/1593:

| 1. *al-Isʿāf al-atamm bi-aḥāsin al-funūn min ḥisāb al-qalam* Cairo ^{1}V, 177.—2. 357
Nukhabat al-zamān fī ṣināʿat al-qabbān, composed in 997/1589, ibid. VI, 206 (autograph).

14 *Astronomy*

1. Muḥammad b. Muḥammad (p. 216) b. Aḥmad b. Muḥammad Badr al-Dīn Sibṭ al-Māridīnī was a *muwaqqit* at al-Azhar in Cairo and died in 934/1527.

Woepcke, *Introduction de l'arithmétique indienne en occident*, Paris 1859, 54, nr. 5, *JA* 1862, I, 103,$_1$. 1. Astronomical tables, with an introduction in 5 chapters, Gotha 1381,$_2$.—2. *al-Maṭlab fī 'l-ʿamal bil-rubʿ al-mujayyab*, on the sine quadrant, Gotha 1425, Krafft 333, Paris 2519,$_3$, Esc. 1926,$_2$, Cairo ^{1}V, 229, 317; commentary by al-Tājūrī, d. 999/1590 (no. 7), Krafft 331.—3. *al-Tuḥfa al-Manṣūriyya fī maʿrifat al-awqāt al-sharʿiyya* Paris 2519,$_7$, Br. Mus. 421,$_2$.—4. *Sharḥ al-Raḥbiyya* I, 491.—5. *al-Lumʿa al-Shamsiyya ʿala 'l-Tuḥfa al-Qudsiyya* p. 154.—6.–9. see Suppl. (7. Garr. 994).—10. *Hidāyat al-ʿāmil fī 'l-muqanṭarāt bil-rubʿ* Berl. *Qu. u. St.* VII, 26, II, 10.—11. *al-Nujūm al-zāhirāt fī 'l-ʿamal bi-rubʿ al-muqanṭarāt* ibid. 27, II, 11.—12. See Suppl. 217,$_{20}$.

| 2. ʿAbd al-Laṭīf b. Ibrāhīm b. Qāsim b. Muḥammad al-Dimashqī al-Umawī b. 469
al-Kayyāl, ca. 950/1543.

1. Two astronomical tables for determining the solar angle, Berl. 5758/9.—2. Other astronomical tables, ibid. 5760/1.

4. ʿAbd al-Qādir Muḥammad al-Manūfī al-Shāfiʿī, who was a *muwaqqit* at the Ghūriyya madrasa in Cairo, wrote, in 980/1572:

Rafʿ al-khilāf fī ʿamal daqāʾiq al-ikhtilāf Cairo ^{1}V, 258, 292.

5. Sulaymān b. Ḥamza b. Ḥashīsh al-ʿUthmānī al-Ḥanafī al-Falakī, fl. ca. 990/1582.

1. *Ṭarz al-ghurar fī ḥall al-durar fī marʿifat al-sāʿāt* Cairo ^{1}VII, 362.—2. *Ẓuhūr al-thurayyā wa-khafāʾ ma kāna wabiyyā*, composed in 988/1580 in response to the plague of spring of that year, ibid. 87, 266.

5a. Yūsuf b. Aḥmad b. Ibrāhīm al-Nābulusī wrote, in 998/1589:

Al-Misk al-ʿāṭir fī ḥall Zīj b. Shāṭir, p. 156.

358 | 7. Abū Zayd ʿAbd al-Raḥmān b. Muḥammad (ʿAbdallāh) al-Tājūrī, who died in 999/1590.

1. *Muqaddima* on calculating the four seasons, the night, the times of prayer, and the *qibla*, Paris $2560_{,14}$, see. Suppl.—2. *Risāla fi ʾl-ʿamal bi-rubʿ al-muqanṭarāt* Cairo V, 287.—3. *Sharḥ al-Maṭlab* see no. 1.—4. *Manāsik al-ḥajj* Gotha 61, 3.—5.–8. see Suppl. (5. Garr. 996).

8. Muḥammad b. ʿUmar b. Ṣadīq (al-Ṣiddīq) b. ʿUmar al-Bakrī al-Fawānīsī, who wrote in the second half of the tenth century.

Suter 193, 475. 1. *Natījat al-afkār fī ʿamal al-layl wal-nahār*, tables regarding the latitude of Cairo, autograph Paris 2545.—2. *Bughyat al-ṭullāb fi ʾl-ʿamal bil-asṭurlāb* ibid. $4580_{,4}$.

9a. Shams al-Dīn Muḥammad b. Abi ʾl-Khayr al-Ḥasanī (Ḥusaynī) al-Ṭaḥḥān al-Urmayūnī al-Mālikī, who wrote in the tenth century in Egypt.

Suter 511. 1. *al-Nujūm al-shāriqāt* see Suppl., RAAD VIII, 765, IX, 378, *Qu. u. St.*
470 VII, 115, vii, 1.—2.–4. | See Suppl. (4. Garr. 1018, Cairo ^{1}V, 319).—5. *Sharḥ Kashf al-qināʿ* p. 157.

10. Jamāl al-Dīn Muḥammad b. Muʿīn al-Dīn al-Hāshimī wrote, in 1004/1595:

Al-Amal al-qawīm fī ḥall al-taqwīm Leid. 1152.

10b. Muḥyi 'l-Dīn ʿAbd al-Qādir b. Muḥammad b. Aḥmad al-Fayyūmī al-ʿAwfī al-Ḥanafī al-Miṣrī, who died in 1022/1614, see Suppl. (3. Cairo [1]V, 292).

12. Muṣṭafā b. Shams al-Dīn b. Aḥmad b. Khiḍr al-Sharkasī al-Ṭāhirī (Ẓāhirī?) al-Khalwatī al-Falakī al-Dimyāṭī al-Shāfiʿī wrote, in 1038/1628:

1. *Kifāyat al-mubtadiʾ* (*Manẓūma fi 'l-rubʿ al-maqṭūʿ*), Cairo [1]V, 283.—2. *al-Durr fi 'l-ghayb al-nafīs fi 'l-rubʿ al-mansūb li-Idrīs* ibid. and VII, 537.—3. See Suppl.

13. Abu 'l-Ḥusayn ʿAbdallāh b. ʿAbd al-Raḥmān b. ʿUmar al-Ṣūfī, who died in 1057/1647.

Kitāb al-mudkhil, from which *Faṣl fī maqādīr al-aflāk wal-kawākib wal-arḍ bil-amyāl* Paris 2330,$_{2}$.

14. ʿAbdallāh b. Aḥmad al-Maqdisī al-Azharī al-Ḥanbalī, ca. 1080/1669.

1. *Tuḥfat al-labīb wa-bughyat al-arīb*, on quadrants and sine, Berl. 5856.—2. See Suppl. (Garr. 2013,$_{10}$).

15. Maḥmūd b. Quṭb al-Maḥallī, ca. 1080/1669.

| 1. *Risāla fī bayān al-murād min ittiḥād al-maṭāliʿ wakhtilāfihā al-masʾūl ʿanhu* 359
min baʿḍ fuqahāʾ al-Shāfiʿiyya Cairo [1]V, 283.—2. *Risāla fi bayān al-waqt alladhī taṭlaʿ fīhi 'l-kawākib al-thābita laylan*, composed in 1077/1666, ibid.—3. *Risāla ʿalā faḍl al-dāʾir* Garr. 1001.—4. See Suppl.—5. *Jadwal mushtamil ʿala 'stikhrāj al-taʾrīkh al-Qibṭī min al-taʾrīkh al-ʿArabī bil-ḥisāb Qu. u. St.* VII, 53, ii, 47, 50.—6. *Jadwal mushtamil ʿala 'stikhrāj daraj al-shams min al-taʾrīkh al-Qibṭī* ibid. 54, ii, 48.

16. ʿAbd al-Wahhāb al-Muqriʾ al-Sirājī wrote, in 1084/1673:

| *Taḥbīr inkishāf al-labs fī taḥrīr inkishāf al-shams*, on the solar eclipse of that 471
year, Munich 867, Cairo [1]V, 231.

17. Shaykh al-Islām Aḥmad al-Bashtakī, who died in 1110/1698.

Jab. I, 68. *Al-Tawqīʿāt al-falakiyya* Cairo ^{1}V, 235.

18. Riḍwān Efendi al-Falakī al-Razzāz lived as a private citizen in Būlāq and died on 23 Jumādā I 1122/21 July 1710.

Jab. I, 74. 1. *Natījat al-afkār fī aʿmāl al-layl wal-nahār*, on astronomical chronology, Berl. 5710.—2. *al-Jawhara al-lāmiʿa*, on chronology, part of which ibid.—3. *al-Durr al-farīd ʿala ʾl-raṣad al-jadīd* Cairo ^{1}V, 245.—4. *Dustūr uṣūl ʿilm al-mīqāt wa-natījat al-naẓar fī taḥrīr al-awqāt* ibid. 246.—5. *Jadāwil al-munḥarifāt*, written with Muḥammad al-Najjāmī, ibid. 296.—6., 7. See Suppl.—8. *al-Zīj al-mufīd ʿalā uṣūl al-raṣad al-jadīd*, following Ulugh Beg, Garr. 1104.

19. Muḥammad al-Ghamrī al-Shāfiʿī al-Falakī, who died after 1124/1712.

1. *al-Qawāʿid al-muqniʿa fī taḥwīlāt al-maqādīr al-arbaʿa*, composed in 1124/1712, Cairo ^{1}V, 187.—2. *Raqāʾiq al-asrār fī ḥisābay daraj wa-daqāʾiq aʿẓam dawwār*, composed in 1111/1699, ibid. 259.—3. See Suppl.—4. *Maknūnāt al-ḍamān* Alex. Ḥurūf 4.

19a. ʿAlī b. Faḍlallāh al-Marʿashī wrote, in 1131/1719:

1. *Risāla fī rubʿ al-muqanṭar fi ʾl-mīqāt* Alex. Fun. 101,$_{10}$.—2. *Sullam al-samāʾ wal-āfāq fi ʾl-rubʿ al-mujayyab*, composed in 1140/1728, ibid. 101,$_{11}$.

20. Ramaḍān b. Ṣāliḥ b. ʿUmar al-Safaṭī al-Khawānakī, who died on 22 Jumādā I 1158/23 June 1745.

Jab. I, 162, on which is based *Khiṭ. jad.* X, 90. 1. *Nuzhat al-nafs bi-taqwīm al-shams* Cairo ^{1}V, 326.—2. *al-Qawl al-muḥkam fī maʿrifat kusūf al-nayyir al-aʿẓam*
472 ibid. 283, 308.—3. *al-Kalām al-maʿrūf fī aʿmāl al-kusūf wal-khusūf* ibid. 270, | 308.—4. *Bulūgh al-waṭar fi ʾl-ʿamal bil-qamar* ibid. 230.—5. See Suppl.

21. Muḥammad b. ʿAlī al-Ḥumaydī (Ḥamīdī?), who died in 1179/1765.

1. *Risāla fi ʾl-āla al-musammāh dhāt al-kursī* Garr. 1006, Cairo ^{1}V, 279, 284, 299.—2. See Suppl., Garr. 1005, Alex. Ḥisāb 56, 3, Qawala II, 277.

22. Ḥasan b. Ibrāhīm b. Ḥasan al-Zaylaʿī al-Jabartī al-Ḥanafī, whose family originated in Jabart, near Zaylaʿ in Abyssinia, was a professor in Cairo who died in 1188/1774.

Jab. I, 386/408 (with a synopsis of the family's history), the source of *Khiṭ. jad.* VIII, 7. 1. *Risāla fi 'l-munḥarifāt* Cairo ^{1}V, 288.—2. *Risāla fi 'l-asṭiḥa* ibid. 305.—3. *Risāla fi 'l-rubʿ al-mujayyab* ibid. VII, 27.—4. *Haqāʾiq al-daqāʾiq ʿalā daqāʾiq al-ḥaqāʾiq* p. 217.—5. *Rafʿ al-ishkāl bi-ẓuhūr al-ʿashr fi 'l-ʿashr fī ghālib al-ashkāl* Cairo ^{1}III, 60, I, 435.—6. *Nuzhat al-ʿayn fī zakāt al-maʿdanayn* Garr. 1864, Cairo ^{1}III, 142, VII, 241/2, ^{2}I, 469.—7. *Iṣlāḥ al-isfār ʿan wujūh baʿḍ mukhaddarāt al-mukhtār* (*Sharḥ Tanwīr al-abṣār*), p. 404.—8.–16. see Suppl. (9. 2031,$_{8}$, Alex. Fiqh Ḥan. 7, Fun. 135, 5, Makram 5; 10. *Ḥāshiya* on al-Ḥifnī's (p. 364) commentary on *al-Risāla al-sharṭiyya* by ʿAbbās Efendi, Garr. 478; 13. Garr. 1007; 16. ibid. 1882).—17. *Risāla fī dāʾirat al-muʿaddil* Alex. Ḥisāb 49.

| 23. ʿAbdallāh al-Muwaqqit bi-Jāmiʿ Qūsūn, who died in Cairo on 12 Dhu 'l-Ḥijja 360
1188/14 February 1775.

Jab. I, 411. *Al-Durr al-thamīn fi 'l-ḥukm ʿalā taḥwīl al-sinīn* Cairo ^{1}V, 245.

24. ʿUthmān b. Ṣāliḥ al-Wardānī devoted himself to astronomy in Cairo, and especially to calendars, and wrote, in 1210/1795:

Al-Sālik al-qawīm fī maʿrifat al-taqwīm min al-Durr al-yatīm or *Jadāwil ḥall ʿuqūd muqawwamat al-qamar bi-ṭarīq al-Durr al-yatīm li-Ibn al-Majdī* (p. 158), Cairo ^{1}V, 261, cf. *Khiṭ. jad.* X, 96.

| 15 *Travelogues and Geographies* 473

1. Muḥammad b. Khiḍr Nāṣir al-Dīn al-Rūmī al-Ḥalabī, ca. 948/1541.

1. *al-Tuḥfa al-laṭīfa fī ʿimārat al-masjīd al-nabawī wal-Madīna al-sharīfa*, composed in 939–44/1532–7, Esc. ^{2}1708,$_{3}$.—2. *al-Mustaqṣā fī faḍāʾil al-Masjid al-Aqṣā* (in Jerusalem), completed on 10 Ṣafar 948/5 June 1541, ibid. 1767.—3. See Suppl.

2. ʿAbd al-Bāsiṭ b. Mūsā b. Aḥmad b. Ismāʿīl al-ʿAlmāwī al-Shāfiʿī was born in Damascus on 15 Rajab 907/25 January 1502, and became the chief *muʾadhdhin* of the Umayyad mosque in 938/1531. After the death of his father, he succeeded the latter as a preacher at the mosque of Barsbay on 28 Jumādā I 940/16 December 1533, and during the holy months he held private religious gatherings for laymen. He died in Shaʿbān 981/December 1573.

RA 170r., *Mukhtasar Tanbīh al-ṭālib wa-irshād al-dāris* p. 165.—2. See Suppl.

3. Abu 'l-Barakāt Badr al-Dīn Abu 'l-Jūd Muḥammad b. Raḍī al-Dīn Muḥammad (p. 366) b. Muḥammad b. Aḥmad b. ʿAbdallāh al-Ghazzī al-ʿĀmirī al-Shāfiʿī al-Azharī al-Dimashqī was born in Damascus on 14 Dhu 'l-Qaʿda 904/24 June 1499. From 18 Ramaḍān 936/17 May 1530 until the end of Dhu 'l-Qaʿda 937/July 1531 he accompanied the *qāḍi 'l-quḍāt* Ibn Furfūr on a trip to Istanbul, which he gives an account of in no. 1. Later he became a professor at al-Muqaddamiyya, al-Shāmiyya, and al-Juwayniyya madrasas in Damascus, as well as at the
361 Taqawiyya in 971/1563. Through the influence of his patron, | the *qāḍi 'l-ʿaskar* Muḥammad b. Maʿlūl, Muḥammad b. al-Ḥijāzī al-Ḥimṣī removed this office from him, but when Muḥammad Čiwizāde became *qāḍi 'l-ʿaskar* six months later al-Ḥimṣī had to step down again. Abu 'l-Barakāt died on 16 Shawwāl 984/7 January 1577.

RA 239v, *TA* 88v. 1. *al-Maṭāliʿ al-Badriyya fi 'l-manāzil al-Rūmiyya*, Br. Mus. Suppl. 680 (autograph), Pet. AM 240.—2. *Manhal al-wurrād fi 'l-ḥathth ʿalā*
474 *qirāʾat al-awrād* | *wa-tuḥfat al-mulūk li-man arāda taḥrīr al-sulūk*, a manual for a way of life pleasing to God, Berl. 8844.—3. *al-Marāḥ fi 'l-muzāḥ*, on jokes, ibid. 5428, *RAAD* XI, 318.—4. Five *rajaz* verses on the ten-fold pronunciation of *al-khātam* Berl. $7069_{,2}$.—5. Some poetry, ibid. 679.—6. *Mukhtaṣar al-siyar* no. 3338.—7.–9. see Suppl.—10. *Jawāhir al-dhakhāʾir fi 'l-kabāʾir wal-ṣaghāʾir*, in verse, Cairo ^{1}VII, 531; a commentary by Raḍī al-Dīn Muḥammad b. Yūnus al-Maqdisī, ibid.—12. *Tafsīr*, in verse, with three titles: a. *al-Taysīr fi 'l-tafsīr* or *Taysīr al-tibyān fī tafsīr al-Qurʾān*, b. *Minḥat al-raḥmān*, c. *Yanbūʿ al-kalām al-muntaẓim min fayḍ majmūʿ jawāmiʿ al-kalim*, composed in 959–62/1552–5, 4 vols., AS 98/9 (vols. 1 and 4, Ritter, *Türkiyat Mecm.* VI–VII [1945], p. 75–7), Mosul $27_{,64}$ (vol. 4, copied in 981 when the author was still alive).

4. Muḥibb al-Dīn Abu 'l-Faḍl b. Taqī al-Dīn Abū Bakr b. Dāʾūd al-Ḥamawī al-Ḥanafī, who died in 1016/1618, see Suppl.

1. *al-Riḥla* or *Hādi 'l-aẓʿān al-Najdiyya ila 'l-diyār al-Miṣriyya*, an account of his trips to Jerusalem, to where he had accompanied the chief *qāḍī* of Damacus in 978/1570 in order to repossess a mosque-turned-into-a-church from the Christians there, to Egypt, where he was a *qāḍī* in Fuwwa for some time, and of his trip from Damascus to Istanbul in 982/1574 at the accession to the throne of Sultan Murād, composed in Maʿarrat al-Nuʿmān, where he was a *qāḍī*, Paris 2293, Alex. Fun. $143_{,1}$, Cairo ^{1}VII, 646.—2.–5. see Suppl. (2. Alex. Fun. $143_{,2}$).

5. Muḥammad b. Aḥmad b. Muḥammad b. Jamāl al-Dīn b. Sukaykir al-Dimashqī, who died in 987/1579.

1. *Zubdat al-āthār fī-mā waqaʿa li-jāmiʿihi fī ʾl-iqāma wal-asfār*, accounts of his trips—from 16 Rabīʿ II 973/11 November 1565 until 13 Muḥarram 976/8 July 1568—from Hama to Aleppo, where he was a preacher at al-ʿĀdiliyya mosque, and to Istanbul, Pet. AM 241.—2. See Suppl.

6. Ḥujayj b. Qāsim al-Wāḥidī made the pilgrimage from Aleppo to Mecca in 992/1584 and wrote on it:

Riḥla, with many digressions on all kinds of sciences, which were actually more interesting to him, Pet. AM 242.

7. Shams al-Dīn Abu ʾl-ʿAbbās Aḥmad b. Muḥammad b. al-Imām al-Buṣrawī wrote, in 1003/1594:

| *Tuḥfat al-anām fī faḍāʾil al-Shām*, Gotha 93,1, Vienna 902, Leid. 816, Paris 823, 475
Br. Mus. 1256, Pet. AM 239, Garr. 753/5, Alex. Taʾr. 44; see Wüstenfeld in *Lüddes Ztschr.* I, 164, *GGA* 1841, p. 1308.

| 8. Muḥammad Ḥāfiẓ al-Dīn al-Qudsī, fl. ca. 1013/1604. 362

Isfār al-asfār wa-abkār al-afkār, a brief description of his trip to Cairo, Jerusalem, and Damascus, as well as a detailed account of his trip by sea from Istanbul to Cairo in thunderstorms and heavy weather in 1013, in rhymed prose, Berl. 6134.

8b. Salāmish b. Kündoghdū al-Ṣāliḥī, who lived in Egypt in the tenth century.

Al-Bustān fī ʿajāʾib al-arḍ wal-buldān, Paris 2212, print. Rome 1584 (Nan. I, 151, Schnurrer 174), *Assemani Globus caelestis Cufico-Arabicus*, Veliterni Musei Borgiani, Padua 1790.

9. Muḥammad Nāṣir al-Dīn al-Sawāʾī al-Shafūnī al-Khaṭīb, who lived ca. 1054/1644.

1. *al-Jawhar al-maknūn fī faḍāʾil ziyārat jabal Qāsiyūn*, in praise of Mount Qasyun and the holy places around Damascus, Berl. 6086/7.—2. *Bahjat al-anām fī faḍāʾil wa-karāmāt al-shaykh Abī Bakr b. Qiwām*, d. 658/1260, ibid. 10100 (as *Bahjat al-aḥbāb*), Alex. Naḥw 34,3, Taṣ. 9.

10. Badr al-Dīn b. Sālim b. Muḥammad Tābiʿ āl al-Ṣiddīq wrote, in 1062/1652:

1. *al-Majāz fī ḥaqīqat riḥlat al-shaykh Zayn al-ʿĀbidīn al-Ṣiddīqī ilā bilād al-Ḥijāz*, print. C., n.d. (Cat. I V, 125).—2. See Suppl.—3. *Qūt al-arwāḥ fī aḥkām al-samāʿ al-mubāḥ*, autograph, Cairo *Nashra* 21, see Farmer, *Sources* 64.

11. Muḥammad b. Yaḥyā b. Taqī al-Dīn b. Ismāʿīl al-Ḥalabī al-Faraḍī Najm al-Dīn was a professor at the Umayyad mosque in Damascus. When his son died he renounced teaching for a number of years, and installed 140 water supply lines at his own expense. Later he took up teaching again, before dying in 1090/1679.

476 | Muḥ. IV, 265. *Al-Ishārāt ilā amākin al-ziyārāt*, on the holy places of Damascus and its surrounding lands, Berl. 6125.

11c. Aḥmad Efendi b. Ṣāliḥ b. Manṣūr al-Ṭarābulusī was a *muftī* in Damietta and *naqīb al-ashrāf* in Cairo, and died in 1159/1746.

Mur. II, 69, A. Taymūr, *RAAD* VII, 226. *Tuḥfat al-adab etc.* See Suppl., abstracts *RAAD* VII, 299/314, al-Maghribī ibid. 346/58, 549/54.

12. Murtaḍā b. ʿAlī b. ʿAlawān, fl. ca. 1120/1708.

1. An account of his pilgrimage to Mecca in 1120/1708, Berl. 6137.—2. A *qaṣīda* ibid. $8018_{,1}$.

13. Murtaḍā Bek b. Muṣṭafā b. Ḥasan al-Kurdī had to leave Damascus in 1127/1715 because of debts; he went to Cairo, where he died sometime after 1133/1721.

1. *Tahdhīb al-aṭwār fī ʿajāʾib al-amṣār*, an account of his journey to Cairo, Berl. 6142.—2. *ʿUqūd al-jumān fī ʿadam ṣuḥbat abnāʾ al-zamān* ibid. 5429.—3. *Hadiyyat al-faqīr li-ḥaḍrat al-wazīr*, an *adab* work dedicated to Ibrāhīm Pāshā, the son-in-law of Sultan Aḥmad, Munich 605, autograph dated 1133/1721, Garr. 232.

14. Muḥammad b. Muḥammad b. Sharaf al-Dīn al-Khalīlī al-Maqdisī was born in Hebron, studied in Cairo, lived in Jerusalem, and died in 1148/1735.

363 | Mur. IV, 95/7. 1. A treatise praising the mosque of Jerusalem, including its merits and blessings, Berl. 6101.—2. A *qaṣīda* in praise of the mosque of Jerusalem, ibid. $8019_{,1}$.

15. Muṣṭafā Asʿad b. Aḥmad b. Muḥammad al-Dimyāṭī al-Laqīmī was born in Damietta in 1105/1693 and made the pilgrimage with his father, during which he attended lectures of scholars in Mecca and Medina. He then continued his studies in Cairo, Damietta, Damascus, and Jerusalem, before living in Cairo. He died in 1178/1759.

Mur. IV, 154/66 (sample poems), Jab. I, 221/42. 1. *Laṭāʾif uns al-jalīl fī taḥāʾif al-Quds wal-Khalīl*, on the merits of Jerusalem and Hebron, Berl. 6102.—2. *Mawāniḥ al-uns bi-riḥlatī li-wādi ʾl-Quds*, on his trip from Damietta to Jerusalem | in 6 months in 1143/1730, composed in 1164/1751, ibid. 6151.—3. *al-Ḥulla al-muʿlama al-bahīja bil-riḥla al-Qudsiyya al-muhīja*, of which a part, ibid.—4. *Dīwān* Br. Mus. 1088,$_1$ (which has Luqaymī). 477

16 *Hunting and Militaria*

1. Al-Darwīsh ʿAlī al-Shādhilī al-Ḥanafī al-Dimashqī, *naqīb* of the archers of Damascus, ca. 1130/1718.

1. *Miftāḥ kanz al-niẓām fī aṣl al-rimāya wa-taʿlīm al-ghulām*, on the origin of archery and a manual on it, Berl. 5544.—2. 33 *rajaz* verses praising the hunters of Damascus, especially the professional huntsman Muṣṭafā b. Ḥasan, ibid. 5545.—3. A hunting poem, ibid. 8020,$_1$.

2. Muṣṭafā Čūrinjī al-Farḥatī, elder of the homeguard in Cairo, who died in 1140/1727.

Kitāb faḍl al-qaws al-ʿArabiyya, on the bow and its use, Gotha 1339.

17 *Music*

ʿAbd al-Qādir b. Muḥammad al-Qādirī, ca. 1050/1640.

1. *Risāla fi ʾl-tawqīʿāt*, composed in 1050/1640, Cairo ¹V, 298.—2. *Risāla fī dhikr al-anghām wa-aṣwātihā*, on melodies and tones, Berl. 5528.

| 18 *Medicine* 364

2. Aḥmad b. al-Ḥājj Sinān b. Sharbatī wrote, in 972/1564:

Risālat uṣūl al-ʿilāj fī taṣḥīḥ al-mizāj, a medical compendium, Berl. 6309.

2a. Shihāb (Sarī) al-Dīn Aḥmad b. Muḥammad al-ʿIlāqī b. al-Ṣayyāgh al-Ḥanafī, the head of the physicians of Egypt,[1] wrote, before 998/1590:

Kifāyat al-arīb etc. see Suppl. II, 1028, 13, Esc. $^{2}891_{,2}$ (manuscript dated 998), see ḤKh. V, $218_{,10776}$, Leclerc III, 317.

478 | 3. Dāʾūd b. ʿUmar al-Anṭākī al-Ḍarīr was born in Antioch, the son of the *raʾīs* of Qaryat Sīdī Ḥabīb al-Najjār. He lived in Damascus and Cairo, dying in 1008/1599 in Mecca, less than a year after he moved to live there.

Muḥ. II, 140/9, Leclerc II, 304, Wüst. *Ärzte* 275, Adnan Adivar, *Osmanli Türklerinde ilim* 96. 1. *Tadhkirat uli ʾl-albāb wal-jāmiʿ lil-ʿajab al-ʿujāb*, a handbook of medicine, Gotha 2009, Munich 836/7, Leid. 1379, Paris 3031/3, 5756/8, 6753, Copenhagen 110, Br. Mus. 989, 1364, 1654, Suppl. 809/10, Cambr. Pr. 49, no. 23, Bodl. I, 588, II, 173, Pet. Ros. 179, Esc. $^{2}837$, Köpr. II, 183, Bursa Haraccizade Ṭibb 10, Meshh. XVI, $7_{,21}$; print. C. 1308, 1309, cf. Leclerc, *Not. et Extr.* 23, p. XIII.—Abstracts: a. al-Jabartī, d. 1237/1821, Cairo ^{1}VI, 39.—b. Khalīl b. Ismāʿīl al-Jazāʾirī, Algiers 1763.—c. Anon., Gotha 108, 2, 2010, $2026_{,16}$, 2084.—2. *al-Nuzha al-mubhija fī tashḥīdh al-adhhān wa-taʿdīl al-amzija* Pet. Ros. 180/1. Bursa, Haraccizade Ṭibb 59.—3. *Nuzhat al-adhhān fī iṣlāḥ al-abdān* Berl. 6312, Munich 835, Gotha 1939 (fragm.), Leid. 1380, Cairo ^{1}VI, 32, 46, VII, 660.—4. *Risāla* on medicine in general, Berl. 6313.—5. *al-Tuḥfa al-Bakriyya fī aḥkām al-istiḥmām al-kulliyya wal-juzʾiyya*, on balneotherapy, Paris 3034.—6. *Unmūdaj fī ʿilm al-falak*, on medical astrology, ibid. $2357_{,7}$.—7. *al-Mufīd* Cairo ^{1}VI, 42.—8. *Risāla fī ʾl-ṭayr wal-ʿuqāb*, on the philosopher's stone, Paris $2625_{,8}$.—9. *Tazyīn al-aswāq bi-tafṣīl (tartīb) ashwāq al-ʿushshāq* I, 431.—10.–31. see Suppl. (27. Patna I, $247_{,2106}$).

4. Madyan b. ʿAbd al-Raḥmān al-Qūṣūnī went to Cairo following the death of Aḥmad b. al-Ṣāʾigh (?) to replace him as chief physician. He died sometime after 1044/1634.

Muḥ. IV, 333, Wüst. *Gesch.* 561. *Qāmūs al-aṭibbāʾ wa-nāmūs al-alibbāʾ fi ʾl-mufradāt*, composed in 1038/1628, Cairo ^{1}VI, 26, see Meyerhof, *al-Andalus* III, 38.

5. Shihāb al-Dīn Aḥmad b. Aḥmad b. Salāma al-Qalyūbī, who died in 1069/1658.

1 Identical with chief physician al-Sarī Aḥmad b. al-Ṣāʾigh, who was succeeded by al-Qūṣūnī (no. 4), Muḥ. IV, 333?

Muḥ. I, 175, followed by *Khiṭ. jad.* XIV, 118, Leclerc II, 303. 1. *al-Maṣābīḥ al-saniyya fī ṭibb al-bariyya*, on therapeutics, Gotha 1961/2, Schluss ibid. 1958/2,
Paris 3034,3, 3044, Upps. | 345, Alex. Ṭibb 44, Cairo ^{1}VI, 40, Sanguinetti, *JA* s. VI. 479
vol. 6 (1865) II, 381.—2. *al-Fawāʾid al-ṭibbiyya al-muwāfiqa li-ṭibb al-bariyya*, a
medical compedium, Berl. 6314.—3. *al-Tadhkira fi ʾl-ṭibb* | Cairo ^{1}VI, 9, print. 365
C. 1305, among others.—4. *al-Aḥkām al-mukhliṣa fī ḥukm māʾ al-ḥimmiṣa* Cairo ^{1}VII, 591.—5. *al-Hidāya min al-ḍalāla fī marʿifat al-waqt wal-qibla bi-ghayr āla* Berl. 5706, Garr. 2096, 2, Alex. Ḥisāb 64.—6. *Muqaddima fi ʾl-fuṣūl al-arbaʿa wa-awqāt al-ṣalawāt wa-ākhir al-layl wa-jihat al-qibla bi-ghayr āla* Gotha 1452/3, Cairo ^{1}V, 303, 318.—7. 500 short prayers for Muḥammad, Berl. 3927, Algiers 1879.—8. *Risāla fī faḍl al-ṣalāt ʿala ʾl-nabī ṣlʿm* Cairo ^{1}I, 199, 212.—9. *Ṣalawāt*, print. Būlāq 1300, Cairo ^{1}I, 205, VII, 174.—10. *Risāla fi ʾl-ṣalāt ʿala ʾl-nabī* ibid. ^{1}VII, 411.—11. *al-Nubdha al-laṭīfa fī bayān maqāṣid al-Ḥijāz wa-maʿālimiha ʾl-sharīfa* ibid. 519, V, 381.—12. *al-Farāʾiḍ al-gharāʾib al-ḥisān fī faḍāʾil laylat niṣf Shaʿbān* Alex. Ḥad. 57,1, Cairo ^{1}VII, 528.—13. *Risāla fī ʿilm al-ḥarf wal-wafq*, games with letters and magical diagrams, Gotha 1269 (= Cairo ^{1}V, 367).—14. *Kitāb al-malāḥim* Cairo ^{1}V, 372.—15. *Taʿbīr al-manāmāt* ibid. ^{1}VI, 126, ^{2}176.—16. *Tuḥfat al-rāghib fī sīrat jamāʿa min ahl al-bayt al-aṭāyib* C. 1307.—17. *Ḥikāyāt gharība wa-ʿajība* or *Ḥikāyāt wa-gharāʾib wa-ʿajāʾib wa-laṭāʾif wa-nawādir wa-fawāʾid wa-nafāʾis*, shortened to *Nawādir al-Qalyūbī*, edited by a later person, Berl. 8428, Gotha 2703/4, Garr. 736, Cairo ^{1}II, 81. *The Book of Anecdotes. Wonders, marvels, pleasanteries, rarities and useful and precious extracts*, ed. W. Nassau Lees and Mawlawi Kabir al Din, Calcutta 1856, 2nd ed. ibid. 1864, lith. C. 1274, 1277, 1279, print. C. 1296, 1297, 1300, 1302, 1304, 1307, 1308, 1311, 1323. On no. 176 see R. Basset, *Mélusine* III, Paris 1886/7, col. 528, and from which W. Ahrens, *Mathematische Unterhaltungen und Spiele* ^{2}II, 136 (Chp. XV, *Das Josephsspiel*).—18.–23. see Suppl. (20. p. 446, 16, 5. c; 21. Garr. 756).—24. *Risāla fī faḍāʾil Makka wal-Madīna wal-Bayt al-ḥarām al-muqaddas wa-shayʾ min taʾrīkhihā* Alex. Taʾr. 71.—25. *Ḥāshiya ʿala ʾl-Waraqāt* I, 487.

7. Ṣadaqa ʿAfīf, ca. 1140/1727.

Jāmiʿ al-gharāʾib wa-dīwān al-ʿajāʾib, a medical compendium, Berl. 6316.

8. Muḥammad b. ʿAbd al-ʿAzīz al-Shāfiʿī al-Ḥalabī al-Mutaṭabbib wrote, in 1153/1740:

| On the properties and uses of animals, Gotha 2066,1. 480

9. Yūsuf b. Jirjī b. ʿAbūdiyya al-Ṭabīb al-Ḥalabī al-Mārūnī wrote, in 1180/1776:

Al-Risāla al-dhahabiyya fī muʿālajat al-ḥummā al-diqqiyya Gotha 1984.

19 *Occult Sciences*

1a. Muḥammad b. ʿAlī b. Muḥammad b. ʿAlī al-Shabrāmallisī, ca. 1021/1612.

366 | Muḥ. IV, 44, from which *Khiṭ. jad.* XII, 124. 1. *Bahjat al-muḥādith fī aḥkām jumla min al-ḥawādith,* on astrology, Berl. 5890, Paris 2597, Alex. Ḥisāb 44, Cairo ^{1}V, 230, 279.—2. *Ṭawāliʿ al-ishrāq fī waḍʿ al-awfāq*, on magic squares, Paris 2698,$_1$.—3. From an untitled work: *Faṣl fī ṣifat tarkīb al-asmāʾ wa-kayfiyyat istikhrājihā min ʿilm al-ḥarf etc.* ibid.,$_2$.—4. *al-Nubdha al-wafiyya fī waḍʿ al-awfāq al-ʿadadiyya* ibid. 3.—5. *Īḍāḥ al-muktatam fī ḥisāb al-raqam* Cairo ^{1}V, 178.—6. *al-Durra al-bahiyya fī waḍʿ khuṭūt faṣl al-dāʾira bil-ṭarīqa al-handasiyya* Ind. Off. 772,$_2$.—7. *al-Irshād lil-ʿilm bi-khawāṣṣ al-aʿdād*, on arithmetic, Berl. 5997.—8. *al-Rajaz al-mafrūḍ fī ʿilm al-ʿarūḍ* ibid. 7138, a commentary, *Kashf al-ghumūḍ*, by ʿAbdallāh b. ʿAlī al-Damlījī, ca. 1217, Berl. 7139, Garr. 512.—9. See Suppl.—10. *Urjūza fī dukhūl shahr al-Muḥarram min ayy yawm min ayyām al-usbūʿ* Alex. Ḥurūf 12.

2. ʿAbd al-Rāḥmān b. ʿAbdallāh al-Iskarī Imām bi-Jāmiʿ Ṭūlūn wrote, in 1034/1624:

1. *Taḥṣīl al-intifāʿ wa-ghāyat al-irtifāʿ fī waḍʿ al-maqāyīs wa-waḍʿ al-arbāʿ* Cairo ^{1}V, 231.—2. See Suppl., Alex. Ḥurūf 8.

3. Muḥammad al-Maqdisī al-Qarqashandī wrote, in 1049/1639:

A work on alchemy, Br. Mus. 1372,$_1$.

4. ʿAbd al-Raḥmān b. Aḥmad Bākathīr wrote, around 1080/1670:

Kashf al-ghubār ʿani ʾl-ishārāt fī-mā baqiya min ʿumr hādhihi ʾl-dār Berl. 2765.

481 5. Muḥammad b. Muhammad al-Fullānī[1] al-Kishnawī al-Sūdānī | studied in his native Sudan and devoted himself for five months to sand divination (*ʿilm al-raml*) in Kāgho, in Bornu. He made the pilgrimage in 1142/1729 and died in Cairo in 1154/1741.

---

1 Often corrupted to Ghilālī, Ghlātī, or Ghlānī.

Jab. I, 159/60. 1. *Bahjat al-āfāq wa-īḍāḥ al-labs wal-ighlāq fī ʿilm al-ḥurūf wal-awfāq* Cairo ^{1}V, 332.—2. *al-Durr al-manẓūm wa-khulāṣat al-Sirr al-maktūm* I, 669, no. 29.—3. *al-Taḥrīrāt al-rāʾiqa*, on Muḥammad's condition and acts after death, completed in Alexandria after his return from the pilgrimage in Rabīʿ I 1156/May 1743 (sic), Berl. 2599, positive reviews by Muḥammad al-Ḥifnawī and Aḥmad al-Mollawī (both died after 1181/1767), ibid. 60.

6. ʿAbd al-Raḥmān b. Muḥammad al-Nīlawī al-Shāfiʿī al-Aḥmadī al-Khalwatī wrote, in 1170/1756:

A work on physiognomy, Berl. 5373.

| 20 *Encyclopaedias and Polyhistors* 367

1. Muḥammad b. ʿAlī b. Muḥammad b. Ṭūlūn al-Ṣāliḥī al-Dimashqī al-Ḥanafī, who was born in al-Ṣāliḥiyya near Damascus in 890/1485 (or, according to others, in 880/1473), studied in Cairo with al-Suyūṭī, returned there in 923/1517, and then became a teacher of grammar, Qurʾānic exegesis, and *ḥadīth* at al-Madrasa al-Ṣāliḥiyya in Damascus, which had been enlarged by Sultan Selīm. He died on 10 Jumādā II 953/9 August 1546.

RA 235v, Wüst. *Gesch.* 522. 1. *Ramz al-sālik li-ʿilm al-madārik*, Berl. 134.—2. *al-Nafḥa al-Zanbaqiyya fi ʾl-asʾila al-Dimashqiyya*, ibid. 297.—3. *al-Luʾluʾ al-manẓūm fi ʾl-wuqūf ʿalā ma ʾshtaghaltu bihi min al-ʿulūm* Br. Mus. $430_{,6}$.—4. *al-Ṭāriʾ ʿalā Zallat al-qāriʾ* (by Nasafī I, 550, V), Berl. 571.—5. *al-Wāḍiḥa fī waṣf al-qarīna al-ṣāliḥa*, a description of the virtuous housewife, ibid. $5595_{,2}$.—6. A *qaṣīda* on various types of martyrs, ibid. $7936_{,3}$.—7. *Taʿlīq wajīz fī tadwīn ʿilm al-kumūn wal-burūz*, on the science of atoms and similar things, ibid. 5104.—8. A treatise on the meaning of words, ibid. 5105.—9. *Kitāb al-masāʾil al-mulaqqabāt fī ʿilm al-naḥw* Leid. 244.—10. *Fatḥ al-qadīr fi ʾl-taʾnīth wal-tadhkīr* ibid. 245.—11. *Tabyīn* | *al-munāsabāt bayna ʾl-asmāʾ wal-musammayāt* ibid. 246 (= 8?).—12. 482
al-Ilmām bi-sharḥ ḥaqīqat al-istifhām ibid. 247.—13. *Minḥat al-afāḍil lil-shurūṭ allatī bihā yataḥaqqaq tanāzuʿ al-ʿāmilayn aw al-ʿawāmil* ibid. 247.—14. *Itḥāf al-nubahāʾ bi-naḥw al-fuqahāʾ* ibid. 249.—15. *Majlis al-mukhāṭaba bayna ʾl-Zajjāj wa-Thaʿlab* from the *Kitāb al-nuzah wal-ibtihāj* of Abu ʾl-Ḥasan ʿAlī b. Muḥammad al-Shimshāṭī, a contemporary of Sayf al-Dawla (*Fihrist* 154, Yāqūt, *GW* III, $320_{,10}$, *Irshād* V, 375), ibid. 250.—16. *al-Asʾila al-muʿtabara wal-ajwiba al-mukhtabara* ibid. 251.—17. *al-Ki(u)nās li-fawāʾid al-nās* Esc. ^{2}545.—18. *al-Ghuraf al-ʿaliyya fī tarājim mutaʾakhkhiri ʾl-Ḥanafiyya*, a continuation of the *Kitāb al-jawāhir al-muḍīʾa* of ʿAbd al-Qādir b. Abi ʾl-Wafāʾ al-Qurashī, d. 775/1373 (p. 97), Br. Mus. Suppl. 645, Šehīd ʿA. 1924; from the end a piece on the

importance and beautiful powers of the letters of the alphabet, Berl. 4133.—19. *al-Tamattuʿ bil-aqrān*, on scholars of the ninth and tenth centuries, an abstract by Ibn al-Munlā, d. 1003/1594, entitled *Mutʿat al-adhhān min al-T.* and another, *al-Ṭayyib al-nashr bil-ṭayy wal-nashr*, Berl. 9888.—20. *Dhakhāʾir al-qaṣr fī tarājim nubalāʾ al-ʿaṣr*, an appendix to the previous work, 136 alphabetically-ordered biographies of people from Damascus, Gotha 1779, cf. Wüstenfeld in *Lüddes Ztschr.* I, 164, *Orient.* II, 162.—21. *Inbāʾ al-umarāʾ bi-anbāʾ al-wuzarāʾ*, biographies of 31 viziers, Berl. 9880.—22. *al-Nuṭq al-munabbiʾ ʿan tarjamat al-shaykh al-Muḥyawī b. al-ʿArabī* ibid. 10098.—23. *Ghāyat al-bayān fī tarjamat*
368 *al-shaykh Arslān* (I, 589), ibid. 10106. |—24. Abstract of a chronicle organised by day (see Suppl.); the author of RA gives several excerpts from it, even though he criticises him for a lack of discernment with regard to *ḥadīth* and for untruthfulness in his representation of contemporary history.—26.–42. see Suppl. (26. *Mulakhkhaṣ T. al-ḥ.* Bursa Ḥü. Čelebī Edeb. 8; 30. *Iʿlām al-sāʾilīn ʿan kutub etc.* Ẓāh. ʿIsh, Taʾrīkh 78; 34. M. Kurd ʿA. *RAAD* V, 216/22; 36. Garr. $2095_{,1}$).—43. *ʿArf al-zaharāt fī tafsīr al-kalimāt al-ṭayyibāt* Garr. 702.—44. *Qaṣd al-sharīd min akhbār Yazīd* Cairo ^{2}V, 300.—45. *Ijāza* Alex. Fun. $183_{,1}$.—46. *al-Naḥla fī-mā warada fi ʾl-nakhla* ibid.$_{2}$.—47. *ʿUnwān al-rasāʾil fī maʿrifat al-awāʾil* ibid.$_{3}$.—48. *Irtiyāḥ al-khāṭir fī maʿrifat al-awākhir* ibid.$_{4}$.—49. *Risāla fi ʾl-fīl* ibid.$_{5}$.—50. *Laqs al-ḥanak fī-mā qīla fi ʾl-samak* ibid.$_{6}$.—51. *Risāla fi ʾl-fakhkh wal-ʿuṣfūr* ibid.$_{7}$.—52. *Ibtisām al-thughūr fī-mā qīla fī nafʿ al-zuhūr* ibid.$_{8}$.—53. *Tuḥfat al-aḥbāb fī manṭiq al-ṭayr wal-dawāb* ibid.$_{9}$.—54. *Araj al-nasamāt fī aʿmār al-makhlūqāt*
483 | ibid.$_{10}$.—55. *al-Mulḥa fī-mā warada fi ʾl-subḥa* ibid.$_{11}$.—56. *Nafaḥāt al-zahr fī dhawq ahl al-ʿaṣr* ibid.$_{12}$.—57. *al-Taʿrīf fī fann al-taḥrīf* ibid.$_{13}$.—58. *al-ʿUqūd al-durriyya fi ʾl-umarāʾ al-Miṣriyya* ibid.$_{14}$.—59. *Taʿlīqāt fi ʾl-tarājim* Ẓāh. ʿIsh, Taʾrīkh 186.

2. Raḍī al-Dīn Muḥammad b. Ibrāhīm b. Yūsuf b. ʿAbd al-Raḥmān b. al-Ḥasan al-Ḥalabī al-Rabaʿī al-Tādhifī al-Ḥanafī al-Qādirī b. al-Ḥanbalī was a descendant of Ibn al-Shiḥna. He was born in Aleppo in 877 and died there on 13 Jumādā I 971/30 December 1563.

RA 278r, Wüst. *Gesch.* 528, Ahlw. Berl. 4954, d. 959? 1. *Dīwān*, compiled by his student Aḥmad b. al-Mollā al-Shāfiʿī, Cairo ^{1}IV, 315, ^{2}III, 78, 107.—2. 10 *qaṣīdas* in praise of Sultan Süleymān, each 10 verses long, Berl. $7939_{,4}$.—3. *al-Rawāʾiḥ al-ʿūdiyya fi ʾl-madāʾiḥ al-Suʿūdiyya* Cairo ^{1}IV, 315.—4. *Ḥadāʾiq aḥdāq al-azhār wa-maṣābīḥ anwār al-anwār*, in honour of the number ten (similar to Sukkardān p. 14, which was in honour of the number seven), dedicated to Sultan Süleymān, Berl. 8419.—5. *Martaʿ al-ẓibāʾ wa-marbaʿ dhawi ʾl-ṣibā*

Cairo ^{1}IV, 315, ^{2}III, 350.—6. *Kanz man ḥājā wa-ʿammā fi ʾl-aḥājī wal-muʿammā*, poetic riddles, with the commentary *Ghamz al-ʿayn ilā kanz al-ʿayn*, Munich 572.—7. *Risāla fi ʾl-aḥājī wal-alghāz* Cairo ^{1}IV, 314.—8. *Risāla tashtamil ʿalā jumlat mā yahwāhu ʾl-sāmiʿ li-qaṣd tashnīf al-masāmiʿ* ibid. 315.—9. *Tuḥfat al-afāḍil fī ṣināʿat al-fāḍil* Br. Mus. 334,$_{2}$.—10. *al-Zubd wal-ḍarab fī taʾrīkh Ḥalab*, an abstract of the work by Ibn al-ʿAdīm (I, 405) with a continuation until 6 Rabīʿ II 951/28 June 1544, Br. Mus. 334, Bodl. I, 836, Pet. AM 203.—11. *Durr al-ḥabab fī taʾrīkh aʿyān Ḥalab*, see Suppl. (read: Abū Dharr), biographies of famous people from Aleppo and those who had a connection with that city, Gotha 1773, Vienna 1184, Paris 2140, 5884, Br. Mus. 1301, Bodl. I, 810, Glasgow 61 (*JRAS* 1899, 754), Yeni 850, NO 3293, Alex. Taʾr. 65, from which 4 biographies in Berl. 10138.—12. *Maṣābīḥ arbāb al-riyāsa wa-mafātīḥ abwāb al-kiyāsa*, a practical guide for judges, Berl. 4954.—13. *Makhāyil al-malāḥa fī masāʾil al-misāḥa*, a commentary on *Ghunyat al-ḥussāb fī ʿilm al-ḥisāb*, see Suppl. I, 860, 9e.—14. *Tadhkirat al-nāsī*, on geometry, Bodl. I, 967, Alex. Fun. 177,$_{1}$.—15. *al-Durar al-sāṭiʿa fi ʾl-adwiya al-qāṭiʿa*, a versification of *Kitāb burʾ al-sāʿa* (I, 269) in 135 *rajaz* verses, Berl. 6308, Br. Mus. 334,$_{3}$.—16.–29. see Suppl. (19. Alex. Fun. 126,$_{7}$; | 20. read: *Qafw*, print. C. 1926; 23. read: *al-Manthūr*; 25. see 1021,$_{48}$).—30. *Kuḥl* 484
al-ʿuyūn al-nujl fī ḥall masʾalat al-kuḥl (*fi ʾl-naḥw*) Alex. Fun. 177,$_{2}$.

3. ʿImād al-Dīn Muḥammad b. Muḥammad b. Muḥammad al-Ḥanafī al-Dimashqī al-ʿImādī, who was a professor at several of the madrasas in Damascus, died on 18 Shaʿbān 986/21 January 1578.

RA 136v. *ʿAsharat abḥāth ʿan asharat ʿulūm*, 10 themes from 10 scientific disciplines, dedicated to Ḥasan Bek, the chief *qāḍī* of Syria, Berl. 88.

4. Aḥmad b. Aḥmad b. ʿAbd al-Ḥaqq al-Sunbāṭī, who died in 990/1582 (or, according to others, in 982/1574).

1. *Rawḍat al-fuhūm fī naẓm Nuqāyat al-ʿulūm* by al-Suyūṭī (p. 200,$_{268}$), with a commentary entitled *Fatḥ al-ḥayy al-qayyūm*, Leid. 14, Alex. Adab 9.—2.–4. see Suppl.—5. Ibid. 1019, 22.

| 5. Marʿī b. Yūsuf b. Abī Bakr b. Aḥmad al-Karmī Zayn al-Dīn al-Maqdisī 369
al-Ḥanbalī was born in Ṭūr al-Karm, near Nablus. He studied in Jerusalem and Cairo, became a Qurʾān reciter at al-Azhar, then a professor of Ḥanbalī *fiqh* at the mosque of Ibn Ṭūlūn, before dying in Rabīʿ I 1033/January 1624.

Muḥ. IV, 358/61, Wüst. *Gesch.* 355. 1. *Qalāʾid al-marjān fī ʾl-nāsikh wal-mansūkh min al-Qurʾān*, composed in 1022/1613 using the commentaries and the writings of Hibatallāh b. Salāma, d. 410/1019 (I, 205), Berl. 480/1, Taymūr *RAAD* IX, 638.—2. *al-Kalimāt al-bayyināt* (*al-saniyyāt*), on sura 2,$_{23}$, composed in 1028/1619, ibid. 980,$_{2}$, Kairouan, *Bull. de Corr. Afr.* 1884, 182 no. 2, Cairo ^{1}VII, 281, ^{2}I, 59.—3. *Iḥkām al-asās fī qawlihi taʿālā inna awwala baytin wuḍiʿa lil-nās* (sura 3,$_{90}$), Cairo ^{1}III, 270.—4. *Farāʾid* (*fawāʾid*) *al-fikar fī ʾl-imām al-mahdī al-muntaẓar* Paris 2026,$_{1}$, Garr. 1527, Cairo ^{1}VI, 161, ^{2}I, 337.—5. *Irshād dhawi ʾl-ʿirfān li-mā lil-ʿumr min al-ziyāda wal-nuqṣān* Berl. 2495, Patna II, 428,$_{2602,6}$.—6. *Naṣīḥa*, pieces of good advice, Berl. 5415.—7. *Dafʿ al-shubha wal-gharar ʿamman yaḥtajj ʿalā fiʿl al-maʿāṣī bil-qadar* Cairo ^{1}VI, 140, ^{2}I, 21.—8. *Jāmiʿ al-duʿāʾ wa-wird al-awliyāʾ wa-munājāt al-aṣfiyāʾ* ibid. ^{1}II, 190.—9. *Risāla fī-mā waqaʿa fī kalām al-Ṣūfiyyīn min al-alfāẓ al-mūhima lil-takfīr etc.* ibid. VII, 546.—10. *Taḥqīq al-burhān fī ithbāt ḥaqīqat al-mīzān* Paris 2026,$_{2}$, Patna II, 428,$_{2602,7}$.—11. *Sulwān al-muṣāb*
485 *bi-firqat al-aḥhāb* ibid.$_{3}$, Garr. 2041,$_{6}$.— | 12. *Ghidāʾ al-arwāḥ bil-muḥādatha wal-muzāḥ* ibid.$_{4}$.—13. *Taḥqīq al-ẓunūn bi-akhbār al-ṭāʿūn*, 20 issues related to the plague, composed in 1028/1619, Berl. 6313, Paris 2026,$_{2}$.—14. *Taḥqīq al-burhān fī shaʾn al-dukhān*, a defence of tobacco-smoking, Gotha 2102,$_{4}$, Qawala I, 424.—15. *Badīʿ al-inshāʾ(āt) wal-ṣifāt fī ʾl-mukātabāt wal-murāsalāt*, on stylistics, Gotha 2828/9, Vienna 243, Leid. 357/8, Paris 4445, Br. Mus. 517,$_{2}$ 1056,$_{2}$, Suppl. 1022/3, Pet. Ros. 162, Cairo ^{1}IV, 211, print. Būlāq 1242, Istanbul 1291, 1299, C. 1305, 1309, 1319, *Mulakhkhaṣ*, print. Mosul, Dominican Press 1866.—16. *al-Ḥikam al-malakiyya wal-kalim al-Azhariyya* Paris 2026,$_{5}$.—17. *Bahjat al-nāẓirīn wa-āyat al-mustadillīn*, on the higher and the lower world, the creation of man and the animals, Paradise, Hell, etc., completed in 1022/1613, Gotha 746, Vienna 1666, Garr. 772, Alex. Mawāʿiẓ 8, cf. Hammer, *Wiener Jahrb.* 83.—18. *Nuzhat al-nāẓirīn fī taʾrīkh man waliya Miṣr min al-khulafāʾ wal-salāṭīn* Berl. 9829/30, Gotha 1642, Munich 395, 899, f. 107, Vienna 920/2, Copenhagen 151/2, Br. Mus. 1233, Bodl. II, 151,$_{3}$, Paris 1826/31, 5920, Pet. Ros. 55, Garr. 607, Alex. Taʾr. 42, cf. Reiske in *Büschings Magazin* V, 371, Venture in Volney, *Voyage* ^{3}I, 244, idem, *Revue d'Egypte* I, 321/48, 385/99, III, 99/112, 143/83.—19. *Qalāʾid al-ʿiqyān fī faḍāʾil mulūk āl ʿUthmān*, completed on 1 Muḥarram 1031/16 November 1621, Vienna 979, Paris 1624, Turkish translation with many additions by Shaʿbān Shifāʾī, Vienna 980, NO 3404, ʿUmūmi 5073.—20. *al-Kawākib al-durriyya fī manāqib al-mujtahid b. Taymiyya* (p. 125), Berl. 10128, Landb. 243 (autograph).—21. *al-Shahāda al-zakiyya fī thanāʾ al-aʾimma ʿalā b. Taymiyya* Landb. 249.—22.–32. see Suppl. (22. Garr. 1847, Patna II, 428,$_{2602,1}$; 24. Patna II, 428,$_{2602,3}$; 28. Garr. 1848, Alex. Taʾr. 3).—33. *Tawfīq al-farīqayn ʿalā khulūd ahl al-dārayn* Patna II, 428,$_{2602,2}$.—34. *Irshād dhawi ʾl-ʿirfān li-nuzūl ʿIsā ʿalayhi ʾl-salām* ibid.$_{8}$.—35. *Taḥqīq al-khilāf fī*

aṣḥāb al-aʿrāf ibid.$_{4}$.—36. *al-Rawḍ al-naḍir fī ʾl-kalām ʿalā Khaḍir* ibid.$_{5}$.—36. *Taḥqīq al-rajaḥān bi-ṣawm yawm al-shakk min Ramaḍān* Taymur, *RAAD* IX, 638,$_{6}$.—37. *Munyat al-muḥibbīn wa-bughyat al-ʿāshiqīn* Alex. Adab 170.

| 6. Muḥammad b. Aḥmad b. Muḥammad al-Ḥattātī al-Miṣrī al-Naqshbandī 370
al-Khalwatī studied in Cairo and Istanbul, then became a *qāḍī* in Asyut and Giza, and was a distinguished poet. He died in 1051/1641.

| Muḥ. III, 366/75 (with sample poems). 1. *al-Dalīl al-hādī wal-ʿaql al-muʿādī,* 486
composed on 5 Rabīʿ II 1035/4 January 1626 (see Suppl.), Cairo ^{1}VII, 390, ^{2}III, 104.—2. *Risāla fī munāqasha maʿa ʾl-Saʿdī wal-qāḍī al-Bayḍāwī fī qawlihi taʿālā wa lladhīna hum li-furūjihim ḥāfiẓūn* (sura 23,$_{5}$, 70,$_{29}$), completed on 10 Rajab 1045/21 December 1635, ibid. ^{1}VII, 390, ^{2}I, 53.—3. *Risāla fī ʾl-munāqasha fī ʾl-istidlāl ʿalā wujūd al-kullī al-ṭabīʿī bi-annahu juzʾ min al-shakhṣ al-mawjūd fī ʾl-khārij,* completed on 8 Jumādā I 1048/18 September 1638, ibid. ^{1}VII, 390, ^{2}I, 186.—4. *Risāla fī mushkilāt al-manṭiq* ibid. ^{1}VII, 390.—5. *Risāla fī mushkilāt al-qisma wal-farāʾiḍ* ibid.—6. *Risāla tashtamil ʿalā munāqashāt fī ʿibārāt waqaʿat fī ʾl-Mawāqif* (by Ījī, p. 269), ibid. ^{1}VII, 391, ^{1}I, 181.—7. *Risāla tashtamil ʿalā jumlat aḥādīth mashrūḥa* ibid. ^{1}VII, 391.

7. Shihāb al-Dīn Aḥmad b. ʿAbd al-Razzāq al-Maghribī al-Rashīdī was born in Rosetta, studied at al-Azhar in Cairo, became a Shāfiʿī shaykh in his hometown, and died there in 1096/1685.

Muḥ. I, 232. 1. *Tījān al-ʿunwān,* 236 *rajaz* verses on Sufism, dogmatics, syntax, principles of law, and legal doctrines, Berl. 91.—2., 3. See Suppl.

8. Muḥammad Sāčaqlīzāde (Ṣačaqlīzāde) al-Marʿashī, who died in 1150/1737, see Suppl.

1. *Tartīb al-ʿulūm,* an encyclopaedia, Berl. 93, Vienna 23, Cairo VI, ^{1}124, ^{2}182, Qawala II, 250; his contemporary Aḥmad al-ʿAlamī wrote *al-Ifhām fī ʾl-ilhām* based on a passage in it, in which al-Marʿashī seemed to espouse questionable views on *al-ʿIlm al-ladunī,* Berl. 94.—2. *Rashīḥat al-naṣīḥ min al-ḥadīth al-ṣaḥīḥ,* completed in 1097/1686, Berl. 1867.—3. *al-Risāla al-ʿādiliyya,* on whether one goes against the true faith if one says that the sultan in power is righteous, composed in 1133/1721, ibid. 2155.—4. *Naṣāʾiḥ* ibid. 4031.—5. *Risāla fī fann al-munāẓara,* on the art of disputation, for his son, for which reason it is also called *al-Risāla al-waladiyya,* Berl. 5329/30, Krafft 401, Pet. 239,$_{4,7}$,

Ros. 197,$_{4}$, Algiers 1407/8, Alex. Adab 59, Fun. 65, Cairo ^{1}II, 277, VII, 264, 415, Qawala II, 250, 304/5.—Commentaries: a. Ḥusayn b. ʿAlī al-Āmidī, ca. 1150/1737, Berl. 5331.—b. ʿAbd al-Wahhāb b. Ḥusayn Walī al-Dīn al-Āmidī, ibid. 5332, Krafft 151, Pet. 239,$_{4}$, Garr. 919, Cairo ^{1}II, 271, Qawala II, 309/10.—c. Ḥusayn b. Ḥaydar al-Marʿashī, Algiers 1407,$_{4}$, Cairo ^{1}II, 270, Qawala 295.—d. Mollā ʿUmarzāde,
487 Cairo ^{1}II, 271.—e., f. see Suppl.—| g. Ḥasan b. Muṣṭafā al-Islāmbulī Nāzikzāde, Qawala I, 310.—h. *Ḥāshiya* by Ḥasan b. Muḥammad al-ʿAṭṭār, d. 1250/1834, Alex. Ādāb al-baḥth 4.—6. *Taqrīr al-qawānīn al-mutadāwala min ʿilm al-munāẓara*, composed in 1117/1705, Berl. 5333, NO 4480/1, AS 4423, Garr. 918, Cairo ^{1}II, 270, VII, 89, Qawala II, 294, Alex. Ādāb al-baḥth 310, Fun. 100, 106.—Glosses by the author himself *Taḥrīr al-Taqrīr* Alex. Ādāb al-baḥth 10.—Abstract by Dāʾūd b. Muḥammad al-Qāriṣī (see below p. 440), with a commentary, composed in 1152/1739, Cairo ^{1}II, 271.—7. *Zubdat al-munāẓara* Cairo ^{1}VII, 265.—8. *Risāla fī dhamm* (*ḥukm shurb*) *al-dukhān* Berl. 5333, Alex. Fun. 158,$_{12}$, Cairo ^{1}VII, 98.—9. *Tahdhīb al-qirāʾa* Rāġib 7.—10. A treatise of the nature of God, Munich 886, f. 231v.—11. *Risāla fi ʾl-īmān* Cairo ^{1}VII, 401.—12. *Tashīl al-farāʾiḍ*, with a commentary, ibid. 143, 401.—13. *Risāla fī tafṣīl masāʾil dhawi ʾl-arḥām* ibid. 143.—14. *Nashr Ṭawāliʿ al-anwār* I, 533.—15.–21., see Suppl. (15. Garr. 1237, Köpr. II, 4, Fātiḥ Waqf Ibr. 29,$_{5}$, print. Konya 1286, on which a *fihrist* by the author, Fātiḥ Waqf Ibr. 29,$_{4}$, commentary ibid. 28 f. 181v/245r; 16. Alex. Fun. 67,$_{6}$; 17. See Suppl. 429, 6,$_{3}$, Sarajevo 136,$_{3}$).—22. *Risāla fi ʾl-dhikr qabl al-dars wa-baʿdahu* Alex. Fun. 165,$_{12}$.—23. *Risāla fī ḥukm al-taghannī* (*al-ghināʾ wal-mūsīqī*) Alex. Fiqh Ḥan. 27, Fun. 64,$_{2}$, 101,$_{7}$.—24. *al-Farāʾid al-fāḍiliyya fī ʿilm al-munāẓara lil-Risāla al-Ḥusayniyya* (p. 468), Alex. Fun. 97,$_{1}$.—25. *Risālat al-tanzīhāt* Alex. Tawḥīd 17.—26. *Risāla fi ʾl-ḍād* Fātiḥ Waqf Ibr. 32.

371 | 9. Aḥmad b. ʿAbd al-Munʿim b. Khayyām b. Yūsuf al-Damanhūrī al-Madhāhibī al-Azhari, who was born in 1101/1689, studied all four *madhhab*s at al-Azhar in Cairo, made the pilgrimage in 1177/1763, became a professor at al-Azhar after the death of al-Ḥifnī, and died on 10 Rajab 1192/4 August 1778.

Autobiography, *al-Laṭāʾif al-nūriyya etc.* (see Suppl.), Garr. 2201. Mur. I, 117, Jab. II, 25/7, on which is based *Khiṭ. jad.* XI, 34. 1. *al-Fayḍ al-ʿamīm fī maʿna ʾl-Qurʾān al-ʿaẓīm* Rāġib 208, Garr. 1311, Cairo ^{2}I, 57.—2. *Tanwīr al-muqlatayn bi-ḍiyāʾ al-awjuh bayna ʾl-sūratayn* Cairo ^{1}VII, 231, ^{2}I, 78.—3. *Nihāyat al-taʿrīf bi-aqsām al-ḥadīth al-ḍaʿīf* Cairo I, ^{1}250, ^{2}8, VII, 345.—4. *Kashf al-lithām ʿan mukhaddarāt al-afhām* Cairo VI, ^{1}181, ^{2}170.—5. *Manʿ al-athīm al-ḥāʾir ʿani ʾl-tamādī fī fiʿl al-kabāʾir* ibid. VII, 230, Alex. Fun. 55.—6. *al-Anwār al-sāṭiʿāt ʿalā*
488 *ashraf al-murabbaʿāt* Cairo ^{1}V, 229.—| 7. *Durrat al-tawḥīd* in 22 *rajaz* verses,

with a commentary entitled *al-Qawl al-mufīd*, composed in 1143/1730, Berl. 5147, Alex. Tawḥīd 28, Cairo ^{1}VII, 39, 298.—8. *Sabīl al-rashād ilā nafʿ al-ʿibād*, an *adab* work, print. Alexandria 1288, C. 1288, 1305.—9. *Irshād al-māhir ilā kanz al-jawāhir*, occult science, Cairo ^{1}V, 331, 360, 368.—10. *ʿIqd al-farāʾid fī-mā lil-thalāth min al-fawāʾid* ibid. 354, Garr. 945.—11. *al-Durra al-yatīma fī ʾl-ṣunʿa al-karīma* Cairo ^{1}V, 380.—12. *al-Nafʿ al-jazīr fī ṣalāḥ al-sulṭān wal-wazīr* ibid. 209.—13. *Ṭarīq al-ihtidāʾ bi-aḥkām al-imāma wal-iqtidāʾ* ibid. VII, 39.—14. *ʿAyn al-ḥayāh fī ʿilm istinbāṭ al-miyāh*, composed in 1153/1740, ibid. Alex. Fun. 93,$_{2}$.—15. *Risāla fī ʾl-mīqāt* Cairo ^{1}VII, 206.—16. *Iqāmat al-ḥujja al-bāhira ʿalā hadm kanāʾis Miṣr wal-Qāhira* ibid. 231, 355.—17. *Ghunyat al-faqīr li-mā lil-Ṭayyiba* (by Ibn al-Jazarī, p. 258) *min al-takbīr* ibid. 345, ^{2}I, 124.—18. *Sharḥ al-Riyāḍ al-khalīfiyya* p. 434.—19. *Sharḥ al-Sullam* Suppl. II, 705.—20. *Sharḥ al-Jawhar al-maknūn* Suppl. II, 706.—21.–29. see Suppl. (25. Alex. Ṭibb 36).—30. *al-Ḥadhāqa fī anwāʿ al-ʿalāqa*, a short work on rhetoric, Garr. 571.—31. *Risāla fī ḥall al-rumūz al-jafriyya* Alex. Ḥurūf 9.

Chapter 2. Al-Jazīra, Iraq, and Bahrain

Even the Ottoman conquest of the year 1048/1638 was not able to resuscitate the lifeless culture of the lands of the Euphrates and the Tigris. The officials of the sultan had to be content with defending, as well as they could, the remains of its material culture against outside pressure from Arab and Kurdish nomads. As such, Arabic literature led a miserable existence in the former centres of
372 intellectual life, Mosul and Baghdad, | dependent as it was on models cherished in Syria and Egypt. The Wahhābī movement of Central Arabia penetrated deep into the south of Iraq, giving rise to theological polemics that sidetracked many for a time.

1 *Poetry*

1. Abu 'l-Ṣafā' b. Abi 'l-Wafā' al-Ḥusaynī al-ʿIrāqī, who wrote his poetry sometime before 1000/1592.

489 | *Dīwān* Garr. 146, manuscript dated 1003, Mosul 228,$_5$.

1b. Abū Aḥmad Nāṣir al-Dīn b. Sikandar b. Suwaydān al-Ḥāṣūrī Arghūn, who flourished around 1015/1606.

Al-Durra al-naqiyya li-ahl al-ʿilm wal-taqiyya, a collection of poems, partly on ʿAlī and his family and partly for the author's friends and acquaintances, Berl. 7957.

1c. Jaʿfar b. Muḥammad al-Ḥaṭṭī al-ʿAbdī, who died in 1028/1619.

Dīwān see *RAAD* VIII, 38/44, 84/90, 100/6.

2. Muḥammad b. ʿAbd al-Ḥamīd al-Baghdādī Ḥakīmzāde, who flourished around 1043/1633.

A collection of poems, several of which were written by himself, Br. Mus. 642.

3. Shihāb al-Dīn al-Mūsawī al-Ḥuwayzī lived in poverty in Basra until he gained the favour of Sayyid ʿAlī Khān al-Mūsawī. He died on 14 Shawwāl 1087/20 December 1676.

Hartmann, *Muw.* 86. *Dīwān*, compiled by his son Maʿtūq, and thus usually called *Dīwān Maʿtūq*, Berl. 8001/2, Leid. 765, Garr. 122, Cairo [1]IV, 248, [2]III, 135, lith. Alexandria 1290, C. 1278, 1280, print. ibid. 1302, 1320, Beirut 1885.

5. ʿUthmān b. ʿAlī b. Murād al-ʿUmarī al-Mawṣilī al-Ḥanafī was born in Mosul in 1134/1721. After a trip to Ṣawrān, in Yemen, he entered the service of Ḥusayn Pāshā and Muḥammad Amīn Pāshā before being given a position in the audit office in Baghdad. But when ʿAlī Pāshā became vizier four years later, he had him incarcerated and sent back to Mosul. In 1176/1762 he went to Istanbul, but when he heard of the death of ʿAlī Pāshā he wanted to return to Baghdad, | 373
but was delayed in Mārdīn, and so went instead to Mosul, and from there to al-Ḥilla. Following the death of Sulaymān Pāshā he represented the latter for a short time in the *wilāyat* of Baghdad, but was removed from office because of his wastefulness. He then went | to Istanbul again, before dying in Aleppo on 490
his way back in 1184/1770.

Mur. III, 164/6, *Khiṭ. jad.* X, 26. 1. *al-Rawḍ al-naḍr fī tarjamat udabāʾ al-ʿaṣr*, an anthology of contemporary poets, some of whom were relatives of the author, completed in 1170/1756, Berl. 7430, Br. Mus. 1110.—2. *Rāḥat al-rūḥ wa-salwat al-qalb al-kaʾīb al-majrūḥ*, a recreational work, Berl. 8436.—3. See Suppl.

6. Muḥammad Amīn b. Ibrāhīm b. Yūnus b. Yāsīn al-Ḥusaynī al-Mawṣilī wrote, in 1202/1789:

Awrāq al-dhahab fī ʿilm al-muḥāḍarāt wal-adab Berl. 8437; in an enlarged edition ibid. 8438.

2 *Philology*

1. Ḥusayn b. Kamāl al-Dīn al-Abzar al-Ḥusaynī al-Ḥillī, ca. 1050/1640.

1. *Durar al-kalām wa-yawāqīt al-niẓām*, a short, practical work on rhetoric, Berl. 7265.—2. See Suppl.

2. Fakhr al-Dīn Muḥammad Ṭarīḥ b. ʿAlī al-Najafī, who died in 1085/1674.

1. *Majmaʿ al-baḥrayn etc.* (see Suppl.), additionally Teh. Sip. II, 262/8.—2. See Suppl.

3 *Historiography*

1. Jamāl al-Dīn Abū ʿAlī Fatḥallāh b. ʿAlawān b. Bishāra al-Kaʿbī al-Qabbānī was born in Qabbān in 1053/1643. He studied, from 1079/1668 onward, in Shiraz, was briefly a *qāḍī* in Basra, and then returned to Qabbān following his father's death in 1080/1669. He wrote, in 1078/1667:

Zād al-musāfir wa-luhnat al-muqīm wal-ḥāḍir fī-mā jarā li-Ḥusayn Bāshā ibn Afrāsiyāb ḥākim al-Baṣra, a *maqāma* on the events that took place during the military confrontation between the ruler of Basra, Ḥusayn Pāshā b. ʿAlī Pāshā Āfrāsiyāb (Suppl. II, 506), and the Ottoman army under Ibrāhīm Pāshā, with a commentary, Br. Mus. 1405/6; ed. Khalaf Shawqī Amīn al-Dāʾūdī, Baghdad 1342/1924.

491 | 2. Aḥmad b. ʿAbdallāh al-Baghdādī died of the plague in 1102/1690 in Baghdad.

ʿUyūn akhbār al-ayʿān bi-mā maḍā min sālif al-ʿaṣr wal-azmān, a universal history up to the year 1098/1687, Berl. 9477, Paris 6677; up to 1102, Br. Mus. 1257/8.

3. Maḥmūd b. ʿUthmān al-Raḥbī, who was a *muftī* in al-Ḥilla around 1150/1737.

374 | *Bahjat al-ikhwān fī dhikr al-wazīr Sulaymān*, containing an introduction, a description of the globe, and the history of the kings of Persia, various empires, the prophets, the vizier Sulaymān, and the prefects of Basra under ʿAlī Pāshā in Baghdad 1136–60/1723–47, Br. Mus. 285.

4. Yaḥyā b. ʿAbd al-Jalīl b. al-Ḥājj Yūnus al-Jalīlī al-Mawṣilī, who died in 1198/1783.

Sirāj al-mulūk wa-minhāj al-sulūk, a universal history until 460/1068, Br. Mus 1259.

5. Abu ʾl-Khayr ʿAbd al-Raḥmān b. ʿAbdallāh (§ 8) b. al-Ḥusayn al-Suwaydī was born in Baghdad in 1134/1721 and died there in 1200/1786.

Mur. II, 330. 1. *Ḥadīqat al-zawrāʾ fī sīrat al-wuzarāʾ*, the history of Ḥusayn Pāshā, 1117–38/1705–22, and of his son Aḥmad Pāshā, 1135–59/1722–46, and their rule in Baghdad, Br. Mus. 949.—2. Some issues in respect of the doings and tricks of juggling dervishes (snake- and fire-eaters, sword-swallowers, contortionists, etc.) from Yemen who appear everywhere and cause problems for the true faith, Berl. 2160.—3. A *maqāma* entitled *Jāmiʿat al-amthāl ʿazīzat al-amthāl*, on popular proverbs and rare expressions, ibid. 8582/3.—4. See Suppl.

6. Muḥammad Amīn b. Khayrallāh al-Khaṭīb al-ʿUmarī hailed from an old family in Mosul. In 1181/1767 he became a preacher at a mosque constructed by his grandfather in that city. He died in 1203/1789.

1. *Manhal al-awliyāʾ wa-mashrab al-aṣfiyāʾ fī sādāt al-Mawṣil al-Ḥadbāʾ*, a history of Mosul, including biographies of its scholars and of the saints buried in its vicinity, composed in 1201/1787, Berl. 9801, Sachau 181 (Syr. Cat. II, 905), Br. Mus. Suppl. 679, Alex. Taʾr. 136, Wehbi Ef. 1146.—2. *Qalāʾid al-nuḥūr wa-bahjat al-nāqid wal-baṣīr, urjūza* on the various sciences, Br. Mus. 639.—3. *Maṭāliʿ al-ʿulūm* | *wa-mawāqiʿ al-nujūm*, an encyclopaedia, Br. Mus. Suppl. 720.—4.–19. 492
see Suppl.—On his younger brother Yāsīn see below, p. 497.

4 *Fiqh*

A The Ḥanafīs

1. ʿAbdallāh al-Suwaydī, ca. 950/1543 (?)

Ṭabaqāt al-sāda al-Ḥanafiyya Berl. 10026.

2. Ghiyāth al-Dīn Abū Muḥammad Ghānim b. Muḥammad al-Baghdādī al-Ḥanafī, ca. 1030/1620.

| 1. *Maljaʾ al-quḍāt ʿinda taʿāruḍ al-bayyināt*, a manual for judges to use in con- 375
troversial cases, Berl. 4838/9, Munich 325, Garr. 1762, Alex. Fiqh Ḥan. 47, 58, 67, Cairo ^{1}III, 111, VII, 551.—2. *Majmaʿ al-ḍamānāt fī ʾl-furūʿ*, composed in 1027/1618, Yeni 545/6, Cairo ^{1}III, 110.—3. See Suppl.

B The Shāfiʿīs

Al-Sayyid Abū Bakr b. Hidāyatallāh al-Ḥusaynī al-Kūrānī al-Kurdī al-Muṣannif, a teacher of Ibrāhīm b. al-Ḥasan al-Kurdī (see below, p. 385), boasted of his encounter, as a mystic, with the prophet Khiḍr. He died in 1014/1605.

Muḥ. I, 110, Sāmī, *Qāmūs al-aʿlām* 691. 1. *Ṭabaqāt al-Shāfiʿiyya* Baghdād 1356.—2. *Sharḥ al-Muḥarrar* I, 493, 25, f (which has al-Shahrazūrī).—The Persian *Sirāj al-ṭarīq* in 50 *bāb* and *Riyāḍ al-khulūd* in 8 *bāb* are mentioned by Muḥibbī.

C The Shīʿa

1. Walī Allāh b. Niʿmatallāh al-Ḥusaynī al-Riḍawī al-Ḥāʾirī wrote, in 981/1573 in Karbala:

1. *Kanz al-maṭālib wa-baḥr al-manāqib fī faḍāʾil ʿAlī b. Abī Ṭālib* Br. Mus. 1308.—2. See Suppl.

2. ʿAbdallāh b. Ṣāliḥ b. Jumʿa al-Baḥrānī, who died in 1135/1723, see Suppl.

1. *al-Fākiha al-Kāẓimiyya lil-firqa al-Imāmiyya*, against deviations from the true Shīʿī faith, named after the shrine of al-Kāẓimayn near Baghdad, Berl.
493 2154. | 2. *al-Wasīla ilā taḥṣīl al-amānī fī ḍabṭ ayyām al-taʿāzī wal-tahānī*, on the days on which Muḥammad, his close relatives, and the imams were born and died, so that his patron Raḍī al-Dīn b. Salāmallāh could celebrate them with a clear conscience as religious holidays, ibid. 2598.—3. a. On the word *nahy*, b. something on Galen, c. a commentary on sura 4,$_{81}$, ibid. 2797.—4. *al-Risāla al-saniyya fī jawābāt al-masāʾil al-Dashtastāniyya*, 35 issues related to prayer, composed in 1132/1720, ibid. 3614.—5. *al-Lumʿa al-Ḥilliyya fī taḥqīq al-masāʾil al-Ismāʿīliyya*, 109 practical, theological questions, ibid. 3615.—6. *al-Masāʾil al-Kāzarūniyya fī baʿḍ al-masāʾil al-dīniyya*, composed in 1133/1721, ibid. 3616.—7. 12 matters concerning religion, ibid. 3617.—8. *al-Masāʾil al-Nāṣiriyya fī baʿḍ al-masāʾil al-ḍarūriyya* ibid. 3618.—9. 32 questions, ibid. 3619.—10. *al-Masāʾil al-Bahbahāniyya fī baʿḍ al-aḥkām al-bayāniyya*, on the washing, dressing, and burial of the dead, composed in 1128/1716, ibid. 4085.—11. *Ḥall al-ʿuqūd ʿan ʿiṣmat al-mafqūd*, composed in 1133/1721 in Kāzarūn, on women, on the inheritance and property of people who have gone missing without a trace, and where there is no one with a legal right to inherit the estate, ibid. 5731.—12. *al-Risāla al-Fahlyāniyya*, 9 general legal questions, ibid. 5004.—13. On whether *ḥadīth* can show that the enveloping of the dead in three pieces of clothing—*qamīṣ*, *miʾzār*, and *izār*—as had been customary until then, was justified, ibid 5452.—14. A *qaṣīda* in praise of the 12 imams, ibid. 8021,$_{1}$.—15., 16. See Suppl.—17. *Aḥkām al-nawāṣib*, in the library of Mahdī Āl al-Sayyid Ḥaydar al-Kāẓimī, *Dharīʿa* I, 302,$_{1580}$.—18. *Fiqh al-athariyyīn* Āṣaf. II, 1182,$_{24}$ (continued in Suppl. II, 504/5, III, 1292).

5 *Sciences of the Qurʾān*

1. Badr al-Dīn Muḥammad b. Muḥammad b. al-Karkhī, who was born in 910/1504 and died in 1006/1597.

376 | 1. *al-Manhaj al-asnā fī āyat al-kursī wal-asmāʾ al-ḥusnā* Cairo ^{1}II, 412 ^{2}I, 363.—2. *Ḥāshiya ʿalā Tafsīr al-Jalālayn* p. 182.

2. Dhu ʾl-Nūn b. Jirjīs al-Mawṣilī, fl. twelfth century.

1. *Risāla fī ʿilm al-tajwīd wal-tartīl* Berl. 534.—2.–4. see Suppl.

494 | 3. Maḥmūd b. ʿUthmān al-Mawṣilī, fl. end of the twelfth century.

Hibat al-mannān fī sharḥ Durrat al-bayān, 127 *ṭawīl* verses on *tajwīd*, with a commentary, Berl. 532.

6 *Dogmatics*

1. Ḥusayn b. ʿAbdallāh al-Shirwānī wrote, in 947/1540 in Mardin:

Al-Aḥkām al-dīniyya, against the Shīʿīs, dedicated to Sultan Süleymān the Magnificent, Leid. 2070, Paris 1458, AS 2172.

2. Muḥammad b. Ḥasan b. Muḥammad b. ʿAlī Mīmīzāde wrote, in 1122/1710:

Ifāḍat al-ʿallām fī-mā yalzam al-mukallaf min al-ʿaqāʾid wal-aḥkām, on the principles of faith, in honour of the vizier ʿAlī Pāshā, Berl. 1850.

3. Al-Sayyid Yāsīn b. Ibrāhīm al-Baṣrī wrote, in 1168/1754:

A refutation, in rhyme, of a poem—by someone from Ṣanʿāʾ—in praise of the founder of the Wahhābī sect, Muḥammad b. ʿAbd al-Wahhāb, Br. Mus. Suppl. 194.

4. ʿAlī b. ʿAbdallāh (§ 9) al-Baghdādī al-Suwaydī, ca. 1170/1756.

1. *al-Mishkāt al-muḍīʾa raddan ʿala ʾl-Wahhābiyya*, Berl. 2156.—2. *al-ʿIqd al-thamīn*, against doubt and unbelief, ibid. 2159.

5. Muḥammad b. ʿAbd al-Raḥmān b. Afāliq al-Aḥṣāʾī al-Ḥanbalī, ca. 1170/1756.

1. A response to a letter by ʿUthmān b. Maʿmar in defence of Ibn ʿAbd al-Wahhāb, Berl. 2158.—2. See Suppl.

7 *Mysticism*

1. ʿAbd al-Qādir b. Aḥmad b. ʿAlī b. al-Mīmī al-Baṣrī, who died in Basra in 1085/1674.

| Muḥ. II, 469. 1. *Risāla* on the necessity of | providing an explanation for some 377 495
obsure phrases that denote aspects of the nature of the Divine, Berl. 2346.—2. *Yatīmat al-ʿaṣr fi ʾl-madd wal-jazr* or *Wary al-zand bil-jazr wal-madd*, on low and high tides, composed in 1084/1673, ibid. 6053.—3. A Sufi *qaṣīda*, ibid. 7996,7.

2. Yūsuf al-Diyārbakrī wrote, in 1121/1709:

Hadiyyat al-ikhwān fī qirāʾat al-mīʿād fī Rajab wa-Shaʿbān wa-Ramaḍān Cairo [1]II, 181.

7a *Philosophy*

Aḥmad b. Muḥammad, the *muftī* of Baghdad, wrote, in 1199/1785:

Ajwibat al-asʾila al-Hindiyya Alex. Fals. 4.

8 *Travelogues*

ʿAbdallāh b. al-Ḥusayn b. Marʿī al-Baghdādī al-Suwaydī Jamāl al-Dīn al-Dūrī was born in 1104/1692 in al-Karkh, on the western side of Baghdad, studied in Baghdad and Mosul, lectured in his hometown at the Marjāniyya, and died in 1174/1760.

Mur. III, 84/6. 1. *al-Nafḥa al-miskiyya fī 'l-riḥla al-Makkiyya*, on a trip to Mecca in the years 1148–50/1735–7, Br. Mus. 972, 1530, cf. v. Kremer, *Denkschr. phil.-hist. Cl. WA* III (1850), 215; a part of which, being an overview of the political situation in Persia and a dialogue on religion with a Shīʿī in the presence of Nādir Shāh (see 5), Berl. 6150.—3. Two *qaṣīdas*, one with a *takhmīs*, Berl. $8043_{,1,2}$.—3. A *maqāma*, in which real proverbs, old and new, are used, ibid. 8577/8.—4. *al-Maqāma al-Jamāliyya* ibid. 8579.—5.–7. see Suppl. (5. See A.E. Schmidt, *Festschrift Barthold*, Tashkent 1927, 73/107; Ritter, *Der Islam* XV, 106, Minorsky *EI* III, 878, see Berl. 2156).—8. *Talkhīṣ al-munāẓara bayna ʿulamāʾ al-sunna wal-Shīʿa* see *RAAD* V, 179/86.

Chapter 3. North Arabia

In this period Mecca was almost equal to the other intellectual centres of the Muslim world. From the tenth/sixteenth century onward | an ever greater num- 496
ber of foreign scholars sought refuge there from troubles in their native countries; not temporarily, but on a permanent basis. | Unsurprisingly, the *fuqahāʾ* 378
were greatest in number among them. In the thirteenth century the orthodox establishment saw its exclusive supremacy threatened by the Wahhābī reformation, a radical offshoot of Ḥanbalī Sunnī extremism[1] that had originated in the Najd. The orthodox managed to stand their ground in the cities of the Hijaz, so that the Wahhābī movement did not initially progress far beyond the desert.

1 *Poetry*

1. ʿAbd al-ʿAzīz b. ʿAlī b. ʿAbd al-ʿAziz al-Zamzamī al-Shāfiʿī ʿIzz al-Dīn was the *muftī* of the Shāfiʿīs in the Hijaz. He died in 976/1568.

1. *Dīwān* a. Praise of the Prophet, b. Praise of scholars and saints, c. Praise of Mecca and the holy places, Paris 3228.—2. *Fayḍ al-jūd ʿalā ḥadīth sayyabatnī Hind* Cairo ¹VII, 147.—3.–6. see Suppl. (3. Alex. Adab 128).

2. ʿAlāʾ al-Dīn b. ʿAbd al-Bāqī al-Khaṭīb wrote, in 1005/1596 in Medina:

ʿIqd al-farāʾid fī-mā nuẓima min al-fawāʾid Berl. 8423.

3. Muḥyi ʾl-Dīn ʿAbd al-Qādir b. Muḥammad b. Yaḥyā al-Ṭabarī al-Makkī was born on 17 Ṣafar 976/12 August 1568. After the death of his father in 1018/1609 he became first imam of the Hijaz. He died in 1033/17 July 1624 in a state of resentment over the fact that Ḥaydar Pāshā had, on 1 Shawwāl, disregarded him in favour of a Ḥanafī to read the festive sermon marking the end of Ramaḍān.

Muḥ. II, 457/64, Wüst. *Ṣūfīs* 198. 1. *Badīʿiyya*, with the commentary *ʿAlī al-ḥujja bi-taʾkhīr Abī Bakr b. Ḥijja* (p. 18), Berl. 7381.—| 2., 3. *Qaṣīdas* ibid. 7961.—4.–7. 497
see Suppl.—8. *al-Araj al-miskī wal-taʾrīkh al-Makkī*, manuscript in Mecca, see Zirikli, *Mā raʾaytu wa-mā samiʿtu* C. 1932, 68.—9. *Rafʿ al-ishtibāk ʿan tanāwul al-tunbāk* Ind. Off. 1861.

1 On the basic aspects of this movement, often misunderstood in the past, see Goldziher, *ZDMG* 52, 156.

4. Ibrāhīm b. Yūsuf al-Mukhtār was a *hijā'* poet in Mecca and died soon after 1040/1630.

Muḥ. I, 53/7. 1. 25 *rajaz* verses, Berl. $8161_{,2}$.—2.–4. see Suppl.

5. Aḥmad b. Masʿūd b. Ḥasan b. Abī Numayy al-Sharīf al-Ḥasanī died in Istanbul in 1041/1631 (see Suppl.).

Wüst., *Scherife* no. 39. 1. Four *qaṣīdas*, Berl. 7966.—2. A *qaṣīda* in praise of the Prophet, with a commentary by ʿAbdallāh al-Shubrāwī, d. 1171/1757, Cairo ^{1}IV, 335, ^{2}III, 397.—3. *Dīwān* Garr. 155.

379 | 6. Aḥmad b. ʿĪsā al-Murshidī al-Makkī was acting *qāḍī* in Mecca and died on 25 Dhu 'l-Ḥijja 1047/11 April 1638.

Muḥ. I, 266/71 (sample poems). 1. A *qaṣīda*, Berl. $7970_{,2}$.—2. See Suppl.

7. After a long period of wandering Fatḥallāh b. al-Naḥḥās al-Ḥalabī al-Madanī settled in Medina and died in 1052/1642.

Muḥ. III, 257/66. 1. *Dīwān*, mostly poems in praise of prominent contemporaries, Berl. 7975/6, Gotha 2325 (incomplete), Paris $3246/7_{,2}$, 4722, Br. Mus. Suppl. 1691/2, Garr. 118, Cairo ^{1}IV, 237, ^{2}III, 13, print. C. 1290; individual poems Berl. 7977, Gotha $1_{,13-5}$, a *rajaz* Berl. $8161_{,3}$.—2. See Suppl.

8. Tāj al-Dīn b. Aḥmad b. Ibrāhīm al-Madanī b. Yaʿqūb, who was born in Mecca, was a professor and a preacher there, and died in 1066/1655.

Muḥ. I, 457/64 (sample poems), Wüst., *Scherife* 62. 1. Three *qaṣīdas*, Berl. $7986_{,2}$.—2.–4. see Suppl.

9. ʿAbd al-ʿAzīz b. Muḥammad b. ʿAbd al-ʿAzīz al-Zamzamī al-Makkī, who was born in 997/1589, and who had Ibn Ḥajar, d. 973/1565 (p. 508), as his maternal grandfather, was the head of the Shāfiʿīs in Mecca. He died in 1072/1662.

498 | Muḥ. II, 426. 1. A *qaṣīda* in 70 verses, Berl. $7992_{,1}$.—2. A poem in praise of the Prophet, with a *takhmīs* by al-Ṣafadī, d. 1100/1688, see p. 433.—3. See Suppl.

10. Aḥmad b. ʿAbdallāh b. ʿAbd al-Raʾūf al-Wāʿiẓ al-Makkī was born in Mecca, became a Sufi, and died in 1077/1666.

Muḥ. I, 226/9. A long *rajaz* on the Prophet, Berl. 8161,4.

11. Darwīsh Muṣṭafā b. Qāsim b. ʿAbd al-Karīm al-Ṭarābulusī was born in Tripoli in 987/1579, went to Damascus in 1014/1605, then to Cairo and Istanbul, before going, in 1027/1618 and 1032/1623, to Medina. After his second visit to the latter he settled permanently there, dying in 1080/1669.

Muḥ. IV, 387/9. 1. A poem in praise of the Prophet, with the commentary *Naṣr min Allāh wa-fatḥ qarīb* by al-Shalūbīn, Paris 3243.—2. See Suppl.

17. ʿAbd al-Raḥmān b. Muḥammad b. ʿAbd al-Raḥmān al-Dhahabī al-Dimashqī b. Sāshū wrote in Mecca, between 1054/1644 and 1120/1708:

1. *Nafaḥāt al-asrār al-Makkiyya wa-rashaḥāt al-afkār al-Dhahabiyya*, a portrayal of contemporary poets, in rhymed prose, Berl. 7424.—2. *Tarājim baʿḍ aʿyān Dimashq min ʿulamāʾihā wa-udabāʾihā* ed. Nakhla Qalfāṭ, Beirut 1886. Cf. Mur. II, 318/24 (sample poems, without date of death).

| 13. Al-Sayyid Jaʿfar b. al-Sayyid Muḥammad al-Baytī al-ʿAlawī al-Saqqāf al-Madanī al-Shāfiʿī was born in 1110/1698 and died in Medina in 1182/1768. 380

1. *Dīwān* Cairo [1]VII, 553, [2]123.—2. *Mawāsim al-adab wa-āthār al-ʿAjam wal-ʿArab* ibid. [1]IV, 335, [2]III, 399, print. C. 1322/6, 3 vols.—14.–16. see Suppl. (14. Garr. 138/9; 15. ibid. 131; 16. ibid. 132).—17. a., b. see Suppl. (also p. 905,1).

2 *Philology*

1. Wajīh al-Dīn b. ʿAbd al-Raḥmān Abū Kathīr al-Shāfiʿī, wrote, ca. 930/1524:

| *Tanbīh al-adīb ʿalā mā fī shiʿr Abi ʾl-Ṭayyib min al-ḥasan wal-maʿīb*, a critical review of al-Mutanabbī, dedicated to Muḥammad b. Numayy b. Barakāt, on the occasion of his succeeding his father as sharif of Mecca in 931/1524 (*Chron. der Stadt Mekka* II, 344), Pet. Ros. 84, Esc. [2]I, 702,3. 499

2. ʿAfīf al-Dīn ʿAbdallāh b. Aḥmad al-Fākihī al-Makkī al-Shāfiʿī al-Naḥwī was born in 899/1493 and died in 972/1564.

1. *Ḥudūd al-naḥw* Cairo [1]VII, 253, see Suppl.—2.–8. ibid.

3. Abu ʾl-Wajāha ʿAbd al-Raḥmān b. ʿĪsā b. Murshid al-ʿUmarī al-Murshidī, who was garrotted in prison in 1037/1628 on the order of Sharif Ibn ʿAbd al-Muṭṭalib, see Suppl.

Muḥ. II, 369/76, Wüst., *Scherife* 34. 1. *al-Tarṣīf fī ʿilm al-taṣrīf* in verse, composed in 1000/1591, Ind. Off. 979$_{,2}$, Cairo [1]IV, 2, [2]II, 52.—Commentaries: a. *Fatḥ al-khabīr al-laṭīf* by Ibrāhīm al-Bājūrī, C. 1310, 1313, 1332.—b. Anon., Br. Mus. 532.—2. *al-Qawl al-mufīd bi-bayān faḍl al-jumʿa al-yawm al-mazīd* Paris 2679$_{,2}$.—3. *Barāʿat al-istihlāl wa-mā yataʿallaq bil-shahr wal-hilāl* Cairo [1]V, 229 (Suppl. 513: Ahlw. V. 175b, a *rajaz* that may be identical with the *Barāʿat al-ist.*).—4. A *qaṣīda* in 78 verses, Berl. 7963$_{,2}$.—5.–12. see Suppl.—13. *al-Fatḥ al-Qudsī fī tafsīr āyat al-kursī* AS 418, *Türkiyat Mecm.* 7–8, II, 84.

4. ʿAbd al-Malik b. Jamāl al-Dīn Ḥusayn b. Ṣadr al-Dīn b. ʿIṣām al-Dīn al-ʿIṣāmī al-Isfarāʾīnī b. al-Mollā ʿIṣām was born in Mecca in 978/1570 and died in Medina in 1037/1627.

Muḥ. III, 87, Wüst., *Ṣūf.* 206. 1. *Tashīl al-ʿurūḍ ilā ʿilm al-ʿarūḍ*, on metrics, composed in 1017/1009, Berl. 7140, Munich 673$_{,4}$, Cairo [1]VII, 161, [2]II, 230.—2. *Risāla fī taḥrīm al-dukhān*, completed in 1035/1626, Alex. Fun. 157$_{,3}$, Cairo [1]III, 178.—3., 4. See Suppl.—5. *Sharḥ abyāt al-dimāʾ* p. 244$_{,13}$.

381 | 5. Muʿīn al-Dīn b. Aḥmad al-Balkhī b. al-Bakkāʾ went from Egypt to Mecca in 980/1572 and died in Medina in 1040/1630.

Muḥ. IV, 406. *Al-Ṭirāz al-asmā ʿalā Kanz al-asmāʾ al-alghāziyya* or *Ṭirāz al-asmā ʿalā Kanz al-muʿammā*, composed in 993/1585, p. 501$_{,5}$.

500 | 3 ***Historiography***

1. Jamāl al-Dunyā wal-Dīn Muḥammad Jārallāh b. ʿAbdallāh Amīn b. Zuhayra al-Qurashī al-Makkī al-Ḥanafī, who came from a very famous Meccan family, completed, in 960/1553:

1. *al-Jāmiʿ al-laṭīf fī faḍāʾil (faḍl) Makka wa-bināʾ al-bayt al-sharīf*, begun in 949/1542, Gotha 1707, Algiers 1609; its preface and some fragments are in Wüstenfeld's *Chron. d. St. Mekka* II, 325ff. cf. p. XXII, no. 14.—2. *Fatāwā* Munich 884$_{,2}$.—3. *Naẓm al-qawāʿid*, with the commentary *al-Bayān al-musāʿid* by Muḥammad b. ʿAlī b. ʿAllān, d. 1057/1647, Qawala II, 64.—Wüst. *Gesch.* 525.

2. Ḥusayn b. Muḥammad b. al-Ḥasan al-Diyārbakrī was a Ḥanbalī (or, according to some, a Mālikī) *qāḍī* in Mecca. He died in 990/1582.[2]

1. *Taʾrīkh al-khamīs fī aḥwāl anfas al-nafīs*, a detailed biography of the Prophet based on Ibn Hishām, with an overview of the history of the caliphs until the accession to power of Sultan Murād III in 982/1574, Berl. 9407/8, Gotha 1798/1800, Vienna 1177/8, Copenhagen 130/2, Pet. Ros. 48/9, Leid. 873/5, Paris 1980/3, 5377, 5435, 5505, Br. Mus. 922/3, 1279, Suppl. 517/8, Nicholson *JRAS* 1899, 907/9, Algiers 1585/6, Köpr. 1035/6, II, 210, Yeni 847, Damad Ibr. P. 897/8, Cairo V, [1]50, [2]173, print. C. 1283, 1302.—2. *Risāla fī misāḥat al-Kaʿba wal-Masjid al-ḥarām*, completed in 943/1536, Berl. 6069, Alex. Fiqh Ḥan. 52. Cairo [1]II, 116.

3. Muḥammad b. ʿAlāʾ al-Dīn ʿAlī b. Shams al-Dīn Muḥammad b. Qāḍī Khān Maḥmūd Quṭb al-Dīn al-Nahrawālī al-Makkī al-Ḥanafī, whose father had come to Mecca from Nahrawālī in Gujarāt, was born in 917/1511. Upon completion of his studies he went to Cairo and Istanbul in 943/1536. On his return to Mecca, he became a professor at the Ashrafiyya. After a second trip to Istanbul in 965/1557 he received a | professorship at the Kanbayātiyya in Mecca, | and in 501 382
Jumādā I 975/November 1567 a professorship of all four orthodox *madhhab*s at the newly-founded Madrasa Sulaymāniyya. He was the *muftī* of Mecca when he died in 990/1582 (or 991).

RA 262r, Wüst. *Gesch.* 534. 1. *al-Iʿlām bi-aʿlām balad* (*bayt*) *Allāh* (*masjid*) *al-ḥarām*, composed in 985/1577 and dedicated to Sultan Murād (982–1003/1574–94), Berl. 6065/6, Gotha 1708/9, Leid. 926/30, Paris 1637/42, 4924, 5932, 5999, Br. Mus. 326/7, Cambr. 42/4, Pet. AM 181, Algiers 1610, Tunis, Zaytūna, *Bull. de Corr. Afr.* 1884, p. 17, no. 46, Fatih 4187, Köpr. II, 205, Yeni 817/8, Ẓāh. ʿIsh, Taʾr. 106, ed. F. Wüstenfeld, *Chron.* I, Leipzig 1857, print. C. 1303, Turkish transl. (see Suppl.) ed. Gottwaldt, Kazan 1286.—2. *al-Barq al-Yamānī fi ʾl-fatḥ al-ʿUthmānī*, a history of Yemen since 900/1494, the time of the first Turkish conquest under vizier Sulaymān Pāshā, the return of the Zaydīs and the second conquest by Great Vizier Sinān Pāshā, with an appendix on his capture of Tunis and Goleta, the work being dedicated to the latter and completed on 1 Ramaḍān 981/3 May 1573, Berl. 9742, Gotha 1616, Vienna 977 (with the title *al-Futūḥāt al-ʿUthmāniyya lil-aqṭār al-Yamaniyya*), Copenhagen 140, Pet. AM 182, Paris 1644/7, 1650, Br. Mus. 1646, Suppl. 588, Bodl. I, 839, Esc. [2]1720/1, Tunis, *Bull. de Corr. Afr.* 1884, p. 27, no. 92, Köpr. 1013/4, NO 3058, Bursa, Hü. Čelebī,

2 ḤKh, reproduced in Wüst. *Gesch.* 566, places his death in 966, but the end of the work, which continues until the year 982, does not seem to be a later addition.

Tarih 50, Alex. Ta'r. 20; cf. de Sacy, *Not. et Extr.* IV (1787), 412/521, *Extractos da historia da conquista da Jaman pelos Othmanos, texto ar. c. trad. e notas p.* D. Lopes, Lisbon 1892.—3. *Muntakhab al-tar'īkh*, a personal history, Leid. 1045 (p. 8).—4. *Timthāl al-amthāl al-sā'ira fī 'l-abyāt al-farīda al-nādira*, verses from various periods, compiled for their use in letters, Leid. 356 = *al-Tamthīl wal-muḥāḍara bil-abyāt al-mufrada al-nādira* Cairo [1]IV, 220, [2]III, 68.—5. *Kanz al-asmā' fī fann al-mu'ammā*, on riddles, Berl. 7346, Esc. [2]556,$_1$, the commentary *al-Ṭirāz al-asmā* by Ibn al-Bakkā' (p. 499), completed in 993/1585, Upps. 63, Paris 3417,$_5$, Esc. [2]536,$_2$.

4. Muḥammad b. 'Abdallāh al-Ḥusaynī al-Samarqandī wrote, in 994/1585:

Tuḥfat al-ṭālib li-ma'rifat man yunsab ilā 'Alī wa-Abī Ṭālib, a genealogy of the Prophet and his relatives, with an appendix on the genealogy of the sharif of
502 Mecca and Medina at the time of the author, | al-Ḥasan b. Numayy, until Qatāda b. Idrīs, ca. 600/1203, a brief listing of the caliphs, the Egyptian Mamlūks, and the Ottoman sultans until Süleymān I, d. 974/1566, Br. Mus. 956, Br. Mus. 956.—2. A *qaṣīda* mourning 'Abd al-Qādir b. 'Alī al-Ṭabarī al-Shāfi'ī al-Makkī, composed in 966/1559, Berl. 7938,$_2$.

383 | 8. Abū 'Alawī Muḥammad b. Abī Bakr b. Aḥmad Jamāl al-Dīn al-Shillī al-Ḥaḍramī hailed from an 'Alid family and was born in Tarīm in the middle of Sha'bān 1030/beginning of July 1621. He studied theology, the profane sciences, and mysticism in his hometown and in Ẓafār, India, and Mecca and Medina. In 1072/1661 he succeeded Shaykh 'Alī b. Abī Bakr b. al-Jamāl and started to give lectures at the Grand Mosque of Mecca. Due to ill-health he had to give up teaching four years later, limiting himself to his activities as a writer. He died in Mecca, on the last day of the year 1093/30 December 1682.

Muḥ. III, 336, Wüst. *Gesch.* 584, Ṣūf. 114. 1. *al-Sanā' al-bāhir bi-takmīl al-nūr al-sāfir fī akhbār al-qarn al-'āshir*, a complement to the work by 'Abd al-Qādir 'Aydārus (see below, p. 419), Br. Mus. 937,$_2$.—2. *'Iqd al-jawāhir wal-durar fī akhbār al-qarn al-ḥādī 'ashar* ibid. 938,$_2$.

9. Al-Sinjārī, who hailed from an old Meccan family close to the sharifs wrote, in 1095/1684:

Manā'iḥ al-karam bi-akhbār Makka wal-Ḥaram, which uses, for ancient times, many hitherto unpublished sources and is extremely well-detailed on the author's own century, | see Snouck Hurgronje, *Mekka*, I, XV, idem, *Bijdr. v. het Kon. Nederlands-Indisch Instituut*, 5.2, Volgreeks II, 344ff. 384

10. ʿAbd al-Malik b. al-Ḥusayn b. ʿAbd al-Malik al-ʿIṣāmī was born in Mecca in 1049/1639, became a professor at the Masjid al-Ḥarām there, and died in 1111/1699.

Mur. III, 139. 1. *Simṭ al-nujūm al-ʿawālī fī anbāʾ al-awāʾil wal-tawālī*, running to the year 1103/1691, Berl. 9478, Br. Mus. Suppl. 492/3, Cairo V, [1]69, [2]220.—2.–5. see Suppl.

| 12. Zayn al-ʿĀbidīn Muḥammad b. ʿAbdallāh al-Khalīfatī al-ʿAbbāsī al-Khaṭīb al-Madanī al-Ḥanafi wrote, in 1171/1757: 503

Natījat al-fikar fī akhbār madīnat sayyid al-bashar Cairo [1]III, 107, [2]V, 383.

13. Jaʿfar b. Ḥasan b. ʿAbd al-Karīm b. Muḥammad Khādim b. Zayn al-ʿĀbidīn al-Barzanjī al-Madanī died in 1179/1765 (see Suppl.).

1. *Mawlid al-nabī* or *ʿIqd al-jawāhir* (*al-ʿIqd al-jawhar*), Berl. 9536, Cairo [1]I, 405, VII, 75, [2]I, 155, II, 415, Ẓāh. ʿIsh, Taʾr. 31, see 33, print. C. 1307 and others—Commentaries: a. *al-Kawkab al-anwar*, by his descendant Jaʿfar b. Ismāʿīl, the *muftī* of the Shāfiʿīs in Medina, completed in 1279/1862 (Alex. Sīra 13), C. 1290, 1307, 1310.—b. *al-Qawl al-munjī* by Muḥammad b. Aḥmad b. Muḥammad ʿUllaysh, d. 1299/1881 (see below p. 486), Cairo [1]II, 75.—c.–h. see Suppl. (e. *Fatḥ al-ʿalīm* Garr. 66).—2. *Qiṣṣat al-miʿrāj* Cairo [1]I, 385, Ẓāh. ʿIsh, Taʾr 38.—3. *Jāliyat al-kadar bi-asmāʾ aṣḥāb sayyid al-malāʾika wal-bashar* Alex. Fun. 147,2, Cairo [1]II, 190, [2]III, 74.—4. *Manāqib sayyid Ḥamza*, d. 624/1225, Berl. 10064,1.—5. *al-Janī al-dānī fī dhikr nubdha min manāqib ʿAbd al-Qādir al-Jīlānī* (I, 560), ibid. 10064,2, Leipz. 268.—6. *Fatḥ al-karīm al-jawād al-mannān bi-wāsiṭat ʿiqd sayyid al-zamān fī baʿḍ manāqib ʿAlī b. ʿAlawān*, d. 665/1266 (I, 584), Berl. 10064,3.—7. *Manāqib Aḥmad b. Yaḥyā al-Masāwī*, d. 841/1437, Berl. 10064,4.—8. *Manāqib Aḥmad b. ʿAlī al-Rifāʿī*, d. 578/1182, ibid. 5. = *Ijābat al-dāʿī fī manāqib al-Rifāʿī* in *Majmūʿa*, Būlāq 1301 (Cairo [2]V, 8).—9. *al-Rawḍ al-wardī fī akhbār al-sayyid al-Mahdī*, autograph dated 1177/1763, Garr. 2013,8.

4 Ḥadīth

1. ʿAlāʾ al-Dīn ʿAlī b. Ḥusām al-Dīn ʿAbd al-Malik b. Qāḍīkhān al-Muttaqī al-Hindī al-Qādirī al-Shādhilī al-Madanī of Burhānpūr in India died in Mecca in 975/1567 (or, according to others, in 977/1569), see Suppl.

1. *al-Burhān fī ʿalāmāt Mahdī ākhir al-zamān*, an adaptation of al-Suyūṭī's
al-ʿArf al-wardī fī akhbār al-Mahdī (p. 192, no. 157), Ind. Off. 1031,$_{2}$, Algiers 857,
504 Garr. 1524.—2. *Talkhīṣ al-bayān fī ʿalāmāt Māhdī ākhir al-zamān*, following |
the same work by al-Suyūṭī, as well as the writings of al-Sulamī, d. 685/1283 (I,
555), and Ibn Hajar al-Ḥaythamī (p. 508), Berl. 2726/30.—3. *al-Burhān al-jalī fī*
385 *maʿrifat al-walī*, ibid. 3368.—4. *Jawāmiʿ al-kalim fi 'l-mawāʿiẓ wal-ḥikam*, | 3,000
sayings and *ḥadīth*, Berl. 8703, Ind. Off. 673/4, Paris 1353, Garr. 1925, Cairo [1]VII,
348, [2]I, 284.—5. *Manhaj al-ʿummāl fī sunan al-aqwāl wal-afʿāl* see Suppl.—6.
Kanz al-ʿummāl fī thubūt sunan al-aqwāl wal-afʿāl NO 1199, 1202, *Dībāja* Gotha
2,$_{110}$, abstract NO 1272.—7. *Niʿam al-miʿyār wal-miqyās li-maʿrifat marātib al-nās*
Ind. Off. 696,$_{2}$.—8. *al-Mawāhib al-ʿaliyya fi 'l-jamʿ bayna 'l-ḥikam al-Qurʾāniyya
wal-ḥadīthiyya* Cairo [1]VII, 347.—9.–20. see Suppl.—21. *Asrār al-ʿārifīn wa-siyar
al-ṭālibīn* Patna II, 344,$_{2539,2}$.

2. Abu 'l-Maʿālī ʿAlāʾ al-Dīn Muḥammad b. ʿAbd al-Bāqī al-Bukhārī al-Makkī wrote, in 991/1583:

Al-Ṭirāz al-manqūsh fī maḥāsin al-Ḥubūsh, on the merits of the Abyssinians, based on al-Suyūṭī and others, Berl. 6118, Gotha 1694, Paris 4631, Br. Mus. 325, 1268, Suppl. 1268, Bodl. I, 859 (abstracts ibid. II, 1363), Cairo [1]VI, 81, [2]V, 255, cf. Flügel, *ZDMG* V, 81, XVI, 696/709.

3. Fakhr al-Dīn Muḥammad b. ʿAlī b. Ibrāhīm al-Ḥusaynī al-Astarābādhī, who died in Mecca on 17 Dhu 'l-Qaʿda 1027/27 October 1619.

Muḥ. IV, 46. 1. *Manhaj al-maqāl fī taḥqīq aḥwāl al-rijāl* (*Majmaʿ al-aqwāl*), on Shīʿī transmitters, composed in 968/1578 in Najaf, Br. Mus. Suppl. 635, adaptation (see Suppl.) entitled *Muntaha 'l-maqāl*, by Muḥammad b. Ismāʿīl b. ʿAbd al-Jabbār, lith. Tehran 1262, 1302.—2. *Talkhīs al-maqāl* (*aqwāl*) *fī taḥqīq aḥwāl al-rijāl*, an abstract of the latter, completed in 988/1580, Ind. Off. 716, Br. Mus. Suppl. 634, Mashh. X, 4, 11/3, cf. Khanikoff, *ZDMG* X, 817.

4. Aḥmad al-Nūbī lived in al-Ṭāʾif and died after 1037/1627.

1. *Tanbīh al-wasnān ilā akhbār Mahdī ākhir al-zamān*, composed in 1021/1612,
Gotha 853.—2. *Ṭayyib al-nashr wal-laṭāʾif fī faḍl al-Ḥibr wal-Ṭāʾif*, in praise
of the city of Ṭāʾif, of ʿAbdallāh b. al-ʿAbbās (al-Ḥibr), and of Muḥammad b.
al-Ḥanafiyya, composed in 1027/1617, Gotha 1535.—3. *Kashf al-aqwāl al-*
505 *mubtadhala fī sabq qalam al-Bayḍāwī li-madhhab al-Muʿtazila* | I, 532.—

4. *Shadd al-ādhān ʿan dhikr al-dukhān*, against tobacco smoking, composed in 1037/1627, Gotha 2102,$_{3}$, Alex. Ṭibb 41.

4b. Aḥmad b. Muḥammad b. Aḥmad b. ʿAlī al-Nakhlī al-Makkī al-Shāfiʿī, eleventh cent. (?).

Mashyakha ʿĀšir I, 442,$_{1}$.

5. Ibrāhīm b. Ḥasan al-Kūrānī al-Shahrazūrī al-Shahrānī al-Shāfiʿī al-Kurdī was born in Shahrazūr in 1025/1616, studied in Baghdad, Damascus, Mecca, and Medina, took up residence in the latter, and died on 28 Jumādā I 1101/10 March 1690.

Mur. I, 5, Jab. I, 67, Afrānī, *Ṣafwa* 210. 1. An inventory of his writings, Berl. 25, 2873,$_{6}$.—2. A course of studies and study certificate, issued on 5 Shawwāl 1086/24 December 1675 to ʿAbd al-Malik b. Muḥammad al-Sijilmāsī, ibid. 220, cf. 221.—3. *Niẓām al-zabarjad fī ʾl-arbaʿīn al-musalsala*, 40 *musalsal* traditions from *al-Mujtabā*, by al-Nasāʾī, d. 303/915 (I, 171), completed in 1085/1674, Berl. 1611.—4. *Masālik al-abrār ilā ḥadīth al-nabī al-mukhtār*, | 57 *musalsal* 386
traditions, ibid. 1612/3, Alex. Fun. 123,$_{3}$ (= *al-Maslak al-mukhtār* Bat. 125,$_{2}$).—5. *al-Maslak al-qarīb ilā suʾālāt al-ḥabīb*, an answer to a query by Sayyid Yāsīn b. al-Sayyid Aḥmad al-Ḥusaynī al-Khaṭīb al-Jazarī on what view to take on the Mahdi who manifested himself in 1075/1664; this was Muḥammad, the 12-year old son of a Kurd named Abdallāh who had many followers until the *wālī* of Mosul had them arrested and sent to Istanbul where they were detained for the rest of their lives, Berl. 2732.—6. *al-ʿAmam li-īqāẓ al-himam*, on the science of *ḥadīth*, Cairo I, ^{1}229, ^{2}69, Alex. Muṣṭ. Ḥad. 17, Ḥad. 53,$_{3}$, Fun. 123,$_{2}$.—7. *Imdād dhawi ʾl-istiʿdād li-sulūk maslak al-sadād* Cairo ^{1}II, 5.—8. *Risāla fī jawāz ruʾyat Allāh taʿālā*, composed in 1083/1672, ibid. VII, 70.—9. *Madd al-fayʾ fī taqrīr Laysa ka-mithlihi shayʾ*, composed in 1092/1681, ibid. 71.—10. *al-Jawāb al-mashkūr ʿani ʾl-suʾāl al-manẓūr*, composed in 1067/1656, ibid.—11. *al-Jawāb al-kāfī ʿan masʾalat iḥāṭat ʿilm al-makhlūq bi-ghayr al-mutanāhī* (author?), ibid.—12. *al-Ilmām bi-taḥrīr qawlay Saʿdī wal-ʿIṣām* (Suppl. I, 739,$_{10\ \text{and}\ 11}$), ibid. 72.—13. *Mashraʿ al-wurūd ilā maṭlaʿ al-jūd*, ibid. 72.—14. *Ishrāq al-shams bi-taʿrīb al-kalimāt al-khams*, composed in 1068/1657, a translation of a Persian commentary by al-Sayyid Niʿmatallāh al-Walī on five | words concerning truth, 506
addressed to his servant Kumayl b. Ziyād al-Nakhaʿī al-Kūfī, d. 82/701 (see *Der Islam* 25, 1938, 85), by ʿAlī, ibid. 83.—15. *Īqāẓ al-qawābil lil-taqarrub bil-nawāfil* ibid. 230.—16. *Qaṣd al-sabīl bi-tawḥīd al-ʿalī al-wakīl* p. 514.—17.–37. see Suppl.

(23. Alex. Fun. 167,$_{24}$; 27. Ibid. 110,$_{1}$; 37. b, ʿĀšir I, 463).—38. *al-Jawāb al-muḥiqq fī-mā huwa ʾl-ḥaqq* Alex. Tawḥīd 42,$_{3}$.—39. *Risāla fī tafsīr qawlihi taʿālā* sura 2$_{180}$, ibid. Fun. 163,$_{2}$.—40. *Nashr al-zahr fi ʾl-dhikr bil-jahr* Ind. Off. 1859.—41. *Itḥāf al-munīb al-rūwāh* (?) *fī faḍl al-jahr bi-dhikr Allāh* ibid. 1860.—42. *Inbāh al-anbāh fī iʿrāb lā ilāha illā ʾllāh* Alex. Naḥw 4.

5a. ʿAbdallāh b. Sālim b. Muḥammad b. ʿĪsā al-Baṣrī al-Makkī, who died in Mecca in 1135/1723.

Al-Imdād fī maʿrifat ʿuluww al-isnād see Suppl., also Garr. 1470, Alex. Fun. 122,$_{5}$, Āṣaf. II, 1710,$_{41}$ (which has *ifrād*).

5c. Muḥammad b. ʿAbd al-Muḥsin al-Qalāʿī, see Suppl.

4. *Tahdhīb al-riyāsa wa-tartīb al-siyāsa* Patna I, 149,$_{1430}$.

6. Muḥammad b. Aḥmad b. Saʿīd b. ʿAqīla Jamāl al-Dīn was born in Mecca, travelled to Syria, Asia Minor, and Iraq, lectured for some time at the Jaqmaqiyya in Damascus, before dying in Mecca in 1150/1737.

Mur. IV, 30. 1. *al-Fawāʾid al-jalīla fī musalsalāt Muḥammad b. Aḥmad b. ʿAqīla* Berl. 1614/5, Alex. Ḥad. 39.—2. *Nuskhat al-wujūd fi akhbār ʿan ḥāl al-mawjūd*, Cairo V, ^{1}167, ^{2}391.—3.–6. see Suppl. (3. Garr. 2069,$_{1}$).

7. ʿAbdallāh b. Ibrāhīm b. Ḥasan Mīrghanī al-Maḥjūb Abu ʾl-Siyāda al-Makkī al-Ṭāʾifī al-Ḥusaynī was born in Mecca and lived there as a Sufi, but because of a dispute he and his family moved to al-Ṭāʾif, where he died in 1207/1792.

Jab. II, 240/1. 1. *al-Muʿjam al-wajīz min kalām al-rasūl al-ʿazīz*, selected for paraenetical purposes from al-Suyūṭī's *al-Jāmiʿ al-ṣaghīr* (p. 186) and from *Kunūz al-ḥaqāʾiq* by al-Munāwī, d. 1031/1622 (p. 394), Berl. 1373, Garr. 1412 (see Suppl.)—2. *al-Anfās al-Qudsiyya fī baʿḍ manāqib al-ḥaḍra al-ʿAbbāsiyya* Cairo
507 V, ^{1}135, ^{2}147.—3.–17. see Suppl. (3. Ẓāh. ʿIsh, Taʾr. 75; 5. ibid.; 6. ibid.; 16. | ibid. 180).—18. *Mishkāt al-anwār fī awṣāf al-mukhtār*, on the life of Muḥammad, with a commentary by the author's grandson Muḥammad b. ʿUthmān (born 1208/1794, lived in Dongola, and died in al-Ṭāʾif in 1268/1852), entitled *Miṣbāḥ al-asrār fi ʾl-kalām ʿalā Mishkāt al-anwār*, C. 1327, see Galthier, *Bull. de l'Inst. franç. d'arch. or.* V, 145/6.

| 5 *Fiqh* 387

A The Ḥanafīs

1. Sinān al-Dīn Yūsuf al-Amāsī al-Wāʿiẓ bi-Makka al-Ḥanafī, who died in 1000/1591.

Tabyīn al-maḥārim, in 98 chapters, following the order of the verses of the Qurʾān, on those verses that contain a prohibition of some kind, composed in 980/1572, Berl. 5000, Br. Mus. 144, Garr. 927, NO 2287/8, Alex. Fiqh Ḥan. 10, Taṣ. 10, Cairo [1]II, 73, Qawala I, 223, Bat. 144.

2. Shaykh al-Islām Muḥammad b. ʿAbd al-ʿAẓīm b. Mollā Farrūkh al-Makkī al-Ḥanafī wrote, in 1051/1641:

Al-Qawl al-sadīd fī baʿḍ masāʾil al-ijtihād wal-taqlīd, Berl. 1843, Paris 816 (which mistakenly has "ca. 950"), Alex. Uṣūl 14, Cairo [1]VI, 177.

3. ʿAbd al-Qādir b. Yūsuf Naqībzāde al-Ḥanafī al-Ḥalabī took up residence in the Prophet's Mosque in Medina in 1060/1650 and died in 1107/1695.

Mur. III, 61. *Wāqiʿāt al-muftīn* Garr. 2097,$_{2}$, Alex. Fiqh Ḥan. 55, 72, Cairo [1]III, 120, 148, Qawala I, 408, print. Būlāq 1301.

7. Abu ʾl-Suʿūd Muḥammad b. ʿAlī Efendi al-Shirwānī wrote, in 1207/1792:

ʿUddat arbāb al-fatwā, a collection of fatwas by his contemporary ʿAbdallāh b. Asʿad, the *muftī* of Medina, print. Būlāq 1304, Cairo [1]III, 80. See Suppl., his refutation of Wahhabism, Manch. 92c.

B The Mālikīs

1. Shihāb al-Dīn Aḥmad b. ʿAbd al-Ghaffār al-Mālikī wrote, in 937/1530:

1. *Izālat al-ghishāʾ ʿan ḥukm ṭawf al-nisāʾ baʿd al-ʿishāʾ*, on the prohibition against women leaving their houses after sunset, | and in particular entering mosques, 508
which he describes as a shameful *bidʿa*, Cairo [1]III, 1532.—2. *al-Munaqqaḥ* see p. 199,$_{256}$.—3. See Suppl.

2. Abū ʿAbdallāh Muḥammad b. Muḥammad b. al-Khaṭṭāb al-Mālikī al-Ruʿaynī Nazīl al-Ḥaramayn, who died on 9 Rabīʿ II 954/30 May 1547.

1. *Tafrīḥ al-qulūb bil-khiṣāl al-mukaffira li-mā taqadamma wa-taʾakhkhara min al-dhunūb*, composed in 945/1538, Bodl. II, $69_{,1}$.—2. *Qurrat al-ʿayn* I, 487.—3.–5. see Suppl.—6. *Hidāyat al-sālik al-muḥtāj ilā bayān afʿāl al-muʿtamir wal-ḥājj* Alex. Fiqh Māl. 16.—7. *Irshād al-sālik al-muḥtāj ilā bayān al-muʿtamir wal-ḥājj* ibid. (but see Suppl. 537, 11, 1).

C The Shāfiʿīs

1. Aḥmad b. Muḥammad b. ʿAlī b. Ḥajar al-Haythamī[1] al-Makkī al-Azharī al-Junaydī al-Saʿdī Abu ʾl-ʿAbbās Shihāb al-Dīn, who died in 973/1565, see Suppl.

388 | *Manāqib b. Ḥajar al-Haythamī* by his student Abū Bakr b. Muḥammad b. ʿAbdallāh b. Bāʿamr, Alex. Fun. $118_{,1}$, *RA* 56v, Rieu Add. 765b, Wüst. *Gesch.* 529. 1. *Thabat* or *Muʿgam*, a study course on his teachers of *ḥadīth*, completed in Ramaḍān 972/April 1565, Berl. 174, Cairo ^{1}I, 251, VII, 527.—2. *Taḥrīr al-maqāl fī ādāb wa-aḥkām wa-fawāʾid yaḥtāj ilayhā muʾaddib al-aṭfāl*, on the question of whether teaching must be rewarded with a salary, on respectable behaviour by the teacher, school-attendance, punishments, and discipline, composed in 957/1550, Berl. 145 (wrongly attributed to a certain ʿAlī al-Makkī, ca. 957), Garr. 789, $2013_{,2}$, Cairo ^{1}II, 148, VII, 119, 195, ^{2}I, 276. Mosul $195_{,85,4}$.—3. *al-Iʿlām bi-qawāṭiʿ al-Islām*, on the terminology by which one declares someone to be an unbeliever, on the occasion of a fatwa on marital affairs he issued in Mecca in 973/1565, which had caused him many problems and much criticism, Berl. 2126/7, Paris 953, Pet. AM 350, Alex. Fiqh Shāf. 6, Cairo ^{1}VII, 194, ^{2}I, 164, 533, Mosul $230_{,63}$.—4. *al-Ṣawāʿiq al-muḥriqa ʿalā ahl al-rafḍ wal-zandaqa*, on the legitimacy of the four imams, written in 950/1543 on the basis of his lectures in
509 Mecca, Berl. 2128/30, Gotha 861 (incomplete), Kazan 34, | Esc. ^{2}1541/2, Br. Mus. Suppl. 192, Ind. Off. 181/4, Stewart 136, Ms. or. oct. 3903, AS 3294, NO 2207, Ẓāh. ʿIsh, Taʾr. 90, Cairo V, ^{1}76, ^{2}241, VI ^{1}153, ^{2}198, Mosul $127_{,106}$, $235_{,147}$, print. C. 1307, 1308, 1324; cf. Goldziher, *SBWA* 78, p. 453. Appendix *Manāqib ahl al-bayt* Br. Mus. Suppl. 193, abstract by Muḥammad Saʿīd b. Hilāl b. Muḥammad Sunbul, Berl. 2131.—(*Tanbīh al-ghabī* by al-Nāshirī, see Suppl., Garr. $2078_{,3}$).—5. *al-Zawājir ʿan iqtirāf al-kabāʾir*, an inventory of 461 major sins, Ind. Off. 185, Stewart 151, Cairo ^{1}II, 160, ^{2}I, 315, Mosul $196_{,99}$, print. Būlāq 1284, C. 1310.—Abstract *Kanz al-nāẓir fī mukhtaṣar al-Zawājir* by Muḥammad b. ʿAlī b. al-Qāsim al-Bayrūtī, Berl. 2643.—6. *al-Qawl al-mukhtaṣar fī ʿalāmāt al-Mahdī al-muntaẓar* Berl. 2725, Cairo ^{1}VII, 196, Patna II, $454_{,2632,5}$.—7. *al-Arbaʿīn al-ʿadliyya* Leid. 1759.—8. *al-Fatḥ al-mubīn fī sharḥ al-Arbaʿīn* (*al-Nawawiyya*) I, 499, print. C. 1307 with glosses by al-Madābighī.—9. *al-Ifṣāḥ ʿan aḥādīth al-nikāḥ*, 130 *ḥadīth* on

---

1 Ahlw. no. 174 favours the reading Haitamī, but without justification.

marriage, Gotha 630.—10. *al-Durr al-manḍūd fi ʾl-ṣalāt ʿalā ṣāḥib al-maqām*
al-maḥmūd, on the merits of prayers and blessings for Muḥammad, Berl. 3923,
Paris 1153/$4_{,1}$, Garr. 1963, NO 2870, Dam. Ẓ. 60, $134_{,1}$, Alex. Ḥad. 23, Qawala I,
232.—11. *al-Jawhar al-munaẓẓam fī ziyārat al-qabr al-mukarram*, composed
after his pilgrimage in 956/1549, Berl. 4052, Paris $1153_{,2}$, Cairo ^{1}VII, 141, print.
C. 1309.—Abstract *al-Luʾluʾ al-muṭahham min al-Jawhar al-munaẓẓam* Berl.
4053.—12. *Risāla fi ʾl-manāhil al-ʿadhba fī iṣlāḥ mā wahiya min al-Kaʿba* Alex.
Taʾr. 134, abstract Gotha $16_{,2}$.—13. *Mablagh al-arab fī fakhr al-ʿArab* Cairo ^{1}VII,
195.—14. *al-Ināfa fī-mā jāʾa fi ʾl-ṣadaqa wal-ḍiyāfa*, ibid.—15. *Tanbīh al-akhyār*
ʿalā muʿḍilāt waqaʿat min kitābay al-Waẓāʾif wa-Adhkār al-adhkār Cairo ^{1}II,
115.—16. *al-Nukhab al-jalīla fi ʾl-khuṭab al-jazīla* ibid. 177, print. C. 1290, 1310.—
17. *al-Taʿarruf fi ʾl-uṣūl* Patna II, $457_{,2632,3}$, with the commentary *al-Talaṭṭuf fi*
ʾl-wuṣūl by ʿAlī b. Muḥammad ʿAllān al-Makkī, d. 1057/1647, Cairo ^{1}II, 241.—18.
Itḥāf ahl al-Islām bi-khuṣūṣiyyat al-ṣiyām Cairo ^{1}VI, 108, ^{2}I, 260. |—19. *Darr* 389
al-ghamāma fī durr al-ṭaylasān wal-ʿadhaba wal-ʿimāma Alex. Fiqh Shāf. 22,
Cairo ^{1}VII, 14, ^{2}I, 514, Patna II, $457_{,2632,4}$.—20. *Taṭhīr al-ʿayba min danas al-*
ghayba, Cairo ^{1}VII, 194, Patna II, $457_{,132,3}$.—21. *Talkhīṣ al-Iḥrāʾ fī ḥukm taʿlīq*
al-ṭalāq bil-ibrāʾ p. $224_{,6}$.—22. *Taḥdhīr al-thiqāt min akl al-kafta wal-qāt* Cairo
^{1}VII, 195, Patna II, $457_{,2632,4}$.—23. *Qurrat al-ʿayn bi-bayān anna ʾl-tabarruʿ lā*
yubṭiluhu ʾl-dayn Cairo ^{1}VI, 196.—24. *Kaff al-raʿrāʿ ʿan muḥarramāt* | *al-lahw* 510
wal-samāʿ, against the *Kitāb faraḥ al-asmāʿ bi-rukhaṣ al-samāʿ* of Ibn Zaghdūn
al-Tūnisī, d. 882/1477 (Suppl. 152), and at the same time against all types of
games, Berl. 5517, Br. Mus. Suppl. $1221_{,iii}$, Ind. Off. 1853, Dam. Z. $60_{,134,2}$, Alex.
Fun. $155_{,3}$.—25. *Tuḥfat al-muḥtāj bi-sharḥ al-Minhāj* I, 496, print. C. 1282, 1290;
on the reputation of this commentary see Snouck Hurgronje, *ZDMG* 53, 142.—
26. *Sharḥ Mukhtaṣar al-fiqh al-Shāfiʿī li-ʿAbdallāh b. ʿAbd al-Raḥmān Bāfaḍl*
al-Ḥaḍramī or *Sharḥ al-Muqaddima al-Ḥaḍramiyya* (see Suppl.), C. 1301, 1305,
Mosul $111_{,107/8}$, $238_{,200}$. Glosses by Ḥusayn b. ʿAlī al-ʿUshārī, Alex. Fiqh Shāf.
19.—27. *al-Fatāwi ʾl-ḥadīthiyya* Yeni 634, print. C. 1307.—28. *al-Fatāwi ʾl-kubrā*
al-Haythiyya al-fiqhiyya Cairo ^{1}III, 250, Mosul $102_{,56,2}$, $108_{,232}$, $239_{,208}$, Patna
I, 97, 987, print. C. 1307.—29. *Mawlid al-nabī*, an abstract of 31, composed in
964/1557, Cairo ^{1}VII, 194, ^{2}V, 395, Ẓāh. ʿIsh, Taʾr. 29, print. C. 1323. Glosses by
ʿAbdallāh b. ʿAlī Suwaydān al-Damlījī, Alex. Sīra 6; by Muḥammad b. ʿUbāda
al-Ṣaʿīdī al-ʿAdawī, d. 1193/1779, Alex. Ḥad. 57_2; by Ḥasan Ḥabbās, Mosul $235_{,143}$.—
30. *Itmām al-niʿma al-kubrā ʿala ʾl-ʿālam bi-mawlid sayyid walad Ādam* Garr.
653, abstract Berl. 9530.—31. *Mukhtaṣar qiṣṣat al-mawlid al-sharīf* ibid. 9531,
Garr. 666.—32. *Ashraf al-madākhil* (*wa-sāʾil*) *ilā maʿrifat* (*fahm*) *al-Shamāʾil* I,
$170_{,3}$, composed 3–8 Ramaḍān 949/12–27 December 1542, additionally Cairo ^{1}I,
267, Tunis, Zayt. II, 238/40, Ẓāh. ʿIsh, Taʾr. 61, Alex. Tawḥīd 30. Glosses by ʿAlī b.
ʿAlī al-Shabrāmallisī, d. 1057/1676, ibid. 244.—33. *al-Khayrāt al-ḥisān fī manāqib*

al-imām al-aʿẓam Abī Ḥanīfa al-Nuʿmān, a defence of Abū Ḥanīfa's honour against al-Ghazzālī, Berl. 10003/5, Cairo V, ^{1}51, 127, ^{2}174, print. 1304, 1311.—34. A smaller work on the same subject, Berl. 10006, Cairo ^{1}VII, 262.—35. *Sharḥ Bānat Suʿād* Suppl. I, 69.—36. *Sharḥ Mishkāt al-maṣābīḥ* I, 449.—37.–57. see Suppl. (38. excise: see p. $70_{,10}$, 79; 48. Garr. 1919, Patna I, $144_{,1398}$; 50 = 32; 55 = 6; 57. Hamb. Or. Sem. 63).—58. *Sawābigh al-madad* Patna II, $458_{,2632,7}$.—59. *Sunan al-ghāra* (?) *fī man aẓhara tahawwunahu fī 'l-khināʿ* ibid. $_{9}$.—60. *al-Isʿāf bi-kashf al-ḥāl* ibid. $452_{,2628,6}$.—61. *Sharḥ Dībājat al-Minhāj* Mosul $103_{,56,5}$.—62. *Tashhnīf al-asmāʿ bi-ḥukm al-samāʿ* Mosul $145_{,66}$.—63. *Jawāb fī 'l-ṭāʿūn ʿalā su'āl warada min al-Yaman* ibid. $166_{,28,2}$.—64. *Fatḥ al-jawād fī sharḥ al-Irshād*
511 Hamb. Or. Sem. 21.—In the catalogues Ibn Ḥajar al-ʿAsqalānī and | Ibn Ḥajar al-Haythamī are sometimes confused; thus Suppl. $75_{,66}$ is attributed to al-Ḥajar al-Haythamī in Patna II, $2633_{,1}$ $75_{,74}$, and in Mosul $106_{,88,1}$.

2. Zayn al-Dīn ʿAbd al-Qāhir b. Aḥmad b. ʿAlī al-Fākihī al-Makkī, who died in 982/1574.

1. *Manāhij al-akhlāq al-saniyya fī manāhij al-akhlāq al-sunniyya*, on ethics, composed in 956/1545 in Mecca, Berl. 5401, Ind. Off. $4573_{,2}$.—2. *Manāhij al-surūr wal-rashād fī 'l-ramy wal-sibāq wal-ṣayd wal-jihād*, dedicated to the sharif of Mecca, Abū Numayy Muḥammad b. Barakāt in the year 947/1540, on the occasion of an attack by infidels (Portuguese?) on its territory, Paris 2834.—3.–5. see Suppl.—6. *Ḥuṣūl al-munā bi-uṣūl al-ghinā* Ind. Off. $4573_{,1}$ (*JRAS* 1939, 365).

3. Muḥammad b. ʿAbd al-Rasūl b. ʿAbd al-Sayyid al-Ḥusaynī al-Shāfiʿī al-Shahrazūrī al-Madanī al-Barzanjī was born in Shahrazūr on 12 Rabīʿ I 1040/20 October 1630 and studied in Hamadan, Baghdad, Damascus, Istanbul, and Cairo. He then settled in Medina where he became a professor. He died there in 1103/1691.

Mur. IV, 65, al-ʿAyyāshī, *Riḥla* II, 57. 1. *Anhār al-salsabīl li-riyāḍ nuwwār al-tanzīl* Cairo I, ^{1}130, ^{2}33.—2. *Sawā' al-sabīl ilā iʿrāb Ḥasbuna 'llāh wa-niʿma 'l-wakīl* (sura $3_{,167}$), composed in 1094/1683 in Medina, Ind. Off. 978.—3. *Bughyat al-ṭālib li-īmān Abī Ṭālib* Berl. 2451.—4. *al-Ishāʿa li-ashrāṭ al-sāʿa*, on the conditions required for the Last Judgement, Berl. 2766/8, Ms. or. oct. 3927, Br. Mus. Suppl. 199, AS 2181, Sbath 491, Cairo ^{1}VI, 112, ^{2}1, App. 37, Garr. 1508, Alex. Mawāʿiẓ 4. Mosul $126_{,86}$, anon. abstract Berl. 2769.—5. *Ilhām al-ṣawāb li-uli 'l-albāb*, a
389 refutation against a repudiation of his *Makhraj etc.* | against tobacco, Berl. 5492, Patna II, $463_{,2635,8}$.—6.–11. see Suppl. (8. Garr. 1526; 11. autograph dated 1093/1682, Lāleli $474_{,4}$).

4. Muḥammad b. Sulaymān al-Kurdī al-Madanī al-Shāfiʿī was born in 1127/1715 in Damascus but moved to Medina before he was one year old. It was there that he grew up and later became a *muftī* for the Shāfiʿīs. In 1172/1758 he passed through Damascus on his way to Istanbul, and died in 1994/1780.

| Mur. IV, 111. 1. *Fatāwī* C. 1307.—2. *Fatḥ al-qadīr bikhtiṣār mutaʿalliqāt nusk* 512
al-ajīr C. 1296, Mecca 1300.—3. *al-Ḥawāshi ʾl-Madaniyya ʿalā sharḥ Ibn Ḥajar lil-Muqaddima al-Ḥaḍramiyya* (p. 510), Rāmpūr I, 229,$_{409}$, Būlāq 1288, C. 1284, 1304, 1307 (see Suppl. 528,$_{26}$, 555,$_{1c}$).—4. *Ajwiba ʿalā asʾila* Patna II, 358,$_{2543,1}$.

| D Ḥanbalīs and Wahhābīs 390

1. Al-Imām Muḥammad b. ʿAbd al-Wahhāb b. Dāʾūd, d. 1206/1791, see Suppl.

J.L. Burckhardt, *Bemerkungen über die Beduinen und Wahaby* (Bertuchs Reisebeschreibungen vol. 57, Weimar 1831) p. 379ff. *Lumaʿ al-shihāb fī sīrat Muḥammad b. ʿAbd al-Wahhāb* Br. Mus. 1262. 1 *Kitāb al-tawḥīd* Br. Mus. 1616, Suppl. 220,$_{2}$, cf. O. Kinealy, *JAS Bengal* 1874, I, 68/72.—Commentary a., b. see Suppl.—c. *Fatḥ al-majīd* by ʿAbd al-Raḥmān b. Ḥasan Qaṣīla, C. 1347.—2. *Kashf al-shubuhāt min al-tawḥīd* Br. Mus. 1262,$_{2}$, Alex. Fun. 123,$_{2}$.—3. *Tafsīr al-Fātiḥa* Br. Mus. 1262,$_{2}$.—4. *Tafsīr al-shahāda* ibid. Suppl. 220,$_{4}$.—5. *Bāb maʿrifat Allāh taʿālā wal-īmān* Br. Mus. 1616,$_{3}$.—6. *Masāʾil khālafa rasūl Allāh ṣlʿm fīhā mā ʿalayhi ahl al-jāhiliyya min al-kitābiyyīn wal-ummiyyīn mā lā ghinā li-muslim ʿan maʿrifatihā* ibid. $_{4}$.—7. On the foundations of Islam, ibid. $_{5}$.—8. On the four differences between Muslims and polytheists, ibid. $_{6}$.—9. *Kitāb al-kabāʾir* Br. Mus. Suppl. 220,$_{3}$.—10. *Kitāb al-sīra*, an abstract of Ibn Hishām, ibid. $_{5}$, Patna II, 309,$_{2554,1}$.—11. An explanation of six passages from the *Sīra*, Br. Mus. Suppl. 220,$_{5}$.—12.–27. see Suppl.—28. *Uṣūl al-īmān* Patna II, 510,$_{2740}$.

6 *Sciences of the Qurʾān*

ʿAbd al-Wahhāb b. Aḥmad Barakāt al-Shāfiʿī al-Aḥmadī wrote, in Mecca in 1149/1736:

Al-Taysīr li-murīd al-tafsīr, a general introduction to and explanation of the Fātiḥa, Gotha 538,$_{1}$.

7 *Dogmatics*

1. Muḥammad ʿAlī b. Muḥammad ʿAllān al-Bakrī al-Ṣiddīqī al-Shāfiʿī was born
in Mecca on 20 Ṣafar 996/21 January 1588, | and issued legal opinions before 513

he was even 24. He gave lectures on Bukhārī in the Kaʿba. He died on 21 Dhu 'l-Ḥijja 1057/18 January 1648.

Muḥ. IV, 18/9, Wüst. *Gesch.* 567. 1. *Mawrid al-ṣafāʾ bi-abaway al-Muṣṭafā* Berl. 54.—2. *al-ʿIqd al-farīd fī taḥqīq al-tawḥīd* ibid. 2446.—3. *al-Mawāhib al-fatḥiyya ʿala 'l-ṭarīqa al-Muḥammadiyya*, completed in 1053/1643; see below, p. 441.—4.–15. see Suppl.—16. *Rafʿ al-albās bi-bayān ishtirāk maʿāni 'l-Fātiḥa wa-sūrat al-Nās* Qawala I, 68.

2. Abu 'l-Ḥasan b. ʿAbd al-Hādī al-Sindī al-Atharī was born in Sind, studied in the Hijaz, and died in Medina in 1136/1723.

Jab. I, 85. Answers to a number of questions—attributed to al-Birkāwī, d. 981/1573 (see below p. 440)—on the doctrine of the unity of God, corrected by an unidentified individual, Berl. 2453.

3. Ḥusayn b. ʿAlī b. ʿAbd al-Shakīr (Shakūr) al-Ṭāʾifī al-Madanī, ca. 1180/1767, see Suppl.

2. *al-ʿUjāla fi 'l-adhkār al-ṣalātiyya* Patna I, 156,$_{1484}$.—3. *al-Fuyūḍāt al-ḥusnā min mashāhid al-ḥabīb al-ḥasnā* ibid.,$_{1486}$.

8 *Mysticism*

1. ʿAbd al-Raḥmān b. Muḥammad b. ʿArrāq al-Ḥijāzī al-Madanī Nūr al-Dīn died in 963/1556.

1. A Sufi treatise in rhymed prose on the concepts of *ḥaqq*, *amr*, and *khalq*, Berl. 3464.—2., 3. See Suppl. (3. as *Nashr al-laṭāʾif fī quṭr al-Ṭāʾif* Alex. Taʾr. 142, in Mecca, see Zurukli, *Aḥsan ma raʾaytu wa-samiʿtu* 99).—4. *Waṣiyyat al-muntaẓir gharīb al-waṭan* Dam. Z. 60,$_{130,1}$ (only Ibn ʿArrāq).

2. Muḥammad b. ʿUmar b. Aḥmad al-ʿĀdilī Badr al-Dīn, ca. 970/1562.

1. *al-Risāla al-ʿĀdiliyya fī bayān al-farq wal-jamʿ fī madhhab al-Ṣūfiyya*, a com-
514 prehensive account of Sufism composed in 971–2/1563–4 | in Mecca, Berl. 3042.—2. *al-Khulāṣa al-ṣughrā fī maqāṣid sālik al-dunyā wal-ākhira* ibid. 3196.—3. *Thamarat al-azhār wa-bahjat al-asrār*, an edifying work, ibid. 8835.

3. Ḥasan b. ʿAbdallāh b. Ḥusayn al-Ḥusaynī al-Makkī al-Madanī al-Samarqandī, who flourished in the second half of the tenth century.

Al-Anwār al-musbala fī baʿḍ khawāṣṣ al-basmala, with the *Khātima ʿala ʾl-ṭibb al-rūḥānī*, composed in 935/1546 in Istanbul, Cairo ^{1}VII, 533.

4. Abu ʾl-Mawāhib Aḥmad b. ʿAlī b. ʿAbd al-Quddūs al-Shinnāwī was born in Maḥallat Rūḥ, west of Cairo, in 975/1567, studied in Cairo and Medina, joined a Sufi order there, and died in 1089/1619.

Muḥ. I, 243/6, Wüst. *Ṣūfīs* 208. 1. *al-Iqlīd al-farīd fī tajrīd al-tawḥīd*, with the commentary *Taḥrīk al-iqlīd fī fatḥ bāb al-tawḥīd* by ʿAbd al-Ghanī al-Nābulusī, d. 1143/1753 (p. 454), Cairo ^{1}II, 73, ^{2}I, 276.—2. *Ṣādiḥat al-azal wa-sāniḥat al-nazal* (*nuzul ?*), a Sufi *qaṣīda*, Berl. $2873_{,11}$, with a commentary ibid. 3419. |—3. 392
al-Ṣuḥuf al-nāmūsiyya wal-sujuf al-nāwūsiyya Cairo ^{1}II, 93.—4. *Fatḥ al-ilāh fī-mā yuqāl dubura kulli ṣalāh* ibid. 213.—5. (see Suppl.) In Garr. 114 attributed to a certain Muḥammad b. Muḥammad b. ʿAlī al-Bakrī al-Ṣiddiqī Abu ʾl-Mawāhib, d. 1037/1627.

5. ʿAlī Khalīfa b. Abi ʾl-Faraj al-Zamzamī, who died in 1063/1653 in Mecca.

Muḥ. II, 133. *Shifāʾ al-muʾminīn* NO 2451.

6. Ṣafī al-Dīn Aḥmad b. Muḥammad b. ʿAbd al-Nabī b. Yūnus al-Badrī al-Qudsī al-Yamanī al-Anṣārī al-Qashshāshī al-Dajjānī (Dajjājī) al-Madanī was born in Medina in 991/1583, studied there and in Mecca, taught in his hometown, and died in 1071/1660.

Muḥ. I, 343/6, Wüst. *Ṣūf.* 210. 1. *al-Simṭ al-majīd al-jāmiʿ li-salāsil* (*fī tartīb talqīn al-dhikr wa-iʿṭāʾ al-bayʿa wal-ilbās wa-salāsil*) *ahl al-tawḥīd*, Ind. Off. $696_{,3}$, Cairo ^{1}II, 88.—2. *Manẓūma fi ʾl-tawḥīd*, with a commentary, *Qaṣd al-sabīl bi-tawḥīd al-ʿalī al-wakīl* by Ibrāhīm al-Kūrānī, d. 1101/1689 (p. 505), composed in 1083/1672, Cairo I, ^{1}37, ^{2}201, Bat. $125_{,1}$.—| 3. *al-Durra al-thamīna fī-mā li-zāʾir* 515
al-nabī ṣlʿm ila ʾl-Madīna Cairo ^{1}VI, 138.—4. *al-Waṣiyya lil-awlād wal-bariyya* Berl. 4019.—5. *Jawāhir al-qalāʾid fī faḍl al-masājid*, on the merits of mosques, especially those of Jerusalem, and on the mischief perpetrated in there, ibid. 6103.—6. *Bustān al-ʿābidīn wa-rawḍat al-ʿārifīn* Cairo ^{1}II, 147.—7.–11. see Suppl. (11. Garr. 1528).—12. See Suppl. III, 1295.

7. ʿAbdallāh b. ʿAlī b. ʿAbdallāh b. ʿAlī b. Aḥmad b. Ḥasan al-Makkī al-Ḥusaynī al-Saqqāf, who died on 10 Rabīʿ II 1125/6 May 1713.

Tanbīh al-sālikīn Cairo ^{1}VI, 48, ^{2}V, 280.—7a., 7b. See Suppl. III, 1295; 8. See Suppl. and III, 1295.

9 *Philosophy*

ʿAlī b. Abi ʾl-Ḥasan al-Ḥusaynī al-Shāmī al-ʿĀmilī Nūr al-Dīn first lived in Damascus, then moved to Mecca, and died in 1068/1657.

Muḥ. III, 132/4. *Manẓūma fi ʾl-manṭiq* Berl. 5207.

10 *Mathematics*

1–3. See Suppl.

(1, 1. Garr. 1040)

4. Ḥasan b. ʿAlī b. Yaḥyā b. ʿUmar al-ʿUjaymī al-Makkī was born in Mecca in 1049/1639, lived as a Sufi in Medina, and died in al-Ṭāʾif on 13 Shawwāl 1113/14 March 1702.

Jab. I, 70. 19. Works Garr. 2008. 1. On a fraction in a treatise called *al-Tuḥfa al-Ḥijāziyya fī nukhabat al-aʿmāl al-ḥisābiyya* by ʿAlī b. Abī Bakr al-Anṣārī (Suppl. II, 230), against a small tract by ʿAbd al-Raḥmān b. ʿAlī b. Ghayth b. Tāj al-Dīn al-Madanī, Berl. 5997.—2.–29. see Suppl.

393 |
11 *Astronomy*

1. Yaḥyā b. Muḥammad b. Muḥammad b. ʿAbd al-Raḥmān al-Maghribī al-Makkī al-Ruʿaynī al-Mālikī al-Khaṭṭāb was born in Mecca in 902/1496 and died there in Rabīʿ I 995/February 1587.

516 | See Suppl. 1. *Risālat wasīlat al-ṭullāb li-maʿrifat aʿmāl al-layl wal-nahār bi-ṭarīq al-ḥisāb*, abbreviated from a work by his father (p. 508), Berl. 5700.—2. *Risāla fiʾstikhrāj al-layl wal-nahār min rubʿ al-dāʾira al-musammā bi-rubʿ al-mujayyab, Risāla fī maʿrifat istikhrāj aʿmāl al-layl wal-nahār bi-rubʿ al-jayb*, following Sibṭ b. al-Māridīnī, d. 881/1475, Berl. 5826, Krafft 327, Alex. Ḥisāb $56_{,2}$, Cairo ^{1}V, 252, Teh. II, $642_{,2}$, anon. comment. Berl. 5827.—3.–12. see Suppl. (11. see Suppl. $526_{,3}$).

2. Ibrāhīm b. Muḥammad b. ʿAbd al-Salām al-Makkī al-Zamzamī al-Khalwatī, who was born in Mecca in 1110/1698, was *muwaqqit* at the Holy Mosque there and possessed an important astronomical library that was squandered by his heirs after his death. He died on 17 Rabīʿ I 1195/14 March 1781.

Jab. II, 69/70. 1. *Manẓūma fi ʾl-awqāt* Cairo ^{1}V, 282 (Suppl., see Garr. $2077_{,1}$).—2. *Wasīlat al-thiqāt bi-fahm ālat al-muqanṭarāt* ibid.

12 *Travelogues and Geographies*

1. Muḥammad b. ʿAbd al-ʿAzīz (p. 224) b. ʿUmar b. Muḥammad b. Fahd al-Qurashī al-Makkī al-Hāshimī Muḥibb al-Dīn Jārallāh, who was a preacher in Jedda, died in 954/1547.

Wüst. *Gesch.* 521. 1. *al-Silāḥ wal-ʿudda fī faḍāʾil bandar Judda*, Berl. 6063, Vienna 891.—2., 3. see Suppl.—4. See Suppl. III, 1295.

2. Muḥammad Kibrīt b. ʿAbdallāh al-Ḥusaynī al-Mūsawī al-Madanī died in 1070/1659.

1. *al-Jawāhir al-thamīna fī maḥāsin al-Madīna* Paris 2252$_{,1}$.—2. *Riḥlat al-shitāʾ wal-ṣayf*, on his trip from Medina to Istanbul during the reign of Murād IV (1032–49/1623–39), Gotha 1543, Cambr. Preston p. 23, no. 158, Kazan 113$_{,2}$, Garr. 219, cf. Tuch, *Die Reise des Scheich Ibr. al-Khijari* (no. 3), p. 1.—3., 4. See Suppl.

3. Ibrāhīm b. ʿAbd al-Raḥmān al-Khiyārī al-Miṣrī al-Madanī al-Shāfiʿī, who was born in Medina on 13 Shawwāl 1037/17 June 1628, became a preacher in the
Prophet's Mosque and | obtained one of the professorships that his father had 517
held there. Because another scholar had succeeded in wrenching this office
away from him, he had to travel to Istanbul. | By way of Damascus he reached 394
Yenishehir, where Sultan Murād was residing and, after the latter had validated his rights, he returned to Medina by way of Istanbul, Damascus, and Cairo. However, although his position was returned to him, he soon died of poison on 2 Rajab 1082/5 November 1671, apparently because he refused to follow the order of the Shaykh al-Ḥarām that he softly pronounce the bismillāh in prayer, as is required by the Ḥanafī rite.

Muḥ. I, 25, Wüst. *Gesch.* 579, *Ṣūf.* 212. *Tuḥfat al-udabāʾ wa-sulwat al-ghurabāʾ*, an account of his trip, Berl. 6135, Gotha 1545, de Sacy 221. Cf. Seetzen in *Zachs Monatl. Correspondenz* XIV, 1806; F. Tuch, *Die Reise des Scheich Ibr. al-Khijari*, Leipzig 1830.

13 *Encyclopaedias and Polyhistors*

1. ʿAbd al-ʿAzīz b. ʿAbd al-Wāḥid al-Miknāsī al-Madanī, shaykh of the Qurʾān reciters in Medina, visited Jerusalem, Damascus, and Aleppo in 951/1544, before dying in Medina in 964/1557.

1. 13 *Urjūzas* on the Islamic sciences, Br. Mus. Suppl. I, 718.—2. See Suppl.

2. ʿAlī b. Sulṭān Muḥammad al-Qāriʾ al-Harawī was born in Herat, lived in Mecca, and died there in 1014/1605.

Muḥ. III, 105, Cod. Landb. Berl. 295, f. 5b. 35 Abh. Garr. 2001, 4, Alex. Fun. $178_{,1-4}$. 1. *Kitāb al-bayyināt fī tabāyun baʿḍ al-āyāt,* which starts with sura $2_{,205}$ and, following al-Bayḍāwī, tries to show that the sense of some near-identical passages in the Qurʾān is actually quite different, Berl. 768, Munich 886, f. 118, Cairo ^{1}VII, 22, ^{2}I, 35, Patna I, $382_{,2562,\ 10}$, $390_{,2569,\ 13}$.—2. *Takhrīj qirāʾat al-Bayḍāwī* NO 61.—3. *Tafsīr al-Qurʾān* AS 224/6, Cairo I, ^{1}152, ^{2}41, Qawala I, 52.—3a. See Suppl.
518 Qawala I, 235.—4. *al-Aḥādīth | al-Qudsiyya* Berl. 1523, Munich 886, fol. 99, Cairo ^{1}I, 263, VII, 26, 135, Alex. Fun. $88_{,2}$, Garr. 2001, 4, print. Istanbul 1316.—4a. *Risāla fī qawlihi* sura $7_{,29}$, *wa-bayān ma qālahu fī tafsīrihi Niẓām al-Dīn Yaʿqūb al-Karkhī* Qawala I, 67.—5. *Sharḥ ʿAqīlat al-atrāb* Suppl. I, 727.—6. *Sharḥ al-Muqaddima al-Jazariyya* p. 259.—7. *Arbaʿūna ḥadīthan fī jawāmiʿ al-kalim* Berl. 1524, Vienna $1661_{,10}$, Garr. $2001_{,6}$, Cairo ^{1}VII, 135, 684, Patna II, $384_{,2568,\ 22}$, $2569_{,4,15}$.—8. *Jamʿ al-arbaʿīn fī faḍl (faḍāʾil) al-Qurʾān al-mubīn* Berl. 1525, Munich 886, f. 85, Cairo ^{1}VII, 26, ^{2}I, 120, commentary by Aḥmad b. ʿAlī al-Qasṭamūnī Cairo ^{1}I, 386.—9. *Khafḍ al-janāḥ bi-rafʿ al-junāḥ bi-arbaʿīna ḥadīthan fī bāb al-nikāḥ,* composed in 1010/1601, Berl. 1526, Munich 886, f. 83b, Garr. $2001_{,8}$ (*Rafʿ al-janāḥ bi-khafḍ al-junāḥ*), Cairo ^{1}I, 334, VII, 46, 133, Patna II, $384_{,3568,\ 1536,\ 56,\ 2569}$ (*Risālat al-Janāḥ*).—10. *al-Hibāt al-saniyya fī tabyīn al-aḥādīth al-mawḍūʿāt* Berl. 1636, Sarajevo 119.—11. *Kitāb al-mawḍūʿāt,* a small collection of works, Berl. 1637/8, Algiers $1552_{,1}$, AS 938/9, Alex. Ḥad. $54_{,2}$, Cairo ^{1}I, 404, VII, 122, 401, 514, Qawala I, 155, Istanbul 1289.—11a. *al-Mawḍūʿāt fī muṣṭalaḥ al-ḥadīth* Alex. Fun. $77_{,5}$, $116_{,1}$, Patna I, $65_{,668}$.—12. *Risālat al-birra fī ḥubb al-hirra,* which declares the tradition according to which the love for cats is a matter to do with faith as inauthentic, Berl. 1639, Munich 886, f. 78b, Cairo ^{1}VII, 26, 132, no. 23, ^{2}I, 118, Qawala I, 118, 237, Patna II, $379_{,2528,\ 3}$, $385_{,32}$.—13. *Iʿrāb al-qāriʾ ʿalā awwal bāb Ṣaḥīḥ al-Bukhārī* see I, 165, with Munich 886, f. 193,
395 Cairo ^{1}VII, 22. |—14. *Tazyīn al-ʿibāra bi-dūn taḥayyuz al-ishāra* Patna II, $324_{,2368,\ 26}$, $467_{,2635,\ 40}$.—15. *Sharḥ Musnad Abī Ḥanīfa* I, 177.—16. *Sharḥ Nukhabat al-fikar* I, 441.—17. *Sharḥ Mishkāt al-maṣābīḥ* I, 448.—18. *Sharḥ Kitāb al-Shifāʾ* I, 455.—19. *Risāla fi ʾl-iʿtiqādiyyāt,* an appendix to his voluminous commentary on *al-Fiqh al-akbar* by Abū Ḥanīfa (I, 177), on all kinds of controversial issues concerning faith, Berl. 1840.—20. *Sharḥ Kitāb Alfāẓ al-kufr* p. 96, 7 and Suppl.—21. *Tashyīʿ fuqahāʾ al-Ḥanafiyya wa-tashnīʿ sufahāʾ al-Shāfiʿiyya,* a defence of the Ḥanafīs against a tract falsely attributed to al-Juwaynī, d. 478/1085 (I, 487), Berl. 2140, Cairo ^{1}VII, 22 (= ibid. 134, no. 35 ?), to which an addendum *Dhayl Tashyīʿ etc.* Berl. 2141, Patna $351_{,2528,\ 4244}$.—21a. *Ṭabaqāt al-Aḥnāf* (i.e. of the Ḥanafīs), based on a commentary on *Musnad Abī Ḥanīfa,* Patna II, $314_{,2451/2}$.—22. *Risālat*

al-ihtidāʾ fi ʾqtidāʾ al-Ḥanafiyya bil-Shāfiʿiyya wa-mā yataʿallaq bi-hādhihi ʾl-qaḍiyya | Berl. 2142/4, Munich 886, f. 71b, Cairo ^{1}VII, 26, 129, Patna II, 386,$_{2568,}$ 519
$_{40}$.—23. *Rīsāla radda bihā ʿalā man nasabahu ilā sabb al-imām al-Shāfiʿī* Cairo ^{1}VII, 135.—24. *al-Muqaddima al-sālima fī khawf al-khātima*, following sura 7,$_{97}$, against Ibn ʿArabī, Berl. 2145/6, 2690, Munich 886, f. 194, Garr. 2001,$_{35}$, Cairo ^{1}VII, 25, Patna II, 384,$_{2568, 19}$.—25. *Sulālat al-Risāla fi ʾl-Rawāfiḍ min ahl al-ḍalāla* Berl. 2147, Cairo ^{1}VII, 25, Patna II, 384,$_{2568, 25, 33}$, 390,$_{2560, 12}$.—26. *Shayam al-ʿawāriḍ fī dhamm al-Rawāfiḍ* Berl. 2148/9, Cairo ^{1}VI, 153, VII, 24, 129.—27. *al-Ajwiba al-muḥarrara fi ʾl-bayḍa al-khabītha al-munkara*, against the custom of sending each other eggs on the occasion of the New Year, which is said to originate with the Christians and the Magi, Berl. 2150, Munich 886, f. 11b. Alex. Fun. 156,$_{9}$.—28. *Risālat al-masʾala fi ʾl-basmala*, on reading sura 9 without the bismillāh, Berl. 2261, Munich 886, f. 180, Garr. 2001,$_{1}$, Cairo ^{1}VII, 24, 130, 399, Patna II, 384,$_{2569, 2}$.—29. *Ṣunʿat Allāh fī ṣīghat ṣibghat Allāh fī taḥqīq al-Bayḍāwī bayyaḍa ʾllāh wajhahu* (*Ṣunʿat ṣibghat Allāh*), on the passage concerning the power of the *ḥamdala* invoked by al-Bayḍāwī, Berl. 2262, Munich 886, f. 124b. Cairo ^{1}VII, 22, 131.—30. *Sharḥ ʿAqāʾid al-Nasafī* I, 548.—31. *Ikhrāj aḥādīth al-N.* ibid.—32. *al-Tajrīd fī iʿrāb kalimat al-tawḥīd* Berl. 2445, Cairo ^{1}IV, 53, VII, 24, 129, 217, ^{2}I, 167, II, 83 Patna II, 384,$_{2569, 3}$.—33. *al-Qawl al-sadīd fī khulf al-waʿīd* Berl. 2494, Cairo ^{1}VII, 23.—34. *Kashf al-khidr fī amr al-Khiḍr*, Berl. 2546/7, Munich 886, f. 161, Alex. Fun. 66,$_{6}$, Cairo ^{1}VII, 133, 621, ^{2}V, 307.—35. *al-Inbāʾ bi* (*fī ḥaqq*) *anna ʾl-ʿaṣā sunnat al-anbiyāʾ*, on the use of the staff by the prophets, Berl. 2548/9, Garr. 2001,$_{12}$, Cairo ^{1}VII, 24, 130, 624, Patna II, 384,$_{2568, 43}$, 390,$_{2560, 10}$.—36. *Taṭhīr al-ṭawiyya bi-taḥsīn al-niyya*, on whether an act has any value in the absence of any intent, Berl. 2635, Munich 885, f. 103, Garr. 200,$_{7}$, Cairo ^{1}VII, 25, 134; abstract *Taḥṣīn al-ṭawiyya fī taḥsīn al-niyya* Berl. 2636, Cairo ^{1}VII, 23.—37. *Risāla fī abaway al-nabī* or *al-abawayn al-sayyidayn al-sharīfayn*, a demonstration that Muḥammad's parents are in Hell, Cairo ^{1}VII, 22,$_{3}$.—38. *Adillat muʿtaqad Abī Ḥanīfa al-imām fī abaway al-rasūl*, on *al-Fiqh al-akbar*, Berl. 10346.—39. *al-Mashhrab al-wardī fī madhhab al-Mahdī* Berl. 2731, Munich 886, f. 168b. Garr. 2001,$_{13}$, Cairo ^{1}VI, 197, VII, 134, Alex. Fun. 97,$_{2}$.—40. *al-Risāla al-wujūdiyya fī nayl masʾalat al-shuhūdiyya*, proof of the heresy of Ibn ʿArabī, Berl. 2853.—41. *Risāla* against the *Fuṣūṣ* of Ibn ʿArabī, Cairo ^{1}II, 86.—42. *Risāla*
fī | *tafāwut al-mawjūdāt*, | on the stations of living beings, Berl. 3369.—43. 520 396
al-Fuṣūl al-muhimma fī ḥuṣūl al-mutimma, on the importance of the right performance of prayer, ibid. 3598, Munich 886, f. 59, Cairo ^{1}III, 97, VII, 24, 131, ^{1}I, 452, Patna 390,$_{2569, 9}$ (*fī uṣūl al-muḥkama*).—44. *al-Burhān al-jalī al-ʿalī ʿalā man summiya min ghayr musammin bil-walī* Berl. 3599, Cairo ^{1}VII, 23.—45. *al-Faṣl al-muʿawwal fi ʾl-ṣaff al-awwal*, on sura 37, Berl. 3600, Munich 886, 226b., Garr. 2001,$_{27}$, Cairo ^{1}VII, 25, 132.—46. *Shifāʾ* (*Īṣāl*) *al-sālik fī irsāl Mālik*, on how

to position one's hands during prayer, Berl. 3601, Cairo II, 22, Patna II, 382$_{,2568, 11, 42}$. Eulogy on this work by Aḥmad b. ʿAbd al-Laṭīf b. Mukayna al-Mālīk, dated 1007/1598, Berl. 46.—47. *Risāla fī taʿyīn al-ʿibāra li-taḥsīn al-ishāra*, on how to keep one's fingers during the *tashahhud* in prayer, Berl. 3603, Ind Off. 1733, a *Dhayl* thereon in Berl. 3604, Garr. 2001$_{,25}$, Cairo ^{1}II, 130, Algiers 724$_{,12}$.—48. *al-Tadhīn lil-tazyīn ʿalā wajh al-tabyīn* Munich 886, f. 160, Cairo ^{1}VII, 24, ^{2}I, 96.—49. *al-Istidʿāʾ fi ʾl-istisqāʾ*, Berl. 3605, Munich 886, f. 69. Garr. 2001$_{,34}$, Alex. Fun. 66$_{,4}$, Cairo ^{1}VII, 23, Patna II, 390$_{,2569, 11}$.—50. *Ṣilāt al-jawāʾiz* (*al-Qawl al-jāʾiz*) *fī ṣalāt al-janāʾiz*, on the admissibility of prayers over corpses in the mosque in Mecca, Berl. 3606, Munich 886, f. 65, Cairo ^{1}II, 23, Patna II, 383$_{,2588, 21}$.—51. *al-Ḥizb al-aʿẓam wal-wird al-afkham*, a collection of prayers, Berl. 3783, Hamb. Or. Sem. 8, Munich 174, Vienna 1707, Ind. Off. 362$_{,1037}$, Garr. 1965, Cairo ^{1}II, 190, 216, 235, ^{2}I, 287, Patna I, 152$_{,1452}$, print. Istanbul 1262, Būlāq 1300.—Commentaries: a. ʿUthmān al-ʿUryānī, d. 1168/1754, Cairo ^{1}II, 199.—b. Ibrāhīm al-Sāqizī, *al-Fayḍ al-arḥam wal-fatḥ al-akram*, abstract by Muḥammad b. Hāshim al-Fallāshī, ibid. II, 228, Alex. Fun. 15, Garr. 1966.—c. Muḥammad al-Nābulusī al-Maqdisī al-Azharī, composed in 1160/1747, Qawala I, 244.—d. *al-Durr al-munaẓẓam* by al-Madanī, d. 1274/1858, ibid. 32.—52. *Sharḥ al-Ḥiṣn al-ḥaṣīn* p. 260.—53. *al-Adab fī* (*faḍāʾil*) *Rajab al-murajjab* Berl. 3820, Cairo ^{1}VII, 21, 134, Patna II, 384$_{,2568, 2}$.—53a. *Risāla fī faḍāʾil Rajab wa-Shaʿbān* Garr. 2001$_{,15}$.—54. *al-Tibyān fī faḍl laylat niṣf Shaʿbān wa-laylat al-qadr fī Ramaḍān* or *Fatḥ al-raḥmān bi-faḍāʾil Shaʿbān* Berl. 3824, Garr. 2001$_{,16}$, print. Būlāq 1307.—55. *Risāla fī-mā yataʿallaq bi-laylat al-niṣf min Shaʿbān* Alex. Fun. 97$_{,3}$, 178$_{,1}$, Cairo ^{1}VII, 133, ^{2}I, 52.—56. *Risāla fī bayān* (*karāhat*) *ifrād al-ṣalāt ʿani ʾl-salām*,
521 on whether it is permissible to merely use the word | *ṣallā* in the blessing for Muḥammad, or whether one has to add *sallama*, as maintained by al-Nawawī, Berl. 3926, Patna II, 387$_{,2568, 48}$, entitled *Taqwiyat baḥth al-imām al-Jazarī maʿa al-imām al-Nawawī* Munich 886, f. 122, with an appendix by ʿAlī b. Muḥammad al-Dāghistānī al-Shirwānī, ibid. 123.—57. *Mawʿiẓat al-ḥabīb wa-tuḥfat al-khaṭīb*, on the sermons by Muḥammad and his successors, composed in 1011/1602, Berl. 3945.—58. *Lubb lubāb al-manāsik wa-ḥubb ʿubāb al-masālik*, on customs surrrounding the pilgrimage, Berl. 4054 (= NO 1647?), Cairo ^{1}III, 116, Turkish translation ibid.—59. *Bidāyat al-sālik fī nihāyat al-masālik* see below p. 416.—60. *al-Ḥaẓẓ al-awfar fi ʾl-ḥajj al-akbar*, in particular about *yawm al-ʿArafa*, composed in 1007/1598 in Mecca, Berl. 4056, Garr. 2001$_{,14}$, Cairo ^{1}VII, 131, 289, Patna II, 384$_{,2568, 17}$.—61. *Wujūb ṭawāf al-bayt ʿala ʾl-anām wa-law kāna baʿd al-inhidām*, on whether the pilgrimage would be void if the Kaʿba collapsed, Berl. 4057, Garr. 2001$_{,23}$, Cairo ^{1}VII, 130, 684.—62. *al-Ṣanīʿa fī taḥqīq al-buqʿa al-manīʿa* Munich 886, f. 13, Garr. 2001$_{,30}$, Cairo ^{1}VII, 23, ^{2}I, 408, Patna II, 284$_{,2568, 23}$.—63. *al-Dhakhīra al-kathīra fī rajāʾ maghfirat al-kabīra*, on whether the

prescribed performance of the pilgrimage entails being forgiven one's major sins, Berl. 4058, Cairo ^{1}VII, 23, 73, 132, 631, ^{2}I, 422, Patna II, 383,$_{2568,\ 14}$.—64. *Bayān fi'l al-khayr idhā dakhala Makka man ḥajja ʿani 'l-ghayr* Berl. 4059, Gotha 1084, | Cairo ^{1}VII, 24, 130, 142, ^{2}I, 496, Patna II, 383,$_{2568,\ 24}$.—65. *Iḥrām al-āfāqī*, 397
on whether a Meccan who was on a journey has any use from returning as a pilgrim and performing the pilgrimage in the month of Dhu 'l-Ḥijja, Berl. 4060.—66. *al-ʿAfāf ʿan waḍʿ al-yad ʿala 'l-ṣadr ḥāl al-ṭawāf*, composed in 1010/1601, Berl. 4061, Garr. 2001,$_{24}$, Cairo ^{1}VII, 24, 130, 684.—67. *al-Iṣṭināʿ fi 'l-iḍṭibāʿ*, on the custom, during the pilgrimage, of walking around with one's cloak held under one's right armpit and slung over one's left shoulder, Berl. 4062, Cairo ^{1}VII, 25, 132, 644, ^{2}I, 401, Garr. 2001,$_{31}$.—68. *al-Ilʿām bi-faḍāʾil al-bayt al-ḥarām* Berl. 4063.—69. *al-Durra al-muḍīʾa fī ziyārat al-raḍiyya*, on visiting the prophet's grave in Medina, Berl. 4064, Munich 886, f. 145, Alex. Taʾr. 7, Cairo ^{1}VII, 45, Patna II, 379,$_{2568,\ 4}$.—70. *al-Qawl al-ḥaqīq fī mawqif al-ṣiddīq* or *al-Wuqūf bil-taḥqīq*, on whether Abū Bakr and ʿAlī, when they were sent by Muḥammad on the pilgrimage in the year 9/630, did or did not execute the *wuqūf* in ʿArafa, Berl. 4064, Cairo ^{1}VII, 23.—71. *Anwār al-ḥujaj fī asrār al-ḥijaj*, Berl. 4066, Cairo ^{1}VII, 23.—72. *Risāla fī bayān al-tamattuʿ fī ashhur al-ḥajj lil-muqīm bi-Makka* Cairo ^{1}VII, 130, 684.— | 73. *al-Maslak al-mutaqassiṭ fi 'l-maslak* 522
al-mutawassiṭ see Suppl. 524, 1b., 1, Vienna 1678.—74. *Fatwā fī suʾāl mansūb ilā buṭlān al-nikāḥ*, on whether the names of the grandparents are necessary for the valid conclusion of a marriage, Berl. 4673.—75. *Risāla fi 'l-nikāḥ* Cairo ^{1}VII, 25.—76. *al-Nisba al-murattaba fi 'l-maʿrifa wal-maḥabba* Berl. 5414, Cairo ^{1}VII, 132, Patna II, 373,$_{2569,\ 39}$.—77. *Maʿrifat al-nussāk fī faḍīlat al-siwāk*, on the toothpick, based on sura 3,$_{29}$, Berl. 5443, Garr. 2001,$_{9}$, Cairo ^{1}VII, 134, Patna II, 386,$_{2568,\ 41,\ 52}$.—78. *al-Taṣrīḥ fī sharḥ al-tasrīḥ* on beards and haircuts, Berl. 5446, Munich 886, f. 80b, Alex. Fun. 97,$_{3}$, Cairo ^{1}VII, 22, 131, Garr. 2001,$_{17}$, Patna II, 386,$_{2568,\ 38}$.—79. (*al-Maqāla al-ʿadhba*) *fī masʾalat al-ʿimāma wal-ʿadhaba*, on the turban, Berl. 5460, Garr. 2001,$_{10}$, Cairo ^{1}VII, 24, 131, 390, Patna II, 386,$_{2568,37}$.—80. *al-Iʿtināʾ bil-ghināʾ*, in defence of music and singing, Berl. 5518, Munich 816, f. 11, Garr. 2001,$_{18}$, Alex. Fun. 97,$_{1}$, Patna II, 379,$_{2568,\ 5,\ 2569,\ 8}$.—81. *Risāla fi 'l-samāʿ wal-ghināʾ* Berl. 5519, Cairo ^{1}VI, 26, 134.—82. *Fatḥ al-asmāʿ fī sharḥ al-samāʿ* Garr. 2001,$_{19}$, Cairo ^{1}VII, 133, *Nashra* 20.—83. *al-Risāla al-ʿaṭāʾiyya fi 'l-farq bayna safada wa-asfada wa-mā mithluhā* Cairo ^{1}II, Patna II, 2, 379,2569, $_{47}$.—84. *Farāʾid al-qalāʾid ʿalā aḥādīth Sharḥ al-ʿAqāʾid* (I, 548), Cairo ^{1}VII, 24.—85. *Tasliyat al-aʿmā ʿan baliyyat al-ʿamā*, 40 *ḥadīth*, Berl. 8847, Alex. Mawāʿiẓ 10, Cairo ^{1}VII, 25, 132, ^{2}I, 97, 279.—86. *Farr al-ʿawn min muddaʿī īmān Firʿawn* see p. 282,$_{7}$.—87. *Risāla fi 'l-karāma li-baʿḍ al-awliyāʾ* Cairo ^{1}VII, 131, 621.—88. *Nāmūs al-maʾnūs* p. 233.—89. *Tabʿīd al-ʿulamāʾ ʿan taqrīb al-umarāʾ* Berl. 5585, Munich 886, f. 87, Patna II, 390,$_{2569,\ 14}$.—90. *Arbaʿūna ḥadīthan fī faḍāʾil*

al-nikāḥ Berl. 5594.—91. *Taḥqīq al-iḥtisāb fī tadqīq al-intisāb*, proof that it is not
shameful to descend from a female slave (in respect of his son Ibrāhīm), Berl.
5600, Munich 886, f. 205b, Patna II, 384,$_{2568,\ 20}$.—92. *Ghāyat al-taḥqīq*
wa-nihāyat al-tadqīq, a treatise on six issues relating to ritual prayer, Gotha 712,
Cairo ^{1}VII, 68.—93. *Kanz al-akhbār fi 'l-adʿiya wa-mā jāʾa min al-āthār* Cairo ^{1}II,
398 209, ^{2}I, 349. |—94. *al-Mawrid al-rawī (rabawī) fi 'l-mawlid al-nabawī* Berl. 8545,
Munich 886 f. 132b, Algiers 724,$_1$, 1694, Garr. 2001,$_2$, Cairo ^{1}VII, 26, ^{2}I, 154, 160.
Patna II, 381,$_{2528,\ 2}$.—95. *Risāla fī awlād al-nabī* Berl. 9645, Cairo ^{1}V, 198.—96.
Istiʾnās al-nās bi-faḍāʾil Ibn ʿAbbās Berl. 9673, Cairo ^{1}VII, 25, ^{2}V, 23.—97.
523 *al-Maʿdin al-ʿAdanī fī faḍāʾil Uways al-Qaranī* | (d. 37/657), Berl. 10067, Munich
886, f. 108, Algiers 724,$_9$, Patna II, 324,$_{2368,\ 27}$, print. Istanbul 1307.—98. *Nuzhat*
al-khāṭir al-fātir fī tarjamat al-shaykh ʿAbd al-Qādir, Algiers 724,$_{18}$, Alex. Taṣ. 45,
Cairo ^{1}VII, 26, ^{2}V, 387.—99. *Sharḥ Bānat Suʿād* Suppl. I, 69.—100.–160. see
Suppl.—161.–72. Suppl. III, 1295.—173. *Risāla fi 'l-jamʿ bayna 'l-ṣalātayn* Patna
II, 382,$_{2568,\ 11,\ 12}$.—174. *Maqāla fī bayān al-Khiḍr* ibid. 389,$_{1569,1}$ (= 34?).—175.
Mirqāt al-mafātīḥ I, 449.—176. *Dhayl martabat al-wujūd* Patna II, 384,$_{2568,\ 16}$.—
177. *Fayḍ al-fāʾiḍ, sharḥ al-Rāʾiḍ fi 'l-farāʾiḍ* (no. 107), ibid. 381,$_{2528,\ 1}$.—178. *Ḥizb*
al-baḥr ibid. 384,$_{2568,\ 28}$.—179. *Risāla fī taḥqīq ḥadīth al-barāʾ fī bāb al-ṣalāt*
ibid. 30,$_{49}$.—180. *Ṭurfat al-himyān fī tuḥfat al-ʿimyān* ibid. 385,$_{31}$.—181. *Risāla fī*
awlādihi wa-azwājihi ṣlʿm ibid. 2569,$_{18,\ 34}$.—182. *al-Azhiya fi 'l-naḥw* Um. 865.

3. Ḥusayn b. Sāmī al-Hattārī al-Madanī, ca. 1100/1688.

1. *Abdaʿ mā kāna wa-ajwad mā yastafīduhu 'l-ṭullāb*, an encyclopaedia, Berl. 92.—2. *Mukhtaṣar etc.* see Suppl., Garr. 1051.—3. *Miʿrāj al-albāb ilā ʿilm al-ḥisāb* Bank. XXII 2426.

Chapter 4. South Arabia

Just as South Arabian culture fell into decay in the first century CE as a result of developments in trade on which its flourishing had been based, the Muslim culture of Yemen too, was adversely influenced by shifts in world trade that occurred around the beginning of the fifteenth century. From the moment that the affluence of the country was no longer sustained from the outside, its capital Zabīd lost its significance for Arabic literature.[1] Nevertheless, this decline was by no means as pronounced as it was in Mesopotamia; indeed, at the court of the Zaydī imams, the poetry, historiography, and theology of this sect were assiduously pursued until the end of the nineteenth century.

| Wüst. *Ṣūf.* = F. Wüstenfeld, *Die Çūfiten in Südarabien in XI (XVII) Jhrh.*, Abh. d. Kgl. Ges. d. Wiss. zu Göttingen, vol. 30 (1883); idem, *Jemen im XI (XVII)*, ibid. vol. 32 (1884). 524

1 *Poetry and Belles Lettres*

1. ʿAbd al-Laṭīf Sirāj al-Dīn b. ʿAlī al-Qāsiʿī, ca. 950/1543.

Al-Sāʾiq al-shāʾiq ila ʾl-sharāb al-fāʾiq al-rāʾiq or *al-Nūr al-bāhir wal-nawr al-zāhir*, poems in praise of the Prophet, of other indivuduals, | of the *Mulḥat al-iʿrāb* (I, 328), the *Alfiyyat b. Mālik* (I, 359), and the *Kitāb al-Shifāʾ* (I, 455), e.g. Leid. 748. 399

2. Sharaf al-Dīn Muḥammad b. ʿAbdallāh al-Mutawakkil ʿala ʾllāh b. Yaḥyā, a grandson of the renewer of the Zaydī dynasty in Yemen, was born in 930/1531 and died in 1011/1601.

Hartmann, *Muw.* 67. *Dīwān*, entitled *al-Rawḍ al-marhūm wal-durr al-manẓūm*, collected by ʿĪsā b. Luṭfallāh b. al-Muṭahhar, d. 1048/1638, Leid. 751, as an appendix to which are the *Muwashshaḥāt*, most of which have an introduction on the occasion of their composition, completed in 1030/1621 after a period of over 20 years, Berl. 8173,2.

3. Shams al-Dīn Muḥammad al-Yamanī al-Sharjī, ca. 999/1590.

Tuḥfat al-aṣḥāb wa-nuzhat dhawi ʾl-albāb, an *adab* work, Berl. 8420 (see Suppl.), Leid 523, Paris 3556, 5984, Br. Mus. Suppl. 1150, Garr. 216.

---

1 See Snouck Hurgronje, *ZDMG* 53, 142, n. 3.

4. Aḥmad b. Abi 'l-Qāsim al-Ḍamrī Shams al-Dīn, ca. 1010/1601.

A poem in praise of the imam al-Qāsim b. Muḥammad, d. 1029/1620, Berl. 7953.

6. Aḥmad b. Aḥmad b. Muḥammad b. al-Hādī al-ʿĀnisī, who died around 1030/1640, see Suppl.

Dīwān Berl. 7972,$_2$.—A *qaṣīda* (by his son?), ibid. 3.

525 | 7. Al-Sayyid Aḥmad b. al-Ḥasan b. Aḥmad b. Ḥamīd al-Dīn lived around 1070/1659 in Kawkabān, Shibām, and Ṣanʿāʾ.

Tarwīḥ al-mashūq fī talwīḥ al-burūq, poems by the author and his friends with an aesthetical and historical commentary, Br. Mus. 1674.

7a. Al-Ḥusayn b. ʿAbd al-Qādir b. al-Nāṣir al-Mutawakkil, who died in 1112/1700 in Shibām, see Suppl.

1. *al-Qawl al-ḥasan etc.* Garr. 124.

7b. ʿAbd al-Bāqī b. ʿAbd al-Raḥīm al-Nāzilī al-Ḥasanī, ca 1074/1663 (?).

Natījat al-fikr etc. Garr. 119.—2. *Badīʿiyya* ibid. 120.

8. Al-Sayyid Fakhr al-Dīn ʿAbdallāh b. ʿAlī b. Muḥammad b. ʿAbd al-ʿĀl al-Wazīrī, who flourished at the beginning of the twelfth century.

1. *Aqrāṭ al-dhahab fi 'l-mufākhara bayna 'l-Rawḍa wa-Biʾr al-ʿArab*, two places near Ṣanʿāʾ, Leid. 442.—2. A *dīwān*, entitled *Jawārish al-afrāḥ wa-qūt al-arwāḥ*, ibid. 768, Gotha 2342/3.—3. *Ṭabaq al-ḥalwāʾ wa-ṣiḥāf al-mann wal-salwā*, a history of Yemen covering the period 1046–90/1636–79, composed in 1118/1706, Br. Mus. Suppl. 592, Landb.-Br. 246.

9. Ibrāhīm b. Ṣāliḥ al-Muhtadī Ṣārim al-Dīn al-Hindī, whose father had emigrated from India to Yemen, died in 1102/1690.

Ibn Maʿṣūm, *Sulāfat al-ʿaṣr* 477/85. 1. *al-ʿArf al-nadī min shiʿr al-Ṣārim al-Hindī*, *Dīwān* compiled by his son, Gotha 2330.—2. *Barāhīn al-iḥtijāj wal-munāẓara fī-mā waqaʿa bayna ʾl-qaws wal-bunduq min al-mufākhara*, a *badīʿiyya* poem in honour of the grandson of the Zaydī caliph of Ṣanʿāʾ, Aḥmad b. al-Ḥasan, together with some other works, Leid. 766.

| 11. Aḥmad b. Aḥmad b. Muḥammad al-ʿĀdawī, ca. 1110/1698. 400

Al-ʿAlam al-mufrad shiʿr al-Mutanabbiʾ Aḥmad, 1. Religious poems, 2. Poems in praise of the descendants of the last ʿAbbāsid caliph, al-Mutawakkil ʿala ʾllāh, d. 945/1538 in Egypt, who played a leading role as *umarāʾ al-muʾminīn* in Yemen between 1094–1114/1683–1703, Paris 3258.

| 11a. ʿImād al-Dīn Yaḥyā b. Ibrāhim b. ʿAlī al-Jaḥḥāfī, ca. 1114/1702. 526

Dīwān see Suppl., under the title *Ghidhāʾ al-arwāḥ* also Berl. or. qu. 2027 (Fischer-Burch. 3).

11b. Al-Qāḍī ʿAlī b. Muḥammad b. Aḥmad al-ʿAnsī, ca. 1120/1708.

1. *Dīwān* Berl. Ms. or. oct. 3770 (Fischer-Burch. 19).—2. See Suppl.

12. Aḥmad b. Muḥammad b. al-Ḥasan b. Aḥmad al-Yamanī al-Kawkabānī al-Ḥaymī completed, in 1143/1730 in Ṣanʿāʾ:

1. *Ṭīb al-samar fī awqāt al-saḥar*, on contemporary poets, with examples of their poems, Berl. 7425/6, Br. Mus. Suppl. 675/6.—2. See Suppl.

13. Ṣafī al-Dīn Aḥmad b. Muḥammad b. ʿAbd al-Hādī al-Qāṭin lived in Ṣanʿāʾ and Kawkabān, spent the years 1171–2/1757–8 in prison, and died on 7 Jumādā I 1199/19 March 1785.

A collection of his poems, Br. Mus. Suppl. 1124.

14. Ḍiyāʾ al-Dīn Shaʿbān b. Sālim al-Rūmī, who died in 1149/1736, see Suppl.

2. *al-Manẓūma fi ʾl-maʾkūlāt* Patna II, $423_{,2594,1}$, $424_{,2594,3}$.—3. *al-Kalima al-muḥkama etc.* ibid. $424_{,2594,\,2}$.

15.—20. See Suppl. (19. Poems, Landb.-Br. 352, wrongly Qānī).

2 *Philology*

1.–3. See Suppl. (to 1, also 917, 28).

4. Ḍiyāʾ al-Dīn Luṭfallāh b. Muḥammad b. al-Ghiyāth, who lived for a time in Mecca and died in 1035/1625 in Ẓafīr.

Muḥ. III, 303/5, Wüst. *Jemen*, 43. 1. *al-Ījāz fī ʿilm al-iʿjāz*, an appendix to *Talkhīṣ al-Miftāḥ* (I, 353), Leid. 339, Ind. Off. 264, no. 954.—2.–4. See Suppl.

5. See Suppl. and 918, 35.

527 | ### 3 *Historiography*

1. Abū ʿAbdallāh ʿAbd al-Raḥmān b. ʿAlī b. Muḥammad b. ʿUmar b. ʿAlī b. Yūsuf Wajīh al-Dīn al-Shaybānī al-Zabīdī b. al-Daybaʿ[1] was born on 2 Muḥarram 866/8 October 1461 in Zabīd, and studied there and in Bayt al-Faqīh. He started his literary activity after his pilgrimage in the year 896/1491. Because of his *History of Zabīd* he gained the acclaim of Sultan Ṣalāḥ al-Dīn al-Malik al-Muẓaffar
401 (al-Ẓāfir) ʿĀmir b. Ṭāhir, | and at the latter's request wrote a separate history of that dynasty in his now-lost *al-ʿIqd al-bāhir* (see Suppl.). In a gesture of gratitude for this he was given a palmgrove near Zabīd and appointed teacher of *ḥadīth* at the town's central mosque. He died in Zabīd on 17 Rajab 944/21 December 1537.

Wüst. *Gesch.* 518. 1. *Bughyat al-mustafīd fī akhbār madīnat Zabīd*, running up to 901/1495, with the autobiography of the author as a *khātima*, Berl. 9763, Copenhagen 141, Pet. Ros. 47, Br. Mus. 1583, Suppl. 586, Cairo V, [1]138, [2]59, Makr. 7, Garr. 625, an appendix, *al-Faḍl al-mazīd*, up to 923/1517, and again to 924/1518, Berl. 9764, Pet. Ros. 47,$_{2,\ 3}$, Cairo V, [1]139, [2]290, Makr. 50.—Abstract: *Historia Jemanae e cod. ms. ar. concinnata ed.* C. Th. Johannsen, Bonn 1828.—2. *Qurrat al-ʿuyūn fī akhbār al-Yaman al-maymūn*, a slightly different adaptation of the same history running to 923/1517, Br. Mus. 1474, Suppl. 587, Cairo V, [1]104, 2294.—3. *Aḥsan al-sulūk fī man waliya madīnat Zabīd min al-mulūk*, a chronological overview in verse until 923/1517, as an appendix to Br. Mus. 1583, Paris 5832.—4. *Tamyīz al-ṭayyib min al-khabīth bi-mā yadūru ʿalā alsinat al-nās min al-ḥadīth* p. 44.—5. *Taysīr al-wuṣūl ilā jāmiʿ al-uṣūl min ḥadīth al-rasūl* I, 439.—6.–8. see Suppl. (8. C. 1345).

---

1 This word is said to mean 'white' in the language of the Nubians, cod. Goth. 2, f. 116v, Muḥ. III, 192, Ulugkhani, *Hist. of Gujarat* I, 49, as a nickname of his grandfather.

2. ʿUmar b. Muḥammad b. Aḥmad b. Abī Bakr Bā Shaybān b. Muḥammad b. Asadallāh b. Ḥasan b. ʿAlī b. Muḥammad al-Ustādh al-Aʿẓam was born in Tarīm in 880/1475 and died in 944/1537.

| Wüst. *Ṣūf.* 81. *Tiryāq asqām al-qulūb fī dhikr ḥikāyāt al-sāda al-ashrāf* Br. Mus. 528
1645.

3. Muḥammad b. Yaḥyā al-Muṭayyab al-Ḥanafī, who lived in Zabīd around 990/1582.

Bulūgh al-marām fī taʾrīkh mawlānā Bahrām, a history of Yemen under Bahrām Pāshā, 977–83/1569–75, Paris 1651, 3.

4. ʿĀmir b. Muḥammad b. Ḥasan al-Duʿāmī was a State Secretary under the princes Shams al-Dīn and ʿIzz al-Dīn who, at the time of the Turkish invasion of Yemen, occupied the Kawkabān fortress near Ṣanʿāʾ. In this capacity he was, in person or by letter, in charge of negotions with Arab princes and their Turkish commanders, and particularly with Pāshā Ḥasan b. al-Ḥusayn, newly appointed in 988/1580, and with whom ʿIzz al-Dīn concluded an alliance. He wrote his memoirs in

Al-Rawḍ al-ḥasan fī akhbār siyar mawlānā ṣāḥib al-saʿāda al-Bāsha Ḥasan fī ayyām wilāyatihi bi-iqlīm al-Yaman, covering the years 988–93/1580–5, Leid.
945, | *Historia Jemanae sub Hasano Pascha ed.* A. Rutgers, Leid. 1838, Wüst. 402
Gesch. 540.

5b. Aḥmad b. Yūsuf b. Muḥammad Fayrūz, fl. tenth century.

Maṭāliʿ al-nīrān, a history of Yemen in the tenth century, Paris 1651,$_1$, cf. de Sacy, *Not. et Extr.* IV, 595.

5c. ʿAbdallāh b. Dāʿir b. Ṣāliḥ.

ʿIqd al-laʾālī, a history of Jaʿfar Pāshā, 1016–35/1607–25, Patna I, 281,$_{2304}$.

5d. The Zaydī imam Muḥammad b. ʿAbdallāh b. al-Ḥusayn al-Muʾayyad wrote, in 1030/1626:

Rawḍat al-albāb wa-tuḥfat al-aḥbāb wa-nukhabat al-aḥsāb fī maʿrifat al-ansāb, on Muḥammad's pedigree, with genealogical tables, Berl, 9402, Ambr. B 7 (*RASO* IV, 94), 18ii (ibid. 99), Cairo ^{2}V, 207.

6. ʿĪsā b. Luṭfallāh b. al-Muṭahhar b. Sharaf al-Dīn Yaḥyā al-Yamanī b. 529 Rasūlallāh was born in Dhumarmar in 986/1578, | joined the victorious Turks, by whom his father had been carried off to Istanbul in 994/1586, and died in 1048/1638.

1. *Rawḥ al-rūḥ fī-mā ḥadatha baʿd al-miʾa al-tāsiʿa min al-fitan wal-futūḥ*, a history of Yemen covering the years 900–1029/1494–1620, Berl. 9743, or. qu. 2033 (Fischer-Burch. 27) volume I, until 963/1558, Garr. 618, Alex. Taʾr. $72,_{2,\,3}$, Br. Mus. Suppl. 590, Cairo V, ^{1}90, 139, ^{2}203, see Suppl.

6a. Shams al-Dīn Aḥmad b. Muḥammad b. Ṣalāḥ al-Sharafī, d. 1055/1646, see Suppl.

Al-Laʾāliʾ al-muḍīʾa etc. additionally Patna I, $278,_{2303}$.

7. Al-Ḥasan b. Aḥmad b. Ṣāliḥ b. Dughaysh al-Ḥaymī al-Kawkabānī al-Shibāmī Sharaf al-Dīn was born in 1018/1608, and travelled from 1 Jumādā II 1057/4 July 1647 until 4 Rabīʿ I 1059/19 March 1649 as an envoy of the Zaydī imam al-Mutawakkil ʿala ʾllāh, from his fortress of Shahāra to the king of Abyssinia, Fāsilādās (1632–70), in Gondar. He died a *qāḍī* in Kawkabān in 1071/1660.

Muḥ. II, 16. *Sīrat al-Qāḍī Sharaf al-Dīn al-Ḥasan b. Aḥmad al-Ḥasan fī dukhūlihi arḍ al-Ḥabasha. Der Gesandtschaftsbericht des H. b. A. al-Ḥ., hsg. v.* F.E. Peiser, Berlin 1894; idem, *Zur Geschichte Abessiniens im 17. Jhrh. Der Gesandtschaftsbericht des H. b. A. El-H.*, Berlin 1898.—2. *Ladhdhat al-wasan*, a collection of poems and letters, Berl. 8430.—3.–5. see Suppl.

8. Al-Muṭahhar b. Muḥammad al-Jurmūzī al-Yamanī al-Ḥasanī, who was born in 1003/1594 and died in 1077/1666.

Muḥ. IV, 406. 1. *al-Jawhara al-muḍīʾa fī taʾrīkh al-khilāfa al-Muʾayyadiyya*, part 2, containing a detailed history of the Zaydī imam al-Muʾayyad billāh Muḥammad b. al-Qāsim, who was born in 990/1582 and died in 1054/1644, Berl. 9744.—2. *al-Nubdha al-mushīra ilā jumal min ʿuyūn al-sīra fī akhbār mawlānā al-Manṣūr billāh al-Qāsim b. Muḥammad*, d. 1029/1620 (p. 534), Br. Mus. Suppl. 543.—3. See Suppl.

530 | 9. Ismāʿīl b. Muḥammad b. al-Ḥasan b. al-Qāsim b. Muḥammad, d. 1079/1668, see Suppl.

Muḥ. I, 416. *Simṭ al-laʾāl fī shiʿr al-āl*, on the poetical achievements of the Zaydī imams, as a commentary to a *qaṣīda* in which he lists their names, Leid. 918, Br. Mus. Suppl. 673/4.

10. Al-Sayyid Jamāl al-Dīn Muḥammad b. Ibrāhīm b. al-Mufaḍḍal b. Ibrāhīm b. ʿAlī b. al-Imām Yaḥyā Sharaf al-Dīn was born in 1022/1613, studied in Ṣanʿāʾ, | Kawkabān, and Shibām, then lived in Wādī Zuhr, before dying in Shibām in 403 1085/1674.

Muḥ. III, 318, Wüst. Jemen, p. 70. *Al-Sulūk al-dhahabiyya fī khulāṣat al-sīra al-Mutawakkiliyya*, on the life of Imam al-Mutawakkil ʿala ʾllāh Sharaf al-Dīn, Br. Mus. Suppl. 542.

11. Yaḥyā b. al-Ḥusayn b. al-Muʾayyad billāh, who died in 1090/1679, see Suppl.

Anbāʾ (*Abnāʾ*) *al-zaman fī akhbār al-Yaman*, a history of Yemen, with due consideration for other countries having relations with it, from the birth of Muḥammad until 1045/1635, Berl. 9745, Patna I, $281_{,2315}$ for abstracts see Suppl. (a. with additions from *Ṭīb al-kisāʾ* no. $13_{,3}$).

12. Yūsuf b. Yaḥyā b. al-Ḥusayn al-Ḥasanī al-Ṣanʿānī Ḍiyāʾ al-Dīn Abū Isḥāq wrote, in 1111/1700:

Nasamāt al-saḥar bi-dhikr man tashayyaʿa wa-shaʿar, 197 biographies of Shīʿī poets from the first century until his own time, Berl. 7423, ʿA. Emīrī Ar. 2207 (autograph).

13. Ḥusām al-Dīn al-Muḥassin b. al-Ḥasan Abū Ṭālib b. Aḥmad, who died after 1161/1748.

1.–2. see Suppl.—3. *Ṭīb ahl al-kisāʾ wal-fulk alladhī ʿalā jūdi ʾl-najāh rasā*, an adaptation of the *sīra* of Imam al-Manṣūr billāh (§ 5, B 5), arranged by year, with additions concerning the lives of his successors, covering the years 1001–1161/1592–1749, Wehbī 1312.

4 Ḥadīth

1. ʿAbd al-Laṭīf b. ʿAlī b. Ibrāhīm al-Dayrabī b. al-Khaṭīb wrote, in 932/1526:

| *Lawāmiʿ al-durar bi-mā lil-siwāk min al-athar*, 180 *rajaz* verses on the tooth- 531 pick, based on a work by Aḥmad b. Abī Bakr b. Muḥammad al-Yamanī al-Shāfiʿī Abu ʾl-ʿAbbās Shihāb al-Dīn (Aḥmad) b. al-Raddād, d. 821/1418, Berl. 5442.

1a. ʿAqīl b. ʿUmar b. ʿImrān al-ʿAlawī, who died in 1062/1652, see Suppl.

3. *Sharḥ al-kabāʾir* Patna I, 122,$_{1229}$ (which has: al-Mālikī).—4., 5. see Suppl. 1002, 58.

2. Shihāb al-Dīn Aḥmad b. ʿĀmir b. al-Ḥusayn al-Saʿdī al-Ḥaḍramī al-Shāfiʿī wrote, in 1087/1666:

Sharḥ al-ṣadr fī asmāʾ ahl Badr Cairo V, ^{1}72, ^{2}221, print. C., n.d.

3. Khālid b. al-Ḥusayn al-Ḥaḍramawtī, ca. 1100/1688.

Fatḥ Allāh al-karīm fī ithbāt anna Muḥammadan lā nabiyya baʿdahu ʿala ʾl-taʿmīm, against the claim that, if Muḥammad's son Ibrāhīm had remained alive, he would have been a prophet, Berl. 2550, Qawala I, 206.

7. Al-Sayyid Muḥammad b. Muḥammad al-Saqqāf al-Bāʿalawī wrote, in 1095/1684:

Manẓūmat Durrat al-ṣafāʾ li-ikhwat al-wafāʾ fī īmān abaway al-Muṣṭafā Alex. Fun. 122, 2.

5 *Fiqh*

A The Shāfiʿīs

1. Qāḍi ʾl-quḍāt Ṣafī al-Dīn Abu ʾl-ʿAbbās Aḥmad b. al-Faqīh Taqī al-Dīn ʿUmar b. Muḥammad b. ʿAbd al-Raḥmān b. Najm al-Dīn b. Abi ʾl-Maḥāsin Yūsuf b. Muḥammad al-Sayfī al-Murādī b. al-Madhḥijī, who died in Zabīd in 930/1523, see Suppl.

404 | 1. *Tajrīd al-zawāʾid wa-taqrīb al-fawāʾid*, Cairo ^{1}III, 201.—2. *Tuḥfat al-ṭullāb*, in verse, completed in 929/1522, ibid. 204.—3. *al-ʿUbāb al-muḥīṭ bi-muʿẓam nuṣūṣ al-Shāfiʿī wal-aṣḥāb* ibid. 244.

1a. Jamāl al-Dīn Muḥammad b. ʿUmar b. Mubārak Baḥraq, d. 930/1524, see Suppl.

532 | 3. *Tarjamat al-mustafīd fi ʾl-tajwīd* additionally Garr. 2070,$_{2}$.

1b. Ṣāliḥ b. Ṣiddīq al-Namāzī, d. 975/1567, see Suppl.

4. *Silsilat al-ibrīz etc.* Berl. 4912 (labelled as '40 Traditions').—5. *al-Qawl al-wajīz*, with a commentary, Ambr. B^ii 35.

2. Wajīh al-Dīn ʿAbd al-Raḥmān b. ʿAbd al-Karīm b. Ibrāhīm b. ʿAlī b. Ziyād al-Ghaythī al-Muqṣirī al-Zabīdī al-Shāfiʿī was born in Rajab 900/April 1495 and died in Zabīd on 11 Rajab 975/11 January 1568.

1. *Īḍāḥ al-nuṣūṣ al-mufṣiḥa bi-buṭlān tazwīj al-walī al-wāqiʿ ʿalā ghayr al-ḥaẓẓ wal-maṣlaḥa*, composed in Rajab 946/November 1539, Cairo ¹VII, 391.—2. *Īrād al-nuqūl al-madhhabiyya ʿan dhawi ʾl-taḥqīq fī Anti ṭāliq ʿalā ṣiḥḥat al-barāʾa min ṣiyagh al-muʿāwaḍa lā al-taʿlīq*, ibid.—3. *al-Fatḥ al-mubīn fī aḥkām tabarruʿ al-madīn* ibid. ²I, 530.—4. *Kashf al-ghiṭāʾ ʿammā waqaʿa fī tabarruʿ al-madīn min al-labs wal-khaṭāʾ* ibid. ¹VII, 391, ²I, 535.—5. *Khulāṣat al-Fatḥ al-mubīn* (no. 3), ibid. ¹VII, 392, ²I, 513.—6. *al-Maqāla al-nāṣṣa ʿalā ṣiḥḥat mā fī ʾl-Fatḥ wal-Dhayl wal-Khulāṣa* ibid. ²I, 540.—7. *Ṣūrat mukātaba*, correspondence on matters of *fiqh* with Raḍī al-Dīn al-Qāzānī al-Miṣrī in Mecca, ibid. ¹VII, 392.—8. *al-Ajwiba al-marḍiyya ʿani ʾl-asʾila al-Makkiyya*, collected by one of his students, ibid.—9. *al-Radd ʿalā man awhama anna tark al-ramy lil-ʿudhr yusqiṭ al-dam* ibid.—10. *Taḥdhīr aʾimmat al-islām ʿan taghyīr bināʾ al-bayt al-ḥarām* ibid.—11. *al-Jawāb al-muḥarrar li-aḥkām al-munshaṭ wal-mukhaddar* ibid.—12. *Iqāmat al-burhān ʿalā kammiyyat al-tarāwīḥ fī Ramaḍān* ibid. ¹VII, 393, ²I, 498.—13. *Taḥrīr al-maqāl fī ḥukm man akhbara bi-ruʾyat hilāl Shawwāl* ibid. ¹VII, 393.—14. *Fatḥ al-karīm al-wāḥid fī inkār taʾkhīr al-ṣalāt ʿalā aʾimmat al-masājid* ibid. ¹VII, 393, ²I, 530.—15. *al-Nuqūl al-ʿadhba al-maʿīna al-mustafād min-hā ṣiḥḥat bayʿ al-ʿīna* ibid. ¹VII, 393, ²I, 545.—16. *al-Jawāb al-matīn ʿani ʾl-suʾāl al-wārid min al-balad al-amīn* ibid. ¹VII, 393, ²I, 508.—17. *Ithbāt sunnat rafʿ al-yadayn ʿinda ʾl-iḥrām wal-rukūʿ wal-iʿtidāl wal-qiyām min ithnayn* ibid. ¹VII, 393, ²I, 495.—18. *Kashf al-jilbāb ʿan aḥkām tataʿallaq bil-miḥrāb*, composed in Dhu ʾl-Ḥijja 970/August 1563, ibid. ¹VII, 393, ²I, 535.—19. *Risāla fī ḥukm mā idhā musikha aḥad al-zawjayn ḥajaran aw ḥayawānan qabl al-dukhūl* ibid. ¹VII, 394, ²I, 516.—20. *Bughyat al-mushtāq ilā taḥrīr al-madārik fī taṣdīq muddaʿi ʾl-infāq* ibid. | ¹VII, 394, ²I, 501.—21. *Kashf al-ghumma ʿan ḥukm al-maqbūḍ* 533
ʿammā fī ʾl-dhimma wa-kawn al-milk fīhi mawqūfan ʿinda ʾl-aʾimma ibid. ¹VIII, 394, ²I, 535.—22. *Muzīl al-ʿanāʾ fī aḥkām mā uḥditha fī ʾl-arāḍi ʾl-mazrūʿa min al-fanāʾ* ibid. ¹VII, 394, ²I, 538.—23. *Ḥall al-maʿqūd wa-aḥkām al-mafqūd* ibid. ¹VII, 394, I, 512.—24. *Faṣl al-khiṭāb fī ḥukm al-duʿāʾ bi-īṣāl al-thawāb* ibid. ¹VII, 394, ²I, 532.—25. *Isʿāf al-mustaftī ʿan qawl al-rajul limraʾatihi anti ukhtī* ibid. ¹VII, 394, ²I, 497.—26. *al-Ajwiba al-muḥarrara ʿani ʾl-masāʾil al-wārida min bilād al-Mahra* ibid. ¹VII, 394, ²I, 495.—27. *Īḍāḥ al-dalāla fī anna ʾl-ʿadāwa al-māniʿa*

min qabūl al-shahāda tujāmiʿ al-ʿadāla ibid. [1]VII, 394, [2]I, 500.—38. *Shadd al-yadayn ʿalā dafʿ mā nusiba ila ʾl-Zuhrī min al-wahm fī ḥadīth al-yadayn* ibid. [1]VII, 395.—29. *al-Mawāhib al-saniyya fi ʾl-ajwiba ʿani ʾl-masāʾil al-ʿAdaniyya* (*ʿurfiyya*) ibid. [1]VII, 395, [2]I, 542.—30. *Simṭ al-laʾāl fi ʾl-kalām ʿalā mā warada fī kutub al-aʿmāl* ibid. [1]VII, 395.—30a. *al-Nukhba fi ʾl-ukhuwwa wal-ṣuḥba*, in verse, ibid.—31. See Suppl.

2b. ʿAbdallāh b. Muḥammad b. Abī Qushayr al-Ḥaḍramī, tenth century.

Aḥkām al-ḥayḍ wal-nifās wal-istiḥāḍa Alex. Fiqh. Shāf. 35, 1. Glosses by Sulaymān b. Ḥajar al-Haythamī (p. 508), ibid. 2.

2c. Barakāt b. Muḥammad b. Ramaḍān b. al-Ḥājj Abū Bakr al-Shighrī wrote, in 1080/1669:

405 | *Zahr al-ghuṣūn*, ca. 4400 *rajaz* verses on Shāfiʿī *furūʿ*, based on the work of al-Murtaḍā Yaḥyā al-Riḍā, Gotha 987 (autograph).

3. Ṭayyib b. Abī Bakr al-Ḥaḍramī, ca. 1135/1723, see Suppl.

2. *Kashf al-ʿiyān fi ʾl-dalīl wal-burhān* Patna II, 430,$_{2606,1}$.

4. Muḥammad b. Ismāʿīl b. Ṣalāḥ al-Amīr al-Kaḥlānī, d. 1182/1769, see Suppl.

9. *al-Masāʾil al-marḍiyya etc.* Garr. 1621.—12. See Suppl. 902,$_{54}$.

5. ʿAbdallāh b. ʿAbd al-Walī b. Muḥammad al-Ward wrote, in 1173/1760:

Al-Jawhar al-aṣīl see Suppl. Garr. 1265.

B The Zaydīs

534 1b. Jamāl (Badr) al-Dīn Muḥammad b. Yaḥyā b. Muḥammad b. Bahrān | al-Baṣrī al-Yamanī al-Ṣaʿdī, d. 957/1550 in Ṣaʿda, see Suppl.

3. *al-Kāfil etc.* Commentaries: *Shifāʾ jahl al-sāʾil ʿammā taḥammalahu ʾl-Kāfil* by ʿAlī b. Ṣāliḥ b. ʿAlī al-Ṭabarī, print. Sanʿāʾ n.d. (Rossi, OM XVIII, 571).—b. *al-Kāshif li-dhawi ʾl-ʿuqūl ʿan wujūh masāʾil al-Kāfil* by Aḥmad b. Muḥammad b. Luqmān b. ʿAlī b. Shams al-Dīn b. al-Imām al-Mahdī li-Dīn Allāh Aḥmad b. Yaḥyā b. al-Murtaḍā, eleventh century, Ṣanʿāʾ 1347 (ibid. 572).—5. *al-Mukhtaṣar etc.* Alex. Adab 129,$_{15}$.

2. Yaḥyā b. Muḥammad b. al-Ḥasan b. al-Ḥumayd al-Zaydī al-Miqrāʿī al-Madhḥijī al-Ḥārithī ʿImād al-Dīn, who died after 972/1564.

1. *Tanqīḥ al-miṣbāḥ*, an exposition and justification of Zaydī doctrine, Berl. 2122.—2. *Miftāḥ al-fāʾiḍ fi ʾl-farāʾiḍ*, on the law of inheritance, abstract *Miṣbāḥ al-rāʾiḍ*, with the commentary *al-Nūr al-fāʾiḍ*, in Berl. 4727, commentary on the introduction, *Tanqīḥ al-fawāʾid wa-taqyīd al-shawārid fī tatimmat al-maqāṣid wa-taṣḥīḥ al-ʿaqāʾid*, completed in 958/1551, ibid. 4728, Garr. 2078,$_{1}$.—3.–7. see Suppl.

3. Al-Mutawakkil ʿala ʾllāh Sharaf al-Dīn Yaḥyā b. Shams al-Dīn b. al-Mahdī Aḥmad b. Yaḥyā b. al-Murtaḍā, who was born in 877/1472 and died in 965/1557.

1. *Kitāb al-athmār wal-azhār*, a Zaydī legal work, an improved version of the *Kitāb al-azhār* (p. 239), see Suppl. Commentaries: a. *al-Mufattiḥ li-akmām al-Athmār* by ʿAlī b. ʿAbdallāh b. ʿAlī b. Rāwiʿ Jamāl al-Dīn, ca. 940/1533, Berl. 4935/6.—b. Jamāl al-Dīn Muḥammad b. Yaḥyā b. Aḥmad al-Bahrān (no. 1b), ibid. 4937/8.—c. see Suppl. (*al-Shumūs wal-aqmār etc.* additionally Berl. Ms. or. qu. 2034, Fischer-Burch. 30).

4b. Shams al-Dīn Aḥmad b. ʿAbdallāh b. al-Wazīr, who died in 985/1577, see Suppl.

2. *al-Risāla al-muḍīʾa etc.* Garr. 2078,$_{4}$.

5. Al-Manṣūr billāh al-Qāsim b. Muḥammad b. ʿAlī b. Rasūlallāh, who died in 1029/1620, see Suppl.

Biography see p. 530. 1. *al-Asās al-mutakaffil bi-kashf al-iltibās*, on dialectic as a means to attain knowledge of God's nature, Berl. 5145, Hamb. Or. Sem. 44, 82.—2. *Mirqāt* | *al-wuṣūl ilā ʿilm al-uṣūl*, a discussion of theological issues, 535
Berl. 10299.—3. Answers to various questions, Br. Mus. Suppl. 214,$_{1-4}$, 215,$_{2}$.—4. *al-Irshād* (*Hādī*) *ilā sabīl al-rashād fī ṭarīq afʿāl al-ʿibād ʿinda faqd al-ijtihād* ibid. 214,$_{5}$.—5. *al-Taḥdhīr min al-fitna* ibid. $_{6}$.—6. *al-Asās li-ʿaqāʾid al-akyās* ibid. 215,$_{1}$.

| 6. His son Sharaf al-Dīn al-Ḥusayn b. Amīr al-Muʾminīn al-Qāsim b. 406
Muḥammad b. ʿAlī was born in 999/1590 and died in 1050/1640 in Ḍamīr.

Muḥ. II, 104. 1. *Ghāyat al-sūl fī ʿilm al-uṣūl* Br. Mus. Suppl. 269. Self-commentary, *Hidāyat al-ʿuqūl*, with glosses by Sharaf al-Dīn al-Ḥasan b. Yaḥyā b. Saylān, ibid. 270.—2. *Ādāb al-ʿulamāʾ wal-mutaʿallimīn*, Ṣanʿāʾ 1344 (Rossi, *OM* XVIII, 571).

6d. ʿAlī b. Sulaymān Shams al-Īmān completed, in 1052/1642:

Ḥayāt al-aḥrār wa-ḥibāʾ al-aḥbār Alex. Firaq 5.

7. ʿAlī b. Ṣalāḥ b. ʿAlī al-Zaydī al-Saʿdī wrote, in 1071/1661:

Īḍāh sabīl al-wuṣūl ilā maʿnā dhawi ʾl-ʿuqūl fī maʿrifat qawāʿid al-uṣūl, with a commentary, Berl. 5146.

9. Aḥmad b. Ṣāliḥ b. Abi ʾl-Rijāl, who died in 1092/1681, see Suppl.

Muḥ. I, 220, Wüst. *Gesch.* 583. (*Taysīr*) *Tafsīr al-sharīʿa* Br. Mus. Suppl. 217$_{,1}$.—2. *Iʿlām al-muwālī bi-kalām sādatihi ʾl-aʿlām al-mawālī* ibid. $_{2}$.—3.–9. see Suppl.

6 *Sciences of the Qurʾān*

1. Muṭahhar (Muṣṭafā) b. ʿAlī b. Nuʿmān al-Ḍamadī al-Yamanī was born in 1004/1595 in Wādī Ḍamad near Ṣanʿāʾ and died after 1070/1659.

Muḥ. IV, 403, Wüst. *Jemen*, 104. *Al-Furāt al-namīr, tafsīr al-kitāb al-munīr* Br. Mus. Suppl. 126.

2. Al-Nāṣir b. ʿAbd al-Ḥāfiẓ b. al-Muḥallā al-Sharafī al-Yamanī studied in Zabīd, then lived at the court of Imam Muḥammad al-Muʾayyad in Ṣanʿāʾ, and died on 1 Ṣafar 1081/28 June 1670.

536 | Muḥ. IV, 44/7, Wüst. *Jemen*, 38. 1. *Kitāb al-muqarrar al-nāfiʿ al-ḥāwī li-qirāʾat Nāfiʿ*, on Nāfiʿ himself and on his two *rāwīs*, Qālūn, d. 220/835, and Warsh, d. 199/814, with regard to the *istiʿādha* and the *basmala*, and then on individual suras, Berl. 645.—2. See Suppl.

3. Muḥammad b. al-Ḥusayn b. Amīr al-Muʾminīn al-Manṣūr billāh al-Qāsim b. Muḥammad b. ʿAlī, eleventh century.

Muntaha ʾl-marām fī sharḥ abyāt al-aḥkām, Ṣanʿāʾ 1342 (Rossi, *OM* XVIII, 571).

4. Abū Saʿīd Muḥammad b. Muḥammad al-Ḥaḍramī, twelfth century.

Risāla fi ʾl-kalām ala ʾl-basmala Qawala I, 68.

|7 *Dogmatics* 407

1. Muḥammad b. ʿIzz al-Dīn b. Muḥammad b. Ṣalāḥ b. Amīr al-Muʾminīn al-Muftī al-Muʾayyadī was appointed *muftī* of Ṣanʿāʾ by Jaʿfar Pāshā and died in 1050/1640.

1. *Wāsiṭat al-darārī*, on *kalām*, with a commentary, *al-Badr al-sārī*, Br. Mus. Suppl. 1212,$_6$.—2., 3. see Suppl. (2. Garr. 2078,$_2$).

8 *Mysticism*

1. Muḥyī (Shams) ʾl-Dīn Abū ʿAbdallāh Muḥammad (ʿAbd al-Hādī b. Muḥammad) b. ʿAlī b. Aḥmad b. Ibrāhīm al-Sūdī (ʿAbd) al-Hādī, who died in 932/1525, see Suppl.

Hartmann, *Muw.* 20. 1. *Dīwān*, with a special section, *Nasamāt al-saḥar wa-nafaḥāt al-zahar*, Berl. 7934/5, Leid. 746.—2. *al-Dhakhīra wa-kashf al-tawaqquʿ li-ahl al-baṣīra* AS 1789.

2. After extensive travels and a long stay in the Hijaz, Ḥātim b. Aḥmad al-Ahdal al-Ḥusaynī settled in Mukhā and died there in 1013/1604.

Muḥ. I, 496/500, Wüst. *Ṣūf.* 114. 1. *Dīwān* Leid. 752, with a supplement ibid., 753.—1a. *al-Muwashshah* Bank. XXIII, 2551.—2. *Kitāb al-naṣāʾiḥ*, a letter to his student Ibn al-ʿAydarūs, d. 1038/1628 (see below p. 418), Āṣaf. I, 382,$_{18,\ 5}$.—3. *Risāla* on mysticism, composed in 1004/1595, with a commentary by ʿAydarūs, *al-Zahr al-bāsim min rawḍ al-ustādh Ḥātim*, with detailed information on al-Ḥusaynī in the introduction, Ind. Off. 683 from which a lemma | on ʿAlī b. 537
ʿUmar, ruler of Mukhā, regarding coffee, Berl. 5479.

3. Sālim b. Aḥmad b. Shaykhān Bā ʿAlawī was born on 7 Rabīʿ II 995/18 March 1587 and died in al-Maʿlāt on 9 Dhu ʾl-Qaʿda 1046/2 April 1637.

Muḥ. II, 200/2, Wüst. *Ṣūf.* 118. 1. *Ghurar* (*Ghurrat*) *al-bayān ʿan ʿumr al-zamān* or *al-ʿArḍ al-kāfī lil-ʿirḍ al-shāfī*, on the amount of time that the earth will continue to exist, Berl. 2764, Qawala I, 206; on which *Kashf al-ghubār ʿani ʾl-ishārāt fī-mā baqiya min ʿumr hādha ʾl-zamān* by ʿAbd al-Raḥmān b. Aḥmad, ibid. 208.—2. *al-Sifr al-manshūr lil-dirāya fi ʾl-dhikr al-manshūr lil-walāya*, a manual on *dhikr*, ibid. 3719.

4. ʿAbdallāh b. ʿAlawī b. Aḥmad al-Ḥusaynī al-Ḥaddādī al-Bāʿalawī, who was born in 1004/1634 in Tarīm in the Hadramawt, journeyed to Mecca and Medina in 1079/1668, and died in 1132/1720.

408 | Mur. III, 91/3. 1. *al-Durr al-manẓūm li-dhawi ʾl-ʿuqūl wal-fuhūm*, a *dīwān*, Cairo ^{1}IV, 231, Bank. XXIII, 62,$_{2557}$, print. Bombay 1883, C. 1302, 1346.—2. Verses on ʿAbd al-Qādir al-Jīlānī, see Suppl.—3. *al-Daʿwā al-tāmma wal-tadhkira al-ʿāmma*, Cairo ^{1}II, 156, print. C. 1304. Commentary see Suppl. (b. Patna I, 134,$_{1323}$).—4. *al-Naṣāʾiḥ al-dīniyya wal-waṣāya ʾl-īmāniyya* C. 1306.—5. *al-Tawassulāt lil-nabī*, on invocations of the Prophet as talismans, Ind. Off. 1037.—6. *al-Durar al-bahiyya fi ʾl-akhlāq al-marḍiyya*, Būlāq 1313.—7.–15. see Suppl. (8. On questions by ʿAbd al-Raḥmān b. ʿAbdallāh, Patna I, 127,$_{1270}$; 12b. Garr. 1599).—16. *Lumʿat al-nibrās fī sīrat al-nabī* Patna II, 458,$_{2632,\ 14}$.—17. *Miftāḥ al-saʿāda wal-falāḥ* ibid. 444,$_{2620,\ 10}$.—18. *Ḥizb al-fatḥ* ibid. $_{11}$.

5., 6., see Suppl.

(6. 2. *Sahm al-saʿāda fī iṣābat al-ḍamīr ʿalā waqf al-irāda* Alex. Ḥurūf 13).

9 *Astronomy*

3. ʿAbdallāh b. ʿAbdallāh b. Aḥmad al-Sharjī, who died in 1097/1686.

Ghāyat itqān al-ḥarakāt lil-sabʿa al-kawākib al-sayyārāt, completed on 10 Rabīʿ I 1080/29 July 1670 in Yemen, Br. Mus. Suppl. 769, see Suppl.

538 | 10 *Occult Sciences*

2. Sharaf al-Dīn b. Ṣalāḥ al-Dīn b. Qāsim b. Muḥammad al-Kawkabānī wrote, in 1111/1699:

Sahm al-jayb etc., see Suppl., and also Hamb. Or. Sem. 1111, Berl. 4237, Garr. 943.

Chapter 5. Oman, East Africa, and Abyssinia

While the literature of the Khārijīs of Oman may actually have started centuries earlier, just as that of other sects did, it is only extant from the eleventh century, and it is unlikely that their colony in East Africa could have seen any literary activity much before that time. The Muslims who pushed forward from Somaliland into Abyssinia have only left us acounts of their battles.

| A *Oman* 409

1. Aḥmad b. al-Naẓar al-Samawʾalī al-ʿUmānī.

Dīwān, 25 alphabetically-ordered poems and rules for prayer, Br. Mus. Suppl. 327 (citation *Qāmūs al-sharīʿa* [see no. 4] V, 65/7). Commentary by Muḥammad b. Waṣṣāf, ibid. 328 (citation ibid. VIII, 307).

2. Darwīsh b. Jumʿa b. ʿUmar al-Maḥrūqī al-ʿIbādī al-ʿAdanī al-ʿUmānī.

Kitāb al-dalāʾil ʿala ʾl-lawāzim wal-wasāʾil Br. Mus. Suppl. 32a, print. C. 1320.

3. ʿAbdallāh b. Ḥalfān b. Qayṣar b. Sulaymān wrote, in 1050/1640:

Sīrat al-imām al-ʿādil Nāṣir b. Murshid b. Mālik, imam of Oman 1034–50/1628–40, Br. Mus. 1252.

4. Jumayyil b. Khamīs al-Saʿdī wrote, during the government of Imam Sultan Ibn Sayf b. Mālik (1059–79/1628–40):[1]

Qāmūs al-sharīʿa, an exposition of *fiqh* according to Ibāḍī doctrine, print. Zanzibar 1297/1304 in 10 rather than 90 volumes.

| 5. Around the year 1140/1728 an anonymous author wrote: 539

Kashf al-ghumma al-jāmiʿ li-akhbār al-umma, a comprehensive history of Ibāḍī Islam in the central, eastern, and western lands, with all relevant theological and biographical data, until the aforementioned year, cf. E. Sachau, *MSOS WAs.* I, 1/19; idem, Uber die religiösen Anschauungen der Ibaditischen Muhammadaner in ʿOmān und Ostafrika, ibid. II, 47/82; Hedwig Klein, *Kap. 33 der anon. ar. Chronik K. al-gh.*, Hamburg 1938.

1 S. Badger, *History of the Imāms and Seyyids of ʿOmān* 78/90, and Suppl.

6. Unknown are the details of the personal life of Abu 'l-Ḥasan b. Muḥammad b. 'Alī al-Basīwī al-'Umānī, whose *Mukhtaṣar al-Basīwī* is held in high esteem as a legal compendium in Zanzibar, as well as on the mainland. It was printed in Zanzibar in 1886 on the order of Sultan Bargas. Cf. E. Sachau, *Muhammedanisches Erbrecht nach der Lehre der Ibāḍitischen Araber von Zanzibar und Ostafrika*, SBBA 1894, VIII.

B *East Africa*

Muḥyi 'l-Dīn, born in 904/1498, wrote, for Sultan Meḥmed b. Ḥusayn b. Süleymān:

Kitāb al-sulwa fī akhbār Kilwa, a history of the island of Kilwa off the East African coast, Br. Mus Suppl. 600, ed. Strong, *JRAS* 1896, 385ff.

410 | C *Abyssinia*

1. 'Arabfaqīh Shihāb al-Dīn Aḥmad b. 'Abd al-Qādir b. Sālim b. 'Uthmān wrote, in Giran in Gimma Abogifarl[1] in 950/1543:

Tuḥfat al-zamān or *Futūḥ al-Ḥabasha*, on the wars against the Abyssinians under Imam Aḥmad b. Ibrāhīm (among the Abyssinians Grañ, left hand), Algiers 1628/9, Br. Mus. Suppl. 599. Cf. Nerazzini, see Suppl.; R. Basset, *Histoire de la conquête de l'Abyssinie (XVIe s.) par Chihabeddin Aḥmad b. 'Abd al-Qādir surnommé Arab-Faqih, Texte ar.*, Fasc. 1, Paris 1897, Fasc. 2, 1898, Fasc. 3 and 4, 1899, Fasc. 5, 1909 (Publ. de l'Ecole des Lettres d'Algiers), *Trad. et Notes*, Fasc. 1, 1897, Fasc. 2. and 3, 1899. *Futuh el Habacha, des conquêtes faites en Abyssinie au*
540 *XVIe s. par l'imam M. a. dit Gragne, vers. franç. de la chronique | ar. du Chahab ad Din, publication commencée par* A. d'Abbadie, *terminée par* Th. Paulitschke, Paris 1898.

2. An unidentified author wrote:

Ta'rīkh al-Ḥabasha, covering the years 1021–54/1612–44, Patna II, 536,$_{2886}$ (26 leaves).

1 After d'Abbadie, op. cit. XI, the manuscripts from Jīzān and Ḥīzān.

Chapter 6. Iran and Tūrān

The flourishing of political power that Iran experienced under the Safavids naturally also positively contributed to literature. However, as was already the case in the previous period, the Arabic language was almost exclusively employed by scholars, especially Shīʿī theologians. It was only at the court of Shah ʿAbbās I (985–1038/1587–1629) that the secular sciences were also pursued to some extent. On the other hand, in Afghanistan and Turkmenistan there was just a handful of people who were interested in Arabic literature and appreciated it.

1 *Poetry and Belles Lettres*

4. Muḥammad Munʿim b. al-Ḥājj Muḥammad Qāsim al-Jazāʾirī, who died around 1720, see Suppl.

1. *Ṭayf al-khayāl etc.*, commentary *Safīnat al-ʿilm*, completed in 1131/1719, Bank. XXIII, 108,$_{2597}$.

1b *Philology*

1. ʿIṣām al-Dīn Ibrāhīm b. Muḥammad b. ʿArabshāh al-Isfarāʾinī, who died in 944/1537, see Suppl.

1. *Mīzān al-adab fi ʾl-ʿulūm al-thalātha al-ṣarf wal-naḥw wal-balāgha* (*fī līsān al-ʿArab*) Berl. 6779/80 (with a commentary by al-Fāḍil al-Tāshkandī, ca. 980/1572), Vienna 238, AS 4421, Alex. Naḥw 43, Fun. 42, Qawala II, 99.—2. *Risāla fī ʿilm al-majāz,* | translated from the Persian by Aḥmad al-Mawlawī, d. 1181/1767, 411
Berl. 7288, Istanbul Univ. A 2803 (see Suppl. Br. H. ^{2}154,$_2$, not mentioned Garr. 580).—3. *Taʿlīqāt ala ʾl-Talwīḥ* p. 277.—4. *Ḥāshiya ʿalā Tafsīr al-Bayḍāwī* I, 531 (see *Türkiyat Mecm.* 6/7, 1945, p. 35–37, Istanbul Univ. A 2172).—5.–17. see Suppl.—18. *Sharḥ al-Shamāʾil* (I, 169), Ẓāh. ʿIsh, Taʾrīkh 60.

| 2. ʿAbd al-Bāqī b. Muḥammad Ḥājjī Ṣadr al-Dīn al-Ṣīrānī wrote, in 950/1543 in 541
Qandahar:

1. *Risāla fī tamām al-mushtarak*, on propositions with double meanings, Esc. ^{2}405,$_6$.—2. See Suppl.

2 *Ḥadīth*

1. ʿAlī b. Muḥammad b. Ḥasan Zayn al-Dīn, who was born in 911/1505 and died after 956/1549.

Biography, Cod. Berl. Pet. 54, 61/6. *Al-Durr al-manthūr min al-maʾthūr wa-ghayr al-maʾthūr*, an explanation of a number of difficult traditions and other phrases, from a Shīʿī point of view, Berl. 1370.

2. ʿAlī b. Abi ʾl-Ḥasan Ibrāhīm al-Anbārī, who died in 988/1580.

Awj al-akhḍar fī manāqib al-aʾimma al-ithnay ʿashar NO 3057.

3. ʿAlī al-Marāghī al-Qabbānī wrote, in 1001/1592:

Al-Nuṭq al-mafhūm min ahl al-samṭ al-maʿlūm (see I, 622, no. 22), Paris 3557/8.

4. Muṣṭafā b. al-Ḥusayn al-Ḥusaynī al-Tafrishī wrote, in 1015/1606:

Naqd al-rijāl, on Shīʿī *ḥadīth*-scholars, in alphabetical order, Br. Mus. Suppl. 636.

5. Ḥājjī Muḥammad b. ʿAlī b. al-Ḥusayn b. Mūsā al-Qummī al-Ardabīlī b. Bābūyā, ca. 1100/1688.

1. *Taṣḥīḥ al-asānīd*, the names of transmitters occurring in Shīʿī *ḥadīth*s, Berl. 9960.—2. A statement on the teachers after whom he cites the works he refers to, ibid. 9961.

(6). Muḥammad Taqī al-Majlisī see Suppl.

1. *Ḥadīqat al-Muttaqīn* additionally Teh. II, 42, abstract *Rawḍat al-muttaqīn* (Kentūrī 1599), Ind. Off. 1831/2, Browne, *Lit. Hist.* IV, 409.

6. His son, Muḥammad Bāqir b. Muḥammad Taqī b. Maqṣūd ʿAlī Akmal al-Majlisī, who died in 1111/1700, see Suppl.

542 | 1. *Mirʾāt al-ʿuqūl fī sharḥ akhbār āl al-rasūl*, a Shīʿī commentary on *al-Rawḍa*, the last part of al-Kulīnī's *al-Kāfī* (Suppl. I, 320), completed in 1076/1665, Berl. 1371.—2. On free will, ibid. 2497.—4.–16. see Suppl.—17.–19. ibid. III, 1297.

7.–19. see Suppl. 9. See also 793, 1.

Ṣaḥīfat al-ṣafāʾ (*fī asmāʾ al-rijāl*) Patna II, 309,$_{2435}$.

3 *Shīʿī fiqh and kalām*

1. ʿAlī b. al-Ḥusayn b. ʿAbd al-ʿĀlī al-Karakī al-Muḥaqqiq al-Thāni, who died in 945/1538 in Najaf, see Suppl.

1. *Risālat nafaḥāt al-lāhūt*, a demonstration of the permissibility of cursing Sunnis as unbelievers, dedicated to Shāh Ismāʿīl, Ind. Off. 471,$_{10}$.—2. Notes to *Kitāb al-nāfiʿ* I, 515.—3.–15. see Suppl.—16.–20. ibid. III, 1297/8.

| 2. Muhadhdhab al-Dīn Aḥmad b. ʿAbd al-Riḍā al-Damamīnī, who died after 412
1084/1673.

1. *Maʿārij al-dīn wa-manāhij al-yaqīn*, on the system of Shīʿī law, completed in 1079/1668 in Mashhad for his son Ilyās, Ind. Off. 290.—2. Treatise on Shīʿī *uṣūl al-dīn* and *furūʿ al-dīn*, composed in 1084/1673 in Aḥmadābād in Gujarāt for the *nawwāb* Muʿaẓẓam Khān, ibid. 291.—4.–22. see Suppl.—23. Ibid. III, 1298.—24. *al-ʿAbqariyya* Patna I, 15, 150, 1431.

3. Muḥammad b. al-Ḥasan al-Ḥasanī al-Ḥurr al-ʿĀmilī, born on 8 Rajab 1033/27 April 1624 in Mashghara in Jabal ʿĀmil, moved to Mecca in 1087/1676, but due to Turkish persecution of the Shīʿa he had to leave it again the very same year. He died in 1099/1688 in Yemen or Iran.

Muḥ. III, 432/5 (misprint: d. 1079). 1. *al-Risāla al-Ithnā ʿashariyya fi 'l-radd ʿala 'l-Ṣūfiyya* Br. Mus. 1197.—2. *Amal al-āmil fī ʿulamāʾ jabal ʿĀmil*, on famous Shīʿis from ʿĀmil, composed in 1097/1685, Berl. 10049.—3.–9. see Suppl.

4 *Sciences of the Qur'ān*

1a. Aḥmad b. Muḥammad al-Bukhārī wrote, in 922/1516:

| *Al-Tajwīd* Patna I, 12, 98 (autograph). 543

3. ʿAbd ʿAlī b. Jumʿa al-ʿArūsī al-Ḥuwayzī wrote, in 1065/1655 in Shiraz:

Nūr al-thaqalayn, a Shīʿī commentary on the Qur'ān based on the work of ʿAlī al-Qummī (I, 205), al-Ṭabarsī (I, 513), and others, Ind. Off. 106.

10. Kalīmallāh b. Nūrallāh al-Ḥanafī, around 1125/1713, see Suppl.

3. *al-ʿUshra al-kāmila* (*fi 'l-taṣawwuf*) Patna II, 376,$_{2560, 2}$.

5 *Mysticism*

1. Muḥammad al-Iṣfahāni wrote around 930/1524.

1. *al-Surūr fi ʾl-sirr al-mastūr*, composed in 930/1524, Cairo ^{1}VII, 645.—2. *al-Nushūr fī sirr al-nūr*, composed in 931/1525, ibid.

3. Abū Naṣr Muḥammad b. ʿAbd al-Raḥmān al-Hamdānī, before 899/1493 (see Suppl.).

(Nallino, *Raccolta di Scritti* II [1940] 121). *Al-Sabʿiyyāt fī mawāʿiẓ al-bariyyāt* see Suppl., also Berl. Ms. or. oct. $3907_{,2}$, Alex. Mawāʿiẓ 21, Patna I, $148_{,1419/20}$, Garr. $2028_{,7}$.

4. Muḥammad Amīn b. Maḥmūd al-Bukhārī Amīr Pādishāh, who died in 987/1579, see Suppl.

1. *Tafsīr sūrat al-Fatḥ* (sura 48), very detailed, Berl. 955.—2. *Risāla fī bayān al-ḥāṣil bil-maṣdar* Berl. 6887/8, Garr. 473.—3. *Risāla fī takfīr al-ḥijaj al-ṣaghāʾir wal-kabāʾir*, a refutation of the view of Shāfiʿī teachers, according to whom all sins are forgiven by a pilgrimage to Mecca, Paris $2679_{,3}$, Cairo ^{1}VII, 521, no. 5.
413 |—4. *Taysīr al-taḥrīr fi ʾl-uṣūl* Patna I, $68_{,5}$. *Faṣl al-khiṭāb fi ʾl-taṣawwuf* AS 1976/9, Fatih 2751, Selīm Aġā 537, Yeni 702, 721/2, see Suppl.—7., 8. Ibid.

5. Muḥammad b. Murtaḍā Mollā Muḥsin al-Fayḍ al-Kāshī, who died after 1090/1679, see Suppl.

1. *al-Kalimāt al-maknūna fī ʿulūm ahl al-ḥikma wal-maʿrifa wa-aqwālihim* Br. Mus. 886.—2.–32. see Suppl. and III, 1300 (5. Ind. Off. 1834, Patna I, $66_{,679,\ 7}$,
544 Patna II, $453_{,2429,\ 3}$; 8. Abstract *Anwār al-ḥikma* in many MSS. | *Dharīʿa* II, $465_{,1674}$; 16. Patna II, $146_{,1405}$; 17. MSS in Tehran and Najaf *Dharīʿa* II, $178_{,656}$, $211_{,824}$; 18. Tehran Sip. II, 388/9; 28. = *Majmūʿat Rasāʾilihi, Dharīʿa* II, $398_{,1595}$.—21. Patna I, $153_{,1456}$).—33. *Risāla fī shakkiyyāt al-ṣalāt* Ind. Off. 1836.—34. *Ahamm mā yuʿmal fi ʾl-yawm wal-nahār wal-usbūʿ wal-sana*, two MSS *Dharīʿa* II, $485_{,1902}$.

6 *Philosophy*

(1) Mīr Ṣadr al-Dīn Abū Naṣr b. Ibrāhīm al-Ḥusaynī al-Shīrāzī, who died in 903/1497.

1. *Ḥāshiyat Ḥāshiyat Kūčak* I, 612 ζ.—2 *Ḥāshiya ʿalā Maṭāliʿ al-anwār* I, 615.

1. Muḥammad Mīrjān al-Tabrīzī Shams al-Dīn, who died around 950/1543.

Al-Maṭālib al-ʿaliyya wal-maqāṣid al-saniyya fī maḥall al-kamālāt al-insāniyya, on metaphysics, Berl. 5141.

2. Muḥammad b. Ibrāhīm Ṣadr al-Dīn (Mollā Ṣadrā) al-Shīrāzī, d. 1050/1640, see Suppl.

8. *al-Maqāla fī taḥqīq al-takhṣīṣ* Patna II, 422$_{,2592,\ 19}$.—11. *Risāla fi ʾl-jabr wal-qadar* Patna II, 459$_{,2633,\ 4}$.—19. ibid. II, 422$_{,2592,\ 8}$, 459$_{,2633,\ 8}$, 459$_{,2633,\ 1}$.—24. ibid. II, 422$_{,2592,\ 9}$.—35. See (I). 1.—37., 38. Suppl. III, 1300.—40. *Risāla fi ʾl-mabāḥith al-iʿtiqādiyya* Patna II, 422$_{,2592,\ 10}$.—41. *Risāla fi ʾl-ḥashr* ibid. 13.—42. *Risāla fī ḥudūth al-ʿālam* ibid. 453$_{,2629,\ 1}$.—43. *Risālat kasr al-aṣnām al-jāhiliyya fī dhamm al-mutaṣawwifīn* ibid. 459$_{,2633,\ 3}$.

8 *Mathematics and Astronomy*

1. Ḥusayn al-Ḥusaynī al-Khalkhālī, a student of Mīrzājān al-Shīrāzī from Khalkhāl, two days' travelling distance from Ardebil, died in 1014/1605.

Muḥ. II, 122. *Sharḥ al-Dāʾira al-Hindiyya*, on an astronomical instrument (see Sédillot, *Mém. prés. par div. sav. à l'A. des Inscr.* s. I, vol. 1, Paris 1844, 98ff.), composed in 1006/1597, Gotha 1417$_{,4}$, Pet. 128$_{,3}$.—2. A discussion of the times of prayer given in sura 17$_{,80}$, Berl. 5701/2, Br. Mus. Suppl. | 761$_{,2}$.—3. A discussion 545
of God's existence and the views of al-Shirwānī, Berl. 2342.—4.–10. see Suppl. (5. *Risāla fī maʿrifat awqāt al-ghurūb* Garr. 997; 6 = 2. ibid. 1307).

2. ʿAbd al-Raḥīm b. ʿAbd al-Karīm al-Qazwīnī al-ʿAjamī, who died in 1026/1617.

1. *al-Zīj fi ʾl-falak* Berl. 5762.—2. *Risāla fi ʾl-kawākib al-thābita* Cairo ^{1}V, 293.

| 10 *Medicine* 414

3. Muḥammad b. Yūsuf b. ʿAbd al-Laṭif, ca. 954/1547, see Suppl.

2. *al-Ṣādiqiyya fī ʿilm al-munāẓara* Patna II, 339$_{,2523,\ 6}$.

4. ʿImād al-Dīn Maḥmūd, who died around 1000/1592 in Isfahan.

Al-Murakkabāt al-Shāhiyya, on composite medicines, dedicated to Shāh Tahmāsp I (930–84/1524–76), Br. Mus. 1363.

11 *Encyclopaedias and Polyhistors*

1. Ghiyāth al-Dīn Manṣūr b. Muḥammad al-Ḥusaynī al-Shīrāzī, who died in 949/1542.

1. *Radd ʿalā Unmūdhaj al-ʿulūm al-Jalāliyya*, a refutation of the encyclopaedia of al-Dawwānī (p. 282), Leid. 15.—2. *Maqālat al-radd ʿalā Unmūdhaj al-ʿulūm al-Jalāliyya* ibid. 16.—3. (*Laṭāʾif*) *al-Ishārāt* ibid. 1597.—4. *Risāla fī ʾl-hudā* ibid. 2071.—5. *Sharḥ Hayākil al-nūr* I, $565_{,5}$.—6.–23. see Suppl. (III, 1301).—24. *al-Lamaʿāt al-kāshifa* Patna I, $125_{,1253}$.

2. Quṭb al-Dīn Abu ʾl-Khayr ʿĪsā b. Muḥammad b. ʿUbaydallāh al-Ṣafawī, who died in 953/1546, see Suppl.

1. *Unmūdhaj al-ʿulūm*, 16 sticking points from the Qurʾān, *ḥadīth*, *fiqh*, and grammar, Vienna 18.—2. *Sharḥ al-Ghurra fī ʾl-manṭiq* p. 271.—3.–5. see Suppl.

3. Ḥabīballāh Mīrzājān al-Shīrāzī al-Baghandī, who died in 994/1586, see Suppl.

546 | 1. *Taʿrīf al-ʿilm*, mostly following al-Jurjānī (p. 280), Ind. Off. $587_{,1}$.—2. Encyclopaedic overview of nine sciences, ibid. 1028.—3.–12. see Suppl.

4. Bahāʾ al-Dīn Muḥammad b. Ḥusayn (Suppl. p. 575) b. ʿAbd al-Ṣamad al-Ḥārithī al-ʿĀmilī al-Jabaʿī al-Bahāʾī, who was born on 17 Dhu ʾl-Ḥijja 953/9 February 1547 in Baalbek,[1] emigrated with his father to Iran. After completing his studies he travelled for 30 years, finally settling permanently in Isfahan, where he enjoyed great respect as Shaykh al-Islām at the court of Shāh ʿAbbās. He died there on 12 Shawwāl 1030/31 August 1621.

Muḥ. III, 440/55, Rieu, *Pers. Cat.* I, 26; Chardin, *Voyage* VI, 326ff; Malcolm, *History of Persia* I, 558, Fr. transl. Paris 1822, II, 362; Goldziher, *SBWA* 78 (1874) 458ff; *RAAD* IX, 348. 1. *Arbaʿūna ḥadīthan*, composed in Ṣafar 995/January 1587 in Isfahan, Berl. 1527/9, Br. Mus. 187, Alex. Ḥad. 31, *Dharīʿa* I, $425_{,2180}$.—2. *Miftāḥ al-falāḥ*, a compendium on daily religious acts, Berl. 3551, Patna I, $157_{,1497/8}$, Persian translation *Ādāb-i ʿAbbāsī* Br. Mus. Pers. Suppl. 8, *Dharīʿa* I, $24_{,127}$.—3. *Risāla fī taḥrīm dhabāʾiḥ ahl al-kitāb*, a refutation of the assertion

1 However, according to al-Ṭālawī in Qazvin.

by Sunnīs, based on sura 57, that eating animals slaughtered by Christians and Jews is allowed, Pet. 247,$_1$.—4. *Risāla fī waḥdat al-wujūd* Cairo ^{1}I, 95.—5. *Jāmiʿ-i ʿAbbāsī*, religious deontology, in Persian, Cambr. Pers. XXV. |—6. *Tashrīḥ* 415
al-aflāk, on the principles of astronomy, Berl. 5703, Hamb. Or. Sem. 123, Br. Mus. 532,$_4$, 1345,$_1$, Suppl. 763,$_1$, Ind. Off. 1043 vi, Garr. 998/9, Alex. Fun. 65,$_3$, Bank. XXII, 2457.—Commentaries: a. Muḥammad al-Ḥusaynī Ṣadr al-Dīn b. al-Ṣādiq (see Suppl.), ca. 1085/1674, Berl. 5704.—b.–f. see Suppl., g., h. Suppl. III, 1301.—7. *Risālat al-ṣafīḥa* (*ṣafḥa*), on the astrolabe, Berl. 5801, Br. Mus. 1346,$_1$ (see *Quellen u. Studien* VII, 23, ii, 7), Persian in Bodl. Pers. 1508.—8. *Khulāṣat al-ḥisāb* (*al-Bahāʾiyya*) Berl. 5998, Ind. Off. 758, Br. Mus. 1345,$_2$, Pet. 243, Cairo ^{1}V, 180, VII, 89, print. Istanbul 1268, lith. Gulistān, Kashmīr 1285, C. 1299; Persian translation Br. Mus. Pers. II, 450a, printed with a commentary Calcutta 1812; German by Nesselmann, Berlin 1843 (cf. Steinhauser, *Ztschr. f. Realschulwesen*
| XIV, 6) French by A. Marre, Paris 1846.—Commentaries: a. ʿIṣmatallāh b. 547
Aʿẓam b. ʿAbd al-Rasūl, completed in 1086/1675, Ind. Off. 759/60, print. Calcutta 1829.—b. Ramaḍān b. Hurayra al-Jazāʾirī, completed in 1092/1681, Cairo ^{1}VI, 180.—c. Ḥājjī Ḥusayn, Ind. Off. 762.—d. ʿAlī al-Khalkhālī, ibid. 763.—e.–n. see Suppl.—9. *al-Fawāʾid al-Ṣamadiyya fī ʿilm al-ʿArabiyya*, dedicated to a certain ʿAbd al-Ṣamad, Berl. 6791.—10. A number of *qaṣīda*s, ibid. 7960.—11. *al-Kashkūl*, an anthology also containing Persian matter, Vienna 421, Bodl. II, 304/5, Ind. Off. 834/40, lith. Tehran 1266, 1296, print. Būlāq n.d. and 1288, C. 1305 (with a commentary by Aḥmad b. ʿAlī al-Manīnī on the *qaṣīda* in praise of the hidden imam Muḥammad al-Mahdī), 1316, cf. Rödiger, ZDMG XVI, 216.—12.–42. see Suppl. (31. Patna I, 36,$_{373}$).—43.–54. Suppl. III, 1301.—55. *Manẓūma fī ʾl-mawʿiẓa* Patna II, 472,$_{2639,\,1}$.—56. *Risāla fī ʾl-muʿammayāt* ibid. 2.

Chapter 7. India

As part of a general increase in Islamic culture, Mongol rule in India also advanced Arabic literature, even though it took a backseat to literature in Persian as it was mainly limited to theology. It was only on the west coast, in Gujarat and Malabar, which were in regular contact with South Arabia and the Hijaz, that it gained increased importance.

1 *Philology*

3. Aḥmad b. Abi 'l-Ghayth b. Mughlaṭāy wrote, in 1116/1704 for Sultan Aʿẓamshāh b. Awrangzīb:

Mulḥat al-badīʿ wa-bahjat al-badīʿ, on rhetoric, in verse with a commentary, Paris 4431.

416 | ### 2 *Historiography*

1. Shaykh Zayn al-Dīn al-Maʿbarī wrote, ca. 985/1577 for Sultan ʿAlī ʿĀdil Shāh of Bījapūr, d. 987/1579:

548 | *Tuḥfat al-mujāhidīn* Br. Mus. 94, Ind. Off. 714, 1044,5, Morley, *Cat. of hist. Mss.* 13; a short history of the spread of Islam in Malabar, the arrival of the Portuguese, and their persecution of the Muslims in the years 904–85/1498–1578. *Tohfut-ul-Mujahideen, an historical Work in the arabic Language transl. into English by* M.I. Rowlandson, London, Or. Transl.-Fund, 1833; *Historia dos Portugueses no Malabar por Zinadim, Manuscripto arabe do seculo XVI, publicado e tradúzido por* D. Lopes, Lisbon 1898. Abstracts in Ferishta, *History of the Rise of the Mahomedan Power in India*, transl. John Briggs, London 1829, vol. IV, 531 (Wüst. *Gesch.* 533).

2. Al-Ḥasan b. ʿAlī b. Shadqam al-Ḥusaynī al-Madanī hailed from Medina, lived in Aḥmadnagar and Khaybar, in Malabar, and died in 1046/1636.

Muḥ. II, 23. *Zahr al-riyāḍ wa-zulāl al-ḥiyāḍ*, a biographical compilation following the example of Ibn Khallikān, composed in 995/1587, vol. III Br. Mus. 365.

3 *Belles Lettres*

1. ʿAbdallāh b. Jumʿa al-Lāhūrī al-Hindī wrote, in 1122/1719:

Munhij al-nufūs wa-mublij al-ʿabūs fī nawādir al-ḥikāyāt wa-gharāʾib al-musāmarāt Pet. Ros. 112.

1a. Muḥammad b. ʿAbdallāh b. Muḥammad b. Jumʿa al-Hindī al-Shāfiʿī, ca. 1132/1720.

Al-Ḥikam al-shawārid min al-amthāl wal-qawāʿid ʿĀšir I, 492 (copy of the autograph dated 1132).

4 *Ḥadīth*

1. Jamāl al-Dīn Muḥammad Ṭāhir b. ʿAlī al-Ṣiddīqī al-Pattānī Malik al-Muḥaddithīn al-Hindī, who died in 986/1578, see Suppl.

1. *Majmaʿ biḥār (al-anwār) fī gharāʾib al-tanzīl wa-laṭāʾif al-akhbār*, in part following the *Nihāya* of Ibn al-Athīr (I, 439), Br. Mus. 1688/9, Ind. Off. 1023, print. India 1283, 1314, Garr 1406/7.—2., 3. see Suppl.

| 5. ʿAbd al-Ḥaqq Miskīn b. Sayf al-Dīn al-Dihlawī Ḥaqqī, who died in 1052/1642, see Suppl. 549

13. ʿAbd al-ʿAlīm Naṣrallāh Khān al-Aḥmādi Khīrajī, whose *Risāla fī 'l-ijtihād wal-taqlīd* is preserved in Patna II, $379_{,2565,2}$.—14. *Ṭayyib al-saʿāda ʿalā takthīr al-ṣalāt* ibid. $377_{,2563,\,2}$.—15. *Asmāʾ rijāl al-Mishkāt* Suppl. I, 262.

5 *Fiqh, Ḥanafī*

| 2. Zayn al-Dīn al-Malībārī, a grandson of the famous Sufi with the same name (p. 287). 417

I. *Qurrat al-ʿayn bi-muhimmāt al-dīn*. Commentaries: 1. Self-commentary *Fatḥ al-muʿīn*, Rāmpūr I, $233_{,438}$, much-used in East India, printings see Suppl.—2. *Nihāyat al-zayn* by Muḥammad al-Nawāwī, C. 1298, see Snouck Hurgronje, *Mekka* II, 366, n. 5.—II., III. See Suppl.

3. Sultan Muḥyi 'l-Dīn Awrangzīb ʿĀlamgīr, who was born in 1029/1620 and reigned in the years 1069–1118/1659–1707, ordered a commission under the leadership of Shaykh Niẓām to collect the:

Fatāwī ʿĀlamgīrī Berl. 4841/2, AS 1601/2, Cairo ^{1}III, 93, print. Calcutta 1251, Būlāq 1276, among others (see Mur. IV, 113).

4. Muḥammad b. Abi 'l-Baqāʾ b. Ḍiyāʾ al-Dīn Abu 'l-Najāʾ al-Ḥanafī:

Munyat al-nāsik fī khulāṣat al-manāsik Patna I, $107_{,1086}$.

6 *Sciences of the Qurʾān*

1. Muḥammad b. Aḥmad Miyānjīw b. Naṣīr wrote, in 981–2/1573–4:

Al-Tafsīr al-Muḥammadī Ind. Off. 103.

2. Fayḍallāh Abu ʾl-Faḍl (Fayḍ) b. al-Mubārak al-Hindī al-Fayḍī was born in 954[1]/1547 and died in Agra in 1004/1594, see Suppl.

1. *Sawāṭiʿ al-ilhām fī tafsīr al-Qurʾān*, which only contains letters without punctuation, completed in 1002/1593 in Lahore, Leid. 1702, Ind. Off. 104/5, Oud. 127, NO 339, Köpr. 113, AS 180 (*Türkiyat Mecm.* 7/8, II, 1945, 85/6), Rāġib 80, Cairo I,
550 ^{1}178, ^{2}54, lith. Lucknow 1306.—|2. *Mawārid al-kalim wa-silk durar al-ḥikam*, a
lexical work with the same artificiality, Berl. Ms. or. oct. 3856, Vienna 354, Köpr. 1399, Cairo ^{1}II 139, Patna I, $151_{,1439}$.

7 *Dogmatics*

1b. ʿAbd al-Ḥakīm b. Shams al-Dīn al-Hindī al-Sālīkūtī (Siyālkūtī) was an adviser to the Mongol sultan Shihāb al-Dīn Shāhjahān (1037–68/1628–58) and died on 18 Rabīʿ I 1067/5 January 1657.

Muḥ. II, 318. 1. *al-Risāla al-Khāqāniyya fī taḥqīq mabḥath al-ʿilm*, on the omniscience of God, composed on the order of the sultan named in the title, Berl. 2344.—2. *ʿAqāʾid* Istanbul 1306.—3. *Zubdat al-afkār*, with glosses by al-Qalanbawī, Kazan 1888, 1901.—4. *Ḥāshiya ʿalā Tafsīr al-Bayḍāwī* I, 532 (*Türk. Mecm.* 7/8, II, 45).—5. *Ḥāshiya ʿalā Sharḥ ʿAqāʾid al-Nasafī* I, 548.—6. *Ḥāshiya ʿala ʾl-Muṭawwal* I, 354.—7.–9. see Suppl.—10. *Risāla fī kayfiyyat ʿilm al-wājib* Patna II, $460_{,2633,\ 7}$.—11. Persian *R. dar maktūb-i Qāḍī Nasī Burhānpūr* ibid. $461_{,2634,\ 3}$.

2. ʿAbd al-Wahhāb al-Qudwāʾī al-Qannawjī Munʿim Khān wrote, in 1125/1713:

418 | 1. *Baḥr al-madhāhib*, on the dogmatic positions of the orthodox, the sectarians, the Sufis, and the unbelievers, Berl. 1851.—2. See Suppl.

3. Quṭb al-Dīn Abū ʿAbd al-ʿAzīz Walī Allāh Aḥmad b. ʿAbd al-Raḥīm al-Dihlawī al-Ḥanafī, who died in 1176/1762, see Suppl.

---

1 Going by the preface of 1. rather than in 944/1537.

1. *al-Iʿtiqād al-ṣaḥīḥ*, with the commentary *al-Intiqād al-rajīḥ* by Muḥammad b. al-Sayyid Ṣiddīq b. Ḥasan Malik Bhūpāl al-Qannawjī (Suppl. 859), composed in 1274/1857, Indian printing Cairo ^{1}II, 5.—2. *al-Fawz al-kabīr* (*wa-fatḥ al-khabīr*) *bi-mā lā budd min ḥifẓihi min ʿilm al-tafsīr* Cairo ^{1}I, 200.—3. *Ḥujjat Allāh al-bāligha*, print. India 1286, Bulaq 1294, ibid. 334.—4.–20. see Suppl.

8 *Mysticism*

1. Muḥammad b. Khaṭīr al-Dīn b. Bāyazīd al-Ghawth al-Hindī was born in 906/1500, a descendant of the Persian poet Farīd al-Dīn ʿAṭṭār. He withdrew for more than 13 years | into the mountains of Qalʿat al-Jabbār, where he wrote his 551
opus maior, which he completed in 928/1522, before publishing it in a revised edition in Gujarāt in 956/1549. He died in 970/1562 and was buried in Gwalior.

Herklots, *Qanoon-e-Islam* 305ff, Garcin de Tassy, *Mémoire sur la religion musulmane* 96. 1. *al-Jawāhir al-khamsa*, on the main points of mysticism (see above), Berl 3041, Ind. Off. 671/2, Paris 1197, 5359, Algiers 923, Cairo ^{1}II, 78, V, 334, Persian translation Stewart 38.—2. *Tadhkirat al-awliyā'* Lahore 1899.

1a. Qāḍī ʿĪsā b. ʿAbd al-Raḥīm al-Aḥmadābādī, who died in 982/1574, see Suppl.

2. *Intiqāl al-muqallid etc.* also Patna II, 492,$_{2625, 11}$.

2. Muḥammad b. Faḍlallāh al-Hindī al-Burhānpūrī lived as a Sufi in Burhānpūr in India and died there in 1029/1620.

Muḥ. IV, 110, Wüst. *Ṣūf.* 218. *Al-Tuḥfa al-mursala ila 'l-nabī*, on the basic principles of faith, composed in 999/1590, Berl. 2040, Alex. Taṣ. 41.—Commentaries: 1. *Itḥāf al-zakī* by al-Kūrānī, d. 1101/1689 (p. 505), composed for the enlightenment of the Javanese in matters of Sufism, Berl. 2041, Ind. Off. 684.—2. *Nukhabat al-mas'ala* by ʿAbd al-Ghanī al-Nābulusī, d. 1143/1730 (p. 458), Berl. 2042, Cairo ^{1}II, 141, Alex. Taṣ. 42,$_{8}$, 49, Fun. 88,$_{8}$, 135, 150,$_{10}$, 157,$_{8}$.—3. *al-Ḥujub al-musbala* by ʿAbd al-Raḥmān b. ʿAbdallāh b. Marʿī al-Dūrī al-Suwaydī, d. 1200/1786, Berl. 2043.—4.–7. see Suppl.

3. ʿAbd al-Qādir b. Shaykh b. ʿAbdallāh b. Shaykh b. ʿAbdallāh b. al-ʿAydarūs Muḥyi 'l-Dīn al-ʿAlawī al-Hindī was born in Aḥmadābād, the capital of Gujarāt, on 20 Rabīʿ I 978/23 August 1570. His father had arrived there from South Arabia
in 958/1551 before dying in 990/1582. | His mother was a woman from India that 419

his father had received as a present from the queen. As a Sufi he attained great eminence and died in 1038/1628.

Muḥ. II, 440, Wüst. *Gesch.* 556, *Ṣūf.* 54, 1. 1. *al-Durr al-thamīn fī bayān al-muhimm min ʿulūm al-dīn*, composed in 994/1586, Berl. 1844.—2. A treatise on
552 the assertion that Muḥammad is the | mediator between God and man, ibid. 2594.—3. *al-Minhāj ilā maʿrifat al-miʿrāj*, completed in 1002/1593, ibid. 2609.—4. *Ghāyat al-qarab fī sharḥ Nihāyat al-ṭalab*, 4 Sufi verses, with a commentary, ibid. 3421.—5. A Sufi *muwashshaḥ*, ibid. 3422.—6. *Asbāb al-najāt wal-najāḥ fī adhkār al-masāʾ wal-ṣabāḥ* ibid. 3718.—7. A poem in verses of three lines each, the first and last of which have the same rhyme while the middle one is the same throughout the poem. The tenor is: life is a voyage for which one has to collect the resources; the best supply is piety. This is explained in a commentary of 10 chapters, ibid. 7964.—8. 26 *rajaz* verses, ibid. $8161_{,1}$.—9. *al-Murāsalāt*, an exchange of letters from Bandar Sūrat and Aḥmadābād with Ḥātim b. Aḥmad al-Ahdal (p. 536) in Mukhā, covering the years 998–1012/1590–1603, ibid. 8633.—10. *al-Maqāla al-nāfiʿa wal-Risāla al-jāmiʿa*, an injunction to piety, ibid. 8848.—11. *al-Nūr al-sāfir fī akhbār al-qarn al-ʿāshir*, with special regard to South Arabia and Gujarāt and the scholars and Sufis living there, completed on 12 Rabīʿ II 1012/20 September 1603 in Aḥmadābād, Br. Mus. $937_{,1}$.—12. *al-Rawḍ al-nāḍir fī man ismuhu ʿAbd al-Qādir*, mostly dealing with the ninth and tenth centuries, Berl. 9890.—13. *Ṣidq al-wafāʾ bi-ḥaqq al-ikhāʾ*, a biography of Aḥmad b. Muḥammad al-Ḥaḍramī Bājābir, d. 1001/1593, ibid. 10139.—14. *al-Muntakhab al-muṣṭafā fī akhbār mawlid al-Muṣṭafā*, ibid. 9535.—15. *Itḥāf al-ḥaḍra al-ʿazīza bi-ʿuyūn al-sīra al-wajīza*, a biography of the Prophet and the ten Companions, ibid. 9660.—16. *Taʿrīf al-aḥyāʾ bi-faḍāʾil al-Iḥyāʾ* Suppl. I, 540.—17.–25. see Suppl.

4. Tāj al-Dīn b. Zakariyyāʾ b. Sulṭān al-Shīrāzī al-Hindī al-Naqshbandī al-ʿUthmānī al-ʿAbshamī lived as a Sufi in Ajmīr, Nagkūr, Jawānpūr, Amruhā, and Kashmir, and then in Mecca, dying there in 1050/1640.

Muḥ. I, 464/70, Wüst. *Ṣūf.* 217. 1. *Risāla fī sulūk khāṣṣat al-sāda*, on the religious views of the Naqshbandiyya, Berl. 2186, Ind. Off. $1038_{,17}$, Alex. Taṣ. 46, Cairo [1]VII, 312, Esʿad $1402_{142b-150a}$. Commentary *Miftāḥ al-maʿiyya fī ṭarīq al-Naqshbandiyya* by ʿAbd al-Ghanī al-Nābulusī (p. 456), Berl. 2188/9, ʿĀšir I, $510_{,2}$, Veliyeddin 1830, Cairo [1]II, 20.—2. *Ādāb al-murīdīn* Berl. 3189, Cairo [1]VII, 312.—3. *Taʿrīb Rashaḥāt ʿayn al-ḥayāt*, a translation of the Persian work by ʿAlī b. Ḥusayn al-Wāʿiẓ al-Kāshifī al-Ṣafī,[1] | d. 909/1503, on the classes of the Naqshbandiyya (Suppl. II, 287), Cairo ¹II, 75, ²V, 202.—4. *Taʿrīb Nafaḥāt al-uns wa-ḥaḍarāt al-quds* p. 266. 553

| 5. ʿAbd al-Karīm b. Muḥammad al-Lāhūrī, ca. 1060/1651. 420

1. *Muntahā maṭālib al-sālikīn*, on the 3 requirements for Sufis, composed in 1062/1653, Berl. 3108.—2. A treatise on the assertion that man approaches God through devoted love, with various anecdotes, ibid. 3109.—3. See Suppl.

6. Muḥammad b. Muḥammad b. Aḥmad al-Fārūqī al- Čishtī, ca. 1100/1688.

1. *Nikāt al-ikhwān bi-ʿawn Allāh al-malik al-mannān*, a short inventory of the points that matter for a Sufi, Berl. 3105.—2. *Marājīn al-ʿushshāq min abḥur al-ashwāq*, a Sufi exposition of the nature of love, the relations between the lover and the beloved, his happiness and suffering in beholding, being united, and separated, ibid. 3106.—3. *al-Jamʿ bayna ʾl-dunyā wal-ʿuqbā bi-ʿināyat Allāh al-ʿulyā*, that the world is a preparatory stage for the Hereafter, is connected to the latter, and is deserving of praise, ibid. 3145.—4. *Risālat man ʿarafa Allāh* ibid. 3231.—5. *Jawāhir al-ʿulūm*, on the nature of revealed knowledge, ibid. 3232.—6. *al-Ḥayra fī dhāt Allāh* ibid. 3233.—7. *Tuḥfat al-sulūk al-mūṣila ila ʾllāh malik al-mulūk* ibid. 3285.—8. Treatise on the *awrād*, the beginning, ibid. 3782.—9. *al-Muflis fī amān Allāh*, a discussion of this Sufi proverb, ibid. 3164.

9 *Philosophy*

1. Muṣliḥ al-Dīn Muḥammad b. Ṣalāḥ b. Jalāl al-Dīn al-Lārī al-Anṣārī was born in Lār, south of Shiraz, and moved to India, where he achieved a high position under Humāyūn (937–63/1530–56). After the latter's death he went as a trader to Aleppo, from where he made the pilgrimage. He then went to Istanbul, but did not receive the reception that he had expected. As such, he retired to Āmid, where he became a professor, before dying in 979/1571.

| *Al-ʿIqd al-manẓūm* 393/400, Rieu, *Pers. Cat.* I, 116. 1. *Baḥth tamām al-mushtarak* Gotha 87,₂, 88,₂.—2. *Fī baḥth al-qudra wal-irāda* ibid. 87,₃, 88,₃.—3. *Fī baḥth al-ḥaraka* Berl. 5100.—4. *Fī taḥqīq al-maʿād wal-mabdaʾ* Leid. 1601.—5.–8. See Suppl. 554

2. Maḥmūd al-Jawnpūrī al-Fārūqī, who died in 1062/1652.

---

1 A *qaṣīda* mourning his death by Aḥmad b. ʿAlī b. Aḥmad al-Buskarī Shihāb al-Dīn, d 1009/1600, in Aḥmadābād (Muḥ. I, 243), is preserved in Berl. 7952.

Afsūs, *ʿArāʾis-i Maḥfil*, Calcutta 1809, p. 92. 1. *al-Ḥikma al-bāligha*, on the structure of philosophy, with a commentary, *al-Shams al-bāzigha*, Ind. Off. $561_{,1}$, print. Lucknow 1280, 1288.—Glosses: a. Mollā Aḥmadallāh, Ind. Off. 562.—b.–d. see Suppl. (d. Patna I, $221_{,1881/2}$, II, $421_{,2591,\ 8}$, $526_{,2827}$).—2 *Risāla fī ithbāt al-hayūlī* Ind. Off. $561_{,2}$.—3., 4. See Suppl.

3. Muḥibballāh b. ʿAbd al-Shakūr al-Bihārī, who died in 1119/1708.

421 | I. *Sullam al-ʿulūm*, on logic, Ind. Off. 563/6, 589, 2, prints in Sprenger, *Cat.* 1878–91.—Commentaries: 1. *al-Munhiya* by Muḥammad Mubārak b. Muḥammad Dāʾim Adhamī Fārūqī (d. 1162/1748), Ind. Off. 567/70, print. Lucknow 1265.—4. Ḥamdallāh al-Sandīlī, Kanpur 1271, 1301, with *Taʿlīqāt* by Muḥammad ʿAbdallāh al-Tūnkī, Lahore 1309, Kanpur 1309, 1322 (see Suppl.).—7. *Fawāʾid* on his commentary by ʿAbd al-ʿĀlī b. Niẓām al-Dīn Baḥr al-ʿUlūm, ibid. $227_{,2000}$.—21. Asadallāh al-Panjābī, Patna I, $227_{,1994}$.—II. *Risāla fi ʾl-jawhar al-fard* Ind. Off. $581_{,9}$.—III. *Musallam al-thubūt*, on the principles of law according to the Ḥanafī and Shāfiʿī rites, composed in 1109/1697, print. Lucknow 1263, Aligarh 1297 (see Suppl.).

10 *Travelogues*

ʿAlī Khān b. Aḥmad b. Muḥammad Maʿṣūm b. Ibrāhīm Ṣadr al-Dīn al-Ḥusaynī al-Ḥasanī al-Madanī was born in Medina on 15 Jumādā I 1052/12 August 1642, a descendant of Ghiyāth al-Dīn al-Shīrāzī (p. 545). He went with his father to Golkonda in 1066/1655, and then in 1068/1667 to Hyderabad (see below). His father died after his patron there passed away in 1083/1672, while ʿAlī Khān himself was incarcerated by the new sultan, Abu ʾl-Ḥasan (1085–98/1672–89).
555 | However, he managed to flee to the court of Awrangzīb who appointed him *khān* and *dīwānī* in Burhānpūr. He died in Shiraz in 1104/1692 (see Suppl.).

Rawḍāt al-jannāt 412, *Ḥadīqat al-ʿālam* (lith. Hyderabad 1266) I, 363/5 (cited by Rieu, Br. M. Suppl. 990), Wüst. *Gesch.* 589. 1. *Sulwat al-gharīb wa-uswat al-arīb*, an account of his trip from Mecca to Hyderabad in the years 1066–9/1655–8, where his father had been appointed earlier, in 1055/1644, by prince Shāhānshāh ʿAbdallāh b. Muḥammad Quṭbshāh, who had given him his daughter in marriage and where he let his entire family join him twelve years later, composed in 1074/1663, Berl. 6136.—2. *Sulāfat al-ʿaṣr fī maḥāsin aʿyān al-ʿaṣr*, on the poets of the eleventh century, in the form of a *dhayl* to the *Rayḥāna* of al-Khafājī (p. 368), completed in 1082/1671, Berl. 7418/9, Vienna 409, Br. Mus. 1647, Garr. 511.—3. *al-Darajāt al-rafīʿa fī ṭabaqāt al-Imāmiyya min al-shīʿa* Berl. 10950.—4. *Badīʿiyya*, with a commentary, *Anwār al-rabīʿ fī anwāʿ al-badīʿ* (with the biographies of those who had written on rhetoric at the end), completed in 1093/1682, Berl. 7384, Leid. 340 (only vol. 2), Garr. 570, Paris 3255, Br. Mus. Suppl. 990/1, Rāġib 1074, Ḥamīdiyye 1216, ʿAlī Emīrī ʿarab. 3563, Cairo [1]IV, 209, Bank. XXIII, 59,3553/6.—5. A poem, Berl. 8006.—6.–8. see Suppl.

11 *Encyclopaedias*

Muḥammad ʿAlāʾ b. ʿAlī b. Qāḍī Muḥammad Ḥāmid b. Muḥammad Ṣābir al-Fārūqī al-Sunnī al-Ḥanafī al-Tahānawī wrote, in 1158/1745:

1. *Kashf iṣṭilāḥāt al-funūn*: *A Dictionary of the Technical Terms used in the Sciences of the Musalmans, ed. by Mawlawies M. Wajih Abdalhaqq and Gholam Kadir under the Superintendence of* A. Sprenger and W. Nassau Lees, 2 vols., Calcutta 1854–62; Istanbul 1317ff.—2. *Aḥkām al-arāḍī* Ind. Off. 1730.

422 | Chapter 8. The Malay Archipelago

From the sixteenth century onwards, Islam also came to the Malay people, seemingly from Malabar, among whom it soon won some of its most fervent adherents.[1] Just as in Malabar, on the Sunda islands the Shāfiʿī rite is predomi-
556 nant, | while the rest of India followed Abū Ḥanīfa. Arabic *fiqh* and mysticism were carefully studied by the Malays, although only a few of them played an active part in furthering its development.

1. Ḥājjī Yūsuf al-Tāj al-Makkī wrote, in 1087/1676, for Abu 'l-Fatḥ, the sultan of Banten on Java:

Zubdat al-asrār, a Sufi work, Bat. 101,$_{2}$.

2. ʿAbdallāh b. ʿAbd al-Qahhār al-Jāwī wrote, in 1161/1748:

Kitāb fī shurūṭ al-ḥajj Bat. 131,$_{4}$.

3. Aḥmad Ṣāliḥ Shams al-Milla wal-Dīn, the sultan of Boni on Celebes, wrote, in 1202/1787 when he was 30 years old:

Al-Nūr al-hādī ilā ṭarīq al-rashād, Bat. 108, 24.

---

1 Cf. T.W. Arnold, *The Preaching of Islam* 294.

Chapter 9. Rumelia and Anatolia

Together with their political power, the central lands of the Ottoman Empire
also gained a certain intellectual ascendancy over the rest of the Muslim world.
In Istanbul, which was from then on regarded as the capital of Islam, scholars from all countries flocked together. Even though they generally remained
only long enough to secure a post in their home country, they nevertheless
provided the educated circles of this city with a lot of energy. | The numer- 423
ous endowments of the Ottoman rulers, which the financial downfall of the
empire only affected towards the end of this period, allowed a host of literati
to devote themselves to scholarly pursuits. The intellectual endeavours of the
Ottoman Empire proved for a large part advantageous to Arabic literature, and
it was only in historiography and belles lettres that Turkish | had pride of place. 557
In books of learning, people employed the Arabic language almost exclusively,
while Turkish only flourished in popular works.

IM. *Al-ʿIqd al-manẓūm fī dhikr afāḍil al-Rūm* by ʿAlī Manuq (§ 2,5), a continuation of the *ShN* (p. 560), in the margin of Ibn Khall. II.

1a *Philology*

1. Jamāl al-Dīn Isḥāq al-Qaramānī, who died in 930/1523.

Al-Tawābiʿ fi ʾl-ṣarf, on morphology, Berl. 6775/6 (attributed to Ibn Kamālpāshā), Upps. 50, 1, NO 4650, Köpr. III, 619.

2. Muṣṭafā b. Muḥammad al-Āynegölī wrote, in 935/1528:

An Arabic dictionary, mostly based on al-Jawharī and al-Fīrūzābādī, Upps. 10,$_1$.

3. Muṣṭafā b. Muḥammad al-Burūsawī Khusrawzāde, who died in 998/1590.

1. *Tanbīh al-anām fī tawjīh al-kalām*, on errors among the masses, Berl. 7099.—
2. *Majmaʿ al-ʿibārāt ʿalā afṣaḥ al-lughāt*, Alex. Lugha 26.

4. Muṣṭafā b. Ibrāhīm, from Gallipoli, died in 1024/1615.

Zubdat al-amthāl, a collection of proverbs based on the work of al-Zamakhsharī, al-Maydānī, and others, composed in 999/1591 and dedicated to Sultan Murād

III, Munich 648, Vienna 339, Copenhagen 242, Leid. 398, Bodl. II, 114, Lee 68, Paris 3967,$_{1}$, Pet. 236,$_{2}$, NO 3932, AS 4025/6.

424 | 5. Khiḍr b. Muḥammad al-Muftī al-Amāsī wrote, in 1060–1/1650–1:

ʿUnbūb al-balāgha fī yanbūʿ al-faṣāha Cairo ^{1}IV, 123, ^{2}II, 177.—2. See Suppl.

5b. Muḥammad al-Tīrawī al-ʿAyshī, who died in 1046/1636.

1. *al-Munaqqaḥāt al-mashrūḥa*, a textbook on rhetoric, Garr. 563, Landb.-Br. 2.—2. *Rūḥ al-shurūḥ* see Suppl. 657, 25b.

558 | 6. Muḥammad b. Muṣṭafā b. Maḥmūd Ḥājibzāde, who died in 1100/1698.

1. *Hadiyyat al-ṣibyān*, on conjugations, Kraft 58.—2., 3. See Suppl.

7. Mollā ʿAbdallāh b. ʿAbd al-Raḥmān b. Mūsā wrote, in 1110/1698:

Al-Muqaddima al-Fakhriyya, a grammar with a commentary entitled *al-Minaḥ al-ilāhiyya*, Leid 258.

8. ʿĪsā b. ʿAlī b. Ḥasan b. Mazyad b. Yūsuf b. ʿAlī al-Būlawī al-Kurdī wrote, in 1113/1701:

Mufīd al-iʿrāb Garr. 476, Alex. Naḥw 41, Cairo ^{1}IV, 96, ^{2}II, 162.

9. Muḥammad Salīm b. Ḥusayn b. ʿAbd al-Ḥalīm Efendi, who died in 1138/1725.

Mawārid al-baṣāʾir li-farāʾid al-ḍarāʾir, on poetical liberty on metrical grounds, Vienna 225, AS 4132, Fātiḥ 4129, Waqf Ibr. 328, Cairo ^{2}II, 242.

10. Shaykh al-Islām Muḥammad Asʿad b. ʿAlī Yanabulī Efendi, who was born in 1096/1684 and died in 1166/1752, see Suppl.

1. *Iṭbāq al-aṭbāq*, aphorisms (cf. I, 349) with a commentary by Muḥammad al-Āqkirmānī, ca. 1167/1753, Vienna 351, Krafft 149.—2. *Bahjat al-lughāt*, an Arabic, Persian, and Turkish dictionary, Krafft 29.

11. Muḥammad Rāghib Pāshā became the governor of Egypt in 1159/1746 and died on 24 Ramaḍān 1176/9 April 1763 as a grand vizier in Istanbul. The

beautiful library, rich in rare items, which he left as a *waqf* to the scholars of Istanbul, bears testimony to his lively literary interest.

Jab. I, 260. 1. *Safīnat al-Rāghib wa-dafīnat al-ṭālib*, an anthology, Vienna 411, Br. Mus. Suppl. 1154, Cairo ¹VI, 149, ²VI, 185, print. Būlāq 1255, 1282, 1288.—2. *Muntakhabāt* Cairo ¹IV, 332, ²III, 385.—3. *Risāla fī 'l-ʿarūḍ*, on which a commentary, Paris 4455 (Turkish *Dīwān* Vienna 737).

| 2 *Historiography* 559

1. Ramaḍān al-Ṭālib wrote, in 928/1521:

Al-Risāla al-fatḥiyya al-Rādūsiyya, on the conquest of Rhodes by Sultan Süleymān, whose physician he was, Paris 1622; cf. Tercier, Mémoire sur la prise de la ville et de l'île de Rhodes, *Mém. de l'Ac. des inscr. anc. rec.* XXVI, 728ff.

1a. See Suppl. III 1303 ad 633.

| 2. Aḥmad b. Qara Kamāl wrote, around 930/1523: 425

Jawāhir al-bayān fī dawlat āl ʿUthmān, Vat. V 870.

3. Sinān al-Dīn Yūsuf b. ʿAlī b. Muḥammad Shāh b. Muḥammad al-Yakānī was a professor in Bursa, then Izniq, then a *qāḍī* in Amasia, a secretary in the ministry of finance, a *qāḍī* in Damascus, again a professor in Bursa and at one of the eight madrasas in Istanbul, and then retired, before dying in 945/1539.

ShN I, 140, 653/6. *Risāla fī 'l-ishāra ilā ghazwat rawāfiḍ al-ʿAjam wastīlāʾ malik al-Rūm ʿalā mamlakat al-Shām*, composed in 922/1516, Pet. 81, 24.

4. Abu 'l-Khayr Aḥmad b. Muṣliḥ al-Dīn Muṣṭafā Ṭāshköprīzāde ʿIṣām al-Dīn was born in Bursa on 14 Rabīʿ I 901/3 December 1495, studied under his father (*ShN* I, 613/7) in Ankara and Bursa, and then in Istanbul and Amasia. At the end of Rajab 931/May 1525 he became a professor at the Dīma Tūqa madrasa, then at the beginning of 933/October 1526, was transferred to the madrasa of Mollā b. Ḥājjī in Istanbul, and then to the Isḥāqiyya, in Üsküb, at the beginning of Dhu 'l-Ḥijja 936/July 1531. On 17 Shawwāl 942/10 April 1536 he again became a professor in Istanbul, at the Qalandarkhāne, and on 21 Rabīʿ II 944/29 September 1537 at the madrasa of the vizier Muṣṭafā Pāshā. On 4 Dhu 'l-Qaʿda 945/25 March 1539 he was transferred to Adrianople, on 23 Rabīʿ I 946/9 August 1539 to one of the eight madrasas in Istanbul, and on 10 Shawwāl 951/| 560

26 December 1544 to the Bāyezīdiyya in Adrianople. On 26 Ramaḍān 952/2 December 1545 he unwillingly became a *qāḍī* in Bursa, but returned to his chair in Adrianople as early as 18 Rajab 954/4 September 1547. On 27 Shawwāl 958/29 October 1551 he became a *qāḍī* in Istanbul. On 17 Rabīʿ I 961/21 February 1554 he was afflicted with an eye infection, as a result of which he lost his eyesight within the space of a couple of months. From then on, he could only dictate. He died in 968/1560.

ShN II, 177/92, *IM* 188/208, *TA* 15r, Hammer, *Gesch. des osm. Reiches* III, 757, Wüst. *Gesch.* 527, Adnan Adîvar, *Osmanlî Türklerinde Ilim* 87/8. An inventory of his writings, Berl. 20. 1. *Nawādir al-akhbār fī manāqib al-akhyār*, alphabetical and within every letter separated according to three sources: Abū Muḥammad al-Andarsakānī (ḤKh III, 637,$_{7315}$), *Siyar al-ṣaḥāba*, Ibn Khallikān and al-Shahrastānī (I, 551), completed on 30 Jumādā I 938/19 January 1532 in Üsküb, Vienna 1181.—2. *al-Shaqāʾiq al-Nuʿmāniyya fī ʿulamāʾ al-dawla al-ʿUthmāniyya*, on 522 *ʿulamāʾ* and Sufis, from the administrations of ʿUthmān until Süleymān, in 10 classes, at the end of which is his own autobiography, completed on 30 Ramaḍān 965/16 July 1558, Berl. 9881/2, Ms. Ar. oct. 3916,
426 Gotha 1765/6, Vienna 1182, Krafft 311, Basel M. III, 217, | Leid. 1038/9, Br. Mus. 364, 1300, 1507, Suppl. 678, Bodl. I, 818, 846,$_{1}$, Cambr. 9, no. 190, Lee 97, Paris 2157/62, Algiers 531,$_{2}$, Pet. 117/8, AM 204/6, Kazan 110, autograph dated 965 Garr. 704/5, MS dated 967 NO 3381, printed in the margin of Ibn Khallikān, Būlāq 1299. Manuscripts in Istanbul, Turkish translations and continuations, see Behcet Gönül, Istanbul kütüphanelerinde al-Sh. an. N. tercüme wezeyilleri, *Türk. Mecm.* 7/8, II, 1945, 136/168. 1). Turkish translation with addenda by Muḥammad al-Majdī, d. 999/1558, Vienna 1125, MSS in Istanbul in B. Gönül 151, print. Istanbul 1269.—2). Ibrāhīm b. Aḥmad al-Amāsī, Br. Mus. Turk., 72. ʿA. Emīrī, Taʾrīkh 727.—3). See Suppl. (read: Köpr. II, 230).—4). Darwīsh ʿAbdallāh Efendi *al-Dawḥa al-ʿirfāniyya fī rawḍat al-ʿulamāʾ al-ʿUthmāniyya* Cairo Fihr. Küt. Türk 205.—5). Sayyid Muṣṭafā, *Ḥaqāʾiq al-bayān fī tarjamat al-Shaqāʾiq al-Nuʿmāniyya* Yîldîz, Tarācim-i Aḥwāl 12.—Abstracts: see Gönül 153–4.—Continuations (*Dhayl*): a. ʿAlī Manuq, see no. 5.—b. ʿAbd al-Qādir Efendi Yîlanğîq, d. 1000/1501, Paris 2164,$_{1}$.—c. Nawʿīzāde, see no. 8.—d. ʿAshiq Čelebī, Paris 2164,$_{2}$, Fātiḥ 4413, Yaḥyā 4597.—e. Anon., Berl. 9885.—f. see Suppl.
561 | —g. ʿĀkif Efendīzāde ʿAbd al-Raḥīm, *al-Majmūʿ fi ʾl-mashhūd wal-masmūʿ*, ʿA. Emīrī ʿArabī 2527.—3. *al-Risāla al-jāmiʿa li-waṣf al-ʿulūm al-nāfiʿa* Berl. 84.—4. *Miftāḥ al-saʿāda wa-miṣbāḥ al-siyāda*, an encyclopaedia of 150 sciences, Vienna 16, Leid. 18, Garr. 1136, Cairo VI, ^{1}200, ^{2}191. *Dībāja* Berl. 85, printed Hyderabad, 2 vols., 1328/9, Turkish translation by his son Kamāl al-Dīn *Mawḍūʿāt al-ʿulūm*, Der Seadet 1312. German translation of the first part by O. Rescher, Stuttgart

[Istbl.] 1937.—Abbreviation by the author, completed on 20 Ṣafar 968/16 November 1560, dictated to his students in Istanbul, anonymous abstract *Madīnat al-ʿulūm* Vienna 17, Cairo ¹VI, 195, *Muntakhabāt* ibid. VII, 115.—5. A treatise on the letter *wāw* in sura 15,₄, Leid. 1701.—6. *Risālat al-ḥamd* (*li llāh*), in a revised version, Berl. 2277.—7. *Risāla fī ʿilm al-farāʾiḍ*, with a self-commentary, completed in 956/1549, Gotha 1110, AS 1608.—8. *Masʾala fiqhiyya*, a discussion of a case of culpability, Berl. 4999.—9. *al-Shuhūd al-ʿaynī fī mabāḥith al-wujūd al-dhihnī*, on the reality of the imagination, ibid. 5106.—10. *al-Qawāʿid al-jaliyyāt fī taḥqīq mabāḥith al-kulliyyāt*, on what it means to be "universal" or "particular", ibid. 5143.—11. *al-Nahal wal-ʿalal fī taḥqīq aqsām al-ʿilal*, on what it means to be a "cause" and on its various kinds, completed on 25 Muḥarram 958/5 February 1551, ibid. 5144.—12. *al-Liwāʾ al-marfūʿ fī ḥall mabāḥith al-mawḍūʿ*, on the nature of the individual sciences and their relations to each other, ibid. 5205.—13. *Risāla fī ʿilm ādāb al-baḥth*, with a self-commentary, Berl. 5323/4, Gotha 2819, Munich 897, f. 58/64, Garr. 907/2, 2099,₃, Alex. Fun. 120,₂, Cairo ¹VII, 106, 419.—Commentary by Aḥmad b. ʿUmar b. Muḥammad b. ʿAlī, completed in 1106/1694 in Sīwās, Berl. 5325, Alex. Fun. 79,₃.—Glosses: a. ʿAbdallāh b. Muḥammad al-Qayṣarī, composed in 1152/1739, Berl. 5326.—b. Khalīl b. Ḥasan al-Sīrawī, Garr. 913.—c. Anon., Berl. 5327.—Versification, ibid. 5328.—14. *Risālat al-shifāʾ fī dawāʾ al-wabāʾ* Leid. 2037, Cairo ¹VI, 152, print. C. 1292.—15. *Munyat al-shubbān fī muʿāsharat al-niswān* Köpr. 1402.—16. *Risāla fī taḥqīq afʿāl al-tafḍīl* Berl. 6889.—17. *Risālat masālik al-khalāṣ fī mahālik al-khawāṣṣ*, on the controversy between al-Taftāzānī (p. 278) and al-Jurjānī (p. 280) on derived and composite metaphors, Berl. 7322, Algiers 228.—18. *al-Inṣāf fī mushājarat al-aslāf*, on the same, Berl. 7323.—19. *Fi ʾl-muḥākama bayna Saʿd al-Dīn wal-Sayyid al-Sharīf*, on a dispute over a passage in the *Miftāḥ* (I, 352), ibid. 7324.—20. *al-ʿInāya fī taḥqīq al-istiʿāra bil-kināya*, on metonymic | metaphors, ibid. 7325, Garr. 572.—21. A *qaṣīda* for Abu ʾl-Suʿūd, Berl. 7939,₂.—22. *Talkhīṣ Tajrīd al-kalām* I, 670.—23., 24. See Suppl.—25. *Risāla fī taqsīm al-ʿilm ila ʾl-taṣawwur wal-taṣdīq* Sarajevo 137,₅. 562

5. ʿAlī Efendi b. Bālī b. Muḥammad Bek Manuq[1] became a teacher at the school for the Janissaries (Khaṣṣakiyya) in 987/1579, before dying in 992/1584.

| Wüst. *Gesch.* 537; Babinger, GO 112; Behcet Gönül, *Türk. Mecm.* 7–8, II (1945), p. 156ff. 1. *al-ʿIqd al-manẓūm fī dhikr afāḍil al-Rūm*, a continuation of the *ShN*, Berl. 9883/4, Vienna 1183, Paris 2163, 5944, Br. Mus. 960 Bursa, Ḥü. Č. Taʾr. 52, manuscripts in Istanbul and translations in Gonül; Cairo V, ¹89, ²270, printed in 427

1 A Turkish term of endearment for a cuddly cat (A. Ateš).

the margin of Ibn Khall., Būlāq 1299, 1310.—2. *Ifāḍat al-fattāḥ fī ḥāshiyat Sharḥ Taghyīr al-Miftāḥ* I, 353, Cairo ^{1}III, 76.

6. ʿAlī Dede b. Muṣṭafā ʿAlāʾ al-Dīn al-Busnawī al-Sigetwārī, Shaykh al-Turba, was born in Mostar in Bosnia, joined the Sufi order of the Khalwatiyya, and was involved in Sultan Süleymān's campaign against Hungary. When the latter perished during the siege of Sigetwār and his heart[2] was buried at the site of the fortress, ʿAlī was put in charge of the guards at his mausoleum. In 1001/1592 Sultan Murād sent him to Mecca with the order to recreate the Maqām Ibrāhīm. It was there that he wrote work no. 2 below. He died in 1007/1598 in the fortress of Szolnik.

Muḥ. III, 200, Wüst. *Gesch.* 545. 1. *Muḥāḍarat al-awāʾil wa-musāmarat al-awākhir*, an augmented abstract of a work by al-Suyūṭī (p. 203, no. 303), Berl. 9371/2, Vienna 822, Pet. AM 194/5, Leid. 1018, Paris 2079/80, 5933, 5996, Ẓāh. ʿIsh, Taʾr. 10, Algiers 1568, NO 4132/7, AS 4251, Köpr. 1381, Bursa Haraččizade Edeb. 39, Cairo ^{1}V, 131, 141, ^{2}V 327 327, print. Būlāq 1300, C. 1311.—2. *al-Risāla al-maqāmiyya al-Makkiyya*, from which abstracts on the *awāʾil* Berl. 9373.—
563 3. *Khawātim al-ḥikam wa-ḥall al-rumūz wa-kashf* | *al-kunūz*, 300 Sufi questions on the wisdom of legal prescriptions etc., completed in Muḥarram 1000/October 1591, Berl. 3479, Welīeddīn 1627, Fātiḥ 2613, NO 2375, Cairo ^{1}VI, 137, ^{2}V 327, 293, App. 41.—4. See Suppl.

7. ʿAbdallāh b. Ṣalāḥ (al-Dīn) b. Dāʾūd b. ʿAlī b. Dāʾir wrote, in 1010/1601 for Sultan Murād III:

1. *Futūḥ al-sulṭān Murād fī bilād al-Yaman*, in a rhetorical style, beginning with the Creation and continuing as a universal history up to the year 1004/1595, autograph Rāġib 979 (Tauer, *AO* VI, 109, note).—2. *Asna ʾl-maṭālib wa-uns al-labīb al-ṭālib*, a geography, NO 2986 (Tauer, *AO* VI, 107).—3. See Suppl. (Wüst. *Gesch.* 541).[3]

8. Muḥammad b. Yaḥyā b. Pīr ʿAlī b. Naṣūḥ Nawʿīzāde ʿAṭāʾallāh ʿAṭāʾī was a secretary in Istanbul, and then a *qāḍī* in Rumelia and then in Üsküb. He died soon after his removal from office in 1045/1635.

---

2 See G. Jacob, *Hilfsbuch f. Vorl.* ^{2}I, 42, n. 2.

3 See p. 528. 5 c (R.).

Muḥ. IV, 263; Wüst. *Gesch.* 562; Behcet Gönül, *Türkiyat Mecm.* 7–8 II (1945 I), 161ff, where we also find the continuations. *Ḥadāʾiq al-ḥaqāʾiq fī takmilat al-Shaqāʾiq*, Turkish, Istanbul 1268. Manuscripts in Istanbul in Gönül.—2. *al-Qawl al-ḥasan fī jawāb al-qawl li-man*, on the theory of litigation, Yeni 532, NO 2057, Köpr. II, 100, III, 100, Alex. Fiqh. Ḥan. 46, Cairo [1]III, 100, 120.

9. Muṣṭafā b. ʿAbdallāh Kātib Čelebī Ḥājjī Khalīfa, the son of an official in the ministry of war, was born in Istanbul in 1017/1609. At the age of 14 he joined the Siliḥdārs and was assigned to the pay-office of the army's administration in Anatolia. In the years 1033–45/1624–35 he was, with the exception of two brief intermissions, on the battlefield in the war against the rebel Abāza Pāshā, present at the failed siege of Baghdad from 11 Ṣafar until 7 Shawwāl 1035/12 November 1625–2 July 1626, and a member of the campaign force sent against Iran in the years 1039–40/1630. After the death of his father in 1035/1626 he was given a post as an aspiring member of the accounting office of the horse regiment. | In 1038/1628 and 1041/1630 he had the opportunity to restart his studies 564
in Istanbul. However, in the years 1043–5/1633–5 he had to join the campaign against Iran that Murād IV led in person. When the army had taken up its winter quarters in Aleppo, he made the pilgrimage to Mecca. Having returned to Istanbul in 1045/December 1635, a number of inheritances allowed him to resign from service and devote himself entirely to the sciences. Although he only resigned in 1055/1645 when he was refused a promotion, he still assumed the post of second *khalīfa* at his old unit three years later. He died, having not even reached 50 years of age, in Istanbul on 17 Dhu 'l-Ḥijja 1067/27 September 1657.

Wüst. *Gesch.* 570, Adnan Adivar, *Ilim* 115/38. 1. *Kashf al-ẓunūn fī asāmi 'l-kutub wal-funūn*, the first volume of which he completed in 1064/1654 after 20 years of collecting, ed. G. Flügel, see I, 3, Būlāq 1274, Istanbul 1310/1. New edition, using the autograph, by Šerefettin Yaltkaya and Kilisli Rifat Bilge, 2 vols., Istanbul 1941/3.—Appendix: *Kešf-el-Zunun Zeyli: Īḍāḥ al-maknūn fi 'l-dhayl ʿalā Kashf al-ẓunūn ʿan asāmi 'l-kutub wal-funūn* by Baghdatlî Ismail Pasha, by the same publishers, Istanbul 1945– . An appendix, *Āthār-i naw* by Aḥmad Ḥanīf Zāde, d. 1180/1766, mainly lists Turkish works of the period after Ḥājjī Khalīfa and revisits some earlier ones, Vienna 36, ed. Flügel, ḤKh, vol. VI.—2. *Taqwīm al-tawārīkh*, a chronological overview, in Turkish, of universal history with tables in Persian, composed in 1058/1648, print. Istanbul 1146/1733, with a continuation of the tables until 1045 and other additions; Arabic translation Br. Mus. 1253. *Cronologia historica scritta in lingua Turca, Persiana et Araba da*

Hazi Halifé Mustafá e trad. nell'idioma Italiano da Giorgio Rinaldi Carli, Venice 1697.—3. *Faḍlaka,* a Turkish history of the Ottoman empire for the years 1003–65/1594–1655, a continuation of a lost abstract of al-Jannābī (p. 387 ḤKh 2198, 3496) and its Turkish translation, As'ad Ef., Vienna 1064/6, Pet. AM 520, print. Istanbul 1286/7.—4. *Tuḥfat al-kibār fī asfār al-biḥār,* composed after the
565 defeat of the Ottoman fleet at the hands of the Venetians at | the Dardanelles in 1067/1656, print. Istanbul 1141/1728. *The History of the maritime Wars of the Turks transl. from the Turkish of Haji Khalifeh by* J. Mitchell, London 1831.—5. *Jihānnumā,* a general geography based on both oriental and occidental sources that had been made available to him by a French defector, composed in 1065/1655 (the first draft Vienna 1282, another version Br. Mus. Or. 1282), unfinished, Istanbul 1145/1732. *Gihan Numah* (On the MSS in Taeschner see Suppl., additionally Paris Fonds turc, Suppl. 215). *Geographia orientalis ex Turc. in Lat. versa a* M. Norberg, Lond. Goth. 1818. *Rumili und Bosna, geogr. beschr. von Mustafa Abdalla Hadschi Chalfa, aus dem Türk. übers. v.* J. v. Hammer, Vienna 1812 (Taeschner, *MOG* II, 308ff), *Description de l'Asie Mineure extr. de la géographie Turque de Hadji Khalfa, surnommé Kiatib-Tchelebi, imprimée sur la traduction mscr. d'*Armain, in *Descr. hist. et géogr. de l'Asie Mineure par* Vivien de St. Martin I, 637, see Adnan, *Ilim* 120ff.—6. *Tuḥfat al-akhyār fi 'l-ḥikam wal-amthāl*
429 *wal-ash'ār,* | composed in 1061/1651, Cairo [1]V, 214, [2]III, 44.—7. *Sullam al-wuṣūl ilā ṭabaqāt al-fuḥūl,* biographies of famous men, composed in 1061/2, autograph Šehīd 'A. Pāshā 1878, Cairo V [1]69, [2]218.—8. *Mīzān al-ḥaqq fi'khtiyār al-aḥaqq,* on the points of controversy between the orthodox and the mystics, in which he distances himself from the rigid orthodoxy of his teacher Qāḍīzāde, composed in Ṣafar 1067/November 1656, Vienna 1032, Rieu 254, print. Istanbul 1281, 1286, 1306, see Adnan Adivar, *Ilim* 118ff.—9.–12. see Suppl.—13. The Turkish *Tārīkh-i Frenjī,* partly printed in *Taṣvīr-i Efkār* no. 35ff., was translated from Carion's *Chronica,* 1531 (see Adnan Adivar, *Ilim* 129).

10. 'Umar al-Isbīrī wrote, around 1150/1737, for a vizier whose librarian he hoped to become:

Farḥat al-fu'ād, a summary of the history of the Ottoman sultans and the scholars of their times up to 974/1567, Munich 425, Babinger, *GO* 242.

11. Abu 'l-Maḥāmid 'Abd al-'Ālim Muḥammad Sa'īd Shahrīzāde, who was born in 1143/1730, wrote, in 1173/1759:

Matn al-tawārīkh, a kind of index to his larger work, *Qurrat al-abṣār fī natāʾij al-tawārīkh wal-akhbār*, with a short autobiography at the end, Pet. Ros. 59 (autograph).

12. Abu ʾl-Barakāt Muḥammad al-Raḥbī wrote, in 1175/1762 for Rāghib Pāshā:

| *Nuzhat al-mushtāq fī ʿulamāʾ al-ʿIrāq*, autograph Rāġib 1050, Medina ZDMG 90, 566
119 (Suppl. III, 1224 to be excised).

3 *Popular Prose*

1. Muḥyi ʾl-Dīn Muḥammad b. al-Khaṭīb Qāsim b. Yaʿqūb was born in Amasia in 864/1459, became a professor in Bursa, Istanbul, Adrianople, at one of the eight madrasas of Istanbul, in Amasia, at the Selīmiyya in Istanbul, again at one of the eight madrasas of that city, at the Bāyezīdiyya in Adrianople, and again at one of the eight madrasas in Istanbul. He died there in 940/1533.

ShN I, 634/8, Mejdī 398. *Rawḍ al-akhyār*, an anthology, mostly from al-Zamakhsharī's *Rabīʿ al-abrār* (I, 349), print. Būlāq 1280, C. 1279, 1292, 1306, 1307.

2. Muḥammad al-Qarabāghī Muḥyi ʾl-Dīn had studied in Iran and then became a professor in Iznik, where he died in 942/1535.

ShN II, 59, Mejdī 455. *Jālib al-surūr wa-sālib al-ghurūr* or *al-Rawḍa*, an abstract by Maḥmūd b. Muḥammad entitled *Laṭāʾif al-ishārāt fi ʾl-muḥāḍarāt wal-muḥāwarāt* (*al-Maqālāt fī ʿilm al-muḥāḍarāt*), Vienna 413, Berl. Oct. 2395, Garr. 2016,$_2$, Cairo ^{1}IV, 327, ^{2}III, 368.

4. ʿAlī b. ʿAbd al-ʿAzīz Ummalwaladzāde, a son of the chief *qāḍī* of Aleppo, | 430
d. 920/1514, became a professor in Bursa, Istanbul, Bursa, at one of the eight madrasas in Istanbul, and then *qāḍī* in Aleppo. He died in 981/1573.

ʿIM 417/30. 1. *al-Risāla al-qalamiyya*, on the glory of the reed-pen, Berl. oct. 2554, Vienna 2003,$_{35}$.—2. *al-Risāla al-shamaʿiyya* Vienna 2003,$_{49}$.—3. *al-Risāla al-sayfiyya* ibid. 50; cf. v. Hammer, *Gesch. der osm. Dichtkunst* II, 350.—Abstracts from the three in *ʿIM* 419ff.

5. Muḥammad Čelebī al-Majdī of Adrianople, who died in 999/1590.

ʿAṭāʾī, Dhayl ShN 334/6, Behcet Gönül, *Türkiyat Mecm.* 1945, p. 151. *Al-Risāla*
567 *al-shamaʿiyya*, extolling the greatness of the | candle, Vienna 2003,32; cf. v. Hammer, *Gesch. der osm. Dichtkunst* 74.—Translation of the *Shaqāʾiq* see above p. 560.

6. Abu ʾl-Fayḍ Muḥammad b. al-Ḥājj Ḥaydar al-Kaffawī, who died in 1053/1643.

Ḥadāʾiq al-akhyār fī ḥaqāʾiq al-akhbār, completed in 1020/1611, NO 2366, Q̊ilïč ʿA. 698.

6a. Aḥmad b. Ibrāhīm al-Rasmī was born on Crete in 1106/1694, went to Istanbul in 1147/1734, became secretary (*rasmī*) to the grand vizier, then head *čawush*, took part in the campaign against the Russians, and then became forage master of the sultan. He died in 1197/1783.

ʿIM I, 78/80. *Al-Maqāma al-zulāliyya al-bishāriyya*, with many proverbs and other *nukat*, Berl. 8581 (Mur. I, 74ff, two riddles).

7., 8. See Suppl.

(7. Garr 226, wrong; 8. Garr. 1929).

7a. Suppl. III, 1303.

4 Ḥadīth

1a. Khayr al-Dīn Khiḍr b. Maḥmūd b. ʿUmar al-ʿAṭūfī al-Marzifūnī, who died in 948/1541, see Suppl.

6. *Ḥiṣn al-āyāt al-ʿiẓām fī tafsīr āwāʾil sūrat al-Anʿām* AS 396,1, 399,1 (Ritter, *Türk. Mecm.* 7–8, II [1945], p. 72).

1(b). ʿAlī b. Ḥasan b. ʿAlī al-Amāsī wrote, in 978/1570:

Tuḥfat dhawi ʾl-albāb fī tarjamat man kharraja lahum al-shaykhān min al-aṣḥāb, Alex. Taʾr. 46, Muṣṭ. Ḥad. 6 (autograph).

1d. Muḥammad Shāhī Oqčizāde was a student of Maḥmūd al-Uskudārī (p. 590) and died in 1039/1629.

Brūsalı̊ II, 178. 1. *al-Naẓm al-mubīn fi 'l-āyāt al-arbaʿīn*, 40 metric verses of the Qur'ān (in Turkish), Heidelberg 217, Köpr. 217.—2. *al-Maqām al-maḥmūd*, edifying *ḥadīth*s, Köpr. 291.

2. Shaykh al-Islām Muḥammad b. Maḥmūd b. Aḥmad Dabbāghzāde, who died in 1114/1702.

| *ʿIlmiyye Sālnāmesi* (Istbl. 1334), p. 489 1. *Rashḥat al-naṣīḥ min al-ḥadīth al-ṣaḥīḥ*, composed in 1096–7/1685–6, AS 1822, NO 2411, Cairo [1]II, 86.—2. *Tartīb jamīl* (to be read thus), p. 279.—3. See Suppl. 568

5 *Fiqh, Ḥanafī*

1. Ḥabīb b. ʿAlī b. Ilyās, ca. 920/1514.

Al-Kifāya, muqaddima fi 'l-ṭahāra wal-ṣalāt, dedicated to Sultan Selīm I (918–26/1512–20), Cairo [1]III, 104.

| 2. Muṣliḥ al-Dīn Mūsā b. Mūsā al-Amāsī Khāzin al-Kutub studied in Asia Minor, Iran, and Arabia, became a Sufi, and then, under Selīm I, a librarian at the Jāmiʿ Bāyezīd in Amasia. 431

ShN II, 14/5, Mejdī 417. *Makhzan al-fiqh* NO 1821, Cairo [1]III, 128, [2]I, 462.

3. ʿAlā' al-Dīn ʿAlī b. Aḥmad al-Jamālī, a student of Muṣliḥ al-Dīn b. al-Ḥusayn who was a professor at the Sulṭāniyya in Bursa, later became the latter's son-in-law, a private teacher, and then a professor in Adrianople. However, when his salary was cut he gave up his cloak. When Bāyezīd II came to power in 886/1481 he ordered al-Jamālī come to him, but when the latter did not heed his call he sent him as a professor to Amasia. Later he went, in the same capacity, to Bursa, then Iznik, then back to Amasia, and finally to Istanbul. While he was on the pilgrimage the *muftī* of Istanbul died, and upon his return he was appointed successor. His manly posture impressed Sultan Selīm to such an extent that he made him *qāḍi 'l-ʿaskar*. He died in 931/1525 while still holding that position.

ShN I, 422/30. 1. *Ādāb al-awṣiyā'*, Yeni 353/4, Cairo [1]II, 4.—2. *al-Mukhtār lil-fatwā*, NO 1808, Alex. Fiqh Ḥan. 61, Cairo [1]III, 126, [2]I, App. 56.—3., 4. See Suppl.

3(a). Yaʿqūb b. Sayyidī ʿAlī ʿAlīzāde al-Rūmī al-Banbānī began his teaching career at the madrasa of Ḥamza Bey in Bursa, then became a professor at | the 569 madrasa of Sultan Bāyezīd there, as well as a *qāḍī*. He then became a professor at one of the eight madrasas of Istanbul, and died in 930 or 931/1524 after returning from the pilgrimage.

ShN. I, 471, Rescher 206, Mejdī 328, Belīgh, *Güldeste-i riyāz-i ʿirfān* 287.—1. *Asrār al-aḥkām* Ind. Off. 1525 and *Mafātīḥ al-jinān wa-maṣābīḥ al-janān*, ibid. 1526, two commentaries on *Shirʿat al-Islām*, I, 464.—2. *Ḥāshiya ʿalā Sharḥ dībājat Miṣbāḥ al-naḥw* I, 352, 29 (with a wrongly-dated alleged autograph).—3. Arabic commentary on Saʿdī's *Gulistān* AS 4401/3.

3b. Shaykh al-Islām Jamāl al-Dīn Isḥāq al-Qaramānī Jamāl Khalīfa, who died in 933/1527, see Suppl.

Tafsīr, Berl. Ms. or. qu. 1591.

3c. See Suppl.

(Son of Muḥammad Aflāṭūn b. Muḥammad Jaʿfar al-Ḥārithī[?]; his *Maqṭar mā al-ḥayāt li-ahl al-ṣalāt* Patna I, 150, 1436).

4. Muḥammad b. ʿUmar b. Ḥamza al-Wāʿiẓ Mollā ʿArab Muḥyi 'l-Dīn was born in Antakya, studied there, in Ḥisn Kayfā, Āmid, and Tabriz, and then worked for a time as a *muftī* and preacher in Aleppo. After making a pilgrimage to Jerusalem and Mecca he studied in Cairo under al-Suyūṭī (p. 180) and al-Shumunnī (p. 99,$_{20}$), before living at the court of the Mamlūk Sultan Qā'itbāy. After the latter's death he went to Bursa and Istanbul, returning to the latter after living for another six years in Aleppo, during which time he participated in the campaign against Iran. He then lived in Sarajevo for 10 years and, finally, in Bursa, where he began the construction of a great mosque, although he died in 938/1531 before it was completed.

ShN II, 3/10, Mejdī 411/5, Belīgh, *Güldeste-i riyāẕ-iʿirfān* 193. 1. *al-Sadād fī faḍl al-jihād*, AS 1985, 1988/9.—2. See Suppl.

432 | 5. Muḥyi 'l-Dīn Muḥammad b. Ilyās Čiwizāde, who died in 954/1547, see Suppl.

570 | *ʿIlmiyye Sālnāmesi*, p. 361. 1. *Fatāwī*, based on a collection begun by his father which had been left unfinished, Köpr. 650, Cairo [1]III, 88.—2. See Suppl.

6. Muḥammad Čelebī b. Quṭb al-Dīn Muḥammad Mīram Kösesi, who was a student of Yaʿqūb b. Sayyidī ʿAlī (p. 568), became a teacher at the madrasa of Aḥmad Pāshā b. Walī al-Dīn in Bursa, and later held that position in Istanbul, Iznik, and Adrianople. He worked as a *qāḍī* in Aleppo, Adrianople, and Istanbul, and was for a time *qāḍi ʾl-ʿaskar* of Anatolia. He then returned to teaching and was awarded a pension after he had completed the pilgrimage. He died in 957/1550.

ShN II, 47/8, Rescher 285. *Risāla fi ʾl-jihād*, Pet. 81,$_{8}$.

7. Burhān al-Dīn Ibrāhīm b. Muḥammad b. Ibrāhīm al-Ḥalabī studied in Aleppo and Cairo before becoming a preacher at the mosque of Sultan Mehmed and a teacher at the Dār al-qirāʾa of the *muftī* Saʿdī Čelebī in Istanbul. He died at the age of 90 in 956/1549.

ShN II, 110/1. 1. *Multaqa ʾl-abḥur*, on Ḥanafī *furūʿ*, Berl. 4613/4, Gotha 1032, Erlangen 38, Munich 317/9, Leipz. 202, BDMG 38, Br. Mus. 217/9, Suppl. 297/8, Ind. Off. 1705, Paris 956/64, 6411, Algiers 1021, Garr. 1739/40, Yeni 576/8, AS 1451/63, NO 1828/51, Köpr. 653, Cairo ^{1}III, 135, lith. with marginal glosses Istanbul 1271 (cf. Worms, *JA* 1842, II, 255ff., Du Courroy, ibid. 1948, II, 1ff.), among others, French transl. H. Sauvaire, see Suppl.—Turkish translation Ḥamdī, Rāġib 459, with a commentary by Muḥammad al-Mawqūfātī, Munich 51, Lund 65/6, print. Būlāq 1254, Istanbul 1269.—Commentaries: a. Qaṣṣābzāde, ca. 1050/1640, Cairo ^{1}III, 451.—b. Derwish Muḥammad b. Aḥmad, composed in 1065/1655, ibid. 86.—c. Muṣṭafā b. Muḥammad, composed in 1068/1657, ibid. 34.—d. Muṣṭafā b. ʿUmar b. Muḥammad, completed in 1066/1655, ibid. 137.—e. *Majmaʿ al-anhur*, by ʿAbd al-Raḥmān b. Muḥammad b. Sulaymān Shaykhīzāde, d. 1078/1667, Paris 965/6, Cairo ^{1}III, 109 (see Suppl.).—f. *al-Durr al-muntaqā*, by Muḥammad b. ʿAlī al-Ḥaṣkafī, d. 1088/1677, Berl. Ms. or oct. 3902, qu. 2077, Algiers 1022, Yeni 472, Alex. Fiqh Ḥan. 25, Cairo ^{1}III, 47.—g. Muḥammad b. Muḥammad Waḥdatī b. Muḥammad Üskübī al-Adranawī, d. 1130/1718, Cairo ^{1}III, 141.—h.–q. see Suppl. (k. Berl. Brill M. 103, Garr. | 1741; o. read: al-Sīwāsī).—r. Anon., Patna I, 571
93,$_{950}$.—13 commentaries in Ahlw. 4610.—2. *Sharḥ Munyat al-muṣallī* I, 478.—3. *al-Rahṣ wal-waqṣ li-mustaḥill al-raqṣ* Cairo ^{1}VII, 603, ^{2}I, 456.—4. *al-Fawāʾid al-muntakhaba min al-Fatāwi ʾl-Tatārkhāniyya* (see Suppl.), Yeni 668, Alex. Fiqh Ḥan. 40, 61, Fun. 97,$_{6}$.—5. *Niʿmat al-dharīʿa fī nuṣrat al-sharīʿa* Yeni 728.—6. *Durrat al-muwaḥḥidīn wa-raddat al-mulḥidīn* Köpr. 720.—7. *al-Qawl al-tamām ʿinda dhikr wilādatihi ʿam*, which refutes objections made against him by some scholars because he did not take the view that every believer must, out

of respect, stand up at the mention of Muḥammad's name, as he argued that only God is entitled to such displays of veneration, Berl. 9546.—8. *al-Ḥilya al-sharīfa*, a depiction of Muḥammad's looks, ibid. 9642.—9. *Risāla fī ḥaqq abawayhi ʿam*, on whether Muḥammad's parents went to Paradise, composed in 931/1524 in Istanbul, ibid. 10345.—10. See Suppl.—11., 12. ibid. III, 1304.—13. *Tasfīh al-ghabī* (Suppl. I, 802). See *Isl. Culture* 1939, p. 446.

8. Shujāʿ b. Nūrallāh al-Anqirawī was a teacher at the Sulṭānsarāy in Adrianople, ca. 965/1587.

Ḥall al-mushkilāt fi 'l-farāʾiḍ, composed in 963–4/1585–6, Leid. 1874, Pet. AMK 929 (anon.), Cairo [1]III, 306, print. Būlāq 1285, C. 1305.

433 | 9. Ḥājjī Rasūl b. Ṣāliḥ al-Āydīnī, who died in 978/1570.

Brūsalı Ṭāhir I, 313. *Al-Fatāwi 'l-ʿadliyya*, composed in 966/1558 on the order of Sultan Süleymān when he was a judge in Marmara, Munich 322, Yeni 646, Alex. Fiqh Ḥan. 41, Cairo [1]III, 11.

10. ʿAlī Čelebī b. Imraʾallāh Qınalızāde[1] al-Ḥāmidī, the son of the *qāḍī* of Isparta,[2] was born in 918/1511. He became a professor in Adrianople, Bursa, Kutāhya and Istanbul, first at a madrasa he himself founded, then at one of the eight, and then at one of the two madrasas that sultan Süleymān constructed next to the
572 mosque that carries his name. He next became *qāḍī* in Damascus,[3] | then in Bursa, Adrianople, and Istanbul, and then *qāḍi 'l-ʿaskar* for Anatolia. When he accompanied the sultan to Adrianople, he died there of blood-poisening caused by his doctor, on 7 Ramaḍān 979/24 January 1572.[4] He was an extraordinarily multi-faceted scholar and also wrote poetry in Turkish and Arabic.

RA 3r, *ʿIM* 375/88, v. Hammer, *Gesch. d. osm. Dichtkunst* II, 341, Wüst. *Gesch.* 532, *EI* II, 1093. 1. *Ṭabaqāt ʿulamāʾ (fuqahāʾ) al-Ḥanafiyyīn*, short accounts of 231 persons, listed in 21 classes, in chronological order until 940/1533, Vienna 1186, Br. Mus. 1302, Bodl. I, 114,$_2$, Garr. 706.—2. *Risāla fī ṭabaqāt al-masāʾil*, on the three periods in the history of Ḥanafī law, Berl. 4868, Leid. 1884, Vat. V, 1460,$_2$.—

1 Also Ibn al-Ḥinnāʾī, Ibn (al-)Ḥinnālī, Ḥinnāwīzāde, Ḥinnāyī, i.e. the son of the henna trader.

2 In Liwā Ḥamīd (= Pisidia), Wüst. Sparta.

3 According to *RA* in Cairo too.

4 *RA* suggests he died as a private individual in Istanbul, in 980 or 981.

3. *al-Istīʿāf fī aḥkām al-awqāf* Algiers 1293,$_{2}$, 1716,$_{6}$.—4. *Risāla fi 'l-ghaṣb* Pet. 81,$_{i}$.—5. *Risāla fi 'l-wujūd al-dhihnī*, on the difference between things as they are and as we imagine them, Berl. 5107.—6. *Risālat al-laṭāʾif al-khams* Leid. 1603.—7. *al-Risāla al-sayfiyya* Berl. 8595,$_{3}$, Vienna 388, Leid. 439.—8. *al-Risāla al-qalamiyya* Leid. 440, Garr. 214,$_{4}$, Copenhagen 231,$_{6}$.—9.–11. see Suppl.—12. *Risāla fī (bayān) dawarān al-Ṣūfiyya wa-raqṣihim* Asʿad 1456, Yi̊ldi̊z Taṣ. 248, Alex. Fun. 172,$_{1}$.

11. Muḥammad b. Mūsā al-Burūsawī Kül Kedisi,[5] who died in 982/1574.

Biḍāʿat al-qāḍī liḥtiyājihi ilayhi fi 'l-mustaqbal wal-māḍī (fi 'l-shukūk al-sharʿiyya) Cairo ^{1}IV, 212, ^{2}III, 36, see Suppl.

12. Ḥāmid b. Muḥammad al-Qasṭamūnī al-Qūnawī, who died in 985/1577.

| *ʿIlmiyye Sālnāmesi* p. 386. *Al-Fatāwi 'l-Ḥāmidiyya* AS 1563, an abstract titled 434
al-ʿUqūd al-durriyya by Muḥammad Amīn b. ʿUmar b. ʿĀbidīn, d. 1252/1836, is preserved in Cairo ^{1}II, 80, ^{2}I, 44, print. Būlāq 1300.

13. Maḥmūd b. Sulaymān al-Kaffawī, who died in 990/1582.

ʿAṭāʾī, *Dhayl ShN* 272/3, Wüst. *Gesch.* 535. 1. *Kātaʾib aʿlām al-akhyār min fuqahāʾ madhhab al-Nuʿmān al-mukhtār*, dedicated | to Sultan Murād III, Berl. 10027, 573
Vienna 1187, Cairo V^{1}, 117, ^{2}303, abstract Berl. 10028.—2. See Suppl.

14. Fuḍayl b. ʿAlī (p. 567, 3) al-Jamālī al-Bakrī al-Rūmī, who died in Istanbul in 991/1583.

ʿAṭāʾī, *Dhayl ShN* 275/8. 1. *al-Ḍamānāt fi 'l-furūʿ al-Ḥanafiyya*, NO 1965/6, Yeni 518, Cairo ^{1}III, 78.—2. *Risālat al-waẓāʾif fi 'l-naḥw*, with a commentary by Ibrāhīm al-Zubayrī, d. 991/1583, Cairo ^{1}IV, 26, ^{2}II, 81.—3., 4. See Suppl.

15. Shams al-Dīn Muḥammad b. Muḥammad (no. 5) b. Ilyās Čiwizāde was born in Istanbul, became *qāḍī* in Damascus in 979/1571, then chief *qāḍī* in Egypt, *qāḍi 'l-ʿaskar* and finally *muftī*, in which capacity he was the successor of Abu 'l-Suʿūd (p. 579). He died in 995/1587.

---

5 I.e. "cinder cat", a nickname for someone with a glacial personality.

RA 259r; *ʿIlmiyye Sālnāmesi* 402. 1. *Majmūʿat al-fatāwī* NO 2020/1.—2. *Risāla fi ʾl-masḥ ʿala ʾl-khuffayn* Leid. 1868, Cairo [1]VII, 613.

16. Muḥammad al-Rūmī al-Qallīnīkī Khwīshī Khālid wrote, in 1000/1591:

Hādi ʾl-sharīʿa, a supplement to the first and the third *fann* of *al-Ashbāh wal-naẓāʾir* (p. 401), Cairo [1]III, 149.

18. Muḥammad b. Aḥmad Nishānjīzāde, who died in 1031/1622.

Brūsalı̊ Ṭāhir III, 141. *Nūr al-ʿayn fī iṣlāḥ Jāmiʿ al-fuṣūlayn* p. 291.

18a. Muṣṭafā b. Sinān al-Ṭūsī, who died in 1032/1623, see Suppl.

Al-Marām etc. additionally Pet. AMK 941, Cairo [2]V, 342.

19. ʿAlī b. Muḥammad al-Riḍāʾī was a well-known Turkish poet in Istanbul. Having held various teaching positions he became a *qāḍī* in Cairo in 1037/1627, where he died on 28 Ṣafar 1039/17 October 1629.

Muḥ. III, 187, ʿAṭāʾī, *Dhayl ShN* 723–4, Brūsalı̊ Ṭāhir I, 313, Wüst. *Gesch.* 557.
574 1. *Naqd al-masāʾil fī jawāb al-sāʾil*, | a collection of fatwas NO 2076, Cairo [1]III, 144.—2. *ʿAwd al-shabāb* I, 385.

20. Muḥammad b. Muḥammad Qāḍīzāde, who died in 1044/1634.

Irshād al-ʿuqūl al-salīma (al-mustaqīma) ila ʾl-uṣūl al-qawīma fī ibṭāl al-bidʿa al-saqīma, against the dancing of dervishes, Köpr. 703, abstract Munich 892, f. 135/40.

435 | 21. Muṣṭafā Bālī b. Sulaymān Bālīzāde, who died in 1069/1658.

1. *Mīzān al-fatāwī*, which he began in 1012/1603 and completed in 1055/1645, Cairo [1]III, 141.—2.–5. see Suppl.

22. Ḥāfiẓ Maḥmūd al-Wārdārī Muftī Wārdār, ca. 1060/1650.

1. *Muʿīn al-muntahī fi ʾl-farāʾiḍ*, composed in 1061/1651, Cairo [1]III, 317.—2. *Tartīb-i zībā*, a concordance to the Qurʾān, composed in 1054/1644, revised by

an unknown individual, AS 83, NO 129/30, Mosul 183,$_{221}$, 293,$_{2}$, Turkish translation AS 84,$_{1}$. NO 131/4.

23. Mollā Ḥusayn b. Iskandar wrote, in 1062/1652:

1. *Majmaʿ al-muhimmāt al-dīniyya ʿalā madhhab al-sāda al-Ḥanafiyya* Cairo ^{1}VII, 589, Mosul 117,$_{115,2}$.—2. *Muqaddima fi ʾl-ʿaqāʾid wal-fiqh ʿalā madhhab al-imām Abī Ḥanīfa*, with a commentary, *Miftāḥ al-falāḥ etc.* Cairo ^{1}VII 586.—3. *al-ʿIbāda wa-wasīlat al-saʿāda* ibid.—4.–7. see Suppl.

24. Muḥammad b. Maḥmūd Ṭuruqjīzāde, c. 1068/1657.

1. *Jāmiʿ al-asʾila al-ʿadīda fī zubdat al-ajwiba al-mufīda*, a handbook for answering legal questions, based on that of Ibn Nujaym (p. 401), Berl. 4840.—2.–4. See Suppl.

25. Yaḥyā b. ʿUmar Minqārīzāde was a professor in Istanbul, became a *qāḍī* in Cairo in 1064/1654 and then in Mecca and Istanbul, was then appointed *qāḍi ʾl-ʿaskar* for Rumelia and then, in 1073/1662, *shaykh al-islām*. He resigned from office because of paralysis in his right hand and retired to Beshikṭāsh, where he died in 1088/1677.

Muḥ IV, 477, *ʿIlmiyye Sālnāmesi* p. 483. 1. *al-Itbāʿ fī masʾalat al-istimāʿ* on sura 7_{203}, Berl. 994.—2. *al-Risāla al-munīra* | *li-ahl al-baṣīra*, on religious duties, 575
ibid. 1846.—3. *Risāla fī lā ilāha illa ʾllāh* ibid. 2450.—4. *Fatāwī* NO 2001/3, 2037, 2056, Köpr. II, 111, Turkish translation AS 82/6.—5., 6. See Suppl.

26. Muṣṭafā b. Mīrzā b. Muḥammad Diḥkī al-Sīrūzī was a *qāḍī* in Istanbul, became *qāḍi ʾl-ʿaskar* in Rumelia in 1081/1670, and died in 1090/1679.

Muḥ. IV, 396. *Lawāzim al-quḍāt wal-ḥukkām fī iṣlāḥ umūr al-anām*, composed in 1085/1674, Yeni 541, Cairo ^{1}III, 107, ^{2}I, 459.

27. Aḥmad b. Ḥusām al-Dīn Ḥasan b. Sinān al-Dīn Yūsuf al-Bayāḍī Kamāl al-Dīn became a *qāḍī* in Aleppo in 1077/1666, then held the same position in Bursa and Mecca. In 1083/1672 he was removed from office and went to Damascus. In 1086/1675 he became *qāḍī* in Istanbul, | and towards the end of that year *qāḍi* 436
ʾl-ʿaskar for Rumelia. He was removed from office after he had had a woman stoned because of adultery with a Jew. He died in 1098/1687.

Muḥ. I, 181. *Mukhtaṣar al-uṣūl al-munīfa lil-imām Abī Ḥanīfa* Mosul $239_{,223}$.—Commentaries: *Ishārāt al-marām min ʿibārāt al-imām* Berl. 1847 (not identifed as a commentary), Landb.-Br. 295, Alex. Tawḥīd 4, Cairo ^{1}II, 4—b. see Suppl.

28. Muḥammad b. Ḥusayn al-Anqirāwī was a professor in Istanbul, then a *qāḍī* in Yenishehir, Cairo, and Istanbul, before being made *qāḍi ʾl-ʿaskar* for Anatolia. It was in this latter capacity that he wrote down the fatwas of Shaykh al-Islām Minqārīzāde (no. 25), who was unable to write himself due to a problem in his right hand. When the latter took leave from office, al-Anqirāwī was made *qāḍi ʾl-ʿaskar* for Rumelia for a period of four years. In 1087/1676, after a trip by the sultan from Adrianople to Istanbul, he was deposed and sent to Ankara to work there as a *qāḍī*, but he was reinstated some years later. After the ousting of vizier Muṣṭafā Pāshā he became *shaykh al-islām*. He died soon after, in 1098/1687.

576 | Muḥ. IV, 214. 1. *Fatāwi ʾl-Anqirāwī* BDMG 40, NO 1973/80, Yeni 628/9, AS 1545/7, Cairo ^{1}III, 87.—2. See Suppl.

29. Ṣādiq Muḥammad b. ʿAlī al-Sāqizī, who died in 1099/1688.

Brūsalī Ṭāhir I, 342. *Ṣurrat al-fatāwī*, composed in 1059/1649, Yeni 619/23, AS 1540, NO 1960/4, Alex. Fun. 36, Cairo ^{1}III, 77, Mosul $131_{,171}$, $181_{,184}$.

30. ʿAbd al-Raḥīm b. Abi ʾl-Luṭf b. Isḥāq b. Muḥammad b. Abi ʾl-Luṭf al-Ḥasanī al-Qudsī was born in Jerusalem in 1037/1627, studied in Cairo, lectured for a time at the Sulaymāniyya in Istanbul, and was then made a professor at the Madrasa Arbaʿīn ʿUthmanī there in 1058/1648. In 1068/1657 he became a *muftī* in Jerusalem and a professor at al-Madrasa al-ʿUthmāniyya there. However, he was fired as early as 1069/1658, and only re-hired in 1072/1661. Later he became a *qāḍī* in Safad, where he was imprisoned for a time. After his release he wanted to raise a complaint in Istanbul but died on the way, in Adrianople, in 1104/1692.

Mur. III, 2/5, Jab. 66. *Al-Fatāwi ʾl-Raḥīmiyya fī wāqiʿāt al-sāda al-Ḥanafiyya* Cairo ^{1}III, 90.—2., 3. See Suppl.

437 | 31. Aḥmad Muḥammad Fiqhī al-ʿAynī wrote, in Istanbul in 1114/1702:

1. *Fayḍ al-ḥayy fī aḥkām al-kayy* Vienna $1463_{,1}$.—2. *al-Fawāʾid al-mumaḥḥaṣa fī aḥkām kayy al-ḥimmaṣa*, on the use of the fontanel, against ʿAbd al-Ghanī

al-Nābulusī (p. 456, no. 34), ibid. $_2$.—3. *Bahjat al-fatāwā*, a (Turkish) revision of a work by Abu ʾl-Faḍl ʿAbdallāh al-Yenishehrī, AS 1527 ter.

32. Muḥammad b. Ḥamza al-Āydīnī al-Güzelḥiṣārī, who died in 1116/1704.

53 *Rasāʾil* Alex. Fun. 295/7,$_{21/74}$. 1. *Risāla fi ʾl-istinān ʿinda ʾl-qiyām ila ʾl-ṣalāt*, completed on 1 Muḥarram 1095/20 December 1683, Cairo [1]VII, 401.—2. *Risāla fī sunniyyat al-siwāk lil-nisāʾ kamā yusann lil-rijāl*, completed on 25 Jumādā I 1105/23 January 1694, ibid.—| 3. *Risāla fī-mā qīla fī masʾalat al-fīl wa-mā rajaḥa minhu bil-riwāya wal-dalīl*, completed on 2 Rabīʿ I 1097/28 January 1686, ibid.—4. *Risāla fī-mā shāʿa bayna ʾl-nās washtahara anna man qāla ʿinda ʾl-taʿajjub Allāh kafara*, completed on 21 Rajab 1116/20 November 1704, ibid. 402.—5. *Risāla fī naẓar al-dhimmiyya ila ʾl-muslima* ibid.—6. *Risāla fi ʾl-shuhūd ʿinda mubāsharat ʿaqd al-nikāḥ* ibid. 402, 404.—7. *Risāla fī-mā qīla min anna qirāʾat al-Fātiḥa ʿaqiba ʾl-ṣalawāt mubtadaʿa* ibid. 402.—8. *Risāla fī-mā baliya wa-khaliqa wa-kharaja ʿani ʾl-intifāʿ bihi min al-maṣāḥif wa-kutub al-dīn*, completed in Dhu ʾl-Qaʿda 1109/5 June 1697, ibid.—9. *Risāla fī ḥayḍ al-marʾa fī khilāl kaffārat al-qatl*, completed on 7 Shaʿbān 1114/28 December 1702, ibid.—10. *Risāla fī maṣraf al-zakāt ʿalā mā naṭaqa bihi ʾl-kitāb wal-sunna wattafaqa ʿalayhi ʾl-aʾimma* ibid.—11. *Risāla fī qawl al-ʿawāmm baʿd al-salām bil-turkiyya ṣabāḥin khair olsun* ibid.—12. *Risāla fī ḥilli mā qatalahu naḥw al-ḥajar min al-ṣayd* ibid. 403.—13. *Risāla fī radd shahādat man kharaja li-qudūm al-amīr* ibid.—14. *Risāla fi ʾl-qadr al-masnūn min al-iʿtikāf*, completed on 9 Jumādā II 1105/7 January 1694, ibid.—15. *Risāla fī ṣalāt al-tarāwīḥ* ibid.—16. *Risāla fī takarrur al-jamāʿa fi ʾl-masjid* ibid.—17. *Risāla fī qirāʾat āyat al-kursī ʿaqiba ʾl-ṣalawāt al-mafrūḍa* ibid.—18. *Risāla fī anna walīmat al-ʿurs sunna wal-ijāba ilayhā wājiba* ibid.—19. *Risāla fi nʿiqād al-ijmāʿ ʿalā anna ʾl-kuffār muʿabbadūn fi ʾl-nār* ibid.—20. *Risāla fī anna ʾl-shahīd nawʿān* ibid.—21. *Risāla fī anna ʾl-sunna fi ʾl-qalansuwa kawnuhā munkhafiḍa lā murtafiʿa* ibid.—22. *Risāla fī man dufiʿat ilayhi zakāt ʿalā annahu faqīr thumma tabayyana annahu ghanī hal yamlikuhā aw lā* ibid.—23. *Risāla fi ʾl-qadr al-masnūn fi ʾl-liḥya* ibid. 404.—24. *Risāla fī anna mutābaʿat al-muqtadī li-imāmihi farḍ* ibid.—25. *Risāla fi ʾl-ghusl* ibid.—26. *Risāla fi ʾl-istinjāʾ* ibid.—27. *Risāla fī-mā zaʿamahu baʿḍ al-nās anna akbar benden kufr* ibid.—28. *Risāla fi ʾl-qiṣāṣ wastīfāʾ al-ḥuqūq yawma ʾl-jazāʾ* ibid.—29. *Risāla fī ʾttifāq al-aʾimma ʿalā anna ʾl-imām yaʾtī bil-tasmīʿ ḥālat al-intiqāl* ibid.—30. *Risāla fi ʾl-ikhtilāf fī lubs al-aḥmar lil-rijāl* ibid.—31.–66. see Suppl.—67. *Fatwā fī bayʿ al-dukhān* Alex. Fun. 157,$_{11}$.

577

33. Muṣṭafā Rifqī b. Ibrāhīm Shaykh Khusrawzāde wrote, after 1134/1721:

438 | *Al-Qurāḍa al-fiqhiyya wal-fukāha al-rifqiyya* Cairo [1]III, 99.

34. Muḥammad Kāmī b. Ibrāhīm b. Muḥammad b. al-Shaykh Sinān b. Maḥmūd al-Adranawī was born in 1059/1649 and died in 1136/1723.

578 | 1. *Mahāmm al-fuqahāʾ*, the Ḥanafīs, in alphabetical order, Cairo V, [1]162, [2]373.—2. See Suppl.

35. Qāḍīzāde Muḥammad, the *muftī* in Erzerum, wrote, in 1148/1735:

Al-Risāla al-fatḥiyya Pet. AM 72.

6 *Sciences of the Qurʾān*

1. In 939/1529, ʿAlam al-Dīn al-Ḥusaynī dedicated to Sultan Süleymān the Magnificent (926–74/1520–66):

Sharh wa-tarjama li-baʿḍ min sūrat al-Baqara AS 398 (Ritter, *Türkiyat Mecm.* 7–8, II [1945], p. 71).

1a. Ṣunʿallāh al-Khālidī wrote, in 937/1531 for Iskender Čelebī:

Tafsīr sūrat al-Ikhlāṣ AS 419 (Ritter, ibid. p. 71).

1b. Saʿdallāh b. ʿĪsā b. Mirḥān al-Ṭaṭāyī Saʿdī Efendi (Čelebī), from Ṭatāy in Wilāyet Qasṭamūnī, was a teacher at the madrasa of Maḥmūd Pāshā in Istanbul as well as at some other madrasas, and was later a *qāḍī* and *muftī* in Istanbul. He died there on 2 Shawwāl 945/22 February 1539.

ShN II, 43, Rescher 283, Mejdī 443, Brūsalī M. Ṭāhir *ʿOM* I, 323. 1. *al-Risāla al-saʿdiyya*, a commentary on the *Fātiḥa*, Sarajevo 60,$_1$.—2. *Ḥāshiya ʿala ʾl-ʿInāya* I, 467.—3. *al-Fawāʾid al-bahiyya*, glosses on Bayḍāwī I, 531, *Türkiyat Mecm.* 7–8, II (1945), p. 38.

1(c). Ḥamdallāh b. Khayr al-Dīn, a preacher at Aya Sofya under Süleymān I, wrote, in 948/1541:

Brūsalī M. Ṭāhir, *ʿOM* I, 274/5. 1. *ʿUmdat al-ʿirfān fī waṣf ḥurūf al-Qurʾān* Leid. 1646, AS 4796,$_1$, a commentary, *Jawāhir al-ʿiqyān*, Ḥamīd. 17.—2., 3. See Suppl.—4. An untitled work, Fātiḥ Waqf Ibr. 36,$_2$.

2a. Qāḍī Muṣliḥ al-Dīn Muṣṭafā al-Niksārī, who died in 969/1561.

ʿAṭāʾī 22, *ʿIM* 212. *Tafsīr sūrat al-Wird*, for Sultan Selīm I, AS 421 (Ritter, *Türk. Mecm.* 7–8, II, p. 77).

| 2b. Aḥmad b. ʿAbd al-Awwal al-Saʿīdī al-Qazwīnī, who died in 966/1558. 579

Tafsīr Fātiḥat al-kitāb Berl. 948, autograph copy completed in 963/1556 in Istanbul.

3. Muṣliḥ al-Dīn Muṣṭafā b. Shabān al-Surūrī was born in Gallipoli as the son of a trader, studied in Istanbul under Ṭashköprīzāde (p. 559), became an acting *qāḍī* there, and then a professor in Gallipoli, Istanbul, and Galata, where he joined the Naqshbandiyya order. However, his patron Qāsim Pāshā built him a madrasa in Galata, thereby forcing him to start lecturing again. Later he became the tutor of prince Muṣṭafā, but when the latter fell out of favour with his father and was murdered al-Surūrī retired from public life. He later assumed an aura of sainthood, especially among sailors. He died in 969/1561.

ʿIM 214/20, Hammer, *Gesch. d. osm. Dicht.* II, 287. 1. *Tafsīr sūrat Yūsuf* Köpr. II, 15, Cairo [1]I, 148, [2]40.—2. *Ḥāshiya ʿala 'l-Bayḍāwī* I, 531.—3. *Sharḥ Gulistān* (of Saʿdī), completed in 957/1550 in Amasia, Berl. 8441/2, BDMG 110, Vienna 554, Upps. 102/3, Paris 3520, 6383, Br. Mus. 1059/60, AS 4104/6, NO 4044/5.—3a. *Sharḥ Dīwān-i Ḥāfiẓ* NO 3963/4.—4. Commentary on the collection of parables called *al-Amthila al-mukhtalifa*, Gotha 190, $220,_2$, Vienna 217, Br. Mus. 499.—5. A Turkish translation of the *ʿAjāʾib al-makhlūqāt*, Suppl. I, 882, Welīeddīn 2462.

4. Abu 'l-Suʿūd Muḥammad b. Muḥammad b. Muṣṭafā al-ʿImādī, the son of the tutor of prince Bāyezīd, was born in 898/1492. He was a student of Ibn Kamālpāshā (p. 596), became a professor in Aynegöl, then at one of the eight madrasas of Istanbul, then in Gajīwīze and Bursa, | before becoming a *qāḍī* 439
in Bursa and Istanbul, and finally *qāḍi 'l-ʿaskar*. He finally died as a *muftī* in Istanbul on 15 Jumādā I 982/3 September 1574.

TA 53r, *RA* 245v, *ShN* II, 81, *ʿIM* 438/68, Hammer, *Gesch. d. osm. Dicht.* III, 352, Brūsalī I, 225. 1. *Irshād al-ʿaql al-salīm ilā mazāya 'l-kitāb al-karīm*, a Qurʾān commentary, | regarded almost as highly as his sources, Bayḍāwī and Zamakhsharī, 580
and dedicated to Sultan Süleymān I, Berl. 902/6, Leipz. 106/7, Dresd. 368, Munich 96, Leid. 1699, Ind. Off. 102, Algiers 351/3, Garr. 1302/4, Sarajevo 64, NO

202/26, AS 135/46 (Ritter, *Türk. Mecm.* 7–8, II [1945], S. 78), Köpr. 68/71, Rāġib 55/7, Yeni 24/30, Cairo I, ^{1}122, 232, Mosul 64,$_{228}$, 125,$_{59}$, 210,$_{51}$, print. Būlāq 1275, among others.—A commentary on the *Dībāja* by Muḥammad b. Muḥammad al-Ḥasanī Zīrakzāde, Leid. 1700.—Glosses: a. ʿAbdallāh Zaytūna, of which an abstract, Algiers 354/5.—b. Anon., *Kalām ḥawl Tafsīr Abi 'l-Suʿūd* Mosul 119,$_{296,}$ 4.—2. *Tafsīr sūrat al-Mulk* (no. 67), Berl. 961.—3. *Tafsīr sūrat al-Kahf* (no. 18), with glosses by Ṭāshköprīzāde (p. 559), AS 359.—4. *Risāla fī (jawāz) waqf al-nuqūd* (*al-manqūl*) Cairo ^{1}VII, 124, 405, Sarajevo 108 (refutation by al-Birkawī p. 583, 12).—5. *Risāla fi 'l-masḥ ʿala 'l-khuffayn* ibid. Cairo ^{1}VII, 613.—6. *Fatāwī* Turkish, compiled by ʿAlī Efendi, Yeni 624/5.—7. Answers to difficult points in law, Gotha 32,$_{1}$.—8. *Tuḥfat al-ṭullāb fi 'l-munāẓara*, in 52 *rajaz* verses, Berl. 8160,$_{3}$.—9. *Maʿrūḍāt*, a Turkish work on numerous legal, religious, and philosophical subjects, dedicated to Sultan Süleymān, Krafft 466. Paul Horster, *Zur Anwendung des isl. Rechts im 16 Jhrh. Die jurist. Darlegungen (Maʿrūżāt) des Scheijch ül-Islām abū S.*, Stuttgart 1935.—10. A *qaṣīda*, Berl. 7940/1, with an anonymous commentary, ibid. 7942, others ibid. 7943—Commentary *al-Manthūr al-ʿūdī etc.* see Suppl., additionally Mosul 164,$_{3,\ 2}$.—11.–19. see Suppl.—20., 21. Ibid. III, 1304.

5. Muḥammad b. Badr al-Dīn al-Aqḥiṣārī Muḥyi 'l-Dīn al-Munshi' became *Shaykh al-ḥaram al-nabawī* in Medina in 982/1574, and died in Mecca in 1001/1593.

Muḥ. III, 400. 1. *Nazīl al-tanzīl* (*Tanzīl al-nazīl*), a Qur'ān commentary in the reading of Ḥafṣ, which he began in Ramaḍān 981/Jan. 1574 in Aqḥiṣār and completed in 999/1590, NO 147, Köpr. 144, AS 282 (Ritter, *Türk. Mecm.* 7–8, II [1945], p. 85), Cairo I, ^{1}128, ^{2}64.—2.–7. see Suppl.

6. ʿAbd al-Muḥsin b. Sulaymān al-Kūrānī, ca. 1050/1640.

Tuḥfat jāmiʿ al-asrār fī tafsīr fātiḥat al-anwār Krafft 406.

7. Muṣṭafā Efendi b. Dā'ūd wrote, in 1076/1665:

Kitāb al-nāsikh wal-mansūkh Köpr. 216.

581 | 8. Muḥammad b. Bisṭām al-Khashshābī Wānī Efendi Wānqūlī, who died in 1096/1685.

Brūsalı̊ Ṭāhir *'OM* II, 50, Belīgh, *Güldeste-i riyāḍ-i 'irfān* 209. *'Arā'is al-Qur'ān wa-nafā'is al-furqān*, legends in the Qur'ān, based on *al-Tha'labī* (I, 429), the main part of which was completed in 1092/1680, Berl. 1030 (fragment), Yeni 100.

| 9. Ismā'īl Ḥaqqī al-Burūsawī, who died in 1137/1724. 440

1. *Tafsīr rūḥ al-bayān* AS 213/6, NO 308/10, Köpr. 100/5, print. Būlāq 1264, Istanbul 1306, among others.—2.–10. see Suppl. (2. Turkish translation, Br. Mus. Turk. 227, xvi; 10. Ḥālet 229).—11. *Tamām al-fayḍ* Ḥālet 244.—12. *Sharḥ al-'aṭā' li-ahl al-ghiṭā'*, an answer to Ḥājj Muḥammad al-Ṣuḥufī, ibid. 250.

10. 'Alī al-Manṣūrī was born in Egypt in Qaḍā' Manṣūra, went to Istanbul in 1088/1677, then became a teacher of the Qur'ān at the madrasa of Köprülüzāde Aḥmad Pāshā in Belgrade. He returned to Istanbul in 1099/1688, became a *mudarris* at the madrasa of Muḥammad Köprülü and then *shaykh al-qurrā'* at the tomb of Ṣāliḥa, the mother of Sultan Süleymān II, near Sulaymāniyya. He died in 1138/1725, and was buried in Skutari.

(Note of Ḥamdī Efendi to Ritter). 1. *Risālat radd al-ilḥād fi 'l-nuṭq bil-ḍād* Selīm Āġā Mağm. 626,$_1$.—2. *Risālat al-ṣalāt* ibid. $_2$.—3. *Risāla fi 'l-su'āl wal-ajwiba* Fātiḥ Waqf Ibr. 28,$_1$.—4. *Taḥrīr al-ṭuruq wal-riwāyāt min ṭarīq Ṭayyibat al-Nashr fi 'l-qirā'āt al-'ashr* Fātiḥ 36, Waqf Ibr. 43, 53,$_1$.—5. *Ḥall mujmalāt al-Ṭayyiba* Fātiḥ Waqf Ibr. 66,$_1$, 53,$_2$.—6. *Risāla fi 'l-takbīr* Fātiḥ 68,$_1$.

10a. Ya'qūb b. Muṣṭafā al-Qusṭanṭīnī al-Khalwatī, who died in Istanbul in 1141/1736.

Natījat al-tafāsīr, on sura Yūsuf, Cairo [1]I, 218, print. Istanbul 1266.

10b. Al-Maghnīsāwī wrote, sometime after 1134/1722:

1. *Risālat al-ḍād al-ṣaḥīḥa* Fātiḥ Waqf Ibr. 32,$_{16}$.—2. *al-Sayf al-maslūl 'alā man yunkir al-manqūl*, on the pronunciation of the letters *ḍād* and *ẓā'*, ibid. 32,$_{15}$.—3. Turkish translation of the *Tamhīd* p. 259,$_9$.

| 10c. Muṣṭafā al-Ḥusaynī al-Ermenākī al-Takkawī, who was born a Greek, wrote, under Sultan Aḥmad III (1113–43/1701–30): 582

Mafāḍ al-fayyāḍ bil-riyāḍāt listirfād fuḍālat al-ḍādāt al-ṭā'iyyāt, on phonology, Fātiḥ Waqf Ibr. 32,$_1$.—2. *Fī makhārij al-ḥurūf* ibid. 32,$_2$.

10d. Abu 'l-Ḥasan Muṣṭafā b. Ḥasan b. Yaʿqūb al-Islambūlī, imam of the Janissaries, wrote, in 1144/1731:

Murshid al-ṭālibīn li-fahm ṭuruq al-Ṭayyiba Fātiḥ Waqf Ibr. $11,_{2}$ (see Suppl. III 1286 ad 454).

11. Muṣṭafā b. ʿAbd al-Raḥmān al-Izmīrī, who died in 1156/1743.

Brūsalī Ṭāhir, *ʿOM* II, 28. 1. *ʿUmdat al-furqān fī wujūh al-Qurʾān*, the readings of the 12 readers, after the *Ṭayyiba* of al-Jazarī (p. 258), Berl. 667, Fātiḥ Waqf Ibr. $20,_{1}$.—2. *Badāʾiʿ al-burhān ʿalā ʿUmdat al-furqān*, an enlargement of no. 1, Cairo I, $^{1}105$, $^{2}16$.—3. *Taqrīb ḥuṣūl al-maqāṣid fī takhrīj mā fi 'l-Nashr min al-fawāʾid* ibid. I, 107.—4. See Suppl.—5. *Risālat al-ḍād* Fātiḥ Waqf Ibr. $32,_{11}$.

11a. Dāʾūd b. Muḥammad al-Qārṣī studied in Istanbul and Cairo and died after 1160/1747.

Brūsalī Ṭāhir, *ʿOM* I, 309. 1. *al-Risāla al-fatḥiyya fī bayān ḍād al-qaṭʿiyya* Fātiḥ Waqf Ibr. $32,_{17}$.—2. *Sharḥ Risālat uṣūl al-ḥadīth* by Birkawī, see Suppl. II, $654,_{3,8}$.—3. *Mukhtār mukhtār al-Ṣaḥīḥ* Suppl. I, 197.—4. *Sharḥ al-ʿArūḍ al-Andalusī* Suppl. I, 544.—5. *Mukhtaṣar Taqrīr al-qawānīn* p. 487.—6. *Risāla fī bayān masʾalat al-irādāt al-juzʾiyya wal-irādāt al-qalbiyya* Selim Āġā $1273,_{4}$, Cairo ^{2}I, 182.—7. *Ḥāshiya ʿalā Sharḥ al-Amthila al-mukhtalifa* p. 579.—8. A commentary on the *Risāla fī uṣūl al-ḥadīth*, p. $584,_{8}$.

12. ʿAbdallāh b. Muḥammad b. Yūsuf b. ʿAbd al-Mannān al-Ḥilmī al-Ḥanafī Yūsuf Effendīzāde, the successor of ʿAlī Manṣūrī as *raʾīs al-qurrāʾ*, died in 1167/1753, see Suppl.

1. *al-Ītilāf etc.* additionally Berl. Ms. or. oct. 2238, Fātiḥ 35, Waqf Ibr. $20,_{2}$, 67.—6. *al-Anwār al-asmāʾiyya fī sharḥ al-asmāʾ al-nabawiyya* Alex. Taʾr. 4.—7. *Radd al-qirāʾa bil-shawādhdh* Fātiḥ Waqf Ibr. $28,_{15}$, Fātiḥ $68,_{2}$.—8. *Tajwīd al-ḍād* Fātiḥ $68,_{6}$, Waqf Ibr. $32,_{6}$.—9. *Bayān marātib al-madd* Fātiḥ $68,_{3}$.—10. A treatise on *qirāʾa* ibid. $_{4}$.—11. *Tuḥfat al-ṭalaba* ibid.$_{5}$.

583 | 13. Aḥmad al-Rushdī Yūsuf Imām Effendīzāde, see Suppl.

Murshid al-ṭalaba ilā īḍāḥ wujūh baʿḍ āyāt al-qurʾāniyya min ṭuruq al-Ṭayyiba autograph Fātiḥ 71.

16. Muḥammad b. Muṣṭafā b. Ibrāhīm b. Aḥmad al-Naʿīmī Kattānīzāde wrote, in 1168/1748:

(mistakenly 1172, Brūsalı̊, *ʿOM* I, 284) *Mutqan al-riwāya fī ʿulūm al-qirāʾa wal-dirāya* Fātiḥ Waqf Ibr. 44.

17. Ḥāmid b. al-Ḥājj ʿAbd al-Fattāḥ al-Bālawī (Pālawī), from Pālū in the *wilāyat* of Diyārbakr, wrote, in 1173/1761:

Zubdat al-ʿirfān fī wujūh al-qirāʾāt Sarajevo 33, commentary *ʿUmdat al-khullān* by Muḥammad Amīn ʿAbdallāh Effendizāde, Mollā Efendi (d. 1275/1858, Brūsalı̊ Ṭ II, 38). Joint lith., Istanbul 1287; a popular textbook.

18. Shākhūrīzāde Aḥmad b. ʿAlī b. Muṣṭafā al-Riḍawī al-Ḥanbalī wrote, in 1195/1781:

Tartīb Ḥanbalī, on the orthography of the 6 *maṣāḥif* ʿUthmān, Fātiḥ Waqf Ibr. 50.

7 *Dogmatics*

1. Nabī (ʿAbd al-Bāriʾ) b. Turkhān b. Ṭurmush al-Sīnūbī wrote, in 936/1529 in Adrianople:

Ḥayāt al-qulūb, against the views of the Khalwatiyya, Vienna 1918, Köpr. 719, Alex. Maw. 14, Cairo ^{1}I, 291, from which chapter 33 is in Gotha 839.

2. Muḥammad Abu ʾl-Luṭf al-Bakrī wrote, under Süleymān I, ca. 950/1543:

1. *Munyat al-ʿibād ila ʾl-istiʿdād li-ayyām al-maʿād*, on the Last Day, Upps. 404,$_{1}$.—2. *Tuḥfat al-aḥbāb fi ʾl-duʿāʾ al-mustajāb* ibid.,$_{2}$.

3. Muḥammad b. Pīr ʿAlī Muḥyi ʾl-Dīn al-Birkawī (Birgili) was born in Bālīkasrī in 929/1523. He joined Mollā ʿAṭāʾallāh, who had a madrasa built for him in Birge and who gave him an allowance. He died in 981/1573.

| *ʿIM* 430/3, Brūsalı̊ Ṭāhir, *ʿOM* I/253/6, *JA* 1828, II, 159, *Ersch u. Grubers Enc.* IX, 584
80. 7 *Rasāʾil* Alex. Fun. 194,$_{1-7}$. 1. *Inqādh al-hālikīn*, on whether it is permitted to receive or pay money for reciting the Qurʾān, Sarajevo 84,$_{4}$, Alex. Fiqh Ḥan. 56, Fun. 78,$_{9}$, Cairo ^{1}VI, 16, VII, 164, 399, 405,$_{2}$, ^{2}I, 269, Turkish translation by

Ekmekjīzāde, Sarajevo 108,$_{6}$, in *Majmūʿa*, Istanbul 1280, p. 1ff, as an abstract, Vienna 1658,$_{2}$.—3. *al-Durr al-yatīm fi ʾl-tajwīd* Garr. 2088,$_{2}$, Fātiḥ 42,$_{2}$, Alex. Fun. 78,$_{7}$, Rāġib 9.—A commentary by Aḥmad al-Rūmī (p. 589,$_{7}$), Garr. 2046,$_{2}$, 2088,$_{1}$, Sarajevo 108,$_{4}$, Fātiḥ Waqf Ibr. 29,$_{1}$, Cairo ^{1}I, 99. Anon. comm., Fātiḥ 42,$_{1}$.—3. *al-Radd ʿala ʾl-shīʿa*, dedicated to Aḥmad Pāshā, Berl. 2132.—4. *Tuḥfat al-mustarshidīn fī bayān madhāhib firaq al-muslimīn* ibid. 2133/4.—5. *Jilāʾ al-qulūb*, on the principles of faith, composed in 971/1563, ibid. 3049/50, Leid. 2175, Algiers 887,$_{1}$, 889,$_{2}$, Garr. 1924, Sarajevo 147,$_{2}$, NO 2355, Alex. Maw. 13, Fun. 78,$_{1}$, Cairo, ^{1}II, 77, 153, VII, 164, 169, 250, 252, 400, 428, 515, ^{2}I, 284, Mosul 129,$_{125}$, abstract Mosul 76,$_{83,\ 2}$.—Commentaries: a. *Ḍiyāʾ al-qulūb* by Isḥāq b. Ḥasan al-Zanjānī al-Tūqātī, completed in 1095/1684, Berl. 3051, Ms. or. oct. 3780,$_{3}$ (Fischer-Burch. 34), Algiers 824,$_{4}$, Alex. Taṣ. 78/9, Cairo ^{1}II, 94, 163, ^{2}I, 320.—b. see Suppl.—6. *Kitāb al-īmān wal-istiḥsān* NO 1194/5.—7. *Dāmighat al-mubtadiʿīn wa-kāshifat buṭlān al-mulḥidīn* Cairo ^{1}II, 21, ^{2}I, 178.—8. *Risāla fī uṣūl al-ḥadīth*, Alex. Fun. 119,$_{2}$, Cairo ^{1}II, 218 ^{2}I, 73 (see Suppl.).—Commentary by Dāʾūd b. Muḥammad al-Qārṣī, completed in 1151/1738, Sarajevo 110.—9.
441 *Muʿaddil al-ṣalāt*, | Berl. 3529/30, Paris 1155, Garr. 2085,$_{3}$, Sarajevo 112,$_{5}$, Alex. Fiqh Ḥan. 56, 65, Fun. 78,$_{12}$, 164,$_{3}$, Cairo ^{1}III, 132, VII, 164, 410, 428, 515.—Commentaries: a. See Suppl.—b. Ismāʿīl Efendi al-Güzelḥiṣārī, Cairo ^{1}III, 67.—c., d. see Suppl. (c. Āṣaf II, 1106,$_{15}$, distorted, d. by Aḥmad Bakr al-Erzerūmī, also Rāġib 527).—10. *Waṣiyya* Berl. 4015., anon. comm., Mosul 174,$_{48}$.—11. *Dhukhr al-mutaʾahhilīn wal-nisāʾ fī maʿrifat al-aṭhār wal-dimāʾ* Berl. 4671, Sarajevo 112,$_{4}$, Alex. Fiqh Ḥan. 26, 54, Cairo ^{1}VII, 164, 409, 429, Garr. 2176,$_{2}$.—Commentaries: a. A self-commentary, *Zād al-mutazawwijīn*, Berl. 4672, Cairo ^{1}VII, 182.—b. Isḥāq b. Ḥasan al-Zanjānī, Alex. Fiqh Ḥan. 54.—12. *al-Sayf al-ṣārim fī ʿadam jawāz waqf al-nuqūd wal-darāhim bi-dūn al-waṣiyya wa-iḍāfa ilā mā baʿd al-mawt* (*fi ʾl-radd ʿalā Abi ʾl-Suʿūd*, p. 579), Garr. 1889, Alex. Fun. 78,$_{2}$, Cairo ^{1}VII, 124, 405, 429,
585 516.—13. *Rāḥat al-ṣāliḥīn wa-ṣawāʿiq al-munāfiqīn fi ʾl-fiqh* Cairo ^{1}VII, 127, ^{2}I, | 300, 422.—14. *Risāla fīmā shāʿa wa-dhāʿa bi-ʿilm al-qurʾān al-ʿaẓīm*, on profiting from the Qurʾān by means of teaching, reading, etc. (cf. no. 1), Berl. 5589.—15. *al-Ṭarīqa al-Muḥammadiyya*, a paraenetic work, Berl. 8836/7, BDMG 28, Gotha 11 (cf. 246), Paris 1321/2, Upps. 455, Garr. 1921/3, Algiers 888/91, Yeni 715, AS 1950/6, NO 2484/93, Damad Ibr. Pāshā 772, Cairo ^{1}II, 94, VII, 399, ^{2}I, 330, Calcutta 562, 642; print. Istanbul n.d. (*BO* II, 1106), among others.—Commentaries: a. ʿAbd al-Nāṣir Khojazāde, a contemporary of the author, Berl. 8838.—b. *al-Wasīla al-Aḥmadiyya* by Rajab b. Aḥmad ca. 1087/1676, Algiers 892, Garr. 1922/3; print. Istanbul (*BO* II, 1107).—c. *al-Hadiyya al-nadiyya* by ʿAbd al-Ghanī al-Nābulusī (p. 454), print. C. 1290 and others—Abstract: *al-ʿUrwa al-wathīqa al-ṣamadiyya* by Aḥmad b. Aḥmad al-Salāwī al-Mālikī al-Shādhilī al-Aḥmadī al-Ṣāwī, Alex. Taṣ. 24.—d. On the section about jealousy, by Muḥammad Qāḍīzāde, ca.

7. DOGMATICS
990/1582, Berl. 8840.—e. Anon., Berl. 8839, Munich 746.—f.–u. See Suppl. (k. Alex. Taṣ. 48).—An abstract, *Miftāḥ al-falāḥ*, by al-Fāḍil Sulaymān Efendi, d. 1134/1722, on which a commentary, Berl. 8841.—16. *Īqāẓ al-nāʾimīn*, on piety being good, but acts performed for the sake of material gain and success reprehensible, Berl. 8842/3, Garr. 2029,₂, 2176,₁, Sarajevo 169,₄, Alex. Fun. 66,₆, 78,₈, Cairo ¹III, 119, 164, 271, 399, 405, 429.—17. *Imtiḥān al-adhkiyāʾ (fī 'l-naḥw)* see I, 533, Köpr. 1455. Turkish glosses by Muṣṭafā b. Ḥamza Adalî (see Suppl.), Pet. 205, Garr. 385, print. Istanbul 1260, 1270.—18. *Kitāb al-irshād* Gotha 711, Leid. 1910.—19. *Rawḍāt al-jannāt fī uṣūl al-iʿtiqād* Istanbul 1305.—20. *Iẓhār al-asrār*, on grammar, Berl. 6781/4, Gotha 209,₂, Munich 708,₂, BDMG 69a, Vienna 172,₂, Pet. 184,₂, 197,₃, Br. Mus. 528, 1397, Cairo ¹IV, 22, ²II, 76, print. Istanbul 1235, 1285, 1301, Būlāq 1279.—Commentaries: a. *Kashf al-asrār* by his student Musliḥ al-Dīn al-Ulāmīshī, Berl. 6783, Pet. Ros. 143,₁, Garr. 468.—b. *Natāʾij al-afkār* by Muṣṭafā b. Ḥamza Adalî, composed in 1085/1674, Berl. 6784, Munich 748, Pet. 204, Br. Mus. Suppl. 979, Garr. 469/70, print. Istanbul 1219, 1251, 1300, 1303.—c. *Ḥall asrār al-akhyār ilā iʿrāb Iẓhār al-asrār* by Zaynīzāde Ḥusayn b. Aḥmad, completed in 1152/1739, Br. Mus. Suppl. 980, Garr. 471, Cairo ¹V, 148, print. Skutari 1218, Istanbul 1224, Būlāq 1279.—d. *Zubdat al-Iʿrāb* by ʿAbdallāh b. Muḥammad, Berl. 6785.—e. *Fatḥ al-asrār* by Muḥammad b. Muḥammad b. Aḥmad, Munich 749, Garr. 472.—f., g. see Suppl.—21. *al-ʿAwāmil al-jadīda* (see I, 341), Berl. 6786/7, Munich 679,₃, Gotha 209,₆, 338, Vienna 172,₃, 209, Pet. 178, 182, Ros. 147, Glasgow 54 II | (*JRAS* 1899, 723), Algiers 48,₆, 50,₃, 52,₃, 54,₃, 180/3, 1436,₂, Sarajevo 167,₂, Alex. Naḥw 33, Cairo ¹VII, 469, print. Istanbul 1235, Būlāq 1279.—Commentaries: a. Sulaymān b. Aḥmad, ca. 1113/1701, Berl. 6788.—b. *Taʿlīq al-fawāḍil* by Ḥusayn b. Aḥmad Zaynīzāde, ca. 1144/1731, Berl. 6789, Vienna 172,₃, 209, Garr. 466/7, print. Istanbul 1220.—c. ʿIṣmat Aḥmad of Qush Atasî, Pet. 178, Garr. 464/5.—d. *Tuḥfat al-ikhwān* by Muṣṭafā b. Ibrāhīm, Pet. 182, print. Skutari 1220. Glosses, see Suppl. (α Alex. Naḥw 35,₁, Istanbul 1298).—e.–h. see Suppl. (e. also Mosul 148,₁₃₄. Superglosses by Mollā Ḥāmid al-Sūsī, ibid. 148, 134,₂; by Saʿdallāh al-Kabīr, ibid. 137,₂₇₄,₇₅; h. Muḥammad Khāliṣ, d. after 1229/1814, Garr. 481; i. Güzelḥiṣārī, Alex. Naḥw 37,₈).—22. *Kifāyat al-mubtadiʾ fī 'l-ṣarf* Krafft 59, Pet. 199,₁, Algiers 229,₆, Cairo ¹VII, 120, 159, 265, ²II, 66.—Commentaries: a. *ʿInāyat al-mubtaghī* by Aḥmad Qush Adalî, | Pet. 200, print. Istanbul 1299.—b. Muḥammad b. Muṣṭafā Ṭāʾūskārī, Pet. 201.—c. Ḥusayn b. Farhād, Munich 747.—d., e. see Suppl.—23. *al-Amthila*, on verb paradigms, Pet. 199,₂.—24. *al-Ṣiḥāḥ al-ʿAjamiyya*, a Persian grammar in Arabic, Br. Mus. 122,₆.—25.–41. see Suppl.—42.–46. ibid. III, 1305 (31. *al-Arbaʿūn*, with a commentary by Muḥammad b. Muṣṭafā al-Āqkirmānī al-Ḥanafī, d. 1174/1760 [Suppl. II, 660, 10b], Sarajevo 107,₁, ₂, 108,₂, print. Tunis 1295, 1316, Istanbul 1323).

4. Muḥammad al-Isbīrī Qāḍīzāde, ca. 990/1582.

1. *Risāla mumayyiza madhhab al-Māturīdiyya ʿani ʾl-madhāhib al-ghayriyya*, on the different views on free will among the orthodox, the Jabriyya, and the Qadariyya, Berl. 2492.—2. *Risāla fī-mā yataʿallaq bi-waʿd allāh wa-waʿīdihi* ibid. 2493.

5. Ashraf Muʿīn al-Dīn Mīrzā Makhdūm al-Ḥasanī al-Shīrāzī, a descendant of Sayyid al-Jurjānī (p. 280), was born in Shiraz and studied there. When he and his mother had completed the pilgrimage he was incarcerated by Shāh Ṭāhmāsp because of his being a Sunnī, while his library, which he had inherited from al-Jurjānī, was plundered as well. When the new shah, Ismāʿīl II, turned on the
587 Shīʿīs after the death of Ṭahmāsp in 984/1574, he called | Ashraf to his court, with a number of other Sunnī scholars. However, in the next year the new shah was poisoned and, when there was another persecution of the Sunnīs, Ashraf fled to Turkish territory, first to Van and then to Istanbul.[1] He was helped into the post of chief *qāḍī* in Diyarbakr by the area's pasha, Darwīsh Pāshā, and the tutor of Sultan Murād. Having worked for another two years as a *qāḍī* in Tripoli, he was then summoned to the court in Istanbul, where he was held in high regard by the sultan because he had been the only one of the *ʿulamāʾ* who succeeded in making it rain after saying a prayer. This was also the reason that he was appointed *qāḍī* in Mecca, although he was removed from that position three years later. When he said in Istanbul that he wished he could retire in Mecca, the sultan first appointed him, for a couple of days, as *qāḍī* of Istanbul, and then as *qāḍi ʾl-ʿaskar*, first for Anatolia and then for Rumelia, after which he received a pension and retired to Mecca, where he died in 995/1587.

443 | *RA* 80r. 1. *al-Nawāqiḍ fi ʾl-radd ʿala ʾl-Rawāfiḍ*, which he began before his first pilgrimage and completed in Istanbul in 987/1579, Berl. 2136, Leid. 2076, Yeni 756, Köpr II, 159. An abstract, perhaps by Muḥammad b. ʿAbd al-Rasūl al-Barzanjī, d. 1103/1691 (p. 511), Berl. 2137, Paris 1459.—2. *Dhakhīrat al-ʿuqbā fī dhamm al-dunyā* NO 2382.

6. Yaḥyā b. ʿAlī b. Naṣūḥ Nawʿī was born in Ṭughra in 940/1533. In 957/1550 he went to Istanbul where he became a professor at one of the eight madrasas there in 995/1587, and was then made a *qāḍī* in Baghdad in 998/1589. But in Rabīʿ II of that year (February 1590) he was summoned back to Istanbul to

1 This information is missing from *RA* but secured by the author's own statement in no. 1.

become the tutor to the sons of the sultan, Murād. When Meḥmed, who had been his student, acceded to the throne in 1003/1595, he became *qāḍi 'l-ʿaskar* and was given the madrasa of | Muḥammad Beg, before dying in 1007/1598. He achieved his greatest fame as a poet in the Turkish language, and was given the same rank as Bāqī because he excelled at both the *ghazal* and the *qaṣīda.* 588

Muḥ. IV, 474/5. 1. *Muḥaṣṣal al-masāʾil al-kalāmiyya wa-mulakhkhaṣ wasāʾil al-ʿaqāʾid al-islāmiyya*, dedicated to Sinān Pāshā, AS 2352.—2. *Risāla fī 'l-farq bayna madhhab al-Ashāʿira wal-Māturīdiyya* Leid. 1882.

7. ʿAlī b. Aḥmad al-Hītī, ca. 1020/1621.

1. *al-Sayf al-bātir li-arqāb al-Shīʿa wal-Rawāfiḍ al-kawāfir*, dedicated to Sultan Aḥmad I (1012–26/1603–17), Berl. 2152/3, Mosul 262,5.

7a. Al-Sayyid Muṭahhar b. ʿAbd al-Raḥmān b. ʿAlī b. Ismāʿīl b. ʿArab Qāḍī, who wrote during the reign of Murād III (982–1003/1574–95).

Mushtamil al-aqāwīl (fī 'l-radd ʿala 'l-Rawāfiḍ wa-ʿaqāʾidihim) Berl. 2135 (which has Ibn ʿAbd al-Salām?), Garr. 1525 (see Suppl.).—2. *Risāla fī tafsīr āya min sūrat al-Aḥzāb* AS 417,2 (Ritter, *Türk. Mecm.* 7–8, II [1945], p. 81/2).

8. Kāfī Ḥasan Efendi al-Aqḥiṣārī was born in Aqḥiṣār in Bosnia in Ramaḍān 951/1544, where he was a *mudarris* and a *qāḍī.* He died on 15 Shaʿbān 1025/29 August 1616.

Babinger, GO 144, ʿAṭāʾī, *Dhayl ShN* 304, Brūsalï Ṭāhir I, 277. 1. *Rawḍāt al-jannāt fī uṣūl al-iʿtiqādāt*, a compendium of orthodox views against innovators, especially the Sufis, completed in 1014/1605, Berl. 1841, Sarajevo 166, 167—A commentary, *Azhār al-rawḍāt*, completed in 1015/1606, ibid. 1842, Leipz. 115,1.—2. *Uṣūl al-ḥikam fī niẓām al-ʿālam*, with a Turkish foreword and paraphrase, Leipz. 231, Dresd. 177,2, 3, 4, see Suppl.

9. Muḥammad b. Muṣṭafā Qāḍīzāde wrote, during the reign of Murād IV (1032–49/1623–40):

Naṣr al-aṣḥāb wal-aḥbāb wa-qahr al-kilāb al-sibāb Cairo [1]VII, 100, [2]I, 211, 370.—2. See Suppl.

10a. Muḥammad Amīn al-Uskudārī, who died in 1149/1736, see Suppl.

589 | 6. *Jāmiʿ al-anwār* Patna I, 153,$_{1448}$ (which has Muftīzāde, not in Brūsalı̊).

11. Ḥusayn b. Yūsuf al-Erzerūmī wrote, in 1154/1741:

Al-Risāla al-munjiya min al-khaṭaʾ al-wāqiʿ bayna ʾl-firqa al-nājiya wa-ghayr al-nājiya Cairo ^{1}VII, 602.

444 | 8 ***Mysticism***

1. Ḥāmid b. Jalāl al-Dīn al-Ḥārithī Shaykhzāde al-Hindī, who died in Istanbul in 959/1552.

Laṭāʾif al-ishārāt fī manāzil al-sāʾirīn wa-maqāmāt al-ʿārifīn, on chapter 9 of Ibn Sīnā's *al-Ishārāt wal-tanbīhāt* (I, 592), Br. Mus. 757.

2. Muḥammad b. Muṣṭafā al-Wānī, who died in 1000/1591.

1. *Tuḥfat al-mulūk*, a (Turkish) collection of prayers, NO 2863.—2.–4. see Suppl.—5. *Sharḥ Durar al-ḥukkām* p. 292.

3. Muḥammad b. Ibrāhīm Bekzāde, ca. 1014/1605.

Rawḍat al-aṣiḥḥāʾ wa-dawḥat al-alibbāʾ Köpr. II, 190.

4. ʿAbd al-Ḥakīm (-Ḥalīm) b. Muḥammad al-Ḥanafī Akhīzāde, a poet who wrote under the pen-name Ḥalīmī, was born in Istanbul in 963/1556. In 978/1570 he began studying in Adrianople, where his father was a *qāḍī*, and then moved to Istanbul. In 982/1574 he became a professor at the newly founded madrasa of Ibrāhīm Pāshā, and after a number of transfers he joined the madrasa of the *wālide* in Skutari in 998/1590. In 1000/1592 he became a *qāḍī* in Bursa and in 1001 held the same position in Adrianople, although he was removed from office in 1003. However, he was made a *qāḍī* in Istanbul in 1004 and *qāḍi ʾl-ʿaskar* for Anatolia in 1005/1596, but was ousted in 1007, before being reinstated in 1008. The following year he left office of his own accord. In Ṣafar 1010/August 1601 he became *qāḍi ʾl-ʿaskar* for Rumelia. He died in office in Istanbul, in Dhu ʾl-Qaʿda 1013/May 1605.

Muḥ. II, 319/22. Brūsalı̊ Ṭāhir, ʿOM I, 228. 1. *Riyāḍ al-sādāt fī ithbāt al-karāmāt* Cairo ^{1}II, 87.—2. *Hadiyyat al-mahdiyyīn (fī ʾl-fiqh)* Garr. 1651.—3. *Rasāʾil* Vat. V. 1395.

| 5. Muḥammad b. Muḥammad Altı̊ Parmaq b. al-Čı̊qrı̊qjı̊ originated in Üsküb, became a preacher at the mosque of Sultan Meḥmed in Istanbul, later settled in Cairo, and died in 1033/1623. 590

Muḥ. IV, 174. 1. *Nuzhat al-jumān wa-nādirat al-zamān*, an Arabic translation of Jāmī's (p. 266) *Nigāristān*, Yeni 907.—2. See Suppl.

6. ʿAzīz Maḥmūd al-Uskudārī Hudāʾī was born in Siwriḥiṣār and studied in Istanbul. In 978/1570 he started working as a private teacher under his own teacher, Nāẓirzāde, at the time the latter was transferred to the newly founded madrasa of the sultan in Adrianople. He also accompanied Nāẓirzāde when he became a *qāḍī* in Cairo and Damascus. In 980/1572 he was granted a professorship in Bursa. However, due to a dream, he gave up this post and became a Jalwatī dervish in Skutari. In 1002/1593 he accepted a position as preacher | and teacher at the mosque of Sultan Meḥmed, before becoming chief preacher in Skutari. He was held in great esteem by the sultan. He died in 1038/1628. 445

Muḥ. IV, 327/9, Brūsalı̊ Ṭāhir, *ʿOM* I, 185/8. 1. *Ḥayāt al-arwāḥ wa-najāt al-ashbāḥ*, on death and resurrection, Berl. 2691.—2. *Fatḥ al-bāb wa-rafʿ al-ḥijāb*, on the talents and merits bestowed upon man, ibid. 3107.—3. *Khulāṣat al-akhbār fī aḥwāl al-nabī al-mukhtār* Leipz. 194, Leid. 2081.—4. *al-Majālis*, a commentary on suras 19ff., compiled after the author's death by Shaykh Ismāʿīl, Glasgow 14 (*JRAS* 1899, 74, 154).—5.–12. see Suppl.

7. Aḥmad b. ʿAbd al-Qādir al-Rūmī, who died in 1041/1631 or 1043, see Suppl.

Ḥadīth from *Maṣābīḥ al-sunna* (I, 448), Berl. 8845/6, Garr. 1506, Mosul 165,$_{15}$.—2., 3. See Suppl.

8. Ismāʿīl b. Aḥmad al-Anqirawī was born in Ankara, became a shaykh at the Mawlawī monastery in Galata, and died in 1042/1632.

Muḥ. I, 418. 1. *al-Risāla al-tanzīhiyya fī shaʾn al-Mawlawiyya* Leid. 1892.—2. *Ḥujjat al-samāʿ fī ḥill istimāʿ al-ghināʾ*, | a defence of music, against which an unidentified author wrote a tract, which al-Anqirawī tried to refute in no. 1; this other person then wrote *al-Barāhīn al-ʿulwiyya ʿalā fusūq al-Mawlawiyya* Berl. 5520, Leid. 1890, *Takmila* Leid. 1891.—3.–11. see Suppl.—12. *Talkhīṣ Risālat shaykh Aḥmad* (Aḥmad b. Muḥammad al-Ṭūsī), on the permissibility of the dancing of the dervishes, Nāfidh 395. 591

9. ʿAlī al-Jisr al-Kutāhī al-Germiyānī al-Qaraḥiṣārī wrote, in 1074/1664:

Al-Minhāj al-Muḥammadī wal-ṭarīq al-Aḥmadī Garr. 1928.

10. Awḥad al-Dīn ʿAbd al-Aḥad al-Nūrī died as a preacher at the Aya Sofya in 1061/1651, see Suppl.

1. *al-Arbaʿīniyyāt*, completed in Jumādā I 1045/October 1635, Cairo [1]VII, 583.—2. *Taʾdīb al-mutamarridīn fī ḥaqq al-abawayn*, on the parents of the Prophet, ibid.—3. *Mirʾāt al-wujūd wa-mirqāt al-shuhūd* ibid.—4. *Risāla fī bayān marātib maʿrifat al-raḥmān* ibid.—5. *Risāla mutaʿalliqa bi-ṭayy al-makān* ibid.—6. *Risāla fī sharḥ kalām amīr al-muʾminīn ʿAlī b. Abī Ṭālib fī ʾl-jawāb ʿan suʾāl Kumayl fī ʾl-ḥaqīqa* ibid.—7. *al-Risāla al-ʿiṭriyya fī ʾl-ḥaqīqa al-qadariyya* ibid.—8. *Ḥujjat al-widād wa-ḥijjat al-fuʾād*, completed in Rabīʿ I 1033/January 1624, ibid.—9. *Qaṣm al-mubtadiʿīn fī ithbāt al-waliyyīn* ibid.—10. *Ithbāt al-ʿilm wal-shuʿūr fī-man kāna min ahl al-qubūr* ibid. 584.—11. *al-ʿAdl wal-isqāṭ bayna*
446 *ʾl-tafrīṭ wal-ifrāṭ* (*fī jawāz al-nāfila bil-jamāʿa*) ibid. |—12. *Risāla fī ʾl-radd ʿalā man ankara intifāʿ baʿḍ al-muʾminīn bi-saʿy baʿḍ ikhwānihim*, completed in Rabīʿ I 1035/December 1625, ibid.—13. *Inqādh al-ṭālibīn ʿan mahāwi ʾl-mughtarrīn al-ghāfilīn* ibid. 14.—*Risāla fī ʾl-kalām ʿalā baʿḍ āyāt min al-Qurʾān al-karīm* ibid.—15. *Riyāḍ al-adhkār wa-ḥiyāḍ al-asrār*, completed Jumādā I 1034/March 1625, ibid.—16. *Risālat al-dawarān li-ghawth hādha ʾl-zamān*, Turkish, ibid.—17.–19. see Suppl.

10a. Ḥusayn b. al-ʿAbbās al-Ḥanafī al-Khalwatī, *khalīfa* of the Khalwatiyya Shaykh al-Nūrī (no. 10), wrote:

1. *al-Risāla al-dawarāniyya*, a defence of the dancing of dervishes, begun in Shawwāl 1092/October–November 1681, Nāfidh 394 (Ritter).—2. *Tuḥfat al-kabīr* Faiḍullāh 53.

11. Nuʿmān Pāshā b. Muṣṭafā Pāshā Köprülü, who died in 1132/1720.

1. *Ikhtiṣār Risālat al-Qushayrī* I, 556.—2. See Suppl.

12. Muḥammad b. Khalīl al-Qaraḥiṣārī, who died in 1142/1729.

592 | *Targhībāt al-abrār wa-tarhībat al-ashrār* NO 2343.

13. Muḥammad Murād al-Üzbekī (Özbekī) al-Naqshbandī, who died in 1142/1729, see Suppl.

1. *Silsilat al-dhahab fi ʾl-sulūk wal-adab*, on the religious views of the Naqshbandiyya, particularly on the nature of prayer, Berl. 2194/6, a commentary, ibid. 2197.—2. *Risāla fi ʾl-samāʿ*, ibid. 3726.

14. ʿUthmān b. Yaʿqūb b. Ḥusayn al-Kämākhī, ca. 1160/1747.

1. *Tuḥfat al-akhyār wa-barakāt al-abrār*, composed for the vizier Aḥmad Pāshā, on religious ethics, Leipz. 183, NO 2096 (*Zakāt al-abrār*).—2.–4. see Suppl.

16. Abū Saʿīd Muḥammad b. Muṣṭafā b. ʿUthmān al-Khādimī, who died in 1176/1762, see Suppl. (III. 1302).

2. Basle, no shelfmark.—4. Under the title *Īḍāḥ ibdāʿ ḥikmat al-ḥakīm min bayān bismillāh al-raḥmān al-raḥīm* Alex. Fun. 100,$_{2}$, see Suppl. 738,$_{4,7}$.—13. *Risāla fī ādāb qirāʾat al-Qurʾān* Patna II, 366,$_{254,2}$.

16a. Ibrāhīm Ḥaqqī b. ʿUthmān al-Faqīrī al-Erzerūmī studied in Erzurum—where his father had moved from Ḥasan Qalʿa—where he also acquired knowledge of Persian under the local *muftī*, Ḥādhiq Muḥammad. In Tellū, near Seʿird, he joined the Qādirī-Naqshbandī shaykh Ismāʿīl Faqīrallāh, adopting his name and marrying his daughter. Most of his works are in Persian and Turkish. He died in 1186/1772.

Brūsalī M. Ṭāhir, *ʿOM* I, 33/6. 1.–4. see Suppl. 1004, 79 (1. Asʿad 1438,$_{8}$, 4. ibid.,$_{1}$).—5. *Miʾat wa-khamsīn ḥikma*, Asʿad 1438,$_{2}$.—6. *Ḥiṣn al-ʿārifīn* ibid.,$_{4}$.—6. *Muntakhabāt al-Mathnawī fī taqlīl al-akl ismuhu Qūṭ-i jān* Persian ibid.,$_{5}$.—7. *Duʿāʾ* ibid. $_{7}$.—8. *al-Insān al-kāmil* ibid.,$_{9}$.—9. A letter, ibid. $_{10}$.—10. *Mustaqṣā fī kamāl al-riḍā* Turkish ibid. $_{11}$.—11. *Maktūb al-sirr* ibid. $_{12}$.—12. *Rōznāme* Turkish ibid.,$_{13}$.—13. *al-Murabbaʿāt al-ʿarabiyya* ibid.—2.–12. *Mufradāt* or *Nafy al-wujūd* ibid.,$_{15}$.—13. *Tartīb al-ʿulūm*, Turkish, ibid.,$_{17}$.—14. *Tafwīḍ al-umūr*, Turkish, ibid.,$_{18}$.—15. Turkish *Risāla* ibid.,$_{19}$.—16. His best-known work is the *Maʿrifetnāme*, a Turkish encyclopaedia, print. Būlāq 1251, 1280, Kazan 1261, Istanbul 1284, 1294, 1310.

| 9 *Politics* 593

1. Qāḍī Ḥusayn b. Ḥasan al-Samarqandī wrote, in 936/1529 for the vizier Ibrāhīm Pāshā:

Laṭāʾif al-afkār wa-kashf al-asrār, a kind of mirror for princes in 5 chapters: 1. *Fī aḥkām al-siyāsa*; 2. *Fī taʾrīkh akābir al-bariyyāt*, a compendium of Islamic history up to the year 936/1529; 3. *Fi 'l-adabiyyāt*; 4. *Fi 'l-akhlāq al-maḥmūdāt*; 5. *Fī ʿājāʾib al-makhlūqāt*, Vienna 885.

2. Burhān al-Dīn (Kamāl al-Dīn) Ibrāhīm b. Bakhshī Dede Khalīfa (Qara Dede) was born in Sūnisa and worked as a tanner in Amasia until the age of 20, when he began studying after he was mocked by a *muftī*. He then became a private teacher in Bursa, then a professor there, then in Amasia, Marzifūn, Āmid, Aleppo, Iznik and, finally, a *muftī*. He died in retirement in 973/1565 (or, according to others, in 975/1567).

ʿIM 286/91, Belīgh, *Güldeste-i riyāḍ-i ʿirfān* 295/6. *Risālat al-siyāsa al-sharʿiyya* Berl. 5626.

447 | **10** ***Astronomy***

1. Maḥmūd b. Muḥammad Mīram[1] Čelebī, a grandson of Qāḍīzāde, was a professor in Gallipoli, Adrianople and Bursa, and then *qāḍi 'l-ʿaskar* in Anatolia. After he was removed from office he made the pilgrimage and died soon after his return to Adrianople in 931/1524.

ShN I, 492/4, Brūsalī M. Ṭāhir, *ʿOM* II, 298/9, Abdülhak Adnān Adîvar, *Ilim* 78, Suter 437. 1. *Risālat al-jayb al-jāmiʿa*, on the sine quadrant, dedicated to Sultan Bāyezīd, composed in 900/1494, Berl. 5855, Gött. ar. 94, f. 80/94, Garr. 2006,$_{20}$.—2.–7. see Suppl.

2. Ghars al-Dīn Ibrāhīm b. Aḥmad al-Ḥalabī was born in Aleppo and studied there, in Damascus, and in Cairo, where he became the tutor to the sons of
594 the Mamlūk sultan Ashraf | al-Ghūrī. When the latter was defeated by the Ottomans in 922/1516 he was imprisoned but later freed in Istanbul. He died there in 971/1563.

ʿIM 247/55. 1. A treatise on sine quadrants, Berl. 5825, Alex. Fun. 65,$_{8}$.—2. *Risāla muʿallaqa ʿalā mawḍūʿāt al-ʿulūm* Br. Mus. 430,$_{4}$.—3.–6. see Suppl. (5. Alex. Fun. 65,$_{7}$).

4. Asʿad b. ʿAlī b. ʿUthmān al-Yāniyawī, who died in 1134/1722, see Suppl.

1 Adnan Adivar, *Ilim* 78, prefers the Turkish pronunciation Mīrim.

Brūsalı̊ M. Ṭāhir, *ʿOM* I, 234, Adnan Adivar, *Ilim* 139/40. 2. *Sharḥ al-anwār fī 'l-manṭiq* NO 2653, written when he was a professor at the Madrasat Abī Ayyūb al-Anṣārī.

11 Medicine

1. Muḥammad b. Muḥammad al-Qawṣūnī (Qayṣūnīzāde) Badr al-Dīn, known by the pen-name Nidā'ī, was born in Ankara into a family that hailed from a village near Cairo. He became the personal physician of Khān Ṣāḥib Girāy in the Crimea, who sent him as an emissary to Selīm I (926–74/1520–66). He later entered the service of the latter and accompanied him in 1565 on his campaign against Szigeth, where he also embalmed his body. He also served Selīm II (974–82/1566–74).

ʿAṭā'ī, *Dhayl ShN* 196, Brūsalı̊ M. Ṭāhir, *ʿOM* III, 239, Hammer, *Gesch. der osm. Dichtkunst* II, 471ff., *Gesch. der Chane der Krim* 55, Adnan Adivar, *Ilim* 94.[1] 1. *Zād al-masīr fī ʿilāj al-bawāsīr*, on haemorrhoids, Gotha 1979, Br. Mus. 453,3, Garr. 1112, Alex. Ṭibb 20.—2. *Maqāla fī jawāz istiʿmāl ḥajar al-bādazahr al-ḥayawānī*, on animal bezoars, Cairo ¹VI, 36, 42.—3.–7. see Suppl.—8. *Manāfiʿ al-nās*, on popular medicine, Istanbul Univers. Yı̊ldı̊z Ṭib. 218, Welīeddīn 2551.

| 2. Ṣāliḥ b. Naṣrallāh al-Ḥalabī Ḥakīmbašı̊ b. Sallūm was born in Aleppo, worked as a phycisian there, then became a *qāḍī* in Istanbul, and finally chief physician to the Ottoman Empire and a confidant of Sultan Meḥmed. He died in Yenishehir in 1080/1670. 595

Muḥ. II, 240/2. Brūsalı̊, *ʿOM* III, 224, Abdülhak Adnan, *La Science chez les Turcs Ottomans*, Paris 1939, 96f., *Ilim* 109. 1. *Ghāyat al-bayān fī tadbīr badan al-insān* Paris Fonds turc 958, AS 3679/80, Köpr. 975, Sbath 604, Istanbul Univers. Ṭib. 230, ibid. TY 7056, 7132, Welīeddin 2521.—1(a). *Ghāyat al-itqān fī tadbīr badan al-insān*, see Suppl., AS 3982, Welīeddīn 2520, 2522, Mosul 33,144, 29,118, 270,39, part IV, *Kitāb al-ṭibb al-jadīd etc.* also Patna I, 253,2149. Turkish translation by Abu 'l-Fayḍ Muṣṭafā b. Muḥammad al-Ṭabīb, *Nuzhat al-abdān fī tarjamat*

1 Adnan, loc. cit., regards the author of no. 8 as a person different, as he calls himself 'Dervish Nidā'ī', and reports that he had been just the teacher (Hoca) of Ṣāḥib Girāy, that he had been accused of slander after his return from his mission to Istanbul, that he had been imprisoned for 7 years, and that he had picked up medicine only afterwards, from a descendant of the Prophet. But we have reports that, as a poet, Qayṣūnīzāde did use the pen-name Nidā'ī, and it is understandable if he somewhat exaggerated the ups and downs of his life in a popular work.

Ghāyat al-itqān, completed in 1141/1729, additionally AS 3681, Istanbul Univ. Yi̊ldi̊z Ṭib. 225, Welīeddīn 2483, print. Istanbul 1303. 1. (*al-Ghāya fī 'l-ṭibb* Berl. 6315 = 1. or 2. ?).—2.,3. See Suppl.—4. *Aqrābādhīn* Mosul 299$_{,1}$.

3. Fayḍī Muṣṭafā Efendi Ḥayātizāde, who died in 1151/1738.

Brūsali̊ Ṭāhir, *ʿOM* III, 232. 1. *al-Risāla al-mushfiya lil-amrāḍ al-mushkila*, on diseases of the lower part of the body in general and how they differ from hypochondria, with which they are often confused, Gotha 1980/1, Turkish ibid. 118, Krafft 385, Welīeddīn 2519.—2. *Khulāṣat al-ṭibb*, Turkish, Rāġib 945.—3. *al-Risāla al-fayḍiyya fī lughāt al-mufradāt al-ṭibbiyya* Welīeddīn 2559.

448 | 12 *Music*

1. Muḥammad b. ʿAbd al-Ḥamīd al-Lādhiqī wrote, during the reign of Bāyezīd II (886–918/1481–1512):

1. *al-Fatḥiyya fī ʿilm al-mūsīqī*, see Suppl., additionally Cairo *Nashra* 12.[1]—2. *Zayn al-iḥsān fī ʿilm al-taʾlīf wal-awzān* NO 3655.

2. Muḥammad Efendi b. Aḥmad b. Maḥmūd b. Muḥammad al-Ganjī b. Abī ʿAṣrūn wrote, around 1150/1737:

596 | 1. *Bulūgh al-munā fī tarājim ahl al-ghināʾ*, on 26 contemporary singers and music in general, Berl. 7427, various pieces in praise of it, ibid. 58, Ẓāh. ʿIsh, Taʾr. 303, see Khalīl Mardam Bek, *RAAD* IV, 57/9.—2. *Rashf al-nabīh fī tajrīd al-tashbīh*, on the theory of similes, completed in 1123/1711, Berl. 7286.

13 *Agriculture*

Khayr al-Dīn b. Tāj al-Dīn Ilyāszāde, ca. 1134/1721.

1. *Falāḥ al-fallāḥ* Berl. 6212.—2. See Suppl.—3. *Bulūgh al-amal fī taḥqīq daʿwa 'l-mushtarī al-ḥabal* Garr. 2002$_{,14}$.

14 *Occult Sciences*

1. Muṣṭafā b. Pīr Muḥammad Muṣliḥ al-Dīn al-Āydinī Bustān Efendī was born in Tīra in 904/1493, became a professor in Bursa, then a *qāḍī* in a small

1 Partial French translation by Baron Rodolphe Erlanger, *La Musique arabe* IV (1939), see H.G. Farmer, Turkish Instruments of Music in the Fifteenth Century, *JRAS* 1940, p. 195–8 (other MSS given there).

town, and a professor again, in Tīra. There he gained the favour of the wife of Sultan Süleymān, through whom he obtained a newly constructed madrasa in Istanbul, and then one of the "great eight" in that city. He then became a *qāḍī* in Bursa, Adrianople, and Istanbul, then *qāḍi 'l-ʿaskar* for Anatolia, and finally for Rumelia. After five years he was removed from office, after which he died, in 977/1569.

ʿIM 335/42. 1. *Najāt al-aḥbāb wa-tuḥfat dhawi 'l-albāb*, on alchemy, Pet. Ros. 206,$_{1}$.—2. *Khazīnat al-asrār wa-hatk al-astār*, ibid.$_{2}$.

2. ʿAlī Bek al-Iznīqī or ʿAlī Čelebī ʿAlāʾ al-Dīn al-Ṣarūkhānī al-Muʾallif al-Jadīd, who flourished around the tenth century.

Hammer, *Gesch. d. Osman Reiches* IV, 607, Adnan, *Ilim* 91/2. 1. *Risāla fī ʿilm al-ilāhī* Pet. Ros. 204,$_{1}$.—2. *Durar al-anwār fī asrār al-aḥjār* ibid.$_{2}$, Vienna 1498,$_{1}$, A. Taymūr, Ṭab. 68,$_{1}$.—3. *Kashf al-asrār fī hatk al-astār*, on alchemy, ibid.$_{3}$, Br. Mus. 1373,$_{1}$, Istanb. Univ. Yildiz Ṭabīʿiyye 226.—4. *Daqāʾiq al-mīzān fī maqādīr al-awzān* Pet. Ros. 205,$_{7}$.—5. *Dīwān-i ḥikmet*, Turkish poems, Vienna 1498,$_{2}$.—6.–13. see Suppl. (12. Taymūr Ṭab. 68, 4; 13. Gotha 1296,$_{3}$).

3. Sultan Muṣṭafā III (1171–87/1757–73) wrote:

| *Al-Nujūm al-zāhira fī ḥawādith Miṣr wal-Qāhira*, on astrology, containing 597
within chapter II predictions on his own government of Egypt, Gotha 1457. Cf. Jab. I, 383/4; Hammer, *Gesch. d. Osm. Reiches* IV, 648.—2. See Suppl.

| 15 *Encyclopaedias and Polyhistors* 449

1. In order to alleviate his loneliness, Muḥammad al-Sharīf b. al-Sayyid al-Muwaqqiʿ Yāʿū al-Qādirī al-Ḥasanī al-Ḥanafī wrote, around 930/1524:

Majmaʿ multaqaṭ al-zuhūr bi-rawḍa min al-manẓūm wal-manthūr, an encyclopaedic overview and description of the various sciences, with an alphabetical index of God's names at the end, Berl. 82.

2. Shams al-Dīn Aḥmad b. Sulaymān b. Kamāl Pāshā served as a young man in the army of Bāyezīd, after which he studied under al-Luṭfī (d. 904/1498) at the Dār al-ḥadīth in Adrianople. He became a professor at the madrasa of ʿAlī Bek there, then in Üsküb, and then again in Adrianople, this time at the Bāyezīdiyyya. He then became a *qāḍī* there and later *qāḍi 'l-ʿaskar* for Anatolia. Having taught again for a while at the Dār al-ḥadīth and the Bāyezīdiyya in

Adrianople, he became Shaykh al-Islām in Istanbul. He died in office in 940/1533.

ShN I, 591/8, Mecdī 381, Mustaqīmzāde, *Dawḥat al-mashāʾikh* 16, *ʿIlmiyye Sālnāmesi* 346ff., Hammer, *Gesch. d. osm. Dichtkunst* II, 205ff., Babinger *GO* 61. An inventory of his writings, Berl. 19. Collections of: 59 treatises, Cairo ^{1}VII, 435/44; 17 treatises, Vienna 1791; 22 mostly Sufi treatises, ibid. 1919; 9 treatises Mosul 117,$_{112}$, 30 Alex. Fun. 169/70, p. 153/4,$_{17-41}$ 165, 176,$_{8-12}$, Laleli 2433, see
598 Suppl.[1] 1. *Risāla fī taḥqīq al-ʿilm*, on science as a notion, Berl. 133.—| 2. *Risāla fī jawāz al-istiʾjār ʿalā taʿlīm al-Qurʾān* Berl. 439, Cairo ^{1}II, 440, no. 40, AS 4794,$_{41}$.—3. *Risāla fī mā yataʿallaq bi-khalq al-Qurʾān* Berl. 446, Vienna 1919,$_{3}$, Leid. 987,$_{37}$, de Jong 157,$_{12}$, Bodl. I, 500,$_{13}$, AS 4794,$_{56}$, 4797,$_{7}$, 4820,$_{26}$, Cairo ^{1}VII, 438,$_{25}$.—4. *Risāla fī anna ʾl-Qurʾān kalām Allāh al-qadīm* Berl. 487, Br. Mus. 861,$_{7}$, AS 4794,$_{13}$, 4820,$_{27}$.—5. *Risāla fī iʿjāz al-Qurʾān* Berl. 729, Vienna 1919,$_{10}$, de Jong 157,$_{37}$, Bodl. I, 500,$_{12}$, AS 4794,$_{57}$, 4797,$_{6}$, Cairo ^{1}VII, 128, 439,$_{31}$.—6. *Tafsīr al-Qurʾān* Ind. Off. 4607 (*JRAS* 1939, 381) AS 80 (*Türk. Mecm.* 7–8, II [1945], p. 73), 125, NO 189/90, Köpr. 63/4, Cairo ^{1}I, 141, ^{2}I, 37.—7. *Risāla fi ʾl-tafsīr* AS 4820,$_{19}$.—8. *Tafsīr sūrat al-Mulk* (no. 67), Berl. 958/9, Vienna 1791,$_{2}$, Leid. 1698, AS 4797,$_{1}$, Cairo ^{1}II, 435,$_{1}$.—8a. *Tafsīr Fātiḥat al-kitāb* Mosul 104,$_{72, 7}$.—8b. *Tafsīr sūrat* 6,$_{159}$, Alex. Fun. 152,$_{5}$.—9. *Tafsīr sūrat al-Nabaʾ* (no. 78), Berl. 966, Cairo ^{1}VII, 436,$_{2}$.—10.
450 *Tafsīr qawlihi*, sura 7,$_{66}$, Cairo ^{1}VII, 436,$_{4}$. |—11. *Risāla fī tasmiyat āyat al-kursī Sayyid al-Qurʾān* (sura 2,$_{256}$), Berl. 983.—12. *Risāla fī maʿrifat anwāʿ ʿilm al-ḥadīth* Berl. 1120, abstract ibid. 1121.—13. *Sharḥ arbaʿīna ḥadīthan* ibid. 1519/20, Gotha 3, Leid. 1757, de Jong 157,$_{22}$, AS 4797,$_{2}$, Cairo ^{1}VII, 436,$_{7}$, with a paraphrase in verse in Turkish, Gotha 3,$_{4}$, Turkish adaptation by Pīr Muḥammad ʿĀshiq Naṭṭāʿī, d. 979/1571, Gotha 36, Vienna 200,$_{5}$.—14. Another collection of 40 *ḥadīth*, with a commentary, Cairo ^{1}VII, 436,$_{8}$, AS 4797,$_{3}$.—15. 30 traditions, Cairo ^{1}VII, 436,$_{9}$.—16. 24 *ḥadīth*, ibid.$_{10}$.—17. *Rasāʾil fi ʾl-aḥādīth al-sharīfa* AS 4794,$_{1}$.—18. *Risāla fī subḥān* Berl. 2287.—19. *Faṣl fī ẓuhūr al-ḥaqq wa-maẓāhir al-ashyāʾ* Berl. 2337,$_{7}$.—20. *Risāla fī waḥdat al-wujūd* Berl. 2239, AS 2258, 4794,$_{7}$.—21. *Risāla fī taḥqīq al-wujūd*, Persian, Cairo ^{1}II, 438,$_{19}$.—22. *Risāla fī taḥqīq ziyādat al-wujūd ʿala ʾl-māhiyya*, on the extent to which existence is accidental to essence, Berl. 2338, Sarajevo 137,$_{7}$, AS 4820,$_{8}$.—23. *Risāla fi ʾl-qaḍāʾ wal-qadar* Berl. 2490/1, Leid. 1596, de Jong 157,$_{4}$, Vienna 1919$_{8}$.—24. *Risāla fi ʾl-jabr wal-qadar* AS 4794,$_{55}$, 4797,$_{9}$, 4820,$_{1}$, Cairo ^{1}VII, 437,$_{12}$.—25. *Risāla fī tafḍīl al-bashar ʿala ʾl-malak* Berl. 2510, AS 4820,$_{12}$.—26. *Risāla fī tafḍīl al-anbiyāʾ ʿala ʾl-malāʾika* Cairo ^{1}VII, 438,$_{2}$.—27. *Risāla fī taḥqīq al-muʿjiza* Berl. 2590, Vienna

1 In the following not all of the smaller treatises could be included, given that titles are often corrupted and information drawn from catalogues does not resolve all outstanding issues.

1919,$_{5}$, Leid. 1294,$_{26}$, AS 4794,$_{58}$, 4797,$_{5}$, Cairo ^{1}II, 439,$_{30}$, Mosul 296,$_{7}$.—28. *Risāla fī anna rasūl Allāh ʿam akmal al-anbiyāʾ wa-afḍal al-rusul* Berl. 2591, AS 4794,$_{5}$, 4797,$_{4}$, Cairo ^{1}VII, 438,$_{23}$.—29. *Risāla fī kawn nabiyyinā ʿam ākhir al-anbiyāʾ* Leid. 2063.—30. *Risāla fī bayān ḥaqīqat al-shafāʿa | wa-sirrihā* Berl. 2592.—31. 599
Risāla fī bayān ḥāl al-rūḥ baʿd mufāraqat al-ajsād ibid. 2593.—32. *Risāla fī tafṣīl mā qīla fī abaway al-rasūl*, on whether Muḥammad's parents died as unbelievers, Berl. 2705/6, Munich 886, f. 296a, Vienna 1919,$_{4}$, Ind. Off. 1037, AS 4794,$_{17}$, 4797,$_{13}$, 4820,$_{14}$, Alex. Fun. 152,$_{4}$, Cairo ^{1}VII, 439.—33. *Fī anna ʾl-jumhūr ʿalā anna ṣaḥāʾif al-aʿmāl tūzanu bi-mīzān* Berl. 2762, Leid. 2065, Vienna 1919,$_{13}$, AS 4794,$_{29}$, 4820,$_{29}$, Cairo ^{1}VII, 438,$_{27}$.—34. *Risāla fī ʾl-maʿād al-jismānī*, on bodily resurrection and the ancients' views regarding it, Berl. 2763, de Jong 157,$_{15}$, Vienna 1919,$_{21}$, AS 4794,$_{8}$, 4797,$_{12}$, 4820,$_{10}$, Cairo ^{1}II, 437,$_{12}$.—35. *al-Āyāt al-ʿashr fī aḥwāl al-ākhira fī ʾl-ḥashr* Cairo ^{1}II, 436,$_{2}$, Mosul 28,$_{83,1}$, 296,$_{13}$.—36. *Risāla fī bayān al-shahīd* Berl. 2790, Leid. 2060/1, Cairo ^{1}VII, 436,$_{5}$, Mosul 296,$_{18}$.—37. *ʿIlm al-ḥaqāʾiq*, on the nature of the term *ḥaqīqa* in relation to Absolute Being, Berl. 2791.—38. *Fī taḥqīq lafẓ al-zindīq wa-tawḍīḥ maʿnāhu ʾl-daqīq* Berl. 2793, Vienna 1919,$_{22}$, de Jong 157,$_{5}$, Br. Mus. Or. 9574,$_{15}$, AS 4794,$_{19}$, 4797,$_{30}$, 4820,$_{18}$, Cairo ^{1}VII, 442,$_{59}$, Cl. Huart, loc. cit. (Suppl.).—39. *Risāla fī ʾl-faqr*, on the saying of the Prophet: *al-faqru fakhrī*, Berl. 3163, AS 4794,$_{32}$, 4797,$_{11}$.—40. *al-Taḥqīqiyya li-ṭālib al-īqān*, against legal experts who forbid the swirling of dervishes and who declare the defence of it a heresy, Berl. 3383.—41. *Risāla* on the power of the dead over their kin who visit their graves, ibid. 4084.—42. *Ishkāl al-farāʾiḍ* Leipz. 211, Mosul 130,$_{39,\,2}$.—43. *Jawāhir al-farāʾiḍ* Paris 861,$_{5}$, Mosul 139,$_{39,\,2}$.—44. *Risāla fī dukhūl walad al-bint fī ʾl-mawqūf ʿalā awlād al-awlād* Berl. 4768/9, Leid. 1867, de Jong 157,$_{8}$, Vienna 1791,$_{5}$, AS 4794,$_{54}$, 4797,$_{15}$, Cairo ^{1}VII, 440,$_{36}$.—45. *Muhimmāt al-muftī* Berl. 4830, Cairo ^{1}III, 141,
Yeni 688, Köpr. 694, Cairo ^{1}III, 141. |—46. *al-Iṣlāḥ fī ʾl-fiqh*, with the commentary 451
al-Īḍāḥ, Köpr. II, 80, Cairo ^{1}III, 9.—47. *Fatāwī* Krafft 468, NO 1967.—48. *Risālat al-riḍā* Vienna 1791,$_{1}$, 1919,$_{20}$.—49. *Fī adab al-qāḍī*, based on the *Hidāya* (I, 466),[2] Berl. 4951, Vienna 1791,$_{9}$.—50. *Risāla fī bayān al-ribā* Berl. 4997, AS 4794,$_{16}$, Cairo ^{1}II, 439,$_{35}$.—51. *Risāla fī ʾl-zakāt* Leid. 1876.—52. *al-Qawl fī ṣiḥḥat mā ajarahu ʾl-jundī min al-mazāriʿ wa-ghayrihā* Gotha 1096.—53. *Risāla fī taḥqīq masʾalat al-istikhlāf*, on whether a *qāḍī* may unilaterally decide to have
someone represent him in specific cases, | Berl. 4998, AS 4794,$_{27}$, 4797,$_{10}$, 600
4820,$_{30}$, Cairo ^{1}VII, 439,$_{34}$, 613.—54. *Risāla fī taḥqīq nawʿay al-ḥuṣūl mā ʿalā sabīl al-tadrīj wa-mā lā ʿalā sabīl al-tadrīj* Vienna 1791,$_{22}$.—55. *Shurūṭ al-ṣalāt* Gotha 765, Pet. 245,$_{5}$.—56. *Kitāb istikhlāfāt al-jumʿa* de Jong 157,$_{7}$, Cairo ^{1}III, 107.—57. *Fī bayān alfāẓ al-kufr* Upps. 405,$_{23}$.—58. *al-Maqālāt fī bayān ahl al-bidaʿ*

2 This is according to Flügel; according to Ahlwardt it is a commentary to an unknown work.

wal-ḍalālāt Gotha 852.—59. *Risāla fī ḥaqīqat al-ṭafra*[3] *wa-ḥaqīqat al-jism*
Vienna 1791$_{,15}$, de Jong 157$_{,13}$, AS 4794$_{,39}$, 4797$_{,25}$ Cairo ^{1}VII, 437$_{,16}$.—60. *Risāla fī*
ʿulūm al-ḥaqāʾiq wa-ḥikmat al-daqāʾiq Berl. 5140, Vienna 1919$_{,2}$.—61. *Risāla fī*
taḥqīq maʿnā jaʿl al-māhiyya AS 4797$_{,17}$, 4820$_{,3}$.—62. *Risālat al-tajrīd*, on plain
speech and metaphorical expressions, Berl. 5203.—63. *Risāla fī ādāb al-baḥth*
ibid. 5337, Vienna 1919$_{,12}$, de Jong 157$_{,12}$, Leid. 2064, Bodl. I, 500$_{,13}$, Alex. Fun.
86$_{,12}$.—64. *Fī baḥth al-rujḥān* AS 4797$_{,20}$.—65. *Fī bayān al-ʿaql* Berl. 5363, de
Jong 157$_{,34}$, Br. Mus. 861$_{,8}$, AS 4794$_{,12}$.—66. *Risāla fī bayān al-nafs al-nāṭiqa* Berl.
5364/5, AS 4794$_{,24}$.—67. *Risāla fi 'l-rūḥ* Leid. 2058/9, Algiers 1384$_{,6}$, AS 4820$_{,9}$,
Alex. Fun. 67$_{,5}$, Cairo ^{1}VII, 437$_{,18}$, Mosul 37$_{,194}$.—68. *Risāla fī taḥqīq al-ḥāl* Leid.
1592, Vienna 1791$_{,13}$.—69. *Maqāl al-qāʾilīn bil-ḥāl min aṣḥābinā wa-aṣḥāb*
al-iʿtizāl de Jong 157$_{,14}$, AS 4794$_{,50}$, 4797$_{,16}$, 4820$_{,4}$.—70. *Fī anna azaliyyat*
al-imkān hal yastalzim imkān al-azaliyya am lā Leid. 1594.—71. *Fī masʾalat*
luzūm al-imkān lil-mumkin Vienna 1791$_{,14}$, AS 4797$_{,21}$.—72. *Fī anna 'l-mumkin lā*
yakūn aḥad al-ṭarafayn AS 4794$_{,52}$.—73. *Fī anna 'l-mumkin mustanid ilā*
muʾaththir am lā AS 4797$_{,22}$.—74. *Risālat al-ghayb* Leid. 2062.—75. *Fī sharḥ*
qawlihi ʿam: sa-ukhbirukum bi-awwali 'mriʾin Krafft 407, de Jong 157$_{,21}$, AS
4794$_{,26}$, Cairo ^{1}VII, 437$_{,11}$, Mosul 296$_{,11}$.—76. *Fī taḥqīq tawqīfiyyat asmāʾ Allāh*
taʿālā de Jong 157$_{,23}$, AS 4794$_{,6}$, Cairo ^{1}VII, 437$_{,26}$, Alex. Fun. 86$_{,10}$.—77. *Fī taḥqīq*
al-khawāṣṣ wal-mazāyā de Jong 157$_{,25}$, AS 4797$_{,29}$, 4820$_{,20}$, Cairo ^{1}VII, 441$_{,53}$, ^{2}II,
200.—78. *Fi 'l-kalām al-nafsī* de Jong 157$_{,29}$, Bodl. I, 500$_{,13}$, AS 4794$_{,43}$.—79. *Fī*
talwīn al-khiṭāb de Jong 157$_{,30}$, AS 4794$_{,47}$, Cairo ^{1}VII, 440$_{,44}$.—80. *Fī taḥqīq al-*
haykal al-maḥsūs (*al-insānī*) de Jong 157$_{,32}$, Vienna 1919$_{,6}$, AS 4794$_{,59}$, 4797$_{,24}$,
Cairo ^{1}VII, 4$_{,101}$, Mosul 296$_{,20}$.—81. *Risāla fī ilāhiyyāt al-Mawāqif* (p. 269),
452 Vienna 1919$_{,7}$, AS 4794$_{,44}$. |—82. *Risāla fī anna arbāb al-kashf wal-ʿiyān hal*
601 *yunkirūn al-māhiyyāt* Cairo | ^{1}VII, 438$_{,20}$.—83. *Risāla fī bayān sirr ʿadam nisbat*
al-sharr ila 'llāh taʿālā Vienna 1919$_{,16}$, AS 4794$_{,38}$, Cairo ^{1}VII, 438$_{,22}$, Mosul
104$_{,33,3}$.—84. *Risāla fī taḥqīq anna mā yaṣdur ʿanhu taʿālā innamā bil-qudra*
wal-ikhtiyār lā bil-karh wal-iḍṭirār Vienna 1919$_{,15}$, AS 4794$_{,37}$, Cairo ^{1}VII, 439$_{,28}$.—
85. *Risāla fī taḥqīq murād al-qāʾilīn bi-anna 'l-wājib taʿālā mūjib bil-dhāt* AS
4794$_{,49}$, 4797$_{,26}$, Cairo ^{1}VII, 439$_{,29}$.—86. *Fī ikfār al-rawāfiḍ* AS 4794$_{,3}$.—87. *Fī*
wujūd al-wājib, Persian, AS 4794$_{,46}$.—88. *Fī taḥqīq al-ʿilla wal-maʿlūl* de Jong
157$_{,5}$, Vienna 1791$_{,12}$, Alex. Fun. 152$_{,2}$.—89. *Fī masʾalat taqdīm al-ʿilla al-tāmma*
AS 4797$_{,23}$.—90. *Risāla fi 'l-wujūd al-dhihnī*, based on a passage from Ṣadr
al-Dīn's glosses on the *Sharḥ al-jadīd* (I, 607), Vienna 1791$_{,6}$, AS 4797$_{,33}$, 4820$_{,7}$.—
91. *Fī khalq al-aʿmāl* AS 4820$_{,11}$.—92. *Sharḥ al-Qaṣīda al-khamriyya* I, 306.—93.
Fī taḥqīq maʿna 'l-aysa wal-laysa, on the notion of existence, Berl. 5381/2, de
Jong 157$_{,3}$, Vienna 1791$_{,1}$, 1919$_{,17}$, AS 4794$_{,51}$, 4797$_{,18}$, 4820$_{,6}$, Cairo ^{1}VII, 437$_{,4}$.—94.

3 A notion debated in scholastic physics, see Ashʿarī, *Maqālāt al-islāmiyyīn* 321–2.

Ḥāshiya ʿalā Tahāfut al-falāsifa p. 298.—95. *Fī madḥ al-saʿy wal-dhamm ʿala
ʾl-baṭāla* Berl. 5413, Vienna 1919$_{,14}$, Leid. 2171/3, de Jong 157$_{,16}$, AS 4794$_{,4}$, 4797$_{,8}$,
Alex. Fun. 69$_{,2}$, 86$_{,12}$, Cairo ^{1}VII, 129, 438$_{,21}$, Mosul 296$_{,14}$.—96. *Risāla fi ʾl-khiḍāb*,
on the permissibility of dying one's hair, Berl. 5445, Munich 884$_{,14}$, de Jong
157$_{,18}$, AS 4794$_{,45}$, Cairo ^{1}VII, 439$_{,35}$.—97. *Fī ṭabīʿat al-afyūn*, on opium, de Jong
157$_{,17}$, Cairo ^{1}VII, 440$_{,41}$.—98. *Bayān ḥadd al-khamr*, on the punishment for
drinking wine, Berl. 5483, Pet. 81$_{,11}$, AS 4794$_{,34}$, 4820$_{,16}$, Cairo ^{1}VII, 440$_{,37}$.—99.
Taʿlīm al-zamr wa-taḥrīm al-khamr AS 4794$_{,35}$, 4820$_{,15}$, Cairo ^{1}VII, 436$_{,61}$, Alex.
Fun. 165.—100. *Fī mā yataʿallaq bil-khamr* AS 4794$_{,36}$.—101. *Risāla fī uslūb
al-ḥakīm* Vienna 1919$_{,18}$, de Jong 157$_{,10}$, AS 4797$_{,27}$, 4820$_{,22}$, Cairo ^{1}VII, 441$_{,50}$.—
102. *Rāḥat al-arwāḥ fī dafʿ ʿāhat al-ashbāḥ* or *Risāla fi ʾl-ṭāʿūn wal-wabāʾ* Vienna
1919$_{,19}$, Leid. 2036, Cairo ^{1}VII, 4, 101, 329, 532, 670.—103. *Rujūʿ al-shaykh ilā ṣibāhi
fi ʾl-quwwa wal-bāh* Welīeddin 2500, Köpr. II, 189, print. Būlāq 1309, C. 1316,
1335.—104. *al-Risāla al-Kamāliyya al-musammāh bil-Fawāʾid*, a theological,
juridical, grammatical, and lexical work, Leid. 2068, Paris 1322, AS 4794$_{,28}$,
4820$_{,2}$.—105. *al-Masāʾil al-sitt min al-masāʾil al-ʿashr li-mawlānā Jalāl al-Dīn
al-Dawwānī* (p. 281), Vienna 1791$_{,10}$.—106. *al-Tanbīh ʿalā ghalaṭ al-jāhil
(al-khāmil) wal-nabīh* (also attributed to al-Birkawī, p. 582), Berl. 6777/8, Alex.
Fun. 69$_{,3}$.—107. *Risālat iṣlāḥ al-saqaṭāt*, on solicisms, Leid. 240, Munich | 892, f. 602
145, Köpr. 1580.—108. *Risāla fī lughat al-Furs wa-maziyyatihā* AS 4794$_{,25}$, Cairo
^{1}VII, 440$_{,39}$,—109. *Risālat al-taʿrīb*, on the spelling of loanwords, Vienna 1919$_{,1}$,
Leid. 239, AS 4794$_{,18}$, 4797$_{,31}$, 4820$_{,5}$, Cairo ^{1}VII, 442$_{,58}$, Mosul 104$_{,73,4}$.—110. *Fī
nisbat al-jamʿ* Berl. 6862, AS 4794$_{,2}$, Cairo ^{1}VII, 441$_{,56}$.—111. *Risāla fī tāḥqīq anna
ṣāḥib ʿilm al-maʿānī yushārik al-lughawī fi ʾl-baḥth ʿan mufradāt al-alfāẓ
al-mustaʿmala fī kalām al-ʿArab* de Jong 157$_{,20}$, Cairo ^{1}VII 163, 441$_{,49}$.—112.
Taḥqīq maʿna ʾl-naẓm wal-ṣiyāgha de Jong 157$_{,11}$, AS 4797$_{,28}$, Cairo ^{1}VII, 441$_{,54}$,
^{2}II, 200.—113. *Risāla fi ʾl-tawassuʿ*, on the expansion of usage (e.g. as a noun
instead of as an adjective), Berl 6881/2, de Jong 157$_{,19,\ 28}$, Br. Mus. 861$_{,5}$, Garr.
2114$_{,2}$ (*al-Risāla al-tawsīʿiyya*), AS 4794$_{,22}$, 4820$_{,24}$, Cairo ^{1}VII, 441$_{,48}$. |—114. *Fī* 453
taḥqīq al-taghlīb Berl. 6883, Br. Mus. 861$_{,6}$, AS 4794$_{,40}$, Cairo ^{1}VII, 440$_{,45}$.—115.
Risāla fī min al-tabʿīḍiyya Berl. 6903, Vienna 1791$_{,7}$, de Jong 157$_{,2}$, AS 4794$_{,20}$,
4820$_{,23}$.—116. *Risālat tafkīk al-ḍamīr* or *Fī dafʿ mā yataʿallaq bil-ḍamāʾir* Leid.
341, de Jong 157$_{,23}$, 208$_{,22}$, Br. Mus. 861$_{,4}$, AS 4794$_{,23}$, 4820$_{,21}$, Cairo ^{1}VII, 441$_{,51}$, ^{2}II,
200.—117. *Risāla fī taḥqīq (waḍʿ) kāda* de Jong 157$_{,9}$, AS 4794$_{,21}$, 4820$_{,25}$.—118.
Risālat al-tafṣīl fī-mā qīla fī amr al-tafḍīl Leid. 2067, de Jong, 157$_{,31}$, Bodl. I, 500$_{,15}$,
AS 4794$_{,10}$, Mosul 257$_{,55}$.—119. *Risāla fī taqsīm al-majāz* Berl. 7287, Br. Mus.
861$_{,3}$, AS 4794$_{,15}$, Cairo ^{1}VII, 441$_{,47}$.—120. *Taḥqīq al-kināya wal-istiʿāra* Berl.
7321.—121. *Risāla fī taḥqīq al-mushākala* ibid. 7343, AS 4794$_{,30}$, Cairo ^{1}VII, 441$_{,46}$,
^{2}II, 200.—122. *Iẓhār al-aẓhār ʿalā ashjār al-ashʿār* AS 3781 (*WZKM* 26, 79).—123.
Risāla fī ṭabaqāt al-fuqahāʾ, in 7 classes, Berl. 9994/5.—124. *Risāla fī ṭabaqāt*

al-mujtahidīn, on the Ḥanafīs, ibid. 10025, Vienna $1537_{,3}$, $1919_{,11}$, AS $4820_{,13}$, Alex. Fun. $164_{,8,\ 67,\ 3}$, Cairo ^{1}VII, 146, cf. Flügel, *Classen der Ḥanaf.* p. 269.—125.–170. see Suppl. (126. Mosul $297_{,46}$; 127. Ibid. $67_{,3}$, Garr. $2059_{,6}$; 164. Garr. 906).—171.–179. Suppl. III, 1306.

3. Muḥammad b. Aḥmad Pāshā al-ʿAjamī Ḥāfiẓ al-Dīn was born in Bardaʿa, studied in Tabriz, and moved to Asia Minor during the unrest caused by the rise to power of Shāh Ismāʿīl. He became a professor in Ankara, Marzifūn, Istanbul, and Iznik, at one of the eight madrasas of Istanbul, and finally at the Aya Sofya. He died in Istanbul in 957/1550.

603 | *SN* II, 49/52. *Madīnat al-ʿilm* Köpr. 1387.

4. Muḥammad b. ʿAlī Sipāhīzāde al-Burūsāwī, who died in 997/1587.

Brūsalī Ṭāhir, *ʿOM* III, 65/6. 1. *Unmūdhaj al-funūn*, on Qurʾānic exegesis, *ḥadīth*, dogmatics, *uṣūl al-fiqh*, rhetoric, medicine, and astronomy, Vienna 19, AS 390.—2. *Awḍaḥ al-masālik ilā maʿrifat al-buldān wal-mamālik* Pet. Ros. 69, NO 4693, Cairo ^{1}V, 16, cf. Dorn, *Caspia* 167/9. Turkish translation, additionally Yeni 787.

5. Muḥammad Amīn b. Ṣadr Amīn al-Shirwānī Mollāzāde joined the military campaign of the vizier Naṣūḥ against Shaḥ ʿAbbās of Iran, went with him to Istanbul, became a *qāḍī* there, and then a professor at the madrasa of Sultan Aḥmad, before dying in 1036/1626.

Muḥ. III, 475, Brūsalī M. Ṭāhir, *ʿOM* II, 23. 1. *al-Fawāʾid al-Khāqāniyya al-Aḥmad Khāniyya*, on 53 sciences following the numerical value of the name Aḥmad. The preface discusses the nature of science and its subdivisions; the 10 sciences dealing with the law take centre stage, the 12 philological sciences are situated on the right, and the 30 philosophical sciences on the left. An appendix discusses the relationship between the sovereign and the sciences. Composed in 1023/1614, Vienna $20_{,1}$, Pet. 26, NO 4132/3, Alex. Fun. 50, Cairo ^{1}IV, 176, ^{2}VI, 186.
454 |—2. *Risāla fī ʾl-madhāhib al-mukhtalifa* NO 2144 (Ritter, *Der Islam* 18, p. 54).—3. *Tafsīr sūrat al-Fatḥ* Cairo ^{1}VII, 599.—4. *Tafsīr sūrat al-Ikhlāṣ* ibid. 600.

6. Abu ʾl-Baqāʾ al-Sayyid Ayyūb b. Mūsā al-Ḥusaynī al-Kaffawī was born in 1028/1619 in Caffa, on the Crimean coast. He succeeded his father as a *muftī*, before being summoned to Istanbul by the grand vizier Muḥammad Pāshā and appointed *qāḍī* in Birka and later in Philippopolis. He later fell into disgrace

and was banished to Caffa. However, after 12 years the khan of the Crimea, Salīm Girāy, was able to obtain a permission for him to settle in Istinya, in Bosnia, where he died in 1094/1683.

Muḥ. II, 121, Brūsalī M. Ṭāhir, *ʿOM* I, 230. 1. *Kulliyyāt al-ʿulūm*, on the technical terms of the sciences, alphabetical, | Vienna 89, Basle (without shelf-mark), 604
Pet. 222, print. Būlāq 1253, 1255, 1281.—2. *Tuḥfat al-shāhān*, a popular work on religious education, in Turkish, Būlāq 1264, Istanbul 1258.

7. Muḥammad al-Āqkirmanī, ca. 1160/1747.

1. *Taʿrīfāt al-funūn wa-tarājim al-muṣannifīn wa-manāqibuhum*, starting with lexicology, Berl. 96.—2. *Sharḥ Iṭbāq al-aṭbāq* p. 558.—3. See Suppl.—4.–7. ibid. III, 1306.

8. Muḥammad b. Muṣṭafā al-ʿAwdānī Yenishehrī, ca. 1168/1754.

1. *al-Risāla al-sittiyya*, a concise overview of the 6 sciences of *ṣarf*, *naḥw*, *bayān*, *badīʿ*, *manṭiq*, and *adab*, completed in Jumādā I 1168/February 1755, Berl. 97.—2. *Risāla fī ḥadd al-ʿilm wa-taqsīmihi* ibid. 139.—3. A demonstration that the abbreviation of God's name is not permissible in prayer, ibid. 3620.

Chapter 10. The Maghreb

While the eastern lands of the Muslim world, though culturally stagnant, lived in relative peace under the Ottomans, North Africa gradually sank into barbarism. From the end of the fifteenth century onward, the Corsairs and their successsors—Turkish pashas, the beys of Tripoli, Tunis, and Algiers—became completely engrossed in their maritime and military exploits. The brisk trade in their ports, fed by their buccaneering practices, received a serious blow when
455 the Christians succeeded in putting a lid on the scourge of piracy. | The Turks were unable to enhance the culture of the Maghreb, which had already sunk low under Berber rule. Under its rulers, life in Morocco was relatively tolerable compared to its eastern neighbours, yet it was too far from the centre of Islamic culture to be able to take part in its intellectual endeavours. At the courts of the
605 sharifs, which were practically army camps, | military concerns outweighed all others. Because the many small changes in the balance of power offered ample subject matter for the literati, it was historiography, of all forms of literature, that prospered most in the Maghreb. Alongside that exception, there are the travelogues inspired by the pilgrimage to Mecca. However, these are so dominated by self-congratulatory biographical anecdotes that their description of places is no more than superficial. As before, poetry was completely out of sync, while scientific literature only barely survived.

NM: Muḥammad b. al-Ṭayyib al-Qādirī (Suppl. 687, 13 b), *Nashr al-mathānī*, a biographical dictionary of the eleventh and twelfth centuries, lith. Fez 1310, 2 parts in 1 volume.

Ṣaf.: Muḥammad al-Ṣaghīr al-Ifrānī (p. 607), *Ṣafwat man intashar min akhbār ṣulaḥā' al-qarn al-ḥādī 'ashar*, a continuation of the *Dawḥat al-nāshir* by Ibn 'Askar (Suppl. 678), without date or place.

1 *Adab*

1. Al-Ḥasan b. Mas'ūd al-Yūsī al-Marrākushī, who died in 1102/1691, see Suppl.

456 | Jab. I, 68, *Ṣaf.* 205/10, Houdas, *Le Maroc* p. 19, n. 1, 'Abdallāh Gannūn, *al-Nubūgh* I, 216. 1. *Dāliyya*, a congratulatory work to his shaykh Abū 'Abdallāh Muḥammad b. Nāṣir al-Dar'ī on the occasion of his return from his second pilgrimage, with a self-commentary, Munich 571,$_1$, Alex. Adab 140, print. Alexandria 1291, Cairo [1]IV, 272, [2]III, 284.—2. *Zahr al-akam fi 'l-amthāl wal-ḥikam*, a valuable collection of proverbs, Pet. Ros. 164.—3. *Ḥāshiya 'alā Kubra 'l-Sanūsī* p. 323.—4. *Kitāb al-muḥāḍarāt* or *Riḥlat al-Yūsī*, Berl. Ms. or. oct. 3955, Munich 571,$_2$, Algiers 1896, print. Fez 1317.—5. *Sharḥ Mukhtaṣar al-manṭiq* p. 325, viii,

I.—6. *Fihrist*, an inventory of his teachers, the main source for al-Ifrānī.—7. *Qānūn ʿalā aḥkām al-ʿilm wa-aḥkām al-ʿālim wa-aḥkām al-mutaʿallim*, an encyclopaedia in 3 chapters, Berl. 95, print. Fez 1310.—8., 9. See Suppl.

2. Abu ʾl-ʿAbbās Aḥmad b. ʿAbd al-ʿAzīz al-Hilālī al-Sijilmāsī, who died in 1175/1762.

| ʿAbdallāh Gannūn, *al-Nubūgh* I, 221/3. *Qaṣīdas*, eulogies, exhortations to piety, on the visiting of the tombs of saints etc., Cairo ²III, 279. 606

2 *Philology*

1. ʿAbd al-Raḥmān b. Muḥammad b. Muḥammad b. Sīdī al-Ṣaghīr al-Akhḍarī al-Banṭiyūṣī al-Maghribī, who flourished around the tenth century.

Al-Jawhar al-maknūn fi ʾl-ṣadaf (sic) *al-thalātha al-funūn*, a didactic poem on rhetoric, Gotha 2791, Br. Mus. $421_{,20}$, *JA* 1854, II, 438, no. 61.

2. Aḥmad b. ʿUmar b. Mukhtār b. Abī Bakr b. ʿAlī al-Jakanī wrote, in 1120/1708:

Al-Sirāj fī ḥadhf al-mubīn (fi ʾl-Qurʾān) Algiers $399_{,1}$, $401_{,1}$, print. Fez 1323 = (?) *al-Sirāj fi ʾl-rasm*, a *manẓūma*, Tunis Zayt. I, 143.

3 *Historiography*

1. Abū ʿAbdallāh Muḥammad b. Ibrāhīm al-Luʾluʾ al-Zarkashī wrote, around 932/1525:

Taʾrīkh al-dawlatayn al-Muwaḥḥidiyya wal-Ḥafṣiyya, running to the year 922, Paris 1874 (cf. *JA* 1848, II, 237, 1849, I, 269), Algiers 1621 (attributed to Ibn Shammāʿ), with an appendix, a chronological table of both dynasties until 839/1435, and a concluding word on Abū Fāris ʿAbd al-ʿAzīz al-Ḥafṣī, print. Tunis 1289 (only until 882/1477 with the same appendix, but without the conclusion), *Trad. franç. d'après l'édition de Tunis et 3 mss par* E. Fagnan, Constantine 1895.

2. Around the year 950/1543 an unidentified person translated from Turkish into Arabic:

Ghazawāt, a romantic chronicle about the corsairs ʿArūj and Khayr al-Dīn, up to the 948/1541 expedition by Charles V, Algiers 1622/3, Paris 1878, print. Algiers 1934, | cf. *Fondation de la régence d'Algiers éd. par* Sander Rang et F. Denis, Paris 457
1837, 2 vols.—An anonymous account of the expedition by Charles V, Algiers

1624, translated by Venture in Rotalier, *Histoire d'Algiers* I, 424 and in *Bull. de la Soc. géogr. d'Oran* 1890, see *Revue Afr.* 1891, 177.

607 | 3. Abū ʿAbdallāh Muḥammad Ṣaghīr b. al-Ḥājj Muḥammad b. ʿAbdallāh al-Ifrānī (Yefrēnī, Wafrānī), who died after 1151/1738, see Suppl.

ʿAbdallāh Gannūn, *al-Nubūgh* I, 217. 1. *Nuzhat al-ḥādī bi-akhbār mulūk al-qarn al-ḥādī*, a history of the Banū Saʿd of Morocco, 917–1081/1511–1670, Paris 4617, 4757, Algiers 1631, Alex. Taʾr. 141. lith. Fez n.d., *Nozhet el hadi, Texte et trad. p.* O. Houdas, 2 vols. Paris 1899 (Publ. de l'École d. lang. or. viv. s. III, v. 2).—2. *Ṣafwa* see p. 604.

4. Abū ʿAbdallāh b. Abi 'l-Qāsim b. Abī Dīnār al-Ruʿaynī al-Qayrawānī wrote, in 1110/1698 (or, according to MS Paris, 1092/1681):

Al-Muʾnis fī akhbār Ifrīqiya wa-Tūnis, Algiers 1630, Paris 1887, print. Tunis 1286. transl. Pélissier and Rémusat in *Exploration scient. de l'Algérie, Sc. hist. et topogr.* VII, Paris 1845 (Wüst. *Gesch.* 586).

5. Abū ʿAbdallāh Muḥammad b. Aḥmad al-Ḥalfāwī al-Tilimsānī wrote, in 1119/1707 (or 1124/1713):

Urjūza, 70 verses on the capture of Wahrān (Oran) by Sultan Abū ʿAbdallāh Muḥammad b. Aḥmad al-Dawlatli Dai Bakdāš,[1] with a commentary by his student Abū Zayd ʿAbd al-Raḥmān al-Jāmiʿī, Berl. 9847, Paris 5113, Br. Mus. 635, 887$_{,6}$.

6. Abū Zakariyyāʾ Yaḥyā b. Abī Rashīd wrote, around 1119/1703:

A poem on the same event, as well as a satire on Ibn al-Qarīḥa, the *faqīh* of Oran, Br. Mus. 887$_{,7}$.

7a. Aḥmad b. ʿAbd al-Ḥayy al-Ḥalabī, who died in 1120/1708, see Suppl.

1. *al-Durr al-nafīs etc.* Alex. Taʾr. 66.—3. *al-Kunūz al-makhtūma fī khaṣāʾiṣ hādhihi 'l-umma al-marḥūma* Fez Qar. 749.

1 Cf. Boulet, *Hist. de l'empire des Cherifs* 138; Rotalier, *Hist. d'Algiers* II, 38; L. Galebert, *l'Algérie* 236.

| 7. An unidentified author wrote, around 1122/1710: 608

Al-Tuḥfa al-marḍiyya fi 'l-dawla al-Bakdāshiyya fī bilād al-Jazā'ir al-maḥmiyya, a history of Muḥammad Bakdāsh (1118–22/1706–10) in rhymed prose, in 16 *maqāmas*, Algiers 1625, cf. *Rev. afr.* II, 34.

8. ʿAlī b. Aḥmad b. Qāsim b. Mūsā Miṣbāḥ al-Dharwīlī, who was born in 1097/1685, wrote, in 1125/1713:

Sana 'l-muhtadī ilā mafākhir al-wazīr Abi 'l-ʿAbbās al-Yaḥmadī, a collection of *qaṣīdas* and *rasā'il* about him, Cairo [1]IV, 263, [2]III, 189, Alex. Adab 81.

| 9. Abū ʿAbdallāh Muḥammad b. al-Ṭayyib al-Sharīf al-ʿAlamī, who died in 1134/1721, see Suppl. 458

NM II, 204. *Al-Anīs al-muṭrib fī man laqiyahu mu'allifuhu min udabā' al-Maghrib*, biographies of some of his contemporaries, lith. Fez 1304, 1315.

10. Hāshim b. ʿAlī b. Aḥmad al-ʿAlamī al-Idrīsī al-ʿArūsī b. Mashīsh wrote, in 1137/1724:

Lāmiyya, in 180 verses, an overview of the most important men in Islam from Muḥammad until his own time, mostly scholars and poets, Berl. 9896.

10a. Abū ʿAbdallāh Muḥammad al-Mashnawī al-Dilā'ī, who died in 1136/1724, see Suppl.

1. *Natījat al-taḥqīq etc.* additionally Basle M. III, 24, 2.

11. Abū ʿAbdallāh Muḥammad b. Muḥammad al-Sarrāj al-Wazīr al-Andalusī wrote, around 1138/1725:

Al-Ḥulal al-sundusiyya fi 'l-akhbār al-Tūnisiyya, a history of Africa, and particularly of Tunis, until the year in which it was written; the first part, in six sections, only stretches until the capture of Tunis by Charles V and actually represents the Introduction to the work itself, in which the author aims to treat the period after 1092/1681 in greater detail, as a continuation of the work by al-Qayrawānī, Munich 418, cf. Haneberg, *Gel. Anz. d. Bayr. Ak. d. Wiss.* 1859, no. 31/3, print. Tunis 1287 (incomplete).

12. Muḥammad b. Khalīl b. Ghalbūn al-Azharī, who died in 1150/1739, see Suppl.

609 | *Al-Tadhkira fī man malaka Ṭarābulus wa-mā kāna bihā min al-akhbār*, a historical commentary on a panegyrical poem on Tripoli (in modern Libya) by Aḥmad b. ʿAbd al-Dāʾim al-Anṣārī, a history of the city from the Muslim conquest until the middle of the twelfth century, Paris 1889,1.

13. Muḥammad al-Ṣaghīr b. Yūsuf of Bejā wrote in 1177/1763, see Suppl.

14. Al-Ḥājj Ḥammūda b. Abī ʿAbdallāh Muḥammad b. ʿAbdallāh b. ʿAbd al-ʿAzīz al-Wazīr al-Tūnisī, who died in 1201/1787.

1. *al-Kitāb al-bāshī*, a history of the pasha of Tunis, Abu ʾl-Ḥasan ʿAlī Bey b. Ḥusayn Bey ʿAlī al-Turkī (r. 1172–88/1758–74), with an overview of the history of the Ḥafṣids until 951/1544 and a general overview of the history of North African life and customs from the beginning of Islam until the author's own lifetime, composed in 1188/1774, Br. Mus. 950/2, see Cherbonneau, *JA* s. IV, v. 18 (1851), 36/53.

15. Muḥammad b. Muḥammad b. ʿAbd al-Raḥmān al-Tilimsānī wrote, in 1193/1779:

Al-Zahra al-nāʾira fī-mā jarā bil-Jazāʾir ḥīna aghārat ʿalayha ʾl-kafara, a history of the Christian campaigns against Algiers, from Khayr al-Dīn until 1189/1775, Munich 419, Algiers 1626, translation by A. Rousseau, *Chroniques de la régence d'Algiers*, Algiers 1841.

459 | 4 ***Popular Prose***

1. Abū Muḥammad ʿĪsā b. ʿAlī b. Aḥmad (or b. Aḥmad b. ʿAlī) al-Lakhmī al-Ishbīlī al-Andalusī, ca. 930/1524.

ʿUyūn al-akhbār, traditions without an *isnād*, aphorisms by wise men, parables, and anecdotes, partly for amusement and partly for edification, Berl. 8417, Paris 3546.

2. Abū Madyan Muḥammad b. Aḥmad b. Muḥammad b. ʿAlī al-Adīb al-Fāsī, who died in 1181/1767, see Suppl.

1. *Tuḥfat al-arīb etc.* additionally Alex. Adab 21.—4. *Khuṭab* Fez Qar. 1538.

| 5 *Ḥadīth* 610

1. Abu ʾl-Ḥasan ʿAlī b. ʿAbd al-Wāḥid b. Muḥammad b. ʿAbdallāh al-Anṣārī al-Sijilmāsī al-Jazāʾirī was born in Tāfilāt, raised in Sijilmāsa, and studied in Fez. In 1040/1630 he made the pilgrimage and continued his studies in Cairo until 1043/1633. After his return to his native country he became a *muftī* in the Jabal al-Akhḍar district, before dying of the plague in al-Jazāʾir at the end of Shawwāl 1057/November 1647.

Muḥ. III, 173, Wüst. *Gesch.* 566. *Al-Durra al-munīfa fi ʾl-sīra al-saniyya al-sharīfa*, on the life of the Prophet, Br. Mus. $159_{,4}$.—In addition he wrote compendia in rhyme (*manẓūmāt*) on almost all of the sciences; these have all been lost.

1a. ʿAbd al-Jalīl b. Muḥammad b. Aḥmad b. ʿAẓẓūm b. Qindār al-Qayrawānī, who died in 971/1563, see Suppl.

1. *Tanbīh al-anām etc.* Berl. 3930, Garr. 1961/2, Dam. Ẓāh. ʿIsh, Taʾrīkh 27, *Mukhtaṣar* Alex. Faw. 26.

1c. Abū Mahdī ʿĪsā b. Muḥammad al-Thaʿālibī al-Jazāʾirī, who died in 1080/1659, see Suppl.

4. *Muntakhab al-asānīd etc.* also ʿĀšir I, $442_{,2}$, Patna II, $538_{,2899}$.—6. *Risāla fi ʾl-khirqa al-ṣūfiyya al-nabawiyya wal-dhikr wal-subḥa* Alex. Fun. $122_{,3}$.—7. *Risāla fī muḍāʿafat thawāb hādhihi ʾl-umma* Garr. $2030_{,7}$.

2. Muḥammad b. Muḥammad b. Sulaymān b. al-Fāsī b. Ṭāhir al-Maghribī al-Rūdānī al-Sūsī was born in 1037/1627 in Tarūdant in the Sūs, studied in Algiers, Morocco, Cairo, and Mecca, and made a trip to Istanbul. In 1081/1670 he joined the retinue of Muṣṭafā Bey, the brother of the vizier Fāḍil, on a journey to Rumelia. After a sojourn of a year in that region he was given a post in Mecca, but in 1093/1682 he was banished to Jerusalem and died the following year in Damascus.

| Muḥ. IV, 204/8, *NM* II, 81/8, *Ṣaf.* 196/8, al-ʿAyyāshī, *Riḥla* II, 30/45. 1. *Ṣilat* 611
al-khalaf bi-mawṣūl al-salaf, on his course of studies, his teachers, and the books he read in class, with *isnāds*, Berl. 208/9, Paris 4470, Garr. 2199.—2. *Risāla* on an astronomical instrument, al-ʿAyyāshī II, 39ff = (?) *Bahjat al-ṭullāb fi ʾl-asṭurlāb*, with a commentary by Muḥammad b. Qāsim al-Mawṣilī al-ʿAbdalī, copied in Damascus in 1113/1701, Mosul $103_{,56,1}$ (which has al-Yardānī), see Suppl.

460 | 3. ʿAbdallāh b. Muḥammad al-Khayyāṭ al-Hārūshī al-Fāsī al-Tūnisī wrote, around 1127/1715:

Kunūz al-asrār fi 'l-ṣalāt ʿala 'l-nabī al-mukhtār, with the commentary *al-Fatḥ al-mubīn wal-durr al-thamīn fī faḍl al-ṣalāt wal-salām ʿalā sayyid al-mursalīn*, Berl. 3928 (imprecise), Cairo [1]II, 211.

4. Muḥammad b. Aḥmad al-Jazāʾirī, who died in 1139/1726.

Al-Mann wal-salwa fi 'l-ḥadīth Köpr. II, 69.

4a. Abū ʿAbdallāh Muḥammad b. ʿAbd al-Raḥmān b. ʿAbd al-Qādir b. Zikrī al-Fāsī, who died in 1144/1731, see Suppl.

ʿAbdallāh Gannūn, *al-Nubūgh* I, 218/20.—4. *al-Minaḥ al-bādiya fi 'l-asānīd al-ʿāliya wal-musalsalāt al-rāsiya wal-ṭuruq al-hādiya al-kāfiya, thabat* following his teacher ʿAbd al-Qādir b. ʿAlī al-Fāsī, d. 1091/1680, Alex. Muṣṭ. Ḥad. 22.

5. Muḥammad b. Abi 'l-Ḥasan b. Muḥammad al-ʿArabī al-Maghribī al-Tilimsāni wrote, in 1156/1743:

Al-Hādī lil-muhtadī Sarajevo III, 113/4, ḤKh VI, 14335.

6b *Fiqh, Mālikī*

1. Abū ʿAbdallāh Muḥammad b. Abi 'l-Ḥusayn al-Ruʿaynī al-Qarawī was born in 891/1486 and died after 944/1537.

Kitāb al-daʿwā wal-inkār Munich 892, Algiers 1292,$_2$.

2. Abū ʿAbdallāh Sīdī Muḥammad al-ʿArbī b. Abi 'l-Maḥāsin Sīdī Yūsuf al-Fāsī, who died in 1052/1642, see Suppl.

Naẓm fi 'l-zakāt Br. Mus. 902,$_5$.

612 | 3. Aḥmad b. ʿAbd al-ʿAzīz al-Sharafī al-Maghribī al-Safāqusī al-Mālikī al-Azharī wrote, in 1089/1669:

Tadhkirat al-ikhwān fi 'l-radd ʿalā man qāla bi-ḥilliyyat al-dukhān Cairo [1]VII, 155.

4. Abū Zayd ʿAbd al-Raḥmān b. Abī Muḥammad ʿAbd al-Qādir b. ʿAlī b. Abi ʾl-Maḥāsin Yūsuf al-Fāsī, who died in 1096/1685, see Suppl.

NM II, 88/92. 1. *al-ʿAmaliyyāt al-Fāsiyya*, a poem of 430 verses on various practical issues in law, with the commentary *al-Amaliyyāt al-fāshiya* by Abu ʾl-Qāsim Saʿīd al-ʿUmarī, Algiers 1278, anon. comm. ibid. 1279/80, see L. Milliot, *Recueil de jurisprudence chérifienne*, Paris 1920, p. 21.—2. *al-Taysīr wal-tashīl fī dhikr mā aghfalahu ʾl-shaykh Khalīl* (p. 101) *min aḥkām al-mughārasa wal-tawlīj wal-taṣyīr* or *al-Taṣrīḥ wal-tasrīḥ fī dhikr aḥkām al-mughārasa* Algiers 1307/10.—3.–23. see Suppl. (4. see 1036,$_6$; 19. edited in part by H.G. Farmer, *Coll. of or. writers on music*, Glasgow 1933, see *Sources* 64).

7 *Sciences of the Qurʾān*

1. Muḥammad b. Aḥmad b. ʿĪsā al-Maghribī al-Mālikī wrote, in 1005/1596:

Ghāyat al-itḥāf fī-mā khafiya min kalām al-Qāḍī (i.e. al-Bayḍāwī), Cairo [1]I, 183.

1b. Aḥmad b. ʿAlī b. ʿAbd al-Raḥmān al-Manjūr, who died in 995/1587, see Suppl.

ʿAbdallāh Gannūn, *al-Nubūgh* I, 185/6.—4. *Sharḥ al-Khazrajiyya* I, 380.—5. See Suppl. 1016,$_{27}$.

| 2. Abū ʿAbdallāh Muḥammad b. Mubārak b. Aḥmad b. Abi ʾl-Qāsim b. ʿAbdallāh 461
al-Sijilmāsī al-Maghrāwī al-Sarghīnī al-Fāsī was, after 1060/1650, imam of the Sharīf mosque in Fez. He died in 1092/1681.

Dāliyya fi ʾl-qirāʾāt; commentaries: a. Idrīs b. Muḥammad b. Aḥmad b. Muḥammad al-Sharīf al-Ḥasanī, d. 1137/1724, Munich 104.—b.–d. see Suppl.

3. ʿAlī b. Muḥammad b. Sālim Shaṭṭār al-Nūrī al-Safāqusī, who died in 1081/1671 (or, according to others, in 1117/1705), see Suppl.

| *Ghayth al-nafʿ fi ʾl-qirāʾāt al-sabʿ* Br. Mus. 78,$_3$, Algiers 369.—2. 4. see Suppl. 613

8 *Dogmatics*

1. ʿAbdallāh b. Fāris al-Tāzī, from Tāza in Morocco, died in Egypt in 869/1574, see Suppl.

Al-Munāẓara wal-muʿāraḍa fī radd al-Rāfiḍa Paris 1461,$_1$.

2. Abū Muḥammad ʿAbd al-Wāḥid b. Aḥmad b. ʿAlī b. ʿĀshir al-Anṣārī al-Andalusī al-Fāsī, who died in 1040/1630 at the age of 51, see Suppl.

NM I, 154/6, ʿAbdallāh Gannūn, *al-Nubūgh* I, 181. 1. *al-Murshid al-muʿīn ʿala ʾl-ḍarūrī min ʿulūm al-dīn* Munich 216, Algiers $537_{,4}$, 605/8, $959_{,3}$, Cairo ^{1}III, 183, lith. Constantine 1262, print. C. 1300.—Commentaries: a. *al-Durr al-thamīn wal-murīd al-muʿīn* by Muḥammad b. Aḥmad b. Mayyāra, d. 1072/1662, completed in 1040/1630, Paris 818, Alex. Fun. 17, Cairo ^{1}II, 164, print. Fez 1292, Tunis 1293, C. 1305, among others.—b.-g. see Suppl.—h. *Manhal al-māʾ al-maʿīn* by Muḥammad b. Muḥammad b. Badr al-Dīn, Alex. Fiqh Māl. 17.—2.-6. See Suppl.

4. Yaḥyā b. Muḥammad al-Shāwī al-Maghribī was born in Milyāna, grew up in
462 Algiers and went to Cairo in 1074/1663 while on pilgrimage. | After his return from Mecca he settled there, lectured at al-Azhar, and became a *qāḍī* of the Mālikī rite. He visited Istanbul twice. He died on his second pilgrimage in 1096/1685. His remains were buried at Rās Muḥammad, and later transferred to Cairo by his son.

Muḥ. IV, 486/8, *Ṣaf.* 199.[1] *Qurrat al-ʿayn fī jamʿ al-bayn* Cairo ^{1}II, 52.—2. See Suppl.

9 *Mysticism*

1. Abu ʾl-ʿAbbās Aḥmad b. Abi ʾl-Maḥāsin Yūsuf al-Fāsī, who died in 991/1583.

614 | *Risāla* on the 5 qualities one should seek to have and the 5 qualities one should seek to avoid, Br. Mus. $645_{,10}$.

2b. Aḥmad b. Muḥammad b. ʿAlī b. Zighlān (Wighlān) b. Namārī b. Mūnis al-Bajāʾī wrote, before 1034/1624:

1. *Ḥadaq al-muqlatayn etc.* see Suppl.—2. *al-Rawḍ al-ansam fī maʿānī ḥurūf al-muʿjam* Esc. ^{2}35, abstracts in Casiri, on which Fr. Codera, *La Ciudad de Dios* XXXIX, $1896_{,21}$.

3. Muḥammad b. (Nāṣir) Muḥammad b. Aḥmad al-Darʿī was the renewer of the Shādhiliyya order in the Maghreb. He died in 1085/1674.

---

1 With the improbable information that he had died in 1097 on his way to Medina, where he was supposedly heading to kill a *faqīh* who had installed a *miḥrāb* in the Prophet's Mosque.

Muḥ. IV, 238, *NM* II, 16/20. 1. *Sayf al-naṣr li-kulli dhī baghy wa-makr*, a prayer for help against enemies, in 59 *rajaz* verses, Berl. 8161,$_5$.—2.–4. See Suppl.

4. Abū ʿAbdallāh Muḥammad al-Mahdī b. Aḥmad b. Abi ʾl-Maḥāsin Yūsuf al-Fāsī, who died in 1109/1698, see Suppl.

1. *Tuḥfat ahl al-ṣādiqiyya bi-asānīd al-ṭāʾifa al-Jazūliyya wal-Zarrūqiyya*, a history of the two renewers of the Shādhiliyya order in the Maghreb, al-Jazūlī (p. 327) and Ibn Zarrūq (p. 328), as well as of their students, composed in 1090/1679, Paris 2046.—2.–4. See Suppl.

5. Aḥmad b. Mubārak al-Sijilmāsī al-Lamaṭī, who died in 1156/1713, see Suppl.

1. *al-Dhahab al-ibrīz min kalām Sīdī ʿAbd al-ʿAzīz*, a collection of assertions by
ʿAlī b. Masʿūd al-Dabbāgh al-Ḥasanī, | whose student he was from 1125/1713 463
onwards, on God, the prophets, angels, the Heavenly Book, the Last Judgement,
and life in the Hereafter, Br. Mus. 174, Algiers 1710, Cairo ^{1}II, 61, print. C. 1278,
1304.—2. *Radd al-tashdīd etc.* see Suppl.—3., 4. ibid.—5. *Izālat al-labs* Fez, Qar.
1582.

9a *Philosophy*

1. Al-Ṣadr ʿAbd al-Raḥmān b. Muḥammad b. ʿĀmir al-Akhḍarī, who died in 953/1546.

Nallino, *OM* I, 570. 1. *al-Sullam al-murawniq fi ʾl-manṭiq* see Suppl. Commentaries:
a. Self-commentary, additionally Garr. 821, Alex. Manṭiq 15, 25,$_3$, 31,$_4$.—Glosses
Y Alex. Manṭiq 20.—b. Alex. | Fun. 110,$_5$.—e. Alex. Manṭiq 25,$_2$, Garr. 822.—f. 615
Alex. Manṭiq 21,$_4$, 25,$_2$, Fun. 108,$_2$, Garr. 823.—k. Garr. 824, Alex. Manṭiq 15,
glosses by al-ʿAṭṭār ibid. 10.—r. Saʿīd Qaddūra al-Maghribī al-Mālikī, Alex.
Manṭiq 15.—s. Glosses by Ibn Ḥasan b. Darwīsh al-Quwaysānī, d. 1255/1839,
ibid. 16, 21, Fun. 1228,$_3$, print. C. 1314.—2. See *JA* 1859, II, 438, 61.—4. Garr. 1041.

2. Abu ʾl-ʿAbbās Aḥmad b. Muḥammad b. Wannān Abu ʾl-Shamaqmaq, who died in 1187/1773, see Suppl.

ʿAbdallāh Gannūn, *al-Nubūgh* I, 249/50. *Sharḥ al-Shamaqmaqiyya lil-sayyid ʿAbdallāh Gannūn al-Ḥasanī*, C. 1354.

10 *Mathematics and Astronomy*

1. Ibrāhīm b. Muḥammad b. Muḥammad al-Maghribī al-Andalusī wrote, in 988/1580:

1. On the determination of the hours, Leid. 1147.—2. *Gharīb al-nāqilīn* (*nāqilayn ?*) *fī aḥwāl al-nayyirayn* ibid. 1148.

2. Muḥammad b. Saʿīd b. Yaḥyā b. Aḥmad al-Sūsī al-Marghīthī was born in 1007/1598, studied in his hometown of Sūs and then in Tāfilāt and Marrakesh. He settled there and gained a large following as a Sufi. He died on 16 Rabīʿ II 1089/7 June 1678.

Muḥ. III, 472, *NM* II, 37/41, *Ṣaf.* 177/9. 1. *al-Muqniʿ fī ʿilm Abī Miqraʿ*, an adaptation of the poem by Abū Miqraʿ (p. 331) on calendars and astrology, in 99 verses, Berl. 5707, Gotha $1456_{,1}$, Algiers $80_{,2}$, $376_{,9}$, $391_{,6}$, $399_{,2}$, $646_{,2}$, Br. Mus. 411/2, Copenhagen $61_{,5}$, Garr. 1002, Alex. Ḥisāb 16/7, Cairo ^{1}V, 371.—Commentaries: a. Self-commentary, α the longer one, *al-Mumtiʿ*, Berl. 5708, Munich 723, Kraft 345, Copenhagen 91, Br. Mus. 411/2, Alex. Fun. $142_{,1}$, $159_{,7}$, print. Fez 1313, 1317 (with a commentary by Muḥammad b. Muḥammad b. ʿAbdallāh al-Warzīzī, see Suppl., in the margin).—β the shorter one, *al-Muṭliʿ*, Berl. 5709, Gotha $1456_{,2}$, Copenhagen $61_{,5}$.—b.–h. see Suppl. (d. Paris $2568_{,1}$).—2.–4. See Suppl.

2a. Abū Muḥammad ʿAbd al-Qādir b. ʿAlī b. Abi ʾl-Maḥāsin Yūsuf al-Fāsī, who died in 1091/1680, see Suppl.

ʿAbdallāh Gannūn, *al-Nubūgh* I, 214.—5. *Urjūza fi ʾl-asṭurlāb*, with a commentary by Muḥammad b. ʿAbd al-Salām al-Qabbānī, Alex. Ḥisāb 50.

616 | 3. ʿAlī b. Muḥammad b. Abi ʾl-Qāsim b. Ibrāhīm b. ʿAlī b. Muḥammad al-Dādasī from Dādas, in the southern Atlas, lived in Fez and Cairo and died after 1094/1683.

Ṣaf. 198. 1. *Bidāyat al-ṭullāb fī ʿilm waqt al-yawm bil-ḥisāb*, in verse, composed in 1047/1637, with the commentary *Itḥāf dhawi ʾl-albāb*, composed in 1048/1638 in Fez, Br. Mus. 409.—2. *Maʿūnat al-ṭullāb*, a poem on the four seasons, ca. 1058/1648, with a commentary by Aḥmad b. Sulaymān al-Taghanāshī, Br. Mus. 410.—3. *al-Yawāqīt li-mubtaghī maʿrifat al-mawāqīt*, in verse, completed in 1058/1648, Cairo ^{1}V, 330, with the commentary *Fatḥ al-muqīt*, Br. Mus. $411_{,3}$.

11 *Travelogues and Geographies* 464

1. Abū ʿAbdallāh Muḥammad al-Quṣumṭīnī Abū Qunfūdh wrote, in 1001/1592 in Damascus while on pilgrimage:

Idrīsiyyat al-nasab (see I, 628) *fī 'l-qurā wal-amṣār wa-bilād al-ʿArab* Cairo ^{1}V, 34, ^{2}19, Rabat 492, ix.

2. Aḥmad b. ʿAbdallāh b. Muḥammad b. ʿAbdallāh al-ʿAbbāsī al-Sijilmāsī, who died in 1031/1622, see Suppl.

ʿAdhrāʾ al-wasāʾil wa-hawdaj al-rasāʾil fī marj al-araj wa-nafḥat al-faraj ilā sādat Miṣr wa-qādat al-ʿaṣr or *Iṣlīt al-khirrīt fī qaṭʿ bulʿūm al-ʿifrīt al-nifrīt*, on his second pilgrimage, Cairo ^{1}IV, 281, ^{2}III, 248.

3. Abū Sālim ʿAbdallāh b. Muḥammad b. Abī Bakr al-ʿAyyāshī al-Mālikī ʿAfīf al-Dīn al-Maghribī was born on 30 Shaʿbān 1037/4 May 1628. He made the pilgrimage several times, studied in Cairo, lived for several years in Mecca and Medina after 1073/1662, then returned to the Maghreb. He died on 10 Dhu 'l-Qaʿda 1091/13 December 1679.

NM II, 45ff, *Ṣaf.* 191/6. 1. *al-Riḥla al-ʿAyyāshiyya*, a description of his pilgrimage, and in particular of his contacts with the scholars of Mecca and Medina and the certificates of study he received from them, ed. Ibrāhīm b. Ḥasan al-Kūrānī, d. 1101/1689 (p. 505), with an abbreviated version of the treatise on Free Will entitled *al-Kashf wal-bayān ʿan masʾalat al-kasb wal-īqān* by Ṣafī al-Dīn al-Qashshāshī, d. 1071/1660, Berl. 1201, Gotha 1545, *Br. Mus. Quart.* XIII, 3, 90, Tunis, *Bull. de Corr.*

Afr. II, 1884, p. 35, no. 139, lith. Fez 1316, 2 vols.—*Voyages dans le sud de l'Algérie* 617
et des états barbaresques de l'ouest er de l'est par el-Aiachi et Moula Ahmed, trad. par Adr. Berbrugger, Exploration scientif. de l'Algerie, Sc. hist. et geogr. IX, Paris 1844ff.—2.–4. See Suppl.

4. Abu 'l-ʿAbbās Aḥmad b. Shaykh al-Islām Muḥammad b. Nāṣir (p. 614) al-Dārī, who died on 19 Rabīʿ II 1129/3 April 1717, see Suppl.

NM II, 116, *Ṣaf.* 221/3 (which has 13 Rabīʿ II 1128 as his date of death). 1. *al-Riḥla al-Nāṣiriyya*, on his trip from Sijilmāsa to Tripoli, with a detour to Biskra, and through Egypt to Mecca and back, in the period 24 Jumādā I 1121/2 August 1709 to 5 Ramaḍān 1122/29 October 1710, Gotha 1546 (fragment), Algiers 1349, 5, 1954, translation by Berbrugger (see no. 3), cf. Seetzen in *Zachs Monatl. Corresp.* XX, 236.—2. See Suppl.

465 | 4b. ʿAbd al-Raḥmān b. Muḥammad b. Kharrūb al-Majjājī wrote, in 1163/1750:

Riḥla from Majjāja to Mecca, Algiers 1564/5.

12 *Medicine*

Ibrāhīm b. Muḥammad al-Maghribī al-Mālikī wrote, in 1068/1658:

Fi 'l-bāh, from a medical point of view, in 18 chapters, the last of which highlights methods by which the chances of conception are improved, Gotha $35_{,6}$.

13 *Warfare*

1. Ibrāhīm b. Aḥmad Ghānim b. Muḥammad b. Zakariyyāʾ al-Andalusī, who had the Spanish name of Arribāsh, was born in Niguelas near Granada. When the Moors were driven from Spain, he moved to Seville, from where he crossed the Atlantic in a Spanish gallion used to transport silver. When the Moors were chased out of Spain for good he was taken prisoner. He then went to Tunis,
618 where | Pāshā ʿUthmān entrusted him with the command of a ship. On a buccaneering raid he was taken hostage and subsequently was a prisoner for 7 years. After his return to Tunis, the governor Yūsuf Dāy entrusted him with the command of Khalq al-Wādi, i.e. La Goulette, the fortress that commands
466 the port of Tunis. | It was here that he wrote a work in Spanish on artillery and its usage, aimed at cannoneers. This work was translated into Arabic by Aḥmad b. Qāsim b. al-Faqīh Qāsim al-Shaykh al-Ḥujrī, entitled:

Al-ʿIzz wal-manāfiʿ lil-mujāhidīn fī sabīl Allāh bi-ālāt al-ḥurūb wal-madāfiʿ Vienna 1412, Algiers 1551/2.

Chapter 11. The Sudan

In the western Sudan, Islam took root at a very early stage (allegedly as early as the fifth century), and it was doing extremely well, particularly after the foundation of Timbuktu at the beginning of the sixth century. Nevertheless, for hundreds of years its population does not seem to have made any active contribution to Arabic literature, to which they owed their intellectual education, and it was not before the eleventh century that Timbuktu saw any literary achievement.[1]

1. Abu 'l-ʿAbbās Aḥmad b. Aḥmad b. Aḥmad b. ʿUmar b. Muḥammad b. ʿAbd al-Qādir Aḥmad Bābā al-Takrūrī al-Ṣanhājī al-Sūdānī, who died in 1036/1627, see Suppl.

Muḥ. I, 170, *Ṣaf.* 52/5, Wüst. *Gesch.* 554, J. Lippert, *MSOS W. As. St.* II, 245, n. 1. 1. *Takmilat (Dhayl) al-Dībāj li-Ibn Farḥūn*, d. 799/1396 (p. 226), biographies of Mālikīs, see Suppl. |—2. *Kifāyat al-muḥtāj li-maʿrifat man laysa fī 'l-Dībāj*, 467 an alphabetical abstract, with an autobiography at the end that was used by Muḥibbī, completed on 15 Ṣafar 1012/26 July 1603, Berl. 10032, Paris 2463.—Manuscripts of both works in Constantine, used by Cherbonneau, *Essai*, see Suppl.—3.–7. Ibid. (4. Berl. Ms. or. oct. 3781, Burch.-Fischer 34 without title).—8. *Tanwīr al-baṣāʾir wal-afhām* | *bi-ḥukm (bi-mā qīla fī) ḥashr al-ajsām baʿd* 619 *al-iʿdām* Berl. or. oct. 3781_{21}.

2. ʿAbd al-Raḥmān b. ʿAbdallāh b. ʿImrān b. ʿĀmir al-Saʿdī was born into a well-established family of Timbuktu scholars on 1 Jumādā II 1004/1 February 1596 and studied there under Aḥmad Bābā. When he was about twenty years old he moved to Jenne, an old trading post on the upper Niger river, and in 1036/1626 became the imam of the Sankore mosque in that town. At the end of 1039/July 1630 he made a trip to Māsina, a vassal of the Songhai Empire to which Jenne and Timbuktu also belonged, and whose centre was the island of Jimballa, situated in the Niger river between these two cities. Having been received with honour, he repeated his visit at the end of 1042/July 1633. At that time he accompanied the sultan of Māsina on a campaign against an unruly vassal, and brokered a peace between the two. At the end of 1044/July 1634 he travelled to Timbuktu to intervene on behalf of one of his brothers, who had beeen banned from Jenne. In 1046/1636 the *qāʾid* removed him from his office of imam, and even though the latter was removed following his complaint with

1 M. al-Fullānī, d. 1154/1741, p. 480–1.

the authorities in Timbuktu, he gave up his post and for the next ten years lived partly as a private citizen and partly as a teacher among the smaller vassals in the south of the Songhai Empire. In 1056/1646 the pasha Muḥammad b. Muḥammad b. ʿUthmān apppointed him state secretary in Timbuktu. It seems that, up to his death, he also exercised this office under Ibn ʿUthmān's successors. As such, he accompanied the pasha on various campaigns, such as, in 1057/1647, against Jurma and Hombori, against Kagho, the former capital of the empire, in 1060/1650, and in 1061/1651 against Bamba. On these campaigns he
468 became familiar with the north and the east of the empire, | of which he had
620 been unaware before then. It was in these years that he wrote | his chronicle
of the Songhai empire, which he completed on 5 Dhu 'l-Ḥijja 1063/28 October 1653. In an appendix he continued his work until 16 Jumāda I 1066/13 March 1656; he probably died soon after that.

Taʾrīkh al-Sūdān, a detailed history of the Songhai Empire from Sunnī ʿAlī onward, including the reign of the Askias and Moroccan supremacy, up to the death of the author, with an introduction on the early history of the major peoples of the empire, the Songhai, Melli, and Tuareg, and on the cities of Jenne and Timbuktu. Spread throughout the work can be found ethnographic descriptions and digressions of a historico-literary character, such as an abstract of Aḥmad Bābā's *Dhayl al-Dībāj*, on the scholars of Timbuktu, in chapter 10. Manuscripts Paris 5147, 5256, 6096. *Texte ar. éd. p.* O. Houdas *avec la collaboration de* E. Benoist, Paris 1898 (Publ. de l'École des langues or. viv. XII, Documents arab. rel. à l'histoire du Soudan I), cf. J. Lippert, *MSOS W. -As. St.* II, 244/53.

3. An unknown author, the grandson of emir Muḥammad b. Sūwū, a Songhai by birth who was born in Timbuktu in 1112/1700, wrote there, in 1164/1751:

Tadhkirat al-nasyān, a continuation of *Taʾrīkh al-Sūdān*, a history of the Moroccan governors of the Songhai empire: *Tedzkiret an-nisiān fī akhbār molouk es-Soudān, texte ar. éd. p.* O. Houdas *avec la collaboration de* E. Benoist, Paris 1899 (Publ. de l'Éc. d. lang. or. viv. IV, 19), based on Paris 6097.

THIRD SECTION

From the Napoleonic Expedition to Egypt in 1798 until the Present Day

Chapter 1. Egypt

With the waning of Ottoman power over Egypt from the end of the 18th century onward, the Mamlūks, who had never been completely subdued, regained their previous strength. But 300 years of dependence had done nothing to improve the political understanding of the Beys. As such, they only used | their 621
power in order to mercilessly extort the people, which not only affected the local population, but the many foreigners who had come to settle in the country too. This was the excuse for Napoleon's campaign to Egypt in 1798 that ended the Mamlūks' dominion. The Egyptians could hardly ignore the superiority of European culture, as it interfered in the Orient for the first time during this episode. A typical example of this is al-Jabartī's (III, 35/6) lively description of the sciences and the technology that were at the service of the supporting units of the occupation army, while his admiration for the orderly proceedings against the murderers of Colbert is no less (ibid. 117).[1] | Yet the French expedition was 470
not able to ensure the permanent influence of European culture. While it is true that Muḥammad ʿAlī, who had emerged victorious from the civil unrest that followed the retreat of French, did liberate his country from a number of insignifcant bloodsuckers by having about 500 Mamlūks slaughtered in Cairo on 2 Ṣafar 1226/11 March 1811 (Jab. IV, 127ff.), his over-ambitious foreign policy goals weighed ever more heavily on the country's finances. His fiscal policies[2] cast the fellahs—who had never had an easy life—into a state of abject poverty (Jab. IV, 109), and when he confiscated all pious endowments and fiefdoms in Dhu 'l-Ḥijja 1227/January 1812 (Jab. IV, 153) he also turned large parts of the middle classes into beggars. His reckless customs policy hit imports from Islamic countries harder than European goods, and led to an | unbearable rise in food 622
prices (Jab. IV, 124, 156, 313). Despite this, these measures were not enough to cover the expenses of his government, and the ever-increasing need for currency forced Muḥammad ʿAlī to degrade the coinage (Jab. IV, 139, 206, 312).

---

1 Cf. also A. Zaynī Daḥlān in Snouck Hurgronje, *Bijdr. t. Taal-, Land- en Volkenkunde v. Nederl. Indië* II, p. 43.

2 Cf. Kremer, *Ägypten* I, 251.

 | DOI 10.1163/9789004326323_004

In order to construct his fleet, he conscripted all carpenters and construction workers to do this work and bought all the timber required at prescribed prices (ibid. 158). On the other hand, his reign did give the country a security of life and property that it had not enjoyed before. Nevertheless, under the jurisdiction of the clergy, abuse continued (ibid. 279) and, whenever he
471 tried to implement the blessings | of the West—which he certainly acknowledged—this was purely to further his own political purposes. The first centre of education that was modelled on a European example was a school for the teaching of mathematics, with the help of study-tools from England (in Dhu 'l-Qaʿda 1231/October 1816, Jab. IV, 255). The inventions of European agriculture were supposed to increase the production of his vast state farms, but since he had no experience in this whatsoever, he had to pay a large number of European swindlers before he found someone who was able to set up his factories.[3] Nevertheless, the public works he started did open the country up to European trade.

Muḥammad ʿAlī, a Macedonian, had no understanding of Islamic culture whatsoever. Reading Turkish only with great difficulty,[4] one could hardly expect him to promote Arabic literature. It was only the printing press, which he introduced in 1821 for practical purposes, that proved useful for intellectual
623 endeavours. The ever-bolder | sense of entrepreneurship among the publishers rendered the treasures of ancient literature, marginalised as they had been by modern compilations, once again accessible to the masses. But this renaissance, which had also been fuelled by European scholarship, was at first more profitable for the latter than for indigenous literature itself, which continued along the all-too-familiar path of scholasticism, while people with a sense of history, such as al-Jabartī, were few and far between. Muḥammad ʿAlī's first successor, ʿAbbās, saw himself forced to dismantle the monopolies, revoke the most onerous of the taxes, and scale back the army and the navy. The people
472 fared better under Saʿīd. | Ismāʿīl on the other hand, followed the course of his grandfather without, however, being his equal in resolution or political acumen, distinguishing himself only in a negative sense by his exorbitant extravagance. Together with military imbroglios and his policy vis-à-vis the sultan, he brought the country to the brink of ruin, and his son Tawfīq was unable to prevent this from coming to pass. As such, the country was ripe for European tutelage, and from September 1882 onward Egypt was, for all intents and purposes, under British rule.

---

3 See v. Prokesch-Osten, *Mehemed Ali*, p. 8.

4 In spite of this, he appears to have been quite fond of the gushing praise of Turkish poets, on which see *Qaṭāʾif al-laṭāʾif* I, 37.

| See Suppl. W. Lane, *Manners and Customs of the modern Egyptians* I, 285/304. 473
A. v. Kremer, *Ägypten* II, 265/336.

1 *Poetry and Rhymed Prose*

1c. The son of a poor pharmacist, Shaykh al-Islām Ḥasan b. Muḥammad al-ʿAṭṭār was born in Cairo sometime after 1180/1766 and completed his studies at al-Azhar. He fled from the French to Upper Egypt, but when peace was restored he returned to his native city. Then he joined the French and tried | 624
to learn from them, travelled to Rumelia by way of Jerusalem and Damascus, and then got married in Skutari in Albania. After all his children there died he returned to Egypt and worked as a teacher at al-Azhar. From 12 Jumādā I 1244/20 November 1828, he edited the national newspaper founded by Muḥammad ʿAlī, *al-Waqāʾiʿ al-Miṣriyya*. Three years later he became head of al-Azhar. Apart from theological and juridical works, he also published poems, which were rather conventional in style. He died in 1250/1834[1] or 1254/1838.[2]

Khiṭ. jad. IV, 38/40, v. Kremer II, 324, Lane I, 297. 1. *Inshāʾ al-ʿAṭṭār*, a collection of stylistic samples and model letters, C. 1270, 1297, 1300, among others.—2. *Dīwān Ibr. al-Isrāʾīlī* I, 323.—3. *Sharḥ al-Samarqandiyya* p. 247.—4. *Ḥāshiya ʿala ʾl-Jawāhir al-muntaẓimāt* p. 423.—5.–7. See Suppl. (5. translation by O. Rescher, *Or. Misz.*).—8. *Sharḥ Jamʿ al-jawāmiʿ* p. 109.

| 2. ʿAlī b. Ḥusayn b. Ibrāhīm al-Miṣrī al-Darwīsh, who died in 1270/1852. 474

Al-Ishʿār bi-ḥamīd al-ashʿār, compiled in 1271/1855 by his student Muṣṭafā Salāma al-Najjārī (see Suppl.), lith. C. 1284.—2. See Suppl.

4. Shihāb al-Dīn Muḥammad b. Ismāʿīl was born in Mecca in 1218/1796.[3] He studied in Cairo under al-Ḥasan al-ʿAṭṭār (no. 1c.), became his assistant at *al-Waqāʾiʿ al-Miṣriyya* and then, when his teacher had retired, succeeded him as editor. In 1252/1836 he became head proofreader at the state printing mill, and was well regarded by Muḥammad ʿAlī's successor ʿAbbās. In 1266/1849 he retired from public life, though he continued to receive his full salary, and died in 1274/1857.[4]

---

1 *Khiṭ. jad.* IV, 38, 10.

2 Ibid., 40, 14.

3 According to v. Kremer, loc. cit., in Ramaḍān 1201/1787; according to al-Sandūbī in 1210.

4 *Khiṭ.* 1273.

625 | *Khiṭ. jad.* III, 30, v. Kremer II, 297, Lane I, 297, H. Gies, *Neuere Versarten* 10. Hartmann, *Muwashshaḥ* 85. 1. *Dīwān* C. 1277.—2. *Safīnat al-mulk wa-nafīsat (dafīnat) al-fulk*, C. 1273, 1281, 1310, see Suppl.

4. ʿAbd al-Raḥmān al-Ṣafatī al-Sharqāwī, who died on 8 Ramaḍān 1264/21 August 1848.

Talāqi ʾl-arab fī marāqi ʾl-adab, his *dīwān*, compiled by his student Muḥammad ʿAyyād al-Ṭanṭāwī (p. 631), Cairo ^{2}III, 67, Patna I, 195$_{,175}$, compiled by Shaykh al-Islām ʿĀrif Ḥikmat, manuscript dated 1285, Alex. Adab 26, Madr. 152 (Dérenbourg, *Homenaje a Fr. Codera*, Zaragoza 1904, p. 590), Leningr. Un. 892.

5. Abu ʾl-Naṣr ʿAlī al-Manfalūṭī, who died in 1298/1880/1, see Suppl.

Dīwān, Būlāq 1300.

6. ʿAbdallāh Bāshā b. Muḥammad b. ʿAbdallāh al-Fikrī was born in 1250/1834 in Mecca, where his father was stationed with the Egyptian troops. In 1267/1850 he entered state service as a scribe, at the same time studying at al-Azhar. In 1279/1861 he became a member of the retinue of Ismāʿīl Bāshā when the latter travelled to Istanbul to receive his royal commission, and was to return there several times more on administrative missions. In 1284/1866 he became a teacher of Islamic sciences to prince Tawfīq and his brothers Ḥasan and Ḥusayn. In 1286/1868 he joined the ministry of finances and was soon entrusted with the establishment of the Khudaywiyya library. In 1288/1870 he became
475 | school inspector of Egypt, and in 1296/1879 minister of education. Being an ally of ʿUrābī Pāshā, he lost this office in 1881 and was even incarcerated for a time, after which he lived privately in Cairo. In 1303/1886 he visited Syria and in 1306/1889 he went as a representative of the Egyptian government to an oriental studies conference in Stockholm. He died in Cairo on 11 Dhu ʾl-Ḥijja 1307/ 27 July 1890.

626 | *Khiṭ. jad.* II, 45/57 (with samples of his poems and style of writing), al-ʿAqqād, *Shuʿarāʾ Miṣr* 78/86, Muḥammad b. ʿAbd al-Ghanī Ḥasan, *ʿAbdallāh Fikrī*, Cairo 1946. 1. *al-Āthār al-Fikriyya*, collected works, poems, letters, *maqāma*s, and speeches, published by his son Amīn, Būlāq 1315, cf. *al-Mashriq* I, 189.—2. *al-Fawāʾid al-Fikriyya lil-makātib al-Miṣriyya*, practical advice and ethics, C. 1307, tenth impression 1317 and others.—3. *al-Fuṣūl al-Fikriyya*, an outline of grammar, C. 1301, 1304, 1307.—4. *Naẓm al-laʾāliʾ*, proverbs and aphorisms,

in alphabetical order, ibid. 1308, 1310.—5. *al-Maqāma al-Fikriyya fī 'l-mamlaka al-bāṭiniyya* C. 1289, see *Āthār* 276ff.—6.–8. See Suppl.

7. As representatives of religious poetry, mention should be made of: 1) Jaʿfar b. Muḥammad ʿUthmān al-Mīrghanī, the son of a Sufi (see Suppl. 809), and 2) ʿAbdallāh b. ʿAlawī.

1) *Riyāḍ al-madīḥ wa-jalāl kulli dhī wudd ṣaḥīḥ wa-shifāʾ kulli qalb jarīḥ fī dhikr al-nabī al-madīḥ*, which was begun in 1282/1864, print. C. 1289 (Suppl. 810).—2) *al-Durar al-bahiyya fī 'l-akhlāq al-marḍiyya* Būlāq 1313 (see Suppl.).

8a. The following authors followed the path of conventional literary poetry: 1) Maḥmūd Efendi Ṣafwat b. Muṣṭafā Āghā al-Zaylaʿī al-Sāʿātī; 2) Yūsuf Efendi al-Shalfūnī; and 3) the Copt ʿAbdallāh Efendi Furayj; while 4) Saʿīd Efendi al-Bustānī tried to portray the life of the Egyptians in comical prose, see Suppl.

1) 1. *Dīwān* ed. Anīs El-Khouri, Beirut 1938.—3. Collection of *muzdawijāt* C. 1287.—2) *Anīs al-jalīs, Dīwān* C. 1291.—3) 1. *Dīwān* C. 1895.—2. *Tarjumān al-mukātaba* C. 1305.—3. *Samīr al-jalīs fī maḥāsin al-takhmīs* C. 1891.—4.–7. See Suppl.—8. *Rashf al-mudām fī 'l-jinās al-tāmm* C. 1894.—4) *Riwāyat dhāt al-khidr* Alexandria 1884, 1904.

9. The poetess ʿĀʾisha ʿIṣmat Khānum bt. Ismāʿīl Bāshā b. Muḥammad Kāshif Taymūr died in 1320/1902, see Suppl.

Al-ʿAqqād, *Shuʿarāʾ Miṣr* 150/4, ʿAbd al-Fattāḥ, *Hilāl* 35, 401/8. 1. *Ḥilyat al-ṭirāz, dīwān* C. 1303, 1306, among others.—2., 3. See Suppl. | 627

10. As an example of modern poetry, easily accessible to people from Europe, mention can be made of the *Qaṣīda bahiyya*, written for King Oscar of Sweden by Ḥamza Fatḥallāh, first inspector for the Arabic sciences | in the ministry of 476
education of Egypt, on the occasion of his participation in the oriental studies conference in Stockholm (Leiden 1889), see Suppl.

11. Besides literary poetry,[5] which was not accessible to the masses, popular poetry written in the colloquial language flourished as before in the form of

5 Whose verbose yet barren style is strikingly satirised in *Qaṭāʾif al-laṭāʾif* 38, and by Muḥammad ʿUthmān Jalāl in his *al-Nisāʾu 'l-ʿālimāt*, ed. F. Kern, p. 74.

the *mawwāl* and the *zajal*. Muḥammad b. ʿUthmān Jalāl[6] b. Yūnus al-Ḥasanī al-Wanāʾī was the first to try to turn this language of songs into a literary genre. Born in 1245/1829 in Cairo as the son of an Egyptian woman and an official of Turkish stock, he learned French, English, and Turkish at the Madrasat al-Alsun in the al-Azbakiyya quarter. In 1261/1844 he joined the translation office (*qalam al-tarjama*) of the government, where he translated Lafointaine's *Fables* (*al-ʿUyūn al-yawāqiẓ fī 'l-amthāl wal-mawāʿiẓ*, C. 1275, 1297, 1313, 1324) and St. Pierre's *Paul et Virginie* (*al-Amānī wal-minna fī ḥadīth Qabūl wa-Ward Janna*, C. 1288) into classical Arabic. When Clot Bey returned from France he accepted him into the Conseil de Médecine and, together with this patron, he published a précis of the history of Muḥammad ʿAlī and an introduction to the French language (*al-Tuḥfa al-saniyya*). In 1280/1863 he joined the war office, and in 1285/1868 the ministry of the interior. When Tawfīq came to power in
628 1296/1879 he appointed | him as a member of his cabinet. He accompanied the *khidīw* on a trip through the Delta and described this journey in rhymed prose in his *al-Siyāḥa al-Khidīwiyya* (Būlāq 1297). At the end of his career he was a judge at the court of first instance in Cairo; he was retired in 1895 and died on 16 January 1898.

After translating the tragedies of Racine into classical Arabic, he tried to
477 transpose the comedies of Molière to the contemporary | Egyptian vernacular and circumstances, but failed to get his pieces a permanent place on the Arab theatrical scene, which at the time was very much in its infancy. The public found the language too common, and because female comedians were lacking his works were either not put on stage at all or, if they were, did not receive the acclaim they deserved.

Autobiography, *Khiṭ. jad.* XVII, 62ff., Vollers, ZDMG 45, 71ff., al-ʿAqqād, *Shuʿarāʾ Miṣr* 112/8. I. Adaptations of Molière.[7] 1. *al-Shēkh Matlūf* (*Le Tartuffe*), 1290/1873, published in transcription by Vollers ZDMG 45, 31ff., cf. Socin, ibid. 46, 131ff.—2. *Arbaʿ riwāyāt min nukhab al-tiyātarāt*, 1307/1890, 1311, containing: a. an improved version of *al-Shēkh Matlūf*. b. *al-Nisāʾu 'l-ʿālimāt* (*Les femmes savantes*), transcription and translation by F. Kern, Leipzig 1898. c. *Madrasit al-azwāg* (*L'école des maris*), transcription etc. by M. Sobernheim, Berlin 1896. d. *Madrasit al-nisāʾ* (*L'École des femmes*).—3. *Riwāyat il-thuqalāʾ* (*Les fâcheux*) 1314/1897.—4. Adaptations of Racine's *Esther*, *Iphigénie*, and *Alexandre le*

6 On the title pages of his works, he mostly just uses the initials M.ʿU. J.

7 The metre of all these pieces is the *rajaz*, contra Socin, *Zur Metrik einiger ins Arab. übersetzter Dramen Molières* (Leipzig, Progr. 1896/7); see M. Hartmann, *DLZ* 1895, 999, *OLZ*, I, 2, Sobernheim *MSOS W. -As. St.* I, 188.

Grand entitled *al-Riwāyāt al-mufīda fī ʿilm al-tarājīda*, 1311/1894, with a eulogy on the family of the viceroy as an appendix.—5.–9. See Suppl.—The adaptations of Corneille's *Cid* and *Trois Horaces* remain unpublished. Finally, there are also three collections of popular poems published under the title *Ḥiml zajal*, Cairo [1]IV, 229.

| 2 *Philology* 629

1. Ḥasan Quwaydir al-Khalīlī, who died in 1262/1846, see Suppl.

1. *Nayl al-arab fī muthallathāt al-ʿArab* (see I, 102), Būlāq 1302. *Dizionario dei triplici, trad. d. E. Vitto*, Beirut 1899.—2. *al-Aghlāl wal-salāsil fī Majnūn ismuhu ʿĀqil* Cairo [1]IV, 205, 309, see Suppl.—3. A *muzdawija* he wrote is in the collection of Maḥmūd Efendi al-Jazāʾirī, C. 1287 and others.—4. See Suppl.

2. Muṣṭafā al-Badrī al-Dimyāṭī, who died in 1268/1851.

1. *Risāla fī ḥukm mā qabl wāw al-jamāʿa al-musnad ilayhi ʾl-fiʿl* Leid. 261.—2.–4. See Suppl.

| 3. Muḥammad al-Damanhūrī, who died in 1288/1871. 478

1. *Risāla ʿalā iʿrāb baʿḍ āyat wa-amthila naḥwiyya* Cairo [1]IV, 53.—2. *Sharḥ al-Kāfī* p. 34.—3., 4. See Suppl.

4. Ibrāhīm b. ʿAbd al-Ghaffār al-Dasūqī, the teacher of E.W. Lane, was born in 1226/1811, studied at al-Azhar and became a teacher of Arabic at the Muhandiskhāne (p. 622) after it had been moved to Būlāq. When this school was dissolved at the beginning of the reign of Saʿīd Pāshā, he became a proofreader at the state printing mill, which also published *al-Waqāʾiʿ al-Miṣriyya*; at the end of his career he was the head proofreader of scientific works there. He died in 1301/1883.

Khiṭ. jad. XI, 9, v. Kremer II, 325 (who is full of praise for his vast knowledge in philology). 1. *Maqāla shukriyya lil-Ḥaḍra al-Ismāʿīliyya ʿalā inshāʾ dār al-wirāqa dhāt al-bahja wal-ṭalāqa* Cairo [1]IV, 327, [2]III, 368.—2. *Ḥāshiya ʿalā Mughni ʾl-labīb* p. 28.—3.–5. See Suppl.

5. Aḥmad b. ʿAbd al-Raḥīm al-Ṭahṭāwī, who died in 1302/1814, see Suppl.

1. *al-Asʾila al-naḥwiyya al-mufīda wal-ajwiba al-ʿArabiyya al-sadīda* Cairo [1]IV, 31, [2]II, 75.—2.–5. See Suppl.

630 | 6. Muṣṭafā Efendi Riḍwān, who died in 1305/1887.

1. *Mukhtaṣar al-bayān*, with a commentary, C. 1296.—2. See Suppl.

7. Ḥusayn b. Aḥmad al-Marṣafī was a professor at al-Azhar, a teacher of Arabic at the Dār al-ʿulūm bil-madāris and, as he was blind himself, at the school for the blind founded by Ismāʿīl. He died in 1307/1889.

Khiṭ. jad. XV, 40. 1. *al-Wasīla al-adabiyya ila ʾl-ʿulūm al-ʿArabiyya* Cairo [1]IV, 343.—2. *al-Kalim al-thamān* (see Suppl.) ibid. VI, 182.

8. See Suppl.

(ad 8c. al-ʿAqqād, *Shuʿarāʾ Miṣr* 22/9, Saʿd Mīkhāʾīl, *Adab al-ʿaṣr* 133/9, Shakīb Arslān in *Radio Araba di Bari* III, 102/6).

9. Finally, mention should be made of three men who were born and raised in the Orient but who settled permanently in Europe, where they contributed to the dissemination of the knowledge of Arabic:

1) Mīkhāʾīl b. Niqūlā Ṣabbāgh, who was born to Christian parents in Acre in 1784, joined the French expedition to Egypt, was obliged to leave the country with it, and died in Paris in 1816.

Biographie univ. XXXIX, 427, Humbert, *Anthologie arabe* 291ff., Sarkis 1192. 1. *Musābaqat al-barq wal-ghamām fī suʿāt al-ḥamām, La Colombe messagère* (on carrier pigeons), text and transl. S. de Sacy, Paris 1805.—2. *Mīkhāʾīl Ṣabbāghs Grammatik der arab. Umgangssprache in Syrien und Ägypten, nach der Munich Hds. hsg. v.* H. Thorbecke, Strasbourg 1886.—3.–4. See Suppl.

2) Ilyās Boqtor, likewise a Christian, was born on 12 April 1784 in Suyūṭ, served as an interpreter in the French army, became a professor of colloquial Arabic at the Bibliothèque du Roi, and died on 26 September 1821.

Biogr. univ. LVIII, Suppl. 408, *Nouv. Biogr. univ.* VI, 314. *Dictionnaire français-ar. publié par* Caussin de Perceval 2 vols., Paris 1827/9, 2nd ed. 1848.

| 3) Muḥammad ʿAyyād al-Ṭanṭāwī, a Muslim and a student of al-Bājūrī 631
(p. 639), was appointed as a teacher of Arabic at the Faculty of Oriental Languages in St. Petersburg, where he died on 29 October 1861.

See Suppl., Jamāl al-Dīn al-Shayyāl, Dr. Perron wal-Shaykhān Muḥammad ʿAyyād al-Ṭanṭāwī wa Muḥammad ʿUmar al-Tūnisī, *Farouk I University, Bulletin of the Fac. of Arts* 2 (1944) 179—221. 1. *Traité de la langue arabe vulgaire* Leipzig 1848.—2. *Naẓm al-Samarqandiyya* p. 247.

3 *Historiography*

1. Ḥusayn b. ʿAbd al-Laṭīf b. Muḥammad al-ʿUmarī b. ʿAbd al-Hādī al-Dimashqī al-Khalwatī, who died in 1216/1802.

Al-Mawāhib al-iḥsāniyya fī tarjamat al-Fārūq wa-dhurriyyatihi Banī ʿAbd al-Hādī al-ʿUmariyya Cairo V, ^{1}163, ^{2}374.

2. ʿAbdallāh b. Ḥijāzī b. Ibrāhīm al-Sharqāwī was born in 1150/1737. He studied at al-Azhar but lived initially in great poverty, until a rich patron took him under his wing. When Shaykh al-ʿArūsī died he became his successor at al-Azhar, and during the French occupation he became, in 1213/1798, chairman of the court dealing with Muslims. When he married the daughter of ʿAlī al-Zaʿfarānī, he moved into real estate: baths, shops, and manors. He died of a stroke in 1127/1812 during a large gathering at al-Azhar.

| *Khiṭ. jad.* XIII, 63, based on Jab. IV, 159/63. 1. *Tuḥfat al-nāẓirīn fī man waliya Miṣr* 480
min al-wulāt wal-salāṭīn, a history of Egypt from Muḥammad until Selīm III and a history of the Napoleonic expedition, Paris 1860, Cairo V, ^{1}31, ^{2}131, print. Būlāq 1286, C. 1281, 1300 (in the margin of al-Masʿūdī).—2. *al-Tuḥfa al-bahiyya fī ṭabaqāt al-Shāfiʿiyya*, from the ninth century onward, Berl. 10041, Cairo V, ^{1}129, ^{2}128.—3. *al-ʿAqāʾid al-mashriqiyya*, with the commentary *al-Jawāhir al-saniyya*, Cairo ^{1}II, 12.—4. *Rabīʿ al-fuʾād fī tartīb ṣalawāt al-ṭarīq wal-awrād* ibid. 83.—5. *al-Fayḍ al-ʿarshī ʿala ʾl-Fatḥ al-Qudsī*, a commentary on the | *Wird* 632
al-saḥar (p. 460), ibid. 101.—6. *Ḥāshiya ʿalā Tuḥfat al-ṭullāb* Suppl. I, 307,$_{7}$.—7. *Sharḥ al-Ḥikam al-ʿAṭāʾiyya* p. 143.—8. *Ḥāshiya ʿalā Sharḥ Umm al-barāhīn* p. 324.—9.–13. See Suppl. (10. Berl. Ms. or. oct. 3907,$_{4}$).

3. Muṣṭafā b. Muḥammad b. Yūsuf al-Ṣafawī al-Qalʿawī was born in 1158/1745, studied at al-Azhar, and at the beginning lived in Qalʿat al-Jabal, up to the time that the pasha had it razed. He died in 1230/1815.

Jab. IV, 237. 1. *Mashāhid al-ṣafā' fi 'l-madfūnīn bi-Miṣr min āl al-Muṣṭafā* Cairo [1]VII, 220.—2. See Suppl. (Garr. 615).

4. ʿAbd al-Raḥmān b. Ḥasan (p. 472) al-Jabartī, who died in 1237/1822, see Suppl.

Lane I, 298, v. Kremer II, 325. 1. *Kitāb ʿajā'ib al-āthār fi 'l-tarājim wal-akhbār*, a history of Egypt in the twelfth and thirteenth centuries, up to 1220 (see Dorn, *Mém. de l'Ac. de St. Pétersbourg* IX, 1865, 722ff.), Berl. 9487/90, Munich 400, Paris 1861/6, Pet. Ros. 60, Br. Mus. 1497/9, Cairo V, [1]83/4, [2]262/3, printed in 4 vols., Būlāq 1290/7, C. 1322/3.[1] *Merveilles biographiques et historiques ou Chroniques du cheikh Abd el Rahman el Djabarti, trad. de l'Ar. par* Chefik Mansour Bey, Abdoulaziz Kahil Bey, Gabriel Nicolas Kahil Bey et Iskender Amoun Efendi, Cairo 1888/94.—2. *Muzhir al-taqdīs bi-dhahāb dawlat al-Fransīs*, a chronicle of Cairo during the French occupation, Br. Mus. Suppl. 571, Cambr. Burckh. p. 12, no. 60, Cairo V, [1]153, [2]349, Garr. 613. Turkish translation by Muṣṭafā Bahjat Efendi, Istanbul 1217 (see Schlechta-Wssehrd, *Denkschr. d. Vienna Ak.* VIII, 13), *Journal d'Abdurrahman Gabarti pendant l'occupation française d'Égypte, trad. de l'Ar. par* A. Cardin, Paris 1838.—3. See Suppl.—4. *Mukhtaṣar Tadhkirat uli 'l-albāb* p. 478.

5. Karīm al-Dīn b. Sirāj al-Dīn completed, in 1263/1846:

481 | *Farā'id al-dahr*, on the most eminent poets and scholars, from the past until modern times, Berl. 7431.

6. Rifāʿ Bek Rāfiʿī b. ʿAlī b. Muḥammad al-Ṭaḥṭāwī al-Badawī was born in Ṭaḥṭā
633 in 1216/1801. In 1241/1826, | Muḥammad ʿAlī sent him and a number of other young Egyptians to France in order to study there.[2] He died in 1290/1873, see Suppl.

Kremer II, 326, J. Heyworth Dunne, *BSOS* 1939, 961/7, *Ḥilyat al-zaman fī manāqib khādim al-waṭan Rifāʿa Bey*, written by his student Ṣāliḥ Muḥammad Bey, Cairo V, [1]45, [2]164.—1. *Anwār tawfīq al-jalīl fī akhbār Miṣr wa-tawthīq Banī*

---

1 Because of his sharp criticism of Muḥammad ʿAlī's government an earlier edition had been confiscated and destroyed; indeed, the government only gave printers and lithographers a concession on the condition that they would not print al-Jabartī's work, v. Kremer, loc. cit.

2 Cf. Jacoub Artin Pacha, *L'Instruction publique en Égypte*, Paris 1898, 82/6, following Goldziher, *WZKM* iv, 237, n. 1.

Ismāʿīl Būlāq 1285.—2. *Takhlīṣ al-ibrīz fī talkhīṣ Bārīs aw al-Dīwān al-nafīs bi-īwān Bārīs* Būlāq 1265 and others, also printed in Turkish translation.—3. *Manāhij al-albāb al-Miṣriyya fī mabāhij al-ādāb al-ʿaṣriyya* Cairo [1]V, 160.—5. *al-Rushd al-amīn lil-banāt wal-banīn* C. 1292.—6. *Muqaddima waṭaniyya Miṣriyya* Cairo [1]IV, 331.—7. *Manẓūma Miṣriyya waṭaniyya* Būlāq 1272, together with two other patriotic poems, Cairo [1]IV, 334, whose popularity, however, hardly reached beyond the walls of the state printing mill, as noted by Kremer (II, 327, where there are also samples in translation).—8.–15. See Suppl.

7. Abu ʾl-Suʿūd ʿAbdallāh Efendi, who died in 1295/1878, see Suppl.

1. *al-Dars al-tāmm fi ʾl-taʾrīkh al-ʿāmm* C. 1289.—2. *Minḥat ahl al-ʿaṣr bi-muntaqā taʾrīkh Miṣr* Cairo [1]V, 161.

8. ʿAlī Bāshā Mubārak was born in Birinbāl in 1239/1823, and came from a
poor family of local judges. He began his studies in the state school of Qaṣr
al-ʿAynī and at Abū Zaʿbal. Having completed his studies at the | polytech- 482
nic (Muhandiskhāne) of Būlāq in 1844, he and a number of other Egyptians
(see no. 6) were sent to Paris to study military science. Back in his native country he was sent to the war office, where he carried out topographical work.
Later he became the director of the cadet school al-Mafrūza, in which capacity
he also wrote some technical course-books. After the war in the Crimea, in
which he had taken part as a member of the Egyptian contingent, he became | 634
a manager for the railways and public works. Later he became minister of the
awqāf and education, and in this position he founded the Khudaywiyya library
in 1870, through which he earned great merit for his preservation of Arabic
literary treasures. Together with the Swiss pedagogue Dr Dor Bey he founded
the Dār al-ʿulūm academy, which was based on the European model and, in
June 1888, he once more assumed responsibility for the ministry of education.
However, soon he was no longer able to cope with the requirements of the age,
and he died in Cairo on 6 Jumādā I 1311/15 November 1893.

Goldziher, WZKM IV, 347, Vollers, ZDMG 47, 720. 1. *al-Khiṭaṭ al-Tawfīqiyya al-jadīda li-Miṣr al-Qāhira wa-muduniha ʾl-qadīma wal-shahīra*, 20 vols., Būlāq 1306; a modern pendant of the work by al-Maqrīzī (p. 47). Parts I–VI, the streets, neighbourhoods, alleyways, mosques, temples, monasteries, mausoleums, public wells, baths, palaces, churches, and shops of Cairo and (part VII) Alexandria, including the biographies of famous persons buried there; Parts VIII–XVII, the famous places of Egypt, in alphabetical order, with corresponding biographies; Part XVIII, the Nilometer; Part XIX, channels and floodgates; Part XX, the minting system. For the biographies he used al-Sakhāwī, al-Shaʿrānī, al-Suyūṭī, al-Muḥibbī, and al-Jabartī; for the very detailed historical and archaeological sections, which also deal at length with antiquity, he used the classics in French translation as well as French works on Egyptology; he also made extensive use of the works of de Sacy and Quatremère.—2. *Nukhabat al-fikr fī tadbīr Nīl Miṣr*, on agriculture in Egypt, C. 1297/8.—3. *Ṭarīq al-hijāʾ wal-tamrīn* (see Suppl.) C. 1306.—4. *al-Mīzān fi 'l-aqyisa wal-awzān* (a special issue of al-Azhar magazine), in which he criticises the work of al-Falakī (p. 642).—5.–13. See Suppl. (12. read: *ʿAlam al-dīn*).

9. See Suppl.—9i. Muḥammad Tawfīq al-Azharī:

Riwāyat anbāʾ al-zamān fī ḥarb al-Dawla wal-Yūnān, C. n.d. (1897).

9k. Nikola Elias

635 | *Riwāyat ḥarb al-ʿUthmān maʿa 'l-Yūnān* C. n.d. (1897).

484 | 10. Works by local scholars on ancient Egypt are entirely based on European works and as such should be excluded here; however, in view of their great historical and cultural importance, it seems appropriate that they be mentioned.

1) (10a) A. Kamāl Pāshā, see Suppl.
2) ʿAlī Efendi Jalāl al-Ḥusaynī, *Maḥāsin āthār al-awwalīn*, on women in ancient Egypt, C. 1308.
3) ʿAlī Efendi Naqīb, the inspector general of the Egyptian museums, *al-Athar al-jalīl li-qudamāʾ wādi 'l-Nīl*, an archaeological work, with many pictures and an appendix containing an overview of the excavations in Egypt in the years 1893/5, 2nd ed. Būlāq 1312.

4 *Popular Prose*

1. Al-Ḥujayj al-Munīr al-Ḥarīrī, who flourished around 1256/1834.

Qiṣṣat al-Miqdād b. al-Aswad al-Kindī, a romanesque tale in ca. 1000 verses in the common vernacular, Berl. 8177/8 (with a detailed table of contents).

2. A final representative of the popular tale (p. 74) is the *Dīwān al-Zīr* (printed in various recensions in Cairo and Beirut). Although this work, too, derives its plot from old-Arabian tribal lore, it is written entirely in the Egyptian

vernacular, while its older counterparts still try to comply with the conventions of literary Arabic.

A detailed table of contents is in v. Kremer II, 307/22.

3e. From *adab* literature, in the strictest sense of the term (see Suppl.), the following must be mentioned:

| Mrs. Rosa Ṣāḥib, *Qaṭāʾif al-laṭāʾif*, C. without publisher and date (1889), 2nd 485
edition ibid. 1894, 2 vols. 1896; short stories and anecdotes in the local dialect, whose subjects are partly derived from the 1001 Nights and partly from Egypt's
more recent past. | Finally, many of the elements belonging to the standard 636
repertoire of European comical literature were taken from French sources.

5 *Ḥadīth*

1. ʿAbdallāh b. ʿAlī Suwaydān al-Damlījī al-Shāfiʿī al-Ashʿarī al-Shādhilī, who died in 1234/1819.

1. *Nūr al-abṣār fī bayān mawlid al-nabī al-mukhtār*, composed in 1205/1791, Gotha 1814.—2. *al-Jawhar al-fard fi ʾl-kalām ʿalā ammā baʿd* Cairo [1]IV, 35, [2]II, 92.—3. *Sharḥ al-Alfiyya* I, 362,$_{18}$.—4. *Sharḥ al-Sullam* Suppl. p. 705,h.—5. *Sharḥ al-Rajaz al-mafrūḍ* p. 480.—6. See Suppl.—7.–10. Ibid. III, 1308.

3. Muḥammad b. Muḥammad al-Amīr al-Ṣaghīr, who died in 1245/1830.

ZDMG 1886, 766. *Risālat musalsal al-ʿĀshūrāʾ al-Amīriyya*, on the traditions about *yawm ʿĀshūrāʾ*, Cairo [1]VII, 21, with glosses by ʿAlī al-Balawī, C. 1305.

4. ʿAlī b. Sulaymān al-Dimnātī al-Bajamʿawī, who died in 1306/1889, see Suppl.

1. *Aghlā masānīd ʿalī al-raḥmān fī aʿlā asānīd ʿAlī b. Sulaymān* C. 1298, cf. Goldziher, *Abh.* II, LXXIII. 2.–11. See Suppl.

5. Muʾmin b. Ḥasan Muʾmin al-Shablanjī, who was born after 1250/1834 in Shabalanja, near Banhāʾ al-Asal, went to al-Azhar in 1267/1851 and died around 1301/1883.

E. Galtier, *Bull. de l'inst. franç. d'archéologie or.* V, 117/21. *Nūr al-abṣār etc.* (see Suppl.) also C. 1317.

6 *Fiqh*

A The Mālikīs

1. Muḥammad b. Aḥmad b. ʿArafa al-Dasūqī al-Mālikī was born in Dasūq and studied in Cairo at al-Azhar, where he lectured afterwards. He died on 21 Rabīʿ II 1230/2 August 1815.

Jab. [1]IV, 231/2, [2]IV, 237/8. 1. *Ḥāshiya ʿala ʾl-Mughnī* p. 28.—2. *Ḥāshiya ʿalā Sharḥ*
637 *al-Dardīr ʿalā Khalīl* p. 103.—3. *Ḥāshiya ʿalā Sharḥ* | *al-Sanūsiyya al-ṣughrā* p. 323.—4. *Manāsik al-ḥajj* Garr. 1859.—5.–7. See Suppl.—8. *Tafsīr* Mosul 231,$_{68}$.

2. Muḥammad b. Muḥammad b. Aḥmad al-Sunbāwī al-Amīr al-Kabīr al-Mālikī was born in Sunbū in 1154/1741 and moved to Cairo at the age of 9. He then joined the Shādhiliyya order and became famous in the Maghreb, from where many students came to him. He died in 1232/1817.

486 | Jab. IV, 285. 1. *al-Majmūʿ fi ʾl-fiqh*, with the commentary *Ḍawʾ al-shumūʿ*, Cairo [1]III, 173, another commentary, *Fatḥ al-qadīr*, see Suppl. Garr. 1839.—2. *al-Manāsik* Cairo [1]III, 185. Commentaries: a. see Suppl.—b. Muḥammad b. Ramaḍān b. Manṣūr b. Muḥammad al-Marzūqī al-Makkī, *al-Fawāʾid al-Marzūqiyya*, Alex. Fiqh Māl. 16.—3. *Maṭlaʿ al-nayyirayn fī-mā yataʿallaq bil-qudratayn* Cairo [1]VII, 37.—4. *Fatāwī* ibid. 278.—5. *Ḥāshiya ʿala ʾl-Shudhūr* p. 30.—6. *Sharḥ Urjūzat al-Saqqāṭ* p. 435.—7. *Masāʾil wa-ajwibatuhā* Alex. Fiqh Māl. 15.—8.–22. See Suppl. (9. also Alex. Fiqh Māl. 15).

3. Abū Yaḥyā Muṣṭafā al-Burullusī al-Mālikī al-Būlāqī was born in 1215/1800. He was a multifaceted scholar and also a poet, who died in 1263/1846.

A. v. Kremer II, 323. 1. *al-Sayf al-Yamānī li-man qāla bi-ḥill samāʿ al-ālāt wal-aghānī* Cairo [1]III, 166.—2. *Ḥāshiya ʿalā Sharḥ al-Sullam* Suppl. p. 705,g.

4. Shaykh al-Islām Abū ʿAbdallāh b. Aḥmad ʿUllaysh al-Mālikī al-Maghribī, whose grandfather hailed from Fez but had stayed in Tripoli while on pilgrimage, was born in Cairo in 1217/1802. In 1270/1853 he became *muftī* of the Mālikīs of Egypt, and died in 1299/1881 (see Suppl.).

Khiṭ. jad. IV, 41ff. 1. *Fiqh al-ʿalī al-mālik fi ʾl-fatwā ʿalā madhhab al-imām Mālik* Cairo [1]III, 175, print. C. 1300, 1301, 1319.—2. *Tadrīb al-mubtadiʾ wa-tadhkirat al-muntahī*, on the law of inheritance, completed in 1283/1866, C. 1301.—3. *Sharḥ Mukhtaṣar Khalīl* p. 103,t.—4. *Muwaṣṣil al-ṭullāb li-minaḥ al-wahhāb fī qawāʿid al-iʿrāb*, a commentary on a grammar written by Yūsuf ʿAbd al-Qādir

al-Barnāwī, C. 1281.—5. *Ḥāshiya ʿalā Risālat al-ṣabbān fī ʿilm al-bayān* p. 372.— 6. *al-Qawl al-munjī*, glosses on the *Mawlid* | by al-Barzanjī (p. 503), C. 1305.— 638
7.–12. See Suppl. (7. See p. 446, 16, 4).

5. Ḥasan al-ʿIdwī al-Ḥamzāwī al-Mālikī was born in ʿIdwa in 1221/1806, studied at al-Azhar, and started teaching there in 1243/1828. He owned a country estate of more than 1000 *faddān*. Since his monthy salary was 1250 piasters, he could spend most of his private income on pious causes. He thus constructed a mosque in his hometown and another one in Cairo that was completed in 1290/1877, next to which he built a public bath and apartments, all of which he donated to the mosque. He died on 27 Ramaḍān 1303/30 June 1886.

Khit. jad. XIV, 371. *Tabṣirat al-ikhwān fī waḍʿ al-yad wa-mā yashhad lahu min al-burhān* Cairo [1]III, 157.—2. *Mashāriq al-anwār fī fawz ahl al-iʿtibār*, on eschatology, Būlāq 1275, C. 1277, 1280, 1297, 1300, 1303, 1307.—3. *al-Nafaḥāt al-nabawiyya fi 'l-faḍā'il al-ʿĀshūriyya* Būlāq 1272, C. 1276, 1278, 1297. |—4. *Kanz al-maṭālib* 487
fī faḍl al-bayt al-ḥarām wa-fi 'l-ḥajar wal-shādhrawān wa-mā fī ziyārat al-qabr al-sharīf min al-ma'ārib Cairo [1]III, 177, lith. C. 1282.—5. *al-Nafaḥāt al-Shādhiliyya Sharḥ al-Burda al-Būṣīriyya* I, 311.—6. *al-Madad al-fayyāḍ ʿalā matn al-Shifā' lil-Qāḍī ʿIyāḍ* (I, 455) lith. 2 vols., C. 1276.—7. *Bulūgh al-masarrāt ʿalā Dalā'il al-khayrāt* p. 328$_4$.—10. See Suppl.

B The Ḥanafīs

See Suppl. (Ad 1. see also ibid. 923, 88a).

C The Shāfiʿīs

1. Shihāb al-Dīn Aḥmad b. ʿAlī al-Dalajī wrote, in 1210/1795:

Kitāb al-falāka wal-maflūkīn, on the poor, who are to be counted among the *fuqarā'* and the Sufis, Berl. 3165.

1b. ʿAbd al-Majīd b. ʿAlī al-Ḥusaynī al-Santamīhī al-Shāfiʿī, who flourished at the end of the nineteenth century.

| *Fatḥ al-malik al-mājid fī faḍl binā' al-masājid* C. 1315, in the margin of *Maʿrifat* 639
mawāqīt al-ṣalāt bil-iqdām, see E. Galtier, *Bull. de l'Inst. franç. d'arch. or.* V, 13ff., Sarkis 1056.

2. Ibrāhīm b. Muḥammad al-Bājūrī al-Shāfiʿī, who was born in 1198/1783 in Bājūr, a village twelve hours from Cairo, began his studies at al-Azhar in

1212/1797. The following year he moved to Giza, away from the French occupation, and it was only after their withdrawal in 1216/1801 that he restarted his studies in the capital. His extremely productive literary career began as early as 1222/1817 with an epistle on the confession of faith (no. 1) addressed to his teacher al-Faḍḍālī (I, 641). Soon after he also started lecturing with great success at al-Azhar, while the last years of his life were spent working exclusively on Fakhr al-Dīn al-Rāzī's (I, 506) Qur'ān commentary. He passed away on 20 Dhu 'l-Qa'da 1276/9 June 1860.

Khit. jad. IX, 2, Kremer II, 322, *WZKM* VII, 52, 58. 1. *Risāla fī 'ilm al-tawḥīd* (see above) Cairo [1]II, 22, print. C. 1289 and others. 2. *Sharḥ Bānat Su'ād* Suppl. I, 69.—3. *Ḥāshiya 'alā Shamā'il al-Tirmidhī* I, 170.—4. *Ḥāshiya 'alā Sharḥ al-Burda* ibid. 310.—5. *Sharḥ al-Burda* C. 1282.—6. *Ḥāshiya 'ala 'l-Fatḥ al-qarīb* I, 492.—7. *Ḥāshiya 'alā Sharḥ al-Samarqandiyya* p. 247i.—8. *Sharḥ al-Durra al-bahiyya* p. 310.—9. *Ḥāshiya 'alā Sharḥ al-Sanūsiyya al-ṣughrā* p. 324,e.—10. *Ḥāshiya 'alā Sharḥ Jawharat al-tawḥīd* p. 412.—11. *Ḥāshiya 'alā Sharḥ al-Raḥbiyya* p. 418.—12. *Ḥāshiya 'alā Sharḥ al-Sullam* Suppl. p. 705.—13. *Ḥāshiya 'alā 'Aqā'id* (*Risālat*) *al-Faḍḍālī* (p. 641, n.p, Cat. Calcutta 90), C. 1296, 1301.—14.–22. See Suppl.—23. *al-Is'ād* see p. 659.

3. 'Abd al-Hādī Najā' al-Abyārī was born in 1236/1821, studied at al-Azhar, became the tutor of the children of Ismā'īl Pāshā, wrote about 40 works, and died in 1305/1887.

Khiṭ. jad. VIII, 29. 1. *Zakāt al-ṣiyām bi-irshād al-'awāmm* Cairo [1]III, 232, print. C. 1303, 1305.—2. *Bāb al-futūḥ bi-ma'rifat aḥwāl al-rūḥ* C. 1304.—3. *Nafḥat*
640 *al-akmām fī* | *muthallath al-kalām* lith. C. 1276 (see Suppl.).—4. *al-Wasā'il*
488 *al-adabiyya fi 'l-rasā'il al-Aḥdabiyya* | Cairo [1]IV, 342, [2]III, 432, print. C. 1301.—
5. *al-Najm al-thāqib fi 'l-muḥākama bayna 'l-Barjīs wal-Jawā'ib* (the Arabic-language newspapers of Paris and Istanbul), Cairo [1]III, 336.—6. *al-Mawākib al-'aliyya fī tawḍīḥ al-kawākib al-durriyya fi 'l-ḍawābiṭ al-'ilmiyya*, varia in *fiqh, adab, ḥadīth*, and astronomy, C. 1304/7.—7.–15. See Suppl. (12. Alex. Balāgha 5).

7 *Dogmatics*

1. Muḥammad b. Aḥmad b. Ḥasan al-Khālidī b. al-Jawharī al-Shāfi'ī was born in 1151/1739, made the pilgrimage with his father (p. 435) in 1168/1756, and then began his teaching career at the Ashrafiyya in Cairo. After his elder brother's death he was offered his position as a Qur'ān reciter at al-Azhar, but refused it. After a second pilgrimage he moved with his family to Mecca in 1187/1775,

but when unrest broke out under the emirs of Cairo, he returned to his native country in that year. When the French invaded the country his house and library were plundered, and he also lost all the money he had invested in various businesses. All this took a toll on his health, and he died in 1215/1800.

Jab. III, 164, 6 treatises Alex. Fun. 171,$_{5}$/$_{10}$. 1. *Marqa 'l-wuṣūl ilā maʿna 'l-uṣūl* Cairo ^{1}II, 264.—2. *Khulāṣat al-bayān fī kayfiyyat thubūt ṣiyām Ramaḍān* ibid. III, 225, Garr. 1861.—3. *Itḥāf uli 'l-albāb bi-sharḥ mā yataʿallaq bi-siyya min al-iʿrāb* Cairo ^{1}VII, 59, ^{2}II, 73.—4. *Sharḥ al-Manẓūma al-Jazāʾiriyya* p. 326.—5. *al-Qawl al-mushfī li-taḥqīq taʿrīf al-shukr al-ʿurfī*, on *shukr* as a notion, Berl. 7059$_{,2}$.—6. *Itḥāf al-rifāq bi-bayān aqsām al-ishtiqāq* Cairo ^{1}VII, 470, ^{2}II, 50.—7.–12. See Suppl. (8. Garr. 2178$_{,1}$; anon. 9. ibid. 2).—13.–18. See Suppl. III, 1309.

2. Muṣṭafā b. Aḥmad al-ʿUqbāwī studied and taught at al-Azhar, | and tried to 489
improve the religious education of the people by giving daily lectures. He died in 1221/1806.

| Jab. IV, 24. 1. *Risāla* or *ʿAqīda*, a profession of faith for ordinary people, com- 641
posed in 1217/1802, Berl. 2059, Cairo ^{1}VII, 324.—2. *Risāla fī dhāt Allāh*, based on the lectures of his teacher Muḥammad al-Amīr, Berl. 2357.

3. Muḥammad b. Muḥammad al-Faḍḍālī al-Shāfiʿī, who died in 1236/1821.

1. *Kifāyat al-ʿawāmm fī-mā yajib ʿalayhim min ʿilm al-kalām* Cairo ^{1}II, 39, on which glosses by his student al-Bājūrī (p. 639), C. 1301.—2. See Suppl.

4. ʿAlī b. Sālim al-Nafrāwī, the son of a professor in Cairo, was highly regarded by the Mamlūk ʿAlī Bek, but after the latter's downfall his house in Giza was destroyed. From then on he lived in miserable circumstances until his death in 1207/1793.

Jab. II, 249/50, *Khiṭ. jad* XVII, 9 (wrongly: d. 1277). *Risāla fi 'l-kalām ʿala 'l-basmala* Cairo ^{1}IV, 54.

8 *Mysticism*

1. ʿUthmān b. Ḥasan b. Aḥmad b. al-Shākir al-Khubuwwī, who died in 1224/1809.

Durrat al-nāṣiḥīn (*wāʿiẓīn*) Cairo ^{1}II, 155, print. Būlāq 1264, 1279, Istanbul 1267, among others.

4. Aḥmad b. Muṣṭafā Ḍiyāʾ al-Dīn al-Jümüshkhānī al-Naqshbandī al-Khālidī wrote, in 1276/1859:

1. *Jāmiʿ al-uṣūl fī ʾl-awliyāʾ wa-anwāʿihim wa-awṣāfihim wa-uṣūl kulli ṭarīq wa-muhimmāt al-murīd waṣṭilāḥihim wa-anwāʿ al-taṣawwuf wa-ghayr dhālik* Cairo [1]II, 77.—2.–8. See Suppl.

490 | 6. Muḥammad Ḥaqqī al-Nāzilī, from Güzelḥiṣār in Āydīn, died in 1301/1884.

1. *Khazīnat al-asrār jalīlat al-adhkār*, C. 1289, 1297, 1302, 1305.—2. A collection of 6 smaller treatises, C. 1299 (Cat. [1]VII, 458), see Suppl.

9 *Paraenesis*

1. Muḥammad b. Maʿdān Jād al-Mawlā al-Shāfiʿī al-Ḥājirī al-Asnawī, a student of al-Sharqāwī (p. 631), was admitted into | the Khalwatiyya order and preached in al-Azhar on Fridays. When the Nile would not rise in 1223/1808 he conducted a prayer for rain in al-Masjid al-ʿĀmm. He died at around 40 years of age in 1229/1814. 642

Jab. IV, 216. *Al-Kawākib al-zahriyya fī ʾl-khuṭab al-Azhariyya* Cairo [1]II, 169, see Suppl.

2. Muḥammad ʿUkkāsha al-Sharqāwī al-Shubrāwī wrote, in 1267/1850:

1. *al-Durra al-saniyya fī ʾl-adʿiya al-nabawiyya wal-ṣalawāt ʿalā khayr al-bariyya*, with a commentary, Cairo [1]II, 211.—2. See Suppl.

3. Ibrāhīm b. ʿAlī b. Ḥasan al-Shāfiʿī al-Saqqāʾ, who died in 1298/1880, see Suppl.

1. *Ghāyat al-umniyya fī ʾl-khuṭab al-minbariyya* C. 1281.—2.–6. See Suppl.

4. ʿAbd al-Majīd b. ʿAlī al-ʿIdwī al-Zaynabī was a guardian at the grave of Zaynab in Cairo who died in 1303/1885.

1. *al-Tuḥfa al-marḍiyya fī ʾl-akhbār al-Qudsiyya*, a collection of edifying tales, C. 1297, 1301, 1304, 1396, 1310.—2. See Suppl.

10 *Mathematics*

Maḥmūd Bāshā al-Falakī visited the polytechnic (Muhandiskhāne) that had been founded by Muḥammad ʿAlī and was then sent to Paris, where he attended the classes of Arago for a number of years. Back in Egypt he was commissioned to make a map of Egypt, and later became a minister of public works and then of education. He died on 30 November 1885.

Th. Neumann, *Das moderne Ägypten*, Leipzig 1893, p. 15, *Tarjamat Maḥmūd Bāshā* by Ismāʿīl Bey Muṣṭafā and Mukhtār Bey, Arabic and French, C. 1886 (special issue of *Bull. de la Soc. de géogr.*).
|| 1. *Natāʾij al-ifhām fī taqwīm al-ʿArab qabl al-islām wa-fī taḥqīq mawlid al-nabī* 643 491
wa-ʿumrihi, translated from the French (*JA*, s. V, vol. 11, 1858, 109/92) by Aḥmad Zekī Efendi (Suppl. III, 281), Būlāq 1305.—2. *Risāla fī ʾl-maqāyīs wal-makāyīl al-ʿamaliyya bil-diyār al-Miṣriyya*, from the French, Istanbul 1290.

11 *Travelogues and Geographies*

1. (2). Muḥammad b. ʿUmar b. Sulaymān al-Tūnisī, who died in 1274/1857, see Suppl.

Kremer II, 324; Jamāl al-Dīn al-Shayyāl, Dr. Perron, and Shaykhān M. ʿAyyād al-Ṭanṭāwī, *Farouk I University, Bull. Faculty of Arts* II (1944), 179–221.

2. Nakhla Ṣāliḥ died on 17 January 1899.

Al-Dalīl al-amīn lil-siyāḥa al-bahiyya fī ʾl-aqṭār al-muqaddasa al-Shāmiyya, on a trip from Cairo to Alexandria, then to Syria and back, in the year 1874, C. 1290.—2., 3. See Suppl.

3. Muḥammad Ṣādiq Bāshā was an Egyptian officer in the engineering corps who had led the Egyptian *miḥmal* to Mecca for a number of years. He published three works on his experiences during the pilgrimage:

1. *Mashʿal al-miḥmal*, 60 pages, C. 1298/1881.—2. *Kawkab al-ḥajj fī safar al-miḥmal baḥran wa-sayrihi barran*, with two blueprints and sketches of maps, Būlāq 1303, 1886.—3. *Dalīl al-ḥajj*, with maps, blueprints, and images, Būlāq 1313/1895.—4., 5. See Suppl.

5. Muḥammad Amīn al-Fikrī, who died in 1317/1899, see Suppl.

1. *Irshād al-alibbā' ilā maḥāsin Ūrūbā*, on the trip during which he accompanied his father to the oriental studies conference in Stockholm (p. 625), C. 1892.—2.–4. See Suppl. (4. Garr. 485).

12 *Encyclopaedias*

1. In gratitude for the special concern given to schooling by the Ottoman government under ʿAbd al-ʿAzīz, Luṭfīzāde Muḥammad Saʿd al-Dīn al-Ḥusaynī published in 1288/1870—initially for the schools in Rosetta—an encyclopaedia
492 on all scienfic subjects, entitled: |

644 | *Al-Riyāḍ al-miskiyya lil-makātib al-Rushdiyya* Berl. 98.

2. Muḥammad Raḥmī.

ʿAsharat al-funūn C. 1306.

Chapter 2. Syria

While, in Egypt, Arabic literature has continued uninterruptedly until the present day, in Syria it was almost extinct at the beginning of the nineteenth century. It was only in Damascus that the learned tradition succeeded in hanging on to a miserable existence. Around the middle of the century, Beirut took a leading role in the intellectual life of the Syrians, albeit under the influence of European education, rather than by itself. From Beirut, the American Mission, a Protestant organisation, was promoting its cause among the Christians. At the same time, it sought to resuscitate scholarship, notably in philology. Nāṣif al-Yāzijī rendered great services in this domain. But from 1869 onward, the Jesuits beat the Americans in competition, and their heavily subsidised printing mill contributed much more to the revival of ancient literature than the Americans had ever been able to. Their newspaper, *al-Bashīr*, and the monthly magazine *al-Mashriq* gained an influence that reached well beyond its intended readership, | and many capable young intellectuals swarmed out 493
from Beirut with the ideal of spreading European culture among their countrymen. However, as their home country was too small for most of them, they migrated to Egypt where they began a career in journalism. The Ottoman government for its part did next to nothing for the promotion and dissemination of Arabic literature, and the Madrasa Ḥamīdiyya that was opened in Tripoli in 1311/1893 produced just one *majmūʿa* | (Tripoli 1311), containing the speeches 645
held at the opening celebration, together with some other documents.

A. v. Kremer, *Mittelsyrien und Damaskus*, Vienna 1853, 135/51.
J. T. Reinaud, De l'état de la littérature chez les populations chrétiennes arabes de la Syrie, *JA*, s. v, vol. 9, 1857, 465/89.

1 *Poetry*

1. Aḥmad b. ʿAbd al-Laṭīf al-Barbīr al-Ḥasanī al-Bayrūtī was born in Damietta in 1160/1748 and died in Damascus in 1226/1811, see Suppl.

1. *Maqāmāt* Cairo ^{1}IV, 328, ^{2}III, 369.—2. *Badīʿiyya*, with a commentary by Muṣṭafā b. ʿAbd al-Wahhāb b. Saʿīd al-Ṣalāḥī and an imitation of the same, Berl. 7388.—3. On the transitory nature of the world, resignation to God's will in adversity, moments of death, etc., ibid. 2633.—4.–6. See Suppl.

2. Ṣāliḥ al-Ḥakawātī al-Shāmī, who died in 1254/1838.

1. *Qiṣṣa ʿala ʾl-rīḥ al-aṣfar wal-ṣalyān wa-Salīm Bāshā*, dated 1246–7/1830–1, a poem in 5 distiches, in colloquial Arabic, with the rhyme occurring in lines 1, 2, 3, and 5, Berl. 8181.—2. *Qiṣṣat al-thalj wal-khafs*, with the same form, dated 1248/1832, ibid. $8182_{,1}$.—3. *Qiṣṣat Jābir*, with the same form, a tale about a poor man of Medina and the miracles that Muḥammad worked on him, ibid. $_{2}$.—4. *Qiṣṣat ʿAlī b. ʿAlīm*, with the same form and edifying in character, ibid. $_{3}$.—5. An edifying story about a conversion, ibid. $_{4}$.—6. A tale in four verses in a single rhyme, on how a female camel is suddenly gifted with the power of speech and thus foils a murderous plot against a Jew, ibid. $_{5}$.

3. Maḥmūd b. Khalīl b. al-ʿAẓm al-Dimashqī, who died around 1285/1868 in Damascus.

1. *Dīwān* Cairo ^{1}IV, 253, ^{2}III, 148.—2. *Sharḥ al-Qaṣīda al-Lāmiyya lil-Maʿarrī* Suppl. I, 453, 1.

4. His son Rafīq Bey, who died in 1343/1925, see Suppl.

1. *al-Bayān fi ʾl-tamaddun wa-asbāb al-ʿumrān* C. 1304.—2.–8. See Suppl.

5. ʿUmar b. Muḥammad Dīb al-Unsī of Beirut, who died in 1293/1875, see Suppl.

Dīwān al-mawrid al-ʿadhb C. 1895 and others.

646 | 6. Fransīs b. Fatḥallāh al-Marrāsh al-Ḥalabī, who died in 1873, see Suppl.

494 | 1. *Mashhad al-aḥwāl* Beirut 1883, in rhymed prose and verse, with a clear European influence, see Hartmann, OLZ I, 239.—2.–7. See Suppl. (6. *Ghābat al-ḥaqq ma-mashhad al-aḥwāl etc.* Alexandria 1298). For his sister Maryāna see Suppl.

7. Abu ʾl-Ḥasan Qāsim al-Kastī al-Bayrūtī, who died in 1324/1906, see Suppl.

1. *al-Dīwān al-musammā Tarjumān al-afkār* Beirut 1299, see Hartmann, op. cit., 229.—2. *Dīwān al-marʾa al-gharība* ibid. 1279/1880.—3. See Suppl.

8. Examples of commemorative poetry written by Syrians are offered by:

a. *al-Mubakkiyāt wa-huwa Majmūʿ mā warada manthūran wa-manẓūman fī taʾbīn faqīd al-ʿilm wal-adab al-maghfūr al-marḥūm Yūḥannā ʿAnḥūrī al-mutawaffā fī* 13 *Ādhār sanat* 1890 *fī madīnat Bārīs*, Beirut 1890.

b. Sallūm Najīb, *Trauerqaṣīde auf den Tod Kaiser Wilhelms I. in transscr. Urtext hsg. und übers. v.* C. Lang, Berlin 1888.

2 Philology

1. Nāṣif al-Yāzijī was born on 25 March 1800 in Kafrshīma in Lebanon, two hours from Beirut. He started working as a secretary for the prince of Lebanon, Emir Bashīr, but when the latter was banished to Malta he went to Beirut to live by his pen, and also worked for the Americans as a teacher of Arabic. In March 1869 he became paralysed on the left side and died on 5 February 1871; see Suppl.

Saʿd Mīkhāʾīl, *Adab al-ʿaṣr* 274/7, v. Kremer, ZDMG XXV, 244/7.

| 2. His son Ibrāhīm, who died on 28 December 1906, see Suppl. 495

3. Buṭrus al-Bustānī was born in 1819 in Dibbiyya | in Lebanon and studied at 647 the Maronite seminary in ʿAyn Warqa. When he was twenty years old he joined the American Mission in Beirut, converted to Protestantism, and became an interpreter at the American consulate. Later he opened a high-school for boys in this same city. In 1870 he founded the newspaper *al-Janna*, a smaller magazine, *al-Junayna*, that only lasted for two years, and finally, the bi-weekly *al-Jinān*. His large dictionary, while dated today, was in its own time a great step forward in Arabic philology. His rather superficial encyclopaedia aimed at spreading European education among his fellow countrymen. He died on 1 May 1883.

M. Hartmann, *Or. Litbl.* III, 226 n. 1. *al-Maṭālib li-muʿallim al-ṭālib*, on grammar, Beirut n.d.—2. *Muḥīṭ al-muḥīṭ*, a lexicon, ibid. 1867/9.—3. *Qaṭr al-muḥīṭ*, an abstract of the former, ibid. 1869.—4. *Dāʾirat al-maʿārif*, an encyclopaedia, Beirut 1876ff; from vol. 7 onwards continued by his brother Najīb, his son Salīm, and his cousin Sulaymān (III, 348), cf. ZDMG 1877, 118ff; 1878, 54; 1879, 142, Fleischer ibid. 34, 579, M. Hartmann, *Or. Litbl.* I, 224.—5.-14. See Suppl. (excise 14. by Fuʾād Afrām al-Bustānī, Suppl. III, 389).—15. *Khuṭba fī adab al-ʿArab*, Beirut n.d. (Alex. Adab 39).

4. Iskandar Āghā b. Yaʿqūb Abkarius, who was of Armenian origin, died in 1303/1885; see Suppl.

1. *Nihāyat al-arab fī akhbār al-ʿArab*, on pre-Islamic poets and princes, Marseille 1852.—2. *Tazyīn Nihāyat al-Arab*, second improved edition Beirut 1867.—3. *Rawḍat al-adab fī ṭabaqāt shuʿarāʾ al-ʿArab* ibid. 1858. |—4. *Nawādir al-zamān* 496

fī waqā'iʿ Jabal Lubnān Cairo v, [1]171, [2]398.—5. English-Arabic Dictionary, third edition Beirut 1892.—6.–10. See Suppl.

3 *Historiography*

1. Niqula b. Yūsuf al-Turk, who died in 1828, see Suppl.

1. *Tamalluk jumhūr al-Fransāwiyya etc.* see Suppl., additionally Berl. Ms. or. oct. 3977, Ẓah. [3]320.—*Ḥawādith al-zamān fī jabal Lubnān* Ẓah. [2]143.

648 | 3. Ḥaydar al-Shihābī was born around 1760 and died in 1835, see Suppl.

1. *al-Ghurar al-ḥisān etc.* Garr. 624, C. 1900, Beirut 1933.

2a. Raslān b. Yaḥyā al-Qārī al-Shājūrī wrote, in 1254/1838:

Safīna, from which *Wuzarā' Dinasha min sanat 922*, Ẓah. [2]143.

6. Khalīl b. Khaṭṭār Sarkīs was born in Abey and died in 1915, see Suppl.

6a. Al-Khūrī Ḥanāniyyā al-Munayyir.

Al-Durr al-marṣūf fī ḥawādith Jabal al-Shūf, from the downfall of the Banū Maʿn until the rise of the Shihāb 1109–1222/1697–1808, Garr. 626a.

9. Ilyās b. ʿAbduh al-Qudsī, who died in 1928, see Suppl.

RAAD VI, 370/2, Lecerf, *Renaissance* 168.

1. See Suppl.—2. *Nawādir fukāhāt*, the Fables of Lafontaine, Damascus 1913.

13. Al-Khūrī Mīkḥā'īl wrote:

Ta'rīkh al-Shām, for the years 1720/82, *Wathā'iq ta'rīkhiyya*, no. 2, Harbasa 1930, continued by Mīkhā'īl al-Dimashqī, *Ta'rīkh ḥawādith al-Shām wa-Lubnān* 1197–1257/1782–1841, ed. L. Cheikho, Beirut 1912.

4 *Islamic Theology and Mysticism*

3. Muḥammad Amīn b. ʿUmar b. ʿAbd al-ʿAzīz b. ʿĀbidīn, who died in 1252/1836, see Suppl.

38. *Tanbīh dhawi 'l-afhām 'alā aḥkām al-tablīgh khalf al-imām* Patna I, 83,$_{835}$.—39. *Muntakhab al-khalq* Suppl. II, 266.

3a. 'Abd al-Fattāḥ b. Muḥammad b. 'Abdallāh b. 'Abd al-Raḥīm al-Jīlī al-Khaṭīb al-Ḥusaynī bi-Dimashq wrote, in 1293/1876:

Shurūq al-anwār fi 'l-mawlid al-mukhtār Ẓāh. ^{2}32.

9a. Muḥammad Abu 'l-Fatḥ b. 'Abd al-Qādir b. Ṣāliḥ b. 'Abd al-Raḥīm al-Khaṭīb fī Dimashq al-Shām died after 1305/1887.

| *Mi'rāj sayyid al-kā'ināt fī ṣu'ūdihi ilā rabb al-samāwāt* Ẓāh. ^{2}38. 649

497 | Chapter 3. Mesopotamia and Iraq

(see Suppl.)

| Chapter 4. Mecca (North Arabia) 498

Up to the present day, the Holy City of Islam has remained completely free of the European influence that is felt everywhere else. As such, even in the nineteenth century Islamic literature in its purest form was still flourishing there. As a place of education, the Ḥaram attracted numerous foreigners, especially Malays, | meaning Mecca offered ample opportunities to energetic teachers. As 499
before, theology was at the heart of the educational enterprise; as far as non-religious literature was concerned, historiography at least found one important representative.

C. Snouck Hurgronje, *Mekka* II, The Hague 1889, p. 200/94

1. Yūsuf al-Baṭṭāḥ al-Makkī wrote, in 1244/1828:

Irshād al-anām ilā sharḥ Fayḍ al-malik al-ʿallām li-ma'shtamala ʿalayhi 'l-nusk min al-aḥkām C. 1299 (Cat. III, 191).

2. Aḥmad b. Zaynī b. Aḥmad Daḥlān was born in Mecca and was, after 1871, *muftī* of the Shāfiʿīs and Shaykh al-ʿUlamāʾ in that place. When, after a dispute with the Turkish governor ʿUthmān Pāshā, Grand Sharif ʿAwn al-Rafīq retired to Medina in 1886 to await the decision by the sultan, Daḥlān accompanied him there. He died there soon after his arrival, in Muḥarram 1304/October 1886. Towards the end of his life he wrote textbooks and commentaries on theology, as well as the history of his hometown as he had witnessed it.

| C. Snouck Hurgronje, Een Rector der Mekkaansche Universiteit, *Bijdr. t. d.* 650
Taal-, Land- en Volkenkunde van Nederl.-Indië 5e Volgr. II, 344/405, *Verspreide Geschriften* III, 67/122 (with two samples taken from 18). 1.-3. See Suppl.—4. *Ḥāshiya ʿalā sharḥ al-Samarqandiyya* p. 248.—5. See Suppl.—6. Four treatises on prayer, C. 1297.—7. A handbook of dogmatics, C. 1298. |—9. *Fatḥ al-jawād* 500
etc. see Suppl., Cairo [1]I, 52.—10. *Tanbīh al-ghāfilīn mukhtaṣar Minhāj al-ʿābidīn lil-Ghazzālī* (I, 542_{38}), C. 1298.—11. *Risāla fī radd Risālat Sulaymān Efendi*, against a Meccan mystic with a large following in the East Indies (Snouck Hurgronje, *Mekka* II, 241f.), Mecca 1302.—12. *al-Durar al-saniyya etc.* see Suppl., C. 1299.—13. *Risālat al-naṣr fī dhikr waqt ṣalāt al-ʿaṣr* (Snouck II, 294) ibid. 1299.—14. *Taqrīb al-uṣūl li-tashīl al-wuṣūl ila 'l-rabb wal-rasūl* ibid. 1304.—15. *al-Sīra al-nabawiyya etc.* see Suppl., C. 1288, 1310 (with no. 16 in the margin).—16. *al-Fatḥ al-mubīn fī faḍāʾil al-khulafāʾ al-rāshidīn wa-ahl al-bayt al-ṭāhirīn* ibid. 1300, 1310.—17. *Asna 'l-maṭālib fī najāt Abī Ṭālib*, on whether the

father of ʿAlī died as an unbeliever, against Ḥasaballāh (no. 6), ibid. 1305.—18. *Khulāṣat al-kalām fī bayān umarāʾ al-balad al-ḥarām min zamān al-nabī ʿam ilā waqtinā hādhā bil-tamām*, an abstract of the chronicle by al-Sinjārī (p. 508) with a continuation until 1884 (Snouck, *Mecca* I, p. XVI), C. 1305, Mecca 1311 (in the margin of 19).—19. *al-Futūḥāt al-islāmiyya baʿd muḍiyy al-futūḥāt al-nabawiyya*, Mecca 1302/3, 1311 (Snouck, op. cit., 354ff.).—20. *al-Jadāwil al-marḍiyya fī taʾrīkh al-duwal al-islāmiyya* C. 1306.—21.–22. See Suppl.

3b. His student and assistant in his activities as a teacher and *muftī* (*muqriʾ* and *amīn al-fatwā*) Muḥammad Saʿīd b. Muḥammad Bābaṣīl, from Hadramawt, wrote:

1. *al-Qawl al-mujdī fi ʾl-radd ʿalā ʿAbdallāh b. ʿAbd al-Raḥmān al-Sindī* (against a Wahhābī theologian), lith. Batavia 1309, see Goldziher, *Die Ẓāhiriten* p. 190, Snouck II, 255.—2.–5. See Suppl.

4. Sayyid Bakrī Abū Bakr ʿUthmān b. Muḥammad Shaṭṭāʾ, whose father had moved from Damietta to Mecca, published the notes of a lecture course that he had given for a number of years:

1. *Iʿānat al-ṭālibīn*, glosses on Zayn al-Dīn al-Malībārī's commentary the *Fatḥ al-muʿīn* on his own *Qurrat al-ʿayn* (p. 549), 4 vols., C. 1300/1883, 1330.—2.–6. See Suppl.

651 | 4c. Sālim b. ʿAbdallāh b. Saʿīd Samīr al-Khuḍrī, see Suppl.

1. *Safīnat al-najāʾ etc.* additionally Berl. Ms. or. oct. 4042/3.

5. Muḥammad al-Ḥaqqī wrote:

Sitt rasāʾil C. 1299, in which he warns against the rise of modern, unlawful customs and the infiltration of the products of modern culture, Snouck II, 219.

6. Muḥammad b. Sulaymān Ḥasaballāh, the son of a Copt, campaiged against the use of tobacco and claimed that the parents and uncle of the Prophet had died as unbelievers, against which Daḥlān wrote his no. 17. The discontented
501 Daḥlān succeeded | in getting him banished from Arabia for half a year, after which he was allowed to continue his teaching.

Snouck II, 238. 1. *al-Riyāḍ al-badīʿa fī uṣūl al-dīn wa-baʿḍ furūʿ al-sharīʿa*, with the commentary *al-Thimār al-yāniʿa*, by Muḥammad al-Nawāwī (no. 7), C. 1301 and others.—2. *Sharḥ Manāsik al-Shirbīnī* p. 417.

7. Muḥammad b. ʿUmar b. ʿArabī al-Nawawī al-Jāwī al-Bantanī was born in Tanara (Banten), the son of a village judge (*pangalu*). He studied under his father, then in Banten and in Purwakarta, in Krawang. Together with his brothers, he made the pilgrimage at a young age and stayed for three years in Mecca. After a brief return to his native country he settled permanently in Mecca in 1855, where he attended the lectures of the city's famous teachers, later working as a teacher himself. From 1870 he limited his classes to mid-mornings so as to have time for his own literary activities. He had a decisive influence on his compatriots, the Sundanese and the Malays, and contributed in no small way to the promotion of piety and learned activity among them. He died after 1888.

| Snouck II, 362ff. 1.–3. See Suppl.—4. *Fatḥ al-majīd Sharḥ al-Durr al-farīd* (by his teacher al-Naḥrāwī) C. 1300.—5.–7. See Suppl.—8. *Targhīb al-mushtāqīn*, a commentary on the *Mawlid* of al-Barzanjī (p. 503), Būlāq 1292.—9.–16. See Suppl.—17. *Sharḥ Bidāyat al-hidāya* (I, 540,$_{26}$) C. 1298, 1308, Būlāq 1309.—18. *Sharḥ Qaṣīdat Zayn al-Dīn al-Malībārī* p. 287.—19.–40. See Suppl. 652

502 | Chapter 5. South Arabia

In the nineteenth century there was no scholarly activity to speak of in the Yemen or in Hadramawt, and though there were men who tried to continue the oral tradition, literary production had no importance whatsoever.

1. ʿAbd al-Raḥmān b. Sulaymān al-Ahdal, who died in 1250/1835, see Suppl. III, 1311.

2. ʿAbd al-Raḥmān b. Muḥammad b. al-Ḥusayn b. ʿUmar Bā ʿAlawī, who was *muftī al-diyār al-Ḥaḍramiyya*, was active as an author in 1251/1836, see Suppl.

3. Ibn Jīʿān, who died in 1256/1841.

Seven Zaydī treatises, Br. Mus. Suppl. 1223.

4. Muḥammad b. Ismāʿīl b. Muḥammad b. Yaḥyā al-Ḥasanī al-Yamanī al-Kibsī, who died in 1307/1890, see Suppl.

1. *al-Laṭāʾif al-saniyya fī akhbār al-mamālik al-Yamaniyya*, composed in 1293/1876, contains a history of Yemen from the beginning of Islam until the time of the author and was written entirely from memory in a short period of time, meaning his information often deviates from that of others, Berl. 9746.—2., 3. See Suppl.

5. ʿAbd al-Qādir b. Muḥammad b. ʿAbd al-Raḥmān al-Naqshbandī, who lived in Aden in 1890.

Al-Nahr al-fāʾiḍ fī ʿilm al-farāʾiḍ Bombay 1304. *Der überfliessende Strom der Wissenschaften des Erbrechts der Ḥanefiten und Schafeiten, ar. Text v. Scheech ʿA. M. übers. u. erläutert v.* L. Hirsch, Leipzig 1891.

23. Abū ʿAbdallāh Ḥumaydān b. Yaḥyā b. Ḥumaydān al-Qāsimī al-Zaydī, date unknown, see Suppl.

653 | 1. Additionally Patna II, $352_{,2539,9}$.—3. Ibid. $_{8}$.—5. Ibid. 351, $3529_{,3}$.—6. Ibid. $_{2}$.—7. Ibid.$_{1}$ (which has *Ḥikāya ʿani ʾl-aqwāl etc.*).—9. *al-Masāʾil al-shatawiyya wal-shubah al-Ḥashwiyya* ibid. $353_{,2539,10}$.—10. *al-Muntazaʿ al-awwal min aqwāl al-aʾimma* ibid. $_{4}$.—11. *al-Muntazaʿ al-thānī* ibid. $_{5}$.—12. *Risāla fī ḥadīth al-siṭl wal-mindīl* ibid. $_{11}$.—13. *Risāla fī ithbāt al-īmān* ibid. 12.

26. In 1281/1864, an unidentified Ismaʿīlī author answered 179 questions by various unnamed individuals regarding various points of the esoteric doctrines of the Ismaʿīlīs, in no systematic order, in:

Masāʾil majmūʿa min al-ḥaqāʾiq al-ʿāliya wal-daqāʾiq wal-asrār al-sāmiya allatī lā yajūzu ʾl-iṭṭilāʿ ʿalayhā illā bi-idhni man lahu ʾl-ʿaqd wal-ḥall ed. R. Strothmann, *Gnosis-Texte der Ismailiten* (Abh. d. Ak. d. Wiss. Göttingen III, 26, 1943, 5/136).

503 ## Chapter 6. Oman

6. Abū Sulaymān Muḥammad b. ʿĀmir b. Rashīd al-Maʿwalī wrote, after 1154/1742:

A Chronicle of Oman; for manuscripts in Zanzibar, see M. Guillain, *Documents sur l'histoire, la géographie et le commerce de l'Afrique orientale,* I, Paris 1856, 473ff., Hedwig Klein (see Suppl. III, 1297, ad 569), 23.

Chapter 7. Persia

See Suppl.

Chapter 8. Afghanistan

See Suppl.

Chapter 9. India

In the nineteenth century, Islam in India was constantly forced into competition with Christianity and local religions while continuing to receive new impulses by continuing contacts with Mecca. As such, the Indian printing houses came to play a significant role in the dissemination of older works, especially collections of *ḥadīth*. Here, too, | theology was at the centre of liter- 654
ary activity. See Suppl.

504 | **Chapter 11. Istanbul**

See Suppl.

Chapter 12. Russia

See Suppl.

506 | Chapter 13. The Maghreb

See Suppl.

508 | 6a. Idrīs b. ʿAbdallāh al-Wadghīrī wrote, in 1231/1816:

Al-Tawḍīḥ wal-bayān fī maqraʾ Nāfiʿ lith. Fez n.d.

18. Muḥammad Abū Ra's b. Aḥmad b. ʿAbd al-Qādir al-Nāṣirī was born on 11 Ṣafar 1165/27 December 1751 in the mountains between Kirsūt and Hūnet. He spent his youth in great poverty in the region of Fehāja, and then went to study in Mascara, Qaytāna (Getna), and Mazūna, surviving as a beggar. He then lived for a number of years with Shaykh ʿAbd al-Qādir b. ʿAbdallāh al-Masharfī in Getna. After a brief career as a *qāḍī* in Wadi Ayzam he returned to Mascara where he became active as a teacher. In 1204/1790 he made the pilgrimage, staying for a while in Cairo on the way. In Shawwāl 1205/June 1791 he took part in the campaign against the Spanish in Oran. After the capture of this city he was appointed a *muftī, qāḍī*, and preacher in Mascara, but was deposed in 1211/1797. In 1214/1800 he travelled to Algiers where he had previously stayed for some time, before he had gone on the pilgrimage. In 1216/1802 he was in Fez, where he was allowed to present his commentary on al-Ḥarīrī to the sultan. An uprising by the Derqāwa sect that had started in Ṣafar 1220/May 1805 kept him from studying for a time. In 1226/1811 he made the pilgrimage for a second time, and while in Mecca he became acquainted with Wahhābī doctrine. On his return
655 he also visited | Jerusalem. He died on Tuesday 15 Shaʿbān 1238/8 May 1823. His writing was extraordinarily productive, and at the end of his autobiography he lists 63 works and compares himself with al-Suyūṭī. Apart from this, another 20 works by him are known as well.

509 | Al-Ḥafnāwī, *Taʿrīf al-khalaf* II 332/3. 1. *Fatḥ al-ilāh wa-minnatuhu fī 'l-taḥadduth bi-faḍl rabbī wa-niʿmatihi*, his autobiography, see G. Faure-Biguet, *JA* s. IX, vol. 14. 304ff., 388ff.—2. *ʿAjāʾib* (*Gharāʾib*) *al-asfār wa-laṭāʾif al-akhbār*, a commentary on his *qaṣīda* on the capture of Oran, *Nafīsat al-jumān*, Paris 4618, Algiers 1632/3, *Bull. de Corr. Afr.* 1884, p. 375, no. 57, translation by Arnaud, *Revue Afr.* 1878, no. 132ff.—3. *al-Qaṣaṣ al-mughrib ʿani 'l-khabar al-muʿrib ʿammā waqaʿa bil-Andalus wa-thughūr al-Maghrib*, a commentary on the poem of nr. 6, mostly on Spanish history, Paris 4619 according Paure Biguet, *JA* s. IX vol. 14 (1899), p. 311.—4. *al-Iṣāba fī man ghaza 'l-Maghrib min al-ṣaḥāba, Bull. de Corr. Afr.* 1885, p. 165, from which *Description et histoire de l'île de Djerba, par Exiga*

dit Kayser, Tunis 1884.—5. *Sharḥ al-Maqāmāt al-Ḥarīriyya* I, 327, 11.—6. See Suppl. Paris 4619.

19. ʿAlī b. Muḥammad al-Mīlī al-Jamālī al-Maghribī al-Mālikī, who died in 1248/1833.

1. *al-Kawākib al-durriyya wal-anwār al-shamsiyya fī ithbāt al-ṣifāt al-saniyya al-qāʾima bil-dhāt al-azaliyya* Cairo [1]II, 39, [2]VI, 204.—2.-8. See Suppl.—9. See Suppl. III, 1313.

39. ʿAbd al-Qādir b. Muḥyi ʾl-Dīn was born in 1222/1807 in Qaytana near Muʿaskar (Mascara). He made the pilgrimage as a child and again in 1828. When his country descended into anarchy after the invasion of the French, he succeeded in uniting the tribes of Hāshim and ʿĀmir under his leadership—as *amīr al-muʾminīn*—and to fill them with enthusiasm for the jihad against the invaders. After 15 years of war with mixed results, he was forced to surrender to the French on the banks of the Moulouya river on 23 December 1847. In spite of promises to allow him to make the pilgrimage he was shipped to Toulon and detained in Amboise. On 2 December 1852, Napoleon III | gave him his 656
freedom again and he settled in Bursa, and after the earthquake of 1855 he moved to Istanbul and later to Damascus. When the Christians were massacred in large numbers there in 1860, he looked after many of the victims. In 1863 he made the pilgrimage again, visited the *Exposition universelle* in Paris in 1867, attended the opening of the Suez canal, and died in Damascus on 19 Rajab 1300/27 May 1883.

Nouv. biogr. gén. I, 67/82, Vapereau, *Dict. univ. des contemporains*, Paris 1880, 3ff., Brockelmann, *Gesch. d. isl. Völker*, 359ff., E. Pröbster, *WI* 22, 132/48.
1. *Dhikr al-ʿāqil wa-tanbīh al-ghāfil*, G. Dugat, *Reflexions de l'intelligent et avis à l'indifferent*, Paris 1858.—2. A poem on the pilgrimage, *ZDMG* XVIII, 615, XIX, 314.—3. *Wishāḥ al-katāʾib. Réglements militaires, texte ar. avec trad. et notes par* F. Patorni, | Algiers 1890, translation by Rosetty in *Spectateur militaire* v. 15. 510
2. 1844.

59. ʿAbdallāh b. Riḍwān

Étude sur le soufisme, texte ar. et trad. franç. par Arnaud, Algiers 1889.

Chapter 14. The Sudan

1. ʿUthmān Danfodiu (b. Fūdyū) b. Muḥammad b. ʿUthmān al-Turūdī, a member of the Fūl tribe and founder of the kingdom of Sokoto, died in 1817.

511 | T.W. Arnold, *The Preaching of Islam* 265ff. *Nūr al-albāb*, against widespread superstition in the Sudan, ed. and transl. Ismāʿīl Hamet in *Revue Afr.* 41st year no. 227, 4th trim. 1897, p. 297, 42nd year no. 228, 1st trim. 1898, p. 58.

11a. Ḥājj Saʿīd, reader to Sultan Alyu of Sokoto, the third successor of ʿUthmān, wrote, in 1855:

Taʾrīkh Sokoto, ed. O. Houdas and E. Benoist in *Publ. de l'École d. lang. or. viv.* IV, 19, 8. 189/220, cf. J. Lippert, MSOS *Afr. St.* III, 229/43.

| Addenda & Corrigenda 657

Volume I

I, 5 Escur.[2] *Les Manuscrits arabes de l'Escurial décrits d'après les notes de H. Derenbourg, revues, mises à jour et complétées par le Dr.* Renaud, II, 2 *Médecine et histoire naturelle,* Paris 1939; II, 3 *Sciences exactes et sciences occultes.* ibid. 1939 (II, 3 not seen).

Halle DMG: H. Wehr, *Verzeichnis der arabischen Handschriften in der Bibliothek der Deutschen Morgenländischen Gesellschaft,* Abh. für die Kunde des Morgenlands XXV, Leipzig 1940.

India Off. II, *Sufism and Ethics* by A.J. Arberry, 1936; idem. Handlist of Islamic Manuscripts acquired by the India Office Library 1936/8, *JRAS* 1939, 353/96.

Löwen: H. Heffening, Die islamischen Handschriften der Universitätsbibliothek Löwen (Fonds Lefort série B and C) mit einer besonderen Würdigung der Mudauwanahdschr. des iv. v. x. xi Jahrhs. *Le Muséon* 50, 85/100.

I, 6 Paris: Inventaire de la collection de manuscrits musulmans de M. Decourdemanche, *JA* 1916.

Philadelphia: *Oriental Manuscripts of the John Fr. Lewis Collection of the Free Library of Philadelphia by* M.A. Simsar. Philadelphia 1937.

Princ. Garr.: *Descriptive Catalog of the Garrett Collection of Arabic Manuscripts in the Princeton University Library by* Philip K. Hitti, Nabih Amin Faris, Butrus Abd-al-Malik, Princeton 1938.

Sarajevo: Fehim Spaho, *Arapski Perzijski i Turski rukopisi hravatskih zemaljskih Muzeja i Sarajevu,* 1942.

Istanbul: Max Krause, *Stambuler Handschriften islamischer Mathematiker,* Quellen und Studien zur Geschichte der Mathematik, Astronomie und Physik, Abt. B. Heft 4, Berlin 1936.

Max Weisweiler, *Istanbuler Handschriftenstudien zur | arabischen Traditions-* 658
literatur, Bibliotheca Islamica 10, Leipzig 1937.

Ẓāh.[2] *Fihris makhṭūṭāt Dār al-kutub al-Ẓāhiriyya: al-Ta'rīkh wa-mulḥaqātuhu, waḍaʿahu Yūsuf al-ʿIsh*, Maṭbaʿat Dimashq 1366/1947 (Maṭbūʿāt al-Majmaʿ al-ʿilmī al-ʿArabī bi-Dimashq).

6, 2 J.M. Abd-el-Jalil, *Brève histoire de la littérature arabe*, Paris 1943.

12. 1 *Taraphae Muallakah cum scholiis Nahs e mss. Leid. ar. ed. vertit explanavit.* J.J. Reiske, Leiden 1742.

Muʿallaqāt AS 4095 dated 545, after a manuscript dating from the year 499, *riwāyat* Aḥmad b. ʿAlī b. al-Sammān.

2a (see Suppl.) Köpr. 1394, Rescher, *MSOS* 1911, 178, mixed, from the *Mufaḍḍaliyyāt* and *Aṣmaʿiyyāt* (Ritter), commentary by al-Anbārī in AS 4099,12.

3. *al-Jamhara* (see Suppl.), Garr. 12, Köpr. 1232 (Rescher, *MSOS* 1912, 7), Āṣaf. I, 1240, 3, Aligarh 126, 1, see D.B. Macdonald, *Proc. AOS*, Dec. 1894, CLXXV–CCXCL. New impression C. 1345/1925.

4. *Ḥamāsa* of Abū Tammām (see Suppl.), commentary by al-Tabrīzī manuscript dated 507 Ind. Off. 4631, *JRAS* 1939, 395, ʿĀšir I, 825/6/7, Ẓāh. Ad. 14, 15 (Plessner, *Islca* IV, 542/3), Patna I, 200,1791.

Page 13, chapter 7: al-Baṭalyūsī, d. ca. 494/1101 (p. 377), Faiẕ. 940.

1. *Sharḥ Dīwān al-Nābigha* by al-Tabrīzī, Faiẕ. 1662,3.

15. 5. *Dīwān ʿAlqama*, C. 1935.

6. *Zaʿāmat al-shiʿr al-jāhilī bayna'Mri'i 'l-Qays wa-ʿAdī b. Zayd li-*ʿAbd al-Mutaʿāl al-Ṣaʿīdī, C. 1934.

16. Line 2, Amīna read: Umayma *Agh.* [2]18, 209, 17. His sister Āmina was the mother of ʿAdī b. Nawfal b. Asad b. ʿAbd al-ʿUzzā, who converted to Islam in the year 8 and whom ʿUmar (or ʿUthmān) appointed governor of Hadramawt, *Agh.* 13, [1]135, [2]129.—*Qaṣīda qāfiyya* Faiẕ. 1662.

2. *Lāmiyyat al-ʿArab* Faiẕ. 1662,4. Commentary 8 (see Suppl.) by Muḥammad b. al-Ḥusayn b. Läjük, autograph dated 686/1288, AS 4145.

| 17. 4. *Dīwān Quṭba* AS 3881. 659

5. A. Fischer, Ein angeblicher Vers des ʿAbīd b. al-Abraṣ, *Mél. Maspéro* III, Cairo 1935, 361/75.

29. D. Künstlinger, *Przeklad i objasnienie 53. sury Qurʾāna, Sourate 53 du Coran, trad. et comt. polonais avec résumé allemand,* Prace Komis. Orj. no. 8, Warsaw 1926.—D. Pesle and A. Tidjani, *Le Qoran* transl. Paris and Rabat 1937.—R. Bell, *The Quran, translated with a critical rearrangement of the Surahs* I, Edinburgh 1937.—*Qurʾān, der Koran ar. u. deutsche Übersetzung mit Erklärung von Maulana Sadruddin,* Berlin, Verlag d. Muslim. Revue 1939.—R. Blachère, *Introduction au Coran* (*Islam d'hier et d'aujourd'hui, Collection publ. par E. Lévi-Provençal,* vol. 3), Paris 1947.—*Le Coran, trad. nouvelle,* ibid. no. 4, 5 excursus ibid. 6.

33. Jābīzāde ʿAlī Fahmī, *Ḥusn al-ṣaḥāba fī sharḥ ashʿār al-ṣaḥāba,* I (Alif-Dāl) Istanbul 1324.—Commentaries 4. Turkish translation by ʿAbdī AS 4087.—6. *Kunh al-murād,* following Garr. 7 (Suppl. no. 12), by ʿAbd al-ʿAzīz b. ʿAlī al-Zamzamī, d. 976/1568 (II, 496).—29. Persian commentary composed in 863/1459, AS 4094.—30. *al-Isʿād* by al-Bājūrī, Qawala II, 186.

36. Line 7, *Dīwān* copied by Yāqūt al-Mustaʿṣimī, AS 3881.—Line 22, *Dīwān* with a commentary, library of Ismāʿīl Ṣāʾib Efendi in Ankara (Dil Fakültesi).

39. ʿAlī b. Abī Ṭālib, *Sad Kalima or Centiloquium with the metrical paraphrase of Rashīd al-Dīn Waṭwāṭ, ed. and transl. by* A.H. Harley, Or. Publ. Inst. Calcutta Muslim Inst. 1927.—*Ṣad Kalimah* with a Turkish translation by Jāmī, Istanbul 1286.—*Ghurar al-ḥikam* (see Suppl.) AS 4151/2, Dāmād Ibr. 947.—*Sharḥ Ṣad Kalimah* by Jamālī Khalwatī AS 4070.—*ʿUyūn al-ḥikam wal-mawāʿiẓ* Teh. Sip. I, 283/6.—*Tuḥfat al-ṣadīq ila ʾl-ṣadīq min kalām amīr al-muʾminīn Abī Bakr al-Ṣiddīq wa-Faṣl al-khiṭāb min kalām al-Khaṭṭāb wa-Uns al-lahfān min kalām amīr al-muʾminīn ʿUthmān b. ʿAffān,* Persian translation by Rashīd al-Dīn Waṭwāṭ, Welīeddīn 2939.

44. Line 4, *Nuzhat al-musāmir fī akhbār Majnūn Banī ʿĀmir* Top Qapu Sarāi 2473.—Kračkovskij, Rannyaya Istoriya povesti o Medžnūne i Leyle v arabskoi literature, in Ali Šir | Navoi, *Sbornik Statei pod red. A.K. Borovkova,* Moscow- 660
Leningrad 1946, 31–67.

58. 4. Sawwār read: Ṣiwār.

61. 20. F. Gabrieli, *RSO* XV, 1934, 26/64, *Dīwān*, *RAAD* XV, 34/58, Khalīl Mardam Bek, *Walīd b. Yazīd*, ibid. 1/33, special issue of *Maṭbūʿāt al-Majmaʿ al-ʿilmī al-ʿArabī* no. 9, Damascus n.d. (1937).

76. 5. The recension of al-Ṣūlī, Mosul 172,$_7$ (following a communication to Ritter by the librarian).

77. 10 (see Suppl.) *Shuʿarāʾ al-Baṣra* quoted by Tabrīzī ad *Ḥamāsa* 465.

78. No. 12 *al-Urjūza al-muzdawija* is cited in Masʿūdī, *Murūj* (C.) I, 42, 6.

79. No. 14 Dawlatshāh *Tadhkira* 23/4.

80. Line 20, *Dīwān* of ʿAbdallāh b. al-Muʿtazz, part IV ed. B. Lewin, *Bibl. Isl.* 17d, 1945.

84. Below: *Dīwān*, manuscript dated 587, Bursa Ḥu. Čelebī, Adab 6.

85. Line 2, the commentary by al-Tabrīzī, Šehīd ʿA. Pāshā 2131, Bursa Kharāğğīzāde Edebiyyāt 91.

No. 4. *Dīwān* Bāyazīd 2592.

87. *Dīwān*, recension by Ibn Jinnī, AS 3966. O. Rescher, *Beiträge zur arab. Poesie, III. Der Dīwān des Motenebbi nach der Ausgabe Okbari, Būlāq 1287 mit Vergleichung der Ed. Jazydjy (Beyrouth) und Wāḥidī (Berlin) I (Qāfiya, Alif bis Rāʾ)* Stuttgart 1940.—ʿAbd al-Wahhāb, *Dhikrā Abi ʾl-Ṭayyib baʿd alf ʿām*, Baghdad 1936.—Ṭāhā Ḥusayn *Maʿa ʾl-Mutanabbī*, C. 1936.

89. Line 12, *Dīwān* Glaser 37, Garr. 31, Patna I, 197,$_{1765}$; ed. Sāmī Dahhān, 3 vols. Beirut 1945.

94. Line 1, *Munshaʾāt wa-rasāʾil* AS 3996, 4194, 2; *Risāla fi ʾl-ʿilm* Patna II, 427,$_{2600,5}$.

95. d. *Munshaʾāt* Paris 6195 (see M. Jawad, *REI* 1938, 286).

103. Line 27–6. *Tasmiyat azwāj al-nabī* Ẓāh.^{2} 70.

104. 11. 4. ʿĀṭif Ef. 2003, 4., 5. Ibid. 3.

| 105. Line 2, *Tafsīr ʿilm al-qawāfī* Bursa, Ḥu. Čelebī Edebiyyāt 33, f. 1–32 v. 661

106. No. 3, with a commentary by al-Bakrī, Fātiḥ 4074, Faiẕ. 1578, Mosul 206, 1.

109. 18.—7. *Risālat Aḥmad b. al-Wāthiq ilā Abi ʾl-ʿAbbās Muḥammad b. Yazīd al-Thimālī yasʾaluhu ʿan afḍal al-balāghatayn shiʿran am nathran wa-jawāb Abi ʾl-ʿAbbās ʿanhā*, ed. G. v. Grünebaum, *Orientalia* X, 1941, 372/81.

111. 21a. Al-Mufajjaʿ Abū ʿAbdallāh Muḥammad b. ʿAbdallāh al-Kātib al-Baṣrī, who had also studied with Thaʿlab and who was active as a Shīʿī poet, died in 320/932.

Fihrist 83, Flügel 223, 1. *Kitāb al-munqidh fi ʾl-aymān* (after the example of Ibn Durayd's *Kitāb al-Malāḥin*), see Yāqūt, GW III, 133,17, 444, 16.—2. *Kitāb al-tarjumān*, cited by Tabrīzī ad *Ḥamāsa* 449,1.

113. Line 31, 17. Anon. *al-Qirāḍ al-Rukniyya*, composed in 661/1263 for Rukn al-Dawla ʿAbd al-ʿAzīz, AS 4072, 3.

115. Line 22, fragm. Ẓāh.² 296.

118. No. 3. 5. *Kitāb al-ayyām wal-layālī* (see Suppl.), Aleppo 1345, together with al-Ajdābī's *Kifāya* and al-Khwārizmī's *al-Wujūh fi ʾl-lugha.*

120. 7. b. *al-Munakhkhal* Faiẕ. 1765.

120. n. 1. See al-Anbārī, *Nuzhat al-alibbāʾ* 437; his commentary on the *Ḥamāsa*, in which he introduces his refutations of earlier interpreters with a verse or a proverb, is often cited by al-Tabrīzī.

122. Line 8, *Ḥilyat al-Faṣīḥ* (see Suppl.) Garr. 252, Qawala II, 3.

126. Line 1, Ẓāh.², 3. No. 2. *Kitāb al-ashriba* ed. M. Kurd ʿAlī, Damascus 1366/1947.—No. 7. AS 3697/70.

No. 5. *Ibn Qotaïba, Introduction au Livre de la poésie et des poètes. Avec introduction, traduction et commentaire par Gaudefroy-Demombynes*, Paris 1947.

137. Below, Plessner, *Islca* IV, 531, Bursa, Kharājjīzāde 21/25, 35.

137. 6. 1. Therefrom (?) *al-Farq mā bayna ʾl-ḍād wal-ẓāʾ* Fātiḥ 5413, 1^b–13^b, see A. Ateš, *Oriens* I, 15.

139, 3a. See Suppl. III, 1196 ad 202, 3b.

662 | 140. Line 9, 4 (see Suppl.), abstract by Abū Bakr Muḥammad b. ʿAlī al-Maḥallī, Ẓāh.^{2} 296.

141. 3. *al-Mīra fī ḥall mushkil al-sīra* by Yūsuf b. ʿAbd al-Hādī, d. 909/1503, Ẓāh.^{2} 22.

142. 13. Ẓāh.^{2} 131, shorter than C. 1343.

143. Line 1, vol. I, Ẓāh.^{2} 15.

5a. Abū Jaʿfar ʿAbdallāh b. Muḥammad b. ʿAlī b. Nufayl al-Ḥarrānī, d. 234/848, *Kitāb al-maghāzī* Ẓāh.^{2} 42.

21. 1. *Akhbār Makka* Ẓāh.^{2} 103, in a different recension 144, 4b. *al-Taʾrīkh wa-akhbār al-Mawṣil* by Abū Dhakwa al-Mawṣilī is cited in al-Masʿūdī, *Murūj* I, 13, 19.

Muḥammad b. Yaḥyā b. Manda (see Suppl.), d. 395/1005, Ibn al-ʿImād, *ShDh* III, 146, *Maʿrifat al-ṣaḥāba* Ẓāh.^{2} 171.

Muḥammad b. Saʿīd al-Qushayrī (ibid.), *Taʾrīkh Raqqa* Ẓāh.^{2} 131.

147. Line 21, *Azwāj al-nabī* Ẓāh.^{2} 71.

2a. Abū Yūsuf Yaʿqūb b. Sufyān al-Fasawī al-Fārisī al-Hamdānī, d. 280/893 (or, according to others, in 288/901), Suyūṭī, *Ḥuff.* IX, 60, Wüst. *Gesch.* 77. *Taʾrīkh* ḤKh 2269, 2343, citation *Fragm. hist.* I, 112, 12.

150. Line 20, *Waqʿat al-jamal* Ẓāh.^{2} 84.

5d. Abū Bishr Hārūn b. Ḥātim al-Tamīmī al-Bazzāz, d. 249/863, Ibn al-Jazarī, *Ghāyat al-nihāya* II, 345. *Taʾrīkh* from ʿAlī until the end of the Umayyads, with the death dates of some of the *ṣaḥāba* and *tābiʿūn*, in 7 folios, Ẓāh.^{2} 93/4.

155. No. 3, 1. ʿAbdallāh b. Muḥammad al-Madanī al-Balawī (see Suppl.), Ẓāh. ^{2}99, ed. M. Kurd ʿAlī, Damascus 1358.

158. 1c. *Qiṣṣat al-Iskandar* AS 3003/4.

159. 2. A fragment of a finely illustrated manuscript in the Ambrosiana, see Löfgren, *Orientalia* N. S. XII, 137, II, 16 (see Suppl.), Ẓāh. ^{2}94.

160. No. 3. *Dhikr b. Abi ʾl-Dunyā wa-ḥālihi wa-mā waqaʿa min aḥādīthihi* by Taqī al-Dīn b. Abī Mūsā Muḥammad b. Abī Bakr ʿUmar b. Aḥmad b. Abī ʿĪsā al-Madīnī, d. 581/1185. Ibn al-ʿImād, *ShDh* IV, 273, Ẓāh.^{2} 219.—46. *Maqtal ʿAlī* Ẓāh.^{2} 82.

| 163. Ad p. 257. *ββ* Abū Ḥudhayfa Isḥāq b. Bishr al-Qurashī, d. 206/821, Ibn 663
al-ʿImād, *ShDh* II, 15. *Kitāb al-mubtadaʾ*, a history of the Prophet, Ẓāh.^{2} 314.

κκ Abū Bakr Jaʿfar b. Muḥammad b. Ḥasan al-Fīryābī, d. 301/914, Ibn al-ʿImād, *ShDh* II, 235, *Dalāʾil al-nubuwwa* (about the miraculous feeding), Ẓāh.^{2} 51.

Abu ʾl-Qāsim ʿAbdallāh b. Muḥammad b. ʿAbd al-ʿAzīz al-Baghawī, d. 317/929, Ibn al-ʿImād, *ShDh* II, 275. *Ḥikāyāt Abī Bisṭām Shuʿba b. al-Ḥajjāj b. al-Ward al-ʿAtakī al-Wāsiṭī wa-ʿan ʿAmr b. Murra* Ẓāh.^{2} 219.

Abū Sulaymān Muḥammad b. ʿAbdallāh b. Aḥmad al-Rabaʿī al-Dimashqī, d. 379/989, Ibn al-ʿImād, *ShDh* III, 95. *Akhbār b. Abī Dhiʾb* Ẓāh.^{2} 219.

(p. 259 *τ*) Yaḥyā b. Maʿīn al-Murrī, Ibn al-Khaṭīb, *Taʾrīkh Baghdād* XIV, 177, Ibn al-ʿImād, *ShDh* II, 79.—1. *al-Taʾrīkh wal-ʿilal* Ẓāh.^{2} 232.—2. *Maʿrifat al-rijāl* ibid. 231.

Abū ʿArūba al-Ḥusayn b. Muḥammad b. Mawdūd al-Ḥarrānī, d. 318/930, Ibn al-ʿImād, *ShDh* II, 275. *Ṭabaqāt* Ẓāh.^{2} 169.

Abu ʾl-Ḥasan Muḥammad b. ʿAbdallāh b. Ḥaywa, d. 366/977, Ibn al-ʿImād, *ShDh* III, 56. *Man wāfaqat kunyatuhu kunyat zawjihi min al-ṣaḥāba* Ẓāh.^{2} 170.

164. *Tarjamat al-Bukhārī* by ʿAfīf al-Dīn ʿAlī b. ʿAbd al-Muḥsin b. al-Dawālībī, d. 858/1454 (*ShDh* V, 293), Ẓāh.^{2} 222.

166. IIIa. Ẓāh.^{2} 202.—c. Ẓāh.^{2} 234.

168. Line 3, II, Ẓāh.[2] 202.—IV. *Rijāl ʿUrwa* ibid. 225.

3a. Ḥammād b. Isḥāq b. Ismāʿīl b. Ḥammād b. Zayd, d. 267/881, Ibn al-ʿImād, *ShDh* II, 152, *Tarikat al-nabī*, transmitted by his son Abū Isḥāq Ibrāhīm b. Ḥammād (Fihrist 200), Ẓāh.[2] 76.

169. Line 9, read: al-Ājurrī. Line 11, V. *Tasmiyat al-ikhwa alladhīna ruwiya ʿanhum al-ḥadīth* Ẓāh.[2] 203.

170. Line 9, 5. Ẓāh.[2] 62.

171. Line 12, 3. Ẓāh.[2] 235.

d. Muḥammad b. Aḥmad al-Dhahabī, d. 748/1347 (II, 57), *al-Mujarrad fī asmāʾ rijāl Kitāb sunan b. Māja* Ẓāh.[2] 214.

664 | 172. 5a. Abū Bakr b. Muḥammad b. Hāniʾ al-Ṭāʾī al-Athram, d. 273/886.

Ibn Ḥajar al-ʿAsqalānī, *Tahdhīb al-Tahdhīb* I, 16, 193. *Kitāb nāsikh al-ḥadīth wa-mansūkhuhu* library of Ismāʿīl Ṣāʾib (Ankara) 1323 (Ritter).

6a. Khaythama b. Sulaymān b. Ḥaydara al-Ṭarābulusī, d. 333/945 (or, according to others, 343 or 365), Ibn al-ʿImād, *ShDh* II, 334. 1. *Faḍāʾil al-Ṣiddīq Abī Bakr* Ẓāh.[2] 83.—2. *Faḍāʾil al-ṣaḥāba* ibid. 169.

6b. Abū ʿAlī Muḥammad b. Hārūn b. Shuʿayb al-Anṣārī, d. 353/964, Ibn al-ʿImād, *ShDh* III, 13. *Ṣifat al-nabī* Ẓāh.[2] 51.

173. Line 2, 2. *Taʾrīkh al-thiqāt* Ẓāh.[2] 204.—6. *Kitāb al-ʿaẓama* vol. 13, ibid. 315.

No. 8, 4. (see Suppl.) Ẓāh.[2] 95, the majority of which was copied by Ibn al-Jawzī.

174. Line 7, 4 (see Suppl.), *al-Ḍuʿafāʾ wal-matrūkūn* Ẓāh.[2] 241.—10. *Faḍāʾil al-ṣaḥāba* ibid. 179.—11. *Akhbār ʿAmr b. ʿUbayd b. Bāb al-Baṣrī al-Muʿtazilī* (Suppl. 338, i, c) *wa-kalāmuhu fi ʾl-Qūrʾān wa-iẓhār bidaʿihi* ibid. 305.

No. 13. *Faḍāʾil Fāṭima* Ẓāh.[2] 71/2.

175. No. 16. 4. *Taʾrīkh Nīsābūr*, Persian translation Bursa Kurshunlu Cami 2047 (Ritter).—5. *Tasmiyat man akhrajahum al-Bukhārī wa-Muslim*, Ẓāh.[2] 208.—

6. *Kitāb al-kunā, talkhīṣ* by ʿAbd al-Ghanī b. ʿAbd al-Wāḥid al-Maqdisī (p. 437), ibid. 210.

176. 19. (see Suppl.) ʿAbdallāh b. Ḥamd al-Baghawī, d. 317/929, Ibn al-ʿImād, *ShDh* II, 275. *Taʾrīkh wafāt shuyūkh al-Baghawī* Ẓāh.[2] 225.

aa. Khalīfa b. Khayyāṭ, d. 204/819, Ibn al-ʿImād, *ShDh* II, 94. *Ṭabaqāt* (the transmitters of Medina) *riwāya* of Abū ʿImrān Mūsā b. Zakariyyāʾ b. Yaḥyā al-Tustarī (*al-Mushtabih* 46, *Mīzān al-iʿtidāl* III, 210), Ẓāh.[2] 199/201.

ab. Abu ʾl-Ḥasan ʿAlī b. ʿAbdallāh al-Madīnī, d. 243/857, *ShDh* II, 81. *Tasmiyat awlād al-ʿashara* Ẓāh.[2] 201.

ac. Abū Jaʿfar Muḥammad b. ʿUthmān b. Abī Shayba, d. 297/910, *ShDh* II, 226, Fihrist 229. *Masāʾil* (*ʿan rijāl al-ḥadīth*) Ẓāh.[2] 235.

d. *Kitāb al-ḍuʿafāʾ* Ẓāh.[2] 236.—e. 4. *Zuhd al-thamāniya min al-ṣaḥāba* ibid. 277.

| i. 1. *al-Kāmil* vol. 3, Ẓāh.[2] 238.—3. *Asmāʾ man rawā ʿanhum al-Bukhārī* 665
ibid. 206.

11. Abū Muḥammad ʿAbdallāh b. Muḥammad b. Jaʿfar b. Ḥibbān b. al-Shaykh, d. 369/980, *ShDh* III, 69. *Ṭabaqāt al-muḥaddithīn bi-Iṣbahān wal-wāridīn ʿalayhā* Ẓāh.[2] 207.

r. read: *al-Muʾtalif* Ẓāh.[2] 190, print. Allāhābād 1327, on which *Ziyādāt* by Abu ʾl-ʿAbbās Jaʿfar b. Muḥammad b. al-Muʿtazz al-Mustaghfirī, d. 432/1041, ibid. 191.—2. ibid. 190.—4. ibid. 96.

177. *Faḍāʾil Abī Ḥanīfa wa-akhbāruhu wa-manāqibuhu* (and of his students) by Abu ʾl-Qāsim ʿAbdallāh b. Muḥammad b. Aḥmad b. Yaḥyā b. al-Ḥārith al-Saʿdī, Ẓāh.[2] 261.

183. Line 4, Tatar translation Kazan 1880.

186. I. 16. While a *qāḍī* in the Maghreb, Asad b. al-Furāt, the conqueror of Sicily, still represented the doctrine of Kufa, i.e. of Abū Ḥanīfa, see *ʿUyūn al-akhbār, Fragm. hist.* II, 370, 11.

3a. Muḥammad b. Waḍḍāḥ al-Qurṭubī al-Andalusī, d. 289/902. *Ittiqāʾ al-bidaʿ* Garr. 2070, entitled *Kitāb al-bidaʿ wal-nahy ʿanhā*, ed. M. Dahmān, Damascus 1349 (*RAAD* XI, 127).

190. Line 6, i.e. Fakhr al-Dīn, see 666/7 (Ẓāh.[2] 249). *Riḥlat al-imām al-Shāfiʿī* (see Suppl.) Ẓāh.[2] 248.

193. 5. *Miḥnat b. Ḥanbal*, by his nephew Abū ʿAlī Ḥanbal b. Isḥāq b. Ḥanbal, Ẓāh.[2] 265.—8. (see Suppl.) *ʿIlal al-ḥadīth* Ẓāh.[2] 232.

194. c. (see Suppl.) *Ṭabaqāt aṣḥāb b. Ḥanbal* Ẓāh.[2] 265.

203. 2a. (see Suppl.) al-Sijistānī's *Kitāb al-maṣāḥif* in A. Jeffery, *Materials for the history of the text of the Qurʾān* (de Goeje Fund XI), Leiden 1937.

206. 1. *ξ* His *Kitāb ʿuyūn al-masāʾil wal-jawābāt* is cited in Masʿūdī, *Murūj* (C.) I, 108, 17.—*o*. A work on Muʿtazilī dogmatics in the library of Ismāʿīl Ṣāʾib Efendi in Ankara (Dīl Fakültesi).

207. Note: The doctrine on the createdness of the Qurʾān is ascribed to Jewish influence in Ibn al-Athīr, C. VII, 24, 6ff; Ṭālūt (Saul), the son of the sister of
666 Labīd al-Aʿṣam al-Yahūdī, a contemporary of the Prophet, supposedly | proclaimed that the Torah was created.—In the year 279/892 the government in Baghdad prohibited the selling of books on *kalām, jadal,* and *falsafa*, Ṭabarī III, 2131,3.

211. No. 7. 10. *Manāqib al-aʾimma* Ẓāh.[2] 84.

216. Line 6, *Bidāyat ḥāl al-Ḥusayn b. Muḥammad al-Ḥallāj wa-nihāyatuhu* by Abū ʿAbdallāh Muḥammad b. ʿAbdallāh b. ʿUbaydallāh b. Aḥmad b. Bākūya al-Shīrāzī, d. 418/1027, Ẓāh.[2] 278.

216. 5, no. 3, library of Ismāʿīl Ṣāʾib (Dil Fakültesi Ankara) 1571,5.—4. ibid. 1.—8. ibid. 4.—33. *Kitāb bayān al-ʿilm* ibid. 2—34. *Masāʾil fi ʾl-niyya wa-ghayrihā* ibid. 3.—35. *Ajwibat masāʾil* ibid. 6.—36. *Fi ʾl-farq bayna ʾl-āyāt wal-karāmāt* ibid. 7.—37. *Kitāb al-ḥuqūq* ibid. 8.—38. *Fī badʾ shaʾn al-muṣannif* (autobiography) ibid. 9.—39. *Masāʾil al-taʿbīr* ibid. 10.—40. *Manāzil al-qāṣidīn ila ʾllāh* ibid. 11 (Ritter).

No. 6c. (see Suppl.) *Miḥnat al-Shāfiʿī* Ẓāh.[2] 248.

218. 10. 3. (see Suppl.) Ẓāh.^{2} 51/2.

219. 12. (see Suppl.) *al-Arbaʿūn* Ẓāh.^{2} 277.

225. I, 14. See *Isl. Culture* 1931, 134/41.

229. Line 17, G. Klinge, Die Bedeutung der syrischen Theologen als Vermittler der griechischen Philosophie an den Islam, *Ztschr. f. Kirchengeschichte* 58 (1939) 346/86.

230. 1. A list of his (50) works, Esc. $^{2}884_{,10}$.

231. XI, 3. *Risāla fī ʿilm al-katif* NO 2840 (*Islca* IV, 557).

247. No. 10, l. 2, ad *al-Badīʿ* (Suppl. 4).—2. *al-Fakhrī* Köpr. 950, see Levi della Vida, *RSO* XIV, 259.

Ibid. no. 9. (see Suppl.) 1. A.P. Luckey, *Math. Annalen* 120 (1948), 245ff.

Ibid. no. 10. (see Suppl.) 4. Instead of *al-Waṣāyā bil-judhūr*, Luckey, *Ber. d. math.-phys. Kl. d. Heid. Ak. d. Wiss.* XCIII, $95_{,5}$, reads *al-Waṣāyā bil-jabr*.

252. 7a. *Zīj al-Rīqānī al-maʿrūf bil-Kirmānī wal-mansūb ilā arṣād al-Battānī*, composed in 489/1096, Bibl. d'Erlanger, see D. Ross, *BSOS* III, 610.

255. No. 14. *Isl. Culture* 1931, 434/41.

| 256. 15. 1. See also Bidez and Cumont, *Les mages hellénisés* II, 233/40. 667

263. No. 11. (A. Madīni) *Il Segistan ovvero il corso del fiume Hindmend* (*sic*) *secondo Abu Ishak el-Farisi el-Istahri, geografo arabo*, Milan 1842.

No. 12. 1. See O. Löfgren, *Über eine neuentdeckte, bessere Textüberlieferung von al-Hamdānīs Iklīl* VIII (Ambr. N. F. D. 284, f. 1–16), *Orientalia* XII, 1943, 135/45.

264. 12. 2. L. Forrer, *Südarabien nach al-Hamdanis Beschreibung der arab. Halbinsel*, AKM XXVII, 2, Leipzig 1942.

265. No. 2. For a fragment of an erotic work, with illustrations, from the turn of the second to the third centuries (ca. 900) in an Egyptian papyrus, see

A. Grohmann and T.W. Arnold, *Denkmäler islamischer Buchkunst*, Munich 1929, 4/5.

270. 19 excise: *de arte etc.* Esc.^{1}797$_{,1}$.

20. *Talkhīṣ li-kitāb Jālīnūs fī ḥīlat al-bur'* Esc.^{2}801, excise: Cmt. etc.

22. Excise: see Esc.^{2} 861.

22. *Risāla fi 'l-talaṭṭuf ilā īṣāl al-nās ilā shahawātihim* (IAUṢ. I, 316) Esc.^{2} 887$_{,1}$.

23. *Risāla fi 'l-bāh* Mosul 34$_{,154,3}$, 10–24. *Fi 'l-nahy ʿani 'l-ḥimya al-mufriṭa* Esc.^{2} 887$_{,2}$ = Suppl. 51?.—28. to be excised.

278. 82. (see Suppl.) *Kitāb al-baḥth fī ṣanʿat al-ṭilasmāt.*

280. 1. *Kitāb al-filāḥa* ʿUm. 4064, Ḥamīd. 1031 (another recension, see *Islca* IV, 553).

281. Line 11, read: Rāġib 963, 5.—Line 22, read: Rāġib 963, 6.—Line 24, read: Rāġib 870, excise 965.

291. B. 1. Dawlatshāh, *Tadhkira* 26/7.

298. 6c. ʿAmīd al-Dīn Asʿad b. Naṣr al-Anṣārī al-Abarzī was the vizier of the Atābek of Fārs, Muẓaffar al-Dīn Abū Shujāʿ Saʿd b. Zangī, and of his son Abū Bakr b. Saʿd. He was imprisoned by the latter in the Ushkunwān fortress, near Iṣṭakhr, accused of high treason, and died there in 624/1227.

Al-Qaṣīda al-Ushkunwāniyya, which he dictated to his son while in prison, with a commentary by Ṣafī al-Dīn Abu 'l-Khayr Masʿūd b. Maḥmūd b. Abi 'l-Fatḥ al-Sīrāfī, whose father had heard the *qaṣīda* from the poet's son, AS
668 4072$_{,1}$ (Ritter), | Meshh. XV, 25, 72 (see Suppl. I, 456, 6c), ed. and transl. Cl. Huart, *L'Ode arabe d'Ochkonwan* n.d. & n.p., printed in a Persian *majmūʿa*, together with the *Muʿallaqāt* and other poems, n.d. & n.p.

304. Line 13, 5. *Ghazawāt al-rasūl naẓman* Ẓāh.^{2} 43.

305. No. 6. Nawā'ī, *Nasā'im al-maḥabba*, Fātiḥ 4060, 139v/140r.

315. Line 9.—6. *Kitāb al-ʿajā'ib wal-ṭuraf* is cited in *Mustaṭraf* II, 41$_{,20}$. No. 4. 2. *Simṭ al-hudā fi 'l-fakhr al-Muḥammadī* Ẓāh.^{2} 16.

320. No. 8. See A.R. Nykl, *Islam* 26 (1942) 16/48.

327. No. 3. *al-Īḍāḥ*, Bibl. d'Erlanger, see Ross, *BSOS* III, 612.

331. 1a. Abu 'l-Qāsim ʿUbaydallāh b. ʿAlī b. ʿUbaydallāh al-Raqqī lived in Baghdad and died in 450/1058. Al-Suyūṭī, *Bughya* 320. *Kitāb al-qawāfī* Fātiḥ 5413 f. 97^{a}–115^{b}, see A. Ateš, *Oriens* I, 16.

333. 8b. (see Suppl. 494 8^{b}) *Muntaha 'l-ṭalab* Lālelī 1941 (*MO* VII, 104), the rest in 14 vols. Faiẕ. 1609/20 (Ritter).

334. No. 10. 3. Ẓāh. Naḥw 147 (Plessner, *Islca* IV, 543).

338. Line 7, Ẓāh.^{2} 297.

343. 8a. Muḥammad b. Abi 'l-Faraj b. Faraj b. Abi 'l-Qāsim Abū ʿAbdallāh al-Mālikī al-Kattānī (al-Kinānī) al-Ṣiqillī al-Dhakī al-Naḥwī was born in 427/1036 in Sicily and died in 515/1121 in Isfahan.

Ibn al-Anbārī, *Nuzhat al-alibbā'* 449/53, al-Suyūṭī, *Bughya* 90. *Muqaddima fi 'l-naḥw* Fātiḥ 5413, f. 71^{b}–88^{b}, see A. Ateš, *Oriens* I, 16.

345. Line 16, Yūsuf Agha $56_{,1}$, $224_{,1}$ (*Islca* IV, 531), Sarajevo 52.

347. Line 3, see A. Socin, *ZDMG* XXXIII, 682/6.

347. II, 5. Library of Ismāʿīl Ṣā'ib, Ankara 1397 (Ritter).

356. 17. Samʿānī, *Ansāb* 466b transcribes Quhunduzī; Yāqūt, *GW* IV, 214 Qahandaz and Quhunduz.

364. 1. Nashwān was a Zaydī, see Abu 'l-Rijāl, *Maṭlaʿ al-budūr* Ambr. B. 131, f. 227a (Löfgren, *Orientalia* XII, 136). 4. Anonymous commentary, Ẓāh.^{2} 158.

381. Line 7, read: Muḥammad b. ʿAbdallāh.

| 385. Line 6, from which *Tarjamat al-Qāḍī al-Fāḍil* Ẓāh.^{2} 299. 669

387. 11. (Suppl.) see ad II, 85.

389. 9a. (see Suppl.) from which the account of the capture of Marqab, translation in M. van Berchem, *Voyage de Syrie* I, 1913, *MIFAO* XXXIII, 310/20.

391. Line 13, in his *Lubāb* he also cites 1. *Faḍāʾil al-khulafāʾ al-rāshidīn* 173, 9.—11. *al-Taʾassī wal-tasallī min al-marāthī wal-taʿāzī*, 294, 9, 410, 7.—12. *Radʾ al-ẓālim wa-radd al-maẓālim* 311, 8.—13. *al-Shaykh wal-shabāb* 377, 4.

395. 2a. *Ṭabaqāt al-Ḥanābila* Ẓāh.^{2} 266.

398. Line 8, Ẓāh.^{2} 306.

399. Line 30, Ẓāh.^{2} 164. A. Müller, *Über Text u. Sprachgebrauch von Ibn Abī Uṣ. Geschichte der Ärzte* Munich 1884, 5, 1885.

401. Line 1, Muḥammad b. Aḥmad b. Muḥammad al-Mālikī al-Andalusī, *Tasmiyat mā warada bihi ʾl-shaykh Abū Bakr Aḥmad b. ʿAlī b. Thābit al-Khaṭīb al-Baghdādī Dimashq min al-kutub min riwāyātihi min al-ajzāʾ al-masmūʿa wal-kibār al-muṣannafa wa-mā jarā majrāhā siwa ʾl-fawāʾid wal-amālī wal-manthūr* Ẓāh.^{2} 309.—1. Ẓāh.^{2} 156.—*Dhayl* b. Ẓāh.^{2} 157, abstract by Aḥmad b. Aybak b. al-Dimyāṭī (see Suppl., with Ṣafadī, *al-Wāfī*, AS 2962, 54).—6. ibid. 192.—20. (see Suppl.) ibid.

401. 1a. Abū ʿAlī al-Ḥasan b. Aḥmad b. al-Bannāʾ, d. 471/1078, Ibn al-ʿImād, *ShDh* III, 339. *Taʿlīqāt* (*bi-ḥawādith ʿaṣrihi fī Baghdād wa-ghayrihā*) Ẓāh.^{2} 156/7.

402. 21. Ẓāh.^{2} 163.—14. Entitled *al-Taḥbīr fi ʾl-muʿjam al-kabīr* Ẓāh.^{2} 181.

403. 2. 1. Ẓāh.^{2} 109/29. *Muntakhab* 129/30.

404. Line 11, 9. *al-Muʿjam al-mushtamil ʿalā dhikr asmāʾ shuyūkh al-aʾimma* Ẓāh.^{2} 226.—10. *Faḍl ʿAlī* ibid. 88.

408. Line 1, Ibn al-ʿImād, *ShDh* III, 231.—4. *Suʾālāt fi ʾl-jarḥ* Ẓāh.^{2} 242.

408. No. 1a. (see Suppl.) al-Ṭaḥḥān. 1 = 2. Ẓāh.^{2} 149.

1b. *Wafayāt* Ẓāh.^{2} 151.

670 | 429. Line 5, Ẓāh.^{2} 321.

434. 1d. (see Suppl.) Ẓāh.[2] 42.—2. Read: *gharāʾib*.

436. No. 8. 1, Ẓāh.[2] 194.—5. ibid. 209.—12. *Maʿrifat al-alqāb* ibid.

437. 11a. Abū Mūsā Muḥammad b. Abī Bakr b. Abī ʿĪsā al-Madīnī, d. 581/1185, Ibn al-ʿImād, *ShDh* IV, 273. *Dhikr Ibn Manda* (d. 395/1005, Suppl. 281, P) *wa-aṣḥābihi* Ẓāh.[2] 227.

438. Line 11, Ẓāh.[2] 211.—*Ikmāl* (see Suppl.) ibid. 212.—*Tahdhīb* ibid. 215, *al-Kāshif* ibid. 213. *Mukhtaṣar Tahdhīb al-kamāl* by Abū Bakr b. Abi ʾl-Majd b. Mājid b. al-ʿImād al-Ṣāliḥī al-Maqdisī al-Ḥanbalī, d. 804/1402, *ShDh* VII, 421, Ẓāh.[2] 215.—9. *Abu ʾl-ʿĀṣ b. al-Rabīʿ* ibid. 174.—10. *Manāqib al-ṣaḥāba* ibid.—11. *Ṣalāt al-nabī fi ʾl-anbiyāʾ laylat al-isrāʾ* ibid. 35.—12. *Ḥadīth al-ifk* ibid. 72.—13. *Faḍāʾil ʿUmar b. al-Khaṭṭāb* ibid. 89.—14. *Talkhīṣ Kitāb al-kunā lil-Ḥākim* (p. 175) ibid. 210.—15. *Akhbār Ḥasan al-Baṣrī* ibid. 306.

439. Line 12 (see Suppl.), 608 n. 1, with 3. Pet. AMK 927 (II, 923_{92}).

15c. Al-Mufaḍḍal b. ʿAlī b. Mufarrij b. Ḥātim al-Maqdisī al-Mālikī, d. 611/1214, Ibn al-ʿImād, *ShDh* V, 47.—*al-Arbaʿūn* Ẓāh.[2] 220/1.

16. Ibn al-ʿImād, *ShDh* V, 133.—3. *al-Istridrāk ʿala ʾl-ansāb al-mutashābiha fī kitāb ʿAbd al-Ghanī b. Saʿīd wal-Dāraquṭnī wa-Aḥmad b. ʿAlī al-Khaṭīb wa-Ibn Mākūlā* Ẓāh.[2] 194.

16a. Abū Manṣūr ʿAbd al-Raḥmān b. Muḥammad b. al-Ḥasan b. ʿAsākir al-Shāfiʿī, d. 620/1223, Ibn Khall. I, 278, no. 374. *al-Arbaʿūn fī manāqib ummahāt al-muʾminīn* Ẓāh.[2] 72.

442. I, b. (see Suppl.) al-Amīr al-Ṣanʿānī, whose *Irshād al-nuqqād ilā taysīr al-ijtihād* is contained in *Majmūʿat al-rasāʾil al-Munīriyya* 1, 1343, 1/47.—VII (see Suppl.), Ẓāh.[2] 249.—X, *Ḥilyat al-Shāfiʿī* ibid. 249.

443. 21. I. *Mashāriq al-anwār*, with a Persian interlinear translation, St Petersburg, *Bull. de l'Ac.* 1911, 255, no. 106.

444. 23. 2. Ẓāh.[2] 73.

445. 1. 1. Ẓāh.[2] 278/80.

446. 10. 10. (see Suppl.) Ẓāh.^{2} 298.—12. *Faḍāʾil al-khulafāʾ* ibid. 86.

671 | 1a. (see Suppl.) Ibn al-ʿImād, *ShDh* III, 249.—3. *Ziyādāt fī Kitāb al-mukhtalif wal-muʾtalif*, based on ʿAbd al-Ghanī b. Saʿīd (166, 16, 2), Ẓāh.^{2} 191.

447. Line 15, 2. Anon. abstract *Bughyat al-sāʾil* vol. 2. *ʿammā ḥawāhu Kitāb al-dalāʾil* (on the life of the Prophet and his qualities), manuscript dated 755, Ẓāh.^{2} 26.

448. Line 11, a. Sarajevo 38 (where the author is referred to as Muḥammad b. ʿAbd al-Laṭīf, see ḤKh ^{1}V, 571, 3, ^{2}II, 1701).

449. Line 2, *Asmāʾ rijāl al-Mishkāt* Ẓāh.^{2} 213.—4. *Maʿālim al-tanzīl* Sarajevo 54/7.

449. 7. 3. (4.) *Dhayl Taʾrīkh Nīsābūr* library of Ismāʿīl Ṣāʾib (Ankara) 1544 (Ritter).

450. 8bb. Abū Masʿūd ʿAbd al-Raḥīm b. Abi ʾl-Wafāʾ ʿAlī b. Aḥmad al-Ḥājjī al-Iṣbahānī, d. 566/1171, *ShDh* IV, 217. *Wafāʾāt jamāʿa min al-muḥaddithīn* Ẓāh.^{2} 226.

9. 13. *Ḥadīth ʿan baʿḍ al-Abhariyyīn* Ẓāh. ^{2}226.

453. 1. 1. *al-Istīʿāb*, merged with the *Maʿrifat al-aṣḥāb* by Abū Nuʿaym (445), perhaps by ʿAfīf b. Saʿīd b. Masʿūd b. Muḥammad b. Masʿūd Abu ʾl-Maḥāmid al-Kāzarūnī (II, 249), Ẓāh^{2}. 173.

454. Line 7, 6. Ẓāh.^{2} 307.—16. *al-Istidhkār fī sharḥ mā rasamahu Mālik fī Muwaṭṭaʾihi riwāyat Yaḥyā b. Yaḥyā al-Laythī*, source of the *Muqaddima, Istinbāṭ* by al-Silafī (450, 9), Ẓāh.^{2} 274.

455. 5. 1. Sarajevo 89/93, Ẓāh.^{2} 53/4.—d. Ẓāh.^{2} 56/7.

456. Line 5, i. Ẓāh.^{2} 63. Anon. abstract Ẓāh.^{2} 69.—5. *Tartīb*, abstract *al-Muntaqā* Ẓāh.^{2} 274.

460. 3. 3. *al-Wujūh wal-naẓāʾir fi ʾl-Qurʾān al-karīm* ḤKh ^{1}VI, 424,$_{14178}$, ^{2}II, 2000, Cairo I, ^{2}66.—4. *Shawq al-ʿarūs wa-uns al-nufūs* ḤKh ^{1} IV, 83,$_{7690}$, ^{2}II, 1067.

4a. His brother Muḥammad b. ʿAbd al-Karīm b. Mūsā al-Pazdawī, d. 493/1100, wrote *Uṣūl al-dīn* (library of Ismāʿīl Ṣāʾib, Dil Fakültesi Ankara 2/1261), see Ritter, *Oriens* I, 56, note 1.

473. Line 4, 2. *Kitāb al-sahm* Ẓāh.^{2} 261.

474. 39. al-Barānīqī, read: al-Baratīqīnī? Zekī Welidi, *Türk. Mecm.* II, 341.

| 475. 43. 3. *Kitāb li-kashf mā ishtabaha ʿala ʾl-sāmiʿīn min al-āy wal-akhbār* 672
mimmā yaḥtaju bihi ahl al-zaygh ʿalā ahl al-sunna (on anthropomorphisms in the Qurʾān and *ḥadīth*), Fātiḥ 3142 (Ritter).

479. 3a. (see Suppl.) E. Lévi-Provençal, *Séville musulmane au début du XIIe siècle. Vie urbaine et corps de métiers* (*Introduction au traité d'Ibn Abdoun et traduction*), Islam d'hier et d'aujourdhui no. 2.

500. XIV. Ẓāh.^{2} 251.

504. 5–15. *al-Ḥikāyāt al-muqtabasa fī karāmāt mashāyikh al-arḍ al-muqaddasa* Ẓāh.^{2} 285.—16. A fragment of a *sīra*, ibid. 46.—17. *Dhikr al-shaykh al-imām al-ʿālim al-zāhid Abī ʿUmar Muḥammad b. Aḥmad b. Qudāma Abī Naṣr al-Maqdisī* (d. 617/1210) *wa-mā kāna ʿalayhi wa-karāmātihi wa-mā ruthiya bihi baʿda mawtihi wa-ghayr dhālika* Ẓāh.^{2} 267 (autograph).—17. *Sīrat al-ʿImād Abī Isḥāq Ibrāhīm b. ʿAbd al-Wāḥid al-Maqdisī al-Ḥanbalī* (d. 614/1217), ibid. 268.

504. (Suppl. 690) 5a. Sayf al-Dīn Abu ʾl-ʿAbbās b. Qudāma al-Maqdisī al-Ṣāliḥī, d. 643/1245, *ShDh* V, 217.—*Taʿālīq* on Jerusalem, Ẓāh. ^{2}133.

505. (see Suppl.) D. 31. Ẓāh.^{2} 173/4, ed. Saʿīd al-Afghānī.

511. 22. lith. n.d. & n.p. (BDMG De 8320, which has *Mīsam*, sic).

518. 94 (see Suppl.). Ẓāh.^{2} 97.—5. *Mathālib b. Abī Bishr* (i.e. al-Ashʿarī), ibid. 305.

524, 3. 9. *Sharḥ Qaṣīdat al-Nābigha* (*JA* s. VI, vol. 12, 360) Basel M. 30, 2.

527. Line 1, Nawāʾī, *Nasāʾim al-maḥabba* Fātiḥ 4060, 114r, 18ff.

537. Line 27, Nawāʾī, *Nasāʾim al-maḥabba* Fātiḥ 4060, 105v/6r.

539. 22. (Suppl.) composed around 1101 in Alexandria: *Al-Ghazālī, Réfutation excellente de la divinité de Jésus-Christ d'après les évangiles, texte établi, traduit et commenté par* Robert Chidias S.J. *Préface de* Louis Massignon (*Bibliothèque de l'École des Hautes Études Sciences Religieuses* LIVe *vol.*), Paris 1939 (manuscripts also AS 2247, Leiden 2084).

546. 6. Nawā'ī, *Nasā'im al-maḥabba* Fātiḥ 4060, 106r, 4ff.

547. 6c. (see Suppl.) *Maqāla etc.* ed. Sv. Dedering, *MOr.* XXV (1931), 35/43.

673 | 549. 6, 1. Garr. 1552.

557. Line 10, read: Garr. 2117, 2.—19. *Naḥw al-qulūb,* incorporated by Ṣarī ʿAbdallāh in his commentary on the *Mathnawī.* S. Nicholson, commentary I, 176, IV, 89/92.—21. *Tarassul al-Qurṭubī* (al-Dānī?) *maʿa 'l-Qushayrī,* Bibl. d'Erlanger, D. Ross, *BSOS* III, 613.

558. Line 9, commentary 9 (see Suppl.), on al-Taybādhkānī, see Nawā'ī, *Majālis al-nafā'is* Fātiḥ 4060, 663 v, 13ff.

559. 6. Nawā'ī, *Nasā'im al-maḥabba* 138r/v.

560. 8. Nawā'ī, *Nasā'im al-maḥabba* 138v 24f.

560. Line 4, Ẓāh. 280.

561. 20. See Suppl. = (?) *Manāqibi ḥaḍrati Ghawth al-aʿẓam,* with a translation in oriental Turkish, Tashkent 1898.

Ibn al-Mulaqqin (II, 113), *Ḥāl al-Jīlī* Ẓāh.[2] 287.—Anon., *Manāqib al-abrār fī manāqib ʿAbd al-Qādir al-Jīlānī* ibid. 294.

565. Line 1, Nawā'ī, *Nasā'im al-maḥabba* 146r 21ff.

566. 15. Nawā'ī, *Nasā'im al-maḥabba* 138r 7ff.

565. *Al-Suhrawardī Shihābaddīn Yaḥyā, Opera metaphysica et mystica,* ed. H. Corbin, Bibl. Isl. XVI. 1945.

568. 20. Nawā'ī, *Nasā'im al-maḥabba* 114r/115v.

569. 22. Nawāʾī, *Nasāʾim al-maḥabba* 125v.

571. 23. When he was twenty years old he engaged in a debate with the head of the Imāmis in Acre, as he reports in his *Kitāb al-ʿawāṣim* (no. 153), see al-Shāṭibī, *Kitāb al-iʿtiṣām* I, 194f.

Line 26, 1. *Isl.* XXV.—Nawāʾī, *Nasāʾim al-maḥabba* 125v, André Regnier, La terminologie mystique d'Ibn Arabi, *Le Muséon* 48, 144/62.—Abu 'l-ʿAlāʾ al-ʿAfīfī, *Min ayna 'staqā Muḥyi 'l-Dīn b. al-ʿArabī falsafatahu 'l-taṣawwufiyya,* al-Jāmiʿa al-Miṣriyya, *Majallat Kulliyyat al-ādāb* I, 1933, 3/46.

583. 27b. (Suppl.) Nawāʾī, *Nasāʾim al-maḥabba* 115v/116r.

28. Nawāʾī, *Nasāʾim al-maḥabba* 117r/v.

29. Nawāʾī, *Nasāʾim al-maḥabba* 142v, 4ff.

585. 32. Nawāʾī, *Nasāʾim al-maḥabba* 140v/141r.

587. 34. 7. *Sharḥ ḥāl al-awliyāʾ* library of Ismāʿīl Ṣāʾib (Ankara) 2916, attributed to ʿAlī al-Maqdisī (II, 404/5) (Ritter).

588. 35b. Abū Bakr b. Qiwām ʿAlī al-Bālisī was born in 584/1188 and died in Aleppo in 685/1286, *ShDh* V, 295. *Manāqib Abī Bakr* Berl. Oct. 3192, Ẓāh2. 293.

| 588. 37. Nawāʾī, *Nasāʾim al-maḥabba* 141r, 14ff. 674

591. G. Gabrieli, *Arch. di Storia delle Science* iv, 1923, 258/70. C. Nallino, Philosophia „orientale" od „illuminativa" d'Avicenna, *RSO* X, 1925, Şemsettin Günaltay, Ibni Sinanin şahsiyet ve milliyetinin meselesi, *Belleten*, Ankara 1940, 1/37. 14b. *Fi 'l-shifāʾ ʿan khawf al-mawt. Jāmiʿ al-badāʾiʿ* 36/43.

593. 26. *Jāmiʿ al-b.* 91/113.

596. 73. *Jāmiʿ al-b.* 152/64.—74. ibid. 116/51.

610. No. 15. (see Suppl.) Muḥammad Bayrām al-Thālith, d. 1259/1843 (Sarkīs 613).

617. 30. 3. Rāġib 843, Asʿad 1926, ʿUm. 3949, 3950, Ğārullāh 1021 (*Islca* IV, 530/1), Istanbul, Üniv. A 2824, Qayseri, Rashid 840.

621. Line 4, 4. (Suppl.) 4 and 8, *Jāmiʿ al-badāʾiʿ* 181/201.—9. *Jawāb ʿan thalāth masāʾil suʾila ʿanhā* ibid. 175/85.

627. Line 4, 3. see F. Cumont, *Syria* XVI, 1933, 46/9. Line 25, read: Ebn.

649. 36. 3. Shortened, with a French translation by Dr. Bishāra Zalzal, Alexandria 1902.

651. 44. ʿAlī b. Yūsuf b. ʿAlī b. ʿAbdallāh b. ʿAlī al-Tanūkhī al-Maqdisī, the grandson of Rashīd al-Dīn Abū ʿAlī Manṣūr b. Abi ʾl-Faḍl al-Ṣūrī, the personal physician of al-Malik al-ʿĀdil (r. 596–615/1199–1218): *Al-Kitāb al-ashraf fī ṣunʿat al-diryāq al-munqidh lil-nufūs al-sharīfa min al-talaf*, composed in 656/1258, Bank. IV, 105.

654. 3. 1. Rāġib 963, 7. 8 (*Islca* IV, 550).—2. Berl. 5567.

655. 5. 1. Berl. Brill M. 184,$_{2}$.

661. Margoliouth, *Isl. Culture* X, 1936, 339/468.—2. Ẓāh.[2] 88.

662. b. 7. Ẓāh.[2] 281/4.—15. Mainly copied from al-Ājurrī (p. 173, 8).—18. Ẓāh.[2] 266.—25. Under the title *Asmāʾ al-ḍuʿafāʾ* ibid. 242.

663, 27. 1. *Kibār al-ḥuffāẓ* Ẓāh.[2] 221.

666. 1. Ẓāh.[2] 249.

675 |***Volume II***

37. line 27.—9. For part of a Turkish commentary on sura 12,$_{15}$ see Birinci, *Türk Dil Kurultayi̊*, Istanbul 1933, 358.

36. 5. Hüsnü, Ibni Arabşah, *Türk. Mecm.* III, 174/82.

43. 9. 1. Ẓāh.[2] 183/5.

44. 20. (see Suppl.) Ẓāh.[2] 258.

45. 3. 6. *Muʿjam* Ẓāh.[2] 228.—7. *Tasmiyat man shahida badran* (?) ibid. 46.

3a. Muḥammad b. Abī Bakr b. Shajara al-Shāfiʿī al-Tadmurī, d. 787/1385, *ShDh* VI, 298. *Al-Sukkariyya fi ʾl-Sukkariyya* (madrasat Taqī al-Dīn b. Taymiyya bil-Qassām) Ẓāh.[2] 134/6.

50. o. Ẓāh.^{2} 97/8.—17. *Binā' al-Kaʿba* Ẓāh.^{2} 105.

51. 9. 2. Ẓāh.^{2} 8.

58. Line 14, a fragment in Ẓāh.^{2} 182.—c. *Dhayl* by Abu 'l-Maḥāsin Muḥammad b. ʿAlī b. al-Ḥasan al-Ḥusaynī al-Dimashqī al-Shāfiʿī, d. 765/1364 (p. 77, 6), ibid. 222.—*al-Iʿlām bi-wafayāt al-aʿlām* ibid. 166.—*Laḥẓ al-alḥāẓ* ibid. 223.—*Dhayl* ibid. 224.

59. 6. *al-Mushtabih* Ẓāh.^{2} 195, on which *Tawḍīḥ al-mushtabih* by Aḥmad b. ʿAlī b. Ḥajar al-ʿAsqalānī, d. 852/1448 (p. 80), ḤKh I, 346, II, 438, ibid. 196.—9. ibid. 244.—18. *Kitāb al-ḍuʿafā'* ibid. 243, on which a *Dhayl* ibid. 244.—8. Ẓāh.^{2} 213.—38. *Manāqib al-Shāfiʿī wa-aṣḥābihi*, abstract by Abū Bakr b. Aḥmad b. Muḥammad b. Qāḍī Shuhba, d. 851/1447 (p. 63), ibid. 253.—39. *al-Mujarrad fī asmā' rijāl Kitāb Sunan Abī ʿAbdallāh b. Māja* ibid. 214.—40. *Ahl al-mi'a fa-ṣāʿidan* ibid. 166.—41. *Tarjamat al-shaykh Raslān* ibid. 285.—42. *Tarjamat al-Ḥallāj* ibid. 286.

60. 6. 1. Ẓāh.^{2} 4/7.

64. Line 9, 6. (see Suppl.) Ẓāh.^{2} 299.—10. *Talkhīṣ li-muqaddimat Ta'rīkh Dimashq* ibid. 137.

65. 1. Ẓāh.^{2} 316.

76. 3. 2. Ẓāh.^{2} 22/3.

77. 6a. Muḥammad b. ʿAlī b. Muḥammad b. Aḥmad b. Sulaymān b. Ḥamza al-Maqdisī b. Zurayq, d. 803/1401, Ibn al-ʿImād, *ShDh* VII, 36. *Man takallama fīhi 'l-Dāraquṭnī* Ẓāh.^{2} 245.

| 79. 8. 1. Ẓāh.^{2} 195. 676

80. 11. 1. Ẓāh.^{2} 246.—2. ibid. 246.—4. (see Suppl.) ibid. 267.

81. Line 10, *Fihrist marwiyyāt b. Ḥajar* Ẓāh.^{2} 310.—1. ibid. 176/7.—12. ibid. 216.

83. 40. Ẓāh.^{2} 182.—41. ibid. 8.

84. 93. *Tarjamat al-Badawī A.* Ẓāh.^{2} 287.

Line 16.—13a. Shihāb al-Dīn Aḥmad b. ʿUmar b. ʿUthmān al-Khwārizmī al-Dimashqī al-Shāfiʿī b. Qara, who was a student of al-Ḥiṣnī and Qāḍī Shuhba, lectured in Damascus, where he constructed a *zāwiya* for dervishes. He died on 10 Jumādā I 868/21 January 1464. Al-Sakhāwī, *al-Ḍawʾ al-lāmiʿ* II, 54. 1. *Nukhabat al-nukhab al-muwaṣṣil ilā aʿla ʾl-rutab*, from al-Bārizī's *Tawthīq ʿura ʾl-īmān* (S. II, 101), which was not based on ʿIyāḍ's *Shifāʾ* (as claimed in ḤKh[2], 503), Ẓāh.[2] 56.—2. *al-Muntaqa ʾl-ʿazīz min faḍāʾil ʿUmar b. ʿAbd al-ʿAzīz min kalām b. Abī Zayd* (I, 187) ibid. 98.—3. *al-Taʿlīq al-naḍr fī tarjamat Abi ʾl-ʿAbbās al-Khiḍr* ibid. 317.—4. *Tarjamat Taqī al-Dīn al-Fāsī Muḥammad b. Aḥmad b. ʿAlī b. al-Khaṭīb* (p. 221) ibid. 275.—5. *Muntaqa ʾl-Mashāriq* see II, 665.

15. Yūsuf b. Ḥasan b. Aḥmad b. ʿAbd al-Hādī, d. 909/1504. Ibn al-ʿImād, *ShDh* VIII, 43. See Suppl. 947, no. 181.—3. Ẓāh.[2] 217.—21. *Maḥḍ al-khalāṣ* ibid. 179.—22. ibid. 74.—34. *al-Mīra fī ḥall mushkilāt al-Sīra* ibid. 22.—35. *Irshād al-sālik ilā manāqib Mālik* ibid. 275.—36. *al-ʿAṭāʾ al-muʿajjal* (on some Ḥanbalis) ibid. 272.—37. *al-Ḍabṭ wal-tabyīn li-dhawi ʾl-ʿilal wal-ʿāhāt min al-muḥaddithīn* ibid. 247.—38. *Tadhkirat al-ḥuffāẓ wa-tabṣirat al-ayqāẓ* ibid. 223.—39. *Taʿlīqāt li-baʿḍ tarājim muʿāṣirīhi* ibid. 185.—40. *Taʿrīf al-ghādī bi-baʿḍ faḍāʾil Aḥmad b. ʿAbd al-Hādī* (his brother) ibid. 287.—41. *Maḥd al-shayd fī manāqib Saʿīd b. Zayd* ibid. 178.—42. *Fihrist kutub b. ʿAbd al-Hādī* ibid. 310.—43. *Taʾrīkh al-Islām*, a fragment, ibid. 9.

85. Line 1, 1. Ẓāh.[2] 54/5.

3. 1. Ẓāh.[2] 18.—Abstract b. ibid. 22.

85. 3a. Shihāb al-Dīn Abū Maḥmūd al-Shāfiʿī al-Maqdisī, who died before 766/1365, may be identical with Aḥmad b. ʿAbd al-Raḥmān al-Ẓāhirī, d. 755/1354, *ShDh* VI, 177. A student of al-Dhahabī and Abū Ḥayyān al-Andalusī, he wrote *al-Mumtiʿ al-muqtaḍab fī sīrat khayr al-ʿAjam wal-ʿArab* Ẓāh.[2] 19 (Suppl. I, 551, 11 wrongly attributed to Abū Shāma).

677 | 86. 5a. See Suppl. II, 1252, ad 77, 3d Ẓāh.[2] 21 (Flügel, loc. cit., gives 742 as the year of death, *Kashf* [2]533, 842, not mentioned in DK, *ShDh*, and *al-Ḍawʾ al-lāmiʿ*).

5b. Fatḥ al-Dīn Muḥammad b. Ibrāhīm b. al-Shahīd, d. 793/1391, *ShDh* VI, 329. *Al-Fatḥ al-qarīb fī sīrat al-ḥabīb* Ẓāh.[2] 20.

87. 8. 1. Ẓāh.[2] 58. Commentary b. ibid. 66.—d. ibid. 66.

88. 1. 10. *al-Muhājirūn min Quraysh* Ẓāh.[2] 175.

89. 2a. (see Suppl.).—6. *Tuḥfat al-ṣadīq bi-faḍāʾil Abī Bakr al-Ṣiddīq* Ẓāh.[2] 89, where it is believed, however, that the author was Abu ʾl-Qāsim ʿAlī b. Balabān ʿAlāʾ al-Dīn al-Maqdisī al-Nāṣirī al-Karakī, who was born in 612/1215 and died in 684/1265, *ShDh* v, 388.

107. Line 26, 17. Commentary by Aḥmad al-Tarmānīnī al-Shāfiʿī al-Azharī, d. 1293/1876, Ẓāh.[2] 25.

110. Line 16, 8a. Ẓāh.[2] 254.

111. Line 32, 7. Ẓāh.[2] 255.

114. Line 7, 13. (see Suppl.) with the title *Ṭabaqāt al-awliyāʾ* Ẓāh.[2] 286.—22. *Ḥāl al-Jīlī* ibid. 287.

118. Line 15, 6. *Asmāʾ ajdād al-nabī* Ẓāh.[2] 77.

126. *Asmāʾ muʾallafāt Ibn Taymiyya li-Ibn Qayyim al-Jawziyya* Ẓāh.[2] 309.

127. C. (see Suppl.) 70a. *Jawāb al-risāla allatī jāʾat min Shhrnql(?) jawāb al-Ṭabarsī* Ẓāh.[2] 269.—70b. *Mā qāma bihi Ibn Taymiyya min kasr al-aḥjār* ibid. 270.—70c. *Jawāb ʿan istiftāʾ ʿani ʾl-mashhad al-mansūb lil-Ḥusayn wa-ʿan mashhad lahu kāna bi-ʿAsqalān* ibid. 151.

129. 6. 7. *Dhayl* Ẓāh.[2] 270.

130. 7a. ʿAlī b. Muḥammad b. Ḥusayn b. ʿUrwa al-Ḥanbalī al-Mashriqī al-Dimashqī b. Zuknūn, d. 837/1434, *ShDh* vii, 222. *Baʿḍ al-sīra al-nabawiyya min mukhtaṣar al-Kawākib al-darārī fī tartīb Musnad al-imām Aḥmad ʿalā abwāb al-Bukhārī* (Suppl. i, 310 line 7), Ẓāh.[2] 20 (wrongly Suppl. i, 263, 39), from which *Fī tafsīr al-Qurʾān al-karīm* Cairo [2]i, 59 (Suppl. ii, 985, 17).

131. Line 1, Ẓāh.[2] 78.

132. 3. Suppl. $133_{,3}$ = $898_{,7}$.

161. 2. 6. *Shuyūkh Burhān al-Fazārī* Ẓāh.[2] 228.

678 | 164. 13. 1 read: Br. Mus. 330/1.

165, 15. 1. *al-Dāris fī taʾrīkh al-madāris* (abstract by an unidentified contemporary), ed. Jaʿfar al-Ḥasanī, Damascus 1948/1367 (*Maṭbūʿāt al-majmaʿ al-ʿIlmī al-ʿArabī bi-Dimashq*).—9. *Mudhākarāt yawmiyya*, a diary, Ẓāh.[2] 139/42, see ʿIsh, *RAAD* VII, 142/54.

166. 2. 2. Ẓāh.[2] 308.

175. 5. 2. (see Suppl.) entitled *Sihām al-samm al-khāriqa fī ʾl-firqa al-mulḥida al-zanādiqa* C. 1295.

179. 6. 11. Ẓāh.[2] 177.

184. 29. Ẓāh.[2] 57.—*Unmūdhaj* ibid.

191. 130. Printed, with a commentary, Kazan 1891.

192. 141. Printed in the margin of ʿAbd al-Raḥīm al-Qāḍī, *Kitāb daqāʾiq al-akhbār fī dhikr al-janna wal-nār* C. 1352.

201. 278. Ẓāh.[2] 10.—279. Ibid. 153.

202. 286. Ẓāh.[2] 262.—290d. (see Suppl.) Ibid. 185.

203. 304. Ẓāh.[2] 2.

204. 337. *Nuzhat al-julasāʾ fī ashʿār al-nisāʾ* Ẓāh.[2] 300.—338. *al-Mustaṭraf min akhbār al-jawārī* ibid.

206. 3. Also Istanbul, Üniv. A 4055 (755 AH after the autograph), A 4189, A 108,$_1$, Šehīd ʿAlī 2234, Köpr 1449,$_1$, Lāleli 2856.—3a. (see Suppl.) 4. *Talkhīṣ majmaʿ al-ādāb* (*ʿalā muʿjam al-asmāʾ fī muʿjam al-alqāb*) in tabular form, vol. 4 Ẓāh.[2] 165.—8. *al-ʿAṭil al-ḥālī wal-murakhkhaṣ al-ghālī* ʿUm. 5542 (= p. 200, 21).

210. C. 2. *Mawʿid al-kirām fī mawlid al-nabī ʿalayhi ʾl-salām* Ẓāh.[2] 68.

221. 4. *Taḥqīq al-nuṣra bi-talkhīṣ maʿālim Dār al-hijra* Ẓāh.[2] 104.

225. 4. al-ʿĀmirī, *Bahjat al-maḥāfil* Ẓāh.[2] 21.

228. Ad line 6: Paris 4727 is the abstract by Yaḥyā b. Abī Bakr al-ʿĀmirī (Suppl. 225), see F. Rosenthal, *Orientalia* XI, 278n.

229. 7. 2. Ẓāh.[2] 89.

236. Line 4. Ẓāh.[2] 258.

239. II. *Muqaddima* library of Ismāʿīl Ṣāʾib (Ankara) 2469.

| 240. X. *al-Jawāhir wal-durar fī sīrat sayyid al-bashar wa-aṣḥābihi wa-ʿitratihi* 679
al-aʾimma (the imams of Yemen until 744 AH), ibid. (Ritter).

242. § 9, read: al-Sharjī.

243. Line 3, Selīm Āġā 542.—Line 7, 5. *al-Ṭarīq al-wāḍiḥa ilā asrār al-Fātiḥa* Br. Mus. Suppl. 827. 1.—6. *al-Jawāb al-shāfī fi ʾl-radd ʿala ʾl-mubtadiʿ al-ghāfī* (against the Yazīdis), Dam. Ẓ. 77, 50, 2.

249. 4. 5. See ad I, 453.

260. 18. *Sharḥ Sīrat al-khulafāʾ min Dhāt al-shifāʾ* by Muḥammad b. Abi ʾl-Ḥājj, completed in 1187/1773, Ẓāh.[2] 91.

264. 3c. 11. *Risāle-i iʿtiqādiyya, Namāz risālesi*, manuscript in Khwārizm, see A. Zeki Velidi, *Türk. Mecm.* II, 315.—12. *Risāla dar jawāzi dhikri jahr* ibid.

267. No. 11. (see Suppl.) Nawāʾī, *Majālis al-nafāʾis* Fātiḥ 4050, 676r.

270. VI. ed. Abu ʾl-ʿAlāʾ al-ʿAfīfī, *Majallat Kulliyyat al-ādāb* II, C. 1934, 133/242.

273. 4. 1. See P. Luckey, *Math. Annalen* 120 (1948), 221ff.

286. § 4. 1a. (Suppl. 310 = 606, 12).

289. § 2. 1. Ẓāh.[2] 27.

1a. Ismāʿīl b. Muḥammad Sharīf, who was a *mudarris* in Aqsarāy, wrote, in 756/1355, *Tadhkirat al-ʿibar wal-āthār fī baḥth al-umam wal-amṣār*, manuscript in Konya, see A. Zeki Validi, ZDMG 95, 367.

302. § 6,$_{9}$ (Suppl. 325 = 641, 3a).

316. *al-Muqaddima*. 1. Berl. 9362/3, Ẓāh.^{2} 1, 2.

319. 8a. Muḥammad b. Ibrāhīm al-Sharrān al-Rammāl al-Gharnāṭī al-Andalusī, who was, in ca. 837/1433, *raʾīs al-kataba* in al-Ḥaḍra al-ʿAliyya.

A. Bābā, *Nayl al-Ibtihāj* Fez 327, C. 311. 1. *al-Urjūza al-manẓūma fī ʾl-farāʾiḍ* Esc. ^{2}853, 5 (on which al-Qalaṣādī wrote a commentary).—2. *Badīʿ al-maqāl fī madḥ man nabaʿa bayna aṣābiʿihi ʾl-zulāl* Būlāq 1319 (Sarkis 570, anon.).

327. 3c. (s. Suppl.) 1. Fez Qar. 1493.

333. Line 4, *Riḥla*, library of Ismāʿīl Ṣāʾib (Ankara) 1477 (Ritter).

340. Line 11, 24 (see Suppl.) also Selīm Āġā 495.

No. 4. *ʿUqūd al-jumān* Ẓāh^{2} 13.

680 | 350. 5. (see Suppl. 383, 6) = p. 570,$_{1}$.

362. 59a. Suppl. see p. 605,$_{2}$.

364. 64. 4. (see Suppl.) Ẓāh.^{2} 47.—5. ibid. 67.

367. 1a. (see Suppl.) 1. *Bahjat al-nāẓirīn* Ẓāh.^{2} 256.

369. 10. 4. *Awj al-taḥarrī ʿan ḥaythiyyat Abi ʾl-ʿAlāʾ al-Maʿarrī* Ẓāh.^{2} 300.

376. 7. 1. Ẓāh.^{2} 187, on which a *Dhayl: Luṭf al-siḥr wa-qaṭf al-ghamr min tarājim aʿyān al-ṭabaqa al-ūlā min al-qarn al-ḥādī ʿashar* by Najm al-Dīn Muḥmmad b. Badr al-Dīn b. Raḍī al-Dīn Muḥammad, d. 1061/1651, ibid. 188.

377. 10b. (see Suppl.) 1. Ẓāh.^{2} 11.

378. 1. Ẓāh. ^{2}188.—3. ibid. 301. A part of the *Dhayl* by Muḥammad al-Maḥmūdī, ibid. 304.—on which a *Tatimma* by Muḥammad b. al-Sammān, ibid. 303.

379. 13. 2. *al-Mūḍiḥa al-qawīma fī faḍl al-khulafāʾ al-arbaʿa al-karīma*, with the commentary *al-Rayḥāna al-shamīma*, Ẓāh.[2] 90.
15. 1. Fragment from a *mukhtaṣar*, Ẓāh.[2] [2]189
17. (Suppl. 405 = 813, 49).

381. 5. 1. Ẓāh.[2] 154.

382. 1. Ẓāh.[2] 159.—3. ibid. 80.—4. ibid. 79.

383. 11. Ẓāh.[2] 276.

387. Line 6, 9. Shihāb al-Dīn Aḥmad b. Budayr al-Budayrī al-Ḥallāj al-Dimashqī wrote *Ḥawādith Dimashq al-yawmiyya min sanat* 1154 (1741) *ilā sanat* 1176 (1763), edited (*tanqīḥ*) by Jamāl al-Dīn Muḥammad Saʿīd b. Muḥammad al-Qāsimī al-Dimashqī, d. 1332/1914 (Sarkis 1483), Ẓāh.[2] 145.

E. 2. Instead of al-Jannābī, Babinger, *Gesch. d. Osm.* 102, no. 90, reads Janābī, without providing any explanation for this.

388. Line 12, Ẓāh.[2] 11.

392. Line 3, 2a. Abu 'l-Fatḥ Shams al-Dīn Muḥammad b. Ibrāhīm b. Muḥammad Muqbil al-Miṣrī al-Shāfiʿī, d. 937/1531, Ibn al-ʿImād, *ShDh* VIII, 224. 1. *al-Rawḍ al-raḥīb fī mawlid al-ḥabīb* Ẓāh.[2] 28.—2. *Rafʿ al-rayb fī khiḍāb al-shayb* Leid. 2658 (in which the author is qualified as a Ḥanbalī).

| 3. al-Ṣāliḥī, see *ShDh* VIII, 250.—2. Ẓāh.[2] 36. 681

394. 13. Ẓāh.[2] 291.

395. 10e. (see Suppl.) 2. *Munawwir al-qulūb*, manuscript dated 1113, Alex. Mawāʿiẓ 46.

395. 11. 1. Ẓāh.[2] 23.—Abstracts: f. ʿAlī b. Ibrāhīm al-Ḥalabī, d. 1044/1634 (Suppl. II, 1249, ad 23), Ẓāh.[2] 24.

399. Line 10, 11. *Tāj al-mulūk al-nafīs bi-tarjamat al-imām al-Shāfiʿī Muḥammad b. Idrīs* Ẓāh.[2] 359.

29a. Muḥammad al-Ḥusaynī al-Shuwaykī wrote, in 1171/1758, *Mawrid al-isʿād wal-imdād fī mawlid ashraf al-ʿibād wal-ʿiyād* (sic) Ẓāh.[2] 30.

29b. Ismāʿīl b. ʿAbdallāh al-Naqshbandī wrote, in 1180/1767, *Manāqib al-ʿashara* Ẓāh.^{2} 178.

411. 26. Muḥammad Amīn b. Sulaymān b. Amīn b. ʿAbd al-Raḥmān al-Ayyūbī wrote *ʿIqd al-tahānī fī tarjamat shaykhihi Muḥammad Saʿīd al-Burhānī* (a *muftī* in Damascus who was born in 1161/1768), Ẓāh.^{2} 263.

429. 15. *Tarājim mashāyikh Abi ʾl-Mawāhib* Ẓāh.^{2} 229.

438. Line 11, 34. *Miʿrāj* Ẓah.^{2} 35.

442. 8. Ẓāh.^{2} 288, *Dhayl* ibid.

444. 43. From which *Fayḍ al-sirr al-mudāwī bi-naql tarājim al-salāṭīn al-arbaʿa* (ʿAbd al-Qādir al-Jīlī, Aḥmad b. Abi ʾl-Ḥasan al-Rifāʿī, Aḥmad al-Badawī, and Ibrāhīm al-Dasūqī) Ẓāh.^{2} 289.

445. 16. 3. Ẓāh.^{2} 29.—4. ibid. 37.

447. Line 2, Ẓāh.^{2} 290.

448. 26. Read: *sayyidinā*, of the Sufis.

452. 38a. Muḥammad b. Ibrāhīm al-Dakdakjī wrote, in 1097/1686, *Ṭabaqāt al-Shādhiliyya*, of which a fragment is in Ẓāh.^{2} 292.

453. (G^1 344) 47. See Suppl. III, 1305, ad 664, 19.

458. 160. *al-Ḥawḍ al-mawrūd fī ziyārat al-shaykh Yūsuf wal-shaykh Maḥmūd* Ẓāh.^{2} 92.

471. 19a. Grandson of Sāčaqlīzāde (486, 8).—3. *Tuḥfat al-aḥbāb fi ʾl-manṭiq* Alex. Fun. 97, 2, Beirut 416, 12.—4. *Sharḥ al-Risāla fi ʾl-majāzāt wal-istiʿārāt* Pet. AMK 932.

682 | 477. § 17. 3. (see Suppl.) *Bulūgh al-munā* Ẓāh.^{2} 303.

479. 20. See Suppl. Ẓāh.^{2} 37.

483. Line 4, read: *fī tarājim muʿāṣirīhi.*

492. § 4. A. 1a. Sharaf al-Dīn Abu 'l-Qāsim b. ʿAbd al-ʿAlīm b. Abi 'l-Qāsim ʿUthmān al-Qurtubī wrote, in 974/1567:

Qalāʾid ʿuyūn al-ʿiqyān fī manāqib al-imām Abī Ḥanīfa al-Nuʿmān (and also of Abū Yūsuf and Muḥammad al-Shaybānī), Ẓāh.[2] 262.

502. Line 6, 4a. Aḥmad b. Muḥammad al-Asadī al-Makkī, d. 1066/1656, Muḥ. I, 327. *Ikhbār al-kirām bi-akhbār al-masjid al-ḥarām* Ẓāh.[2] 107.

502. 10. 6. *Risāla fī taḥrīm al-dukhān* Alex. Fun. 157,3.

502. 11. An unidentified author wrote, in 1154/1741:

Qiṣaṣ wa-akhbār jarat bi-ʿUmān Ẓāh.[2] 159/60.

507. § 5A. 2c. (see Suppl. = ibid. 647, 27) 1. b. (Suppl. 524) 1. Sulaim. 419/20 (Suppl. II, 948, 4).

508. C. 1. *Nafāʾīs al-durar fī tarjamat shaykh al-islām Ibn Ḥajar*, by Abū Bakr b. Muḥammad b. ʿAbdallāh b. al-Faqīh ʿAlī Bā ʿAmr al-Nrnī(?), Ẓāh.[2] 359 = *Mānaqib*.

513. 12. Ẓāh.[2] 106.

Suppl. II, 871,4, *Chronika Muhammeda Tahira al-Karahi o Dagestanskich Voinach v period Šamilya, Arabskij Tekst podgotovlennij A. M. Barabanovym pod redakziei I. Ju. Kračkovskogo*—Trudi Instituta Vostokovedenija XXXVII, Moscow-Leningrad 1946.

683 ## Indices

Supplement III, 503ff.

507b. ʿAbd al-Ḥamīd al-Kassī S II, 918.
512b. ʿAbdallāh b. Hilāl al-Ahwāzī G I, 239/40.
515b. ʿAbdallāh b. Muḥammad b. Abi ʾl-Shaykh N G I, 176 (5665).
517b. ʿAbdallāh b. ʿUbaydallāh al-Wāfī al-Fayyūmī S II, 724.
519b. ʿAbd al-Munʿim b. Muḥammad al-Abarqūhī G I, 357.
521b. ʿAbd al-Qādir b. Shaykh b. ʿAbdallāh b. ʿAydarūs G II, 551, S II, 617.
524a. ʿAbd al-Raḥmān b. ʿAlī b. al-Rabīʿ al-Shaybānī al-Yamanī G II, 186.
526b. ʿAbd al-Raḥmān b. Muḥammad b. ʿAsākir S I, 610.
530b. ʿAbd al-Wahhāb b. Aḥmad b. Maḥmūd al-Rūmī G I, 446.
533b. Aḥmad b. ʿAbd al-ʿAzīz b. Muḥammad al-ʿAjamī S I, 512 N (III, 1213).
537b. Aḥmad b. ʿAlī al-Manīnī G II, 145.
539a. Aḥmad al-Bulqīnī al-Shāfiʿī G I, 493.
542b. Aḥmad b. Ibrāhīm b. Khalīl al-Ḥalabī G II, 159.
543a. Aḥmad b. Ismāʿīl al-Isfarāʾinī S II, 259.
545b. Aḥmad b. Muḥammad al-Asadī G II, 512 N.
547b. Aḥmad b. Muḥammad al-Malīnī G II, 100.
548a. Aḥmad b. Muḥammad al-Matbūlī G II, 186.
548a. Aḥmad b. Mūsā al-ʿIrrīf G I, 559.
551b. Aḥmad b. ʿUthmān b. Qara al-Shāfiʿī G II, 119.
555a. Aḥmad b. Yūsuf al-Samīn G I, 521.
557b. ʿAlwān b. ʿAlī b. ʿAṭiyya al-Ḥamawī G I, 447.
558b. ʿAlī b. ʿAbd al-Muḥsin al-Dawālībī G I, 164 N (p. 663).
565a. ʿAlī b. Muḥammad b. Ghānim G II 168, 7d.
565b. ʿAlī b. Muḥammad al-Laythī al-Wāsiṭī S I, 714 N (III, 1228).
571a. Al-Amīr al-Kabīr Muḥammad b. Muḥammad G II, 486, S II, 738.
588a. Dhu ʾl-Wizāratayn Muḥammad b. Masʿūd G I, 454.
594b. Jaʿfar b. Muḥammad al-Fīryābī I, 163 N (S 668).
598a. Al-Jumaḥī Muḥammad b. Sallām S I, 165.
601 Hārūn b. Yaḥyā G I, 260, 5a, S I, 406.
601b. Al-Harawī al-Qāriʾ G II, 517.
602a. Abū Hiffān S I, 117.
605b. Abū Ḥāmid b. Abī Dharr al-Ghifārī S N II, 518, 850.
684 606b. Ḥāmid b. Samḥūn Abū Bakr S I, 884.
606b. Ḥammād b. Isḥāq S I, 266.
607b. Al-Ḥasan b. Aḥmad al-Aʿrābī al-Ghandajānī G I, 120.
616b. Al-Ḥusayn b. ʿAbdallāh b. Muḥammad al-Ṭībī G II, 76.

617a. Al-Ḥusayn b. Muḥammad b. Mawdūd Abū ʿArūba al-Ḥarrānī G (p. 663) N I, 163.
618b. Abu ʾl-Khayr ʿAlī Nūr al-Dīn S II, 1020.
619a. Khaythama b. Sulaymān b. Ḥaydara al-Aṭrābulusī G I, 172 N (p. 664).
621b. Ibn Akhī Ḥazzām al-Khuttalī S I, 433.
623a. Ibrāhīm b. ʿAbd al-Raḥmān al-Bilbaysī G I, 493.
625b. Ibrāhīm b. Muḥammad al-ʿAjamī G I, 167.
626b. Ibrāhīm b. Muḥammad al-Saʿdī al-Mālikī G I, 456.
638a. Al-Kurlānī Jalāl al-Dīn S I, 645.
641a. Al-Maḥallī Jamāl al-Dīn S II, 140.
645b. Ibn al-Manlā Muḥammad b. Aḥmad b. Muḥammad al-Ḥaṣkafī II, 179.
647b. Al-Marrāsh Fransīs b. Fatḥallāh S II, 755.
649b. Al-Māzinī Ibrāhīm ʿAbd al-Qādir S III, 157.
653b. Al-Mujaddid al-Sirhindī S II, 536.
655b. Muḥammad b. ʿAbdallāh al-Azraqī S I, 209.
Muḥammad b. ʿAbdallāh b. al-Ḥusayn al-Muʾayyad II, 528.
656b. Muḥammad b. ʿAbdallāh al-Khwārizmī G I, 540.
662b. Muḥammad b. Aḥmad b. Jābir al-Huwārī I, 360.
666b. Muḥammad b. Aḥmad al-Shāsī S I, 307.
Muḥammad b. Aḥmad Abū Shuʿla al-Mawṣilī G I, 521.
668a. Muḥammad b. ʿAlī al-Adfīnī al-Buḥayrī G I, 491.
669b. Muḥammad b. ʿAlī al-Kharfūshī G I, 362.
675b. Muḥammad b. Abī Bakr b. ʿAjāna al-ʿAdnānī G I, 480.
681b. Muḥammad b. Hārūn b. Shuʿayb al-Anṣārī G I, 172 N (664).
682a. Muḥammad b. Humām al-Dīn G I, 538, S II, 91.
689b. Muḥammad b. Ibrāhīm al-Shīrāzī Abū Naṣr G II, 544.
690a. Muḥammad b. ʿĪsā b. Muḥammad Aṣbagh G I, 384.
696b. Muḥammad b. Muḥammad b. ʿAbdallāh b. Manṣūr al-Ahwāzī S II, 1023 N (*Sharḥ al-Maqāla al-ʿāshira min Kitāb Uqlīdīs* Patna II, 553, 2928, 2. *Risāla fī ʿilm al-mīzān* ibid. 3).
703b. Muḥammad b. Muḥammad al-Shābī G I, 489, S I, 674.
709a. Muḥammad b. ʿUthmān b. Abī Shayba G I, 176 N (p. 664).
712a. Muḥammad b. al-Shaykh Maḥmūd al-Ḥubūbī S III, 482.
721a. Muḥammad b. Yūsuf b. al-Mughīra G I, 458.
| 723b. Al-Mundhirī Muḥammad b. Abī Jaʿfar G I, 129. 685
726b. Muṣṭafā b. Ismāʿīl al-ʿIbādī S II, 893.
729b. Najīb ʿAzīz S III, 384.
730b. Ibn al-Naḥwī Yūsuf b. Muḥammad al-Tawzarī G I, 316, S I, 473.
733a. Niʿmatallāh b. Küčük al-Samarqandī S II, 945 N (*Kanz al-uṣūl fī maʿrifat ḥadīth al-rasūl* Patna I, 36, 364)

733a. Al-Nīsābūrī Abū Isḥāq al-Thaʿlabī G I, 429.
739a. Pārsā Khwāja S II, 283.
740a. Al-Qāḍī Mīr Ḥusayn G II, 272, S II, 294.
743b. Al-Qasṭallānī Aḥmad b. Muḥammad G II, 87.
744b. Ibn Qudāma Sayf al-Dīn Abu ʾl-ʿAbbās G I, 504 N (S. 672).
744b. Al-Qūhī Abū Sahl S I, 399.
745b. Qyrq Emre G II 292, S II, 316.
746a. Ibn al-Rafʿa Aḥmad b. Muḥammad b. ʿAlī G I, 543, II, 165.
747b. Al-Rashīd b. al-Zubayr G I, 314.
747b. Rashīd al-Dīn Waṭwāṭ S I, 486.
752b. Salīm ʿAbd al-Ghanī Ramaḍān S III, 384.
755b. Al-Sijāʿī Aḥmad b. Aḥmad S II, 445.
756a. Al-Sirmīnī ʿAbdallāh G I, 491, S I, 676.
765a. Al-Shurunbalālī Ḥasan b. ʿAmmār G II, 406, S II, 430.
767a. Ibn al-Ṣalāḥ ʿĪsā b. Luṭfallāh S II, 550.
776b. Wajdī Muḥammad Farīd S III, 324.
786a. Zayn al-ʿĀbidīn b. ʿAbd al-Raʾūf al-Munāwī G II, 574.
787b. Zakariyyāʾ b. Muṭīʿ b. ʿAbd al-Nūr S II, 926.
787b. Al-Zankalūnī G II, 497.

789b. *ʿĀbir fi ʾl-anṣār wal-muhājir* S II, 746.
789b. *ʿĀbir sabīl* S III, 147.
815a. *Awj al-taḥarrī ʿan ḥaythiyyat Abi ʾl-ʿAlāʾ al-Maʿarrī* G II, 369, N (p. 680).
823b. *Bayān al-aḥkām al-mutaʿalliqa bil-malāʾika wal-mursalīn* G I, 554.
832a. *Dall wa-Taynān* S III, 25.
845b. *Dustūr al-ʿulamāʾ* S II, 628.
861b. *Fatḥ al-raʾūf al-jawād* S II, 417, 32.
882a. *Ghāyat al-bayān fī tadbīr badan al-insān* G II, 447.
891b. *al-Ḥaqāʾiq al-Muḥammadiyya* S II, 307.
Ḥaqāʾiq al-taʾwīl wa-daqāʾiq al-tanzīl G II, 262.
904b. *Khulāṣat al-Nihāya* G I, 466, II, 97.
938a. *Kashf al-niqāb wal-rān* G II, 414, S II, 438.
946a. *Laṭāʾif al-maʿārif* G I, 338, II, 129, S II, 129.
950a. *al-Lumʿa al-Dimashqiyya* G I, 131, S II, 131.
686 | 986a. *al-Misk al-ʿāṭir* S II, 485 N (III, 1291).
1025b. *al-Nūr* S I, 427.
1028a. *Nuzhat al-awzān* S II, 715.
1028a. *Nuzhat al-julasāʾ* G II, 204 N (p. 675).
1029a. *Nuzhat al-nufūs wal-afkār fī maʿrifat al-nabāt wal-ashjār* S II, 171.
1044a. *al-Raḥbiyya* G I 490, S I, 675.

1045b. *Rashf al-sirr al-ghāmiḍ* S I, 463 N (III 1209).
1046b. *al-Rawḍ al-ʿāṭir fī-mā tayassara etc.* G II, 374.
1047a. *al-Rawḍ al-nasīm wal-durr al-yatīm* G II, 388.
1071b. *al-Risāla al-sharṭiyya* S II, 487, 797.
1085a. *al-Sirājiyya* G I, 470.
1089b. *al-Shamaqmaqiyya* G II, 615, S II, 706.
1098a. *Shifāʾ al-asqām fī ziyārat khayr al-anām* II, 107.
1134a. *Tawḍīḥ al-Mushtabih* G II, 59 N (S. 675).
1146a. *Ṭārif al-majd* S II, 516 n.
1160b. *Wiqāyat al-sālik* G I, 542.
1162b. *Zād al-musāfir wa-luhnat al-muqīm wal-ḥāḍir* G II, 490.

687 # Postscript

Now that printing is complete it is my pleasure to once again thank all those who helped me in my work: H.G. Farmer, who sent me the proofs of his *Sources* even before the work had appeared in print; Fritz Meier in Basle, now Alexandria, from whom I received valuable information on the manuscript holdings of the municipal library of Basle; a special word of thanks must go to H. Ritter, who never tired of informing me of manuscripts in Istanbul and who corrected the last pages of the second volume, not accessible to me, and thereby enriched their content on many occasions.

As before, I included in the Addenda all I had available. The inclusion of every new collection of manuscripts, such as that of the late Ismāʿīl Ṣāʾib Efendi, now in Ankara, will further extend the scope of the present work. The Indices of the Supplements will also be adequate for this volume as the page numbering of the first edition has been reproduced in the margin.

The Appendix to Supplement II has not been continued, even though I have a lot of material available. In the same way in which several of the authors mentioned there could already be identified in the present work, it is to be expected that further research will also clarify the lifetime and origin of other writers, whom the catalogues now mention by name alone.

Halle, June 1948 C. Brockelmann